TWO VOLUMES IN ONE

THE BOOK OF JUDGES

WITH INTRODUCTION AND NOTES

and

NOTES

ON

THE HEBREW TEXT

OF THE

BOOKS OF KINGS

WITH AN INTRODUCTION AND APPENDIX

THE LIBRARY OF BIBLICAL STUDIES

Edited by

Harry M. Orlinsky

TWO VOLUMES IN ONE

THE BOOK OF JUDGES

WITH INTRODUCTION AND NOTES

and

NOTES

ON

THE HEBREW TEXT

OF THE

BOOKS OF KINGS

WITH AN INTRODUCTION AND APPENDIX

BY

C. F. BURNEY

PROLEGOMENON BY

WILLIAM F. ALBRIGHT

KTAV PUBLISHING HOUSE, INC.

NEW YORK

1970

FIRST PUBLISHED 1903, 1918

SBN 87068-002-1

Library of Congress Catalog Card Number: HE 66-1489
Manufactured in the United States of America

WESTERN ASIA IN THE

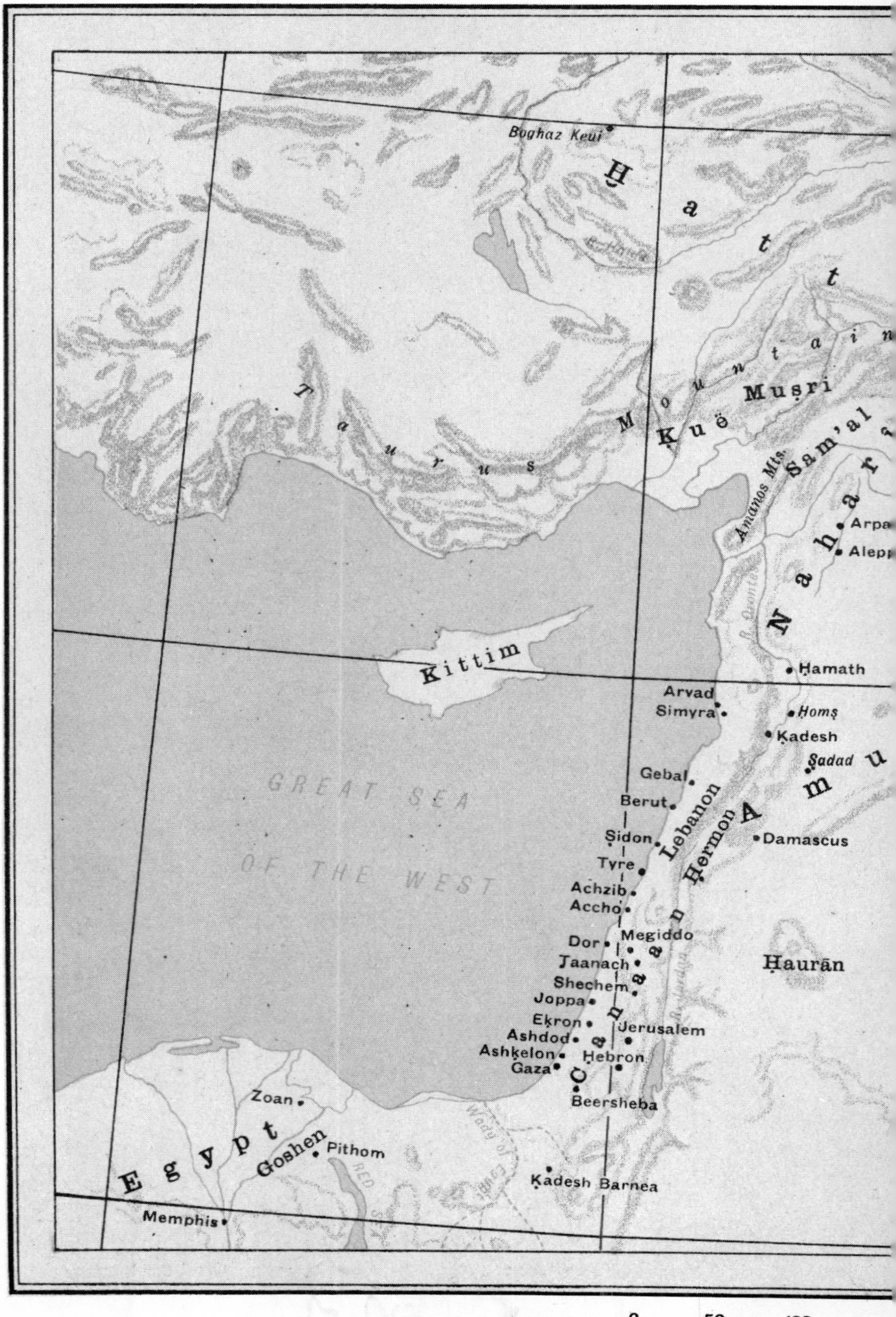

SCALE 1 : 7,000,000 0 50 100

COND MILLENNIUM B.C.

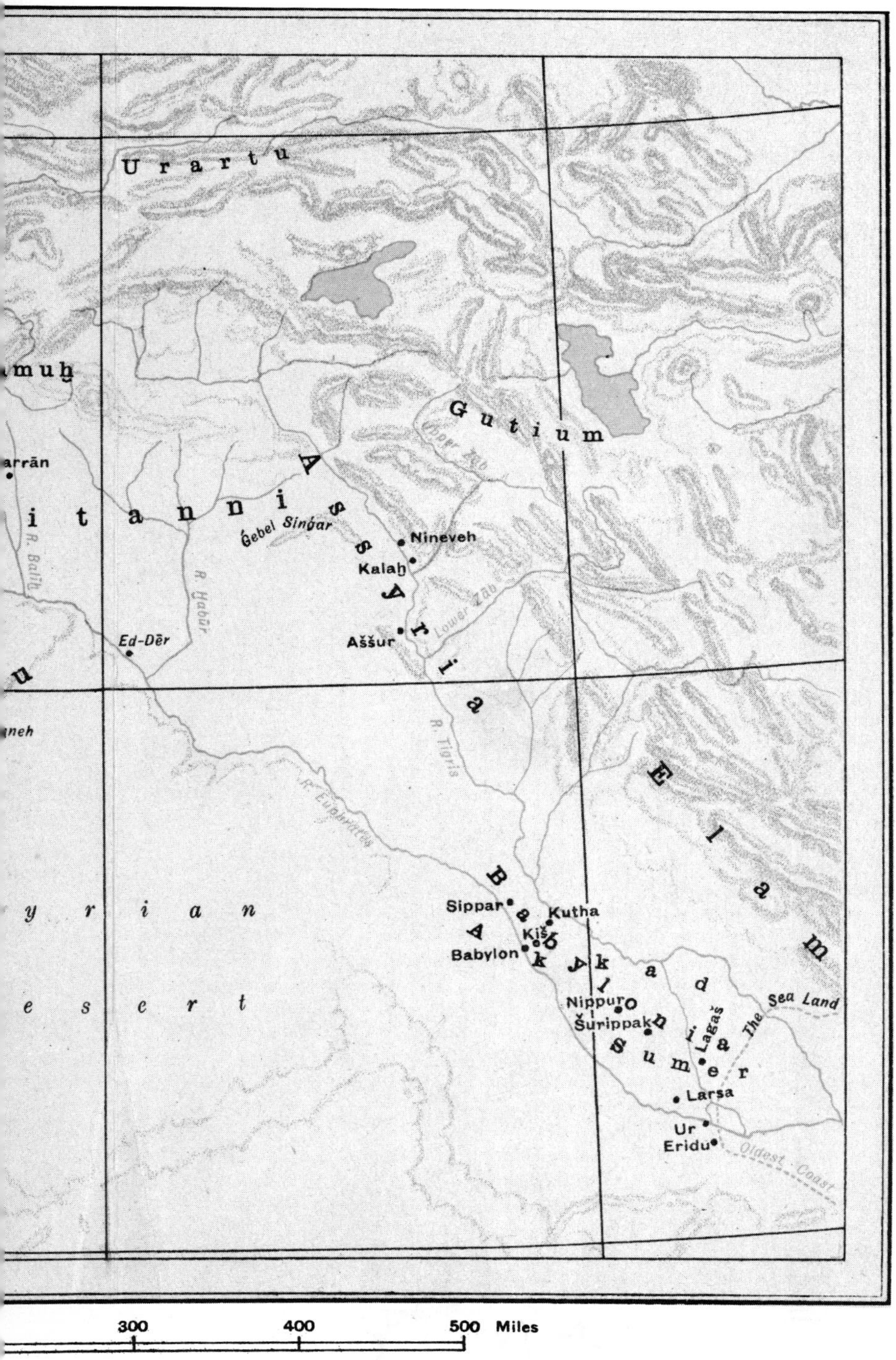

THE BOOK OF JUDGES

WITH INTRODUCTION AND NOTES

EDITED BY

THE REV. C. F. BURNEY, D.Litt.

ORIEL PROFESSOR OF THE INTERPRETATION OF HOLY SCRIPTURE
IN THE UNIVERSITY OF OXFORD,
CANON OF ROCHESTER,
AND FELLOW OF ST. JOHN BAPTIST'S COLLEGE, OXFORD

FIRST PUBLISHED 1918

TO MY WIFE

CONTENTS

	Page
PROLEGOMENON	1
ADDENDA,	xiii
PRINCIPAL ABBREVIATIONS EMPLOYED,	xxii
TRANSLITERATION OF SEMITIC WORDS,	xxxi
INTRODUCTION :—	
§ 1. Title, Scope, and Place in the Canon,	xxxiii
§ 2. Structure,	xxxiv
§ 3. The Old Narratives,	xxxvii
§ 4. The Editors,	xli
§ 5. Chronology,	l
§ 6. External Information bearing on the Period of Judges,	lv
§ 7. The Permanent Religious Value of Judges,	cxviii
§ 8. Hebrew Text and Ancient Versions,	cxxii
TRANSLATION AND COMMENTARY,	1
ADDITIONAL NOTES :—	
External Evidence for the Use of the Terms 'Cana'an' and 'The Land of the Amorite,'	41
Ṣedeḳ as a Divine Name,	41
The Meaning of the Name Ḳiriath-Arba',	43
The Conquest of the Negeb,	44
The original Form of J's Account of the Settlement of the Tribes of Israel in Cana'an,	47
A Detailed Examination of the Rhythm of the Song of Deborah,	158
The Climactic Parallelism of the Song of Deborah,	169
The Language of the Song of Deborah,	171
Yahweh or Yahu originally an Amorite Deity,	243

	PAGE
EARLY IDENTIFICATION OF YAHWEH WITH THE MOON-GOD,	249
THE USE OF WRITING AMONG THE ISRAELITES AT THE TIME OF THE JUDGES,	253
HUMAN SACRIFICE AMONG THE ISRAELITES,	329
THE WOMEN'S FESTIVAL OF JUDGES 11 40,	332
THE MYTHICAL ELEMENTS IN THE STORY OF SAMSON,	391
THE ORIGIN OF THE LEVITES,	436
DESCRIPTION OF THE PLATES,	495
NOTE ON THE MAPS OF PALESTINE,	498
INDICES:—	
I. GENERAL INDEX,	503
II. INDEX OF GRAMMATICAL AND PHILOLOGICAL OBSERVATIONS,	520
III. INDEX OF FOREIGN TERMS:—	
HEBREW (INCLUDING CANA'ANITE),	522
BABYLONIAN AND ASSYRIAN (INCLUDING SUMERIAN),	524
ARAMAIC (INCLUDING SYRIAC),	525
ARABIC,	526
GREEK,	527
LATIN,	527
IV. INDEX OF PASSAGES FROM OTHER BOOKS DISCUSSED,	527
MAPS:—	
WESTERN ASIA IN THE SECOND MILLENNIUM B.C.,	*Frontispiece*
THE DISTRICT ROUND GIBE'AH,	*to face p.* 465
PALESTINE (*five Maps*),	*End of Volume*
PLATES,	,, ,,

ERRATA.

p. xxi, l. 26. For 'Ǵel-a'y' read 'el-Ǵa'y.'

p. lxxix, l. 10. For 'erdanu' read 'Šerdanu.'

,, footnote || After '*op. cit. supra*' add 'p. 73.'

CONTENTS

	Page
PROLEGOMENON	1
ADDENDA,	xiii
PRINCIPAL ABBREVIATIONS EMPLOYED,	xxii
TRANSLITERATION OF SEMITIC WORDS,	xxxi
INTRODUCTION :—	
§ 1. TITLE, SCOPE, AND PLACE IN THE CANON,	xxxiii
§ 2. STRUCTURE,	xxxiv
§ 3. THE OLD NARRATIVES,	xxxvii
§ 4. THE EDITORS,	xli
§ 5. CHRONOLOGY,	l
§ 6. EXTERNAL INFORMATION BEARING ON THE PERIOD OF JUDGES,	lv
§ 7. THE PERMANENT RELIGIOUS VALUE OF JUDGES,	cxviii
§ 8. HEBREW TEXT AND ANCIENT VERSIONS,	cxxii
TRANSLATION AND COMMENTARY,	1
ADDITIONAL NOTES :—	
EXTERNAL EVIDENCE FOR THE USE OF THE TERMS 'CANA'AN' AND 'THE LAND OF THE AMORITE,'	41
ṢEDEḲ AS A DIVINE NAME,	41
THE MEANING OF THE NAME ḲIRIATH-ARBA',	43
THE CONQUEST OF THE NEGEB,	44
THE ORIGINAL FORM OF J'S ACCOUNT OF THE SETTLEMENT OF THE TRIBES OF ISRAEL IN CANA'AN,	47
A DETAILED EXAMINATION OF THE RHYTHM OF THE SONG OF DEBORAH,	158
THE CLIMACTIC PARALLELISM OF THE SONG OF DEBORAH,	169
THE LANGUAGE OF THE SONG OF DEBORAH,	171
YAHWEH OR YAHU ORIGINALLY AN AMORITE DEITY,	243

PAGE

Early Identification of Yahweh with the Moon-God, 249

The Use of Writing among the Israelites at the Time of the Judges, ... 253

Human Sacrifice among the Israelites, ... 329

The Women's Festival of Judges 11 40, . . . 332

The Mythical Elements in the Story of Samson, . 391

The Origin of the Levites, ... 436

DESCRIPTION OF THE PLATES, ... 495

NOTE ON THE MAPS OF PALESTINE, ... 498

INDICES:—

I. General Index, ... 503

II. Index of Grammatical and Philological Observations, ... 520

III. Index of Foreign Terms:—

Hebrew (including Cana'anite), . . . 522

Babylonian and Assyrian (including Sumerian), 524

Aramaic (including Syriac), ... 525

Arabic, ... 526

Greek, ... 527

Latin, ... 527

IV. Index of Passages from other Books discussed, . 527

MAPS:—

Western Asia in the Second Millennium B.C., . *Frontispiece*

The District round Gibe'ah, . . . *to face p.* 465

Palestine (*five Maps*), ... *End of Volume*

PLATES, ... ,, ,,

ERRATA.

p. xxi, l. 26. For 'Ǵel-a'y' read 'el-Ǵa'y.'

p. lxxix, l. 10. For 'erdanu' read 'Šerdanu.'

,, footnote || After '*op. cit. supra*' add 'p. 73.'

PROLEGOMENON
TO

C. F. BURNEY

THE BOOK OF JUDGES WITH INTRODUCTION AND NOTES

and

NOTES ON THE HEBREW TEXT OF THE BOOK OF KINGS

I. THE BOOK OF JUDGES

A. The Book of Judges.

1. Burney followed the trend of his time and found JE material in the early part of the Book. That there is material in Judges which is also found in the Tetrateuch (Genesis-Numbers) is certain; for example, see *YGC* (American ed., 1968), pp. 38 ff. On the other hand, the current tendency, exemplified by the latest work of such scholars as the late Martin Noth and Sigmund Mowinckel, is to recognize continuing tradition, both written and oral, which was crystallized in the "J" document and its northern recension, "E." Whatever the exact situation may turn out to have been, it is reasonably certain today that the prose tradition of Israel's beginnings had already been written down in substantially its still preserved form before the

Division of the Monarchy, *c.* 922 B.C. We shall discuss the problem of Judges 1 below.

2. In 1943 a most important discovery was published by Martin Noth (*Überlieferungsgeschichtliche Studien* I, Halle [Salle]), that the books of Deuteronomy, Joshua, Judges, I and II Samuel, and I and II Kings belong to a single work written by a Judaean historian who may conveniently be called the Deuteronomist. Naturally, most of his work was careful collecting and editing of older written material, though he was fortunately not averse to the use of oral tradition in the absence of written sources. There is no sense in speaking of a "Deuteronomic School," since the total length of this compilation was incomparably less than that of almost any of the great one-man historical works of antiquity, quite aside from medieval and modern times. One thinks immediately of Livy, Tabarī, Gibbon, and Toynbee. This in no way detracts from the intrinsic historical value of the material—quite the contrary. It is clear that the Deuteronomist was extremely careful to omit material that lacked good validation, and the accuracy of his information is being confirmed over and over again by the progress of archaeology and its ancillary disciplines.

To be sure, in his zeal for collecting material, the Deuteronomist sometimes brought too much together. For example, his list in Joshua 12 of thirty-one kings of towns in Western Palestine which were conquered by Joshua, includes towns which were not inhabited at the time of the Conquest, as in the case of Ai (v. 9) and Arad (v. 14). On the other hand, he does not mention the king of Bethel, obviously supposing that Bethel was ruled from Ai. Since Bethel was destroyed about the middle of the thirteenth century B.C., while Ai had been in ruins for many centuries, the two towns (less than two miles apart) had evidently been closely associated by tradition. The town of Arad is not actually mentioned in either the A or B recensions of the LXX in Judg. 1:16, but only the Descent of Arad (*YGC* [Am. ed., 1968], p. 40, n. 82). Both references are thus basically correct.

3. Burney's treatment of textual—mainly Septuagintal—problems is excellent; he was admirably prepared for work in this field, in which he followed such guides as Paul de Lagarde and G. F. Moore. It has been recognized for centuries that the Greek text of Judges offers an extraordinary enigma. The two recensions, A and B, often differ radically in wording and sometimes even in content. There is nothing quite comparable elsewhere in the Bible. Following Lagarde and Moore, Burney recognized that the A recension is much closer to the Lucianic text—so far as it was then known—than the B recension. Like them, he concluded that both are independent translations from Hebrew into Greek. Subsequent scholars have tended to disagree, and to regard the Hebrew text as basic and the two Greek recensions as quite secondary; but the discovery of the Qumran material from Cave IV has drastically altered the situation. F. M. Cross, Jr. (who is charged with the publication of the fragments of the Bible in Cave IV) has established definitively that the Scroll material includes many examples of what he calls the Old Palestinian or Proto-Lucianic text. (See Cross, *The Ancient Library of Qumran* [New York, 1958], pp. 124 ff.; *HTR,* 57 [1964], pp. 281-299; *IEJ,* 16 [1966], pp. 82-95.) While there is little of Judges preserved among the fragments from Qumran, material available in I and II Kings further illustrates the correctness of this point of view; see J. M. Miller, *JBL,* 86 (1967), pp. 276-288, and Fr. James D. Shenkel *Chronology and Recensional Development in the Greek Text of Kings* (Cambridge, Harvard U. Press, 1968); for an example of the historical importance of recognizing the reliability of the Greek of Judges, see *YGC* (Am. ed., 1968), p. 40, n. 82. Cf. further H. M. Orlinsky's forthcoming study of "The Hebrew *Vorlage* of the Septuagint of the Book of Joshua" (in the Rome Congress Volume, *Supplements to Vetus Testamentum,* 1969).

B. Burney's Use of Material of Archaeological Origin.

As pointed out in his General Introduction, Burney's extensive use of material that derived from the ancient Orient, including Babylonia, Assyria, Egypt, and Phoenicia, as well as the conventional literary and textual approaches, was not appreciated by professional Old Testament scholars of his day. The Germans left Burney's work severely alone, and the Americans followed suit. My own teacher, Paul Haupt, never referred to Burney in any of his publications, even when he was dealing with subjects which had been examined in detail by Burney. There was not a single copy of Burney's *Judges* either in the Johns Hopkins library or in Haupt's private library; in fact, I was introduced to Burney in 1920 by my British archaeological friends in Jerusalem and by a copy of his *Judges* which I found in the library of the British School of Archaeology. The reason for this astonishing neglect is simple: Wellhausen was very skeptical about the value of any material of archaeological origin. Up to late in his life, he doubted that cuneiform had really been deciphered; and he seldom even mentioned Egyptian discoveries. So far as I know, he never referred to the Amarna Tablets in any of his standard works. Non-epigraphic archaeology remained completely foreign to the purview of Wellhausen and of virtually all members of his school, who referred scornfully to it as "Scherbenwissenschaft." On the other hand, S. R. Driver, who was an older teacher and colleague of Burney and afterwards a close friend of his, was most sympathetic to his approach—another illustration of the basic humility of the older scholar. After all, Driver had written some very trenchant criticisms of the work of A. H. Sayce and Fritz Hommel, and had scored the weaknesses of the early Palestinian archaeologists, so he might not be expected to sympathize with Burney's approach—and yet he was so intellectually honest that he was willing to meet Burney more than halfway.

Burney's full discussions make his commentary a comprehensive treatment of the whole of early Israelite historical tradition. For the first time a major specialist in Old Testament tried intelligently to create a synthesis of Biblical tradition and the new data from all then-known Near Eastern sources. How tremendous the break in scholarly approach was, may be gauged by the fact that when German Biblical criticism began its triumphal march with Eichhorn and De Wette just before and after the beginning of the nineteenth century, little was known about the ancient world in which Israel grew to maturity except for isolated and sometimes distorted fragments preserved by late compilers such as Josephus and Eusebius. This state of affairs continued substantially through the nineteenth century. De Sacy refused to accept the decipherment of Egyptian by Champollion; Ernest Renan and Alfred von Gutschmidt, followed by many contemporaries, refused to accept the decipherment of cuneiform. Archaeology proper remained a book of seven seals, so far as Biblical scholars were concerned, well down into the present century. Burney himself had a good command of cuneiform, though he also accepted some notions of his teacher, C. J. Ball, about the Semitic origin of Sumerian. Fortunately, these ideas were nearly always quite irrelevant to his work on Judges. Burney was particularly careful in his use of the Amarna Tablets, where he was able to follow Knudtzon's excellent edition without the misunderstandings which defaced the work of secondary scholars, such as the late Samuel Mercer, who undertook to publish an English translation of the Amarna Tablets without any real knowledge of cuneiform. Burney dug deeply into the Amarna Tablets and related sources at a time when virtually no German Old Testament scholars were even referring to them. Of course, Burney could not know anything about Ugarit and Mari, with their epoch-making contributions to our understanding of the Old Testament.

C. *The Chronology of Judges.*

Burney was careful not to attempt any detailed analysis of the chronology of Judges, though he did mention a number of then current reconstructions of the chronological tradition which appears in the Hebrew Bible. He recognized that the early material was partly based on the use of a forty-year period as a general term, though he could not have understood that Hebrew *dôr* in the early books of the Bible means "life-time," in the sense of Etruscan-Roman *saeculum* or early Greek *genea*, and that forty years was the conventional numerical equivalent for "generation" among Phoenicians as well as Israelites. On these points see my observations in *BASOR*, 163(1961), pp. 50 f. and *CAH*[2] II, Chap. XXXIII (1966), pp. 39 f.

Burney's approach to the chronology was impaired by what was then a common view, that Amraphel of Gen. 14 was to be identified with Hammurapi of Babylon—which was entirely erroneous, since the true form of the latter name is now known from Ugaritic inscriptions to have been *'Ammurapi'*. (For my latest views in regard to the identification of Amraphel, see *BASOR*, 163 [1961], pp. 49 f., n. 67, and *YGC* [Am. ed., 1968], p. 68.) At that time Babylonian chronology was still greatly inflated, following the erroneous ideas of some neo-Babylonian scholars, and so cautious modern historians were dating Hammurapi about 2100 B.C. Now we know that Hammurapi's accession fell in the eighteenth century—in my own opinion, in or about 1728 B.C. I take much the same view of the fundamental historicity of Patriarchal tradition that was taken by Burney in 1918, but date the westward migration of Abraham some three centuries after the date allowed by Burney, or, according to my own chronology, some five centuries before the Exodus.

Burney was very cautious about trying to date the Exodus, but he obviously tended to prefer a date in the thirteenth century B.C. to one in the fifteenth. In my opinion we must still date the Exodus in the early years of Ramesses the Great, as I have been dating it for nearly fifty years. But the approximate year has fluctuated according to the latest plausible astronomical-calendrical results of specialists in this area of Egyptology. I see little escape today from a date about 1297, at the lowest ebb of Egyptian control of Asia after the disastrous defeat at Kadesh-on-the-Orontes in the fifth year of Ramesses II. The Egyptian chronology, which seems now to be correct, has been proposed by M. B. Rowton and is rather reluctantly accepted by R. A. Parker, who is the foremost authority today on such problems. For a fuller account of my reasons for this date, see *YGC* (Am. ed., 1968), pp. 156-164, 273 f.

The date of the Conquest is more problematical, since it took a much longer time than might be assumed from some of the traditions in Joshua (see below on Judges 1). The critical phase of the Conquest was almost certainly the occupation of the towns of the Shephelah about 1234 B.C. This date can be fixed closely by the fact that ancient Lachish fell after a bowl was inscribed with a hieratic text relating to the collection of tribute, and almost certainly dated in the fourth year of Merneptah, that is (according to the new Rowton chronology in *CAH*²), in or about the year 1234 B.C. This bowl was found by J. L. Starkey in the ash-filled debris from the destruction of the last Bronze Age occupation of the town. Since practically all the sherds of this broken bowl were found in an area about a meter square, there can be no question of sherds out of context or of a bowl which had been moved from one place to another. The bowl was actually found in the debris from the destruction of the level of occupation in question.

We now have an admirable general survey of the relation between archaeological finds and the traditions of the Conquest by Paul W. Lapp, "The Conquest of Palestine in the Light of Archaeology" (*Concordia Theological Monthly* 38 [1967], pp. 283-300). There is also new evidence of significance for the duration of the Israelite occupation of Transjordan before the Conquest of Western Palestine began. For some of this, see the article by Otto Eissfeldt, "Protektorat der Midianiter über ihre Nachbarn im letzten Viertel des 2. Jahrtausends v. Chr.," *JBL*, 87 (1968), 383-393. I fully accept Eissfeldt's approach and expect to publish an article on the Midianite caravan trade in the Herbert Gordon May anniversary volume (see my observations as quoted by Eissfeldt in the article to which I have referred). In my opinion, the "Mosaic" occupation of Eastern Palestine lasted for several decades—possibly for as much as half-a-century. This was well remembered by early Israelite tradition as preserved in later documentary compilations in Numbers 22 ff. Individual stages in the chronology of Judges may now be fixed roughly by archaeological means. For example, Philistine influence in the hill-country began to grow after the early twelfth century; the fall of Dan (Laish) is in the process of being fixed, by the excavations of A. Biran, about the late twelfth century B.C. The destruction of Shechem by Abimelech may also be dated toward the end of the twelfth century; the destruction of Shiloh by the Philistines (confirmed in Ps. 78 and especially in two passages in Jer.) may be dated about the middle of the eleventh century B.C. or a little later, as we know from the results of H. Kjaer's excavations at Seilun. Joseph A. Callaway's article on the chronology of Iron Age Ai (*JBL*, 82 [1968], 312-320) illustrates the error into which an excellent archaeologist may be led by overlooking evidence; by failing to utilize already published evidence from Shiloh, as well as the results of the work of J. L. Kelso and the writer at Bethel (now published by Kelso and Swauger), he has actually dated the destruction of pre-Israelite Ai by Joshua well after the destruction of Shiloh by the Philistines in the middle of the eleventh century B.C. or later; the pottery evidence for this is very clear. I directed the most relevant excavations at Bethel and Gibeah myself, and was a frequent visitor at the excavations at Shiloh and Ai; the collar-rimmed store-jars of all these sites fall into two classes, identical in shape, just as stated by Callaway. The second of these two series was characteristic of the period of Saul at Gibeah and had not yet come into use at all before the destruction of Shiloh by the Philistines. The Hebrew and Syriac texts agree in Josh. 8:17 that "there was no man left in Ai and Bethel who did not go out after Israel." The omission of "and Bethel" by the Greek recensions is to be judged on the same basis as

so many other omissions in either Hebrew or Greek texts of the Pentateuch and Former Prophets (Joshua—II Kings), now especially well documented by the Qumran MSS of Samuel, where the original text was substantially longer than any of the recensions. (See also immediately below, § D on Chapter I.)

D. Judges 1 (Burney, pp. lv-cxix, 1-34).

The whole question of the original occupation of Palestine by the ancestors of Israel is now much more complex than Burney could ever have imagined. In the first place, we now have an increasingly impressive body of clear-cut evidence that the higher culture of early Israel was derived almost entirely from Mesopotamia (including Babylonia) in such areas as cosmogony, customary law of two principal types, and tribal traditions. In *YGC* (1968, Chapter II) important new attestations of parallels between the cosmogonies of Mesopotamia and Israel, published in the past two or three years, are referred to or described in detail, and striking new light on the Patriarchal family laws of mixed Hurro-Babylonian type is also easily available in the work of E. A. Speiser (see especially his Anchor *Genesis* [1964]). Most remarkable, however, is the new light on the ancestral affiliations of different groups of the Patriarchal Hebrews. It is now clear, for example, thanks especially to the work of A. Finet, that both the *Banū-sim'al*, "Children of the North," and *Banū-yamīna*, "Children of the South," were identified with the *'Apiru/'Abiru* (which was still written by all scholars *Ḫabiru* in Burney's time). Moreover, the principal tribes of the southern branch of the Mesopotamian *'Apiru* were the *'Awnanum, Yaḫrurum* or *Yaḫurrum* (still called *Ya'uru* by the Assyrians in the 13th century B.C.), the *Ub-rapi'u*, and the *Yama'ammu*, which correspond to the extinct early Israelite groupings *'Awnan* (Onan,) *Ya'or* (Er), and *Raphe'* (Rapha), and in the last case apparently to the tribe from which the pre-15th dynasty Hyksos chieftains with Semitic names (e.g., *Ya'qub-'Al*) sprang. It is interesting to note that these three names are attached to tribes which had no offspring, that is, they had become extinct but were remembered in tradition. If we combine the evidence of the Testament of Jacob in Gen. 49 (*YGC* [Am., ed., 1968], pp. 266 f. and 270 f.), it becomes clear that the original Hebrew settlement in Palestine was a long-continuing movement, and that a number of—if not most of—the later tribes were already living in or near territory, later assigned to them after the Conquest proper, quite early in the Patriarchal age. When members of the same tribes came up from Egypt with the Mosaic body, they naturally settled, whenever possible, beside their kinsmen. This explains why Judah was already settled in the hill-country of that tribe in the traditions of Jacob, and why Jacob and Ephraim himself are said to have occupied parts of central Palestine in the Patriarchal age. This is confirmed by the fact that the little state of Shechem, ruled by Lab'ayu in the Amarna period, was almost certainly Hebrew long before the Conquest, just as affirmed by Biblical and early post-Biblical tradition.

In all such movements of extremely mobile tribes and clans we must expect to see a great deal of shifting, splitting, and regrouping, as clearly happened in the case of the clans of Manasseh, judging from the Biblical lists and traditions, confirmed or corrected by the Ostraca of Samaria. In Arab tribal history, notably in Palestine, we find the same sort of thing happening. Details of the Testament of Jacob (Gen. 49) make it clear that the situation of the different tribes was very different at the time that the oldest tribal sayings were put into form. Some tribes apparently had previously been seminomadic, whereas others were apparently already quite settled; some seem to have been engaged largely in tribal raids and banditry, while others were quiet, peaceful wage earners. Especially in the stories of Abraham and in the Testament of Jacob, we find clear indications that some were donkey-caravaneers while others appear as vintagers. But these early Hebrews were as a rule far from being barbarians, even though they may not have been particularly peace loving, and they may often have been landless. This follows from the fact that practically all trade was then conveyed on donkey-back, and that donkey caravaneers formed a very large class in all the countries of the ancient East. It has, however, been a great surprise to learn that the First Dynasty of Babylon, that of Hammurapi, and the contemporary Assyrian dynasty of Shamshi-adad I, from whom practically all subsequent Assyrian kings seem to have descended, were closely related by blood and ties of alliance with such Hebrew tribes as the *'Awnanum* and *Yaḫrurum*. In fact, both their genealogical trees include these two Hebrew tribes among their ancestors.

In Burney's time it was still impossible to foresee any of these or many other important discoveries bearing on the issue. It was equally impossible to realize the great antiquity of the tribal traditions of Israel. Yet Burney saw much farther and more correctly than most of his contemporaries and successors.

In the light of the preceding remarks, it becomes clear that past efforts to define the exact movements of the tribes in Palestine after the first migration, no later than the nineteenth century B.C., are futile. In most cases the geographical distances are so small that they may perfectly well have wandered back and forth over the country for generations before deciding to take up permanent residence in a given area. Usually these pre-Conquest settlements were determined by the basic considerations of availability of water, grazing land, bush country, and scrub forest where there was a measure of security. But there were also such important considerations as proximity to trade routes and opportunity for planting vineyards, where Hebrew groups could have easy access to caravan routes for normal caravaneering or for raiding caravans, after which they could find shelter in suitable hilly terrain with plenty of vegetation, with caves and rock fortresses, and especially with forest cover conveniently accessible. As M. B. Rowton has pointed out (see *Studies in Honor of Benno Landsberger,* Chicago, 1965, pp. 375-387), all over southwestern Asia the *'Apiru* seem to have preferred wooded and scrub country for security reasons, to more open country where they could be more easily attacked by royal security troops or avenging local raiders. In such areas, vineyards and winepresses were a natural means of livelihood.

In the light of archaeology, it is decidedly unlikely, in my opinion, that Judges 1 is always more original than the relevant chapters of Joshua. This was pointed out cogently by G. Ernest Wright ("The Literary and Historical Problem of Joshua 10 and Judges 1," *JNES,* 5 [1946], 105-114). I do not mean for a moment that the chapter is not independently valuable. I have no idea what its immediate documentary source may have been, but it would seem to have been found by the Deuteronomist historian somewhere, and he correctly recognized that there were elements in this text which were not found in other material at his disposal. This would explain why it was included and why it repeats a number of stories which are told in almost the same language in Joshua. Under the circumstances, there is no way that I can see of dating such events mentioned in the chapter as the conflict between the men of Judah and Simeon and the mysterious Adonibezek. This episode does not suit the time of Joshua at all, and the events in question may well have occurred some time during the previous century or two. Most significant is the account of the destruction of Bethel (vv. 22-26), which is clearly more original than the account in Josh. 8, where the men of Bethel are also mentioned together with those of Ai (see above, § C).

E. The Early Judges of Israel (Burney, pp. 35-77).

1. Virtually nothing more is known now about the oppressions of Cushan-Rishathaim and Eglon than was known in Burney's time. Burney suggested for the former name an

impossible Cossaean (Kassite) derivation, which he credits to his former teacher, C. J. Ball. Since then a good many other suggestions have been made, including some of my own, which are historically more plausible, but are equally impossible to demonstrate. On the antiquity of the poetic quotation from the time of Caleb and Othniel—or very soon afterwards—which we find in Joshua 15 and Judges 1, see my discussion in *YGC* (Am. ed.), pp. 47 f. It seems likely, therefore, that the mysterious figure of Cushan was somehow embedded in the Othniel tradition. But this does not clarify the identity of this particular oppressor or his ethnic background. I refrain from repeating or adding to previous conjectures.

2. Nor is there anything new about the figure of Eglon, king of Moab. By this time Moab was certainly an independent state, and it is entirely reasonable to suppose that it was in the process of expanding its borders after it had been freed from Midianite domination (see O. Eissfeldt, *JBL,* 87 [1968], 383 ff.).

3. Shamgar ben-Anath (Judges 3:31) was considered by Burney to be an historical figure, but he had only a few speculative observations to make about him. That Shamgar was historical he recognized from the fact that he is referred to in the Song of Deborah as having flourished shortly before Deborah (Judg. 5:6). Incidentally, I myself suspect that we should read *Yabîn* instead of *Ya'el* in that verse; some early scribe—possibly rhapsodist—confused the name with that of the heroine Jael mentioned later in the Song of Deborah. This Jabin was probably not king of Hazor, which had been destroyed by Joshua and was not thereafter a Canaanite capital, as we know from the excavations of Y. Yadin. The Jabin of the prose narrative was presumably a Canaanite prince of another important town in the north, possibly Taanach (see below). However this may be, the name Shamgar was plausibly identified by the late Martin Noth with a Hurrian Shimikari, though a Canaanite origin of the name is not impossible. My former view that he was prince of Beth-Anath, and hence, accord-

ing to a usage common among Aramaeans and Israelites in the tenth-eighth centuries B.C., called "son of Anath," remains entirely possible, but there are now indications that the name "Ben-Anath" may have been fairly common among Canaanites. It would mean "son of (the goddess) Anath," who was commonly represented in Canaanite art as suckling kings and other important people at her own breasts. (This is confirmed by references in the Ugaritic epics.)

Since 1921 (*JPOS*, I [1921], 55 ff., where I proposed this interpretation of the patronymic) I have also suggested that Shamgar may have been a Canaanite hero of the war against the invading Sea Peoples. According to the revised chronology of the *Cambridge Ancient History*, this would locate him somewhere in the period of the first Philistine raids or invasions, between *c.* 1235 and 1175 B.C. Since the Sea Peoples were the common enemy of both Canaanites and Israelites, it would not be surprising to find a Canaanite champion also accepted as an Israelite hero in the course of time.

F. The Song of Deborah (Burney, pp. 78-176).

1. Burney's treatment of Judges 5 was far ahead of his time. As I wrote in my own first paper on the subject ("The Earliest Forms of Hebrew Verse," *JPOS*, 2 [1922], 69-86), "To him [Burney] we owe the first clear explanation of the unique poetic style of the Song, and the invention of the term 'Climactic parallelism.'" In this respect Burney's treatment of the Song is in striking contrast to Haupt's (*Wellhausen Festschrift*, Giessen, 1914, pp. 191-226). Where Haupt had eliminated all repetition of words and phrases from the entire Song of Deborah, Burney recognized that the repetition itself was the most characteristic feature of its style. Here Haupt has proved to have been entirely wrong, and Burney's chief weakness was that he could not at that time understand the exact nature of the style, so he failed to insert repetitions where they had

accidentally dropped out by haplography. On the subject of repetitive style, see now the first chapter of *YGC* (1968). Stylistically, the Song of Deborah is intermediate between the Song of Miriam (Ex. 15) and the so-called Song of Moses (Deut. 32), which I date, following Eissfeldt, about the third quarter of the eleventh century B.C. There is a much closer relation in time between the Song of Miriam and the Song of Deborah than there is between the Song of Deborah and Deut. 32. The resemblance between Deborah and Miriam appears in verse structure, repetitive style, and such stylistic features as similarity in the words spoken by the enemy in Ex. 15. A date for the Song of Deborah after the middle of the twelfth century seems unlikely, and I continue to attribute the composition of the poem roughly to about 1150 B.C. or a little earlier. There is no need to go into detail about my own present historical interpretation of the poem here. It must be noted, however, that the name Sisera is no longer an enigma, since it has turned up as the name of a Luvian prince Sisaruwa in the Ugaritic tablets of the thirteenth century B.C. (For the name [Greek *Sisara*] see *YGC* [1968], p. 251, n. 127.) Now that the name appears from its form to be Luvian, the question arises as to whether Sisera was a Luvian in Canaanite service, or was the head of an invading band of Philistines or other Sea Peoples. That the Philistines spoke a Luvian dialect is now virtually certain; see *CAH*^{2} II (1966), Chap. 33, p. 30. For the general historical background see most recently my brief survey in *The Biblical Period from Abraham to Ezra* (Harper Torchbook 102), 38-40.

2. Burney's experiment in transcribing the Song of Deborah in its original phonetic form (pp. 160 ff.) is a remarkable tour de force for its time. As observed above, the metrical reconstruction is weaker than either the phonology or the translation. In this respect Haupt was superior, in spite of the Procrustean bed into which he tried to force the meter (which was undoubtedly mixed, though structurally regular).

Burney's phonology was based on a systematic analysis of the Canaanite forms and glosses in the Amarna Tablets, in the light of what was then known about comparative Semitic grammar and early Northwest Semitic spelling. Naturally, during the War years in which Burney wrote his volume, not nearly enough was known about the precise regularities of accentual and other phonetic shifts. The latter gradually emerged, largely from my own research, beginning in the twenties and continued actively to the present. It is brought together in my own publications and those of Zellig S. Harris, *Development of the Canaanite Dialects* (New Haven, 1939), as well as of Frank M. Cross and D. N. Freedman (especially in their *Early Hebrew Orthography* New Haven, 1952). Basic material will be found also in my *Vocalization of the Egyptian Syllabic Orthography* (New Haven, 1934) and *The Proto-Sinaitic Inscriptions and Their Decipherment* (Cambridge, Mass., 1966). The results of the former monograph are now accepted by all competent scholars. On the other hand, general acceptance of some positions taken in the latter will have to await future archaeological discovery. It is, however, true that my views with regard to the consonantal shift at the end of the Bronze Age, as well as on the earlier and later shifts in accent and vowel quantity, have already been confirmed by the progress of Ugaritic and related investigation since the early thirties of this century.

Of course, new Northwest Semitic words and forms are being recovered all the time. The latest example to come to my attention is *šabayu*, "captive(s)," in a new cuneiform tablet from Taanach, corresponding exactly to Massoretic *šebyĕkā* (Judg. 5:12), in spite of the usual emendation to *šôbekā* (followed by Burney).

G. *The Midianite Invasion, Gideon and Abimelech (Burney, pp. 176-289).*

1. In Judg. 6-9 we have what may well be described as

the earliest example of historical composition in prose in the Hebrew Bible. There are some poetic quotations, and a short poem in prose transmission is quoted in the name of Jotham son of Gideon. Burney's discussion of these chapters (pp. 176-289) is still one of the best studies to appear on the subject. New archaeological evidence has, however, clarified the picture greatly. It is probable that the events in question took place quite early in the period of the Judges, and that my own past tendency to date them between *c.* 1100 and 1050 B.C. was too low for the evidence. In my present opinion it is more likely that these events must be dated entirely in the twelfth century, chiefly in its second half. The raids of the Midianites and their North Arabian allies stand in striking contrast to the war between the Israelites in Transjordan and the Midianites described in Num. 31 (see the discussion by O. Eissfeldt, with contributions from the present writer, in *JBL,* 87 [1968]). In the latter the Midianites are portrayed with vast numbers of donkeys, but without camels; in Judg. 6 they appear with innumerable camels, but no donkeys are mentioned. In other words, either one set of traditions was entirely wrong, or there was a dramatic shift from donkey nomadism to camel nomadism between the lifetime of Moses and that of Gideon, a century or more later. I have maintained since the late thirties that the effective domestication of camels in southwestern Asia began no earlier than the twelfth or thirteenth century B.C., and that the references to the great camel raids of Gideon's time are the first clear-cut evidence found anywhere for the full domestication of camels. Subsequent discoveries have only strengthened the evidence for this late dating of the introduction of camels as an important economic factor in Near Eastern history. So far not one Assyro-Babylonian inscription, among economic texts of all sorts and letters by the tens of thousands, has yielded a single mention of the domesticated Arabian camel in cuneiform texts before the ninth century B.C. (The only exceptions are in vocabularies devoted chiefly to wild animals.) The first absolutely unquestionable representation of the camel in art dates from late tenth-century Carchemish. The first rock-cut representations of camels from central Arabia have just been published by E. Anati, *Rock-art in Central Arabia,* I (Louvain, 1968), *passim.* Anati has found that all representations of camels during the epigraphic stage, after the beginning of the first millennium B.C., are of domesticated camels, wherever a decision can be made. In the earlier "herding-hunting stage" which came to an end with the introduction of writing, toward the end of the second millennium B.C., camels were in a wild state and were being hunted. This is in complete agreement with the evidence of our excavations in South Arabia, as well as with the scattered evidence all over southwestern Asia and Egypt. Camels were, of course, perfectly well known in the wild state from the earliest times on down to the late second millennium B.C., if not later.

In view, however, of the great utility of camels for their milk and hair as well as for their flesh and hide, it is more than likely that they were often kept in a semi-domesticated state and it may well be that the now famous "kites" (enclosures formed by dry stone walls converging toward a narrow passage which leads into a pocket surrounded by the same type of wall) were used in part for rounding up herds of semi-wild camels in order to milk them and cut their hair, etc. But Num. 31 shows clearly that in an extremely tenacious early tradition (which cannot possibly have been invented in the seventh century B.C.) the Midianites were provided with donkeys at the general ratio of five donkeys to one man, which I have shown elsewhere (*BASOR,* 163 [1961], pp. 41 f.) to have been the normal number of donkeys per man in donkey caravans of the Twelfth Egyptian Dynasty in the early second millennium B.C. I have been collecting evidence, which will be presented in the Herbert Gordon May anniversary volume, on the Midianites as donkey caravaneers in the third quarter of the second millennium B.C. As of now, the evidence indicates that the importation of spices from South Arabia by donkey caravans began no later than the 15th century

B.C. and continued actively until taken over, about the twelfth century, by camel caravaneers. At first sight such early donkey caravans in Arabia may sound surprising, but a little consideration should alter the impression. West Arabia was much better watered, relatively speaking, than the rest of the peninsula, since the north-south mountain chains catch the rain and enable the ground to be watered both by rainfall and by deflector-dam irrigation. In fact, there are no extensive stretches of waterless desert to interrupt normal communications at any point along the watershed ridges of West Arabia. Where no convenient wells or springs were available, water could be carried on donkey-back, just as it was carried, according to the Mari Letters, across the North Syrian desert.

2. The Gideon narrative contains extremely important evidence for the missionary activity of the comparatively small Yahwist minority in the new tribal confederation. Burney's discussion is still useful, though naturally out of date as the result of archaeological discoveries in Palestinian sites of Late Bronze and Early Iron Ages, as well as because of the extraordinary finds at Ugarit, which throw so much light on our knowledge of Canaanite religion and enable us to get a much more balanced idea of the relation between Yahwism and Baalism in this period. (See my discussion in *YGC* [1968], Chapters III and IV.)

3. In spite of the importance of the figure of Gideon in early Hebrew history, it would seem that in its extant form in Judges it serves mainly as a prelude to the account of Abimelech's attempt to establish a kingdom in Israel with its capital at Shechem. The whole problem of Shechem has been greatly illuminated by the excavations carried on there by G. Ernest Wright and his associates. (See especially his *Shechem: The Biography of a Biblical City* [New York, 1965]; and the reports of each campaign in *BASOR*, including especially the account of the fifth campaign in No. 180 [1965], pp. 7-41.) The excavations at Shechem prove that the town had not been destroyed by the Israelites in the general period of Joshua, and we may therefore safe-

ly accept the total absence of any mention of a destruction of Shechem in the book of Joshua, as well as the clear tradition that Joshua made Shechem the center of the Israelite confederation, as historically correct.

In the sacred area which formed a fortified *temenos* on the north side of the town, the excavators—continuing and correcting the results of previous German work—uncovered the remains of successive temples and cultic installations beginning in Middle Bronze II B (about 1700 B.C.) and continuing down to the destruction of the final cultic installation on the site in the late twelfth century B.C. This destruction is no doubt identical with the destruction by Abimelech which must, therefore, be dated no later than about 1100 B.C. and perhaps as early as *c.* 1125. This sacred area seems to have borne the name *Al-ili,* "City of God," in the Amarna Letters (*CAH*[2] II, Chap. 20, p. 19). In Hebrew tradition the name of the same area is *Migdal Šekem,* literally, "Fortress of Shechem," which was presumably the name of the area before the town walls included the lower city as well. The identity of Baal-Berith and El-Berith is still uncertain, but the most plausible explanation is that it identifies Yahweh as lord of the tribal confederation with the old chief divinity of the city, whose earlier name is not otherwise known.

H. Jephthah and the Ammonites (Burney, pp. 295-333).

The Ammonites were late in settling down, as may be inferred from the absence of any specific reference to them in the account of the Conquest of Eastern Palestine by Israel. Edomites, Moabites, the Amorites of Sihon, and the kingdom of Bashan are all mentioned frequently, but there is scarcely a word about the Ammonites. It was not until later that the Ammonites found their way into the tradition. What there is sounds strangely elusive, and almost certainly reflects later editorial additions—nearly all Deuteronomic. The reason for late settlement of the Ammonites is probably, as I pointed out in *Miscellanea Biblica B.*

Ubach (Montserrat, 1953), pp. 131-136, that they were unable to gain sufficient strength from nesting on the edge of the Syrian desert, squeezed between it and greater Gilead, to attack Israel. As pointed out then, "More than any other Syrian state, Ammon was dependent on caravan trade for its continued prosperity." Donkey caravaneering was not feasible for the Ammonites, who were separated from the old north-and-south trade routes by stretches of true desert, which were not feasible for donkey caravans. Camel caravan trade would normally expand very rapidly after its effective introduction in the twelfth century B.C. We do not hear of any invasion of Israel by the Ammonites until the time of Jephthah, which later tradition placed 300 years before the Israelite conquest of Gilead and Moab (Judges 11:26). In Gen. 15, the fourth *dôr* in verse 16 is obviously equivalent to the 400 years of verse 13; see my discussion in *BASOR* 163, (1961), pp. 50 f. on the older meaning of *dôr,* "lifetime" (= Old Assyrian *dârum*). If Jephthah flourished, as seems likely, in the eleventh century, this would carry us back three lifetimes or 200 years plus to about the early thirteenth century.

The statement attributed to Jephthah that Chemosh was the chief divinity of Ammon has generally been understood as confusion, on the part of the later Israelite editor of Jephthah's speech, between the chief god of Moab, Chemosh (or, as we find on the Mesha Stone, Ashtar-Chemosh), and Milcom, the chief god of Ammon. It is, however, very doubtful whether this inference is quite correct. In the first place, the story of Lot's daughters shows clearly that Moab and Ammon were believed to be very close in tribal ancestry. Furthermore, these divinities are already mentioned in the Ugaritic lists of gods as *Kmš* and *Mlkm*. The later vocalization is certain in both cases: *Kammush* and *Milkum* (for older *Malikum*). Both these names were designations of Nergal and his Northwest Semitic counterpart Resheph. It is, therefore, probable that both peoples worshipped the same divinity under both names, and that the names became specialized as time went on. On the nature of the divinity Ashtar-Chemosh, identified with the morning star as lord of heaven, see my discussion in *YGC* (Am. ed. 1968), pp. 239 ff.

No new light has been shed by recent discovery on the meaning of the sacrifice of Jephthah's daughter, whether she was condemned to perpetual virginity, or was to be a human sacrifice. The arguments on both sides are perhaps equally weak.

I. Samson (Burney, pp. 340-408).

The story of Samson is definitely based on a popular narrative which was largely, if not entirely, in poetic form. See *YGC* (Am. ed., 1968), pp. 22 f., where I render the passage Judg. 15:16:

"With the jawbone of a donkey
Have I mightily raged,
With the jawbone of a donkey
Have I slain a thousand men!"

Note that Burney was fully aware of the stylistic character of this verse but that his translation was rather eccentric, in the absence of sufficient external linguistic evidence:

"With the red ass's jawbone I have reddened them bright red.
With the red ass's jawbone I have smitten a thousand men."

The first line sounds much more like Old English verse than it does like any conceivable Hebrew poetry of that period. Burney exaggerates the mythological elements in the story of Samson, much as I was inclined to do at the beginning of my scholarly career (which coincided approximately with the writing of Burney's *Judges*). It must always be remembered that, as Hugo Winckler used to insist, in all oral tradition there is a tendency to fuse mythological motives with historical events when there seems to be striking similarity—in detail or wording—between them.

I overemphasized this point in my discussion of "Historical and Mythical Elements in the Story of Joseph," *JBL,* 37 (1918), 111-143, where I followed Winckler's approach quite closely in essential respects. After fifty years of archaeological research, it can now be said that the story of Samson is faithful to actual conditions in or about the late twelfth century B.C. in the Shephelah and adjacent Philistine plains. It is highly unlikely that Samson was a mythical figure, though his name is probably a kenning (Arabic *kunyah*) like the name of Gideon (see *YGC* [Am. ed., 1968], p. 199, n. 101). One reason for my increasingly conservative point of view is precisely that the poetic quotations in the story of Samson are definitely archaic in type—intermediate in form between normal Canaanite repetitive style of the thirteenth century (found also in the Song of Miriam) and the various tenth-century poetic styles with which we are now increasingly familiar.

J. The Final Narratives of Judges (Burney, pp. 408-494).

1. The story of Micah and the Danites (Judges 17-18) is extremely important from the standpoint of early Israelite history, and it is well treated by Burney. The excavations recently carried out by A. Biran at Tell el-Qâḍī have brought to light important occupation of the Middle Bronze Age, less important of the Late Bronze, followed by a destruction in the middle of Iron I—say about 1100 B.C. This work has established the historicity of the tradition in question, which contains many elements of extraordinary value for our understanding of early Israelite religious life and organization. On the mysterious problem of the ephod, see my discussion in *YGC* (Am. ed., 1968), pp. 200 ff., where I propose a new interpretation of this enigmatic object, based largely on Ugaritic material as well as on the important work of Hermann Thiersch, *Ependytes und Ephod: Gottesbild und Priesterkleid im alten Vorderasien* (Stuttgart, 1936). In my opinion the ephod was a surrogate for the image of Yahweh (which no Israelite was al-

lowed to make or to see). On the analogy of Phoenician as well as Mesopotamian parallels, the divinity of heaven was often represented as clad in the *astrochitōn,* which was a garment of precious metal studded with stars representing the starry firmament. Since the representation was itself of base metal or wood, covered with gold or silver leaf, it would naturally stand by itself, and so it was possible for the ephod to function as a symbolic image without being a representation of Yahweh. The original ephod, as known from Old Assyrian commercial documents of the Patriarchal age and from Ugaritic references, was a wraparound robe of conical shape which would stand by itself and might be variously decorated. It may be recalled that cult images, among both pagans and Christians, have always shown a tendency to become more and more elaborately adorned, so that the dress itself frequently attracts more attention than the anthropomorphic figure of the divinity clad in the robe or tiara, or both. How plausible this explanation of the ephod is, from the standpoint of Israelite religion, may be seen from the conceptual analogy between it and the image of a young bull (*'ēgel*) on which the invisible figure of Yahweh stood at the sanctuaries of Bethel and Dan.

2. The story of the Levite of Bethlehem and the civil war which broke out after the atrocity of Gibeah (Judges 19-21) is more enigmatic, and the extremely high figures for the men of Israel given in it point to a late date in the history of Israel—presumably no earlier than the Divided Monarchy and possibly as late as the seventh century. The composition and redaction of these chapters are very hard to analyze, and I am skeptical of most efforts to do so. Burney's detailed treatment contains much of value to the contemporary student, because of the continuing obscurity of the problems involved. Archaeology has shed extremely little light on these chapters. It is true that remains of a pre-Saulide occupation of the town later called Gibeah of Saul were found in the excavations carried out by me in 1922 and 1933, and resumed by Paul Lapp recently. But there is no completely satisfying proof that Gibeah of

Benjamin, which was so thoroughly destroyed according to this narrative, was really located at Tell el-Fûl, where there was only a very small village at that time. On the other hand, the attempt to identify it with Geba, modern Jeba', is contrary to the explicit indications of 19:11-15, which definitely suggest that the first village on the watershed-ridge road running northward from Jerusalem is intended. Perhaps the most reasonable supposition is that the site in question was actually Tell el-Fûl, but that the original story was considerably exaggerated during long oral transmission. In any case, it is almost impossible to imagine the tribes of Israel allied to attack a single unfortified Benjaminite village. In such cases, the progress of knowledge often shows that details which seem most suspect are quite correct and that portions of the narrative which seem to us reasonable actually come from some other source—in this case probably one of the Patriarchal narratives such as the story of Lot and his daughters at the destruction of Sodom. I cannot accept the often-expressed view that the story of Sodom is modeled after the episode of Gibeah—and yet it may be correct. In the absence of direct evidence, it is imprudent to make conjectures without strong indirect reasons—e.g., from style.

II. THE BOOK OF KINGS

A. Structure and Text of Kings (Burney, pp. ix-xliv).

1. There has been no significant addition to our understanding of the structure of the books of Kings during the past two-thirds of a century. The reason is simply that we do not have any substantial additions to early Hebrew literature, and so cannot go beyond the indications of the text. Form-criticism has indeed been developed as a separate branch of investigation, but results are only significant, as a rule, when we have sufficient identity of form to make parallels in meaning significant.

The most important recent contribution to our understanding of *Kings* as a whole is Martin Noth's convincing demonstration that the historical books from Deuteronomy to II Kings inclusive are chiefly the work of a single author who compiled and edited already existing material. Since we have discussed Noth's contribution in our Prolegomenon to Burney's *Judges,* it is not necessary here to go into details, except to point out that there is a difference of opinion as to when the work of the Deuteronomist proper came to an end and how much of the latter part of II Kings is to be considered as supplementary matter added to bring the work up to date. I consider it incredible that the numerous sources, both written and oral, used by the Deuteronomist can possibly have been available to any considerable extent after the destruction of Jerusalem and the complete devastation of Judah. The most reasonable *Sitz im Leben* for the work is precisely the reign of Josiah, with the king's well-attested interest in earlier Hebrew history and institutions. As I have pointed out, with illustrations from different lands of the Near East (*FSAC,* Baltimore, 1940, pp. 240 ff.; 1957, pp. 314 ff.), there was a great revival of interest in antiquity in several countries during the seventh-sixth centuries B.C., an interest which gave rise to a considerable body of what today would be called antiquarian or archaizing literature. While it is difficult to say just where the original Deuteronomist may have concluded his work, a very good place to end would be II Kings 23:25. There may possibly have been a series of additions, but in the light of the complex relationship between the end of Kings and chapter 52 of Jeremiah, there were probably different additions in different early manuscripts—as we now know to have been true in the case of the book of Job.

2. In his *Kings,* Burney followed his teacher, S. R. Driver, closely and did not go astray. Later scholars were to abandon the correct interpretation of the textual evidence which had already been given by Paul de Lagarde and G. F. Moore, as well as by S. R. Driver in his *Notes on the Hebrew Text . . . of the Books of Samuel.* An admirable discussion of the whole question of the text of

Kings was given by J. A. Montgomery with the assistance of H. S. Gehman and the latter's student, J. W. Wevers, as well as of H. M. Orlinsky. Montgomery's treatment of the Lucianic recension on pp. 18-21 of his volume (1951) is very good, but since Montgomery himself died early in 1949, shortly before the Dead Sea Scrolls had become generally known, it was left for F. M. Cross, Jr. and his pupils to carry on the work of analyzing and evaluating the Lucianic text. (Cf. for the publications of Cross and his pupils my Prolegomenon to Burney's *Judges,* Section A, 2.) In the case of the book of Kings there is still a great deal to be done because of the paucity of our sources. It has become clear, thanks to the discovery of an intermediate fragmentary text at Qumran which shows similarities both to the Hebrew Kings and the Hebrew Chronicles, that Chronicles is a more important source for the text of Kings than has commonly been recognized. Burney is careful not to mention the text of the Chronicler—a procedure which was probably wise two-thirds of a century ago, but which is no longer tenable. Quite aside from the discoveries at Qumran, which make the usual late date of the Chronicler increasingly improbable, there is the continued discovery of data from archaeological sources which confirm details in the transmitted text of the Chronicler. This includes whole bodies of material which have previously been relegated to the realm of legend. I refer especially to such matters as the tribal and clan genealogies of I Chronicles, to the lists of functionaries, both royal and cultic, in the same Book, and to the validation of a host of historical and textual details. The cultic material, as well as the legal information, has also been greatly underestimated—note, for example, my treatment of the musical guilds of David in *ARI*[5] (1968), pp. 119 ff., and of the judicial reform of Jehoshaphat in the *Alexander Marx Jubilee Volume* (New York, 1950), pp. 61-82. Father J. D. Shenkel's treatment (*Chronology and Recensional Development in the Greek Text of Kings* [Cambridge, 1968]) of the chronology of Kings, from a strictly textual point of view, is a valuable supplement to Burney's synopsis in this volume, pp. xli ff. It is increasingly absurd to prefer the evidence of late versions and still later recensions of Kings to the early evidence of Chronicles.

B. Conclusions of the Court History of David's Succession, I Kings 1:1-2:46 (Burney, pp. 1-27).

Burney's treatment of the text follows the example of Driver's *Notes on the . . . Text of Samuel,* but includes more archaeological and historical data. It may, however, be considered as essentially a commentary and treated this way. Very little can be added to what has been said by scholars in the past about the unusual character of the account of David's last years and the succession to his throne. As pointed out by many scholars–notably by the great historian of antiquity, Eduard Meyer—this narrative is unique in the ancient world before Herodotus and is in some ways superior to the latter. Both the care with which the story is told and the dramatic skill of its style are worthy of this masterpiece of historical writing. It is, therefore, not surprising that there is scarcely any new light on the meaning of the text—disregarding the many conjectures which have been made by scholars with regard to the historical background of particular episodes.

C. History of the Reign of Solomon, I Kings 3:1-11:43 (Burney, pp. 27-173).

1. It is difficult to check details in the account of Solomon's reign because of the lack of independent historical sources and the almost total absence of any inscriptions from tenth-century Israel, aside from a few graffiti which *may* date from this period. The only real exception is the agricultural calendar of Gezer, on which see *ANET,* 320. The most significant information from it is the fact that there were boys' schools in Israel about 925 B.C., and that

the spelling was North Israelite, not the later Judaean orthography; also that simple poetic ditties were used for mnemonic purposes and writing practice. This is interesting in connection with the almost certain fact that there was a great upsurge of literary activity during the latter part of this century. Since this period was characterized by an inexplicable decline in the power of both Egypt and Assyria, it is not surprising that no references to David or Solomon have been found in the inscriptions of these countries. If it were not for the Gezer calendar one might indeed imagine that Israel was not yet literate at the time, since not a single inscribed seal or seal impression of this period has yet turned up. Nor are there any ostraca like those of Samaria from the eighth century, or like those of Lachish and Arad from the seventh-sixth centuries B.C. The reason for the lack of ostraca is probably that there was no general destruction of Israelite cities in the time of David or Solomon, and that public buildings then constructed were still in use after their time. Shishak's invasion *c.* 918 B.C. brought a certain amount of destruction, but nowhere does it seem to have been complete. Yet at any time discoveries in Jerusalem or elsewhere may yield monuments of this early period, since it is very hard to believe that a century which has yielded so many Phoenician and North Syrian inscriptions should not also have witnessed the erection of triumphal steles celebrating the victories and building operations of such powerful rulers as these two kings of Israel.

2. The material preserved in chapter 4 is quite fragmentary. There have been important additions to our knowledge of the later administrative divisions of Israel and, following a highly original study by A. Alt in 1913, now reprinted in *KSGVI,* II, pp. 76-89, there have been a number of significant studies using considerably expanded material discovered since then. In 1925 I published a long article, based on much additional material of archaeological and topographical nature, in *JPOS,* 5, 17-54. Most recently, G. E. Wright has prepared an important study, which should appear shortly.

On the wise men of I Kings 5.9 ff. (4:29 ff. in the English Bible), see my discussion in *ARI,* pp. 125-129, as well as in *YGC* (Am. ed., 1968), pp. 249 ff.

3. Burney devotes a good deal of attention to details of the building of the temple and its furnishing, including some illustrations and line drawings. Our comparative archaeological data have increased enormously in extent: see *ARI,* 142 ff., and especially G. E. Wright, *Biblical Archaeology* (Philadelphia and London, 1957), pp. 129-145. There are still many moot questions connected with the temple and its furnishings, since very few remains of comparable Syro-Phoenician buildings from the same period have been found. Continuing discoveries, however, do clarify details more and more; so we may hope before long for clarification of the principal aspects of temple construction and furnishings. When one stops to think about it, the progress in comparative archaeology which has been made during the two-thirds of a century since this volume of Burney's appeared, is really remarkable.

4. The information about Solomon's other building operations in chap. 9 has been considerably amplified, and in some cases further confused, by archaeological discoveries. Of the fortress cities built by Solomon, specifically Solomonic fortifications and other constructions have been found at Megiddo, Hazor, and now also at Gezer, just as indicated in I Kings 9:15. There is, however, some ambiguity with reference to the mention of Gezer, since Solomon's building of Gezer is mentioned again in verse 17 after a passage which deals with the reported attack on the city by the king of Egypt whose daughter Solomon married, in order to provide a dowry. This is extremely odd, since the population is said to have been Canaanite, though the entire Philistine plain (which had previously been conquered by David and was presumably subject to Solomon) lies between Egyptian territory along the northern coast of Sinai and native Israelite territory around the site of Gezer. For these and other reasons, I suggested in 1924 (*JPOS,* 4, 143 f.) that there had been an error in reading here, and

that the Gezer of vss. 15 and 16 was really Gerar, southeast of Gaza (see below), and the Gezer of verse 17 is in its proper place before Beth-horon the Nether. This suggestion has not generally been accepted, and still remains *sub judice,* though I cannot see any serious objection to it so far. The identification of Tell Jemmeh with Gerar by previous scholars, including the excavator, Sir Flinders Petrie, has proved to be wrong, and the true location of Gerar is at Tell Abu Ḫureirah, discovered about twenty years ago by a young Israeli but not yet excavated. This site agrees extraordinarily well with the Biblical and patristic evidence for Gerar, and the identification is almost certainly correct. Tell Abu Ḥureirah is about twelve miles east-southeast of Tell Jemmeh and nearly as far northeast of Sharuhen (Tell el-Fâr'ah). It was thus well outside of Philistia proper and close to the Egyptian frontier.

Juxtaposed with the first reference to the building of Gezer we also find mention of the building of Hazor and Megiddo. Several verses below there is a general reference to towns for chariots and horses (not horsemen). At Megiddo a magnificent layout of stables and storage-quarters for chariots and harness was excavated by P. L. O. Guy and his colleagues, who attributed them to the Solomonic period. There seems to be little doubt, judging from the explicit statements of the excavators and my own observations at the time, that there were successive levels of hydraulic lime plaster pavement (which is hard but not waterproof). It is not disputed that the latest phase of the stables is post-Solomonic and that they were finally destroyed about 815 B.C., probably in connection with the Syrian invasion mentioned in I Kings 13.

5. The account of the Queen of Sheba's visit to Solomon was apparently not taken seriously by Burney, since he has no comment on it. Today, however, there is no longer any real difficulty with its historicity, though there may be some exaggeration in the tradition as it stands. It is also possible that the lady was merely a wealthy noblewoman and not actually a reigning queen. In Burney's time the chronology

of the South Arabian inscriptions tended to be much too high (early), because of the tendency of many scholars, including especially Eduard Glaser, to date the Minaean kingdom before the early Sabaean instead of the reverse. This led to the dating of the older South Arabian inscriptions as far back as *c.* 1600 B.C., and it was easy to date the rise of Saba' to the end of the second millennium B.C. and the beginning of the first. The work of the expeditions organized by Wendell Phillips in 1950 and following years forced a very considérable reduction of dates and confirmed the low chronology according to which the Minaean kingdom followed the old Sabaean state, and not the other way around. But it also became clear as the result of the first two campaigns, both at Timna', capital of Qatabân, and at Hajar Bin Ḥumeid, that the beginnings of irrigation culture in the Western Aden Protectorate (now South Yemen) came no later than *c.* 1400 B.C., and that the foundation of the earliest towns along the old caravan route in Qatabân fell not far from 1000 B.C. (See my paper in the Eissfeldt *Festschrift, Von Ugarit nach Qumran* [Berlin, 1958], pp. 1-8.) In the Prolegomenon to Burney's *Judges,* I have discussed the succession of donkey-caravaneering and camel-caravaneering in Western Arabia. The former began no later than the 14th century B.C. and probably a century or two earlier; the latter began about the twelfth century B.C. By the time of Solomon, camel-caravan trade between Sheba and Palestine was in any case well developed, and the expedition of the "Queen of Sheba" can easily be explained as a step in the direction of organizing this trade, which was so profitable to both parties. Thanks to the work of A. J. Lundin, A. Jamme, and H. von Wissmann, it is now reasonably certain that the succession of Sabaean eponyms is preserved in the inscriptions as far back as the eighth or ninth, and possibly as early as the tenth or eleventh century B.C. on public inscriptions found at Ṣirwâḥ, which had been saved by Eduard Glaser's squeezes made at the end of the late nineteenth century.

6. In Burney's time it was quite impossible to say much

about the location of Ophir, which was a source of most of Solomon's precious metals, ivory, and monkeys. (On the supposed "peacocks" [*tukkîyîm*], see my remarks quoted by Bodenheimer in the *Interpreter's Dictionary of the Bible*, art. "Fauna," vol. II, p. 252a; see also *ARI*[5], 212, n. 16.) There is no basis whatever for the translation "peacock" or for the idea that Ophir was in India. Almost certainly it was roughly equivalent to Egyptian Punt, which included Eritrea and Somalia. Outside of Biblical references, Ophir appears only on an ostracon scratched into a large amphora sherd found during B. Maisler (Mazar)'s excavations at Tell el-Qasîleh on the 'Auja (Yarqon) near Tel Aviv. It reads "gold of Ophir for the temple of Horon—30 shekels." The date is somewhere in or about the first half of the eighth century, and the destination of the gold was perhaps the temple of Ḥaurôn/Horon at Jamnia, which is otherwise attested.

D. The Divided Monarchy

1. Here we are on firm historical ground from any rational standpoint, since there is so much overlapping with cuneiform sources. For details see the Histories of Israel by Martin Noth and John Bright, as well as the commentaries by J. A. Montgomery and John Gray; very useful is the recent book by Y. Aharoni, *The Land of the Bible* (Hebrew, 1962; now also in English). The chronological framework is in the process of being cleared up by new work on the early recensions of Kings (including Chronicles—see above). Burney's efforts were on the right track, but there were not enough synchronistic data available from other sources.

2. Burney correctly emphasized the importance of the LXX for the synchronisms between kings of Israel and Judah after the Division of the Monarchy. J. D. Shenkel, a pupil of F. M. Cross, Jr., in his book *Chronology and Recensional Development in the Greek Text of Kings*

(1968), has developed this field of research still farther, with emphasis on the importance of the Greek variants, especially those of proto-Lucianic (Old Palestinian) origin. My own tentative reconstruction of the chronology of the Divided Monarchy is based on several postulates (*BASOR,* 100 [1945], pp. 16-22): (a) that the dating of the kings of Israel in terms of regnal years of the kings of Judah tended to be more original than the absolute lengths of the reigns; (b) that Thiele's rearrangement of the chronology of Tiglath-pileser III and his reidentification of Azriyau or Izriyau with Azariah/Uzziah was correct, at least in principle; (c) that the recensional tradition of the Chronicler is sometimes more accurate than that of Kings; (d) that the Biblical and Phoenician synchronisms between Hiram and David and Solomon are reliable; (e) that the reign of Hezekiah began in 715 and not 14 years earlier; (f) that it is idle to speculate on coregencies, though they may have been more common than we usually suppose.

Since that time the discovery of a new Phoenician king in the cuneiform texts (*Mélanges Isidore Lévy,* Brussels, 1955, 1-9), the clarification of Egyptian synchronisms (*BASOR,* 130 [1953], 4-10; 141 [1956], 23-27; 171 [1963], 64-67 [by Hans Goedicke]), and the publication of the Nebuchadnezzar Chronicle with the exact date of the end of the reign of Jehoiachin, have filled out the picture in detail (D. J. Wiseman, *Chronicles of Chaldaean Kings,* London, 1956). Contrary to appearances for several years, the numbers on the ostraca of Samaria had not been misinterpreted by earlier scholars, so there is no need to change the dates of several late kings of Israel in order to agree with a supposed new identification of the numerical signs for regnal years (see Y. Aharoni, *BASOR*, 184 [1966], pp. 13-19, and *The Land of the Bible* [London, 1966], p. 323).

An important new synchronism appears in the stele of Ninurta-eresh (scarcely to be read *Nergal-eresh*), found by David Oates at Tell er-Rimâh in eastern Mesopotamia, and published by Stephanie Page in *Iraq* (1968), pp. 139-153.

The date of the stele is not preserved (so!) but can easily be inferred from its contents. The supposed date in the first year of Adad-nirari III (809-782 B.C.) is quite wrong, since *ina ištēt šatti* does *not* mean "in the first year" but "in one year, in a single year" (cf. W. von Soden, *Grundriss der akkadischen Grammatik,* p. 91, and *Akkadisches Handwörterbuch,* p. 400.) The lands reported to have been conquered, according to this text, are all in Syria and Palestine; they include Damascus, Samaria, Tyre, Sidon, Arvad "in the midst of the sea," and Lebanon. If we compare the statements in the Expedition List (preserved from the middle of the ninth century to the end of the eighth), we see immediately that the only one which fits is the eponymy of Asshur-baltu-nishê (802 B.C.—formerly dated a year earlier, like all the earlier eponyms). In that year the king (or his general—presumably Ninurta-eresh, who had been eponym the previous year) conducted a campaign *ina elī tãmtim,* "upon the sea," which clearly refers to his capture of Arvad, mentioned specifically in the stele. Island Tyre, also mentioned, may have been included.

There has been some uncertainty about the exact form of the name of the ruler of Samaria; it must be *Ya-'u-su* (with the normal Assyrian sibilant shift), pronounced *Ya'ōš,* not *Ya-'a-šu,* since the sign in question has the values *a', i', u',* and *'a, 'i, 'u.* No other vocalization will suit the facts of Hebrew historical phonology. The name thus had two forms, *Ya'ōšyahu,* "May Yahweh Grant," or *Yahu'âš,* "Yahweh Has Granted." For the fluctuations note the various forms of the name Jehoiachin (*Yahu-yakîn* [=*Yaukîn*] and *Yekon-yahu*). There is evidence of similar doublets in several other royal names, e.g., Jotham and Josiah (*Ya'ōšyahu*).

The date of the accession of Joash of Israel is thus fixed to the year 802 B.C. My previous approximate date for him, *c.* 801-786, is one year too late, and E. R. Thiele's exact date, 798-782/81 (*The Mysterious Numbers of the Hebrew Kings* [Chicago, 1951]), is quite wrong. The solution is given by J. Maxwell Miller, *JBL,* 86 (1967), pp.

276-288, who shows that Jehu's rebellion may have taken place anywhere between 844 and 842, if the Old Palestinian (Proto-Lucianic) readings are combined with the Assyrian evidence. This is a year or two higher than I was allowing, and we can now safely date the rebellion in 843/42—in which case the year 802/1 emerges directly from the Biblical synchronisms, as I have shown. In a number of other known cases, change of rulers is connected with an Assyrian invasion. (I expect to deal with this synchronism at length elsewhere.)

Father Shenkel has been able to show that textual evidence of probably Lucianic origin furnishes another apparent confirmation of my chronological reconstruction. E. R. Thiele's treatment of the chronological material suffers from a doctrinaire approach. In general he disregards the Greek variants and rejects the divergent materials in Chronicles. As a result, he has to defend the Massoretic Hebrew text of Kings throughout against all other evidence, ancient and modern. He also assumes an improbable series of shifts in the calendars and dating methods of North and South in order to obtain precise results—to an accuracy that assumes transmission of correct numbers in an otherwise often corrupt text.

3. It is interesting to note the steady increase in the number of kings of Judah and Israel who are mentioned in extra-Biblical sources. These sources are mostly cuneiform inscriptions but also alphabetic inscriptions, ostraca, and seals from Palestine:

Judah		Israel	
Uzziah-Azariah	seal & cuneiform	Omri	cuneiform, etc.
Jotham	seal	Ahab	"
(Jeho) ahaz	cuneiform	Jehu	"
Hezekiah	"	Joash	"
Manasseh	"	Jeroboam II	seal

Judah		Israel	
Josiah	ostraca	Menahem	cuneiform
Jehoiachin-Yaukin	cuneiform and seals	Pekah	"
		Hoshea	"

Charles Fox Burney was born November 4th, 1868, the son of Charles G. Burney, paymaster-in-chief of the Royal Navy. Like so many other boys from navy families he attended the Merchant Tailors School, from which he went predictably, to Oxford, receiving his B.A. in 1890. His scholastic record was unusually good, but he also engaged in athletics and other extra-curricular activities. Being strongly drawn toward theology, he turned to a teaching career in the Church; in 1893 he became deacon and lecturer in Hebrew at Oxford, and the following year he was ordained priest and received his M.A. This was followed by a post as librarian (1897-1908), and then by election as fellow (1899). It was not until 1914 that he was appointed "Oriel Professor of the Interpretation of Holy Scripture." Aside from two honorary doctorates (Oxford and Durham), he did not receive any special academic honors, either at home or abroad. For instance, when he died on the 15th of April, 1925, he had not been elected to membership in the British Academy, founded in 1901. In view of the scope and originality of his work, combined with sound learning and a scholarly method far ahead of his time in important respects, one might feel justified in regarding him as a frustrated man. But of this there is no evidence. He lived a rich and happy life, much loved by his family and friends, and he bred horses and indulged in gardening on the side. In 1950 I used to hear many stories about him from his niece, who was the wife of a high British official in the Western Aden Protectorate.

His chief publications were: *Notes on the Hebrew Text*

of the Book of Kings (1903); *Israel's Settlement in Canaan* (1918, 3rd ed. 1921); *The Book of Judges* (1918, 2nd. ed. 1920); and *The Aramaic Origin of the Fourth Gospel* (1922).

William F. Albright
W. W. Spence Professor Emeritus
of Semitic Languages
The Johns Hopkins University

March 7, 1969

LIST OF ABBREVIATIONS

ANET- ed. Pritchard, J.B.: *Ancient Near Eastern Texts Relating to the Old Testament,* second edition (Princeton, 1969).

ARI^5- Albright, W.F.: *Archaeology and the Religion of Israel,* fifth edition (Baltimore, 1956).

BASOR- *Bulletin of the American Schools of Oriental Research.*

CAH^2- *Cambridge Ancient History,* second edition (Cambridge, 1968).

FSAC- Albright, W.F.: *From the Stone Age to Christianity,* second edition (Baltimore, 1957).

HTR- *Harvard Theological Review.*

IEJ- *Israel Exploration Journal.*

JBL- *Journal of Biblical Literature.*

JPOS- *Journal of the Palestine Oriental Society.*

KSGVI- Alt, A.: *Kleine Schriften zur Geschicte des Volkes Israels,* 3 vols., (Münich, 1953-1959).

YGC- Albright, W.F.: *Yahweh and the Gods of Canaan* (Garden City, N.Y., 1968).

PREFACE

A NEW commentary upon one of the books of the Old Testament seems to call for a few words in justification of its appearance, and for an indication of the special features which it aims at offering. The Book of Judges is not a book which has suffered from neglect on the part of scholars in the past: indeed, the last thirty years have witnessed the accession of much valuable work devoted to its elucidation. The Commentary by Professor Moore (1895)—to cite but a single example—is, by general consent, one of the most thorough and scholarly volumes even of so eminent a series as the *International Critical Commentary*. Biblical science, however, does not stand still. We are—or should be—daily widening the basis of our research. Fresh knowledge of the languages, literature, and antiquities of the peoples who were kindred to Israel, by race or by environment, is constantly being brought within reach; and the Old Testament scholar who would keep abreast of the possibilities of Biblical interpretation must spread his nets wide if he is to gather in the available material for his studies.

For myself, I can say with truth that such first-hand acquaintance with the Babylonian and Assyrian language and literature as I have been able to acquire during the past fourteen years or so, has revolutionized my outlook upon Old Testament studies. The possibilities for fresh investigation offered within this sphere, together with an instinctive preference for study of the Biblical sources themselves, prior to consultation of that which has been written about them by other scholars, have, I hope, imparted some measure of originality to my work; though originality, as an end in itself, was not what I was striving after. I have, so far as I was able, made myself acquainted with the work of my predecessors in the same field; and I trust that I have regularly discharged the duty incumbent upon every scholar by making due acknowledgment to them whenever I have cited their opinion. An apparent exception to this rule may be found in the introductory discussions on the composition and sources of the various narratives contained in the book; but here I have always worked out my own conclusions and argued them in detail, and anything like a regular citation of my agreement with, or divergency from, other scholars must have led to undue prolixity, and would only have tended to confuse the reader.

I trust that the somewhat lengthy § 6 of my Introduction, on 'External information bearing on the period of Judges,' may not be deemed superfluous to the purpose of the commentary. The Book of Judges occupies a position on the borderland between history and legend. In order to place our feet on firm ground, and gain as much as may be for veritable history, it is most important to examine the external sources, so far as they are accessible, which bear upon the condition of Canaʿan and its inhabitants at and before the period covered by the book. It is important also—in view of the frequent reference made in the commentary to Babylonian influence and analogy—to understand how it was that such influence had permeated Canaʿan to so large an extent at this early period. Throughout my work I have had in view, not merely the elucidation of the text of Judges, but as thorough an investigation as I could make of the early period of Israel's residence in Canaʿan for which Judges forms our principal text-book. My volume, therefore, may perhaps be described as a collection of material for this early history rather than as a commentary pure and simple; and if this view is taken of it I shall be content.

Since the basis of correct exegesis of the Old Testament consists in a sound philological knowledge of Hebrew, and such knowledge is mainly advanced through comparative study of the cognate Semitic languages, considerable attention is devoted in the notes to questions of comparative philology. In discussions which fall under this head I have adopted the plan of transliterating both the Hebrew words and those from cognate languages which are brought into comparison with them, in order that the Hebrew student who is unacquainted with the cognate languages may be able, to some extent at least, to appreciate the argument. A table explaining the method of transliteration is given on pp. xxxi f., and an index of the transliterated forms will be found at the end of the volume. The use of Hebrew and other Semitic types has been minimized as far as possible, in the hope that the commentary may prove useful, not merely to Hebrew scholars, but to the larger class of Biblical students who are ignorant of the language. Whenever a quotation is made in the original it is accompanied by a translation.

Among the notes on the text there will be found some which are of very considerable length, *e.g.* those on the Ashera (p. 195), the Ephod (p. 236), the representation of Samson as a Nazirite (p. 342), the line of the Midianites' flight, and the site of Abel-meḥolah (p. 219), as well as some of the other geographical notes, and many of the textual notes upon the Song of Deborah. Notes such as these have been expanded without compunction, because I believed that I had new light to throw upon very difficult problems; and readers who are really desirous of getting to the bottom of such problems will not, I think, quarrel with me upon this score.

It is possible that one of the Additional Notes—that on the use of writing in the time of the Judges, and the antiquity of the Alphabetic Script (p. 253)—may be thought to hang upon rather a slight peg in the reference to writing in *ch.* 8^{14}, so far as the necessities of the commentary are concerned; but the many-sided interest of the subject and the manner in which it has entered into recent discussions (some of them not untinged with controversial bias) seemed to call for an explicit statement of the facts, and of such deductions from them as appear to be justified. The notes on 'Yahweh or Yahu originally an Amorite Deity' (p. 243), and 'Early identification of Yahweh with the Moon-god' (p. 249), form integral parts of my theory as to the Ashera; and I am unaware of any source of information which brings together the facts which I was desirous of marshalling.

Among those to whom I owe thanks for assistance rendered in the preparation of this commentary, there are two whose help has been of a very special character. Dr. Driver read through the whole of my new translation of the text of Judges (which I completed before beginning to write the notes upon it), and made many suggestions which materially improved it. He also saw, in one form or another, all or most of what I have written on *chs.* 1-8; and since he was without stint accessible to all who desired to consult him, I was accustomed constantly to discuss points of difficulty with him, and many of my conclusions and theories embodied in the commentary have, needless to say, much profited through his advice and revision. Dr. C. J. Ball has undertaken the heavy task of reading the whole of my proof-sheets and discussing them personally with me. All that my book owes to him it is impossible for me adequately to estimate; a small part of it may be seen in the number of fresh suggestions which he has allowed me to include in my notes.*

When all has been said, however, my debt to these two scholars for actual co-operation in the work put into my book is but a tithe of what I and the book owe to them in a wider sense. Enjoying as I did the close friendship of Dr. Driver from the year that I came up

* Cf. pp. 114, 119, 122, 129, 144, 148, 250, 325, 421, 476 f.

to Oxford as an undergraduate until the year of his death, I cannot but feel that most of what I have learned in method and thoroughness of scholarship is due to his teaching and example. Under Dr. Ball I began as a schoolboy to study the elements of Hebrew; under him some twenty years later I began to grapple with Assyriology, and the marvellous gifts which he possesses as a teacher caused the early stages of a study which might otherwise have seemed tedious and repellent to appear in the light of an easy and fascinating pastime.

I have also to express my grateful thanks to Professor L. W. King for much advice upon matters connected with Babylonian studies. He has read, in particular, § 6 of my Introduction and all my Additional Notes which deal with the influence of Babylonian civilization upon Cana'an; and my confidence in the lines which I have taken in dealing with this side of my subject has been greatly strengthened by his approval and support. Professor R. W. Rogers of Drew Theological Seminary, Madison, New Jersey, whose regular visits for research in the Bodleian Library have made him as much a son of Oxford as of the United States, was in residence here during the greater part of the years 1913-14. During our long friendship we have grown accustomed to discuss the Biblical questions in which our common interests lie; and I owe much to his judicial mind and expert knowledge of Assyriology.

With my wife I have talked over many of the points, both small and great, which have arisen in the course of my researches; and the book owes not a little to her quick apprehension, sound common sense, and unerring feeling for style and lucidity.

Finally, I must thank the Trustees of the British Museum for permission to reproduce the seal-cylinder impressions figured in Plate III., and the two reliefs from the Report on excavations at Carchemish, edited by Dr. D. G. Hogarth, which appear in Plate V.;

M. Leroux, the publisher of Delaporte's *Catalogue des Cylindres orientaux . . . de la Bibliothèque Nationale*, for a similar permission in the case of the seal-cylinder impressions given in Plate II.; the Committee of the Palestine Exploration Fund for kindly allowing me to make the sketch-map of the district round Gibeʿah (opposite p. 465) upon the basis of their large survey-map; and the British Academy for permission to make use of the map of Western Asia which has been prepared for my Schweich Lectures.

C. F. B.

OXFORD,
Easter 1918.

ADDENDA

p. 17. *Ch.* 1[17]. Against the identification of Ṣephath with Sebaita (Esbeita), cf. Lawrence in *PEF. Annual*, iii. (1914-15), p. 91, who points out that the site Esbeita cannot have existed before the Christian era.

p. 29. *Footnote* *. The disappearance of the *k* in אַכְזִיב 'Akzîb = ez-Zîb is highly remarkable. Kampffmeyer (*ZDPV.* xv. p. 31) suggests that, as a first stage, *k* may have been weakened into *ḫ* (as in Mikmash = modern Muḫmâs) and then into א, the first syllable being eventually treated as though it were the Ar. Article (cf. ed-Dâmiyyeh for 'Adam, er-Restân for Arethusa, etc.).

p. 62. *Note* on 'the Ḥittites . . . mount Lebanon.' Meyer, *IN.* pp. 332 ff., defends the 𝕳 text in Judg. 3[3], Josh. 11[3], which places the Ḥivvites in the Lebanon district, and proposes to substitute חֹרִי 'Ḥorites,' on the authority of 𝕲 in Gen. 34[2], Josh. 9[7], passages which, as they stand in 𝕳, place the Ḥivvites in central Cana'an (Shechem and Gibe'on). The introduction of the Ḥorites into these latter passages is opposed by Kit., *GVI.*[2] i. p. 37, *n*[1], upon good grounds.

p. 69. *Footnote* on אטר. The common biliteral element DAR, ṬAR, etc., underlying a series of triliteral roots has been noted and further illustrated by Ball, *Semitic and Sumerian* (*Hilprecht Anniversary Volume*, pp. 41 f.).

p. 88. *Ch.* 4[7]. The root-meaning of Heb. *náḥal* is stated by BDB. to be unknown. It seems obvious that the root נחל must be allied to חלל in the sense 'to pierce,' and that *náḥal* therefore properly denotes a *cutting* or *boring*: cf. especially Job 28[4], if *náhal* is there rightly understood as meaning a *mine-shaft.* Other instances of allied פ"נ and ע *doubled* verbs (*i.e.* of the same biliteral differently triliteralized) are נטף 'to drip,' and New Heb. טפף whence טִפָּה 'drop'; נסך 'to weave' and סכך 'to intertwine'; נפץ and פצץ 'to break in pieces'; נצח and צחח 'to shine, be brilliant'; נקב and קבב 'to curse.' Similarly, פ"נ and ע"ו, נפח and פוח 'to breathe'; נפץ 'to break in pieces,' and פוץ 'to be dispersed' (by breaking); נצץ and צוץ 'to shine, blossom'; נקר and קור 'to bore, dig.'

p. 95. Add to the list of authorities, P. Haupt, *Die Schlacht von Taanach*, pp. 193-225 of *Studien zur semit. Philol. u. Religionsgesch. Julius Wellhausen . . . gewidmet*, 1914. (He treats the text of Judg. 5 with the greatest freedom, subjecting it to a drastic rearrangement.)

p. 96. On the analogy to Hebrew poetry offered by the old Anglo-Saxon poetry, and by *Piers Ploughman*, cf. Gray, *Forms of Hebrew Poetry* (1915), pp. 128 ff.

p. 158. The extreme variation in the number of unstressed syllables which may accompany a stressed syllable in Hebrew poetry, according to our theory, is well illustrated by the passage from *Piers Ploughman* quoted by Gray, *Forms of Hebrew Poetry*, p. 130:—

> ‘On Good Friday I fynde | a felon was y-saved,
> That had lyved al his life | with lesynges and with theftę;
> And for he beknede to the cros, | and to Christ shrof him,
> He was sonner y-saved | than seint Johan the Baptist;
> And or Adam or Ysaye | or any of the prophetes,
> That hadde y-leyen with Lucifer | many longe yeres,
> A robbere was y-raunsoned | rather than thei alle,
> Withouten any penaunce of purgatorie | to perpetual blisse.’

Here we find not merely ⏓⏓⏓–́⏓ (‘and for he béknede,’ ‘that hadde y-léyen’), but even ⏓⏓⏓⏓⏓–́⏓ (‘withouten any pénaunce’). The resemblance is rather striking between the line

> ‘Withouten any pénaunce of púrgatorie | to perpétual blísse’

and *v.*[9b] of the Song of Deborah,

> *hammithnaddabhím báʿám | barrakhú Yahwáh.*

p. 210. *Ch.* 7 [5.6]. Mez, *ZATW.* xxi. (1901), pp. 198-200, notes the fact that Ar. *karaʿa*, which is formally identical with Heb. *kāraʿ* ‘bend down’ (used in our passage in the description of one form of drinking), has the meaning ‘drink with the muzzle in the water,’ *i.e.* by sucking the water in, as is done by ruminants, and animals such as the horse and ass, in contrast to Ar. *walaġa* ‘lap with the tongue’ (equivalent in meaning to Heb. *lāḳaḳ*), the method of drinking practised by the dog, as well as by the wolf and other beasts of prey. His conclusion is that ‘those that bent down (כרעו) upon their knees to drink water’ put their mouths into the water like cattle; whereas the lappers (המלקקים) were those who flung the water into their mouths with their hands—this being (in his opinion) the nearest approach to lapping, the actual practice of which is impossible for a human being. These latter, he thinks, were chosen on account of this dog-like or wolf-like characteristic as betokening their fitness for the enterprise; and he seeks to fortify this inference by quotation of two Ar. proverbs which compare a razzia with the licking of a wolf, *i.e.* in respect of its lightning-rapidity, as appears from another proverb, 'more swiftly than a dog licks its nose.' Mez's arguments are reproduced, with additional remarks, by McPherson, *JAOS.* xxii. (1901), pp. 70-75; and the two articles are cited as authoritative in Gesenius-Buhl, *Handwörterbuch*[16] (1915) *s.v.* כרע. BDB., *s.v.* כרע, compares the Ar. verb, and offers (with a query) the suggestion that it may bear a derivative sense, the ground-meaning being 'kneel to drink.'

Objection may be made to the identification of Heb. *kāra'* in our passage with Ar. *kara'a* on several grounds.

1. The phrase אשר יכרע על ברכיו לשתות 'who bendeth down upon his knees to drink' is very different from the Ar. usage of *kara'a*, in which the verb is always followed by the prep. فى 'in'—'drink with the muzzle *in* the water, or, *in* a vessel' (cf. the Dictionaries of Freytag, Lane, Kazimirski). McPherson, who perceives this difficulty, thinks that על ברכיו may be a later scribal expansion, אשר יכרע לשתות מים meaning 'who drinks putting his mouth to the water.' Such an English rendering would seem to require an original אֲשֶׁר יִשְׁתֶּה כָּרֹעַ, the Heb. sentence as given by McPherson meaning rather 'who puts his mouth in the water as regards drinking.' But, if כרע really has the meaning of the Ar. verb, לשתות is obviously redundant; whereas, on the other hand, the omission of במים, which is demanded on the analogy of the Ar. فى الماء, appears to be fatal to the theory. It cannot be doubted that the expression יכרע על ברכיו is original, and has the meaning which it possesses elsewhere (1 Kgs. 8[34], 2 Kgs. 1[13], Ezr. 9[5]).

2. The philological analogue of Heb. *kāra'* appears to be the Ar. *raka'a* (as rightly recognized by Ges., *Thes.*, Ges.-Buhl, though not by BDB.), with transposition of radicals (cf., probably, the converse transposition in Ar. *ḳara'a*, which is surely to be compared with Heb. *rāḳa'*, and not with *ḳāra'* as in BDB.). If, however, *kara'a* bears a derived sense 'kneel to drink,' we are faced by the phenomenon that the root with more primitive meaning has undergone transposition, whereas the presumably later derived form has not. Again, if the point of connexion between Heb. *kāra'* and Ar. *kara'a* is that the latter properly means 'kneel to drink' (BDB.), such a posture is true of the camel only, but not of the ox, sheep, goat, horse, ass, or of the wild ruminants. We must suppose, therefore, that *kara'a* got its specialized sense through observation of the camel only; but of this there seems to be no trace in Ar. Such a sense as 'bow the head *or* neck' (true for the other animals mentioned) would be expressed by another verb.

3. Mez's theory, in postulating that Heb. *kāra'* denotes the putting the mouth into the water, is obliged to assume that the lappers, in contrast, put their hands to their mouths (retaining, therefore,

בידם אל פיהם in the position which it occupies in 𝔐). But no amount of special pleading can make it appear that the scooping of water into the mouth with the hand has any resemblance to lapping 'as the dog lappeth.'

If these arguments are sound, the resemblance between Heb. *kāraʿ* and Ar. *karaʿa* is probably merely fortuitous; and the comparison with *karaʿa* should be expunged from Heb. Lexicons, or at any rate marked as highly precarious.

p. 214. *Note on ch.* 7[15]. In explaining Heb. *šibhrô*, 'its elucidation,' by comparison of Bab. *šabrû*, *šabrâtu*, it is of course not intended to affirm that *šébher* is actually the formal equivalent of *šabrû*, *i.e.* a Shaphʿēl from a so-called triliteral form (ברה), since such a form would naturally exhibit a ל״ה nominal termination. What is affirmed is that there are in Heb. originally-biliteral forms which have been triliteralized by prefixed שׁ in the sense 'make,' which is the preformative employed in this sense in the Shaphʿēl. This has already been pointed out by Ball in his article *Semitic and Sumerian* in the *Hilprecht Anniversary Volume*, pp. 54 f. שׁ־בר '*to make* the action of *seeing*' is precisely on the analogy of שׁ־כב '*to make* the action of *reclining*,' from root KAB = כב in כפף 'to bend, bow down' (cf. also גבב, נגף); שׁ־קל 'to weigh,' properly '*to make light*' (cf. קלל), *i.e.* 'to heave, lift.' We may add the ordinary Heb. שׁ־בר (not included in Ball's list) '*to make* the action of *breaking*' (cf. Ar. *bara* 'to fashion by *cutting*,' Heb. פרר, Bab. *parâru* 'to break *or* shatter').

The distinction between שׁבר, properly 'make + see' or 'make + bright' (cf. בר־ר 'to make bright,' Bab. *barâru* 'to be bright'; שׁ־פר 'to make bright,' or, internally, 'to show brightness'),* and the ordinary Heb. שׁבר, properly 'make + break,' is the same as exists between Bab. *ka-pâru* 'to be bright *or* brighten,' Piʿel *kuppuru*, Heb. כִּפֶּר properly 'to make bright, purge,' so 'to atone' (cf. the evidence adduced by the present writer in *ET.* xxii. pp. 325 ff.), and Bab. *ka-pâru* 'to cut.' The identity in form combined with diversity in meaning is explained by the fact that there is a Sumerian BAR, PAR with the idea of 'brightness' (standing in syllabaries for *barû* 'to see,' *barâru* 'to shine,' *namâru* 'to be bright,' *nûru* 'light,' etc.), and another Sumerian BAR, PAR which is distinct (at least as known to us) in meaning, and carries the idea of 'breaking, splitting,' etc. (standing in syllabaries as the equivalent of *parâru* 'to break,' *kapâru* 'to cut,' *palâku* 'to divide,' *ḫasâsu* 'to cogitate—*animam dividere*,' *parâsu* 'to decide,' etc.).

* For the connexion between *seeing* and *brightness*, cf. Heb. אור 'to be bright' = Bab. *amâru* 'to see' (a relation in form like that between Heb. נור Bab. *namâru*, both 'to shine'). When a man *sees clearly* again after faintness, his eyes are said to *become bright*: cf. 1 Sam. 14[27.29], Ps. 13[3] (𝔐 [4]).

p. 221. Discussion of 1 Kgs. 4 [12]. The writer, having independently suggested that the words 'which is in proximity to Ṣarĕthan' have been accidentally transposed and should properly refer to 'Abel-meḥolah,' now notices that the same conjecture has been put forward with a query by Prof. Moore in *JBL.* xiii. (1894), p. 79, *n* [9].

pp. 253 ff. Since the printing of *Addit. note* on 'The use of writing, etc.' there has appeared a valuable article by J. H. Breasted entitled *The Physical Processes of Writing in the Early Orient and their Relation to the Origin of the Alphabet*, in *AJSL.* xxxii. (July 1916), pp. 230-249. Breasted deals, on pp. 241 ff., with Assyrian Reliefs depicting scribes writing cuneiform on a clay tablet (cf. our *Addit. note*, p. 255), and he regards the second scribe, who is occasionally present, using pen, ink, and scroll, as an Aramaean (cf. our *Addit. note*, p. 256, *footnote*; *Description of the Plates*, p. 495).

p. 255. *Footnote* *. The form of the stylus used for writing cuneiform, and the method of using it, have been discussed by P. Zehnpfund, *Ueber babylonisch-assyrische Tafelschreibung*, in *Actes du* 8e *Congrès International des Orientalistes tenu en* 1889 *à Stockholm et à Christiania* (1893), pp. 265-272; J. de Morgan, *Note sur Procédés techniques en Usage chez les Scribes babyloniens* in *Recueil de Travaux*, xxvii. (1905), pp. 240 f.; A. T. Clay, *Documents from the Temple Archives of Nippur* (1906), pp. 17-20; L. Messerschmidt, *Zur Technik des Tontafelschreibens* in *OLZ.* (1906), cols. 185-196, 304-312, 372-380. The fact that the wedges were made by impression merely, without drawing, which is emphasized by the present writer, is confirmed by Clay: 'To produce long horizontal wedges for the purpose of filling out lines, as was frequently done, it is not necessary to draw the stylus over the soft clay. By simply lowering the handle it is possible to make a wedge as long as the stylus' (p. 20).

p. 332. *Addendum to Additional Note on the Women's Festival of Judg.* 11 [40]. The conclusion that the myth of Demeter and Kore is to be connected, in its origin, with the myth of Ištar and Tammuz may be substantiated by the following facts:—

(1) The brilliant discovery of Ball (*PSBA.* xvi., 1894, pp. 195 ff.) that the Sumerian name of Tammuz, DUMU.ZI* (Bab. *Du'ûzu*, *Dûzu* ‡) is identical with the Turkish *dōmūz* 'pig,' and that there is thus an 'original identity of the god with the wild boar that slays him in the developed legend,' is confirmed, quite independently and along

* Usually explained to mean 'Son of life,' or as an abbreviation of DUMU.-ZI.ABZU, 'True son of the deep water.' It is possible that one or the other of these meanings may have been read into the name after its original signification had been forgotten.

‡ On the evolution of the name-forms in Sumerian and Semitic, cf. Zimmern, *Der Bab. Gott Tamûz*, pp. 703 f.

b

totally different lines, by Robertson Smith's scarcely less brilliant conjecture that the pig was originally regarded as the theriomorphic representative of the deity. 'My own belief,' says this latter writer, 'is that the piacular sacrifice of swine at Cyprus on April 2 represents the death of the god himself, not an act of vengeance for his death. . . . Adonis, in short, is the Swine-god, and in this, as in many other cases, the sacred victim has been changed by false interpretation into the enemy of the god' (*Religion of the Semites*,[1] p. 392, *n*[1]; *id.*[2] p. 411, *n*[4]). Among the Greeks 'the pig is the victim specially consecrated to the powers of the lower world' (Farnell, *The Cults of the Greek States*, iii. p. 32). The ceremonial of the Thesmophoria, celebrated by women in the cult of Demeter and Persephone, is especially noteworthy in this connexion. Lucian's scholiast states that 'At the Thesmophoria it is the fashion to throw living pigs into the underground sanctuaries . . . and certain women called ἀντλητρίαι descend and bring up the decaying remnants and place them on the altars: and people believe that the man who takes (part of them) and mixes them up with his grain for sowing will have an abundant harvest. And they say that there are serpents down below about the vaults, which eat the greater part of the food thrown down' (quoted from Farnell, *op. cit.* p. 89; cf. also Miss Harrison, *Prolegomena to the Study of Greek Religion*,[2] *ch.* iv.). Here it is questioned whether the swine were regarded merely as gifts to the earth-goddess, or as incarnations of the divinities themselves. The former view is taken by Frazer (*Spirits of the Corn*, ii. pp. 16 ff.); while Farnell regards the evidence as insufficient to establish it, and supposes that 'as these goddesses may be supposed to have partaken of the swine's flesh that was thrown down to them, the remnant would be regarded as charged with part of their divinity, and would be valuable objects to show (? strew) over the fields. But no Greek legend or ritual reveals any sense of the identity between Demeter and the pig' (*op. cit.* pp. 90 f.). We may remark, however, that, at any rate from the Semitic side, the method of sacrifice—the *throwing down* of the *living* animal—is wholly in favour of the theriomorphic conception. The slaying of the victim by a method which avoided bloodshed, or which might be interpreted as an act of self-immolation, suggests that it was a totem-animal too sacred to be slaughtered by any individual worshipper (cf. Robertson Smith, *Religion of the Semites*,[2] pp. 418 ff.).* The term μέγαρον, or μάγαρον, which is used to describe the underground caves (τὰ μέγαρα) into which the pigs were thrown, and also the adytum of the temple at Delphi where the oracular responses were

* The reference in Isa. 65^{4}, 66^{17} to the eating of swine's flesh by the renegade Palestinian Jews or Samaritans, probably in early post-exilic times, reprobates the practice not simply because the animal was regarded as unclean upon arbitrary or sanitary grounds, but as a definite act of idolatry; and there can be little doubt that the allusion is to the ceremonial partaking of the flesh of the totem-animal in Tammuz-ritual. Cf. Cheyne, *Prophecies of Isaiah, ad loc.*

received, seems to be distinct from the Homeric term *μέγαρον*, which denotes a large chamber, hall, or palace, and has been supposed with considerable probability to be the Phoen. and Heb. *meʿârā*, Ar. *muġâra*, 'cave,' with *γ* for rough ע in transliteration, as in Γαζα = עזה, etc.* ; and, if this is so, the Semitic connexions of the rites of which we are speaking receive further substantiation.

(2) One of the titles most frequently applied to Tammuz in Sumerian dirges is AMA.UŠUMGAL.ANNA. This means lit. 'Mother, great serpent, heaven,' *i.e.* 'the divine Mother who is the great serpent.'‡ Tammuz is also occasionally equated with the goddess KA.DI. Now KA.DI (as has been noted by Jensen, *KB.* vi. 1, p. 565) is stated in iv.[2] R. 30, No. 2, Obv. 18 and Rev. 6 to be a deity of the Underworld; according to v. R. 31, 30 she is identical with the divine Serpent (*ilu ṣîru*); from a text published by Scheil (*Textes Élam.-Sémit.*, 1e série, p. 91, l. 23) we gather that the Serpent is the 'child' (*mîru*), or, it may be, the 'messenger' (*šipru*) of KA.DI; while, according to v. R. 46, 29, the constellation of the Serpent represents the goddess Ereškigal, the counterpart of the Greek Persephone as mistress of the Underworld. For the Greeks also, however, the serpent is the incarnation of the earth-goddess Ge, the prototype of Demeter (cf. Farnell, *op. cit.* pp. 9 f.); and, as is clear from the passage relating to the Thesmophoria which we have already quoted, 'this animal that was once the incarnation of the earth-spirit remains the familiar representative of the chthonian goddesses of the Olympian period' (Farnell, *op. cit.* p. 91). Further comment is needless.

p. 340. *Note* on Ṣorʿah. The city *Ṣa-ar-ḫa*, mentioned in the T.A. Letters, together with *A-ia-lu-na*, *i.e.* Aijalon (Kn. 273), can hardly be other than the Biblical Ṣorʿah. It may be questioned, in view of the concurrence of the vocalization of *Ṣa-ar-ḫa* with the modern Ṣarʿah, whether the Biblical form ought not likewise to be vocalized not צָרְעָה but צַרְעָה Ṣarʿah. Cf. 𝕲 Σαραα.

p. 351. *Note* on *ch.* 14[6]. To the parallels adduced for the method employed by Samson in rending the lion, add the duplicated figure rending a lion on the seal-cylinder impression figured in *Revue d'Assyriologie*, xxx. (1916), Plate 1, fig. 6.

p. 359. Since the *footnote* dealing with the *βουγονία*-myth was written, there has appeared an article on the subject by A. E. Shipley in *Journal of Philology*, xxxiv. (1915), pp. 97-105.

p. 408. J. Halévy, *RÉJ.* xxi. (1890), pp. 207-217, treats the narrative

* Cf. Robertson Smith, *Religion of the Semites*,[2] p. 200; Lagarde, *Symmicta*, ii. p. 91; Muss-Arnolt, *Semitic Words in Greek and Latin*, in *Trans. of the American Philol. Assoc.* xxiii. (1892), p. 73; Boisacq, *Dict. Étym. de la Langue Grecque*, p. 617.

‡ Cf. Zimmern, *Der Bab. Gott Tamūz*, p. 7, *n*[2]; Langdon, *Tammuz and Ishtar*, pp. 114 ff.

of Judg. 17, 18 as a single document, and regards it as probably the work of a Judaean patriot and convinced partisan of the Temple at Jerusalem, who aimed at defaming the rival Israelite sanctuaries of Bethel (Micah's temple) and Dan by imputing to them a discreditable origin—both of them owed their origin to a theft; whereas the site of the Temple at Jerusalem was honestly purchased by David at a high price (2 Sam. 24 [27]). Halévy's arguments are ingenious but not convincing.

J. A. Bewer (*The Composition of Judges, Chaps.* 17, 18, in *AJSL.* xxix. (1913-14), pp. 261-283) attacks the critical theories of compilation or of interpolation in this narrative, maintaining that 'the story is a unity throughout with very few redactional touches (17 [6], 18 [1a.bβ], and possibly 18 [29aβ-b]). His arguments do not lead the present editor to modify his conclusions, as expressed in pp. 442 ff., in any respect.

The credit must, however, be given to Bewer of recognizing the Levite's name in והוא גר שם of 17 [7], which he emends וְהוּא בֶּן־גֵּרְשֹׁם 'and he was a son of Gershom'—thus anticipating the suggestion made independently by the present writer in his *note ad loc.* Bewer also favours the emendation הָאָרוֹן for הָאָרֶץ, which has been adopted in 18 [39].

p. 430. *Footnote* ‡ on Nephtoaḥ = Liftâ. Another instance of the change of *n* to *l* in a modern Ar. name as compared with its ancient equivalent is seen in Shunem = Sôlem. On the loss of the final *ḥ* after a long vowel cf. Kampffmeyer, *ZDPV.* xv. p. 26, who cites the similar disappearance of the ע in אֶשְׁתְּמֹה (Josh. 13 [50]) by the side of the normal אֶשְׁתְּמֹעַ.

p. 442. *Chs.* 19 [1]-21 [25]. To the authorities named add J. A. Bewer, *The Composition of Judges, Chap.* 19, in *AJSL.* xxx. (1914-15), pp. 81-93; *The Composition of Judges* 20, 21, *id.* pp. 149-165. The narrative is regarded as 'derived from one old, in the main reliable, source, which was worked over by a late theocratic editor. It is not improbable that a still later annotator, imbued with the same spirit as the editor, inserted a few characteristic interpolations.'

p. 462. *Ch.* 19 [9] *note* on 'the day hath waned, etc.' The connexion of Heb. רפה with Bab. *rabû* or *rapû* 'to sink' (of the sun setting) has been affirmed (since the printing of our note) by Haupt in *AJSL.* xxxiii. (Oct. 1916), p. 48. Haupt also connects *rᵉphā'îm* with *rapû* as meaning 'those who have "sunk" into their unseen abode' (as is done by the present writer in *note* on 'Teraphim,' p. 421, after the suggestion of Ball), though he denies connexion between *rᵉphā'îm* and *Tᵉrāphîm.* Since Haupt makes no reference to Ball's remarks in *Proc. Brit. Acad.* vii. p. 16 (a paper read before the British Academy on June 3, 1915, and published shortly afterwards), we must assume that the two scholars have independently reached similar conclusions.

p. 486. *Ch.* 20 [45]. *Note* on 'the crag of Rimmon.' The ordinary identification with Rammôn, three and a half miles east of Bethel, is opposed by W. F. Birch (*PEF. Qy. St.*, 1879, pp. 127-129), who makes a strong point of the use of *séla*ʿ 'crag' or 'cliff' as denoting 'a rock more or less perpendicular' (cf. 2 Chr. 25 [12], Jer. 51 [25], Ps. 141 [6]). He states that there is no such cliff at Rammôn, which Stanley (*Sinai and Palestine*, p. 214) describes as 'a white chalky height,' and Rob. (*BR.*[3] i. p. 440) as 'a conical chalky hill'; and maintains that this want is a fatal defect in the identification of this site with 'the crag of Rimmon.' All that is left, therefore, in favour of the identification is the identity of name: but modern place-names indicating the presence of a pomegranate tree (*Rummâneh*) or group of such trees (*Rummân*), happen to be extremely common in Palestine (the present writer has counted eighteen such in *SWP. Great Map*); thus by itself identity of name argues nothing.

The claims of Rammôn to be the site mentioned in our narrative were investigated by Finn (*Byeways in Palestine*, 1868, pp. 205 ff.), who visited the spot in order to inquire for a cavern which might be capable of containing six hundred men for four months. He saw four (not large) caverns, and was told of two others; and his conclusion was that 'all the refugees might sleep in these places if there was no village at the time, which seems probable.' On Finn's return from Rammôn, the guide told him of a vast cavern in the Wâdy Suwênîṭ capable of holding many hundred men, near which there is a watercourse half-way down the precipice (cf. p. 208). This cave, which is known as Muġâret Ǵel-aʿy, has been carefully investigated and described by H. B. Rawnsley (*PEF. Qy. St.*, 1879, pp. 118-126). It occupies a precipitous position on the south-west side of the Wâdy Suwênîṭ, and is near a spring which affords an adequate supply of water. There is a current tradition in Ǵebaʿ that the cave will hold six hundred men, and the main entrance-cave is said to afford shelter for sixteen flocks of one hundred sheep each. Rawnsley thought that six hundred men might hide there in case of emergency; while three hundred could find ample lodging.

This is the site which Birch (in the article above mentioned) advocates as the real 'crag of Rimmon.' If he is correct, we have an explanation of the question raised by *ch.* 20 [43], why the pursuit of the Benjaminites ceased when they had reached a point to the east of Gebaʿ, viz. the fact that at this point they would disappear over the side of the Wâdy Suwênîṭ, and reach their refuge. It certainly seems improbable that, when the fugitives could reach such a stronghold as this at a comparatively short distance (four or five miles) from Gibeʿah, and were at any rate in its immediate neighbourhood when they came 'east of Gebaʿ,' they should have travelled double the distance in order to reach Rammôn, which can in no way be compared as a defensive position.

PRINCIPAL ABBREVIATIONS EMPLOYED

I. Texts and Versions

$\mathfrak{H}$ . . The Hebrew consonantal text, as represented by all MSS. and printed editions.

$\mathfrak{M}$ . . The same as supplied with vowels and accents by the Massoretes. Ordinarily, $\mathfrak{H}$ represents the Massoretic text, unless the reading in question depends upon vowels or accents, when $\mathfrak{M}$ is employed.

Variation in reading between $\mathfrak{H}$ and $\mathfrak{M}$ is represented in the usual way, viz. by

Kt. . . *K^{e}thîbh*, the 'written,' *i.e.* consonantal, text.

Ḳ^{e}rê . . The 'read' text, *i.e.* the emendation of the Massoretes.

$\mathfrak{G}$ . . The Greek (Septuagint) version (ed. Swete, 1887). Different MSS. are represented by $\mathfrak{G}^A$ (Alexandrinus, edd. Brooke and McLean, 1897); $\mathfrak{G}^B$ (Vaticanus), etc. $\mathfrak{G}^L$ = the recension of Lucian as edited by Lagarde (cf. p. cxxvi.).

'A. . . The Greek version of Aquila;

Σ. . . " " Symmachus;

Θ. . . " " Theodotion;

cited from Field, *Origenis Hexaplorum quae supersunt* (1875).

$\mathfrak{L}$ . . The Old Latin (pre-Hieronymian) version, fragments of which have been collected and edited by Sabatier (*Bibliorum . . . Latinae Versiones*, vol. i. 1751), and Vercellone (*Variae Lectiones Vulg. Lat. Bibl.*, vol. ii. 1864). $\mathfrak{L}^L$ = Codex Lugdunensis (ed. Ul. Robert, 1881-1900), as cited by Kit. *BH.*

$\mathfrak{S}^h$ . . The Syro-hexaplar version (ed. Lagarde, *Bibliothecae Syriacae*, 1892).

$\mathfrak{S}^P$ . . The Syriac (Peshiṭṭâ) version.

$\mathfrak{T}$ . . The Targum of Jonathan on the Prophets (ed. Lagarde, *Prophetae Chaldaice*, 1872; Praetorius, *Das Targum zum Buch der Richter*, 1900). This Targum is sometimes cited as $\mathfrak{T}^J$. $\mathfrak{T}^O$ = the Targum of Onkelos on the Pentateuch.

𝔙 . . The Latin version of Jerome (Vulgate).
Ar. . . The Arabic version (based on 𝔖^P).
Copt . . The Coptic version.
A.V. . . The Authorized version.
R.V. . . The Revised version.
O.T. . . Old Testament.

2. Sources.

D . . The Deuteronomist.
D^2 . . A later hand influenced by the former.
E . . The Elohistic narrative in the Hexateuch, Judg., and 1 Sam.
E^2 . . Later work by a member (*or* members) of the Elohistic school.
H . . The Law of Holiness in Leviticus.
J . . The Jehovistic (*or* Yahwistic) narrative in the Hexateuch, Judg. and 1 Sam.
JE . . The combined narrative of J and E—a symbol used when it is not possible, or not necessary, to distinguish the sources.
R^D . . The Deuteronomic redactors of Kgs. and of JE in Josh.
R^{E2} . . Redactor of the school of E^2, the principal editor of Judg. (cf. pp. xli ff.).
R^{JE} . . Redactor of J and E in the Hexateuch, Judg., and 1 Sam.
R^P . . Redactors of the Priestly school (influenced by the Hexateuchal document P) of Judg. and Kgs.
P . . The Priestly document in the Hexateuch.
X . . An unknown source in Judg. 20, 21 (cf. p. 457 f.).

3. Authorities.

[See also the literature cited at the head of the various sections of the Commentary. The works there mentioned are cited, within the section to which they refer, by the authors' names only.]

AJSL.—The American Journal of Semitic Languages and Literatures (vols i.-xi., entitled *Hebraica*, 1884-95).

AJTh.—American Journal of Theology (1897 ff.).

Bach.—J. Bachmann, *Das Buch der Richter* (1868).
Vol. i. on *chs.* 1-5 is all that ever appeared.

Baethgen, *Beiträge.*—F. Baethgen, *Beiträge zur Semitischen Religionsgeschichte* (1888).

BDB.—F. Brown, S. R. Driver, and C. A. Briggs, *A Hebrew and English Lexicon of the Old Testament* (1891-1906).

Ber.—E. Bertheau, *Das Buch der Richter und Ruth* (2nd ed., 1883): *Kurzgef. Exeget. Handbuch zum A.T.*

Black—J. S. BLACK, *The Book of Judges* (1892): *The Smaller Cambridge Bible for Schools.* Containing suggestions by W. Robertson Smith (RSm).

Bochart, *Hierozoicon.*—S. BOCHARTUS, *Hierozoicon; sive Bipertitum Opus de Animalibus Sacrae Scripturae*, cum notis E. F. C. Rosenmüller (1793-6).

Böhl, *KH.*—F. BÖHL, *Kanaanäer und Hebräer: Untersuchungen zur Vorgeschichte des Volkstums und der Religion Israels auf dem Boden Kanaans* (1911).

Br.—R. E. BRÜNNOW, *A Classified List of all Simple and Compound Cuneiform Ideograms* (1887-9).

Breasted, *AR.*—J. H. BREASTED, *Ancient Records of Egypt* (5 vols., 1906-7).

—— *Hist. Eg.*—*A History of Egypt* (1906).

Bu., [*Comm.*].—K. BUDDE, *Das Buch der Richter* (1897): *Kurzer Hand-Commentar zum A.T.* herausg. von K. Marti.

—— *RS.*—*Die Bücher Richter und Samuel, ihre Quellen und ihr Aufbau* (1890).

Buhl, *Geogr.*—F. BUHL, *Geographie des Alten Palästina* (1896).

Burch.—M. BURCHARDT, *Die Altkanaanäischen Fremdworte und Eigennamen in Aegyptischen* (1909-10).

Camb. Bib.—*The Cambridge Bible for Schools and Colleges.*

CH.—J. ESTLIN CARPENTER and G. HARFORD-BATTERSBY, *The Hexateuch according to the Revised Version . . . with Introduction, Notes, etc.* (1900).

CH.^{J}, CH.^{E}, etc., refer to the lists of Words and Phrases characteristic of J, E, etc., as contained in vol. i. pp. 185 ff. In such references the number following is the number in the list.

CIS.—*Corpus Inscriptionum Semiticarum* (1881 ff.).

Le Clerc—J. CLERICUS, *Veteris Testamenti Libri Historici* (1708).

Cooke—G. A. COOKE, *The Book of Judges* (1913): *Cambridge Bible.* Often cited as Cooke, *Comm.* in the notes on *chs.* 4 and 5, when supplementary to, or divergent from, the monograph noticed on p. 78.

—— *NSI.*—*A Text-book of North-Semitic Inscriptions* (1903).

Cor.—C. CORNILL, *Introduction to the Canonical Books of the Old Testament*, trans. by G. H. Box (1907).

COT.—E. SCHRADER, *The Cuneiform Inscriptions and the Old Testament*, 2nd ed., trans. by O. C. Whitehouse (1885-88).

CT.—*Cuneiform Texts from Babylonian Tablets, etc., in the British Museum* (1896 ff.).

Davidson, *Syntax.*—A. B. DAVIDSON, *Hebrew Syntax* (1894).

DB.—*A Dictionary of the Bible*, ed. by J. Hastings (1898-1902).

Delitzsch, *Paradies.*—FRIED. DELITZSCH, *Wo lag das Paradies? Eine Biblisch-Assyriologische Studie* (1881).

—— *Prolegomena.*—*Prolegomena eines Neuen Hebr.-Aram. Wörterbuchs zum AT.* (1886).

—— *HWB.*—*Assyrisches Handwörterbuch* (1896).

Doorn.—A. VAN DOORNINCK, *Bijdrage tot de Tekstkritiek van Richteren*, i.-xvi. (1879).

Dozy—R. DOZY, *Supplément aux Dictionnaires Arabes* (1881).

Driver, *Tenses.*[3]—S. R. DRIVER, *A Treatise on the Use of the Hebrew Tenses* (3rd ed., 1892).

—— *LOT.*[9]—*An Introduction to the Literature of the Old Testament* (9th ed., 1914).

—— *NHTS.*[2]—*Notes on the Hebrew Text and the Topography of the Books of Samuel* (2nd ed., 1913).

—— *Schweich Lectures.*—*Modern Research as illustrating the Bible* (*Schweich Lectures*, 1908).

EB.—*Encyclopaedia Biblica*, ed. by T. K. Cheyne and J. Sutherland Black (1899-1903).

Ehr.—A. B. EHRLICH, *Randglossen zur Hebräischen Bibel* (vol. 3, 1910).

ET.—*Expository Times* (1889 ff.).

Ew., *HI.*—H. EWALD, *The History of Israel* (Eng. trans. of vols. i.-v., 1869-74).

—— *DAB.*—*Die Dichter des Alten Bundes* (2nd ed., 1854-67).

Field, *Hex.*—F. Field, *Origenis Hexaplorum quae supersunt* (1875).

Frankenberg—W. FRANKENBERG, *Die Composition des Deuteronom. Richterbuches* (*Richter ii.* 6—*xvi.*) *nebst einer Kritik von Richter xvii.-xxi.* (1895).

Garstang, *Hittites.*—J. GARSTANG, *The Land of the Hittites* (1910).

Ges., *Thes.*—W. GESENIUS, *Thesaurus Philologicus Criticus Ling. Hebr. et Chald. Veteris Testamenti* (1826-58).

G.-K.—*Gesenius' Hebrew Grammar as edited and enlarged by the late E. Kautzsch*, 2nd English ed. revised in accordance with the 28th German ed. (1909) by A. E. Cowley (1910).

Grä.—H. GRÄTZ, *Emendationes in Plerosque Sacrae Scripturae Veteris Testamenti Libros*, ed. G. Bacher : (fasc. tert. 1894).

Gress.—H. GRESSMANN, *Die Anfänge Israels* (1912-14), Part I. 2 of *Die Schriften des Alten Testaments*, edited by various scholars.

Hall, *NE.*—H. R. HALL, *The Ancient History of the Near East* (1913).

Holzinger—H. HOLZINGER, *Richter* 2^{6}-16^{31} *untersucht*, as quoted from the manuscript by Budde in his Commentary.

Hommel, *AHT.*—F. HOMMEL, *The Ancient Hebrew Tradition as illustrated by the Monuments*, trans. by E. McClure and L. Crosslé (1897).

Hommel, *Grundriss.—Grundriss der Geographie und Geschichte des Alten Orients* (1904).

Houb.—C. F. HOUBIGANTIUS, *Notae Criticae in Universos Veteris Testamenti Libros* (1777).

HP.—R. HOLMES and J. PARSONS, *Vetus Testamentum Graecum cum Variis Lectionibus* (1798-1827).

ICC.—The International Critical Commentary.

JAOS.—Journal of the American Oriental Society (1851 ff.).

Jastrow, *RBA.*—M. JASTROW, jr., *Die Religion Babyloniens und Assyriens* (1905-12).

—— *RBBA.—Aspects of Religious Belief and Practice in Babylonia and Assyria* (1911).

JBL.—Journal of Biblical Literature and Exegesis (1890 ff.).

Jensen, *Kosmologie.*—P. JENSEN, *Die Kosmologie der Babylonier* (1890).

Jos.—FLAVIUS JOSEPHUS (*Opera* ed. Niese, 1888-94).
—— *Ant.—Antiquitates Judaicae.*
—— *BJ.—De Bello Judaico.*
—— *C.Ap.—Contra Apionem.*

JQR.—Jewish Quarterly Review (1888 ff.).

JTS.—Journal of Theological Studies (1900 ff.).

KAT.[3]—H. ZIMMERN and H. WINCKLER, *Die Keilinschriften und das Alte Testament* (1903).

Published as the 3rd ed. of E. Schrader's work which bears the same title (see under *COT.*), though really an entirely new work in plan and contents.

KB.—Keilinschriftliche Bibliothek: Sammlung von Assyrischen und Babylonischen Texten in Umschrift und Übersetzung, ed. E. Schrader in collaboration with various scholars (vols. i.-vi. 2 (1), 1889-1915).

Ke.—C. F. KEIL and F. DELITZSCH, *Biblical Commentary on the Old Testament*—vol. iv., *Joshua, Judges, Ruth*, ed. by Keil, trans. by J. Martin (1865).

Kennicott—B. KENNICOTT, *Vetus Testamentum Hebraicum cum Variis Lectionibus*, 2 vols. (1776-80).

Kent—C. F. KENT, *Narratives of the Beginnings of Hebrew History* (1904).

Kimchi—Rabbi DAVID KIMCHI (A.D. 1160-1235), Commentary on Judges as printed in Buxtorf's Rabbinic Bible.

King, *Hammurabi.*—L. W. KING, *Letters and Inscriptions of Hammurabi* (1898-1900).
—— *Chron.—Chronicles concerning Early Babylonian Kings* (1907)
—— *Sum. and Akk.—A History of Sumer and Akkad* (1910).
—— *Bab.—A History of Babylon* (1915).

Kit.—R. KITTEL, *Das Buch Richter* (*Die Heilige Schrift des A. T.*, ed. E. Kautzsch, 3rd ed. 1909, pp. 340-377).

—— *BH.*—*Biblia Hebraica* (*Liber Judicum*, 1905).

—— *HH.*—*A History of the Hebrews*, trans. by J. Taylor (1895-6).

—— *GVI.*[2]—*Geschichte des Volkes Israel* (2nd ed., 1909-12).

Kn[udtzon]—*Die el-Amarna-Tafeln, mit Einleitung und Erläuterungen*, herausgegeben von J. A. KNUDTZON : *Anmerkungen und Register*, bearbeitet von O. WEBER und E. EBELING (1907-15).

König, *Syntax.*—F. E. KÖNIG, *Historisch-comparative Syntax der Hebräischen Sprache: Schlusstheil des Historisch-kritischen Lehrgebäudes des Hebräischen* (1897).

Kue., *Ond.*—A. KUENEN, *Historisch-kritisch Onderzoek naar het Ontstaan en de Verzameling van de Boeken des Ouden Verbonds* (2nd ed., 1885-89); *German Trans.* (1890-92).

La.—M. J. LAGRANGE, *Le Livre des Juges* (1903).

—— *ÉRS.*[2]—*Études sur les Religions Sémitiques* (2nd ed. 1905).

Lane—E. W. LANE, *An Arabic-English Lexicon* (1863-93).

Levi ben-Gershon—Rabbi LEVI the son of Gershon (A.D. 1288-1344), Commentary on Judges as printed in Buxtorf's Rabbinic Bible.

Maspero, *Mêlées.*—G. MASPERO, *Les Premières Mêlées des Peuples* (Part II. of *Histoire Ancienne des Peuples de l'Orient Classique*), 1897.

MDOG.—*Mitteilungen der Deutschen Orient-Gesellschaft* (1898 ff.).

Meyer, *IN.*—E. MEYER, *Die Israeliten und ihre Nachbarstämme* (1906).

—— *GA.*[2]—*Geschichte des Altertums* (2nd ed., vol. i., 1907-9).

Mo., [*Comm.*].—G. F. MOORE, *A Critical and Exegetical Commentary on Judges* (*International Critical Commentary*), 2nd ed., 1903.

—— *SBOT.*—*The Book of Judges; Critical Edition of the Hebrew Text*, 1900; *A New English Translation*, 1898 (*The Sacred Books of the Old Testament*).

Müller, *AE.*—W. MAX MÜLLER, *Asien und Europa nach Altägyptischen Denkmälern* (1893).

Muss-Arnolt, *Dict.*—W. MUSS-ARNOLT, *A Concise Dictionary of the Assyrian Language* (1894-1905).

MVAG.—*Mitteilungen der Vorderasiatischen Gesellschaft* (1896 ff.).

NHTK.—C. F. BURNEY, *Notes on the Hebrew Text of the Books of Kings* (1903).

NHTS.[2]—See under Driver.

No.—W. NOWACK, *Richter, Ruth u. Bücher Samuelis* (1902): *Handkommentar zum A.T.* herausg. von W. Nowack.

Oet.—S. OETTLI, *Das Deuteronomium und die Bücher Josua und Richter* (1893): *Kurzgefasster Kommentar*, edd. H. Strack and O. Zöckler.

OLZ.—Orientalistische Litteratur-Zeitung (1878 ff.).

Oort—*Textus Hebraici Emendationes quibus in Vetere Testamento Neerlandice vertendo usi sunt A. Kuenen, I. Hooykaas, W. H. Kosters, H. Oort*, ed. H. OORT (1900).

OS.—Onomastica Sacra, ed. P. de Lagarde (1887). This contains the 'Name-lists' of Eusebius and Jerome.

OTLAE.—A. JEREMIAS, *The Old Testament in the Light of the Ancient East*, trans. by C. L. Beaumont, ed. by C. H. W. Johns (1911).

PEF.—Palestine Exploration Fund (founded 1865).

—— *Qy. St.—Quarterly Statement* (1869 ff.).

Petrie, *Hist. Eg.*—W. M. FLINDERS PETRIE, *A History of Egypt.* Vol. 1. *Dynasties i-xvi* (1894) ; Vol. 2. *Dynasties xvii-xviii* (1896) ; Vol. 3. *Dynasties xix-xxx* (1905).

PSBA.—Proceedings of the Society of Biblical Archaeology (1878 ff.).

i.-v. R.—H. C. RAWLINSON, *The Cuneiform Inscriptions of Western Asia*, i.-v. (1861-84, iv.², 1891).

Rashi—Rabbi SHELOMO YIṢḤAḲI (A.D. 1040-1105), Commentary on Judges as printed in Buxtorf's Rabbinic Bible.

RB.—Revue Biblique (1892 ff.).

RÉJ.—Revue des Études Juives (1880 ff.).

Reuss—E. REUSS, *La Bible : Traduction Nouvelle avec Introductions et Commentaires* (1874).

Riehm, *HWB.*²—E. K. RIEHM, *Handwörterbuch des Biblischen Alterthums* (2nd ed. 1893-4).

Rob., *BR.*³—E. ROBINSON, *Biblical Researches in Palestine and the Adjacent Regions : a Journal of Travels in the Years* 1838 *and* 1852 (3rd ed., 1867).

Rogers, *CP.*—R. W. ROGERS, *Cuneiform Parallels to the Old Testament* (1912).

—— *HBA.*⁶—*A History of Babylonia and Assyria* (6th ed., 1915).

Ros.—E. F. C. ROSENMÜLLER, *Scholia in Vetus Testamentum—Judices et Ruth* (1835).

de Rossi—J. B. DE ROSSI, *Variae Lectiones Veteris Testamenti.* 4 vols. (1784-8).

RSm.—W. ROBERTSON SMITH, as cited by Black, *q.v.*

Sayce, *HCM.*—A. H. SAYCE, *The 'Higher Criticism' and the Verdict of the Monuments* (1894).

—— *Archaeology.—The Archaeology of the Cuneiform Inscriptions* (1907).

SBOT.—The Sacred Books of the Old Testament, edited by various scholars, under the editorial direction of P. Haupt.

Smith, *HG.*—G. A. SMITH, *The Historical Geography of the Holy Land* (13th ed., 1906).

Smith, *DB.*[2]—*A Dictionary of the Bible*, edited by Sir W. Smith and J. M. Fuller (2nd ed. of vol. i., 1893).

Stade, *GVI.*[2]—B. STADE, *Geschichte des Volkes Israel* (2nd ed., 1888-9).

Stu.—G. L. STUDER, *Das Buch der Richter grammatisch und historisch erklärt* (2nd ed., 1842).

SWP.—*Survey of Western Palestine.*

—— *Great Map.*—*Map of Western Palestine in 26 Sheets, from Survey conducted for the Palestine Exploration Fund by Lieutenants C. R. Conder and H. H. Kitchener, R.E., during the Years* 1872-77. *Scale One Inch to a Mile* (1897).

—— *Name Lists.*—*Arabic and English Name Lists* to above (1881).

—— *Mem.*—*Memoirs* to above in 3 vols. (1881-3).

T.A. Letters.—The letters in cuneiform discovered at Tell el-Amarna.

TB.—*Altorientalische Texte und Bilder zum Alten Testaments*, ed. H. Gressmann in collaboration with A. Ungnad and H. Ranke (1909).

Thomson, *LB.*—W. M. THOMSON, *The Land and the Book* (ed. of 1861).

Vincent, *Canaan.*—H. VINCENT, *Canaan d'après l'Exploration Récente* (1907).

Wellh., *Comp.*[3]—J. WELLHAUSEN, *Die Composition des Hexateuchs und der Historischen Bücher des Alten Testaments* (3rd ed., 1899).

—— *TBS.*—*Der Text der Bücher Samuelis* (1871).

—— *Prolegomena.*—*Prolegomena to the History of Israel* (trans. by J. S. Black and A. Menzies, 1885).

Westm. Comm.—*Westminster Commentaries.*

Winckler, *GI.*—H. WINCKLER, *Geschichte Israels* (1895-1900).

—— *KT.*—*Keilinschriftliches Textbuch zum A.T.* (1892).

—— *AF.*—*Altorientalische Forschungen* (1893-1906).

When cited for the T.A. Letters the reference is to *KB.* vol. v.

ZA.—*Zeitschrift für Assyriologie und Verwandte Gebiete* (1886 ff.).

ZATW.—*Zeitschrift für die Alttestamentliche Wissenschaft* (1881 ff.).

ZDMG.—*Zeitschrift der Deutschen Morgenländischen Gesellschaft* (1846 ff.).

ZDPV.—*Zeitschrift des Deutschen Palästina-Vereins* (1878 ff.).

4. Other Abbreviations and Signs.

Ar., . . .	Arabic.
Aram., . .	Aramaic.
Assyr., . .	Assyrian.
Bab., . .	Babylonian.
Eg., . . .	Egyptian.
Heb., . .	Hebrew.
New Heb., .	New Hebrew, the language of the Mishna, etc.
al., . . .	*et aliter* or *et alii.*
וג׳ . . .	וְגוֹמֵר 'and the rest'; used when a Heb. quotation is incomplete.
׳ . . .	Sign of abbreviation in Heb. words.

The sign † after a series of Biblical references means that all occurrences in the O.T. of the word or phrase in question have been cited.

Biblical references are given in accordance with the numeration of chapter and verse in the English versions. When this varies in the Hebrew, the variation is usually noted: thus, Hos. 14^{2}, 𝔐 ^{3}.

The first and second halves of a verse are specified as, *e.g.*, $v.^{1a}$, $v.^{1b}$, the guide to such division being the Heb. accent *Athnaḥ*, which halves the verse. When it is necessary to refer to quarter-verses, these are specified as, *e.g.* $v.^{1a\alpha}$, $v.^{1a\beta}$, $v.^{1b\alpha}$, $v.^{1b\beta}$, the dividing factor being usually the accent *Zāḳeph*, which commonly halves the *Athnaḥ*- and *Silluḳ*-clauses.

In the translation of the Hebrew text the following signs are employed as indications of correction:—

Emendations are placed between ⌜ ⌝.

Additions are placed between ⟨ ⟩.

Excisions are indicated by [ ].

Italics are used in the ordinary way to mark *emphasis*; and not, as in A.V., R.V., as an indication that the words so marked are not represented in the original.

A small superlinear figure attached to the title of a work (*e.g.* Driver, *Tenses* ^{3}) denotes the *edition* to which reference is made.

TRANSLITERATION OF SEMITIC WORDS

Consonants.

Arabic.

ا	ʾ	ف	*f*
ب	*b*	ق	*ḳ*
ت	*t*	ك	*k*
ث	*ṯ*	ل	*l*
ج	*ǵ*	م	*m*
ح	*ḥ*	ن	*n*
خ	*ḫ*	ه	*h*
د	*d*	و	*u, w*
ذ	*ḏ*	ي	*i, y*
ر	*r*		
ز	*z*		
س	*s*		
ش	*š*		
ص	*ṣ*		
ض	*ḍ*		
ط	*ṭ*		
ظ	*ẕ*		
ع	ʿ		
غ	*ġ*		

Hebrew and Aramaic.

א	ʾ		
בּ	*b,*	ב	*bh*
גּ	*g,*	ג	*gh*
דּ	*d,*	ד	*dh*
ה	*h*		
ו	*w, v*		
ז	*z*		
ח	*ḥ*		
ט	*ṭ*		
י	*y*		
כּ	*k,*	כ	*kh*
ל	*l*		
מ	*m*		
נ	*n*		
ס	*ṡ*		
ע	ʿ		
פּ	*p,*	פ	*ph*
צ	*ṣ*		
ק	*ḳ*		
ר	*r*		
שׂ	*s*		
שׁ	*š*		
תּ	*t,*	ת	*th*

Babylonian.

Non-gutturals as in Hebrew

ʾ

ḫ

Vowels.

	Long.	*Short.*	*Half-vowels.*
Hebrew / W. Aramaic	*â, ā, ê, ē, î, ô, ō, û*	*a, e, i, o, u*	*ă, ĕ, ŏ* or $^{a, e, o}$
Syriac . .	*â, î, û*	*a, e*	
Arabic . .	*â, î, û*	*a, i, u,* and modifications to *e* and *o* where usual.	
Babylonian	*â, ê, î, û*	*a, e, i, u*	

In Hebrew place- and personal names the familiar forms of A.V. and R.V. are usually retained; except that צ is always represented by ṣ and not z, certain letters are marked by diacritic points (thus ח = ḥ, ט = ṭ, ס = ṡ, ק = ḳ), and ע is regularly marked by ʿ, except where it already stands as g (*i.e.* ġ = غ) through the influence of 𝔊, as in עַזָּה = Γαζα, Ġaza). א is occasionally represented by ʾ. The divine name יהוה is regularly represented by Yahweh.

INTRODUCTION

§ 1. Title, Scope, and Place in the Canon.

THE title of the Book is in 𝔐 שפטים, *Šōphᵉṭîm*, whence comes our English title 'Judges.' The principal versions render 𝔊 ΚΡΙΤΑΙ; 𝔙 *Liber Judicum, Hebräice Sophetim*; 𝔖ᴾ ܣܦܪܐ ܕܕܝܢܐ ܕܒܢܝ ܐܝܣܪܝܠ . ܕܡܬܩܪܐ ܥܒܪܐܝܬ ܫܘܦܛܐ 'The book of the Judges of the children of Israel, which is called in Hebrew *Šōphᵉṭîm*.'

The title *Šōphᵉṭîm* is doubtless derived from *ch.* 2 $^{16 \text{ ff.}}$, which is due to the main editor (R^{E2}; cf. § 4), who employs the term 'Judges,' not in the sense in which we are accustomed to use it in English of officials who *decide* legal cases and act as *arbitrators* between man and man, but with the meaning '*Vindicators*,' or '*Deliverers*' from the power of foreign oppressors.* There exist, however, passages in the Book, not due to this editor, in which the term is used in the more general sense of 'Arbitrators' or 'Magistrates' (cf. further, on this distinction in usage, p. 1, *footnote*). In this latter sense, the Carthaginian title *sufes* (*suffes*), plur. *sufetes* (*i.e.* שׁוֹפֵט, שׁוֹפְטִים), as cited by Livy and other Latin writers, has been aptly compared. On the occurrence of the term in Phoenician inscriptions, cf. Cooke, *NSI.* pp. 115 f.‡

The Book of Judges deals with the period during which the tribes of Israel were still struggling to maintain their footing in Canaʿan, before they had attained such an amount of cohesion among themselves as entitled them to rank as a nation rather than as a collection of separate units, and enabled them to establish their independence against the foreign races by whom they were surrounded. During this period we repeatedly find one or more of the tribes falling under the foreign yoke for a time, until the uprising of some one of sufficient personality to revive and unite the

* In some passages Heb. *Môšîaʿ* 'Saviour' is used by the editor as an alternative title (cf. *ch.* 3 $^{9.15}$); and we also find the verb *hôšîaʿ* 'to save' similarly used as a synonym of 'to judge.'

‡ Jensen (*ZA.* iv., 1889, pp. 278 ff.) quotes evidence in proof that in Assyr. *šâpiṭu* was used to denote the commander of a host. Cf. *KAT.*³ pp. 647, 650.

scattered energy of the clans, and thus to enable them to shake themselves free. Such leaders (the *Šôphᵉṭîm*, 'Judges'), after the success of their efforts, seem generally to have continued to hold a position of authority which, though doubtless merely local and uninvested with the prerogatives of the kingship of later times, yet represents a stage of development preparatory to the monarchy; just as their partial success in uniting the tribes to take common action against the foe is a stage towards the later unity which made possible the ideal of a nation organically combined under the rule of one king.

Of the three divisions of the Hebrew Canon—the Law, the Prophets, and the *Kᵉthûbhîm*, 'Writings' (Hagiographa)—the Book of Judges finds its place among the Prophets. This second division is sub-divided into two parts, each of which is reckoned as containing four books—'the Former Prophets,' consisting of Joshua', Judges, Samuel, and Kings; and 'the Latter Prophets,' comprising Isaiah, Jeremiah, Ezeḳiel, and 'the Twelve.'

The justification of this inclusion of Judges among the Prophets is found, as in the case of the other books assigned to 'the Former Prophets,' in the fact that the mere compilation of an historical record was not the purpose with which the book was put into shape, but rather the inculcation of the religious truths which were to be deduced from Israel's past history. It is abundantly evident that the ancient narratives (for the most part) which form the basis of the history, and also—and especially—the editorial framework into which these older narratives have been fitted, are the work of the Prophetical schools or guilds of Israel which, in pre-exilic times, were the chief literary conservators of the records of national history. The lines along which the religious bearing of Israel's past history is worked out in Judges are indicated in the sections which follow.

§ 2. Structure.

The Book of Judges opens with a section extending from *ch.* 1^{1} to 2^{5}, which describes the settlement of the tribes of Israel in the promised land, and pictures this settlement as very gradual and partial, and as effected, in the main, through the independent efforts of individual tribes. The facts which are thus narrated are stated in *v.*^{1} to have taken place 'after the death of Joshua''; but it is clear that the standpoint of *v.*^{1} is not the standpoint of the main part of the narrative, which pictures the tribes as starting their movements from 'the City of Palms,' *i.e.* Jericho (*v.*^{16}), or from Gilgal in the near neighbourhood (2^{1}); *i.e.* from the position in which they were stationed after their first crossing of the Jordan, and which formed their headquarters during their invasion of the hill-country, as narrated in Josh. 4^{19} P, 9^{6}, $10^{6.7.9.15}$ JE, 10^{43},

14^{6} R^{D}. It is obvious, moreover, that the narrative of *ch.* 1 cannot be correlated with the narrative of the conquest of Canaʿan under Joshuaʿ, as this now stands in the Book of Josh.; since this latter pictures the conquest as the work of the tribes of Israel as a whole, and as much more complete and far-reaching than is pictured in Judg. 1. Clearly, therefore, Judg. 1^{1} to 2^{5} cannot originally have stood as the proper sequel of the closing chapter of Josh., which pictures the death of Joshuaʿ as taking place subsequently to the dispersion and settlement of the tribes throughout the land of Canaʿan; but is out of place in its present connexion, and really offers another account of the original settlement in the land, in many respects different from that which is found in Josh. as that Book now stands.

Looking, however, at the next section of the Book, which runs from *ch.* 2^{6} to 3^{6}, we seem at once to discern the true sequel to Josh. 24; this section opening, in *vv.*$^{6\text{-}9}$, with an actual repetition of the words of Josh. $24^{28\text{-}31}$, with one slight variation in order. That these *vv.*$^{6\text{-}9}$ are not a later insertion from Josh., but stand in proper connexion with the narrative which immediately follows them in Judg. 2, requires no proof. While *v.*^{6} reiterates the mention of Joshuaʿ's dismissal of the people to their homes after his final exhortation to them at Shechem, as narrated in Josh. $24^{1\,ff.}$, *v.*^{7} states that they remained faithful to his injunctions during his lifetime, and the lives of the elders who survived him, and *vv.*$^{8.9}$ give a summary account of his death and burial. The narrative is immediately taken up by *v.*^{10}, which states that, after the death of the surviving elders mentioned in *v.*^{7}, there arose a new generation that did not know Yahweh nor the work which He had done for Israel, and thus were guilty of defection from His service, as related in *vv.*$^{11\,ff.}$

In these latter verses the narrator propounds his philosophy of Israel's history in general terms. We are told that defection from Yahweh and the worship of the deities of Canaʿan (the Baʿals and ʿAshtarts) led to divine punishment which took the form of deliverance into the hand of foreign oppressors; punishment was followed by repentance and appeal to Yahweh for deliverance; Yahweh thereupon raised up a 'Judge,' *i.e.* a saviour or vindicator (cf. § 1), who effected deliverance by the help of Yahweh; but, when the Judge died, defection from Yahweh again ensued, and the same cycle of punishment, repentance, and deliverance was re-enacted.

If we examine the narratives which follow after this introductory section, forming the main body of the Book, we find that this 'pragmatic' scheme of history (as it has been styled),* which has been stated in general terms in the introduction $2^{11\,ff.}$, is applied

* The term 'pragmatic' is used as defined in *The Concise Oxford Dictionary of Current English*: 'treating facts of history with reference to their practical lessons.'

to particular cases as they occur, the striking phraseology of the general introduction being, for the most part, repeated practically *verbatim* in the introductions to particular narratives (cf. pp. 54 ff. of the *notes*). Of such a character are the introductions to the narratives of ʿOthniel, 3 $^{7\,ff.}$, Ehud, 3 $^{12\,ff.}$, Deborah and Baraḳ, 4 $^{1\,ff.}$, Gideʿon, 6 $^{1\,ff.}$, Jephthaḥ, 10 $^{6\,ff.}$ (perhaps originally intended as an introduction to the judgeship of Samuel; cf. *note ad loc.*), and Samson, 13 ^{1}. Corresponding to these introductions to the narratives, we find that more or less stereotyped formulae are employed at their close, referring to the subjugation of the foreign oppressor, and the length of the period during which 'the land had rest': so, after the victories of ʿOthniel, 3 ^{11}, Ehud, 3 ^{30}, Deborah and Baraḳ, 4 ^{23}, 5 ^{31b}, Gideʿon, 8 ^{28}. Elsewhere, as a variation, the length is given of the period during which the Judge 'judged Israel': so of Jephthaḥ, 12 ^{7a}, Samson, 15 ^{20}, repeated in 16 ^{31b}, the so-called 'minor' Judges, 10 $^{2a.3}$, 12 $^{8.11.14}$; cf., in 1 Sam., ʿEli 4 ^{18}, Samuel 7 ^{15}.

It will readily be noticed that the religious pragmatism of the main introduction and the special headings is not characteristic of the histories as a whole. In these the religious motive, in so far as it is put forward, is of a much more ingenuous and primitive character. Yahweh commissions men to act as deliverers, and His Spirit incites them to deeds of valour; but, if we except certain special sections, such as 6 $^{7-10}$ and 10 $^{6-16}$ (this latter a much expanded form of the ordinary introduction to a narrative), we find that the conceptions of sin, punishment, and repentance, so far from being prominently brought forward, are altogether ignored and unmentioned. In the history of Samson, in particular, the conception of the hero as a divinely appointed deliverer of his people seems little suited to the narrative; since his actions, so far as his personal volition is concerned, are wholly dictated by his own wayward inclinations, and he does not in any way effect deliverance or even respite from the foreign yoke.

We observe also that, whereas the stereotyped introduction to the various narratives speaks as though the apostasy of Israel from time to time, and their ensuing punishment, were *national* and *general*, the actual illustrations adduced in the narratives themselves are, at any rate in most cases, merely *local*, some particular tribe or group of tribes falling temporarily under the dominion of a foreign oppressor, but Israel as a whole (*i.e.* the entity of twelve tribes, which is clearly intended by 'the children of Israel' of the introductory formula) being unaffected.

It is obvious, therefore, that the main narratives of the Judges and their exploits cannot emanate from the author who was responsible for the framework in which they are set, which enforces the lesson already sketched in a preliminary way in *chs.* 2 ^{6}-3 ^{6}, containing (as we have noticed above) the original introduction to the Book. Clearly, the main narratives represent older material, which has been utilized by a later editor for the working out of the religious philosophy which he reads into Israel's past history.

The work of the editor who was responsible for the pragmatic introduction, 2^{6}-3^{6}, and the framework of the narratives following, extends no further than the history of Samson, the last of the Judges. The final narratives of the Book, viz. the story of Micah and the Danites, *chs.* 17, 18, and the story of the outrage at Gibeʿah with its consequences, *chs.* 19-21, though in the main of the same literary character as the other old narratives, do not serve to illustrate this editor's scheme as laid down in his general introduction, and altogether lack traces of his hand as seen in the stereotyped introductions and conclusions to the stories of the Judges. We must conclude, therefore, that these two stories, though derived ultimately from the same history-book (*or* books) as the other old narratives, were not embraced within the main editor's Book of Judges. There is reason for supposing that this editor also omitted, as alien to his purpose, the story of Abimelech, *ch.* 9 (substituting in its place the brief summary which is found in *ch.* 8^{33-35}; cf. p. 266), and such exploits of Samson as are now related in *ch.* 16 (cf. p. 338). These stories must have been re-inserted into Judg. at a later period—very possibly by the editor who added the later Introduction to the Book which we now find in *chs.* 1^{1}-2^{5}. This later editor appears also to have been responsible for the brief notices of the 'minor' Judges contained in 10^{1-5}, 12^{8-15} (the reasons for supposing that the 'minor' Judges did not belong to the main editor's scheme are given on pp. 289 f.). The notice of Shamgar, *ch.* 3^{31}, seems to have been inserted at a still later period (cf. p. 76).

§ 3. The Old Narratives.

From examination of the old narratives which form the basis of the history of Judg. the fact at once emerges that the main editor is dependent, not upon a single source, but upon two main sources, sections from which have been pieced together without any thoroughgoing attempt to harmonize existing inconsistencies in detail; much as different documents have been combined into a single history in the Pentateuch and Josh., and in 1 Sam. The proof of this fact has been sufficiently established in the special Introductions to the various sections of the Book which follow in the Notes. The most noteworthy illustration is the history of Gideʿon, *chs.* 6^{1}-8^{28}; but a similar combination of two different narratives may also be traced in the stories of Ehud, *ch.* 3^{7-30}, Abimelech, *ch.* 9, Jephthaḥ, *chs.* 10^{17}-12^{7}, and (in the Appendix to Judges) in the narratives of *chs.* 17, 18, and 19-21.*

* The prose-history of Deborah and Baraḳ, *ch.* 4, likewise exhibits combination with elements derived from another narrative, relating probably to different events. It is not unlikely, however, that this combination was effected when the story was still in the oral stage: cf. pp. 81 ff.

It is generally recognized that the main characteristics of the old narratives thus combined in Judges are similar to those of the old 'Prophetical' narrative which runs through the Pentateuch and Josh. (the Hexateuch); and which is formed, likewise, by combination of two main documents, one of which must be supposed to have emanated from the Kingdom of Judah, and probably took shape as a written document *cir.* B.C. 850 (the reign of King Jehoshaphaṭ); while the other is doubtless the work of the prophetic schools of the Northern Kingdom, and should probably be dated, in the main, somewhat later, *i.e. cir.* B.C. 750 (the reign of king Jeroboʿam II. and the period of the writing prophets, ʿAmos and Hoseaʿ). The former of these two narratives, owing to its predilection for the divine name Jehovah or Yahweh, is commonly known as the Jehovistic or Yahwistic narrative, and cited under the symbol J; while the latter, which exhibits a preference for the divine title *Elōhîm* ('God'), is termed the Elohistic narrative, and is cited as E.*

Since J and E carry the history of Israel from the earliest times down to the death of Joshuaʿ, and were certainly not put into writing until some centuries after the latter event, there is no *a priori* reason why they should be supposed each to have terminated with the narrative of Joshuaʿ's death: but, on the contrary, when we find in Judg. and 1 Sam. a similar combination of two old narratives possessing much the same characteristics as J and E, the question is at once raised whether these narratives should not be regarded as the proper continuation of J and E in Josh.; J and E thus representing, in their original forms, continuous prophetic histories of the nation of Israel down to the foundation of the monarchy, if not further.‡ Observing, moreover, that the closing verses of Josh., *ch.* 24 $^{28\text{-}31}$ E, are repeated practically *verbatim* in Judg. 2 $^{6\text{-}9}$, the point at which the main editor opens his history, and that these verses point both backwards and forwards—Israel served Yahweh in accordance with the injunctions of Joshuaʿ's speech, which is detailed at length in Josh. 24 ^{1} ff. E, during the lifetimes of Joshuaʿ and the elders who survived him; but the setting of a period to this service immediately raises the question

* For the evidence upon which these approximate dates are assigned to J and E, cf. CH. i. pp. 107 f., 117 ff.

‡ The purpose of the present argument being merely to suggest that the old narratives of Judg. are essentially of a piece with J and E in the Hexateuch, we are not here concerned to inquire whether these same two narratives continue later than 1 Sam. 12, which forms the close of the history of the circumstances which led to the institution of the monarchy in Israel. 1 Sam. 1-12 stands in essential connexion with the history of Judg., and examination of the old narrative of Judg. cannot be carried out apart from some consideration of these earlier chapters of 1 Sam. With regard to 1 Sam. 13 ff. it will be sufficient here to remark that a similar combination of two narratives runs on to the end of the book; whereas 2 Sam., on the contrary, consists, in the main, of a single very early source narrating the court-history of David.

what happened *after* the elders were dead, which forms the subject of the book of Judg. as a whole (cf. the direct transition from Judg. 2 $^{6-9}$ to *v.*^{10}, on which see p. 52)—we may fairly claim that the fact that the document E of the Hexateuch continues beyond the end of Josh., and provides material for the history of Judg., seems to be placed beyond the range of controversy.

A similar conclusion must be drawn with regard to the companion-document J. The fact is generally admitted that the old document which forms the basis of the later introduction to Judg., *chs.* 1 ^{1}-2 ^{5}, is derived from J (cf. pp. 1 f., 47 ff.), and that the concluding portion of this old account of the settlement of the tribes of Israel in Canaʿan has been utilized by the main editor in his own introduction, *ch.* 2 ^{23a}, 3 $^{2a.5a.6}$ (cf. pp. 52, 55). These concluding verses, however, tell us that, as the result of the survival of some of the races of Canaʿan, 'the children of Israel dwelt in the midst of the Canaʿanites; and they took their daughters to themselves for wives, and their own daughters they gave to their sons; and they served their gods'; and this seems to indicate that some account of Israel's defection from Yahweh, and the consequences thereby entailed, must have followed in J. Since, therefore, the main editor knew and employed the J document thus far, the inference is that he also made use of its material for his subsequent history.

The fact that the main editor thus appears to have utilized both J and E in his introduction to Judg. does not, however, amount to a demonstration that the old narratives which follow must necessarily be derived from the same documents. Such a conclusion can only be based upon detailed examination of each separate story, and this has been attempted in the Introductions prefixed to each section of the book in the Notes. It may be freely acknowledged that the evidence which can be adduced in proof of it is not of equal cogency throughout. Close connexion with J is undeniable in 6 $^{11-24}$ (p. 177), 13 $^{2-25}$ (pp. 336 f.), the main narrative in 19 (pp. 443 ff.), and parts of 20 (pp. 455 ff.); and the same is true of E in the main thread of 2 ^{6}-3 ^{6} (pp. 52 ff.), 6 $^{7-10}$ (p. 177), 8 $^{22.23.27a\beta b}$ (pp. 183 f.), 10 $^{6-16}$ in the main (p. 294), 11 $^{12-28}$ (pp. 303, 310-317). In other parts of the composite narrative the criteria are frequently very slight; while occasionally they are practically non-existent, and the only ground which we have for assigning a narrative to J is the fact that the parallel narrative seems to emanate from E, or *vice-versâ*. This, however, is a state of affairs which we find also in the Hexateuch, where it frequently happens that, while the fact is clear that we are dealing with a narrative composed of elements derived from the two Prophetical sources, yet criteria for accurate distinction of these sources are hardly to be discovered.*

* This is especially the case with the JE narrative contained in Josh. 1-12. Cf. CH. ii. pp. 305 ff.; Driver, *LOT.*^{9} pp. 104 ff. (who with characteristic caution does not attempt to separate the two sources).

It is scarcely necessary to emphasize the fact that when we refer to J and E we must think, in each case, rather of a school of historians than of a single historian. Clearly, neither J nor E in the Hexateuch is homogeneous throughout; both of them must have made use of pre-existing material, written as well as oral, the product of very various ages, and embodying divergent and sometimes conflicting traditions.*

Illustrations from Judg. of the use of earlier material in J are seen in the Samson-stories, *chs.* 14-16, which have been edited and fitted with a strongly characteristic introduction, *ch.* 13 (pp. 337 f.), and in one of the narratives in *chs.* 19-21, which appears to be constructed throughout upon a basis of earlier J narratives (p. 456). Similarly, the Song of Deborah, *ch.* 5, is obviously much older than the accompanying prose-narrative, *ch.* 4, though both appear to belong to E (p. 83); and the inference that the former was excerpted from an ancient written source (probably a collection of poems such as 'the Book of the Wars of Yahweh' mentioned in Num. 21 [14]), is confirmed by the fact that the prefixed statement as to the occasion on which the song was composed, seems to have been excerpted with it from the old source (cf. *note* on *v.*[2]). Again, the E^2 element which is so clearly marked both in Judg. and in 1 Sam. 1-12 (originally a part of the history of the Judges; cf. p. 294), can never have formed an independent document, but presupposes the earlier history of E, to which it forms a religious expansion and interpretation. This incorporation of earlier material and the existence of more than one hand in J and E are sufficient to explain the unequal distribution of characteristic phraseology, and also the occurrence in certain sections of striking words and phrases which are not found elsewhere in the histories.‡

While, however, J and E undoubtedly embody the work of *two schools* of prophetic historians, it is natural to suppose that the work of these schools has survived through being gathered together into two continuous prophetic histories; and that it was these *two*

* Cf. CH. i. pp. 108 ff., 119 ff. Skinner (*Genesis* (*ICC.*), pp. 181 f.) points out that J seems to embody a tradition which knew nothing of the Flood, and also (cf. pp. 418, 450, 570) one which ignored the sojourn in Egypt and the Exodus. The discussion in *Addit. note*, pp. 44 ff. leads us to the conclusion that J has embodied an ancient Calibbite tradition narrating the conquest of the Negeb by a northward movement from Ḳadesh-Barnea', and that this has been modified in J as we know it by later influences. Such examples of composite authorship might be multiplied.

‡ Such are not frequent; but we may notice that the Divine title 'Yahweh Ṣᵉbhā'ôth,' which occurs in 1 Sam. 1 [3.11], 4 [4], 15 [2], 17 [45], as also in 2 Sam., is not found at all in the Hexateuch and Judg.; and 'Belial,' which occurs in Judg. 19 [22], 20 [13]; 1 Sam. 1 [16], 2 [12], 10 [27], 25 [17.25], 30 [22], is only found in the Hexateuch in Deut. 13 [14], 15 [9]. The instances from Judg. of words not found in JE in the Hexateuch which are cited by Kit., *Studien und Kritiken*, 1892, pp. 57, 61; König in *DB.* ii. pp. 811b-812b, would not be significant enough to tell against our theory even if that theory involved the supposition that J and E were respectively the composition of a single hand throughout.

documents, and not two collections of disconnected narratives, which were wrought into one by the redactor R^{JE}. There is thus a sense in which it is perfectly legitimate to speak of 'the J writer' and 'the E writer,' *i.e.* the actual individuals who were responsible for the composition of the continuous history-books; and since, as we have seen, evidence points to an original uninterrupted sequence between the Hexateuch narratives of J and E, and the narratives of J and E in Judg., we may without excessive boldness maintain that, when we use the symbols J and E in Judg., they have for us no less definite meaning than they possess for us as titles of documents in the Hexateuch.*

§ 4. The Editors.

The portions of Judg. which we assign to the main editor, who, as we have seen (§ 2), is responsible for the pragmatic setting of the book, are as follows:—

Introduction: *ch.* $2^{6b\text{ (in part)}.11a.14ab\alpha.16.17}$.

Framework: *chs.* 3^{7-11}, 3^{12-15a} (working up extracts from the old narrative), 3^{20}, 4^{1-4} (working up old extracts), $4^{23.24}$, 5^{31b}, 6^{1-6} (working up old extracts), $8^{28.33-35}$, $10^{6a\alpha}$‡, 11^{33b}, 13^{1}, 15^{20}.

Modern critical scholars unanimously regard this editor as a member of the Deuteronomic School, *i.e.* as influenced by the standpoint and phraseology of Deuteronomy: thus the signature which is generally adopted for him is R^{D} (Deuteronomic Redactor). The present writer has, however, convinced himself that this view is not correct. Deuteronomy was (in his opinion) unknown to our

* That we have in Judg. the continuation of the documents contained in the Hexateuch was maintained by J. J. Stähelin, *Specielle Einleitung in die kanon. Bücher des A.T.* (1862), pp. 66 ff., and by E. Schrader in de Wette's *Einleitung in die Bibel, A. u. N.T.* (1869), pp. 337 ff. The subject was first systematically worked out for different parts of Judg. by Ed. Meyer, Stade, and Böhme in articles in *ZATW.* (cf. references in the present Commentary, pp. 1, 176, 293, 335). The merit of attempting to distinguish J and E throughout the book belongs, however, to Budde in his *Richter und Samuel* (1890); and Budde's view has been accepted in the main by Cornill, Moore, Nowack, and Lagrange. Kue. (*Ond.* § 19^{13}) speaks with some scepticism of the theory, and it is opposed by Kittel in *Theol. Studien und Kritiken*, 1892, pp. 44 ff.; *HH.* ii. pp. 14 ff.; *GVI*². ii. pp. 15 ff., and by König, *Einleitung in das A.T.*, pp. 252 ff.; *DB.* ii. pp. 811b-812b. The arguments advanced by these two latter scholars, however, would for the most part only be valid if J and E were to be regarded as each the work of a single individual—a view which is maintained by no one. Cf. *e.g.* Kittel's argument that the history of Abimelech cannot be from E, because in it Shechem is a Cana'anite city, whereas in Josh. 24 E^2 it is Israelite; or, again, that in view of Gen. 22 E, the story of Jephthah's sacrifice of his daughter can hardly belong to the same source.

‡ It is impossible in 10^{6-16} to be sure how much is due to the main editor and how much to his source, E^2: cf. p. 294. Most scholars assign a larger portion of the section to the editor.

editor. The influence which really moulded his thought and diction was the influence of the later Ephraimitic school of prophetic teachers, whose work is generally marked as E^2. Thus the signature which is adopted in the present commentary to mark the work of the main editor is R^{E2} (Redactor of the late Ephraimitic School). The grounds upon which this view is based have now to be stated.

The passages in Judg., 1 Sam. 1-12, which are characteristically the work of E^2 are as follows:—Judg. $2^{6\ (\text{in part}).7\text{-}10.13.20.21}$, $6^{7\text{-}10}$, $8^{22.23.27a\beta b}$, $10^{6\text{-}16\ (\text{in the main})}$, 1 Sam. $7^{1\text{-}14}$, $8^{1\text{-}22}$, $10^{17\text{-}27a}$, $12^{1\text{-}25}$.* These passages are united together by a common phraseology and theological outlook, the characteristics of which, so far as they distinguish the passages in Judg., are noticed on pp. 55, 177, 183 f., 294; cf. further Bu., *RS.* pp. 180 ff., Driver, *LOT*[9]. p. 177. Their connexion with Joshua's last address, as related in Josh. 24 (generally assigned, except for a few minor details, to the later stratum of E, *i.e.* E^2) is very close; and more especially is this the case with 1 Sam. 12, which relates Samuel's last address before his retirement from the office of judge after the election of Saul as king. The following comparison illustrates the closeness of connexion between the two chapters:—

Josh. 24 ^{1} And they took their stand before Yahweh.
1 Sam. 12 ^{7} And now take your stand, that I may plead with you before God.

Josh.^{5} And I sent Moses and Aaron.
Sam.^{8} And Yahweh sent Moses and Aaron. (Cf.^{11} And Yahweh sent Jerubba'al, etc.).

Josh.^{6} And I brought forth your fathers out of Egypt.
Sam.^{8} And they brought forth your fathers out of Egypt.

Josh.^{7} And they cried unto Yahweh.
Sam.^{10} And they cried unto Yahweh.

Josh.^{8} And they fought with you. ^{9a} And he fought with Israel.
Sam.^{9b} And they fought with them.

Josh.^{10b} And I delivered you from his hand.
Sam.^{11b} And he delivered you from the hand of your enemies.

Josh.^{14} And now fear Yahweh, and serve him in integrity and in truth.
Sam.^{24a} Only serve Yahweh, and serve him in truth with all your heart. ^{14}. If ye will fear Yahweh and will serve him.

Josh.^{16} Far be it from us to forsake Yahweh.
Sam.^{23} Far be it from us to sin against Yahweh.

* Omitting, in Judg., $6^{25\text{-}32,\ 35b}$, $7^{2\text{-}7}$, passages which, though assigned to E^2 upon adequate grounds, have not the same special characteristics as the passages above cited.

Josh.^{17} For Yahweh our God, he it is that brought up us and our fathers from the land of Egypt, from the house of bondmen.

Sam.^{6} Yahweh . . . that brought up your fathers from the land of Egypt.

Josh.^{17} And who did these great signs before our eyes.

Sam.^{16} Behold the great thing which Yahweh is about to do before your eyes.

Josh.^{22}. And Joshuaʿ said unto the people, Ye are witnesses against yourselves. And they said, We are witnesses.

Sam.^{5}. And he said unto them, Yahweh is a witness against you, and his anointed is a witness . . . And ⌈they⌉ said, He is a witness.

This correspondence between the phraseology of the two addresses —which is so close as to make it obvious that they must both have assumed their present form at the hands of the same author, or else that 1 Sam. 12 must have been modelled upon Josh. 24— is of the first importance in proof that 1 Sam. 12, and the sections in Judg. and 1 Sam. which are similar to it, are rightly to be regarded as *pre-Deuteronomic.** The fact is familiar that JE in Josh. has been edited by a redactor of the Deuteronomic School (R^{D}), and the portions of Josh. which are the work of this redactor bear unmistakably the impress of the thought and phraseology of D. Now though there already existed in his source the farewell-address of Joshuaʿ which belongs to E^{2} (*ch.* 24), R^{D} was so little satisfied with this as an adequate expression of the Deuteronomic ideal that he inserted side by side with it (*ch.* 23) another address of his own composition in which he enforces that ideal in language which repeats and echoes the language of D almost sentence by sentence. It is worth while to give a full summary of the D phrases in this address in order to exhibit what is properly to be understood as the influence of D upon the members of its 'school':—

Josh. 23^{3}. 'Ye have seen all that Yahweh your God did.' Cf. Deut. 29^{2} ($\mathfrak{H}^{1}$), 3^{21}, 4^{3}; 'That which Yahweh thy God did,' Deut. 7^{18}, 24^{9}, cf. $11^{4.5}$.

v.^{3}. 'For Yahweh your God, He it is that fighteth for you.' So *v.*^{10}, Deut. 3^{22} †.

v.^{5}. 'As Yahweh your God spake unto you.' So v.^{10}. Cf. Deut. 1^{21}, 2^{1}, $6^{3.19}$, 9^{3}, 10^{9}, 11^{25}, 12^{20}, 15^{6}, 18^{2}, $26^{18.19}$, 27^{3}, 29^{13} ($\mathfrak{H}^{12}$), 31^{3}; Josh. $13^{14.33}$, 14^{12}, 22^{4}, all R^{D}; Judg. 2^{15} D^{2}, 1 Kgs. $5^{5.12}$ ($\mathfrak{H}^{19.26}$), 8^{20}; 2 Kgs. 24^{13}, all R^{D}.‡

* That the presentation of Samuel as we have it in this narrative in 1 Sam. was familiar to Jeremiah and his hearers is clear from Jer. 15^{1}, where Samuel is coupled with Moses as a typical *intercessor* on behalf of Israel; for he only appears in this light in 1 Sam. $7^{8\,ff.}$, $12^{19.23}$, and not in the older narrative with which this is combined. Cf. Cornill as cited by Bu., *RS.* p. 178; Driver, *LOT.*^{9} p. 178.

‡ In several of these passages R.V. renders 'promised' for 'spake'; but the verb is in every case the same in the Hebrew.

v.^{6}. 'All that is written in the Book of the Law of Moses' (a direct reference to the Deuteronomic Code). Cf. Josh. 1$^{7.8}$, 8$^{31.34}$ R^{D}; 1 Kgs. 2^{3}; 2 Kgs. 14^{6} R^{D}.

v.^{6}. 'So as not to turn aside therefrom to the right hand or to the left.' Cf. Deut. 17^{20}; also 5^{32} (𝕳^{29}), 17^{11}, 28^{14}; Josh. 1^{7} R^{D}; 2 Kgs. 22^{2} R^{D}.

v.^{8}. 'Cleave to' (דבק ב, of adherence to the worship of Yahweh). Cf. Deut. 4^{4}, 10^{20}, 11^{22}, 13^{4} (𝕳^{5}), 30^{20}; Josh. 22^{5} R^{D}; 2 Kgs. 18^{6} R^{D}. Of adherence to idolatry, or to the representatives of it, *v.*^{12}; 1 Kgs. 11^{2}; 2 Kgs. 3^{3} R^{D}.

v.^{9}. 'And Yahweh hath dispossessed from before you nations great and mighty.' Cf. Deut. 4^{38}, 9^{1}, 11^{23}.*

v.^{11}. 'And ye shall take great heed to yourselves.' Cf. Deut. 2^{4} †.

v.^{11}. 'To love Yahweh your God.' Cf. Deut. 10^{12}, 11$^{13.22}$, 19^{9}, 30$^{6.16.20}$; Josh. 22^{5} R^{D}.

v.^{13}. 'Until ye perish.' Cf. Deut. 28$^{20.22}$.

v.^{13}. 'Which Yahweh your God hath given you.' Cf. *vv.*$^{15.16}$; Josh. 18^{3} R^{D}; with 'about to give you' (*or* 'thee,' 'us,' 'them'), constantly in Deut.

v.^{14}. 'With all your heart and with all your soul.' Cf. Deut. 11^{13}, 13^{3} (𝕳^{4}); Josh. 22^{5} R^{D}; 'with all thy heart, etc.,' Deut. 4^{29}, 6^{5}, 10^{12}, 26^{16}, 30$^{2.6.10}$; 'with all his heart, etc.,' 2 Kgs. 23^{25} R^{D}; 'with all their heart, etc.,' 1 Kgs. 2^{4}, 8^{48} (=2 Chr. 6^{38}) R^{D}; 2 Chr. 15^{12}; 'with all the heart, etc.,' 2 Kgs. 23^{3} (=2 Chr. 34^{31}) R^{D}.

v.^{14}. 'There hath not fallen one word out of all the good words, etc.' Cf. Josh. 21^{45} (𝕳^{43}) R^{D}; 1 Kgs. 8^{56} R^{D}.

v.^{15}. 'Until He destroy you.' Cf. Deut. 28^{48}; 'to destroy you' (Yahweh as subj.), Deut. 9$^{8.19.25}$, 28^{63}.

v.^{16}. 'Shall go and serve other gods, and worship them.' So 1 Kgs. 9^{6} (=2 Chr. 7^{19}) R^{D}; cf. Deut. 11^{16}, 17^{3}: 'serve other gods,' Josh. 24$^{2.16}$ E; Judg. 10^{13} E^{2}; 1 Sam. 8^{8}, 26^{19}; Deut. 7^{4}, 13$^{6.13}$ (𝕳$^{7.14}$), 28$^{36.64}$; Jer. 16^{13}, 44^{3}; 'other gods,' with 'serve' closely following with suffix of reference, Deut. 8^{19}, 13^{2} (𝕳^{3}), 28^{14}, 30^{17}, 31^{20}; Judg. 2^{19} D^{2}; 1 Kgs. 9^{9} (=2 Chr. 7^{22}) R^{D}; 2 Kgs. 17^{35} R^{D}; Jer. 11^{10}, 13^{10}, 16^{11}, 22^{9}, 25^{6}, 35^{15}; 'other gods,' without 'serve,' Ex. 20^{3} E, 23^{13} E; 2 Kgs. 5^{17} (Ephraimitic); Hos. 3^{1}; Judg. 2^{17} R^{E2}; Deut. 5^{7}, 6^{14}, 11^{28}, 18^{20}, 31^{18}; Judg. 2^{12} D^{2}; 1 Kgs. 11$^{4.10}$, 14^{9}; 2 Kgs. 17$^{7.37.38}$, 22^{17} (=2 Chr. 34^{25}) all R^{D} †.

v.^{16}. 'And the anger of Yahweh be kindled against you.' Cf. Deut. 7^{4}, 11^{17}.

v.^{16}. 'And ye perish quickly from off the good land which He hath given you.' Cf. Deut. 11^{17}. 'The good land,' Deut. 1^{35}, 3^{25}, 4$^{21.22}$, 6^{18}, 8^{10}, 9^{6}.

The close and constant echo of the phraseology of D as seen in this address—which is equally characteristic of other portions of

* Heb. *hôrîš*, translated 'hath dispossessed,' is rendered by R.V., sometimes 'possess,' sometimes 'drive out.' Cf. *note* on 1^{19}.

Josh. belonging to this redactor, and also of the handiwork of the Deuteronomic redactor of Kgs.*—sufficiently illustrates what is properly to be taken as the work of 'the Deuteronomic School.' It is evident at a glance that it is to the pre-Deuteronomic address Josh. 24 E^2, and not to Josh. 23 R^D, that the address in 1 Sam. 12 and the kindred sections in Judg. and 1 Sam. exhibit a close affinity; and that therefore we have not erred in marking them as E^2, and in regarding them as dating from a period *prior to* the promulgation of Deuteronomy. It is true that the religious ideas of E^2 and D are in many points closely kindred, and that there are a certain number of phrases which are common to them (such *e.g.* as 'Yahweh your God,' 'other gods,' 'forget Yahweh,' etc.); but the explanation of this surely is that the thought and phraseology of E^2 have exercised a well-marked influence upon D. Had the opposite been the case—*i.e.* had our so-called E^2 been modelled under the influence of D, it would be difficult to explain why only a limited number of characteristic D phrases were employed, whereas the most striking ones (as seen in R^D in Josh. and Kgs.) are wholly absent. As a matter of fact, a large number of the ideas and phrases which characterize E^2 are already to be found in Hosea‘ ‡; and it is doubtless to the influence of Hosea‘ and his school that we owe the presenta-

* Cf. the long list of phrases characteristic of R^D in Kgs. which is given by the present writer in his article 'Kings I. and II.' in *DB.* ii. pp. 859 ff.

‡ The following is a rough list of phrases and thoughts contained in Hosea‘ which have influenced E^2, as well as somewhat later thought (D and Jeremiah):—

Defection from Yahweh characterized as whoredom, 1^{2}, 2^{2-5} (𝔐 $^{4-7}$), $4^{12.15.18}$, $5^{3.4}$, 6^{10}, 9^{1}.

'The Ba‘als,' $2^{13.17}$ (𝔐 $^{15.19}$), 11^{2}; 'the Ba‘al,' 13^{1}.

'Go after,' of adherence to false worship, $2^{5.13}$ (𝔐 $^{7.15}$); of following Yahweh, 11^{10}.

Verb 'love' (אהב) applied to Yahweh's feeling for Israel, 3^{1}, 9^{15}, 11^{1}, 14^{4} (𝔐 ^{5}); cf. subs. 'love,' 11^{4}.

'Yahweh, their God,' 3^{5}, 7^{10}; 'Yahweh, thy God,' 12^{9} (𝔐 ^{10}), 13^{4}, 14^{1}(𝔐 ^{2}).

'Forget,' of defection from Yahweh,' 2^{13} (𝔐 ^{15}, 'Me she forgat'), 4^{6} ('Thou hast forgotten the *tôrā* of thy God'), 8^{14} ('Israel forgat his maker'), 13^{6} ('they have forgotten Me').

'Practices' (מעללים) with *evil* connotation, 4^{9}, 5^{4}, 7^{2}, 9^{15}, 12^{2} (𝔐 ^{3}); cf. Judg. 2^{19} E^2; Deut. 28^{20}; eighteen occurrences in Jer.

'They have forsaken to observe Yahweh,' 4^{10}.

'Return unto Yahweh,' of repentance, 6^{1}, 7^{10}, $14^{1.2}$ (𝔐 $^{2.3}$); 'unto God,' 5^{4}.

'I desire mercy (חסד) and not sacrifice;
And the knowledge of God more than burnt offerings,' 6^{6}; cf. 1 Sam. 15^{22} E^2.

Verb 'cry,' of supplication to Yahweh, 7^{14}, 8^{2}.

'Transgress covenant,' 6^{7}, 8^{1}.

'Provoke' (הכעים, obj. 'Yahweh' understood) 12^{14}; characteristic of D.

Reference to the deliverance from Egypt, 2^{15} (𝔐 ^{17}), 11^{1}, 12^{9} (𝔐 ^{10}), 13^{4}.

Depreciatory reference to the paraphernalia of cultus, 3^{4}, $10^{1.2}$.

Depreciatory reference to the existing form of kingship as opposed to the Theocratic ideal, $8^{4.10}$ (as emended; cf. p. 184), 10^{3}, $13^{10.11}$ (cf. Judg. $8^{22.23}$ E^2; 1 Sam. $8^{6.7}$, 10^{19}, $12^{17.19}$ E^2).

Antipathy to bull-worship of Northern Kingdom, $8^{5.6}$, 10^{5}, 13^{2} (cf. R^D in Kgs.).

tion of Israel's early history as it appears in E^2, and (it may well be) ultimately the Deuteronomic revival itself.*

Now, even a cursory examination of the phraseology of the main editor of Judg. makes it clear that this is modelled upon the E^2 sections which we have been discussing. The address of 1 Sam. 12 especially, which properly rounds off the history of the Judges with the final address of Samuel, the last of their number, after the election of the first king, seems to have been used by our editor as the type to which he sought to conform his pragmatic setting of Judg. Examination of his phraseology in detail yields the following results :—

1. 'Did that which was evil in the sight of Yahweh,' Judg. 2^{11}, $3^{7.12}$, 4^{1}, 6^{1}, 10^{6}, 13^{1}, all R^{E2}. Elsewhere, Num. 32^{13} JE ?; 1 Sam. 15^{19} E^2; 2 Sam. 12^{9}; Deut. 4^{25}, 9^{18}, 17^{2}, 31^{29}; twenty-two occurrences in R^{D}'s framework to Kgs., and parallel passages in 2 Chr.; Jer. 32^{30}, 52^{2}; Isa. 65^{12}, 66^{4}; Ps. 51^{4} (𝔥 ^{6}).

2. 'And they forsook Yahweh, and served the Ba'als and the 'Ashtarts,' Judg. 2^{13} E^2 (worked in by R^{E2}). Cf. 1 Sam. 12^{10} E^2, 'We have sinned, because we have forsaken Yahweh, and have served the Ba'als and the 'Ashtarts'; so very similarly (exc. om. 'and the 'Ashtarts'), Judg. 10^{10} E^2; with inverted order, 'and they served the Ba'als and the 'Ashtarts . . . and forsook Yahweh,'

* The present writer is of the opinion that the origin of Deuteronomy is to be sought in the prophetic school, not of the Southern, but of the *Northern* Kingdom, and that we have a gradually developing stream of thought represented by E, Hosea', E^2, and finally D. If this view is correct, the composition of D must have taken place some time *subsequently* to the fall of Samaria and the end of the Northern Kingdom. Sargon only claims to have carried captive 27,290 of the inhabitants of Samaria, and definitely states that he allowed the remainder to retain their possessions (? *inušunu*, of doubtful meaning), set his officers as prefects over them, and laid upon them the tribute of the former kings (cf. Winckler, *Sargon*, p. 101; Rogers, *CP.* p. 331). Doubtless (as was the case with Nebuchadnessar's first deportation from Jerusalem; 2 Kgs. $24^{12\text{-}14}$) those whom he removed were the politically influential and the skilled artificers; and he would have no reason for interfering with the members of the prophetic order, who belonged to the poorer classes, and would hardly have been clustered in and about the capital city. During the period after B.C. 722, Samaria remained the centre of an Assyrian province, with a population to some extent leavened by foreign settlers (cf. Winckler, *Sargon*, pp. 5, 21; Rogers, *CP.* p. 326). The mainly late narrative of 2 Kgs. $17^{24\text{-}41}$, which reads almost as though the foreign element were in sole possession and the religion of Yahweh had died out, is without doubt coloured by bitter antipathy to the Samaritans of later times. But, in fact, a not inconsiderable body of Israelites had survived the conquest; amongst whom the prophets of the north may be supposed to have continued their literary labours quietly and unobtrusively, setting their hopes upon a future when the whole of Israel (both of the north and of the south) should be united in faithful worship of Yahweh at one common centre. The grounds upon which this theory is based have not yet been published by the writer, but he hopes to produce them in the near future in a work entitled *The Prophetic School of Northern Israel and the Mosaic Tradition.*

Judg. 10^{6} E^{2}; 'served the Ba'als and the 'Ashtarts' coupled with 'forgat Yahweh' (cf. No. 3), Judg. 3^{7} R^{E2}.

(*a*) 'Forsook Yahweh' occurs elsewhere in Judg. 2^{12} D^{2} (based on E^{2} *v.*^{13}), Josh. 24^{16} E^{2}; Isa. 1^{4}; 1 Kgs. 9^{9}; 2 Kgs. 21^{22}, both R^{D}; Jer. 2$^{17.19}$; 2 Chr. 7^{22}, 21^{10}, 24$^{20.24}$, 28^{6}; cf. 'forsakers of Yahweh,' Isa. 1^{28}, 65^{11}; 'forsook Him' (Yahweh as obj.), 2 Chr. 13^{10}, 24^{25}; 'shall forsake Him,' 1 Chr. 28^{9}; 2 Chr. 15^{2}; 'His forsakers,' Ezr. 8^{22}; 'Thy forsakers,' Jer. 17^{13} (both referring to Yahweh); 'ye (they) have forsaken Me' (Yahweh as speaker), Judg. 10^{13} E^{2}; 1 Kgs. 11^{33}; 2 Kgs. 22^{17} both R^{D}; Jer. 1^{16}, 5$^{7.19}$, 16^{11bis}, 19^{4}; 2 Chr. 12^{5}, 34^{25}; 'hast forsaken Me,' Deut. 28^{20}; 'shall forsake Me,' Deut. 31^{16} (source ?).

Similar phrases are 'forsook to observe Yahweh,' Hos. 4^{10}; 'forsook the covenant of Yahweh,' Deut. 29^{25} (ℌ^{24}); Jer. 22^{9}; 'forsook the commandments of Yahweh,' 1 Kgs. 18^{18} R^{D}; 'forsook my *tôrā*,' Jer. 9^{13} (ℌ^{12}).

(*b*) 'The Ba'als and the 'Ashtarts,' 1 Sam. 7^{4} E^{2} (obj. of 'put away').

'And the 'Ashtarts,' coupled with 'put away the foreign gods from your midst,' 1 Sam. 7^{3} E^{2}.

'The Ba'als' alone, Judg. 8^{33} R^{E2} (obj. of 'went a whoring after'), Hos. 2$^{13.17}$ (ℌ$^{15.19}$), 11^{2} (obj. of 'sacrificed to'), 1 Kgs. 18^{18}; Jer. 2^{23}, 9^{14}, ℌ^{13} (in each case obj. of 'went after'); 2 Chr. 17^{3}, 24^{7}, 28^{2}, 33^{3}, 34^{4}.

3. 'And they forgat Yahweh their God,' Judg. 3^{7} R^{E2}, based on 1 Sam. 12^{9} E^{2}.

'Forget Yahweh' occurs elsewhere, Deut. 6^{12}, 8$^{11.14.19}$; Jer. 3^{21}; Isa. 51^{13}; 'forgat (*or* forgattest) Me' (Yahweh as speaker), Hos. 2^{13} (ℌ^{15}), 13^{6}; Jer. 2^{32}, 13^{25}, 18^{15}; Ezek. 22^{12}, 23^{35}; 'forgotten Thee' (Yahweh as obj.), Ps. 44^{17} (ℌ^{18}).

4. 'And the anger of Yahweh was kindled against Israel,' Judg. 2^{14}, 3^{8}, 10^{7} R^{E2}, based on 2^{20} E^{2}. Elsewhere, Num. 25^{3} E or J, 32^{13} JE ?; 2 Kgs. 13^{3} R^{D}.

'The anger of Yahweh was kindled' occurs again in Num. 11^{10} J ?, 12^{9} E, 32^{10} JE ?; Deut. 29^{27} (ℌ^{26}); Josh. 7^{1} R^{P}; 2 Sam. 6^{7} =1 Chr. 13^{10}; 2 Chr. 25^{15}; Ps. 106^{40}; cf. 'and Yahweh heard, and His anger was kindled,' Num. 11^{1} E; 'and the anger of God was kindled,' Num. 22^{22} J revised; 'and the anger of Yahweh (*or* my anger) shall be kindled,' Deut. 7^{4}, 11^{17}, 31^{17}; Josh. 23^{16} R^{D}.

5. 'And He gave them into the hand of spoilers, and they spoiled them,' Judg. 2^{14} R^{E2}.* Cf. 2 Kgs. 17^{20} R^{D}, 'and He gave them into the hand of spoilers.'

'Give into the hand' (of delivering up enemies; Yahweh as subj.) is found again in R^{E2}, Judg. 6^{1} (of Midian), 13^{1} (of Philistines), and is frequent elsewhere both in pre- and post-Deut. literature.

* It is doubtful whether this phrase belongs to R^{E2}. It may be later: cf. p. 55.

6. ‘He sold them into the hand of,’ Judg. 2^{14}, 3^{8}, 4^{2} R^{E2}, based on Judg. 10^{7} E^{2}, 1 Sam. 12^{9} E^{2}; cf. Judg. 4^{9} E. ‘Sold them’ (*sc.* ‘to their enemies’; subj. ‘their Rock,’=‘Yahweh’), Deut. 32^{30}.

7. ‘Their enemies round about,’ Judg. 2^{14}, 8^{34} R^{E2}, based on 1 Sam. 12^{11} E^{2}; cf. 2 Sam. 7^{1}; Deut. 12^{10}, 25^{19}; Josh. 23^{1} R^{D}.

8. ‘And the children of Israel cried unto Yahweh,’ Judg. (2^{16}),* $3^{9.15}$, 4^{3}‡, 6^{6} R^{E2}, based on Judg. 10^{10} E^{2}; ‘and your fathers cried unto Yahweh,’ 1 Sam. 12^{8} E^{2}; ‘and they cried unto Yahweh,’ 1 Sam. 12^{10} E^{2}; Josh. 24^{7} ‡ E, Ex. 14^{10} E (source of preceding). Elsewhere, with Israel as subj., Ps. $107^{6\ddagger.13.19.28\ddagger}$; cf. 2 Chr. 13^{14} ‡; Hos. 8^{2}; Mic. 3^{4}.

9. ‘Yahweh raised up judges,’ Judg. 2^{16} R^{E2}, 2^{18} D^{2} (based on *v.*^{16}); ‘Yahweh raised up a saviour,’ Judg. $3^{9.15}$ R^{E2}. No close parallel. הקים is used, with Yahweh as subj., of *raising up* men to fill particular positions in Deut. $18^{15.18}$ (a prophet), Josh. 5^{7} R^{P} (the sons of those who died in the wilderness), § 1 Sam. 2^{35} (a faithful priest), 2 Sam. 7^{12}=1 Chr. 17^{11} (thy seed as king), 1 Kgs. $11^{14.23}$ (an adversary), 1 Kgs. 14^{14} (a king), Am. 2^{11} (prophets and Nazirites), Jer. 6^{17} (watchmen), 23^{4} (shepherds), 23^{5} (a righteous sprout), 29^{15} (prophets), 30^{9} (a king), Ezek. 34^{23} (a shepherd), Zech. 11^{16} (*id.*).

10. ‘Went a whoring after’ (of intercourse with deities other than Yahweh), Judg. 2^{17}, 8^{33} R^{E2}, 8^{27} E^{2}, Ex. $34^{15.16}$ J, Deut. 31^{16} (source ?), Lev. 17^{7}, 20^{5bis} (both H), Ezek. 6^{9}, 20^{30}, 1 Chr. 5^{25}.¶

11. ‘They turned aside quickly from the way,’ Judg. 2^{17} R^{E2}. Cf. Ex. 32^{8} E ?, source of Deut. $9^{12.16}$.†

12 (*a*) ‘Was (were) subdued,’ Judg. 3^{30} (Moab), 8^{28} (Midian), 11^{33} (the children of ʿAmmon), all R^{E2}, based on 1 Sam. 7^{13} E^{2} ‘and the Philistines were subdued.’ The verb (נכנע Niphʿal) is used elsewhere in a *passive* sense in 1 Chr. 20^{4}, 2 Chr. 13^{18}, Ps. 106^{42}. In other occurrences the sense is *reflexive* (‘humble oneself’).

(*b*) ‘God subdued’ (הכניע Hiphʿîl) Judg. 4^{23} R^{E2} (Jabin, king of Canaʿan). Cf. Deut. 9^{3}, 1 Chr. 17^{10}, 2 Chr. 28^{19}, Ps. 81^{14} (𝔥 ^{15}); with David as subj., 2 Sam. 8^{1}=1 Chr. 18^{1}.

13. ‘And the land had rest’ (ותשקט הארץ), Judg. $3^{11.30}$, 5^{31}, 8^{28} R^{E2}. Cf. Josh. 11^{23}, 14^{15} R^{D} (והארץ שקטה ממלחמה), Isa. 14^{7}, Zech. 1^{11}, 1 Chr. 4^{40}, 2 Chr. $14^{1.6}$ (𝔥 13^{23}, 14^{5}).

As the result of these statistics, it appears that phrases Nos. 2, 3, 6, 8, 10, 12 appear definitely to be modelled upon 1 Sam. 12 or other sections of E^{2}, or at least to be drawn from a similar source

* Restored here upon the analogy of parallel passages.

‡ With the variant spelling ויצעקו for ויזעקו.

§ Here, however, the context seems to demand הקמים ‘that arose,’ in place of הקים.

¶ Cf. the characteristics of Hoseaʿ given in *Footnote* ‡, p. xlv.

of inspiration; and Nos. 4, 7, 9, 11, 13, while too general to form the basis of any inference, at the same time fully fit in with the theory of E^2 influence. There remain Nos. 1 and 5, which, taken by themselves, may seem to support the theory of D influence. We observe, however, that No. 1, while frequent in Deut. and R^D in Kgs., is by no means the creation of the D school, as the occurrences in 1 Sam. and 2 Sam. show; while No. 5, which is doubtfully assigned to R^{E2}, is paralleled merely by the single occurrence from R^D in Kgs., and no weight can be laid upon the connexion. Evidence thus surely indicates that the main editor of Judg. did his work under the influence of E^2 prior to the promulgation of D; such connexion with D as he exhibits being due to the fact that he contributes to the stream of prophetic thought which resulted ultimately in the latter work. Some traces of the work of a genuine Deuteronomic hand are to be found in the introductory section to Judg. (cf. 2 $^{12.14b\beta.15.18.19}$, 3 $^{1a.3}$, marked as D^2); but these are clearly distinct from, and later than, the work of R^{E2} (cf. p. 55).

It is clear that R^{E2}, though the principal editor of Judg. as we know the book, was not the first editor who brought together the old narratives of J and E and combined them into a continuous whole. The story of Abimelech, *ch.* 9 $^{1-57}$, which was known to R^{E2} and omitted by him from his work as alien to his purpose, was already a composite narrative, containing elements from the two ancient sources (cf. pp. 267 f.); and the same is true at any rate of the story of Micah and the Danites, *chs.* 17-18, which undoubtedly belonged to the original history of the period of the Judges, though it was not utilized by R^{E2}. We must conclude, therefore, that there existed a composite history of the Judges prior to the work of R^{E2}; and since we have found reason to believe that the double strand of ancient narrative in Judg. is of a piece with JE in the Hexateuch (cf. § 3), it is natural to assume that J and E in Judg. were first brought together as part of a continuous history of the origins of Israel by the redactor of the same sources in the Hexateuch, R^{JE}. The handiwork of this redactor is also to be traced in the combination of the two strands in 1 Sam. 1-12, which doubtless originally formed the concluding part of the history of the period of the Judges.

Traces of R^{JE}, as we find them in Judg., are for the most part harmonistic merely,* and he does not seem to have been dominated by any definite pragmatic purpose akin to that of R^{E2}. Whether he set the narratives of individual Judges in a stereotyped framework is doubtful. It may be noticed, however, that the closing formula in the narratives of Jephthah (12 ^{7a}) and Samson (16 ^{31b}), 'And he judged Israel *x* years,' occurs in the same form at the close of the judgeship of 'Eli, 1 Sam. 4 ^{18b} (cf. also of Samuel, 1 Sam. 7 ^{15}), and is therefore presumably prior to R^{E2} (whose regular concluding formula is 'and the land had rest *x* years'); while, on the other

* Cf. references in *Index* to R^{JE} under 'Redactors of Judges.'

hand, the fact that the statement generalizes the scope of the Judges' influence (over *Israel*, and not merely over one or more tribes) is an indication that it is later than the old narratives themselves, and therefore in all probability redactional.*

The date of the redaction of Judg. can only be approximately determined. E^2, which exhibits strongly the influence of Hoseaʿ, must be subsequent to that prophet, who flourished *cir.* B.C. 750-735, but not necessarily very long subsequent. It is reasonable to suppose that R^{JE} may have done his work of combining J and E (including E^2) *cir.* B.C. 700 or a little later. R^{E2} may then be placed *cir.* B.C. 650. The book took its final form at the hands of the editor (or school of editors) imbued with the priestly conceptions of post-exilic times, for whose work we use the symbol R^P. The extent of R^P's work has been sufficiently indicated in the final paragraph of § 2. Cf. also references in the *Index* under 'Redactors of Judges.'

§ 5. Chronology.

In attempting to estimate the length of the period covered by the Book of Judg. we turn naturally to examine the chronological data supplied by the editors, which may seem at first sight to afford us an exact basis for our calculations. Unfortunately, however, this is not the case.

In 1 Kgs. 6 1 we find a statement from the hand of the priestly reviser of the book ‡ that the period from the Exodus until the building of the Temple in the fourth year of Solomon was 480 years. Addition of the data which we possess for this period gives the following result:—

Wanderings in the wilderness, ...	40 years.
Conquest under Joshuaʿ, ...	Not stated.
Oppression of Cushan-rishʿathaim (3 8), . .	8 years.
Interval after deliverance by ʿOthṇiel (3 11), .	40 ,,
Oppression of ʿEglon (3 14), ...	18 ,,

* A difference is to be discerned in the use of *šāphaṭ* 'to judge,' *šōphēṭ* 'judge' by R^{E2} and R^{JE}. For R^{E2} a 'judge' is so termed as a *vindicator* or *deliverer* (cf. *ch.* 2 16.17.18, 3 10); but in the passages above noticed which we assign to R^{JE} 'to judge' means simply *to exercise the judicial functions of a magistrate* or *ruler*. This latter usage is also found in the mention of the periods covered by the minor Judges (*ch.* 10 2.3, 12 9.11.14), where R^P seems to have copied the formula of R^{JE}, since it is scarcely possible that the brief notices of these Judges, the whole conception of which belongs to the post-exilic school of thought, should have existed in R^{JE}'s Book of Judges (cf. pp. 289 f.). We assign to R^{E2} the notice of *ch.* 15 20, which states that Samson 'judged Israel . . . twenty years'; but this simply means that R^{E2}, when he deliberately rejected the Samson-stories which now stand in *ch.* 16, concluded his narrative with R^{JE}'s formula which we find in *ch.* 16 31b.

‡ Evidence is conclusive that the verse in question belongs to the latest additions to Kings. Cf. *NHTK.* pp. 58 f.

Interval after deliverance by Ehud (3 [30]),	.	80 years.
Oppression of Jabin (4 [3]),	. . . . .	20 ,,
Interval after deliverance by Deborah (5 [31]),	.	40 ,,
Oppression of Midian (6 [1]),	. . . .	7 ,,
Interval after deliverance by Gideʿon (8 [28]),	.	40 ,,
Reign of Abimelech (9 [22]),	. . . . .	3 ,,
Tolaʿ's judgeship (10 [2]),	. . . . . .	23 ,,
Ja'ir's judgeship (10 [3]),	. . . . . .	22 ,,
Oppression of ʿAmmon (10 [8]),	. . . .	18 ,,
Jephthaḥ's judgeship (12 [7]),	. . . . .	6 ,,
Ibṣan's judgeship (12 [9]),	. . . . .	7 ,,
Elon's judgeship (12 [11]),	. . . . .	10 ,,
ʿAbdon's judgeship (12 [14]),	. . . . .	8 ,,
Oppression of the Philistines (13 [1]),	. .	40 ,,
Samson's judgeship (15 [20], 16 [31]),	. . .	20 ,,
ʿEli's judgeship (1 Sam. 4 [18]),	. . . .	40 ,,
Samuel's judgeship,	. . . . . .	Not stated.
Reign of Saul,	. . . .	,,
Reign of David (1 Kgs. 2 [11]),	. . . .	40 years.
Portion of Solomon's reign (1 Kgs. 6 [1]),	.	4 ,,

Here we have a total of 534 years, exclusive of three periods of unstated length, representing the domination of Joshuaʿ, Samuel, and Saul.

As regards the first of these indefinite periods—we find that, at the beginning of the wilderness-wanderings, Joshuaʿ first appears in the old narrative of E, Ex. 17 [8 ff.], as the leader of Israel in the battle with the ʿAmaleḳites at Rephidim, and subsequently, in the same E narrative, as Moses' attendant (cf. Ex. 24 [13], 32 [17], 33 [11]), being described in 33 [11] by the Hebrew term *naʿar* which can hardly denote more than a youth approaching man's estate. If we are justified in combining these two representations—a warrior, and yet a very young man—we may picture him as about 20 years old at the time of the Exodus; and adding to this the 40 years of the wanderings, we get an approximate 60 years; which, subtracted from his age at his death, 110 years (Josh. 24 [29] = Judg. 2 [8] E), gives 50 years as the period of his leadership in the conquest of Canaʿan. According to *ch.* 2 [7-10], however, a further period of indefinite length has to be assumed between the death of Joshuaʿ and the oppression of Cushan-rishʿathaim; since we are here informed that Israel remained faithful all the days of the elders that outlived Joshuaʿ, and apostasy only began after the death of the latter.

The length of Samuel's judgeship must have been considerable. According to 1 Sam. 7 [15], 'he judged Israel all the days of his life'; and it was not until he was an old man that he appointed his sons in his place, and their mismanagement of affairs led to the demand for a king (1 Sam. 8 [1 ff.], probably E^2). We have no data, however, for forming an approximate estimate of the duration of this judgeship; and, similarly, we are unable to arrive at the length of Saul's reign by any reference, direct or indirect, in the O. T. Such a note of time was desiderated by the scribe who added the gloss which stands in 1 Sam. 13[1], framed upon the analogy of the recurring formula in Kgs. :—'Saul was *x* years old when he began to reign, and he reigned *y* years over Israel.'*

If we add 50 years for Joshua''s judgeship to the 534 years, the result is 584 years, without reckoning the two (or, if we take account of *ch.* 2[7.10], *three*) periods of undetermined length, which, upon the lowest computation, can scarcely have amounted together to much less than 50 or 60 years.‡ This is far too long to have formed the basis for the calculation of 480 years for the period given in 1 Kgs. 6[1]. Yet it is probable that the author of this late addition to Kgs. had precisely the same data as we now possess.

Thus Nöldeke (*Untersuchungen zur Kritik des A. T.*, 1869, pp. 173 ff.) supposes that the calculator followed the oriental practice of ignoring periods of oppression and usurpation, and so cut out of his reckoning the periods during which Israel is said to have served Cushan-rish'athaim, 'Eglon, Jabin, Midian, 'Ammon, the Philistines, and the reign of Abimelech—in all a total of 114 years.§ Subtracting this from the 534, and allowing 40 years (evenly or unevenly divided) for Joshua' and Saul, and 20 for Samuel, Nöldeke reaches the total of 480 years.

Moore (*Comm.* xli. f.) agrees with Nöldeke in his omissions; but differs in thinking that, for the Judaean author of the chronology, the rule of Saul, like that of Abimelech, was regarded as illegitimate and so not reckoned; and that for 'Eli's judgeship we should follow 𝔊 rather than 𝔐, and read 20 years and not 40 years. Then, upon the supposition that Joshua''s life fell into three periods

* The formula as it stands in 𝔐 is simply a skeleton, both of the requisite numbers being omitted, as in the rendering given above. The word וּשְׁתֵּי is probably corrupt dittography of the following שנים 'years'; and we are scarcely justified in rendering '*x* and two years,' since this would require וּשְׁתַּיִם שָׁנָה . . .

‡ The history of 'Eli's family during the periods of Samuel and Saul requires a considerable lapse of time. The death of 'Eli synchronizes with the death of his son Phineḥaṡ in the battle of Aphek (1 Sam. 4). Since Phineḥaṡ was still an able-bodied man, his son Aḥiṭub must have been a young man at most at this date. Yet according to 1 Sam. 14[3], it is Aḥiṭub's *son* Aḥijah (apparently = Aḥimelech of *ch.* 22[11]) who is priest in the early or middle part of Saul's reign; and at the slaughter of the priests of Nob, Abiathar, the son of Aḥimelech and *grandson* of Aḥiṭub, escapes to David carrying the Ephod with him, and is old enough to exercise the priestly office on David's behalf by manipulation of the sacred lot.

§ Wellh. (*Prolegomena*, p. 230) has noted the striking fact that, after making the necessary assumption that the 40 years of Philistine domination coincide with the judgeship of 'Eli, and include that of Samson, the total of the remaining foreign dominations, viz., 71 years, nearly coincides with the total assigned to the minor Judges, viz., 70 years; and he infers that the latter were intended to take the place of the former in the scheme of reckoning.

of 30+40+40 years, he assigns 40 years for the conquest of Cana'an under Joshua'; and gives 40 years for Samuel's judgeship on the ground of the importance of his work, and the fact that he is represented as an old man when he died, and is said to have 'judged Israel all the days of his life.' This produces the required total of 480 years.

These and similar calculations can only, however, possess a relative importance; since it is evident that the author of the statement in 1 Kgs. 6[1] must have been employing an artificial method of reckoning. We know that the Exodus probably took place under Mineptah, the successor of Ra'messe II. (cf. p. civ); and, on the other hand, we are able, by aid of Assyrian chronology, to determine approximately the date of Solomon's accession.* These data force upon us the conclusion that the period which we are considering cannot really have occupied much more than 250 years; or possibly, if the Exodus took place not under Mineptah, but subsequently to his death, an even shorter space of time.

Evidence also leads us to conclude that the instances of the oppression of the Israelites by various foreign races, and of deliverance and respite effected by the Judges, were in most, if not in all, cases, local rather than general. Thus, supposing that the terms of years mentioned are based upon accurate information, it is highly probable that they not infrequently coincide with or overlap one another. Thus, *e.g.*, the south Palestinian tribes may have been suffering from the oppression of the Philistines while the east Jordan tribes were exposed to the encroachments of the 'Ammonites. The period

* Mineptah's reign is dated by Petrie B.C. 1234-1214, and by Breasted B.C. 1225-1215. Solomon's accession must be placed *cir.* B.C. 970. This latter date is obtained by back-reckoning from the earliest O.T. date fixed by Assyrian chronology, viz. B.C. 854, the date of Ahab's presence at the battle of Karkar in alliance with Bir-idri of Damascus, the Biblical Ben-Hadad II. Ahab is most likely to have been allied with Ben-Hadad at the end of his reign, when, as we are informed by 1 Kgs. 22[1], after the treaty concluded between the two kings as related in 1 Kgs. 20[33.34], 'there continued three years without war between Aram and Israel.' It may be plausibly assumed that this period of three years was really less. 1 Kgs. 22[2] states that 'in the third year' Ahab determined to recover by force of arms from Ben-Hadad the city of Ramah of Gile'ad which he had failed to cede in accordance with his compact. It is not unlikely that the first of the three years as reckoned was really the remnant of the year which elapsed after the treaty of 20[33 f.], so that there remains only one full year for the working of the alliance in the form of a combined resistance to Assyria. Now Ahab reigned 22 years according to the Biblical reckoning; therefore 854 must have been his 21st year, 853 according to the predating method (*i.e.* the reckoning of the still unexpired portion of the year in which a king came to the throne as his first reigning year) being his 22nd year and also the 1st year of Ahaziah. Back-reckoning from B.C. 854 according to the chronology of 1 Kgs., with reduction of the length of each reign by one year to allow for predating (which comparison of the synchronisms of the reigns of the two kingdoms proves to have been the historian's method of reckoning) gives B.C. 931 for the accession of Jerobo'am and Rehobo'am, and B.C. 970 for the accession of Solomon whose reign is given as lasting 40 years.

of the Philistine oppression extended not merely over the judgeship of Samson, but also over that of 'Eli; and, at any rate partially, into the periods of Samuel and Saul. Possibly Samson and 'Eli may have been contemporaries. This is a consideration which by itself suggests to us the futility of any attempt to construct a chronology of the period upon the evidence which we possess.

But are the data given in the Biblical sources to be relied upon as defining with accuracy the various periods to which they are referred? The fact can scarcely escape notice that the number 40 or its multiple occurs with singular frequency. Thus, 40 years represents the length of the wilderness-wanderings, of the peace enjoyed after the victories of 'Othniel, Deborah, and Gide'on, of the Philistine oppression, of 'Eli's judgeship, and of the reigns of David and Solomon. Ehud's judgeship occupies twice 40 years, and that of Samson half 40. This fact suggests to us that 40 years may be employed as a round number, representing approximately the length of a generation. Bearing this in mind, we notice that the 480 years of 1 Kgs. 6 [1] is also a multiple of 40, viz. 40 × 12, *i.e.* twelve generations. That twelve generations were supposed, as a matter of fact, to cover the period in question appears from the genealogy of Aaron and his successors in 1 Chr. 6 [3-10] (𝔐 5 [29-36]), where twelve names are given between Ele'azar the son of Aaron and 'Azariah, who is specified as 'he that executed the priest's office in the House that Solomon built in Jerusalem.' These twelve generations might naturally be reckoned as follows: (1) Moses, (2) Joshua', (3) 'Othniel, (4) Ehud, (5) Baraḳ, (6) Gide'on, (7) Jephthaḥ, (8) Samson, (9) 'Eli, (10) Samuel, (11) Saul, (12) David, these being the twelve national leaders who were specifically divinely-appointed; and that this scheme—or something like it—was in the mind of the chronologist is suggested by the facts that six of these generations (viz. 1, 3, 5, 6, 9, 12) are actually reckoned as 40 years, and a seventh, viz. Joshua', may also have been so reckoned if we suppose that his 110 years fell into periods of 30 + 40 + 40 years. Such a scheme, however, if it was ever fully worked out, may have been subsequently vitiated by various influences, *e.g.* the desire to exclude Saul as illegitimate, and the raising of the number of Judges within the Book of Judges to twelve by the addition of the minor Judges in an attempt to find representatives for each of the twelve tribes of Israel.

This discussion may suffice to illustrate the hopelessness of any attempt to construct a chronology of our period from the Biblical sources available. We can only, as we have already noticed, conjecture that the total length of the period from the Exodus to the fourth year of Solomon was approximately 250 years; but for the formation of a chronological scheme within this period, or even for a conjectural estimate of the length of that portion of it which is covered by the Book of Judges, we are absolutely without data.

§ 6. External information bearing on the period of Judges.

Our knowledge of the history of Canaʿan at this period, as derived from extra-Biblical sources, is for the most part such as can be drawn by inference from evidence which properly concerns an earlier period.

We possess no certain evidence as to the earliest settlement of Semitic peoples in Canaʿan. The earliest Semites of whom we have authentic knowledge in Babylonia were settled in Akkad in the north. The recently published dynastic lists from Nippur prove the existence of an early tradition relating to a succession of dynasties in Babylonia from post-diluvial times, which had their seats at Kiš, Erech, Ur, Awan, and other cities.* There is obviously a large element of myth in the tradition; ‡ but, if we may judge from the royal names that are preserved, it would seem that the earliest rulers of Kiš, Erech, and Ur were non-Semitic. Unfortunately, the lists are too fragmentary to admit of any estimate of the date at which Semites made their appearance in Babylonia. We first find them enjoying full political power in the north, under the famous Semitic dynasty of Akkad, which was founded by Šarru-kîn or Sargon I.,§ around whose name a number of traditions clustered in later times. It is related that 'he subdued the country of the West (sun-setting) in its full extent,'‖ *i.e.* the Mediterranean sea-board including Canaʿan; and this tradition has now been proved to have an authentic basis.¶ Other famous rulers of the

* Cf. Poebel, *Historical Texts* (*Univ. of Pennsylvania Mus. Publ.*, Vol. iv. No. 1, 1914), pp. 73 ff.

‡ In addition to the occurrence of the names of gods and demigods among the early rulers, the chronological calculations of the early scribes of Nîsin, who compiled the lists in the twenty-second century B.C., present a striking resemblance to the chronological system of Berossus with its mythical and semi-mythical dynasties: cf. King, *Bab.* p. 114, *n* 1; pp. 116 f., *n* 5.

§ The name Sargon is the Biblical form (used in Isa. 20 1 of the Assyrian king of the 8th century B.C.) of the Babylonian name Šarru-ukîn or Šarru-kîn. A not quite complete list of the early Semitic rulers of Akkad (and of other Babylonian dynasties) was published by Scheil, *Comptes rendus de l'Acad. des Inscriptions et Belles-Lettres*, 1911 (Oct.), pp. 606 ff., and *Revue d'Assyr.*, ix. p. 69. This document proves the correctness of the Neo-Babylonian tradition that Šarru-kîn, or Sargon, was the founder of the Dynasty of Akkad. It used to be assumed that he and two other early Semitic rulers were kings of Kiš, on the strength of the title *šar* KIŠ which they bear in their inscriptions; but it is now clear that this should always be read *šar kiššati*, 'king of the world,' a title to which they laid claim in virtue of their power as kings of the dynasty of Akkad (cf. King, *Britannica Year-Book*, 1913, pp. 256 ff.). The powerful king Šar-Gani-šarri (or Šar-Gali-šarri), with whom Sargon I. used to be identified, was not the founder, but a later ruler, of the Dynasty of Akkad.

‖ For the inscription, cf. King, *Chron.* ii. pp. 3 ff.; Rogers, *CP.* pp. 203 ff.; *TB.* i. pp. 105 ff.

¶ Cf. the highly important series of inscriptions of kings of Agade (Akkad) recently published by Poebel (*op. cit.* ch. vi.). In one of these Sargon, in ascribing his conquests to the god Enlil, says, 'and he gave him the upper land, Mari, Yarmuti, and

same dynasty were Narâm-Sin,* and Šar-Gani-šarri, who was probably his grandson. We have contemporary evidence of the activity of the latter in Amurru or the West-land.‡

While Akkad in the north of Babylonia was thus dominated by Semites, Sumer in the south was still occupied by the people who are known to us, from their habitat, as Sumerians; a non-Semitic race possessing an advanced civilization, to which the Semites who succeeded them owed an incalculable debt. The date at which the Semites gained the ascendancy in Akkad is a matter of uncertainty. It may have been at some time in the fourth millennium B.C.; and was at any rate not later than the earlier decades of the third millennium.§

The early common home of the Semites, prior to their dispersion throughout western Asia, was probably central Arabia;|| and the fact that the first Semites who are known to us as occupying Babylonia are found to be settled in the north and not in the south, lends colour to the theory that they may represent a wave of Semitic immigration into Babylonia which first entered the country not from the south but from the north-west.¶ If this was so, these Semites, after quitting their early home, may have first traversed Cana'an and northern Syria, leaving in all probability settlements

Ibla, as far as the cedar-forest and the silver mountains. Unto Šarru-kîn, the king, Enlil did not give an adversary' (pp. 177 ff.). Here 'the upper land' is the West-land, so-called, apparently, as reached by going up the Euphrates. Poebel adduces reasons for taking 'the cedar-forest' to be the Lebanon and Anti-Lebanon, and 'the silver mountains' the Taurus (cf. pp. 222 ff.).

* According to the Neo-Babylonian tradition, Narâm-Sin was the son of Sargon. This is possible; but it may be noted that two other members of the house probably occupied the throne between Sargon and Narâm-Sin; and if so, eighty or ninety years separated Narâm-Sin's accession from that of his father.

‡ A tablet of accounts from Tello is dated 'in the year in which Šar-Gani-šarri conquered Amurru in Basar.' Cf. King, *Sum. and Akk.* p. 225.

§ The date which was formerly accepted by scholars is that which is given by Nabonidus, the last king of Babylon (B.C. 550), who states that, when digging in the foundations of the temple of the sun-god at Sippar, he discovered the foundation-memorial which had been laid by Narâm-Sin 3200 years previously (for the inscription, cf. *KB.* iii. 2, pp. 102 ff.). This would place Narâm-Sin's date B.C. 3750. Modern investigation, however, has tended to discredit Nabonidus' statement; and though the reduction of a thousand years or more which at one time was suggested is doubtless too drastic (cf. the discussion in Rogers, *HBA.*[6] i. pp. 494 ff.), it is quite possible that Nabonidus' calculation is a good deal too high (resulting, it may be, in part from the reckoning of early contemporaneous dynasties as though they were consecutive). Indeed, the evidence of the recently-discovered dynastic lists has been interpreted by King as supporting the view which would place Sargon's accession not so very much before the end of the fourth millennium B.C. But, in the present very partial state of excavation in Babylonia, it is possible that we may still be totally uninformed with regard to a period of considerable length in these early times.

|| For a summary of the views which have been put forward on this subject, and the authorities who support them, cf. Barton, *Semitic Origins*, pp. 1 ff.; Rogers, *HBA.*[6] i. pp. 452 f.

¶ Cf. King, *Sum. and Akk.* p. 55.

in these districts in their wake; or they may have come up from Arabia along the western bank of the Euphrates, where in later times we find settlements of Aramaeans, and may have left the further west, including Canaʿan, wholly untouched.*

Be this as it may, we cannot point to a period, within the range of our historical knowledge, when Canaʿan was unoccupied by a Semitic population. Excavation of ancient sites in Palestine has revealed the fact that the earliest inhabitants were neolithic cave-dwellers who burned their dead, and who were therefore probably non-Semitic; ‡ but how long this race continued to occupy the country cannot be estimated with any approach to certainty.§

We stand on surer ground in speaking of a later wave of Semitic migration northwards and westwards from Arabia, which founded

* Evidence is lacking in justification of any definite theory as to the approximate date of the earliest migrations of the Semites northward and westward. The use of the Semitic Babylonian language in the inscriptions of the early rulers of Akkad implies the lapse of a period of indefinite length (probably many centuries) since the first departure of their ancestors from Arabia, to allow for the development of this language. We may contrast, in this respect, the later immigration into Babylonia of the 'Amorites' who founded the First Dynasty of Babylon (cf. pp. lviii ff.); the West Semitic language spoken by these immigrants (as evidenced by their proper names), with its Arabian affinities, implying a much less remote separation from the parent-stock. An interesting point in connexion with the earliest settlement of Semites in Babylonia, is the fact that the closely shaven Sumerians always represent their deities as *bearded*, and therefore, apparently, as Semites (cf. figures in King, *Sum. and Akk.* pp. 47 f.; Hall, *NE.* plate xiv. p. 204). The significance of this fact is as yet unelucidated; but the theory (put forward by Ed. Meyer, *Semiten und Sumerier; Abhandl. d. k. p. Akad.*, 1906) is somewhat plausible that these Sumerian deities may have been Semitic in origin, and that there may therefore have been a Semitic population in Babylonia even prior to the coming of the Sumerians. This theory is criticized by King, *Sum. and Akk.* pp. 47 ff.; and favoured by Jastrow, *Heb. and Bab. Traditions*, pp. 8 f. A further fact which admits of no doubt is the ultimate linguistic connexion between Sumerian and many of the primitive biliterals which can be proved to underlie Semitic triliteral roots (cf. Ball, *Semitic and Sumerian* in *Hilprecht Anniversary Volume*; *Shumer and Shem* in *Proceedings of the British Academy*, 1915). This must carry back the connexion between Sumerians and Semites to a hoary antiquity; but the study of the subject is not at present sufficiently advanced to admit of any theory in explanation.

‡ Cf. Vincent, *Canaan*, pp. 73 ff., 208 ff.

§ The primitive inhabitants of the hill-country of Seʿir, to the south of Canaʿan, who were dispossessed by the children of ʿEsau, are called *Ḥôrîm* in Deut. 2 [12.22] (cf. Gen. 14 [6], 26 [20-30]); and the view has frequently been advocated that this name is connected with Heb. *ḥôr* 'hole,' and denotes 'Troglodytes' or 'cave-dwellers'; but this is highly precarious. More probably *Ḥôrîm* is to be connected with the name Ḫaru, which was a designation applied by the Egyptians to a portion of southern Palestine. Cf. Müller, *AE.* pp. 137, 148 ff., 240; Jensen, *ZA.* x. pp. 332 f., 346 f.; Hommel, *AHT.* p. 264, *n* 2; Paton, *Syria and Palestine*, p. 37; Meyer, *IN.* pp. 330 f.; *GA.*[2] I. 2, p. 600; Kit., *GVI.*[2] i. p. 36; Lehmann-Haupt, *Israel*, p. 37, *al.* Connexion of *Ḥôrîm* and *Ḫaru* with *Ḫarri*=Aryans, proposed by Winckler, *MDOG.* xxxv. pp. 49 ff., and adopted by Gemoll, *Grundsteine zur Geschichte Israels*, p. 17, is very improbable. Cf. Meyer, *GA.*[2] I. 2, p. 601; Kit., *GVI.*[2] i. pp. 37 f. The Ḥorite genealogies in Gen. 36 [20-30] consist of Semitic names.

a dynasty at Babylon, and was also responsible for peopling the region to the west of the Euphrates, including the Mediterranean sea-board, with a race who were doubtless the ancestors of the Amorites of Biblical times.*

The First Babylonian Dynasty, which probably lasted from *cir.* B.C. 2225 to 1926,‡ consisted of eleven kings. The fourth and fifth of these kings bear good Semitic Babylonian names, Apil-Sin ('son of Sin,' the moon-god) and Sin-muballiṭ ('Sin gives life'); but the remaining names are foreign, and present close analogies to Arabic and Hebrew. Thus three of them, Ḫammurabi or Ammurabi, Ammiditana, and Ammizaduga, contain the element *Ammu* or *Ammi* which is familiar to us from its occurrence in Arabic and Hebrew. Cases of its occurrence in Hebrew proper names are ʿAmmiʾel, ʿAmmihud, ʿAmmizabad, ʿAmminadab, ʿAmmishaddai, and perhaps ʿAmram. The meaning of this *ʿamm* in Arabic is 'paternal uncle'; in Hebrew perhaps more generally 'kinsman' (on the father's side), since the term is used in the plural in the expression וַיֵּאָסֶף אֶל־עַמָּיו 'and he was gathered to his kinsmen,' Gen. 25^{8}, *al.*§

If proof were needed that these *Ammi*-names were foreign to the Babylonians, it would be found in the fact that a list exists in which a Babylonian scribe has explained the names Ḫammurabi and Ammizaduga by what seemed to him to be their Babylonian equivalents; the former by *Kimta rapaštum*, 'a widely-extended kindred,'

* We say 'Amorites' because they are thus described ('men of the land of Amurru') by the Babylonians (cf. p. lix); but the use of this term does not imply the holding of any theory as to a racial distinction between 'Amorites' and 'Canaʿanites' (such *e.g.* as that the Canaʿanites were in origin the earliest Semitic settlers in Syria-Palestine, prior to the coming of the Amorites). Since the name Amurru applied to Syria-Palestine is certainly older than the flowing into this region of the Semitic wave of which we are speaking (cf. Böhl, *KH.* p. 33), the name 'Amorite' would be equally suitable to the (assumed) earlier Semitic population inhabiting it. We are wholly in the dark as to the original *racial* distinction (if such existed) between Canaʿanite and Amorite; and speculations on the subject are of the nature of guess-work pure and simple. On the geographical and literary distinctions in the usage of the two terms, cf. p. 3 (O.T.), p. 41 (extra-Biblical).

‡ This reckoning results from King's discovery that the so-called 'Second' Babylonian Dynasty (of 'the Country of the Sea,' *i.e.* Lower Babylonia), which lasted three hundred and sixty-eight years, was partly contemporary with the First Dynasty and partly with the Third (Kaššite) Dynasty: cf. *Chron.* i. pp. 93-113. Previously, the three dynasties had been assumed to have been successive, and the beginning of the First Dynasty was placed *cir.* B.C. 2440. In view of this new evidence, King assumed, as the most probable conclusion, that the Third Dynasty immediately succeeded the First (cf. *op. cit.* pp. 136 f.; followed by Meyer, *GA.*[2] I. ii. pp. 341 ff.; Hall, *NE.* pp. 28, 192 ff.), and so dated the First Dynasty B.C. 2060 to 1761. Now, however, in the light of further evidence, he concludes (as already conjectured by Ungnad, *ZDMG.* lxi. pp. 714 ff., and Thureau-Dangin, *ZA.* xxi. pp. 176 ff.) that the Second Dynasty, though partly contemporary with the First and the Third, yet dominated Babylonia for a period of about one hundred and sixty years. Cf. the full chronological discussion in *Bab. ch.* iii.

§ On ʿ*Ammi*-names in Semitic, cf. Gray, *EB.* 138 ff.

and the latter by *Kimtum kettum* 'a just kindred.'* More probably the names really contain a predicative statement:—Ḫammurabi, 'the (divine) kinsman is great,' Ammizaduga, 'the (divine) kinsman is just.' Both names, so far as the form is concerned, might have occurred in Hebrew, the former as ʿAmmirab or ʿAmrab, the later as ʿAmmiṣadoḳ. ‡

Space forbids our examining in detail the remaining names of this dynasty; but we may notice in passing that Abi-eshu' (the name of the eighth king) is the exact equivalent of the Hebrew Abishuaʿ, and that in the seventh name Samsu-iluna, 'Samsu is our god,' we have the Arabic form of the suffix of the 1st plural in *iluna*, the Babylonian form being *iluni*. The second name Sumu-la-ilu, is only satisfactorily to be explained from Arabic, the *la*, as in Arabic, giving emphasis to the predicative statement—'The Name (κατ' ἐξοχήν) indeed is god.'

In addition to the evidence afforded by these king-names, we have abundant evidence in the proper names contained in the documents belonging to this dynastic period, which proves the influx into Babylonia of a very large foreign element. § Many of these display the same characteristics as we have found in the king-names—a close resemblance to Hebrew, and more particularly to Arabic; especially to the forms of southern Arabic which are known to us from inscriptions (Minaean and Sabaean). ||

The question which we now have to ask is, Who were these foreign immigrants, and from what region did they enter Babylonia? There exists a tablet belonging to the reign of Zabum (the third king of the dynasty) which deals with a dispute between two contending parties about a certain piece of property. In this document the names are of the characteristically foreign type of which we have been speaking, and they are described as 'men as well as women, children of Amurru' (*ištu zikarim adi sinništum mârê A-mur-ru-um*). ¶ The Babylonian name Amurru (=Sumerian MAR.TU, 'West-land') was applied by the Babylonians to the whole region west of the Euphrates including Syria and Palestine, and bounded on the west by the Mediterranean (cf. *Addit. note*, p. 41). We infer, therefore, that the First Babylonian Dynasty was founded by foreign conquerors from Amurru, the country to the west of the Euphrates, who entered Babylonia probably from the north-west, just as the earlier wave of Semitic immigration appears to have

* Cf. v. R. 44, col. 1, ll. 21, 22.

‡ עמצדק is known as a South Arabian name: cf. Ranke, *Early Bab. Personal Names*, p. 27. According to Weber, the name עמרב occurs in a South Arabian inscription: cf. *OLZ.* x. (1907), 146 ff.; *MVAG.*, 1907, 2, pp. 95 ff.

§ Cf. Ranke, *Early Bab. Personal Names*; Thureau-Dangin, *Lettres et Contrats de l'Époque de la Première Dynastie Babylonienne.*

|| Cf. Hommel, *AHT.* ch. iii; *Grundriss*, pp. 129 ff.; Ranke, *Early Bab. Personal Names*, pp. 27 ff.

¶ Cf. Ranke, *Early Bab. Personal Names*, p. 33.

done. The presence of two Babylonian names among the foreign names of the other kings is no doubt due to the fact that the immigrant settlers gradually tended to assimilate their language and civilization to the superior civilization into the midst of which they entered. *

The language spoken by these immigrants, which we have seen to be illustrated by their proper names, has been variously described

* It is worth while here to call attention to the later prevalence and persistency of the Semitic Babylonian language as proof of the deep-seated influence of the *first* Semitic settlement; just as we have already (p. lvii, *footnote* *) called attention to the development of this language as we first know it (in the inscriptions of the early rulers of Akkad), as proof of the long-prior antiquity of the separation of this branch of Semites from the parent-stock. Neither of these facts, it may be thought, has received sufficient attention; and they are most strikingly overlooked by Myres in *The Dawn of History*—a little book which, for all its imaginative power and grace of style, is somewhat superficial and unreliable when dealing with *facts* as they concern Sumerians and Semites (*chaps.* 4 and 5). It is not 'possible to discover with certainty the period of emigration' from Arabia (p. 106) of the first Semitic wave which entered Babylonia; such records as we possess of the dynasty of Akkad do not suggest a recent occupation of the country, nor does it appear that Sargon of Akkad was leader of a horde of 'Mesopotamian nomads' (p. 111). The remarks (p. 106) as to the modifications which produced the different Semitic languages are somewhat obscure, but they certainly seem to *suggest* that these modifications took place in the course of ages *at the fountainhead*, i.e. *ex hypothesi* in central Arabia (it is difficult to attach any other meaning to the statements that 'the intervals between' the successive Semitic migrations from Arabia 'have been sufficient to ensure that the characteristics of "Semitic" speech, which is common to all emigrants from Arabia, should have had time to alter slightly,' and that 'these successive groups of dialects retained their peculiarities—and if anything added to them—after their separation from the parent language'), while each offshoot from the parent-stock as it were registered and retained the particular stage of linguistic development which had been reached at the date of its breaking off, with such later modifications as are implied by the parenthesis, 'and, if anything, added to them.' If this statement were at all true to fact, then Arabic (whether we call it the latest offshoot or the residuary representative of the parent-language) ought to exhibit the most advanced condition of phonetic decay—whereas it is a commonplace that the reverse is true, and that in many respects this language exhibits the most primitive formations. Clearly the truth is that the parent-stock, owing to its comparative immunity from outside influences ensured by the monotony of the desert, remained in a relatively unmodified condition through incalculable ages; whereas the offshoots, so soon as through migration they became subject to such influences, underwent a more or less rapid modification. This is the reason why (as already noted, p. lvii, *footnote* *) we must conclude that the Semitic Babylonian of the dynasty of Akkad, which is substantially the Semitic Babylonian of later times, indicates that the users of the language, when we first meet with them, had long been separated from the parent-stock; whereas the language of the Western Semites who founded the First Dynasty of Babylon (as evidenced by their proper names; cf. pp. lviii f.), which exhibits striking resemblances to South Arabian, as known to us some 1500 years and more later, indicates that *this* branch of Semites, when they come into the light of history, must have left the common home comparatively recently. The influence of environment upon a Semitic language is most strikingly illustrated by Aramaic, which from the accident of its position has experienced the most rapid development (or decay), and has been most receptive of external influences. Lastly, Myres' statement that

as South Arabian, Canaʿanite, Amorite, or West Semitic. Of these titles, the two latter are no doubt the most suitable.*

It cannot be doubted that this Amorite or West Semitic tongue was the ancestor of the Hebrew language of later times, which, as is well known, was not the speech of the Israelites only, nor shared by them only with other 'Hebrew' races, which are represented in Genesis as closely related to them—*e.g.* the Moabites, whom we know from Meshaʿ's inscription (*cir.* B.C. 850), to have spoken a language which only differed dialectically from the Hebrew of the Old Testament; but, as is apparent from the 'Canaʿanite glosses' of the Tell el-Amarna Letters to which we shall shortly refer, and from the Phoenician inscriptions of much later times, was but one form of the common language of at least the southern portion of the Mediterranean sea-board.‡ This is a fact which seems to be recognized in Isa. 19 [18], where the Hebrew language is designated as 'the language (lit. "lip") of Canaʿan.'

There is evidence which suggests—if it does not certainly prove—that from the time of Ḫammurabi onwards the First Babylonian Dynasty ruled not only over Babylonia, but also over Amurru.§ The whole of Sin-muballiṭ's reign and a great part of that of Ḫammurabi were occupied with a long struggle with the Elamites for the possession of southern Babylonia.‖ Kudur-Mabuk, king of western Elam (Emutbal), having conquered the city of Larsa, installed his sons, Warad-Sin and Rîm-Sin, successively as its rulers; and the power of Elam was gradually extended over the neighbouring city-states until it embraced eventually the whole of southern and central Babylonia. It was not until Ḫammurabi's thirtieth year that he was able to effect a turn in the tide; but his success was then so decisive that he not only captured Larsa but even invaded the land of Emutbal and defeated the Elamites upon their own ground. Now we know that the Elamite Kudur-Mabuk styled himself ADDA of Amurru,¶ just as he styled himself ADDA of Emutbal. Precisely how much the claim to this title implied we are unable to affirm; but, however much or little of an historical element we may find in the much-debated *ch.* 14 of Gen., it can

'the second wave of emigration . . . overflowed and washed out, as it were, whatever was left of the first' (p. 113) is seen to be very wide of the truth when we consider that the language of the first wave (Semitic Babylonian) became the dominant language of Babylon and Assyria as long as these kingdoms lasted.

* 'Amorite' (or more correctly 'Amurrite': cf. p. 168) is a proper designation of the language of Amurru, as also of its people.

‡ That Aramaic, which, as known to us from the close of the ninth century B.C. and onwards, was the speech of the Semitic races inhabiting the more northerly portion of the Mediterranean sea-board (north and north-east of the Lebanons) was also at an earlier period merely a dialectical form of the language of Amurru, is suggested in the discussion of *Addit. Note*, pp. 173 ff.

§ Cf., on this question, Winckler, *AF.* i. pp. 143-152.

‖ Cf. the detailed account given by King, *Bab.* pp. 150 ff.

¶ Cf. i. R. 2, No. 3; *CT.* xxi. 33; Rogers, *CP.* pp. 247 f.

hardly be denied that it affords ground for the assumption that Amurru, even as far south as south-eastern Canaʿan, was at one time under the suzerainty of Elam and subject to a yearly tribute.* After Ḫammurabi's successes and the consolidation of his power, we find him claiming a like suzerainty over Amurru. The Diarbekir-stele, which bears a portrait of him, describes him as 'King of Amurru' without any further title. Ammiditana, a subsequent king of the same dynasty, is likewise termed 'King of the land of Amurru.' ‡ Ḫammurabi was not merely a conqueror, but in the best sense an organizer and ruler; and it is probable that any region over which he claimed the title of 'king' was not a mere sphere for occasional razzias aimed at the collection of booty and tribute, § but would experience, at least to some extent, the benefits of his good government and civilizing influence. ||

* The name of Chedorlaʿomar (Kudur-Lagamar), who is represented as leader of the confederation, is genuinely Elamite in formation, though the bearer of it is otherwise unknown (on the supposed discovery of the name, cf. King, *Hammurabi*, i. pp. liv f.). The name of the goddess Lagamal occurs fairly frequently in proper names on contract-tablets of the First Dynasty period (so several times on tablets in the library of St. John's College, Oxford; cf. also Ungnad, *Babylonische Briefe*, No. 249; *Beiträge zur Assyr.* vi. 5, p. 95). 'Amraphel, King of Shinʿar' is generally accepted as Ḫammurabi. 'Arioch, King of Ellasar' may be Warad-Sin of Larsa, since Warad-Sin might be represented in Sumerian form by ERI.AGU (cf., however, King, *Hammurabi*, i. pp. xlix ff.). 'Tidʿal, king of peoples' (Heb. *gôyîm*), may have been a Ḥittite chieftain. His name has been plausibly connected with Dud-ḫâlia, a name which is borne in later times by one of the last rulers of the Ḥittite empire (cf. Sayce's note in Garstang, *Hittites*, p. 324, *n* 4). The term *gôyîm* may represent the Bab. *umman Manda*, i.e. semi-barbarian hordes from the north. On the historical probability of such an alliance as is pictured, cf. King, *Bab.* p. 159; Rogers, *HBA.*[6] ii. pp. 83 f.: Skinner, *Genesis* (*ICC.*), pp. 257 ff. The Larsa Dynastic list recently published by Clay (*Miscellaneous Inscriptions in the Yale Babylonian Collection*, 1915, pp. 30 ff.), seems to prove that Warad-Sin was considerably anterior to Ḫammurabi.

‡ Cf. Winckler, *AF.* i. pp. 144-146; King, *Hammurabi*, pp. 195 f., 207 f.; Jeremias, *OTLAE.* i. p. 322; Böhl, *KH.* p. 35.

§ Against the view of Hogarth, *The Ancient East*, pp. 24 f.

|| The list of cities mentioned in the prologue to Ḫammurabi's Code enables us to form an estimate of the extent of his empire during the latter years of his reign. It includes the principal religious centres not only of Akkad and of Sumer as far south as Eridu, but stretches northward to Aššur and Nineveh and westward to Aleppo—if, as is generally supposed, this city is to be understood by Ḫallabim (KI). Both Aleppo and also, probably, 'the settlements on the Euphrates,' which he claims to have subdued, would be reckoned as part of Amurru. The fact that no more southerly cities of Amurru are enumerated is, it must be confessed, a point which may be advanced against the view which is advocated above. May we, however, explain the omission by the fact that in Amurru, which, as contrasted with Sumer and Akkad, was a comparatively new and uncivilized country, there existed no ancient and celebrated centres of culture, the deities of which Ḫammurabi was concerned to propitiate? At any rate he specially distinguishes the west Semitic deity Dagan as 'his creator' (*banišu*).

A striking example of the influence of the Semitic Babylonian *language* upon the language of Canaʿan (Hebrew), which it is difficult to assign to any other period than

We have, then (it may be assumed), in the First Dynasty of Babylon a dynasty of 'Amorite' origin, bearing sway both over Babylonia and (from the time of Ḫammurabi) over Amurru to the west as far as the Mediterranean sea-board. This dynasty, as facts abundantly prove, must have fallen rapidly under the influence of Babylonian civilization. It will be sufficient, in this regard, to allude to the legal Code of Ḫammurabi, in which the far-reaching and highly-detailed character of the legislation proves (as indeed we know from extraneous evidence) that the great king was not the initiator of the whole system, but embodied earlier elements, many, if not most, of which were doubtless due to Sumerian civilization.* These facts help us to understand two phenomena

that of the First Babylonian Dynasty, is seen in the uses of the Bab. Permansive (in form identical with the Heb. Perfect) and Praeterite (in form identical with the Heb. Imperfect), as compared respectively with the uses of the Heb. Perfect and Imperfect with *wāw consecutive*. The Bab. Permansive, like the Heb. Perfect, essentially regards an action as existing apart from any idea of time-relations; whereas the Bab. Praeterite, like the Heb. Imperfect with *wāw consecutive*, comes into use as soon as an action can be brought into a time-relation, *i.e.* can be regarded as springing out of a defined point in time. A good illustration of the two usages in Bab. may be seen in the opening lines of the Creation-epic, where Permansives describe the condition of things prior to creation (*la nabû, la zakrat, la kiṣṣura, la šeʾ, la šupâ*, etc.), but Praeterites are employed so soon as the actions of creation begin to *take their start* out of conditions as defined by the Permansives (so *iḫikû-ma, ibbanû-ma*, etc.). Since the mode of thought thus defined in language is peculiar to Babylonian and to Hebrew (with which we may group the inscriptions of Meshaʿ and of Zakir: cf. p. 174), and is otherwise unknown in Semitic, it is reasonable to explain the connexion as due to the influence of the older civilization upon the younger at a specially formative period in the history of the latter.

* Cf. *e.g.* what is known as to the reforms of Urukagina, Sumerian *patesi* of Lagaš, *cir.* B.C. 2800: King, *Sum. and Akk.* pp. 178 ff. The fragment of a Sumerian code of laws (published by Clay, *Miscellaneous Inscriptions in the Yale Bab. Coll.*, 1915, pp. 18 ff.) also contains instructive evidence upon this point. The fragment preserves nine laws. Two of these, which fix compensation for injury resulting in miscarriage, are condensed in Ḫammurabi's Code; the latter also adds other laws on the subject to suit the peculiar conditions of Babylonian society under the First Dynasty. Another law, dealing with compensation for the loss of a hired boat, is amplified to form four laws in the Code. Two of the newly-recovered Sumerian laws, relating to the loss of a hired ox, are practically reproduced in the Code; while others on unfilial conduct, elopement, and seduction find Semitic Babylonian parallels in certain features, but no precise equivalents. One law, which provides for the payment of his portion to a son who renounces his sonship, and which enacts his subsequent legal separation from his parents, is not paralleled in the Code, but, as Clay points out, is strikingly illustrated by the parable of the prodigal son in Luke 15 [11]. The Sumerian Code bears the title 'the law of Nisaba and Ḫani.' Nisaba was patroness of writing, and Ḫani in later periods is described as 'lord of the seal' and 'god of the scribes': they may well have been patrons of law under the Sumerians. It is noteworthy that Nisaba is here mentioned before her consort, a fact which suggests that he was a deity of less consideration. The divine name Ḫani occurs in proper names of the Dynasty of Ur and the First Dynasty of Babylon; and we know of a West Semitic kingdom of Ḫana (later Ḫanî) on the middle Euphrates not far from the mouth of the Ḫâbûr (cf. King, *Bab.* pp. 129 ff.). If the Sumerian god

which, in later times, are very striking: (i) the influence of Babylonian civilization upon Canaʿan, and, eventually, upon Israel, both in regard to legislation and also to legends and early traditions; * and (ii) the use of the Babylonian language and the cuneiform script in Syria and Canaʿan as a medium of communication in the fourteenth century B.C. (as witnessed by the T.A. Letters), and probably also in later times. ‡

The empire of Ḫammurabi was maintained, on the whole, unimpaired under his son and successor Samsu-iluna. This king, however, experienced considerable trouble in the south, both from the Elamites and also from the people of the Sea-country on the borders of the Persian Gulf, where a ruler named Iluma-ilu appears as the founder of an independent dynasty. After Samsu-iluna the power of the First Dynasty gradually declined. Its fall was hastened, if not actually brought about, by a raid of the Ḫittites, § an Anatolian people from beyond the Taurus, who now for the first time appear upon the arena of western Asia. || The reins of government in Babylon seem then to have been seized by the dynasty of the Sea-country to which we have already alluded (reckoned as the Second Babylonian Dynasty in the Kings' list; cf. *Footnote* ‡, p. lviii). This dynasty may be inferred to have been, in the main, Sumerian, perhaps with a certain Semitic admixture. ¶

After a lapse of some 160 years the Sea-country rulers were

Ḫani was ultimately of West Semitic origin—a possibility which these facts seem to suggest, we have recovered a very noteworthy result of Sumerian contact with the west prior to the age of Ḫammurabi. It should be added that, though the Sumerian Code is undated, both script and contents suggest a rather earlier date than that of the First Dynasty.

* It does not of course follow that the 'Amorites' were in all respects debtors to the earlier Babylonian civilization, and contributed nothing of their own. Certain elements, both in their civilization and in their traditions, may be, so far as we know, distinctively Amorite in origin. If it were possible to analyse the sources of the traditions which are unmistakeably common in origin to the Babylonians on the one hand and to the Canaʿanites and Hebrews on the other, we should, in all probability, distinguish three successive sources from which, in turn, material has been drawn:—(i) Sumerian, (ii) Semitic Babylonian, (iii) Amorite. Clay, in his book *Amurru, the Home of the Northern Semites* (1909), seeks to prove that Amurru was the cultural centre of the Northern Semites, and that 'the influence of Babylonian culture upon the peoples of Canaan was almost *nil*' (p. 91); but this is a paradox.

‡ Cf. Hommel, *AHT*. pp. 45 f.

§ A chronicle published by King states that 'against Samsu-ditana the men of the land of Ḫatti <marched>, against the land of Akkad.' King connects this statement with the fact that in later years the Kaššite king Agum-Kakrime brought back the images of the god Marduk and his consort Ṣarpanitum from the Ḫittite state of Ḫanî in northern Syria, and installed them again in the temple of Esagila at Babylon. Cf. *Chron.* i. pp. 148 f.; ii. p. 22.

|| For possibly older references to the Ḫittites (time of Ḫammurabi) cf. *Footnote* * on Gen. 14, p. lxii, and Garstang, *Hittites*, p. 323.

¶ The names of the first three kings and of the last king are Semitic, while the remaining seven are Sumerian.

driven out of Babylon by Kaššite invaders from the east who founded a new dynasty (the Third Dynasty) which lasted for the long period of 576 years, and is to be dated *cir.* B.C. 1760-1185. The latter part of this period is therefore coincident with part of the period covered by the Book of Judg.; and it is possible that in Judg. 3 7-11 we may have the echo of a Kaššite raid upon the west in which the name of the raiding chieftain has been perverted by late Jewish ingenuity (cf. p. 64). The fact seems to be established that the Kaššites were, in origin, Indo-Germanic;* but they speedily adapted themselves to the Semitic Babylonian civilization, though their king-names remain, with few exceptions, Kaššite throughout the dynastic period. The Kaššite success in conquering Babylon was probably due in large measure to their possession of horses and chariots; and the foundation of their dynasty marks the introduction of the horse into Babylonia, and thence very speedily into Syria and Egypt.‡

The domination of Egypt by the Hyksos, and their subsequent expulsion, have an important bearing upon the history of Cana'an at the period of Babylonian history with which we have been dealing. That the Hyksos were Asiatic Semites may be regarded as certain; but that they were uncivilized nomads pouring into Egypt directly from Arabia is unlikely. If Manetho's explanation of the name Hyksos as 'shepherd-king' (from *Hyk*='king' and *sos*='shepherd')§ be approximately correct,|| it was probably applied by the Egyptians to the invaders in contempt and derision. The fact that, according to Manetho, the first Hyksos king, Salitis, rebuilt and fortified the city of Avaris in the Delta (probably the modern Tell el-Yahudiyyeh in the Wâdy Ṭûmîlât¶) because he

* Cf. Hall, *NE.* p. 201.

‡ Bab. *sîsû* 'horse,' is regularly written ideographically ANŠU.KURRA; and the accepted conclusion is that this Sumerian equivalent means 'ass of the mountain,' and preserves record of the fact that the horse was introduced into Babylonia from the high-lying steppes of central Asia, across the eastern mountains. Though it is, of course, an elementary fact that ANŠU means 'ass,' and that KURRA may mean 'mountain,' the analogy of parallel cases in which ANŠU is prefixed as a determinative before the names of other beasts of burden (the mule and camel) serves to cast doubt upon this explanation, and to suggest that ANŠU.KURRA is properly to be understood as 'ass-like animal (*i.e.* beast of burden) called KURRA.' KURRA is then, in all probability, a foreign name for the horse, introduced into Babylonia together with the animal which bore it. It is tempting to associate the name with Persian *ghour*, Hindi *ghor-khur*, Baluchi *ghur* or *ghuran*, Kirghi *koulan*—names which are applied to the onager. The transference of a name from one animal to another of kindred (or even of diverse) species is not without analogy.

§ Cf. Jos., *C. Ap.* I. 14.

|| On this interpretation *sos* is probably the Egyptian *šasu*, a term applied to the Asiatic Bedawin. Breasted (*Hist. Eg.* p. 217) objects to this explanation, and suggests that the real meaning of Hyksos is 'ruler of countries'—a title which Ḫyan, one of the Hyksos kings, often gives himself on his monuments. Cf. Griffith in *PSBA.* xix. (1897), pp. 296 f.; W. M. Müller in *MVAG.*, 1898, 3, pp. 4 ff.

¶ Cf. Petrie, *Hyksos and Israelite Cities*, pp. 9 f.

feared the incursion of 'the Assyrians' (a term loosely used to denote the dominant power in Babylonia at the time)* seems to be an indication that the Hyksos had connexions beyond the borders of Egypt in a north-easterly direction, *i.e.* throughout Cana'an and northern Syria; and inasmuch as we find them, after the reduction of Avaris by Aḥmosi I., next making a stand in Sharuḥen (*i.e.* no doubt the city of that name mentioned in Josh. 19[6] as assigned to Sime'on in southern Judah) where they are besieged for three years, and finally defeated by Aḥmosi in northern Syria,‡ we have good ground for concluding that they were, in origin, the more or less civilized people of Amurru, and that their line of retreat lay, as was natural, into the land occupied by their kindred.§ This conclusion is strengthened by the fact (accepted by Egyptologists) that it was they who introduced horses and chariots into Egypt, and that Aḥmosi succeeded in expelling them by turning this powerful engine of warfare against them. As we have already noticed, it was the Kaššites who introduced the horse into western Asia, and the peoples of Amurru must speedily have obtained it through their Mesopotamian connexion. The name of the most important Hyksos king known to us, Ḫyan, is certainly Semitic,‖ and among the scarab-names of kings or autonomous chieftains collected by Petrie¶ there occurs *Y pk-hr* or *Y ḳb-hr* which may represent a Semitic Ja'cob-el—a name which raises speculation on account of its Israelite connexions. Another name, *'nt-hr*, seems to represent 'Anath-el.**

The length of the period covered by the Hyksos invasion and domination of Egypt is most uncertain. Petrie‡‡ accepts and defends Manetho's statement that five hundred and eleven years elapsed from their first invasion to their ultimate expulsion; but

* Cf. Hall, *NE.* p. 215, *n* 3.

‡ Cf. the autobiographies of the two Egyptian officers named Aḥmosi, who took part in this war: Breasted, *AR.* ii. §§ 1 ff.

§ The cause originally conducing to the invasion of Egypt by the Western Semites can only be conjectured. Hall may be correct in supposing that the almost contemporary incursion of the Kaššites from Irân and the Ḥittites from Asia Minor into Mesopotamia and northern Syria 'must have caused at first a considerable displacement of the Semitic population, which was pressed south-westwards into southern Syria and Palestine,' with the result that it 'burst the ancient barrier of Egypt': *NE.* p. 212. Cf. also Luckenbill, *AJTh.* xviii. (1914), p. 32.

‖ The name is borne by an Aramaean king of Ya'di in northern Syria in the ninth century B.C., and is written Ḫa-ia-ni in the annals of Shalmaneser III. (cf. *KB.* i. p. 170), and חיא in the inscription of Kalumu, the succeeding king of Ya'di (on which cf. p. 174).

¶ Cf. Petrie, *Hyksos and Israelite Cities*, pp. 68 f. and Pl. LI.; Hall, *NE.* p. 217.

** Cf. Spiegelberg in *OLZ.* vii. (1904), 131; Hall, *NE.* p. 217. There seems to be no justification for Spiegelberg's proposal to interpret the Hyksos name *Smḳn* as Sime'on (*loc. cit.*; *Aegypt. Randglossen zum A.T.* p. 12), since the equivalent *ḳ*=ע appears to be unproven (on the equivalents of Eg. *ḳ*, cf. Burch. §§ 113 f.).

‡‡ Cf. *Hist. Eg.* pp. 204, 228; *Historical Studies*, p. 14.

Ed. Meyer and his followers * allow conjecturally no more than a hundred years. Hall ‡ seems to have good sense on his side in arguing for a figure between these two extremes—perhaps about two hundred years. The accession of Aḥmosi I., who expelled them from Egypt, is dated *cir.* B.C. 1580. §

Invasion of Palestine and Syria, thus begun by Aḥmosi I., was carried further by subsequent kings of the Eighteenth Egyptian Dynasty. It is a moot point whether Amenḥotp I. (*cir.* B.C. 1559), the successor of Aḥmosi, undertook a Syrian campaign; but his successor, Ṭhutmosi I. (*cir.* B.C. 1539), advanced victoriously through Syria as far as Naharîn, *i.e.* the district between the Orontes and the Euphrates (cf. *note* on 'Aram-naharaim,' ch. 3 [7]), and set up a boundary-tablet on the bank of the Euphrates to mark the northern limit of his kingdom.|| Such incursions of Egyptian kings into Syria, though productive of booty, failed to bring the Western Semites permanently under the Egyptian yoke or to ensure payment of a regular tribute.

It was Ṭhutmosi III. (*cir.* B.C. 1501), the most famous king Egypt ever had, who, after a long period of inaction enforced upon him by the powerful Queen Ḥatšepsut, with whom he was associated as ruler, began on her death a series of seventeen campaigns in Syria (*cir.* B.C. 1479-1459), resulting in its thorough conquest and consolidation as a part of the Egyptian Empire.¶ In the first of these he met a confederation of north Palestinian kinglets, under the leadership of the Prince of Ḳadesh—possibly an immigrant Ḥittite from the north; a combination which reminds us of the league of the kings of northern Cana'an under Sisera, as recorded in Judg. A battle at Megiddo, graphically described, resulted in his complete success, and Megiddo was invested and soon fell into his hands. The list (on the walls of the Temple of Amon, at Karnak) of 'the people of Upper Retenu [southern Syria, including Palestine] whom his majesty shut up in wretched Megiddo' contains a hundred and nineteen names, and is of great geographical interest. ** Among the names occur *Y-ʿ-ḳ-b-'â-rạ* and *Y-š-p-'â-rạ* (Nos. 102

* Cf. Meyer, *GA.*[2] I. ii. p. 293; Breasted, *Hist. Eg.* p. 221.

‡ Cf. Hall, *NE.* pp. 23 ff., 216 f., 218.

§ The accession-dates given for Egyptian kings are those of Breasted, whose chronological table at the end of his *History of the Ancient Egyptians*, 1908 (an abbreviation of the *History of Egypt*, 1906) may usefully be consulted. The only deviation is in the dates given for Amenḥotp I. and Ṭhutmosi I., where a complicated question of succession arises, involving the reign of Ṭhutmosi II. (who for our purpose is a nonentity) in relation to that of Ṭhutmosi III. Cf. Hall, *NE.* pp. 286 ff., whose conclusions are assumed, and whose dates, as given in the Table, p. 228, have been adopted.

|| Cf. Breasted, *AR.* ii. §§ 79, 81, 85.

¶ *Ibid.* ii. §§ 391 ff.

** Cf. Müller, *AE.* pp. 157 ff.; *Die Palästinaliste Thutmosis III.*, *MVAG.*, 1907, 1. Petrie, *Hist. Eg.* ii. pp. 320 ff., attempts to find a systematic arrangement in the list, and offers identifications, many of which must be deemed highly precarious.

and 78), which have been read respectively as Ja'cob-el and Joseph-el.* The remainder of this campaign was occupied with the reduction of three cities on the southern slopes of the Lebanon.

The second, third, and fourth campaigns seem to have been fully spent in consolidating the conquests of the first. During the course of the second campaign it is interesting to note that Ṭhutmosi received a present (which he describes as 'tribute') from the far-off kingdom of Assyria, which at this period was beginning to rise into prominence. Northern Syria, however, with Ḳadesh on the Orontes as a centre of disaffection, still remained untouched; but the fifth campaign made substantial progress towards this objective through the reduction of the coast-cities of Phoenicia. The sixth campaign is highly important as marking the first transport of the Egyptian army by sea to Syria. The establishment of a base in the Phoenician harbours meant that thenceforward Ṭhutmosi could get within striking distance of northern Syria after a few days' sail; and the hold of Egypt upon the coast-land of western Asia was thus materially strengthened. In the sixth campaign Ḳadesh was captured after a long siege. The account of this campaign is interesting as preserving record of Ṭhutmosi's policy for securing the future allegiance of Syria. The sons of the conquered chieftains were carried back to Egypt to be educated, in order that, imbued, as it was hoped, with Egyptian ideals and sympathies, they might in time succeed their fathers as faithful vassals of their suzerain.

After a seventh campaign directed against Arvad and Simyra, Ṭhutmosi reached, in his eighth campaign, the climax of his successes. Advancing into Naharîn, he met and defeated 'that foe of wretched Naharîn,' *i.e.*, probably, the king of Mitanni,‡ captured Carchemish, and crossing the Euphrates, set up his boundary-tablet upon its eastern bank beside that of Ṭhutmosi I. 'Ḫeta the Great,' *i.e.* the Hittites of Cappadocia, now sent him presents; and it is even possible that he may have received them from Babylon.§ Ṭhutmosi's remaining campaigns in Syria were occupied in quelling revolts and generally consolidating the broad territory which he had won.

Egypt's Asiatic Empire was maintained unimpaired under the

* The latter equivalence is very doubtful, since the sibilants do not correspond. Nos. 35 and 18, which have been read *Š-m-'-n* and understood as Sime'on, appear to lack the ' (ע). W. M. Müller (*Die Palästinaliste Thutmosis III.*) transcribes both as *Ša-ma-na*. Cf. his remarks on p. 15.

‡ Cf. Breasted, *AR.* §§ 476, 479; Hall, *NE.* p. 241. W. M. Müller regards the view that the king of Mitanni was overlord of the whole of Naharîn as questionable: cf. *AE.* p. 251.

§ It is a disputed question whether we should find allusion to 'tribute of the chief of Shin'ar,' or whether the reference is to Singara, *i.e.* the modern Ǵebel Singar, north-west of Nineveh. Cf. Breasted, *AR.* ii. § 484 (*footnote*); Hall, *NE.* p. 242.

next two Pharaohs, Amenḥotp II. (*cir.* B.C. 1448) and Thutmosi IV. (*cir.* B.C. 1420), though both these monarchs had to quell rebellions which broke out in northern Syria and Naharîn at or shortly after their accessions.* The authority of Egypt was, however, effectively maintained by official representatives and garrisons in the larger towns; and the system of allowing the Syrian cities a large measure of autonomy under their petty chieftains proved, on the whole, to be justified. The marriage of Thutmosi IV. with the daughter of Artatama, king of Mitanni in northern Mesopotamia, ‡ was a judicious measure which gained for Egypt an ally upon the north-eastern limit of her Asiatic kingdom; and it was probably owing to this that Amenḥotp III., the son of Thutmosi by his Mitannian queen, succeeded to the empire without having to meet any insurrection on the part of the turbulent elements in Naharîn.

For the reigns of Amenḥotp III. (*cir.* B.C. 1411) and his successor Amenḥotp IV. (*cir.* B.C. 1375), we possess the evidence of the correspondence discovered at Tell el-Amarna in Egypt in 1887,§ which is of unique importance for the history of Syria and of the surrounding countries of western Asia in their relation with Egypt. At this period (as the T.A. Letters first proved to us ||) the language of diplomacy and commerce in western Asia was Babylonian, and correspondence was carried on in the cuneiform script, written upon clay tablets. Many of these letters are addressed to the king of Egypt by the independent rulers of the neighbouring kingdoms of western Asia—Babylonia or Karduniaš (to give the kingdom its Kaššite name), Assyria, Mitanni, etc.—who were naturally concerned to preserve good diplomatic relations with Egypt. These,

* Cf. Breasted, *AR.* §§ 780 ff.; 816 ff.

‡ Cf. T.A. Letters, Knudtzon, No. 29, ll. 16 ff.

§ The most recent edition of the T.A. Letters is that of J. A. Knudtzon, *Die el-Amarna Tafeln* (1908-15), which takes the place of H. Winckler's edition (*KB.* v, 1896) as the standard edition for scholars. The cuneiform text of the Berlin collection of tablets has been published by Abel and Winckler, *Der Thontafelfund von El-Amarna* (1889), and that of the British Museum collection of tablets by Bezold in Budge and Bezold, *Tel el-Amarna Tablets in the Brit. Mus.* (1892). All the original tablets were exhaustively collated by Knudtzon for his transliteration and translation of the texts. Böhl, *Die Sprache der Amarnabriefe* (1909) is important for philology.

|| Since the discovery of the T.A. Letters a few cuneiform tablets have been found at various Palestinian sites which have undergone excavation (cf., for the more important ones, Rogers, *CP.* pp. 278 ff.). The most important evidence for the widespread use of cuneiform Babylonian is found in the great store of tablets discovered by Winckler in his excavation of the site of the ancient Hittite capital (Ḫatti) at Boghaz Keui east of the river Halys in Asia Minor. The first instalment of autographs of these documents has been published very recently (H. H. Figulla and E. F. Weidner, *Keilschrifttexte aus Boghazköi*, parts 1 and 2, Oct. 1916); but prior to this we possessed only Winckler's account of them in *MDOG.* xxxv. (Dec. 1907), containing extracts from some few which appeared to the discoverer to be among the more important. A fairly full abstract of this account has been translated into English in the *Annual Report of the Smithsonian Institution*, 1908 (some misprints in proper names).

though of first importance for the history of the times, do not here concern us, except incidentally. It is interesting, however, to notice the way in which such constant correspondence could be conveyed backwards and forwards through Syria, together with the valuable presents with which the letters were often accompanied, apparently without great risk of miscarriage.* There exists a passport-letter, addressed by an unnamed king—very possibly the king of Mitanni ‡—'to the kings of Canaʿan, the servants of my brother' (*i.e.* the king of Egypt), exhorting them to see that his messenger, Akiya, receives no hindrance, but is safely and speedily forwarded on his way to the Egyptian court (cf. Kn. 30).

It is the correspondence of the subject-kinglets which brings most vividly before us the condition of Syria at the time, and the causes which were leading to the gradual weakening of Egypt's hold upon her Asiatic possessions. In the reign of Amenḥotp III. the Egyptian empire was at its zenith, and the luxury and magnificence of the kingdom had never been surpassed. This, however, was due to the continuous efforts of the Pharaoh's warlike ancestors: he seems himself to have been content to enjoy the fruits of past achievement, and not to have been greatly concerned with the maintenance of the tradition of empire-building. Thus already in his reign we discern the beginning of movements which were destined ultimately to bring about the decline of Egypt's suzerainty over Syria.

It was under Amenḥotp IV., however, that the crisis became acute. This king is remarkable as the introducer into Egypt of a new form of religion, a kind of philosophic monotheism which centred in the worship of the solar disc (called in Egyptian Aton). Repudiating his own name, he adopted the name Aḫnaton ('Spirit of Aton'); and having removed his capital from Thebes, where the power and influence of the old religion were naturally at their strongest, he founded a new capital, some three hundred miles lower down the Nile and about one hundred and sixty miles above the Delta, to which he gave the name Aḫetaton ('Horizon of Aton'). This is the modern Tell el-Amarna. Wholly absorbed in his religious speculations and in domestic life, the king cared little about the fate of his Asiatic provinces; and letters from the native princes and governors of Syria speak again and again of the growing spirit of disaffection towards Egypt, or beg for assistance in the face of open revolt.

* There are, as might be expected, some complaints of molestation and robbery. Thus we find that the caravan of Ṣalmu, the messenger of Burnaburiaš, king of Karduniaš, was twice plundered on the way to Egypt in Egyptian territory (Syria-Palestine), and compensation is demanded of the Egyptian king (Kn. 7). On a later occasion (during the unsettled period of the north Syrian revolt) the merchants of Burnaburiaš were robbed and murdered (Kn. 8). Ašur-uballiṭ, king of Assyria, says that Egyptian messengers have been waylaid by the Sutû, a nomad people (Kn. 16). Some of the Syrian chieftains express their willingness to provide provisions and safe escort for caravans (cf. Kn. 226, 255).

‡ Cf. Weber's discussion in Knudtzon, pp. 1072 ff.

The trouble arose principally from the encroachments of the Ḥittites upon northern Syria. As we have already remarked, in alluding to an incursion of this people into Babylonia some five hundred years earlier (cf. p. lxiv), the Ḥittites were an Anatolian race whose principal centre lay west of the Taurus, in the region which is known to us later on as Cappadocia. Our knowledge of them has been placed on a new footing in recent times (1907) through the excavations of Winckler at an ancient site near the modern village of Boghaz Keui, which proved to have borne the name of Ḥatti, and to have been the capital of the Ḥittite kingdom.* We are still, however, at a loss as to the racial origin of the Ḥittites. Their physiognomy, as depicted on their own and on Egyptian monuments—a prominent nose, high cheek-bones, and a retreating forehead and chin—are closely reproduced at the present day among the Armenians. They were certainly non-Semitic; and it does not seem probable (as has been variously suggested) that they were of Iranian or Mongolian origin. The inscriptions upon rock and stone, which are assumed (with practical certainty) to be Ḥittite work, are written in a peculiar pictographic script, and are still undeciphered. Attempts at decipherment have been made by several scholars upon different lines; ‡ but they have not met with general acceptance or yielded results which are capable of utilization. The Ḥittite language, as written in cuneiform on tablets found at Boghaz Keui, and in the Arzawa letters which were found among the T.A. correspondence, cannot be connected with any known language.§ Fortunately, a large number of the documents from Boghaz Keui are written in Babylonian; and it is these which have so largely extended our knowledge.||

* Cf. *MDOG.* xxxv. pp. 12 ff.

‡ Cf. especially the articles by Sayce in *PSBA.* xxv.-xxvii. (1903-5).

§ Knudtzon has argued from the Arzawa letters that the language is Indo-Germanic (*Die zwei Arzawa-Briefe, die ältesten Urkunden in indogermanischer Sprache, mit Bemerkungen von S. Bugge und A. Torp*, 1902); but the theory has failed to gain acceptance (cf. *e.g.* the criticism of Bloomfield in *American Journal of Philology*, xxv. pp. 12 ff.), and, according to Weber (Kn. p. 1074), the author of it himself had some misgivings with regard to it. F. Hrozný (*MDOG.* lvi., *December* 1915, pp. 17-50) maintains the same conclusions upon the evidence of the Ḥittite documents from Boghaz Keui, which he is engaged in transcribing; but until some part at least of the rich material from Boghaz Keui has become the common property of scholars, it is impossible to pass judgment upon the theory. Hrozný has been criticized by Bork, *OLZ.*, Okt. 1916, 289 ff., and by Cowley in a paper read before the Royal Asiatic Society in December 1916, which is as yet unpublished: cf. brief abstract in *JRAS.* for January 1917, pp. 202 f. The important Sumerian-Akkadian-Ḥittite vocabularies from Boghaz Keui, published in transcription by Delitzsch for the Berlin Academy (*Abhandl. k. p. Akad.*, 1914, 3), though of the greatest value for our interpretation of Ḥittite words, have not thrown any further light upon the linguistic affinities of the Ḥittite language.

|| The fullest and most recent book on Ḥittite excavation and history is Garstang, *The Land of the Hittites* (1910). See also King, *Bab.* pp. 225-41; Hall, *NE. ch.*

Of the early history of the Ḫittites we know nothing. Probably they formed at first a collection of semi-independent tribes, loosely united by the bond of a common extraction, and only temporarily acting together under one leader on such occasions as the raid on northern Syria and Babylonia which brought about the downfall of the First Babylonian Dynasty, *cir.* B.C. 1926 (cf. p. lxiv). Ḫattušili I., who was king of the city of Kuššar * (*cir.* B.C. 1400), was succeeded by his son Šubbiluliuma, who bound the Ḫittite clans into a strong confederation, and whose reign of probably some forty years (*cir.* B.C. 1385-1345) was a career of conquest resulting in the creation of an empire which lasted under one dynasty for nearly two hundred years.

In the latter years of Amenḥotp III. we find Šubbiluliuma crossing the Taurus, and leading his forces to the attack of northern Syria. The safe retention of Naharîn as an Egyptian province depended, as we have noticed (p. lxix), largely upon the goodwill of the king of Mitanni; and the alliance which had been contracted through the marriage of Ṭhutmosi IV. with a Mitannian princess had been further cemented by the union of Amenḥotp III. with Gilu-Ḫipa, sister of Tušratta, the reigning king of Mitanni, and subsequently with Tadu-Ḫipa, Tušratta's daughter, who, after the death of Amenḥotp III., became a wife of his successor, Aḫnaton.‡ Tušratta, however, had succeeded to a kingdom weakened by internal intrigues, his brother, Artaššumara, who reigned before him, having been assassinated. He was strong enough to repel the Ḫittites from Mitanni for the time being,§ but could not prevent Šubbiluliuma from invading Naharîn, where the projects of the Ḫittite king were furthered by another brother of Tušratta, named (like his grandfather) Artatama. This prince, having very possibly been implicated in the murder of Artaššumara, had been obliged to fly from Mitanni to Naharîn, and, with his son Šutatarra, and grandson Itakama, of whom we hear later on as prince of Kinza or Kidša (*i.e.* the district of which the principal city was Ḳadesh on the Orontes) welcomed the opportunity of intriguing with the Ḫittites against Tušratta. Further south, in the district of the Lebanons, Abd-

viii.; Hogarth, article 'Hittites' in *Encyc. Britann.*[11] vol. xiii.; Weber in Kn., pp. 108 ff.; Ed. Meyer, *Reich und Kultur der Chetiter* (1914); Luckenbill, *AJTh.* xviii. (1914), pp. 24 ff. For the Boghaz Keui documents, cf. Winckler, *MDOG.* xxxv.; *OLZ.* xiii. (1910), 289 ff. For an account of the excavations at Boghaz Keui, cf. Puchstein, *Boghazköi: die Bauwerke* (1912).

* The site of this city is unknown.

‡ Unlike the Mitannian wife of Ṭhutmosi IV., who was the mother of Amenḥotp III., both Gilu-Ḫipa and Tadu-Ḫipa occupied the position of inferior wives only. The influential Tii, who was chief wife of Amenḥotp III. and mother of Aḫnaton, seems to have been of Semitic origin on her father's side. Nefertiti, the queen of Aḫnaton, is now known to have been his full sister (the daughter of Tii); and Petrie's view (*Hist. Eg.* ii. p. 207) that she is identical with Tadu-Ḫipa is thus disproved; cf. Hall, *NE.* pp. 255 f., 258, *n*².

§ Cf. Kn. 17.

Aširta, who was chieftain of Amurru,* perceived that his own interests would best be served by making common cause with the Ḥittites, and attacking the rulers of the Phoenician coast-cities, who were loyal to Egypt. For a time this Amorite prince and his son Aziru managed with amazing astuteness to pass themselves off as faithful vassals of Egypt, in spite of the urgent representations of Rib-Adda, the governor of Gebal, who displayed the utmost energy in the Egyptian cause. Amenḥotp III. seems at length to have been convinced of the true state of affairs and to have despatched an army; and the tension was temporarily relieved.‡ Under Aḫnaton, however, no such help was forthcoming; and the Phoenician cities fell one after another into the hands of the Amorites.§

Meanwhile in the south affairs were little better; local dissensions were rife among the petty Cana'anite princes, and we find them engaged in active intrigue against their suzerain, and at the same time sending letters to the Pharaoh full of protestations of loyalty and accusations against their neighbours. So far as we can judge, ARAD-Ḫiba, the governor of Jerusalem, stood faithfully for the interests of the Egyptian king; but he seems to have stood almost alone. His letters make urgent and repeated requests for the despatch of Egyptian troops, and state that unless they can speedily be sent the whole country will be lost to Egypt. The part played by the Ḥittites and Amorites in the north is filled in the south by a people called Ḫabiru.‖

The Ḫabiru are mentioned under this name in the letters of ARAD-Ḫiba only.¶ He states that they have plundered all the king's territory and occupied his cities; unless the king can send troops before the end of the year, the whole of his territory will certainly fall away to them. Certain of the vassals, notably one Milkili and the sons of Labaya, are accused of conspiring with the Ḫabiru and allowing them to occupy the king's territory; and the district of Shechem ** seems to be specified as having thus passed into their hands. The cities of Gezer, Ashḳelon, and Lachish

* On the sense in which the term Amurru is used in the T.A. Letters, cf. p. 41.

‡ Cf. Kn. 117, ll. 21 ff.

§ For a fully detailed account of the movements of Subbiluliuma, and the north Syrian rebellion, cf. the admirable section in Hall, *NE.* pp. 341 ff., whose view of the relation of Artatama and his descendants to the reigning king of Mitanni is followed above.

‖ Most writers refer to this people as Ḫabiri; but, as Knudtzon points out (cf. p. 45, *n*), out of the seven (or eight) passages in which they are mentioned the form is *Ḫabiru* in the two cases in which the name stands as a Nominative, Ḫabiri (with the Genitive termination) being in all occurrences an oblique form. So Dhorme, *RB.*, 1909, p. 67, *n* 2.

¶ This series of letters has been translated into English by Ball, *Light from the East*, pp. 89-93, and by Rogers, *CP.* pp. 268-278.

** (*Mâtu*) *Ša-ak-mi*, according to Knudtzon's reading (289, l. 23). Winckler (185) fails to make satisfactory sense of the passage.

appear to have been implicated in assisting them.* Indeed, ARAD-Ḫiba states that he has been obliged to tax the king's own high commissioner with playing into their hands, and that on this account he has been slandered to the king. In this last reference (Kn. 286, ll. 16 ff.) the question addressed to the commissioner—'Wherefore lovest thou the Ḫabiru, and hatest the city-governors?'—sets them in contrast to the latter,‡ who represented the delegated authority of Egypt.

The question of the identity of the Ḫabiru has aroused greater interest and keener discussion than any other point raised by the T.A. Letters. Were they, as has often been alleged, identical with the *Hebrews*, *i.e.* with the clans which are pictured in Gen. as the descendants of Abraham the Hebrew, who may very well have been pressing into Cana'an at about this period? Were they even (as has been more boldly suggested§) the tribes of Israel engaged under Joshua' in the invasion and conquest of the Promised Land? The acceptance of this latter view involves the abandonment of the commonly received conclusion as to the date of the Exodus, and the placing of this event at least some two hundred years earlier (cf. pp. cxvi f.).

The philological equivalence of (*amêlûtu*) *Ḫa-bi-ru* ‖ with עִבְרִי *'ibhrî*, 'Hebrew'—or rather, since the form is not a gentilic, with עֵבֶר, 'Ebher, 𝕲 Εβερ (Gen. 10 [21], 11 [14], *al.*)—is perfect. About this there can be doubt at all.¶

* This is an inference only; though a fairly certain one. In the letter in question (Kn. 287) there comes a break of about eight lines, after which ARAD-Ḫiba continues, 'let the King know that all the states are leagued in hostility against me. Behold, the land of Gezer, the land of Ashkelon, and Lachish gave unto them food, oil, and everything that they needed; so let the King have a care for his territory, and despatch bowmen against the men who have done evil against the King my lord.' Here it can scarcely be doubted that the object implied in 'gave unto them' is the Ḫabiru, who must have been mentioned in the missing passage. So Weber in Kn. p. 1337.

‡ The term *ḫazan(n)u*, *ḫazianu*, plur. *ḫazanûtu*, is doubtless the same as New Heb. *ḥazzān*, which means *inspector* or *overseer*. Cf. the reference to Ja'cob as a 'city-overseer' (*ḥazzan māthā*) under Laban, quoted by Buxtorf, *Lexicon*, s.v. from *Baba meṣia*. The ordinary New Heb. usage of *ḥazzān* to denote a synagogue-overseer or minister is technical and secondary. Besides the title *ḫazanu*, the ordinary title by which the Syrian and Palestinian vassal-chieftains describe themselves to the Egyptian king, and are described by him (cf. Kn. 99), is *amêlu*, 'man' of such and such a city. To outsiders they are *šarrâni* 'kings' (cf. Kn. 30), a title which is familiar to us as applied to them in the O.T., and which was doubtless always claimed by them when independent of the suzerainty of Egypt.

§ So, most recently, Hall, *NE.* pp. 409 ff.

‖ *Amêlûtu* 'men,' or sing. *amêlu* 'man,' are used as Determinatives before the names of tribes or classes.

¶ Handcock (*The Latest Light on Bible-lands*, pp. 79-81) is mistaken in supposing that 'the crucial point' in the identification is whether the Heb. ע can be equated with the Bab. *Ḫ*, and in concluding that such an equation 'is totally at variance' with 'the ordinary rules of philological transmutation'; and his pronouncement—

Discussion of the identity of the Ḫabiru with the Hebrews is closely bound up with another question of identification. As we have observed, the (*amêlûtu*) *Ḫa-bi-ru* (or *-ri*) are only mentioned in this form (*i.e.*, their name only occurs spelt out syllabically) in the letters of ARAD-Ḫiba. Many other letters, however, mention a people whose name is written ideographically (*amêlûtu*) SA.GAZ, who occupy a position as freebooters and aggressors against constituted authority identical with that occupied by the Ḫabiru. The question is whether SA.GAZ is merely the ideographic method of writing *Ḫabiru*, and the reading *Ḫabiru* to be assumed wherever the ideogram occurs. The importance of this is to be found in the widespread character of the aggressions of the SA.GAZ. If the Ḫabiru are identical with them, they must have permeated not merely southern and central Cana'an, but also Phoenicia and northern Syria; for the SA.GAZ are mentioned, *e.g.*, with especial frequency in the letters of Rib-Adda of Gebal as employed by

coming as it does in a popular work—is liable to mislead. Granted that the ע in עִבְרִי is probably soft (as may be assumed from the 𝔊 form 'Εβραῖος), we have, in addition to *Kinaḫḫi*=כְּנַעַן (rightly cited by Handcock) the following examples of Bab. *ḫ*=Heb. soft ע among the Cana'anite 'glosses' in the T.A. Letters:—*ḫi-na-ia*= עֵינַי; *ḫa-pa-ru* (also *a-pa-ru*)=עָפָר; *ḫa-zi-ri*=עָצוּר (עָצִיר); *zu-ru-uḫ*=זְרוֹעַ (cf. references in Böhl, *Die Sprache der Amarnabriefe*, p. 15). Cf. also *ba-aḫ-lum*= בַּעַל in the proper names *Pu-ba-aḫ-la* (Kn. 104, l. 7), and *Mu-ut-ba-aḫ-lum* (Kn. 255, l. 3); and the place names (*âlu*) *Ṣa-ar-ḫa* (Kn. 273, l. 21)=צָרְעָה, 𝔊 Σαραα; (*âlu*) *Ḫi-ni-a-na-bi* (Kn. 256, l. 26)=עֵין עֲנָב, the עֲנָב of Josh. 11^{21}, 15^{50}; (*âlu*) *Ša-am-ḫu-na* (Kn. 225, l. 4) perhaps=שִׁמְעוֹן, Jos. (*Vita*, 24) Σιμωνιάς, modern Semûniyyeh, five miles west of Nazareth, perhaps the Biblical שִׁמְרוֹן, Josh. 11^{1}, 12^{20}, 19^{15}, which appears in $𝔊^{B}$ as Συμοων (cf. Buhl, *Geogr.* p. 215); (*âlu*) *Ta-aḫ-[nu-ka]* (Kn. 208, l. 14)=Ta'anakh (Tell Ta'annuk). Were it necessary to go outside the T.A. Letters, we might add to this list by such Amorite proper names in First Dynasty tablets as *Ḫammurabi*, where the first element in the West Semitic עַמּוֹ (cf. *Ḫa-mu-ni-ri* by the side of *Am-mu-ni-ra* in the T.A. Letters); *A-bi-e-šu-uḫ* (by the side of *A-bi-e-šu-'*)=אֲבִישׁוּעַ; *Ya-di-iḫ-el*=יְדִיעֲאֵל (cf. 1 Chr. $7^{6\,ff.}$, 11^{45}, 12^{21}, 26^{2}); *Ya-aš-ma-aḫ-(ilu)-Da-gan*=יִשְׁמַעְדָּגָן, etc.

As for the vowels—they offer no difficulty. Dhorme's statement (*RB.*, 1909, p. 72) that *Ḫabiru* is a participial form is unwarranted (we never find it written *Ḫa-a-bi-ru*, i.e. *Ḫâbiru*). *Ḫabiru* is of course not a gentilic form like Heb. sing. *'ibhrî*, plur. *'ibhrîm* (the Bab. gentilic form would be *Ḫabirâ*; cf. p. lxxxi), but a substantive form like עֵבֶר *'ēbher* (the eponym of *'ibhrî*) with the nominative case-ending. The short *i* vowel in *Ḫabiru* might very well vary: cf. *Armu*, *Aramu*, *Arimu*, *Arumu*=Heb. אֲרָם *'Arâm*. A good analogy for *Ḫabiru*=עֵבֶר may be seen in *Bît Adini*= בֵּית־עֶדֶן, Beth-'Eden (probably עֶדֶן should be עֵדֶן, but is differentiated by 𝔐 from the עֵדֶן of Gen. 2: cf. Müller, *AE.* p. 291, *n* 4).

Abd-Aširta and Aziru in the reduction of the Phoenician cities.* The view that SA.GAZ is to be read as *Ḫabiru*, which has always been regarded with favour by the majority of scholars, is now generally supposed to have been placed beyond question by Winckler's discovery of the interchange of the two terms in documents from Boghaz Keui. This scholar states ‡ that, besides mention of the SA.GAZ-people, there is also allusion to the SA.GAZ-gods, and that as a variant of this latter there exists the reading *ilâni Ḫa-bi-ri, i.e.* 'Ḫabiru-gods.' This discovery, while certainly proving a general equivalence of the Ḫabiru with the SA.GAZ, does not, however, necessarily involve the conclusion that SA.GAZ in the T.A. correspondence was always and everywhere *understood and pronounced* as *Ḫabiru*: indeed, the contrary can be shown to be the case.

In a syllabary given in ii. R. 26, 13 *g-h*, (*amêlu*) SA.GAZ is explained by *ḫab-b[a-tum]*, 'robber' or 'plunderer.' In another tablet the ideogram is glossed by *ḫab-ba-a-te.* § No doubt the common Bab. verb *šagâšu*, which means *to destroy, slay*, and the like, is a Semiticization of the Sumerian ideogram; and the element GAZ, which in its pictographic form clearly represents a cutting or striking weapon, has by itself the values *dâku*, 'to kill, fight, strike,' *maḫâṣu*, 'to smite, wound' (Heb. מחץ), etc. || Possibly the root *ḫabâtu*, from which *ḫabbatum* is derived, though it regularly means 'to plunder,' may have an original connexion with the root *ḫbṭ* which runs through Heb., Aram., and Ar., with the sense 'to strike or beat,' in which case the root-sense of *ḫabbatum* would be 'cut-throat' rather than 'thief' (the two actions are commonly united among the nomad tribes of the Arabian desert). That (*amêlu*) SA.GAZ has its normal value in the T.A. Letters is placed beyond a doubt by the occurrence in a letter from Yapaḫi of Gezer (Kn. 299, l. 26) of the form (*amêlu*) SA.GAZ.MEŠ(*-tum*).¶ Here *-tum* is a Phonetic Complement,** pointing to a Bab. equivalent which ends with this syllable, a fact which indicates *ḫabbatum* and excludes *Ḫabiru* (or *-ri*). In view of this we may infer that in a passage in

* A summary of all allusions to the SA.GAZ is given by Weber in Kn. p. 1147.

‡ Cf. *MDOG.* xxxv. p. 25, *n.* For the former, cf. Figulla and Weidner, *Keilschrifttexte* 1, No. 1, Rev. l. 50; No. 3, Rev. l. 5; for the latter, No. 4, Rev. col. iv. l. 29.

§ Cf. R. C. Thompson, *The Reports of Magicians and Astrologers of Nineveh and Babylon*, i. No. 103, Obv. 7.

|| Cf. Br. 4714 ff.

¶ MEŠ, which means 'multitude,' is used as the sign of the plural.

** A Phonetic Complement is often used in cuneiform in order to obviate doubt as to the precise Bab. word or form denoted by an ideogram. Thus, *e.g.*, the name Uta-napištim, which is commonly written ideographically UD.ZI, often has the syllable *-tim* added to indicate that ZI has the value *napištim.* MU, which means 'to speak' in Sumerian, and so can be used for the Bab. *zakâru* with the same meaning, may be written MU (*-ar*), MU (*-ra*) to indicate the precise form of the verb *izakkar, izakkara.* Thus perfect clearness is gained without the labour of writing the forms syllabically *i-zak-kar, i-zak-ka-ra.*

a letter from Dagan-takala (Kn. 318) in which he begs help of the King of Egypt—'Deliver me from the mighty foes, from the hand of the (*amêlûtu*) SA.GA.AZ.MEŠ, the robber-people (*amêlûtu ḫa-ba-ti*), the Šutû (*amêlûtu Šu-ti-i*)'—we have, not the specification of *three* distinct classes of foes, but of two only, *amêlûtu ḫa-ba-ti* being simply an explanatory gloss on (*amêlûtu*) SA.GA.AZ.MEŠ.*

We conclude, then, that wherever the ideogram SA.GAZ stands in the T.A. Letters, the equivalent that was *understood and read* was not *Ḫabiru* but *ḫabbatum*, 'the robber-people' or 'brigands.' It is a different question whether the Ḫabiru were included among the people who could be classed as *ḫabbatum*. That this is to be affirmed appears to be certain from the equivalent 'SA.GAZ-gods'='Ḫabiru-gods' discovered by Winckler in the documents from Boghaz Keui (cf. p. lxxvi). When, further, while ARAD-Ḫiba refers exclusively to the encroachments of the Ḫabiru and does not mention the SA.GAZ, other princes in the south refer in a similar connexion and in similar terms to the encroachments of the SA.GAZ and make no allusion to the Ḫabiru, the inference is inevitable that the terms Ḫabiru and SA.GAZ refer in these letters to one and the same people.‡

We must notice next that SA.GAZ, though meaning *ḫabbatum*, 'robbers,' is not, as used in the T.A. Letters, a *mere* class-term (*i.e.* applicable to any body of people, of whatever race, who might

* It is true that *amêlûtu ḫa-ba-ti* is not preceded by the diagonal wedge which as a rule marks a gloss; but this is sometimes omitted (cf. Kn. 148, l. 31; 288, l. 34. In 288, l. 52, the wedge *follows* the gloss at the beginning of the next line). The fact that Dagan-takala (or his scribe) did not know the ideogram GAZ, and so was obliged to write GA.AZ (which only occurs in this passage), favours the view that he may have glossed the ideogram in order to avoid misunderstanding. Dhorme (*RB.*, 1909, p. 69) compares Kn. 195, ll. 24 ff., where Namyawaza offers to place his SA.GAZ and his Sutû at the disposal of the Pharaoh. 'These in fact are the two designations which describe the soldiers of the irregular and rebel army. There is no ground for regarding the *Ḫa-ba-ti* as a third group. Everything thus favours reading GAZ or SA.GAZ as *Ḫabbatu*.' In Kn. 207, l. 21, we actually find (*amêlu*) GAZ-MEŠ followed by the diagonal wedge and then the syllable *ḫa-*, after which the tablet is broken and illegible.

‡ Cf. especially ARAD-Ḫiba's statement, 'Behold, this deed is the deed of Milkili and the sons of Labaya, who have given up the King's territory to the Ḫabiru' (Kn. 287, ll. 29 ff.), with the statement of Biridiya of Megiddo, 'Behold, two sons of Labaya have gi[ven] their money to the SA.GAZ' (Kn. 246, ll. 5 ff.). Cf. also the words of Labaya, 'I do not know whether Dumuya has gone with the SA.GAZ' (Kn. 254, ll. 32 ff.); and of Milkili, 'Let the King my lord know that hostility is mighty against me and Šuwardata; and let the King deliver his land out of the hand of the SA.GAZ' (Kn. 271, ll. 9 ff.); and of Bêlit-UR.MAḪ.MEŠ (Ba'alath-Leba'oth? Cf. Josh. 15^{32}, 19^{6}. UR.MAḪ.MEŠ means 'lions'), 'the SA.GAZ have sent to Aijalon and Sor'ah, and the two sons of Milkili were nearly slain' (Kn. 273, ll. 18 ff.). The fact that Labaya and Milkili should themselves represent their relations with the SA.GAZ somewhat differently from ARAD-Ḫiba and Biridiya is only to be expected. The statements of ARAD-Ḫiba—'Let the King hearken unto ARAD-Ḫiba thy servant, and send bowmen, and bring back the King's territory to the King. But if there be no bowmen, the King's territory will certainly fall away to the Ḫabiru'

adopt a bandit-life), but is definitely employed of a tribe or tribes from *a particular locality*, and united by racial affinity. This is clear from the fact that the ideogram is followed in two of its occurrences by the affix KI, 'country *or* place,'* which is used both with the names of countries and districts and with the names of tribes emanating from such districts. In one occurrence of Ḫabiru we likewise find KI added,‡ marking the term similarly as racial and not merely appellative. We may assume, then, with confidence that the connexion between the Ḫabiru and the SA.GAZ was a racial one; though it does not necessarily follow that *all* the SA.GAZ were Ḫabiru—since, on the evidence which we have reviewed, there is nothing to forbid the theory that the Ḫabiru may have been but a single clan of a larger body of people called SA.GAZ.§

Is it probable, then, that the Ḫabiru were merely the southern branch of the racial movement into western Syria represented by the aggressions of the SA.GAZ? That they had gained a footing not only in the extreme south (the district round Jerusalem) but also in central Cana'an is clear from the facts that they are mentioned as in occupation of Shechem (cf. p. lxxiii), and that the prince of Megiddo expresses anxiety as to their movements (cf. p. lxxvii, *footnote*). But there is another reference in one of ARAD-Ḫiba's letters which seems to identify them with the SA.GAZ still further north. 'When there was a ship (*or* a fleet?) at sea,' he writes, 'the king's strong arm held the land of Naḫrima and the land of Kapasi (?); but now the Ḫabiru hold all the king's cities' (Kn. 288, ll. 33 ff.).|| Here the allusion undoubtedly is to the Egyptian fleet which, since the victorious campaigns of Ṭhutmosi III. had possessed a base in the Phoenician harbours (cf. p. lxviii), and enabled the Pharaoh to reach Naharîn (Naḫrima) with little delay and suppress any inclination to revolt in the extreme northern part of his Asiatic empire. Now, however, in the absence of this fleet, the Ḫabiru are in the ascendant, and are holding either the cities of Naḫrima in the north, or (more probably) the Phoenician cities which it was necessary for Egypt to hold in order to maintain her footing in the ports. Adopting this latter hypothesis, we see at once that the SA.GAZ to whom Rib-Adda of Gebal so constantly alludes as employed by the Amorite chieftains Abd-Aširta and Aziru for the reduction of

(Kn. 290, ll. 19 ff.); 'Should there be no bowmen this year, the King my lord's territories are lost' (Kn. 288, ll. 51 ff.)—are strikingly similar to the statement of Bayawa, 'Unless Yanḫamu [the Egyptian plenipotentiary] arrives this year, the entire territories are lost to the SA.GAZ' (Kn. 215, ll. 9 ff.); and it can hardly be doubted that the reference in each case is to the same peril.'

* Kn. 215, l. 15; 298, l. 27.

‡ Kn. 289, l. 24.

§ So Dhorme, *RB.*, 1909, p. 69.

|| The rendering here adopted is that which is generally accepted (cf. Winckler, Ball, Rogers, etc.), from which there seems no reason to depart. It is difficult to believe that Knudtzon's rendering is correct; still less that of Ungnad in *TB.* i. p. 133.

the Phoenician cities were Ḫabiru, as well as the southern aggressors. This is a point of the first importance for the elucidation of the Ḫabiru-question.

The close connexion of the SA.GAZ-Ḫabiru with the people called Sutû is evident. Both peoples are in the service of Namyawaza as mercenaries (Kn. 195, ll. 27 ff.); both commit aggressions upon Dagan-takala (Kn. 318), and, apparently, upon Yapaḫi of Gezer (Kn. 297-99). Rib-Adda of Gebal, who complains repeatedly of the aggressions of the SA.GAZ, also states that one Paḫura has sent Sutû who have killed his erdanu mercenaries (Kn. 122, ll. 31 ff). Concerning the Sutû we happen to be fairly well informed. We learn from a chronicle that the Kaššite king Kadašman-Ḫarbe I. (*cir.* end of the fifteenth century B.C.) 'effected the conquest of the marauding Sutû from east to west, and destroyed their power, built fortresses in Amurru,' etc.* Adad-Nirari I. of Assyria (*cir.* B.C. 1325) states that his father Arik-dên-ili 'conquered the whole of the widespreading Ḳutû, the Aḫlamû, and Sutû.' ‡ The Aḫlamû are known to have been an Aramaean nomadic or semi-nomadic people. The Ḥittite king Hattušili II. makes 'the Aḫlamû-peril' his excuse for having ceased diplomatic relations with the king of Karduniaš (Kadašman Enlil II. §). Tiglath-Pileser I. (*cir.* B.C. 1100) tells us that he defeated 'the Aramaean Aḫlamû' who inhabited the district in the neighbourhood of Carchemish. || It is clear from these references that the Sutû must have been a nomad tribe inhabiting the northern part of the Syrian desert to the west of the upper Euphrates ¶; and with this agrees the statement of Ašur-uballiṭ that the Sutû have detained the messengers of Aḫnaton (Kn. 16, ll. 37 ff.), since the Egyptian envoys would have to cross the desert on their way to Assyria.

Now the Egyptian term for the Semitic nomads of the Asiatic desert is *šasu*, a word which seems to be foreign to the language, and which has been plausibly connected with the West Semitic root שָׁסָה *Šāsā*, 'to plunder.'** The *Šasu*, then, are simply 'the plun-

* Cf. Winckler, AF. i. p. 115. Winckler makes Kadašman-Ḫarbe the second king of that name (*cir.* B.C. 1252); but cf. King, *Bab.* p. 243, *n* 1.

‡ Cf. Tablet, ll. 19 f. in *KB.* i. p. 4; Budge and King, *Annals of the Kings of Assyria*, p. 6; and, for the reading Arik-dên-ili and not Pudi-ilu, King and Hall, *Egypt and Western Asia*, p. 396.

§ *MDOG.* xxxv. p. 22. Text in Figulla and Weidner, *Keilschrifttexte* 1, No. 10, Obv. ll. 36 f.

|| Cf. Annals, v. ll. 44 ff. in *KB.* i. p. 32; Budge and King, *op. cit. supra.*

¶ It is generally supposed the Shoa' and Ḳoa' of Ezek. 23 23 are the Sutû and Ḳutû. On the Sutû in relation to the Aramaeans, cf. Streck, *Ueber die älteste Geschichte der Aramäer*, in *Klio*, vi. (1906). pp. 209 ff.

** Cf. Müller, *AE.* p. 131; Meyer, *IN.* p. 324. The Semitic root is only known to occur in Heb. where it is fairly frequent. Meyer (*loc. cit.*, *n* 1) notices the interesting fact that it is used in 1 Sam. 14 48, which relates Saul's conquest of the Amalekite Bedawin on the border of Egypt:—'he smote 'Amalek, and delivered Israel from the hand of his plunderer' (שֹׁסֵהוּ).

derers *or* brigands'; and the agreement of this designation with the Bab. *ḫabbatum*, which, as we have seen, is the equivalent of the ideogram SA.GAZ, can hardly be merely accidental (cf. p. lxxxviii). While, therefore, the meaning of SA.GAZ favours the conclusion that the appellation belongs to a nomad people, the connexion of the SA.GAZ with the Sutû suggests that, like these latter, they belonged to the north Syrian desert, the region which both cuneiform and Biblical records associate with the Aramaeans. These facts should be taken in connexion with the further facts that the SA.GAZ are principally mentioned as employed by Abd-Aširta and his sons, and that the land of Amurru, over which these chieftains held sway, extended (as Winckler has proved from the Boghaz Keui documents*) from the Lebanon eastward across the Syrian desert to the Euphrates, thus embracing precisely the northern part of the desert inhabited by Aramaean nomads. Thus the conclusion that the SA.GAZ—and therefore the Ḫabiru—were Aramaean nomads seems to be raised to a practical certainty.‡

Now the O. T. definitely connects the ancestors of the Hebrews with the Aramaeans. Abraham is not himself termed an Aramaean, but he has Aramaean connexions. Rebeḳah, the wife of his son Isaac, is brought from Aram-naharaim, and is the daughter of Bethuel, the son of Naḥor, his brother (Gen. 24 J.). Bethuel is termed 'the Aramaean' (Gen. 25 [20] P, 28 [5] P), and so is his son Laban, the brother of Rebeḳah (Gen. 31 [20.24] E). Ja'cob's wives are Aramaeans (the daughters of Laban), and he himself is called 'a vagabond Aramaean' (אֲרַמִּי אֹבֵד, Deut. 26 [5]). On his return from Paddan-Aram he re-enters Cana'an bearing the new name Israel (Gen. 32 [28] J, 35 [10] P), together with his many sons (or *clans*), and takes up his abode at or near Shechem, concerning his relations with which city variant traditions are extant.§ The mere fact, then, that the situation pictured in the T.A. Letters is that Aramaean nomads are flocking into Syria-Palestine and taking

* *MDOG.* xxxv. pp. 24 f. Cf. also King, *Bab.* pp. 237 f.

‡ That Abd-Aširta and his sons were aspiring to raise Amurru to the status of an independent kingdom like the powerful kingdoms on its borders was the opinion of Rib-Adda, as appears from Knudtzon's reading of three passages in his letters, as interpreted by Weber (cf. Kn. p. 1101; so Dhorme, *RB.*, 1909, p. 69). In Kn. 76, ll. 11 ff., Rib-Adda says, 'Who is Abd-Aširta, the dog, that he should seek to take for himself all the cities of the King, the Sun? Is he the king of Mitanni, or the king of Kaššu [Karduniaš] that he should seek to take the King's land for himself?' In Kn. 104, ll. 17 ff.; 116, ll 67 ff., we find similar rhetorical questions with regard to the sons of Abd-Aširta, the last passage adding comparison with 'the king of Ḫata,' *i.e.* the Hittites. Comparison of these three passages one with another proves that this interpretation is correct, rather than that offered by Winckler, which suggests that Abd-Aširta and his sons were acting *in the interests of* the king of Mitanni, etc. The passages, then, indicate the wide scope of Abd-Aširta's schemes, and also suggest that he and his sons were largely responsible for organizing the flow of the Aramaean tribesmen westward into Syria-Palestine.

§ Cf. *note* on 'Shechem,' pp. 269 f.

forcible possession of many of its cities might by itself lead us plausibly to infer that the southern wing of this immigration probably included the ancestors of Israel—more especially since ARAD-Ḫiba states that they (the Ḫabiru) are in possession of the land of Shechem (cf. p. lxxiii). When, moreover, we add to this the fact that the equivalence between the names 'Ḫabiru' and 'Hebrew' is perfect (p. lxxiv f.), the inference is surely raised to a high degree of probability.

The only fact which should make us hesitate in assuming the identity of the Ḫabiru with the Hebrews as proved beyond the possibility of a doubt is the occurrence of the term *Ḫa-bir-a-a*, *i.e.* a gentilic form 'Ḫabiraean,' in two Babylonian documents; in each case in application to men who bear *Kaššite* names—Ḫarbišiḫu * and Kudurra.‡ If, as it is reasonable to suppose, *Ḫa-bir-a-a* is the gentilic of *Ḫabiru*,§ the fact that the only two names of Ḫabiru-people that are known to us should be Kaššite is certainly remarkable; and the conclusion that the Ḫabiru were Kaššites has been adopted by several scholars.|| Recently, Scheil has published a tablet bearing a brief memorandum which mentions the Ḫabiru (*amêlu Ḫa-bi-ri* exactly as in the T.A. Letters) at Larsa in the reign of Rîm-Sin, six centuries earlier than the T.A. Letters.¶ This scholar's conclusion (based on this occurrence and on the Kaššite names above-mentioned) is as follows:—'The Ḫabiru were in origin an Elamite, Kaššite, or Lower Mesopotamian people. . . . In any case they served among the forces of the Elamite dynasty at Larsa. Without doubt they were also employed in the far countries to the west, where the supremacy of Kudur-Mabuk, Ḫammurabi, Ammiditana, etc., maintained itself with more or less authority, thanks to the presence of armed troops.' The proof that Kaššite troops were stationed by these monarchs in Amurru (Syria-Palestine) is, however, non-existent; and still less (apart from the

* Cf. iv.[2] R. 34, 2; and, for a transliteration and translation of the document, Winckler, *AF.* i. pp. 389-396. The letter, written by an unnamed Babylonian king, mentions a king of Assyria named Ninib-Tukulti-Ašur, who seems to have reigned towards the end of the thirteenth century B.C. (cf. Johns, *Ancient Assyria*, pp. 66 ff.), *i.e.* during the latter part of the Kaššite period in Babylon.

‡ Cf. Scheil, *Recueil de Travaux*, xvi. (1894), pp. 32 f. The name occurs on a boundary-stone of the time of Marduk-aḫi-erba of the Fourth Babylonian Dynasty (B.C. 1073).

§ Hommel, however, regards the similarity between Ḫabiru and Ḫabirâ as purely fortuitous, taking the latter to mean an inhabitant of the land of Ḫapir or Apir, *i.e.* that part of Elam which lay over against eastern Arabia. Cf. *AHT.* p. 236; *Grundriss*, p. 7.

|| So Halévy in *Journal Asiatique* (1891), p. 547; Scheil in *Recueil de Travaux*, *loc. cit.*; Hilprecht, *Assyriaca* (1894), p. 33, *n.*; Reisner in *JBL.* (1897), pp. 143 ff.; Lagrange in *RB.* (1899), pp. 127 ff.

¶ *Revue d'Assyriologie*, xii. (1915), pp. 114 f. The memorandum runs: 'There are 4 (*or* 5?) garments for the officers of the Ḫabiru which Ibni-Adad . . . has received. Levied (?) on the property of the temple of Šamaš by Ili-ippalzam. [Month of] Nisan, 11th day, [year of] Rîm-Sin, King.'

assumption that the Ḫabiru were Kaššites) can the presence of such troops in the west be proved for six centuries later.*

* It is true that ARAD-Ḫiba speaks of the outrages committed by the Kaši people, who seem on one occasion nearly to have killed him in his own house (Kn. 287, ll. 32 f., 71 ff.); and Biridiya of Megiddo apparently couples them with the SA.GAZ as in the pay of the sons of Labaya (Kn. 246, ll. 5 ff.: the reading is uncertain, as the tablet is broken; but traces of *Ka-* can be seen after *amêlût mât*). Since, however, Rib-Adda of Gebal more than once begs the Pharaoh to send him Kaši troops to protect Egyptian interests in Phoenicia (Kn. 131, l. 13; 133, l. 17; conjecturally restored in 127, l. 22), and in one of these passages (133, l. 17) *Ka-*[*ši*] is a gloss upon [*Me-lu-*]*ḫa*, *i.e.* Ethiopia (Heb. כּוּשׁ *Kuš*), it can scarcely be doubted that the people of identical name mentioned by ARAD-Ḫiba and Biridiya were likewise Sudanese mercenaries at the disposal of the Egyptian high-commissioner, who may well have proved themselves hostile and troublesome to the governors of Jerusalem and Megiddo. It must be recollected that ARAD-Ḫiba actually charged the high-commissioner with favouring the Ḫabiru and hating the city-governors (Kn. 286, ll. 16 ff.). The identity of the Kaši with the Sudanese mercenaries in all these passages is assumed by Weber (Kn. pp. 1100 f.). There is the same ambiguity in regard to the term (Kushite or Kaššite) in cuneiform as exists in the case of the Heb. כּוּשׁ (cf. p. 64, *footnote*).

Sayce (*ET*. xv., 1903, pp. 282 f.) bases his theory that the Ḫabiru were 'Hittite condottieri' upon a discovery which he claims as the result of his attempted decipherment of the Hittite inscriptions, viz. that the name Kas was used throughout the Hittite region, the kings of Carchemish, for example, calling themselves 'kings of the country of Kas.' He takes references in the T.A. Letters to the land of Kaššu (Kašši in oblique forms) to refer to the land of the Hittites, alleging that reference to Babylonia (ordinarily assumed) is out of the question, since this is called Karduniaš —in answer to which it is sufficient to remark that the full title claimed by the kings of the Third Babylonian Dynasty, as appears from a short inscription of Kara-indaš I. (*cir.* B.C. 1425) is 'King of Babylon, King of Sumer and Akkad, King of Kaššu (*Ka-aš-šu-u*), King of Karduniaš' (cf. iv.[2] R. 36 [38], No. 3; Delitzsch, *Paradies*, p. 128). Sayce then claims that the Kaši people of ARAD-Ḫiba's letter are identified with the Ḫabiru in the passage in which the writer, having accused Milkili and the sons of Labaya of giving the king's land to the Ḫabiru, then goes on to say, 'Behold, O King my Lord, I am righteous as regards the Kaši people: let the King ask the high-commissioner whether [or no] they have dealt very violently and brought serious evil to pass' (Kn. 287). Most readers, however, must surely infer that the passage, on the contrary, distinguishes between the two peoples. Why should the writer apply different appellations to one people in successive sentences? Obviously ARAD-Ḫiba, having made his own accusation against his enemies, then proceeds to deal with an accusation which *they* have made against *him*—probably resistance to the Sudanese troops of Egypt involving bloodshed, as we may infer from his later statement that they had nearly killed him in his own house. The letters from the Cana'anite princes are full of such mutual recriminations. Equally groundless is the statement that the sons of Arzawa—who must certainly have been Hittites (cf. pp. lxxxiii f.)—mentioned in one letter (Kn. 289 = Winckler 182 + 185) take the place of the Ḫabiru in other letters. The passage in question says, 'Behold, Milkili, does he not revolt with the sons of Labaya and the sons of Arzawa to give up the King's territory to them'? Here, if the sons of Arzawa are Ḫabiru, we should surely draw the same inference with regard to the sons of Labaya. In two of the three other passages in question, however (Kn. 287, 290, 289, ll. 21 ff. = Winckler, 180, 183, 185), the sons of Labaya are distinguished from the Ḫabiru, for the former are associated with Milkili in giving up the King's territory to the latter.

There is no reason, so far as we can say, why Rîm-Sin should not have employed Aramaean (Hebrew) tribesmen as mercenaries *cir.* B.C. 2100. Abraham 'the Hebrew,' who is assigned to this period in Gen. 14, is earliest associated with the city of Ur (Gen. 11 28.31, 15 7) on right bank of the Euphrates and bordering on the Syrian desert, with which Larsa on the left of the river was closely connected.* There were SA.GAZ in Babylonia in Ḫammurabi's reign, and their overseer bore a Semitic Babylonian name, Anum-pî-Sin.‡ If such tribesmen came later on into the regular employ of the Kaššite kings, it would not be strange if some of them adopted Kaššite names.§ We find, then, in this last mentioned evidence, no insuperable objection to the identification of the Ḫabiru with the Hebrews in the widest sense of the term.||

Another fact which we have learned from the T.A. Letters, and which is of high interest for the history of Cana'an in the period prior to the Israelite settlement, is that a large and influential portion of the population of Syria-Palestine at this time was non-Semitic. That part of this foreign element was Ḥittite is now placed beyond a doubt. We have already alluded to 'the sons of Arzawa' and 'the sons of Labaya' as leagued with the Ḫabiru in rebellion against the constituted authority of Egypt. There exists among the T.A. correspondence the copy of a letter addressed by Amenḥotp III. to Tarḫundaraba, king of Arzawa (Kn. 31). This letter is written for the most part in a language which we must infer to be the language of the addressee; and the fact that this is Ḥittite has now been certainly proved by the discovery of a number

Lastly, Sayce's statement that *Ḫabiru* (*-ri*) cannot be a proper name because it is not *Habirâ* (a gentilic form) is directly contradicted by the fact that we have *Sutû* (*-tî*), *Aḫlamû* (*-mî*) which are certainly tribal names and yet are not gentilics (on these people, cf. p. lxxix); his explanation of the name as meaning 'confederates' (like Heb. *ḥābhēr*, plur. *ḥ^abhērîm*, the ordinary philological equivalent for which in Bab. is *ibru*, which occurs in the T.A. Letters, Kn. 126, l. 16) is ruled out by the occurrence of the gentilic *Ḫabirâ* with the two Kaššite names which we have already noticed (p. lxxxi), since such a gentilic can only be formed from a proper name, and is excluded no less by the occurrence once of (*amêlûtu*) *Ḫa-bi-ri* (KI) which marks the name as racial (a tribe from a particular district: cf. p. lxxviii); and his finding in this last-mentioned method of writing the name an indication of the association of the 'confederates' with the city of Ḥebron (assumed to mean 'confederate-city') takes no account of the fact that we cannot dissociate *Ḫabiri* (KI) from the two occurrences of SA.GAZ (KI) which we have discussed with it.

* A regular part of the title claimed by Rîm-Sin is 'he that cared for Ur.' Cf. Thureau-Dangin, *Die Sumerischen und Akkadischen Königsinschriften*, pp 216 ff.

‡ Cf. King, *Hammurabi*, no. 35; Ungnad, *Babylonische Briefe*, no. 26, with *note* b.

§ Cf. Winckler, *KAT.*³ p. 197, *n* 1. Knudtzon (p. 47, *n* 8) maintains (against Scheil) that the name of Kudurra's father, which is read as *Ba-ṣi-is*, seems not to be Kaššite.

|| Discussions of the Ḫabiru and SA.GAZ which take fullest account of available evidence are Winckler, *GI.* i. (1895), pp. 16-21; *AF.* iii. (1902), pp. 90-94; *KAT.*³ (1903), pp. 196 f.; Knudtzon, pp. 45-53; Weber in Knudtzon, pp. 1146-1148, 1336; Dhorme in *RB.*, 1909, pp. 67-73; Böhl, *KH.* (1911), pp. 83-96.

of documents in the same language among the Boghaz Keui documents. The precise position of Arzawa is at present unascertained; but it seems to have been a subordinate Hittite kingdom in Asia Minor.* 'The sons of Arzawa' can hardly mean anything else than 'men from the land of Arzawa.' ‡ Labaya, on the other hand, seems to be a personal name. There are three letters from Labaya (Kn. 252-254); and the first of these, though mainly written, like the others, in Babylonian, is so much coloured by a curious foreign jargon that in places it is incomprehensible. Another letter, written wholly in the Arzawa language and undeciphered (Kn. 32), mentions the name of Labaya three times; and the position of the earliest occurrence of the name in the first line leaves little doubt that the writer was Labaya himself.

Other non-Semitic names in the Syrian and Palestinian letters—Šuwardata, Yašdata, Zirdamyašda, Artamanya, Ruṣmanya, Manya, Biridašwa, Biridiya, Namyawaza, Teuwatti, Šubandu, Šutarna, etc.—appear to be Aryan; and some of them have certainly been identified as such.§ They are found throughout Canaʿan as well as to the north of the Lebanons. Šuwardata, who was in antagonism to ARAD-Ḫiba of Jerusalem, was chieftain of Kelti, *i.e.* in all probability the Biblical Ḳeʿilah (1 Sam. 23 [1], *al.*) some eight miles north-west of Hebron. Biridiya and his brother (?) Yašdaṭa were princes of Megiddo. Ruṣmanya was prince of the city of Šaruna, a name which is identical with the Biblical Sharon, the maritime plain north of Joppa. The presence of this Aryan element in Syria and Palestine is doubtless to be connected with the fact that the kingdom of Mitanni was at this period dominated by an aristocracy who described themselves as *Ḫarri*, *i.e.* Aryans, bore Aryan-sounding names, and venerated the Aryan deities Mitra, Varuna, Indra, and the Nâsatya-twins. ‖ The bulk of the Mitannian population appears, however, to have been related to the Hittites, and very possibly owed its origin to the Hittite invasion of western Asia in

* Cf. Winckler in *OLZ.* ix. p. 628; *MDOG.* xxxv. p. 40; and especially the detailed discussion of Knudtzon, *Die zwei Arzawa-Briefe* (1902), pp. 16 ff.

‡ Similarly the appellation *Arzawiya* applied to the chieftain of Ruḫizzi (probably in central Syria) seems to mean 'the Arzawan' (cf. Kn. 53, 54, *al.*).

§ Hall (*PSBA.* xxxi., 1909, p. 234; cf. also *NE.* p. 410, *n* [5]) identifies Šuwardata or Šuyardata with the Aryan Surya-dâta, *i.e.* 'Sun-given' (Ἡλιοδῶρος). Böhl (*KH.* p. 17, *n* [1]) quotes G. J. Thierry as comparing Biridašwa with Sanskrit *Bṛhad-ašwa* '(He who owns a) great horse.' Biridiya appears to contain the same first element. The element *Arta* in Artamanya is seen in the names Artaššumara and Artatama of the Aryan dynasty of Mitanni: cf. the Old Persian Artakhšatrâ (Artaxerxes) from *arta* 'great' and *khšatrâ* 'kingdom.' The second element appears in Manya and Ruṣmanya. Šutarna, the father of Namyawaza, bears a name which is also borne by a member of the Mitannian dynasty. Namyawaza may be compared with Mattiuaza of the Mitannian dynasty. Cf. Hommel, *Sitzungsberichte der k. böhm. Gesellsch.*, 1898, vi.; E. Meyer, *Zeitschr. f. vergl. Sprachforschungen*, xlii (1909), pp. 18 ff.; Weber in Kn. *passim.*

‖ Cf. Winckler, *MDOG.* xxxv. pp. 37 ff., 51; *OLZ.* xiii. 289 ff. The names occur in Figulla and Weidner, *Keilschrifttexte* 1, No. 1, Rev. ll. 55 f.; No. 3, Rev. l. 24.

the 20th century B.C., which, as we have seen (p. lxiv), brought about the end of the First Babylonian Dynasty;* or, it may be, to a still earlier settlement of Ḥittites, superimposed upon an older population. This Ḥittite population was governed, but not absorbed, by its Aryan conquerors, just as the Semitic population of Babylonia was governed by the Kaššite aristocracy who doubtless belonged to the same wave of Indo-European invasion that founded the Aryan Dynasty of Mitanni. The language of Mitanni appears to be neither Ḥittite nor Indo-European, but is said to have connexion with the Vannic or Caucasian type.‡

Now it seems to be clear that prior to the conquests of Ṭḥutmosi I. and Ṭḥutmosi III. the kingdom of Mitanni extended south-west of the Euphrates, and included Naharîn, if not some portion of Syria still further south. We have noticed, in speaking of the campaigns of Ṭḥutmosi III., that the leader of the forces of Naharîn was probably the king of Mitanni (cf. p. lxviii). The glosses which occur in the letter from the inhabitants of Tunip prove that Mitannian was the language which was ordinarily spoken in this Syrian city.§ The inference is plausible that the cessation of the West Semitic Babylonian predominance in Amurru, which is marked by the fall of the First Babylonian Dynasty *cir.* B.C. 1926, laid this region open to Mitannian (*i.e.* Ḥittite-Aryan) influence and occupation, the permeation of this strain in the population extending ultimately up to the frontier of Egypt. The campaigns of the Pharaohs of the Eighteenth Dynasty curtailed and eventually destroyed Mitannian claims to suzerainty in Amurru, confining the Mitannian kingdom to the eastern side of the Euphrates. The Ḥittite-Aryan strain still, however, formed a well-marked element in the population of Syria and Cana'an; and there should be no doubt that it is this strain which is denoted in the O.T. by the term 'Ḥittites,' when this term is used in enumeration of 'the seven races' inhabiting Cana'an at the time of the Israelite occupation (cf. *ch.* 3 [5] *note*).||

* The Ḥittite state of Hanî on the middle Euphrates was apparently the outcome of this invasion. Cf. King, *Bab.*, p. 210, *n* [4].

‡ Cf. Jensen, *ZA.* v. (1890), pp. 166-208; vi. pp. 34-72; Brünnow, *ZA.* v. pp. 209-259; Sayce, *ZA.* v. pp. 260-274; *PSBA.* xxii. (1900), pp. 171-225; Messerschmidt, *MVAG.*, 1899, 4; Bork, *MVAG.*, 1909, 1 and 2.

§ Cf. Messerschmidt, *MVAG.*, 1899, 4, pp. 119 ff. Tunip has been placed as far south as Ba'albek in the Lebanon-district, and as far north as Tinnab, some 25 miles to the north of Aleppo. The largest consensus of opinion would locate it in the neighbourhood of Ḳadesh on the Orontes. Cf. Weber's discussion in Kn. pp. 1123 ff.; and, for Egyptian evidence, Müller, *AE.* pp. 257 f.

|| The proved existence of Ḥittites in southern Cana'an in the 14th century B.C. is not, of course, a proof that they were there 700 years earlier in the time of Abraham (assuming this to have been the period of Ḫammurabi), as is pictured in Gen. 23 P where they appear as inhabitants of Ḥebron; nor can this be regarded as proved until it can be shown that there is good ground for believing Gen. 23 to be based on *contemporary* information, or until external contemporary information has been brought to light. For if (as there is reason to believe) Gen. 23 owes its composition (or even its

The existence of this Ḥittite-Mitannian element in Canaʿan seems to throw light upon the origin of another people enumerated among 'the seven races,' viz., the Jebuṡites of Jerusalem. The fact that ARAD-Ḫiba the governor of Jerusalem bears a name of this class seems to be clear. The Sumerian ideogram ARAD 'servant,' which forms the first element in his name, proves that the second element Ḫiba (also written Ḫeba) is a divine name. There can be little doubt that this is the Ḥittite-Mitannian goddess Ḫipa or Ḫepa, who figures in the names of the Mitannian princesses Gilu-Ḫipa and Tadu-Ḫipa (cf. p. lxxii), and in that of Pudu-Ḫipa, the wife of the Ḥittite king Ḫattušili II.; and who is enumerated among the great deities in the Boghaz Keui documents.* The name of the Jebuṡite of David's time, אֲרַוְנָה Arawna (2 Sam. 24 [20.22.23.24]) or אֲרַנְיָה Aranya (*Kt.*, 2 Sam. 24 [18]), which is certainly non-Semitic, is Ḥittite in appearance: we may perhaps compare the Ḥittite king-names Arandaš and Arnuanta for the first element in the name.‡ On the other hand, Adoni-ṣedeḳ of Josh. 10 (cf. Judg. 1 [5-7])

present form only) to an age much later than the time to which it refers, the possibility that the author or editor may have assumed the conditions of a later age for the more or less remote period of which he is writing has obviously to be taken into account. Cf. the way in which the Philistines are represented in Gen. 26 (J in the main) as inhabitants of the maritime plain in the Patriarchal period, although evidence leads us to conclude that they did not settle in Palestine until a much later date (cf. pp. xciiff.). While making this criticism of Prof. Sayce's contention that the historical fact that there were Ḥittites at Hebron in Abraham's time can now be proved (cf. *ET.* xviii. pp. 418 ff.; *HCM.* pp. 143 f.; and elsewhere), the fact should be noted that, while the historical existence of Ḥittites in southern Palestine at *any* period has been called in question by many scholars, Prof. Sayce has the merit of having all along maintained its truth upon evidence which might have been patent to all at least since the discovery of the Boghaz Keui documents (which certified the fact that the Arzawa language was a Ḥittite dialect), if not since that of the T.A. Letters. There is no *a priori* reason (so far as we know) why there should not have been Ḥittite clans in southern Canaʿan before 2000 B.C.; and evidence that such was the case may yet come to light. Sayce's evidence (*Biblical World*, Feb. 1905, pp. 130 ff.; cf. *Archaeology*, p. 206) in proof that the Ḥittites were already settled in southern Palestine at least as early as the Twelfth Egyptian Dynasty (*cir.* 2000-1788 B.C.) breaks down under the criticism of Breasted, *AJSL.* xxi. (1905), pp. 153-158. Cf. also W. M. Müller, *OLZ.* xii. (1909), 427 f.

* Cf. *MDOG.* xxxv. p. 48. The reason why we transcribe the first element of ARAD-Ḫiba's name according to its value as a Sumerian ideogram is that if, as the honorific mention of Ḫipa implies, he was a Ḥittite-Mitannian, the ideogram probably stands for the Ḥittite or Mitannian word for 'servant,' which is unknown to us. Hommel (*Sitzungsberichte der k. böhm. Gesellsch.*, 1898, vi, p. 10) and Dhorme (*RB.*, 1909, p. 72) propose the form Arta-Ḫepa (cf. Artaššumara, Artatama, Artamanya); while Gustavs (*OLZ.*, 1911, 341 ff.) offers the form Put-i-Ḫepa, the Mitannian root, *put* being interpreted by Bork (*MVAG.*, 1909, 1, p. 126) in the sense 'to serve.' Cf. Weber in Kn. pp. 1333 f. The ordinarily-accepted form Abdi-Ḫiba is based upon the assumption that the man was a Semite, which is very improbable.

‡ It is likely that the termination in Aran-ya may be hypocoristic, the name bearing the same relation to a fuller form such as Aran-daš as Aki-ya does to Aki-Tešub, Aki-izzi, Gili-ya to Gilu-Ḫepa, and Biridi-ya to Birid-ašwa.

is good Semitic, and so is Malki-ṣedeḳ (Gen. 14 [18]), if this can be accepted as the genuine name of a king of Jerusalem.

Now Ezeḳiel, in characterizing figuratively Jerusalem's idolatrous career from the earliest times, states at the opening of his description, 'Thy father was the Amorite, and thy mother a Ḥittite' (Ezek. 16 [3]; cf. *v.*[45]). This statement has been often understood to be merely metaphorical—*morally* considered, Jerusalem may be said to have affinity with the early heathen races of Cana'an. In the light, however, of the facts which we have just noticed, viz.: the mixture of Ḥittite and Semitic names among the pre-Israelite inhabitants of Jerusalem as known to us, it becomes highly probable that Ezeḳiel's words preserve an ethnographical fact, and that the Jebušites of Jerusalem actually derived their origin from the amalgamation of two strains, Amorite and Ḥittite.*

By the end of Aḫnaton's reign Egypt had practically lost her hold upon the whole of her Asiatic dominions. North of the Lebanons Šubbiluliuma had thoroughly consolidated the Ḥittite domination. Aziru's duplicity in posing as the supporter both of Egyptian and of Ḥittite interests had at length proved disastrous to him, and the Ḥittite king had attacked and defeated him and reduced Amurru to vassalage.‡ The murder of Tušratta in a court-conspiracy, producing anarchy in Mitanni, gave Šubbiluliuma the opportunity of intervening in the affairs of that kingdom; and having placed Mattiuaza, an exiled son of the late king, upon the throne, he married him to his daughter and assumed to himself the rôle of suzerain.§ Šubbiluliuma seems not to have attempted to extend his domination to Cana'an; and here the Ḫabiru and other turbulent elements in the population were left to work their will unchecked by any effective control by Egypt. The death of Aḫnaton was speedily followed by the sweeping away of the new religion which he had endeavoured to impose upon Egypt, and the restoration of the ancient cultus. The reigns of the succeeding Pharaohs of the Eighteenth Dynasty, Sakere, Tut'anḫaton, and Ay, cover in all a period of not more than eight years (*cir.* B.C. 1358-1350), during which the power was really in the hands of the Amon-priesthood at Thebes, and the reigning monarchs themselves were little more than figureheads. Tut'anḫaton (the change of whose name to Tut'anḫamon marks the re-establishment of Thebes as the seat of government and the triumph of the god Amon), may possibly have attempted an expedition into Cana'an as well as into Nubia; for under him envoys from Syria are represented, together

* Cf. Sayce, *Archaeology*, p. 205; Hommel, *Grundriss*, p. 55; Jeremias, *OTLAE.* i. p. 340; Böhl, *KH.* p. 26; Luckenbill, *AJTh.* xviii. pp 57 f.

‡ Cf., for the circumstances, *MDOG.* xxxv. p. 43; Weber in Kn. pp. 1134 f.; Hall, *NE.* p. 350; Böhl in *Theologisch Tijdschrift*, 1916, pp. 206 ff. Text in Figulla and Weidner, *Keilschrifttexte* 1, No. 8.

§ Cf. *MDOG.* xxxv. p. 36; Böhl in *Theologisch Tijdschrift*, 1916, pp. 170 ff. Text in Figulla and Weidner, *Keilschrifttexte* 1, Obv. ll. 48 ff.

with Ethiopians from the south, as bringing tribute,* and Ḥaremḥeb is described, when commander-in-chief of the Egyptian forces, as 'king's follower on his expeditions to the south and north country.' ‡

It is doubtful, again, whether Ḥaremḥeb, § who succeeded Ay (*cir.* 1350), attempted to wage war in Syria. The name of Ḫeta (the Ḥittites) appears in a list of names belonging to his reign, and the captives whom he is represented as presenting to the gods of Egypt may include some Asiatics.|| It was probably Ḥaremḥeb who concluded the treaty with Šubbiluliuma (written *S'-p'-rw-rw* in Egyptian) to which reference is made in the treaty of Raʿmesse II. with Hattušili (cf. p. xci).

Raʿmesse I., the founder of the Nineteenth Dynasty, must have been an old man at his accession (*cir.* B.C. 1315), and his reign of two years or less was uneventful. His son and successor, Sety I. (*cir.* B.C. 1313), early turned his attention to the recovery of Egypt's Asiatic dominions. At the beginning of his reign he received a report of the condition of affairs in Canaʿan:—'The vanquished Šasu, they plan rebellion, rising against the Asiatics of Ḫaru. They have taken to cursing and quarrelling, each of them slaying his neighbour, and they disregard the laws of the palace.' ¶ This report, which summarizes the situation in Canaʿan as we have it in the T.A. Letters, is of high interest as indicating that the SA.GAZ-Ḫabiru of the latter were identical with the people whom the Egyptians called Šasu, i.e. Asiatic Bedawin.**

Pushing through the desert without delay, Sety easily routed the outposts of the Šasu, and then marched through the whole length of Canaʿan, conquering or receiving the submission of various fortified cities on his route. A boundary-stone discovered by G. A. Smith, at Tell eš-Šihâb, 22 miles due east of the southern end of the sea of Galilee, proves that he must have extended his arms east of Jordan to the Ḥaurân.‡‡ His main object, however, was to regain possession of the Phoenician coast-cities, in order that,

* Cf. Breasted, *AR.* ii. §§ 1027 ff. The fact that the tribute of the north is represented as presented to the Pharaoh by the two viceroys of Nubia creates suspicion that it may have been added, in imitation of earlier representations, as the conventional pendant of the tribute of the south.

‡ Cf. Breasted, *AR.* iii. § 20.

§ Ḥaremḥeb, who first rose to position as a general and administrator in the reign of Aḫnaton, seems to have been the real wielder of power during the reigns of the weaklings who succeeded this monarch. On the death of Ay he succeeded to the kingship as the nominee of the priesthood of Amon (to whose worship he seems all along to have adhered), and his position was legitimized by marriage with a princess of the royal line. Cf. Breasted, *Hist. Eg.* pp. 399 ff.; Hall, *NE.* pp. 310 ff.

|| Cf. Breasted, *AR.* iii. § 34.

¶ Cf. Breasted, *AR.* iii. § 101.

** Cf. the remarks on p. lxxix as to the identity in meaning of Šasu with SA.GAZ=*ḫabbatum.*

‡‡ Cf. *PEF. Qy. St.*, 1901, pp. 347 ff.; 1904, pp. 78 ff.

following the example of Ṭhutmosi III., he might obtain a naval base for the provision of reinforcements in a future campaign against the further north. This successfully accomplished, he returned to Egypt with his captives and spoil.

Resolved in a second (undated) campaign to try conclusions with the Ḥittites—whose king, Muršili (Eg. *M-r'-s'-r'*), the son of Šubbiluliuma, had succeeded to the throne after the brief reign of his brother Arandaš—Sety advanced between the Lebanons, and for the first time Egyptian and Ḥittite forces met in conflict. Sety claims to have reached Naharîn; but since he did not gain any decisive success against the Ḥittites, we may suspect that this is an exaggeration. After this campaign Sety concluded a treaty with Muršili,* the terms of which probably left Cana'an and Phoenicia to Egypt, and the whole of Syria north of the Lebanons to the Ḥittites. During the remainder of Sety's reign (which lasted some 21 years in all) we hear of no further campaign in Syria. It is interesting to note that Sety (like Ra'messe II.) mentions a district called *'A-sa-ru*, corresponding to the hinterland of southern Phoenicia ‡—precisely the position assigned in the Old Testament to the Israelite tribe of Asher (cf. *ch.* 1[31] *note*).

His successor, Ra'messe II. (*cir.* B.C. 1292), was fired with the ambition of recovering Egypt's Asiatic empire as it had existed at the end of the reign of the great conqueror Ṭhutmosi III. This was a task more difficult than ever before. The Ḥittite king Muršili, and his son and successor Muwattalli (Eg. *Mw-ṭ-n-r'*), profiting by the long period of peace, had occupied Ḳadesh on the Orontes as a frontier-fortress, and rendered it a very formidable obstacle to be overcome by an Egyptian army advancing northward between the Lebanons. Of Ra'messe's earliest moves we know no more than the fact that a limestone stele, cut in the rock at the mouth of the Nahr el-Kelb near Bêrût, bears the Pharaoh's name, and is dated the fourth year of his reign.§ This shows that, like his father Sety, his initial move was to follow the policy of Ṭhutmosi III. and to make sure of his hold upon the Phoenician cities; but whether this cost him any fighting we have no means of determining. In any case, his ulterior object was sufficiently obvious to forewarn the Ḥittite king; and when next year he advanced against northern Syria in order to try conclusions with the Ḥittites, Muwattalli ‖ had

* Mentioned in the treaty of Ra'messe II. with Ḫattušili. This speaks of a treaty with Muwattalli; but there can be no doubt that the name is an error for Muršili; cf. Breasted, *AR.* iii. § 377, note *c*.

‡ Cf. Müller, *AE.* pp. 236 ff.

§ Another stele in the same place has been thought to be dated 'year 2' (so Petrie, *Hist. Eg.* iii. p. 46), but the date should more probably be read 'year 10.' There was but one campaign before that against Ḳadesh in 'year 5.' Cf. Breasted, *AR.* § 297.

‖ Hall makes Muršili the Ḥittite king whom Ra'messe met at Ḳadesh, and supposes that he died shortly after, 'crushed by the disaster that had befallen his armies' (*NE.* p. 361); but the treaty of Ḫattušili with Ra'messe certainly speaks as

mustered an army of some 20,000 including his north Syrian dependants and allies from Asia Minor, among whom we recognize Dardanians (Dardeny), Lycians (Luka), Mysians (Mesa), Kataonians (Kaṯawaden), and Cilicians (Kelekeš). The bad strategy displayed by Raʿmesse nearly involved him in defeat, his first and second divisions (the first led by the king himself) encountering a surprise-attack from behind the city of Ḳadesh, whilst the third and fourth divisions were still straggling some miles in the rear. The second division appears to have been cut to pieces in the first onset of the Ḥittites, while the first division (already in camp) was largely put to flight; but the personal bravery of Raʿmesse (rallying no doubt his own bodyguard and some part of the first division) succeeded in holding the foe at bay until reinforcements arrived, when the aspect of affairs was changed and the Ḥittites were beaten off with heavy losses. Next day both armies seem to have been too exhausted to renew the combat; and Raʿmesse had to be content to return to Egypt without attempting to reduce the fortress of Ḳadesh.*

It is easy to see that this campaign, though much magnified by Raʿmesse on account of the personal part which he played in retrieving the issue of the battle, must have been somewhat disastrous to the prestige of Egypt in Syria. We are not surprised, therefore, to find that within the next year or so the whole of Canaʿan, stirred up doubtless by Ḥittite influence, was in revolt; and in his eighth year Raʿmesse had to undertake a campaign for its reconquest, and was obliged to lay siege to and reduce even a city so far south as Ashḳelon.

Pushing northward, he then captured a number of cities in the district of Galilee, among which we recognize the name of Beth-ʿAnath (cf. *ch.* 1[33] *note*), and seems also to have extended his arms into the Lebanon-district, for he records the conquest of a city named Dapur 'in the land of Amor' (Amurru), which was garrisoned by Ḥittites.‡ Possibly the stele discovered by Schumacher at

though peace had been broken in the time of Muwattalli (Breasted, *AR.* iii. § 374), and this is the view which is taken by Breasted (*Hist. Eg.* pp. 423 ff.), Garstang (*Hittites*, p. 343), Luckenbill (*AJTh.* xviii. p. 49), and King (*Bab.* p. 235).

* The fullest accounts of this battle (with plans and Egyptian reliefs) will be found in Breasted, *AR.* iii. §§ 298 ff.; *The Battle of Kadesh* (*Decennial Publications of the University of Chicago*, 1904); *Hist. Eg.* pp. 425 ff.; Petrie, *Hist. Eg.* iii. pp. 47 ff.

‡ The view commonly held (cf. Petrie, *Hist. Eg.* iii. p. 61; Breasted, *AR.* iii. §§ 356 f.; *Hist. Eg.* p. 436; Hall, *NE.* p. 362) that Dapur is the Biblical Tabor in the plain of Esdraelon is not very probable. Heb. ת is not usually represented by Eg. *d* (no instances cited by Burch.), nor ב by Eg. *p* (very rare; cf. Burch. § 50); and the fact that this city alone is distinguished as 'in the land of Amor' surely dissociates it from the group in which it occurs. No Ḥittite remains have been discovered further south than Restân, north of the Lebanons. Elsewhere Dapur is associated with Ḳadesh: cf. Müller, *AE.* p. 221. We find Tabor normally spelt among the Asiatic names in the great list of Raʿmesse III. at Medinet Habu: cf. W. M. Müller, *Egypt. Researches* (1904) Pl. 65, No. 27; Burch. No. 1083.

Šêẖ Saʿd in the Ḥaurân,* about three miles north of Tell ʿAštarâ, may have been set up during this campaign.

The records for the following years are scanty, but it is clear that they witnessed a long and arduous struggle to recover northern Syria from the Ḥittites. Raʿmesse must have advanced into Naharîn as far as Tunip, conquered this city, and then lost it again; for in a subsequent campaign we find him once more capturing it, together with Katna and Arvad, and claiming to have subdued the whole of northern Syria and Naharîn.‡ It is unlikely that he retained possession of his conquests for any length of time. Muwattalli, though he might be temporarily worsted, was by no means beaten, and probably wrested back most if not all of the captured territory as often as Raʿmesse returned with his army to Egypt. At length, in or shortly before the twenty-first year of Raʿmesse's reign, Muwattalli died and was succeeded by his brother Ḫattušili II. (Eg. *Ḫ-t'-s'-r'*), who immediately proposed a treaty of peace which the Egyptian king was not loath to accept. The Egyptian text of this treaty is engraved on the walls of Karnak and the Ramesseum, and has long been known §; and parts of a copy in cuneiform Babylonian were discovered among the Ḥittite archives at Boghaz Keui.‖ It is a diplomatic document of the highest interest, dealing in legally phrased clauses with obligations of alliance and the mutual right of extradition of emigrants and political refugees. Both parties are placed upon a footing of exact equality—a fact which proves that neither had any permanent advantage to claim as the result of many years of conflict. There is no definition of the boundary line between the two kingdoms; and our inference must be that it remained as defined or recognized in the earlier treaties of Šubbiluliuma (cf. p. lxxxviii) and Muršili (cf. p. lxxxix), to which the present treaty refers. Thirteen years later Raʿmesse married the eldest daughter of Hattušili, and the Ḥittite king actually accompanied his daughter to Egypt for the ceremony.¶

During the remainder of Raʿmesse's long reign of sixty-seven years he was never again obliged to take the field in Syria.** His son Mineptaḥ was an elderly man when he succeeded him (*cir.* B.C. 1225), and his accession seems to have been the signal for a revolt in Canaʿan, which he quelled in his third year. Mineptaḥ's reference

* Cf. *ZDPV.* xiv. pp. 142 ff.

‡ Cf. Breasted, *AR.* iii. §§ 363 ff.

§ Cf. Breasted, *AR.* iii. §§ 367 ff.; Petrie, *Hist. Eg.* iii. pp. 63 ff.

‖ Cf. *MDOG.* xxxv. pp. 12 f.

¶ Cf. Breasted, *AR.* iii. §§ 416 ff.

** To the reign of Raʿmesse II. is assigned the composition of the document contained in *Papyrus Anastasi* I., which gives an imaginative and satirical description of the perils and difficulties attendant upon travel in Palestine. This document, which is of the highest interest on account of the typographical and descriptive information which it offers, has been most recently edited by A. H. Gardiner, *Egyptian Hieratic Texts, Series I. Part I.* (1911).

to this campaign is, from the Biblical point of view, of the highest interest, for in it we find Israel mentioned among Palestinian localities—Pe-kanan (*i.e.* 'the Cana'an'), Ashkelon, Gezer, Yeno'am, Ḫaru (*i.e.* southern Palestine)—as plundered and subdued.* Mineptaḥ's statement is 'Israel (*y-s-r-'-r*) is desolated, his seed is not,' ‡ and the name Israel is marked by the Determinative which means 'men,' showing that it denotes a people and not a country.

The next event which is of interest for Biblical history is the settlement of the Philistines in Cana'an. Already in the reign of Mineptaḥ we can trace the beginning of a migratory movement among the peoples of the north-eastern Mediterranean. Mineptaḥ was obliged, in his fifth year, to repel an extensive invasion into the western Delta on the part of the Libyans, together with various peoples who came by sea to assist in the raid, those who are named being the 'Aḳaywaša, Turuša, Luka, Šardina, and Šakaluša.§ After a lapse of nearly thirty years we find that history repeats itself, and the Libyans, profiting by the period of confusion and weakness which ensued in Egypt after the death of Mineptaḥ (*cir.* B.C. 1215), again invaded the western Delta in force in the fifth year of Ra'messe III. of the Twentieth Dynasty (*cir.* B.C. 1193), assisted by sea-rovers called Pulasati and Ṯakkara,‖ some of whom joined the land forces of the Libyans, whilst others entered the Nile-mouths in their ships. Ra'messe claims a decisive victory against these

* The inscription in which this reference occurs was discovered by Petrie in 1896, and a full account of it was given by him in the *Contemporary Review* for May of the same year. Cf. also Petrie, *Hist. Eg.* iii. p. 114; Breasted, *AR.* iii. §§ 602 ff.

‡ In the expression 'his seed is not,' *seed* seems to mean *posterity*; and the phrase does not mean 'their crops are destroyed,' as explained by Petrie and many scholars after him. This is clear from the fact that the same expression is used five times elsewhere of other conquered foes (cf. Breasted, *AR.* iii. § 604), *e.g.* of the sea-peoples who endeavoured to invade Egypt in the reign of Ra'messe III., of whom this king says, 'Those who reached my border are desolated, their seed is not.' Here reference to 'crops' is obviously out of the question.

§ Cf. Breasted, *AR.* iii. §§ 569 ff. The 'Aḳaywaša are probably the 'Αχαιϝοί, *Achivi*, or proto-Greeks; the Turuša may be the Τυρσηνοί or Tyrrhenians, whose migration from Asia Minor to Italy probably took place at about this period; the Luka, as we have already noticed (p. xc), are certainly the Lycians; the Šardina were perhaps originally from Sardis in Asia Minor, and subsequently gave their name to Sardinia (some of them had been in the employ of Egypt as mercenaries since the days of Aḫnaton: they appear in the T.A. Letters as *amêlu Šerdani*; cf. Kn. 122, l. 35); the Šakaluša were probably from Sagalassos in Asia Minor (Sagalassian mercenaries are perhaps intended by *ṣâbê âlu Šeḫlali*, 'soldiers of the city of Seḫlal'), mentioned by Abd-Aširta in one of his letters, Kn. 62; so Hall in *PSBA.* xxxi. p. 231, *n* 86). Cf. Müller, *AE.* pp. 357 f., 372 ff.; Hall, *NE.* pp. 68 ff., 377. On the *-ša* and *-na* terminations of many of these names as nominal suffixes in Asia Minor (illustrated by the Lycian *-äzi*, *-aza*, etc.), cf. Hall, *Oldest Civilization of Greece*, pp. 178 f.

‖ Or Zakkala, if Hommel (*PSBA.* xvii., 1895, p. 205; *Grundriss*, pp. 28, 32, *n* 4) is right in connecting with the city-name Zaḳḳalû, mentioned in a Babylonian inscription of the Kaššite period (the same that has already been cited for the name Ḫarbišiḫu: cf. p. lxxxi).

combined forces.* But a greater peril awaited him. In his eighth year he had to meet a threatened invasion of the sea-peoples, which was clearly no casual raid, but a migration on a large scale. The invaders came both by land, moving down the coast of Syria, and also by sea, the land-contingent bringing their families and possessions in heavy two-wheeled ox-carts. 'The isles were disturbed,' Raʿmesse tells us, and 'no one stood before their hands,' even the Ḥittites being mentioned as wasted before their advance. 'They set up a camp in one place in the land of Amor [Amurru]. They desolated his people and his land like that which is not. Their main support was Pulasati, Ṯakkara, Šakaluša, Danauna, Wašaša. These lands were united, and they laid their hands upon the land as far as the Circle of the Earth. Their hearts were confident, full of their plans.' ‡ Raʿmesse equipped a fleet to meet the invaders, and marched into Canaʿan himself at the head of his land-army, which was composed partly of Egyptians and partly of Šardina mercenaries. Somewhere upon the coast of Phoenicia a battle was fought in which Raʿmesse was victorious; and his army, having accounted for their foes by land, turned their arrows to the assistance of the Egyptian ships which were engaged in a naval battle inshore in one of the harbours. § Raʿmesse thus succeeded for the time in checking the southern progress of the tide of invasion; but it cannot have been long afterwards—whether later in this Pharaoh's reign or in the period of national decay which supervened at his death—that the immigrant tribes pressed on and occupied the whole of the maritime plain of Canaʿan from Carmel to the border of Egypt, extending ultimately, as it seems, across the plain of Esdraelon to Beth-she'an (cf. p. 24).

However much doubt may attach to the identification of the other invading tribes, ‖ it is certain that the Pulasati (written *Pw-r'-s'-ṯ* or *Pw-r'-s'-ty*) are the *P*^{e}*lištîm* of the O.T. The Philistines were recognized by the Israelites as immigrant settlers, and their earlier home is said to have been כַּפְתּוֹר Kaphtor (Deut. 2^{23}, Am. 9^{7}),

* Cf. Breasted, *AR.* iv. §§ 35 ff.

‡ Cf. Breasted, *AR.* iv. § 64.

§ Cf. the Egyptian relief as figured by Rosellini, *Monumenti dell' Egitto*, i. Pl. cxxxi.; Maspero, *Mêlées*, p. 469; Macalister, *Schweich Lectures*, p. 119.

‖ The name Ṯakkara has been connected by Petrie (*Hist. Eg.* iii. p. 151) with the place-name Zakro in eastern Crete, and this view is favoured by Hall (*NE.* p. 71). The older identification with the Τευκροί of the Troad, adopted by Lauth, Chabas, Lenormant, and ultimately by Brugsch (cf. references in Maspero, *Mêlées*, p. 464, *n* 3) may also connect this people originally with Crete, whence the Trojan Teucer is said to have come (Virgil, *Aen.* iii. ll. 102 ff.): cf. Hall, *Oldest Civilization of Greece*, p. 176. Maspero (*Revue Critique*, 1880, p. 110) and Breasted (*Hist. Eg.* p. 477) think of the pre-Greek Sikeli or Sicilians. The Danauna may have been the Δαναοί, as is commonly thought, in spite of the fact that there was a settlement of them in Canaʿan some two hundred years before this date (cf. p. xcv). On the Šakaluša as the Sagalassians, cf. p. xcii. Most difficult of all to identify are the Wašaša, who Hall thinks may be 'the people of Ϝαξός (Waxos), the 'Οαξός of Herodotus and 'Αξός of later days, a prominent city of Crete' (cf. *op. cit.* p. 177).

which is defined in Jer. 47 [4] by the term אִי *'î*, always applied to the islands and coast-lands of the Mediterranean. The identity of Kaphtor with the Egyptian Keftiu,* and of both with the island of Crete, admits of no reasonable doubt; but it is not unlikely that the ancestors of the Philistines had at one time or another connexion with the mainland of Asia Minor, especially with Lycia and Caria (which may, indeed, be included under the term Keftiu, if, as Hall states, it is derived from an Egyptian word meaning 'behind,' and so denotes somewhat vaguely 'the back of beyond'). ‡ The term כְּרֵתִי *Kᵉrêthî*, which is often applied in the O.T. to a section of the Philistines (especially David's foreign bodyguard), bears a close

* The absence of the final *r* in Keftiu as compared with Kaphtor is explained by Spiegelberg (*OLZ.* xi. 426 f.) as due to elision; and this seems more probable than the rival explanation offered by Wiedemann (*OLZ.* xiii. 53) that Kaphtor is the Egyptian *Kaft-ḥor* 'Upper Kefti' (like *Retenu-ḥor* 'Upper Retenu'), since it is more likely that the Israelites learned the name directly from the Philistines themselves than through an Egyptian medium. W. M. Müller (*MVAG.*, 1900, p. 6) cites the Ptolemaic form *Kpt'r* with retention of *r*.

‡ The men of Keftiu figured on Egyptian tombs of the Eighteenth Dynasty period bear striking resemblance to the Minoans, the remains of whose civilization have been excavated at Knossos and other sites in Crete, and the vases which they carry are identical in workmanship. It is impossible, however, to regard the Philistines as identical with these Keftians. The former, as represented in Egyptian reliefs, are quite unlike the latter, and always wear a high feathered headdress, such as, according to Herodotus (vii. 92) was worn at the battle of Salamis by the Lycians (περὶ δὲ τῇσι κεφαλῇσι πίλους πτεροῖσι περιεστεφανωμένους), whom the same writer believes to have come originally from Crete (i. 173). Cf. the feathered headdress worn by the figures depicted on an Assyrian relief from Kuyunjik of the seventh century B.C.: Layard, *Monuments of Nineveh, 2nd Series*, Plate 44. Herodotus also states that the Carians came to the mainland from the islands, and were originally subjects of King Minos (i. 171; cf. also Strabo, xiv. 2, 27), and he ascribes to them, among other inventions borrowed by the Greeks, the fastening of crests on helmets—which, however, were clearly quite different from the feathered skull-caps of the Lycians and Philistines. A head with feathered headdress, identical with that of the Philistines, forms one of the pictographs upon the clay disk discovered by Pernier in the palace of Phaestos in Crete. The human figures included among the pictographs on this disk are non-Minoan in outline and costume, and the signs as a whole differ considerably from those of the Minoan signary. Whether the disk should 'be regarded as a record of a peaceful connexion between the Minoan lords of Phaestos and some neighbouring race enjoying a parallel form of civilization,' or as 'the record of an invading swarm, the destroyers perhaps of Phaestos itself,' is a question which cannot at present be settled. Cf. Evans, *Scripta Minoa*, i. pp. 22-28, with Plates xii. and xiii.

The Aegean pottery which has been discovered at sites in Palestine which come within the Philistine sphere (Tell eṣ-Ṣâfiyyeh, Gezer, 'Ain-šems) is of the inferior style called 'Late Minoan III.' *i.e.* belonging to the period subsequent to the destruction of Knossos which marks the end of 'Late Minoan II.' *cir.* B.C. 1400. Late Minoan III. style, which follows immediately on Late Minoan II., was very possibly the inferior imitation of Minoan art already developed in south-western Asia Minor by the invaders of Crete, who may have been the ancestors of the Philistines.

On the Keftian and Philistine questions, cf. Hall in *Annual of the Brit. School at Athens*, viii. (1901-2), pp. 157-188; *NE.* pp. 68-74; Macalister, *The Philistines; their History and Civilization* (*Schweich Lectures*, 1911, published 1914), chap. i.

resemblance to 'Cretan,' and is so rendered by 𝔊 in Ezek. 25^{15}, Zeph. 2^{5}; and an allied tribe, also employed as mercenaries by the Judaean kings, bore the name כָּרִי *Kârî* (2 Sam. 20^{23} *Kt.*, 2 Kgs. $11^{4.19}$), *i.e.* Carians.

The O.T. tells us nothing as to the other sea-peoples allied with the Philistines; but we gather from the narrative of the Egyptian Wenamon (cf. p. xcvi), that there was a Ṯakkara settlement at Dor a little south of Carmel about eighty years after the invasion. It is possible that the Danauna may have settled on the sea-coast to the north of Phoenicia, where, as we learn from a letter of Abimilki of Tyre to Aḫnaton, there was a settlement of them some 200 years earlier.* So late as the latter half of the 9th century B.C. Kalumu king of Ya'di in northern Syria was harassed by the king of the Danonim (מלך דננים), and was obliged to hire the assistance of the king of Assyria ‡—a fact which favours the inference that this people is to be looked for somewhere upon the north Syrian littoral.

After having successfully repulsed another invasion of the Libyans (this time in alliance with the Mašawaša, a north African people dwelling to the west of the Libyans), which took place in his eleventh year, Ra'messe III. undertook (probably within the next year or two) a second campaign in Syria concerning which our very scanty information is derived solely from pictorial reliefs.§ He seems to have stormed and captured several fortified cities, one of which is described as 'in the land of Amor,' whilst another, which is represented as surrounded by water, is probably Ḳadesh. Two others are pictured as defended by Ḥittite troops, and one of these bears the name Ereṯ.

After the death of Ra'messe III. the Twentieth Dynasty was continued by a series of nine rulers, all of whom bore the name Ra'messe (IV-XII). The total period covered by their reign was under 80 years (B.C. 1167-1090); and since in the whole line there was not one monarch possessing the slightest vigour or initiative, the power of the empire suffered a swift and irretrievable decline. Early in Ra'messe XII.'s reign we find that a Tanite noble named Nesubenebded has made himself ruler of the whole Delta-region,

* Cf. Kn. 151, ll. 49 ff. Abimilki's words are, 'The King my lord has written to me, "What news hast thou of Cana'an? Send me word." The king of the land of Danuna is dead, and his brother has become king in succession, and the land is at rest.' It is generally assumed that the O.T. references to the Philistines as occupying the maritime plain of southern Cana'an in Patriarchal times (Gen. $21^{32.34}$ R, 26 J; cf. also Ex. 13^{16} E, 15^{14} J) are necessarily anachronistic; but the fact that there were Danauna in Syria some two hundred years before the days of Ra'messe III. should give us pause before we assert this categorically, since for aught we know there *may* have been an earlier Philistine settlement just as there was an earlier Danauna settlement. The existence of such an earlier Philistine settlement has been argued by Noordzij (*De Filistijnen*, p. 59), mainly on the ground that by the time of Samson and Saul the Philistines were already largely Semitized.

‡ Inscription of Kalumu, ll. 7 f. Cf. references p. 174, *footnote* *.

§ Cf. Breasted, *AR.* iv. §§ 115-135.

while at Thebes the supreme power is in the hands of the high-priest of Amon, Ḥriḥor by name.

A document dated in the fifth year of this reign (*cir.* B.C. 1114) is of the highest interest to us as illustrating Egypt's total loss of power and prestige in Syria.* This is the report of a certain Wenamon, an official despatched by Ḥriḥor to Phoenicia in order to procure timber from the Lebanon for the sacred barge of Amon. The report, which is a chapter of misfortunes, is undoubtedly authentic, and was apparently drawn up to explain the emissary's waste of time and ill-success in accomplishing his errand.

Starting from Thebes in charge of an image of the god named 'Amon-of-the-Way,' Wenamon goes to Tanis, and on exhibition of his credentials Nesubenebded and his wife Tentamon give him a passage on board a trading-vessel commanded by a Syrian in order that he may reach Gebal and obtain the timber from Zakar-baʿal (Eg. *Ṯ'-k'-r'-b-ʿ-r*), the Phoenician prince of that city. In the course of the voyage the ship touches at Dor, which belongs to a settlement of the Ṯakkara under a prince named Badyra, or, it may be, Bod'el (Eg. *B'-dy-r'*). ‡ Whilst the ship is in harbour one of the crew steals Wenamon's money, amounting to 5 *deben* of gold and 31 *deben* of silver, § and decamps. Wenamon interviews Badyra and endeavours to make him responsible for the robbery, on the ground that it took place in his harbour; but the Ṯakkara prince not unnaturally disclaims all obligation to make good the money, while politely promising to search for the thief. After waiting in harbour nine days without result, Wenamon is obliged to continue his journey. Unfortunately at this point there comes a lacuna in the MS.; but we are able to gather from what remains || that the ship put in at Tyre, and that either here or at some other port Wenamon met some Ṯakkara travellers bearing a bag of silver amounting to 30 *deben*, and incontinently seized it as surety for his own money.

Arrived at Gebal, Zakar-baʿal refuses to see him, and sends a message, 'Begone from my harbour!' Wenamon waits patiently for nineteen days, in spite of daily orders to depart; then one of the youths in the prince's retinue falls into a prophetic frenzy, and demands that the god, and the messenger of Amon who has him in

* The Golénischeff papyrus, discovered in 1891 at El-Ḫibeh in Upper Egypt. For translation and discussion, cf. W. M. Müller in *MVAG.*, 1900, 1, pp. 14-29; Erman in *Zeitschr. für aegypt. Sprache*, xxxviii (1900), pp. 1-14; Breasted, *AR.* iv. §§ 557 ff.; Maspero, *Contes populaires de l'Égypte* (4e éd. 1911), pp. 214-230; *Popular Stories of Ancient Egypt* (trans. of preceding by Mrs. Johns, revised by Maspero, 1915), pp. 202-216.

‡ In favour of taking the name as Semitic בדאל we may compare the Phoenician names בדעשתרת Bod-ʿAštart, בדמלקרת Bod-Melḳart, בדתנת Bod-Tanith. בד is probably a shortened form of עבד 'servant of': cf. Cooke, *NSI.* p. 41.

§ That is (according to Petrie, *Hist. Eg.* iii. p. 197) about £60 in gold and £12 in silver.

|| Maspero (*op. cit.*) offers a conjectural restoration of the missing section.

his care, shall be brought into the presence of Zakar-ba'al. Thus Wenamon, who, having abandoned hope of accomplishing his mission, is loading his belongings on to a ship bound for Egypt, is stopped by the harbour-master and ordered to remain until the morning. He is then granted an interview with Zakar-ba'al, who, in spite of the prophecy, is by no means disposed to receive him with open arms, but demands his credentials which he has foolishly left in the hands of Nesubenebded and Tentamon, and asks why he and his god have been sent, not in a special ship, but in a mere merchant-vessel, in which he might easily have been wrecked and have lost the image of the god.* On Zakar-ba'al's inquiring his business, he replies, 'I have come after the timber for the great and august barge of Amon-Re, king of gods. Thy father did it, thy grandfather did it, and thou wilt also do it.' Zakar-ba'al admits that this is true, and professes himself quite willing to do business at a price; then sending for the journal of his fathers he proves from it that they were paid in full for all the timber which they supplied, and were under no obligation to supply anything freely to Egypt as overlord.‡ This documentary evidence is clinched by an argument which is very noteworthy as proving how utterly the Phoenician cities had shaken off the Egyptian suzerainty. 'If,' says Zakar-ba'al, 'the ruler of Egypt were the owner of my property, and I were also his servant, he would not send silver and gold, saying, "Do the command of Amon." It was not the payment of ⌜tribute⌝ which they exacted of my father. As for me, I am myself neither thy servant nor am I the servant of him that sent thee. If I cry out to the Lebanon, the heavens open, and the logs lie here on the shore of the sea.'§

Wenamon blusters in vain; even the production of the image of Amon, and the solemn assurance that the life and health which the god is able to bestow is of far greater value than a mere money-payment, are without effect. He agrees, therefore, to send his scribe back to Egypt with a request to Nesubenebded and Tentamon to despatch various goods in payment for the timber; and, as an earnest that he is ready to perform *his* side of the bargain, Zakar-ba'al embarks a small part of the timber on the ship by which the messenger sails. The goods arrive from Egypt in due course, and Zakar-ba'al immediately gives orders that the timber shall be felled and dragged down to the shore. When all is ready for embarka-

* The precise meaning of Zakar-ba'al's remarks about the ship seems to be open to doubt. The interpretation adopted above is based on the rendering of Breasted.

‡ The keeping of this journal by Zakar-ba'al and his ancestors, coupled with the fact that among the goods supplied him from Egypt in payment for the timber are 500 rolls of papyrus, is of the first importance in proof of the high antiquity of the use in Cana'an of an alphabetic script written upon papyrus or leather, alongside of the use of cuneiform Babylonian written upon clay tablets. Cf. *Addit. Note* on 'The use of writing in Cana'an at the time of the Judges,' p. 258.

§ The actual quotations here given are derived from Breasted's translation.

tion he sends for Wenamon, and points out that he himself has done as his fathers did, whereas the Egyptian can scarcely make the same claim. Then somewhat sarcastically he congratulates Wenamon on being more fortunate than his predecessors—certain messengers of Ḫamwese (probably Raʿmesse IX.) who were detained in the land seventeen years until their deaths: and he suggests that Wenamon should go and see their tomb!

Wenamon, however, having secured his timber, is only bent on embarking it as soon as possible and setting sail; but, unfortunately for him, before he can accomplish this, eleven ships of the Ṯakkara appear outside the harbour with the object of stopping his departure and arresting him—doubtless on account of his seizure of the silver belonging to the Ṯakkara travellers.* Wenamon is in despair; but Zakar-baʿal manages to enable him to embark and slip through their fingers. His ship is then driven by a contrary wind to the land of Alasa (probably Cyprus); and here he is (or fancies that he is) in imminent danger of death at the hands of the islanders, and only escapes through finding some one who understands Egyptian, and who interprets his words to the queen of the country. At this point, unfortunately, the MS. breaks off; and we do not know what further adventures Wenamon encountered before he managed to reach Egypt.

This narrative of Wenamon—lengthy as it is even when reduced to a mere summary—has seemed worthy of inclusion both on account of its intrinsic interest as exemplifying Egypt's loss of even the shadow of authority in her former Asiatic dominion, and also because, illustrating as it does most vividly the condition of civilization in Canaʿan, it falls into the middle of the period covered by the Book of Judges, and happens to be the solitary piece of extra-Biblical evidence known to us which belongs to that period. The reason why—whilst earlier centuries have proved comparatively rich in extra-Biblical material bearing on the history of Syria and Palestine—the period of the Judges of Israel is thus so barren is not far to seek. We have arrived at an age in which no external great power was strong enough or free enough to interfere in the affairs of Canaʿan. This period extends from the early middle part of the twelfth century B.C. (end of the reign of Raʿmesse III.) down to the middle of the ninth century B.C. when the co-operation of Aḥab of Israel in the league against Shalmaneser III. of Assyria (B.C 854) foreshadows the speedy interference of this great power in the affairs of the small kingdoms of Canaʿan.‡

* The narrative here suggests that a previous attempt to arrest Wenamon had been made by the Ṯakkara, and that the account of this has disappeared in the lacuna in the middle of the MS.

‡ The incursion into southern Canaʿan of the Pharaoh of whom it is recorded in 1 Kgs. 9[16] that he captured Gezer and presented it as a dowry to his daughter on her marriage with Solomon (early middle part of the tenth century B.C.), and the invasion of Judah and Israel by Shishaḳ (Sheshonk I.) in the reign of Rehoboʿam of

The decline of Egyptian power we have outlined. The Ḥittite empire, shaken to its foundations by the irresistible movement of the sea-peoples of which we have already spoken (cf. p. xciii), appears to have been wiped out, perhaps some two decades later (*cir.* B.C. 1170) through the invasion of a people whom the Assyrians called Muškaya,* the Meshech of the Old Testament (Gen. 10^{2}, *al.*), and the Μόσχοι of Herodotus (iii. 94; vii. 78), who were probably akin to the Phrygians of later times. Thenceforward Carchemish became the chief centre of Ḥittite civilization; but there were other independent or semi-independent principalities throughout northern Syria, extending apparently as far south as Ḳadesh on the Orontes, the former frontier-city of the great Ḥittite empire.‡ The rulers

Judah (latter half of the same century), as recorded in 1 Kgs. 14^{25} and upon the walls of the temple of Amon at Karnak, are isolated incidents merely, and do not mark a recrudescence of Egyptian power in Palestine.

* Tiglath-Pileser I. tells us that in the first year of his reign (*cir.* B.C. 1120) he attacked and defeated 20,000 Muškaya and their five kings who fifty years previously had held the lands of Alzi and Purukuzzi, and after a course of unbroken victory had 'come down' and seized the land of Kummuḫ (Commagene, south of the Taurus and north of Mesopotamia): cf. Budge and King, *Annals of the Kings of Assyria*, pp. 35 f.; *KB.* i. p. 18. In later times their land, to the north-west of Kummuḫ on the borders of Cappadocia, is known as Mušku or Musku: cf. for collected references Delitzsch, *Paradies*, pp. 250 f. It is on Tiglath-Pileser's information as to this Muškaya-movement—coupled with the facts that Arnuanta, who must have reigned *cir.* B.C. 1200 or a little earlier, is the last Ḥittite king whose archives have been found at Boghaz Keui, and that both Boghaz Keui and Carchemish exhibit signs of destruction and subsequent reconstruction at a period not much later than Arnuanta—that the conclusion is based that the Muškaya were the destroyers of the Ḥittite empire. Cf. Hogarth, *The Ancient East*, p. 38; Garstang, *Hittites*, p. 53; King, *Bab.* p. 241.

‡ This conclusion depends on the emendation of 2 Sam. 24^{6}, according to which the northern limit of David's kingdom extended 'to the land of the Ḥittites, unto Ḳadesh' (reading אֶרֶץ הַחִתִּים קָדֵשָׁה after 𝔊^L in place of the unintelligible אֶרֶץ תַּחְתִּים חָדְשִׁי 'land of Taḥtim Ḥodshi' of 𝔐). There is no reason for doubting the restoration 'unto Ḳadesh'—with Driver (*NHTS.*² *ad loc.*) and others—on the ground that David's kingdom could not have extended so far north, the ordinary northern limit of the kingdom of Israel being Dan (probably Tell el-Ḳâḍy, south of Ḥermon; cf. *notes* on 'Laish,' *ch.* 18^{7}, and on 'from Dan, etc.,' *ch.* 20^{1}), which is one hundred miles south of Ḳadesh, if, as is probable, the latter city is to be located on the Orontes at a point a little south of the lake of Ḥomṣ (cf. Maspero, *Mêlées*, pp. 140 f.). The ideal northern limit of the kingdom, which was realized in the reigns of David and Solomon and again in that of Jerobo'am II., was 'the entry of Ḥamath' (cf. *ch.* 3^{3} *note*), which is clearly proved by *ch.* 3^{3}, Josh. 13^{5} to have been the *northern* and not the southern end of the pass (el-Buḳâ') between the Lebanon and Anti-Lebanon ranges. The attempt to identify 'the entry of Ḥamath' with Merǵ 'Ayyûn, the southern mouth of el-Buḳâ' (so *e.g.* van Kasteren, *RB.* 1895, pp. 23-36; cf. Buhl, *Geogr.* p. 66), produces the ridiculous result that the *terminus a quo* in these two passages ('mount Ba'al-Ḥermon,' *ch.* 3^{3} = 'Ba'al-Gad,' Josh. 13^{5}) and the *terminus ad quem* are in the same locality, or at most separated by five or six miles only; and how 'all Lebanon' can be said to lie between these two points, or, so situated, to be 'eastward' of 'the land of the Gebalites,' passes comprehension.

of these principalities are 'the kings of the Ḥittites,' mentioned in 1 Kgs. 10^{29}, 2 Kgs. 7^{6}.

Lastly, Babylon and Assyria were, during the period of the Judges as also two centuries earlier, so much engaged in mutual suspicions or open hostilities, that they had no scope for raids of conquest in the west. The Synchronistic History of Babylonia and Assyria * is a record of boundary-treaties and their violation, of invasions and counter-invasions, sufficiently preoccupying to absorb the main output of each kingdom's energy so long as their power remained, upon the whole, fairly evenly balanced. Taking a comprehensive survey of the four centuries from B.C. 1400 to B.C. 1000,‡ we observe that the tendency of Babylon is towards decline of power, whereas the tendency of Assyria is towards the gathering of strength and energy, which gives promise of the predominant position which she was to attain in western Asia from the ninth until nearly the close of the seventh century B.C. This may be largely explained by difference of temperament, the strong infusion of Sumerian and Kaššite strains in the Semitic blood of the Babylonians apparently tending towards a peace-loving and mercantile disposition; whereas such infusion as entered into the more purely Semitic blood of the Assyrians seems to have been furnished, at the beginning of their national history, by an Anatolian strain, which has been plausibly supposed to account for the lust of war and ruthlessness which distinguished them so markedly in comparison with their southern kinsmen.§

With the rejection of the southern end of el-Buḳâ' as 'the entry of Ḥamath,' and acceptance of the northern end, van Kasteren's attempt to trace a line south of the Lebanons for the ideal description of Israel's northern boundary in Num. $34^{7\,ff.}$ P, Ezek. $47^{15\,ff.}$ breaks down entirely. Furrer's attempt (*ZDPV.* viii., 1885, pp. 27-29) to find the line north of the Lebanon-region and including it is probably approximately correct, except that he goes too far north in placing 'the entry of Ḥamath' at er-Restân (Arethusa), nearly fourteen miles north of Ḥomṣ (which would bring Ḳadesh—if it is to be sought at the site above indicated—nearly thirty miles within the border), and in identifying Ziphron of Num. 34^{9} with Safrâneh, by the expedient of placing it *before* and not *after* Ṣedad of *v.*[8], *i.e.* the modern Ṣadad. Probably the boundary crossed the Orontes near Riblah (modern Ribleh) some twenty miles south of Ḥomṣ (cf. Ezek. 6^{14}, reading מִמִּדְבָּר רִבְלָתָה), ran east-south-east to Ṣadad, and then to the modern Zifrân, described by Wetzstein (*Reisebericht über Haurân und Trachonen*, p. 88) as an extensive ruined site fourteen hours north-east of Damascus. That such a northern extension of territory could be and was claimed by David as the result of his successful wars with the Aramaeans and his treaty with To'i, king of Ḥamath (2 Sam. 8, 10) is extremely probable—more especially if the territory of Aram-Ṣobah is to be placed approximately in the neighbourhood of Ḥomṣ (cf. Nöldeke in *EB.* 280).

* This chronicle has been edited by Peiser and Winckler in *KB.* i. pp. 194 ff.

‡ Cf., on this period of Assyrian and Babylonian history, Budge and King, *Annals of the Kings of Assyria*, pp. xxiv-lvi; King, *Records of the reign of Tukulti-Ninib I.*; *Bab.*, chaps. vii., viii.; Rogers, *HBA.*[6] pp. 109-132, 144-179; Johns, *Ancient Babylonia*, pp. 94-106; *Ancient Assyria*, pp. 50-78; Hall, *NE.* pp. 368-370, 384-389, 398 f.

§ Cf. King, *Bab.* pp. 139 ff.

In the first half of the thirteenth century B.C. the rise of Assyrian power was remarkably rapid, culminating in the reign of Tukulti-Ninib I. (*cir.* B.C. 1275), who actually conquered Babylon and held it for seven years. This monarch's reign, however, terminated in rebellion and civil war which brought about a period of retrogression, during which Assyria had to suffer at least one serious invasion by the Babylonians.* In the reign of Ašur-dân I. (*cir.* B.C. 1167) the power of Assyria began to revive,‡ and reached a height never before attained in the reign of Tiglath-Pileser I. (*cir.* B.C. 1120), the first really great empire-builder of this kingdom. Tiglath-Pileser's conquests, however, extensive as they were (including Babylon, and great tracts of country to the north and north-west of Assyria, even as far as the land of Ḳumanî in the Taurus region), did not reach so far south-west as the land of Canaʿan, where at this period the tribes of Israel were slowly gaining their footing under the Judges; though he came into conflict with Aramaean tribes in the neighbourhood of Carchemish and drove them westward across the Euphrates, and the fact that he claims to have set sail on the Mediterranean in ships of Arvad, and to have slain a great dolphin or whale, § indicates some extent of penetration into northern Syria. After Tiglath-Pileser I. we possess practically no knowledge of the course of Assyrian history for a hundred and thirty years; and the silence of the Synchronistic History as to Assyrian victories is a sure indication that the kingdom must have undergone a long period of decline. ||

Failing thus the interference of any great power in Syria and Palestine for a period of some three centuries, a unique opportunity was afforded to the smaller peoples of the country to settle down and consolidate their power. In the north the Aramaeans, whose gathering force and westward migratory movements came into evidence in the period of the T.A. Letters, now spread both eastward across the Euphrates into the district of Ḫarran and south-westward into Syria, north and east of the Lebanons, founding in northern and central Syria a number of small principalities interspersed among the principalities which, as we have seen, were the survivals of the great Ḥittite Empire.¶ South of the Lebanons

* According to the Synchronistic History, Adad-šum-naṣir of Babylon slew Enlil-kudur-uṣur of Assyria in battle, and besieged the city of Aššur (*cir.* B.C. 1213). It is probable that this reassertion of Babylonian power was continued under his immediate successors: cf. King, *Bab.* p. 244; Rogers, *HBA.*[6] p. 125; Hall, *NE.* p. 385.

‡ He attacked Babylonia and captured several cities from Zamama-šum-iddin, the last king of the Kaššite Dynasty. This defeat of Babylon was doubtless contributory to the fall of the Third Dynasty, which took place shortly after at the hands of the Elamites.

§ Cf. 'Broken Obelisk,' col. iv. ll. 2f. (Budge and King, *op. cit.*, p. 188.)

|| Cf. Budge and King, *op. cit.* p. lvi.

¶ Our knowledge of north Syrian history is far too scanty to enable us even to draw inferences as to the relative strength and persistency of the Ḥittite and

opportunity favoured the southern branch of the Aramaean stock which is known as the Hebrews, among whom the tribes of Israel formed an important element. It is a fact worthy of notice that the Book of Judges, in recording the experiences of Israel in their struggle to obtain a footing in Cana'an, makes no sort of allusion to any collision with, or aggression at the hands of, a great power such as Egypt or Assyria—as might well have happened had the information embodied in the book been merely vague and anachronistic. The absence of such allusion—which, as we have seen, is in strict accord with the historical circumstances of the period—should considerably strengthen our confidence that the course of history as described is in the main based upon a trustworthy tradition. The historical value of this tradition is discussed in the special introductions to the various sections of the book.*

Aramaean elements. Even the evidence of proper names is fallacious, since it is likely that, where Aramaean influence was strong, the Ḥittites may eventually have undergone Semiticization and have adopted Semitic names, just as we know that the Philistines did. It is at any rate a fair conjecture that it was in the far north (neighbourhood of Carchemish) that the Ḥittites longest retained their individuality, while further south Aramaean influence more speedily prevailed, as much by peaceful penetration as by conquest. Ḥamath, which—until the recent discovery of a Ḥittite inscription at er-Restân (cf. Garstang, *Hittites*, p. 85, n^2)—was the most southerly site at which Ḥittite remains were known, is a state concerning which it is possible to bring together a few facts bearing on this question. Originally an important Ḥittite centre (on the Ḥittite remains, cf. Garstang, *Hittites*, pp. 93 ff.), it was probably still purely Ḥittite in David's time (B.C. 1000), since its king To'i or To'u was anxious to secure David's support against the encroachments of the Aramaeans (2 Sam. 8^{9f}=1 Chr. 18^{9f}). The name To'i may well be identical with the name which appears in the T.A. Letters as Tuḫi, and is borne by the regent of Mitanni during the minority of Tušratta (Kn. 17, l. 12); cf. Luckenbill, *AJTh.* xviii. p. 57. The next king known to us is Irḫulêni, mentioned by Shalmaneser III. as allied against him with Bir-idri (Ben-Hadad II.), Aḥab, etc., at the battle of Ḳarḳar (B.C. 854). His name is not convincingly Semitic, though we cannot affirm it to be Ḥittite. Zakir, King of Ḥamath (a little before B.C. 800), whose inscription we possess (cf. p. 173), bears a Semitic name and writes in Aramaic, though some at any rate of the seven kings with whom he is at war are also Aramaeans ('Bar-Hadad the son of Hazael'=Ben-Hadad III. of 2 Kgs. 13^{24}; ברגש='Bar-Gus, probably='Arami the son of Gus' mentioned by Shalmaneser III., *KB.* i. p. 170—a fact not hitherto noticed; and 'the King of Sam'al'). Later Kings of Ḥamath are Eniel (who paid tribute to Tiglath-Pileser IV., B.C. 738), and Ilu-bi'di or Ya'u-bi'di (subdued by Sargon, B.C. 720), both of whom bear Semitic names. Here, then, from the time of Zakir onwards, we have evidence for the Semiticization of Ḥamath; but whether this implies an Aramaean conquest or merely a gradual assimilation it is impossible to determine.

* Taking a comprehensive and summary survey of Judges as a whole, we may confidently conclude that the figures of Deborah and Baraḳ, Gide'on-Jerubbaal, 'Abimelech, and Micah are historical, and that the narratives concerning them contain a very solid substratum of fact. The same may be affirmed with considerable probability of Ehud and Jephthaḥ; though in the case of the narrative of the latter it remains ambiguous whether the enemy was 'Ammon or Moab. Balance of probability inclines (in the opinion of the present writer) against the historical character of Samson; though in any case the picture which is drawn of relations between

Thus we conclude our survey of the condition of affairs in Canaʿan and the surrounding countries prior to and during the period of the Judges of Israel. It is probable that the reader may notice a seeming omission: viz. that throughout we have advanced no theory as to the relation of Israel's early traditions to the course of history with which we have been dealing. This has been intentional. Throughout the section our aim has been to bring together relevant information derived from sources contemporary with the events to which they refer. The early traditions of the O.T. (and here we are speaking of the traditions of Gen. to Josh.) are embodied in sources which, in their written form, are certainly many centuries later than the events which they narrate. Opinions vary greatly as to their historical value; but, whatever view be held upon this question, it can hardly be disputed that, for our present purpose, the wiser course is not to mix contemporary historical evidence with other evidence into the interpretation of which the theoretical element is bound to enter in a greater or less degree.

This principle, however, calls for a certain qualification. External history of Canaʿan, though unfortunately very barren of information bearing directly upon the early movements of the tribes of Israel, *does* offer a few facts which call for correlation with the O.T. traditions; and the interpretations of these facts—especially in their chronological relation to the Exodus and the settlement in Canaʿan—has its bearing upon the historical period covered by the Book of Judges. The facts in question have been mentioned as they occur. It may be convenient here to tabulate them:—

Jaʿcob-el, the name of a Hyksos chieftain, before B.C. 1580 (cf. p. lxvi).

Israelites and Philistines possesses a real historical interest. ʿOthniel and the five minor Judges, Tolaʿ, Ja'ir, Ibṣan, Elon, and ʿAbdon, are undoubtedly not individuals but personified clans. Shamgar, the son of ʿAnath, is proved to be an historical name by the allusion in *ch.* 5 6; though, since this bare allusion is probably all that the author of the late insertion in 3 31 had to go upon, it is at least as likely that he was a foreign oppressor as a deliverer (cf. p. 113). Comparison of the contemporary Song of Deborah with the parallel prose-narrative in *ch.* 4 affords incontrovertible evidence of the large amount of genuine history which may be found in the old prose-sources (cf. p. 82), even though (as we must probably assume) they were handed down orally for many generations before being committed to writing; and it is a fair inference that other old narratives which contain intrinsic evidence of their appropriateness to the circumstances of the period (*e.g.* the J narrative of Gideʿon, and the stories of Abimelech and Micah) are no less historical. The only narrative which appears not to possess any historical value is the story of the outrage at Gibeʿah and the ensuing vengeance taken by Israel on the tribe of Benjamin; since the oldest form of the story (which we assign to J) is clearly constructed in close imitation of earlier J narratives, and appears to offer marked evidence of a special motive, viz. animosity to the memory of Saul. Even here, however, it would be bold to assert categorically (especially in view of the Shiloh-story in 21 19ff.) that no historical elements at all have entered into the narrative.

Ja'cob-el and Joseph-el (?), place-names in Cana'an, *cir.* B.C. 1479 (cf. pp. lxvii f.).

Ḫabiru pressing into Syria-Palestine, *cir.* B.C. 1375 (cf. pp. lxxiii ff.).

Šamḫuna, a place-name in Cana'an, *cir.* B.C. 1375, possibly = Sime'on (cf. p. lxxv, *footnote*).

The name Asher occurs in western Galilee, *cir.* B.C. 1313 (cf. p. lxxxix).

Mineptaḥ defeats a people called Israel in Cana'an, *cir.* B.C. 1223 (cf. p. xcii).

The question of prime importance to us here is the *terminus a quo* which we are to assign to the period of the Judges. This depends upon the date at which the Exodus is placed; and on this point, fortunately, we possess reliable information. Ex. 1^{11} J states that the Israelites, under the system of forced labour imposed upon them, 'built for Pharaoh store-cities, Pithom and Ra'amses'; and Naville has proved that the site of Pithom (called in Egyptian P-etôm, *i.e.* 'the abode of Etôm,' a form of the Sun-god) was the modern Tell el-Masḫûṭa, in the east of the Wâdy Ṭûmîlât, near the ancient frontier of Egypt, and that the founder of the city was Ra'messe II.* Thus, granted the historical truth of the Israelite tradition (and in such a matter there is no reason to suspect it), it follows that Ra'messe II. (*cir.* B.C. 1292-1225) was the Pharaoh of the oppression, and his successor Mineptaḥ (*cir.* B.C. 1225-1215), probably the Pharaoh of the Exodus.‡

If this is so, however, we observe at once that the external allusions above noted, which seem to refer to the presence of Israelite tribes in Cana'an, are all prior to the Exodus; and that at any rate the last two appear to postulate the existence there of Israelite elements which must have been distinct from those that made their escape from Egypt under Mineptaḥ. Asher is occupying in the reigns of Sety I. and Ra'messe II. the precise position in Galilee which, according to later Biblical tradition, was allotted to him *after* the settlement in Cana'an effected through the conquests of Joshua'; and a people named Israel forms a tribal element in Cana'an (as is implied by its mention in the midst of Cana'anite

* Cf. Naville, *The Store City of Pithom and the Route of the Exodus* (ed. 1, 1885; ed. 4, 1903); W. M. Müller in *EB.* 3782 ff.; Sayce in *DB.* iii. pp. 886 f.; McNeile, *Exodus* (*Westm. Comm.*), p. xciii; Driver, *Exodus* (*Camb. Bib.*), pp. xxx, 4.

‡ So at least we infer from Ex. 2^{23}, 4^{19} J, which indicate that, in the view of the narrator, the Pharaoh of the Exodus was the next after the great oppressor. Obviously, however, we cannot postulate the same degree of accuracy for this conclusion as for the statement of Ex. 1^{11}. Mineptaḥ's reign was not very long (about ten years); and supposing that the Exodus took place not under him but in the period of weakness and anarchy which immediately followed his reign, we cannot be sure that the J writer would have known of this, or, knowing it, would have thought it necessary to make the point clear. In any case, however, it is obvious from the Hebrew narrative that the Exodus followed at no long interval after the death of the Pharaoh of the oppression.

place-names *) at a date nearly coincident with (or rather earlier than) the Biblical Exodus.

The conclusion that the historical Exodus from Egypt did not include the whole of the tribes which were subsequently known as 'Israel' is not, however, to be drawn from these external references merely, but is inherent in the earliest traditions of the O.T. itself, if they be read between the lines. It is clear that the conception of Israel as a unity of twelve tribes, effecting the conquest of Cana'an in a body under the leadership of Joshua', can only have arisen long after these twelve tribes had been welded into a political whole under the monarchy. Indeed, we can trace, in the different strata of the Biblical narrative, the growth and hardening of this conception.

The oldest account of Israel's settlement in Cana'an, as we have it in Judg. 1^{1}-2^{5} from the narrative of J, representing as it does Israel's occupation as very gradual and partial, effected largely by the individual efforts of each of the tribes rather than by a great united movement, differs widely from the impression produced by R^{D} in Josh., according to which the whole of Cana'an, except the maritime plain and the Lebanon district (cf. Josh. 13^{1-6}), was conquered by the combined tribes under the leadership of Joshua'; and the impression produced by the theory of R^{D} has been heightened and stereotyped in the document which forms the main part of Josh. 13^{15}-21^{42}, in which a post-exilic priestly writer (P) represents the detailed allocation of the whole of Cana'an among the tribes as the work of Joshua' subsequent to the conquest (cf. pp. 1 f.). In choosing between these differing conceptions of the conquest of Cana'an, we cannot hesitate for an instant in selecting the presentation of J as nearer to the truth, and in explaining that of R^{D} and P as coloured by the circumstances of later times. It is true that even J, as we have the historian's work in Judg. 1 (cf. the original form of the narrative as reconstructed in *Addit. note*, p. 47), seems to represent the tribes as assembled at Gilgal (2^{1}) or at Jericho (1^{16}), and as starting their individual efforts from this point largely under the direction of Joshua' (cf. *ch.* 1^{3}, *note*); but that this conception sits very lightly upon the narrative is clear. Careful examination of the movements of separate tribes in the light of all available Biblical information proves *e.g.* that Judah must have conquered his inheritance, not by moving southward from Jericho, but by moving northward from Ḳadesh-Barnea' into the Negeb, and subsequently into the district of Ḥebron (cf. *Addit. note*, p. 44)—therefore independently of Joshua'. The settlement of half-Manasseh east of Jordan, in northern Gile'ad, which the later

* In view of the grouping in which the reference to Israel occurs, the alternative explanation which suggests itself—viz. that we may have here Mineptaḥ's version of the Exodus, the disappearance of Israel in the waterless desert being, from the Egyptian point of view, regarded as equivalent to their extinction—may be dismissed as out of the question.

sources in the Biblical narrative assume to have been decided upon by Moses and confirmed by Joshua' (cf. Deut. 3^{13}, Num. 32^{33} R^{P},* Josh. 13^{29-31} P), is shown by the J narrative of the settlement (if Josh. 17^{14-18} as slightly modified, and, in sequence, Num. $32^{39.41.42}$, Josh. 13^{13}, are rightly assigned to it: cf. pp. 49 ff.) to have been really an overflow-movement from the west of Jordan owing to want of room in the latter district; and though the J narrator himself assumes that the movement was made at the advice of Joshua', the reference to the Machir-clan of Manasseh in Judg. 5^{14} as still west-Jordanic in the time of Deborah leads us to infer that it did not take place until some time after Joshua''s death (cf. *note* on 'Machir,' pp. 134 f.).

Concluding, therefore, as we seem bound to do, that the representation of Joshua' as the head of a united body of twelve tribes, their leader in the conquest of the main part of Cana'an, and the subsequent arbiter as to the precise extent of their heritages, is a comparatively late conception, finding little or no support in the earliest information which we possess, the way is prepared for the further inference that the tribes which he *did* lead across Jordan to the conquest of a footing in Cana'an were probably a part merely and not the whole of the elements which went to form united Israel in later times; and, since tradition is doubtless correct in making him the successor of Moses in the leadership of Israel, that therefore the Israelites whom Moses led out of Egypt at the Exodus were not the whole of Israel, as the term was subsequently understood; but that certain elements which eventually formed part of the nation must have gained their heritages in Cana'an by other means and at other periods.

This inference, which, as we have seen, is pressed upon us by the extra-Biblical evidence which seems to postulate the existence of Israelite tribes already settled in Cana'an at the period when the tribes eventually delivered from bondage by Moses must have been still in Egypt, is further borne out by the evidence of the O.T. The tribe Asher, which appears from Egyptian evidence to have been settled in its permanent heritage by the reign of Sety I., *i.e.* about one hundred years before the Exodus, belongs to the group of tribes which Israelite tradition represents as descended from the sons of handmaids and not full wives—a tradition which can hardly mean anything else than that these tribes were regarded in later times as holding an inferior position in the Israelite confederacy, perhaps because they were not purely Israelite by race. The terms in which Dan—another member of the same tribal group—is mentioned in the old poem called 'The Blessing of Ja'cob,' Gen. 49^{16}, are best explained as meaning that full tribal rights in the con-

* Num. 32, which appears to be a mixed narrative formed by combination of JE and P (cf. Driver, *LOT.*^{9} pp. 68 f.; Gray, *Numbers* (*ICC.*), pp. 425 ff.) deals throughout with the negotiations of Gad and Re'uben alone. It is only in v^{33} that half-Manasseh is introduced—evidently by a very late hand.

federacy, though eventually won, were not won until some little time at least had elapsed after the final settlement of all the tribes in Cana'an (cf. p. 392). Other facts which make in the same direction are the detachment of the handmaid-tribes Gad, Dan, and Asher from the common interests of Israel in the time of Deborah, as evinced by their failure to respond to the call to arms (Judg. 5 17 *); and the names of these same three tribes, which point to their primitive adhesion to forms of cultus other than pure Yahweh-worship (cf. pp. 197, 392).‡ In J's account of the settlement, Asher, Naphtali, and Dan are very far from appearing in the light of recent and successful invaders. The two former 'dwelt in the midst of the Cana'anites,' *i.e.* it is the Cana'anites who hold the predominance, both in numbers and in power §; while the last-named is actually ousted from his territory and driven up into the hills (*ch.* 1 31-34).|| Gad is unmentioned.

* Naphtali, the remaining handmaid-tribe, forms an exception—probably because, owing to his geographical position, his interests were directly concerned.

‡ If there was a god Asher who was a form of the Moon-god (as is suggested by the evidence brought together on pp. 196 ff.), he may also have been regarded as a particular aspect of the God Yahweh (cf. p. 197, *footnote* *; *Addit. note*, p. 249) by the Cana'anite worshippers of that Deity; and this may explain why the symbol of his (assumed) consort Ashera was so often set up by the side of Yahweh's altar, and also the keen antipathy with which the Ashera was regarded by the exponents of the ethical (Mosaic) form of Yahweh-religion. For the theory of two forms of Yahweh-religion, one long indigenous in Cana'an and marked by naturalistic characteristics, the other, highly ethical in character, owing its origin to Moses (or rather to the revelation vouchsafed to him), and introduced into Cana'an by the Israelite tribes who came under Moses' influence, cf. the present writer's article in *JTS.* ix. (1908), pp. 321 ff. If Dan, however, is a title of the Sun-god (cf. p. 392), then here we can trace no connexion with Yahweh, however remote; and it is open to conjecture that this tribe may not have embraced the worship of Yahweh until their migration to the north and forcible appropriation of Micah's *sacra* and his Yahweh-priest, whose worth had been proved for them by the oracle indicating the success of their undertaking. If the interpretation of *ch.* 18 5 suggested in the *note ad loc.* is correct, the Danite spies do not ask for an oracle *from Yahweh* in the first place, but from the Teraphim (*'ĕlōhîm*); and it is the latter which returns the answer as from Yahweh. As to Gad, the god of Fortune, in relation to Yahweh we can affirm nothing.

§ Contrast the statement with regard to Ephraim (*ch.* 1 29), from which we learn that, though this tribe 'did not dispossess the Cana'anites that dwelt in Gezer,' yet 'the Cana'anites dwelt in the midst of Ephraim,' and not *vice-versâ*.

|| Steuernagel (*Die Einwanderung der israelitischen Stämme in Kanaan*, pp. 28 f.) has suggested with some plausibility that, since Naphtali and Dan were originally one tribe (Bilhah), and Dan at first dwelt south-west of Ephraim, Naphtali's earliest home was probably in the same neighbourhood, and he, like Dan, eventually had to seek a new home further north. Thus, in the statement of Judg. 1 33 that 'Naphtali did not dispossess the inhabitants of Beth-shemesh and Beth-'anath,' the reference may be to the *southern* Beth-shemesh ('Ain-šems). The mention of these two cities in the north in Josh. 19 38 P is then a later assumption based on the fact that Naphtali later on occupied a northern position. This view gains some support from the blessing of Naphtali in Deut. 33 23—'Possess thou the Sea and the South' (ים ודרום ירשה). Here Naphtali (according to Steuernagel) appears, like Dan, to

Not merely the four handmaid-tribes, however, but probably also some of the tribes which were reckoned as full members of the Israelite confederacy, may be conjectured to have taken no part in the historical Exodus. The northern tribe Zebulun stands in J's narrative (*ch.* 1 [30]) on much the same footing as the handmaid-tribes Asher, Naphtali, and Dan; *i.e.* so far as the information offered us is concerned, he is *there* in Canaʿan maintaining a precarious footing among the Canaʿanites, and nothing is told us as to how he *came to be* there. Another northern tribe, Issachar, is unmentioned in the document as we know it; and the same is true of the trans-Jordanic Re'uben. In fact, the only tribes of which the J writer records *conquests* fall into two groups: (1) Judah and Simeʿon, and (2) the house of Jośeph. We have found reason to believe that the conquests of the first group took place not under Joshuaʿ from the east of Jordan, but by a northward move from Ḳadesh-Barneaʿ. The house of Jośeph, on the other hand, is explicitly connected with Joshuaʿ in the part of the narrative which now stands in Josh. 15 [14. 18]; and there are indications which suggest that the southern campaign as described by JE in Josh.—viz. the conquest of Jericho, ʿAi, and Bethel, and the defeat of the Amorite league at the descent of Beth-ḥoron—was really carried out by these Jośeph-tribes under Joshuaʿ's leadership, and not by united Israel (cf. 1 [22] *notes*).

It is clear that the tradition which connects the Jośeph-tribes with Egypt is primitive and authentic. Whether they were the only tribes which suffered under Egyptian bondage and were delivered by Moses is a further question. We find in early times certain Israelite or related clans dwelling in the south of the Negeb close to the borders of Egypt. These are the north Arabian clans which ultimately went to form the tribe of Judah (Ḳenites, Jeraḥme'elites, etc.; cf. p. 45); the remnant of Simeʿon which, after a tribal disaster in central Canaʿan, appears to have sought a home in the extreme south, in the neighbourhood of the Judah-clans (cf. *ch.* 1 [3] *note*); and probably the remnant of Levi—as we may conjecture from the early association of this tribe with Simeʿon in the raid on Shechem with its disastrous results, and from its subsequent association chiefly with the tribe of Judah (cf. *Addit. note*, pp. 436 ff.). Whether any of these Israelite clans crossed the frontier into Egypt we cannot say for certain; but considering the comparatively hard conditions of existence in the region south of the Negeb, and the readiness with which permission

be hard-pressed by foes, and the wish is expressed for him that he may exert his power and conquer the Philistine maritime plain (*yām*) and the *dārôm*, *i.e.* the Shephelah, which is so designated in late Jewish usage (cf. Neubauer. *Géographie du Talmud*, pp. 62 f.; Buhl., *Geogr.* p. 85, and references to Daroma in *OS.*, where we find cities such as Eleutheropolis, 'Anab, Eshtemoaʿ, and Ṣiḳlag assigned to the region). On the ordinary assumption that Naphtali is here pictured as occupying his final northern position, 'sea' is explained as the sea of Galilee; but no commentator has succeeded in offering a plausible explanation of *dārôm*.

to pass into the region of Goshen (the Wâdy Ṭûmîlât) was granted by Egyptian kings of the Empire-period to similar tribes when impelled by stress of famine,* it is highly probable that they may have crossed and recrossed on more than one occasion—as often in fact as the pinch of hunger compelled them to seek a more fertile pasture-land, or the return of favourable seasons lured them back to the nomadic life to which they were accustomed. Evidence that Sime'on was in Egypt at the period of the oppression may perhaps be found in the Joseph-story, according to which Sime'on is the brother selected to be bound and retained as a hostage (Gen. 42 [24.36] E). That Levi, at least in part, was also there, seems to follow with the acceptance of the traditional view of the identity of the earlier secular tribe with the later priestly body (the view maintained in *Addit. note*, p. 436), since Moses was a Levite, and the Egyptian names borne by him and by Phineḥas offer valid evidence both for the historical existence of the bearers and for their Egyptian connexions (cf. *ch.* 20 [28] *note*, and *footnote*). Tradition is clear that some of the elements which subsequently went to form the tribe of Judah (*e.g.* the Ḳenites) were not in Egypt but in the wilderness (Midian); though it is conceivable that other elements of the tribe may have taken part in the Exodus. In any case there is good reason to believe that the Joseph- and Judah-groups were associated at Ḳadesh-Barnea' for a considerable period, and together came under the influence and teaching of Moses (cf. *Addit. note*, pp. 439 f.).

Another point, which for our purpose it is important to notice, is the fact that the O.T. traditions represent the migration of Israel's ancestors from their early home in the east westward into Cana'an, not as a single movement completed in a short space of time, but as a series of movements extending over a very considerable period. Assuming (as we are bound to do) that these early traditions deal in the main with the movements of *tribes* under the guise of individuals,‡ the earliest of these tribal move-

Cf. the inscriptions mentioned on p. 439, *footnote* *.

‡ The explanation of individuals as personified tribes, and of their doings as tribal movements, which is in fact forced upon us in regard to much that is related in the patriarchal narratives (cf., as typical instances, the accounts of Abraham's descendants by his second wife, Ḳeṭurah, Gen. 25 [1ff.], and of the relations of Ja'cob's 'sons' with Shechem, Gen. 34), must of course not be pressed to account for every detail in the stories; since some elements may possibly be due to the admixture of reminiscences as to actual individuals (tribal leaders, etc.), and a good deal in the setting of the stories (especially of those which are most picturesque and lifelike) undoubtedly belongs to the art of the story-teller. The literature which deals with this subject is endless. It is sufficient here to refer to the Introduction to Skinner's *Genesis* (*ICC.*), pp. iii-xxxii, and to Kittel, *GVI.*² i. pp. 386-455, as offering markedly sane and judicious estimates of the character of the Genesis-narratives. Guthe (*Gesch. des Volkes Isr.* pp. 1-6) lays down canons for the interpretation of the narratives in their historical reference to tribal movements which are helpful so long as the qualifications above suggested are borne in mind.

ments is represented by the journey of Abraham (Abram) and his nephew Lot from Ḫarran into southern Canaʿan—a movement which tradition regarded as responsible for the formation of the different divisions of the 'Hebrew' race, Jaʿcob, Edom, Moab, and ʿAmmon, not to mention various Arabian tribal groups to whom Israel acknowledged a relation more or less remote. Now the tradition embodied in Gen. 14 makes Abraham contemporary with Ḫammurabi (Amraphel), dating him therefore *cir.* B.C. 2100. The traces of lunar worship in early Hebrew religion centre primarily round the Abraham-tradition, and undoubtedly connect Abraham with Ur and Ḫarran, and with the First Dynasty period (cf. the facts cited in *Addit. note*, pp. 249 ff.). Whether, therefore, we regard Abraham as an historical clan-chieftain or as the ideal personification of the clan itself, there is good ground for believing in the historical truth of a Semitic clan-movement at this period from Ur to Ḫarran, and thence to southern Canaʿan (Be'er-shebaʿ). And since, as we have seen (pp. lxxxi, lxxxiii), there were Ḫabiru in Babylonia as early as the time of Ḫammurabi and Rîm-Sin, it is reasonable to conclude that this migration was (as the O.T. tradition represents it) the beginning of the Hebrew westward movement—itself but a part of the larger Aramaean movement which indisputably continued during a period of many centuries.

A subsequent accession from the east seems to be represented by the arrival of the Aramaean tribe Rebeḳah, who, by union with Isaac, Abraham's 'son,' produces the two tribal groups. ʿEsau-Edom and Jaʿcob. These for a while dwell together in southern Canaʿan, until the hostile pressure of the former compels the latter to cross the Jordan in the direction of his ancestral home, where, in course of time, he unites with fresh Aramaean elements (Jaʿcob's wives). Ultimately the whole tribal body thus formed moves once more towards Canaʿan, impelled as it appears by the westward pressure of other Aramaeans (the pursuit of Laban), with whom eventually a friendly treaty is formed, fixing the tribal boundary at or near Miṣpah in Gileʿad.* When this Hebrew group, thus modified by fresh accessions, once more enters Canaʿan, it no longer bears the common name of Jaʿcob, but is known as Israel.‡

We may now observe that this tribal interpretation of early Israelite traditions—taken in broad outline *as they stand*, and with-

* Cf., for the interpretation of early tradition embodied in this paragraph, Steuernagel, *Die Einwanderung der israelitischen Stämme in Kanaan* (1901), §§ 6 ff. Steuernagel's book is a far-seeing and suggestive examination of early Israelite tradition which merits careful study.

‡ It is possible, as Steuernagel assumes, that the Le'ah- and Zilpah-tribes may have been in Canaʿan earlier than the Bilhah- and Jaʿcob-Rachel-tribes, and, coming subsequently to be regarded as 'brothers' of the latter, were not unnaturally traced back to a common 'father.' Thus, owing to priority of settlement, Le'ah comes to be regarded as the earlier wife, while Rachel is the more closely united and better-loved wife. Cf. *op. cit.* p. 54.

out any shuffling or rearrangement to fit in with a preconceived theory—offers us a chronological solution of most of the facts derived from extra-Biblical evidence (pp. ciii f.) which seem to have a bearing upon the history of Israel's ancestors. If the Hebrew immigration into Cana'an represented by Abraham really took place as early as *cir.* B.C. 2100, it is natural that a tribe called Ja'cob, descended from Abraham, should have given its name to a site Ja'cob-el in southern or central Cana'an by B.C. 1479.* And if the Ja'cob-tribe, having again crossed the Jordan eastward, returned to Cana'an at a later period increased by fresh Aramaean accessions, this may well have been in process of happening, *cir.* B.C. 1375, when, as we know from the T.A. Letters, an Aramaean people called Ḫabiru were pressing into Cana'an, and gradually gaining a footing there upon a semi-nomadic basis (*i.e.* transitional between the nomadic and the settled stage), much as Ja'cob-Israel and his 'sons' are represented in Gen. as doing.‡ The fact that Ja'cob, in making his westward migration, is pressed by the Aramaean Laban agrees with the T.A. presentation of the Ḫabiru-movement as of a part with a widespread Aramaean movement as represented by the SA.GAZ and the Sutû; and the seizure of the district of Shechem by the Ḫabiru (cf. p. lxxiii) may well be identified with the events of which we have an echo in Gen. 34, 48$^{21.22}$. Indeed, the latter passage can hardly be explained except upon the assumption that the Shechem-district, which eventually came in post-Exodus times to form part of the possession of the Joseph-tribes, had been captured at an earlier period by another section of Israel. Finally, the allusion to *Israel* as a people in Cana'an in the reign of Mineptah, *cir.* B.C. 1223, agrees with the Biblical tradition that Ja'cob on his second entry into Cana'an assumed the new name Israel. If it be merely a coincidence that prior to the Ḫabiru-invasion we have external evidence for Ja'cob in Cana'an, while subsequently to it we have like evidence for Israel, it is certainly a remarkable one.

A further question upon which we have not yet touched concerns the period at which the Joseph-tribes broke off from the rest of Israel and migrated to Egypt. It has commonly been

* The name Ja'cob (*Ya'^{a}ḳōb*), like Isaac (*Yiṣḥāḳ*), Joseph, etc., is a verbal form implying the elision of -*'ēl*, 'God,' as subject of the verb. Cf. the personal and place-name *Yiphtāḥ* (Judg. 11^{1} ff., Josh. 15^{43}) with the place-name *Yiphtaḥ'ēl* (Josh. 19^{14,27}), and the place-name *Yabneh* (2 Chr. 26^{6})=*Yabn^{e}'ēl* (Josh. 15^{11}). Other examples of tribal-names thus formed are *Yisrā'ēl* and *Yišmā'ēl* (but probably not *Y^{e}raḥm^{e}'ēl*; cf. p. 252). Other place-names so formed are *Yizr^{e}'ēl*, *Y^{e}ḳabṣ^{e}'ēl* (Neh, 11^{25}=*Ḳabṣ^{e}'ēl*, Josh. 15^{21}, 2 Sam. 23^{20}) *Yoḳth^{e}'ēl* (Josh. 15^{38}, 2 Kgs. 14^{7}), *Yirp^{e}'ēl* (Josh. 18^{27}). On the transference of tribal names to places or districts, cf. Burch. ii. p. 84. The West Semitic names *Yaḫḳub-el*, *Yaḳub-el* (without expression of ע, which is represented in the first example by *ḫ*), *Yaḳubum* (hypocoristic, exactly like Ja'cob) occur in early Bab. documents; though we cannot be quite sure of their equivalence to Ja'cob, since the syllable *ḳub* may also stand for *ḳup*, *kub*, *kup*. Cf. Ranke as cited by Gressmann, *ZATW*. xxx. (1910), p. 6.

‡ Cf. Kit. *GVI.*^{2} i. p. 410.

assumed that this must have taken place during the Hyksos domination. This conclusion is based partly upon the assumption that the entry of Semitic tribes into Egypt would have been most likely to have occurred under the Hyksos, who were themselves in all probability Asiatic Semites; partly upon the fact that the duration of Israel's sojourn in Egypt, as given in Ex. 12 [40] P, viz. 430 years, if reckoned backward from the probable date of the Exodus in the reign of Mineptah—say, from B.C. 1220, gives B.C. 1650 as the date of entry, which falls well within the Hyksos-period, whether we adopt the long or the short scheme of reckoning that period (cf. p. lxvi). If, however, we are correct in identifying the immigration of Israel and his 'sons' into Canaʿan with the invasion of the Ḫabiru, *cir.* B.C. 1400, and if, again, it is the fact that the O.T. traditions preserve a substantially correct recollection of the *order* of events (as we gathered from our preceding discussion), then it appears that Joseph did not break off from his brethren and go down into Egypt until *after* the Ḫabiru-invasion, *i.e.* perhaps two centuries after the expulsion of the Hyksos by Aḥmosi I., the founder of the Eighteenth Dynasty. It is remarkable, indeed, that if the Pharaoh under whom Joseph is represented as rising to power was a member of the Hyksos-dynasty, the 'new king, who knew not Joseph' (Ex. 1[8]), and instituted an era of oppressive measures in order to check the increase of Israel, is found, not in Aḥmosi I., who expelled the hated Semitic invaders, but in Raʿmesse II. of the Nineteenth Dynasty, nearly 300 years later. The Biblical estimate of 430 years for the duration of the sojourn in Egypt belongs to the latest stratum of the narrative, and is clearly bound up with a purely artificial system of calculation (cf. p. cxvi). A different tradition is preserved in the 𝕲 text of the passage, where the addition of the words καὶ ἐν γῇ Χαναανmakes the 430 years include the whole patriarchal period as well as the sojourn in Egypt; and since on the Biblical reckoning the former lasted 215 years, the latter is therefore reduced to a like period. This reckoning would give us B.C. 1435 as the date of the entry, *i.e.* during the reign of Amenḥotp II.

Increasing knowledge of the history of Egypt during the Empire proves beyond a doubt that the period of the Eighteenth Dynasty, from the reign of Ṭḥutmosi III. onwards, when Canaʿan was a province of Egypt and the intercourse between the two countries was (as we learn from the T.A. Letters) close and constant, is in all respects suited to the condition of affairs which, according to the Genesis-tradition, brought about the entry of Israel's ancestors into Egypt. The Egyptian inscription noticed on p. 439 *footnote*, in which Asiatic refugees crave, and receive, admission into Egypt,* belongs either to the reign of Ḥaremḥeb or to that of one of the successors of Aḫnaton under whom Ḥaremḥeb held the position of

* Cf. Breasted, *AR.* iii. §§ 10 ff.

general. Here the Asiatics beg the Pharaoh to grant them a home within the border of Egypt 'after the manner of your fathers' fathers since the beginning'—a statement which indicates that it had long been customary for the Pharaohs to grant such admission. Under Amenḥotp III., when the power and luxury of the Empire were at their height, the development of trade between Syria and Egypt left its mark upon the Egyptian language through the introduction of a large Semitic vocabulary.* The Semitic population of Egypt must have been considerable, partly drawn thither by trade and partly as slaves, the captives of Asiatic campaigns. 'As this host of foreigners intermarried with the natives, the large infusion of strange blood made itself felt in a new and composite type of face, if we may trust the artists of the day.'‡ Some of these Semitic foreigners rose to important positions of trust and authority in the state. Such were Dûdu and Yanḫamu, two high officials bearing Semitic names who are often mentioned in the T.A. Letters.§ Indeed, the position of the latter, who was high commissioner over Yarimuta, a great corn-growing district,‖ offers several points of analogy to the position of Joseph as pictured in Gen., and he has been thought with some plausibility to be the historical figure round whom the story of Joseph's rise to power in

* Cf. Breasted, *Hist. Eg.* p. 337.

‡ Cf. Breasted, *Hist. Eg.* p. 339.

§ On the name Dûdu, cf. p. 291. Yanḫamu may stand for ינעם, which is known as a Sabean proper name: cf. Weber in Kn. p. 1171.

‖ Yarimuta was reached by sea from Gebal, and thence the Gebalites imported the necessities of life, especially corn, for which, when reduced to straits, they were obliged to barter their sons and daughters, and the furniture of their houses (a fact which reminds us of Gen. 47 [18ff.]): cf. references given by Weber in Kn. p. 1153. The view that Yarimuta lay in the Delta, and was possibly identical with the land of Goshen, is favoured by Niebuhr in *MVAG.*, 1896, 4, pp. 34-36; W. M. Müller in *MVAG.*, 1897, 3, pp. 27 f.; Weber in Kn. p. 1153; Dhorme, *RB.*, 1909, p. 370; Hall, *NE.* p. 346. If, however, it is the same as Yarmuti in 'the upper land' to which Sargon of Akkad lays claim in the inscription recently published by Poebel (cf. p. lv, *footnote* ¶), it can hardly have lain in the Nile-Delta, but must be sought upon the Syrian seaboard. Poebel suggests 'the plain of Antioch, along the lower course and at the mouth of the Orontes river' (*op. cit.* pp. 225 f.). The resemblance of the Biblical name ירמות Yarmuth is striking; and so is that of the Benjaminite clan-name ירימות Yᵉrîmôth or Yᵉrêmôth. The former was a Cana'anite city of some importance (associated with Jerusalem, Ḥebron, etc., in Josh. 10 [3.5.23] JE), and situated in the Shephelah (Josh. 15 [35] P)—a fact which would seem to exclude comparison with the maritime Yarimuta, unless (as is not impossible) the name was extended to denote not merely the city but the southern maritime plain which afterwards belonged to the Philistines, and which was, and still is, an excellent corn-growing country: cf. the description of it by Eshmun'azar, king of Ṣidon (quoted on p. 387, *footnote* *), which suggests that Ṣidon was dependent upon the district for its corn-supply. Whether, however, Yarimuta actually lay within the borders of Egypt or not, the fact that Yanḫamu was constantly in Egypt and in close touch with the Pharaoh as a high official of the court remains undoubted: cf. the conspectus of allusions to him given by Weber in Kn. pp. 1169 ff.

Egypt was constructed.* If, then, we may assume that the entry of the Joseph-tribes into Egypt took place during the flourishing period of the Empire,‡ it is likely that the change of policy under Ra'messe II., which led him to take measures to oppress and to check the increase of the Hebrews, may have been dictated by the fact that the loss of Egypt's hold upon her Asiatic empire, which resulted from the weakness of Aḫnaton and his successors, tended to make the presence of a considerable body of Semitic aliens upon the north-east border of Egypt a menace to the safety of the state.§

While, however, our theory places the entry of the Joseph-tribe into Egypt considerably later than the Hyksos-period, this does not forbid the view that earlier ancestors of Israel may have been in Egypt with the Hyksos. If Abraham represents a Hebrew migration to Cana'an some centuries before the Hyksos-invasion of Egypt, and if this invasion was a southward movement of the people of Amurru (cf. p. lxvi), it seems not at all unlikely that some of Israel's ancestors, who (as tradition informs us) occupied southern Cana'an,

* Cf. J. Marquart, *Chronologische Untersuchungen* (*Philologus Zeitschr. für das class. Alterthum: Supplementband* vii. 1899), pp. 677-680; Winckler, *Abraham als Babylonier, Joseph als Ägypter* (1903), p. 31; Cheyne in *EB.* 2593; Jeremias, *OTLAE.* ii. pp. 72 ff.; Weber in Kn. p. 1171.

‡ Evidence does not allow of our fixing a more exact date. We naturally infer that it was after the invasion of Cana'an by the Ḫabiru had begun, if this is rightly identified with the entry of the tribes of Israel into that country; but the T.A. Letters, though they show us this invasion in full flow, afford no evidence as to the date at which it began. The theory that the people (marked as foreigners by a Determinative) called '*Apuriu* or '*Apriu* in Egyptian inscriptions were the Hebrews, which was first advanced by Chabas (*Mélanges Égyptologiques*, I. Ser., 1862, pp. 42-55; II. Ser., 1864, pp. 108-165), accepted by Ebers (*Aegypten und die Bücher Mose's*, 1868, p. 316; *Durch Gosen zum Sinai*², 1881, pp. 505 f.), and then generally contested and rejected by Egyptologists, has been revived by Hommel (*AHT.* p. 259), and supported with strong arguments by Heyes (*Bibel und Ägypten*, 1904, pp. 146-158), and is regarded as plausible by Skinner (*Genesis* (*ICC.*), pp. 218 f.). Driver, *Exodus* (*Camb. Bib.*) pp. xli f.), and other Biblical scholars; though among modern Egyptologists Maspero (*Mêlées*, p. 443, *n*³; *Contes populaires*, p. 119, *n.*³) and Breasted (*AR.* iv. § 281, *n*ᵉ) definitely reject it, while W. M. Müller (*EB.* 1243) more guardedly refuses to decide either for or against it. The chief objection to the identification seems to be found in the representation of Heb. *b* by Eg. *p*; but that this interchange, though rare, does actually occur is proved by Heyes (cf. *op. cit.* p. 148; his best instance is Eg. *ḫurpu* = Heb. *ḥérebh*, 'sword'): cf. also Burch. § 50. The '*Apuriu* find mention in inscriptions ranging from the reign of Thutmosi III. to that of Ra'messe IV. (*cir.* B.C. 1167): thus, if they were really the Hebrews, the inference must be that some Hebrews (not necessarily *Israelites*) remained behind in Egypt after the Exodus. Cf. the discussion by Kit. (*GVI.*² i. p. 453, *n*²), who concludes that, though they may have been Hebrews in the wider sense, they can hardly have been Israelites. The inscriptions picture them as performing (like the Hebrews of Ex. 1 ¹¹ᶠᶠ·) heavy manual labour in connexion with the building operations of the Pharaohs, especially the quarrying and transportation of stone. Driver (*op. cit.*) gives a convenient conspectus of the passages in which they are mentioned.

§ Cf. Spiegelberg, *Der Aufenthalt Israels in Aegypten* (1904), pp. 35 ff.

may have been implicated in it. The tradition of Gen. 12^{10-20} J, which brings Abraham and his wife and followers to Egypt in time of famine, looks not unlike an echo of the Hyksos-period; and the way in which the patriarch is represented as escorted out of the land may not impossibly amount to the placing of the best interpretation upon a dismissal which may really have been an expulsion —possibly based on a vague recollection of the actual expulsion of the Hyksos by Aḫmosi I. If this is so, it is not impossible that the Hyksos-chieftain Jaʿcob-el may have been a representative of the Jaʿcob-tribe.

Thus the only extra-Biblical allusion to Israel's ancestors for which, on our interpretation of the Biblical tradition, we fail to find an explanation is the supposed occurrence of Jošeph-el as a place-name in Canaʿan, *cir.* B.C. 1479; since, on our theory, the Jošeph-tribe can scarcely have been in Canaʿan at this date. The interpretation of *Y-š-p-'â-rạ* as Jošeph-el is, however, as we have noticed (p. lxviii), of very doubtful validity.

The view which makes Raʿmesse II. the Pharaoh of the oppression, and Mineptaḥ, or one of his immediate successors, the Pharaoh of the Exodus, though favoured by the majority of scholars, is not universally accepted. The fact is certainly remarkable that, if we take the Biblical scheme of computation as it stands, and adding 480 years to B.C. 967 (which is fixed with approximate certainty for the fourth year of Solomon: cf. p. liii, *footnote*), in accordance with the statement of 1 Kgs. 6^1 R^P, obtain B.C. 1447 (in the reign of Amenḥotp II.) as the date of the Exodus; then add 430 years for Israel's residence in Egypt (cf. Ex. 12^{40} P), and obtain B.C. 1877 (in the Hyksos-period according to Petrie's longer scheme of chronology, though earlier according to Breasted and Hall) for the entry into Egypt; then add 215 years for the Patriarchal period (according to Gen. 12^{4b}, 21^5, 25^{26b}, 47^{9a}, all P*), and obtain B.C. 2092 for Abraham's departure from Ḫarran; this last date falls within the reign of Ḫammurabi (*cir.* B.C. 2123-2081) in accordance with the tradition of Gen. 14. Thus Hommel ‡ adopts the reign of Amenḥotp II. for the Exodus.

It should not, however, escape our notice that the one fact which makes this computation remarkable is the approximate correctness of the exterior dates, viz. that 1125 years appear accurately to represent the period from a date in Ḫammurabi's reign to a date in Solomon's reign. This is probably not the result of accident, but may well be due to the fact that a Jewish chronologist living in Babylon during the exile may easily have obtained from Baby-

* According to this scheme Abraham is seventy-five on his departure from Ḫarran, and one hundred at the birth of Isaac; Isaac is sixty at the birth of Jaʿcob, and Jaʿcob is one hundred and thirty when he enters Egypt with his sons.

‡ *ET.* x. (1899), pp. 210 ff. Hommel assigns in each case a date nine years later than those given above. Orr, *Problem of the Old Testament* (1908), pp. 422-424, adopts the conclusions of Hommel.

lonian sources the figure which represented the period from Ḫammurabi to his own day.* This, however, argues nothing for the correctness of the sectional periods within the external limits. The back-reckoning to Solomon is of course based upon the (approximately correct) chronology of Kgs.; but the Babylonians could supply no information as to the date of the Exodus, or of Israel's entry into Egypt, or of the lives of the patriarchs. As we have seen (§ 5) in discussing the period assigned in 1 Kgs. 6 [1] for the Exodus to the fourth year of Solomon, 480 years is a purely artificial computation, based on the theory of twelve generations of forty years each, and worked out within the period by the use of suspiciously recurrent periods of forty years. If, however, we cannot find even an approximately historical basis for the Biblical chronology of *this* period, why should we pin our faith to the correctness of the earlier periods given for Israel's sojourn in Egypt (based, apparently, on the assumption of four generations of one hundred years each!‡), and for the lives of the patriarchs? The reign of Amenḥotp II., when Egypt's hold upon her Asiatic empire was at its strongest immediately after the victorious reign of Ṭhutmosi III., may well be thought to be the least probable period for the Exodus and settlement in Cana'an by force of arms.

Another view as to the date of the Exodus is represented by Hall (*NE.*, pp. 403 ff.), who attempts to revive the theory of Josephus (*C. Ap.* I. 14) by connecting the Exodus with the expulsion of the Hyksos; and further supposes that the aggressions of the Ḫabiru, as we read of them in the T.A. Letters, are identical with the invasion of Cana'an by the Israelites under the leadership of Joshua'. This theory is obliged to do great violence to the Biblical tradition; for not only are the circumstances of Aḥmosi's expulsion of the Hyksos widely different from the Biblical account of the Exodus, but, in order to dispose of the inference (based on Ex. 1 [11]) that Ra'messe II. was the Pharaoh of the oppression, the names Pithom and Ra'amsēs have to be explained as 'the interpretations of a scribe who knew their names as those of Egyptian cities which existed in his time in and near the land of Goshen' (p. 405), and, to bridge the interval between Aḥmosi I. and Amenḥotp III., the 'forty' years in the wilderness (probably intended to represent the length of a generation §) have to be expanded to nearly two hundred years (p. 408), and thus the possibility of a real historical connexion between Joshua' and Moses is necessarily excluded. On the identification of Joshua''s conquests with the Ḫabiru-invasion we cannot, as Hall confesses (p. 410), identify any of the persons mentioned in the one source with those who are mentioned

* The care and accuracy with which the Babylonians preserved their chronological data, even back to the earliest period of their history, are familiar facts. Cf. Rogers, *HBA.*[6] i. pp. 470 ff.

‡ Cf. Driver, *Exodus* (*Camb. Bib.*), p. xlv, and notes on 6 [27], 12 [40].

§ Cf Num. 14 [26-35] JEP, 32 [13] P, Deut. 2 [14], and the remarks on p. liv.

in the other.* The question whether the character of the Ḫabiru-aggressions closely resembles the Biblical narrative of Israel's doings as depicted in Josh. must be largely a matter of individual opinion. In the view of the present writer the position of Ḫabiru and SA.GAZ in Cana'an is more nearly analogous to that of the floating, semi-nomadic population which has at all times formed a feature of Palestine—a population living at peace with the settled inhabitants of cities and villages when the country is under a strong government, though even then ever ready to seize the opportunity for blackmail and petty aggression; but a really dangerous element when affairs are unsettled and the government is weak or non-existent, and without scruple as regards selling their services for warfare and intrigue to the highest bidder. Such a relation towards the Cana'anites—normally peaceful, but sometimes aggres-

* Orr (*The Problem of the Old Testament*, pp. 423 f.) likewise holds that the invasion of the Ḫabiru 'synchronises very closely with the conquest of Cana'an by the Israelites,' and finds in this 'a coincidence of much importance.' It is curious that this writer, whose book is a defence of the historical character of the O.T. against the attacks of criticism (cf. especially *ch.* iii.), and who rightly (in the opinion of the present writer) objects to the sweeping statement of Kuenen that 'the description of the Exodus from Egypt, the wandering in the desert, and partition of Canaan . . . to put it in a word, are *utterly unhistorical*' (cf. p. 57), should fail to observe that the identification of the Ḫabiru-invasion with that of Israel at once cuts at the roots of the historical character of the old narratives in Josh. Comparison of the names of Cana'anite kings in Josh. and the T.A. Letters, where we have information from both sources, yields the following result:—

	Book of Josh.	*T.A. Letters.*
Jerusalem	Adoni-ṣedeḳ (10^3)	ARAD-Ḫiba (Kn. 285 ff.).
Lachish	Yaphia' (10^3)	Yabni-el (Kn. 328). Zimrida (Kn. 329).
Gezer	Horam (10^{33})	Yapaḫi (Kn. 297 ff.).
Ḥaṣor	Yabin (11^1)	Abdi-Tirši (Kn. 228).

Here, since the T.A. names, as derived from actual contemporary letters, must necessarily be correct, the Biblical names, if referred to identically the same period, are *ipso facto* declared to be false; and if this is the fact with every name which can be tested, what ground have we left for holding that any names, or indeed any facts, mentioned in the Biblical account of the conquest of Cana'an are of the slightest historical value? The only supposed historical *gain* arising from identification of the Ḫabiru-invasion with the conquests of Joshua', is that it fits in well enough with the late Biblical scheme of chronology which we have already discussed (p. cxv); yet, while we can attach a real historical value to an ancient narrative in which the main outline (*i.e.* as concerns names, scenes, and actions) appears to be approximately true to fact, even though chronological data are lacking (as in J and E upon the view which we maintain), it is difficult to see what importance can be attached to the maintenance of a chronological scheme which (on the test of external evidence) at once wrecks the historical character of the narratives to which it is applied. To do Dr. Orr justice, it is probable that he did not realize the further implications of his argument as they are here pointed out; yet, if this is so, what is the value of an argument which, basing itself upon the supposed identity between two sets of circumstances as pictured in Biblical and extra-Biblical sources, neglects so obvious a precaution as the comparison of the names of some of the principal actors?

sive—appears more nearly to correspond to the position of Israel in Canaʿan in patriarchal times (cf. for the aggressive side, Gen. 34), than to the invasion of the Joseph-tribes under Joshuaʿ which, when we have made all allowance for the exaggerations of R^D, was still a definitely organized campaign of conquest. In any case, since, as we have seen (cf. pp. lxxv ff.), it is impossible to separate the Ḫabiru from the SA.GAZ, or to deny that the former were, at least to a large extent, identical with the latter, the Ḫabiru-invasion must have extended over a far wider (more northerly) area than did Israel's career of conquest even as interpreted by the later editors of the old narratives in Josh.

The outstanding advantage which seems to accrue from Hall's theory of the Exodus, as also from that of Hommel, is that we gain a far longer period for the course of events from the Exodus to the fourth year of Solomon, for which, as we have seen, the late author of 1 Kgs. 6^1 assigns 480 years, but which, if we place the Exodus under Mineptaḥ, cannot really have covered much more than 250 years (cf. p. liii). Considering, however, the facts noticed on pp liii f., no valid reason can be advanced in proof that a longer period than 250 years is required. On the other hand, supposing that we identify Joshuaʿ's conquest of Canaʿan with the Ḫabiru-invasion, we are faced by the very real difficulty that the Syrian campaigns of Sety I. (which dealt primarily with the Ḫabiru-aggressions; cf. p. lxxxviii), Raʿmesse II., Mineptaḥ (who actually defeated *Israel*), and Raʿmesse III. all fall within the period of the Judges; yet, while much is told us in Judg. of the aggressions of comparatively petty antagonists, not a word is said as to any collision with the great power of Egypt. Such an omission, which, on the theory of the Exodus which we adopt, is an argument from silence which may be taken to favour the general authenticity of the narratives of Judg. (cf. p. cii), must surely be deemed very strange if we are to throw Israel's occupation of Canaʿan under Joshuaʿ back to the period of the T.A. Letters.

§ 7. The Permanent Religious Value of Judges.

The religious value of any O.T. Book may be considered under a twofold aspect—(1) its place in the record of Revelation, *i.e.* the historical evidence which it affords as to the evolutionary process through which the religion of Israel attained its full growth; and (2) the extent to which its teaching is fitted to awaken a response in the human conscience of to-day. The value of the first aspect may be defined as *evidential*; that of the second as *spiritual*. Both these aspects are to be discerned in most of the O.T. writings; though it goes without saying that each aspect is not equally prominent in all. Without doubt the Prophetic writings exhibit the fullest combination of the two aspects, invaluable as they are, both as marking stages in the development of Israel's religion, and also as making a direct appeal, whether it be to the collective or to the individual conscience, which can never become obsolete.

It should not, however, escape our notice that here there exists some amount of interaction between the two aspects. The spiritual value of the teaching of the Prophets has (as the outcome of modern critical study of the O.T. Scriptures) been greatly enhanced through the understanding of the circumstances of the times which called it forth, and of the relation which it bears to earlier thought.

In other parts of the O.T. literature we observe the one aspect greatly predominating over the other. Thus, *e.g.* a very large number of the Psalms, owing to an entire absence of historical allusions or any similar criteria of date, are difficult to place in their historical, or even in their logical, position in the line of religious development; yet at the same time their abiding spiritual worth, as evidenced by the manner in which they *touch* men's souls to-day, causing them to vibrate in spiritual sympathy, and voicing their highest and deepest aspirations in relation to God, is as great as that of any part of the O.T. Conversely, some portions of the historical literature—and perhaps most markedly the Book of Judges—are insignificant in their direct spiritual value as compared with the Prophets and the Psalms; yet their importance for the understanding of the historical evolution of Israel is unique.

Taking the O.T. as a whole, however, we notice, in part as compared with part, the same kind of interaction between the two aspects of religious value as we observed especially in the Prophetic writings when considered by themselves. The Psalm which voices the most inward feelings of Christian faith, invaluable as it is in itself, attains an enhanced value when the fact is clearly recognized that it is the product of a stage in a long line of religious development, for the tracing of which the historical books, as analysed and understood by modern critical methods, are of prime importance. For the question is at once raised how, out of beginnings exhibiting elements that are crude, primitive, and it may be even repulsive, there can have sprung to being thoughts and aspirations which, as the expression of all that we understand by *Religion*, have never been surpassed; and the only possible answer is found in the recognition of an inward Principle of Divine Inspiration, guiding and determining the course of Israel's religious evolution. Conversely, such a record of Israel's early history as the Book of Judges, which, taken by itself, might (so far as its religious aspect is concerned) be deemed to possess a value not much deeper than that represented by the interests of the anthropologist or student of comparative mythology, becomes, in the light of that which O.T. Religion *taken as a whole* has produced (*e.g.* the level of faith and practice represented by the Prophets and Psalms), of deep, if not of vital, importance for the study of the antecedents of historical and practical Christianity.

(1) The value of Judg. for the history of Israel's social and religious evolution is obvious. The Book covers a period of transition from the unsettled and disintegrated tribal life to the more or less organized federation of tribes on the way to be moulded into a nation. The extent of the disintegration of the tribal units which afterwards went to form the nation can only be gathered from Judg., and would hardly be realized by us if we only possessed the records contained in the Pentateuch and Josh. in the form in which they have come down to us. We see the tribes acting to a large extent independently of their fellows, settling down as best they could in the midst of an alien population, which for the most part they seem to have been unable to subdue, adopting forms of religious cultus which were coloured by the beliefs and practices of their heathen neighbours, if not identical with them. When, however, a period of oppression at the hands of a foreign foe and of desperate misfortune supervenes, the man whom the crisis produces as leader and deliverer, and who at least in some cases (witness the Song of Deborah) succeeds in rousing the scattered tribes to such a measure of common action as foreshadows the later unity of Israel as a nation, acts in the name and at the instigation, not of some local Canaʿanite or Israelite Baʿal, but of Yahweh, the warrior-God whose ancient seat was found, not within Canaʿan, but at Mount Ṣinai in the desert-region of Seʿir, external to the land of Israel's settlement (cf. *ch.* 5 [4]).

Here, then, are raised problems which press for solution before we can attain any really satisfactory grasp of the development of the early religion of Israel. How did Yahweh, whose earlier sphere of influence appears to have been conceived as extraneous to the land of Canaʿan, come to be regarded as asserting and maintaining His influence over Israel, and in Israel's favour, when the tribes were settled in the land of their inheritance? What was there in Yahweh's character and claim which enabled Him at times of special crisis to exercise a *unifying* influence over the scattered and somewhat heterogeneous elements out of which the nation of Israel was eventually produced? How was it that, when evidence points to the recognition of 'gods many and lords many,' and that not merely among the earlier Canaʿanite inhabitants, but among the tribes of Israel themselves, in spite of all, the worship of Yahweh, fostered apparently by crisis and misfortune, emerged as the dominant religion, and came (amid such unpromising surroundings) to be of the lofty spiritual and ethical character which we find exemplified in the Prophetical writings of the eighth century B.C. and onwards? Biblical history, as we know it, claims to supply answers to these questions. A special Providence, a chosen people, a unique Revelation made at an early period in the history of the race to a leader and teacher endowed with exceptional qualifications for his office—these are factors which tradition pictures as guiding and determining the evolution; and however much modern scientific study may modify our conceptions of the *process*, it will be found that, apart from the recognition of such factors, the history of Israel's religious development remains an insoluble enigma.

(2) While, however, it is true that there is nothing in Judg. which makes a direct spiritual appeal to men's consciences at the present day at all comparable to that which is made by the teaching of the later Prophets, the fact must not be overlooked that the book is placed in the Hebrew Canon among 'the Former Prophets,' and occupies this position because it is history written with a purpose, and that purpose a religious one (cf. § 1). This religious purpose stands out very prominently in the main redactor's philosophy of history, according to which neglect of Yahweh's ordinances and the worship of strange gods lead to punishment, but true repentance is followed by a renewal of the Divine favour. The fact that God deals with nations in accordance with their regard or disregard for His moral laws offers a lesson the emphasizing of which can never become superfluous, especially at such a crisis as that through which the world is passing at the present time (1918). If it be objected that the editor of Judg. is reading into past history the standpoint of his own much later time, and drawing conclusions as to Yahweh's moral government which could not have been drawn by Israel in the time of the Judges, it may be replied, firstly, that the lesson as deduced by the editor would remain for the instruction of subsequent ages, fortified by the teaching of the later Prophets and of our Lord Himself, as well as by the experience of history, even if the historical data upon which it is based were only susceptible of such an interpretation in the light of more developed experience of Yahweh's moral dealings with His people; but, secondly, that it is by no means certain (in view of what has been said above on the personality of Moses and his inculcation of ethical Yahwism as of the nature of historical postulates in the evolution of Israel's religion) that at any rate some part of Israel (*e.g.* those, such as the Joseph-tribes, who had incontestably come under the influence of Moses) were unconscious that, in rejecting Yahweh and following the Baʿals and the ʿAshtarts, they were lapsing from a higher form of religion to a lower, and infringing the covenant into which Israel had entered with Yahweh as the outcome of the signal deliverance from Egypt, and the events which immediately followed it. It should be noticed that the doctrine of sin, chastisement, repentance, and salvation is not confined to the main redactor's pragmatic setting, but is worked out and emphasized by the lessons of past history in portions of the book which belong to the later school of E—*ch.* $6^{7\text{-}10}$, $10^{6\text{-}16}$, and in parts of 1 Sam. which seem to emanate from the same hand, and doubtless originally belonged to the same connected work—1 Sam. $7^{2\text{-}14}$, $8^{7.8}$, $10^{18.19a}$, $12^{1\text{-}25}$. These passages,

as we have already noticed (§ 4), are closely connected in thought with the formulæ of R^{E2}, and seem to have supplied their model.

If we go back to the most ancient parts of the narrative, we find the utmost emphasis laid upon the fact that the Judges act in the Divine strength which inspires and supports them, enabling them to gain the victory against odds which, from the human point of view, might seem to be insuperable. It is Yahweh who commissions them either by a prophetic message (4^{6}) or by a Self-manifestation ($6^{11ff.}$, $13^{3ff.}$), who promises His presence and support ($6^{14.16}$), and vouchsafes special signs in confirmation of His promise ($6^{17ff.36ff.}$, $13^{19ff.}$). His Spirit 'comes upon' them (11^{29}; cf. 3^{10} R^{E2}), or 'clothes itself in' them (6^{34}), or 'rushes upon' them ($14^{6.19}$, 15^{14}), or strengthens them in answer to prayer ($15^{18.19}$, $16^{28ff.}$). He goes forth before His host in the visible manifestations of nature ($5^{4.5}$; cf. 4^{14}), discomfits (4^{15}) and gives into their hands their foes (3^{28}, $6^{9.15}$, $8^{3.7}$, 11^{30}, 12^{3}; with 'before me' in place of 'into my hand,' 11^{9}), and gives them victory (15^{18}).

It is this fact that the achievements of the Judges were wrought in reliance upon the Divine guidance and power which impresses the writer of the Epistle to the Hebrews, and enables him to regard them as the heroes of Faith:—'the time will fail me if I tell of Gideʿon, Baraḳ, Samson, Jephthaḥ; . . . who through faith subdued kingdoms, . . . from weakness were made strong, waxed mighty in war, turned to flight armies of aliens' (Heb. 11^{32-34}). Without inquiring too closely into the ethical character of this 'faith' as viewed from the Christian standpoint, it is sufficient for us to reflect that it fulfilled, in relation to the age which produced it, the function which is fulfilled by the quality as we understand it at the present in the full light of Revelation; and thus we are still able to number these ancient heroes among the 'great cloud of witnesses' whose example and inspiration may help us to 'run with patience the race that is set before us.'

§ 8. Hebrew Text and Ancient Versions.

Hebrew Text. If we except the Song of Deborah, the Heb. Text ($\mathfrak{H}$) of Judg. may be said to be well preserved, being comparable in this respect with the narrative-portions of Josh. and Kgs., and superior to Sam. Such corruptions as occur are due to the ordinary causes which have affected the Heb. Text of the O.T. as a whole, and a rough classification of them may be not without value for the purposes of textual criticism; though the fact must be borne in mind that, from the nature of the subject, anything like an exhaustive and well-defined classification is out of the question. Reference is made throughout to the pages of the Commentary where the points in question are discussed.

1. *Alteration.*

Confusion of letters:—ב for כ‡, pp. 122, 136; ב for מ, p. 114; ד for ב*, pp. 123, 149, 486; ד for מ, p. 231; ד for ר*, pp. 39, 119, 225, 428, 434; ה for י*, pp. 212, 383, 461; ה for יו‡, pp. 479, 485; ה for ש, p. 366; ו for כ*, p. 157; ו for ת, p. 62; ט for מ‡, p. 112; י for ו‡, pp. 122, 123, 131, 186, 273; כ for ו*, p. 388, 483; ל for ג, p. 156; ל for מ, p. 122; ל for ת, p. 226; מ for א, p. 364; מ for ב, p. 390; מ for ל, p. 123; נ for ד, p. 419; נ for ל*, p. 328; נ for ת, p. 115; ס for ם‡, p. 232; ס for ר, p. 365; ע for ש, p. 233; פ for ג*, p. 112; צ for כ, p. 212; צ for נ (or ץ for ון‡), p. 435; צ for ע‡, p. 282 (cf. p. 207); צ for פ, p. 366; צ for ק, p. 128; ר for ד,*, pp. 33, 219, 365 (cf. pp. 65, 122); ר for ק, p. 217; ת for א*, p. 281 (cf. p. 325); ת for ל, p. 319.

Here the examples marked * are most likely to have arisen in the ancient script, and those marked ‡ in the square script. Many examples, however, can hardly be explained as due to similarity, and may have arisen from such an accident as the obliteration or illegibility of a letter, combined with the influence of the context in determining what the original word in which it occurs may have been. Such a case is no doubt to be seen in the substitution of ד for original מ in החריד for החרים, ch. 8^{12}.

Transposition of letters:—pp. 33, 119, 120, 128, 129, 133, 225, 312, 326, 491 (cf. p. 208).

Transposition of clauses:—pp. 102, 120, 124, 210, 387, 417.

Confusion of similar words and forms:—pp. 65, 74, 119, 129, 132, 227, 228, 277, 279, 280, 323, 361, 429, 459, 463, 471, 474, 478, 479, 480, 484, 485.

Substitution through propinquity:—pp. 137 (יששכר for נפתלי), 369 (בקמות for בשדות), 376 (הלילה for היום), 474 (שבטי for שבט).

Wrong division (a) of words:—pp. 119 f., 136, 150, 230, 474, 484; (*b*) *of sentences:*—p. 130.

Error due to the use of abbreviation in writing:—pp. 119 f., 123 f., 129, 149, 150, 307, 466.

Error in vocalization:—pp. 90, 93, 114, 120, 130, 147, 152 f., 188, 230, 278, 287, 316, 317, 326, 334, 372, 488, 492, 493.

Grammatical solecisms:—Masc. for Fem., pp. 93, 321, 493 (cf. p. 129); Fem. for Masc., p. 383 *bis*, 463; Sing. for Plur., pp. 226, 229, 463, 474, 492; Plur. for Sing., pp. 61, 68, 285, 287, 310, 347, 348, 480, 483; False Tense, pp. 73, 214, 383, 483.

Intentional perversion:—pp. 5, 58, 64, 65 f., 228, 434, 461 (cf. p. 32).

2. *Insertion.*

Dittography (a) of words:—pp. 61, 225, 475, 482 (cf. p. 68); (*b*) *of letters:*—pp. 90, 114, 316, 470, 482 (cf. p. 35).

Doublets:—pp. 57, 130, 139, 232, 327, 350, 351 f., 415, 423 f., 474, 485.

Other marginal notes inserted in the text:—pp. 113, 350, 382, 415, 428 (cf. p. 484).

Insertions explicative of an already corrupt text:—pp. 148, 151, 327, 366, 470.

Unclassified:—pp. 142, 152, 273.

3. *Omission.*

Homoeoteleuton:—pp. 380, 470.

Haplography of letters:—pp. 282, 472.

Unclassified omissions (*a*) *of single words or parts of words:*—pp. 17, 205, 319, 326, 369, 427 f., 473; (*b*) *of sentences or parts of sentences:*—pp. 22, 38, 140, 209, 490.

The Septuagint. The fact has long been remarked that in the 𝔊 version of Judg. the uncial MSS. A and B exhibit a divergency which is without parallel in any other part of the O.T., and which raises the question whether they should not be ranked as two distinct translations from the Hebrew. The learned Septuagint scholar J. E. Grabe, writing in 1705 to Dr. John Mill, Principal of St. Edmund Hall, Oxford, deals with the subject of this divergency, remarking 'Omnibus mediocriter tantum Graecae linguae peritis primo intuitu patet Vaticano et Alexandrino codice duas diversas dicti libri versiones, vel saltem duas editiones saepissime ac multum inter se discrepantes contineri.' This *Epistola ad Millium*, which runs to 56 quarto pages, aims at establishing the fact that Cod. A represents the genuine 𝔊 text; while Cod. B offers the recension of Hesychius, which, as we know from the often-quoted statement of Jerome, was current in Egypt at the time when he wrote. Whatever view be taken as to Grabe's conclusions, the fact can hardly be disputed that he raised a very genuine problem when he emphasized the divergency of A and B in Judg.—a problem which calls for serious consideration before 𝔊 can satisfactorily be employed for the elucidation of the text of the book.

The divergency between the two 𝔊 versions of Judg. was most thoroughly exemplified by P. de Lagarde in his *Septuaginta Studien*, Erster Theil, 1891, in which he printed the two texts of *chs.* 1-5 on opposite pages, thus exhibiting their variation in as striking a manner as possible. Lagarde did not rest content with reproducing merely the texts of the two uncials A and B. Together with A he grouped the Aldine and Complutensian editions, the five cursive MSS. which appear in the notation of HP. as 108, 19, 54, 118, and 29, and the Armenian (Arm.), Old Latin (𝔏), and Syro-hexaplaric ($𝔖^h$) versions. With B he associated the text of the Sixtine edition, the *Codex Musei Britannici Add.* 20,002, the *Catena Nicephori*, and the short extant fragments of the Sahidic and Bohairic versions. Lagarde printed the texts of A and B *in extenso*, and recorded in footnotes the variants which are found in his other authorities for each respective version of the 𝔊 text.

Professor Moore, in the course of his studies in preparation for his Commentary on Judg., had reached independently the same conclusions as Lagarde in a paper read before the *Society of Biblical Literature* in May 1890; and when his Commentary appeared in 1895 he offered an enriched conspectus of the MS. and other authorities which represent each version respectively. His summary conclusion as to the 𝔊 versions is as follows:—'I say versions; for Lagarde has demonstrated in the most conclusive way, by printing them face to face through five chapters, that we have two Greek translations of Judges. It would probably be going too far to say that they are independent; the author of the younger of them may have known and used the older; but it is certain that his work is not a recension or revision of his predecessor's, but a new translation.'*

The editors of the Larger Edition of the Cambridge Septuagint, Messrs. Brooke and M'Lean, have decided that it would be impossible to present the textual evidence for the 𝔊 text of Judg. clearly if the text of B alone were taken as a standard, the readings of MSS. which contain the A recension being treated as variants. They are therefore proposing to follow the plan inaugurated by Lagarde, and to print the text of A and B on opposite pages.‡ Pending the preparation of this edition, they have published (1897) a trustworthy edition of the text of A in Judg. which forms the most available source for purposes of collation. The *primâ facie* conclusion of these scholars as to the relationship of the two versions is as follows:—'No final verdict can as yet be pronounced, but a preliminary investigation of the earlier chapters leads to the surmise that the true text of the Septuagint is probably contained neither in the one nor in the other exclusively, but must

* Moore's notation is as follows:—

1. Older 𝔊 version: Uncials:
   - $𝔊^{A}$ = *Cod. Alexandrinus.*
   - $𝔊^{P}$ (or $𝔊^{Cs}$ in *SBOT.*) = *Cod. Coislianus* = HP. X.
   - $𝔊^{V}$ (or $𝔊^{Bs}$ in *SBOT.*) = *Cod. Basiliano-Vaticanus* = HP. XI.
   - $𝔊^{S}$ ($𝔊^{Sr}$ in *SBOT.*(= *Cod. Sarravianus* = HP. IV, V.

   Cursives in three groups:
   - $𝔊^{L}$ = HP. 19, 108, 118, the Complutensian Polyglot, and Lagarde's *Libr. V. T. Canon. pars prior*, 1883 (cf. p. cxxvi).
   - $𝔊^{M}$ (or $𝔊^{Lp}$ in *SBOT.*) = HP. 54, 59, 75, 82, and the fragments of a Leipzig uncial palimpsest.
   - $𝔊^{O}$ (or $𝔊^{Vn}$ in *SBOT.*) = HP. 120, 121, and the Aldine edition (Venice, 1518).
2. Younger 𝔊 version: Uncials:
   - $𝔊^{B}$ (or $𝔊^{V}$ in *SBOT.*) = *Cod. Vaticanus.*
   - $𝔊^{G}$ (or $𝔊^{Bm}$ in *SBOT.*) = *Cod. Mus. Brit.* 20, 002.

   Cursives:
   - $𝔊^{N}$ = HP. 16, 30, 52, 53, 58, 63, 77, 85, 131, 144, 209, 236, 237, and the text printed in the *Catena Nicephori* (Leipzig, 1773).

‡ Since the above was written, the part containing Judges has appeared (1917). The editors have not carried out their original intention, but have printed the text of B in full, and have given prominence to the variant readings of the A-text by the use of Clarendon type.

be sought for by comparing in detail, verse by verse, and word by word, the two recensions, in the light of all other available evidence, and especially of the extant remains of the Hexapla.'

So much may suffice to illustrate the stage at which the question of the two 𝔊 texts of Judg. has arrived at the present time. We may now proceed to statement of the main results which seem to accrue from examination of the two texts.

The outstanding fact is that the text of Cod. A, together with other members of the same family as noted by Lagarde and Moore, is really identical with that text of 𝔊 which Lagarde has, with high probability, argued to be the recension which was the work of Lucian, the presbyter and martyr of Antioch—a recension which Jerome states to have been current in Constantinople and Asia Minor, as far west as Antioch.

The stages by which the recovery of Lucian's recension was effected were as follows. Vercellone, in his *Variae Lectiones Vulgatae Latinae Bibliorum Editionis*, Tom. ii. (1864), p. 436, had remarked that the four 𝔊 MSS. which appear in HP. notation as 19, 82, 93, and 108 exhibited a text which very frequently coincided with the extant remains of 𝔏; and that this is also the case with the 𝔊 text of the Complutensian Polyglot, which has been shown to be based substantially upon HP.108. When Wellhausen published his *Text der Bücher Samuelis* (1871), he commented on the fact that the same four MSS. frequently offered readings which are intrinsically more probable than those contained in Cod. B. Ceriani in 1863 had suggested (*Hexapla*, p. lxxxvii) that the recension of Lucian was contained in these MSS.; but it was not till 1883 that Lagarde published his *Librorum Veteris Testamenti Canonicorum, pars prior*, containing the 𝔊 text of the O.T. from Genesis to Esther based upon these four MSS. with the addition of HP. 118. In his preface to this work the editor pointed to the numerous agreements between the readings of these five MSS. and the Biblical quotations of St. Chrysostom, who, since he was a priest of Antioch and bishop of Constantinople, may be presumed to have made use of that recension of 𝔊 which was current in Antioch and Constantinople, viz., as Jerome informs us, the recension of Lucian.

Of the five MSS. upon which Lagarde bases his text of Lucian, 118 is complete for Judg., while 19 and 108 exhibit considerable lacunae. 82, which is also available for Judg., is placed by Moore in another group of the A version family, which he distinguishes by the signature $𝔊^{M}$. We have already noticed that the three Codd. 19, 108, and 118 are cited by Lagarde for his A group in *Septuaginta Studien*, together with the Complutensian (based upon 108), and 𝔏, the correspondence of which with Lucian's recension in the other historical books has been noted.*

* Cf. the examples cited by Driver for Samuel in *NHTS.*² pp. lxxvii-lxxx and by the present writer for Kings in *NHTK.* pp. xxxvi-xl.

Adequate discussion of the characteristics of the two 𝔊 versions and their relation one to the other demands a separate treatise. It is only possible here to state summarily the conclusions which seem to result from comparison of the two texts.

1. They are distinct translations, in the sense that each presupposes the independent use of a Heb. original.

2. The two Heb. originals, while possessing much in common which differentiated them from ℌ, yet varied in many important particulars. That used by 𝔊^{B} was the nearer to ℌ. That used by 𝔊^{AL} exhibited many readings which possess the stamp of originality.*

3. Though the two 𝔊 texts may be classed as distinct translations in the sense above specified, they exhibit identities in rendering which cannot be the result of chance, and which indicate that the younger translation (whichever that may have been) was made by the aid of reference to the older.

4. Both translations, and perhaps especially that represented by 𝔊^{AL}, have been extensively worked over, and contain many doublets.

The *Vulgate* (𝔙), *Peshiṭtâ* (𝔖^{P}), and *Targum* (𝔗) are of but slight critical value as compared with the two 𝔊 texts, since all represent recensions of the original Heb. much more closely akin to ℌ; and their main importance lies in the early traditions of interpretation which they embody. The principal characteristics of these versions may be gathered from modern works and articles (such as those of *DB.*) which deal with the textual criticism of the O.T., and need not be noticed here. It is worth while, however, in the case of 𝔖^{P}—a version of which we possess no authoritative critical text, and of the origin of which little is known—to point out certain affinities with other versions which are apparent in the text of Judges.

1. Affinities with 𝔊 are fairly frequent, especially with the version represented by 𝔊^{AL}.‡

2^{1}. אעלה וג׳. 𝔖^{P} prefixes ܘܗܟܢܐ ܐܡܪ ܡܪܝܐ. Cf. 𝔊^{B} *τάδε λέγει κύριος*.

5^{8}. אז לחם שערים. 𝔖^{P} ܘܗܘܝܢ ܠܚܡܐ ܕܣܥܪܐ. Cf. 𝔊^{AL} *ὡς ἄρτον κρίθινον*, 𝔏 'velut panem hordeaceum,' 𝔖^{h} ܐܝܟ ܕܠܠܚܡܐ ܕܣܥܪܐ.

* This version (as represented by 𝔊^{AL}, 𝔖^{h}, 𝔏) preserves superior readings to ℌ and to 𝔊^{B} in the following passages in Judg.:—$5^{4.14}$, $7^{5.6}$, 8^{4}, 10^{11}, $11^{20.34}$, $12^{2.3}$, 13^{23}, $14^{11.19}$, 15^{6}, $16^{19.24}$, 17^{3}, $19^{2.3.30}$, $20^{15.33}$. In 5^{12}, $11^{26.35}$, 18^{16}, 16^{25}, 18^{9} the readings of the version have claims to consideration, though they are not actually adopted in the present commentary Cf. *notes ad loc.*

‡ The same phenomenon has been noted in the 𝔖^{P} text of Sam. by Driver, *NHTS.*^{2} p. lxxi, and in that of Kgs. by the present writer in *NHTK.* p. xxxii. In citations from 𝔖^{P} the text of Walton's Polyglot has been collated with that of Ceriani's facsimile of the Codex Ambrosianus.

5^{11}. פרזונו. 𝔖^{P} ܕܐܣܓܝ 'which he multiplied.' Cf. 𝔊^{B} *αὔξησον*.

7^{5}. At end of verse 𝔖^{P} adds ܐܩܝܡܝܘܗܝ ܐܒܪܝܐ (תציג אותו לבד). So 𝔊^{AL}, 𝔖^{h}.

7^{22}. ובכל המחנה. 𝔖^{P} omits ו, with 𝔊^{B}, 𝔏^{L}.

9^{48}. הקרדמות. 𝔖^{P} ܢܪܓܐ (הקרדם). So 𝔊^{AL}, 𝔖^{h}, 𝔙.

10^{1}. בן דודו. 𝔖^{P} ܒܪ ܕܕܗ (understanding דודו to mean 'his uncle'). Cf. 𝔊 *υἱὸς πατραδέλφου αὐτοῦ*, 𝔙 'patrui Abimelech.'

10^{11}. 𝔖^{P} agrees with 𝔊^{AL}, 𝔖^{h}, 𝔏^{L}, 𝔙 in omitting מן and taking list of nations as subj. of לחצו.

10^{34}. ממנו. 𝔖^{P} ܠܒܪ ܡܢܗ (ממנה). So 𝔊^{AL}, 𝔖^{h}.

11^{35}. 𝔖^{P} sides with 𝔊^{B}, 𝔙 (cf. *note ad loc.*).

12^{3}. כי אינך מושיע. 𝔖^{P} ܕܠܝܬ ܡܢ ܕܦܪܘܩ ܠܟ (כי אין מושיע). So 𝔊^{AL}, 𝔖^{h}.

14^{3}. עמי. 𝔖^{P} ܒܥܡܟ (עמך). So 𝔊^{L}.

14^{7}. וירד וידבר. 𝔖^{P} ܘܢܚܬܘ ܘܡܠܠܘ. So 𝔊 *καὶ κατέβησαν καὶ ἐλάλησαν*.

14^{15}. השביעי. 𝔖^{P} ܪܒܝܥܝܐ (הרביעי). So 𝔊^{BA}, 𝔏^{L}.

15^{3}. עמם. 𝔖^{P} ܒܥܡܟܘܢ (עמכם). So 𝔊^{AL}, 𝔙.

15^{6}. ואת אביה. 𝔖^{P} ܘܠܒܝܬ ܐܒܘܗ (ואת בית אביה). So ℌ$^{MSS.}$, 𝔊^{AL}, 𝔖^{h}.

20^{16a}. 𝔖^{P} omits מכל העם . . . בחור with 𝔊, 𝔙.

2. There are clear instances of affinity with 𝔗—and this of a character which is not to be explained merely by the fact that both versions are Aramaic, or by the probability that both may have been influenced by a similar Jewish tradition of exegesis, but which suggests actual connexion between the two.*

3^{3}, *al.* סרני. 𝔖^{P} ܛܘܪܢܐ. 𝔗 טורני.

3^{19}. דבר סתר לי אליך המלך. 𝔖^{P} ܡܠܬܐ ܕܟܣܝܬܐ ܐܝܬ ܠܝ ܠܡܐܡܪ ܠܟ ܡܠܟܐ. 𝔗 פתגמא דסתרא אית לי למללא עמך מלכא.

3^{25}. ויחילו עד בוש. 𝔖^{P} ܘܟܬܪܘ ܣܓܝ. 𝔗 ואוריכו עד סגי.

5^{25}. בספל אדירים. 𝔖^{P} ܒܣܦܠܐ ܕܓܢܒܪ̈ܐ. 𝔗 בפילי גבריא.

5^{28}. רכבו. 𝔖^{P} ܡܪܟܒܬܗ ܕܒܪܝ. 𝔗 רתיכוהי דסיסרא ברי.

6^{26}. במערכה. 𝔖^{P} ܒܣܕܪܐ. 𝔗 בסדרא.

7^{18}. ליהוה ולגדעון. 𝔖^{P} ܚܪܒܐ ܠܡܪܝܐ ܘܠܓܕܥܘܢ. 𝔗 חרבא מן קדם יי ונצחניא על ידי גדעון.

18^{6}. נכח י׳ דרככם. 𝔖^{P} ܡܪܝܐ ܢܬܩܢ ܐܘܪܚܟܘܢ. 𝔗 אתקין יי אורחכון.

20^{48}. מעיר מתים. 𝔖^{P} ܘܡܕܝܢ̈ܬܐ ܐܢܫ ܡܢ ܩܘܪ̈ܝܐ. 𝔗 מקרויהון גמרינין.

* Cf. for Sam. *NHTS.*^{2} pp. lxxi f. and for Kgs. *NHTK.* pp. xxxiv f.

THE BOOK OF JUDGES

I. 1–2. 5. *Survey of Israel's settlement in Cana'an.*

Besides the Commentaries, etc., cited throughout the book, cf. Eduard Meyer, *Kritik der Berichte über die Eroberung Palaestinas*, *ZATW.* i. (1881), pp. 117-146; L. B. Paton, *Israel's Conquest of Canaan*, *JBL.* xxxii. (1913), pp. 1-53.

This section was added by a post-exilic editor of the Priestly school of thought (R^P) as a fresh introduction to his new edition of the history of the Judges. The introduction is composed in the main of extracts culled from the old Judaean document (J) of the ninth century B.C. J's narrative originally gave an account of the first settlement of the tribes of Israel in Cana'an, describing the gradual and partial manner in which it was effected. Extracts from the same narrative are found in the Book of Joshua', several of them being parallel to passages in Judg. 1, and, where not identical in wording, appearing in a more original form. Thus Josh. 15 [14-19] = Judg. 1 [20.10b (in part). 11-15]; Josh. 15 [63] = Judg. 1 [21]; Josh. 16 [10] = Judg. 1 [29]; Josh. 17 [11-13] = Judg. 1 [27.28]. Further extracts from the same narrative, not contained in Judg. 1, are found in Josh. 13 [13], 17 [14-18], 19 [47], and probably in Num. 32 [39.41.42]. The original form of J's narrative of the settlement in Cana'an has been very skilfully reconstructed by Bu.: cf. *Additional note*, p. 47.

The reason why the old narrative of J did not appear in full in Josh. doubtless was that, as picturing the settlement in Cana'an as the work of individual tribes, and as only very partially effected, it conflicted with the view taken by the Deuteronomic editor (R^D) of JE in Josh., according to which practically the whole of the promised land, with the exception of the maritime plain, was summarily conquered by all Israel in a series of campaigns under the leadership of Joshua'; and was even more sharply opposed to the presentation of affairs as given by the Priestly writer (P) in Josh., which makes the accurate delimitation of the conquered territory among the twelve tribes to have been settled by Joshua' after the conquest. Cf. further *Introd.* pp. xxxiv f.

In utilizing J's matter for his introduction to Judges, R^P regards it as referring, not to the first settlement in Cana'an, but to the outcome of events 'after the death of Joshua'' (*v.* [1]). Thus, in order to illustrate (from his point of view) the slackness of Israel in failing to carry out what they *might* have accomplished in obedience to Yahweh's command, he alters in several passages J's statement that they '*could not* dispossess' the Cana'anites into '*did not* dispossess.' So in *vv.* 21.27 as compared with the parallel passages in Josh.; and doubtless also in *v.* 19 (cf. *note*). R^P also adds statements with regard to the conquest of Jerusalem (*v.* 8) and the Philistine cities (*v.* 18) which actually conflict with statements from J which he incorporates (*vv.* 21.19). Cf. further *notes* following.

The standpoint of *ch.* 2 1-5 is clearly that of R^P. The severe censure of Israel as a whole on the ground that they have *wilfully* neglected Yahweh's command by failure to extirpate the inhabitants of Cana'an is of a piece (Bu. *RS.* p. 20) with the deliberate alteration of 'could not dispossess' into 'did not dispossess' noticed above. The representation of the tribes of Israel as apparently assembled in one body at Bethel (cf. *note* on 2 1) is at variance with the narrative of J in *ch.* 1, which represents them as scattered throughout the land, and each making its own settlement as best it could. The speech which is put into the mouth of the Angel of Yahweh appears to be a free composition by R^P, based upon reminiscence of passages in the Pentateuch and Josh. (cf. *notes ad loc.*). Wellh., however, is doubtless correct in recognizing (*Comp.*[3] p. 210) that in *vv.* 1a.5b we have genuine fragments of the old narrative of J, describing the removal of the religious centre of Israel from Gilgal to Bethel after the conquest of the latter city by the house of Joseph, as narrated in 1 22 ff.

The purpose of R^P's introduction is to explain the unsettled condition of affairs as related in the narrative of Judges, by the addition of details known to him which had not been incorporated by the main editor (R^{E2}) in *his* introduction, *ch.* 2 6-3 6.

The following words and phrases are to be noticed as characteristic of J:—'the Cana'anites,' as a general term for the inhabitants of Palestine, 1 1 (see *note*); 'the Cana'anites and the Perizzites' coupled, 1 5 (*note*); 'at the first' (בתחלה), 1 1; 'deal kindly with' (lit. 'do kindness with,' עשה חסד עם), 1 24; 'dependencies' (lit. 'daughters,' בנות), 1 27, five times; 'and it came to pass, when' (ויהי כי), 1 28; 'dwelt in the midst of' (ישב בקרב), 1 29.30.32.33; 'prevailed' (lit. 'was heavy,' כבד), 1 35; 'the Angel of Yahweh' (מלאך יהוה), 2 1.(4). Cf. CH^J.

I. 1. R^P Now after the death of Joshua', J the children of

1, 1. *after the death of Joshua'.* As related in Josh. 24 29.30 (E). R^P assumes that he is taking up the history from the point reached in the closing chapter of Josh. The proper continuation of Josh. 24 is found, however, in R^{E2}'s introduction to Judg., contained in *ch.* 2 6ff., where *vv.* 6-9 are nearly verbally identical with Josh. 24 28.31.29.30. So far from dealing with events which happened subsequently to Joshua's death, the old narrative of J pictures Israel as still at Gilgal (2 1), or

Israel enquired of Yahweh, saying, 'Who shall go up for us first against the Canaʿanites to fight against them?' 2. And Yahweh said, 'Judah shall go up: behold, I have given the land into his hand.' 3. And Judah said to Simeʿon his brother, 'Go up with me into my lot, that we may fight against the Canaʿanites,

close by at Jericho (1 [16]), shortly after the passage of the Jordan and before the tribes had entered upon their inheritances.

the children of Israel enquired, etc. Literally translated, *v.* [1] runs, 'And it came to pass, after the death of Joshuaʿ, and the children of Israel enquired, etc.', the use of 'and' to introduce the sentence to which the time-determination refers being idiomatic in Hebrew. Thus, apart from R^{P}'s note of time, the sentence is to be rendered, 'And the children, etc.' This may have formed the commencement of J's narrative of the tribal conquests: cf. *Additional note*, p. 47.

enquired of Yahweh. The reference doubtless is to consultation of the oracle by means of the sacred lot; cf. the use of the phrase in 1 Sam. 14 [37], 22 [10], 23 [2], 30 [8], etc. This lot was cast by means of Urim and Tummim, as appears from the undoubtedly original form of 1 Sam. 14 [41], preserved by 𝔊. Here Saul's address to Yahweh runs, 'O Yahweh, God of Israel, wherefore hast thou not answered thy servant to-day? If this iniquity be in me, or in Jonathan my son, O Yahweh, God of Israel, give Urim; but if it be in thy people Israel, give Tummim.' Cf. also 1 Sam. 28 [6]. Thus Urim and Tummim were apparently two concrete objects employed in connexion with the Ephod. Cf. 1 Sam. 14 [18], where $𝔊^{BL}$ preserves the true reading 'Ephod' in place of 'Ark of God' in 𝔐. On the nature of the Ephod, cf. *note* on *ch.* 8 [27].

Who shall go up. From the Jordan valley, which is the point of departure in *v.* [16], into the hill-country to the west. The expression *ʿālā* 'go up' is used, however, in a general way of a military expedition. Cf. *ch.* 12 [3], 18 [9], 1 Sam. 7 [7], Isa. 36 [10], *al.*

against the Canaʿanites. The use of 'Canaʿanite' as a general term to describe the inhabitants of the country west of Jordan is characteristic of J; while E uses 'Amorite' in the same general sense. When greater accuracy is deemed desirable, the Canaʿanites are defined as the dwellers in the lowlands, *i.e.* the maritime plain and the Jordan valley, and the Amorites as inhabitants of the hill-country which lies between. So in Num. 13 [29] (prob. R^{JE}), Josh. 11 [3] (R^{D}); cf. Deut. 1 [7.19.20], Josh. 5 [1], 13 [3.4] (both R^{D}). The inhabitants of the mountain-range east of Jordan and north of the Arnon are described as Amorites by E and by writers influenced by this source (R^{JE} and school of D). Upon the evidence as to the use of the terms from extraneous sources, cf. *Additional note*, p. 41.

3. *into my lot.* J, like E and R^{D} and P in Josh., doubtless represented the partition of Canaʿan among the tribes of Israel as decided

and I also will go up with thee into thy lot.' So Sime'on went with him. 4. R[P] And Judah went up; and Yahweh gave the Cana'anites and the Perizzites into their hand; and they smote them in Bezeḳ—ten thousand men. 5. J And they came upon

by lot under the direction of Joshua'. Cf. *Introd.* p. cv. The position and (ideal) extent of Judah's 'lot' is described in Josh. 15 [1-12] P. It was bounded on the east by the Dead Sea and on the west by the Mediterranean, while the northern border ran from the Jordan near its junction with the Dead Sea, and passing close to the south of Jerusalem (which fell within the territory of Benjamin), terminated at the Mediterranean near Jabne'el (Yebnâ). The southern border is noticed under *v.* [36] 'from the Crag.'

So Sime'on went with him. The cities assigned to Sime'on in Josh. 19 [1-8] (P) fall within the territory of Judah; and most, if not all, of them are reckoned to Judah in Josh. 15 [26-32.42] (P). The tribe of Sime'on seems to have been very small. The story of Gen. 34 (J and P combined) probably reflects an early attempt made by this tribe and the tribe of Levi (*Additional note*, p. 437) to settle in central Palestine; when an attack made upon the Cana'anite city of Shechem, in violation of friendly treaty, provoked (as we may infer from Gen. 49 [7] J) such reprisals on the part of the Cana'anites as decimated the aggressors and caused the dispersion of the remnant of their clans to seek a settlement in other parts of the land. As to when this Shechem-incident may have occurred, cf. *Additional note*, pp. 437 ff. In the so-called 'Blessing of Moses,' Deut. 33 (E), dated by Driver (*Deut.*, *ICC.*, p. 387) either shortly after the rupture under Jerobo'am I., or during the middle and prosperous part of the reign of Jerobo'am II. (*c.* 780 B.C.), Sime'on is not mentioned at all; unless we follow the suggestion of 𝔊[AL] in *v.* [6b], and read, 'and let Sime'on be few in number' (שמעון for מתיו. The rendering πολὺς ἐν ἀριθμῷ rests on a false interpretation of מספר as implying a *large* number).

4. The verse seems to be a summary statement by R[P] of the result of the campaign, based upon the information afforded by J in the following verses.

5. *And they came upon Adoni-bezeḳ in Bezeḳ.* The name Adoni-bezeḳ is open to grave suspicion, since nowhere else do we find a Hebrew proper name which describes a man as 'lord' of his city or country. The form of name which we should expect as a compound of Adoni is 'such and such a deity is lord': cf. Adonijah, 'Yah *or* Yahweh is lord,' Adoniram, 'the High one is lord,' and in Phoenician Adoni-eshmun, 'Eshmun is lord,' etc. It is conceivable that Bezeḳ may have been the name of a local Cana'anite deity; but such a deity is otherwise quite unknown, and it is scarcely possible that the city should bear the name of the deity, without some such prefix as Beth, 'house of' (cf. Beth-'anath, Beth-dagon). Moreover, no city

Adoni-bezeḳ in Bezeḳ, and they fought against him, and smote

named Bezeḳ in southern Palestine is mentioned elsewhere in the O. T.; and the Bezeḳ of 1 Sam. 11 [8] (the modern Ḫirbet Ibzîḳ, seventeen miles N.N.E. of Nâblus on the road to Bêsân) cannot be the place intended, since Judah and Simeʿon are represented as moving in a westerly or south-westerly direction from Jericho (*v.* [16]), into the territory allotted to Judah. A site Ḫirbet Bezḳeh, six miles S.E. of Lydda, has been advocated by Conder (*SWP. Mem.* iii. 36), but this seems too far to the west to have been the scene of action.

The mention of Jerusalem in *v.* [7], as the city to which the king was taken, apparently by his own followers (cf. *note*), after his mutilation by the Judaeans, makes it probable that we have here to do with Adoni-ṣedeḳ, king of Jerusalem, who is named in Josh. 10 [1] (E) as the head of the confederacy against Joshuaʿ in southern Palestine; in which case we would seem to have an account of his fate different from that given by E in Josh. 10 [22] ff. The view that, in Adoni-ṣedeḳ, Ṣedeḳ is the name of a Canaʿanite deity is plausible, but the evidence is inconclusive. Cf. *Additional note*, p. 41. Adoni-ṣedeḳ may denote 'my lord is righteous' (lit. 'is righteousness'; in accordance with the common substitution of substantive for adjective in Heb.), or 'lord of righteousness.'

If Adoni-ṣedeḳ be the original form of the name in our passage, the form Adoni-bezeḳ, unless merely due to accidental corruption, is probably an intentional perversion made by a late scribe in order to cast ridicule upon the name of a heathen deity. Ṣedeḳ, either the deity's name, or ascribing 'righteousness' to the heathen divine 'lord,' is changed into *bezeḳ*, a word unknown to us in Heb., but very likely existing with the meaning 'pebble' or small 'fragment' of stone, as in Syr. *bezḳâ*, Aram. *bizḳā*, perhaps in jesting allusion to the material and helpless idol: cf. Hab. 2 [19], where the idol is described as a 'dumb stone.' Such perversion of the title of a heathen deity is most probably seen in Baal-zebub, 'lord of flies,' 2 Kgs. 1 [2.3.6.16], for an original Baal-zebul (cf. Βεελζεβουλ, Mk. 3 [22] and parallels, Matt. 10 [25]), 'lord of the mansion' (temple, or heavenly abode; applied to Yahweh's abode in 1 Kgs. 8 [13], Isa. 63 [15]: cf. Cheyne in *EB.* col. 407 f.); and in the substitution of *bōšeth*, 'shameful thing,' for Baʿal where it occurs in proper names, as in Ishbosheth in 2 Sam. 2 [8], etc., for Eshbaʿal, 1 Chr. 8 [33], 9 [39], and in other cases: cf. the present editor's *Outlines of O. T. Theology*, pp. 27 f. Similar instances of the perversion of names in jest are noticed in *ch.* 3 [8] *note.* The form Αδωνιβεζεκ has been adopted by 𝕲 in Josh. 10 (2 codd. Αδωνιζεβεκ; so Josephus and other writers: cf. Mo., *Comm.*, p. 17).

Upon this view of the origin of the name Adoni-bezeḳ, it is probable that the words 'in Bezeḳ' were added still later as an explanatory gloss, when the proper name had come to be understood as 'lord of Bezeḳ.' The statement 'they came upon Adoni-

the Cana'anites and the Perizzites. 6. And Adoni-bezeḳ fled; and they pursued after him, and captured him, and cut off his thumbs and his great toes. 7. And Adoni-bezeḳ said, 'Seventy kings, with their thumbs and their great toes cut off, used to pick up food under my table: as I did, so hath God requited me.' And they brought him to Jerusalem, and he died there.

8. R^P And the children of Judah fought against Jerusalem, and

Ṣedeḳ' does not necessarily postulate mention of the locality where the encounter took place, though this may have existed in the full narrative of J. Bu. would supply 'the king of Jerusalem' after the proper name.

The Cana'anites and the Perizzites. The two terms are so coupled only in J, Gen. 13 [7], 34 [30] †: the occurrence in *v.* [4] (R^P) being adopted directly from J in *v.* [5].

The view that the Perizzites were a remnant of the pre-Cana'anitish inhabitants of Palestine (cf. Kautzsch in Riehm, *HWB.*[2] ii. p. 1211) is based upon insufficient grounds. More probably the term, like *pᵉrāzî* in 1 Sam. 6 [18], Deut. 3 [5], denotes the dwellers in unwalled hamlets; just as the term Ḥivvites appears to denote communities of tent-dwellers (cf. *note* on *ch.* 10 [4]).

6. *cut off his thumbs and his great toes.* Le Clerc and commentators after him compare the statement of Aelian (*Var. Hist.* II. 9) that the Athenians voted to cut off the thumb of the right hand of every one of the Aeginetans, that they might be unable to carry a spear, but able to propel an oar. Similar mutilations of prisoners of war are noticed by Mo. *ad loc.* Probably, however, La. is correct in concluding, with Calmet, that the mutilation was intended to degrade the captive to the position of a punished slave, rather than to prevent the bearing of arms; though the latter motive may also have been operative.

7. *Seventy kings.* A large round number. Cf. *note* on *ch.* 8 [30].

as I did, etc. There is perhaps an etiological connexion between the tradition of Adoni-ṣedeḳ's speech and the name which he bears; the idea of 'measure for measure' being suggested by 'the Lord is righteous' (*i.e. just*; cf. use of term in Deut. 25 [15], *al.*).

they brought him to Jerusalem. The subject of the verb must be Adoni-ṣedeḳ's own followers; since J, the author of the narrative tells us in *v.* [21] = Josh. 15 [63] that the Judaeans were unable to conquer Jerusalem. It is likely, however, that R^P referred the verb to the victorious Judaeans, and so introduced his statement as to the conquest of Jerusalem in the verse following.

8. *And the children of Judah fought against Jerusalem, etc.* This statement by R^P is obviously incorrect. So far from the city having been captured and set on fire, we are told by J in Josh. 15 [63] that the

took it, and smote it at the edge of the sword, and the city they set on fire. 9. And afterward the children of Judah went down to fight against the Cana'anites dwelling in the hill-country and the Negeb and the Shephelah. 10. And Judah went against

sons of Judah *were unable to dispossess* the Jebuśites dwelling in Jerusalem (so *v.*[21], with the variation 'did not dispossess' noticed in the opening section). With this failure to capture Jerusalem agree the facts of history as otherwise known to us. In the old story of Judg. 19 Jerusalem or Jebuś is a 'city of the Jebuśites, . . . the city of foreigners who are not of the children of Israel' (*vv.*[10-12]). And in 2 Sam. 5[6 ff.] the capture of the city from its Jebuśite inhabitants is related as one of the great achievements of David. Even R[D] in Josh., who relates in 10[28 ff.] the capture and destruction of the cities of three of the kings who took part in the southern confederacy (10[3] E), viz. Lachish, 'Eglon, and Ḥebron, makes no statement as to the capture of Jerusalem; though it is true that the king of Jerusalem is included (*v.*[10]) in the list of vanquished kings given in Josh. 12.

at the edge of the sword. Lit. 'according to the mouth of the sword' (ל *of norm* in לְפִי, as in לְפִי אָכְלוֹ, lit. 'according to the mouth of his eating,' Ex. 16[18]), *i.e.* 'as the sword devours,' viz. *without quarter.*

9. *the children of Judah went down.* Jerusalem is 2593 feet above the Mediterranean sea-level, Ḥebron (*v.*[10]) 3040 feet; and the intervening country rises slightly on the whole rather than falls. Thus the expression 'went down' would be in this respect inappropriate. The writer, however, is thinking, not merely of the much lower Negeb and Shephelah, but also of the fall in the hill-country from the central plateau on which Jerusalem stands, both westward towards the Shephelah, and towards the wilderness of Judah in the direction of the Dead Sea.

the Negeb. The arid steppe-region extending from a little south of Ḥebron, where the hill-country gradually sinks, to Ḳadesh-Barnea' about fifty miles south of Be'er-sheba' on the border of the desert. The root נגב in New Heb. and Aram. means 'to be dry *or* parched'; and Negeb accordingly must denote 'the dry region': cf. *v.*[15] where springs of water are named as a desideratum. From the standpoint of Palestine 'the Negeb,' or, 'towards the Negeb,' is a common designation of the south. Negeb is in R.V. always rendered 'the South' (with capital S); but its application to a particular region of southern Palestine requires the retention of the Hebrew term.

the Shephelah. A term meaning 'lowland,' and, according to Smith (*HG.* pp. 201 ff.), properly applied to the low hills or downs lying between the Judaean hill-country to the east and the maritime plain (called *'ēmeḳ*, 'the Vale,' by J in *v.*[19]) to the west—a region which, as distinct both from hill-country and plain, was constantly debatable ground between the Israelites and Philistines. Smith

the Cana'anites who dwelt in Ḥebron: (now the name of Ḥebron

clearly proves the distinct character of this region, as separated from the hill-country of Judah by a series of valleys running southward from Aijalon, a distinction which does not exist north of Aijalon, where the hill-country slopes down directly into the maritime plain. Yet there are indications that the use of the term Shephelah was not always or at all times thus limited in its application. As Buhl (*Geogr.* p. 104, *n* 164) remarks, the specification of the cities in the Shephelah in Josh. 15 33 ff. points to a wider application, especially *vv.* 45-47 which include the Philistine cities with their neighbouring villages as far west as the sea and as far south as the wâdy of Egypt (wâdy el-'Arîš); these latter verses indicating the linguistic usage of the term at the period at which they were penned, even if they be regarded as a later interpolation. The same inference may be drawn from the 𝔊 rendering πεδίον or ἡ πεδινή, and from Eusebius' statement (*OS.* 296 10) that the term includes all the low country (πεδινή) lying about Eleutheropolis (Bêt-Ǵibrîn) to the north and west.* On the other hand, the fact must not be overlooked that Ob. 19, 2 Chr. 28 18 appear expressly to distinguish the Shephelah from the territory of the Philistines (the maritime plain); and the same seems to be true of Zech. 7 7, which refers to the period when the Shephelah was inhabited by Judah. The usage of the term thus appears to have fluctuated between a wider and narrower application, the wider and looser usage probably being relatively later.

10. *And Judah went, etc.* J's account of the conquest of Ḥebron and Debir is found in Josh. 15 14-19. There, after a statement by a late Priestly writer (*v.* 13) that Caleb was given Ḥebron or Ḳiriatharba' as his portion, we read:—'14. And Caleb dispossessed from thence the three sons of 'Anaḳ, Sheshai, and Aḥiman, and Talmai. 15. And he went up thence against the inhabitants of Debir, etc.,' *vv.* 15-19 being verbally identical with Judg. 1 11-15, except for the variation וילך 'and he went,' Judg. 1 11, for ויעל 'and he went up,' Josh. 15 15, and the addition הקטן ממנו, 'who was younger than he,' in Judg. 1 13, after the words 'the brother of Caleb.' The parallel to *v.* 14 of Josh. is found in Judg. 1 20 b and the names of the sons of 'Anaḳ at the end of *v.* 10.

Judg. 1 20 a, 'And they gave Ḥebron to Caleb, as Moses had said,' is J's statement upon which Josh. 15 13 is based by a late redactor who inserted the narrative of J into the midst of the P document in Josh. The original form of J's narrative is found if we place Judg. 1 20 a before Josh. 15 14-19: cf. *Additional note*, p. 48. The dislocation in Judg. 1 by which *v.* 20 comes later on instead of prior to *v.* 10 end is due to R^P, who, by his insertion of *vv.* 9.10 down to 'and they smote,'

* Buhl's further objections to Smith's view appear to be satisfactorily met by the latter writer in *Expositor*, 1896, pp. 404 ff.

formerly was Ḳiriath-arba῾:) and they smote J Sheshai and Aḥiman,

doubtless intended to represent the whole tribe of Judah as acting in concert.

Hebron. The modern el-Ḫalîl, *i.e.* 'the Friend,' an abbreviation of 'Town of the Friend of God' (the Mohammedan title for Abraham), about eighteen miles a little west of due south of Jerusalem.

now the name of Hebron formerly, etc. So exactly Josh. 14 15 (in a section 14 6-15 R^D, but probably a later note). The statement that Ḳiriath-arba῾ was the same as Ḥebron is also found in Gen. 23 2, 35 27, Josh. 15 13.54, 20 7, 21 11 (all P), and the name appears in a list of cities inhabited by the children of Judah in Neḥemiah's time, Neh. 11 25 †.

Ḳiriath-arba῾. The name means 'City of Four'; and there can be little doubt that 'Four,' like 'Seven' in Be'er-sheba῾, 'Well of Seven,' is a divine title. Probably both 'Four' and 'Seven' represent aspects of the Moon-god, the former referring to the four phases of the moon, the latter to one quarter, or the seven-day week. For the evidence upon which this view is based, cf. *Additional note*, p. 43. The view generally adopted that 'City of Four' means Tetrapolis, fourfold city or city of four federated tribes, is based merely upon conjecture; and no evidence can be adduced in support of it, unless it be found in the fact that the name Ḥebron may possibly be explained as 'association' or 'federation.' The Priestly writer in Josh. 15 13, 21 11 𝔐 would appear to suppose Arba῾ to have been the ancestor of the ῾Anaḳite clans originally inhabiting Ḥebron; and in Josh. 14 15 𝔐 Arba῾ is stated to have been 'the greatest man among the ῾Anaḳites.' In all these passages, however, 𝔊 reads 'the metropolis of ῾Anaḳ,' *or* 'of the ῾Anaḳites' (μητρόπολις = אֵם 'mother,' *i.e.* 'mother-city,' as in 2 Sam. 20 19); and Mo. argues with reason that this was the original reading, and that the alteration in 𝔐 is due to a scribe who misunderstood the sense in which the term 'mother' is used.

Sheshai, and Aḥiman, and Talmai. Described in *v.* 20 as 'the three sons of ῾Anaḳ'—a statement with which the three proper names were originally connected in J's account. Cf. the first *note* on *v.* 10. The reference is to three ῾Anaḳite clans rather than to three individuals. In Num. 13 22 (JE) the spies, and notably Caleb (cf. *note* on *v.* 12), come across the same three in their reconnaissance of Ḥebron —a fact which perhaps has its bearing upon the question of Caleb's conquest of Ḥebron (cf. *Additional note*, p. 46). Mo. speaks of the ῾Anaḳite names as 'of distinctively Aramaic type'; but it is more to the point to observe that they seem to exhibit the influence of North Arabia. It should be noticed that names with the termination *-ai*, as in Talmai and Sheshai, appear to have been specially numerous among the Judaeans, and not least among the Calibbite and Jeraḥme'elite elements of this mixed tribe. Cf. the genealogy of 1 Chr. 2, and notice besides Ḥushai, 2 Sam. 15 32, *al.*, and the Gittite Ittai, 2 Sam. 15 19, *al.* The name Talmai occurs in 2 Sam. 3 3, 13 37 as

and Talmai. 11. ⌜And they went up⌝ thence against the inhabitants of Debir. (Now the name of Debir formerly was

borne by a king of the Aramaean state Geshur (probably north of Gile'ad), and Talmî has been found in inscriptions from el-'Olâ near Têmâ as the name of two kings of Liḥḥyân (D. H. Müller, *Epigraphische Denkmäler aus Arabien*, p. 5, quoted by Sayce, *HCM.* p. 189 *n.*). The Nabaṭean form is Talmû or Talimû : cf. *CIS.* ii. 321, 344, 348. The name is closely akin to Bab. *talîmu*, Sam. *t^elîm*, 'uterine brother'; cf. Aram. Bar-tulmai (Bartholomew). Shēshai (שֵׁשַׁי, 𝔊^L Σεσει, ^B Σεσσει. Josh. 15[14] 𝔊^BL Σουσει, ^A Σουσαι. Num. 13[22] 𝔊^L Σεσει, ^B Σεσσει. Cf. Shāshai, שָׁשַׁי, Ezr. 10[40] 𝔊^BA Σεσει, identical with 𝔊^B Σεσεις, ^A Σεσσεις of 1 Esdr. 9[34]) is apparently a variation of the name Shîsha or Shavsha (שִׁישָׁא, שַׁוְשָׁא) borne by a Judaean of the time of David and Solomon (1 Kgs. 4[3], 1 Chr. 18[16]); and names with this termination *-ā* (with final א) are likewise characteristic of Judah (cf. 1 Chr. 2), and point to North Arabian influence, which may thus be supposed to have been operative in southern Cana'an as early as the time of the 'Anaḳites. Shavsha (more original than Shîsha : cf. *NHTK.* p. 38) undoubtedly stands for Shamsha, *i.e.* 'the Sun'; cf. Aram. Ki-šavaš (כישויש) for Bab. Ki-šamaš in an inscription of B.C. 504: *CIS.* ii. 65 (cited by Cheyne in *EB.* 4433). Shēshai, which, as the 𝔊 variants indicate, may have been originally Shavshai, Shashshai, or Shishshai (שַׁוְשַׁי, שַׁשַּׁי, שִׁשַּׁי), may be compared with the late Bab. *šaššu* for *šamšu*, 'sun.' It is worth noticing that the Heb. Samson (properly Shimshôn; Bab. Šamšânu, BDB. *s.v.*) perhaps 'Sun-man,' and the place-name Beth-shemesh, 'House of the Sun,' also belong to southern Palestine.

In Aḥiman the element *mān* is probably the name or title of a deity, perhaps Měnî, the god of *fate* or *destiny* mentioned in Isa. 65[11]. Cf. the goddess Manôthû in the Nabaṭean inscriptions; Ar. Manât, Ḳurân 53[20]. The name belongs to the familiar class which claims relationship to a deity:—'Brother of Mān,' or 'Mān is my brother.' The occurrence of the name (וַאֲחִימָן) in the list of Levites in 1 Chr. 9[17] is probably an erroneous dittography of the following וַאֲחֵיהֶם, 'and their brethren.'

11. *And they went up.* Reading וַיַּעַל with 𝔊^B and ‖ Josh. 15[15], in place of 𝔐 וַיֵּלֶךְ. The singular verb is taken by R^P to refer, as a collective, to the tribe of Judah mentioned by him in *v.*[10]; but in the original narrative of J it referred to Caleb. Cf. the first *note* on *v.*[10].

Debir. The site commonly accepted for Debir is eẓ-Ẕâhariyyeh, which lies about eleven miles south-west of Ḥebron, and which 'may

Ḳiriath-sepher.) 12. And Caleb said, 'He that smiteth Ḳiriath-

be regarded as the frontier town between the hill-country and the Negeb' (Smith, *HG.* p. 279; cf. Trumbull, *Kadesh-Barnea*, pp. 104 f.). This identification depends merely upon conjecture. It suits the connexion in which Debir stands in Josh. 15 [48-51] with Socoh (the modern Šuwêkeh), 'Anab ('Anâb), and Eshtemoh (elsewhere Eshtemoa', probably the modern es-Semû'), which are all in close proximity, and the narrative of *vv.* [14ff.] (cf. *note* on *v.* [15]); but is opposed by the fact noticed by Sayce (*DB.* i. p. 578a) that Petrie found no traces at eẕ-Ẕâhariyyeh of anything older than the Roman period.*

It may also be observed that, while Ḥebron stands 3040 feet above the sea, the elevation of eẕ-Ẕâhariyyeh (2150 feet) is nearly 900 feet lower, and the descent from the former site to the latter appears, in the main, to be gradual and continuous.‡ Thus, if the reading 'And *they went up from thence* (*i.e.* from Ḥebron) to Debir' is correct, the identification of Debir with eẕ-Ẕâhariyyeh would seem to be excluded, unless we regard the expression 'went up' as used in the general sense of making a campaign (cf. *note* on *v.* [1]), an explanation which the precise 'from thence' (מִשָּׁם) may be thought to render somewhat improbable. The only site south of Ḥebron which seems to stand on a higher elevation is Yuṭṭâ (3747 feet); but this corresponds in name at least with the Biblical Juṭṭah, Josh. 15 [55], 21 [16].

Ḳiriath-sepher. As vocalized, the name appears to mean 'book-city': 𝔊[AL] πόλις γραμμάτων (and so 𝔊[BAL] in Josh. 15 [15.16], and in 15 [49], where 𝔐 reads Kiriath-sannah, probably a textual error); 𝔏 'civitas litterarum'; 𝔖[h] 'city of writings'; 𝔗 'archive-city.' Upon this slight basis, merely, Sayce builds the theory that the city 'must have been the seat of a library like those of the great cities of Babylonia and Assyria,—a library which doubtless consisted in large measure

* Conder's statement (*Tent Work*, p. 245) that the name Debir 'has the same meaning' as eẕ-Ẕâhariyyeh is wholly incorrect. It may be true that the name of the modern village is 'derived from its situation on the "back" of a long ridge.' *Ẕahr* means 'back,' and *ẕahâr* is applied to 'the exterior and elevated part of a stony tract' (so Lane), both words being derived from a verb *ẕahara*, 'to be outward, exterior, apparent.' But Debir, on the contrary, can only be explained from Ar. *dabara*, 'to be behind,' whence *dabr* and *dubr*, 'hindmost *or* back part,' and is the same, apparently, as the Heb. word used in 1 Kgs. 6 [16] *al.* as the older name of the most holy place in Solomon's temple, which, upon this etymology, may be rendered 'shrine.' The contrast in sense between the two roots is clearly seen if we compare *ẕâhir*, 'exterior' (commonly opposed to *bâṭin*, 'interior') with *dabr*, 'the location *or* quarter that is behind a thing' (so Lane).

‡ Cf. *SWP. Great Map*, xxi. Smith (*loc. cit.*), though regarding the identification of eẕ-Ẕâhariyyeh with Debir as probable, describes the journey from Ḥebron as *a descent* 'over moors and through wheat-fields, arranged in the narrower wadies in careful terraces, but lavishly spread over many of the broader valleys.'

ṡepher, and taketh it, I will give him ʿAchṡah my daughter as wife.' 13. And ʿOthniel, the son of Ḳenaz, the R[P] younger

of books on clay which may yet be brought to light' (*HCM.* p. 54). If the name really meant 'city of books,' or rather 'records,' we should expect the form קִרְיַת סְפָרִים (Ḳiriath-ṡᵉphārîm : cf. Ḳiriath-yᵉʿārîm); and it is possible that the plur. ספרים may have been written in the abbreviated form ספר׳, which came to be mistaken for the singular (cf. *footnote* § on p. 124). 𝔊[B] in this passage reads Καριασσωφαρ, *i.e.*, apparently, Kiriath-ṡōphēr, 'city of the scribe'; a name which W. M. Müller would recognize in the Egyptian *Bai-ti-ṯu-pa-ïra*, 'house of the scribe' (*AE.* p. 174). This vocalization of the Heb. name is in itself more probable.

12. *And Caleb said.* The statement evidently points back to an earlier mention of Caleb in J's original narrative. Cf. the first *note* on *v.*[10]. Caleb is called 'the son of Jephunneh the Ḳenizzite' in Num. 32[12] (P), Josh. 14[6.14] (R[D]). In JE's narrative of the mission of the spies to explore the Negeb (Num. 13, 14) he is the only spy mentioned by name, and the only one among the number who maintains the possibility of the conquest of the ʿAnaḳites inhabiting the region (Num. 13[30]). In the later narrative of P, which is interwoven with that of JE in these two chapters, and in which the twelve spies (one for every tribe, and all named) explore the whole of Canaʿan, Joshuaʿ is associated with Caleb (the representative of Judah) in urging the immediate conquest of the land. Cf. for the analysis of the narrative, Gray, *Numbers* (*ICC.*), pp. 128 ff. In Josh. 14[6-15] (R[D] based on JE) Joshuaʿ grants Ḥebron to Caleb in response to his request, and in remembrance of the promise of Moses made to Caleb after the return of the spies.

Caleb's clan of the Ḳenizzites appears from Gen. 36[11] to have belonged to the Edomites, and, like the allied clan of the Jeraḥme'elites (1 Chr. 2[9.18.42]), still remained distinct from Judah in the early days of David: cf. 1 Sam. 27[10], 30[14]. Evidence seems to indicate that the Ḳenizzites, like other elements which went to form the mixed tribe of Judah, really entered and settled in the Negeb by advancing northward from the neighbourhood of Ḳadesh-Barneaʿ, and that the tradition which makes the granting of Ḥebron and Debir to Caleb subsequent to and dependent upon the invasion and conquest of Canaʿan under Joshuaʿ, represents a later adjustment of facts. Cf. *Additional note*, p. 44.

13. *ʿOthniel, the son of Ḳenaz.* The reference is probably, as in the case of Caleb, to a Ḳenizzite family rather than an individual. ʿOthniel is named in *ch.* 3[9] as the deliverer of Israel from a foreign oppressor.

the younger brother of Caleb. The sentence may be construed grammatically as referring either to Ḳenaz (so 𝔊) or to ʿOthniel

J brother of Caleb, took it: and he gave him ʿAchśah his daughter as wife. 14. And when she came, ⌜he⌝ incited ⌜her⌝ to ask of her father a field: and she lighted down from off the ass; and Caleb said to her, 'What wouldest thou?' 15. And she said to him, 'Grant me a present; for thou hast set me in the land of the Negeb; so give me springs of water.' And Caleb gave her the upper spring⌜⌝ and the nether spring⌜⌝.

(so 𝔙); but, since Caleb is himself called 'the Ḳenizzite' (cf. *note* above), it seems clear that he too is regarded as a descendant or 'son' of Ḳenaz, and that Caleb and ʿOthniel are ranked as brothers. This was the view of R^P, who added, after 'the brother of Caleb,' the words 'who was younger than he' (so *ch.* 3^{9}), in order to explain how the fact that ʿOthniel married his own niece did not imply a great disparity in age. R^P's addition is not found in the parallel narrative of J in Josh. Cf. the first *note* on *v.*^{10}.

he gave him ʿAchśah, etc. Probably the story implies the union of two families of the Ḳenizzites.

14. *when she came.* Apparently, as Mo. suggests, ʿAchśah is pictured as arriving to meet her father and her future husband from some place of safety, such as Ḥebron, where she had been left during the attack on Debir.

he incited her. Reading וַיְסִיתֶהָ with 𝔊, 𝔏, $𝔖^h$, 𝔙 here, and 𝔙 and some MSS. of 𝔊 in ‖ Josh. 15^{18}, in place of 𝔐 'she incited him.' The correction is necessary in view of the fact that the request, as narrated, comes from ʿAchśah.

15. *a present.* Lit. 'a blessing,' in the tangible form of a gift. The expression is so used in Gen. 33^{11} (E), 1 Sam. 25^{27}, 30^{26}, 2 Kgs. 5^{15}.

thou hast set me, etc. The character of the district (Negeb, 'the dry region'; cf. *v.*^{9} *note*) justifies the request.

springs of water. The Heb. word *gullôth*, here rendered 'springs,' is otherwise unknown, and the meaning can only be inferred from the context.* It may perhaps be an old Canaʿanite word which dropped into disuse in later Hebrew; or, as Mo. thinks, 'a proper name of alien origin' (so Bu.).

the upper spring and the lower spring. Reading גֻּלַּת sing. with the old fem. termination, as is demanded by the sing. adjectives עִלִּית and תַּחְתִּית. This old termination, as seen in *gullath*, is frequent,

* Cf., however, גַּל in Cant. 4^{12b}, which, if not merely a corruption of גַּן, 'garden,' which occurs in the first half of the verse (as presupposed by 𝔊, 𝔙, $𝔖^P$), probably means 'spring': גַּל נָעוּל parallel to מַעְיָן חָתוּם

16. And ⌜Hobab the⌝ Ḳenite, the father-in-law of Moses,

as Bu. remarks, in Cana'anite place-names, *e.g.* Ṣephath, Ba'alath, Ṣarephath: cf. *NHTK.* p. 42 f. || Josh. 15^{19} has the plur. 'the upper springs, etc.' The springs in question have been plausibly identified with the springs of Seil ed-Dilbeh between Ḥebron and eẓ-Ẓâhariyyeh, 'on the north, the 'Ain Heǵireh with a shadoof for irrigation, and on the south the 'Ain Dilbeh, a square pool covered with weeds' (Smith, *HG.* p. 279, n^2). Cf. *SWP. Mem.* iii. p. 302. Mo. notices the fact that these springs are somewhat nearer to Ḥebron than to eẓ-Ẓâhariyyeh, and appositely remarks that the story 'is told to explain or establish the claim of 'Achsah, a branch of the Ḳenizzite clan 'Othniel of Debir, to waters which by their situation seemed naturally to belong to the older branch, the Calebites of Ḥebron.'

16. *And Ḥobab the Ḳenite.* Reading וְחֹבָב הַקֵּינִי with Mo., Bu., No. (cf. *ch.* 4^{11}), in place of $\mathfrak{H}$ וּבְנֵי קֵינִי, 'And the children of Ḳenite,' which cannot be original, since the gentilic adjective 'Ḳenite' cannot be used of an individual without the Article, which is tacitly inserted in R.V. The words, 'the father-in-law of Moses,' which follow, seem to demand mention of the proper name. $\mathfrak{G}^{AL}$, $\mathfrak{S}^{h}$ read, 'And the children of Ḥobab the Ḳenite,' a text which suits the pl. verb עָלוּ, 'went up,' in *v.* ^{16a}, but not the sing. וַיֵּלֶךְ וַיֵּשֶׁב, 'and he went and dwelt,' in *v.* ^{16b}. $\mathfrak{G}^{B}$ reads 'Jethro' in place of 'Ḥobab.' These variations suggest that the original of $\mathfrak{G}$ already lacked the proper name, and that the lacuna was differently supplied in different MSS. (Stu., Meyer); though it is possible that the reading 'Jethro' represents the substitution of the better known name of Moses' father-in-law, in place of Ḥobab (Mo., La.). The reading of $\mathfrak{G}^{AL}$ is adopted by La., Kit., and may be original: but the sing. verbal forms in *v.* ^{16b} favour the reading adopted above; and it is easy to suppose that the pl. verb in *v.* ^{16a} has been altered from sing. עָלָה to suit the subject as it stands in $\mathfrak{H}$. Meyer (*IN.* p. 90) emends וְקַיִן simply, and thus reads, 'And Ḳain, the father-in-law of Moses, went up, etc.'; but, as Mo. notices, the mention of 'Ḥobab the Ḳenite' in *ch.* 4^{11}, whether it be original or a later gloss, depends upon and substantiates the reading in our passage, Moses' father-in-law being elsewhere described not as a Ḳenite but as a Midianite.

Ḳain occurs as the tribal name of the Ḳenites in *ch.* 4^{11}, Num. 24^{22} (JE). The name may denote a worker in metal, and perhaps indicates that this form of industry was characteristic of the tribe. For the theory that the story of Cain (Ḳain) and his descendants (Gen. 4 J) was intended to explain the nomadic life of the Ḳenites and their skill as artificers, cf. Cheyne, *EB.* 621 f.; Skinner, *Genesis* (*ICC.*), pp. 111 ff.

⌐went up from the City of Palms with the children of Judah into the wilderness of Judah which is in the Negeb of ʿArad; and

the father-in-law of Moses. Moses' father-in-law, when first introduced in Ex. 2 [18] (J), is called Reʿuel. The document E, which takes up the narrative in Ex. 3, speaks of him by the name Jethro; and this name is uniformly employed elsewhere in E. Num. 10 [29] (J) mentions 'Ḥobab, the son of Reʿuel, the father-in-law of Moses.' Here it is ambiguous whether the title 'father-in-law' refers to Ḥobab or Reʿuel; and, if this passage stood alone in mentioning Ḥobab, we should naturally refer the title to Reʿuel in agreement with Ex. 2 [18], and regard Ḥobab as brother to Ṣipporah, Moses' wife, and brother-in-law to Moses. But from Judg. 4 [11] the title 'father-in-law' is clearly seen to refer to Ḥobab. It is true that R.V. *text*, in order to solve the difficulty, renders 'brother-in-law'; but this is quite unwarrantable. The Heb. term employed, *ḥōthēn*, is the same as the Ar. *ḫâtin*, properly 'circumciser,' the original reference being to the nomadic custom by which the father-in-law performed the rite of circumcision upon the bridegroom (Heb. *ḥāthān*, 'the circumcised') shortly before marriage. Probably Ḥobab is the true name of Moses' father-in-law according to J, and Reʿuel is a remoter ancestor—perhaps the clan-name.

went up. Cf. *note* on *v.* [1], 'who shall go up.' The 3rd sing. עָלָה is read in place of pl. עָלוּ in 𝔐. Cf. the first *note* on this verse.

the City of Palms. Mentioned again in *ch.* 3 [13], Deut. 34 [3], 2 Chr. 28 [15] †, the two latter passages showing the reference to be to Jericho. Jos. (*BJ.* IV. viii. 3) alludes to the 'many kinds of date-palms, differing from each other in flavour and name,' which flourished in his day in the neighbourhood of Jericho, owing to the fertilizing influence of Elishaʿ's fountain. Other references are collected by Smith, *HG.* p. 266, *n* [4]. At the present day the palms have entirely disappeared. The site of Jericho is undoubtedly the modern Tell es-Sulṭân, a large mound which lies in the Jordan valley five miles east of Jordan, and at the foot of the central range of hills, close to the mouth of the Wâdy el-Ḳelt, which affords a passage into the hill-country of Ephraim, and is thought to be the ancient valley of ʿAchor. Just below Tell es-Sulṭân lies the ʿAin es-Sulṭân, which must be identified as Elishaʿ's fountain. The modern Jericho (Erîḥâ) is a squalid village lying one and a half miles to the south.

with the children of Judah. Num. 10 [29ff.] (J) records Moses' invitation to Ḥobab to throw in his lot with Israel, and join in the occupation of Canaʿan.

into the wilderness of Judah which is in the Negeb of ʿArad. The description is somewhat obscure, and the text may be suspected; but the case for its rejection is not convincing. Mo. regards the statement as 'self-contradictory,' because 'the wilderness of Judah, the

he went and dwelt with ⌜the ʿAmaleḳites⌝. 17. And Judah went

barren steeps in which the mountains break down to the Dead Sea, and the Negeb are distinct regions.' The fact that in Josh. 15^{21-62} (P), the territory of Judah is divided into 'the Negeb' (*vv.* $^{21-32}$), 'the Shephelah' (*vv.* $^{33-47}$), 'the Hill-country' (*vv.* $^{48-60}$), and 'the Wilderness' (*vv.* $^{61.62}$), would seem at first sight to draw such a distinction; but the precise term, 'the wilderness of Judah,' only occurs once again in the O. T. in the heading of Ps. 63, and is there applied to the scene of David's wanderings during his outlaw life, including doubtless 'the wilderness of Ziph' (1 Sam. 23^{14}, 26^{2}; Tell Zîf), 'the wilderness of Maʿon,' in the 'ʿArabah south of Jeshimon' (1 Sam. 23^{24}, 25^{1} $\mathfrak{G}^{B}$; Tell Maʿîn), close to Carmel (1 Sam. 25^{2}; el-Kurmul, about one mile north of Maʿîn), 'the wilderness of ʿEn-gedi' (1 Sam. 24^{1}; ʿAin Ǵidî). Ziph, Maʿon, and Carmel are assigned in Josh. 15^{55} not to 'the Wilderness' but to 'the Hill-country.' The wilderness of Ziph and of Maʿon may be thought of, then, as the region immediately eastward of these cities breaking down towards the Dead Sea; but, if this part of the Wilderness actually took its name from two cities in the Hill-country, it might be said to extend into the Hill-country, and (conceivably) to be 'the Wilderness of Judah which is in the Hill-country.' ʿArad is to be identified with Tell ʿArâd, 'a barren-looking eminence rising above the country around' (Rob. *BR*^{3}. ii. p. 101), which lies seventeen miles nearly due south of Ḥebron, and about half that distance due south of Maʿon. Some eight miles south-west of Tell ʿArâd is el-Milḥ, which is probably the City of Salt (Heb. *ʿîr hammélaḥ*) mentioned in Josh. 15^{62} as one of the six cities in 'the Wilderness.' ʿEn-gedi, the only other one of these six cities which can be identified, lies approximately twenty miles north-east of Tell ʿArâd, and the three sites are so placed that a line drawn from ʿEn-gedi to el-Milḥ would fall upon Tell ʿArâd (cf. Map IV). Thus it would seem that ʿArad (though assigned to the Negeb in the possibly composite passage, Num. 21^{1} JE) might have been included in 'the Wilderness' if it had been enumerated among the cities of Judah in Josh. 15. Just as the wilderness of Ziph and Maʿon appears to denote not precisely the region in which these cities were situated, but the barren country to the east which bordered upon them, so the Negeb of ʿArad may denote that part of the Negeb bordering upon ʿArad to the south, into which the wilderness of Judah might be said to exteṇd (cf. 'the Negeb of the Ḳenites,' 1 Sam. 27^{10}).

All suggested emendations of the passage base themselves, to some extent, upon $\mathfrak{G}$. $\mathfrak{G}^{B}$ reads *εἰς τὴν ἔρημον τὴν οὖσαν ἐν τῷ νότῳ* Ιουδα, *ἥ ἐστιν ἐπὶ καταβάσεως* Αραδ. $\mathfrak{G}^{AL}$, $\mathfrak{S}^{h}$ (besides omitting *ἥ ἐστιν*) transpose Ιουδα and place it after *ἔρημον* as in $\mathfrak{V}$; but the word is marked with an asterisk in $\mathfrak{S}^{h}$, and it seems clear that $\mathfrak{G}^{B}$ represents the more original form of $\mathfrak{G}$. Hence La. reaḍs בַּמִּדְבָּר אֲשֶׁר בַּנֶּגֶב יְהוּדָה בְּמוֹרַד עֲרָד, 'into the wilderness which is in the Negeb of

with Simeʿon his brother, and they smote the Canaʿanites who inhabited Ṣephath, and devoted it to destruction. And the name

Judah at the descent of ʿArad'; van Doorninck (*Theol. Literatur-zeitung*, 1884, p. 211), followed by Bu. (*RS.* p. 10) מִדְבַּר יְהוּדָה אֲשֶׁר בְּמוֹרַד עֲרָד, 'into the wilderness of Judah which is at the descent of ʿArad.' It is not clear, however, considering the site of Tell ʿArâd, to what 'the descent of ʿArad' could refer. The Heb. term rendered 'descent' is used in Josh. 10^{11}, Jer. 48^{5}, and probably also in Josh. 7^{5}, of a steep pass between mountains. La.'s contention that 'if Tell ʿArâd is on a plain, the plateau descends not far off from it, towards the east,' is not very convincing as to the appropriateness of the expression in this connexion. Examination of the rendering of 𝔊^{B} can scarcely fail to suggest that the words τὴν οὖσαν ἐν τῷ νότῳ and ἥ ἐστιν ἐπὶ καταβάσεως represent a double rendering of a single phrase in the Hebrew; in which case במורד or במרד (ἐπὶ καταβάσεως) is simply a corruption of בנגב (ἐν τῷ νότῳ), the resemblance between the two words in the ancient character being not remote. Mo. regards במורד as an old error for במדבר, 'into the wilderness,' as in Josh. 8^{24} 𝔊. In his view בְּמִדְבַּר עֲרָד 'into the wilderness of ʿArad' represents the original text; אשר בנגב, 'which is in the Negeb,' is a gloss to ʿArad from Num. 21^{1} introduced into the text in the wrong place (*i.e. before* instead of *after* 'ʿArad'); and במדבר, 'into the wilderness (of),' being thus left without a genitive, has finally been explained by the addition of יהודה, 'into the wilderness of Judah.' Mo.'s view is adopted by No., Kit., and approved by Bu. in his *Comm.*, except that Bu. favours retention of the words אשר בנגב after ערד, thus reading, 'into the wilderness of ʿArad which is in the Negeb.'

with the ʿAmaleḳites. Reading אֶת־הָעֲמָלֵקִי with all recent commentators. The reading occurs as a doublet (μετὰ τοῦ λαοῦ Αμαληκ) in 𝔊^{N}, 𝔏^{L}, Copt. The Ḳenites are found among the ʿAmaleḳites in 1 Sam. 15^{6}, and are associated with them in Balaʿam's prophecy (Num. $24^{20.21}$ JE). 𝔐, 'and he went and dwelt with the people,' gives no intelligible sense. Heb. *hā-ʿām*, 'the people,' is doubtless a remnant of the original reading *hā-ʿămālēḳī*.

17. *Ṣephath.* Only mentioned here. The ruined site Sebaita, nearly thirty miles south of Be'er-shebaʿ, is favoured by many; but there is no philological connexion between this name and the Heb. Ṣĕphath. In this respect nothing can be alleged against Rob.'s finding of the name (*BR*^{3}. ii. p. 181) in naḳb eṣ-Ṣafâ ('pass of the smooth rock'), a steep pass upon the route from Petra to Ḥebron, east-north-east of the ǵebel el-Madêrah; though no trace has been discovered of a city bearing the name.

and devoted it to destruction. The Heb. verb is the Hiphʿîl (causative) modification of a root *ḥāram* which does not occur in

of the city was called Ḥormah. 18. R^P And Judah took Ġaza

Heb. in the simple stem, but the sense of which may be illustrated from Ar. In Ar. *ḥaruma* means 'to be forbidden, prohibited, unlawful,' then 'to be sacred *or* inviolable.' Hence, in the first sense, *ḥarîm* denotes the forbidden or private part of a house, *i.e.* the women's apartments; *maḥram* is a female relation who comes within the prohibited degrees, and whom therefore it is unlawful to marry; *el-Muḥarram* is the first month of the Mohammedan year, during which fighting is prohibited. In the second sense we may notice *ḥaram*, the sacred territory of Mecca, *el-mesǵid el-ḥarâm*, the sacred mosque. In Heb. the causative *heḥᵉrîm* means to make a thing unlawful or *taboo*, by devoting it to God, and is commonly applied, as in this passage, to Israel's action in their religious wars, when the foes and their cities were devoted to wholesale destruction, and sometimes the cattle also (cf. Josh. 6 21, 1 Sam. 15 3), though not always (cf. Deut. 2 34.35, 3 6.7). Inanimate objects coming under the sacred ban were destroyed by fire; or, as in the case of gold and silver, and utensils of metal, dedicated to Yahweh's sanctuary (Josh. 6 24: the latter half of the verse appears, however, to be an addition by R^D to the older narrative). Everything so devoted was called *ḥérem*, 'devoted thing'; and appropriation of any such *ḥérem* was thought to incur Yahweh's dire displeasure, and could only be expiated by death, as in the case of 'Achan (Josh. 7 1 ff.). The verb is used in a precisely similar sense by Mesha', king of Moab, when relating his treatment of a captured Israelitish city:—'And Chemosh said to me, "Go, take Nebo against Israel"; and I went by night, and fought against it from break of dawn until noon, and I took it and slew the whole of it, 7000 men, and . . ., and women, and . . ., and damsels; for to 'Ashtar-Chemosh had I devoted it (החרמתה, *heḥᵉramtīhā*); and I took thence the vessels of Yahweh, and dragged them before Chemosh' (*Moabite Stone*, ll. 14-18).

And the name of the city was called Ḥormah. Tradition connects the name with the root *ḥāram* in the sense 'devoted to destruction.' Possibly the original meaning of the name may have been 'sanctuary' or 'sacred area.' Cf. Ar. *ḥaram* noticed above. The site of Ḥormah has not been identified. This narrative seems to be a duplicate of Num. 21 1-3 (JE), which is probably the immediate sequel of Num. 14 40-45 (JE), and which places the conquest and extermination of the Cana'anites inhabiting a district of the Negeb, and hence the origin of the name Ḥormah, immediately after the mission of the spies, who, according to JE, were sent out from Ḳadesh-Barnea'. Probably the position of the narrative in Num. is the more original, and points to the capture and settlement of a portion of the Negeb by Judaeans (Calibbites) who advanced northwards from Ḳadesh at some time prior to the occupation of Cana'an by the Israelite tribes who entered from the east under Joshua'. Cf. further *Additional note*, p. 44.

and the border thereof, and Ashḳelon and the border thereof, and ʿEḳron and the border thereof. 19. J And Yahweh was with Judah, and he gained possession of the hill-country; for ⟨he was⟩ not ⟨able⟩ to dispossess the inhabitants of the Vale, because they

18. *And Judah took Ġaza, etc.* The three Philistine cities here specified (the modern Ġazzeh, ʿAsḳalân, and ʿÂḳir) are all situated in the maritime plain, *i.e.* 'the Vale,' the inhabitants of which *v.*[19] tells us Judah could not dispossess. Josh. 13[3] (R^D) informs us that these three cities, together with Ashdod and Gath, remained uncaptured by Joshuaʿ; and in Judg. 3[3] 'the five lords of the Philistines' are included among 'the nations which Yahweh left to test Israel by them' (3[1]). There is no suggestion that Judah first captured the cities and then failed to hold them; and it thus seems probable that *v.*[18], like the statement as to the capture of Jerusalem in *v.*[8], is a mistaken editorial insertion. 𝕲 corrects to καὶ οὐκ ἐκληρονόμησεν.

ʿEḳron. The 𝕲 form is Ακκαρων, while the name appears in the Assyr. inscriptions as Amḳaruna; and these two facts taken together suggest that the Heb. vocalization should be ʿAḳḳaron for ʿAmḳaron, the double *ḳ* representing assimilated *m*, or the *m* arising through dissimilation of double *ḳ*.

19. *he gained possession.* The Heb. verb *hôrîš* (causative of *yāraš*) means 'to cause to inherit *or* possess,' with the collateral idea of causing succession to the inheritance of the previous owner, and so disinheriting or dispossessing him. This double sense is illustrated by the present verse, where 'gained possession of' and 'to dispossess' are both represented by the same verb in the Heb. In *v.*[27] a single occurrence of the verb is applied, by a kind of zeugma, both to cities (Beth-she'an, Taʿanach), for which the rendering 'gain possession of' would be the more suitable, and to the inhabitants of cities (Dor, Ibleʿam, Megiddo), with regard to whom this rendering is impossible, and the sense postulated is 'dispossess.'

he was not able to dispossess. 𝕳 has simply 'not . . . to dispossess,' the governing verb יָכֹל, 'was able,' being absent. It is theoretically possible to translate the Heb. as it stands 'was not for dispossessing,' *i.e.* 'could *or* did not dispossess' (cf. Driver, *Tenses*, § 204); but since we know, from the parallel narrative in Josh., that in *vv.*[21.27] an original 'could not dispossess' has been altered by R^P into 'did not dispossess' for dogmatic reasons (cf. *introd. note* to section), it is reasonable to conclude that such an alteration was intended by R^P in this case also, and that he has carried it out imperfectly by simple excision of the verb יָכֹל (we should have expected emendation to a perfect הוֹרִישׁ, as in *vv.*[21.27]).

the Vale. The Heb. ʿ*ēmeḳ*, lit. 'depression,' is applied to a wide and

had chariots of iron. 20. And they gave Ḥebron to Caleb, as Moses had said: and he dispossessed from thence the three sons of ʿAnaḳ. 21. But the Jebuśites dwelling in Jerusalem the

open vale or lowland country, and here denotes the maritime plain to the west of the hill-country of Judah, or, more accurately, to the west of the low foothills which lie between the Hill-country and the Vale (cf. *note* on 'the Shephelah,' *v.*[9]). Cf. further, p. 203, *footnote*.

chariots of iron. These are also mentioned as forming the most effective part of the military equipment of the Canaʿanites inhabiting the vale (*ʿēmeḳ*) of Jezreel: Josh. 17[16] (J); cf. Judg. 4[3]. Among the steep and narrow passes of the Judaean hill-country they would have been useless: though in 1 Sam. 13[5] the Philistines are described as bringing them up into the central hill-country as far as Michmash, doubtless through the pass of Aijalon. Here the incredibly large number of 30,000 chariots given by 𝔐, appears in 𝔊[L], 𝔖[P] as 3000. The Aramaeans in later times found chariots ineffective among the hills surrounding Samaria: 1 Kgs. 20[23-25].

20. *And they gave Ḥebron to Caleb.* Cf. Josh. 14[6-15] (R[D] based on JE).

as Moses had said. Referring back to Num. 14[24] (JE): cf. Deut. 1[36], Josh. 14[9].

the three sons of ʿAnaḳ. Sheshai, Aḥiman, and Talmai, mentioned in *v.* [10 end], which is the proper sequel to *v.*[20] in the original form of J's narrative (cf. the first *note* on *v.*[10]). Heb. *ʿănāḳ* means 'neck'; and it may be inferred that *b^enê ʿănāḳ* properly denoted 'long-necked (*i.e.* tall) men.' Cf. the spies' description of their size and stature in Num. 13[33] (JE), and the rendering of 𝔊 *υἱοὺς γιγάντων* in Deut. 1[28].

21. *the Jebuśites.* Nothing is known of this people beyond the fact that they appear as the inhabitants of Jerusalem here and in || Josh. 15[63], and in the narrative of David's capture of the city, 2 Sam. 5[6 ff.] 'Araunah the Jebuśite' still lived at or just outside of Jerusalem after David had captured it and made it his capital (2 Sam. 24[16 ff.]); and very possibly the Jebuśites, after their expulsion from the stronghold of Ṣion (the south-east hill), which became the city of David, were still allowed to dwell upon the (presumably unwalled) south-west hill, which is styled 'the cliff (lit. "shoulder") of the Jebuśites' in Josh. 15[8], 18[16] (P). In Judg. 19[10.11], 1 Chr. 11[4.5] the name Jebuś is given to Jerusalem as an earlier name of the city. In the Tell el-Amarna tablets, however, we find the name Urusalim regularly employed so early as *cir.* B.C. 1400. Cf. further, on the Jebuśites, *Introd.* pp. lxxxvi f.

the children of Judah. Reading 'Judah' in place of 'Benjamin' with || Josh. 15[63]. The alteration in 𝔐 has been made in accordance with Josh. 18[16] (P), which, in describing the lot of the children of Benjamin, makes the border run south of Jerusalem so as to include the city, and mentions it among the cities belonging to the tribe in *v.*[28].

children of ⌜Judah⌝ did not dispossess: and the Jebuṡites dwelt with the children of ⌜Judah⌝ in Jerusalem, unto this day.

22. And the house of Joṡeph also went up to Bethel: and

did not dispossess. An alteration of ‖ Josh. 15^{63} 'were not able to dispossess.' Cf. *introd. note* to section.

dwelt . . . unto this day. To what period does this note of time refer? We can scarcely imagine Jebuṡites and Judaeans dwelling side by side in Jerusalem prior to the capture of the ancient stronghold by David; and in fact in the old narrative of Judg. $19^{11.12}$ Jebuṡ is described as 'the city of foreigners who are not of the children of Israel,' and so likely to prove inhospitable to the Levite in need of a night's lodging. On the other hand, the fact that Jebuṡites remained at Jerusalem after the capture of the city by David (cf. *note* on 'the Jebuṡites' above) appears to have been due rather to David's clemency than to the inability of the Judaeans to dispossess them. This consideration, however, may have been overlooked by the writer of J; and it seems the more probable view that the note refers to a period subsequent to David's capture of the city.

22. *the house of Joṡeph.* So *v.*^{35}, Josh. 17^{17} (J), 2 Sam. 19^{20}, 1 Kgs. 11^{28}, Am. 5^{6}. The reading of 𝔊, *οἱ υἱοὶ* Ιωσηφ, is probably an alteration under the influence of the plural verb 'went up' (וַיַּעֲלוּ). The term may be used to include not merely Ephraim and Manasseh, but also Benjamin. Cf. 2 Sam. 19^{20}, where Shimeʿi, the Benjaminite (16^{11}), speaks of himself as belonging to the house of Joṡeph.

went up to Bethel. Sc. from Gilgal: cf. *v.*^{1} *note*; *ch.* 2^{1}. Bethel is the modern Bêtîn,* about ten miles north of Jerusalem; and ʿAi, the first city captured in the hill-country, according to Josh., lay immediately to the east of Bethel (Josh. 7^{2}, $8^{9.12}$ JE; cf. Gen. 12^{8} J). The narrative seems to picture an independent attack made by the Joṡeph-tribes upon the hill-country; and it is not improbable that it originally formed part of a longer account in which this section of Israel carried out its campaign under the leadership of Joshuaʿ. This is the view of Bu., who suggests that J's narrative originally ran 'went up to ʿAi,' and then followed on with an account of the capture of ʿAi, as in Josh. 8, before mentioning the reconnaissance and capture of Bethel (*v.*^{23}). Cf. *RS.* pp. 57 f., and see further *Additional note*, p. 48. The mention of the men of Bethel in Josh. 8^{17} as joining with the men of ʿAi in repelling Israel's attack upon the latter city is clearly a late gloss, which finds no place in 𝔊, and is out of harmony with the context. We have no account in Josh. of the capture of Bethel, but Josh. 12^{16} (R^{D}) mentions the king of Bethel in the list of kings smitten by Joshuaʿ.

* For the modification of the final *-ēl* to *-în*, cf. Zerʿîn for Jezreʿel, Isrâʾîn for Israʾel (in Birket Isrâʾîn at Jerusalem), Bêt Ǵibrîn, 'House of Gabriel,' and Wâdy Ismaʿîn (Ishmaʿel).

Yahweh was with them. 23. And the house of Joseph made a reconnaissance at Bethel. (Now the name of the city formerly was Luz.) 24. And the watchers saw a man coming out of the city, ⟨and they laid hold on him⟩ and said to him, 'Show us, we pray thee, the way to enter the city, and we will deal kindly with thee.' 25. So he showed them the way to enter the city, and they smote the city at the edge of the sword; but the man and

and Yahweh was with them. Cf. *v.*[19], 'and Yahweh was with Judah' (with את = 'with' in place of עמם *v.*[22]). 𝔊[AL.] καὶ Ιουδας μετ' αὐτῶν. Bu. (*RS.* pp. 58 f.; *Comm.* p. 11, followed by Kit. *HH.* i. p. 269; *GVI.*[2] i. p. 570) makes out a good case for the suggestion that under both readings, 'Yahweh' and 'Judah,' there lies an original 'Joshua'.' If, as is generally acknowledged, Josh. 17[14-18] belongs to this narrative, some mention of Joshua' is to be expected. A sufficient reason for the excision of the name of Joshua', and the substitution of the reading of our text, is furnished by the fact that R[P] professes to be giving an account of events which happened 'after the death of Joshua'' (cf. *introd. note* to section).

23. *made a reconnaissance.* The same Heb. verb *tûr* is used of the *exploration* of Cana'an by the *spies* (*hat-târîm*, Num. 14[6]) in the parts of Num. 13, 14 which belong to P. In this passage we have the Hiph'îl (causative) modification of the verb, which, if not merely an error for the simple stem (ויתירו for ויתורו), may mean 'caused a reconnaissance to be made.' 𝔊[L] καὶ παρενέβαλον (so 𝔊[BA] with doublet καὶ κατεσκέψαντο), 𝔙 'cum obsiderent,' suggest a reading וַיַּחֲנוּ וג׳, 'and the house of Joseph encamped against Bethel.' Cf. the rendering of 𝔊 in *ch.* 9[50].

now the name of the city formerly was Luz. Cf. Gen. 28[19], 35[6], 48[3], Josh. 18[13], all P, or redactional notes based on P—a fact which has led Mo. (*SBOT.*), No. to mark the statement here as due to R[P]. The reference to Luz, however, in *v.*[26] J clearly points back to an earlier mention of the name in the same document. For conjectures as to the meaning of the name Luz, cf. *EB.* 2834.

24. *and they laid hold on him.* So 𝔊 καὶ ἔλαβον αὐτόν, *i.e.* וַיֹּאחֲזוּ בוֹ or וַיֹּאחֲזֻוהוּ (cf. *v.*[6]), which, as Bu. remarks, may easily have fallen out before וַיֹּאמְרוּ, 'and they said.'

the way to enter. So Mo. The Heb. *m[e]bhô* (lit. 'place *or* act of entry') might mean 'entrance' (so R.V.), as in 2 Kgs. 11[16], 16[18] *al.*; but, as the position of the city-gate must have been obvious to the spies, the expression probably means, as Mo. remarks, 'the most advantageous point for an assault or surprise.'

25. *at the edge of the sword.* Cf. *v.*[8] *note.*

all his clan they let go. 26. And the man went to the land of the Ḥittites, and built a city, and called its name Luz: that is its name unto this day.

27. And Manasseh did not dispossess Beth-she'an and its

26. *the land of the Ḥittites.* The Ḥittite principalities (relics of the earlier mighty empire which embraced a great part of Asia Minor and northern Syria) extended as far south as Ḳadesh, near the sources of the Orontes in the Anti-Lebanon. The northern limit of the kingdom of Israel in David's time seems to have extended 'to the land of the Ḥittites unto Ḳadesh' (2 Sam. 24[6], reading אֶרֶץ הַחִתִּים קָדֵשָׁה after 𝔊[L] in place of the unintelligible text of 𝔐). On the Ḥittites, cf. further *Introd.* pp. lxxi f., lxxxiv ff., xcix f.

called its name Luz. The site of this northern Luz is unascertained. As Mo. notices, modern names compounded with the Ar. *lauz*, 'almond,' are not infrequent, and any attempt at identification must therefore be wholly unreliable.

27. *And Manasseh did not dispossess, etc.* Upon the use of the verb *hôrîš*, here rendered 'dispossess,' cf. *note* on *v.*[19]. Beth-she'an, which received the Greek name Scythopolis in Macedonian times (cf. 𝔊's gloss ἥ ἐστιν Σκυθῶν πόλις), is the modern Bêsân, situated above the Jordan valley at the mouth of the Wâdy Ǵâlûd, which descends south-east from the plain of Esdraelon; Ta'anach, now called Ta'annuk, lies some seventeen miles a little north of due west of Bêsân, upon the southern edge of Esdraelon, and about eight miles north-north-west of the Wâdy Bel'ameh, which probably preserves the name of the ancient Ible'am;* Megiddo, coupled with Ta'anach in *ch.* 5[19], Josh. 12[21], 17[11], 1 Kgs. 4[12], is now identified with Tell el-Mutesellim ('the mound of the governor'), five miles north-west of Ta'annuk, an important site commanding the pass from the plain of Sharon to the plain of Esdraelon, which the recent excavations of the German Palestine Exploration Society (vol. i. of the Report 1908) have shown to have been a fortified city of the Cana'anites many centuries before the Israelite occupation of Palestine. The statement of Josephus that Dor was situated on the Mediterranean seacoast, near Carmel (*Ant.* VIII. ii. 3; cf. *C. Ap.* ii. 116), is confirmed by the Egyptian narrative of Wenamon, the envoy of Ḥriḥor of Thebes (*cir.* B.C. 1114), who in his voyage from Egypt to Phoenicia puts in at the harbour of Dor (Breasted, *AR.* iv. § 565; cf. *Introd.* p. xcvi).

* The modern Yebla, north-west of Bêsân, proposed by Conder (*SWP. Mem.* ii. p. 98) as the site of Ible'am, is philologically less probable. The dropping of the final syllable with its guttural ע might be paralleled, however, by the modern el-Ǵib for Gibe'on. For the dropping of the preformative י of יִבְלְעָם in Bel'ameh, cf. the form בִּלְעָם Bile'am 1 Chr. 6[70] (𝔐 [55]), and Zer'in for יִזְרְעֶאל.

dependencies, and Ta'anach and its dependencies, and the inhabitants of Dor and its dependencies, and the inhabitants of

OS. places the site eight Roman miles from Caesarea (283 [3]), and this tradition is preserved in the identification with the modern Ṭanṭûrah, which lies north of Caesarea at a little less than eight English miles. The term *Nāphath* (*Nāphôth*) *Dôr* (Josh. 11 [2], 12 [23], 1 Kgs. 4 [11]), if rightly explained to mean 'the heights of Dor,' is difficult to account for upon this identification, unless it is applied to the outlying flanks of the Carmel-range some distance inland from Ṭanṭûrah.

As the text stands, it is rather strange that Dor, lying in the extreme west, should be interposed between the two cities Ta'anach and Ible'am, which occupy a central position in near neighbourhood to one another. Thus it is probable (as Mo. suggests) that the mention of Dor originally stood last, as in 1 Chr. 7 [29], which is probably based upon this passage. With this change, the cities are mentioned approximately in their geographical order from east to west; and it is noticeable that they must have formed, with their dependencies, a strong belt of fortresses separating the central tribes of Israel from the tribes in the north. We learn from the narrative of Wenamon that the inhabitants of Dor at this period were not Cana'anites but Ṯakkara, a western people who invaded Cana'an at the same time as the Philistines, and who were probably allied to them (cf. *Introd.* pp. xcii f.). This fact, coupled with the fact that we find Beth-she'an in the hands of the Philistines at the end of Saul's reign (1 Sam. 31 [10]), suggests the possibility that the whole series of cities extending from Sharon across the plain of Esdraelon may have belonged to these western invaders in the times of the Judges.

The account of the inheritance of West Manasseh, as given in Josh. 17 (J and P combined), is somewhat perplexing. This much, however, is clear, as stated by P (*vv.* [9.10]). It was bounded on the west by the Mediterranean; on the north by the territory of Asher, which, we are told in Josh. 19 [26] P, extended as far as Carmel; on the south by the territory of Ephraim, the boundary line being the Wâdy Ḳana, *i.e.* it need not be doubted, the modern Wâdy Kâna* running into the Nahr el-'Auǵa, which reaches the sea a few miles north of Joppa. The eastern boundary is stated to have been the territory of Issachar; and it is here that our information is too slight and perplexing to allow of any certain inferences as to the delimitation. According to J in Josh. 17 [11], the towns along the southern edge of the plain of Esdraelon which Manasseh was unable to conquer were (though rightly belonging to Manasseh) 'in Issachar and in Asher.'

dependencies. Lit. 'daughters,' a term applied to smaller cities or hamlets dependent upon the larger fortified cities. The use of the expression is characteristic of J. Cf. CH.[J] 88.

* The Ar. name is spelt with *K*, but it seems likely that this is a transcriptional error for *Ḳ*, which is found in the Heb. name.

Ible'am and its dependencies, and the inhabitants of Megiddo and its dependencies; but the Cana'anites persisted in dwelling in this land. 28. And when Israel was waxen strong, they impressed the Cana'anites for labour-gangs, and did not dispossess them at all.

29. And Ephraim did not dispossess the Cana'anites who

persisted. The Heb. verb (הוֹאִיל) is used in this special sense in || Josh. 17[12] and in *v.*[35] † of this chapter. Elsewhere, when used of an action undertaken of one's own accord, it has the sense *to resolve*: cf. Gen. 18[27.31] (R.V. 'I have taken upon me'), Deut. 1[5] (R.V. 'began'); and we may infer therefore for the special usage with which we are dealing the sense *to carry out one's resolution*, so *persist.* When the verb is employed of an action undertaken at the instance of some one else, *to consent* is the appropriate rendering: cf. *ch.* 17[11], 19[6], 2 Sam. 7[29], 2 Kgs. 5[23], 6[3] (R.V. 'be content' in all passages except 2 Sam. 'let it please thee').

28. *labour-gangs.* The Heb. term *maś* denotes a levy of men impressed for task-work, rather than the task-work itself (as in R.V.): cf. especially the phrase *maś 'ōbhēdh*, 'toiling labour-gang,' Gen. 49[15], Josh. 16[10], 1 Kgs. 9[21]. Such a levy was imposed upon the Israelites in Egypt (cf. Ex. 1[11], where, as Mo. points out, the term שָׂרֵי מִסִּים should be rendered 'gang-foremen' rather than 'taskmasters' R.V.), and by Solomon not merely upon the Cana'anites (as stated in 1 Kgs. 9[15-22]) but also upon the Israelites for the purposes of his extensive building operations: cf. 1 Kgs. 5[13] ([27] 𝔐).

and did not dispossess them at all. The Heb. construction (וְהוֹרֵישׁ לֹא הוֹרִישׁוֹ, Infinitive Absolute emphasizing the finite verb) lays stress upon the fact that the expulsion of the Cana'anites was left absolutely unaccomplished. R.V., by its rendering 'and did not utterly drive them out,' suggests that the expulsion was partially but not completely accomplished, a sense which is directly at variance with the meaning of the Heb.

29. *Ephraim.* The account of Ephraim's heritage as given in Josh. 16[5ff.] P is somewhat confused and perplexing: cf. Hogg in *EB.* 1319. Here we need only notice that the tribe occupied the central part of Cana'an, its northern boundary marching with that of Manasseh along by the Wâdy Ḳana (cf. *note* on Manasseh, *v.*[27]) to the sea, while the southern boundary, starting from the Jordan near Jericho, met the territory of Benjamin and Dan, apparently turning north or north-west at Gezer. Cf. further p. 222.

Gezer. The modern Tell Ǵezer, situated in a commanding position to the east of the maritime plain of Philistia, upon an outlying spur of the low hills of the Shephelah, about eighteen miles west-north-west

dwelt in Gezer; but the Cana'anites dwelt in the midst of them in Gezer.

30. Zebulun did not dispossess the inhabitants of Ḳiṭron, nor

of Jerusalem. The identity of the site with the ancient Gezer, inferred from the identity of the modern Ar. with the ancient Heb. name, was placed beyond doubt by the discovery in 1871 by Clermont-Ganneau of the inscription 'the boundary of Gezer,' cut in ancient Heb. characters upon several of the rocks at a short distance from the site: cf. Macalister, *Bible Sidelights from the Mound of Gezer*, pp. 22 ff.; Driver, *Schweich Lectures*, p. 46. The site of Gezer has been excavated by Mr. Macalister under the auspices of the Palestine Exploration Fund (1903-1905, 1907-1909), and a detailed Memoir has recently (1912) appeared. For a convenient summary of the discoveries, cf. Driver, *op. cit.*

The excavations have shown that Gezer was inhabited by a race of cave-dwellers as early as *cir.* B.C. 3000. It is first mentioned in history as captured by Ṭhutmosi III. (*cir.* B.C. 1501-1447). Among the Tell el-Amarna letters (*cir.* B.C. 1400) there are several from Yapaḫi, king or governor of Gezer, who appeals for help against a people whose name is written ideographically SA.GAZ, and who are generally supposed to be identical with the Ḫabiru (cf. *Introd.* pp. lxxv ff.). Mineptaḥ claims to have captured Gezer upon the celebrated 'Israel' stele: cf. Breasted, *AR.* iii. § 617. This must have been *cir.* B.C. 1223, a few decades before the Israelite invasion of Cana'an under Joshua'. The failure of the Ephraimites to capture Gezer is confirmed by 1 Kgs. 9[16], where we learn that the city was still in the hands of the Cana'anites in the days of Solomon, when it was taken and burnt by the Phara'oh who was king of Egypt at that time, and given as a dowry to his daughter on the occasion of her marriage with Solomon. These facts are for us difficult to reconcile with the statement of R^D in Josh. 10[33] that, when Horam king of Gezer came to the assistance of Lachish, 'Joshua' smote him and his people until he had left him none remaining.'

but the Cana'anites . . . Gezer. 𝔊 adds καὶ ἐγένετο (αὐτῷ) εἰς φόρον. ‖ Josh. 16[10b], 'but the Cana'anites dwelt in the midst of Ephraim unto this day, and became toiling labour-gangs': probably the more original form of J's statement. The words 'unto this day,' if they 'do not necessarily imply a time prior to the destruction of the city by the Egyptians' (Mo.), at any rate seem to point to the earlier monarchic period. Cf. *note* on the same expression in *v.*[21].

30. *Zebulun.* The description of Zebulun's territory given in Josh. 19[10ff.] P is obscure. The southern boundary was contiguous with the territory of Issachar along a line which ran east and west across the plain of Esdraelon in the neighbourhood of Mount Tabor; while on the south-west the boundary marched with the territory of Manasseh,

the inhabitants of Nahalol; but the Cana'anites dwelt in the midst of them, and became labour-gangs.

31. Asher did not dispossess the inhabitants of 'Acco, nor the

north-west with the territory of Asher, and north, and apparently east, with that of Naphtali. Jos., however, states (*Ant.* v. i. 22) that their inheritance included the land which reached as far as Gennesaret, as well as that which lay about Carmel and the sea (cf. Gen. 49 [13]).

Ḳiṭron . . . Nahalol. Neither site has been identified. Nahălōl (perhaps meaning 'watering-place' of flocks; cf. plural נַהֲלֹלִים, Isa. 7 [19]) appears in Josh. 19 [15], 21 [35] as Nahălāl. G[B] Δωμανα in the present passage must have read Dimnah, which is coupled with Nahălāl in Josh. 21 [35]. In Josh. 19 [15] Ḳaṭṭāth seems to stand in place of Ḳiṭrōn; but neither name occurs elsewhere. The Jerusalem Talmud (*Megillah*, i. 1) identifies Nahălāl with Mahlûl; and for this the modern Ma'lûl, 3½ miles west of Nazareth, has been advocated by Schwarz and others,* and 'Ain Mâhil, about the same distance north-east of Naẓareth, by Conder.

In the same passage in the Talmud Ḳaṭṭāth is said to be Ḳĕṭînîth or Ḳĕṭônîth ‡ (cf. 𝔊[B] Κατανaθ in Josh. 19 [15]), a site which may be the modern Ḫirbet Ḳuteineh to the west of the plain of Esdraelon §: cf. Neubauer, *Géographie du Talmud*, p. 189. The view put forward in the Babylonian Talmud (*Megillah*, 6[a]) that Ḳiṭrôn is the same as Ṣippôrî (Sepphoris), *i.e.* the modern Ṣeffûriyyeh, 3½ miles north of Naẓareth, is opposed by Neubauer (*op. cit.* pp. 191 f.) upon the ground of a tradition (preserved in the same passage in the Talmud) that the tribe of Zebulun complained that, while Naphtali had been granted fields and vineyards, they had only been granted mountains and hills. Ṣippôrî, however, was famed for its fertility; and hence Neubauer argues that it must have belonged not to Zebulun but to Naphtali.

31. *Asher.* The tribe is mentioned as inhabiting western Galilee in the lists of the Egyptian kings, Sety I. and Ra'messe II., prior to

* The substitution of Ar. ' for Heb. *h* requires substantiation; and this is also needed as regards the interchange of *n* and *m* in Nahălāl, Mahlûl, if the two forms are to be regarded as philologically connected.

‡ Editions vary as to the form. Ḳeṭonith (or Ḳeṭunith) is given by Neubauer *loc. cit.*, and by Mo. and Cheyne (*EB.* 2654) following him. The Krotoschin edition (1866) has קטונית, Ḳeṭonith, but the Jitomir (1866) and Petrokov (1899) editions read קטינית, Ḳeṭinith. The reference given by Neubauer from the Tosefta (*Sotah, ch.* 15) to איש קטונית, 'a man of Ḳeṭonith,' should be, as a matter of fact (Pazewalk edition, 1881), בן קיטנית, 'a son of Ḳiṭnith,' with *var. lect.* קטנית, Ḳiṭnith or Ḳaṭnith.

§ The Heb. Ḳĕṭînîth corresponds exactly to the Ar. Ḳuṭeineh if this latter is to be regarded as a diminutive. Cf. for the vowel change modern Ar. *kefîfah* for *kufeifah*, 'little basket': Wright, *Comparative Grammar*, p. 89.

Ḳaṭṭāth may very likely have arisen from an original Ḳaṭṭant or Ḳaṭṭint: cf. *bath* from *bint*, and, for the lengthening of the *a*, *'ām* for *'amm*.

inhabitants of Ṣidon, nor Aḥlab, nor Achzib, nor Ḥelbah, nor

the Israelite invasion under Joshua'; cf. *Introd.* p. lxxxix. The position of Asher's inheritance is described in Josh. 19 [24ff.] P. It seems to have been a strip of country reaching southward to Carmel, where it joined the territory of Manasseh, and apparently bordering the sea as far north as Achzib and Maḥaleb (cf. *note* following on Aḥlab). Farther north the western boundary must have been formed by the territory of the Ṣidonians, while the east and south-east boundary-line was formed by the territory of Naphtali and Zebulun. Probably the limits thus defined are largely ideal, a considerable portion of the territory which they include belonging properly to the Phoenicians; cf. *note* on *v.* [32].

'Acco. The modern 'Akkâ, situated on a rocky promontory at the northern extremity of the bay of 'Akkâ, the south side of which is formed by the promontory of Carmel. The town received the name Ptolemais during the Greek period; cf. *OS.* 224 [75]. The Acre of the Crusaders is a modification of the modern Ar. name; cf. Smith's article in *EB.* 3967 ff. 'Acco is wanting in the text of 𝔐 in Josh. 19 [24-31], but should probably be restored in place of 'Umma in *v.* [30].

Ṣidon. The modern Ṣaida, about twenty-five miles south of Beirût.

Aḥlab . . . Ḥelbah. The two names are so similar that they look like variations of the same name. Schrader (*COT.* i. p. 161) and Delitzsch (*Paradies*, pp. 283 f.) compare the name *Maḫalliba* mentioned by Šennacherib in a list of Phoenician cities which capitulated to him in his third campaign: *Taylor Cylinder*, Col. ii. l. 38; cf. *KB.* ii. p. 90. Šennacherib names 'Great Ṣidunnu (cf. צִידוֹן רַבָּה, Josh. 19 [28]) little Ṣidunnu, Bît-zitti, Ṣariptu (Ṣārĕphath, 1 Kgs. 17 [9.10], Ob. [20], Σαρεπτα Lu. 4 [26]; the modern Ṣarafand), Maḫalliba, Ušû, Akzibi, Akkû'; and the order running from north to south should place Maḫalliba somewhere between Ṣarafand, which lies eight miles south of Ṣidon, and Achzib (cf. *note* following), some thirty miles farther south. Mo. hazards the conjecture that the name may have been 'the old name of the *Promontorium album* of Pliny, the modern Râs el-Abyaḍ, midway between Tyre and Achzib,' a suitable site for an important town. The name may be connected with Heb. *ḥālābh*, 'milk,' in allusion to the whiteness of the headland.

The strange מֵחֶבֶל of Josh. 19 [29] (*mēḥĕbel*; R.V. 'by the region'; *marg.* 'from Ḥebel'.) is almost certainly a corruption of מַחֲלֵב, Maḥălēb (cf., in support of the transposition, 𝔊[B] ἀπὸ Λεβ); and this fact lends support to the view of Müller (*AE.* p. 194, *n* [4]), La. that the name should be so read in our passage, as against that of Mo. that Maḫalliba, Aḥlab, Ḥelbah were existing variations of the same name.

Aphiḳ, nor Reḥob: 32. but the Asherites dwelt in the midst of the Canaʿanites inhabiting the land; for they did not dispossess them.

33. Naphtali did not dispossess the inhabitants of Beth-

Achzib. The Εκδιππα of *OS.* 224[77], a form in which the δ seems to preserve the Aram. pronunciation. The modern identification is ez-Zîb, eight and a half miles north of Accho.*

Aphiḳ. Mentioned (in the form Aphēḳ) with Reḥob among the cities of Asher in Josh. 19[30]. That the Aphēḳ of 1 Sam. 29[1] is the same (as suggested by Bu., La.) is scarcely likely, as this latter is probably to be sought in northern Sharon ‡ (Smith, *HG.* p. 350), and would therefore lie too far to the south. On the other hand, as Mo. points out, the modern Afḳâ, north of Bêrût (probably the Apheḳ of Josh. 13[4]), 'is much too far north for the present context and that of Josh. 19[30].' The name Apheḳ appears to have been by no means uncommon.

Reḥob. The site is unknown. Müller cites the occurrence of the name in Egyptian lists; *AE.* p. 153. That the Beth-reḥob of *ch.* 18[28], 2 Sam. 10[6], inhabited by Aramaeans (probably the Reḥob of Num. 13[21]), cannot be the same as the Asherite Reḥob is perhaps too positively asserted by Mo. The identity is assumed by Nöldeke in *EB.* 279.

32. *the Asherites dwelt, etc.* In the case of Asher it is not claimed that the Canaʿanites eventually became a subject people. The maritime cities mentioned in *v.*[31] belonged to Phoenicia throughout the period covered by the history of the kingdom of Israel. In the Song of Deborah (*ch.* 5) the reference to Asher in *v.*[17] ('Asher sat still by the shore of the seas, dwelling beside his creeks') seems to indicate that the Asherites dwelt among the Phoenician Canaʿanites in a condition of dependence; and being thus unmolested by the central Canaʿanites, refused to make common cause against them with the other Israelite tribes.

33. *Naphtali.* The territory of Naphtali is described by P in Josh. 19[32-39]. It lay to the north of Zebulun, and was bounded by the territory of Asher on the west and by the Jordan on the east. The predominance of the foreign element in the region of Naphtali and Zebulun, as in that of Asher, is indicated by the title *Gᵉlîl hag-gôyîm*, 'the District (circuit) of the Nations' applied to it in

* If the name comes from the Heb. root כָּזָב, Aram. כְּדַב, as is suggested by the form Εκδιππα (cf. the word-play of Mic. 1[14] in the case of the southern Achzib), we should expect ed-Dîb. The substitution of *z* for *d* in modern Ar. is, however, not unparalleled.

‡ Probably Josh. 12[18] ought to read מֶלֶךְ אֲפֵק לְשָׁרוֹן אֶחָד, 'The king of Apheḳ pertaining to Sharon, one'; cf. Buhl, *Geogr.* p. 213, *n* 674.

shemesh, nor the inhabitants of Beth-ʿanath; but they dwelt in the midst of the Canaʿanites inhabiting the land; and the inhabitants of Beth-shemesh and Beth-ʿanath became labour-gangs for them.

34. And the Amorites pressed the children of Dan into the

Isa. 9[1] (𝔐 8[23]), or, in short form, *hag-Gālîl*, Josh. 20[7], 21[32]; 1 Kgs. 9[11]; 1 Chr. 6[76] (𝔐[61]), whence the name Galilee. Cf. also 'Ḥarosheth of the nations,' *ch.* 4[2.13.16], probably in Zebulun; cf. *note ad loc.*

Beth-shemesh . . . Beth-ʿanath. Both sites are unidentified (cf., however, *Introd.* p. cvii, *footnote* ||). Beth-ʿanath occurs in the Egyptian lists of the Eighteenth and Nineteenth Dynasties; cf. Müller, *AE.* pp. 193, 195, 220. ʿAnāth is the name of a goddess, possibly the same as the Babylonian Antum or Anatum, consort of Anu, the god of heaven, and chief of the first triad of gods (Anu, Enlil, and Ea); cf. Jastrow in *DB.* v. p. 538 b, and *RBA.* i. p. 143. Further traces of the cult of this goddess in Canaʿan are preserved in the southern ʿAnāthôth (ʿAnâta, two and a half miles north-north-east of Jerusalem), and in the proper name Shamgar ben-ʿAnāth, *ch.* 3[31], 5[6]. She was worshipped in the fifth century B.C. by the Jewish garrison stationed at Elephantiné on the southern border of Egypt. We meet with the compound name ʿAnath-bethel, in which the deities ʿAnath and Bethel (treated as a divine name) are probably equated;* and ʿAnath-yahu also occurs. Probably she was 'the queen of heaven,' who, according to Jer. 44[15 ff.], was worshipped by the Jews who dwelt in Pathros, *i.e.* in Upper Egypt, where Elephantiné was situated. Our information as to this Jewish garrison and its religious cultus is derived from recently discovered Aram. papyri which were edited in 1911 by Sachau under the title *Aramäische Papyrus und Ostraker aus einer jüdischen Militär-Kolonie zu Elephantine.* Cf. the present editor's article in *Church Quart. Rev.*, July 1912.

but they dwelt. 𝔊[AL], 𝔖[h] καὶ κατῴκησεν Ισραηλ, very possibly the original text; cf. *note* on Josh. 13[13], which belongs to the same narrative, in *Additional note*, p. 51.

34. *the Amorites.* The term is used, here and in *v.*[35], as a general name for the pre-Israelite inhabitants of Palestine, who elsewhere in this section (*vv.*[1.3.5.17.27.28.29.32.33]; cf. also *vv.*[4.9] from the editor R^P) are described as Canaʿanites, in accordance with the regular practice of J. Such a use of 'Amorites,' on the contrary, is characteristic of E (cf. *note* on *v.*[1]); and the difficulty of accounting for this deviation in usage on the part of J has led Meyer (*ZATW.* i. p. 126) to conclude that *vv.*[34-36] are the work of a later hand. So Stade, *GVI.* i. p. 138 *n.* Against this view Bu.'s arguments (*RS.* pp. 15 ff.) are cogent; notice

* Such a compound deity is seen in ʿAshtar-Chemosh, mentioned on the Moabite Stone, l. 17.

hill-country; for they did not suffer them to come down into

J's phrases in *v.*^{35}—'persisted in dwelling,' as in *v.*^{27}, Josh. 17^{12}, 'became labour-gangs,' as in *vv.*$^{30.33}$, Josh. 16^{10}; and the fact that *v.*^{34} clearly forms the lowest grade in a descending scale—in *vv.*$^{27-30}$ the Canaʿanites remain in the midst of Israel, and eventually become subject; in *vv.*$^{31-33}$ Asher and Naphtali dwell in the midst of the Canaʿanites, the inference being that these latter retained the predominance, whether in power or in numbers (cf. *notes* on *vv.*$^{32.33}$); in *v.*^{34} the 'Amorites' actually oust the Danites from their territory. It is probable that J originally wrote 'Canaʿanites' in these two verses* (Χαναναῖος is the reading of HP. 55 in *v.*^{35}), and that the substitution of 'Amorites' is due to a later hand, under the influence, it may be conjectured, of the textual corruption 'Amorites' for 'Edomites' in *v.*^{36}.

pressed the children of Dan, etc. Josh. 19$^{41-46}$ P assigns sixteen or seventeen (𝔐) cities to Dan, all of which, so far as they can be identified, lie in the Shephelah and vale-country to the east of the territories of Benjamin and northern Judah. Out of this list, however, Ṣorʿah, Eshta'ol, ʿEḳron, and Timnah are assigned by P to Judah in Josh. 15$^{33.45.57}$. In the narrative of Samson the Danites appear to be confined to a small district about Ṣorʿah and Eshta'ol, immediately contiguous to the hill-country, while Timnah is occupied by Philistines just as ʿEḳron is elsewhere. We may infer that the Amorites or Canaʿanites who, as our narrative informs us, forced the Danites into the hills, were themselves suffering from the encroachments of the Philistines on the west. The Philistines, who entered Canaʿan about the same time as, or a very short time before, the Israelite invasion under Joshuaʿ (cf. *Introd.* pp. xcii ff.), must naturally have driven such of the original Canaʿanite inhabitants of their territory as escaped extirpation (cf. Deut. 2^{23}) eastward towards the hill-country, where they would come into conflict with the Danites, who may have made their settlement prior to Joshuaʿ's invasion (cf. *Introd.* pp. cvi f.). Josh. 19^{47}, which originally formed part of J's narrative, informs us that finally a large portion of the tribe of Dan, if not the main portion, finding their district too narrow (read וַיֵּצַר . . . מֵהֶם, 'was too strait for them,' in place of 𝔐 וַיֵּצֵא . . . מֵהֶם, R.V. 'went out beyond them'), migrated to the extreme north of Palestine, conquered the city of Leshem (or perhaps Lêshām: cf. *ch.* 18^{7} *note*), and established themselves in and about the city, which they renamed Dan. This migration is further related in *ch.* 18, where the conquered city is called Laish (*vv.*$^{7.27}$), and seems already to have taken place at the period to which the Song of Deborah relates (cf. *note* on *ch.* 5^{17}). Thenceforward Dan figures in the common phrase 'from Dan to Beershebaʿ' as the northernmost limit of Palestine.

* Meyer appears now to incline to this view: cf. *IN.* p. 525, *n* 1.

the Vale. 35. And the Amorites persisted in dwelling in Har-ḥereś, in Aijalon, and in Sha'albim: yet the hand of the house

the Vale. Cf. *v.*[19] *note.*

35. *persisted in dwelling.* Cf. *v.*[27] *note.*

Har-ḥereś. The name means 'hill of the Sun,' and the fact that *ḥereś* = *šemeš* has led Stu. and others after him to identify the site with Beth-shemesh ('house *or* temple of the Sun'), *i.e.* the modern 'Ain-šems ('spring of the Sun') which occupies an elevated site to the south of the Wâdy Ṣarâr (vale of Soreḳ), where it opens out upon the Shephelah. This identification is favoured by the fact that Beth-shemesh is mentioned with Sha'albim in 1 Kgs. 4[9], and 'Ir-shemesh ('city of the Sun,' doubtless the same as Beth-shemesh) with Sha'albim and Aijalon in Josh. 19[41.42], just as Har-ḥereś is in our passage.

𝔊^AL represents בְּהַר חֶרֶס by ἐν τῷ ὄρει τοῦ Μυ[ρ]σινῶνος (so 𝔖^h), 𝔊^B by ἐν τῷ ὄρει τῷ ὀστρακώδει* (with the doublet ἐν τῷ Μυρσινῶνι), *i.e.*, in the first case הֲדַס *hadaś*, 'myrtle,' in the second חֶרֶשׂ *ḥereś*, 'potsherd' in place of חֶרֶס *ḥereś*; both variations being possibly attempts to get rid of the reference to the Sun with its idolatrous implications (so La.). Why such a reference should have been found more objectionable in the case of *ḥereś* than in that of *šemeš* is not obvious: but it cannot be merely accidental that Timnath-ḥereś of Judg. 2[9] appears in || Josh. 24[30] and in Josh. 19[50] as Timnath-śeraḥ (סרח a transposition of the consonants of חרס). ‡

Aijalon. The identification of Rob. (*BR*[3]. ii. pp. 253 f., iii. pp. 144 f.) with the modern Yâlô, seven miles north-north-east of 'Ain-šems and in the south of the 'vale' into which the pass of Beth-ḥoron opens out ('the vale of Aijalon,' Josh. 10[12]) is universally accepted. The name 'Ayyālôn perhaps means 'haunt of deer' (*'ayyāl*). How 𝔊 arrived at the rendering αἱ ἄρκοι is obscure, unless this may be regarded as a corruption of οἱ δόρκοι § (for the normal αἱ δορκάδες). 𝔊, however,

* Cf. the gloss 'quod interpretatur testaceo,' which appears in 𝔙.

‡ It must be considered doubtful whether *'îr ha-hereś*, 'city of destruction,' in Isa. 19[18] 𝔐 is also to be considered as an alteration of an original *'îr ha-ḥereś*, 'city of the Sun,' *i.e.* Heliopolis. The phrase 'one shall be called' implies that one of the five cities mentioned is to be distinguished by a name which denotes its special character as representative of the worship of Yahweh; and this consideration weighs in favour of the view that the reading of 𝔊, πόλις ασεδεκ, *i.e.* עִיר הַצֶּדֶק, 'city of righteousness' (as it were 'the Egyptian Jerusalem': cf. Isa. 1[26]), is likely to be the original reading. Cf. Gray's acute discussion of the passage in *Isaiah* (*ICC.*) *ad loc.* This, however, may have been afterwards altered to *'îr ha-ḥereś* in allusion to Heliopolis, and the reading of 𝔐, *'îr ha-hereś*, may represent a still later stage.

§ ὁ δόρκος is found in Nicolaus of Damascus (B.C. 16), 46, 47; Dioscorides (*cir.* A.D. 60), 2, 85; Testamenta XII. Patriarcharum 1121 D: cf. Sophocles, *Greek Lexicon s.v.*

of Joseph prevailed, and they became labour-gangs. 36. And the border of the ⸢Edomites⸣ was from the ascent of ʿAḳrabbim,

confines δορκάς to the Heb. *ṣᵉbî*, 'gazelle,' with which the *'ayyāl* is often coupled, but never confused.

Shaʿalbim. Site unknown. The name appears in Josh. 19^{42} as Shaʿălabbin, and probably means 'foxes': cf. Assyr. *šêlibu*, Ar. *ṯaʿlab*, and the rendering of 𝔊 αἱ ἀλώπεκες. Apart from this place-name, the fact that the word was used in Heb. would be unknown to us, the ordinary Heb. word for 'fox' being *šûʿāl*.

prevailed. Lit. 'became heavy.'

36. *the border of the Edomites.* Reading הָאֲדֹמִי in place of 𝔐 הָאֱמֹרִי 'the Amorites' with Bu., Kit. (*HH.* i. p. 268), Buhl (*Edomiter*, p. 25), No., La., etc. The reading τὸ ὅριον τοῦ Ἀμορραίου ὁ Ἰδουμαῖος is found in $𝔊^{AL}$, the group of MSS. cited by Mo. as $𝔊^{M}$, Arm., Eth., $𝔖^{h}$ (with obelus before ὁ Ἰδ.), and this is adopted by Hollenberg, *ZATW.* i. p. 103. But the writer's interest is centred upon the footing gained by the tribes of *Israel* in Palestine, and the frontier between Amorites and Edomites would scarcely concern him in this connexion; while such a use of the term 'Amorite' is contrary to the practice of J: cf. $v.^{34}$ *note.* It cannot be doubted that he is indicating the line along which the frontier of the southern-most tribe (Judah) marched with the frontier of *Edom.* האמרי is an easy corruption of האדמי, and the versions as cited above present a doublet. A similar confusion occurs between אֱדֹם 'Edom' and אֲרָם 'Aram': 2 Sam. $8^{12.13}$ (cf. $v.^{14}$, 1 Chr. $18^{11.12}$, Ps. 60 *heading*), 2 Chr. 20^{2}, 2 Kgs. 16^{6}.

from the ascent of ʿAḳrabbim. Usually identified with the Naḳb eṣ-Ṣafâ, a steep pass which runs up northward out of the Wâdy el-Fiḳrah: cf. *note* on Ṣephath $v.^{17}$. An obvious objection to this identification lies in the fact that the frontier of Edom cannot be said to commence *from* this point, since this would leave out of account the twenty-five miles or so which intervene between the mouth of the Naḳb eṣ-Ṣafâ and the southern extremity of the Dead Sea at which the frontier is stated to begin in Num. 34^{3}, Josh. 15^{2} P. The same objection applies, in an enhanced degree, to the more westerly Naḳb el-Yemen, advocated by Trumbull (*Ḳadesh-Barnea*, p. 111). More probably we should find the ascent in the Wâdy el-Fiḳrah, which Trumbull (*op. cit.* pp. 94 f.) describes as 'a wâdy which ascends south-westerly from the ʿArabah, from a point not far south of the Dead Sea, and which separates Palestine proper from the 'Azâzimeh mountain tract, or Jebel Muḳrâh group. The northern wall of this wâdy is a bare and bold rampart of rock, forming a natural boundary.' Scorpions (*ʿaḳrabbîm*) are said to abound in this district, from the Crag and upwards.

from the Crag. Here we seem to have a second starting-point for the frontier-line between Judah and Edom, *i.e.* upon the most natural hypothesis, the other extremity of the frontier, farthest removed from the ascent of ʿAḳrabbim. The identification of *has-ṣelaʿ*, 'the Crag,' has caused difficulty. Clearly the reference cannot be to the city of Petra,* which was the capital of the Nabataeans from *cir.* B.C. 300 until the second century A.D.; for Petra lies some fifty miles a little east of due south of the southern end of the Dead Sea, among the mountains of Seʿir to the east of the ʿArabah; whereas the researches of Trumbull in connexion with his identification of the site of Ḳadesh-Barneaʿ at ʿAin-Ḳudês, nearly fifty miles south-south-west of Be'er-shebaʿ (generally accepted), have proved beyond a doubt that the territory of Edom must have extended for a considerable distance west of the ʿArabah: cf. Trumbull, *Ḳadesh-Barnea*, pp. 106 ff.; Buhl, *Edomiter*, pp. 23 ff. The course of the southern boundary of Judah is described in detail in Num. 34 3-5, Josh. 15 1-4 P. From these passages we gather that its eastern extremity was the southern 'tongue' of the Salt Sea, and that thence it took its start (וְיָצָא Josh. 15 3) to the south of the ascent of ʿAḳrabbim (*i.e.* upon the identification of the ascent proposed above, upon the south side of the Wâdy el-Fiḳrah; the wâdy, or at least its north side, being claimed by Judah: cf. the analogy of Deut. 3 16, 'the middle of the wâdy being also a boundary'), made a turn (וְנָסַב Num. 34 4) south of this ascent and passed on to Ṣin (an unknown site), and reached its extremity in this direction (תּוֹצְאֹתָיו Num. 34 4) south of Ḳadesh-Barneaʿ. It then took a new start (וְיָצָא Num. 34 4), presumably to the west or north-west, and passing on by a number of unidentified sites, took a turn (וְנָסַב) to the 'Wâdy of Egypt,' *i.e.* the Wâdy el-ʿArîš, and found its end (תּוֹצְאֹתָיו) at the sea (the Mediterranean; Num. 34 5). Here the line along which the frontier of Judah marched with that of Edom was, it must be assumed, in its course west-south-west from the Dead Sea along the Wâdy el-Fiḳrah, and then south-south-west to a point just south of Ḳadesh-Barneaʿ; and it is noteworthy that, in the narrative of Moses' embassy to the king of Edom (Num. 20 14 ff. JE), he states that the Israelites are 'in Ḳadesh, a city in the extremity of thy border.' The natural inference

* Whether Ṡelaʿ (without the article) in Isa. 16 1, 42 11 is the name of a city is very doubtful. Cheyne (*EB.* 4344) takes the word as a collective term, referring to the country as a whole—'the rocks.' In 2 Kgs. 14 7, which relates Amaziah's defeat of the Edomites in the Valley of Salt and the capture of has-Ṡelaʿ, the reference, if it stood alone, might most naturally be explained as referring to a city; but ‖ 2 Chr. 25 12 takes has-Ṡelaʿ to be 'the crag' from the top of which the captured Edomites were cast headlong.

2. 1. And the Angel of Yahweh went up from Gilgal unto

is that *has-sela'*, 'the Crag' of our passage, which formed one extremity of the frontier-line between Judah and Edom, is the same as *has-sela'* 'the Crag' at or close to Ḳadesh, which tradition regarded as the crag which was smitten by Moses (Num. 20[8.10.11] JEP). This conclusion, reached independently by the present editor, is also that of Buhl (*op. cit.* 25) and La.

Bu., Mo. regard the מ in מהסלע as due to dittography of the preceding מ in עקרבים, and emend הַסֶּלַע 'to Sela'.' Mo. conjectures that the site of has-Sela' may have been the modern eṣ-Ṣâfiyyeh, near the southern end of the Dead Sea; but his description of this as 'a bare and dazzling white sandstone promontory a thousand feet high' (derived from Buhl, *op. cit.* p. 20) is stated by La. to be incorrect; and moreover, if, as he supposes, the ascent of 'Aḳrabbim is the Naḳb eṣ-Ṣafâ, the boundary-line between the two points as specified extends for not more than twenty-five miles, and the description must be regarded as merely fragmentary.

and upwards. Upwards towards the first point of departure, the ascent of 'Aḳrabbim. As La. remarks, 'On indique deux points de départ, c'est-à-dire les deux extrémités de la frontière nord, et מעלה marque tout le reste d'une façon indéterminée.'

If the emendation 'to Sela'' noticed above be adopted, the sense in which ומעלה is used is inexplicable, since Mo.'s rendering 'and beyond' cannot be justified. Bu. emends וָהָלְאָה in this sense.

2, 1-5. Upon the relation of these verses to the preceding narrative cf. *introductory note* to 1 [1ff].

1. *the Angel of Yahweh.* The expression is characteristic of J. E's phrase being 'the Angel of God.' So used, it is always definite (not '*an* angel of Y.'; still less a human messenger—𝕿 'the prophet of Y.'), and denotes Yahweh Himself in manifestation to man. That this is so appears from a number of passages, both in J and E. Thus in *ch.* 6 'the Angel of Y.' of *vv.*[11.12.21.22] ('the Angel of God, *v.*[20])='Yahweh' of *vv.*[14.16.23]; in Ex. 3 'the Angel of Y.' of *v.*[2]= 'Yahweh' of *vv.*[4a.7], and 'God' of E's narrative, *vv.*[4b.6.al.]; in Gen. 16 'the Angel of Y.' of *vv.*[7.9.10], who appears to Hagar speaks as Yahweh in the 1st person ('I will greatly multiply thy seed,' *v.*[10]), and is referred to as 'Yahweh' in *v.*[13]; and in E's narrative of Hagar in Gen. 21, 'the Angel of God,' *v.*[17], makes a similar promise in his own name, *v.*[18]; in Gen. 22, 'the Angel of Y.' of *v.*[11] speaks as Yahweh in *v.*[12]; in Gen. 31 [11.13], 'the Angel of God' says 'I am the God of Bethel'; in Gen. 48 [15.16] E, Jacob's reference to 'the Angel who delivered me from all evil' is parallel to 'the God before whom my fathers walked,' etc. To these passages we may add the account of

the appearance of the Angel of Y. to Manoaḥ in *ch.* 13, if it be assumed that R.V. is right in rendering in *v.*^{22} 'We must surely die, for we have seen God.' Possibly, however, *'ĕlōhîm* may here denote no more than 'a god' 'or divine being': cf. *note ad loc.* and *ch.* 6^{22}.

There are, however, a few passages in which a distinction appears to be drawn between Yahweh and His Angel. So in Gen. 24, Yahweh sends His Angel before Abraham's servant *vv.*$^{7.40}$ (yet in *vv.*$^{27.48}$ the servant acknowledges that it is Yahweh who has led him); in Num. 22^{31} Yahweh uncovers Bala'am's eyes so that he sees the Angel of Y. In Ex. 23^{23} Yahweh promises to send His Angel before Israel, who is described in 23^{20} as 'an Angel' (מַלְאָךְ indef.; but, according to 𝔊, 𝔙, Sam., 'mine Angel' as in *v.*^{23} 𝔐). Similarly 'mine Angel' of Ex. 32^{34} is described as 'an Angel' in 33^{2} (𝔊 'mine Angel'), and appears to be something less than Yahweh's full manifestation; since Yahweh says in *v.*^{5} 'If I go up into the midst of thee for one moment, I shall consume thee,' and it is only as the result of importunate intercession on the part of Moses that Yahweh promises 'My Face shall go' (33^{14}), *i.e.*, clearly, Yahweh Himself as distinct from His Angel.*

It must be observed, however, that both in Ex. 23 and 32, 33, the narrative largely consists of redactional matter which is relatively late as compared with J and E (cf. the analysis of CH. *ad loc.*); and probably at the period to which this redaction belongs, the tendency to modify reference to Yahweh's self-revelation to Israel by the introduction of an intermediary was already operative. It is not unlikely, indeed (as suggested by the alternation of 'the Angel of Y.' with 'Yahweh' in the passages first noticed), that the original conception of the Angel represents an early attempt (imperfectly carried out) to interpose such an intermediary, where the primitive narratives simply spoke of Yahweh Himself as appearing and holding direct intercourse with men. If this is so, we may trace a very early anticipation of the far more drastic introduction in the Targums of the 'Memra' ('Word') of Yahweh in passages where reference to Yahweh's direct communication with man was offensive to the taste of later times.

from Gilgal. Gilgal was the headquarters of Joshua' and the Israelites during the invasion of the hill-country, and before the tribes

* If Isa. 63^{9}, as the passage stands in 𝔐, could be relied upon as original, it might be argued that the Angel of Yahweh has the same meaning as His Face, since 'the Angel of His Face' can scarcely mean anything but 'the Angel who is His Face,' *i.e.* His manifestation (so Davidson in *DB*. i. p. 94 b: 'One in whom His face (presence) is reflected and seen'). The rhythmical structure of the section in which this passage occurs, however, confirms the text of 𝔊 *οὐ πρέσβυς οὐδὲ ἄγγελος, ἀλλ' αὐτὸς ἔσωσεν αὐτούς*, *i.e.* לֹא צִיר וּמַלְאָךְ ⟨כִּי⟩ פָּנָיו הוֹשִׁיעָם, 'It was not an envoy or angel, but His Face that saved them.' Thus 'His Face' is contrasted with any other form of manifestation, such as that of an angel.

⌜Bethel⌝. R^P And he said, '⟨I visited you indeed, and⟩ brought

had effected a settlement in the land: cf. Josh. 4^{19} P, 9^{6}, $10^{6.7.9.15}$ JE, 10^{43}, 14^{6} R^D. The name is preserved in the modern Birket ('pool') Ǵilǵûliyyeh, three miles east-south-east of the ancient site of Jericho, and about the same distance west of the Jordan. Several other places in Palestine bore the same name: cf. *EB. s.v.* Gilgal, which in Heb. always has the definite article prefixed, '*the* Gilgal,' doubtless denotes 'circle' (cf. Heb. *galgal*, 'wheel'), and seems to refer to a circle of stones of a primitive religious character. The Gilgal of our passage was probably so named from the stones which tradition related to have been set up by Joshua at the first 'lodging place' (Josh. $4^{3.8}$ J) after the passage of the Jordan, which is stated (4^{19} P) to have been Gilgal. The explanation of Josh. 5^{9} J, which connects the name with the 'rolling away' of the reproach of uncircumcision (Heb. *gallôthî*, 'I have rolled away,' from root *gālal*), is merely a play of words, such as is frequent in J's narrative.

unto Bethel. 𝕳 'unto hab-Bochim': but (1) it is unnatural that the name should be given before the occasion which was its cause is related, and (2) 𝕲 preserves the name Bethel in the doublet ἐπὶ τὸν Κλαυθμῶνα καὶ ἐπὶ Βαιθηλ, and since there can have been no reason for the introduction of this latter if ἐπὶ τὸν Κ. (*i.e.* the reading of 𝕳) already stood in the text, we may infer (with most moderns) that 'unto Bethel' was the reading of 𝕲's original. Adopting this reading, the passage comes into connexion with the narrative of *ch.* $1^{22\,ff.}$, which relates the capture of Bethel by the house of Joseph. The Ark, which was the visible symbol of Yahweh's presence, was carried up from Gilgal and found a resting-place at Bethel, where sacrifices were offered to Yahweh (*v.* ^{5b}). The Ark is still at Bethel in the narrative of *ch.* 20^{27}: cf. also 20^{18}, 21^{2}. Of the circumstances which led to its removal to the Ephraimite sanctuary of Shiloh, where it appears in 1 Sam. 3^{3}, we have no information.

After ἐπὶ Βαιθηλ 𝕲 has the addition καὶ ἐπὶ τὸν οἶκον Ισραηλ. It is probable that this is merely an accidental doublet of בית אל (so Mo.), the אל in an imperfectly legible MS. being mistaken for a contraction of ישראל such as י״ל. A similar process has taken place in Deut. 32^{8} 𝕳, where למספר בני ישראל 'according to the number of the children of Israel,' appears in 𝕲 as κατὰ ἀριθμὸν ἀγγέλων θεοῦ (בני אל), which probably represents the original text.* Bu., regarding the addition as genuine, would restore וְאֶל־בֵּית יִשְׂרָאֵל; and so Kit., La. If this is correct, it is likely, as Bu., No. suggest, that יִשְׂרָאֵל is an alteration

* If the passage pictures the 'Sons of God,' or subordinate angelic powers, as guardians of the foreign nations, the contrast offered by the following clause, 'But Yahweh's portion is his people,' becomes more pointed and effective.

you up from Egypt, and brought you in unto the land which I

of an original יוֹסֵף, and the passage notes the fact that it was 'unto the house of Joseph' that the Angel of Yahweh went up, *i.e.* they had the charge of the sacred Ark.

I visited . . . up. Reading פָּקֹד פָּקַדְתִּי אֶתְכֶם וָאַעֲלֶה אֶתְכֶם in place of 𝔐 אַעֲלֶה אֶתְכֶם. The restoration is purely conjectural; but the use of the Heb. Imperfect in 𝔐 is inexplicable, since a future signification 'I will bring you up' is impossible; nor is it natural to explain the tense here as used pictorially to describe the event as still in progress—a usage which is not uncommon 'in the language of poetry and prophecy' (cf. Driver, *Tenses*, § 27), but is scarcely suited to a plain statement of fact such as the present. That an omission in the text was suspected by the Massoretes is perhaps indicated by the פסקא or lacuna in 𝔐 before אעלה.* It is natural to suppose that ו *consecutive* originally stood before the Imperfect, in continuation of some event of which the statement has fallen out of the text of 𝔐. This missing statement was supplied by Böttcher (*Neue exeget. Krit. Aehrenlese*) from Ex. 3^{16}, Gen. 50^{24}, his restoration running פָּקֹד פָּקַדְתִּי אֶתְכֶם וָאֹמַר אַעֲלֶה, 'I visited you indeed and said, "I will bring you up, etc."'; ‡ and this suggestion has the advantage of accounting for the omission by homœoteleuton, the scribe's eye passing from ויאמר to ואמר. The text adopted above is that of Doorn. (who followed Böttcher in part), and is favoured by Bu., Oort. It makes, with its continuation, a statement in nearly identical terms of the fulfilment of the promise of Gen. 50^{24} E: 'God will indeed visit you, and bring you up out of this land unto the land which he sware to Abraham, to Isaac, and to Jacob.' Cf. Ex. 13^{19} E.

Other suggestions have been made as to the text. Stu. simply inserts אָמַרְתִּי '*I said*, "I will bring you up,"' and cites in favour of this *v.*[3], 'And furthermore I said.' So also Ber. La. substitutes the Perf. for the Imperf., reading אָנֹכִי הֶעֱלֵיתִי 'It was I who brought you up'—a cutting of the knot. Mo. thinks that, since the speech of the Angel is 'a cento of quotations and reminiscences,' it is possible that the author copied Ex. 3^{17a}, 'I will bring you up,' without correct-

* 𝔊^B supplies this lacuna by the words Τάδε λέγει Κύριος, and the same words are found in 𝔖^P, Ar. This, however, does not solve the difficulty of the Heb. tense. 𝔊^AL, 𝔖^h Κύριος ἀνεβίβασεν κ.τ.λ. turn the verbs into the 3rd person, but inconsistently preserve 1st person καὶ ἐγὼ εἶπα in *v.*[3]—a fact which tells against the originality of the preceding variations from 𝔐.

‡ Böttcher offers the alternative בָּחַרְתִּי בָכֶם וָאֹמַר אַעֲלֶה 'I made choice of you and said, etc.'

sware unto your fathers; and I said, "I will never break my covenant with you. 2. And ye—ye shall not make a covenant with the inhabitants of this land; their altars ye shall break down." But ye have not hearkened to my voice: what have ye done? 3. And furthermore I said, "I will not drive them out from before you, but they shall be ⌜adversaries⌝ to you, and their gods shall be a trap to you."' 4. And it came to pass,

ing the tense: but we have no reason to suspect R^P of such gross carelessness.

the land which I sware unto your father. Cf. Ex. 33 [1] JE, Num. 14 [23] JE, 32 [11] P, Deut. 1 [35], 10 [11], 31 [20.21.23], 34 [4] JE, Josh. 1 [6] JE.

I will never break, etc. For the expression, cf. Lev. 26 [44] H. The precise reference, however, is not to H, but to the covenant of Ex. 34 [27] J: 'for after the tenor of these words I have made a covenant with thee and with Israel.' Cf. note following.

2. *And ye, etc.* A quotation from Ex. 34 [12.13a]: 'Take heed to thyself, lest thou make a covenant with the inhabitants of the land whither thou goest, lest it be for a snare in the midst of thee: but their altars ye shall break down.'

3. *And furthermore I said.* The reference is to Josh. 23 [13] R^D, Num. 33 [55] P.

adversaries. Reading לְצָרִים with 𝔊, 𝔏, 𝔙, 𝔗, 𝔐[mg], Stu., Ber., Doorn., Mo. (in *SBOT.*), No., Kit., Ehr., in place of 𝔐 לְצִדִּים. Cf. Num. 33 [55b] P וְצָרֲרוּ אֶתְכֶם 'and they shall act as your adversaries.' According to the regular meaning of צִדִּים in Heb., the statement of 𝔐 can only be rendered 'they shall be to you *as sides.*' R.V. expands this into 'they shall be [as thorns] in your sides,' with marg. ref. to Num. 33 [55]. Such a sense cannot possibly be inherent in 𝔐 as the text stands, though it is legitimate to suppose, with Mo. (*Comm.*), Bu., La., that לְצִדִּים may be the remnant of an original reading לְצְנִינִים בְּצִדֵּיכֶם as in Num. 33 [55a]: cf. Josh. 23 [13] R^D . . . וְהָיוּ לְשֹׁטֵט בְּצִדֵּיכֶם, 'and they shall be . . . as a scourge on your sides.' Delitzsch (*Prolegomena*, p. 75) compares צִדִּים with Assyr. *ṣaddu*, 'net, snare, trap'; but this word is not elsewhere found in Heb., and the improbability of its occurrence here is enhanced by the fact that we expect to find in this passage (as elsewhere in the speech) a reference to an earlier warning. Grätz emends לְצְנִינִים 'as thorns.'

a trap. The metaphor is that of bird-catching, and the Heb. term *môḳēš*, lit. 'fowling instrument,' is commonly parallel to *paḥ*, *i.e.* probably a form of clap-net still employed in Palestine, and bearing

as the Angel of Yahweh spake these words unto all the children of Israel, that the people lifted up their voice, and wept. 5. So they called the name of that place Bochim. J And they sacrificed there to Yahweh.

the same name *faḫ* in Ar.: cf. Baldensperger in *PEF. Qy. St.* 1905, p. 38. BDB. and Driver on Am. 3^{5} explain *môḳēš* as the *lure* or *bait*, a rendering suggested by Am. 3^{5} 𝔐 (where the text, however, is almost certainly at fault*), but impossible in Job 40^{24}, 'pierce his nose with *môḳ^ešîm*,' and in Ps. 64^{5} 'they tell of hiding *môḳ^ešîm* (a *bait* or *lure* is to be *displayed* not *hidden*), and inappropriate (to say the least) in Ps. 18^{5}, where the *môḳ^ešê māweth* (|| 'nooses of She'ol') are a terror and not an attraction. Since the root *yāḳaš* is evidently connected with *nāḳaš* 'strike,' the two verbs being variant triliterals of the biliteral קשׁ, it is probable that *môḳēš* denotes some form of trap in which the release of a spring or support caused the *striking* (knocking down or piercing) of the victim.‡

5. *Bochim.* Meaning 'weepers.' Stu. is probably correct in suggesting connexion with the *'Allôn bakhûth*, 'oak of weeping,' which is stated in Gen. 35^{8} E to have been 'below Bethel.'

And they sacrificed, etc. Cf. *note* on Bethel, *v.* ¹.

* As the text stands in 𝔐, the passage runs—

Shall a bird fall into a *paḥ* upon the ground,
When there is no *môḳēš* for it?
Shall a *paḥ* spring up from the ground,
Without surely capturing?

It is impossible, however, to think that Amos could have written anything so awkward as the repeated *paḥ*; and as a matter of fact the word is omitted by 𝔊 in the first clause: εἰ πεσεῖται ὄρνεον ἐπὶ τὴν γῆν ἄνευ ἰξευτοῦ. With this omission there disappears the necessity of explaining *môḳēš* as something in the nature of a lure.

‡ Dr. Driver has privately communicated the following note:—'As to *môḳēš*, the last words of my note in *Am.* p. 158 leave, I fear, an incorrect impression on the reader: but I have corrected it in *Exodus* (*Camb. Bib.*) on 10^{7}. It seems to me to be something like what we should call a *trigger*, with a bait upon it, which, whether touched by the bird, or pulled by the fowler, caused the trap, or net, to close upon the bird (cf. the illustration, *Am.* p. 157). The *môḳēš* certainly was destructive; but it seems certainly to have acted as a lure to entice to disaster (Ex. 10^{7}, 23^{33}, 1 Sam. 18^{21}); and it is this double aspect of it which suggests to me that it was the trigger properly, but often spoken of as including the bait upon it as well. Job. 40^{24} suggests that it had a sharp point—possibly it *struck* the bird with this: it was sufficient to be the means of catching a bird, but not to pierce the nostril of the hippopotamus. *n^eḳaš* in Aram. is *to strike*; and hence the idea that it was a boomerang: cf. BDB. *s.v.* נקשׁ: but the view in this article seems to me doubtful. I see that BDB. under *môḳēš* do say "prop. a bait or lure"; but "prop." seems to me to be wrong; this is only a secondary idea.'

EXTERNAL EVIDENCE FOR THE USE OF THE TERMS 'CANA'AN' AND 'THE LAND OF THE AMORITE'

(cf. *ch.* 1[1] *note*)

For the Egyptians Pe-kanan, *i.e.* 'the Cana'an,' denoted 'the entire west of Syria-Palestine' (Breasted, *AR.* iii. § 87), while the corresponding ethnographical term seems to have been extended beyond the low-lying maritime region to the population of Western Syria as a whole, as in the usage of J. The Egyptian term Amor was applied to the mountainous district of Lebanon.

The early Babylonians, as far back as the time of Sargon of Akkad (about the end of the fourth millennium B.C.: cf. *Introd.* p. lvi, *footnote* §), knew Syria and Palestine generally as Amurru.* In the T.A. Letters (*cir.* B.C. 1400) the term Kinaḫḫi, or Kinaḫna, Kinaḫni (*i.e.* Cana'an), is applied to the Phoenician coast-land, while Amurru (the land of the Amorites) is not applied to Palestine as a whole, but denotes the 'Hinterland' of the northern Phoenicians, *i.e.* the mountainous district of the Lebanons, and also, as now appears from the cuneiform documents recently discovered at Boghaz Keui, the region still farther east, *i.e.* the Syrian desert and its surrounding districts, as far as the border of Babylonia: cf. Winckler in *MDOG.* xxxv., Dec. 1907, pp. 25 f. Possibly these facts may have a bearing on the distinction of usage between J and E; the former embodying the tradition of the south which lay outside the sphere of the Amorites, while the latter presents the tradition of the northern tribes: cf. Winckler, *GI.* i. pp. 52 ff. See further, on the extra-Biblical evidence as to the usage of the two terms, Jastrow in *EB.* 638 ff.; Meyer, *GA.*^{2} i. §§ 354, 396; Böhl, *KH.* pp. 2 ff., 31 ff.; Müller, *AE.* pp. 177, 205 ff., 218 ff., 229 ff.; Weber in Kn. pp. 1132 ff.

ṢEDEḲ AS A DIVINE NAME (cf. *ch.* 1[5] *note*)

The view that, in אדני צדק Adoni-ṣedeḳ, מלכי צדק Malki-ṣedeḳ, Ṣedeḳ is the proper name of a Cana'anite deity is commonly held, but the evidence cannot be said to be conclusive. The following occurrences of Ṣidḳ or Ṣedeḳ in compound proper names may be noticed: צדקמלך Ṣidḳi-milk on a Phoenician coin, *cir.* B.C. 449-420, Cooke, *NSI.* p. 349; Sabaean צדקאל Ṣidḳi-el, Hommel, *Süd-ar. Chrestom.* quoted by Cooke, *loc. cit.*; Aram. צדקרמן Ṣidḳi-Rammân, *CIS.* ii. 73

* The name Amurru is commonly represented by the Sumerian MAR.TU, 'west land'; but evidence shows that from the earliest times MAR.TU was read and pronounced as Amurru among the Semitic Babylonians: cf. Böhl, *KH.* pp. 32, 33.

(letters דק not quite certain), cf. *EB.* 'Names,' § 36; Phoenician צדקדכר Ṣidḳi-dakar, quoted by Baethgen, *Beiträge zur Sem. Religionsgesch.* p. 128 (without ref. to source); and the following instances from cuneiform literature quoted by Zimmern in *KAT.*[3] p. 474: Ṣidḳâ, king of Ashḳelon, a contemporary of Ḥezeḳiah, *KB.* ii. 91; Rab-Ṣidḳi in T.A. Letters, Knudtzon, no. 170 (given as Ben-Ṣidḳi by Winckler, no. 125 in *KB.* v.); Ṣidḳi-ilu as the name of an eponym, B.C. 764, cf. Winckler, *KT.* p. 59; Ṣubi-ṣidḳi, Johns, *Deeds*, no. 6, rev. 3. From these we can scarcely separate the Israelite צדקיהו Ṣidḳi-Yahu or צדקיה Ṣidḳi-Yah.

The conclusion that Ṣedeḳ is the proper name of a deity is based upon a statement of Philo of Byblos that the Phoenicians had a deity named Συδυκ. This writer (quoted by Eusebius, *Praep. Evan.* i. 10), in the course of a lengthy account of the Phoenician Pantheon, based upon information derived professedly from Sanchuniaton, remarks that Ἀπὸ τούτων [Αμυνος καὶ Μαγος] γενέσθαι Μισωρ καὶ Συδυκ, τουτέστιν εὔλυτον καὶ δίκαιον. Οὗτοι τὴν τοῦ ἁλὸς χρῆσιν εὗρον. Here Συδυκ and Μισωρ are shown to correspond to the Heb. words *ṣedeḳ* 'justice,' and *mêšār* 'uprightness.' The statement that these deities 'discovered the use of salt'* seems to indicate no very profound acquaintance with their origin and characteristics; and definite information thus failing us, it is natural to suspect the influence of Babylonian thought, in view of the fact that for the later Babylonians *kettu* ‡ 'justice,' and *mêšâru* 'uprightness' appear as the 'sons' of Šamaš the Sun-god (cf. *KAT.*[3] pp. 224 *n*[1], 370), a theory which would seem to imply hardly more than that these attributes were characteristic of Šamaš, or at most that they might be venerated in connexion with his worship: cf. the manner in which Ḫammurabi pictures himself as deriving his legal code, the embodiment of Justice, directly from Šamaš. Not very dissimilar are certain statements in the Psalms with regard to Yahweh: 'Righteousness (*or* Justice, *ṣedeḳ*) shall walk before him,' 85 [13]; 'Righteousness (*ṣedeḳ*) and Judgment are the foundation of thy throne,' 89 [14], cf. 97 [2]; 'Righteousness (*ṣedeḳ*) and Peace have kissed,' 85 [10].

But, granted the existence of a W. Semitic deity Ṣedeḳ § = Bab. Kettu, the inference by no means follows that, where Ṣedeḳ occurs

* Possibly we may trace connexion with the ברית מלח 'covenant of salt' (Num. 18 [19] P, 2 Chr. 13 [5]), in which *ṣedeḳ* 'righteousness,' and *mêšār* 'uprightness' would naturally be involved. Cf. La., *ÉRS.*[2] p. 421. Upon the ceremonial use of salt in covenants, cf. Gray's note on Numbers *loc. cit.*

‡ *Kettu* for *kentu*, √ *kânu* = Heb. כון. *Kettu* is the Bab. equivalent of the W. Semitic *ṣedeḳ*.

§ צדק, *i.e.* Ṣedeḳ or Ṣiddiḳ, occurs as a masc. proper name in Sabaean (cf. *CIS.* iv. no. 287, ll. 2, 11, 15, etc.); and this is perhaps to be explained as contracted from צדקאל, a form which we have noticed above as occurring in

in compound proper names either predicatively or in the genitival relation, it must refer to this deity. 'Justice' or 'Righteousness' cannot have been pictured as the exclusive possession of the son of Šamaš, and it is reasonable to assume that the attribute may have been predicated of other deities. Thus few would dispute that Ṣidḳi-Yahu means, not 'Yahu is the god Ṣedeḳ,' but simply 'Yahu is righteousness' (*i.e.* righteous), the name corresponding in form precisely to Ḥizḳi-Yahu, 'Uzzi-Yahu, 'Yahu is strength' (strong). Analogously it may be inferred that Ṣidḳi-Rammân denotes 'Rammân is righteousness.' It would seem to follow, therefore, that where Ṣedeḳ is coupled, not with a proper name, but with an honorific title such as *'adoni*, *melekh*, or *'el*, it is at least as probable that the meaning intended is 'the (unnamed) Lord, King, *or* God is righteous' as that we are to find reference to (the god) Ṣedeḳ described as Lord, etc.

THE MEANING OF THE NAME ḲIRIATH-ARBA'

(cf. *ch.* 1 [10] *note*)

The evidence which goes to prove that in Ḳiriath-arba', *i.e.* 'City of Four,' 'Four' is a divine title is as follows. The name naturally suggests comparison of the Assyrian Arbela between the Upper and the Lower Zab. The name of this city is written in cuneiform (*âlu*) *Arba' ilu*, '(city) Number Four God.' Here it is beyond doubt that the numeral Four is employed as a divine name or title. The inference that Ḳiriath-arba' is to be explained similarly is strengthened by comparison of the place-name בֵּית אַרְבֵאל 'Beth-Arbel' of Hos. 10 [14] (perhaps situated near Pella on the east of Jordan), where we find the name Arba-ilu apparently taken directly from the Assyrian or Babylonian, since the ע of the Hebrew אַרְבַּע is wanting.* Winckler (*GI.* ii. pp. 39 ff.), who adopts this explanation of Ḳiriath-arba', further explains Be'er-sheba' in like manner as 'Well of Number Seven God.' Thus fresh light is thrown upon the subject. A god *Sibitti*, *i.e.* 'Number Seven,' was known to the Babylonians at the period of the First Dynasty. Thus, for example, we find such names

Sabaean. It is worthy of observation that, in the inscription cited, the name צדק stands in close conjunction with מראשמם, *i.e.* according to Derenbourg, 'Vir Solis' (Ar. امرؤالشمس *Imru-eš-šems*), to be explained as 'vir Solis cultor': cf. discussion in *CIS. loc. cit.*

* Cf. בֵּל, Isa. 46 [1], Jer. 50 [2], 51 [44], taken directly from Bab. *bêlu*=Aram. בְּעֵל, Heb. בַּעַל.

as Warad (ilu) Sibittim, *i.e.* 'servant of (God) Sibitti': Thureau-Dangin, *Lettres et Contrats de l'époque de la première dynastie Babylonienne*, p. 50: cf. further references in Jastrow, *RBA*. i. p. 173.

The meaning of Four and Seven as divine titles is elucidated by the well-known fact that the name of Sin, the Moon-god, is commonly written in cuneiform as '(God) Number Thirty,' thirty days being the conventional length of the lunar month. It is probable that, as Winckler thinks (*op. cit.* p. 48), Four and Seven represent different phases of the Moon-god, the former the four phases of the moon, the latter the seven-day week as a lunar quarter. Evidence that the worship of *Sibitti* extended to the West is to be found in the fact that, in the list of kings of the West whom Tiglath-Pileser IV. mentions as paying tribute, the king of Gebal bears the name Sibittibi'li, *i.e.* 'Number Seven is lord': cf. Rost, *Tiglath-Pileser*, p. 26. The evidence here brought together is based upon the present editor's note in *JTS*. xii. pp. 118 f.

THE CONQUEST OF THE NEGEB (cf. *ch.* 1 $^{16.17}$ *notes*)

The account of the conquest of 'Arad in the Negeb which is given in Judg. 1 $^{16.17}$ cannot be considered apart from the very similar account which is found in Num. 21 $^{1-3}$ (J). This latter narrative states that, during the period of Israel's sojourn in the wilderness, the king of 'Arad advanced against them, apparently because they were encroaching upon his territory, fought against them, and took some of them prisoners. Israel thereupon vowed a vow that, if Yahweh would deliver up the Cana'anites into their hand, they would place their cities under a ban (*ḥérem*), and utterly destroy every inhabitant. Success attended their arms; the vow was carried out; and the name of the district was thenceforth known as Ḥormah, a name in which there is an assumed connexion with *ḥérem*.

This narrative, which implies a northward advance of Israel from Ḳadesh-Barnea' into the Negeb, is at variance with the preceding narrative (Num. 20 $^{14-21}$ JE), which apparently pictures the whole of the Israelites as turning southwards from Ḳadesh, in order to compass and avoid the land of Edom. It is also difficult to understand why an immediate settlement in the conquered territory was not effected by at least a portion of the Israelites, when the whole of the Cana'anites inhabiting it had been put to the sword.

The author of the introduction to Deut., who apparently bases his information upon E, gives, in 1 $^{41-46}$, an account of a disorganized attempt made by the Israelites to conquer the Negeb, after the failure of the mission of the spies, and against the express command of Moses. This was repulsed by 'the Amorite who inhabited that hill-country,' Israel being put to the rout, and beaten down 'in Se'ir as far as Ḥormah.' This narrative corresponds with Num. 14 $^{40-45}$, which apparently combines elements from J as well as from E, and in which the foe appears not as 'the Amorite,' but as 'the 'Amalekite and the Cana'anite' (*v.* 45 a). No mention is made in Deut. of Israel's subsequent success, and their extirpation of the inhabitants of the district; and we are probably correct in inferring that these details were not contained in the E source.

The question is further complicated by the account of the conquest of 'Arad which occurs in Judg. 1 16.17. Here it is the tribes of Judah and Sime'on, together with the Ḳenites, who are related to have effected the conquest, moving southwards from the City of Palms (*i.e.* Jericho) subsequently to the passage of the Jordan under Joshua'. As in the narrative of Num., however, the origin of the name Ḥormah is explained by the fact that the Cana'anites inhabiting a city (previously named Ṣephath) were smitten, and the city placed under the ban and utterly destroyed.

The narratives of Num. 21 and Judg. are obviously parallel, and cannot, as they stand, be reconciled. It is easy to supply a reason for the occurrence of the narrative in Judg. as a duplicate to that in Num., viz., the view that the conquest of Cana'an under Joshua' was the first settlement in the land of any of the tribes of Israel: but, if the narrative of Judg. be taken to be correct in its present position, it is not easy to divine why the narrative of Num. should have come in at that particular place.

Adopting, then, the view that the conquest of 'Arad in the Negeb took place through a tribal movement northward from the neighbourhood of Ḳadesh, the inference becomes plausible that this movement was effected, as related in Judg., by the tribes of Judah and Sime'on in alliance with the Ḳenites. It is a well-known fact that the tribe of Judah consisted of mixed elements: the genealogy of 1 Chr. 2 includes among the descendants of Judah the North Arabian tribes of the Ḳenites and Jeraḥme'elites, and the clan of Caleb which was of Ḳenizzite, *i.e.* of Edomite, origin (cf. Gen. 36 11). Whether or not these clans originally formed an integral part of the tribe of Judah, it is clear that so early as the days of David they were regarded as standing in a very intimate relation to the tribe. In 1 Sam. 27 7 ff., which relates David's stay as an outlaw with Achish king of Gath, we read that David made pretence to Achish that his occasional raids were directed 'against the Negeb of Judah, and against the Negeb of the Jeraḥme'elites, and against the Negeb of the Ḳenites'; and Achish remarks to himself with satisfaction, 'He hath made *his people Israel* utterly to abhor him; therefore he shall be my servant for ever.' Again, in 1 Sam. 30 26-31, David sends presents 'of the spoil of the enemies of Yahweh' to the Judaeans of the Negeb, including the Jeraḥme'elites and the Ḳenites.

If, then, clans which originally inhabited the region south of the Negeb are subsequently found occupying the Negeb and forming part of the tribe of Judah, what is more probable than that this change of locality was effected through conquests gained in the

Negeb in a movement directly northwards, as is suggested by the narrative of Num. 21?

We seem, in fact, to be upon the track of a Calibbite tradition, embodied in the Judaean document J, which originally narrated the way in which this northward movement was effected by the clan of Caleb, and probably other kindred clans. It may be conjectured that this tradition lies at the bottom of the older (JE) narrative of the spies which is combined with the P narrative in Num. 13 and 14.* In this older narrative (in contrast to that of P) it is the Negeb only which is explored; Caleb is the only spy who is mentioned by name; and it is Caleb only who maintains, against the opinion of the other spies, that the conquest of the district is quite a feasible undertaking, in spite of the race of giants—the sons of ʿAnaḳ—inhabiting it:—'We can easily go up and possess it, for we are well able to overcome it' (Num. 13^{30}).

As a matter of fact, the conquest of these sons or clans of ʿAnaḳ and their cities is directly ascribed to Caleb in Josh. $15^{14\text{-}19}$ = Judg. $1^{20.10b \text{ (in part)}.11\text{-}15}$ from the narrative of J. Is it not, then, at least a plausible theory that the original Calibbite story related that Caleb, after first spying out the Negeb, then proceeded to go up and conquer it?

It seems probable that the present form of the combined JE narrative of the spies, which makes the project of conquest fail in spite of Caleb's protests, is due to the theory that the conquest of any part of Canaʿan did not take place until the country as a whole was invaded by a combined movement from the east made by the whole of the tribes under the leadership of Joshuaʿ. This theory, as we have seen, accounts for the present form of Judg. $1^{16.17}$, which makes the conquest of the Negeb to have been effected through a movement which took its start from Jericho.

It is the Judaean document J which embodies the Calibbite tradition in Num. 21: cf. 'the Canaʿanite' in *v.*[1]. The Ephraimite E, on the other hand (which is naturally the principal repository of the Joshuaʿ-tradition), from which is drawn the narrative which is found in Deut. $1^{41\text{-}46}$ (cf. 'the Amorite' in *v.*[44]), while mentioning the defeat of the Israelites, knows nothing, or at any rate will have nothing, of the subsequent victory as narrated by J.

Our inference, then, is that clans which went to form the tribe of Judah (including North Arabian clans then or subsequently embodied in the tribe) advanced northward from Ḳadesh-Barneaʿ; and, in combination with the remnant of the tribe of Simeʿon (which, after a disastrous attempt to effect a settlement in Central Palestine, appears to have moved southward: cf. *note* on 1^3), conquered the territory of ʿArad, and settled down in it, afterwards advancing their conquests

* In Gray's *Numbers* (*ICC.*), pp. 130 ff., the two narratives of the spies are arranged in parallel columns, and will be found each to read nearly continuously.

still farther north, into the country which is known to us later on as the hill-country of Judah.

If this inference be true, it will help to explain to us a very striking fact in the later history, viz. the isolation of Judah and Sime'on from the rest of the tribes. From the Song of Deborah, which celebrates the great victory over the forces of Ṡiṡera, it is clear that an organized attempt was made on that occasion to unite the tribes of Israel against the Cana'anites. Ten tribes, including the tribes from the eastern side of Jordan, are mentioned, either for praise as having taken part in the contest, or for blame as having held aloof: Judah and Sime'on alone remain unnoticed. We must infer, therefore, that at that period they were so far isolated from the rest of the tribes that they were not even expected to take part in the common interests of Israel, and therefore received no call to arms.

This single instance is in itself so striking, that we need do no more than allude briefly in passing to the fierce rivalry which is pictured as existing between the men of Israel and the men of Judah in the days of David (2 Sam. $19^{41\text{-}43}$), and to the fact that the superficial union between Judah and the rest of the tribes which was effected under Saul, David, and Solomon, was readily dissolved at the commencement of Reḥobo'am's reign.

THE ORIGINAL FORM OF J'S ACCOUNT OF THE SETTLEMENT OF THE TRIBES OF ISRAEL IN CANA'AN

Bu. has displayed great skill and critical insight in reconstructing J's narrative in the form in which it may be supposed originally to have stood: cf. *RS.* pp. 84 ff. The following reconstruction is indebted to him throughout, but exhibits in detail such variations as have been adopted in the notes on the text, with citation of Bu.'s readings in the footnotes.

Judg. $1^{1a\beta b}$ And the children of Israel enquired of Yahweh,
saying, 'Who shall go up for us first against the
1^{2} Cana'anites to fight against them?' And Yahweh
said, 'Judah shall go up: behold, I have given the
1^{3} land into his hand.' And Judah said to Sime'on his
brother, 'Go up with me into my lot, that we may
fight with the Cana'anites, and I also will go up with
{ 1^{5} emended after Josh. 10^{1} } thee into thy lot.' So Sime'on went with him. And
they came upon Adoni-ṣedeḳ,[a] the king of Jerusalem,
and they fought against him, and smote the Cana'an-
1^{6} ites and the Perizzites. And Adoni-ṣedeḳ[a] fled; and
they pursued after him, and captured him, and cut
1^{7} off his thumbs and his great toes. And Adoni-ṣedeḳ[a]

[a] Bu. 'Adoni-bezeḳ.'

said, 'Seventy kings, with their thumbs and their
great toes cut off, used to pick up food under my
table: as I did, so hath God requited me.' And
they brought him to Jerusalem, and he died there.
1[19] And Yahweh was with Judah, and he gained possession of the hill-country; for he was not able to
dispossess the inhabitants of the Vale, because they
1[21] after Josh. 15[63] had chariots of iron. But the Jebusites dwelling in
Jerusalem the children of Judah could not dispossess;
and the Jebusites dwelt with the children of Judah in
Jerusalem, unto this day.

1[20.10bβ] || Josh. 15[14] [b]And they gave Ḥebron to Caleb, as Moses had
bidden[b]: and he dispossessed from thence the three
sons of 'Anaḳ, Sheshai, and Aḥiman, and Talmai.
1[11] after Josh. 15[15] And he went up thence against the inhabitants of
Debir. (Now the name of Debir formerly was
1[12] || Josh. 15[16] Ḳiriath-ṡepher.) And Caleb said, 'He that smiteth
Ḳiriath-ṡepher, and taketh it, I will give him 'Achṡah
1[13] || Josh. 15[17] my daughter as wife.' And 'Othniel, the son of
Ḳenaz, the brother of Caleb, took it: and he gave
1[14] || Josh. 15[18] him 'Achṡah his daughter as wife. And when she
came, he incited her to ask of her father a field: and
she lighted down from off the ass; and Caleb said
1[15] || Josh. 15[19] to her, 'What wouldest thou?' And she said to him,
'Give me a present; for thou hast set me in the land
of the Negeb; so give me springs of water.' And
Caleb gave her the upper spring and the lower spring.

1[16] And Ḥobab the Ḳenite, the father-in-law of Moses,
went up from the City of Palms with the children
of Judah into the wilderness of Judah which is [c]in
the Negeb of 'Arad[c]; and he went and dwelt with
1[36] the Amaleḳites. And the border of the Edomites
was from the ascent of 'Aḳrabbim,[d] from the Crag
and upwards.[d]

1[17] And Judah went with Sime'on his brother, and
smote the Cana'anites who inhabited Ṣephath, and
devoted it to destruction. And the name of the city
was called Ḥormah.

1[22] And the house of Joṡeph also went up to 'Ai: and
1[23a] Joshua' was with them. . . .[e] And the house of
Joṡeph made a reconnaissance at Bethel. (Now the

[b—b] Bu. 'And to Caleb, the son of Ḳenaz, there was given an inheritance among the children of Judah, namely Ḥebron.'

[c—c] Bu. 'at the descent of 'Arad.'

[d—d] Bu. 'to Petra and beyond.'

[e] Here Bu. is probably right in supposing that the document originally related the conquest of 'Ai, as in Josh. 8.

1[24] name of the city formerly was Luz.) And the
watchers saw a man coming out of the city,[f] and
they laid hold on him,[f] and said to him, 'Show us,
we pray thee, the way to enter the city, and we will
1[25] deal kindly with thee.' So he showed them the way to
enter the city, and they smote the city at the edge of
the sword; but the man and all his clan they let go.
1[26] And the man went to the land of the Ḥittites, and
built a city, and called its name Luz: that is its
name unto this day.
2[1a] [g]And the Angel of Yahweh went up from Gilgal
2[5b] unto Bethel: and they sacrificed there to Yahweh.[g]
{1[27] || Josh. 17[11.12]} And Manasseh could not dispossess Beth-she'an and
its dependencies, and Ta'anach and its dependencies,
and the inhabitants of Ible'am and its dependencies,
and the inhabitants of Megiddo and its dependencies,
[h]and the inhabitants of Dor and its dependencies[h];
but the Cana'anites persisted in dwelling in this land.
{1[28] || Josh. 17[13]} And when Israel was waxen strong, they impressed
the Cana'anites for labour-gangs, and did not dispossess them at all.
{1[29] || Josh. 16[10]} And Ephraim did not dispossess the Cana'anites
who dwelt in Gezer: but the Cana'anites dwelt in the
midst of Ephraim [j]unto this day,[j] and became toiling
labour-gangs.
Josh. 17[14] [k]And the house of Joseph spake unto Joshua',
saying, 'Why hast thou given me but one lot and
one territory for an inheritance, seeing that I am

f–f Not adopted by Bu. The passage is supplied from 𝔊: cf. *note ad loc.*

g–g This is placed by Bu. at the close of the narrative, after mention of the settlement of the other tribes.

h–h Bu. follows the order of 𝔐. For the reasons for the transposition, cf. *note ad loc.*

j–j Omitted by Bu.

k The fact that Josh. 17[14-18] was originally derived from the J narrative is clearly shown by the phraseology: cf. Bu. *RS.* p. 32. That the subject in *v.*[14a] should be 'the *house* of Joseph' and not 'the *children* of Joseph' appears from *v.*[17] and from the singulars לִי 'to me,' וַאֲנִי 'and I,' etc., in *v.*[14b] and elsewhere. It is impossible, however, to derive any consistent sense from the section as it stands in 𝔐. The house of Joseph complain that they have only received *one* lot, which is insufficient for their numbers, the extent of this lot being further diminished owing to the fact that part of it falls in the vale, where the Cana'anites are too strong to be ousted by them owing to their possession of iron chariots (cf. Judg. 1[19], 4[3]). Joshua', in acknowledging the justice of their protest, recommends them to 'go up' into the forest and cut down for themselves (*v.*[15]), this forest being further described as הַר 'hill-country' in *v.*[18]. That the reference, however, cannot be to any part of the hill-country west of Jordan appears to be clear. The situation presupposed is that the west Jordan

a great people, forasmuch as hitherto Yahweh hath
Josh. 17 ^{16} blessed me? The hill-country doth not suffice for
me: and all the Cana'anites that dwell in the land of
the vale have chariots of iron, both they that are in
Beth-she'an and its dependencies, and they that are
Josh. 17 ^{17} in the vale of Jezre'el.' And Joshua' said unto the
house of Joseph, 'Thou art a great people, and hast
Josh. 17 $^{18a\alpha}$ great power: thou shalt not have one lot only. For
Josh. 17 $^{15a\beta b}$ the hill-country of Gile'ad shall be thine: get thee up
into the forest and cut down for thyself there; since
the hill-country of Ephraim is too narrow for thee.'
Num. 32 ^{39} *l* Then Machir the son of Manasseh went to Gile'ad,
and took it,*l* and dispossessed the Amorites that were

country has already been allotted among the tribes, and the house of Joseph have not found the difficulties of gaining a footing in the portion of hill-country (in contrast to the vale) allotted to them to be insuperable. Thus Bu. suggests, with great plausibility, that the hill-country which Joshua' invites them to conquer is the hill-country of *Gile'ad,* which is appropriately described as יַעַר forest or jungle-land: cf. 2 Sam. 18 $^{6.8.17}$. As the result of Joshua''s suggestion there follows the conquest of districts in Gile'ad by different clans of Manasseh, as described in the passages from Num. given above, which may plausibly be taken as the continuation of our narrative. If Bu.'s view of the situation be correct, 'Gile'ad' in Josh. 17 ^{18a} may be supposed to have been excised by the priestly redactor of this section of Josh., to whom is due the general dislocation of the J passage in question. Marks of his hand are to be seen in the plurals *v.* ^{14}, 'And the children of Joseph spake' (an alteration, noticed above), *v.* ^{16a}, 'And the children of Joseph said' (addition necessitated by the dislocation of *v.* ^{15}), לָנוּ 'to us' (alteration of לִי 'to me'), in the explanatory 'to Ephraim and to Manasseh,' *v.* ^{17}, and in the P phrase תֹּצְאֹתָיו 'its goings out,' *v.* ^{18a}. The main part of this final verse, with its five times repeated כִּי and its apparent ascription of iron chariots to the Cana'anites inhabiting the hill-country, appears in its present form to be due to this editor as a weak summary of *his* view of the situation, viz. that what is contemplated is a further extended conquest west of Jordan. The words of *v.* ^{15} בארץ הפרזי והרפאים 'in the land of the Perizzites and the Rephaim,' which are wanting in 𝔊, are probably merely a corrupt doublet of the following כי אין לך הר אפרים, 'since the hill-country of Ephraim is too narrow for thee.'

Bu., to whom is due the merit of this reconstruction, varies in the following details. In *v.* ^{16a} he retains לָנוּ 'to us' of 𝔐, and reconstructs *v.* ^{16b} by the help of *v.* ^{18b}:—'And the Cana'anites which dwell in the vale I cannot dispossess, since they are too strong for me. For they have chariots of iron, both they that are in Beth-she'an,' etc. After *v.* ^{15b} he adds the words of *v.* ^{18a}, 'and its goings out shall be thine.'

l–l 𝔐 וַיֵּלְכוּ בְּנֵי מָכִיר . . . וַיִּלְכְּדֻהָ. 𝔊, however, καὶ ἐπορεύθη υἱὸς Μαχειρ . . . καὶ ἔλαβεν αὐτήν, points to the text adopted above, which is favoured by the singular verb וַיּוֹרֶשׁ in 𝔐, and by the parallelism of *vv.* $^{41.42}$.

Num. 32 41 therein. And Ja'ir the son of Manasseh went and
took the tent-villages thereof, and called them the
Num. 32 42 tent-villages of Ja'ir. And Nobaḥ went and took
Ḳenath and its dependencies, and called it Nobaḥ
Josh. 13 13 after his own name. But the children of Israel[m] did
not dispossess the Geshurites and the Ma'acathites;
but Geshur and Ma'acath dwelt in the midst of
Israel, unto this day.

1 30 . . . . . .[n]

Zebulun did not dispossess the inhabitants of
Ḳiṭron, nor the inhabitants of Nahalol; but the
Cana'anites dwelt in the midst of them, and became
labour-gangs.

1 31 Asher did not dispossess the inhabitants of 'Acco,
1 32 nor the inhabitants of Ṣidon, nor Maḥaleb,[o] nor
Achzib, nor Aphiḳ, nor Reḥob: but the Asherites
dwelt in the midst of the Cana'anites inhabiting the
land; for they did not dispossess them.

1 33 Naphtali did not dispossess the inhabitants of Beth-
shemesh, nor the inhabitants of Beth-'anath; but they
dwelt in the midst of the Cana'anites inhabiting the
land; and the inhabitants of Beth-shemesh and Beth-
'anath became labour-gangs for them.

1 34 And the Cana'anites[p] pressed the children of Dan
into the hill-country; for they did not suffer them to
Josh. 19 47 come down into the vale. [q]So the border of the
children of Dan was too strait for them[q]; and the
children of Dan went up, and fought with Lesham,
and took it, and smote it at the edge of the sword,
and took possession of it, and dwelt therein; and
they called Lesham, Dan, after the name of Dan
1 35 their father. But the Cana'anites[p] persisted in
dwelling in Har-ḥereś, in Aijalon, and in Sha'albim:

[m] Possibly the original may here have read 'the children of Manasseh.' The reading 'in the midst of Israel' (with reference to the clans of Manasseh) in the latter half of the verse is favoured by the analogy of 𝔊L in Judg. 1 33 which reads, with reference to Naphtali, *καὶ κατῴκησεν* Ισραηλ, in place of 𝔐 וַיֵּשֶׁב simply. Cf. *RS.* p. 39.

[n] Here Bu. supposes a lacuna for the account of the settlements of Benjamin and then Issachar.

[o] Bu. reads Aḥlab, and adds Ḥelbah after Achzib, as in 𝔐.

[p] Bu. 'Amorites,' as in 𝔐.

[q—q] Reading וַיֵּצֶר, in place of 𝔐 וַיֵּצֵא, Bu., following 𝔊, reads וַיָּצִיקוּ מֵהֶם גְּבוּל נַחֲלָתָם 'so they made the border of their inheritance too strait for them.'

yet the hand of the house of Joseph prevailed,[r] and
they became labour-gangs.
2^{23a} So Yahweh left these nations, not expelling them
3^{2a} quickly, only on account of the generations of the
3^{5a} children of Israel, to teach them war.[s] And the
children of Israel dwelt in the midst of the Cana'an-
3^{6} ites; and they took their daughters to themselves
for wives, and their own daughters they gave to
their sons; and they served their gods.

2. 6–3. 6. *Introduction to the History of the Judges.*

This section forms the introduction to the Book of Judges as it left the hand of the main editor (R^{E2}): cf. *Introd.* p. xxxv. That it is not homogeneous is clear even from a cursory examination; but the analysis is difficult, and scholars are not agreed upon points of detail.

The narrative of the Book of Joshua' is resumed in 2^{6-9} by repetition of Josh. 24^{28-31}. The two passages are identical except for small verbal variations, and for the different order in which the verse occurs which states that the people (Josh. 'Israel') served Yahweh during the lifetime of Joshua' and the elders who survived him (in Josh. 24^{31} after the mention of Joshua''s death, in Judg. 2^{7} before it). Critics are agreed in assigning this section to E, with the exception of Judg. 2^{7} = Josh. 24^{31}, which is regarded as editorial. That this verse should belong to E is demanded, however, by the E narrative in Josh. 24^{16-24}: cf. especially *vv.* $^{18b.19.21.22.24}$. If, according to E, the people, in response to Joshua''s last appeal, pledged themselves to serve Yahweh, the narrative of E (upon the assumption that it went on to relate the history of the Judges: cf. *Introd.* p. xxxviii) *must* have stated that this promise was carried out up to a certain point. Such a statement is found in Judg. 2^{7}.

The same conclusion as to the origin of this verse appears to be demanded by what follows. Judg. 2^{10}, which forms the natural continuation of *v.* ^{9} in the E narrative, certainly presupposes *v.* ^{7}: cf. especially *v.* ^{7}, 'who had seen (Josh. 'known') all the great work of Yahweh which he had wrought for Israel,' with *v.* ^{10}, 'who knew not Yahweh nor yet the work which he had wrought for Israel.' To assign *v.* ^{10} as well as *v.* ^{7} to the main editor (whether we call him R^{D}, or, according to our theory, R^{E2}) seems to be forbidden by the fact that *v.* ^{10} is a necessary link in the introduction to E's narrative of the Judges, which, as appears below, can be traced in the verses which follow, and which may be expected to read continuously, since there is no reason to suppose that R^{E2} felt the need of excising any portion of it. Moreover, if *v.* ^{7} be editorial and *not* part of E, it is not clear

[r] Bu. adds 'against the Amorites.'

[s] Here Bu. adds the list of nations given in 3^{3}, which we assign to R^{D}.

how it came to be incorporated both in Josh. and Judg.; for in each case the editor was presumably drawing directly from the pre-Deuteronomic work of R^{JE}.*

The small variations between the two recensions of these verses may be dismissed in a few words. It is clear from the narrative of Josh. 24 that *v.* 28 was originally intended by E to round off and conclude the account of Joshua's last words which precedes; and for this purpose the statement that 'Joshua dismissed the people every man to his inheritance,' is obviously sufficient. In Judg. 2 6, however, this sentence, which *concludes* a section of E, is taken by R^{E2} to *introduce* what he has to narrate about the events which followed the settlement. It may be assumed, therefore, that the expanded form of *v.* 6b represents an adaptation due to R^{E2}. The disappearance from *v.* 8 of the E phrase, 'and it came to pass after these things,' which occurs in the corresponding *v.* 29 of Josh. 24, is of course due to the fact that the 'things' referred to have no place in Judg. If Judg. 2 10 be rightly regarded as forming part of E, it follows that 2 7 is in its original position with regard to its context, since the connexion between 2 10 and 2 9 cannot be broken. The position of Josh. 24 31 must therefore have been altered by the redactor.‡

In the verses which follow, a difference in the point of view is evident. In *vv.* 11-19 Israel's punishment for idolatry is that they are delivered into the hands of the *surrounding* nations; as we find, in fact, to be the case in the narrative of the Judges which follows. In *vv.* 20.21, however, the punishment consists in Yahweh's refusal to interpose any further in order 'to dispossess any from before them of the nations which Joshua left when he died'; obviously meaning the races still remaining *within* the land after the settlement of the tribes and their merely partial conquest. This aspect, then, of Yahweh's relation to Israel is not strictly apposite to what follows in Judg., in so far as it cannot have been specially framed in order to introduce the events which follow in the book; these events, as we have noticed above, serving rather to illustrate the former point of view.

Moreover, the purpose for which the nations still remaining after Joshua's death are here stated to have been left by Yahweh is not that of 2 11-19, where the surrounding nations are employed in order to *punish* idolatrous Israel. It is stated in 2 22, 3 1.4 to be 'in order

* The only solution, upon the assumption of the Deuteronomic origin of the verse, would seem to be that it may have been inserted in Josh. by a later hand in order to make Josh. 24 28-31 square exactly with Judg. 2 6-9. The converse process (insertion from Josh. into Judg.) is excluded by the facts noticed above.

† The only reason for the assigning of *v.* 7 to the editor appears to be the occurrence of the D phrase 'who had prolonged days'; but there is no reason why this phrase should not have been adopted by the D school from E (just as other phrases, *e.g.* אלהים אחרים 'other gods,' have been), and in fact it cannot be proved that the similar phrase 'that thy days may prolong themselves' in Ex. 20 12 did not originally belong to E.

‡ In $\mathfrak{G}^B$ of Josh. the verse stands in the same position as in Judg.

to prove Israel by them.' The method of 'proof,' however, is explained in two different ways. In 2^{22}, 3^{4} it is a *religious* probation—to test the adhesion of Israel to Yahweh's precepts ('the ways *or* commands of Yahweh'); but in $3^{1.2}$ it is explained simply as directed towards keeping the successive generations of the children of Israel exercised in the use of arms, and is therefore, it may be inferred, *devoid of any strictly religious purpose.* These remaining nations, again, which form Yahweh's instrument of probation, appear, as mentioned in 3^{3}, to be (with the exception of 'all the Cana'anites') *surrounding* nations, inconsistently with 2^{20-23}, but in accordance with 2^{11-19}, where it is these nations that form Yahweh's instrument of punishment. Once more, 3^{5} harks back to the point of view of 2^{20-23}, and it is the races *within Cana'an* with whom the writer is concerned.

Looking once more at 2^{11-19}, the existence in these verses of a duplication of statement can hardly escape notice. Thus *v.*[13] repeats *v.*[12], and *vv.*[18.19] are in substance the same as *vv.*[16.17]. If, however, we remove one set of duplicates, viz. *vv.*[12.18.19], it will be found that the remainder, with the exception of *vv.*[14bβ.15], is nearly identical in wording with the pragmatic framework of the book as seen in the introductions to the histories of the various judges. The closeness of the parallel may best be seen by a comparison with 3^{7-9}:—

2^{11}	And the children of Israel did that which was evil in the sight
3^{7a}	And the children of Israel did that which was evil in the sight
2^{12}	of Yahweh, and they forsook Yahweh and served the
3^{7b}	of Yahweh, and they forgat Yahweh their God, and served the
2^{14a}	Ba'als and the 'Ashtarts. And the anger of Yahweh was
3^{8}	Ba'als and the 'Ashtarts. And the anger of Yahweh was
2^{14a}	kindled against Israel, and he delivered them into the hand
3^{8}	kindled against Israel,
2^{14a}	of spoilers and they spoiled them, and he sold them into
3^{8}	and he sold them into
2^{14a}	the hand of their enemies round about.
3^{8}	the hand of Cushan-rish'athaim, king of Aram-naharaim : and
—	
3^{8}	the children of Israel served Cushan-rish'athaim eight years.
2^{16}	<And the children of Israel cried unto Yahweh,> and Yahweh
3^{9}	And the children of Israel cried unto Yahweh, and Yahweh
2^{16}	raised up judges, and they saved
3^{9}	raised up a saviour for the children of Israel, and he saved
2^{16}	them from the hand of their spoilers.
3^{9}	them . . .

This framework is due to the main editor, who appears (as has been argued in the *Introd.* pp. xli ff.) to have been a representative of the later school of E.

The words in $2^{14a.16}$, which find no parallel in $3^{7.9}$ ('and he delivered them into the hand of the spoilers and they spoiled them'; 'from the hand of their spoilers'), may be by a later hand (D^2; cf. 2 Kgs. 17^{20}); but it is more likely that they belong to R^{E2}, who in referring to Israel's enemies generally at the commencement of his history, may be expected to use some emphasis and even repetition (2^{14a}). The clause missing in 𝔐, 'And the children of Israel cried unto Yahweh,' seems necessary to complete the nexus, and has been supplied in accordance with $3^{9.15}$, 4^3, 6^6, 10^{10}.

The verses, however, which appear not to have originally formed part of this writer's scheme, viz. *vv.* $^{12.14b\beta.15.18.19}$, are just the verses which exhibit very markedly the phraseology of Deuteronomy*; and we can hardly err therefore in regarding them as additions made in later times by a member of the Deuteronomic school (D^2).

2^{20}-3^6 is very difficult to analyse with any certainty. If, as seems probable, E's narrative in 2^{6-10} is continued by *v.* ^{13} (notice E's expression 'the Ba'als and the 'Ashtarts'), *vv.* $^{20.21}$ form the appropriate sequence. Notice the opening phrase, 'So the anger of Yahweh was kindled against Israel,' which has formed the text of the editorial expansion of R^{E2} in *vv* $^{14a.16.17}$.

Of the two methods of probation noticed above, that which consists in religious proving (3^4) may be regarded as due to E (נִסָּה in this sense is characteristic: cf. $CH.^{JE}$ 192 a). The somewhat awkwardly inserted interpolation 2^{22}, which also refers to this religious probation, is marked by its phraseology as Deuteronomic. The alternative method of probation ('to teach them war,' 3^{2a}) as devoid of religious purpose, may be judged to be older than the other, and is therefore probably to be assigned to J. This seems to connect on to 2^{23a}; which may very well be the sequel to the J narrative in 1^1-2^5, which gives a detailed account of the foreign races within Palestine which the different tribes were unable to expel. Notice the expression 'these nations,' clearly referring to nations just previously mentioned. The immediate sequel to 3^{2a} is $3^{5a.6}$, which relates how Israel settled down among the Cana'anites, intermarrying with them and adopting their religious practices ('Cana'anites,' J's general term for the inhabitants of Palestine: cf. 1^3 *note*. Notice also the J phrase 'dwelt in the midst of'). 2^{23b} (back-reference to 2^{21b}), and 3^{5b} (list of races) exhibit the hand of the redactor of J and E.

The summary of nations 'which Yahweh left to prove Israel by them,' $3^{1a.3}$, must be due to D^2: cf. the similar Deuteronomic summary in Josh. 13^2 ff. Finally, the awkwardly placed explanatory glosses in $3^{1b.2b}$ seem to be due to the latest hand of all (R^P).

* Cf. especially the phrases 'go after other gods,' *vv.* $^{12.19}$, 'vex Yahweh,' *v.* ^{12}, 'as Yahweh had spoken and as Yahweh had sworn to them,' *v.* ^{15a}. Cf. $CH.^D$ 85, 91, 107^b; phrases of R^D in Kings in *DB.* ii. pp. 860 f., nos. 32, 39.

6. E So Joshuaʿ dismissed the people, R^{E2} and the children of Israel went E every man to his inheritance R^{E2} to possess the land. 7. E And the people served Yahweh all the days of Joshuaʿ, and all the days of the elders who outlived Joshuaʿ, who had seen all the great work of Yahweh which he had wrought for Israel. 8. And Joshuaʿ the son of Nun, the servant of Yahweh, died, aged one hundred and ten years. 9. And they buried him within the boundary of his inheritance, in Timnath-ḥereś, in the hill-country of Ephraim, on the north of mount

2, 6. *dismissed the people.* From Shechem; where, according to Josh. 24$^{1-28}$ E, they had been assembled by Joshuaʿ to receive his final charge.

7. *the elders.* The sheikhs of the various tribal clans who were the representatives of permanent official authority in matters social and religious. They appear from the earliest times, both in J (Ex. 3$^{16.18}$, 12^{21}) and E (Ex. 17$^{5.6}$, 18^{12}, 19^{7}, 24$^{1.9.14}$).

outlived. Lit. 'prolonged days after.' Upon the use of the phrase in this passage, cf. *footnote*, p. 53.

who had seen, etc. ‖ Josh. 24^{31} 'who had known, etc.' So in our passage 𝔊 ἔγνωσαν, 𝔙 'noverant.' The expression 'all the great work of Yahweh' probably includes (as Mo. notices) not merely the conquest of Canaʿan, but also the wonderful events of the Exodus and wilderness-wanderings. Cf. Deut. 11^{7}, where the same phrase is employed with regard to these latter.

8. *the servant of Yahweh.* This title, which is only applied to Joshuaʿ here and in ‖ Josh. 24^{29}, is very frequently used with reference to Moses: so in Deut. 34^{5}, Josh. 1^{1} (both E), Josh. 1$^{13.15}$, 8$^{31.33}$, 11^{12}, 12^{6}, 13^{8}, 14^{7}, 18^{7}, 22$^{2.4.5}$ (all R^{D}), 2 Kgs. 18^{12} (R^{D}), 2 Chr. 1^{3}, 24^{6} (cf. 'servant of God,' 2 Chr. 24^{9}, Neh. 10^{29}, 𝔐^{30}, Dan. 9^{11}). It is applied to David in the headings of Pss. 18 and 36, and to the nation of Israel in Isa. 42^{19}†. Similarly, 'my servant' or 'my servants' (in Yahweh's mouth), 'his servants' are employed as a description of the outstanding figures of Israel's history, especially the prophets, and the idealized representative of Israel in Isa. 40 ff.; the idea embodied being that of vocation to a special mission: cf. the editor's *Outlines of O. T. Theology*, pp. 112 ff.

9. *Timnath-ḥereś.* ‖ Josh. 24^{30} and 19^{50} Timnath-śeraḥ, doubtless an intentional metathesis made by a later scribe: cf. *note* on Har-ḥereś, *ch.* 1^{35}. The same alteration appears in a few MSS. of 𝔐, and in 𝔙, $𝔖^{P}$ in our passage.

The site of this city is uncertain. Christian tradition, as represented by Eusebius and Jerome, identifies it with the Timnah of Gen. 38^{12} (*OS.* 261^{33} Θαμνα), *i.e.* the modern Tibneh, ten miles north-west of Bethel. About three miles to the east of Tibneh is Kefr Išûaʿ,

Ga'ash. 10. And also all that generation were gathered unto their fathers; and there arose another generation after them who knew not Yahweh, nor yet the work which he had wrought for Israel.

11. R^{E2} And the children of Israel did that which was evil in the sight of Yahweh, [ ] 12. D^2 and forsook Yahweh the God of their fathers, who had brought them out of the land of Egypt; and they went after other gods, of the gods of the peoples who were round about them, and bowed themselves down to them; and they vexed Yahweh. 13. ^{E} And they forsook Yahweh, and

i.e. 'Joshua''s village.' Samaritan tradition, however, claims as the site the modern Kefr Ḥâris, some nine miles south-south-west of Nâblus, which is said to have been the burial-place of both Joshua' and Caleb. Cf. Buhl, *Geogr.* p. 170.

mount Ga'ash. The site is unknown. 'The wâdys of Ga'ash' are mentioned in 2 Sam. 23^{30} = 1 Chr. 11^{32}; and these Buhl conjectures to be the valleys close to Tibneh on the west: *Geogr.* p. 101.

10. *were gathered unto their fathers.* Elsewhere the expression used (in every case in P) is 'gathered unto his kindred' (עַמָּיו); so Gen. $25^{8.17}$, 35^{29}, 49^{33}, Num. 20^{24}, Deut. 32^{50}; cf. Num. 27^{13}, 31^2.

11. At the end of the verse, 𝔐 (with the Versions) adds 'and they served the Ba'als,' a statement which is redundant by the side of *v.* 13, and probably represents an early accidental repetition.

12. *went after . . . round about them.* A reminiscence of Deut. 6^{14}.

13. *the Ba'als.* Reading plur. לַבְּעָלִים (cf. *v.* 11b 𝔐) in place of the sing. לַבַּעַל.* The title Ba'al signifies 'owner' or 'possessor,' and was applied by the Western Semites to a deity as owner of a special sphere of influence, whether in the heavens, *e.g.* Ba'al-zebul, 'owner of the (heavenly) mansion' (cf. 1^5 *note*), and, among the Phoenicians and Aramaeans, Ba'al-shamêm, 'owner of the heavens'; or of a special locality or city where his worship was practised, *e.g.* Ba'al-Ḥermon, and Phoenician Ba'al-Ṣidon, Ba'al-Lebanon, etc.; or of a special property, *e.g.* Ba'al-berîth, 'owner of a covenant' worshipped at Shechem, *ch.* 8^{33}, 9^4; Ba'al-Gad, the name of a locality where the Ba'al was worshipped as the god of fortune, Josh. 11^{17}, 12^7, 13^5. The plur. 'the Ba'als' refers to the different local Ba'als among the Cana'anites. Upon the use of the title as applied to Yahweh in early times, cf. the present editor's *Outlines of O. T. Theology*, pp. 27 ff.

* Mo. emends 'served the Ba'als, etc.,' into 'burned incense (ויקטרו) to the Ba'als, etc.,' on the ground that 'עבד ל' for עבד with accus. is unexampled.' But, as Bu. rightly remarks, even if the occurrence of the verb with this constr. in Jer. 44^3 be regarded as a gloss (as by Mo.), the constr. is found twice over in 1 Sam. 4^9 (probably E): פן תעבדו לעברים כאשר עבדו לכם.

served the Ba'al⌜s⌝ and the 'Ashtarts. 14. R^E2 So the anger of Yahweh was kindled against Israel, and he gave them into the hand of spoilers, and they spoiled them, and he sold them into the hand of their enemies round about, D² and they were not

Ba'al being thus not the proper name of a deity, but a title applied to many local Cana'anite deities, it is impossible to define any special characteristic which may have been common to all. We can only infer from such passages as Hos. 2 5.8.12 (7.10.14 𝔐) that the Ba'als were commonly regarded as the givers of agricultural fertility, and were therefore worshipped in a round of agricultural festivals: cf. *ch.* 9 27. This view is confirmed by the common connexion of the Ba'als with the 'Ashtarts, on which see *note* following.

the 'Ashtarts. The local forms of the goddess 'Ashtart. The vocalization 'Ashtoreth, which meets us everywhere in 𝔐, is an intentional alteration made by the introduction of the vowels of *bōšeth*, 'shame' or 'shameful thing,' in order to indicate that this word is to be substituted in reading. 𝔊, however, always renders ἡ Ασταρτη, which doubtless nearly preserves the true pronunciation.* The same substitution of the vowels of *bōšeth* has been made in Molech for Melech, 'king,' the god in whose worship the Israelites made their children to pass through the fire; and the word *bōšeth* is substituted for Ba'al in Hos. 9 10, Jer. 3 24, 11 13, and in the proper names Ishbosheth, Mephibosheth, Jerubbesheth: cf. *note* on 'Jerubba'al, *ch.* 6 32.

There can be no doubt that a principal (if not *the* principal) conception embodied in the Cana'anite 'Ashtart was that of the mother-goddess, to whom was due the fecundity of nature. This may be inferred from the expression *'ašt^erôth ṣônékhā*, *i.e.* either the '*breeding ewes*' or 'the *offspring* of thy flock,' Deut. 7 13, 28 4.18.51 †; and also from the special characteristics of the numerous small figurines, apparently of this goddess, which have been unearthed in the excavation of city-sites in Palestine: cf. Driver, *Schweich Lectures*, pp. 56 ff.; Vincent, *Canaan*, *ch.* iii.; *TB.* ii. pp. 81 ff. Whether the *ḳ^edhēšîm* and *ḳ^edhēšôth*, *i.e.* the temple-prostitutes of both sexes belonging to the Cana'anite religion, were specially devoted to the service of 'Ashtart is not certain. The Bab. Ištar, however, had her female prostitutes, who bore the title *ḳadištu* or *ḫarimtu*: cf. *KAT.*³ p. 423.

Old Testament writers seem to regard 'Ashtart as specially a Phoenician deity: so 1 Kgs. 11 5.33, ''Ashtart the goddess of the Ṣidonians': cf. 2 Kgs. 23 13. Her worship was, however, very widely diffused among the Semites. She is the Bab. Ištar, the one goddess

* An original 'Ashtart may have come to be pronounced 'Ashtárath or 'Ashtéreth. בְּעֶשְׁתְּרָה Bĕ'eshtĕrā for בֵּית עֶשְׁתְּרָה Beth-'Eshtĕra in Josh. 21 27 probably preserves one original form of the name.

able any more to stand before their enemies. 15. Whithersoever they went out the hand of Yahweh was against them for evil, as Yahweh had spoken, and as Yahweh had sworn to them; and they were in sore straits. 16. R[E2] ⟨And the children of Israel cried unto Yahweh,⟩ and Yahweh raised up judges, and they saved

who holds her position as it were in her own right, and not merely as the somewhat shadowy consort of a god. Different localities in Babylonia were famous for the worship of Ištar, who thus appeared, under various localized forms, as the Ištar of Erech, of Nineveh, of Arbela, etc. The principal aspects under which she was regarded were as the goddess of war (she is spoken of as *bêlit taḫâzi*, 'mistress of battle,' and her chief epithet is *ḳarittu*, 'warrior': see references in Muss Arnolt's *Dict.*, and, for a representation of the goddess under this aspect, *TB.* ii. p. 80) and goddess of love or mother-goddess (cf. Herodotus' statement (i. 131. 199) that the Assyrians called her Μυλιττα, *i.e. muallidat*, 'she who causes to bear'). This latter aspect of the Cana'anite 'Ashtart we have already noticed: of the existence of the former in Cana'an we have no evidence; though it may be noticed that the Philistines, after their victory over Israel and the death of Saul, hung Saul's armour in the temple of 'Ashtart (1 Sam. 31^{10}).

The plur. *ištarâti* came to be used in Babylonian in the general sense 'goddesses' (a point of resemblance to the Heb. plur. *'Aštārôth*); and even the sing. Ištar is sometimes employed to denote 'goddess,' alongside of *ilu*, 'god,' especially in the penitential psalms: cf. *ilšu u ištaršu zenû ittišu*, 'his god and his goddess are angry with him': Muss Arnolt, *s.v. ištaru*.

The same deity is seen in the Sabaean 'Athtar, the Aram. 'Attar, and in the Moabite compound form 'Ashtar-Chemosh. With regard to 'Athtar, Barton (*Semitic Origins*, pp. 123 ff.) has made out a plausible case in proof that the mother-goddess came to be transformed into a male deity; but his argument that the same phenomenon is to be observed in the Moabite deity (only mentioned once in Mesha''s inscription, l. 17) is not equally convincing: cf. *op. cit.* pp. 141 ff.

15. *Whithersoever they went forth.* *Sc.* to battle. So Le Clerc 'quamcumque expeditionem aggrederentur'; Mo. 'in every campaign,' and similarly Stu., Bach., Bu., La. For יצא 'go forth' in this military sense, cf. *ch.* 5^4, 2 Kgs. 18^7, Deut. 28^{25}.

as Yahweh had spoken, etc. Cf. Deut. 28^{25}, and, generally, the whole tenour of that chapter.

16. *And the children of Israel cried unto Yahweh.* This clause is not found in 𝔐 or Verss., but forms elsewhere a regular element in the pragmatic scheme of R[E2], and can scarcely be dispensed with in the present connexion. Cf. *introd.* to the section.

judges. The two verbs *šāphaṭ* 'judge,' and *hôšîa'* 'save,' are used interchangeably by R[E2] with reference to Israel's deliverers.

them from the hand of their spoilers. 17. But even unto their judges did they not hearken; for they went a whoring after other gods, and bowed themselves down to them: they turned aside quickly from the way wherein their fathers had walked, obeying the commandment of Yahweh: they did not do so. 18. D² And when Yahweh had raised up judges for them, Yahweh would be with the judge, and would save them from the hand of their enemies all the days of the judge: for Yahweh would be moved to pity because of their groaning by reason of them that crushed and oppressed them. 19. But when the judge died they would turn back, and deal more corruptly than their fathers, in going after other gods to serve them and to bow themselves down to them: they did not let fall any of their practices or of their stubborn way. 20. E So the anger of Yahweh was kindled against Israel, and he said, 'Because this nation have transgressed my covenant which I commanded their fathers, and have not hearkened to my voice, 21. I also will no more expel any from before them of the nations which Joshua left when he died':

and they saved them. 𝔊 καὶ ἔσωσεν αὐτοὺς Κύριος. Possibly original (so La.); cf. *v.*[18], where Yahweh is similarly subject of the verb.

17. *went a whoring.* A frequent metaphor for intercourse with other deities and unfaithfulness to Yahweh. So again in *ch.* 8[27.33].

they turned aside quickly, etc. For the phrase, cf. Ex. 32[8] (E?), Deut. 9[12.16].

18. *would be with, etc.* The verbal sequence in the Heb., in this and the following verse, describes what happened on repeated occasions.

would be moved to pity. R.V. 'for it repented the Lord' does not adequately express the sense of the verb. Cf. the use of the same verb (נִחַם) in *ch.* 21[6.15], Jer. 15[6], Ps. 90[13].

20. *have transgressed my covenant.* *I.e.* the divine constitution given to Israel by Yahweh at Ḥoreb or Ŝinai, upon the basis of which (*i.e.* upon condition of the faithful performance by Israel of the ordinances of the constitution) Yahweh undertook to make Israel his peculiar people. The two sides of the covenant are tersely summarized in Deut. 26[17-19].

21. *left when he died.* Lit. 'left and died.' The Heb. constr. is very peculiar. 𝔊, in place of וימת 'and died,' reads ἐν τῇ γῇ· καὶ ἀφῆκεν (in connexion with the verse following τοῦ πειράσαι κ.τ.λ.). Here ἐν τῇ γῇ is most likely only an insertion explanatory of the

22. D[2] in order to prove Israel by them, whether they would keep the way of Yahweh to walk ⌈therein⌉, as their fathers kept it, or not. 23. J So Yahweh left these nations, not expelling them quickly, R[JE] and did not give them into the hand of Joshua'.

3. 1. D[2] Now these are the nations which Yahweh left to prove Israel by them, R[P] even all who had not experienced all the wars of Cana'an ; 2. J only on account of [ ] the generations of the

preceding κατέλιπεν : but καὶ ἀφῆκεν = וַיַּנַּח, *i.e.* the opening word of *v.*[23] 'and [Yahweh] left,' which must have stood in immediate connexion with *v.*[21] before D[2]'s insertion (*v.*[22]) was made. It is possible, therefore, that D[2] took up this word to introduce his insertion (meaning perhaps to write וַיַּנִּיחֵם), and explained 'So he left them in order to prove Israel,' etc. This may then be supposed to have become subsequently corrupted into וימת in 𝔐. Such a repetition by an editor of the words of the older source as the text of his expansive comment is seen in R[E2]: 'So the anger of Yahweh was kindled against Israel'; a statement which introduces *vv.*[14.16.17] prior to the occurrence of the same phrase in *v.*[20] E.

La. emends וַיַּנַּח for וַיָּמֹת, and connects the verb closely with the preceding sentence : 'que Joshué a laissé subsister "en repos"' ; but this is scarcely possible.

22. *therein.* Reading sing. בָּהּ with some MSS. and 𝔊, 𝔏, 𝔙, 𝔖, in place of 𝔐 plur. בָּם.

3, 2. *on account of the generations, etc.* *I.e.* the generations successive to the one which had been responsible for gaining the first footing in Cana'an ; as is explained by R[P]'s gloss, 'such namely as formerly knew nothing thereof.' The text adopted is that of 𝔊, πλὴν διὰ τὰς γενεὰς υἱῶν Ισραηλ κ.τ.λ. So 𝔏. 𝔐 inserts דַּעַת after לְמַעַן, and this can only be rendered with 𝔖[P], 𝔗, R.V. 'only that the generations of the children of Israel might know' ; what they were to know being left to be understood inferentially from the context, viz., the art of war, as the following sentence states. But the constr. 'that they might know (*sc.* war) to teach them war' is impossibly harsh, and the fact that דַּעַת 'to know' is omitted by 𝔊 points to its being merely an erroneous dittography of דֹּרוֹת 'generations' (so Oort, No., Kit., Ehr.).

Mo. (and so Bu.) would prefer to read דַּעַת instead of דֹּרוֹת, and to regard ללמדם as a gloss on the former word, thus obtaining the text רַק לְמַעַן דַּעַת בְּנֵי יִשְׂרָאֵל מִלְחָמָה 'merely in order that the children of Israel might have experience of war.' This of course

children of Israel, to teach them war, $^{R^P}$ such namely as formerly knew nothing thereof:—3. $^{D^2}$ the five lords of the Philistines, and all the Cana'anites, and the Ṣidonians, and the ⌜Ḥittites⌝ dwelling in mount Lebanon, from mount Ba'al-Ḥermon unto the

simplifies the passage, and says all that is required to convey the writer's meaning; but it may be doubted whether we are justified in so far altering the text against the evidence of 𝔊, which gives us a quite comprehensible construction.

knew nothing thereof. Lit. 'had not known them.' The 'them' refers to R^P's previous 'all the wars of Cana'an' in *v.*[1]; and he uses the plur., regardless of the fact that the sing. 'war' intervenes in the old source (*v.*[2a]).

3. *the five lords of the Philistines.* The rulers of the five principal Philistine cities are always distinguished by the title *śéren*—a title never used in any other connexion. The word is not, so far as we know, susceptible of a Semitic derivation; the old view (cf. Ges. *Thes.*) that it is the same as the Heb. *śéren*, 'axle' of a wheel (1 Kgs. 7[30], and in the cognate languages), and that the princes are so called as being, as it were, the axles or pivots of the state, being both unlikely in itself, and also (presumably) precluded by the fact that we do not find the title used elsewhere among the Hebrews or other Semitic peoples.

This being so, it is likely that the title may be of native Philistine origin. $𝔖^P$ ܛܘܪ̈ܢܐ, 𝔗 טרני render *τύραννοι*, and it is thus a plausible conjecture that *śéren* is simply *τύραννος* reproduced in a Hebraïzed form. 𝔊 renders *σατράπαι*, *σατραπεῖαι*, *ἄρχοντες* (most usual in $𝔊^B$), and *στρατηγοί* (once); 𝔙, satrapae, reguli, principes.

Upon the Philistines and their origin, cf. *Introd.* xcii ff.

the Ḥittites dwelling in mount Lebanon. 𝔐 and all Verss. 'the Ḥivvites.' In Josh. 11[3] we find mention of 'the Ḥivvites under Ḥermon in the land of Miṣpah.' In this latter passage $𝔊^B$ reads 'Ḥittites,' making the opposite change (Ḥivvites for Ḥittites) in the list of races dwelling in the central hill-country of Palestine which immediately precedes. In other passages in which the Ḥivvites are mentioned in such a way that they can be more or less definitely localized, they appear as inhabitants of Central Palestine: so in Gen. 34[2] (P) the term is used of the Shechemites, and in Josh. 9[7] (J) of the Gibe'onites. Thus, in both passages where Ḥivvites are mentioned in 𝔐 as dwelling in the neighbourhood of Lebanon and Ḥermon,* modern scholars take the view that the true reading should be Ḥittites (החתי may easily have been confused with החוי; cf. $𝔊^B$

* 'The land of Miṣpah' in Josh. 11[3] seems to be the same as 'the valley (Heb. *biḳ'ā*) of Miṣpeh' in *v.*[8]; *i.e.* probably the southern portion of the great plain between the two Lebanons now called el-Buḳâ' in Ar.: cf. Warren in *DB.* iii. p. 402.

entry of Ḥamath. 4. E And they served to prove Israel by them, to know whether they would hearken to the commandment of Yahweh, which he commanded their fathers by the hand of Moses. 5. J And the children of Israel dwelt in the midst of the Canaʿanites, R^{JE} the Ḥittites, and the Amorites, and the Perizzites, and the Ḥivvites, and the Jebuṡites. 6. J And they took their daughters to themselves for wives, and their own daughters they gave to their sons; and they served their gods.

in Josh. 11 [3]). The Ḥittite principalities extended as far south as Ḳadesh in the neighbourhood of the Anti-Lebanon (cf. *Introd.* p. xcix); and it is likely that Ḥittite clans may have penetrated into the Lebanon-district, which is ideally reckoned as part of the promised land.

from mount Baal-Ḥermon . . . Ḥamath. The northern extremity of Israel's inheritance, which still remained unconquered after the campaigns of Joshuaʿ, is described in Josh. 13 [5] (R^D) as 'all Lebanon eastward [*sc.* of the land of the Gebalites], from Baʿal-Gad under mount Ḥermon unto the entry of Ḥamath.' Josh. 11 [17], 12 [7] (R^D) mentions Baʿal-Gad as the extreme northern limit of the territory subdued by Joshuaʿ. Here Baʿal-Gad is probably the same as Baʿal-Ḥermon, and this is supposed to be the modern Bânyâs (Greek Paneas, *OS.*, 217 [40]; in N. T., Caesarea Philippi), a grotto near the sources of the Jordan where the ancient worship of Gad was superseded in later times by the worship of Pan; cf. Rob. *BR.*[3] iii. pp. 409 ff. Ḥamath, frequently mentioned in the Assyrian inscriptions as Amattu or Ḫammâtu, is the modern Ḥamâ, situated on the Orontes about 115 miles north of Damascus. 'The entry of Ḥamath' is mentioned several times as the ideal northern limit of the kingdom of Israel (Num. 13 [21], 34 [8]; Josh. 13 [5], 1 Kgs. 8 [65] = 2 Chr. 7 [8], 2 Kgs. 14 [25], 1 Chr. 13 [5], Am. 6 [14], Ezek. 47 [20], 48 [1] †); probably because it represented the actual northern limit of the kingdom as Solomon inherited it after the conquests of David (1 Kgs. 8 [65]), and as it was regained in later times through the victories of Jeroboʿam II. (2 Kgs. 14 [25]). It is doubtless (as Rob. *BR.*[3] iii. p. 568, points out) the *northern* extremity of the pass between the Lebanon and Anti-Lebanon ranges. The descriptions here and in Josh. 13 [5] are obviously intended to cover all the Lebanon-district from south to north. Cf. *Introd.* p. xcix, *footnote* ‡.

5. *the Canaʿanites, etc.* To the term 'Canaʿanites' used by J as a general designation of the inhabitants of Canaʿan (cf. 1 [3] *note*) R^{JE} adds the catalogue of races which, when complete, enumerates the 'seven nations' of Canaʿan: cf. Deut. 7 [1], Josh. 3 [10], 24 [11].* Here the Girgashites are missing. On the races mentioned, cf. references in *Index*.

* Driver, on Deut. 7 [1] (*ICC.*), gives a conspectus of all the passages in which the enumeration occurs, noticing the order and omissions.

3. 7-11. ʻOthniel.

This narrative exhibits throughout the characteristic phraseology of R^{E2}'s pragmatic scheme. Indeed, R^{E2} appears to have possessed no further information than the names of the oppressor and deliverer, and the length of the periods of oppression and subsequent peace. The name Cushan-rishʻathaim, signifying 'Cushan of double wickedness,' or, as we might say, 'the double-dyed barbarian,' excites suspicion; and, if genuine, can scarcely be preserved in its original form. The subjugation of Canaʻan by a kingdom so remote as that of Mesopotamia might have been expected to have left further traces than we here possess: and it is strange that the deliverer from this foe from the north-east should have been found in a Ḳenizzite from the extreme south; a member of a clan whose connexion with the northern and central tribes of Israel appears at this time to have been of the slightest (cf. pp. 44 ff.). Hence many critics have supposed that the editor was altogether without authentic information, and, in order to fill up a blank in his scheme of history, chose the name of ʻOthniel, which had the advantage of being well known, and, at the same time, of giving a Judge to Judah. Such an hypothesis does not explain the origin of Cushan-rishʻathaim, a name which can scarcely be the product of mere invention.

Of the attempted explanations of this name which have been put forward, the most plausible is that suggested by Ball (*ET.* xxi. Jan. 1910, p. 192), who compares the Kaššite name Kashsha-rishat (cf. Ranke, *Early Babylonian Personal Names*, p. 244, *n.*[7]). The Kaššites were foreign invaders of Babylonia, probably from Elam and the farther East, who founded the Third Babylonian Dynasty, which lasted from *cir.* B.C. 1760 to *cir.* 1185: cf. *Introd.* p. lxv. Their name appears in cuneiform as *Kaššu*; and there can be little doubt that this is the Heb. כּוּשׁ *Kûš* (Cush) mentioned in Gen. 10[8] as the 'father' of Nimrod, whom the writer regards as the founder of civilization in Babylonia.* The name Kashsha-rishat happens, in the occurrence cited, to belong to a woman; but both elements in the name are familiar in other names, both masc. and fem. Thus the element Kash is seen in Kash-tiliash, which occurs twice among the king-names of the dynasty. Such a name would have been represented in Heb. as כַּשׁ־רִישַׁת or כּוּשׁ־רִישַׁת, and would thus readily have lent itself to the jesting modification which is found in 𝔐. As Ball remarks, 'on any computation, the period of the

* The passage belongs to J; and it is probable that this writer's Kûš is unconnected with the Ḥamitic Kûš of P in *v.*[6]. Cf. Skinner (*Genesis*, *ICC.*, p. 208), who remarks that 'it is conceivable that in consequence of so prolonged a supremacy, Kaš might have become a name for Babylonia, and that J's knowledge of its history did not extend farther back than the Kaššite dynasty. Since there is no reason to suppose that J regarded Kaš as Ḥamitic, it is quite possible that the name belonged to his list of Japhetic peoples.'

7. R[E2] And the children of Israel did that which was evil in the sight of Yahweh, and forgat Yahweh their God, and served the Baʿals, and the ⌈ʿAshtarts⌉. 8. And the anger of Yahweh was kindled against Israel, and he sold them into the hand of Cushan-rishʿathaim, king of Aram-naharaim: and the children of

Judges, that is to say, the period of the settlement of Israel in Canaan, falls within that of the Cassite or "Cushite" domination in Babylonia. Although nothing is known at present of any expedition westward on the part of these Babylonian Cushites, it is quite possible that the story of Cushan-rishʿathaim's oppression of Israel may preserve an indistinct memory of such an historical episode.' *

The only other suggestion as to Cushan-rishʿathaim which needs be noticed is that proposed by Klostermann (*GVI.* p. 119), who, working upon the suggestion of Grä. that Aram should be Edom (confusion of ארם and אדם as in 2 Sam. 8[12.13], 2 Chr. 20[2], 2 Kgs. 16[6]: in this case 'naharaim' must be regarded as a later gloss; notice its omission in *v.*[10]), supposes that there may have been an Edomite king named Cushan,‡ and that *rishʿathaim* may represent an original *rôsh hat-têmānī*, *i.e.* 'chieftain of the Temanites' (רשעתים from רֹשׁהַתֵּימָנִי). This king, he thinks, may be identical with 'Ḥusham (חֻשָׁם) of the land of the Temanites' mentioned in Gen. 36[34]. This view is favoured by Marquart, *Fundamente israelitischer und jüdischer Geschichte*, p. 11; Cheyne, *EB.* 969; and (as regards the emendation 'Edom') by La. Granted that the emendations based upon the proper name are highly precarious, it is at any rate possible that an encroachment upon southern Palestine by the Edomites may have occurred at this period; and, if so, the deliverer might naturally be found in a clan (the Ḳenizzites) which was allied to or incorporated with the tribe of Judah.

3. 7. *the ʿAshtarts.* Reading הָעַשְׁתָּרוֹת with two MSS. and 𝔙 ('the 'Ashtarts' are regularly mentioned elsewhere by E or R[E2] in connexion with 'the Baʿals': cf. 2[13], 10[6], 1 Sam. 7[4], 12[10]) in place of 𝔐 הָאֲשֵׁרוֹת 'the *'Ashērôth.*' The plur. of 'Ashera (on which cf. *ch.* 6[25] *note*) is usually 'Asherim (nineteen occurrences); while 'Asheroth is only found twice besides: 2 Chr. 19[3], 33[3].

8. *Cushan-rishʿathaim.* See introduction to the section. A similar distortion of the name of an enemy in order to cast ridicule upon him

* In the passage cited by Ball from the T.A. Letters which appears to connect *Kaš* with *Naḫrima* (*i.e.* the Biblical Aram-naharaim), 'as by rights belonging to the Pharaoh's empire' (according to Winckler's reading in *KB.* v. 181, l. 35: cf. also *KAT.*[3] 195), the mention of *Kaš* cannot be substantiated, since the actual reading is *Ka-pa-si*: cf. Knudtzon, *Die el-Amarna Tafeln*, 288, l. 36.

‡ Cf. the use of Cushan as a tribal name parallel to 'the land of Midian' in Hab. 3[7].

Israel served Cushan-rishʿathaim eight years. 9. And the children of Israel cried unto Yahweh, and Yahweh raised up a saviour for the children of Israel, and he saved them, to wit ʿOthniel the son of Ḳenaz, Caleb's $^{R^P}$ younger $^{R^{E2}}$ brother. 10. And the spirit of Yahweh came upon him, and he judged Israel; and he went forth to war, and Yahweh gave into his hand Cushan-rishʿathaim, king of Aram; and his hand prevailed against Cushan-rishʿathaim. 11. And the land had rest forty years. And ʿOthniel the son of Kenaz died.

is probably to be seen in the Aram. name טבאל, Isa. 7 [6], properly Ṭab'ēl, *i.e.* ''El is wise' (cf. Ṭabrimmon, 'Rimmon is wise,' 1 Kgs. 15 [18]), but vocalized by 𝔐 as Ṭab'al in order to suggest to Jewish readers the Heb. meaning 'good for nothing.' Other instances of a like perversion are perhaps to be seen in Zebaḥ and Ṣalmunna (*ch.* 8 [5] *note*), and Adoni-bezeḳ (*ch.* 1 [5] *note*).

Aram-naharaim. 'Aram of the two rivers,' mentioned elsewhere, Gen. 24 [10] (J), Deut. 23 [4] ([5] 𝔥), 1 Chr. 19 [6], Ps. 60 title†. The two rivers (if the dual form be correct) are the Euphrates and possibly the Chaboras (Heb. Ḥabor, 2 Kgs. 17 [6], 18 [11]). The land of Naḫrima or Narima is repeatedly mentioned in the T.A. Letters, and the same designation is found in the Egyptian Naharîn, which seems to have been used of the district both east of the Euphrates and west as far as the valley of the Orontes: cf. Müller, *AE.* pp. 249 ff. Possibly, as Mo. suggests, the dual form in Heb. may be a later artificiality (cf. יְרוּשָׁלַיִם for יְרוּשָׁלֵם), and the original form may have been a plur. *Nᵉhārîm*, 'Aram of the rivers,' *i.e.* the upper watershed of the Euphrates.* R.V. 'Mesopotamia' (as 𝔊^{AL}, 𝔙) is too wide, since this term appears to have been used by the Greeks to cover the whole vast district between the Euphrates and Tigris: cf. references cited by Mo.

9. *ʿOthniel, etc.* Cf. 1 [13] *notes.*

10. *And the spirit of Yahweh came upon him.* The divine incentive to deeds of superhuman valour. The same expression is used of Jephthaḥ in *ch.* 11 [29], and, with emphatic and pictorial description of the force of the divine access, of Gideon, 6 [34] (it 'clothed itself in him'), and Samson, 13 [25] (it 'began to impel *or* smite him'), 14 [6.19], 15 [14] (it 'rushed upon him': the same verb *ṣālaḥ* is used of the rapid onslaught of fire in Am. 5 [6]).

judged Israel. Avenged and vindicated them, as the verse goes on to relate.

11. *forty years.* *I.e.* for a whole generation: cf. *Introd.* p. liv.

* The reason adduced by Mo. (followed by Cooke), viz. that there is no trace of a dual form in the Egyptian Naharîn, is based on the argument of W. M. Müller, *AE.* pp. 251 f. In *EB.* 287, however, the same authority states that the form might equally well be read as Naharên, *i.e.* a dual form.

3. 12-30. *Ehud.*

An ancient narrative is introduced by R^{E2} in *vv.* $^{12\text{-}15a}$, in which we find the editor's characteristic phraseology combined with material derived from his source. R^{E2} also closes the narrative in his usual manner in *v.* ^{30}. That the old narrative is not a unity, but combines elements derived from two sources, was first recognized by Winckler (*Alttest. Untersuchungen*, pp. 55 ff.); and this view is also taken by Mo., Bu. (*Comm.*), No. The most striking evidence for this is found in *vv.* $^{18\text{-}20}$. In *v.* ^{19b} 'Eglon is surrounded by his retinue, and Ehud manages to gain a private interview by stating that he has a secret communication (דבר סתר) to make to the king, thus securing the dismissal of the bystanders. In *v.* ^{20}, however, Ehud comes in unto him (בא אליו), apparently from outside, and *finds him sitting alone* in his roof-chamber; whereupon he announces that he is the bearer of a divine communication (דבר אלהים). Having noticed this indication of a double narrative, we can scarcely fail to observe that *v.* ^{19a} interrupts the connexion between *v.* ^{18} and *v.* ^{19b}. Clearly Ehud, after dismissing his own retinue (*v.* ^{18}), at once takes steps to secure a private audience (*v.* ^{19b}). If *v.* ^{19a} were really part of this narrative, we should expect *v.* ^{19b} to be introduced by the statement that he re-entered the king's presence. As the narrative stands, the sequence is somewhat abrupt. The natural sequence to *v.* ^{19a} is *v.* ^{20}. This, when directly connected with *v.* ^{19a}, may have run ויבא אל המלך 'And he came in unto the king.'

Other traces of a double source may be seen in *v.* ^{22b} by the side of *v.* ^{23a}, and in *v.* ^{28} following upon *v.* ^{27}. In *v.* ^{27} Ehud musters his forces, and we are told that 'they went down with him from the hill-country' into the Jordan valley. In *v.* ^{28} he invites them to come down, only then explaining the purpose of the muster; and we are again told that 'they went down after him.' Traces of two accounts of Ehud's escape have been supposed to exist in *v.* ^{26}; but these are not so obvious.

Beyond these points, it is difficult to discover further indications which might aid in discrimination of the sources; and phrases peculiarly characteristic of either J or E do not happen to occur in the narrative. Bu. (*RS.*) notices that the verb הִתְמַהְמָהּ 'tarry' in *v.* ^{26} is confined to J when it occurs in the Pentateuch (Gen. 19 ^{16}, 43 ^{10}; Ex. 12 ^{39}). Rather more significant as a mark of J is the expression in *v.* ^{28} which relates the holding of the fords of the Jordan against Moab, as compared with *ch.* 12 ^{5a}:

וילכדו את מעברות הירדן למואב
וילכד גלעד את מעברות הירדן לאפרים

Cf. also *ch.* 7 ^{24} (also J), as emended in our text, ולכדו להם את מעברות הירדן. Here the use of the ל as a kind of *dativus incommodi*

12. R[E2] And the children of Israel again did that which was evil in the sight of Yahweh: and Yahweh strengthened ʿEglon king of Moab against Israel, because they had done that which was evil in the sight of Yahweh. 13. And he gathered unto him the children of ʿAmmon and ʿAmaleḳ; and went and smote Israel; and ⌈⌉took possession of the City of Palms. 14. And the

(ʻagainst' or ʻto the detriment of') is rather striking. It must be acknowledged, however, that criteria upon which to base a detailed analysis are wanting; and nothing can be affirmed with even approximate certainty as to the composition of the narrative beyond the fact of the existence of a few fairly clear indications that two sources have been employed. The old narrative as a whole is therefore marked in the text as JE.

3. 12. *Yahweh strengthened ʿEglon.* The same verb (*ḥizzēḳ*) is used in Ezek. 30[24] of Yahweh's ʻstrengthening' the arms of the king of Babylon as an instrument of punishment.

13. *ʿAmaleḳ.* A marauding Bedawi people dwelling in the south of the Negeb (Num. 13[29], 14[25] R[JE. 43.45] JE), in the neighbourhood of the Ḳenites (*ch.* 1[16] *note*, 1 Sam. 15[6]) and the tribe of Simeʿon (1 Chr. 4[43]). Israel is related (Ex. 17[8 ff.] E, Deut. 25[17-19]) to have first come into conflict with them soon after the Exodus upon arriving at Rephidim, which must have been close to Ḥoreb or Sinai—a fact which tells in favour of the location of the holy mountain somewhere in the neighbourhood of Ḳadesh-Barneaʿ in the south of the Negeb: cf. *note* on *ch.* 5[4]. David, whilst dwelling at Ṣiḳlag in the Philistine country, made forays against the ʿAmaleḳites (1 Sam. 27[8]), and suffered reprisals in his turn (1 Sam. 30). 𝔐 in *ch.* 5[14], 12[15] suggests that ʿAmaleḳites may at one time have been found in Central Palestine; but cf. *note* on the former passage. The ʿAmaleḳites are again mentioned as invading Israelite territory during the period of the Judges in *ch.* 6[3.33], 7[12], where they appear in conjunction with the Midianites and ʻall the children of the East,' nomadic peoples like themselves with whom it is natural to find them associated. In the present narrative there is no further allusion to ʿAmmon or ʿAmaleḳ; and it is possible that R[E2] may have amplified the account of the invasion by the addition of the names of these peoples. Nöldeke (*EB.* 128) suggests that ʿAmaleḳ in this passage may have arisen from an ancient dittograph of ʿAmmon (עַמּוֹן ועמלק).

and took possession of. Reading sing. וַיִּירַשׁ with 𝔊, 𝔙, in place of 𝔐 (and so 𝔗) plur. וַיִּירְשׁוּ. 𝔖[P] has plur. verbs throughout *v.*[13b], ʻthey went and smote, etc.'

children of Israel served ʿEglon king of Moab eighteen years. 15. And the children of Israel cried unto Yahweh, and Yahweh raised up for them a saviour, to wit Ehud the son of Gera, the Benjaminite, a left-handed man: JE and the children of Israel

the City of Palms. Jericho, as in ch. 1^{16} (cf. *note*). The mention of Jericho in this connexion suggests that the city can scarcely have remained unbuilt and unfortified after its destruction by Joshuaʿ until the days of Aḥab, as might be inferred from 1 Kgs. 16^{34} taken in connexion with Joshuaʿ's curse in Josh. 6^{26} (JE); for the allusion to its capture by ʿEglon seems to imply that it was a fortified city, the possession of which was employed as a vantage-ground for the oppression of the surrounding country.

15. *Ehud the son of Gera.* Gera appears as a son (*i.e.* clan) of Benjamin in Gen. 46^{21} (P), and as a grandson in 1 Chr. 8^{3}; while Ehud himself is found in the obscure genealogical lists of 1 Chr. 7^{10}, 8^{6} (7^{10} would make him the great grandson of Benjamin, but here the name is probably due to an erroneous marginal gloss: cf. Curtis, *ICC. ad loc.*). These facts need not be weighed against the historical truth of our narrative, as though Ehud were simply a clan-name of Benjamin round which the narrator had woven his story; since it is much more probable either that the name has been introduced by the Chronicler into his genealogy directly from Judg., or that a clan in subsequent ages traced its descent from the individual Ehud (so Bu. *RS.* p. 100; Mo.). The fact, however, that Ehud is called 'son' of Gera very likely means that he was member of a clan of that name, and not that Gera was actually the name of his father. Similarly, in David's time, Shimeʿi the Benjaminite was a 'son of Gera,' 2 Sam. 16^{5}, 19$^{16.18}$, 1 Kgs. 2^{8}.

left-handed. Lit. 'bound (*i.e.* restricted) as to his right hand.' The adj. *'iṭṭēr*,* 'bound,' is used by itself in New Heb. in the sense 'left-handed' or 'lame' (restricted in the use of a foot), and belongs in form to the class of words descriptive of bodily defects, *e.g.* *ʿiwwēr*

* The verbal form אטר is not, as stated by Mo., cognate with אטם, but rather belongs to a series of triliteral roots from an original DAR, ṬAR, TAR, ṢAR, ŚAR, ZAR, with the sense 'go round,' 'surround,' and hence, in some instances, 'bind' (a form of surrounding). So דור (Ar. *dâra* and its derivatives, *e.g.* *dâr*, 'dwelling,' or properly circle of buildings round a court; Bab. *dûru*, 'wall' as encircling; Heb. *dôr* 'generation' as periodic, *dûr* 'ball' as *being round*), probably ד־ר־ר (whence *derôr* 'swallow,' perhaps as flying round in circles), ח־דר, ג־דר ; טור, א־טר, ע־טר, ק־טר (Ezek. 46^{22}); תור, כ־תר ; צור, צר־ר, א־צר, ע־צר, ח־צר, ק־צר (bind harvest); א־סר ; זור (compress), א־זר, ח־זר (Aram.). Notice, especially in the ṢAR series, the ascending scale of initial gutturals employed to differentiate the modifications of the original sense of the biliteral root.

sent by his hand tribute to ʿEglon king of Moab. 16. And Ehud made himself a sword with two edges, a cubit long; and he girded it under his raiment on his right thigh. 17. And he presented the tribute to ʿEglon king of Moab: now ʿEglon was a very fat man. 18. And when he had finished presenting the tribute, he sent away the people who were carrying the tribute.

'blind,' *'illēm* 'dumb,' *pissē*^{a}*ḥ* 'lame,' etc.; but that the peculiarity did not involve any defect in skill appears from the reference to the 700 left-handed Benjaminites in *ch.* 20[16]. 𝔊 renders ἀμφοτεροδέξιον (—δέξιοι), 'ambidextrous,' in both passages; and similarly 𝔙 here 'qui utraque manu pro dextera utebatur,' but in 20[16] 'sinistra ut dextra proeliantes.' Cf. the description of the Benjaminites in 1 Chr. 12[2].

tribute. The Heb. *minḥā* is used elsewhere in this sense in 2 Sam. 8[2.6], 1 Kgs. 4[21] (𝔐 5[1]), 2 Kgs. 17[3]. In other passages the word has the meaning of a *present* offered voluntarily in order to gain the favour of the recipient: cf. Gen. 32[13], 𝔐[14], 2 Kgs. 8[8], 20[12]. In the sacrificial terminology of the Priestly Code *minḥā* denotes the *meal-offering.*

16. *two edges.* Lit. 'two mouths': cf. the expression 'a sword of mouths,' Prov. 5[4], Ps. 149[6], and the phrase noticed in *ch.* 1[8].

a cubit long. The Heb. term *gōmedh* (only here in O.T.) is explained by the Jewish interpreters as a short cubit, *i.e.* the length from the elbow to the knuckles of the closed fist: cf. Mo. in *JBL.* xii. p. 104. The measure thus corresponds to the Greek πυγμή, approximately $13\frac{1}{2}$ inches. 𝔊 renders σπιθαμῆς τὸ μῆκος αὐτῆς, 'a span long'; but, as Mo. (following Stu.) appositely points out, 'the description of ʿEglon's corpulence (*v.*[17]) is pertinent only in relation to the fact that a long dirk was buried, hilt and all, in his belly.' 𝔙 offers a curious and obscure paraphrase, intended to explain the character of the sword: 'gladium ancipitem, habentem in medio capulum longitudinis palmae manus,' interpreting *gōmedh* as a hand-breadth and referring it to the hilt. 𝔖ᴾ ܓܡܕ ܐܘܪܟܗ is interesting as reading *gāmadh* (cf. Ar. *ǵamada*, 'cut off'; Aram. *g*^{e}*madh*, 'contract') in place of *gōmedh*: '*he curtailed* its length.' Such a proceeding on the part of Ehud, for the purpose of more effectively concealing the weapon under his raiment, would be perfectly intelligible: still, the consideration noticed above seems to demand a precise mention of the length of the sword, as in 𝔐.

under his raiment. Heb. *maddîm* is the loose outer garment, outside of which the sword was usually worn: cf. 1 Sam. 17[39].

18. *he sent away the people, etc.* The tribute was doubtless paid in kind (most probably in farm-produce) and would require a number of bearers. In later times, when Moab was subject to Israel, the tribute consisted in the wool of one hundred thousand rams and one

19. But he himself returned from the graven images which are near Gilgal; and he said, 'I have a secret communication for thee, O king.' And he said, 'Silence!' And there went out from him all who stood by him. 20. And Ehud came in unto him: now he was sitting by himself in his cool roof-chamber.

hundred thousand lambs: 2 Kgs. 3[4]. A representation of a train of envoys of Jehu, king of Israel, bearing tribute to the Assyrian king, is to be seen upon the black obelisk of Shalmaneser III. (cf. Driver, *Schweich Lectures*, p. 17), and in this case the tribute is very costly (consisting largely in vessels of gold: cf. *NHTK*. p. 377), in accordance with the resources of the kingdom of Israel in Jehu's time.

19. *graven images.* This is the meaning which is regularly borne by the Heb. *p^{e}sîlîm* elsewhere (twenty-one occurrences). In itself the term simply denotes 'carved things,' and might refer to figures in low relief carved upon standing stones, possibly some of the stones from which Gilgal derived its name (cf. *note* on *ch.* 2[1]). The connexion in which the *p^{e}sîlîm* are mentioned is, however, rather striking: it is when Ehud reaches this point that he dismisses his retinue; and later on (*v.*[26]) when he has passed it he gets clear away, and so escapes. Both references, especially when taken together, can scarcely fail to suggest a comparison with the sculptured *boundary-stones* which have been found in Babylonia (cf. *OTLAE*. i. p. 11; Jastrow, *RBBA*. pp. 230, 385 f.), and to raise the possibility that the *p^{e}sîlîm* may have marked the limit of the sphere of Moab's influence, beyond which comparative safety was attained. Such a theory could not hold if the narrative were a unity; since, according to *v.*[13], Jericho, three miles west-north-west of Gilgal, was in the possession of Moab. But, as we have noticed, the story clearly seems to have been derived from two sources, and the source to which the references to the *p^{e}sîlîm* belong may have differed as to this point; or the words 'which are near Gilgal' may be a later and erroneous identification of the site of the *p^{e}sîlîm*.

A.V., R.V. render 'quarries,' apparently following 𝔗 מחצביא. 𝔊 ἀπὸ τῶν γλυπτῶν, 𝔙 'ubi erant idola,' support the ordinary meaning of the word. 𝔖^P ܦܣܝܠܐ employs the same word as 𝔥.

a secret communication. Lit. 'a word of secrecy.'

Silence! The command (Heb. *hăs*, onomatopoetic, like English 'hush!' or 'ssh!') is addressed by 'Eglon to his retinue.

20. *roof-chamber.* The Heb. *'ăliyyā* is explained by the same term *'ulliyya*, *'illiyya* in Ar., in which it denotes a room built on the top of the flat roof of a house, with windows on every side for the free passage of air. Cf. Mo., who quotes authorities for the use of such roof-chambers in the modern east. The purpose of this *'ăliyyā* is

And Ehud said, 'I have a communication from God for thee.' And he rose up from his seat. 21. And Ehud put forth his left hand, and took the sword from his right thigh, and thrust it into his belly. 22. And the hilt also went in after the blade, and the fat closed over the blade; for he drew not the sword out of his belly. And he went out into the vestibule. 23. And Ehud

further defined by the term *ham-mᵉḳērā* (עֲלִיַּת הַמְּקֵרָה), lit. 'roof-chamber of coolness.' The size and character of the windows in such a chamber is indicated by 2 Kgs. 1[2], where we are told that king Aḥaziah accidentally fell through the lattice-window (הַשְּׂבָכָה) in his *'ăliyyā*.

a communication from God. Lit. 'a word of God.'

he rose up, etc. The action seems to have been intended as a mark of reverence for the divine oracle.

21. *put forth, etc.* The movement of the left hand to the right side was unlikely to arouse suspicion.

22. *the hilt also went in.* As Mo. remarks, 'the dirk was doubtless without either guard or cross-piece.'

into the vestibule. Heb. *hap-paršᵉdhônā* only here. The precise rendering 'vestibule' is conjectural, but there is no reason for doubting the originality of the Heb. word. There is an Assyr. word *parašdinnu*, the exact meaning of which is similarly unknown; but (according to Delitzsch, *HWB.* p. 546) we have the equivalents *pa-ra-aš-din-nu* = KIRRUD.DA in Sumerian, *i.e.* some form of cavity or opening. *Paršᵉdhônā* may therefore be assumed to denote a means of exit; though exactly what we cannot say. La., adopting this explanation, assumes that the term denotes the *window.* But the form of the Heb. word (with ה locative) implies that it was something *into* which and not simply *through* which Ehud passed; and, moreover, there seems no reason why the writer should not have used the ordinary word *ḥallôn*, 'window,' if this had been his meaning.

The rendering which we have adopted is given by 𝔊, τὴν προστάδα (from which apparently R.V. marg. 'the ante-chamber'), 'A. παραστάδα, Σ. εἰς τὰ πρόθυρα. We cannot, however, certainly assume that the meaning of the word was familiar to the translators, since it is not unlikely that the rendering may have been dictated by the accidental resemblance of the Greek word to the Heb.*

* This is a consideration which appears not infrequently to have influenced the 𝔊 translators. Driver (*NHTS.*[2] p. 270) notices ἐσχαρίτην for אֶשְׁפָּר probably read as אֶשְׁכָּר 2 Sam. 6[19], δρέπανον for דָּרְבָן 1 Sam. 13[21], τόκος for תֹּךְ Ps. 72[14] *al.*; to which we may add τοπάζιον for פָּז Ex. 28[17] *al.*; σκηνοῦν for שָׁכֵן Judg. 5[17], 6[11].

went out into the colonnade, and shut the doors of the roof-chamber upon him, and lock⌜ed⌝ them. 24. Now when he had gone out, his servants came; and they looked, and, behold, the

𝔙, 𝔗* seem to have read or understood *hap-péreš* (Ex. 29[14]; Lev. 4[11], 8[17], 16[27]; Num. 19[5], Mal. 2[3]†) in place of *hap-paršᵉdhônā*: 'and the *faeces* came out' *sc.* from the anus, as is said to be the ordinary consequence of a wound in the abdomen (cf. Mo.). This emendation is adopted by Nöldeke, Mo., Bu., Kent; but the objections advanced against it by No. are valid;‡ and in any case it can scarcely stand in view of the support given to 𝔐 by the Assyr. parallel.

𝔖ᴾ 'and he went out *hastily*' (ܘܢܦܩ ܒܣܘܪܗܒܐ) is a bad guess. R.V. 'and it came out behind' depends upon a mere conjecture made by a number of the older commentators (cf. Mo.'s enumeration), and involves a violation of grammar (הַחֶרֶב 'the sword' is fem., and can scarcely be the subject of the masc. וַיֵּצֵא 'and it came out').

23. *into the colonnade.* Or 'portico.' Heb. *ham-misdᵉrônā* only here. The meaning of the term is almost as obscure as the meaning of that last discussed, to which it probably corresponds in the parallel narrative. The Heb. root *śādhar* means 'to arrange in order *or* in a rank,' and is so used in New Heb., Assyr., and Aram. We have cognate substantives in all these languages meaning 'arrangement,' 'rank,' or 'row' (in Assyr. 'line of battle'); and it may thus be inferred that *misdᵉrôn*, in accordance with its form (substantives with preformative מ commonly denote the *place* of the action implied by the verbal form), may mean 'place of rows' (*sc.* of pillars), *i.e.* 'colonnade.' This is the rendering of Sᴾ *ksûsṭᵉrôn*, *i.e.* ξυστός. 𝔊 τοὺς διατεταγμένους recognizes the meaning of the root, but is at a loss for an intelligible rendering. 𝔙 'per posticum' (perhaps an error for 'per porticum'). 𝔗 לְאַכסדרא, *i.e.* ἐξέδρα. R.V. 'into the porch.'

and locked them. The Heb. construction (וְנָעַל, Perfect with Weak *wāw*) is irregular. We should expect וַיִּנְעֹל; but it is quite possible that the form intended is the *infinitive absolute* וְנָעֹל in continuation

* 𝔗's rendering, however, אכליה שפיך 'cibus ejus ejectus,' is merely an illustration of the Rabbinic method of explaining an incomprehensible word by analysis (פֶּרֶשׁ 'dung' and שְׁדָה 'to cast out'), as is rightly noticed by Stu., Ber., No. The translator therefore had the same reading before him as that of 𝔐.

‡ 'Schon Holzinger hat darauf aufmerksam gemacht, dass diese Aenderung in הפרש nicht ohne Bedenken ist, insofern הפרש gewöhnlich den Thiermist, nicht aber den Menschenkoth bezeichnet, man würde auch ein ממנו oder doch das Suff. am Subj. erwarten; endlich ist es auch nicht leicht zu verstehen, wie unter dem Einfluss von המסדרנה das urspr. הפרש in הפרשדנה verderbt werden konnte.' No. offers no explanation of the difficult word.

doors of the roof-chamber were locked: and they said, 'Surely
he is covering his feet in the closet of the cool apartment.'
25. And they waited till they were ashamed; and, behold, he
opened not the doors of the roof-chamber: so they took the key
and opened them, and, behold, their lord was fallen down on
the ground dead. 26. But Ehud had escaped while they tarried,
and had passed the graven images, and escaped to Se'irah.
27. And when he arrived, he blew the trumpet in the hill-
country of Ephraim, and the children of Israel went down with
him from the hill-country, and he before them. 28. And he
said unto them, '⌜Come down⌝ after me, for Yahweh hath given

of the preceding imperfect with *wāw* consecutive: lit. 'and locking,' for 'and locked.' For this idiomatic construction, cf. Davidson, *Hebrew Syntax*, § 88; G-K. § 113 *z*. A precisely similar construction is found in *ch.* 7^{19}, וַיִּתְקְעוּ בַּשּׁוֹפָרוֹת וְנָפוֹץ הַכַּדִּים, 'and they blew the trumpets and brake (lit. "and breaking") the pitchers.' Adopting this slight change of one vowel-point, there is no reason to suppose, with Mo., that the words 'are, as the false tense proves, the addition of a scribe, who, observing that the doors were locked (*vv.* $^{24.25}$), missed an explicit statement here that Ehud locked them.'

24. *he is covering his feet.* The same euphemism is found in 1 Sam. 24^{3}.

25. *till they were ashamed.* Or, 'to the point of confusion': Heb. עַד־בּוֹשׁ. The expression here implies the perplexity and apprehension caused by an occurrence which is inexplicable. As we might say, they were *at their wit's end.* There are two other occurrences:—2 Kgs. 2^{17}, 'they urged him till he was ashamed' (such was the importunity of the disciples that Elisha' had no longer the *face* to refuse their request); 2 Kgs. 8^{11}, 'And he steadied his countenance, and set (it on him) till he was ashamed' (Elisha' looked Ḥazael *out of countenance*).

the key. A flat piece of wood with projecting pins corresponding to holes in the wooden cross-bolt into which the pins of the socket fall when the door is locked. When the key is inserted into a hollow in the bolt and pushed upwards, the pins of the key push up the pins of the socket, and the bolt is released. For a full description and illustrations, cf. *DB*. ii. p. 836.

26. *had passed, etc.* Cf. *note* on *v.* ^{19}.

Se'irah. The site is unidentified.

28. *come down after me.* Reading רְדוּ אַחֲרַי with 𝔊 Καταβητε ὀπίσω μου (cf. the following, 'and they came down after him'), in place of 𝔐 רִדְפוּ אַחֲרַי, which can only mean 'pursue after me.'

your enemies, even Moab, into your hand.' So they went down after him, and took the fords of the Jordan against Moab, and suffered no man to pass over. 29. And they smote of Moab at that time about ten thousand men, every stout and every valiant man; and there escaped not a man. 30. R^{E2} So Moab was subdued that day under the hand of Israel. And the land had rest eighty years.

R.V. renders 'Follow me'; but such a meaning for the verb cannot be paralleled.

took the fords, etc. Cf. *ch.* 7 [24] (*note*), 12 [5]. The *coup* was designed to prevent the escape of the Moabites who occupied Israelite territory west of Jordan (cf. *v.* [13b]), and at the same time to prevent the despatch of assistance to them from the land of Moab.

29. *And they smote, etc.* The statement implies that the army of occupation west of Jordan was cut to pieces, but scarcely (as R^{E2} seems to imply in *v.* [30]) that the land of Moab was invaded and subdued.

30. *eighty years.* A round number representing, approximately, two generations.

3. 31. *Shamgar.*

It is quite clear that this brief notice formed no part of the Book of Judges as it left the hand of R^{E2}. The story of Ehud must have been directly connected by R^{E2} with *ch.* 4 [1]: 'And the children of Israel again did that which was evil in the sight of Yahweh, when Ehud was dead.' We miss, moreover, R^{E2}'s pragmatic introduction and conclusion, and no hint is given as to the length of the period of oppression or of the subsequent period of tranquillity.

The name of Shamgar the son of ʿAnath is, however, certified as historical by its occurrence in the Song of Deborah, which alludes to the desolate condition of the country 'in the days of Shamgar the son of ʿAnath' (*ch.* 5 [6]); though, for all this passage tells us, Shamgar may have been a foreign oppressor (see below as to his name) and not an Israelite judge. The exploit recorded of Shamgar bears striking resemblance to that of one of David's heroes, Shammah the son of Agee (2 Sam. 23 [11 ff.]), and also to Samson's feat with the jawbone at Ramath-leḥi (*ch.* 15 [14 ff.]). In all three cases the success is recorded to have been gained against the Philistines. It should be noticed, also, that the Song of Deborah, though mentioning Shamgar, says nothing about any encroachment of the Philistines, who seem at this point to appear too early in the narrative. It may be added that, since the Song deals with the Canaʿanite aggressions in N. Palestine, it is the less natural to connect Shamgar with the Philistines in the south.

The name Shamgar is certainly non-Israelite. It bears close resemblance to the Ḥittite Sangara or Sangar (*KB.* i. pp. 107, 159), which we find as the name of a king of Carchemish in the reigns of Ashurnaṣirpal and Shalmaneser III. (ninth century B.C.). It is perhaps worth noticing that some codd. of 𝔙 read Sangar; and so Jos. *Ant.*, v. iv. 3 Σανάγαρος. 'Anath as the name of a goddess has been noticed under *ch.* 1^{33}. The use of the name as a masc. proper name, without such a prefix as *'ébhedh* ('servant of 'A.': cf. Baethgen, *Beiträge*, pp. 52, 141), may seem strange to us, but is certainly not unusual (as stated by Mo.), since Anatum occurs several times among the names of the period of the first Babylonian dynasty: three occurrences are cited by Ranke, *Early Babylonian Personal Names*, p. 66, and three (one probably the name of a woman) by Thureau-Dangin, *Lettres et Contrats de l'époque de la première dynastie Babylonienne*, p. 15.* The name also occurs at the close of one of the T.A. Letters; *ana Anati šulma kibi*, 'To Anatu speak salutation' (No. 125 in Winckler's ed., *KB.* v. p. 236; No. 170 in Knudtzon's ed.).

Granted that *ch.* 3^{31} forms no part of R^{E2}'s history, it is a further question whether this allusion to Shamgar as a judge of Israel is due to the same hand as introduced the five 'minor' judges in *ch.* 10^{1-5}, 12^{8-15} (R^P: cf. *note* on 10^{1-5}). It is noteworthy that, according to R^P's scheme, the number of judges is twelve (the tribal number) without Shamgar; since R^P, who reintroduced the story of Abimelech into the book (pp. 263, 266, 268), clearly intended him to rank as a judge: cf. *ch.* 10^1, 'And there arose after Abimelech to judge Israel, etc.' Moreover, as Mo. remarks, the verse which tells Shamgar's brief story exhibits 'none of the distinctive formulas of the list 10^{1-5}, 12^{8-15}; and what is more conclusive, Shamgar is not embraced with them in the final chronological scheme of the book; neither the period in which he wrought deliverance for Israel nor its duration is given.' ‡ Thus it seems likely that the verse is an insertion made subsequently to the work of R^P; possibly, as Bu. suggests (*RS.* p. 166, and *Comm.*), by a scribe who wished to dispense with the reckoning of the wicked Abimelech among the twelve judges. Notice, as a mark of the later hand, the גַּם־הוּא, '*he also* saved Israel.' This interpolator probably extracted the name Shamgar the son of 'Anath from the Song of Deborah, upon the supposition that he was an Israelite hero, and may have based his exploit upon the similar

* If the termination *-atum* is really an hypocoristic affix, as is supposed by Ranke (*op. cit.* pp. 14 f.), it is possible that 'Anath, Anatum, used as a personal name, may be not really the name of the goddess, but an hypocoristic abbreviation of a personal name compounded with the name of the *god* Anu, *e.g.* Anummalik, 'Anu counsels,' Anum-gamil, 'Anu spares,' etc. Cf. Sinatum, Sinnatum (Ranke, *op. cit.* pp. 153, 162), by the side of Sin-malik, Sin-gamil, etc.

‡ Jos. (*Ant.*, v. iv. 3) states that he died within a year of his election as judge, an assertion which is clearly intended to explain the absence of the usual chronological note.

31. G1 And after him came Shamgar, son of ʿAnath, who smote of the Philistines six hundred men with an ox-goad. And he also saved Israel.

exploit of Shammah the son of Agee which we have already noticed.

Mo. (*Journal of the American Oriental Society*, 1898, p. 159) notices that certain recensions of 𝔊 (codd. 44, 54, 56, 59, 75, 76, 82, 106, 134 HP.; *sub obel.* 121), together with 𝔖h, Arm., Slav., have the account of Shamgar's exploit a second time after 16 31. Here it appears with the introductory formula καὶ ἀνέστη μετὰ τὸν Σαμψων Σεμεγαρ υἱὸς Εναν, which corresponds closely to the formula of *ch.* 10 1, 'And there arose after Abimelech to save Israel,' etc. Comparing this with 'the awkward and unparalleled' ויהי אחריו (𝔊 ἀνέστη) of 3 31, Mo. infers that the position and form of the reference to Shamgar, as it stands in 16 31 in the authorities cited, is the more original:—'There is thus good reason to think that the verse at first stood after the story of Samson, and was subsequently, for some reason, removed to a place between Ehud and Barak.' More probably the notice, as it stands in 3 31 𝔐 (depending, as we have seen, upon the allusion in 5 6), was subsequently moved to a position after 16 31 because it seemed to refer to the period of the Philistine domination; and the introductory formula was at the same time squared with that which is found in 10 1.3.

Nestle (*JTS.* xiii. pp. 424 f.) cites a chronicle (published by Lagarde, *Septuaginta Studien*, ii. pp. 21 ff.) which originated in the Vandalian Church of Africa in A.D. 463, as stating both that Shamgar of 3 31 was an oppressor of Israel, and that Shamgar the Judge succeeded Samson.* These statements are (according to Nestle) of much greater antiquity than A.D. 463, that which places the judge Shamgar after Samson being at least as old as Julius Africanus (*cir.* 140 A.D.).

ox-goad. Heb. *milmadh hab-bāḳār.* The word *malmēdh* (assumed Absolute form) occurs only here, and must be supposed to denote literally 'instrument of instruction *or* training.' In Hos. 10 11 the verb from which it is derived, *limmēdh*, is used of *training* a heifer to the yoke. Elsewhere the word for 'goad' is *dorbhān*, 1 Sam. 13 21 (also used in New Heb.), *dorbhōnā*, Eccles. 12 11. The modern Palestinian ox-goad is a wooden pole eight or nine feet long, shod at one end with a metal point and at the other with a metal blade for cleaning the ploughshare. Cf., for figures, *EB.* p. 78; *DB.* i. 49.

𝔊AL, ἐκτὸς μόσχων (τῶν) βοῶν, 𝔖h, 𝔏, read מִלְּבַד for במלמד.

* After allusion to Ehud, the chronicle states, 'deinde servierunt regi Semegar annis xx. hic occidit ex alienigenis in aratro boum octingentos viros et defendit filios Israel.' The reference to Samson is followed by a second allusion to Shamgar, this time as Judge:—'Deinde Sampson filius Manoe . . . qui plus occidit in morte sua quam quod in vita sua. deinde Samera iudicavit eos anno uno. hic percussit ex Allophylis sescentos viros praeter iumenta et salvum fecit et ipse Israel. deinde pacem habuerunt annis xxx.'

4. 1–5. 31. *Deborah and Baraḳ.*

Besides the Commentaries, etc., quoted throughout the book, cf. Cooke, *The History and Song of Deborah*, 1892; Driver, in *Expositor*, 1912, pp. 24 ff., 120 ff.

R^{E2}'s hand is seen in the introduction, 4^{1-4}, which contains certain facts derived from the old narrative, and in the conclusion, $4^{23.24}$ 5^{31b}.

In the material employed by R^{E2} we are fortunate in possessing not merely a prose-narrative of presumably the same date as the other lengthy narratives relating to the exploits of the Judges (*ch.* 4), but also a poetical description which is generally accepted as a contemporary document (*ch.* 5),* and which must therefore be regarded as a peculiarly valuable picture of the condition of affairs during the period which followed the settlement in Cana'an.

In both accounts the main facts are the same. Each opens with reference to a drastic oppression of Israel on the part of the Cana'anites. Deborah, the 'mother in Israel' of the poem, is clearly the instigator of the effort to shake off the foreign yoke, just as Deborah the 'prophetess' is in the prose-narrative. In both Baraḳ is leader of the Israelite troops against Ṡiṡera the leader of the Cana'anites. In both, again, the battle and the rout of the Cana'anites takes place in the plain of Megiddo, Ṡiṡera subsequently meets his death at the hand of a woman named Ja'el, and a period of pastoral prosperity follows upon Israel's victory.

There exist, however, a certain number of somewhat remarkable discrepancies between the two narratives, which we must proceed to notice. According to the prose-narrative, the principal oppressor of Israel was Jabin, king of Ḥaṣor in North Palestine, a city probably situated near the lake Ḥûleh (doubtfully identified with the waters of Merom), and about three and a half miles south-south-west of Ḳedesh of Naphtali. This narrative states that the captain of Jabin's army was Ṡiṡera 'who dwelt at Ḥarosheth of the nations,' *i.e.* probably el-Ḥâriṯiyyeh on the right bank of the lower Ḳishon, and north-west of Megiddo. The fact is remarkable, however, that no mention of Jabin occurs in the poem, in which Ṡiṡera only is named. It is clear, too, that Siṡera is there regarded not merely as the captain of the Cana'anite army and the viceregent of a higher power, but as himself of kingly rank. His mother, when she is pictured as anxiously

* Cf. Wellh. *Comp.*[3] p. 218, *n.*: 'In proof that the Song is a contemporary composition, we may cite in the first place 5^8, where the whole number of the fighting men of Israel is given as 40,000 (in the Pentateuch 600,000), and also the fierceness of the passion 5^{25-27}, and the exultation over the disappointed expectation of the mother, 5^{28ff}. "Only some one actually concerned, who had experienced the effrontery of an insolent oppressor directed against himself, could express himself with this glowing hatred over a dead foe; not a poet living some centuries later" (Studer, p. 166).' Such arguments as have been advanced against the contemporary character of the poem are insignificant: cf. Mo. pp. 129 f.; La. p. 114.

awaiting his return after the battle, is attended by princesses (5 [29]); and, if the emendation which is adopted in the last clause of *v.* [30] may be regarded as correct, it is stated that he will bring back with him 'two dyed embroideries for the neck of *the queen*,' *i.e.* for his mother or wife. Kings of Cana'an are represented as taking part in the battle (*v.* [19]); but they only receive brief mention, and are obviously subordinate to Ṡiṡera, whose fate occupies nearly a third of the whole poem.

There is also a striking difference in the two narratives as to the tribal connexions of Deborah and Baraḳ. According to the prose-narrative, Deborah dwells between Ramah and Bethel in the hill-country of Ephraim, far to the south of the scene of action; while Baraḳ belongs to Ḳedesh of Naphtali, west-north-west of lake Ḥûleh and not far from Ḥaṣor. In the poem, however, *v.* [15], though admittedly somewhat obscure, at any rate seems to indicate that both Deborah and Baraḳ belonged to the tribe of Issachar, which, as occupying a region which extended southward from the plain of Megiddo (Josh. 19 [17-23]), was naturally a principal sufferer from the aggressions of the Cana'anites.

Again, there is a difference as to the Israelite tribes which are said to have taken part in the battle. According to the prose-narrative, Baraḳ is enjoined to take with him 10,000 men of the tribes of Naphtali and Zebulun only (*v.* [6]); but from the poem we gather that a grand muster of all the tribes was attempted, with the exception of Judah and Sime'on in the south, which were probably at this time remote from the interests of the other tribes (cf. p. 47). Those which responded to the summons, and bore their part in the combat, were the tribes surrounding the great plain, viz. Ephraim with Benjamin, Machir (*i.e.* West Manasseh), Zebulun, Issachar, and Naphtali (5 [14.15.18]).

It is also supposed by some scholars that there is a slight difference as to the scene of the battle. In the prose-account Baraḳ sweeps down from Mount Tabor to the north of the plain, and the battle takes place on the right bank of the Ḳishon (*vv.* [14-15]). According to the poem, the scene is 'at Ta'anach by the waters of Megiddo' (*v.* [19]), *i.e.*, if regarded as a precise definition, on the left bank. This, however, if really a discrepancy, is a very minor point, and need not be taken seriously into account.

Lastly, a point which Wellh. (*Comp.*[3] p. 217) regards as 'die Hauptdifferenz' between the two narratives, and which has been made much of by a large number of scholars, is probably no discrepancy at all. According to the prose-narrative, when Ṡiṡera after his flight arrives at the tent of Ḥeber the Ḳenite, Ja'el, Ḥeber's wife, welcomes him with protestations of friendship, his request for a drink of water is met by the offer of curdled milk, and Ja'el allows him to lie down and sleep in the tent, undertaking herself to stand at the tent-door and put any chance pursuer off the track of the fugitive. As soon, however, as Ṡiṡera is fast asleep, Ja'el takes a tent-peg and mallet, and going softly to him so as not to wake him, hammers the peg through his temples so forcibly as to pin his head to the ground. Most modern critics think that we have in the poem a different description of the death of Ṡiṡera. Here it is supposed that Ja'el is pictured as approaching him from behind as he is eagerly drinking, felling him with a blow from a mallet, and then beating his head to pieces. This view is based principally upon the line rendered in R.V. 'at her feet he bowed, he fell, he lay,' where the three verbs would accurately describe Ṡiṡera's coming down on his knees under the blow, falling forward on his face, and lying prone. It necessitates, however, a very forced explanation of the peg, יתד (a point rightly emphasized by Kue., La., and Kit., *GVI.*² ii. 79 *n* ¹), making it to denote the wooden handle of 'the workman's mallet' (if that be the meaning of the Heb. expression). The statement 'She smote Ṡiṡera, crushed his head, shattered and struck through his temples' (*v.*²⁶; see *note*) agrees well with the prose-account as describing the effects of driving a wooden peg through her victim's temples; whilst, had Ṡiṡera been struck down from behind, he would naturally have fallen on his face, in which case the smashing and piercing of his temples is not so easily explained. It may be added that the Heb. בין רגליה scarcely admits of the rendering 'at her feet.' It properly means 'between her feet' (*or* 'legs': cf. the only other sense in which the expression is used, Deut. 28⁵⁷), and rather describes Ja'el's straddling over Ṡiṡera's recumbent body in order to deliver the fatal blow than the idea that he fell prone '*at* (*i.e.* before) her feet.' Probably the expression is intended to emphasize the indignity of his death. Thus it appears that it is unnecessary to find variation between the prose and poetical accounts as regards this event, beyond that which may naturally be referred to the licence of poetry.

Looking now at the prose-narrative alone, we cannot fail to notice that it contains serious internal discrepancies. Ṡiṡera, the captain of the host of Jabin, lives at a great distance from him (assuming that Ḥarosheth and Ḥaṣor are rightly identified), thirty-four miles in a direct line without taking account of the detours which are necessary in traversing a rugged and difficult country. Deborah, living between Ramah and Bethel (the former five miles, the latter ten miles, north of Jerusalem), sends to Baraḳ at Ḳedesh of Naphtali, more than ninety miles to the north. Baraḳ musters his troops at Ḳedesh in the heart of the enemy's country, and must have marched them unmolested close past the gates of Ḥaṣor in order to reach Mount Tabor, thirty miles to the south. After the rout of the Cana'anites, Baraḳ pursued the fugitives up to (עד) Ḥarosheth, twelve miles or more west-north-west. Ṡiṡera meanwhile flees north-north-east towards Ḥaṣor, thirty miles distant; but instead of seeking safety in the fortified city of his sovereign Jabin, he prefers to find it in the tent of a stranger, although this is quite close to Ḳedesh (*v.* 11), and he must therefore have passed by Ḥaṣor in his flight. Here he meets his death; and Baraḳ, in spite of the delay which his pursuit of Śiśera's army in a different direction might have been expected to cause, seems all the time to have been close on his heels; for the narrative apparently pictures him as arriving at Ja'el's tent shortly after the murder.

These difficulties for the most part disappear with recognition of the fact that Jabin king of Ḥaṣor has really no place in our narrative, but belongs to quite a different narrative which has been erroneously interwoven with it. The shadowy figure of Jabin plays no real part in the story. His position was plainly something of a puzzle to R^{E2}; for whereas the old narrative makes him 'king of Ḥaṣor' according to the theory of R^{E2} he was 'the king of Cana'an, who reigned in Ḥaṣor' (*v.* 2), *i.e.*, apparently, a kind of superior monarch who was overlord of the many petty kings of the Cana'anite cities. Yet we never hear elsewhere of Cana'an as a political unit. Kings of separate cities such as Jerusalem, Jericho, 'Ai, etc., are constantly mentioned, but never a king of Cana'an.

We meet with Jabin king of Ḥaṣor in Josh. 11^{1-9}, where he appears as head of a coalition of Cana'anite kings in North Palestine which was defeated by Joshua' near the waters of Merom. This narrative is derived in the main from JE (whether J or E is doubtful), but has been amplified by R^{D} in his usual manner (*vv.* 2 and 8b), in order to intensify the magnitude of the coalition and the thoroughness of Joshua''s conquest. It seems probable that the references to Jabin in Judg. 4 are reminiscent of the victory recorded in Josh. 11. Possibly the original form of this narrative may have made Zebulun and Naphtali the chief actors in the defeat of Jabin, *i.e.* it may have related a separate tribal movement akin to those which are recorded in the J document in Judg. 1, and possibly originally forming part of it. If this is so, a parallel may be found in the account of the conquest of Adoni-ṣedeḳ in Josh. $10^{1ff.}$ as compared with that of Judg. $1^{5ff.}$ (cf. *note* on *v.* 5).

We have already noticed the discrepancy between the prose and poetical narratives as to the homes of Deborah and Baraḳ. It is not unlikely that in *ch.* 4^{5} we may have a gloss introduced by a late hand confusing Deborah with another Deborah, Rebeḳah's nurse, who is recorded in Gen. 35^{8} to have been buried under an oak below Bethel. There was a city named Dāběrath belonging to Issachar, Josh. 21^{28}, 1 Chr. 6^{72} (𝕳 *v.* 57), one of the boundary-points between Issachar and Zebulun, Josh. 19^{12}, and this is identified with the modern Debûriyyeh at the west foot of mount Tabor. Possibly there may have been a connexion between the name of this city and the name of the prophetess. The fact that the name Ḳedesh ('sanctuary') was applied to several different places has led some scholars to suppose that, while Baraḳ's city is rightly named Ḳedesh, an error has arisen as to the particular Ḳedesh in question. Thus Wellh., Reuss, Cooke think that the reference is properly to Ḳedesh of Issachar (Josh. 12^{22}, 1 Chr. 6^{72}, ℌ *v.*^{57}), *i.e.* the modern Tell Abû Ḳudîs, two and a half miles south-east of Tell el-Mutesellim (Megiddo), and about the same distance north of Ta'anach. Smith's objection (*HG.* p. 396 *n.*) that this Ḳedesh 'was too near the battle and too much under the hills of Manasseh for Sisera to flee there' is not very weighty; but a consideration which appears to be fatal to this theory is the strong improbability that Baraḳ could have ventured with impunity to muster a large force of poorly armed Israelites (*ch.* 5^{8b}) within so short a distance of Ta'anach and Megiddo, two of the most important of the Cana'anite fortified cities (*ch.* 1^{27}; cf. *ch.* 5^{19}), and could then have marched his army across the open plain to Tabor thirteen miles to the north-east; this too at a time when travel was beset with the utmost danger and difficulty even for the peaceful and inoffensive wayfarer (*ch.* 5^{6}). Conder (*Tent Work*, p. 69), mainly on the ground of a highly precarious identification of Baṣ'annim with the modern Beṣṣûm (cf. *note* on *ch.* 4^{11}), suggests that 'the Ḳedesh of the narrative where Baraḳ assembled his troops' is the modern Ḳadîš* 'on the shore of the sea of Galilee, only twelve miles from Tabor'; and this view is favourably regarded by Smith (*loc. cit.*). But, taking into consideration the proximity of Ḳedesh of Naphtali to Ḥaṣor, the conclusion which most commends itself is that Ḳedesh properly belongs to the history of the Jabin-campaign which took place in the farther north (cf. Josh. $11^{1\,ff.}$), and is therefore unconnected with our narrative. Indeed, the character of Baraḳ's force of mountaineers, and the fact that they 'deployed' upon mount Tabor (cf. *note* on *ch.* 4^{6}), make the supposition probable that this mountain (or possibly Daberath at its foot) was their first mustering place, and that they arrived at it in their tribal detachments, and (as mountaineers would naturally do) in open skirmishing order under cover of the night.

Supposing the view taken above to be the true explanation of the discrepancies between the prose and poetical narratives, the course of events appears to become reasonably clear. As Driver remarks, 'this view of the relation of Judg. 4 to Josh. 11 does not materially modify the picture which we form from Judg. 4 and 5 respecting Deborah and Baraḳ, and their victory over Sisera: it leaves the general representation untouched, and merely bids us disregard a few elements in *ch.* 4 which have properly no connexion with Sisera.' There is no essential difference between the two accounts. The scene of action is laid in and about the plain of Megiddo. The Cana'anites with their strong cities in and bordering on the plain (*ch.* 1^{27}) oppress the surrounding Israelite tribes. A deliverer is

* خربة قديش (*sic*); cf. *SWP. Name Lists*, p. 128.

found in the tribe which, owing to its situation, had been the greatest sufferer. Possibly Barak̦ had at one time been a captive in the hands of the Cana'anites (cf. *ch.* 5^{12b} *note*), and therefore his call to action and readiness to obey the summons are the more easily to be understood.

As to the source from which the prose-narrative was derived—the indications of phraseology, so far as they go, seem to point to E. Thus we may notice *v.*^{4} אשה נביאה, lit. 'a woman, a prophetess'; cf. איש נביא 'a man, a prophet' in *ch.* 6^{8}: *v.*^{9}, 'for *into the hand of* a woman *shall Yahweh sell* Ṡiṡera' (the phrase is generally characteristic of R^{E2}, but is found in 1 Sam. 12^{9} E^{2} with which R^{E2}'s connexion is very close: cf. *Introd.* xli ff.): ויהם י' 'and Yahweh discomfited'; cf. 1 Sam. 7^{10}, Ex. 14^{24}, Josh. 10^{10} (all E), Ex. 23^{27} (JE or E), Deut. 2^{15}. Cf. also the phrase, 'and all the people that were with him' with the same phrase in *ch.* $7^{1a\alpha}$ (apparently characteristic of the E narrator; cf. also $7^{2a.19}$, 8^{4}). It should further be noticed that 1 Sam. 12 (E^{2}) presupposes a narrative of the oppression of Ṡiṡera (*v.*^{9}), and also probably alludes to the deliverance effected by Barak̦ (if we follow 𝔊, $\mathfrak{S}^{P}$ in reading Barak̦ in *v.*^{11} in place of the unknown Bedan). In *v.*^{11} the allusion to Ḥobab (J's name) is doubtless a gloss derived from *ch.* 1^{16}.

The fragments of the Jabin-narrative *may* be derived from J (as noticed above); but it is at least as probable that the combination of reminiscences of this campaign with the account of the victory of Deborah and Barak̦ was effected when the story was still in the oral stage—in which case the narrative as a whole must be assigned to E.* We may notice that in 1 Sam. 12^{9} (E^{2}) Ṡiṡera is already described as 'captain of the host of Ḥaṣor'; but the assumption is open that these words may be a later gloss. Ps. 83^{9} combines Jabin with Ṡiṡera, but is probably not earlier than the post-exilic period.‡

The poetical narrative, which was probably at first preserved in written form in a collection of poems compiled in the northern kingdom, may be reasonably supposed to have been subsequently incorporated in E.

4. 1. R^{E2} And the children of Israel again did that which was evil in the sight of Yahweh, when Ehud was dead. 2. And

4, 1. *when Ehud was dead.* R^{E2}'s narrative connects immediately on to the end of the story of Ehud, 3^{30}. Cf. *note* on 3^{31}.

* An attempt at analysis has been made by Bruston, 'Les deux Jéhovistes,' *Revue de Théol. et Philos.* 1886, pp. 35 ff., but has not met with acceptance: cf. Bu. *RS.* 70, *n* 2.

‡ Similarly 'Oreb and Ze'eb are combined with Zebaḥ and Ṣalmunna in *v.*^{11}, as in the present form of the Gideon-narrative. The Psalm is plausibly regarded by Cheyne as referring to the events narrated in 1 Macc. 5: cf. *Origin of the Psalter*, pp. 97 f.

Yahweh sold them into the hand of Jabin the king of Cana'an, who ruled in Ḥaṣor; and the captain of his host was Śiśera, and he dwelt in Ḥarosheth of the nations. 3. And the children of

2. *Jabin the king of Cana'an, etc.* R^{E2} states his view that Jabin was not simply 'king of Ḥaṣor,' as might be inferred from *v.*[17] (cf. Josh. 11[1ff.]), but 'king of Cana'an,' *i.e.* overlord of the various city-kings of northern Cana'an, whose royal city was Ḥaṣor. This statement is intended to explain the perplexing relationship of Jabin to Śiśera: cf. *introd.* to the narrative, p. 81.

Ḥaṣor. This city is named in Josh. 19[36] among the cities assigned to Naphtali, and immediately precedes Ḳedesh in the list. The name is very possibly preserved in the modern name of the valley Merǵ ('meadow') el-Ḥaḏîreh, south-south-west of Ḳedesh on the northern side of the Wâdy 'Auba which runs into the lake of Ḥûleh, and in Ǵebel ('hill') Ḥaḏîreh immediately to the east of the 'meadow.' There are no traces of an ancient city upon this hill, and it is therefore supposed that Ḥaṣor may have been one of the ruined sites upon the hills still further east: cf. Buhl, *Geogr.* p. 236.

and the captain of his host, etc. The statement gives the narrator's view of the relationship of 'Śiśera' of the one narrative to 'Jabin' of the other.

Śiśera. The name has the appearance of being Ḥittite in origin. Cf., with the same termination, Sangara (noticed under *ch.* 3[31]), and Tarḫulara, the name of a king of Gurgum in northern Syria who was a contemporary of Tiglath-pileser IV.: Rost, *Tiglath-pileser*, p. 13, *al.*; *KB.* ii. p. 21.* The resemblance of the name to Bab. *seseru*, *sisseru*, 'child *or* youth,' is rather striking (Delitzsch, *Prolegomena*, p. 199, *Rem.* 3), but may be merely accidental. The name Śiśera occurs again in Ezr. 2[53] = Neh. 7[55] in a list of Něthînîm (foreign Temple-slaves) who returned to the land of Judah after the Exile.

Ḥarosheth of the nations. Probably el-Ḥâritiyyeh, a large double mound on the northern bank of the Ḳishon, commanding the narrow passage between Carmel to the south and the hills of Galilee to the north, which connects the plain of Esdraelon with the plain of Acre: cf. Thomson, *LB.* pp. 436 f.. Buhl's objection to this identification (*Geogr.* p. 214), on the ground that according to 4[13] the city cannot have been situated near the Ḳishon, hardly seems to carry weight; and the circumstances of Śiśera's rout as depicted in 5[21] are entirely in favour of such a site: cf. *note ad loc.* The name Ḥarosheth is probably connected with Heb. *ḥōreš* (1 Sam. 23[15.16.18.19], 2 Chr. 27[4]), Assyr.

* We cannot follow Mo. and Cooke in adding the Ḥittite names cited by Müller (*AE.* 332) from Egyptian sources which appear to end in *-sira*, Ḫ-tà-sì-ra, Maṷ-ra-sì-ra, etc., since we now know from the cuneiform tablets discovered at Boghaz Keui (cf. *MDOG.* Dec. 1907) that the name which appears in Egyptian as Ḫ-tà-sì-ra is really Ḫattušili, and Maṷ-ra-sì-ra Muršili.

Israel cried unto Yahweh: for he had nine hundred chariots of iron; and he oppressed the children of Israel with rigour twenty years.

4. And Deborah a prophetess, the wife of Lappidoth—she was

ḫuršu or *ḫursu*, 'wooded (?) mountain-ridge' (cf. Delitzsch, *Prolegomena*, p. 180)—an appropriate description of the wooded hills of Galilee below which el-Ḥâriṯiyyeh is situated.*

The city was doubtless called Ḥarosheth *of the nations*, as a Cana'anite city which formed, as it were, the gateway into the maritime plain which remained in the possession of the Phoenicians (*ch.* 1 31.32). Cf. the name 'district of the nations' noticed in *note* on *ch.* 1 33.

3. *chariots of iron.* Cf. ch. 1 19 *note.*
twenty years. Approximately half a generation.

4. *Deborah.* The name means 'bee.' Mo. compares the Greek name Μέλισσα, which was applied to the priestesses of Delphi, and to those of Demeter, Artemis, and Cybele: cf. references in Liddell and Scott *s.v.* On the possible connexion of Deborah with the city of Daberath, cf. *introd.* to section, p. 81.

the wife of Lappidoth. The fact that Lappidoth means 'torches,' or possibly 'lightning-flashes' (cf. Ex. 20 18), while Baraḳ is the ordinary term for 'lightning,' led Hilliger (*Das Deborah-lied*, Giessen, 1867) to make the precarious suggestion that Lappidoth and Baraḳ are one and the same man, and that in the original form of the tradition Baraḳ was the husband of Deborah. This view is favoured by Wellh. (*Comp.*3 p. 218), Bu. (*RS.* p. 69), Cooke.

she was judging. The verb *šāphaṭ* is here used (as commonly elsewhere in Heb.) in the sense in which we normally speak of 'judging,' *i.e.* (as explained in *v.* 5) of deciding cases between man and man. Since, however, R^{E2} regularly uses the verb in the sense 'vindicate,' or 'save' from a foreign oppressor (cf. *notes* on 2 16, 3 10), Mo. believes that this must have been the original sense in this passage; and since the participle שֹׁפְטָה (expressing continued action—'was judging') would be inappropriate in this sense, he proposes to vocalize as a perfect, שָׁפְטָה—'it was she that judged (*i.e.* saved) Israel at that time.' But if this sense had been intended, R^{E2}, who does not unnecessarily vary his phraseology, might naturally have

* The modern name Ḥâriṯiyyeh appears to mean 'ploughed *or* cultivated land,' the Heb. and Assyr. word noticed above being apparently unknown in Arabic. This fact, however, is no obstacle to the explanation of the Heb. name which is given in the *note*, or to the identification with el-Ḥâriṯiyyeh; since the substitution of a similarly sounding name for an old name of unknown meaning may very easily occur: cf. *note* on 'the rills of Megiddo,' *ch.* 5 19.

judging Israel at that time. 5. Gl. And she used to sit under the palm tree of Deborah between Ramah and Bethel in the hill-country of Ephraim, and the children of Israel came up unto

been expected to have written וַיָּקֶם י׳ שֹׁפְטָה, 'And Yahweh raised up a judge': cf. *ch.* 2[16], 3[9.15].

5. *she used to sit.* The verb *yāšabh* is used in the sense of presiding as judge. Cf. 1 Kgs. 21[8], 'who presided (lit. *sat*) with Naboth' (so *v.* [11]); Isa. 28[6], 'for him that presides (*sits*) over the judgment'; Ps. 9[7] (𝕳 *v.* [8]), 'Yahweh *sitteth* for ever' (cf. the parallel clause, 'He hath prepared his seat for the judgment'); Am. 6[3], 'the *seat* of violence' (*i.e.* of unjust judgment). R.V.'s rendering, '*she dwelt* under the palm-tree' is therefore inadequate and misleading. The tree was doubtless a sacred tree under which the oracle of Yahweh might be expected to be ascertained. Such a tree is seen in the *êlôn môré*, 'terebinth of the oracle(*tôrā*)-giver' near Shechem, Gen. 12[6]J, which is perhaps the same as the *êlôn mᵉ'ônᵉnîm*, 'terebinth of the soothsayers' mentioned in Judg. 9[37].

the palm-tree of Deborah. Deborah, Rebeḳah's nurse, is stated in Gen. 35[8]E to have been buried under an oak (Heb. *'allôn*) below Bethel; and hence the tree became known in later times as *'allôn bākhûth*, 'the oak of weeping' (cf. 2[5] *note*). This tree, as Ewald points out (*HI.* iii. p. 21, *n* [4]), appears to be alluded to again in 1 Sam. 10[3] as 'the terebinth (Heb. *'êlôn*) of Tabor'; since it can scarcely be doubted that 'Tabor' (תבור) is an error for 'Deborah' (דבורה). The context shows that the tree was on the way to Bethel and not far from Ramah; whereas Tabor lies more than fifty miles to the north. The difference between *'allôn* and *'êlôn* is one of vowel-points merely.

We have already noticed that the allusion in our passage to 'the palm-tree of Deborah between Ramah and Bethel' seems to be based upon a late confusion between the two Deborahs (cf. *introd.* to section). Whether the palm-tree (Heb. *tōmer*) of Deborah can be the same as the famous tree of the two other passages is somewhat more doubtful. Evidence seems to show that, throughout the O.T., the words *'allôn*, *'allā* are generally used to denote the oak (of various species), and *'êlôn*, *'êlā*, the terebinth (cf. *EB.* 4975); but it is not impossible that these terms may have been used at times to describe other kinds of tall and conspicuous trees. In favour of such a possibility it may be noticed (1.) that the Aram. *'îlānā* (the equivalent of Heb. *'êlôn*) denotes 'tree' in general; and (2.) that the name *'êlîm* (the plur. of *'êlā*), which occurs as a place-name in the narrative of the wilderness-wanderings (Ex. 15[27]), is apparently so-called because there were seventy *palm-trees* there. Cf. Wellh., *Prolegomena*, p. 234 *n.*

Ramah. The modern er-Râm, five miles due north of Jerusalem.

Bethel. Cf. *note* on *ch.* 1[23].

her for judgment. 6. E And she sent and called Baraḳ the son of Abinoʿam from Ḳedesh of Naphtali, and said unto him, 'Hath not Yahweh the God of Israel commanded, "Go, and open out upon mount Tabor, and take with thee ten thousand men of the

6. *Baraḳ.* Cf. *note* on Lappidoth, *v.*[4]. The Punic Barcas, the surname of Hamilcar, has been compared; and also the Sabaean ברקם and Palmyrene ברק. Cf. references in BDB. p. 140.

Ḳedesh of Naphtali. The modern Ḳadîs, four miles west-north-west of the lake of Ḥûleh, and about three miles north-east of Merǵ el-Ḥaḍîreh (cf. *note* on Ḥaṣor, *v.*[2]).

open out. The Hebrew verb *māšak* means to *draw out* or *extend*, and is used both intransitively and transitively. The passages in which the verb is intransitive are Job 21[33], R.V., 'and all men shall draw after him,' where the idea seems to be that of a long-extended or never-ending line (cf. Shakespeare, *Macbeth*, iv. 1, 'What! will the line stretch out till the crack of doom?'); and the present passage and *ch.* 20[37], where the expression is used in a military sense. In the latter passage the meaning can scarcely be mistaken, for here the verb is used of the manner in which the ambush advanced against the city of Gibeʿah in order to capture it. *Extension into column* would be out of place as a fighting formation; therefore *extension* or *opening out into line* must be what is intended; *i.e.* into loose skirmishing order such as would be best adapted for the attack of light-armed mountain troops. The modern military term is *deploy*, from the French *déployer*=Latin *displicare.* The verb *māšak* in this sense has been conjecturally restored in *ch.* 5[14a].

The same verb is used in its transitive sense in *v.*[7], 'And *I will draw out* unto thee, etc.' Here the sense may be 'cause to advance in a similar extended order,' or, more probably, 'draw forth' or 'attract.'

upon Mount Tabor. The rendering 'open out *upon*, etc.' preserves the ambiguity of the preposition ב in the Hebrew; the sense being either 'advance in open order (so as to come) upon mount Tabor' (prep. of rest after verb of motion), *i.e.* mount Tabor is the objective of the movement described by the verb: or 'when upon mount Tabor, open out'; *i.e.* mount Tabor is the point from which this strategic movement preparatory to advancing into the vale is to commence.

Mount Tabor is doubtless the modern Ǵebel eṭ-Ṭôr ('mountain') on the north-east side of the plain of Esdraelon. Its altitude is only 1843 feet, and it rises 1312 feet above the plain; but it forms a very conspicuous object owing to its isolation and its peculiar domed shape which is noted by Jerome (*OS.*, 156[33]); 'est autem mons in medio Galilaeae campo mira rotunditate.' As Smith remarks *HG.* p. 394), 'It is not necessary to suppose that Baraḳ arranged his

sons of Naphtali and of the sons of Zebulun? 7. And I will draw out unto thee unto the wâdy Ḳishon Ṡiśera, the captain of Jabin's host, with his chariots and his multitude, and I will give him unto thine hand."' 8. And Baraḳ said unto her, 'If thou

men high up Tabor; though Tabor, an immemorial fortress, was there to fall back upon in case of defeat. The headquarters of the muster were probably in the glen, at Tabor's foot, in the village Debûriyyeh.'

of the sons of Naphtali, etc. The poem, *ch.* 5, differs in describing a general muster of the tribes. Cf. *introd.* to the present narrative, p. 79.

7. *the wâdy Ḳishon.* The Hebrew term which is here represented by the Ar. *wâdy* is *náḥal.* Both the Arabic and Hebrew terms denote a winter-stream or torrent (𝔊 χειμάρρους), or the valley-bed of such a stream, which may vary from an insignificant depression to a precipitous ravine (such as is seen, *e.g.*, in the wâdy Ḳelt), which marks the action of water at a period when the rainfall of Palestine was much heavier than it is at present.

It is only the larger streams of this character (*e.g.* the Yarmuḳ, Jabboḳ, and Arnon) which constantly contain an abundant flow of water. Many of them fail in the summer-months, leaving the valley-bed dry, or nearly so; but in winter they may possess considerable volume, and are liable after storms or lengthy rains to swell suddenly to the dimensions of swift and dangerous torrents. Many wâdys, again (*e.g.* the Ḳidron), though of considerable depth, are now quite dry, or only occasionally contain a little water. A.V., R.V., render *náḥal* variously by 'brook,' 'stream,' 'river,' 'flood,' 'valley.' The Ar. term *wâdy* is here adopted as preserving the same ambiguity as is possessed by the Hebrew term. Cf. further, *Addenda*, p. xiii.

The character of the wâdy Ḳishon is described by Thomson (*LB.* p. 435). Its higher reaches are fed by the winter-streams which descend from the hill-country to the south of the great plain; but the most important source is the perennial spring of Ǵenîn (ʿEn-Gannim), which, however, is insufficient to provide a constant flow during summer and autumn. 'I have crossed,' says Thomson, 'the bed of the Kishon (even after it enters the plain of Acre) in the early part of April, when it was quite dry. The truth is, that the strictly permanent Kishon is one of the shortest rivers in the world. You will find the source in the vast fountains called Sa'adîyeh, not more than three miles east of Haifa. They flow out from the very roots of Carmel, almost on a level with the sea, and the water is brackish. They form a deep, broad stream at once, which creeps sluggishly through an impracticable marsh to the sea; and it is *this* stream which the traveller crosses on the shore. Of course, it is largely swollen during the great rains of winter by the longer river from the interior.'

wilt go with me, I will go; but if thou wilt not go with me, I will not go.' 9. And she said, 'I *will* go with thee: howbeit, glory shall not accrue to thee upon the course which thou art taking; for into the hand of a woman shall Yahweh sell Ṡiṡera.' So Deborah arose, and went with Baraḳ to Ḳedesh. 10. And Baraḳ summoned Zebulun and Naphtali to Ḳedesh; and there went up after him ten thousand men: and Deborah went up with

8. '*If thou wilt go, etc.*' 'The presence of the prophetess will not only ensure to him divine guidance (*v.*^{14}), but give confidence to him and his followers' (Mo.). 𝔊 makes Baraḳ add a reason for his demand: ὅτι οὐκ οἶδα τὴν ἡμέραν ἐν ᾗ εὐοδοῖ τὸν ἄγγελον Κύριος μετ' ἐμοῦ.

The fact that this sentence is clearly an incorrect* translation of כִּי לֹא יָדַעְתִּי אֶת־יוֹם הַצְלִיחַ מַלְאַךְ יְהוָה אִתִּי 'for I know not the day whereon the Angel of Yahweh shall prosper me,' proves that the translator must have had a Hebrew original before him; but Bu., Mo. (*SBOT.*), No. are probably right in regarding this as an early gloss, intended to obviate an unfavourable interpretation of Baraḳ's demand. 𝔗's paraphrase of *v.*$^{14a\beta}$ is very similar: הלא מלאכא דיהוה נפק לאצלחא קדמך 'Hath not the angel of Yahweh gone forth to make [thy way] prosperous before thee?' The phrase, 'the Angel of Yahweh' (a J phrase) is somewhat unexpected, if the narrative is rightly assigned to E; and seems, moreover, to presuppose 5^{23a}, where metrical reasons compel us to regard it as due to textual alteration. The passage is accepted by Houbigant, Grätz, Stu., Frankenberg, La.

9. *howbeit, glory, etc.* In spite of Mo.'s contention that the context betrays no sign of disapproval, it is difficult to escape the common impression that the unpalatable information is produced by the prophetess at this juncture in consequence of Baraḳ's want of alacrity in accepting the divine mandate. As La. paraphrases, 'You wish for a woman's help, and it is a woman (though a different one) who shall have the honour.'

to Ḳedesh. Upon the view that the Ḳedesh here referred to is not Ḳedesh of Naphtali, but another Ḳedesh nearer to the scene of the battle, cf. *introd.* to chapter, p. 82.

10. *after him.* Lit. 'at his feet,' *i.e.*, as we might say, 'at his heel.' So 5^{15}, 8^{5}, *al.*

* The translator reads מַלְאָךְ (*St. Absol.*) and treats it as object of the verb, making יהוה the subject; while regarding אתי (accus. 'me') as the prep. 'with me.'

him. 11. Now Ḥeber the Ḳenite had separated himself from Ḳain, Gl. from the sons of Ḥobab, Moses' father-in-law, E and had pitched his tent as far away as the terebinth of ⌈Baṣʿannim⌉ which is near Ḳedesh. 12. And they told Śîsera that Baraḳ the son of Abinoʿam had gone up to Mount Tabor. 13. And Śîsera summoned all his chariots, even nine hundred chariots of iron, and all the people who were with him, from Ḥarosheth of the nations unto the wâdy Ḳishon. 14. And Deborah said unto Baraḳ, 'Arise; for this is the day whereon Yahweh hath given Śîsera into thine hand: hath not Yahweh gone forth before

11. *had separated himself from Ḳain.* The statement explains how a member of a clan which normally inhabited the Negeb (cf. 1 [16]) came to be found in northern Canaʿan.

Ḥobab, Moses' father-in-law. R.V. *text* 'brother-in-law,' quite unwarrantably: cf. *note* on 1 [16].

the terebinth of Baṣʿannim. Vocalizing 𝔥 אֵלוֹן בַּצְעַנִּים, in place of 𝔐 א' בְּצַעֲנַנִּים (cf. Josh. 19 [33]), R.V. 'the oak (*marg.* terebinth) in Zaʿanannim,' where ב is regarded as the preposition. If this had been intended, however, we should have expected הָאֵלוֹן (with the article) 'the (well-known) terebinth';* not simply אֵלוֹן, which can only mean '*a* terebinth.' The locality (otherwise unknown) is described in Josh. 19 [33] as on the border of Naphtali; a fact which suggests, as Mo. remarks, that Ḥeber the Ḳenite belonged originally to the story of Jabin.

Conder (*SWP. Mem.* i. pp. 365 f.; *Tent Work*, p. 69) identifies Baṣʿannim with the modern Beṣṣûm, four miles west of the Ḳadîš which is south-west of the sea of Galilee. There is not, however, any philological connexion between the names; and the proposed identification depends partly upon the view with regard to Ḳedesh which we have noticed in the *introd.* to the chapter (viz. that it is not Ḳedesh in Naphtali, but another Ḳedesh nearer to the scene of the battle), and partly upon the fact that A.V. renders *'êlôn* 'terebinth' erroneously as 'plain,' and there is a plain (Ar. *sahel*) called el-Aḥmâ close to the south of Beṣṣûm.‡

14. *hath not Yahweh gone forth before thee?* The scene gains

* Mo. compares הָאֵשֶׁל בָּרָמָה 'the tamarisk in Ramah,' 1 Sam. 22 [6], 31 [13], הָאֵלָה אֲשֶׁר בְּעָפְרָה 'the terebinth which is in ʿOphrah,' *ch.* 6 [11], etc.

‡ Driver (*Expositor*, Jan. 1912, p. 32, *n* [2]) exposes the manner in which the extraordinary error which identifies 'the plain (!) of Ẓaanaim' with the plain called Sahel el-Aḥmâ has penetrated into several modern maps.

thee?' So Baraḳ went down from mount Tabor, and ten thousand men after him. 15. And Yahweh discomfited Ṡiṡera, and all his chariots, and all his army, at the edge of the sword before Baraḳ; and Ṡiṡera alighted from his chariot, and fled away on foot. 16. And Baraḳ pursued after the chariots and after the army as far as Ḥarosheth of the nations: and all Ṡiṡera's

much in vividness if we may suppose (with Thomson, *LB.* p. 436) that Deborah, as she speaks, points to the gathering storm, which appears to have burst in the face of the foe at the commencement of the battle: cf. *ch.* 5[4.5.20.21] (*notes*); Jos. *Ant.* V. v. 4. Yahweh's connexion with the phenomena of the storm, especially when He goes forth to battle before His people, is well marked in the O.T.: cf. Josh. 10[11], 1 Sam. 7[10], Ps. 18[9 ff.], etc., and the present editor's discussion in *JTS.* ix. p. 326.

15. *at the edge of the sword.* The phrase לפי חרב (on which cf. *note* on 1[8]) may possibly here be a corrupt dittography of the following לפני ברק, 'before Baraḳ'; but Mo. goes too far when he states that it 'appears incongruous with the verb' (ויהם, 'discomfited').*

16. *And Baraḳ pursued, etc.* The circumstances of the rout appear to have been as described by Thomson (*LB.* p. 436):—'The army of Sisera naturally sought to regain the strongly fortified Harosheth of the Gentiles, from which they had marched up to their camping-ground a short time before. This place is at the lower end of the narrow vale through which the Kishon passes out of Esdraelon into the plain of Acre, and this was their only practicable line of retreat. The victorious enemy was behind them; on their left were the hills of Samaria, in the hand of their enemies; on their right was the swollen river and the marshes of Thora; they had no alternative but to make for the narrow pass which led to Harosheth. The space, however, becomes more and more narrow, until within the *pass* it is only a few rods wide. There, horses, chariots, and men become mixed in horrible confusion, jostling and treading down one another; and the river, here swifter and deeper than above, runs zigzag from side to side of the vale, until, just before it reaches the castle of Harosheth, it dashes sheer up against the perpendicular base of

* In the other occurrences of the phrase, it is used with the following verbs:— הִכָּה 'smite,' Num. 21[24]; Deut. 13[16a], 20[13]; Josh. 8[24b], 10[28.30.32.35.37.39], 11[11.12.14], 19[47]; Judg. 1[8.25], 18[27], 20[37.48], 21[10]; 1 Sam. 22[19]; 2 Sam. 15[14]; 2 Kings. 10[25]; Jer. 21[7]; Job 1[15.17]; הָרַג 'slay,' Gen. 34[26]; חָלַשׁ (? הֶחֱלִישׁ) 'render prostrate,' Ex. 17[13]; הֶחֱרִים 'ban' or 'utterly destroy,' Deut. 13[16b]; Josh. 6[21]; 1 Sam. 15[8]; נָפַל 'fall,' Josh. 8[24a], Judg. 4[16]†. It therefore appears not inappropriate after המם 'discomfit.'

army fell at the edge of the sword; there was not left so much as one. 17. But Ṡiṡera fled away on foot unto the tent of Ja‘el, the wife of Ḥeber the Ḳenite: for there was peace between Jabin king of Ḥaṣor and the house of Ḥeber the Ḳenite. 18. And Ja‘el came out to meet Ṡiṡera, and said unto him, ‘Turn in, my lord, turn in unto me; fear not.’ So he turned in unto her into

Carmel. There is no longer any possibility of avoiding it. Rank upon rank of the flying host plunge madly in, those behind crushing those before deeper and deeper into the tenacious mud. They stick fast, are overwhelmed, are swept away by thousands. Such are the conditions of this battle and battle-field that we can follow it out to the dire catastrophe.’ Doubtless the storm (cf. *note* on *v.*[14]) was responsible for the sudden swelling of the Ḳishon, and the reduction of the plain surrounding it to a quagmire, in a manner which has frequently been observed by travellers. Cf. also Smith *HG*. p. 395; Ewing in *DB*. iii. p. 5*a*.

17. *unto the tent of Ja‘el.* Ṡiṡera's refuge cannot have been greatly remote from the scene of the battle; especially since *v.*[22] represents Baraḳ as not far behind in pursuit, though having previously accomplished the rout of the Cana‘anite army before Ḥarosheth. Cf. the discussion in *introd.* to the chapter, pp. 80 f.

18. *Turn in.* Or, perhaps, more correctly, ‘Turn aside.’ Ja‘el persuades Ṡiṡera to desist in his flight, and take shelter in the tent, without his previously having asked admission.

a fly-net. The Heb. word, *s^e^mîkhā*, is a ἅπαξ λεγόμενον, and the meaning adopted is based upon philological considerations, and accords with the context.* A net to keep off the flies would be more essential for the rest and comfort of a hot and weary man than anything of the nature of a rug or coverlet. 𝔊[B] ἐπιβολαίῳ, 𝔊[AL] ἐν τῇ δέρρει αὐτῆς ‘with her leathern covering’ (a rendering commonly used elsewhere to translate יריעה ‘tent-curtain’; so 𝔖[h] ܒܡܫܟܬܐ ܕܝܠܗ), 𝔏 ‘in pelle sua,’ 𝔙 ‘pallio,’ 𝔖[p] ܒܡܟܣܝܬܐ ‘with the coverlet,’ 𝔗 בגונכא, *id.*, Ar. بالقطيفة *id.*; A.V. ‘mantle,’ *marg.* ‘rug *or* blanket,’ R.V. ‘rug.’ All these appear to be guesses guided by the context. Grä.'s emendation בַּמִּכְסֶה, ‘with a coverlet,’ is unnecessary.

* An original biliteral סך, שׂך ‘interweave,’ ‘intertwine,’ appears both as the ע״ו form סוך, שׂוך, and as the ע doubled סכך, שׂכך. There can be no doubt that the √שׂבך, whence שְׂבָכָה ‘net-work’ (as interwoven) represents the same root internally triliteralized by the labial ב which is akin to ו; cf. שׁוּל and שֹׁבֶל, both meaning ‘skirts,’ from an original biliteral של. שְׂמִיכָה, from √שׂמך, may exhibit the same root שׂך internally triliteralized by מ, which is also close akin to ו: cf., for the same internal triliteralization, Bab. *namâru* by the side of Heb. נור, both meaning ‘shine.’

the tent, and she covered him with a fly-net. 19. And he said unto her, 'Give me, I pray thee, a little water, for I am thirsty': and she opened her bottle of milk, and gave him to drink, and covered him. 20. And he said unto her, 'Stan⌜d⌝ at the door of the tent, and it shall be, if any man come and ask thee, and say, "Is there any man here?" that thou shalt say, "No."' 21. Then Ja'el the wife of Ḥeber took a tent-peg, and took a hammer in her hand, and approached him softly, and struck the peg into his temple, and it went down into the ground; for he was fast asleep ⌜and exhausted⌝: so he died. 22. And, behold,

19. *a bottle of milk.* The beverage is described in 5 [25], in one clause as milk, in the other as *ḥem'ā* 'curds,' *i.e.* the *leben* which is the choicest drink of the modern Bedawin, and is said to be most delicious and refreshing, but to possess a strongly soporific effect: cf. Conder, *Tent Work*, pp. 69 f.

20. *Stand.* Reading fem. עִמְדִי in place of masc. עֲמֹד. Ehr.'s proposal to point as Infin. Absol. עָמֹד, used, as occasionally elsewhere, in place of the Imperative, is possible: cf. Davidson, § 88 *b*; G-K. § 113 *bb*.

21. *Then Ja'el, etc.* On this account of the death of Ṡiṡera, as compared with that which is given in the poem, 5 [26.27], cf. the discussion in *introd.* to chapter, pp. 79 f.

a tent-peg. The peg would be made of wood, and the hammer would be a heavy mallet, also of wood, as at the present day. 'Among the Bedawin, pitching the tent is woman's business, and so no doubt it was in ancient times; the mallet and pin were accustomed implements, and ready to hand' (Mo.).

for he was fast asleep. In place of this 𝔊[AL] renders *καὶ αὐτὸς ἀπεσκάρισεν* ('made a convulsive movement') *ἀνὰ μέσον τῶν γονάτων* (𝔊[L] *ποδῶν*) *αὐτῆς*. This seems to represent a paraphrastic attempt at interpretation of the somewhat uncommon נרדם (𝔊[B] *ἐξεστώς*) in the light of *ch.* 5 [27].

and exhausted. Vocalizing וַיָּעֵף with Mo., Bu., No., in place of 𝔐 וַיָּעַף or וַיָּעָף, which, in spite of the prevalent accentuation*

* According to Kit., *BH.*, 4 MSS. place the pause upon נרדם and connect ויעף with וימת. A.V. renders the sentence 'for he was fast asleep and weary. So he died,' and similarly R.V. *marg.* (with the variation 'in a deep sleep'): but it must be emphasized that, *as* וַיָּעַף *is pointed in* 𝔐, it cannot denote a state existing coincidently with that which is described by the participle נִרְדָּם 'fast asleep'; but only some further resultant state, the ו *consec.* having the force '*and so.*'

as Barak̦ was pursuing Ṡiṡera, Ja'el came out to meet him, and said to him, 'Come, and I will show thee the man whom thou art seeking.' And he came in unto her; and, behold, Ṡiṡera was fallen down dead, and the peg was in his temple. 23. R^{E2} So God subdued on that day Jabin the king of Cana'an before the children of Israel. 24. And the hand of the children of Israel bore more and more severely upon Jabin the king of Cana'an, until they had destroyed Jabin the king of Cana'an.

(connecting with the preceding והוא נרדם rather than with the following וימת), can only be understood (as by R.V. *text*) in connexion with what follows: '*so he swooned* and died.' But to speak of a man whose head had been practically shattered by the tent-peg as swooning before death ensued, appears almost ludicrous.

23. *So God subdued, etc.* The concluding formula of R^{D2}. In this passage only we get the active verb with subject God (*'ĕlōhîm* a mark of the E school; but variants exist in 𝔊: cf. Kit., *BH.*) in place of the passive, 'was (were) subdued,' *ch.* 3^{30}, 8^{28}, 11^{33}.

24. *until they had destroyed, etc.* It can scarcely be doubted that R^{E2} (like R^{D} in Josh.) tends to exaggerate the far-reaching effects of the victory. So far as the old narrative is concerned, it does not even mention the capture of the city of Ḥarosheth.

5. 1-31. *Deborah and Barak̦: the triumph-song.*

Besides the Commentaries, etc., quoted throughout the book, and the authorities cited at the head of the *introd.* to 4^{1}-5^{31}, cf.* C. F. Schnurrer, *Dissertatio inauguralis philologica in Canticum Deborae*, 1775; republished in *Dissertationes philologico-criticae*, 1790, pp. 36-96 (his discussions are marked by learning and good sense): J. B. Köhler in Eichhorn's *Repertorium für Biblische und Morgenländische Litteratur*, vi. 1780, pp. 163-172 (a criticism of Schnurrer. Translation and very brief notes): J. G. von Herder, *Briefe das Studium der Theologie betreffend* (1780), 4e Ausg. 1816, i. pp. 65-75 (a literary appreciation); *Vom Geist der ebräischen Poesie* (1783), 3e Ausg. von K. W. Justi, 1825, pp. 237-243 (translation with scanty notes): G. H. Hollmann, *Commentarius*

---

* The compilation of a list of nineteenth-century authorities upon the Song necessarily goes back to Schnurrer at the end of the eighteenth century; since this scholar's work is very outstanding, and has had considerable influence upon his successors. For earlier writers, cf. Justi, as noticed above, and Bachmann, pp. 298 f. Reuss, in his *Geschichte der heil. Schrift. A. T.*, names a considerable number of additional nineteenth-century writers on the Song; but the present editor has not been able to find their works, either in the Bodleian Library, or in Dr. Pusey's library, which Dr. Darwell Stone, Principal of Pusey House, has kindly made accessible to him. The fact, however, that these writers are either not cited at all, or only very occasionally cited, by subsequent scholars, may perhaps justify the assumption that their contributions to the study of the Song are of no special importance.

philologico-criticus in Carmen Deborae, 1818 (very scholarly and thorough): K. W. Justi, *National-Gesänge der Hebräer*, ii., 1820, pp. 210-312 (he gives, pp. 117-225, a full list of earlier writers on the subject from the commencement of the eighteenth century; and his commentary offers a serviceable conspectus of their opinions): H. Ewald, *Die Dichter des Alten Bundes* (1839), neue Ausarb. 1866, pp. 178-190 (his translation often happily reproduces the original rhythm. Very brief notes): G. Boettger, *Commentarius exegetico-criticus in Deborae canticum*, in Käuffer's *Biblische Studien*, i. pp. 116-128, ii. pp. 81-100, iii. pp. 122-148 (down to *v.* 23), 1842-4 (he adds little or nothing to the work of earlier scholars); J. von Gumpach, *Alttestamentliche Studien*, 1852, pp. 1-138 (lengthy, but not very discriminating): J. G. Donaldson, *Jashar*, 1854, pp. 237-240, 261-289 (comments of no special value): E. Meier, *Uebersetzung und Erklärung des Debora-Liedes*, 1859 (his comments are often suggestive): G. Hilliger, *Das Deborah-Lied übersetzt und erklärt*, 1867 (he makes no special contribution of his own): A. Müller, *Das Lied der Deborah; eine philologische Studie*, in *Königsberger Studien*, 1887, pp. 1-21 (a protest against the attempt to extract a rendering from a corrupt text at all costs—having mainly in view the second edition of Bertheau's commentary on Judges, which appeared in 1883); M. Vernes, *Le cantique de Débora*, in *RÉJ.* xxiv. 1892, pp. 52-67, 225-255 (he regards the Song as a very late production—not earlier than the fourth or third century B.C.—based upon the prose-narrative in *ch.* 4): C. Niebuhr, *Versuch einer Reconstellation des Deboraliedes*, 1894 (highly fanciful*): H. Winckler, *AF.* i. (1893-97), pp. 192 f., 291 f.; *GI.* ii., 1900, pp. 127-135 (many original, but not very convincing, emendations); P. Ruben, *JQR.* x. (1898), pp. 541-558 (emendations based on very rash philologizing): K. L. Stephan, *Das Debora-Lied*, 1900 (his original suggestions are not happy): A. Segond, *Le cantique de Débora*, 1900 (painstaking, but fails at crucial points): V. Zapletal, *Das Deboralied*, 1905 (he deals somewhat arbitrarily with the text in order to produce a uniform scheme of three-beat stichoi; and his Hebrew forms and constructions are often very curious): Ed. Meyer, *IN.* pp. 487-498.

On the metrical form of the poem, cf. J. Ley, *Die metrischen Formen der hebräischen Poesie systematisch dargelegt*, 1866, pp. 160-171; *Grundzüge des Rhythmus, des Vers- und Strophenbaues in der hebräischen Poesie*, 1875, pp. 214-219: G. Bickell, *Carmina Veteris Testamenti metrice*, 1882, pp. 195-197; *Dichtungen der Hebräer*, i., 1882, pp. 27-31: C. J. Ball, *The formal element in the Hebrew Lyric*, 1887: H. Grimme, *Abriss der biblisch-hebräischen Metrik*, in *ZDMG.* 1896, pp. 572-578: J. Marquart, *Fundamente israelitischer und jüdischer Geschichte*, 1896, pp. 1-10: D. H. Müller, *Der Aufbau des Debora-Liedes*, in *Actes du XIe Congrès Internat. d'Orientalistes*, 1897 (1898), iv. pp. 261-272: E. Sievers, *Studien zur hebräischen Metrik* (part i. of the writer's *Metrische Studien*, 1901), pp. 418 ff.: J. W. Rothstein, *Zur Kritik des Deboraliedes und die ursprüngliche rhythmische Form desselben*, in *ZDMG.*, 1902, pp. 175-208;

---

* The poem, in its original form, is thrown back by Niebuhr into the fourteenth century B.C. Šišera becomes a king of Egypt—Sesu-ra, the (supposed) last representative of the Eighteenth Dynasty; who revived Aḫnaton's cult of the Solar-disk, which had been abandoned for the old religion of Egypt under Sesu-Ra's predecessors, Amen-tut-anḫ and Ay; and whose accession was signalized by a combined attempt of the kings of Cana'an to throw off the Egyptian yoke ('⟨Sisera, king of Egypt⟩, chose new gods; then was there war at the gates ⟨of Egypt⟩'). Sesu-Ra is supposed to have quelled the Cana'anite opposition; but subsequently to have suffered defeat at the hands of the Hebrew tribes under Baraḳ. It goes without saying that the text of the poem has to undergo somewhat violent treatment before this view of affairs can be extracted from it.

437-485; 697-728; 1903, pp. 81-106; 344-370; N. Schlögl, *Le chapitre V du livre des Juges*, in *RB.*, 1903, pp. 387-394 (a common-sense criticism of Rothstein): E. G. King, *Early Religious Poetry of the Hebrews*, 1911, pp. 8-14: G. A. Smith, *The early Poetry of Israel* (*Schweich Lectures*, 1910), 1912, pp. 80-90.

The historical circumstances presupposed by the Song, as compared with the prose-narrative of *ch.* 4, have already been discussed in the general *introd.* to 4^{1}-5^{31}. It remains to say something about the metrical form of the poem. As a preliminary, we may notice that, while *v.*[1] and *v.*[31 b] are obviously the work of editors, the former being due, in all probability, to R^{JE}, and the latter to R^{E2}, *v.*[2] also, which is usually regarded as the opening couplet of the poem, is more probably an ancient introduction, extracted, together with the poem itself, from the old song-book in which it was contained (cf. *note ad loc.*). The poem thus possesses two introductions of a different date in *v.*[1] and *v.*[2], and its true commencement is found in *v.*[3].

The fact may now be regarded as well established that Hebrew poetry, besides such long-recognized characteristics as parallelism in thought, etc., possesses a definitely marked metrical or (perhaps more accurately) rhythmical system. Attempts which have been made to discover a strict form of scansion by feet may be said to have resulted in failure: investigation has rather proved that ancient Hebrew possessed no regularly quantitative system of metre, but rather a system in which so many *ictûs* or rhythmical beats occur in each stichos, while the number of intervening unstressed syllables is governed merely by the possibilities of pronunciation.*

The existence of such a system in the poetry of an ancient Semitic

* This system is exactly illustrated in English by Coleridge's *Christabel*, on the rhythm of which the poet writes:—'I have only to add that the metre of Christabel is not, properly speaking, irregular, though it may seem so from its being founded on a new principle: namely, that of counting in each line the accents, and not the syllables. Though the latter may vary from seven to twelve, yet in each line the accents will be found to be only four. Nevertheless, this occasional variation in number of syllables is not introduced wantonly, or for the mere ends of convenience, but in correspondence with some transition, in the nature of the imagery or passion.' In illustration of this system, as worked out in the poem, we may quote

'They crossed the moat, and Christabel
Took the key that fitted well;
A little door she opened straight,
All in the middle of the gate;
The gate that was ironed within and without,
Where an army in battle array had passed out.
The lady sank, belike through pain,
And Christabel with might and main
Lifted her up, a weary weight,
Over the threshold of the gate:
Then the lady rose again,
And moved, as she were not in pain.'

language is well illustrated by the Babylonian epic poems, where the regular rhythmical form appears to consist in four beats to the line.* Thus, *e.g.*, we may cite (*Gilgameš-epic*, xi. 9. 10):

luptéka Gílgameš amát niṣírti
u pirísta ša ilấni kấša lukbíka

'I will unfóld to thee, Gílgameš, a wórd of sécrecy,
And a decísion of the góds will I téll thee—e'en thée.'

Or, with a fewer number of syllables to the line (*id.* xi. 21. 22):

kíkkiš kíkkiš ígar ígar
kíkkišu šimḗma ígaru ḫissás

'Reéd-hut, reéd-hut! wáll, wáll!
Reéd-hut, lísten! wáll, atténd!'

This four-beat measure is well recognizable in Hebrew, and is prominent in the Song of Deborah, about three-eighths of the poem being so composed. The rhythm, as it appears in the original, may be illustrated from *v.*[5]:

hārī́m nāzᵉlū́ mippᵉnḗ Yahwéh
mippᵉnḗ Yahwéh ᵉlōhḗ Yisrā́'ēl

The measure appears to be especially characteristic of such examples of Hebrew poetry as may be supposed (upon other grounds) to be among the most ancient; and the influence of the Babylonian pattern may here be conjectured to have been operative, or even a more remote tradition common to both peoples. As illustrations from other early poems we may cite Ex. 15[1b]: ‡

'āšī́rā lᵉ Yahwéh kī gā́'ō gā́'ā
sū́s wᵉrōkhᵉbhṓ rāmā́ bhayyā́m

'I will síng to Yahwéh, for he hath tríumphed, hath tríumphed;
The hórse and his ríder hath he whélmed in the séa';

* Cf. Zimmern, *Ein vorläufiges Wort über babylonische Metrik*, in *ZA.* 1893, pp. 121-124; *Weiteres zur babylonischen Metrik*, in *ZA.* 1895, pp. 1-20. In the latter article, the author publishes a neo-Babylonian text in which the stichoi are divided by three vertical lines into four parts. This division can, in his opinion, serve no other purpose than to indicate the four verse-members (feet); and thus we have an actual proof that the Babylonians consciously reckoned lines of four beats in one species of their poetry.

‡ The major part of this poem is so composed. Sievers (*op. cit.* pp. 408 f.) contrives to fit nearly the whole of it to this measure.

and 2 Sam. 1[22] from David's lament over Saul and Jonathan, which is mainly composed in this measure:

middám ḥ^alālī́m meḥḗlebh gibbōrī́m
ḳéšeth Y^ehônāthā́n lō nāsṓgh 'āḥṓr
w^eḥérebh Šā'ū́l lō thāšū́bh rêḳā́m

'From the bloód of the slaín, from the fát of the stróng
The bów of Jónathan túrned not báck,
And the swórd of Saúl retúrned not voíd.'

Together with the four-beat measure we also find, in the Song of Deborah, a three-beat measure into which about five-eighths of the poem is cast. We may instance *v.*[4]:

Yahwéh b^eṣêth^ekā́ missḗ'ī́r
b^eṣá'dh^ekhá miss^edhḗ 'Edhṓm

This is the most frequent form of Hebrew measure, the Book of Job and a great number of the Psalms being written in it. Couplets of this form may account for the term 'hexameter' as used by Josephus.*

The three-beat measure appears, like the four-beat measure, to be of considerable antiquity. We find it, for instance (combined with an opening line of four beats), in the ancient 'Song of the Sword' which is ascribed to Lamech in Gen. 4[22ff.], and evidently celebrates the invention or acquisition of weapons of bronze and iron by a people in the nomadic stage:

* Jos. applies the term (*Ant.* IV. viii. 44) to the 'Song' (Deut. 32) and 'Blessing' (Deut. 33) of Moses, in both of which the three-beat measure is well marked. He also states (*Ant.* II. xvi. 4) that Ex. 15 is composed 'in hexameter verse,' a statement which is true only of a very minor portion of the poem (cf. *vv.*[2.8bc.16cd]), the greater part being composed, as we have already noticed, in the four-beat measure. David is said (*Ant.* VII. xii. 3) to have composed 'songs and hymns to God of several sorts of metre: some of those which he made were trimeters, and some were pentameters.' Here the trimeter of course is the three-beat measure considered as a stichos and not as a couplet (hexameter); while the pentameter is the so-called *Ḳînā* (elegiac) measure which is well exemplified, *e.g.* by Ps. 42-43; cf. *v.*[2]:

'Thírsteth my sóul for Gód,
For the Gód of my lífe,
Whén shall I cóme and behóld
The fáce of Gód.'

The former measure is reckoned either as trimeter or hexameter because each three-beat stichos is complete in itself, and the two lines of the couplet are usually parallel in sense; whereas in the pentameter (3+2) the second line completes the sense of the first.

'Adhā́ w^e Ṣillā́ š^e má'an ḳôlī́
n^e šê Lémekh ha'^a zḗnnā 'imrāthī́
kī 'î́š hārághtī l^e phiṣ'ī́
w^e yéledh l^e ḥábbūrāthī́
kī šibh'āthάyim yúḳḳam Ḳáyin
w^e Lémekh šibh'î́m w^e šibh'ā́

''Áda and Ṣílla, heár my voíce;
Wives of Lámech, give eár to my wórd:
For a mán have I sláin for my wóund,
And a bóy for the sáke of my bruíse:
If séven times Cáin be avénged,
Then Lámech full séventy and séven.'

Occasionally we find couplets in the Song of Deborah composed of a four-beat line followed by a three-beat line (4 + 3); cf. *vv.* 4b.15b-18.26b.27a. Instances of the reverse order (3 + 4) occur in *vv.* 6a.9. Combination of these two forms of measure is found similarly in Ex. 15. Other metrical forms employed in Hebrew poetry do not come under consideration in the present connexion.

The fact that Hebrew vocalization, as known to us from 𝔐, represents a somewhat artificial system of pronunciation which is due to the method of cantillation practised in the Synagogue from early times, does not invalidate the conclusions above illustrated as to the metrical form of Hebrew poetry; since there is no reason to suppose that the number and position of the accentual beats were essentially altered to suit the pronunciation of 𝔐. We are not altogether without evidence as to the pronunciation of Hebrew as a spoken language, but can draw well-founded inferences, partly from comparative philology, and partly from evidence derived from the transliterations of Amorite and Hebrew words which are found in Babylonian and Assyrian inscriptions (Amorite proper names on Babylonian First Dynasty Tablets; 'Canaanite glosses' on the T.A. Tablets; Biblical names in Assyrian Annals), and of proper names and place-names in 𝔊. Such evidence indicates that the main difference between the original and the traditional pronunciations consisted in the occurrence of short vowels in positions in which we now find either tone-long vowels or else vocal *sh^e wa*. Such a couplet as that quoted above from the Song of Deborah, *v.* 5, was probably pronounced in some such form as

harrî́m nazalû́ mippanáy Yahwáh
mippanáy Yahwáh 'elāháy Yisra'él

This, however, does not, for our purposes, vary essentially from the pronunciation of 𝔐. Cf. further, *Additional note*, p. 158.

The theory of Hebrew rhythm here exemplified is substantially that which has been expounded in detail by Sievers (*op. cit.*), and which is now very generally adapted by scholars.* Sievers gives (pp. 418 ff.) his view of the rhythmical form of the Song of Deborah, which agrees throughout with that which has been arrived at by the present writer (prior to consultation of Sievers' version), except in a few minor particulars which depend upon individual views as to the original form of certain passages. The translation which follows aims at reproducing the rhythm of the original, in so far as this can be done consistently with a strictly accurate translation. Here and there a faithful reproduction of the rhythm (which might have been

* Ball's rendering of the Song (published nearly thirty years ago) proceeds upon the assumption of a more strictly metrical method, his lines falling into regular iambic feet, with an occasional anapaest or trochee. Such a theory must now give way in favour of that which is adopted above; yet the writer's method deserves notice, if only as a tribute to his exceptional command of English style in his reproduction of what he conceives to be the metrical form of the original. We may cite, by way of illustration, *vv.* 25 ff., the account of Ṡiŝera's murder:—

Maim shá'al, ḫálab náthaná;
Basífl 'addírim híqribá ḫem'áh:
Yadáh [samól] layyáthed tíshleḫénn
Wimínah lálmuth 'ámilím;
Wahálăma Sís'ra máḫaqá roshó,
Umáḫaçá waḫálăfa ráqqathó.

Bein ráglaihá kará', nafál, shakáb;
Bein ráglaihá kará', nafál:
Bāshér kará', shám⌜mah⌝ nafál shadúd.

'He asked but water, milk she gave;
In lordly platter she presented curds.
Her left hand to the tent-pin soft she lays,
And to the workmen's maul her right;
Then smote she Sisera and brake his head;
She struck, and pierced withal his temples through.

'Betwixt her feet he bowed, he fell, he lay;
Betwixt her feet he bowed, he fell;
E'en where he bowed, he fell, slain violently.'

A similar system of syllable-reckoning is found in the Syriac metres, the invention of which is ascribed by tradition to Bardesanes (born 154 A.D.).

Bickell counts syllables in the same way as Ball; but his feet (in contrast) are trochaic, and he takes great liberties with the Hebrew forms in order to fit them into his system. Thus *vv.* 24 ff. run, according to this system, as follows:—

Téborákh minnášim Já'el,
Mínnaším b'ohl t'bórakh!
Májm saál, chaláb natána;
B'séfl -ddir híqr'ba chém'a.
Jádah, l'játed tíšlachänna;
Vímináh lehálmutí 'amélim.

obtained through a paraphrase) has to give way in favour of a faithful rendering into English.

That the poem was intended to exhibit a kind of strophic arrangement is very probable. On examination of its contents, it appears to fall into the following divisions :—

(1) *vv.*$^{3-5}$. Introduction—Praise of Yahweh, who is pictured as setting forth from His earthly seat to the help of His people (9 stichoi).

(2) *vv.*$^{6-8}$. Israel's oppression by the Canaanites prior to the rising of the tribes (11 stichoi).

(3) *vv.*$^{12.9-11}$. Summons to a retrospect of Yahweh's 'righteous acts' in giving victory to His people (11 stichoi).

(4) *vv.*$^{13-15a}$. Muster of the clans—The patriotic tribes (9 stichoi).

(5) *vv.*$^{15b-18}$. Reproach of the recreant tribes, who are contrasted with Zebulon and Naphtali, whose bravery was most conspicuous (10 stichoi).

(6) *vv.*$^{19-21}$. The battle (9 stichoi).

(7) *vv.*$^{22.23}$. Flight of the foe (6 stichoi).

(8) *vv.*$^{24-27}$. Ja'el's deed extolled—The fate of Ṡiṡera (11 stichoi).

(9) *vv.*$^{28-30}$. The poet gloats over the anxiety and vain expectation of Ṡiṡera's mother (11 stichoi).

v.^{31a}. A concluding couplet (supposed by some to have been added to the poem in later times).

V'hál'ma Sís'ra', mách'qa róšo,
V'mách'ça v'chál'fa ráqq'to.
Bén ragläha kára', náfal,
Vé-šakháb *laáreç*,
Bén ragläha kára', náfal ;
Báašér kará', šam náfal šádud.

This typically German rhythm lends itself admirably to his translation :—

'Jahel sei von Frau'n gepriesen,
Von den Frau'n im Zelte!
Statt des Wassers gab sie Milch ihm,
Rahm in mächt'ge Schale.
Ihre Hand griff nach dem Pflocke,
Und den Hammer fasste ihre Rechte.

'Und sein Haupt zerschlug sie hämmernd,
Quetschte seine Schläfe.
Sisara fiel, stürzte nieder,
Lag zu ihren Füssen,
So vor ihr dahingestrecket,
Blieb er, wo er fiel, zerschmettert liegen.'

Marquart's system likewise takes such liberties with the position of the *ictus* as would be capable (by the aid of emendation, where deemed necessary) of producing almost any desired result from any Hebrew poem to which it might be applied.

Here we notice that, out of the nine divisions or strophes into which the poem falls, four, viz. Nos. 2, 3, 8, and 9, are of exactly the same length, viz. eleven stichoi. Every strophe, except Nos. 5 and 7, contains a single line; and in Nos. 4, 6, 8, and 9 these single lines correspond with a break in subject, rounding off the strophe. Such a measure of uniformity suggests that, in its original form, the poem may have been more completely uniform. Thus, *e.g.*, it seems probable that *v.*[12] in strophe 3 originally stood before *vv.*[9-11]—an arrangement which brings the single stichos *v.*[11c] to the end of the strophe. This gives a very natural order:—Deborah, Baraḳ, the military commanders, 'the people' or rank and file of the fighting men, and then typical representatives of the community in time of peace—the sheikhs, the wayfarers, and the village-maidens. We must not, however, lay too great stress upon such an arrangement, since it seems fairly clear that it was not hard and fast throughout the poem. Few would doubt that strophe 1 stands substantially in its original form. In this case the strophe may be said to fall into two parts, 1a (*v.*[3]) and 1b (*vv.*[4.5]); and it is 1a, and not 1b, that the poet has rounded off with the single stichos.

The variation in length of strophes 1, 4-7, and more especially the very marked comparative brevity of No. 7, suggests that the poem has undergone a certain amount of mutilation in transmission—a conclusion which is also rendered highly probable by the very corrupt condition of the text in the middle part of the poem (*vv.*[8-15]), which has been the despair of a multitude of commentators.

It is perhaps needless to remark that the emendations adopted in the translation are not claimed as offering more than a reasonably possible solution of textual difficulties which are in some cases so considerable that they may well be regarded as beyond the reach of remedy.* When confronted by difficulties of such a character there are three courses which are open to the translator. He may endeavour to force a meaning out of 𝔐 as it stands, in defiance of the ordinary rules which govern Hebrew philology; he may abandon the passage as hopeless, and leave a lacuna in his translation; or he may seek, by aid of the ancient Versions, or (in default of such aid) by means of reasonable conjecture, so to emend the text that it may satisfy at once the demands of the Hebrew language and the requirements of the context. The third course has been adopted as most appropriate to a commentary of which the aim is the elucidation of the Biblical text by all the aids which modern research has placed within our reach.

* The very corrupt condition of portions of the poem may be taken as an indication that it was derived by E, not from *oral* tradition, but from an ancient *written* source which may already have been partially illegible when it was drawn upon by the historian. Cf. the similar phenomenon in David's lament over Saul and Jonathan, 2 Sam. 1[17ff.], and Solomon's words at the dedication of the Temple, 1 Kgs. 8[12.13]—poems which we know to have been extracted from an ancient song-book, viz. the Book of Jashar.

5. 1. R^{JE} Then sang Deborah and Baraḳ the son of Abinoʿam on that day, saying,
2. E (When long locks of hair were worn loose in Israel; when the people volunteered.)

Bless ye Yahweh!

3. Attend, ye kings; give ear, ye rulers:
I — to Yahweh I will sing,
Will make melody to Yahweh, the God of Israel.
4. Yahweh, in thy progress from Seʿir,
In thy march from the field of Edom,
Earth quaked, yea, heaven ⌜rocked⌝,
Yea, the clouds dropped water.
5. The mountains ⌜shook⌝ before Yahweh,
[] Before Yahweh, the God of Israel.

6. ⌜From⌝ the days of Shamgar ben-ʿAnath,
⌜From⌝ the days of ⌜old, caravans⌝ ceased.
And they that went along the ways used to walk [] by crooked paths.
7. Villag⌜es⌝ ceased in Israel;
. . . . ceased;
Till thou didst arise, Deborah,
Didst arise as a mother in Israel.
8. ⌜Armourers had they none;⌝
⌜Armed men failed from the city:⌝
Was there seen a shield or a lance
Among forty thousand in Israel?

12. Awake, awake, Deborah!
Awake, awake, sing paean!
Rise up, Baraḳ, and lead captive
Thy capt⌜ors⌝, O son of Abinoʿam!
9. ⌜Come, ye⌝ commanders of Israel!
Ye that volunteered among the people, bless ye Yahweh!
10. ⌜Let⌝ the riders on tawny she-asses [⟨review it,⟩]
And let the wayfarers [⟨⌜recall it to mind!⌝⟩]
11. [] Hark to ⌜the maidens laughing⌝ at the wells!
There they recount the righteous acts of Yahweh,
The righteous acts of his ⌜arm⌝ in Israel.[]

13. Then down ⸢to the gates gat⸣ the nobles;
Yahweh's folk ⸢gat them⸣ down mid the heroes.

14. From Ephraim ⸢they spread out on the vale⸣;
'After thee, Benjamin!' mid thy clansmen.
From Machir came down the commanders,
And from Zebulun men wielding the truncheon [].

15. And ⸢thy⸣ princes, Issachar, were with Deborah;
And ⸢Naphtali⸣ was leal ⟨to⟩ Baraḳ:
To the vale he was loosed at his heel.

⟨Utterly reft⟩ ⸢into⸣ factions was Re'uben;
Great were ⸢his searchings⸣ of heart.

16. Why sat'st thou still amid the folds,
To hear the pastoral pipings? []

17. Gileʿad beyond the Jordan dwelt,
And Dan [] abideth by the ships.
Asher sat still by the shore of the seas,
Dwelling beside his creeks.

18. Zebulun is the folk that scorned its life to the death,
And Naphtali on the heights of the field.

19. On came the kings, they fought;
Then fought the kings of Canaʿan;
In Taʿanach, by the rills of Megiddo;
The gain of money they took not.

20. From heaven fought the stars;
From their highways they fought with Ṡiṡera.

21. The torrent Ḳishon swept them off;
[]⸢It faced them⸣, the torrent Ḳishon.
⸢Bless thou⸣, my soul, the might ⟨of Yahweh!⟩

22. Then loud beat the hoofs of the horse⸢s⸣;
⸢Off⸣ gallop⸢ed⸣, ⸢off⸣ gallop⸢ed⸣ his chargers.

23. Curse ye, ⸢curse ye⸣ Meroz! []
Curse ye, curse ye her towns-folk!
For they came not to the help of Yahweh,
To the help of Yahweh mid the heroes.

24. Most blessed of women be Ja'el, [ ]
Of tent-dwelling women most blessed!

25. Water he asked; milk she gave;
In a lordly dish she proffered curds.

26. Her hand to the peg she put forth,
And her right to the maul of the workmen;
And she smote Ṡiśera—destroyed his head,
Shattered and pierced through his temples.

27. 'Twixt her feet he bowed, he fell down, he lay prone;
'Twixt her feet he bowed, he fell down.
Where he bowed, there he fell down undone.

28. Out through the window she leaned and exclaimed,
The mother of Ṡiśera out through the lattice:
'Wherefore delayeth his car to come?
Wherefore tarrieth the clatter of his chariots?'

29. Her wisest princesses mak⌜e⌝ answer,
Yea, she returneth her reply: [ ]

30. 'Are they not finding—dividing the spoil?
A damsel—two damsels for every man:
A spoil of dyed stuffs for Ṡiśera,
A spoil of dyed stuffs embroidered;
Two dyed embroideries for the neck of ⌜the queen.⌝'

31. So perish all thy foes, Yahweh:
But be ⌜thy⌝ friends like the sun going forth in his might.

R^{E2} And the land had rest forty years.

5, 1. *Then sang Deborah.* That the poem was actually composed by Deborah does not appear to be probable: cf. *note* on *v.*[7b].

2. *When, etc.* The view which is taken in the translation given above is that this statement forms no part of the poem, but simply states the *occasion* on which it was composed, viz. when the Israelites consecrated themselves with unshorn locks (see below) to fight the battle of Yahweh, and made spontaneous offering of their service. The *form* of the sentence (Infinitive Construct with ב in a temporal clause) is exactly like that which is employed in stating the supposed occasions of several of the Psalms in the 'David' collection. So Ps. 3, 'When he fled from Absalom his son' (בְּבָרְחוֹ וג'); Ps. 34, 'When he changed his conduct before Abimelech, etc.' (בְּשַׁנּוֹתוֹ וג'): Ps. 51, 'When Nathan

the prophet came unto him, etc.' (בְּבוֹא וג׳); cf. also Pss. 52, 54, 57, 59, 60, 63.*

Bārᵉkhû Yahweh, 'Bless ye Yahweh!' may then be regarded as the *title* of the poem, indicating that it is *a song of thanksgiving*; just as in certain Psalms we find a prefixed *Halᵉlû Yāh*, 'Praise ye Yah!' which is not strictly part of the Psalm itself, but indicates its contents, viz. *a song of praise*: cf. Pss. 106, 111, 112, *al.* Title and note of occasion appear to have been taken over by the E writer from the old song-book (perhaps 'the Book of the wars of Yahweh,' Num. 21[14]) in which the poem was contained. The ordinary view, which makes this verse the opening couplet of the poem, is opposed by its somewhat abrupt character, in contrast to *v.*[3] which forms a natural opening (cf. Ex. 15[1b], 'I will sing to Yahweh, etc.'); and also (and especially) by the difficulty of finding a suitable rendering which does justice to the Hebrew construction. It is very doubtful whether the rendering of R.V., 'For that, etc., bless ye Yahweh' (*i.e.* Thank Yahweh that such spontaneous service was rendered) can be justified, no parallel to the use of the Infinitive Construct with ב in such a sense seeming to exist.‡ The only natural rendering of בפרע וג׳ is that which makes it a temporal clause: 'When, etc., bless ye Yahweh'; *i.e.* when Israel offers spontaneous service, bless *Yahweh* as the true source of the noble impulse, just as He is the true giver of victory; and (implicitly) do not ascribe the movement to human merit (cf. *ch.* 7[2]). The impulse described by the verb *hithnaddēbh*, i.e. voluntary service in Yahweh's

* Since writing the above note, the present editor has discovered that a similar view was put forward by William Green, Fellow of Clare Hall, Cambridge, in 1753 (*The Song of Deborah, reduced to metre*). Green treats *v.*[2] as a statement of the occasion of the poem, and renders *vv.*[1,2],

'Then sang Deborah and Barak
The son of Abinoam, on that day,
When they set Israel free, (and)
The people willingly offered themselves,
saying, Bless ye Jehovah.'

His note on the passage runs as follows:—'The second Period contains the title and occasion of the Song, as may be seen by comparing it with the titles of the Psalms, many of which run as this does. See titles of the 3rd, 34th, 51st, and other Psalms. The Song plainly begins at Period the third.'

‡ We should expect עַל with the Infin. Constr. (cf. Ex. 17[7] עַל־נַסֹּתָם אֶת־י׳ 'on account of their trying Yahweh,' Am. 1[3] עַל־דּוּשָׁם 'on account of their threshing'), or עַל־אֲשֶׁר, or אֲשֶׁר alone, with the finite verb (cf. Ex. 32[35] עַל־אֲשֶׁר עָשׂוּ 'because they had made,' Ps. 144[12] אֲשֶׁר בָּנֵינוּ כִּנְטִיעִים 'For that our sons are like young plants'). Bu. asserts (against Mo.) that it is permissible to render ב 'on the ground that' after ברך; but he quotes no illustration of such a usage.

cause, is ascribed to the influence of Yahweh in 1 Chr. 29 [14]. It would be precarious, however, to argue from so late a passage to the passage with which we are dealing; and, in any case, such an explanation involves reading more into our verse than perhaps it may reasonably be supposed to contain. Mo. suggests that the pref. ב might here be rendered 'with':—'with long streaming locks in Israel, with free gifts of the people, praise ye Yahweh'—a rendering which, even if it be possible, does not commend itself as at all probable.

When long locks of hair were worn loose. Heb. *biphroaʿ peraʿôth.* The construction is literally that of an impersonal active verb: 'When one let loose long locks, etc.'

Much discussion has taken place over the meaning of substantive and cognate verb. The grounds upon which the rendering given above is adopted are as follows. In Bab. *pirtu* (plur. *pirêtu*, *pirîtu*) means 'long hair' (of the head): cf. *Gilgameš-epic* I. col. ii. 36, where it is said of the wild man Engidu that 'his long hair is arranged like a woman's' (*uppuš pirîtu kîma sinništi*; lit. 'he is arranged as to the long hair, etc.'). The same subs. is seen in the Ar. *farʿ* 'long hair' of a woman, 'full *or* abundant hair' (Lane). In Heb. *péraʿ* occurs in Num. 6 [5] with reference to the Nazirite: R.V. 'All the days of his vow of separation no razor shall come upon his head: until the days be fulfilled in which he separateth himself to the Lord, he shall be holy, he shall let the locks (*péraʿ*) of the hair of his head grow long. Similarly, Ezek. 44 [20]: R.V. 'Neither shall they (the priests the sons of Ṣadoḳ) shave their heads, nor suffer their locks (*péraʿ*) to grow long; they shall only poll their heads.' In all these cases (Bab., Ar., and Heb.) the meaning of the substantives is undisputed.

A plur. form *parʿôth*, Construct State of *peraʿôth* in our passage with fem. termination (cf. Bab. *pirtu*, plur. *pirêtu*), is found in Deut. 32 [42]; and the meaning has been held to be equally ambiguous in Deut. and Judg. In the passage of Deut. (where Yahweh is the speaker) Driver renders as follows:—

'I will make mine arrows drunk with blood,
And my sword shall devour flesh,
With the blood of the slain and of the captives,
From the long-haired heads of the foe.'

The Heb. phrase in the last line is *rôš parʿôth*, lit. 'head of long locks.'

There is no dispute that the *verb pāraʿ* has the meaning *let loose, unbind long hair* in other passages: cf. Lev. 10 [6], 21 [10], 13 [45], Num. 5 [18]. It is also used metaphorically in the sense of *letting loose* people by removing restraint from them, in Ex. 32 [25] (twice). Syr. *peraʿ* means 'to sprout,' and late Ar. *faraʿa* is quoted in this sense * (cf. references in BDB. *s.v.* פרע II.).

* The roots פרע and פרח 'sprout' may be ultimately connected.

This is the case for the rendering which has been adopted in the text with some confidence. As Black remarks (after W. Robertson Smith), 'The expression . . . refers to the ancient and widespread practice of vowing to keep the head unshorn until certain conditions had been fulfilled (cf. Acts 18[18]). The priests [cf. the passage from Ezek. already cited] were prohibited from making such vows because they might interfere with the regular discharge of the priestly functions; but with warriors in primitive times the unshorn head was a usual mark of their consecration to the work which they had undertaken, and their locks remained untouched till they had achieved their enterprise or perished in the attempt (cf. Ps. 68[21]). War among most primitive peoples is a sacred function, and this was specially the case in Israel where Jehovah was the God of Hosts.'

This interpretation, which was probably intended by Σ. ἐν τῷ ἀνακαλύψασθαι κεφαλάς (cf. 𝔊[B] Ἀπεκαλύφθη ἀποκάλυμμα), is also adopted by Cassel, Wellh. (*Isr. u. Jüd. Gesch*[2]. p. 97), Vernes, No., La., Cooke (*Comm.*), Gress., and, on Deut. 32[42] (according to Driver), by Schultens, Knobel, Keil, and by R.V. *marg.* 2.

The principal rival interpretation is 'For that (*or* when) the leaders led.' This appears in 𝔊[AL], Θ., ἐν τῷ ἄρξασθαι ἀρχηγούς, and is adopted by R.V., Schnurrer, Herder (1780), Hollmann, Ges., Ros., Donaldson, Meier, Ewald, Hilliger, Bach., Reuss, Ber., Oet., Bu., Stephan, Kit., Zapletal, Kent, Smith, and apparently given the preference by Mo. on Judg.; and in Deut. by R.V. ('From the head of the leaders of the enemy'), Schultz, Kamphausen, Dillmann, Oet., Steuernagel. It depends upon the fact that in Ar. the verb *faraʿa* has the sense *overtop* or *surpass in height*, and then *become superior in eminence*, *nobility*, etc.; and hence is derived the subs. *farʿ*, *noble* or *man of eminence* (Lane).*

If this rendering is correct, it is at any rate remarkable that, where so many occasions for mentioning *leaders* or *chieftains* occur in the O.T., both in poetry and prose, this particular term should be found only in the two passages specified, and should in both of them be open to a considerable measure of ambiguity.

Other explanations may be dismissed in a few words. Kimchi, and several older modern commentators (Köhler, Herder (1825), etc.),

* There can be little doubt that this root is the same as that from which the subs. 'long hair' is derived, the common idea being that of *luxuriant growth*.

Cooke makes a mistake in attempting (with some of the older commentators) to connect the Aram. פּוּרְעָנִים, which is used in 𝔗[O] Deut. 16[18] to translate the Heb. שֹׁטְרִים 'officers' (in subordinate position); since the sense here intended is *vindices* (from פְּרַע 'to avenge'), alongside of Heb. שֹׁפְטִים, Aram. דַּיָּנִין 'judges.' Cooke adds a reference to Ex. 20[5] in 𝔗[J]; but this is quite off the point, פּוּרְעָן here having the sense 'vindictive,' in the phrase, 'a jealous and vindictive God.'

following the rendering of 𝔖ᴾ, 'For the vengeance wherewith Israel was avenged,' explain 'For the vengeance (lit. vengeances) which was taken in Israel,' *i.e.* the avenging of their wrongs. Similarly, in Deut. 32 [42] R.V. *marg.* offers the rendering, 'From the beginning of revenges upon the enemy.' But this sense of the verb פרע, though common in Aram., cannot be paralleled in Heb., in which *nāḳam* is the regular term for 'avenge.' Lastly, Le Clerc, Michaelis, Justi, Stu., von Gumpach, assuming the meaning of the root to be *to loosen* in a general sense, would render 'For the freedom (freedoms) which was wrought in Israel.' Such a sense, however, cannot be supported.

volunteered. The Heb. *hithnaddēbh,* which is used, as here, in 2 Chr. 17 [16], Neh. 11 [2], in the sense of offering one's self willingly to perform certain services, occurs in 1 Chr. 29 (*passim*), Ezr. 1 [6], 2 [68], 3 [5] † with the meaning *offer freewill offerings* (*nᵉdhābhôth*) for the Temple. Cf. also, in Bib. Aram., Ezr. 7 [13.15.16] †.

3. *ye rulers.* Heb. *rōzᵉnîm,* which is connected with an Ar. root meaning 'to be weighty, grave, firm in judgment,' is only employed in the O.T. in poetical or elevated diction. It is parallel to 'kings' (as here) in Hab. 1 [10], Ps. 2 [2], Prov. 8 [15], 31 [4], and to 'judges of the earth' in Isa. 40 [23] †. Cf. Bab. *urzunu* (*ruzzunu*?), *ruṣṣunu,* 'mighty, dignified,' cited by Dyneley Prince, *JBL.*, 1897, pp. 175 ff. ; Langdon, *AJSL.*, 1912, pp. 144 f.

I— unto Yahweh I will sing, The first 'I' is a *nominativus pendens.* R.V., 'I, even I will sing, etc.,' is incorrect.

will make melody. Heb. *zimmēr* is used of playing an instrument (cf. Ps. 33 [2b], 144 [9b], 147 [7b], *al.*), as well as of singing. Hence the rendering adopted is preferable to the more specific rendering of R.V., 'I will sing praise.'

4. *Yahweh, when, etc.* Yahweh is pictured as marching to the assistance of Israel from His ancient seat in the south (as rightly observed by Hollmann), which is placed by the poet in 'Seʿir' or 'the field of Edom.' That this seat can be no other than Ṡinai (of J and P) or Ḥoreb (of E and D), as is assumed by the author of the ancient gloss 'This is Sinai' in *v.* [5b], cannot be doubted. The old poem called 'the Blessing of Moses,' Deut. 33, is very explicit. It opens with the quatrain—

'Yahweh came from Ṡinai,
And beamed forth unto them from Seʿir ;
He shone forth from mount Paran,
And came from ⌜Meribath-Ḳadesh.⌝'

Here Ṡinai is grouped with Seʿir, *i.e.* the mountain-range of Edom which runs north and south, from the Dead Sea to the Gulf of ʿAḳaba ; with a mountain (or mountain-range) belonging to Paran—perhaps Ǵebel Fârân, among the mountains to the south-east of

Ḳadesh ; and with Meribah of Ḳadesh,* *i.e.* Ḳadesh-Barneaʿ, which was close to the border of Edom : cf. Num. 20^{16b}, and *note* on 'from the Crag,' Judg. 1^{36}.

The evidence of the 'prayer' of Habaḳḳuḳ is similar. This opens with the statement—

'God came from Teman,
And the holy one from mount Paran.'

Teman, which etymologically means 'the right hand side,' or South country, from the standpoint of Canaʿan, is the name applied to a district of Edom, as appears from Ezek. 25^{13}, Ob. ^{9}.

If the site of Mount Sinai is to be sought among the mountains of Edom, not far from Ḳadesh—possibly in the Ǵebel el-Maḳrah group to the south-east of ʿAin Ḳudês (cf. *Map* V.), this is consonant with several other statements contained in the O.T. For instance, Moses comes to Mount Ḥoreb when feeding the flock of his father-in-law, the priest of Midian (Ex. 3^{1} E) ; and Midian appears to have been situated north-east of the Gulf of ʿAḳaba, in the neighbourhood of the hill-country of Seʿir.‡ Israel's first conflict with the ʿAmaleḳites is at Rephidim close to Sinai (Ex. $17^{8ff.}$ E) ; and the ʿAmaleḳites are mentioned elsewhere as inhabiting the region immediately south of the Negeb, in the neighbourhood of the Ḳenites and Simeʿonites : cf. *note* on 'ʿAmaleḳ' *ch.* 3^{12}. The story of Moses striking the rock at Ḳadesh is given as the origin of the name Meribah in Num. 20^{1-13} (JEP), and is closely parallel to the story of his striking the rock at Rephidim close to Sinai, Ex. 17^{1b-7} (JE), where the name Meribah is similarly given ; and it is impossible to think otherwise than that the two narratives are duplicates of the same tradition. Cf. further Sayce, pp. *HCM.* 262-272.

The traditional site of Sinai is Ǵebel Mûsâ in the south of the peninsula of Sinai, more than 150 miles south of Ḳadesh (ʿAin Ḳudês), and considerably over 100 miles from the southernmost district of Edom, and from the land of Midian. The only evidence

* 𝔐 reads מֵרִבְבֹת קֹדֶשׁ, *i.e.* 'from ten thousands of holiness,' which is paraphrased by R.V., 'from the ten thousands of holy ones.' 𝔊, however, renders σὺν μυριάσιν Καδης, and it is clear that a place-name is required by the parallelism with the three preceding stichoi. This can be scarcely other than מִמְּרִיבַת קָדֵשׁ: cf. Deut. 32^{51}, Ezek. 47^{19}, 48^{28}; Ps. 106^{32}.

‡ The statement of Ex. 3^{1} that Moses 'led his flock *to the back* of the wilderness' implies that the mountain of God lay to the *west* of Midian. The Μοδιανα or Μαδιαμα of Ptolemy (vi. 7), *i.e.* the Madyan of the Arabic geographers, lies east of the gulf of ʿAḳaba and south of the mountain-range of Seʿir ; but the land of Midian may in all probability have extended further northwards along the eastern side of Seʿir. Thus a mountain west of Midian might be situated in Seʿir to the east of the ʿArabah : but the tradition which associates Sinai with Ḳadesh and Paran, seems rather to favour the district of Edom which lay to the west of the ʿArabah.

in the O.T. which may be said to tell in its favour, in so far as it is incompatible with the evidence given above associating Sinai with Ḳadesh, is the statement of Deut. 1 [2] that 'it is eleven days from Ḥoreb by way of the hill-country of Se'ir to Ḳadesh-Barnea'.' It may be noticed also that P in Num. 33 [16-36] places twenty stations between Sinai and Ḳadesh; but this is discounted by the fact that the old narrative JE knows nothing of these stations, and only mentions Tab'erah (Num. 11 [3]), Ḳibroth-hatta'avah (Num. 11 [34]), and Ḥaṣeroth (Num. 11 [35]), as intervening.*

The tradition which connects Sinai with Ǵebel Mûsâ cannot be traced beyond the monastic period. It seems to have been in the fourth century A.D. that Christian communities began to settle in the Sinai peninsula, and monasteries were established in the neighbourhood of Ǵebel Mûsâ, and also of Ǵebel Serbâl in the west of the peninsula, which, in the opinion of many authorities, possesses the earlier claim to have been considered the traditional Sinai. Upon this question, cf. Driver, *Exodus* (*Camb. Bib.*), pp. 186 ff. ‡

the field of Edom. The phrase שְׂדֵה אֱדוֹם (parallel to 'Seir,' a mountain-district: cf. preceding *note*) suggests an original connexion between Heb. *sādhé*, ordinarily rendered 'field,' and Bab. *šadû*, 'mountain.' § Cf. also *v.* [18], 'on the heights of *the field*'; Num. 23 [14], 'unto *the field* of the watchmen' (Ṣophim), further explained by 'unto the top of Pisgah,' mentioned as a point of view; Deut. 32 [13], 'produce

* Ḳadesh is not mentioned at the end of Num. 12 or the beginning of 13. Num. 12 [16] says that 'the people journeyed from Ḥaṣeroth and pitched in the wilderness of Paran,' and *ch.* 13 then at once commences to relate the mission of the spies. But that it was Ḳadesh from which, according to the old narrative, the spies were sent forth is clear from 13 [26], where they return to Ḳadesh, and from 32 [8], where they are definitely stated to have been sent forth from Ḳadesh-Barnea'.

‡ An expansion in 𝔗's paraphrase of *v.* [5] shows that the translator must have supposed Sinai to be a very small mountain, and therefore could not have known the tradition identifying it with Ǵebel Mûsâ or Ǵebel Serbâl. The passage runs, 'Mount Tabor, Mount Ḥermon, and Mount Carmel were in a fury one with another, and were saying one to another, the one of them, "Upon *me* shall His *Shĕkhînā* dwell; and *me* it becometh"; and another, "Upon *me* shall His *Shĕkhînā* dwell; and *me* it becometh." He caused His *Shĕkhînā* to dwell on Mount Sinai, which is weaker and smaller than all the mountains.'

§ Heb. שׂ=Bab. *š* is seen also in שָׂבֵעַ=*šebû* 'be sated', שֶׂה=*šu'u* 'sheep', שׂוּט=*šâṭu* 'rebel', שֵׂיב=*šêbu* 'hoary', שִׂיחַ 'plant'=*šiḫtu* 'shoot' from *šâḫu* 'grow', שְׂמֹאל=*šumêlu* 'left side', שֵׂעָר 'hair'=*šârtu* 'hairy skin', שַׂק=*šaḳḳu* 'sack', שָׂרַף=*šarâpu* 'burn', שַׂר 'prince'=*šarru* 'king', and in other cases in which the connexion is not so obvious. Cf. the way in which loan-words in Hebrew from Assyrian represent *š* by ס; *e.g.* סַרְגוֹן for *Šargânu*, etc.: cf. the present editor's note in *JTS.* xi. p. 440.

of *the field*,' parallel to 'the heights of the earth'; 2 Sam. 1[21a], where we should perhaps read '*ye fields* of ⸢death⸣' (שְׂדֵי מָוֶת), parallel to 'ye mountains of Gilboa''; Jer. 18[14], 'Shall the snow of Lebanon fail from the rock of *the field?*' In all these cases the more original meaning 'mountain' appears to be prominent. Cf. Barth, *Etymologische Studien*, pp. 65 f.; Winckler, *AF.* i. p. 192; Peters, *JBL.*, 1893, pp. 54 ff. The reason why *sādhé* came to denote more generally 'field,' i.e. *open country*, usually uncultivated pasture or hunting-ground, probably was that the usage sprang up in Palestine where this type of country is found in the hills as opposed to the vale (*'ēmeḳ*), which doubtless was then, as it is now, appropriated for arable purposes. A parallel may be found in the fact that, for the Babylonians, the same Sumerian ideogram KUR stands both for *šadû*, 'mountain,' and *mâtu* (Aram. *māthā*), 'country'; a fact which points the inference that for the original users of the ideogram their 'country' was a mountain-country.

Earth quaked. The reference is not to Yahweh's manifestation in storm and earthquake at the giving of the Law on Sinai or Ḥoreb (Ex. 19[16ff.], Deut. 4[11.12], 5[22 ff.]), as has been supposed by many scholars—a fact which would have no special significance in the present connexion, but to his appearance in these natural phenomena upon the occasion with which the poem deals. As we have already noticed (4[14] *note*), the fact that a thunder-storm burst in the face of the foes, and materially assisted in their discomfiture, may be inferred both from the poetical and prose-narratives. The statement that 'the earth quaked' need not be taken more literally than the companion-statement that 'the heaven rocked'; and may well be a poetical description of the apparent effect produced by the rolling peals of thunder.

rocked. Reading נָמוֹגוּ with 𝔊[LNal] ἐταράχθη (cf. 𝔊[A] ἐξεστάθη), 𝔏 'turbatum est,' Bu., Mo., Oort, No., in place of 𝔐 נָטָפוּ which means 'dropped' or 'dripped,' and is the word used in the following stichos—a fact which doubtless accounts for its erroneous occurrence in our passage. The Heb. root *mûgh*, suggested by the Versions above cited, is the same as the Ar. *mâǵa*, which, as applied to the sea, means 'be in a state of commotion,' 'be agitated with waves,' 'be very tumultuous' (Lane). Marquart, Ehr. read נָמוֹטוּ 'were shaken.'

5. *shook.* Vocalizing נָזֹלּוּ (as in Isa. 63[19], 64[2]) with 𝔊 ἐσαλεύθησαν, 𝔖[h] ܐܠܗܘ, 𝔏 'commoti sunt,' 𝔖[p] ܙܠܗܘ, 𝔗 זעו, Ar. يزعزعت, and most moderns, in place of 𝔐 נָזְלוּ 'flowed down,' which has the support of 𝔙 'fluxerunt.'*

* It is possible that נָזְלוּ as vocalized by 𝔐 may be intended as a weakened form of נָזֹלּוּ; cf. יָזְמוּ for יָזֹמּוּ, נָבְלָה for נָבֹלָּה in Gen. 11[6.7]; G-K. § 67 *dd*.

Before Yahweh, etc. 𝕳 opens the clause with the words זֶה סִינַי, *i.e.* if part of the original, 'Yon Ṡinai before Yahweh, etc.' The use of the pronoun זֶה *deiktikōs* can be paralleled (cf. BDB. s.v. זה 2); but, as Mo. remarks, 'would only be natural if Sinai were in sight.' The chief objection, however, to the originality of the words is the fact that they are metrically superfluous, since they make the stichos to contain five beats;* whereas, with their omission, the verse is perfectly balanced. It can hardly be doubted that זה סיני is simply a scribe's marginal note which has crept into the text, and which is to be understood predicatively, 'This is Ṡinai' (cf. Σ. τουτέστι τὸ Σινα), *i.e.* 'This refers to Ṡinai,' viz. the mention of the mountains in the first stichos of *v.*[5]. The inclusion of this gloss in the text must have happened fairly early, since it appears in the same position in all the Versions, and also in Ps. 68[8], which is copied from our passage.‡ This view is adopted by von Gumpach, Donaldson, Ball, Mo., Bu., Oort, No., La., Kit., Cooke, Gress. Winckler and Marquart read רָגַז סִינַי 'Ṡinai trembled,' and modify Yahweh's title in order otherwise to shorten the stichos (Winck. 'before Yahweh'—tautologous with parallel stichos; Marq. 'before him'—three beats only in the stichos). Kit., *BH.* proposes (after Grä.) to read זָע for זֶה—'Ṡinai quivered,' and to delete יהוה.

6. *In the days of Shamgar, etc.* Cf. *note* on 3[31], where the fact is remarked that the name Shamgar is non-Israelite, and may very likely be Ḥittite in origin. We have also noticed (4[2] *note*) that Ṡiṡera may very possibly be a Ḥittite name; and these two inferences, taken together, lend colour to the theory, propounded by Marquart, and afterwards worked out by Mo. (*JAOS.*, 1898, pp. 159 f.), that Shamgar may have been a foreign oppressor, and Ṡiṡera his immediate successor, if not his son: both being members of a Ḥittite dynasty ruling in Cana'an, to which the Cana'anite city-kings, at least in the vicinity of the great plain, were vassals.

From the days of old. 𝕳 reads 'In the days of Ja'el'; but this can scarcely represent the original text. As Mo. appositely remarks, 'it is singular that the name of this Bedawi woman should be coupled with that of Shamgar. And how can the period before the rise of Deborah be called *the days of Ja'el*, when the deed which made her famous was only the last act in the deliverance which Deborah had already achieved? The best that can be said is that, although Shamgar and Ja'el, both of whom in different ways wrought deliverance for their people, were living, they did nothing to free Israel from the tyranny of the Cana'anites until Deborah

* זה סיני would count as one beat only.

‡ Ps. 68 is probably not earlier than the Maccabaean period. Ball has made out a strong case for finding its occasion in the events narrated in 1 Macc. 5[9 ff.], *cir.* B.C. 165: cf. *JTS.* xi. (1910) pp. 415 ff.

appeared.' The difficulty is enhanced if Shamgar was not really an Israelite Judge, as supposed by the author of the gloss in 3 [31], but (as is suggested by his name: cf. *note*) a foreign oppressor. Many commentators would escape the difficulty by excising the words 'in the days of Ja'el' as a gloss suggested by *vv.* [24 ff]. Here, however, we find ourselves upon the horns of a dilemma. If we excise no more than these words, with Geddes, Bickell, Cooke, Marquart, Bu., Mo. (*Comm.*, but not *SBOT.*), No., we then have a stichos consisting of two beats only, חדלו ארחות 'caravans ceased'—which is scarcely possible. If, on the other hand, we also excise 'the son of 'Anath' from stichos *a* (with Kit.), and then read *a b* as a single stichos, 'In the days of Shamgar caravans ceased' (rhythmically correct), we are unable to point to the source whence 'the son of 'Anath' was derived by the late author of 3 [31].

Assuming the correctness of the suggestion noticed above, that Shamgar was a foreign oppressor preceding Sisera, it is feasible to regard the י of יעל as due to dittography of the final letter of בימי, and to find in על the first two letters of עָלָם 'old time' (so Ball, privately). Then, reading in both stichoi מִימֵי for בִּימֵי (confusion of מ and ב is frequent; cf. examples cited by Driver, *NHTS.*[2] p. lxvii.) we obtain the text adopted above. It may be objected to this that מימי עלם suggests too remote an antiquity. Yet cf. the expression חרבות עולם 'the desolations of old time,' Isa. 58 [12], 61 [4], an expression covering a period of not more than fifty to seventy years. It would be natural for the poet, after the great victory, somewhat to exaggerate the duration of the oppression.

Suggested substitutions of another proper name for the name Ja'el (*e.g.* 'Ja'ir,' Ewald, *HI.* ii. p. 365; ''Othniel,' Grä.) do not call for comment.

caravans. Vocalizing אֹרְחוֹת with most moderns, in place of אֳרָחוֹת 'ways' or 'paths' of 𝔐.* *'Ōrᵉḥā* (cf. Gen. 37 [25], Isa. 21 [13]) is the active participle fem. sing. of *'āraḥ* 'to journey,' and is used collectively to denote a travelling company. The aggressions of the Cana'anites put a stop to commercial intercourse in Israelite territory. חָדְלוּ אֳרָחוֹת of 𝔐, *i.e.* 'the ways ceased,' is interpreted by R.V. 'the highways were unoccupied'; ‡ but to make 'ceased' to mean 'ceased

* The same change has to be made in Job 6 [19], where אָרְחוֹת תֵּמָא 𝔐 should be אֹרְחוֹת ת'. Similarly, in Job 31 [32] we must read לָאֹרֵחַ 'for the wayfarer' (|| גֵּר 'a sojourner') in place of לָאֹרַח 𝔐, which can only mean 'for the way.'

‡ R.V. *marg.* offers the rendering 'the caravans ceased'; but it should be noted that this involves a tacit adoption of our emendation, and cannot be got out of 𝔐 as it stands.

to be used' is a forced expedient which cannot be justified. Such an idea would have been more naturally expressed by a different verb: cf. Isa. 33[8], 'The highways lie desolate (נָשַׁמּוּ מְסִלּוֹת), the wayfaring man ceaseth.'

They that went, etc. Even the private wayfarer could only find safety by taking 'crooked,' *i.e.* devious and roundabout, paths.

crooked paths. Lit. 'crooked ones,' 'paths' being naturally inferred from the context. So in Ps. 125[5] עֲקַלְקַלּוֹתָם 'their crooked (ways).'

𝔐 inserts אֳרָחוֹת 'paths' before עֲקַלְקַלּוֹת, but this spoils the rhythm by introducing a fifth beat into the stichos. The omission is favoured by Mo. (who quotes Briggs, Ley, Grimme), Bu., No., La., Cooke.

7. *Villages.* Reading פְּרָזוֹת with four MSS. of 𝔐, 𝔖[P] ܦܨܝܚܐ 'open (*i.e.* unwalled) places,' 𝔗 קרוי פצחיא 'village-towns,' and many moderns. *P*[e]*rāzôth* (cf. Ezek. 38[11], Zech. 2[4] (𝔐[8]), Est. 9[19] †) are the unwalled hamlets which the Israelites dwelling round about the plain of Esdraelon were compelled to inhabit owing to their failure to capture the fortified cities of the Cana'anites: cf. *ch.* 1[27 ff]. Such hamlets, being unprotected, were speedily swept out of existence by the foe; and we are left to infer that, as happened during other periods of oppression (cf. *ch.* 6[2], 1 Sam. 13[6]), the Israelite inhabitants must have been driven to take refuge in the caves and fastnesses of the hills.

𝔐 פְּרָזוֹן, which occurs again in the suffix-form פִּרְזוֹנוֹ in *v.*[11], has been explained as a collective 'peasantry,' 'rural population' (hence R.V. *marg.* 'villages'); but the coupling of the plur. verb חָדְלוּ, 'ceased' with the sing. collective subject is extraordinarily harsh, and can scarcely be justified.* Bu., who retains פרזון, feels constrained to alter the verb into the sing. חָדַל (cf. 𝔊[AL] ἐξέλιπε φραζων). צדקת פרזונו in *v.*[11] is likewise only susceptible of a very forced explanation:—'the righteous acts of (*i.e.* pertaining to) his peasantry,' *i.e.* 'his righteous acts towards the peasantry.' The rendering of 𝔊[B] δυνατοί *v.*[7], 𝔙 'fortes' *vv.*[7.11], Ber., La., and several of the older commentators,‡ R.V. *text*, 'rulers' (or 'judges') *v.*[7], 'his rule' *v.*[11], may be

* A parallel may perhaps be found in 1 Kgs. 5[3] (𝔐[17]), הַמִּלְחָמָה אֲשֶׁר סְבָבֻהוּ 'the state of warfare (sing.) which surrounded (plur.) him,' which can only be explained upon the supposition that the writer, in speaking of *warfare*, had implicitly in his mind the *foes* (plur.) who were its cause, and so lapsed into the plur. verb. Cf. *NHTK. ad loc.*

‡ This interpretation is given by Rabbi Isaiah (in Buxtorf, Rabbinic Bible): ויש לפותרו לשון ממשלה שחדלו מהיות להם ממשלה 'and it is possible to interpret it in the sense of "rule," viz. that they ceased to have rule.'

compared with פְּרָזָו in Hab. 3[14], where the meaning 'his chief men,' 'rulers,' or 'warriors' is given by 𝔊, 𝔙, 𝔖[P], 𝔗, and is agreeable to the context. Such an explanation is not without philological support* (as stated by Mo.); yet if the root פרז was really employed in Heb. in the sense 'decide' or 'judge,' it is somewhat strange that no clear occurrences of it are to be found.

. . . *ceased*. As 𝔐 stands, the word is connected with the preceding stichos: 'Villages ceased in Israel, they ceased'; and the Versions all presuppose the same text. Since in *v.*[7b], however, we have a perfectly balanced distich, it seems obvious that *v.*[7a] must originally have formed a similar distich, the first stichos beginning, and the second ending, with חדלו 'ceased' (cf. the similar structural arrangement in the distichs *vv.*[21a. 24]); though what the subject of the second חדלו was we have no means of conjecturing.

Till thou didst arise. קַמְתִּי is doubtless intended by 𝔐 for 1st pers. sing., as rendered by 𝔖[P], 𝔗, A.V., R.V., 'until I arose.' The objection that, inasmuch as the poet addresses Deborah in *v.*[12], it is scarcely possible that she can here be the speaker, is sufficiently answered in the words of Herder, who, writing of *v.*[12], remarks, 'Just as Pindar so often arouses himself, his 'φίλον ἦτορ,' just as David so often summons heart and soul, when both are preparing themselves for the highest flights of their song; so Deborah wakes herself as she now commences the actual description of the battle, and as it were endeavours once more to fight the valiant fight.' A real objection to taking קמתי as the first pers. has, however, been advanced by Houb., viz. that, if this had been intended, we should have expected the 1st pers. pronoun, אני דבורה, instead of דבורה simply (cf. Dan. 10[7], 12[5]): and it is perhaps preferable, therefore, to take the verb as the older form of the 2nd pers. fem. sing. (for קַמְתְּ: cf. Jer. 2[20], where שָׁבַרְתִּי, נִתַּקְתִּי must be regarded as 2nd fem. sing.; Mic. 4[13], וְהַחֲרַמְתִּי: G-K. § 44 *h*), as is done by most moderns. 𝔊 ἕως οὗ ἀνέστη ([B], according to Swete, ἀναστῇ), 𝔏 'donec surrexit,' 𝔙 'donec surgeret,' presuppose קָמָה, or possibly קָמַת. If this is original, we must suppose that it was altered into קַמְתִּי (intended as the 1st pers. sing.) in 𝔐 under the influence of the heading in *v.*[1], 'Then sang Deborah and Baraḳ' (so Wellh.).

* Ar. *faraza* means to *separate, divide,* and then, apparently, *decide*: cf. Lane *s.v.* 2.8. Bab. *parâsu* (with which cf. Heb. *pāraš*, 'divide') means to *decree, judge, give decision*; and *piristu*=*decision*. Sum. GAR.ZA, MAR.ZA=Bab. *parṣu, i.e.* a divine *decree* or *institute* in Temple-worship: cf. Br. 5647, 5836; Muss-Arnolt, *Dict.* p. 836 *b*. We thus have evidence that the sense *divide*, and thence *decide*, runs through the differently modified Semitic root *prs* (*prš*), *prṣ*, *prz*.

8. *Armourers, etc.* Reading

חָסְרוּ לָהֶם חָרָשִׁים
אָזְלוּ חֲמֻשִׁים מֵעִיר

The text of 𝔐 here offers perhaps the greatest crux in the poem. As it stands, it can only be rendered, 'One chooses (*or* shall choose) new gods (*or* God chooses new things); then battling (??) of gates.' The rendering of A.V., R.V., 'They chose new gods; then was war in the gates,' proceeds upon the assumption that the verb יבחר is an impersonal Imperfect used pictorially of a past event, and that לחם is employed in place of the ordinary מִלְחָמָה in the sense 'war'; 'war of gates' being interpreted as 'war in the gates.' If לָחֶם or לָחֵם* is really intended to convey this sense, it is best to regard the form as an Infinitive Pi'el, used in place of a substantive, in accordance with the explanation of Schnurrer, 'tunc factum est τὸ oppugnare urbes (Israëliticas).' The meaning then is that apostasy from Yahweh to the service of strange gods was punished by the siege of Israel's cities by the Cana'anites; a thought which is akin to the pragmatism of R^{E2}. It is true that the 'new gods' may be paralleled by Deut. 32 [17], 'They sacrificed . . . to gods whom they knew not, to new ones that came up recently'; and the idea of *choice* of gods other than Yahweh is found in *ch.* 10 [14] (E^2).‡ But, apart from the difficulty of construing the Hebrew in this sense, the stage depicted as 'war in the gates' hardly suits the condition of abject submission already described in *vv.* [6.7], or the statement as to the absence of weapons among the Israelites in *v.* [8b]. Still less probable is the explanation of Ewald (and so Meier), who regards אֱלֹהִים as referring to *judges*, so called as God's representatives § ('heilige Richter'), and somewhat prosaic-

* The common reading is לָחֶם; but thirty-six MSS. read לָחֵם or לָחֶם (Kit., *BH.*). We should expect the Infin. Pi'el to be לַחֵם; but no other instance of the Pi'el of this verb exists.

‡ Possibly a scribe may have endeavoured to restore an illegible text under the influence of these two passages (Cooke, Mo.).

§ Cf. the present writer's *Outlines of O.T. Theology*, pp. 15 f. The use of *'ĕlōhîm* in the passages quoted from Ex. 21 [6], 22 [8.9] ('The Book of the Covenant'), is susceptible, however, of a different and probably preferable explanation, viz. the household-gods (Teraphim), which were possibly connected with the practice of ancestor-worship, and whose cultus appears to have existed among the Israelites in early times apart from any conception that the allegiance due to the national God Yahweh was thereby contravened. Laying these passages aside, the only *certain* instance of the employment of *'ĕlōhîm* to denote judges is Ps. 82 [6].

ally makes the passage state that the outbreak of hostilities was coincident with the appointment of new judges (Deborah and Baraḳ).

The evidence of the Versions is somewhat conflicting. 𝔊ᴮ, 𝔗 support substantially the text of 𝔓, and the interpretation of it given by A.V., R.V. 𝔊ᴮ renders *ἐξελέξαντο θεοὺς καινούς, ὅτε ἐπολέμησαν πόλεις ἀρχόντων*. Here *ὅτε* is probably a corruption of *τότε* (as in HP. 58), and *πόλεις* a corruption of *πύλας*. *πύλας ἀρχόντων* is most likely to be the result of a doublet (שְׁעָרִים 'gates'; שָׂרִים 'princes'); the second rendering coming into the text from the margin as *ἄρχοντας*, and then being altered to the genitive to make sense.* *ἐπολέμησαν* may be a rendering of לָחֶם of 𝔐, regarded as Infin. Constr. Pi'el; or it may represent an original לָחֲמוּ (or לחמ׳ regarded as an abbreviated plural); unless it be considered as a corruption of *ἐπολέμησεν*, as is suggested by 𝔙, 'et portas hostium ipse [Dominus] subvertit,' where the translator had before him a text identical with 𝔓, but treated לחם as the Perfect לָחַם. The lengthy paraphrase of 𝔗 appears to have behind it a text in no way different from 𝔐:—'When the house of Israel desired to serve new errors [*i.e.* idols], which had lately been made, with which their fathers had not concerned themselves, the peoples came against them and drave them from their cities, etc.' Here the description of the idols clearly points to the fact that the paraphraser had Deut. 32 [17] in his mind. The same text and interpretation are offered in stichos *a* by 𝔊ᴬᴸ *ᾑρέτισαν θεοὺς καινούς*. The rendering of this stichos which makes 'God' the *subject* of the verb is offered by 𝔖ᴾ ܓܒܐ ܐܠܗܐ ܚܕܬܐ, 'God chooses a new thing,' 𝔙 'Nova bella elegit Dominus'; and has been adopted by a few of the earlier commentators, who understand חדשים 'new ones,' either as 'new judges,' or 'new things' (properly חדשות; cf. Isa. 42 [9], 48 [6]; sing. Isa. 43 [19], Jer. 31 [21])—*i.e.* a new mode of action, viz. deliverance through the agency of a woman.‡ This rendering, however, is opposed by the fact that 'Yahweh,' and not 'God,' is employed elsewhere throughout the poem with reference to the God of Israel.

Another interpretation of the stichos *b* is offered by 𝔊ᴬᴸ *al.* *ὡς ἄρτον κρίθινον*, 𝔏 'velut panem hordeaceum' (so 𝔖ʰ); 𝔖ᴾ ܐܝܟ ܠܚܡܐ ܕܣܥܪܐ; *i.e.* the last two words of 𝔓 are vocalized as לֶחֶם שְׂעֹרִים 'barley-bread.' This has led Bu. to propose the emendation אָזַל לֶחֶם שְׂעֹרִים

* HP. cite four Codd. Arm. as reading *ἄρχοντες πόλεων*.

‡ Kemink (as quoted by Donaldson) seeks to find the clue to the passage in this conception; but emends חדשים into הַנָּשִׁים—'God makes choice of women' (Deborah and Ja'el).

'The barley-bread was spent,' upon the view that the ל of אזל has been omitted through haplography. The verb אזל is employed in this sense in 1 Sam. 9 [7]; and barley-bread is typical of the Israelite peasantry in the Midianite's dream, *ch.* 7 [13], doubtless as forming their staple sustenance. In harmony with this suggestion, Bu. conjectures that stichos *a* may have run זִבְחֵי אֱלֹהִים חָדֵלּוּ 'The sacrifices of God ceased,' *i.e.* through lack of the wherewithal to provide them. Apart, however, from the objection to the use of 'God' instead of 'Yahweh,' which we have already noticed, such a distich, though not at variance with what follows in the next distich, yet stands in no necessary connexion with it. Such a connexion has been sought by Lambert (*RÉJ.* xxx. p. 115) in his emendation of stichos *b* אָז לַחֲמֵשׁ עָרִים; according to which the sentence would run on into the following distich:—'Then unto five cities was there seen a shield, etc.' But such an overrunning between distich and distich is contrary to analogy. La., Schlögl, Kent, in following Lambert, reject stichos *a* altogether; and combine stichos *b* with the following distich in such a way as to form a single distich of the whole:—

'Then there was not seen a shield for five cities,
Or a lance among forty thousand in Israel.'

The emendation adopted above has been made at the suggestion of Dr. Ball, who observes that the only guide which we possess as to the original sense of the distich is found in the succeeding distich, 'Was there seen a shield, etc.' This immediately recalls the similar account of the drastic disarmament effected by the Philistines at the commencement of Saul's reign, as recorded in 1 Sam. 13 [19-22], which relates that 'no armourer (*or* smith, חָרָשׁ) was found throughout all the land of Israel: for the Philistines said, Lest the Hebrews make them swords or spears'; but all the Israelites were obliged to go down to the Philistines in order to sharpen their agricultural implements. 'So it came to pass in the day of battle that there was neither sword nor spear found in the hand of any of the people that were with Saul and Jonathan: but with Saul and with Jonathan his son there was found.' The resemblance between חדשים 'new things' and חרשים 'armourers' is patent; יבחר may have arisen through transposition of the letters of חסרו, and אלהם from לחם or אֱלֵהֶם. As a parallel clause we have the statement that 'Armed men failed from the city'—a natural result of the absence of armourers and the vigorous oppression exercised by the Cana'anites. חֲמֻשִׁים is the term employed of the armed warriors in the Midianite camp, *ch.* 7 [11]. Possibly אָזְלוּ חֲמֻשִׁים may have been written in abbreviated form 'אזל' חמש (cf. *footnote*, p. 124); while the letters of מעיר may be supposed to have suffered transposition ערים.

Marquart already has our חֲרָשִׁים ;* but rearranges *vv.*$^{7a-8a}$ in a manner which scarcely commends itself. Supposing *v.*^{7b} to be a later gloss, he follows *v.*^{7a} (as in ℌ) by the first two words of stichos *a* of *v.*^{8a} in the form יִבְחֲרוּ אֹהָלִים : 'Village-life ceased in Israel; They fled into tents . . .' His next distich then runs, 'The barley-bread was spent; Armourers ceased in the land' (חָדְלוּ חָרָשִׁים ⟨בָּאָרֶץ⟩). Here the first word is from *v.*^{7a}, the second from *v.*^{8a}, and the third supplied by conjecture. Other suggested emendations need not here be noticed.

Was there seen, etc. The Imperfect יֵרָאֶה is frequentative—whenever and wherever one might look, this condition of affairs existed. The curious reading of 𝔊^{L} (occurring with variations in other recensions of 𝔊), σκέπη νεανίδων ἂν ὀφθῇ καὶ σιρομάστης, has undoubtedly arisen from an original text σκέπην ἐὰν ἴδω καὶ σιρομάστην, reading אִם אֶרְאֶה 'Do I see,' for אִם יֵרָאֶה, which may be original (so Marquart, Gress.). In its present form 𝔊^{L} seems to have undergone the following process. A scribe noted the variant ἂν ὀφθῇ (the reading of 𝔊^{B}) upon the margin of his MS. This was subsequently copied into the text; and since ἐὰν ἴδω was superfluous by the side of ἂν ὀφθῇ, σκέπην ἐὰν ἴδω was corrupted into σκέπη νεανίδων, thus supplying a nominative to ὀφθῇ; and, in accordance with this, σιρομάστην became σιρομάστης.

Among forty thousand. Hollmann comments upon the contrast between the number of able-bodied men in Israel as here given, and the large numbers of the Pentateuchal narrative: Ex. 12^{37b}, Num. 11^{21} (J) 600,000; Num. 1^{46} (P) 603,550. The modest assessment of our passage is, as he remarks, a strong argument for the contemporaneousness of the poem with the events which it celebrates. So Wellh. as already quoted (p. 78, *footnote*).

12. This verse is placed before *vv.*$^{9-11}$ for the reasons noted on p. 102.

Awake, awake, Deborah! On the supposed incompatibility of this address with Deborah's reputed authorship of the Song, cf. *note* on *v.*^{7}, 'Till thou didst arise.' The variation of accent—here *ûrî ûrî*, but in the next stichos *ûrî ûrî*—is a rhythmical device: cf. G-K. § 72 *s*.

Thy captors. Vocalizing שֹׁבֶיךָ, with 𝔖^{P}, Michaelis, Wellh., Stade, Black, Bu., Kit., No., Marquart, Segond, La., Ehr., Smith, Cooke (*Comm.*), Gress.: cf. Isa. 14^{2} וְהָיוּ שֹׁבִים לְשֹׁבֵיהֶם 'and they shall be captors to their captors.' 𝔐 שֶׁבְיְךָ, *i.e.* 'thy band of captives' rather than 'thy

* The same emendation was offered by von Gumpach in 1852.

captivity' (R.V.), offers a sense which is perfectly legitimate, and can be paralleled elsewhere (cf. Num. 21[1], 2 Chr. 28[17], Ps. 68[18], 𝔐[19]); but misses the fine paradox which is gained by the easy emendation. It is by no means improbable that Baraḳ, like Gideʿon (cf. *ch.* 8[18ff.]), may have had his own private wrongs to avenge as well as those of his people.

A number of interesting variants are offered by this verse by 𝔊[AL al.], 𝔖[h]. Taking 𝔊[AL] as typical, it runs *ἐξεγείρου, ἐξεγείρου, Δεββωρα,* [A]*ἐξεγείρου* ([L] *ἐξέγειρον*) *μυριάδας μετὰ λαοῦ, ἐξεγείρου, ἐξεγείρου* ([A] adds *λάλει*) *μετ' ᾠδῆς· ἐνισχύων* [A] *ἐξανάστασο* Βαραχ ([L] *ἐξαναστὰς ὁ* B.) *καὶ* [A] *ἐνίσχυσον* ([L] *κατίσχυσον*) *Δεββωρα τὸν Βαραχ, καὶ αἰχμαλώτιζε αἰχμαλωσίαν σου, υἱὸς Αβινεεμ.* Other noteworthy variants are the addition of *σου* after *μετὰ λαοῦ,* and *ἐν ἰσχύϊ* in place of *ἐνισχύων.* Here we must eliminate the doublet of stichos *b*, *ἐξεγείρου, ἐξεγείρου, λάλει μετ' ᾠδῆς*, which represents insertion of the 𝔐 tradition (cf. 𝔊[B]); and, since La. is probably right in regarding *ἐνισχύων*, with variant *ἐν ἰσχύϊ*, and *ἐνίσχυσον* as doublets of an original *ἐν ἰσχύϊ σου* in stichos *c*, we can scarcely err in also excising *καὶ ἐνίσχυσον . . .* Βαραχ, the addition of Δεββωρα τὸν Βαραχ being an attempt to explain the corrupt *ἐνίσχυσον*. Thus, the original Heb. which lies behind this recension of 𝔊 may have run as follows :—

עוּרִי עוּרִי דְּבוֹרָה
הָעִירִי רְבָבוֹת בָּעָם
בְּעֻזֵּךְ קוּם בָּרָק
וּשֲׁבֵה שֶׁבְיֵךְ בֶּן־אֲבִינֹעַם

'Awake, awake, Deborah !
Arouse myriads among the people !
In thy strength arise, Baraḳ !
Lead captive thy captive-band, son of Abinoʿam !'

So La., with the addition of בַּשִּׁיר, *μετ' ᾠδῆς*, at the end of stichos *a*. Mo. (*SBOT.*) reads עָם (? עַמֵּךְ) for בָּעָם, and חֲזַק 'Take courage' in place of בְּעֻזֵּךְ.

It is a moot point whether such a text is superior to 𝔐, as Mo., No., La., Zapletal, Cooke (*Comm.*) think. Mo. rests his argument mainly upon the fact that 'Here Deborah is not summoned to sing a song—whether of battle or of victory—but to arouse the myriads of her countrymen, which certainly agrees better with the words addressed to Baraḳ.' This is true, if we suppose that the poet pictures himself as addressing the chief actors *prior to the battle* ; but the obvious inference to be drawn from 𝔐, as it stands, is that he is rather addressing them as he voices his song, i.e. *subsequently to the victory*, calling upon Deborah to recount the main facts in poetic strain, and upon Baraḳ to fight his battles o'er again. Nor is it any objection to this view that in such a case the verse should stand at the commencement of the poem (where it is placed by Niebuhr): cf. the words of Herder already cited under *v.*[7] *note* on 'Till thou didst arise.' A point which should not escape notice is that it is somewhat strange if the poet here alludes to 'myriads among the people,' even in hyperbole, when previously (*v.*[8]) he has placed the whole available fighting strength of Israel at the moderate assessment of forty thousand. רבבות may quite easily have arisen as a corruption of דבורה or of דברי, and בעם (among the people) come in later in explanation of the 'myriads.' It thus appears that there is no sound ground for abandoning the lucid text of 𝔐.

9. *Come, ye commanders.* Reading לְכוּ מְחֹקְקֵי, as privately suggested by Ball. 𝔐 לִבִּי לְחוֹקְקֵי 'My heart is to the commanders,' *i.e.* (presumably) it *turns* or *goes out* towards them: cf. 𝔙 'Cor meum diligit principes Israel.' The ellipse of the verb is illustrated by Schnurrer from Ps. 141[8] אליך יהוה עיני 'Unto Thee, Yahweh, (are) mine eyes.' Such a use of 'heart,' as denoting sympathetic attraction, is perhaps not quite without parallel in Hebrew (cf. 2 Kgs. 10[15]), though 'soul' (*népheš*) is more usual in such a sense (cf. 1 Sam. 18[1], Gen. 34[3.8], *al.*): but the invitation, 'Bless ye Yahweh!' of stichos *b* favours the supposition that the commanders *are addressed* in stichos *a*; and the imperative לכו forms a natural and appropriate opening to the invitation to thanksgiving.

commanders. *Mᵉḥôḳᵉḳîm* are the imposers of *ḥuḳḳîm*, 'statutes' or 'enactments.'

that volunteered. Cf. *v.*[2] *note.* 𝔊[AL] *οἱ δυνάσται* reads הַנְּדִיבִים.

10. *Let the riders, etc.* Reading

רֹכְבֵי אֲתֹנוֹת צְחֹרוֹת יָשִׂיחוּ
וְהֹלְכֵי עַל־דֶּרֶךְ יָשִׁיבוּ עַל־לֵב

As the verse stands in 𝔐, it offends against parallelism and rhythm. The imperative שִׂיחוּ (rendered by R.V. 'Tell *of it*') comes at the end of stichos *c* of a tristich referring to three classes of people previously mentioned; and the rhythmical form of the tristich is 3 + 2 + 3 beats. Moreover, stichos *b*, יֹשְׁבֵי עַל־מִדִּין, which affords the only instance of a two-beat stichos in the poem, cannot, as it stands, be explained with any approach to probability. The substantive *madh*, to which the plur. *middîn* must be referred, is derived from a verb *mādhadh*, 'to measure,' and denotes 'measure' (Jer. 13[25], *lit.* 'the portion of *thy measures'*), or more usually 'garment,' as in *ch.* 3[16], so-called as *lengthy* or *wide* (cf. Ar. *madda*, 'to extend *or* stretch'). R.V. 'rich carpets,' however, has no more basis than the mere supposition that a word which usually means a spreading garment may also denote any spreading piece of woven material, and that such a rendering is suitable to the context. But even the appropriateness of this assumption may be questioned. The two other classes mentioned are travellers along the roads, which, in contrast to their former condition (*v.*[6]), may now be used with impunity. These classes appear to cover all the population—the wealthy magnate who rides, and the plain man who walks. Is it appropriate that between these two classes there should be interposed reference to a third class of persons who are vaguely defined as those who sit (presumably indoors) upon carpets? It is true that some have explained *middîn* as 'saddle-cloths' or 'housings,' thus making the clause a further description of the riders; but this is excluded by the fact that the verb *yāšabh*, 'sit,' is never used in Hebrew of riding an animal.

The Versions afford no help towards elucidation. 𝕲[BL] καθήμενοι ἐπὶ κριτηρίου (so 𝕾[h]), 𝖁 'et sedetis in judicio,' 𝕿 ומתחברין למתב על דינא, 'and are associated in order to preside over judgment,' read מָדוֹן, which may mean 'strife,' but scarcely 'judicial procedure.' 𝕲[A] represents מדין by λαμπήνων, 'covered chariots,' 𝕷 'in lecticis,' apparently a guess influenced by the context;* 𝕾[P] ܘܬܒ̈ܝ ܒܒ̈ܬܐ 'and ye who sit at home'—a guess.

The emendation offered above proceeds upon the assumption that the strophe *vv.*[12.9-11] contains an invitation to a *retrospect* of the past deliverance; as is evident from *vv.*[11.12]. If, then, the word שִׂיחוּ at the end of *v.*[10] means 'review' *sc.* the past deliverance, whether in thought or in speech (see *note* below); and having regard to the fact that so much of the remainder of the verse as can be translated contains reference to two classes of persons which, as we have noticed, appear to include the whole population; it is reasonable to assume that the complete verse was originally a *distich*, in which the two classes are mentioned in parallel stichoi, and summoned to take part in the retrospect. In other words, we may expect to find in the obscure ישבי על מדין a parallel to שיחו 'review.' The resemblance to the phrase יָשִׁבוּ עַל־לֵב, 'let them recall it to mind,' is obvious; the only real difference—that between לב and מדין—being accounted for by the fact that the resemblance between ב and ד is very close in the old character, and that between ל and מ not remote. לב read as מד may

* Or possibly reading צַבִּים; cf. Isa. 66[20], Num. 7[3] ἐν λαμπήναις is the 𝕲 rendering of this word in the Isa. passage.

have been taken for מד׳, an abbreviated form of the plural (cf. *foot-note* § below).

If we have in יִשְׁבוּ a jussive, 'let them recall,' etc., it is probable that in place of the imperative שִׂיחוּ we should likewise have a jussive form יָשִׂיחוּ 'let them review.' But if ישבו על לב belongs to stichos *a* and ישיחו to stichos *b*, the former contains five beats and the latter three beats. We may assume therefore that an erroneous transposition has taken place, the rectification of which gives us four beats in each stichos. That such errors of transposition have often occurred in copying MSS. cannot be doubted. The explanation is that a scribe erroneously copied the latter part of stichos *b* in place of the corresponding part of stichos *a*; and then, in order to avoid spoiling the appearance of his MS., transposed the omitted part of stichos *a* to stichos *b*. Such an erroneous transposition has clearly taken place in Ps. 35 [5.6], where *v.* [5a], 'Let them be as the chaff before the wind,' should be followed by *v.* [6b], 'And the Angel of Yahweh pursuing them'; and *v.* [6a], 'Let their way be dark and slippery,' by *v.* [5b], 'And the Angel of Yahweh pushing them down.'* Similarly, in *v.* [7] of the same Psalm, 'a pit' has been transposed from stichos *b*, where 'digged' now has no object, to stichos *a*, where 'they have hid' already has its proper object 'their net.' Cf. also the transposition which is rectified in Judg. 7 [6], with *note ad loc.*

tawny she-asses. A.V., R.V., 'white asses.' The adjective *ṣᵉḥôrôth* occurs only here in Heb., but comparison of the Ar. shows that it denotes light reddish-grey, or white flea-speckled with red (*ṣuḥra* the colour, *ṣaḥûr* a she-ass so coloured). ‡ Asses of this colour are rare and highly prized at the present day in the East; and their mention in this passage implies that their owners are persons of rank and means, travelling at their ease in a time of peace. The she-ass is preferred for riding purposes as more tractable than the entire male. §

* דחה always means to *push* or *thrust* for the purpose of casting down: cf. BDB. *s.v.* R.V.'s rendering, 'driving *them* on,' is intended to give a suitable meaning, as the half-verse now stands (clearly 'chaff before the wind' cannot be 'pushed down'); but is quite unwarranted by the usage of the verb elsewhere.

‡ Lette (quoted by Hollmann) cites Firuzabadius: صاحور ابل واتان فيها بيض وحمرة '*ṣaḥûr* is used of a camel or she-ass in which there is white and red.'

§ The reading of 𝔊ᴮ ἐπὶ ὄνου θηλείας μεσημβρίας is interesting as seeming to *prove* that אתנות צחרות must have stood in the Heb. MS. used by the translator in the *abbreviated form* אתנ׳ צחר׳, which was read as אתנ׳ צהר׳ and then interpreted as אָתֹן צָהֳרָיִם. Similar abbreviations of plural terminations are presupposed in *v.* [8aβ] (אזל׳ חמש׳), *v.* [10] (לב misread as מד, and then treated as shortened plur. מד׳), *v.* [11] (מצחק׳), *v.* [22b] (דהר׳ דהר׳). On the use of abbreviation in Heb. MSS., cf. Ginsburg, *Introd. to Mass.-Crit. Bible*, ch. v.

review it. The verb שִׂיחַ may mean *to talk* about anything or to any one, as in Ps. 69 [12] ([13] 𝔐), 'They that sit in the gate *talk* about me'; Job 12 [8], '*Speak* to the earth, and it shall instruct thee'; or *to muse* or *meditate* upon some topic, as in Ps. 77 [6] ([7] 𝔐), 'I will *muse* with my heart'; Ps. 119 [78], 'I will *muse* upon thy precepts'; *al.* Hence in our passage the verb may mean 'think about it' (𝔖[P] ܙܢܘ) or 'talk about it' (𝔊[B] διηγεῖσθε, [A] φθέγξασθαι, [L] ἐφθέγξασθε, 𝔙 'loquimini,' 𝔗 ומשתעין), and the rendering 'review it' is adopted as applicable either to thought or speech, and therefore equally ambiguous.

The Heb. leaves the *object* of the verb to be understood from the context, both here and in the corresponding expression in the parallel stichos; but English idiom obliges us to supply it as 'it.' Obviously it is the recent deliverance, which is defined in *v.*[11] under the term 'the righteous acts of Yahweh.' There is not the slightest ground for doubting the originality of the verb שיח, as has been done by some scholars.

recall it to mind. *Lit.* 'bring it back to (*or* upon) heart,' the *heart* being regarded by the Hebrews as the seat of the intellectual or reflective faculty. The same expression, with על 'upon,' as here, occurs in Isa. 46 [8]; but is more frequent with אל 'unto':* cf. Deut. 4 [39], 30 [1], 1 Kgs. 8 [47], Isa. 44 [19], Lam. 3 [21].

11. *Hark . . . wells!* Reading

קוֹל מְצַחֲקוֹת בֵּין מַשְׁאַבִּים

As 𝔐 stands, מִקּוֹל מְחַצְצִים can only be explained upon the most improbable assumptions. The difficulty is twofold. In the first place, it seems impossible to assign a satisfactory sense to מִן. The suggestions which have been put forward may be grouped as follows: מִן has been explained as denoting (1) *Separation*; 'Away from *or* Far from' (cf. for this usage, BDB. *s.v.* **1 b**); (2) *Substitution*; 'Instead of' (as though for מִהְיוֹת: this is an explanation which is of very doubtful justification, תַּחַת being commonly used in such a sense); (3) *Comparison*; 'More than' (BDB. **6**); (4) *Origin*; 'By reason of' (BDB. **2 e**); (5) *Partition*; 'Something of' (BDB. **3**).

Secondly, we have no clue to the meaning of מְחַצְצִים, which can only be conjectured.‡ The rendering of A.V., R.V., 'archers,' is that which is adopted by Kimchi and Levi ben-Gershon, and by Luther,

* The prepositions על and אל are frequently used interchangeably after a verb of motion. Cf. cases cited in *NHTK.* p. 10.

‡ Several of the modern explanations of the word were already debated by the mediæval Jewish commentators. Cf. Tanchum, as cited by Ges., *Thes.* p. 511.

Ges., Justi, Ke., Ber., Oet., Cooke, etc. It appears to go back to the interpretation of 𝔗, מְחַצְצֵי גִירִין, 'those who shoot arrows,' which, though occurring in *v.*[8] (or as a gloss to *v.*[8]; cf. note to Praetorius' edit.), is doubtless based upon our passage, and interprets מחצצים as a denominative from חֵץ 'arrow.' Adopting this explanation, the rendering least open to objection is that of R.V., 'Far from the noise of the archers.' Justi renders somewhat similarly, 'Instead of the noise of the archers'; and, in favour of this, Hollmann cites Gen. 49[22.23]—a passage which seems similarly to refer to the disturbance of pastoral peace by the attacks of hostile archers (there described as בַּעֲלֵי חִצִּים, lit. 'owners of arrows'). Hollmann rightly objects, however, to the use of מִן in place of תַּחַת.

Other interpretations of מחצצים base themselves upon the root-sense of the verb חצץ, which is that of *dividing*. Among these, the most widely adopted is 'those who divide the spoil' (Schnurrer, Köhler, Hollmann, Hilliger, Stu., von Gumpach, Bach., Bickell, Kent). All that can be said in favour of this interpretation has been said by Hollmann, who compares the Ar. verb *ḥaṣṣa*, which means in Conj. III., 'share a portion with some one else, give to some one else'; Conj. IV., 'give (to some one else) one's portion'; and the substantive *ḥiṣṣah*, 'portion.' As parallels for such a sense, Hollmann cites Isa. 9[3], 𝔐[2] ('as men exult when they divide spoil'; already cited by Ges.), Isa. 33[23.24], Ps. 68[12], 𝔐[13]; and giving מִן a comparative meaning, he renders 'prae jubilo sortientium . . . ibidem canant laudes Dei.' An obvious objection (noted by Meier) is that the crucial word שָׁלָל 'spoil' has to be supplied by conjecture, and that the ordinary term for 'dividing' spoil (occurring with object שָׁלָל in all the passages cited by Hollmann, and also in *v.*[30] of the Song) is חִלֵּק.

Some commentators, again (Menaḥem quoted by Rashi, Boettger, La.), have been attracted by the use of the verb in Prov. 30[27]—R.V. 'The locusts have no king, yet go they forth all of them *by bands*' (חֹצֵץ, lit. 'dividing [themselves] into companies or swarms,' BDB.). Thus מחצצים is thought to mean 'those who range themselves' in battle-array, or 'divide' the army into companies. Whatever sense, however, is attached to מִן in this connexion, it remains an enigma why these military operations should be carried out at the places of drawing water.

From this point of view, the explanation of Ros., 'those who divide (the flocks) at the watering places,' is more comprehensible. Vernes, who also adopts this explanation, paraphrases the verse, '"Chantez par-dessus la voix des distributeurs aux auges," c'est-à-dire : chantez de tous vos poumons, plus fort encore que ne crient ceux qui distribuent et font ranger les troupeaux près des auges où ils vont s'abreuver à la tombée du jour.' Having thus expressed his idea of the meaning of the passage, Vernes refers to the rivalry existing between shepherds in watering their flocks, which leads to frequent disputes. But such a comparison of the singing of the praise of Yahweh with the angry shouts of rival shepherds is altogether grotesque.

Herder thinks that מחצצים may have the sense, 'those who apportion,' *sc.* water to their flocks; and having rendered שיחו in the preceding verse 'denkt auf ein Lied,' he gives to מן a partitive sense, and makes the clause resumptive of שיחו:—'Ein Lied zum Gesange der Hirten die zwischen den Schöpfebrunnen Wasser den Heerden theilen aus.' A similar connexion with שיחו (already suggested by 𝔊^B διηγεῖσθε ἀπὸ φωνῆς κ.τ.λ., 𝔊^L ἐφθέγξασθε φωνήν κ.τ.λ., 𝔖^P, Ar. as noticed below) is sought by Meier, who quotes, as a parallel to such a partitive usage of מן, Ps. 137 [3], 'Sing us *one of the songs* (מִשִּׁיר) of Zion.'* Such an overrunning from the one distich to the other is, however, in the highest degree improbable: and, moreover, since the words, 'There they recount, etc.,' in stichos 2 cf *v.* [11] can only refer to what goes on at the places of drawing water, the gist of the passage (according to this interpretation) is that the classes of people mentioned in *v.* [10] are summoned to relate (שיחו) how another class of people are relating (יתנו), etc.—a very awkward and unpoetical conception.

Lastly, as probably based on the idea of *division* inherent in the verb חצץ, we may notice the rendering of 𝔊, ἀνακρουομένων, *i.e.*, apparently, 'singers' or 'players' (cf. the use of the verb elsewhere in 𝔊: 2 Sam. 6 [14.16], 1 Chr. 25 [3.5], Ezek. 23 [42])—an interpretation which suggests that חצץ may have had the sense of *marking the intervals* of the musical scale: cf. the use of the Lat. *dividere* by Horace, *Odes* I. xv. 15, 'Imbelli cithara carmina divides'; and the 'septem discrimina vocum' of Virgil, *Aen.* vi. 646, *i.e.* probably the seven notes of the scale. So also Shakespeare, *I. Henry the Fourth*, iii. 1:

'ditties highly penn'd,
Sung by a fair queen in a summer's bower,
With ravishing division, to her lute.'

Romeo and Juliet, iii. 5:

'Some say the lark makes sweet division;
This doth not so, for she divideth us.'

Ewald, who adopts the rendering 'singers' upon the authority of

* Meier does not, however, agree with Herder as to the meaning of מחצצים; but he revocalizes the form as מְחַצְּצִים (a supposed derivative of מחץ), and renders 'Feindezerschmettrer'!

𝔊, offers a very improbable explanation of the ground-sense of the verb, *those who keep time* or *order*, and hence *rhythm*; quoting in support of his view חֵצֶץ of Prov. 30[27], which has already been noticed above: cf. *HI.* ii. p. 355 *n*[1]; *DAB.* i. p. 180.

The other Versions were evidently very puzzled by the stichos. 𝔙's rendering, 'ubi collisi sunt currus, et hostium suffocatus est exercitus,' is obscure. 𝔖[P] (connecting with שיחו) renders ܪܢܘ ܥܠ ܡ̈ܠܐ ܕܒܨܘ̈ܝܐ ܕܒܝܢܝ ܡܠܦ̈ܢܐ 'Meditate upon the words of the researchers, who are among the learned'; and this appears in Ar. as 'Consider some of the words of those who investigate the books of the learned.' Here the idea of *dividing* which is proper to חצץ appears to be understood as referring to *investigation* (as in Heb. בִּקֵּר); and 'the places of drawing water' seem to be metaphorically explained as the founts of knowledge. The paraphrase of 𝔗 clearly understands the verse to mean that the scenes of former hostile outrages are now consecrated to the praises of Yahweh; but the rendering is too vague and diffuse to admit of detailed elucidation.*

This survey of the interpretation of the stichos may serve to show that every artifice has been employed by scholars, ancient and modern, to extract a suitable meaning from 𝔥, and that the best suggestions possess only the slightest of claims to serious consideration. It is probable, therefore, that the text has suffered corruption. The emendation offered above is based upon the acute suggestion of Bu. (adopted by Marquart) קוֹל מְצַחֲקִים 'Hark! the merry-makers.' Here the change in the verbal form is but slight; and the rejection before קול has the support of 𝔊[A] φθέγξασθε (𝔊[L] ἐφθέγξασθε) φωνήν, *i.e.* apparently שיחו קול. קול, properly 'a sound of . . . !' is then employed as in Gen. 4[10], Isa. 13[4], 40[3.6], 52[8]; Jer. 4[15], 10[22], 25[36], 50[28]; Cant. 2[8], 5[2]: cf. G-K. § 146 *b*.

The reason why we have adopted the fem. form מְצַחֲקוֹת, 'laughing maidens,' in preference to the masc., is because it appears more natural to find the *girls* of the village (*haš-šōᵓᵃbhôth*, 'the maidens who draw water'; cf. Gen. 24[11.13]) at the *mašᵓabbîm*, 'places of drawing water,' than representatives of the male portion of the community (unless it be supposed that the מצחקים are the shepherds,

* It has not been deemed necessary to discuss the Rabbinic interpretation of מחצצים advocated by Schultens (as quoted by Ros., etc.), which, regarding the word as a denominative from חֵץ, explains it as meaning 'those who cast lots with arrows'; nor the suggestion (also current in Rabbinic circles) which surmises a connexion with חָצָץ 'gravel,' in the sense 'gravel-treaders.'

watering their flocks). A fem. form is as likely as a masc., if it may be supposed that the plur. was written in abbreviated form מצחק׳ (cf. *footnote* §, p. 124); and the fact that the masc. plur. verbal form יתנו, 'they recount,' follows in the next clause, does not militate against such a supposition, since there are many cases in which the masc. form of the 3rd plur. Imperfect is employed in preference to the fem. with reference to a fem. subject preceding (cf. the cases collected in G-K. § 145 *u*). Other suggested emendations need not be noticed.

at the wells. Lit. 'between *or* among the places of drawing water.' The subs. *maš'abbîm* is a ἅπαξ λεγόμενον, but there is no ground for doubting its genuineness; since it is a regularly formed derivative from the verb *šā'abh*, 'draw water,' which is of frequent occurrence. For בֵּין, usually 'between,' in the more general sense 'among,' cf. Hos. 13 [16], Ezek. 19 [2], 31 [3], Cant. 2 [2.3].

they recount. The verb *tinnā*, which occurs again in a similar sense in *ch.* 11 [40] ('to *commemorate* the daughter of Jephthaḥ') is doubtless the same as the Syr. *tannī*, which corresponds to the Ar. *ṯanna*, 'celebrate'; the root-idea being 'do a second time.' The normal Heb. equivalent of the Syr. and Ar. should be *šinnā*; and a Heb. *šānā* (the Ḳal or simple stem-form) does occur several times in the sense 'repeat,' as the regular equivalent of the Ar. and Aram. verb. The form *tinnā* must therefore be regarded as a pronounced Aramäism; but is not on that account necessarily to be condemned, since it is reasonable to suppose that the North Israelite dialect was to some extent tinged by Aramaic influence. Cf. further *Additional note*, p. 171.

𝔊 δώσουσιν, 𝔏 'dabunt,' 𝔖[P] ܢܬܠܘܢ, vocalize the form as יִתְּנוּ, which is adopted by Marquart; but this is very improbable. 𝔙, 'ibi narrentur justitiae Domini,' takes the form as a passive, and makes צדקות י׳ the subject. 𝔗, יודון על זכותא דיי, supports 𝔐.

the righteous acts of Yahweh. The acts by which Yahweh manifests His covenant-faithfulness—in this case by vindicating His people against the national foe. The meaning of the expression is best illustrated by its occurrence in 1 Sam. 12 [7], with the description of Yahweh's dealings with Israel which follows, in substance corresponding with the pragmatism of R^{E2}. Cf. also the use of the same phrase in Mic. 6 [5].

his arm. Reading זְרֹעוֹ as suggested privately by Ball, in place of 𝔐 פִּרְזוֹנוֹ, the difficulties of which have already been noticed under *v.* [7] *note* on 'Villages.' The phrase *the arm of Yahweh*, as descriptive of His might exhibited in the deliverance of His people, is familiar in the O.T. Cf. Ex. 15 [16], 'By the greatness of thine arm they [Israel's foes] are as still as a stone'; the characteristic phrase of Deut., 'with a mighty hand and with a stretched out arm'; Isa. 51 [9], 'Awake, awake, put on strength, O arm of Yahweh'; *al.*

At the end of the verse 𝔊 adds an additional stichos, אָז יָרְדוּ לַשְּׁעָרִים עַם־יְהוָה 'Then down to the gates gat the people of Yahweh.' This clearly belongs to the description of the tribal muster, which commences with *v.* [13]; and the similarity of the stichos to stichos *a* of that verse, which, as it stands, is obviously somewhat corrupt, proves it to be a marginal variation which has been subsequently copied into the text. We observe similar variants of a single stichos in *vv.* [15b.16b].

12. For the notes on this verse, cf. pp. 120 f.

13. *Then down . . . heroes.* Reading

אָז יָרְדוּ לַשְּׁעָרִים אַדִּירִים
עַם־יְהוָה יָרַד־לוֹ בַּגִּבּוֹרִים

It is not clear what 𝔐 intends by the vocalization of the twice repeated יְרַד. Jewish interpreters explain the form as apocopated Imperfect Pi'el of רָדָה 'to have dominion' (from full form יְרַדֶּה), the Pi'el, which does not occur elsewhere in Heb., being employed causatively, 'cause to have dominion.'* That this was intended by 𝔐 seems very probable, since we may thus explain the awkward and ungrammatical connexion of עם with אדירים, as due to the necessity of making יהוה the subject of the verb in stichos *b*, just as He must have been assumed to be in stichos *a* :—

'Then may He cause a remnant to have dominion over the nobles—the people ;
'May Yahweh cause me to have dominion over the heroes.'

Or possibly it may have been supposed that the apocopated form has the sense of a full Imperfect : 'Then He shall cause, etc.'

The awkwardness and improbability of this need not be laboured. It may suffice to remark that, since *vv.* [14.15] describe the advance of the tribes in ordinary narrative-form, employing Perfect tenses, we naturally expect to find the same method adopted in the present passage. This is a consideration which sufficiently refutes the alternative explanation of יְרַד as Imperative Ḳal of יָרַד 'go down'

* We should expect יַרְדְּ (apocopated Imperf. Hiph'îl) in such a sense (cf. Isa. 41 [2])—a form which is here adopted by von Gumpach.

(in place of the normal Imperative רֵד), as adopted, *e.g.* by Hollmann, who regards the verse as the words of Deborah prior to the battle :—'Tunc ego : "Descendite residui nobilium populi, Jehova descende mihi cum heroibus."' A further difficulty is found in the use of the word שָׂרִיד 'remnant,' a term ordinarily applied to a survivor (or survivors) after a defeat in battle ; but here, it must be supposed, employed to denote Israel's exiguous forces, implicitly contrasted with what they might have been but for the long-continued aggressions of the Cana'anites.

It need not be doubted that the true text of the verse is indicated by *v.*^{11c}, which we have already noted as a marginal variation to *v.*^{13}. This variation appears, in fact, to represent the combination of two originally separate marginal notes ; *viz.* אָז יָרְדוּ לַשְּׁעָרִים as a variant of אָז יְרַד שָׂרִיד, and עַם יהוה 'the people of Yahweh,' a variant of the separated עָם יהוה which is found in 20 MSS. of 𝔐. 𝔊^{B}, though agreeing with 𝔐 in reading שָׂרִיד, supports the vocalization of ירד as a Perfect, and the view that עם goes with יהוה and forms the subject of stichos *b* ; and further reads לוֹ (*i.e.* the 'ethical' dative, referring to the subject of the verb—cf. BDB. *s.* לְ. **5h**—rather than 'for Him,' *i.e.* Yahweh) in place of לִי in stichos *b*—a correction which is obviously to be adopted :—

τότε κατέβη κατάλημμα τοῖς ἰσχυροῖς·
λαὸς Κυρίου κατέβη αὐτῷ ἐν τοῖς κραταιοῖς.

The restoration of the verse as given above is, as regards stichos *b*, generally adopted by moderns, and is scarcely open to doubt. Stichos *a* may perhaps be held to be open to criticism as regards the sense which it yields. Since the verb יָרְדוּ 'went down,' as employed in *v.*^{14}, refers to Israel's downward onset from mount Tabor (cf. *ch.* 4^{14b}), the meaning must be the same in the present passage ; and 'to the gates' can therefore only refer to the gates of the foe—it was down to the very gates of such Cana'anite cities as Ta'anach and Megiddo (cf. *v.*^{19}) that the Israelites advanced in their first spirited onslaught. If this interpretation be held to be improbable, it is difficult to see how the text can otherwise be explained.

Other conjectural emendations of stichos *a* have been made. Thus Mo. (followed by Bu., No., Gress.) thinks that שריד ל represents an original יִשְׂרָאֵל, and, supplying כ before אדירים, he obtains the sense, 'Then Israel went down like the noble.' Kit., in *BH.*, offers the suggestion אָז יְרַד שָׂרִיד לְרֹדֵיהֶם 'Then let a remnant dominate those who dominated them.'

14. *From Ephraim . . . vale.* Reading

מִנִּי אֶפְרַיִם מְשָׁכוּ בָעֵמֶק

𝔐, as it stands, is incredibly concise. The literal rendering is 'From Ephraim their root in 'Amaleḳ'; which is explained, by inferring the necessary verb from *v.* 13, 'From Ephraim *came down those* whose root *is* in 'Amaleḳ.' The explanation of 'their root in 'Amaleḳ' is also a grave stumbling-block. The Bedawi people called 'Amaleḳ in the O.T. appear elsewhere as inhabiting the desert-region south of the Negeb (cf. *note* on *ch.* 3 12); and it is to this region that Saul marches in order to carry out his commission to destroy 'Amaleḳ, as recorded in 1 Sam. 15. In the present passage we seem to be told that the 'root' of the tribe of Ephraim (or a portion of it), which inhabited central Palestine, was 'in 'Amaleḳ,' *i.e.* we must infer that they dwelt in the midst of the 'Amaleḳites. Yet elsewhere, in enumerations of the foreign races inhabiting Canaan, we find no allusion to the 'Amaleḳites; though, in view of the bitter hostility which existed between Israel and them (cf. Ex. 17 15.16 E; 1 Sam. 15 2.3), it is scarcely possible that they should have been unmentioned if they had inhabited Cana'an in any considerable numbers. It is true that they are pictured in *ch.* 6 3.33, 7 12 as invading the land together with the Midianites and 'children of the East'; but here they appear in their normal character as roving nomads, making periodical forays at the time when the Israelites' crops were ready for reaping, and bringing their camels and tents with them, as Bedawi tribes would naturally do. The only passage which can be adduced as possibly supporting the allusion to 'Amaleḳ in our passage, is the reference in *ch.* 12 15 to Pir'athon (probably the modern Far'atâ) as situated 'in the land of Ephraim, in the hill of the 'Amaleḳite.' How this locality obtained its name is unknown to us. It may have been so named as the scene of an encounter with Amaleḳite clans which had entered Cana'an upon such a foray as is described in the story of Gide'on. But even on the supposition that it was so named as the settled abode of 'Amaleḳites, the very nature of the reference compels us to regard it as a very limited district in comparison with the whole territory occupied by Ephraim; and though, upon this view, it might be possible to speak of 'Amaleḳ as having his root in Ephraim, the converse statement, as we find it in 𝔐, seems to be out of the question.

In face of this difficulty, we may obtain help from 𝔊AL, Θ., which, in place of שָׁרְשָׁם בַּעֲמָלֵק 'their root in 'Amaleḳ,' read ἐτιμωρήσατο (𝔊L ἐτιμωρήσαντο) αὐτοὺς ἐν κοιλάδι, *i.e.* שֵׁרְשָׁם בָּעֵמֶק, ἐτιμωρήσατο *αὐτούς* being doubtless a somewhat free rendering of the verbal form 'rooted them out,' * which is rendered more literally by 𝔊^B *ἐξερίζωσεν αὐτούς*. Here בָּעֵמֶק 'in the vale,' affords excellent sense (cf. *v.*[15]); and though we can scarcely accept שָׁרְשָׁם, it can hardly be doubted that the translator is right in assuming that a verbal form is here needed.‡ שרשם may easily have arisen as a corruption of מָשְׁכוּ 'they spread out *or* deployed,' the verb which is actually used of the skirmishing advance of the Israelite tribes upon this occasion in *ch.* 4[6] (cf. *note*). Winckler (followed by Marquart, Bu., No., Kit., Zapletal) proposes שָׁרוּ 'they travelled *or* passed along,' from the root שׁוּר, which is well known in Assyr. as *šâru* and in Ar. as *sâra*, but only occurs once in Heb., viz. Isa. 57[9], and there very doubtfully.§ La.'s suggestion שָׁלִישִׁים 'captains'—'From Ephraim (there were) captains in the vale'—is opposed by the facts that it fails to supply the desiderated verb; and that שלישים, so far as can be judged by the occurrences of the term, appear to have been a class of officers *connected with chariots* (cf. *NHTK*. p. 139), of which the Israelites possessed none at this period.

'*After thee, Benjamin!*' The words אַחֲרֶיךָ בִנְיָמִין are viewed with suspicion by many recent commentators; but, as it seems, without just cause. They occur again in Hos. 5[8], where the prophet is describing the hasty preparations for battle, in face of the Assyrian invasion:—

'Blow the horn in Gibeʿah,
The trumpet in Ramah;
Raise the battle-cry, Beth-aven,
"After thee, Benjamin!"'

Here the sense which we attach to the verb הָרִיעוּ 'Raise the battle-cry,' is that which it possesses in Josh. 6[5.10.16.20], 1 Sam. 17[20.52], Isa. 42[13], 2 Chr. 13[15]; cf. Judg. 15[14]; and the natural inference is that the words 'After thee, Benjamin!' which immediately follow, represent the old Benjaminite battle-cry; both in Hoseaʿ, and also,

* It can scarcely represent שִׁכֵּלָם (*sic* for שִׁכְּלָם), as La. supposes.

‡ שרשם is similarly treated as a verbal form by 𝔙, 'delevit eos in Amalec'; and apparently by the paraphrase of 𝔗, 'From the house of Ephraim arose Joshuaʿ the son of Nun at the first—he made war with the house of ʿAmaleḳ; after him arose king Saul of the house of Benjamin—he destroyed the house of ʿAmaleḳ.'

§ Cheyne, Marti, Box emend וַתָּסֻכִי 'And *thou didst anoint thyself* to (the god) Melek with oil,' in place of וַתָּשֻׁרִי 'And thou didst journey.'

by inference, in the Song of Deborah. So G. A. Smith, *The Twelve Prophets*, on Hos. 5 [8]. If this be so, the meaning may be, 'Benjamin (the tribe) takes the lead; let others follow!' or, 'After thee, Benjamin (the eponymous ancestor), we (the tribesmen) follow!' For אַחֲרֵי 'after' used of following a leader in battle, cf. *ch.* 4 [14], 1 Sam. 11 [7]. As the battle-cry stands in the Song, the precise sense may be '(The cry) "After thee, Benjamin!" (was) among thy clansmen'; or, 'Those from Ephraim spread themselves in the vale "after thee, Benjamin,"' *i.e.* the Benjaminites headed the Ephraimites, as their war-cry would have them do.

Many scholars (Hollmann, Köhler, Justi, Ros., Stu., Kit., Ber.) explain אחריך ב׳ 'After thee (Ephraim) *came* Benjamin'; but, apart from the improbability that the same expression should occur here and in Hosea in different senses, it is unlikely that the poet should address the tribe mentioned in the previous stichos (and there alluded to in the 3rd pers.), and not the tribe with which the present stichos deals.

In place of אַחֲרֶיךָ, 𝔊^AL al. offer the reading ἀδελφοῦ σου (connected with κοιλάδι in the preceding line), *i.e.* אָחִיךָ '*Thy brother*, Benjamin, among thy (Ephraim's) clansmen.' This is adopted by Bu., No., La., Kent, Cooke (*Comm.*), but is in no way preferable to 𝔐.*

thy clansmen. עֲמָמֶיךָ. The plur. form regularly denotes 'kinsmen'; as *e.g.* in the phrase 'he was gathered to his kinsmen' (עַמָּיו), Gen. 25 [8], *al.* Upon the view that עֲמָמֶיךָ (for עַמֶּיךָ) is a mark of Aram. influence, cf. *Additional note*, pp. 171 ff.

Machir. Mentioned in Josh. 17 [1b.2] R^P as the first-born son of Manasseh, and in Num. 26 [29] P as the only son—a description which implies that Machir was the predominant clan of the tribe of Manasseh. Both passages associate Machir with the land of Gileʿad east of Jordan; in Josh. he is 'the father of Gileʿad' (הַגִּלְעָד *i.e.* clearly *the district*, and not a person), and is termed 'a man of war,' possessing 'the Gileʿad and the Bashan'; in Num. the fact that Machir inhabited this region is expressed by the statement that he 'begat Gileʿad.' In the same passage of Num. (*vv.* [30 ff.]) six grandsons (sons of Gileʿad) are assigned to Machir, of whom at any rate Shechem ‡ and Îʿezer, *i.e.* Abiʿezer (cf. Josh. 17 [2] R^P) pertained to the territory of the *western* division of Manasseh. In Josh. 17 [1b.2] we find that the

* Bu. supposes that אחיך came to be altered into אחריך owing to the influence of Hos. 5 [8]. Winckler and Marquart reject אחריך ב׳ altogether (as a gloss from Hos.), much to the detriment of the poetry.

‡ Vocalized שֶׁכֶם, whereas the city is always שְׁכֶם; but the identity of the two cannot be doubted.

six *grandsons* of Machir, according to P in Num., are set down as his younger *brothers*.

Supposing that this late evidence were all the information which we possessed with regard to Machir, we should naturally infer that this predominant section of Manasseh settled first in Gileʿad, and that it was only subsequently that some of its clans made their way into central Canaʿan west of Jordan. If, however, the reconstruction of the original J narrative of the tribal settlement in Canaʿan, which we have adopted from Bu., is substantially correct, and Num. 32 [39.41.42] forms the sequel of Josh. 17 [16ff.], which certainly belongs to this narrative; then Manasseh first of all effected a settlement in the hill-country *west* of Jordan, and it was only subsequently to this that the clan of Machir, together with Ja'ir and Nobaḥ, finding their west Jordanic territory too exiguous, pushed their way to the east of Jordan and made settlements there (cf. *Additional note*, pp. 49 ff.).

In our passage in the Song, it can hardly be doubted that Machir refers to *west* Manasseh. If this is not the case, there is no other allusion to this part of Manasseh; and supposing that a tribe so intimately associated with the scene of battle had refused its aid, it would certainly have been bitterly censured in the Song. On the other hand, Gileʿad east of Jordan *is* mentioned, independently of Machir, and is censured for holding aloof (*v.* [17]); the reference probably being to the tribe of Gad, which inhabited the southern portion of Gileʿad. We seem therefore to have choice of two hypotheses: either the term 'Machir' is used in the Song, by poetic licence, of Manasseh as a whole, and here refers to west Manasseh to the exclusion of Machir in Gileʿad; *or*, the Manassite settlements at this period were *west of Jordan only*; and the migration of Manassite clans (Machir, Ja'ir, Nobaḥ) to the east of Jordan, which the J document already referred to supposes to have been carried out under the direction of Joshuaʿ, really only took place *later than the victory of Deborah*. This latter hypothesis seems to be preferable; since we have already noticed (p. 45) that the J document, as we know it, adopts the view that the whole tribal settlement of the Israelites took place under the direction of Joshuaʿ.

Ultimately Machir was closely, and probably exclusively, associated with the east of Jordan. According to the genealogy of 1 Chr. 7 [14-16],* Machir is the son of Manasseh by an Aramaean concubine; and Machir's son Gileʿad takes a wife named Maʿacah, *i.e.* the Aramaean clan of the Maʿacathites, which, together with the Geshurites, the children of Israel were unable to expel from Gileʿad (Josh. 13 [13] J). This means, without a doubt, that ultimately the Machir-section of Manasseh became closely fused by intermarriage with the Aramaeans

* The text of this passage, as it stands in 𝔐, is somewhat confused and corrupt; but the solution is fairly transparent: cf. Curtis, *ICC. ad. loc.*

who remained dwelling in the territory east of Jordan; cf. the way in which the genealogy of 1 Chr. 2 includes North Arabian clans, such as Jeraḥme'el, among the descendants of Judah.

the commanders. Heb. *mᵉḥôḳᵉḳîm*, as in *v.*[9] (*note*).

men wielding. The Heb. verb *mōšᵉkhîm* is here satisfactorily explained from Ar. *masaka*, 'to grasp and hold,' which is in like manner construed with the prep. ב, cf. Ges., *Thes. s.v.* 2. The explanation favoured by Mo., La., Smith, '*drawing* the truncheon' (cf. for constr. with ב, 1 Kgs. 22 [34], ואיש משך בקשת 'and a man drew a bow') is hardly so natural; and still less so the interpretation of Ges. (doubtfully), Cooke, No., Kit., '*marching along with* the truncheon,' in supposed accordance with the use of *māšak* noticed under *ch.* 4 [6].

the truncheon. Vocalizing בַּשֵּׁבֶט and omitting סֹפֵר. Heb. *šēbheṭ* here denotes the wand of office—a term which, in two other poetical passages (Gen. 49 [10], Num. 21 [18]), has for its parallel *mᵉḥôḳēḳ* (the word which, in the plur., is rendered 'commanders' in the parallel stichos), in the sense *commander's staff.*

After *šēbheṭ* 𝔐 adds *sōphēr*—'the truncheon *of the muster-master*' (lit. *enumerator*)—an addition which is correct as regards sense, but spoils the rhythm by the introduction of one beat too many; and must therefore be regarded as a gloss.

15. *And thy princes, Issachar.* Reading וְשָׂרַיִךְ יש׳: cf. 𝔏 'Principales tui, Issachar.' Such a direct address to the tribe imparts vigour and life to the description of the muster; cf. *vv.* [14aβ. 16a]. 𝔐 וְשָׂרַי בְּיִשׂ׳ 'And my princes in Issachar,' is an awkward expression, and can scarcely be original. The force of '*my* princes' is obscure; since it is unlikely that the poet, who elsewhere sinks his individuality, intends thus to identify himself specially with the tribe of Issachar. Ew., Ros., in defence of 𝔐, treat Deborah as speaking; but in this case the words 'with Deborah' which follow are superfluous; since it is impossible that the prophetess should, in one breath, allude to herself both in the first and third persons. Ges. and Hollmann follow Kimchi in taking שָׂרַי as a poetical plur. form for the ordinary שָׂרִים; but the existence of such forms is more than doubtful, the cases cited being otherwise explicable (cf. G-K. § 87 *g*). 𝔊[B], καὶ ἀρχηγοὶ ἐν Ισσαχαρ, seems to presuppose the vocalization וְשָׂרֵי בְיִשׂ׳, a variant which is found in some Heb. MSS. *teste* Ginsburg. Such a use of the Construct State before the prep. ב may be illustrated by הָרֵי בַגִּלְבֹּעַ 'Ye mountains in Gilboa',' 2 Sam. 1 [21]; שִׂמְחַת בַּקָּצִיר 'joy in harvest,' Isa. 9 [2]: cf. G-K. § 130 *a*. This reading, which is favoured by Rabbi Tanchum, has been adopted by the majority of

moderns (Schnurrer, Justi, Stu., Ber., Müller, Cooke, Oet., No., La., Kit., etc.).

𝔙 'duces Issachar,' 𝔖ᴾ ܘܣܝܥܬܐ ܕܝܫܫܟܪ, 𝔗 ורברבי יששכר seem to have read 'וְשָׂרֵי יש simply, and this is adopted by Michaelis and Mo.; but it is hardly likely that so simple and obvious a reading should, if genuine, have suffered the alteration which we find in 𝔐. Bu. connects 'ושרי ביש with ספר from the preceding stichos; and thus obtains the reading 'סִפְרוּ שָׂרֵי בְיִשׂ, 'Count the princes of Issachar' (*sc.* if you can !). This emendation (followed by Marquart) of course necessitates the taking of the words עם דברה into the next stichos (see *note* following). Such an emphasis upon the innumerable princes or leaders of Issachar (not to speak of their followers) is scarcely, however, in accord with the poet's moderate assessment of the whole fighting force of Israel in *v.*[8]. Winckler's emendation of ושרי into וְשָׂרוּ 'and they journey' is altogether improbable; cf. *note* on the supposed occurrence of this verb in *v.*[14], 'From Ephraim . . . vale.'

with Deborah. Bu. reads עַם in place of עִם of 𝔐—'the people (*i.e.* clansmen) of Deborah,' comparing the use of עַם in *v.*[18a] So Marquart.

and Naphtali was leal to Barak. Reading וְנַפְתָּלִי כֵּן לְבָרָק. Naphtali is here conjecturally restored in place of Issachar. That Naphtali, 'le nom le plus essentiel de cette histoire' (Reuss: cf. *v.*[18]), should be altogether unmentioned in the strophe which describes the heroic response of the patriotic tribes, appears highly improbable; and it is equally unlikely that the poet should have been guilty of the prosaic inelegancy which is occasioned by the repeated mention of Issachar in the parallel stichoi. If the statement of the prose-narrative that Baraḳ belonged to Ḳedesh of Naphtali is part of the original story, and not due merely to the combination of the Jabin-tradition (cf. p. 82), the mention of Naphtali in connexion with Baraḳ is what we should expect. The substitution of Naphtali for Issachar is also favoured by Stu., A. Müller, Mo. (*SBOT*), D. H. Müller, No., Driver, Kent, Cooke (*Comm.*), Gress.

כֵּן in the sense 'steadfast,' and so 'reliable' or 'honest,' is found several times in Heb.: cf. especially Gen. 42 [11.19.31.33.34], where Joseph's brethren say כֵּנִים אֲנַחְנוּ 'we be *honest*'; Prov. 15 [7], 'The heart of a fool is *not reliable*' (לֹא־כֵן: || 'The lips of the wise disperse knowledge'); and the expression דְּבָרִים אֲשֶׁר לֹא־כֵן 'things which were *not right*,' 2 Kgs. 17 [9]. The adj. *kênu* is also very frequent in Assyr. in the sense 'reliable' or 'faithful,' and in Syr. *kîn* has the meaning 'steadfast,' 'just.' On this interpretation of כֵּן we obtain, with no more serious alteration of the text than the addition of ל before ברק, the sense 'leal to Baraḳ' as an excellent parallel to 'with Deborah' in stichos *a*.

The view that כֵּן is the substantive which elsewhere in the O.T. has the meaning 'base' or 'pedestal,' here used metaphorically in the sense 'support' or 'reliance,' is as old as the Jewish commentators *; and has been adopted by many of the earlier modern commentators (Köhler, Herder, Hollmann, Justi, Stu., etc.). Schnurrer likewise regards כֵּן as a substantive; but connects it with the Ar. verb *kanna*, 'to cover *or* protect' (cf. Heb. *gānan*), and so explains in the sense 'bodyguard' or 'escort.' This root, however, is not otherwise known in Heb. (Ps. 80^{16} is scarcely an instance).

The explanation of כֵּן as the adverb 'so' or 'thus' appears to be impossible, as 𝔐 now stands. R.V. renders 'As was Issachar, so was Baraḳ'; but this meaning cannot be extracted from the Heb. without the addition of כְּ before יששכר; and even so it is, as Mo. remarks, 'difficult to imagine a worse anticlimax.' Scarcely less feeble is the sense which is gained by No. through the insertion of עִם before ברק: 'and Naphtali was similarly with Baraḳ.' $\mathfrak{G}^{B}$ omits ויששכר; and connecting כן ברק with the following stichos, offers the rendering οὕτως Βαρακ ἐν κοιλάσιν ἀπέστειλεν ἐν ποσὶν αὐτοῦ. Following this suggestion, von Gumpach, Grä., Grimme combine the stichoi and read כֵּן בָּרָק בְּעֵמֶק שֻׁלַּח בְּרַגְלָיו. Since, however, it is difficult to believe that ברגליו has here any other meaning than 'at his heel' (cf. 4^{10} *note*), we may in this consideration find evidence for the view that the expression refers back to the mention of Baraḳ in the *preceding* stichos, as in 𝔐.

$\mathfrak{G}^{L}$, $\mathfrak{S}^{h}$, omitting all traces of stichos *b*, represent stichos *c* by ἐξαπέστειλε πεζοὺς αὐτοῦ εἰς τὴν κοιλάδα, *i.e.* בָּעֵמֶק שִׁלַּח רַגְלָיו. On the supposition that this is original, the active verb and the suffix of the object demand a subject, which might be found in כֵּן בָּרָק of 𝔐 (so La., but reading וּבָרָק). Or it is conceivable that the letters כנברק might conceal an original וְנַפְתָּלִי; and stichos *b* would then run, 'And Naphtali despatched his footmen to the vale.' Such a

* Cf. the statement of R. Tanchum (*apud* Schnurrer); 'Some think that כן signifies those upon whom Baraḳ *relied*, and whom he had as his followers; from that meaning of the word כן which is found in Ex. 30^{18} 'כִּיּוֹר וְכַנּוֹ' ['a laver and its base'].

stichos, however, does not offer so good a parallel to stichos *a* as that which we have adopted with but little alteration of 𝔐; and we may reasonably doubt a reconstruction which involves the annihilation of the single stichos at the close of the strophe which appears elsewhere to be characteristic of the poem (cf. p. 102).

he was loosed. The subject of the verb is the tribe mentioned in the preceding stichos, which we have assumed to be Naphtali, Baraḳ's own contingent. The verb שִׁלַּח (used similarly in the active, of releasing a bird, Gen. 8 7.8, Deut. 22 7, or beast, Ex. 22 4, Lev. 16 22; or pent up waters, Job 12 15) vividly describes the sudden onrush of the tribe at the moment when Baraḳ's word of command unleashed it, as it were, from restraint.

at his heel. Lit. 'at his feet': cf. 4 10 *note.*

Utterly reft into factions, etc. Reading

נִפְרֹד נִפְרַד לִפְלַגּוֹת רְאוּבֵן
גְּדוֹלִים חִקְרֵי לֵב

𝔐 offers an isolated four-beat stichos, which may be rendered 'In the clans (*or* districts) of Re'uben great were the resolves of heart.' As this stands, Heb. *pᵉlaggôth*, lit. 'sections,' may be compared with the use of *pᵉluggôth* in 2 Chr. 35 5 of the 'divisions' of the priestly families for the purpose of Temple-service. So 𝔗 renders בזרעית 'in the family.' The cognate Bab. *pulug[g]u* and *pulukku* denote a 'division' or 'district' of a country; Phoenician פלג *id.* This seems to be the meaning intended by 𝔊B in *v.* 15 εἰς τὰς μερίδας (*v.* 16 εἰς διαιρέσεις, 'A. *id.*, 𝔊L *v.* 15 ἐν ταῖς διαιρέσεσιν are ambiguous), 𝔖P ܠܦܠܓܘܬܐ, Ar. الي قسمة. R.V.'s rendering of *pᵉlaggôth* by 'water-courses' depends on the use of the term in Job. 20 17, and the meaning of the cognate *pᵉlāghîm*, 'canals' (lit. 'cuttings'), which is found in Isa. 30 25, Ps. 1 3, *al.* This meaning, however, is not so likely in the present connexion as that given above. חִקְקֵי (which occurs again in this uncontracted form in Isa. 10 1; cf. עֲמָמֶיךָ for עַמֶּיךָ *v.* 14), from an assumed sing. חִק (Ar. *ḥikk*) = the normal חֹק 'statute,' *i.e.* 'action prescribed,' must here be taken to mean *actions prescribed for oneself*, i.e. *resolves* (so BDB.). Such a usage of the term is, however, unparalleled elsewhere. The stichos recurs in *v.* 16c, where it is clearly a marginal note offering two variations, which has crept into the text. One of these variations is חִקְרֵי 'searchings' or 'questionings,' in place of חִקְקֵי; and this is probably correct, and has been adopted above. 'Searchings of heart' must be taken to mean, not (as we might use the phrase) anxious self-questionings, but the ascertaining of the views of others, or, as we should express it, *interchanges of opinion.* The trait of indecision and ineffectuality is noted as characteristic of Re'uben in Gen. 49 [4a]. The other variation לפלגות appears, as the text stands, to be less natural than בפלגות, though it is possible to explain ל in the sense 'at'; cf. לחוף ימים, 'at the shore of the seas,' in *v.* [17ba].

It may be regarded as certain that this single stichos cannot originally have stood by itself without a parallel, at the commencement of the strophe which deals with the tribes which failed to respond to the summons to arms: and if it was composed, as we now find it, as a four-beat stichos, we must suppose that a similar corresponding stichos, which originally preceded it, has wholly disappeared from the poem. The possibility that the stichos represents the remains of *two parallel stichoi* cannot, however, be overlooked: and since the characteristic rhythm of the other couplets of the strophe is clearly 4 + 3 beats, it may be inferred that this measure was also employed in the opening couplet. חקרי לב (or חקקי לב) forms a single beat; but, if we add a suffix to לב, we obtain two beats—*ḥiḳrê libbô*, lit. 'the searchings of his heart,' *i.e.* 'his searchings of heart.' Thus it is reasonable to suppose that גדולים חקרי לבו may represent the three-beat stichos *b*; and, if this is so, we have the last two beats of stichos *a* in לפלגות ראובן. Now, 'Great were his questionings of heart' suggests, as a parallel, *divisions* of counsel in regard to the summons to arms on the part of the clansmen of Re'uben; and this is just the sense which may properly be attached to לפלגות '*into divisions*,' *i.e.* into divergent opinions, or into parties giving opposed counsels, or, as we should say, *factions* (so 𝔙 renders 'diviso contra se Ruben'): cf. Syr. *pulâgâ* 'division,' which may mean *hesitation*, and also σχίσμα.

What is desiderated, therefore, to supply the first part of the stichos is some verb meaning *was divided* or *was rent asunder*; and this may very likely have been נִפְרַד, which may well have been emphasized by a preceding Infinitive Absolute נִפְרֹד. The emphatic נִפְרֹד נִפְרַד supplies a suitable parallel to גְּדוֹלִים in stichos *b*; both statements laying stress upon the *extent* of Re'uben's fruitless discussions and differences of opinion. The use of the prep. ל 'into' after a verb expressing *division* can be abundantly illustrated (cf. חָצָה ל 'divide into,' Gen. 32 [8]; נִתַּח ל 'cut up into,' Judg. 19 [29]; קָרַע ל 'rend into,' 2 Kgs. 2 [12]; הִכָּה ל 'smite into,' Isa. 11 [15]). לפלגות may therefore be regarded as the more original reading; and בפלגות may be thought to be a correction—as more naturally expressing the sense 'in' or 'among,' which seems to be required by 𝔐.

16. *the folds.* Heb. *mišpᵉtháyim.* The meaning assigned to the word is purely conjectural. It suits the context here (cf. the stichos following), and in the one other occurrence, Gen. 49^{14}, where the tribe of Issachar is compared to 'an ass of strength (lit. bone) lying down amid the *mišpᵉtháyim.* And he saw rest that it was good, and the land that it was pleasant, etc.' In Ps. 68^{14} (apparently based upon our passage) a cognate term is used:—'Will ye lie (*or* When ye lie) among the *šᵉphattáyim*?' Both forms are duals, and may refer to some kind of double pen, with an inner and outer enclosure: Roediger in Ges., *Thes.* 1471, compares *Gᵉdhērôtháyim*, used as a proper name in Josh. 15^{36}, and meaning 'two fences,' or 'double fence.' *Gᵉdhērôth* is a term employed of sheep-folds (cf. Num. $32^{16.36}$, 1 Sam. 24^{4}, *al.*) constructed for permanent use out of solid material (cf. Num. 32^{16}, 'We will *build* sheep-folds'); and it is possible, as Roediger suggests, that *mišpᵉtháyim* may have been the name applied to temporary folds made of hurdles. This explanation of the term, which is as old as David Kimchi, is adopted by the majority of moderns.

The rival interpretation is 'ash-heaps,' such as are found in close proximity to modern Palestinian villages. This is based on the fact that there is a subs. *'ašpōth*, meaning 'ash-heap,' or 'refuse-heap,' occurring in 1 Sam. 2^{8}, Ps. 113^{7}, Lam. 4^{5}, *al.*, which is supposed to be cognate. The advocates of this interpretation do not seem, however, to have explained the connexion of the village ash-heap with pastoral amenity and the tending of flocks; nor the use of the dual, which appears, upon this view, to be quite anomalous. Were there, regularly, *two* ash-heaps to each village or encampment?

The Versions were puzzled by *mišpᵉtháyim*, and seem to have guessed at its meaning. 𝔊^{B} τῆς διγομίας; 𝔊^{L} transliterates τῶν μοσφαθαιμ (^{A}μοσφαιθαμ); 'A. τῶν κλήρων (so 𝔊 in Gen. 49^{14}, Ps. 68^{14}; 𝔙 in the latter passage 'inter medios cleros'); Σ. τῶν μεταιχμίων; 𝔙 'inter duos terminos'; 𝔖^{P} ܒܝܬ ܫܒܝ̈ܠܐ 'between the footpaths' (so in Gen.); Ar. بين الطرق *id.*; 𝔗 בין תחומין 'between the boundaries' (similarly in Gen.).

the pastoral pipings. Heb. *šᵉrîḳôth 'ădhārîm*, lit. 'the hissings *or* whistlings of (*i.e.* for) the flocks.' In Latin *sibila*, 'hissings' or 'whistlings' is used similarly of *piping* to flocks upon a mouth-organ of reeds: so Ovid, *Met.* xiii. 784 *f.*:

> 'Sumptaque arundinibus compacta est fistula centum;
> Senserunt toti pastoria sibila montes.'

Cf. also 'sibila cannae,' Statius, *Thebais* vi. 338. The Latin term is also employed by Columella, *De Re Rust.*, ii. *cap.* 3, of *whistling* to oxen to induce them to drink more freely after work:—'Quem [cibum] cum absumpserint, ad aquam duci oportet, sibiloque allectari, quo libentius bibant.' Cf. the way in which whistling or music will cause cows which are difficult milkers to yield their milk more freely (a fact noted *e.g.* by Hardy, *Tess of the D'Urbervilles*, *ch.* 17).

These parallels suggest that Heb. *šᵉrîḳôth* here refers to playing to flocks upon a mouth-organ or pipe—probably the *'ûghābh*, which is explained by 𝔗 *'abbûbhā*, 𝔙 'organon,' as a reed-pipe—the purpose being to conduce, in one way or another, to their physical well-being by the *charm* of the shrill music (*'ûghābh* probably gains its name from its *sensuous* effect: cf. the meaning of the root in Heb. and Ar.). Thus the indolent Re'ubenite is pictured as charmed into inaction by the music of the shepherd's pipe.

The Heb. root does not occur elsewhere in connexion with flocks; but the verb *šāraḳ* is used in Isa. 5 [26], 7 [18], Zech. 10 [8], of the employment of hissing or whistling, as a *signal*. Hence some have thought that the reference in our passage is to whistling (*not* piping) in order to call the flocks together. But why should the sound of such shepherd's calls be represented as keeping Re'uben at home?

Heb. *šᵉrîḳôth* bears striking resemblance to the Greek σῦριγξ, which has been supposed by Lagarde and Lewy (cf. references in BDB.) to be derived from the same Semitic root *šrḳ*; but it is more likely that both words are independently onomatopoetic from the sound which they describe. Cf. the English word *shriek*.

17. *Gile'ad.* The reference appears to be to the tribe of Gad, and *not* to East Manasseh (cf. *note* on 'Machir,' *v.* [14]). The history of Jephthaḥ (10 [17]-12 [7]) shows us Gile'adites, who presumably were Gadites, inhabiting the southern portion of Gile'ad, in proximity to the land of 'Ammon. On the use of the term 'Gile'ad,' cf. *ch.* 10 [17] *note*. Gad is read in place of Gile'ad by 𝔖ᴾ, Arm., Goth., and a few codd. of 𝔊; while Ar. interprets Gile'ad as referring to Re'uben.

And Dan abideth by the ships. Omitting לָמָּה before the verb with two Heb. MSS., 𝔙, 𝔗, Ar., and with 𝔖ᴾ as it now stands.* 𝔐, which has the support of 𝔊, offers a fine and vigorous line with its rhetorical query, 'And Dan—wherefore abideth he by the ships?' But elsewhere throughout the strophe the scheme of rhythm in the couplets appears to be 4 + 3 beats; and, if we adopt the reading of 𝔐, we have here, exceptionally, a stichos *b* containing *four* beats instead of three, which is improbable.

* 𝔖ᴾ reads ܘܕܢ ܠܠܡܐܢܐ ܢܓܪ ܣܦܝ̈ܢܐ 'And Dan to the harbour draws ships'; but the resemblance of ܠܠܡܐܢܐ 'to the harbour' to ܠܡܢܐ 'wherefore?' suggests that this latter may have been the original reading, and that the alteration may have been induced by the context.

The reference to Dan in connexion with *ships* may be taken to indicate that clans of this tribe had already made their migration to the extreme north of Cana'an, as related in *ch.* 18, Josh. 19 [47] J; since, if the tribe was still dwelling only in the south, it is difficult to understand how they can have become seafarers (cf. *note* on *ch.* 1 [34]). Even the supposition that the Danites carried on trading by sea from their northern home (though supported, as Mo. notes, by the following couplet with regard to Asher) is not without its difficulties; since *ch.* 18 [7.28], informs us that Laish, which they conquered, was isolated, not merely from Aram on the east, but from Ṣidon on the west; though it is true that 18 [7] at the same time compares the habit of life of the people of Laish with that of the Ṣidonians. It is reasonable, however, to suppose that the Danites, living on friendly terms with the Phoenicians, may shortly after their settlement have entered into close relationship with them, and taken service on board their ships (so Stu.). It was probably the protection extended by the Phoenicians to the tribes of Asher and Dan (in return, we may infer, for service rendered) which made these tribes unconcerned to throw in their lot with the central Israelite tribes, and respond to the summons to battle. Bu., who formerly (*RS.* p. 16) proposed to emend אֳנִיּוֹת 'ships' into נְאוֹתָיו 'his pastures,' now (*Comm.*) adopts the view which we have advocated, and retains the reading of 𝔐.

Asher sat still, etc. Cf. *note* on *ch.* 1 [32], 'the Asherites dwelt, etc.'

his creeks. Heb. *miphrāṣāw*, which only occurs here in Heb., is elucidated by its philological connexion with Ar. *furḍah*, 'a gap *or* breach in the bank of a river, by which ships *or* boats ascend'; *firâḍ*, 'the mouth of a river' (Lane). The verb *faraḍa* means 'to make a notch *or* incision.' It is possible to explain the possessive suffix of *miphrāṣāw* as '*its* creeks,' referring to 'the shore of the seas' in the preceding stichos (so Mo.).

18. *that scorned its life, etc.* The expression is unique, and must be regarded with suspicion. The verb *ḥērēph* elsewhere properly denotes *verbal* taunting or reproach (cf. BDB.: properly, 'to say sharp things about'; connected with Aram. *ḥarrēph*, 'sharpen'); though it is true that there are passages in which it is used metaphorically *of insulting* God by injustice to the poor (Prov. 14 [31], 17 [5]), or idolatry (Isa. 65 [7]). This latter usage, however, hardly supports the conception implied in 'insulting' one's own life by exposing it to risk of death. The Ar. parallels cited by Ros. are not very apposite ('We *count* our lives *of light value* (*lanurḫiṣu*) in the day of battle,' *Ḥamasa*, p. 47, ed. Freytag; *tahâwana nafsahu*, 'he *held* his life *of light worth*'); since the expressions there used, so far from appearing forced and strange, are familiar all the world over.

Phrases used elsewhere in O.T. of risking one's life are 'he cast his life in front' (וַיַּשְׁלֵךְ אֶת־נַפְשׁוֹ מִנֶּגֶד) *ch.* 9 [17]; 'I placed my life in my hand' (וָאָשִׂימָה נַפְשִׁי בְכַפִּי) *ch.* 12[3], cf. 1 Sam. 19[5], 28[21]; 'he poured out his life unto death' (הֶעֱרָה לַמָּוֶת נַפְשׁוֹ) Isa. 53[12]. It is conceivable that this latter phrase (הֶעֱרָה נַפְשׁוֹ לָמוּת) may have been the original reading in our passage; cf. the use of the Piʿel of the same verb in Ps. 141[8], 'Pour not out my life' (אַל־תְּעַר נַפְשִׁי), *i.e.* 'Give me not over unto death.' So Ball, who, as an alternative, suggests the emendation הֶחֱרִים for חרף—'*devoted* his life to death' (on *heḥ*[e]*rîm* 'devote' to a deity, usually by destruction, cf. *note* on *ch.* 1[17])—a striking and vigorous expression which may very well have been employed, though no close parallel can be cited. Cf., however, the words of St. Paul in Rom. 9[3]: ηὐχόμην γὰρ ἀνάθεμα εἶναι αὐτὸς ἐγὼ ἀπὸ τοῦ Χριστοῦ ὑπὲρ τῶν ἀδελφῶν μου, κτλ. Ἀνάθεμα is the regular rendering of 𝔊 for Heb. *ḥērem* 'devoted thing,' and ἀναθεματίζειν for the verb *heḥ*[e]*rīm*.

to the death. Lit. '(so as) to die.'

on the heights of the field. Cf. *note* on 'the field of Edom,' *v.* [4]. The use of the expression here is somewhat enigmatical, in view of the fact that the scene of the battle was the low-lying plain of Esdraelon (called *ʿēmeḳ*, 'vale,' lit. 'depression,' in *vv.* [14.15]). It can hardly mean (Cooke, *Comm.*) that 'the two tribes came fearlessly down from their mountain-homes prepared to sacrifice all for the cause,' because it was not *on the heights* of their mountain-homes that they risked their lives. Mo. thinks that the phrase 'may perhaps be employed here of the mounds and hillocks in the plain, which, however inconsiderable, were positions of advantage in the battle, especially as rallying points for the hard pressed Canaʿanites before the rout became complete. These elevations, where the enemy fought with the ferocity of desperation, Zebulun and Naphtali with reckless hardihood stormed and carried.' It may be doubted whether any part of the plain itself would have been described as *sādhé* (*v.*[4] *note*): yet it is quite likely that the battle may have raged round about the cities of Taʿanach and Megiddo on the edge of the hill-country; or that many of the Canaʿanites, finding their escape to Ḥarosheth barred by the flooded Ḳishon (cf. *note* on 4 [16]), may have been driven into the hills of Galilee, which come down to the right bank of the river, and there made their last desperate stand.

19. *the kings of Canaʿan.* *I.e.* the petty chieftains of the fortified Canaʿanite cities such as Taʿanach and Megiddo, who appear as a rule to have been mutually independent (cf. the condition of affairs in earlier times as gathered from the T.A. Letters; *Introd.* pp. lxx ff.); but are here united for action under the leadership of Sīsera, who was, presumably, the king of Ḥarosheth. Cf. the alliance among the Amorite city-kings of the south against Joshuaʿ, as related in Josh. 10.

The use of the term 'king of Cana'an' as applied to Jabin in *ch.* 4^2 by R^{E2} is different; in that it pictures him as overlord of northern Cana'an as a whole—a conception which gains no support from the older narrative. Cf. *note ad loc.*

In Ta'anach, etc. On the sites of these cities cf. *ch.* 1^{27} *note.*

the rills of Megiddo. Lit. 'the waters of M.' The reference doubtless is to the numerous small tributaries of the Ḳishon which flow down from the hills to the south-east of Megiddo. The modern Ar. name for the Ḳishon is Nahr el-Muḳaṭṭa', *i.e.* 'River of the ford *or* shallow.' While there is no philological connexion between Megiddo and Muḳaṭṭa', we are probably right in inferring that the modern name was bestowed owing to its assonance with the old city-name of unknown meaning. So Smith, *HG.* p. 387, *n* [1]. A similar phenomenon is noted as regards the Heb. name Ḥarosheth compared with the modern Ar. el-Ḥâriṯiyyeh (*ch.* 4^2 *note*).

The gain of money they took not. Most commentators interpret this statement as meaning that they were baulked in their expectation of spoil. So Mo.: 'it was a most unprofitable campaign for them; a sarcastic meiosis. The gains of war were in the ancient world one of the principal causes of war; cf. Ex. 15^9.' This explanation is described by La., not unjustly, as 'pensée très banale et qui devance le cours des événements'; and it may be added that, if the reference is to hoped-for *spoil*, the description of this spoil as 'money' or 'silver' simply is not very natural: contrast *v.* [30]. La. himself adopts the explanation offered by Rashi and Levi ben-Gershon, that the kings did not fight for payment like mercenaries, but with the whole-heartedness of men who are protecting their own interests. This is more probably correct. A third explanation, which is not impossible, is given by Kimchi, viz. that they did not accept money as ransom from the Israelites who fell into their hands, but slew them without quarter—the statement thus emphasizing the fierceness of the combat. Cf. the way in which Trojan combatants, when vanquished, are pictured as offering the Greeks a price for the sparing of their lives. Thus, in *Iliad*, vi. 46 ff., Adrestus addresses Menelaus:—

ζώγρει, Ἀτρέος υἱέ, σὺ δ' ἄξια δέξαι ἄποινα.
πολλὰ δ' ἐν ἀφνειοῦ πατρὸς κειμήλια κεῖται,
χαλκός τε χρυσός τε πολύκμητός τε σίδηρος·
τῶν κέν τοι χαρίσαιτο πατὴρ ἀπερείσι' ἄποινα,
εἴ κεν ἐμὲ ζωὸν πεπύθοιτ' ἐπὶ νηυσὶν Ἀχαιῶν.

Il. x. 378 ff., xi. 131 ff. are similar.

Several commentators follow Tanchum in understanding *bėṣa'* in the sense 'fragment,' or, as we should say, 'bit' of money (cf. Ar. *baḍ'a*, Aram. *biṣṣuá*); primitive money taking the form of uncoined ingots, the value of which was tested by weight. Since, however, there is no parallel for such a meaning elsewhere in the Heb. of the O.T., in which *béṣaʿ* occurs with frequency in the sense 'gain made by violence, unjust gain, profit' (BDB.), it seems preferable to acquiesce in the ordinary meaning, which is quite suitable to the context.

20. *From heaven fought the stars, etc.* The bręak between the stichoi is obviously to be placed upon הכוכבים, which gives 3 + 3 beats to the distich; and not, as by 𝔐, on נלחמו (so R.V., 'They fought from heaven, The stars in their courses fought, etc.'); since this offends against rhythm by offering 2 + 4 beats.

From their highways. Winckler proposes to emend מִמְּסִלּוֹתָם into מִמַּזְּלוֹתָם 'from their stations.' The term proposed, *mazzālôth* (cf. 2 Kgs. 23^{5}), is elucidated from Bab., in which *manzazu* denotes a 'place of standing,' from *nazâzu* 'to stand'; and a fem. form *manzaltu* (= *manzaztu*) is found, *e.g.* in iii. R. 59, 35*a*: 'The gods in heaven in *their mansions* (*manzaltišunu*) set me.' These heavenly *mansions* or *stations* are identified by Delitzsch (*Prolegomena*, p. 54) with the zodiacal stations; while Jensen (*Kosmologie*, pp. 347 f.) thinks that they denoted rather the stations of certain fixed stars and planets, lists of which are found in the Bab. inscriptions. In Ar. *manzil* denotes a 'lodging place' or 'mansion'; and the plur. *al-manâzil* is used of the twenty-eight *mansions* of the moon. Thus the occurrence of מִמַּזְּלוֹתָם in our passage would be appropriate to the context; and it is possible that the reading of 𝔐 may represent the easy substitution of a common term for the more unusual word: but since מִמְּסִלּוֹתָם of 𝔐 yields a good sense, the alteration is unnecessary.

21. *The torrent Ḳishon, etc.* Cf. Thomson's description of the probable circumstances of the rout, as cited under *ch.* 4^{16}. A description of the Ḳishon is given under *ch.* 4^{7}.

swept them off. The Heb. verb *gāraph* does not occur elsewhere; but the meaning which it bears is elucidated by the usage of the Ar. verb *ǵarafa*. Thus Ar. says جَرَفَتْهُ السُّيُولُ 'the torrents *swept it away*'; جَرَفَ النَّاسَ كَجَرْفِ السَّيْلِ '*it swept away* men like *the sweeping away* of a torrent' (Lane). The sense attached to Aram. *gᵉraph* (here employed by $𝔖^{P}$) is similar. $𝔊^{B}$ ἐξέσυρεν αὐτούς, $𝔊^{AL}$ ἐξέβαλεν αὐτούς, 𝔙 'traxit cadavera eorum,' render with approximate accuracy. 𝔗, more freely, תברנון 'shattered them.'

It faced them, the torrent Ḳishon. Reading קִדְּמָם נַחַל קִישׁוֹן. As 𝔐 stands, נַחַל קְדוּמִים is a source of great difficulty. The root *ḳdm* in Semitic has the meaning 'to be in front *or* before.' Hence, in Heb., the subst. *ḳédhem* means, locatively, *what is in front* (opposed to *'āḥôr, that which is behind*), Ps. 139 ^{5}, Job 23 ^{8}; and, especially, the *East*, this being the region which (possibly as the direction from which the sun rises) was regarded as *in front* in reckoning the quarters of the compass *; *or*, temporally, *what is before*, *i.e.* 'ancient *or* former time' (Bab. *ḳudmu* is employed in both these senses). From *ḳédhem* comes the denominative verb *ḳiddēm*, which means *to be in front* and also *to confront* in a hostile sense (cf. the Ar. *'aḳdama*, 'cause to advance against the enemy').

The substantival form *ḳ^{e}dhûmîm* only occurs in our passage; and, in accordance with the sense of the root, the main explanations of *naḥal ḳ^{e}dhûmîm* are two: (1) '*torrent of antiquity*' (lit. *of ancient times*) is adopted by 𝔊^{B} χειμάρρους ἀρχαίων (perhaps 'men of old time'), 𝔗 ('the torrent at which signs and mighty acts were wrought for Israel from ancient times'), Kimchi ('the torrent that was there from ancient times'), R.V. ('that ancient river'), Michaelis, Justi, Boettger, Bach., Reuss, Oet., Vernes, etc.; (2) '*torrent of* (*hostile*) *encounters*,' suggested by Abulwalid, and adopted by Schnurrer, Köhler, Hollmann, Ros., von Gumpach, Donaldson, Ber., Kit., etc.

Why the Ḳishon, rather than any other stream, should be spoken of as an *ancient* torrent is not clear. The only obvious explanation is that in the mind of the poet it had a *long history* behind it; and this explanation is also demanded by the rival rendering 'torrent of encounters,' which would seem to imply that many historical battles had taken place in the neighbourhood of the Ḳishon. At the present day such a title as 'torrent of battles' would be appropriate to the Ḳishon; since we know that, as a matter of fact, the vale of Esdraelon is the historical battle-field of Palestine: cf. Smith, *HG.* pp. 391 ff. But the inference that the Hebrew poet knew of traditions of ancient battles in this locality, such as that of Ṭhutmosi III. against the prince of Ḳadesh and his allies (cf. *Introd.* p. lxvii), appears somewhat precarious.

Other explanations of *naḥal ḳ^{e}dhûmîm* have been offered. Thus Meier, Cooke, Grimme, Driver render '*the onrushing torrent*,' and, similarly, Smith, Segond, 'the torrent of spates.' It is doubtful, however, whether such a sense can be maintained. The verb *ḳadama* in Ar. may mean 'to advance,' and 'to be bold in attack'; but always with the implied idea of *going in front of* (leading), or *coming in front of* (meeting), *some one else*; and the transference of this idea to an onrushing stream is somewhat remote. Still less probable is the

* Similarly, *mē'āḥôr*, 'behind'='on the west,' Isa. 9 ^{12}, 𝔐 ^{11}; *yāmîn*, 'the right'='the south,' Ps. 89 ^{12}, 𝔐 ^{13}, *al.*

sense, '*winding* (*i.e. self-confronting*) *torrent*,' adopted by Herder. The fact (noted by Mo.) is, however, worthy of observation that in Ar. *ḳadûm* (identical with our form) means a man who is *first in attacking the foe*, and so, *brave*, *courageous*. Thus the Heb. phrase would mean '*the torrent of heroes*,' if, as might be the case, the word was employed in Heb. in the Ar. sense.*

The Versions not already noticed are not helpful: 𝔙 'Cadumim'; 𝔖[P] ܪܩܕܘܡܝܡ (with ܪ erroneously for ܕ), Ar. *id.*; 𝔊[A], Θ. *καδησειμ*; 𝔊[L] *καδημειμ*; 'A. *καυσώνων* (connecting with קָדִים 'east wind').

The emendation adopted above follows the private suggestion of Ball; and has been independently adopted, as regards קִדְּמָם, by Ehr.‡ It assumes that it is natural to find in the stichos a verbal parallel to נְרָפָם of stichos *a*; and that the first occurrence of נַחַל is an erroneous insertion, made to explain the *substantive* קְדוּמִים, when this latter had taken the place of the verbal form קִדְּמָם. The *form* of the distich, with its identical term and inverted order in the parallel stichoi, may be compared with *v.*[24].

It is true that the sense obtained through the emendation involves something of a hysteron-proteron; since, strictly speaking, the torrent 'came in front of' the Canaʿanites in their flight before it 'swept them away' in their attempt to cross it: yet we have no right to demand an accurately logical sequence from the poet; and it is legitimate to explain the second verb as to some extent explanatory of the first—the torrent swept them away *because* it confronted them in their flight.

The numerous other emendations which have been offered need not be noticed.

Bless thou, my soul, the might of Yahweh! Reading תְּבָרְכִי נַפְשִׁי עֹז יְהוָה. 𝔐 תִּדְרְכִי נַפְשִׁי עֹז is barely intelligible. The Imperfect תִּדְרְכִי has been taken as a pictorial description of past events (R.V. *marg.* 'thou hast trodden down'; properly, 'thou treadest down': cf. the use of the Imperf. in Ex. 15[5] תְּהֹמֹת יְכַסְיֻמוּ 'The deeps cover them'!—where the tense, in describing a past event, emphasizes 'the process introducing it and preliminary to its complete execution': Driver, *Tenses*, § 27*a*); or as a Jussive in place of the Imperative (so R.V. *text* 'March on'). עֹז is taken either as the direct

* On nouns of this form used in Heb. in an active sense, cf. G-K. § 84[a] *m*. It is worth while to remark that, in *miphrāṣ v.*[17], *gāraph v.*[21], we have instances of words of which the meaning would be obscure, were it not for the clear elucidation offered by Ar.

‡ So also (since the writing of the above *note*) Gressmann in *Die Anfänge Israels*, p. 186. Rothstein adopts the same verbal form in the plur.; but emends the remainder of the line beyond recognition—קִדְּמוּ מַיִם מַרְכְּבֹתָם 'The waters confronted their chariots.'

accusative (R.V. *marg.*), and explained as abstract 'strength' for concrete 'the strong' (so 𝔙 'Conculca anima mea robustos'); or as an adverbial accusative 'with strength' (R.V. *text*, 𝔗 בתקוף : cf. G-K. § 118*q*). Upon either interpretation we have, if not 'simple bathos' (Mo.), at any rate a very weak conclusion to the strophe; and, as Mo. rightly remarks, 'most inappropriate as the conclusion of *vv.*$^{20.21}$, which tell how heaven and earth conspired to destroy Sisera.' On the other hand, the sense offered by the stichos as restored above, viz. an ejaculation of thanksgiving to *Yahweh* as the controller of the powers of nature which assisted Israel, is very suitable to the context; and may be compared with Ex. 15^{6}, where, after allusion to the overwhelming of the Egyptian hosts by the Red Sea (as the Cana'anites were overwhelmed by the Ḳishon), the poet exclaims—

'Thy right hand, O Yahweh, is glorious in power;
Thy right hand, O Yahweh, dasheth in pieces the enemy.'

The use of the *Jussive* (תברכי) in place of the Imperative is scarcely to be termed 'rare' (Mo., referring to תדרכי): cf. *ch.* 7^{17a}, Hos. 14^{2}, 𝔐^{3} (תשא Juss. coupled with the Imperat. קח); Ps. 51$^{8.9}$, 𝔐$^{9.10}$ (Juss. three times, alongside of the Imperat. four times in the two following verses); Ps. 71^{2a} (Juss. twice; parallel to Imperat. twice in *v.*^{2b}); 71$^{20.21}$. It is possible, however, that the Imperative may have been originally written: cf. בָּרְכִי נַפְשִׁי in Ps. 103$^{1.2}$.

The corruption of תברכי into תדרכי is likely; ב and ד being very similar in the old character. עז יהוה may have been written עז י׳, and the י׳ subsequently omitted through accident. That יהוה was sometimes thus abbreviated into י׳ is proved by Jer. 6^{11}, where חמת יהוה of 𝔐 is read as חמתי by 𝔊; and by Judg. 19^{18}, where בית יהוה is clearly an error for ביתי. Cf. Driver, *NHTS.*^{2} p. lxix. *n*^{2}.

Mo.'s suggestion, combining part of the preceding stichos, נַחַל קְדוּמִים דָּרַךְ נַפְשֵׁי עֹז (similarly La.) is condemned, if by nothing else, by the monstrosity נַפְשֵׁי.* The emendation of Ruben (adopted by Cheyne, *JQR.* x. p. 566; *EB.* 2652) is an example of how not to use the Assyr. dictionary.

22. *loud beat.* Lit. 'hammered' (*sc.* the ground). Cf. the English expressions, 'the hammer of countless hoofs'; 'to hammer along the road,' used of pushing a horse to a fast pace on the hard road. R.V. and most moderns render 'did stamp.' The Versions treat הָלְמוּ either as passive (𝔊^{B} ἐνεποδίσθησαν, ^{AL} ἀπεκόπησαν, Θ. ἀνεκόπησαν, 𝔗 אשתלפא 'were drawn off,' *i.e.* possibly pulled *or* broken off) or

* The fem. subst. נפש occurs some forty-nine times in the O.T. in the plural with the fem. termination, and never with the masc. termination; the form נפשים in Ezek. 13^{20} being clearly an error for חפשים 'free.'

intransitive (𝔙 'ceciderunt,' 𝔖[P] ܢܦܠܘ, Ar. سقطوا—all meaning 'fell,' or, as we should say 'stumbled'; cf. the rendering of 𝔊[B]). Similarly, Kimchi explains that the form is 'a stative; as though he said, the horses' hoofs were battered (נהלמו) through excessive galloping in the battle.' The same view is taken by other Jewish interpreters, and is adopted by A.V., 'Then were the horsehoofs broken, etc.' Mo., who favours this interpretation, vocalizes the verb as a passive הֻלְּמוּ (Pu'al not elsewhere found). Against it, we may remark that horses' *hoofs* are not very likely to be injured by excessive galloping,* more especially on a plain which must have been largely in the condition of a swamp owing to the heavy rain-storm (cf. *ch.* 4[14] *note*); and further, if the poet meant that they were *broken* or *bruised*, he would scarcely have expressed this by stating that they were *hammered* through themselves striking the ground.

Probably a passive sense is given to הלמו by the Versions and early interpreters owing to the prep. מן 'from' or 'through' of the succeeding stichos as it stands in 𝔐, which seems to denote the *source* of the action denoted by הלמו. Cf., however, the *note* following.

Smith, who adopts the vocalization as a *passive* הֻלְּמוּ, renders as an *active* 'thudded'; but this term, which commonly denotes the dull, dead fall of a heavy body, is not very happy.

the horses. Reading plur. סוּסִים with Bu., Kit. *BH.*, Gress., by taking over the מ from the commencement of the following stichos. Cf. 𝔊[L], 𝔖[h].

off galloped, off galloped. Reading דָּהֲרוּ דָּהֲרוּ, as suggested by Kit., *BH.* Cf. 𝔊[B] σπουδῇ ἔσπευσαν. The verb דהר occurs again of a galloping horse in Nah. 3[2]. 𝔐 reads מִדַּהֲרוֹת דַּהֲרוֹת 'through the galloping, galloping' (Suspended Construct State: cf. Gen. 14[10]). It seems likely, however, that the מ belonging to סוסים at the end of the preceding stichos came erroneously to be prefixed to דהרו דהרו, and this was then treated as מדהרו' דהרו', *i.e.* as an abbreviated plur. substantive (on the use of such abbreviations, cf. *footnote* §, p. 124). Adopting our emendation, the couplet offers two stichoi *parallel in sense*, and it may be noticed that such parallelism (either synonymous or climactic: cf. *Additional note*, p. 169) is characteristic of the poem;

* The modern Syrian horse has particularly good legs and feet, and is usually shod with plates; but in ancient times horses appear to have gone unshod. Isa. 5[28] refers to the hardness of the hoofs of the Assyrian horses ('like flint'), as a proof of their power to resist wear and tear; but whether this implies that trouble was common with the feet of ordinary horses is doubtful.

whereas the synthetic form of parallelism, which is offered by 𝔐 in this distich, is comparatively rare (cf. *vv.*[8b.16a.19b]).

The repeated *daharû daharû* is intended to represent the three-fold beat of a horse's gallop; and does so most accurately with the main *ictus* on the third beat; as in the final movement of the overture to Rossini's *Guillaume Tell.* Virgil represents the gallop by the familiar dactylic line, *Aen.* viii. 596,

> 'Quadrupedante putrem sonitu quatit ungula campum';

and this dactylic rhythm is adopted by Charles Kingsley in *My Hunting Song*:

> 'Hark to them, ride to them, beauties! as on they go,
> Leaping and sweeping away in the vale below';

but the dactylic measure is not quite so true as the anapaestic. In Ps. 68[11] 𝔐[12] we find the measure ⏓⏓⏓ (⏑́); *yiddṓdhūn yiddṓdhūn*, 'Kings of hosts *are running*, *are running*,' which is again intended to represent the sound of a cavalcade galloping away in the distance. This reminds us of the rhythm of Browning's *How they brought the Good News from Ghent to Aix*:

> 'I sprang to the stirrup, and Joris, and he;
> I galloped, Dirck galloped, we galloped all three.'

his chargers. Heb. *'abbîrāw*, lit. 'his strong ones.' The term is used elsewhere of horses in Jer. 8[16], 47[3], 50[11]. Horses at this period were employed in chariots, and not (so far as we know) for riding purposes; but since the functions of chariotry in warfare were akin to those of cavalry in later times, the rendering 'chargers' may be held to be justified.

23. *Curse ye, curse ye Meroz!* Reading אוֹרוּ מֵרוֹז אָרוֹר, in place of 𝔐 אוֹרוּ מֵרוֹז אָמַר מַלְאַךְ יְהוָה '"Curse ye Meroz"! said the Angel of Yahweh,' which is plainly unrhythmical (five beats). Such an allusion to the Angel of Yahweh in this ancient poem is also somewhat unexpected (cf. *ch.* 2[1] *note, end*). Probably ארור became corrupted into אמר 'he said'; and the natural query 'Who said?' was answered by supplying a subject—'the Angel of Yahweh.'

Meroz is only mentioned here, and the site is unidentified. The modern Muraṣṣaṣ, four miles north of Bêsân, which is doubtfully advocated by Buhl (*Geogr.* p. 217) after Guérin, is not philologically connected with the Heb. name; and conjectures that Meroz is the corruption of some better known name (cf. the suggestions cited by Mo. *SBOT.*) are necessarily futile, since we have no guide as to the locality of the city. It is highly probable that the curse took practical effect, and the city with its inhabitants was destroyed by the Israelites, and never subsequently rebuilt. Cf. the fate of Penuel (*ch.* 8 [8.9.17]) and Jabesh of Gile'ad (*ch.* 21 [8-12]) in similar circumstances.

For they came not to the help of Yahweh. Possibly Meroz was situated somewhere upon the line of the enemy's flight; and, like Ṣuccoth and Penuel on the occasion of Gide'on's rout of the Midianites closed its gates when it might have aided by cutting off the fugitives, or by supplying the pursuers with much needed refreshment.

mid the heroes. Heb. *bag-gibbôrîm* as in *v.*[13]. So R.V. *marg.* 'among the mighty.' R.V. *text* 'against the mighty' is less probable.

24. *Most blessed of women be Ja'el.* 𝔐's addition of 'the wife of Ḥeber the Ḳenite,' which spoils the balance of the couplet, is a prosaic gloss derived from *ch.* 4 [17].

tent-dwelling women. Lit. 'women in the tent.' Cf. the phrase 'the tent-dwellers' applied to the Bedawin on the farther east of Jordan in *ch.* 8 [11]. Mo. compares the Ar. expression *'ahlu-lwabar*, 'the people of the hair-cloth tents.'

a lordly dish. Lit. 'a dish of (*i.e.* fit for) nobles.' Heb. *ṣêphel* occurs once again in *ch.* 6 [38] to denote the dish or basin into which Gid'eon wrung the dew from the fleece. The word is used in the cognate languages in a similar sense. Cheyne's emendation (*EB.* 2313) 'a bowl of *bronze*' (ארד deduced from Bab. *urudû*) is uncalled-for.

curds. Cf. *ch.* 4 [19] *note.*

26. *Her hand to the peg, etc.* Against the view that this description of Ṣîsera's death is essentially different from that of *ch.* 4 [21 ff.], cf. pp. 79 f. Cooke's contention (*Comm.*) that 'according to the parallelism of Hebrew poetry *her hand* and *her right hand* mean the same thing; and so should *nail* and *workmen's hammer*,' cannot be substantiated. Cf. Prov. 3 [16]:

'Length of days is in her right hand;
In her left hand are riches and honour.'

So also Cant. 2 [6], 8 [3]. The only difference in our passage is that the poet has chosen to use *yādhāh* 'her hand' instead of *s*^e^*mōlāh* 'her left hand.' 𝔊^BA^, 𝔏, 𝔙, Ar. explain correctly as 'her left hand.'

she stretched forth. Heb. תִּשְׁלַחְנָה, apparently a plur. form, but probably intended for a sing.*

* The view that in this and a few other cases we have the remains of an emphatic form of the Imperfect, akin to the Ar. *modus energicus* I, *yaḳtulanna*

the maul of the workmen. Heb. *halmûth ʿămēlîm.* The expression has caused difficulty. The term *halmûth*, from *hālam* 'to hammer,' should represent the implement described under the term *maḳḳébheth* in *ch.* 4[21], *i.e.* a hammer or heavy wooden mallet; but elsewhere in Heb. substantives ending in *-ûth* are secondary formations denoting abstract qualities*; cf. G-K. § 86 *k*. The real existence of a *concrete* derivative from *hālam* is, however, a reasonable assumption; and possibly the true form of the subst. should be *ḥalmath.* The Heb. verb *ʿāmal*, from which *ʿămēlîm* is derived, commonly means *to toil* (i.e. *to labour*, with the accessory idea of *weariness* or *painful endeavour*); and all its occurrences are, with possibly one exception (see below), very late. The subst. *ʿāmāl*, which occurs both in early and late literature, usually denotes, in its earlier occurrences, *trouble*; and the sense *toil* or *labour* is only found in the later literature, especially Ecclesiastes. The subst. *ʿāmēl* (of which our form is the plur.) means a *labourer* in Prov. 16[26], and is coupled with the cognate verb:—'The appetite of the labourer laboureth for him.' This passage occurs in the central section of Prov., which many scholars regard as pre-exilic; though a considerable body of opinion views the whole book as the product of post-exilic times. The word occurs twice in Job in the sense *sufferer*; and, in an adjectival sense, *toiling*, five times in Ecclesiastes†. Hence the occurrence of *ʿămēlîm* in our passage is commonly regarded with grave suspicion. Mo. remarks, 'עמלים does not mean *artisans* (smiths, carpenters), but men who are worn out, or wear themselves out, with toil and hardships; "hammer of hard-working (or weary) men" is a singular metonymy for a heavy hammer!'

Such a statement overlooks the fact that the cognate languages prove that the root can be used in the general sense of *work*, apart from the connotations noticed above. Thus Ar. *ʿamila* means 'to

for the ordinary *yaḳtulu*, is rejected by G-K. § 47 *k*; yet seems, at least in our passage, to be by no means improbable. Cf. the Phoenician form יעמסן, occurring in the inscription on the sarcophagus of Eshmunʿazar king of Ṣidon (*CIS.* I. i. no. 3, ll. 5 f.):—ואל יעמסן במשכב ז עלת משכב שני 'and let him not superimpose upon this resting-place the chamber of a second resting-place.' יעמסן, which recurs in ll. 7.21, may be compared with the Ar. *modus energicus* II. *yaḳtulan.* Cooke (*NSI.* pp. 34 f.) treats יעמסן as a suffix-form 'carry me'; an explanation which involves a highly forced and unnatural treatment of the context.

If תשלחנה be not an energetic form, the alternative is to vocalize it as a suffix-form תְּשַׁלְּחֶנָּה, and to treat יָדָהּ as an *accusativus pendens*:—'her hand, to the peg she stretched it forth.'

* The forms are mostly late. A complete list of them is given by König, *Lehrgebäude der hebräischen Sprache*, ii. 1, pp. 205 f.

work *or* make,' '*amal* 'work *or* occupation,' '*amil* 'artisan'; Aram. '*ămal* 'to labour'; Bab. *nîmelu** 'the produce of work,' *i.e.* 'gain *or* possession.' There is no difficulty, therefore, in supposing that '*ămēlîm* may denote 'workmen' generally, *without* the connotation of toil or weariness.

The meaning of the phrase is correctly elucidated by 𝔖[P] ܠܐܪܙܦܬܐ ܕܢܓܪ̈ܐ 'to the carpenter's mallet,' Ar. *id.*, 𝔗 לארזפתא דנפחין 'to the mallet of the smiths,' 𝔙 'ad fabrorum malleos' (treating הלמות as a plur.). 𝔊[B], 'A. εἰς σφῦραν κοπιώντων interpret עמלים in accordance with customary Heb. usage. 𝔊[AL] εἰς ἀποτομὰς κατακοπῶν ([L] κατακοπτῶν) misunderstands.

she smote. Lit. 'hammered.'

destroyed. Heb. *māḥᵃḳā*, which only occurs here in the O.T., is explained from New Heb. and Aram. 'wipe out *or* erase,' *Ar. maḥaḳa* 'utterly destroy, annihilate.'

pierced through. The Heb. verb *ḥālaph* commonly means to *pass on*, or *pass away*; but is here used transitively 'passed (i.e. *pierced*) through.' This usage is substantiated by Job 20 [24], 'The bow of bronze *pierces him through*' (*taḥlᵉphēhû*), where 'bow' is used metonymically for the arrow which is shot from it. Mo. explains 'demolishes,' lit. 'causes to pass away,' quoting Isa. 24 [5] חָלְפוּ חֹק in support of the causative usage. This, however, probably means 'they have *passed by* (*i.e.* overstepped) the ordinance' (cf. ‖ עָבְרוּ תוֹרוֹת 'they have transgressed the laws') and not 'they have abolished' it.

27. *'Twixt her feet, etc.* The passage is discussed on p. 80.

undone. Driver's rendering. Heb. *šādhûdh* means lit. 'treated with violence.'

28. *and exclaimed.* Heb. וַתְּיַבֵּב. The verb *yibbēbh*, which only occurs here in O.T., is explained from Aram., in which *yabbēbh* means 'blow the trumpet,' and also 'raise a shout'; being used in this latter sense by 𝔖[P] to translate Heb. הֵרִיעַ in *ch.* 7 [21], 1 Sam. 4 [5], 17 [20]; Ps. 47 [2], 66 [1], *al.* In New Heb. the verb means 'to lament' over a corpse. Thus 𝔙 renders 'et ululabat,' 𝔖[P] ܘܡܒܒܐ, Ar. جلبت. 𝔊[AL], however, renders καὶ κατεμάνθανεν, 𝔖[h] ܡܬܒܩܝܐ ܗܘܬ, 𝔗 ומדיקא

* With *nîmelu* with preformative *n* from √עמל, cf. *nîmeḳu* from √עמק, *nîmedu* from √עמד.

the maul of the workmen. Heb. *halmûth 'ămēlîm.* The expression has caused difficulty. The term *halmûth*, from *hālam* 'to hammer,' should represent the implement described under the term *makkébheth* in *ch.* 4[21], *i.e.* a hammer or heavy wooden mallet; but elsewhere in Heb. substantives ending in *-ûth* are secondary formations denoting abstract qualities*; cf. G-K. § 86 *k*. The real existence of a *concrete* derivative from *hālam* is, however, a reasonable assumption; and possibly the true form of the subst. should be *halmath.* The Heb. verb *'āmal*, from which *'ămēlîm* is derived, commonly means *to toil* (i.e. *to labour*, with the accessory idea of *weariness* or *painful endeavour*); and all its occurrences are, with possibly one exception (see below), very late. The subst. *'āmāl*, which occurs both in early and late literature, usually denotes, in its earlier occurrences, *trouble*; and the sense *toil* or *labour* is only found in the later literature, especially Ecclesiastes. The subst. *'āmēl* (of which our form is the plur.) means a *labourer* in Prov. 16[26], and is coupled with the cognate verb:—'The appetite of the labourer laboureth for him.' This passage occurs in the central section of Prov., which many scholars regard as pre-exilic; though a considerable body of opinion views the whole book as the product of post-exilic times. The word occurs twice in Job in the sense *sufferer*; and, in an adjectival sense, *toiling*, five times in Ecclesiastes†. Hence the occurrence of *'ămēlîm* in our passage is commonly regarded with grave suspicion. Mo. remarks, 'עמלים does not mean *artisans* (smiths, carpenters), but men who are worn out, or wear themselves out, with toil and hardships; "hammer of hard-working (or weary) men" is a singular metonymy for a heavy hammer!'

Such a statement overlooks the fact that the cognate languages prove that the root can be used in the general sense of *work*, apart from the connotations noticed above. Thus Ar. *'amila* means 'to

for the ordinary *yaktulu*, is rejected by G-K. § 47 *k*; yet seems, at least in our passage, to be by no means improbable. Cf. the Phoenician form יעמסן, occurring in the inscription on the sarcophagus of Eshmun'azar king of Ṣidon (*CIS.* I. i. no. 3, ll. 5 f.):—ואל יעמסן במשכב ז עלת משכב שני 'and let him not superimpose upon this resting-place the chamber of a second resting-place.' יעמסן, which recurs in ll. 7.21, may be compared with the Ar. *modus energicus* II. *yaktulan.* Cooke (*NSI.* pp. 34 f.) treats יעמסן as a suffix-form 'carry me'; an explanation which involves a highly forced and unnatural treatment of the context.

If תשלחנה be not an energetic form, the alternative is to vocalize it as a suffix-form תִּשְׁלָחֶנָּה, and to treat יָדָהּ as an *accusativus pendens*:—'her hand, to the peg she stretched it forth.'

* The forms are mostly late. A complete list of them is given by König, *Lehrgebäude der hebräischen Sprache*, ii. 1, pp. 205 f.

work *or* make,' *'amal* 'work *or* occupation,' *'amil* 'artisan'; Aram. *'ămal* 'to labour'; Bab. *nîmelu** 'the produce of work,' *i.e.* 'gain *or* possession.' There is no difficulty, therefore, in supposing that *'ămēlîm* may denote 'workmen' generally, *without* the connotation of toil or weariness.

The meaning of the phrase is correctly elucidated by 𝔖ᴾ ܠܡܪܙܦܬܐ ܕܢܓܪܐ 'to the carpenter's mallet,' Ar. *id.*, 𝔗 לארזפתא דנפחין 'to the mallet of the smiths,' 𝔙 'ad fabrorum malleos' (treating הלמות as a plur.). 𝔊ᴮ, 'A. εἰς σφῦραν κοπιώντων interpret עמלים in accordance with customary Heb. usage. 𝔊ᴬᴸ εἰς ἀποτομὰς κατακοπῶν (ᴸ κατακοπτῶν) misunderstands.

she smote. Lit. 'hammered.'

destroyed. Heb. *māḥᵃḳā*, which only occurs here in the O.T., is explained from New Heb. and Aram. 'wipe out *or* erase,' *Ar. maḥaḳa* 'utterly destroy, annihilate.'

pierced through. The Heb. verb *ḥālaph* commonly means to *pass on*, or *pass away*; but is here used transitively 'passed (i.e. *pierced*) through.' This usage is substantiated by Job 20 [24], 'The bow of bronze *pierces him through*' (*taḥlᵉphēhû*), where 'bow' is used metonymically for the arrow which is shot from it. Mo. explains 'demolishes,' lit. 'causes to pass away,' quoting Isa. 24 [5] חָלְפוּ חֹק in support of the causative usage. This, however, probably means 'they have *passed by* (*i.e.* overstepped) the ordinance' (cf. || עָבְרוּ תוֹרוֹת 'they have transgressed the laws') and not 'they have abolished' it.

27. *'Twixt her feet, etc.* The passage is discussed on p. 80.

undone. Driver's rendering. Heb. *šādhûdh* means lit. 'treated with violence.'

28. *and exclaimed.* Heb. וַתְּיַבֵּב. The verb *yibbēbh*, which only occurs here in O.T., is explained from Aram., in which *yabbēbh* means 'blow the trumpet,' and also 'raise a shout'; being used in this latter sense by 𝔖ᴾ to translate Heb. הֵרִיעַ in *ch.* 7 [21], 1 Sam. 4 [5], 17 [20]; Ps. 47 [2], 66 [1], *al.* In New Heb. the verb means 'to lament' over a corpse. Thus 𝔙 renders 'et ululabat,' 𝔖ᴾ ܘܝܒܒܬ, Ar. جلبت. 𝔊ᴬᴸ, however, renders καὶ κατεμάνθανεν, 𝔖ʰ ܘܡܣܬܟܠܐ ܗܘܬ, 𝔗 ומדיקא

* With *nîmelu* with preformative *n* from √עמל, cf. *nîmeḳu* from √עמק, *nîmedu* from √עמד.

'and looked attentively'; *i.e.*, apparently, וַתַּבֵּט or וַתִּתְבּוֹנֵן. This latter verb is adopted by Klostermann, Marquart, No., La., Zapletal, and is favoured by Bu. and Cooke (*Comm.*).

the lattice. Heb. *hā-'ešnābh.* The precise meaning of the term is uncertain. It occurs again in Prov. 7 [6] (‖ *ḥallôn* 'window,' as in our passage); and in Ecclus. 42 [11] †, where it is mentioned as a means of gazing on the street. The conventional rendering, which we have adopted, is that which is given by 𝔊[AL], Θ., διὰ τῆς δικτυωτῆς (so, in Prov., 𝔙 'cancellos'). 𝔗 אעיתא, apparently 'wood-work,' perhaps has the same meaning. 𝔊[B], however, renders ἐκτὸς τοῦ τοξικοῦ 'through the loop-hole'; while 𝔙 'de coenaculo,' 𝔖[P] ܥܠ ܟܣܣܛܘܢ think of an upper chamber or colonnade (ξυστός).

tarrieth. On the Heb. form אֵחֱרוּ (for אֵחֲרוּ or אֵחֲרוּ), cf. G-K. § 64 *h.*

the clatter. Heb. *pa'amê*, lit. 'strokes,' here no doubt refers to the *hoof-beats* of the chariot-horses.

29. *Her wisest princesses.* As Mo. remarks, 'there is a fine irony in the allusion to the wisdom of these ladies, whose prognostications were so wide of the truth.'

make answer. Reading plur. תַּעֲנֶינָה, in place of 𝔐 תַּעֲנֶנָּה 'answereth her' (sing. with suffix), which is impossible after the plur. חַכְמוֹת שָׂרוֹתֶיהָ. An equally possible alternative is to emend חַכְמַת for חַכְמוֹת—'The wisest one of her princesses answereth her.' So 𝔙 'Una sapientior ceteris uxoribus ejus'; 𝔖[P] ܚܟܝܡܬ ܟܠ ܟ̈ܠܬܗ̇; Ar. *id.*

Yea, she returneth her reply. She tries to quiet her anxiety by making herself the most reassuring answer. 𝔐 adds לָהּ 'to herself,' which destroys the balance of the couplet by adding a fourth beat to the stichos.

30. *A damsel, two damsels.* Heb. *râḥam* (which elsewhere in O.T. means 'womb') occurs in plur. with the meaning 'girl-slaves' in the inscription of the Moabite stone, l. 17.

for every man. Lit. 'for the head of a man'; *i.e.*, as we might say, 'per head.'

of dyed stuffs embroidered. Lit. 'of dyed stuffs, embroidery,' the two substantives being in apposition.

Two dyed embroideries. Lit. 'a dyed piece of two embroideries.' This may be understood as the dual of what would be in the sing. 'a dyed piece of embroidery' (צֶבַע רִקְמָה), the dual termination of the second (genitival) subst. sufficing to throw the whole compound expression into the dual. Cf. sing. בֵּית אָב 'a father's house *or* family,' plur. בֵּית אָבוֹת 'families': G-K. § 124 *r*. R.V.'s rendering, 'of divers colours of embroidery on both sides' (the explanation of Kimchi and Levi ben-Gershon), can hardly be correct.

The manner in which the terms meaning 'dyed stuff' and 'embroidery' are repeated and combined in the three final stichoi of the strophe is somewhat strange; and various alterations and omissions have been proposed. We need only notice the reconstruction suggested by Bu., which reduces the three stichoi to two, each containing three beats :—

שְׁלַל צֶבַע צְבָעַיִם לְסִיסְרָא
שְׁלַל רִקְמָה רִקְמָתַיִם לְצַוָּארִי

'Spoil of a piece or two of dyed stuff for Sisera;
Spoil of a piece or two of embroidery for my neck.'

Here צב' צב' and רק' רק' are brought into exact analogy with רחם רחמתים 'a damsel or two.' It may be questioned, however, whether this rearrangement is not too precise and formal to represent the original. 𝔊, as it stands, is susceptible of the rendering which we have given in the text; and in its repetition, which may be paralleled by *v.* [27], it exhibits affinity to the climactic parallelism which is so marked elsewhere in the Song (cf. *Additional note*, pp. 169 f.). It may be intended to represent the way in which the women's thoughts run on in prospect of the spoil. Cf. the passage from Virgil, *Aen.* xi. 782, cited by Ros. and others :—

'Femineo praedae et spoliorum ardebat amore.'

for the neck of the queen. Reading שֵׁגָל 'queen' (cf. Ps. 45 [9], 𝔊 [10], Neh. 2 [6]), after the suggestion of Ewald, in place of 𝔐 שָׁלָל 'spoil.' So Ber., Wellh., Stade, Oet., Oort, Schlögl, Kit., Driver, etc. The reading of 𝔐 can only mean 'for the neck of the spoil,' which fails to yield sense; since it is impossible to follow Michaelis, Schnurrer, Ros., and several of the older commentators in explaining 'the spoil' as referring to the beasts of burden captured from the foe, which are to be led in triumph decked with the dyed raiment, etc.; nor is it likely that Justi is right in suggesting (after Mendelssohn) that 'the spoil' refers to the captured damsels previously mentioned. Levi ben Gershon explains as בעלי שלל 'owners of spoil'; and similarly Hollmann supposes an ellipse of איש before שלל—'man of spoil' (cf. A.V. '*meet* for the necks of *them that take* the spoil'): but such an ellipse is impossible. It would be easier to follow W. Green (1753) in vocalizing as an active participle שֹׁלֵל 'spoiler'; as is suggested by the rendering 𝔖ᴾ ܟܠ ܒܙܘܙ ܢܣܒܘܢ (Ar. *id.*). Kimchi explains 'for the necks of the spoil' as equivalent to 'on the head of the spoil,' the sense intended being that 'the garments are placed on the head of the spoil to give them to the captain of the host.' He thus seems to regard 'the spoil' as referring to the *captives* generally; an explanation which is without analogy. R.V., 'on the necks of the spoil,' apparently assumes that the passage means that the garments are on the necks of the spoil (captives or slain?) before they become a booty; but the explanation of ל as 'on' ('belonging to') is very harsh and improbable.

𝔊ᴮ *τῷ τραχήλῳ αὐτοῦ* (ᴬ *περὶ τράχηλον αὐτοῦ*) *σκῦλα*; 𝔏 'circa cervices ejus spolia'; 𝔗 בזת ציורי צבעינין על צוריה; *i.e.* לְצַוָּארוֹ (לְצַוָּארָיו) שָׁלָל 'for his (*i.e.* Ṡiṡera's) neck as a spoil'; and this is adopted by Meier, Hilliger, Stu. 𝔊ᴸ *περὶ τὸν τράχηλον αὐτοῦ*, *i.e.* לְצַוָּארוֹ, omitting שָׁלָל: so No., La., Kent. The original of 𝔙, 'supellex varia ad ornanda colla congeritur,' is not clear.

Further, Donaldson, Reuss, Grä., Smith, etc., read לְצַוָּארִי שָׁלָל 'a spoil for my neck'; while Bu., Cooke adopt the reading לְצַוָּארִי 'for my neck' simply.

31. *So perish, etc.* The couplet is regarded by Meier, Winter (*ZATW.* ix. 223 ff.), Bu., etc., as an addition, in the style of the Psalms, made to the poem in later times. It cannot be doubted, however, that it forms a most effective conclusion. As Mo. remarks, the single word '*So*' brings the whole course of events before our eyes again, culminating in Ṡiṡera's 'death by a woman's hand, disgrace worse than death; the anguish and dismay of those who loved him,' which the poet, with consummate art, leaves to the imagination of the reader. It is true that the idea embodied in the phrase 'thy friends' (lit. 'those that love thee') first comes into *prominence* at a later age (Ex. 20[6], the explanatory extension of the Second Commandment, probably E[2]; Hosea', and Deuteronomy); but it by no means follows that it was wholly unthought of in much earlier times.

thy friends. Reading אֹהֲבֶיךָ with 𝔙, 𝔖ᴾ, in place of 𝔐 אֹהֲבָיו 'his friends.'

An echo of the couplet is probably to be found in the first three verses of Ps. 68, which later on (*vv.*[7.8.13]) shows traces of the influence of the poem.

A DETAILED EXAMINATION OF THE RHYTHM OF THE SONG OF DEBORAH.

A more detailed presentation of the rhythmical scheme of the Song of Deborah, and the extent to which this scheme is reproduced in our English rendering, may be of interest, as illustrating the method of early Hebrew poetical composition. As we have already remarked (p. 96), ancient Hebrew poetry, like English poetry, possesses no regularly quantitative system of metre; but is characterized by the occurrence of so many *ictûs* or rhythmical beats to the line, the intervening unstressed syllables being governed by the possibilities of pronunciation rather than by any strict rule. It is feasible, however, both in Hebrew and English, to divide the stichoi into 'feet,' with a view to a more accurate observation of the correspondence which may be obtained between the original and its translation; and an attempt has been made to do this in the comparison which is offered below.

Such a division of the Hebrew original into 'feet' also serves to illustrate the position of the *ictus* and its relationship to the accompanying unstressed syllables. It may be noticed that the Song contains, in all, 298 'feet.' Of these, by far the most frequent concatenation of stressed and unstressed syllables is ⏓⏓–́, *i.e.* the anapaest,* this 'foot' occuring 115 times. Closely similar to this is the 'foot' which contains an additional syllable as a weak (unstressed) ending, *i.e.* ⏓⏓–́⏓; and this is found 13 times. Further, we find, with an additional unstressed syllable before the *ictus*, ⏓⏓⏓–́, 31 times; and, with a weak ending, ⏓⏓⏓–́⏓, twice. Rarely, four unstressed syllables precede the *ictus*; ⏓⏓⏓⏓–́, 4 times; but there is no instance of such a 'foot' with an additional syllable as a weak ending. Next to the 'anapaest,' the most frequent 'foot' is the 'iambus,' ⏓–́, this occurring 77 times; and, corresponding to this with a weak ending, ⏓–́⏓, 25 times. Not infrequently, a word of a single syllable may bear the *ictus*, unaccompanied by any unstressed syllable; –́, 12 times. Such an *ictus* may be followed by a weak ending, –́⏓, 19 times.‡

It thus appears that, out of the 298 'feet' in the poem, 192, or nearly two-thirds, are either ⏓⏓–́ or ⏓–́ in form; and it will be found that this proportionate relationship of stressed to unstressed

* The term 'anapaest' is used loosely to denote two unstressed syllables followed by the stress, and not necessarily two *short* syllables followed by a *long*; since it is possible in Hebrew for an unstressed syllable to be long by nature.

‡ In this analysis, *Furtive Pathaḥ* is not reckoned as a weak ending. Thus *maddû*^{a}ʿ is reckoned as ⏓–́, not as ⏓–́⏓.

syllables is (speaking generally) characteristic of other examples of Hebrew poetry. The reason why an anapaestic or iambic 'foot,' with such variations as we have noted, is characteristic of Hebrew rhythm, depends upon the fact that the Hebrew tonic syllable is always either the ultimate or penultimate syllable of a word, the accented ultimate being by far the most frequent (in the Song 239 instances, as against 59 instances of the accented penultimate); while the throwing of the accent farther back than the penultimate syllable is wholly unknown. It is thus impossible to find a dactylic 'foot,' –́⏓⏓; while the trochaic 'foot,' –́⏓, is, as we have seen, comparatively uncommon. In English, on the contrary, the accented penultimate or antepenultimate syllable greatly prevails over the accented ultimate; and a dactylic or trochaic measure is therefore natural, and indeed, at times, unavoidable. The comparative prevalence of dactylic or trochaic 'feet' in our English rendering of the Song will be found to be the feature which most markedly militates against close approximation to the Hebrew original. Fortunately, however, the English language is rich in weighty monosyllables; and the use of these enables us largely to reproduce the effect of the Hebrew rhythm by bringing the *ictus* down to the final syllable of the 'foot.'*

The fact is familiar to students that the system of Hebrew vocalization, as known to us from 𝔐, represents the artificial product of the synagogue-system of cantillation; and only preserves the original pronunciation of living Hebrew in a very modified form. We are able, however, partly by the help of comparative philology, and partly by the aids to which reference has been made on p. 99, to infer with a fair approximation to certainty what the spoken pronunciation of the language must have been like; and an attempt has been made to reproduce this pronunciation in the transliteration of the Hebrew original. It should be remarked that this transliteration only claims substantial accuracy in so far as it substitutes full short vowels in open syllables for the tone-long vowels and vocal *sh*^{e}*wa* of 𝔐: but the evidence at our disposal is not sufficient to enable us to dogmatize as to the *precise vocalization* of many word-forms at the period represented by the Song; and many of the forms which are

* The conclusions here adopted assume that the practice of spoken Hebrew, as regards the position of the tone, is substantially preserved in 𝔐. We must not, however, overlook the possibility that the synagogue-system of cantillation may to some extent have affected the *position* of the tone-syllable, tending to throw it forward to the end of the word; and it is conceivable that, when Hebrew was a spoken language, the practice with regard to the tone conformed to that of Arabic, viz. that the accent was thrown forward till it met a long syllable, and if no long syllable occurred in the word, the accent rested on the first syllable. Such a system would to some extent modify our conclusions as to the different types of 'feet' represented in the Song; and, leading as it would to a multiplication of 'feet' of the form –́⏓ and even –́⏓⏓, would result in a closer approximation of the Hebrew rhythm to the English rendering.

given must be regarded as only approximately accurate (cf. the philological remarks which are added at the close of this note).

It is, however, the relationship of the unstressed syllables to the *ictus*-bearing syllable, and not the precise quality of the vowels of such syllables, which is of importance to us in our presentation of the rhythmical form of the Song; the latter question, though of supreme importance to philology, being only of subordinate interest as regards our present subject.

Lastly, it may be observed that the short vowels which take the place of tone-long vowels and vocal *shᵉwa* in our transliteration, though represented as full vowels, may very likely have been pronounced in some cases with extreme brevity (as in Arabic), and in others very possibly slurred together in utterance. The effect of such a slurring would be to diminish the number of unstressed syllables (making *e.g.* ⏓⏓⏓–́ sound as ⏓⏓–́), but would in no way essentially alter the character of the rhythm.

It will be noticed that, in the four-beat stichoi, we have placed a double line of division, halving the stichos. This indicates the caesura, which is characteristic of this form of rhythm; and which ordinarily marks a break in sense, sometimes considerable, as in *vv.*[3a.4bα], where the first half of the stichos is parallel to the second; but at other times very slight, and amounting to little more than the taking of breath at the half-way point. Stichoi also occur occasionally in which the caesura is purely formal, *sense* requiring a connexion rather than a break. So in *v.*[10a] (caesura between subst. and adj.), *vv.*[17aα.31b] (between Constr. St. and its following genitive).

Lest it should be thought that the fact that the caesura is purely formal in *v.*[10a], where we have re-arranged the text, is an argument against the arrangement, it may be remarked that the occurrence of such formal caesuras can be substantiated elsewhere. Thus we have Ps. 45[2b]:

לשוני עט | סופר מהיר

'My tóngue is the pén | of a reády wríter.'

---

3. *šumuʿū́ | malakhī́m || haʾzī́nu | rōzinī́m*
ʾanōkhī́ | lYahwáh || ʾanōkhī́ | ʾašī́ra
ʾazammér | lYahwáh || ʾelāháy | Yisraʾél

4. *Yahwáh | baṣēthikhá | misSeʿī́r*
baṣaʿdikhá | missadhḗ | ʾAdhṓm
ʾáraṣ | raʿā́ša || gam-šamḗm | namṓghū
gam-ʿabhī́m | naṭaphū́ | máyim

5. *harrī́m | nazalū́ || mippanáy | Yahwáh*
mippanáy | Yahwáh || ʾelāháy | Yisraʾél

Ps. 89 16b:

יהוה באור | פניך יהלכון

'Yahwéh, in the líght | of thy coúntenance shall they wálk.'

Ps. 10 13a:

על־מה נאץ | רשע אלהים

'Whérefore contémneth | the wícked, Gód?'

Similarly, Babylonian, which ordinarily marks the caesura very clearly, offers occasional instances of a formal kind merely. Thus, *Gilgameš-epic* xi. 121:

ki áḳbi ina púḫur | ilâni limútta

'When I decreéd in the assémbly | of the góds an evil thíng.'

Id. xi. 182:

átta abkál | ilâni ḳurádu

'Thóu, O ságe | of the góds, thou wárrior.'

Creation-epic iv. 11:

zananútum îršat | parák ilâni-ma

'Abúndance is the desíre | of the sanctuary of the góds.'

Id. iv. 31:

alík-ma ša Tiámat | napšátuš purú'ma

'Gó, and of Tiámat | her lífe cut óff.'

It may be noted that, in the English rendering, the ordinary English accentuation of proper names has been adopted, rather than that of the Hebrew, in cases in which the latter would appear scarcely tolerable in the conventionalized forms to which the English reader is accustomed. In other cases, in which this difficulty is less acute or non-existent, the Hebrew accentuation has been retained.

---

3. Atténd, | ye kíngs; || give eár, | ye rúlers:
Í— | to Yahwéh || Í | will síng,
Will make mélody | to Yahwéh, || the Gód | of Ísrael.
4. Yahwéh, | in thy prógress | from Se'ír,
In thy márch | from the fiéld | of Edóm,
Eárth | quáked, || yea, heáven | rócked,
Yea, the cloúds | drópped | wáter.
5. The moúntains | shoók || befóre | Yahwéh,
Befóre | Yahwéh, || the Gód | of Ísrael.

6. *miyyamáy | Šamgár | ben-ʿAnáth*
miyyamáy | ʿōlám || ḥadhalū́ | ʾōraḥṓth
whōlikháy | nathībhṓth || yēlakhū́ | ʿaḳalḳallṓth

7. *ḥadhalū́ | parazṓth | bYisraʾél*
. . . . ḥadhalū́
ʿádh | šaḳḳámti | Dabhōrá
šaḳḳámti | ʾém | bYisraʾél
8. *ḥašarū́ | lahúm | ḥarrašī́m*
ʾazalū́ | ḥamušī́m | meʿī́r
maghén | ʾim-yirraʾé | warúmaḥ
bʾarbāʿī́m | ʾálaph | bYisraʾél

12. *ʿū́rī | ʿū́rī | Dabhōrá*
ʿū́rī | ʿū́rī | dabbari-šī́r
ḳū́m | Baráḳ | wašabhḗ
šobháyka | bén | ʾAbhinū́ʿam
9. *lakhū́ | muḥōḳaḳáy | Yisraʾél*
hammithnaddabhī́m | baʿám || barrakhū́ | Yahwáh
10. *rōkhibháy | ʾathōnṓth || ṣaḥōrṓth | yasīḥū*
whōlikháy | ʿal-dárakh || yašī́bhu | ʿal-lébh
11. *ḳṓl | muṣaḥḥaḳṓth || béyn | masʾabbī́m*
šám | yutannū́ || ṣadhaḳṓth | Yahwáh
ṣadhaḳṓth | zurōʿṓ | bYisraél

13. *ʾaz-yaradhū́ | lašaʿarī́m | ʾaddīrī́m*
ʿam-Yahwáh | yaradh-lṓ | baggabbōrī́m
14. *minni-ʾEphrḗm | mašakhū́ | baʿémeḳ*
ʾaḥaráyka | Binyamī́n | baʿamamáyka
minni-Makhī́r | yaradhū́ | muḥōḥaḳī́m
umizZabhūlū́n | mošikhī́m | bašébheṭ
15. *wasaráyka | Yissakhár | ʿim-Dabhōrá*
waNaphtáli | kén | laBharáḳ
baʿémeḳ | šulláḥ | baraghláw

naphrṓdh | naphrádh || laphalaggṓth | Reʾubhén
gadhōlī́m | ḥeḳeráy | libbṓ
16. *lámma | yašábhta || béyn | hammašpatḗm*
lašamṓᵃʿ | sarīḳṓth | ʿadharī́m
17. *Galʿádh | baʿébher || hayYardén | šakhín*
waDhán | yaghū́r | ʾoniyyṓth
ʾAšér | yašábh || laḥóph | yammī́m
waʿál | maphraṣáw | yaškún
18. *Zabhūlū́n | ʿam-ḥarráph || naphšṓ | lamū́th*
waNaphtalí | ʿal-marōmáy | sadhḗ

6. From the dáys | of Shamgár | ben-ʿAnáth,
From the dáys | of óld, || cáravans | ceásed
And they that wént | along the wáys || used to wálk | by crooked páths.
7. Víllages | ceásed | in Ísrael;
. . . . ceásed;
Till thoú | didst aríse | Deboráh,
Didst aríse | as a móther | in Ísrael.
8. Ármourers | hád they | nóne;
Ármed men | faíled from the | cíty:
Was there seén | a shiéld | or a lánce
Amóng | forty thoúsand | in Ísrael?

12. Awáke, | awáke, | Deboráh!
Awáke, | awáke, | sing paéan!
Ríse | Barák̦, | and lead cáptive
Thy cáptors, | O són | of Abinóʿam!
9. Cóme, | ye commánders | of Ísrael!
Ye that volunteéred | among the péople, || bléss ye | Yahwéh!
10. Let the ríders | on táwny || she-ásses | reviéw it,
And lét | the wayfárers || recáll it | to mínd!
11. Hárk | to the maídens || laúghing at | the wélls!
Thére | they recoúnt || the righteous ácts | of Yahwéh,
The righteous ácts | of his árm | in Ísrael.

13. Then dówn | to the gátes | gat the nóbles;
Yahweh's fólk | gat them dówn | mid the héroes.
14. From Ephráim | they spread oút | on the vále;
'After theé, | Benjamín!' | mid thy clánsmen.
From Machír | came dówn | the commánders,
And from Zebulún | men wiélding | the trúncheon.
15. And thy prínces, | Issachár, | were with Deboráh;
And Naphtáli | was leál | to Barák̦:
To the vále | he was loósed | at his heél.

Útterly | réft into || fáctions was | Re'úben;
Greát were | his seárchings | of heárt.
16. Why sát'st | thou stíll || amíd | the fólds,
To heár | the pástoral | pípings?
17. Gileʿád | beyónd || the Jórdan | dwélt,
And Dán | abídeth | by the shíps.
Ashér | sat stíll || by the shóre | of the séas,
Dwélling | besíde | his créeks.
18. Zebulún | is the fólk || that scorned its lífe | to the deáth,
And Naphtalí | on the heights | of the fiéld.

19. *bā'ū | malakhīm | nalḥămū*
'az-nalhamū́ | malakháy | Kanáʿan
baTaʿnákh | ʿal-máy | Magiddṓ
báṣaʿ | káśaph | lo-laḳăḥū
20. *min-šamḗm | nalḥamū́ | hakkōkhabhī́m*
mimmašillōthám | nalḥamū́ | ʿim-Šišará
21. *náḥal | Ḳīšṓn | garaphám*
ḳaddamám | náḥal | Ḳīšṓn
Tubarrakhí | naphšī́ || ʿóz | Yahwáh

22. *'az-halamū́ | ʿaḳibháy | šušī́m*
daharū́ | daharū́ | 'abbīráw
23. *'úrrū | Merṓz | 'arṓr*
'úrrū | 'arṓr | yōšibháyha
ki-lō-bā'u | laʿezráth | Yahwáh
laʿezráth | Yahwáh | baggabbōrī́m

24. *tuburrákh | minnašī́m | Yaʿél*
minnašī́m | baʿúhul | tuburrákh
25. *máyim | šaʾál || ḥalábh | nathắna*
bašéphel | 'addīrī́m || haḳrī́bha | ḥemʾá
26. *yadháh | layathídh | tašlaḥánna*
wyamīnáh | lhalmáth | ʿamīlī́m
whalamá | Šīšará || maḥaḳá | rōšṓ
umaḥaṣá | waḥalaphá | raḳḳathṓ
27. *beyn-raghláyha | karáʿ || naphál | šakhábh*
beyn-raghláyha | karáʿ | naphál
baʾšér | karáʿ || šam-naphál | šadhū́dh

28. *baʿádh | haḥallṓn || našḳaphá | wattuyabbábh*
'ém | Šīšará || baʿádh | haʾešnábh
maddū́aʿ | bōšéš || rakhabhṓ | labhṓ
maddū́aʿ | 'aḥḥarú || paʿamáy | marḳabhōtháw
29. *ḥakhamṓth | sarrōtháyha | taʿnáyna*
'aph-hī́ | tašī́bh | 'amaráyha
30. *halṓ | yamṣuʾū́ || yuḥallaḳū́ | šalál*
ráḥam | raḥmathḗm || larṓš | gábar *
šalál | ṣabhaʿī́m | laŠīšará
šalál | ṣabhaʿī́m | riḳmá
ṣábaʿ | riḳmathḗm || laṣawwaráy | šeghál

31. *kén | yobhadhū́ || kol-ʾoyabháyka | Yahwáh*
wʾōhabháyka | kaṣéth || haššámaš | baggabūrathṓ

* Possibly this couplet should be regarded as consisting of trimeters rather than tetrameters :—

halō-yamṣuʾū́ | yuḥallaḳū́ | šalál
ráḥam | raḥmathḗm | larōš-gábar.

19. On came | the kíngs, | they foúght ;
Then foúght | the kíngs | of Caná'an ;
In Tá'anach, | by the ríIls | of Megíddo ;
The gaín | of móney | they toók not.
20. From heáven | foúght | the stárs ;
From their híghways | they foúght | with Ṡíṡera.
21. The tórrent | Ḳishón | swept them óff ;
It fáced them, | the tórrent | Ḳishón.
Bléss thou, | my soúl, || the míght | of Yahwéh !

22. Then loúd beat | the hoófs | of the hórses ;
Off gálloped, | off gálloped | his chárgers.
23. Cúrse ye, | cúrse ye | Meróz !
Cúrse ye, | cúrse ye | her tówns-folk !
For they cáme not | to the hélp | of Yahwéh,
To the hélp | of Yahwéh | mid the héroes.

24. Most bléssed | of wómen | be Já'el,
Of tént-dwelling | wómen | most bléssed !
25. Wáter | he ásked ; || mílk | she gáve ;
In a lórdly | dísh || she próffered | cúrds.
26. Her hánd | to the pég | she put fórth,
And her ríght | to the mául | of the wórkmen ;
And she smóte | Ṡíṡera || —destróyed | his heád
Sháttered | and piérced | through his témples.
27. 'Twixt her feét | he bówed, || he fell dówn, | he lay próne ;
'Twixt her feét | he bówed, | he fell dówn.
Whére | he bówed, || there he fell dówn | undóne.

28. Oút | through the wíndow || she leáned | and exclaímed,
The móther | of Ṡíṡera || oút | through the láttice :
'Whérefore | deláyeth || his cár | to cóme ?
Whérefore | tárrieth || the clátter | of his cháriots' ?
29. Her wísest | princésses | make ánswer,
Yea, shé | retúrneth | her replý :
30. 'Áre they not | fínding || —divíding | the spoíl ?
A dámsel— | two dámsels || for évery | mán :
A spoíl | of dýed stuffs | for Ṡíṡera,
A spoíl | of dýed stuffs | embroídered ;
Twó dyed | embroíderies || for the néck | of the queén.'

31. So pérish | áll || thy foés | Yahwéh :
But be thy friénds | like the sún || going fórth | in his stréngth.

The following notes are offered in explanation of the Heb. forms adopted in the transliteration.

3. *šumu'û*, for 𝔐 *šimᵉ'û*. Comparative philology points to such a form: cf. Bab. *ḳuṭulû*; and Ar. *uḳtulû*, where the need for the prosthetic vowel was the direct result of the slurring away of the first short *u* vowel. That Heb. *ḳᵉṭōl* was once pronounced *ḳuṭúl* may also be inferred from Origen's translit. of לְחַם, Ps. 35[1] by λοομ (*o* in translit. answering to *ŭ*).

malakhîm, with two *ă*'s in open syllables, for 𝔐 *mᵉlākhîm*. So throughout the poem, *parazôth*, *ḥakhamôth*, etc.

ha'zînû; or possibly *ha'zanû*. The origin of the *ī* of the Hiph'îl is obscure.

rōzinîm. The *ō* of the Act. Particip. (from an original *â*; cf. Ar. *ḳâtil*) was of early development in Heb.: cf. the T.A. 'glosses'* *zûkini*=סֹכֵן, *ûbil*=אֹבֵל, where the *û* is the nearest approach to the representation of *ō* in cuneiform script.

'anōkhí; perhaps originally accented *'anókhi*. Cf. אנך of the Moabite stone and Phoenician inscriptions.

6. *lYahwáh*. It is here assumed that, before the weak letter י, the short vowel of the preposition is merged by crasis with the following short vowel. Cf. T.A. *badiu*=בְּיָדוֹ (gloss on Bab. *ina ḳâtišu*). A similar crasis is assumed before the weak ה in *whōlikáy*, etc. Whether such a crasis took place before ע is perhaps more doubtful. A possible instance is to be seen in the Precative Particle בִּי, if this really stands for בְּעִי 'supplication'; and, similarly, the name רוּת is usually regarded as a contraction of רְעוּת (cf. Syr.

* The so-called 'Cana'anite glosses' in the T.A. Letters (which might preferably be termed 'Amorite,' as relics of the language of Amurru: cf. *Introd.* pp. lx f.) are words and phrases in the language which is the prototype of Hebrew, occurring in the letters which were written in the cuneiform script and in the Babylonian language by the petty kings and governors of Cana'anite cities to their suzerain, the king of Egypt. We may infer that the scribes who were responsible for the writing of these letters were themselves Cana'anites, to whom the Babylonian was a foreign language, acquired (as evidence shows) not always very perfectly. Thus, they often employ a Cana'anite word as an explanation or gloss of the equivalent term in Babylonian which precedes it in the letter; or even occasionally substitute a Cana'anite term for the Babylonian, for which they were probably at a loss. These 'glosses' are of great value, not only as forming the earliest relics of the Hebrew language which are known to us, but also because (inasmuch as they are written syllabically in the cuneiform script) they embody the vocalization as well as the consonants of the forms. A complete list of the T.A. glosses will be found in Böhl, *Die Sprache der Amarnabriefe*, pp. 80 ff.; cf. also *KAT.*[3], pp. 651 ff.

ܙܢܘܬܐ). The crasis is of regular occurrence in Bab., where *e.g.* *bêlu* stands for the West Semitic *beʿēl*, *báʿal*.

'azammér. The last vowel probably *ĕ* or *ă*. The *ē* of the Piʿel in 𝔐 is a late and artificial development. So late as the time of Origen this vowel is regularly represented in translit. by ε and not by η (contrast the Act. Particip. Ḳal, where η always appears : *e.g.* Νωσηρ).

'eláhây, for 𝔐 *'elōhê*. For *â* in place of *ō*, cf. Ar. *ilâh*, Syr. *'elâhâ*. That *ê* was originally the diphthong *ay* is clear from comparative philology.

4. *baṣêthiká*, *baṣaʿdikhá*. The connective vowel before the suffix is given as *ĭ*, the Genitive case-ending after the preposition, as in Bab. and Ar.

missadhê. That שָׂדֶה was originally שַׂדַי might be conjectured from the sporadic occurrence of the latter form in 𝔐 as a poetical archaism. The early existence of the more familiar form is, however, witnessed by the T.A. *šatê* = שָׂדֶה as a gloss to the Bab. *ugari*.

'Adhom. For the initial short vowel, cf. Bab. *Adumu*.

'áraṣ, for 𝔐 *'éreṣ*. It must be regarded as an open question whether the segholate nouns were pronounced at this period with a helping vowel after the second consonant (as in 𝔐, and in the form which we have adopted), or in the monosyllabic form (*e.g.* *'árṣ*) which is assumed to be the original (cf. Ar. *'arḍ*, the philological equivalent of אֶרֶץ). Origen uniformly represents this type of noun as monosyllabic : *e.g.* αρς = אֶרֶץ, δερχ = דֶּרֶךְ, etc. ; the only exceptions being formed by words which have a guttural as second or third radical ; *e.g.* ιααδ = יַחַד, ρεγε = רֶגַע, etc. On the other hand, the much earlier evidence of 𝔊 exhibits a uniform representation of the helping vowel ; *e.g.* Ιαφεθ = יֶפֶת, Λαμεχ = לֶמֶךְ, etc. Among the T.A. glosses we find *baṭnu* = בֶּטֶן, *ṣu'ru* = צַהַר, *šaḫri* = שַׁעַר, segholate forms with case-ending, just like Ar. *'arḍun*. Taking, however, a Hebrew proper name of the classical period such as חִזְקִיָּהוּ (meaning, apparently, 'Yahu is strength, *or* my strength'), where the first element *ḥizḳi* must be assumed to be a segholate noun of the form *ḥĕzeḳ* (for the normal *ḥŏzeḳ* ; cf. fem. *ḥezḳā* by the side of *ḥozḳā*), we find that the helping vowel after the *z* which appears in the 𝔊 translit. Εζεκιας is confirmed by the Assyr. translit. in Sennacherib's inscription,* where the name is spelt out as *Ḫa-za-ḳi-ia-u* or *Ḫa-za-ḳi-a-u*. In face of this conflict of evidence, it appears preferable to retain the helping vowel in

* The Taylor Cylinder, col. ii. l. 71 ; col. iii. ll. 11, 29 ; cf. *KB.* ii. pp. 92, 94.

segholate forms,* vocalizing, as 𝔊 suggests, form 1 as in *'áraṣ*; form 2 as in *šéphel*, *v.* [25]; form 3 as in *'úhul*, *v.* [24] (cf. 𝔊 forms Βαραδ, Εζερ, Ζογορ).

raʿáša. The pausal form is retained, here and elsewhere (*nalhámû*, *laḳáḥû*, *v.* [19]; *nathána*, *v.* [25]), as probably characteristic of the original pronunciation. Origen recognizes such pausal forms in his transliterations; *e.g.* ιδαββηρου = יְדַבֵּרוּ. The existence of the pausal accent in Bab., as indicated by the doubling of the succeeding consonant, also seems to be clear; cf. Delitzsch, *Assyr. Gramm.* § 53 *c*. In Ar. the pause introduces certain formal modifications.

šamém, in place of 𝔐 *šāmáyim*. For the dual termination *-êm*, cf. Phoenician שמם.

naṭaphú, in place of 𝔐 *nāṭᵉphú*, as in Ar.; and so in similar verbal forms throughout the song. Possibly such a form may sometimes have been pronounced *naṭphú*: cf. T.A. gloss *maḫṣu* for *maḫaṣu* (מחצו). The Bab. Permansive form is similar.

máyim; or possibly *mêm*: cf. T.A. gloss *mîma*, *mêma* (spelt out *mi-ma* and *mi-e-ma*). Moabitic, however, represents the י in מין, a fact which perhaps indicates a pronunciation such as we have adopted (*i.e.* the pronunciation of 𝔐).

5. *harrím*, for 𝔐 *hārîm*. Similarly, ר is doubled in *yirraʾé*, *v.* [8], *barrakhú*, *v.* [9], etc. It cannot be doubted that ancient Heb. found no more difficulty about the pronunciation of double ר than does Bab. and Ar. Cf. the T.A. gloss *ḫarri* = הַר with Genitive case-ending; and the 𝔊 transliterations 'Αμορραῖος = אֱמֹרִי pronounced *'Amurri* (native of the land of Amurru); Χαρραν = חָרָן, cf. Bab. *Ḫarrânu*.

7. *'ém*; or possibly *'imm* (Origen, εμ). Similarly, *maghén*, *v.* [8], may have been pronounced *maghínn*, *ʿóz*, *v.* [21], *ʿuzz* (Origen, οζ), etc.

9 ff. *muḥōḳaḳáy*, *muṣaḥḥaḳóth*, *yutannú*. The short preformative vowel of the Piʿel is represented by *u*, as in Ar. Cf. the T.A. gloss *yukabid* = יְכַבֵּד.

11. *zurōʿó*. For vowel of first syllable, cf. T.A. gloss *zurûḫ*.

13. *baggabbōrím*; or possibly *baggabbârím* as in Ar.: but it is probable that original *â* had already in most, if not in all, cases become *ō*; as it certainly had in the case of the Act. Particip. Ḳal: cf. *note* on *rōzinîm*, *v.* [3]. The original *a* of the sharpened first syllable of the subst. was probably not yet thinned to *i*, as in 𝔐.

* It is, as a matter of fact, difficult to conceive that a form like *'arṣ* can ever have been pronounced without a helping vowel under the *r*, supposing this *r* to have been trilled; and, in the same way, *šiphl* cannot be pronounced as a true monosyllable, but naturally becomes *šiphel*.

Many instances may be drawn from 𝕲 showing that the thinning of an original *a* in a toneless closed syllable into *i* is a late development: cf. Μαριαμ = מִרְיָם, Μαχμας = מִכְמָשׁ, Γαλααδ = גִּלְעָד, etc.

15. *naphrôdh naphrádh.* On the analogy of the fact noticed in the preceding *note* with regard to substantives, it may be assumed that the original *a* of the preformative of Niphʿal was unthinned to *i* (so *nalḥamú*, *v.* 19; *naškaphá*, *v.* 28; cf. the T.A. glosses *naḳṣapu*, [*na*]*aḳṣapti*); and the same inference may be drawn with regard to the preformative vowel of the Perf. Hiphʿîl (*hakríbha*, *v.* 25), and the sharpened first syllable of the Perf. Piʿel (*ḥarraph*, *v.* 18; *ḳaddamám*, *v.* 21; *'aḥḥarú*, *v.* 28). In the case of the preformative vowel of the Imperf. Ḳal we have evidence from the T.A. glosses that the original *a* of the preformative was, at that period, preserved as in Ar., *yazkur* standing for יִזְכֹּר. Hence, in *v.* 17 we vocalize *yaškún* for יִשְׁכֹּן of 𝕸, and in *v.* 30 *yamṣú'ú* for יִמְצְאוּ.

26. *tašlaḥanna*, vocalized upon the analogy of the Ar. *modus energicus I.* Cf. *footnote*, p. 152.

rôšô. That an original *ra'š* (as presupposed by the Ar. *ra's*) had already developed into *rôš* in Heb. is proved by the T.A. gloss *rušunu* 'our head,' where the *u* of the syllable *ru* represents *ô*.

THE CLIMACTIC PARALLELISM OF THE SONG OF DEBORAH.

The purpose of this note is to call attention to a characteristic of the Song which is somewhat infrequent in Hebrew poetry, viz. the recurrence of a form of parallelism which has been not inaptly termed *Climactic.* In this form, stichos *b* of a distich does not offer a more or less complete echo of stichos *a* in different words (Synonymous parallelism); nor, on the other hand, is it merely formally parallel to stichos *a*, while in matter it offers an advance in thought (Synthetic parallelism). Instances of such forms of parallelism are to be found in the Song; but do not call for special comment.* In Climactic parallelism, however, stichos *b* is partially parallel to stichos *a*, but adds something further which completes the sense of the distich, thus forming, as it were, a climax. In the following examples this principle is carried out to a varying extent, in a manner which adds to the vigour and movement of the poetry. In order that the method may be the more clearly observed, the stichoi are divided into sections upon the basis of parallel and non-parallel parts; and the

* On the various forms of Hebrew parallelism, cf. Driver *LOT.*[9] pp. 362 ff.

parallel parts are placed one beneath the other, while the non-parallel sections stand separately. It may thus be observed that the non-parallel portion of stichos *b* is intended to round off and complete the whole distich.

5. The mountains shook | before Yahweh,
Before Yahweh, | the God of Israel.

6. From the days of Shamgar ben-ʿAnath
From the days of old, | caravans ceased.

7*b*. Till thou didst arise, | Deborah,
Didst arise | | as a mother in Israel.

9. Come, | ye commanders of Israel,
Ye that volunteered among the people, | bless ye Y.

11. There they recount | the righteous acts of Y.,
The righteous acts of his arm | in Israel.

12*a*. Awake, awake, | Deborah;
Awake, awake, | sing paean!

12*b*. Rise up, Baraḳ, | and lead captive
O son of Abinoʿam, | | thy captors!

18. Z. is the folk | that scorned its life to the death,
And N. | on the heights of the field.

19*a*. On came the kings, | they fought
the kings | Then fought | of Canaʿan.

20. From heaven fought | the stars
From their highways they fought | | with Ṡiṡera.

23. For they came not | to the help of Y.
To the help of Y. | mid the heroes.

28. Out through the window | leaned and exclaimed
out through the lattice | | the mother of Ṡ.

30. A spoil of dyed stuffs | for Ṡiṡera,
A spoil of dyed stuffs | | embroidery,
Dyed stuff | for the neck of the queen | two embroideries.

Cf. also *v.*[27], where the single word שדוד 'undone' in stichos *c* forms the climax to the description of Ṡiṡera's death and humiliation.

Driver (*LOT.*[9] p. 363) remarks that 'this kind of rhythm is all but peculiar to the most elevated poetry'; and quotes, as instances occurring elsewhere, Ps. 29[5], 92[9] 𝔐[10], 93[3], 94[3], 96[13], 113[1]. 'There is something analogous to it, though much less forcible and distinct, in some of the "Songs of Ascents" (Ps. 121-134), where a somewhat emphatic word is repeated from one verse (or line) in the next, as Ps. 121 [1b.2] (help); *v.* [3b.4]; *v.* [4b.5a]; *v.* [7.8a]; 122 [2b.3a], etc.'

Observation of this structural device cannot fail to suggest that the emendations and excisions proposed by some scholars, *merely for the sake of removing repetitions*, should be received with the utmost caution. Thus, *e.g.* when Rothstein emends נלחמו in *v.* [19aα] into [ו]ערכו '[and] they set the battle in array,' on the ground that 'das natürliche rhythmische Empfinden sträubt sich dagegen, in beiden Halbversen das gleiche Verbum zu lesen,' he is proceeding upon an assumption which belies the most salient characteristic in the parallelism of the Song.

THE LANGUAGE OF THE SONG OF DEBORAH.

In considering the language of the Song, one broad general principle has first to be laid down; viz. that, since Hebrew literature, as known to us from the O.T., is extremely exiguous, the Hebrew vocabulary which we possess doubtless represents only a somewhat limited part of the vocabulary which must have been in regular, if not in common, use in the written and spoken language. This is a consideration which is substantiated by the large number of ἅπαξ λεγόμενα which occur throughout the O.T.; and its importance is enhanced when it is applied to one of the very few monuments of the earliest period of the literature which happen to have survived. In discussing the text of the Song, we have noticed a number of words, the meaning of which can only be elucidated by recourse to the evidence supplied by the cognate languages. Thus, משך 'grasp,' *v.* [14], מפרצים *v.* [17], נרף *v.* [21], מחק *v.* [26], and possibly קדומים *v.* [21], are explained from the Arabic; פלגות *v.* [15] possibly from Babylonian and Phoenician usage, but more probably from Aramaic; עמלים *v.* [26] in a sense common to Arabic, Aramaic, and Babylonian, but *not* to early Hebrew as otherwise known to us; יבב *v.* [28] from Aramaic and New Hebrew; and רחם *v.* [30] from Moabitic. משאבים *v.* [11] is elucidated only by our knowledge of the meaning of the verb in Hebrew; while the signification of משפתים *v.* [16] can only be vaguely guessed. These facts do not, of course, imply that *e.g.* the list of words which are explained from the Arabic are to be regarded as Arabisms, *i.e.* that their use in the Song is *due to the influence of Arabic*; but simply that Hebrew and Arabic being from a common stock, and our knowledge of the Arabic vocabulary being much more extensive than our knowledge of the Hebrew, Arabic helps us to explain some of the otherwise unknown Hebrew words, which may have been, and very likely were, in common daily use at the early period represented by the Song.

Further, the fact urged by Vernes, in his argument for the late date of the Song, that a number of the words employed in it occur elsewhere, mainly or exclusively, in the third division of the Hebrew Canon—the *Kᵉthûbhîm*, is really destitute of significance as bearing upon the date. Hebrew poetry, like the poetry of other languages, has its choice words and expressions which are not commonly employed in prose; the great bulk of the Hebrew poetry known to us in the O.T. is contained in the *Kᵉthûbhîm* (Pss., Job, Cant., Lam.); and at least two-thirds of the words cited by Vernes in proof of his thesis are cited because they occur in these poetical books.*

There are, however, a few forms in the Song which are to be regarded as dialectical. Of those which have frequently been cited by scholars in time past, the termination ִ—ין in מִדִּין *v.*[10], and the supposed Absol. plur. termination ַ—י in שָׂרַי *v.*[15], have disappeared under our criticism of the text; but there remain the Relative שֶׁ *v.*[7] for the ordinary אֲשֶׁר; קַמְתִּי *v.*[7], if rightly regarded as 2nd fem. sing., for the normal קַמְתְּ; the form עֲמָמֶיךָ *v.*[14] (cf. Neh. 9[22.24]) with dissimilated ם, for עַמֶּךָ; and, most remarkable of all, יְתַנּוּ *v.*[11], where comparison of the cognate forms in Arabic and Aramaic, and the actual occurrence of the normal form in Hebrew (שָׁנָה 'to do a second time'), lead us to expect יְשַׁנּוּ. It should be observed that the Song is not the only example of pre-exilic literature in which these forms occur. The Relative שֶׁ is found again in *ch.* 6[17], 7[12], 8[26], in 2 Kgs. 6[11] (if the text is sound), and throughout Cant. (which, however, may be post-exilic). Instances of forms resembling קַמְתִּי for קַמְתְּ have been quoted in *note ad loc.* from Mic. 4[13], Jer. 2[20]. Forms from verbs ע *doubled* exhibiting dissimilation, like עֲמָמֶיךָ, are seen in חִקְקֵי Isa. 10[1] (as in the variant for חִקְרֵי in the Song, *v.*[15]); הֲרָרֵי Num. 23[7], JE, *al.*, הֲרָרֵי Jer. 17[3], הֲרָרֶיךָ Deut. 8[9]; צְלָלֵי Jer. 6[4]. יְתַנּוּ is substantiated by לְתַנּוֹת in *ch.* 11[40] (if original; cf. *note*).

The claim that these forms are proofs of the late date of the

* Most of the remainder occur in the prophets, who also naturally at times employ terms which would not be used in plain prose. In citation of his references to various books, Vernes frequently does not state all the facts, or states them incorrectly. Thus רַעַשׁ, which is assigned to Pss. and Ezek., occurs also in the pre-exilic prophets Am. 9[1], Nah. 1[5], Jer. 4[24], 8[16], 10[10], 50[46], 51[29]; מָגֵן, assigned to Pss., Prov., Chron., is, needless to say, very frequent also in the earliest literature; סֵפֶל, assigned to Chron., Neh., Pss. (where it does *not* occur), is only found again in Judg. 6[38] E; and so on.

Song (Vernes), and the assertion that they are late alterations of the text, (Rothstein), are, therefore, equally unwarranted; and scholars generally recognize the fact that the Hebrew of northern Cana'an must have exhibited certain dialectical peculiarities—as indeed is seen to be the case in the lengthy narratives in Kings which must have emanated from the prophetic schools of the Northern Kingdom: cf. *NHTK.* pp. 208 f.

Many scholars, however, while admitting the existence of such dialectical forms, express their doubts as to the possibility of so marked an Aramaïsm as יְתַנּוּ in an early poem, and are inclined to regard it as a textual corruption; and it is somewhat surprising to find so learned and judicious a scholar as Mo. asserting roundly that 'as equivalent of Heb. שׁנה the word is not conceivable in old Hebrew.'

Such a statement appears to imply a preconceived conclusion as to the sharp differentiation between early Hebrew and early Aramaic which, in default of evidence, we are scarcely justified in drawing. Indeed, it may be claimed that such evidence as we *do* possess as to the relationship between the two languages at a later period (and therefore, *a fortiori*, at this period) tends all in the other direction; *i.e.* it is more likely that, if we possessed ample evidence as to the character of the Hebrew or Cana'anite,* and the Aramaic, which were spoken at this period, we should find that both languages existed in dialectical forms exhibiting so many common characteristics that we should (at any rate in some examples) find it difficult, if not impossible, to draw a distinction between the two, and to say, 'This is Hebrew (Cana'anite), and this Aramaic.'

The discoveries of recent years have given us some insight into the character of the language spoken, at about the eighth century B.C., by some of the small Aramaean states which lay to the north of Israel. Thus, we have the Hadad-inscription of Panammu, king of Ya'di in northern Syria, dating from about the middle of the eighth century B.C., and the two inscriptions of his son Bar-rekub (towards the end of the same century), who seems to have been king of Sam'al as well as of Ya'di (unless the two places are to be regarded as identical). These were discovered near Zenǵîrly in the years 1889-91.‡ Next, an inscription of Zakir, king of Ḥamath and La'ash, *cir.* 800 B.C. or a little earlier, was discovered in 1903 by Pognon, and published by him in 1907.§ And, most recently, an

* The fact is well recognized that Hebrew is 'the language of Can'aan' (*cf.* Isa. 19 18); and that Phoenician, Moabitic, etc., are examples of the same language, with dialectical variations.

‡ Cf. E. Sachau in *Ausgrabungen in Sendschirli*, 1893, D. H. Müller, *Die altsemitischen Inschriften von Sendschirli*, 1893; Cooke, *NSI.* pp. 159-185.

§ Pognon, *Inscriptions Sémitiques de la Syrie, de la Mésopotamie, et de la région de Mossoul*, 1907, pp. 156-178; cf. also Driver in *Expositor*, June 1908, pp. 481-490; Lidsbarski, *Ephemeris*, iii. pp. 1-11.

inscription of Kalumu, an earlier king of Ya'di of the latter half of the ninth century B.C., has also been discovered in the neighbourhood of Zenǵîrly.*

The language of the inscriptions of Panammu and Bar-rekub, kings of Ya'di during the eighth century B.C., is clearly Aramaic of a kind, though distinguished by certain marked characteristics which connect it with Hebrew (Cana'anite) rather than with later Aramaic. Into these characteristics we cannot here enter in detail; but it may be noticed that, in the three ordinary equations, Ar. ذ = Aram. ד = Heb. ז; Ar. ث = Aram. ת = Heb. שׁ; Ar. ظ = Aram. ט = Heb. צ, it is to Hebrew and not to Aramaic that the Zenǵîrly dialect conforms. The use of שׁ where Aramaic ordinarily employs ת (*e.g.* ישׁב for יתב, שׁקל for תקל) is, we may observe, the converse of the employment of the form יְתַנּוּ in the Hebrew of the Song, where we should expect יְשַׁנּוּ.‡

Turning, however, to the inscription of Kalumu, who may have preceded Panammu as king of Ya'di by nearly a century,§ we find that his language is Cana'anite throughout, closely resembling Phoenician as known to us from inscriptions of the fourth century B.C. and later, though marked by a few Aramaïsms such as the use of בַּר 'son' in place of בֵּן.

The language of Zakir's inscription associates itself most closely with Aramaic, though offering points of contact with Cana'anite similar to those which are found in the inscriptions of Panammu and Bar-rekub; and in addition so remarkable a Hebraïsm as the use of the Imperfect with ו *consecutive*, a construction which is elsewhere only found in Biblical Hebrew and in the inscription of Mesha', king of Moab.

These facts—and more especially the remarkable alteration in the

* First edited by F. von Luschan in *Ausgrabungen in Sendschirli*, 1911; cf. also E. Littmann, 'Die Inschriften des Königs Kalumu,' in *Sitzungsberichte der Königl. Preuss. Akad. der Wiss.*, 1911, pp. 976-985; M. Lidsbarski, 'Eine phönizische Inschrift aus Zendschirli,' in *Ephemeris für Semit. Epigraphik*, iii. pp. 218-238 (he gives a list of other writers on the inscription, p. 220 *n.*). Kalumu is mentioned in the shorter inscription of Bar-rekub, in a passage which, prior to the discovery of his inscription, was not unnaturally unintelligible to editors. Bar-rekub says (ll. 15 ff.), 'And a good house my fathers, the kings of Sam'al, did not possess; they had only the house of Kalumu, and it was their winter-house and their summer-house: so I built this house.'

‡ Cf. further on the dialect of these inscriptions, Cooke, *NSI.* pp. 184 f.

§ Kalumu's father, Ḫayân the son of Gabar, paid tribute to Shalmaneser III. in B.C. 854 (cf. *KB.* i. pp. 170 f.); and seems to have been succeeded by his son Sha'il, before the accession of Kalumu. Bar-rekub states that his father Panammu, as well as himself, was a contemporary of Tiglath-Pileṡer, who reigned from 745-727 B.C.

language used by the kings of Ya'di in the course of a century or so —are sufficient to make us surmise that, if the characteristics of so-called Aramaic in the 8th and 9th centuries B.C. were such as we have noticed; in the 12th century B.C. (*i.e.* at about the period of the Song of Deborah) Aramaic may scarcely as yet have been differentiated from Hebrew as a separate language, but the two may have appeared as somewhat closely related dialectical forms of the one language which was known to the Assyrians as 'the tongue of Amurru.'

Before, therefore, we pass an opinion as to the possibility or impossibility of 'Aramaïsms' in the Song of Deḇorah, we have to take account of the following facts :—

(1) Evidence shows that even so much as three hundred years later than the date of the Song, the 'Aramaic' spoken by states in northern Syria was more nearly related to Cana'anite or Hebrew than was the Aramaic of later times.

(2) The northern, or, more accurately, central, Palestinian Hebrew of some three hundred years later, albeit that we know it as the literary language of the prophetic schools (1 Kgs. 17—2 Kgs. 10), offers certain dialectical peculiarities akin to Aramaic.

(3) The Song is probably the only existing instance of a piece of literature belonging to this early period which emanates from the extreme north of Palestine, and was perhaps composed by a member of a tribe (Issachar?) which may have been in Canaan without a break from its earliest settlement in the west; and had not, like the Joseph-tribes, undergone the segregation from external Semitic influences involved in the sojourn in Egypt (cf. *Introd.* pp. cvi ff.).

(4) In any case, the northern tribes of Israel dwelt in close association (cf. *ch.* 1 [30 ff.]) with the Cana'anites of the north, who may have been considerably influenced linguistically by their Aramaean neighbours, just as these latter were doubtless influenced by them.

(5) There were Aramaean clans closely contiguous to Israel not only on the north, but east of Jordan—the Geshurites and Ma'acathites—clans which ultimately became united to East Manasseh by intermarriage (cf. *note* on 'Machir' 5 [14] at *end*). Some of these clans may already have used the later Aram. ת for Heb. שׁ in cases in which the Ar. equivalent is ث, and may have passed on some of their terms as loan-words to the Israelites.

(6) Judg. 12 [6] is actual proof that there existed dialectical peculiarities among the Israelites in regard to the pronunciation of the sibilant שׁ (*sibbóleth* for *shibbóleth*).

Bearing these facts in mind, we may recognize the existence of 'Aramaïsms' in the Song as a natural phenomenon, and may well pause before we condemn a form such as יְתַנּוּ as impossible in a very early example of northern Israelite literature.

6. 1–8. 28. *Gideʿon.*

Besides the Commentaries, etc., quoted throughout the book, cf. W. Böhme, *Die älteste Darstellung in Richt.* 6 11-24 *und* 13 2-24, *und ihre Verwandtschaft mit der Jahveurkunde des Pentateuch, ZATW.* v. (1885) pp. 251-274; H. Winckler, *Die Quellenzusammensetzung der Gideonerzählungen, AF.* i. (1893) pp. 42-59.

The narrative of the oppression of Midian and the deliverance effected by Gideʿon is highly composite throughout. In no other section of Judges is the existence of two documents bearing the characteristics of J and E more clearly evident, and the criteria for determining the main lines of analysis are fairly decisive; though in details there remains considerable scope for difference of opinion.

6 1-6. Here R^{E2}, whose regular introductory formulae occur in *vv.* 1.6b, opens the narrative with a statement of facts derived from his old sources. We notice certain similarities to the narrative of J in 1 Sam. 13 5.6, to which *ch.* 7 12 J ('like the sand which is upon the sea-shore for multitude') is also related. The fact, however, that there is some duplication of statement (cf. *v.* 3 'there would come up Midian' with *v.* 5, 'For they and their cattle used to come up'; *v.* 4, 'And they encamped against them, and destroyed the produce of the land' with *v.* 5, 'with their tents, . . . and they came into the land to destroy it'), and the somewhat curious combination of tenses in the Heb.,* suggest that elements from more than one source have been combined; and these it is useless to attempt to unravel.‡

* After וְהָיָה . . . וְעָלָה . . . וְעָלוּ in *v.* 3 we should expect וְחָנוּ . . . וְהִשְׁחִיתוּ in *v.* 4a, more especially as these statements are continued by וְלֹא יַשְׁאִירוּ in *v.* 4b. The frequentative construction continues the narrative in *v.* 5a יַעֲלוּ . . . וּבָאוּ, and this is followed in *v.* 5b by an imperfect with ו *consecutive* וַיָּבֹאוּ 'and they came into the land, etc.', which, as summarizing in brief the result of these repeated raids, might stand in the same narrative in continuation of preceding frequentatives; but at the same time is just as likely to have been taken from another narrative which spoke of a single invasion, or viewed the repeated invasions as a single fact (cf. וַיַּחֲנוּ . . . וַיַּשְׁחִיתוּ, *v.* 4).

‡ It is possible (cf. Bu. *RS.* p. 107) that the narrative may contain later glosses. Thus ואת המערות 'and the caves' may be explanatory of את המנהרות 'the crevices,' or erroneous dittography of it. In *v.* 3b it is not unlikely that the text originally ran ועלה מדין עליו 'then would come up Midian against them' simply, and that later insertion of ועמלק ובני קדם necessitated the

6^{7-10}. The retrospect of Israel's past history and the polemic against their idolatry are in the style of the later strata of E which closely approximates to the style of R^{E2}, and, indeed, appears to have formed its model (cf. *Introd.* pp. xli ff.). We may compare generally Josh. 24, 1 Sam. 10^{17-19}, 12. Cf. especially the phraseology of *vv.* $^{8b\alpha.9a}$ with 1 Sam. 10^{18}. The phrases 'bring up *or* bring out from Egypt,' 'from the house of bondmen,' 'oppressors,' 'Yahweh your God,' 'Amorite' used as a general designation of the inhabitants of Cana'an, are characteristic of the school of Hosea'; cf. *Introd.* p. xlv. Possibly *v.* ^{7} may be due to R^{E2}; cf. *v.* ^{7a} with *v.* ^{6b}: still, the phrase, 'cried unto Yahweh,' is originally due to E^2; cf. 1 Sam. 12^{10}, Josh. 24^{7}. Moreover, the expression עַל אֹדוֹת 'on account of' in *v.* ^{7b} is characteristic of E: cf. $CH.^{E}$ 111.*

6^{11-24}. This section clearly stands in no original relationship to the foregoing. Contrast, in *v.* ^{13}, Gide'on's unconsciousness of any apparent cause for Israel's misfortunes, with the unnamed prophet's denunciation of Israel's idolatry as the crying cause of these misfortunes. The narrative generally has close affinities with *ch.* 13 and Gen. 18^{1} ff., which belong to J. Special J phrases are 'the Angel of Yahweh,' *vv.* $^{11.12.21.22}$ ('the Angel of God' in *v.* ^{20} is probably an accidental variation: cf. *note ad loc.*); 'If now I have found grace in thy sight,' *v.* ^{17}; 'Oh, my lord' (בי אדני), *v.* ^{15}: cf. $CH.^{J}$ 4, 31a, 56b.

It is probable (as supposed by Bu., Mo., etc.) that this narrative may have undergone some later modifications and additions, the main purpose of which was to imply that the divine character of Gide'on's visitor was evident from the first, and was at once recognized by Gide'on: cf. *notes* on the text. The precise extent of these secondary additions being highly debatable, no attempt has been made to indicate them in the text. Winckler's theory that two distinct narratives are here combined throughout does not commend itself.

6^{25-32} is clearly distinct in source from the foregoing. In 6^{24} Gide'on builds an altar to Yahweh, which is still, when the narrator writes, to be seen in 'Ophrah of the Abi'ezrites, and was, we may certainly infer, the only altar to Yahweh there. In *v.* ^{26}, however, he

awkward resumption ועלו. Adoption of this conclusion does not, however, oblige us to suppose that the similar detailed description of the foe in *v.* ^{33a}, $7^{12a\alpha}$ is likewise due to later interpolation; though it is possible that this may be so.

* Stade (*GVI.* i. p. 182) remarks that the introduction of *anonymous* persons, such as the prophet of this section, into the narrative, is always a mark of late date. This consideration has weight as regards the lateness of the narrative in comparison with the earlier parts of E; but by no means compels us to regard the section as later than E^2, in face of the evidence connecting it with E^2 which is noticed above.

is commanded to build an altar to Yahweh in place of the Ba'al-altar, as though no other Yahweh-altar existed in the place, though (if *vv.* 25 ff. are really the sequel of 6 11-24) he had only just previously built such an altar to Yahweh. Since 6 11-24 belongs to J, we may infer, therefore, that 6 25-32 comes from E; and with this agrees the polemic against Ba'al-worship which characterizes it, and which perhaps justifies us in regarding the section as belonging to the same stratum of E as 6 7-11, *i.e.* E^2. In addition to the phrase 'Yahweh thy God' in *v.* 26 (cf. *v.* 10), Bu. notes as an E phrase, 'rose up early in the morning' (וישכימו בבקר), *v.* 28. The name Jerubba'al, which first appears here, seems to belong to E: notice 7 1, 8 29, 9 1.2.5.16.19.24.57, 1 Sam. 12 11. R^{E2} combines Jerubba'al Gide'on 8 35a: cf. R^{JE}'s gloss, 'that is, Gide'on' in 7 1a.

6 33, describing the incursion of Midian, etc., as in *v.* 3b (cf. *footnote*), 7 12a, belongs in all probability to E: cf. *note* on 7 1. J's narrative, in 6 11-24, presupposes that the Midianites are already on the spot, and ravaging the country, at the time of Gide'on's commission.

6 34, describing Gide'on's muster of his small force from the clan of Abi'ezer only, is to be assigned to J; while

6 35, which pictures the muster of a large force from all Manasseh, Asher, Zebulun, and Naphtali, presupposes the narrative of 7 2-7 (on which see below), and must therefore, in its present form, be assigned to E^2. It seems likely, however, that the verse is composite (cf. the repeated וּמַלְאָכִים שָׁלַח 'and he sent messengers'); and that the first half, which speaks of a muster from the tribe of Manasseh, belongs to the original narrative of E, which may have been closely akin to J in assuming that Gide'on drew his force from purely local sources. The גַּם־הוּא 'it also' (the tribe of Manasseh) is R^{JE}'s link with the preceding *v.* 34.

6 36-40, which gives an account of a request by Gide'on for a sign of God's favour, can scarcely belong to the narrative 6 11-24 which contains the account of the Theophany. This latter also narrates the request for and the granting of a sign (*vv.* 17 ff.); and in face of this the second sign appears less marvellous and also superfluous. Probably it belongs to a narrative in which the call of Gide'on was related as taking place in a different manner, perhaps through the medium of a vision. Since 6 11-24 belongs to J, we shall scarcely err in assigning 6 36-40 to E, especially in view of the fact that throughout it uses 'God' (*hā-'ĕlōhîm vv.* 36.39, *'ĕlōhîm v.* 40) and not 'Yahweh.' It may be observed, however, that Gide'on's words in *v.* 39a bear close resemblance to the words of Abraham in Gen. 18 30.32, usually assigned to J.*

* According to Bu. (*RS.* p. 111) the words are probably a gloss derived from this passage. La. remarks that the words 'and I will speak only this once' are more appropriate to the Genesis-passage where the conversation is prolonged.

7 [1] appears to belong to E. Notice the connexion with 6 [33]. The invaders arrive and make their encampment as specified; Gideʿon then musters his force, and they make *their* encampment: it then remains to notice the relative positions of the two camps. 'The vale' of 7 [1b] is 'the vale of Jezreʿel' of 6 [33b].

7 [2-7]. Looking at the account of the muster (6 [35]), and the methods employed to reduce the large force from 32,000 to 10,000, and finally to 300, and reading it in the light of the narrative which follows, we can scarcely fail to trace indications of discrepancy. Thus, in 7 [23] we are informed that, on the flight of the Midianites, 'the men of Israel were called to arms from Naphtali, and from Asher, and from all Manasseh,' and joined in the pursuit. Yet these are the very tribes which, according to 6 [35], had already been mustered by Gideʿon, and the great bulk of whose representatives must, according to 7 [2-7], have been dismissed, and scarcely have had time even to reach their homes. It should be noticed, again, that in 8 [2], where Gideʿon contrasts the achievement of his own small force with that of the Ephraimites, he speaks of his force as 'Abiʿezer.' It is of course possible that under this title he may be simply referring to himself as representative of the clan; yet the allusion can scarcely fail to convey the impression that his army as a whole was composed largely if not solely of Abiʿezrites. Reading this in connexion with 6 [34] which narrates the muster of the clan, the theory becomes plausible that the original narrative may have made Gideʿon draw his force from his own clan only; and that this may account for the smallness of its numbers, until reinforced, when the pursuit was taking place, by accessions from the other clans of Manasseh, as well as from the other tribes mentioned (cf., however, *note* on 7 [23]). Thus, the passages which narrate the first muster from Manasseh, Asher, Zebulun, and Naphtali (6 [35]), and the reduction of the large force to a very small one, must, upon this view, be supposed to belong to another and a later narrative.

We have assigned 6 [35] partly to the original E (the muster of Manasseh), and partly to E [2] (the muster of the other tribes mentioned). The latter half of this verse, as narrating the muster of a large force from several tribes, is obviously intended to pave the way for the narrative of 7 [2-7], which is to be assigned in like manner to E [2]. That the narrative of E [2] has been fitted into, and is to some extent dependent upon, the older E, may be inferred from the echo of the phrase of *v.* [1], 'all the people that were with him,' in *v.* [2], 'the people that are with thee.'

7 [8]. The first part of this verse (down to 'their trumpets') is obviously intended to explain how Gideʿon came to have so many trumpets and pitchers (if the emendation adopted in the text be accepted) as are presupposed by 7 [16]; and since, in the narrative of the night-attack, there is good reason to believe that the trumpets

belong to one account and the pitchers to the other, this portion of 7^{8} must be regarded as due to the redactor of the two main narratives, *i.e.* R^{JE}. The rest of the verse is to be assigned to E^{2}; the latter half being resumptive of the narrative of the older E which was broken at 7^{1b} by insertion of the later intervening narrative.

7^{9-14}. The older narrative of E, resumed, as we have noticed, in 7^{8b}, is here continued. The relative positions of the two camps having been defined, the Midianite camp as *below* that of Gide'on *in the vale*, the way is paved for the narration of Yahweh's command, 'Go down into the camp, etc.'* Cf. 6^{25} for the introductory formula of *v.*[9], 'And it came to pass the same night, etc.'

7^{15-22}. The account of the night-attack is very involved, and it is impossible to regard it as a unity. Bu. remarks, 'To carry a burning torch in a pitcher turned upside down over it requires two hands; thus there is no hand left for the trumpet, or *vice-versâ*. In the same way, it is impossible at once to blow a horn and to raise the battle-cry' (*Comm.* p. 60). These objections to the integrity of the narrative are to some extent answered by La.; ‡ yet the fact remains that throughout the narrative there occur repetitions which can only be accounted for by the supposition that two parallel accounts have been closely interwoven. Thus *v.*[17a] is repeated by *v.*[17bβ]; *vv.*[19bα.20aα] by *v.*[22aα]; *v.*[21b] gives an account of the effects of the night-alarm which differs from that which is given by *v.*[22aβ]; and *v.*[22b] can scarcely be anything else than the combination of two variant accounts of the line of flight. Probably, therefore, the view is correct which regards the pitchers and torches as belonging to one account, and the trumpets to the other. The ruse connected with the pitchers and torches has about it an air of originality and verisimilitude, and Gide'on's small force (according to J's account) would be more likely to find pitchers or

* The obvious transition from 7^{1b}, as noticed above, seems to be the only safe argument upon which this section is assigned to E. Bu. (*Comm.*), who takes the same view as to the source of the narrative, adduces as evidence the night-scene, the dream, and its interpretation; though rightly remarking (against Winckler) that the use of *ha-'ĕlōhîm* 'God' (not Yahweh) in the mouth of a Midianite in *v.*[14] is destitute of significance as a criterion. Such evidence, however, is not very weighty. A night-scene from J immediately follows in one of the narratives of the night-attack; and though it is true that E in the Hexateuch seems to display a fondness for the narration of revelations vouchsafed in nightly visions, this fact by no means renders improbable the occurrence of a like incident in J. The section is assigned to J by Mo., though the majority of scholars appear to be of the opinion of Bu.

‡ La. suggests that, if the pitcher had a hole in it, the torch could be passed through the hole and held by the hand underneath the pitcher; and moreover, even if both hands were needed for this operation, the trumpet might at the same time be suspended from a bandolier. When the pitcher is broken, one hand is surely sufficient to carry the torch, and it is then that the trumpet is blown. Further, it goes without saying that it is possible to desist from blowing the trumpet in order to raise the battle-cry (p. 136).

jars ready to their hand than a sufficient supply of trumpets (the statement of *v.*[8] must be regarded as the work of R^{JE}): hence we shall probably be right in assigning the pitchers and torches to J, and the trumpets (perhaps under the influence of Josh. 6[12ff.]) to the later narrative of E. We may then make the following allocation. To J belong *v.*[16] with the exception of 'trumpets and' inserted by R^{JE} in joining the two narratives (notice as a J phrase 'three bands,' lit. 'heads' רָאשִׁים, as in *ch.* 9[34.37], I Sam. 11[11], 13[17f.], all probably J) *v.*[17a], *v.*[20] (from 'and they brake,' etc.) with the modification which is due to the insight of Bu. (substituting בַּחֶרֶב for הַשּׁוֹפָרוֹת לִתְקוֹעַ, and omitting חֶרֶב after וַיִּקְרְאוּ; cf. *v.*[18bβ]), 'and in their right hand the sword; and they cried, "For Yahweh and for Gideʿon!"' This is directly continued by *v.*[21]; and, possibly with some small intervening omission, by *v.*[22bβ] which recounts the direction of the enemy's flight. To E must be assigned *v.*[15] (continuing the previous E narrative), *v.*[17b], which is continued by *v.*[18] down to 'all the camp,' *v.*[19] down to 'the trumpets,' and *v.*[22] down to 'Beth-shiṭṭah,' which relates in due sequence how all the three hundred took up the trumpet-call of Gideʿon's band (read וַיִּתְקְעוּ שְׁלֹשׁ הַמֵּאוֹת בַּשּׁוֹפָרוֹת), and the effect which the demonstration had upon the foe. All that remains over appears to be the work of R^{JE} in joining and harmonizing the two narratives. Thus, mention of the trumpets had to be inserted in *v.*[16] and in *v.*[20] ('the trumpets to blow,' leading to the alteration of J's account above noticed); and mention of the battle-cry and the breaking of the pitchers from J needed to come into *vv.*[18.19], which are otherwise derived from E; just as mention of the trumpet-blowing by the three bands had to be duplicated from E's account in *v.*[22a], and inserted at the beginning of *v.*[20], which is derived from J. If this scheme be adopted, it will be found that the two accounts run parallel, and are each nearly continuous, as may be seen from the connected narrative of each which is given in the *notes ad loc.* This view of the combination of J and E assumes, as we have already noticed, that the statement of *v.*[8], which (if the emendation adopted in the text be correct) mentions both pitchers and trumpets, is the work of R^{JE}.

7[23]. This mention of the call to arms of the neighbouring Israelite tribes is inconsistent with E's narrative in 6[35], 7[2-7]; since according to this narrative these are the tribes whose representatives had been summoned in the first place, and then, for the most part, dismissed (cf. under 7[2-7]). This objection does not hold against assigning the verse to J; though, as a matter of historical fact, it may be doubted whether Gideʿon, who seems to have planned his attack in the first instance with the aid of his own clan of Abiʿezer only, would have been able, in the course of a hurried pursuit towards the south-east, to have summoned the tribes of Naphtali and Asher who dwelt to the north of the scene of action. Possibly, therefore, the verse may be a later gloss, or may have originally mentioned only 'all Manasseh.'

7^{24}-8^{3}. The difficulty noticed under the preceding verse does not apply to the summoning of Ephraim which is here narrated; since the position occupied by this tribe would enable them to intercept the fugitives in time, as is related. The source of the narrative seems to be indicated by Gideʿon's allusion in 8^{2} to his achievement as 'the vintage of Abiʿezer,' from which we are justified in assuming that we have the sequel of the account which pictures the rout of Midian as, in its inception, the unaided work of the clan of Abiʿezer; *i.e.* the account of J.* It is clear, however, that 7^{25} is, in part at least, the work of R^{JE}; the statement that the heads of ʿOreb and Ze'eb were brought to Gideʿon *beyond the Jordan* being obviously an attempt to harmonize the narrative with $8^{4ff.}$ which comes from a different source. Probably the statement 'and they pursued Midian' is also due to the same hand, with allusion to 8^{4ff}. According to J's narrative, the task of Ephraim seems to have been simply to hold the fords; and there is no indication that the pursuit was pushed across the Jordan. On the other hand, *v.*$^{25b\alpha}$, 'and the heads of ʿOreb and Ze'eb they brought unto Gideʿon,' appears to belong to J; more especially if the opening of 8^{1}, 'said *unto him*' (with back-reference to Gideʿon's name in 7^{25b}) is in its original form.

8^{4-21}. The impression which 8^{1-3} leaves upon us is that the rout of Midian is completed and pursuit at an end. The capture and execution of ʿOreb and Ze'eb may be said to constitute the chief honours of the victory. A lull in the proceedings of victorious Israel affords occasion for the recriminations of the Ephraimites. Yet in $8^{4ff.}$ we find Gideʿon crossing Jordan, and in hot pursuit of two Midianite kings, Zebaḥ and Ṣalmunnaʿ, previously unnamed. And not only so, but his chance of success appears so remote to the men of Succoth and Penuel, upon whom he calls for refreshment for his weary force, that they meet his request with a taunting refusal (*v.*^{6}). The conclusion is irresistible that the narrative of 8^{4-21} belongs to a different account from that of 7^{24}-8^{3}, and that Zebaḥ and Ṣalmunnaʿ in the one account take the place of ʿOreb and Ze'eb in the other. If 7^{24}-8^{3} is rightly assigned to J, the assumption is that 8^{4-21} belongs to E; and in favour of this conclusion there may be cited the incredibly large numbers in *v.*^{10}, which accord with the narrative of 7^{2-7} where Gideʿon's large force is reduced to 300 in order that his victory may partake of a miraculous character.‡ As a mark of E's

* La. recognizes that this section belongs to J, but other scholars very strangely assign it to E.

‡ It is not unlikely that the older narrative of E has been amplified by E^{2} in this section also, though evidence decisive of such amplification is lacking. Cf., however, the E section *vv.*$^{22-27}$ which follows.

narrative we may notice the phrasing of *v.*[4], 'And the three hundred men that were with him,' compared with 7 [1aα.2a.19]. The mention in *v.*[21] of 'the crescents that were upon the necks of their camels' is a point of connexion with *v.*[26], which belongs to a section which undoubtedly comes from E.

As we read this section, we can scarcely fail to notice that it presupposes the prior narration of incidents which have disappeared altogether from the Gide'on-narrative as known to us. Gide'on's inquiry of the Midianite kings as to the fate of his brethren (*v.*[18]) demands that some account of their murder must originally have existed in this narrative, and supplies a new motive for Gide'on's taking action against the Midianites, viz. the prosecution of the blood-feud which naturally devolved upon him. Such a motive, however, is by no means inconsistent with his *rôle* as the divinely appointed deliverer of Israel. Similar personal considerations enter into the actions of Samson which are ascribed to him as 'Judge' or vindicator of Israel; and may possibly have also influenced Baraḳ, if, as seems likely, he was at one time a captive in the hands of the Cana'anites (cf. 5 [12], *note*). We have already noticed (cf. under 6 [36-40]) that in E the account of Gide'on's call is missing, that which is derived from J (6 [11-24]) having taken its place. Probably E's account of the call was closely combined with the account of the personal outrage which is presupposed by 8 [18] ff. This is a further point which connects our narrative with E rather than J; since, if it belonged to the latter, we might reasonably expect to find some reference to the family-feud in J's account of Gide'on's call in 6 [11-24]; and Gide'on would scarcely have professed to regard himself as the man least suited for the task entrusted to him (*v.*[15]). It may be added that the obviously sincere description of Gide'on's kingly bearing given by the Midianite kings in 8 [18] is hardly consonant with his position as we gather it from J's narrative in 6 [11-24].

8 [22-27]. This section seems clearly to exhibit the hand of E^2 in *vv.*[22.23.27aβb]. In *v.*[22], the fact that 'the men of Israel' (*i.e.* the tribes as a whole; cf. *note ad loc.*) join in requesting Gide'on to become their king, invests his victory with a wider importance than it seems to have possessed in either of the older accounts. Cf., as a mark of E^2, the use of the verb הוֹשַׁעְתָּנוּ 'thou hast saved us.' In *v.*[23], the idea that the appointment of a human ruler is inconsistent with the true conception of the Theocracy, is characteristic: cf. 1 Sam. 8 [6.7],*

* The view put forward in this passage, that Israel's request for a king amounts to *a definite rejection of Yahweh's kingship*—'They have not rejected *thee*, but they have rejected *me*, that I should not be king over them'—stands in striking contrast to the standpoint of the parallel and older narrative from J, where Yahweh Himself grants a king as a mark of favour and pity: cf. 9 [16], where Samuel is instructed with regard to Saul, 'Thou shalt anoint him to be leader over my people Israel, and he shall save my people out of the hand of the Philistines: for I have looked upon my people, because their cry is come unto me.'

10[19], 12[17] (all E^2); and passages in Hosea' in which the appointment of a king appears to be regarded as a wilful act, closely bound up with Israel's defection from Yahweh—Hos. 8[4.10],* 10[3], 13[10f.] As a matter of fact, Gide'on's sons *do* seem to have become hereditary sheikhs of Shechem, by virtue of the office transmitted by their father: cf. *ch.* 9[2], where the verb *māšal*, 'rule,' is the same as is employed in 8[23], 'I will not rule over you, etc.' The polemic against the Ephod in *v.*[27], with the special term employed to describe defection from Yahweh, וַיִּזְנוּ 'and they went a whoring,' is also characteristic of E^2: cf. *Introd.* p. xlv.

There is no reason, however, to doubt that the main part of *vv.*[22-27] belongs to an older narrative: and since the verses which we assign to E^2 are *based upon* this older narrative, the inference is clear that the latter must be assigned to the older stratum of E. The connexion between *v.*[26b] and *v.*[21bβ] has already been remarked.

8[28]. The concluding summary of R^{E2}, couched in his usual style and phraseology.

6. 1. R^{E2} (JE) And the children of Israel did that which was evil in the sight of Yahweh: and Yahweh gave them into the hand of Midian seven years. 2. And the hand of Midian pre-

6. 1. *Midian.* On the situation of the land of Midian, as lying to the east or north-east of the gulf of 'Aḳaba, in the northern part of the modern Ḥiĝâz, cf. *footnote*, p. 110. The nomadic Arabian clans of Midian were regarded by the Israelites as related to themselves, though somewhat remotely. Midian is reckoned in Gen. 25[1-6] J as one of the sons of Abraham by his second wife, or concubine (*v.*[6], 1 Chr. 1[32]), Ḳeṭurah; just as Ishma'el is also Abraham's son by the concubine Hagar. The Midianites of our narrative are classed as Ishma'elites in *ch.* 8[24]; and similarly, in the story of Jošeph and his brethren, Gen. 37[25ff.], while the J narrative relates that Jošeph was sold, at Judah's suggestion, to Ishma'elite traders, the E narrative makes him to have been kidnapped by passing Midianites. It thus appears that some amount of vagueness existed in the minds of Israelite historians in their definition of these Arab tribes: and with this inference agrees the fact that, whereas the land of Midian which formed the home of Moses during his exile from Egypt lay far to the south of Cana'an (cf. also 1 Kgs. 11[18]), Gen. 25[6] describes Abraham as sending away the sons of the concubines (including Midian) 'eastward, into the land of the east'; and similarly, one of the Bala'am-

* Hos. 8[10] should almost certainly be emended (after 𝔊) וְיֶחְדְּלוּ מְעַט מִמְּשֹׁחַ מֶלֶךְ וְשָׂרִים 'that they may cease for a little from anointing a king and princes.'

vailed against Israel: because of Midian the children of Israel made themselves the crevices which are in the mountains, and the caves, and the strongholds. 3. Now it used to be that, when Israel had sown, there would come up Midian, and ʿAmaleḳ, and the children of the East; they would come up against them. 4. And they encamped against them, and destroyed the produce of the land as far as Ġaza; and they would leave no means of sustenance in Israel, neither sheep, nor ox, nor ass. 5. For they

narratives embodied in Num. 22-24 (JE) pictures 'elders of Midian' as forming the retinue of Balaḳ, king of Moab ($22^{4.7}$; cf. also the late narrative of P in Num. 31^{1-12}). See further, on this point, Skinner, *Genesis* (*ICC.*), p. 349.

2. *because of Midian, etc.* The limestone-hills of Palestine are full of caves of various shapes and sizes, which are partly natural and partly artificial. The writer of our narrative traces the origin of these caves to the Israelite refugees, for whom they formed welcome hiding-places. Cf. 1 Sam. 13^{6} J.

crevices. Heb. *minhārôth*, a ἅπαξ λεγόμενον, is explained from the Ar. *minhara* or *minhar*, lit. a place hollowed out by water.

3. *Now it used to be, etc.* The Heb. tenses employed in *vv.*$^{3-5}$ for the most part denote recurrence; but there are some exceptions which probably point to a combination of two originally separate narratives. Cf. *footnote* * p. 176.

there would come up Midian, etc. The Arab tribes from the east of Jordan commit similar depredations upon the peasant-proprietors west of Jordan at the present day, pitching their tents in the Wâdy of Jezreʿel and the Wâdy Šerrâr a little further north, as is described in our narrative, $7^{1.12}$. Cf. Thomson, *LB.* pp. 447 f.

and ʿAmaleḳ, and the children of the East. Possibly a later insertion in the narrative: cf. *footnote* ‡ p. 176. On ʿAmaleḳ, cf. *ch.* 3^{12} *note.* The expression 'children of the East' is used again in 1 Kgs. 4^{30} 𝔥 5^{10} (cited for their proverbial wisdom), Isa. 11^{14}, Jer. 49^{28} (|| Ḳedar), Ezek. $25^{4.10}$, Job 1^{3}, as a general description of the Arab tribes to the east of Jordan, extending as far as the Euphrates; but in Gen. 29^{1} E 'the land of the children of the East' is applied to the district of N. Mesopotamia in which Ḥaran was situated.

4. *as far as Ġaza. I.e.*, as far as the south-western extremity of the Philistine territory. According to this statement, the Midianite incursions must have extended over the greater part of Palestine. The remainder of the narrative, however, appears to confine them to central Palestine; and Gideʿon's exertions rid the country of them at one blow. Possibly, therefore, the reference may be due to a later editor, who was thinking of incursions of Arab tribes from the south (ʿAmaleḳites?); and it may have been this hand which was responsible

and their cattle used to come up, with their tents, ⌜and⌝ would come in like locusts for multitude; and both they and their camels were without number: and they came into the land to destroy it. 6. And Israel was brought very low by reason of Midian; and the children of Israel cried unto Yahweh.

7. E² And when the children of Israel cried unto Yahweh by reason of Midian, 8. Yahweh sent a prophet unto the children of Israel: and he said to them, 'Thus saith Yahweh, the God of Israel, "*I* brought you up from Egypt, and I brought you forth from the house of bondmen, 9. and I rescued you from the hand of Egypt, and from the hand of all your oppressors; and I drave them out from before you, and gave you their land. 10. And I said to you, 'I am Yahweh your God; ye shall not fear the gods of the Amorites in whose land ye are dwelling': but ye have not hearkened to my voice."'

11. J And the Angel of Yahweh came, and sat under the

for the allusion to ''Amaleḳ and the children of the East,' in addition to Midian, in the earlier part of the verse.

5. *with their tents.* Lit. 'and their tents.' In the verbal form which follows, 'and would come in,' we adopt the reading of *Ḳᵉrê* וּבָאוּ. 𝔊^AL, 𝔖^h, Θ., 𝔏 presuppose יָבִאוּ, which would govern וְאָהֳלֵיהֶם 'and their tents they would bring in, etc.' Since this reading, however, seems to make the following 'like locusts for multitude' refer to the tents and not to the Midianites (as in 7 ¹²), it must be regarded as inferior to that which is adopted above. It is possible, however, that *Kt.* may indicate the Ḳal יָבֹאוּ 'they used to come in,' the *asyndeton* being due to careless piecing together of the parallel narratives.

8. *a prophet.* Lit. 'a man, a prophet' or 'a prophet-man.' Cf. 'a prophetess-woman,' *ch.* 4 ⁴.

***I** brought you up, etc.* It is characteristic of E² to base admonition and rebuke upon a retrospect of God's mercies as vouchsafed to Israel in their past history. Cf. Josh. 24 ²ᶠᶠ·, Judg. 10 ¹¹ᶠ·, 1 Sam. 2 ²⁷·²⁸,* 10 ¹⁷ᶠᶠ·, 12 ⁷ᶠᶠ. This method is further developed in Deuteronomy; probably owing to the influence of the school of thought represented by E². Cf. *Introd.* p. xlv.

11. *the Angel of Yahweh.* Upon the conception involved in this title, and its alternation with 'Yahweh' simply in *vv.* ¹⁴·¹⁶·²³, cf. *note* on *ch.* 2 ¹.

* 1 Sam. 2 ²⁷⁻³⁶ is commonly regarded as later than E², though without adequate reason.

terebinth which was in ʿOphrah, which belonged to Joash the Abiʿezrite; and Gideʿon his son was beating out wheat in the wine-press, to save it from Midian. 12. And the Angel of Yahweh appeared unto him, and said unto him, 'Yahweh is with thee, thou mighty man of valour.' 13. And Gideʿon said unto him, 'Oh, my lord, if Yahweh *is* with us, why, then, hath

the terebinth. Heb. *hā-'ēlā*; possibly 'the (sacred) tree,' without specification of its species: cf. *note* on 'the palm-tree of Deborah,' *ch.* 4[5]. The terebinth or turpentine-tree (*Pistacia terebinthus*, *L.*) is frequent in Palestine, where it often grows to a large size; and, since it usually stands in isolation, it forms a prominent landmark. Many of these trees are regarded as objects of veneration at the present day. Cf. Tristram, *Nat. Hist.* pp. 400 f.

ʿOphrah. The site is unknown. It may be inferred from *ch.* 9[1.2] that it was not far from Shechem. Neither Farʿatâ, six miles west-south-west of Shechem (*SWP. Mem.* ii. p. 162), nor Farʿah as preserved in the name of the wâdy to the east of Shechem (Bu.), are philologically probable; the former name accurately corresponding to the Biblical Pirʿathon. The designation 'ʿOphrah of the Abiʿezrites' (*v.*[24], 8[32]) is perhaps intended to distinguish the city from the Benjaminite ʿOphrah mentioned in Josh. 18[23] P (so Kimchi).

which belonged, etc. The reference is to the terebinth, and not to the city of ʿOphrah.

the Abiʿezrite. Abiʿezer is named in Josh. 17[2] as a clan of Manasseh—a fact which also appears from *v.*[15] of our narrative. The clan is referred to the Machir-division of Manasseh in Num. 26[30] P, 1 Chr. 7[18]: cf. *note* on 'Machir,' *ch.* 5[14].

was beating, etc. The Heb. *ḥābhaṭ* 'beat out' (with a stick) is similarly used of threshing grain in a small quantity in Ru. 2[17]. The ancient wine-press (Heb. *gath*) was a trough hewn out of the solid rock, in which the grapes were trodden by the foot; the expressed juice flowing down a channel into another trough at a slightly lower level, the wine-vat (Heb. *yéḳebh*). The use of a wine-press in a sheltered situation for the beating out of wheat was less likely to attract the attention of marauding Midianites than the ordinary process of threshing with a wain drawn by oxen (or an ox and an ass), upon a threshing-floor in an exposed situation open to the wind.

13. *If Yahweh* **is** *with us.* Heb. וְיֵשׁ י׳ עִמָּנוּ. The use of וְ before יֵשׁ—lit. '*And is* Y. with us'—imparts a touch of sarcasm to Gideʿon's response which it is difficult adequately to reproduce in English. Cf. 1 Kgs. 2[22], 'Why, *pray*, askest thou Abishag the Shunammite for Adonijah?' (ולמה, lit. '*And* why'); 2 Kgs. 7[19], '*Pray*, if Yahweh were to make windows in heaven, could this thing

all this happened to us? and where are all his wondrous works which our fathers recounted to us, saying, "Did not Yahweh bring us up from Egypt?" But now Yahweh hath cast us off, and given us into the hand of Midian.' 14. And Yahweh turned unto him, and said, 'Go in this thy strength, and save Israel from the hand of Midian: have not I sent thee?' 15. And he said unto him, 'Oh, my ⌜l⌝ord, whereby can I save Israel?

come to pass?' (והנה, lit. '*And* lo'). Other instances are cited in *NHTK.* p. 20.

which our fathers recounted to us. Cf., for the phrase, Ps. 44^{1} (𝔥 ^{2}), 78^{3}. The injunction is laid upon Israelite fathers to recount to their children the facts of the deliverance from Egypt in Ex. $12^{26.27}$, $13^{8.14.15}$ (R^{JE}?), Deut. 6^{20ff}. It is possible that Gide'on's speech, as it stood originally in J, may have been expanded by a later hand in *v.* ^{13b}.

14. *Yahweh.* 𝔊^{BAL} ὁ ἄγγελος Κυρίου. Cf. *v.* ^{16} *note.*

have not I sent thee? Since these words embody a direct commission from Yahweh, it is supposed by many scholars that Gide'on must at once have recognized that he was being addressed by Yahweh or His Angel; and that the passage is therefore inconsistent with *v.* ^{22}, where it is stated that it was only *after the miracle of v.* ^{21} that Gide'on recognized who his visitor was. The whole section, *vv.* $^{11-24}$, having clearly undergone some amount of re-editing (cf. *notes* following), it is quite likely that this passage may be due to the later hand; as also the words 'I will be with thee' in *v.* ^{16}, which recall Ex. 3^{12} E. While, however, the narrative assumes that Yahweh, in order to appear visibly to Gide'on, clothes Himself in human form, it does not necessarily follow from this that He should dissemble His presence by couching His commission in the form in which it would be delivered by an intermediary, such as a prophet ('Hath not Yahweh sent thee?'). On the other hand, even though Yahweh should give His commission *directly*, as He is represented as doing, here and in *v.* ^{16}, by the narrative as it now stands, it would obviously require something more surprising than this direct commission (viz. the portent of *v.* ^{21}) to convince Gide'on that he was actually the spectator of a Theophany.

While, therefore, we may *suspect* conflation of the narrative in the passages under discussion, it is a mistake to speak dogmatically and to say that they *cannot* originally have stood alongside of *v.* ^{22}.

15. *my lord.* Vocalizing אֲדֹנִי, in place of אֲדֹנָי of 𝔐, *i.e.* 'my (divine) Lord.' The vocalization of 𝔐 is intended to indicate that Gide'on by this time recognized that his visitor was Yahweh Himself; but it is clear from *v.* ^{22} that this was not the case until the occurrence of the events narrated in *v.* ^{21}. The form which we have adopted is

behold my family is the weakest in Manasseh, and I am the least in my father's house.' 16. And Yahweh said unto him, 'I will be with thee, and thou shalt smite Midian as one man.'

the ordinary title of respect (like our 'sir'), and is so vocalized by 𝕸 in *v.*[13].

behold, my family, etc. Mo. compares 1 Sam. 9[21]; and remarks that 'the protestation is, no more than that of Saul, to be taken too literally. Both the following narratives imply that the hero's family was one of rank and influence in the clan.' The word rendered 'family' properly means 'thousand' (Heb. *'éleph*); and occurs in connexion with tribal organization in 1 Sam. 10[19] ('by your tribes and by your thousands'), the following *vv.*[20.21] showing it to be synonymous with *mišpāḥā*, the ordinary term for a *clan* or *family* within the tribe. Cf. also the use of the word in Mic. 5[2] ('the thousands of Judah,' among which Bethlehem is a small 'thousand' or 'clan').

the weakest. Heb. הַדַּל, which R.V. renders 'the poorest.' The adj., however, suggests not merely poverty, but also paucity of numbers and lack of influence in the affairs of the tribe as a whole.

16. *And Yahweh . . . 'I will be with thee.'* 𝕲[BA] καὶ εἶπεν πρὸς αὐτὸν ὁ ἄγγελος Κυρίου, Κύριος ἔσται μετὰ σοῦ. If this had originally stood in the Heb. text, it is very unlikely that it would have been altered into the reading of 𝕳; and we should rather regard the readings of 𝕲, here and in *v.*[14], as due to the harmonizing tendency which is elsewhere frequently manifested in this Version. 𝕲[L] 𝕾[h] agree with 𝕳 in the present passage. As we have already remarked (*ch.* 2[1] *note*), it is not unlikely that the original narrative spoke throughout of Yahweh Himself as appearing to Gideʿon and holding intercourse with him; and that the introduction of 'the Angel' represents an early attempt to modify the text which has not been thoroughly carried out in 𝕳.

'I will be with thee.' Cf. *note* on 'have not I sent thee?' *v.*[14]. The precise words כי אהיה עמך are found in Ex. 3[12], E's narrative of the Theophany to Moses at Mount Ḥoreb: cf. also Josh. 1[5] R[D]. In each of these passages, the writers, in using the verbal form *'ehyeh* 'I will be,' probably have in view the significance of the name Yahweh as denoting *progressive revelation*, as is explained in Ex. 3[14] in the formula *'ehyeh 'ăšer 'ehyeh* 'I will be (*or* become) what I will be.' While, however, the latter formula refers to the revelation *as a whole*, as it is to be unfolded throughout the history of the chosen people, and the course of this revelation is intentionally left undefined,* in the former expression we have a particular phase of the

* Cf. the similar phrase 'I will have mercy upon whom I will have mercy,' Ex. 33[19] J, which implies that God refuses to define beforehand a course of action which will be determined by his sovereign will. Similarly, *'ehyeh 'ăšer*

17. And he said unto him, 'Prithee, if I have found grace in thy sight, make me a sign that thou art speaking with me. 18. Depart not hence, prithee, until I come unto thee, and

revelation clearly stated—Yahweh promises that He *will be with* each of three chosen servants, Moses, Joshua', and Gide'on.

R.V. renders 'Surely I will be with thee' (so in Ex. 3[12], 'Certainly, etc'); but it is preferable to regard the כִּי as simply introducing the direct narration, like ὅτι *recitativum* in Greek. Such a use of כִּי is frequent: cf. examples collected in *NHTK.* p. 6; BDB. *s.v.* 1b.

as one man. For the expression, cf. *ch.* 20[1.8.11], Num. 14[15], 1 Sam. 11[7], 2 Sam. 19[14], 𝔐 [15], Ezr. 3[1], Neh. 8[1] †.

17. *Prithee, if I have found, etc.* Here 'prithee' represents the Heb. precative particle *nā*, which comes in the protasis of the sentence after the conjunction 'if,' and is rendered 'now' by A.V., R.V.—'If now I have found grace, etc.' Such a rendering, however, can scarcely be held adequately to represent the precative force of the particle*; and the rendering 'prithee' has therefore been adopted, the fuller 'I pray thee,' sometimes employed as a rendering by A.V., R.V., (cf. *v.* [39], 8[5], *al.* ‡) being less suitable as making too much of the monosyllabic particle. It is obvious that, so far as the particle expresses *entreaty*, it properly refers to the request which is formulated in the apodosis; but its use at the commencement of the protasis is probably intended to place the speaker in the attitude of a suppliant from the moment that he opens his mouth.

make me a sign that thou, etc. As the narrative stands, the request seems to indicate Gide'on's dawning consciousness that his visitor is a supernatural being, and his inability (owing to his uncertainty) to

'ehyeh implies that God is absolutely self-determined, and that what He *will be* is to be revealed at His own good pleasure. Cf. the present editor's criticism of Dr. Davidson's interpretation of the two phrases (*Theology of the O.T.*, p. 56), in *JTS.* vi. p. 466.

* For the use of 'now' in the rendering of A.V., R.V., cf. the illustrations collected in the Oxford *New Eng. Dict.*, vi. *s.v.* II. 9, where the adverb is used 'In sentences expressing a command or request, with the purely temporal sense weakened or effaced': *e.g.* Shakespeare, *Love's Labour's Lost,* II. i. 124, 'Now faire befall your maske'; *Tempest,* III. i. 15, 'Alas, now pray you worke not so hard . . . pray now rest yourselfe.' The usage is similar in modern colloquial speech, in such a form of request as 'Now, don't forget!'

‡ In *v.* [39] A.V., R.V. the rendering 'I pray thee' stands side by side with the rendering 'now'—'Let me prove, *I pray thee,* but this once with the fleece; let it *now* be dry only upon the fleece.' In 7[3] A.V., R.V. *nā* is rendered 'Go to,' as in Isa. 5[5], Jer. 18[11] (on the use of this obsolete expression, cf. *DB.* ii. 194*a*); apparently because the rendering 'I pray thee' was felt to be unsuitable in the mouth of Yahweh. There is no reason, however, why 'prithee' should not be employed in these passages also as the *conventional* introduction of a request (or a command couched as such), which is what *nā* amounts to in Heb.

bring my present, and set it before thee.' And he said, 'I will abide until thou returnest.' 19. And Gide'on went in, and made ready a kid of the goats, and unleavened cakes of an ephah of

express himself clearly through fear of giving offence. He desires confirmation of his surmise, but does not quite know how to phrase his request, or what kind of sign to expect, because he is not yet clear as to the character of the stranger.

In what follows, however, in *v.*[18] there is no reference to a *sign*, the sign of *v.*[21] being clearly unexpected by Gide'on; and the act of grace which is asked of the stranger is to stay while a meal is prepared for him, the conversion of which into a sacrifice does not seem to be *anticipated.* It is likely, therefore, that, as Mo., Bu., etc., think, *v.*[17b] may be an editorial addition,* and that originally *v.*[17a] was directly connected with *v.*[18a]—an arrangement which would make the passage closely parallel to Gen. 18[3] J, 'Prithee, if I have found grace in thy sight, prithee pass not away from thy servant.'

18. *my present.* The Heb. *minḥā* frequently denotes a gift voluntarily offered (cf. *note* on 'tribute,' *ch.* 3[15]); but it is somewhat strange to find it applied to hospitality offered in the form of a meal. It is possible, therefore, that the term is intended to denote (*sacrificial*) *offering* (so 𝔊 τὴν θυσίαν, 𝔙 'sacrificium'), and that its employment is due to editorial alteration in view of the fact that the meal actually *did* become a sacrifice: cf. *note* preceding. Bu. conjectures that, in place of 'and bring my *minḥā*,' the original narrative may have used the words 'and bring unto thee a morsel of bread': cf. Gen 18[5].

19. *made ready, etc.* If we regard this description as referring to the preparation of an ordinary meal, we must suppose that the cakes are unleavened as necessarily prepared in haste; and that the broth is probably the liquid in which the meat was boiled (Kimchi), which, as containing much of its nutritiousness, would not be wasted. Böhme, however, finds in the ingredients of the meal the three forms of sacrificial offering—flesh-offering, meal-offering, and drink-offering,—and therefore regards *v.*[19aβ] ('the flesh . . . pot') and *v.*[20] as a later addition to the narrative, inserted for the purpose of giving to the meal the character of a religious offering. This view is also favoured by Bu. Against it, Mo. remarks, 'if the object was to convert Gide'on's hospitality into a sacrifice, it would have been done unmistakably. In no ritual that we know was meat presented in a basket (as unleavened cakes were) or a libation made of broth. It is conceivable that such rites existed in this early time; but not that such a description proceeds from a later edition. I find in the words, how-

* The unusual relative particle שׁ, as in 8[26], is thought to mark the passage as a gloss.

meal: the flesh he put in a basket, and the broth he put in a pot; and he brought it out unto him under the terebinth, and presented it. 20. And the Angel of God said unto him, 'Take the flesh and the unleavened cakes, and set them on yonder crag, and pour out the broth': and he did so. 21. And the Angel of Yahweh stretched forth the end of the staff which was in his hand, and touched the flesh and the unleavened cakes; and fire went up from the rock, and devoured the flesh and the

ever, no certain evidence of a sacrificial intention; even וַיַּגֵּשׁ ['and presented it'] is properly used of bringing food to one, putting it within his reach (Gen. 27^{25}).' The question must be held to be doubtful; cf. *note* following.

an ephah. A dry measure, corresponding to the liquid measure called *bath*, each containing the tenth part of a *ḥômer*: cf. Ezek. 45^{11}. Its content was probably about a bushel. Such a quantity of flour—weighing some 45 lb., and sufficient to make about twenty-three of our ordinary loaves—is hugely in excess of the needs of the occasion; and possibly this consideration should be held to weigh in favour of the opinion that the writer has in view a religious offering rather than an ordinary meal prepared for a single individual.

20. *The Angel of God.* The expression is that which is commonly employed by E (cf. *ch.* 2^{1} *note*); J's phrase, which is elsewhere employed throughout this narrative, being 'the Angel of Yahweh' (so here $\mathfrak{G}^{AL}$, $\mathfrak{S}^{h}$, $\mathfrak{L}^{L}$). Probably the present variation is merely due to transcriptional accident (Mo.), and does not indicate a difference of source.

'*Take the flesh, etc.*' This ritual as here prescribed can scarcely fail to suggest to us the ancient rock-altar with cup-marks on its surface for receiving libations, such as have been discovered in the excavations of various ancient sites in Palestine: cf. Driver, *Schweich Lectures*, pp. 66 f.; Vincent, *Canaan*, pp. 94 ff.; *TB*. ii. pp. 2 f. Possibly, therefore, the origin of the legend should be traced to the fact that such a rock-altar existed at ʿOphrah in later times, and that its consecration as such was popularly ascribed to the occasion here related. If this is so, however, why are we told in *v.*^{24} that Gideʿon subsequently *built* an altar to Yahweh on the site? Perhaps we should find in these facts (as Wellh. thinks) an indication of the composite character of the narrative.

21. *stretched forth . . . in his hand.* We may note the verbal similarity to 1 Sam. 14^{27}—also J.

and fire went up, etc. The supernatural fire is a token of the Divine acceptance of the offering as well as of the power of the Deity: cf. 1 Kgs. $18^{22ff.}$, Lev. 9^{24}, 2 Chr. 7^{1}. In the similar narrative of *ch.* $13^{19.20}$ it seems that Manoaḥ kindles his sacrifice in the ordinary way.

unleavened cakes: and the Angel of Yahweh departed from his sight. 22. And Gide'on perceived that he was the Angel of Yahweh; and Gide'on said, 'Alas, Lord Yahweh! forasmuch as I have seen the Angel of Yahweh face to face.' 23. And Yahweh said to him, 'Peace be to thee; fear not. Thou shalt not die.' 24. So Gide'on built there an altar to Yahweh, and called it *Yahweh shālôm*. Unto this day it is still in 'Ophrah of the Abi'ezrites.

from the rock. The fact that 'the crag' (*has-sélaʿ*) of *v.*[20] is here called 'the rock' (*haṣ-ṣûr*) is noted by several commentators; but it scarcely seems necessary to infer diversity of source from this small variation.

and the Angel of Yahweh departed, etc. Cf. *ch.* 13[20], where the Angel ascends in the flame from the altar, and disappears.

22. *And Gide'on perceived, etc.* Here we have a clear indication that it is only after the portent related in *v.*[21] that Gide'on recognizes the supernatural character of his guest. Cf. *note* on 'my lord,' *v.*[15].

'*Alas, etc.*' For the idea that no human being can see God and survive, unless through an exceptional manifestation of the Divine favour, cf. *ch.* 13[22f.], Gen. 16[13] J,* 32[30] 𝔐[31] J, Ex. 24[9-11] J, 33[18-23] J. E in Ex. 20[19] extends the danger of death to the hearing of the voice of God: cf. Deut. 4[33], 5[25.26]. We may notice also the words of Isa'iah in Isa. 6[5]. On the other hand, Ex. 33[11] E states that 'Yahweh used to speak unto Moses face to face (פָּנִים אֶל־פָּנִים, as in our passage), as a man speaketh unto his friend.'

23. *And Yahweh said, etc.* It is rather strange to find Yahweh again speaking after the departure of His visible representative (*v.*[21bβ]); and there is no indication that the voice is to be understood as coming from heaven, as inferred by Kimchi and Levi ben-Gershon. It seems likely, therefore, that *vv.*[22-24] may be due to a later hand, in explanation of the name of the altar, *Yahweh shālôm*. Cf. the inference already drawn, in the *note* on 'Take the flesh, etc.' *v.*[20], as to *vv.*[20.21] in relation to *vv.*[22-24].

24. *Yahweh shālôm.* The meaning is 'Yahweh is peace,' *i.e.* 'is *peaceful*' or '*well-disposed*.' For this use of *šālôm* (substantive in place of adjective), cf. Ps. 120[7],

'I am peace; but when I speak,
They are for war.'

* In this passage we ought probably to follow Wellh. in emending Hagar's words, הֲגַם אֱלֹהִים רָאִיתִי וָאֶחִי אַחֲרֵי רֹאִי 'Have I actually seen God and lived after my vision?'

25. E² And it came to pass the same night, that Yahweh said to him, 'Take ⌜ten men of thy servants⌝, and a bull [] of seven

25. *And it came to pass the same night.* Cf., for the exact phrase, *ch.* 7⁹, 2 Sam. 7⁴, 2 Kgs. 19³⁵. 'The same night,' if the expression is an integral part of the source (E²; cf. the same phrase in *v.*⁴⁰ E), probably refers to the night following the day on which the unnamed prophet uttered his denunciation (*vv.*⁷⁻¹⁰). It is possible, however, that the phrase may be the redactional formula of R^{JE}, and may refer to the Theophany which immediately precedes in the narrative as it at present stands.

'*Ten men . . . years old.* The text of 𝔐 is here incomprehensible, and can only be naturally rendered 'the bull of the ox which belongeth to thy father, and the second bull of seven years old.' Only one bull, however, is mentioned in *vv.*²⁶·²⁸; and apart from the difficulty involved in the expression 'the bull of the ox,'* it is impossible to divine why Gide'on should be ordered to take this first mentioned animal, seeing that it is not utilized in any way in the narrative which follows. R.V. (in agreement with Ew., Stu., Ke., etc.) explains the conjunction ו 'and' in the sense 'even,' thus making the reference to be to one animal only; but it is more than doubtful whether such a rendering is legitimate.‡

Clearly the text of 𝔐 must have suffered corruption; but the Versions seem to have had practically the same text before them, and thus afford us little or no help.

𝔊ᴮ, τὸν μόσχον τὸν ταῦρον ὅς ἐστιν τῷ πατρί σου καὶ μόσχον δεύτερον ἑπταετῆ, agrees in all respects with 𝔐. The only important variations offered by 𝔊ᴬᴸ are τὸν μόσχον τὸν σιτευτόν in place of τὸν μόσχον τὸν ταῦρον, and the omission of καί before the second μόσχον. This at any rate yields an intelligible sense; 'the second bull of seven years old' being taken as a further definition of 'thy father's fatted bull,' and the reference thus being to one animal only; though why the

* A somewhat similar collocation is seen in Ps. 69³¹, 𝔐³², מִשּׁוֹר פָּר 'more than an ox-bull.' Here, however, parallelism and rhythm compel us to divide the stichoi at מִשּׁוֹר, and, probably, to read מִפָּר in place of פָּר :—

'And it shall please Yahweh more than an ox;
<More than> a bull that hath horns and parted hoofs.'

‡ A few cases can be cited in which the conjunction ו appears to have such an explicative force; but they are rare, and in most cases the text is open to suspicion. Cf. 1 Sam. 17⁴⁰, 'and he put them into the shepherd's bag which he had, *even* into the scrip' (וּבַיַּלְקוּט); 1 Sam. 28³, 'and they buried him in Ramah, *even* in his city' (וּבְעִירוֹ.) See further BDB. *s.v.* ו, 1 b; G-K. § 154, *n* 1b.

years old, and pull down the altar of Baʿal which belongeth to thy father, and cut down the Ashera which is by it. 26. And

animal in question should be described as 'the second,' with assumed reference to an unnamed 'first' bull, remains obscure. It should be noticed, however, that τὸν μόσχον τὸν σιτευτόν simply represents the rendering of 𝔊^{AL} in *v.*^{28}, *i.e.* הַפַּר הַשֵּׁנִי 'the second bull' read as הַפַּר הַשָּׁמֵן 'the fatted bull.' It seems obvious, therefore, that the text of 𝔊^{AL} has suffered correction after *v.*^{28}, and that we have no real elucidation of 𝔐's פַּר־הַשּׁוֹר 'the bull of the ox.' Some MSS. of 𝔊 represent ופר השני וג׳ by καὶ μόσχον ἑπταετῆ with omission of δεύτερον ; and this word is marked with an asterisk in 𝔖^{h}.

𝔙 'taurum patris tui,' 𝔖^{P} ܠܬܘܪܐ ܕܐܒܘܟ 'the bull of thy father,' omitting either פר or השור ; or possibly rendering the difficult compound expression by a single term, just as is done by R.V., 'thy father's bullock,' cutting the difficulty. 𝔗 simply represents the text of 𝔐.

In face of this difficulty, the most satisfactory course seems to be to follow Kue. (in Doorn., p. 70 *n.*) and to restore the text after *v.*$^{27a\alpha}$, קַח עֲשָׂרָה אֲנָשִׁים מֵעֲבָדֶיךָ וּפַר שֶׁבַע שָׁנִים, omitting השני 'the second' as an insertion made subsequently to the textual corruption which introduced apparent mention of *two* bulls : cf. for this latter point, the evidence from the Versions above cited. Gideʿon is commanded to take ten men of his servants, and in *v.*^{27} it is stated, with no more than the necessary variation in wording, that he took them. Such detailed repetition is characteristic of Heb. story-telling, as of Babylonian ; and is a feature which, so far from appearing tautologous, adds a certain vivid picturesqueness to the narrative. It will be sufficient here to compare *ch.* 7$^{10b.11b}$: '"Go down, thou and Purah thy lad, unto the camp" . . . So he went down, he and Purah his lad, etc.'

Kue.'s emendation is favoured by Bu., Oort, Mo. (*Comm.*), Kit., Gress. ; but Mo. (*SBOT.*), La. prefer to read simply קַח אֶת־הַפַּר הַשָּׁמֵן 'Take the fatted bull.'

the Ashera. The *'ăshērā* (plur. usually *'ăshērîm* ; in two late passages, 2 Chr. 19^{3}, 33^{3} *'ăshērôth* ; Judg. 3^{7} probably a textual error for *ʿashtārôth* ; cf. *note ad loc.*) was an idolatrous object, the precise character of which is very doubtful. The most lucid reference is Deut. 16^{21}, where it is enjoined, 'Thou shalt not plant an Ashera—any kind of tree (*or* wood) beside the altar of Yahweh.' We thus gather that the Ashera was a wooden object (cf. *v.*^{26} of the present context), possibly a tree-trunk or pole, which was 'planted,' or, as 2 Chr. 33^{19} has it, 'set on end' in the ground beside an altar (cf. the present passage). This inference is borne out by the various verbs which are employed to describe the destruction of the Ashera, *e.g.* it might be 'cut down' (*v.*^{25}, 2 Kgs. 18^{4}, 23^{14}), 'chopped down' (Deut. 7^{5}, 2 Chr. 14^{3}, 𝔐^{2}, 31^{1}), 'plucked up' (Mic. 5^{14}, 𝔐^{13}), 'pulled down' (2 Chr. 34^{7}), or 'burnt' (Deut. 12^{3}, 2 Kgs. 23^{15}). It is commonly supposed, upon this evidence, that the Ashera was a symbol of, or substitute for, the sacred tree which was regarded by the early Semites as the abode of a deity; much as the *maṣṣēbhā* or standing stone preserved the idea that the deity was accustomed to inhabit stones or rocks. Upon the unsatisfactory character of this inference, cf. Mo. in *EB.* 331.

There are passages in the O.T. in which Ashera seems to be used as the name of a Cana'anite *goddess.* Thus, in 2 Kgs. 21^{7} mention is made of 'the graven image of the Ashera' placed by Manasseh in the Temple. 2 Kgs. 23^{7} perhaps speaks of women weaving 'shrines' (*bāttîm*, lit. 'houses') for the Ashera; and the Ba'al and the Ashera are coupled together as the objects of idolatrous worship: 1 Kgs. 18^{19}, 2 Kgs. 23^{4}.

We find the name Aširtu or Ašratu in Babylonian as the name of a goddess, who was doubtless of Amorite origin. In an inscription dedicated to Ašratum on behalf of Ḫammurabi, in which this king is specially designated as king of Amurru (the west land), the goddess appears as 'bride of the king of heaven' (*kallat šar šamê*), and as 'mistress of sexual vigour and rejoicing' (*bêlit kuzbi u ulṣi*): cf. Hommel, *Aufsätze und Abhandlungen*, ii. p. 211. The name Abd-Aširta = 'servant of Ashera' is borne by the chieftain of Amurru who figures prominently in the T.A. Letters (cf. *Introd.* p. lxxii ff.); and the name (ilu) Ašratum-ummi = '(the goddess) Ašratum is my mother' is found three times as a feminine name on contract-tablets of the First Babylonian dynasty: cf. Thureau-Dangin, *Lettres et Contrats de l'époque de la première dynastie Babylonienne*, p. 16. Special interest attaches to a passage in one of the Bab. tablets discovered at Ta'anach, which runs, 'If the finger (= omen) of Aširat point, then let one mark and follow': cf. Rogers, *CP.* p. 282; *TB.* i. p. 128. The S. Arabian goddess Aṯirat is doubtless the same as Ashera, and appears, according to Hommel, to have been consort of the moon-god (cf. *op. cit.* pp. 207 ff.). In an Aram. inscription from the N. Arabian Têma her name is Ašîra (Cooke, *NSI.* pp. 195 ff.; La., *ÉRS.*^{2} pp. 122, 502 f.).

The relation of the Ashera-cult to Yahweh-worship, and the connexion of the Ashera as a wooden symbol (pole or tree-trunk) with the goddess of this name are very obscure questions; but the following theory may be advanced. Evidence goes to prove that the God Yahweh was known and worshipped by the 'Amorite' immigrants into W. Syria (Amurru), whose original home was probably S. Arabia, and who founded the First Dynasty at Babylon (cf. *Additional note*, p. 243). The presumption is at any rate very strong that Yahweh was identified with the moon-god Sin, whose predominance at this period is attested by the preponderance of proper names compounded with Sin in the First Dynasty tablets (cf. *Additional note*, p. 249). But, as we have just observed, Aṯirat seems to have been the consort of the moon-god in S. Arabia; and the same conclusion may be drawn as to Ašratum from her title 'bride of the king of heaven' in the inscription of Ḫammurabi above quoted. Quite possibly, therefore, Ashera may have been worshipped among the Amorites inhabiting Cana'an as the consort of Yahweh; and this fact would account both for the setting up of her symbol beside the altar of Yahweh, and also for the bitter hostility with which her cult was regarded by the prophets as exponents of the true (Mosaic) Yahwism.

The use of the normal expression הָאֲשֵׁרָה '*the* Ashera' in O.T. is strange as applied to a goddess; but the explanation probably is that it was employed to designate the *symbol* of the goddess (the pole or tree-trunk), which was perhaps not usually carved to represent her features; though this may occasionally have been the case (cf. 'the graven image of the Ashera,' 2 Kgs. 21 [7], noticed above), as with the stone pillars of Ḥatḥor at Serabit (cf. Petrie, *Researches in Sinai*, plates 95, 101, 102, 103, 111), and the totem-poles of certain savage tribes at the present day.* Possibly the 'horrible object (Heb. *miphléṣeth*) for an Ashera' erected by the queen-mother in the reign of Aṡa (1 Kgs. 15 [13]) was a pole carved with certain features which were more than usually revolting to the exponents of the purer form of Yahwism.

Whether the Amorite אשרה 'Ashera stood in any connexion with the originally Babylonian עשתרת 'Ashtart (Ištar), or was quite distinct from her, is a question which cannot at present be settled. The two names are unconnected.‡ The name Ashera probably designates the goddess as the giver of *good fortune*: cf. the sense attaching to the root אשר in Heb. In this connexion it is worth while to recall the passage above cited from the Ta'anach tablet, where the finger of Ashera points the way to the *right* or *prosperous* course.

There can be little doubt that, as has often been remarked, the tribal name Asher was originally connected with the deity of good fortune (a masc. form of Ashera?), just as the name Gad is derived from a similar deity. Indeed, it seems highly probable that, just as the latter name is explained by בְּגָד 'with (the help of) Gad!' in Gen. 30 [11] J, so the somewhat strange expression בְּאָשְׁרִי 'in my good luck!' (*i.e.* by somewhat forced inference, 'I am in luck!'), Gen. 30 [13] J,

* The reason why no example of an Ashera has been unearthed in excavation, whereas the occurrence of *maṣṣēbhôth*, or standing stones, has proved very frequent, doubtless is that the former was always made of wood, which necessarily perishes in the damp climate of Palestine.

‡ Haupt's attempt to connect the two names (*JAOS*. xxviii. pp. 112 ff.) does not commend itself. Cf. the criticisms of Barton (*JAOS*. xxxi. pp. 355 ff.).

build an altar to Yahweh thy God upon the top of this stronghold in due form, and take the bull [], and offer it up as a burnt offering with the wood of the Ashera which thou shalt cut down.' 27. So Gideʿon took ten men of his servants, and did as Yahweh had spoken unto him; and, because he feared his father's household and the men of the city, so that he could not do it by day, he did it by night. 28. And the men of the city rose up early in the morning, and, behold, the altar of Baʿal was broken down, and the Ashera which was by it was cut down, and the bull [] was offered up upon the altar which had been built. 29. And they said one to another, 'Who hath done this thing?' And when they had enquired and searched, they said, 'Gideʿon the

is an intentional alteration of an original בְּאֲשֵׁרָה 'with (the help of) Ashera!'*: cf. Ball *ad loc.*, *SBOT.* p. 84. This passage, then, would suggest that part of the 'good fortune' brought by Ashera was connected with success in child-bearing; a characteristic which connects the goddess, at least in *function*, with Ištar under the aspect of Mylitta, *i.e. muallidat*: cf. p. 59 *note.* ‡

26. *this stronghold.* The Heb. *māʿôz* (from the root *ʿûz* 'to take *or* seek refuge') seems here to denote a natural fastness, *i.e.* an inaccessible crag, rather than a fortification. Cf. *ṣûr māʿôz*, 'rock of fastness,' Isa. 17 [10], Ps. 31 [2], 𝕳 [3].

in due form. Heb. *bam-maʿarākhā*, *i.e.*, apparently, lit. 'in the (proper) arrangement.' The verb *ʿārakh*, from which the substantive is derived, when used in a sacrificial connexion, may mean *to arrange* the logs of wood upon an altar (Gen. 22 [9]), or the portions of the sacrificial victim upon the wood (Lev. 1 [8.12] 6 [5]). The altar-pyre thus

* Or possibly בְּאָשֵׁר 'With (the help of) Asher!' *i.e.* the masc. form of Ashera. Hommel (*op. cit.* p. 209) is inclined to think that traces may be found in O.T. of Asher as a surname of Yahweh in several old poetical passages, especially in Deut. 33 [29], which he renders,

'[Yahweh] is the shield of thine help,
And Asher the sword of thine excellency.'

Such an explanation certainly relieves the difficulty of וַאֲשֶׁר חֶרֶב גַּאֲוָתֶךָ, where אֲשֶׁר, as vocalized in 𝔐, is taken for the relative pronoun; R.V. 'And that is the sword, etc.'—a very awkward and unpoetical construction.

‡ The view that the name Ashera is connected with Bab. *aširtu* 'temple,' perhaps so called as a 'place of favour,' and that the Ashera was simply a pole which marked the precincts of such a sanctuary, does not seem to be probable. If this was the only significance which the Ashera possessed, why should it have excited so much animosity upon the part of the adherents of the purer form of Yahwism?

son of Joash hath done this thing.' 30. And the men of the city said unto Joash, 'Bring forth thy son, that he may die; because he hath broken down the altar of Ba'al, and because he hath cut down the Ashera which was by it.' 31. And Joash

arranged is termed *ma'arākhā* in Ecclus. 50 [12ff.], where, in speaking of Simon the son of Onias, the writer says:

'When he received the pieces from the hand of his brethren,
While himself standing *by the pyres*;
Round about him a crown of sons,
Like cedar-plants in Lebanon;
And they encompassed him like poplars of the wâdy,
All the sons of Aaron in their glory,
With the fire-offerings of Yahweh in their hand,
Before all the assembly of Israel;
Until he finished serving the altar,
And setting in order the pyres of the Most High.

Here the first phrase italicized is על מערכות, and the second ולסדר מערכות עליון.

In Num. 23 [4], 'The seven altars *have I arranged*,' the verb may be used as in the cases noticed above, of setting in order the altar-pyres; but it is possible that it refers to the arranging of the stones of the altars, *i.e.* to the building of them.

In our passage, the context forbids us to interpret *ma'arākhā* of the altar or pyre as duly arranged; but it is natural and legitimate to understand the word as denoting the *act of arrangement* (whether of the altar-stones or the pyre), as prescribed by custom.

The explanation of *bam-ma'arākhā* here adopted is that which is offered by 𝔏 'in ordinatione,' 𝔖[P] ܒܣܕܪܐ, 𝔗 בסדרא 'in order'; and is probably intended by 𝔊 ἐν τῇ παρατάξει. 𝔙 paraphrases 'super quem ante sacrificium posuisti'—a rendering which seems to accord with the view put forward by Kimchi, who, having explained the *mā'ôz* as the crag upon which Gide'on offered the flesh and the unleavened cakes, then goes on to interpret *ma'arākhā* as the level place on the top of the crag upon which it was possible to arrange the stones of the altar. Levi ben-Gershon explains similarly.

take the bull. Omitting הַשֵּׁנִי 'the second'; here and in *v.* [28], as a later gloss. Cf. *note* preceding.

30. '*Bring forth, etc.*' The voluntary surrender of Gide'on by his father would have obviated the blood-feud which must have been entailed if the townsmen had slain him without such consent (Mo., Cooke). Mo. quotes a parallel from the life of Mohammed:—'So the Qoreish at Mecca tried to persuade Mohammed's uncle, Abū Ṭālib, to withdraw from him his protection, that they might kill the

said to all who stood by him, 'Will *ye* contend for Ba'al? or will *ye* save him? Whosoever will contend for him shall be put to death at morning: if he be a god, let him contend for himself, because he hath broken down his altar.' 32. So they called him

pestilent agitator without incurring the vengeance of his family' (Ibn Hishām, ed. Wüstenfeld, pp. 167-169).

31. '*Will* **ye**, *etc.*' The pronoun is very emphatic in the original, the contrast being between the assumed power of the god as contrasted with his would-be avengers. Mo. appositely cites 'deorum injuriae dis curae,' Tacitus, *Annals* i. 73.

Whosoever . . . at morning. These words interrupt the connexion between the first and last parts of the verse (cf. *note* preceding); and are probably, as Bu. thinks, the insertion of a zealot for Yahweh who, not satisfied with so mild a method of procedure as is suggested by Joash (the leaving of the god to take care of himself if he can), puts into his mouth the statement that the service of a false god deserves the death-penalty (cf. Deut. 13).

at morning. I.e., we may infer, the morning of the next day. The outrage perpetrated upon Ba'al's altar was discovered in the early morning (*v.* 28), but the investigations implied by *v.* 29 must have taken some time; and it was possibly not until the evening that the deed was brought home to Gide'on.

The phrase עַד־הַבֹּקֶר commonly means 'until the morning' (*ch.* 19 25, Ex. 16 23.24, 29 34, *al.*); but since this sense is here unsuitable, we must take the force of the pref. עד to be *at* (lit. *up to*) the time indicated—much as we speak of arriving *up to time* in the sense *at* the fixed time. Cf., in a spatial connexion, the use of the prep. אל 'unto' where we should expect 'at'; 1 Kgs. 6 18, 2 Kgs. 10 14, Ezek. 31 7, 47 7 (cf. *note* in *NHTK.* on 1 Kgs. 6 18). This explanation of עד seems more probable than the view that it should be taken in the sense '*while* the morning (lasts)'; cf. עַד הִתְמַהְמְהָם 'whilst they delayed,' *ch.* 3 26.

If, however, such passages as *ch.* 16 2 עַד־אוֹר הַבֹּקֶר, 1 Sam. 1 22 עַד־יִגָּמֵל הַנַּעַר, really imply an ellipse of some such word as 'wait,' and should be rendered 'Till the morning dawns!' 'Till the lad be weaned!' (cf. *note* on the former passage); it would be possible in the present passage to treat עד הבקר similarly as an independent sentence, placing a break on יומת preceding:—'Whosoever will contend for him shall be put to death. (Wait) till the morning! If he be a god, etc': *i.e.* if Ba'al is really a god, he will at any rate have taken action to avenge himself by the next morning; therefore it is reasonable to ask for a suspense of judgment until that time.

Jerubba'al on that day, saying, 'Let Ba'al contend with him, because he hath broken down his altar.'

32. *Jerubba'al.* The meaning, as explained by the narrator, is 'Let Ba'al contend,' an Imperf. יָרוּב (Jussive יָרֹב)* being employed for the normal יָרִיב (Jussive יָרֵב), which would yield the form יְרִבַּעַל Jeribba'al. Why, in face of the explicit statement of *v.* 32b, Mo. should say that 'by an ingenious etymology the name is made to signify, Adversary of Ba'al,' is not clear.

It is probable that, while the meaning of the name may really be 'Let Ba'al contend,' or 'Ba'al contends,' Ba'al is here, as often elsewhere (see below), a title of *Yahweh*; and the original purpose of the name was to place the bearer of it under the guardianship of the Deity:—'Let Ba'al contend,' *sc.* for the bearer of the name, *i.e.* be his advocate. Such a meaning appears to attach to the name Merib-ba'al (1 Chr. 8[34], 9[40]), which is compounded with the participial form of the verb:—'Ba'al is an advocate,' *sc.* of his nominee; and, similarly, we have the name Jeho-yarib, *i.e.* 'Yahweh contendeth,' 1 Chr. 9[10], *al.* Cf. passages in which the verb *rîbh* is used of Yahweh's *taking sides* on behalf of His servants, or *pleading their cause*: so in 1 Sam. 25[39], David, on hearing of the death of Nabal, says, 'Blessed be Yahweh, who hath pleaded the cause of my reproach (אֲשֶׁר רָב אֶת־רִיב חֶרְפָּתִי) from the hand of Nabal'; Mic. 7[9], 'Till He (Yahweh) shall plead my cause' (יָרִיב רִיבִי); Jer. 50[34], 'Their Avenger is strong; Yahweh Ṣebha'oth is His name; He shall surely plead their cause' (רִיב יָרִיב אֶת־רִיבָם).

Wellh. (*TBS.* p. 31) suggests that the name should properly be יְרֻבַּעַל Jerûba'al, which is supposed to mean 'Founded by Ba'al,' or 'Foundation of Ba'al' (the first element from the root ירה: for form, cf. פְּנוּאֵל Penuel, 'Face of God'); and with this he compares יְרוּאֵל Jeruel, 2 Chr. 20[16]; יְרִיאֵל Jeriel, 1 Chr. 7[2]. This suggestion has been favoured by several scholars (Mo., Bu., No., etc), but is in no way superior to the explanation adopted above.‡

That the title *Ba'al, i.e.* 'Master' or 'Owner,' was actually applied to Yahweh in early times cannot be doubted. Thus we have the name Esh-ba'al or Ish-ba'al, *i.e.* 'man of Ba'al,' a son of Saul, who always appears as a loyal worshipper of Yahweh (1 Chr. 8[33], 9[39]); Merib-ba'al, son of Jonathan, noticed above; Ba'al-yadha', *i.e.* 'Ba'al knows *or* takes notice' (*sc.* of the bearer of the name; 1 Chr. 14[7]), a

* Cf., for this form, Prov. 3[30] *Kt.*, and Infin. Constr. רוב Judg. 22[22] *Kt.*

‡ As a matter of fact, the sense to be attached to the element *yerû* in *Yerû'ēl* is highly uncertain.

33. E And all Midian and ʿAmaleḳ and the children of the East assembled themselves together; and they passed over, and encamped in the vale of Jezreʿel. 34. J And the spirit of Yahweh

name borne by one of David's heroes; Baʿal-ḥanan, *i.e.* 'Baʿal is gracious' (1 Chr. 27 [28]), one of David's officers; and—most striking instance of all—Baʿal-ya, *i.e.* 'Ya *or* Yahweh is Baʿal' (1 Chr. 12[5], 𝔐[6]), one of David's heroes. These names, where they occur in Sam., have been disguised by a later hand in order to remove the reference to Baʿal which was (wrongly) taken to refer to a false god. Thus we find, in Ish-bósheth for Esh-baʿal, Mephibósheth for Meribbaʿal, the substitution of *bṓšeth*='shame' or 'shameful thing'; cf. Hos. 9 [10], Jer. 3 [24], 11 [13], where allusions to the Baʿal have been similarly disguised. Baʿal-yadhaʿ appears in 2 Sam. 5 [16] as El-yadhaʿ, *i.e.* 'God takes notice.' Hos. 2 [16.17], 𝔐 [18.19], is a passage which witnesses to such an application of the title Baʿal to Yahweh; and also to a dislike of it on the part of the prophets of the higher form of Yahwism, which was doubtless ultimately instrumental in bringing about a discontinuance of the usage:—'And it shall be in that day, saith Yahweh, that thou shalt call me *'îšî* (my husband); and shalt call me no more *baʿalî* (my Baʿal *or* Master). For I will take away the names of the Baʿals out of her mouth, and they shall no more be mentioned by their name.'

The reason why the name Jerubbaʿal was not similarly disguised by later scribes doubtless was because it is essential to the point of the narrative, which is polemical to idolatry. In 2 Sam. 11 [21], however, we find the altered form Jerub-bésheth. Cf. further the present editor's *Outlines of O.T. Theology*, pp. 27 ff.

33. *And all Midian, etc.* Cf. *v.* [3] *note.*

passed over. I.e. crossed the Jordan.

the vale of Jezreʿel. The name of Jezreʿel is preserved in the modern Zerʿîn, situated upon an outlying spur of the Gilboaʿ-range overlooking the plain (for the termination *-în* for *-ēl*, cf. *footnote* p. 21). According to Macalister, however, the modern site cannot actually represent the ancient city, since the strata do not exhibit an antiquity so remote as O.T. times (cf. *PEF. Qy. St.* 1909, p. 175).

'The vale (*ʿēmeḳ*) of Jezreʿel' here denotes (as is clear from *ch.* 7 [1.8b.12]) the part of the great plain immediately to the north of Gilboaʿ, where it begins to narrow down before its descent into the Jordan valley. There are two other occurrences of the term in O.T.: Josh. 17 [16] J, where the children of Joseph state that the Canaʿanites inhabiting the vale of Jezreʿel are too strong for them, owing to their possession of iron chariots; and Hos. 1 [5], where the vale is mentioned as a battle-field: 'I will break the bow of Israel in the vale of Jezreʿel.' In these passages 'the vale of Jezreʿel' seems to mean the whole extent of the modern Merǵ ibn ʿÂmir, just as 'the great plain

clothed itself in Gide'on, and he blew a trumpet; and Abi'ezer was called to arms after him. 35. E And he sent messengers

of Esdraelon'* does in Judith 1 [8]; cf. also 3 [9], 4 [6], 7 [3]. 'The valley of Megiddo' (*bik'ath M^egiddo*) is a different designation for the same plain in 2 Chr. 35 [22], Zech. 12 [11]. ‡

34. *clothed itself in Gide'on.* The same striking phrase occurs in 1 Chr. 12 [18], 𝔥 [19], 2 Chr. 24 [20]. The meaning seems to be that the divine spirit took complete possession of Gide'on, so that he became, as it were, its incarnation, and was thus employed as its instrument. For the different terms used in this book to describe the access of the spirit of Yahweh upon a 'Judge,' cf. *ch.* 3 [10] *note*.

and Abi'ezer. Gide'on's own clan, 'the weakest in Manasseh' (*v.* [15]), musters the three hundred who form his sole force, according to the earlier and more authentic tradition preserved in J: cf. p. 179.

was called to arms. Heb. וַיִּזָּעֵק. The passive (Niph'al) form of the verb זעק or צעק, meaning 'to cry out *or* call,' always denotes a summons to battle or armed resistance; the original reference of the verb probably being to the loud, excited shout of a messenger who has little time to spare. R.V.'s rendering, 'was gathered together,' is weak and inexpressive.

35. *And he sent messengers, etc.* On the summoning of the tribes here mentioned, cf. pp. 178 f.

* Esdraelon, the Graecized form of Jezre'el, is written Εσδραηλων, Εσδρηλων, Εσρηλων, with other variants which are doubtless due to textual corruption. Cf. the full list in *EB.* 1391, *n* 1.

‡ Smith (*HG.* pp. 384 ff.) would restrict the O.T. usage of 'the vale of Jezre'el' to the south-eastern portion of the plain denoted in our passage (see above); while supposing that the whole wide open plain was properly termed *bik'ā*, as in the phrase *bik'ath M^egiddo*. This view is based upon the assumption that, while *bik'ā* (which he renders 'Plain or Opening') may denote a broad open valley surrounded by hills, *'ēmek* (rendered 'Vale or Deepening') is 'never applied to any extensive plain away from hills, but always to wide avenues running up into a mountainous country like the Vale of Elah, the Vale of Hebron, and the Vale of Aijalon.' Such a conclusion as regards *'ēmek* (though quoted with approval by many scholars, *e.g.* Cooke here; Gray on Num. 14 [25], *ICC.*; Driver in *DB.* iv. 846a) can scarcely be maintained. In *ch.* 1 [19] (cf. *note*) *'ēmek* denotes the whole of the maritime plain to the west of the hill-country of Judah; and the usage in 1 [34] is similar, and can scarcely be restricted to the vale of Sorek or the vale of Aijalon. In the Song of Deborah, *ch.* 5 [15c] (and *v.* [14a] as emended), *'ēmek* denotes the widest and most open part of the great plain, through which the Kishon flows. The words of the servants of the king of Aram, 1 Kgs. 20 [23], 'Their gods are gods of hills; therefore were they stronger than we: but let us fight against them in the plain (Heb. *bam-mîšôr*, lit. 'upon the level ground'); surely we shall be stronger than they' (cf. also *v.* [25]), are paraphrased by the man of God (*v.* [28]), 'Because the Aramaeans said "A god of hills is Yahweh, and not a god of vales"' (*'ămāķîm*). Here it would be absurd to say that the reference is to the valleys running up into the hills, and not to the low-lying and level country generally. Similarly, the *'ēmek* in which the horses are pictured as

throughout all Manasseh, and they R[JE] also E were called to
arms after him; E[2] and he sent messengers throughout Asher
and Zebulun and Naphtali, and they came up to meet them.
36. E And Gideʿon said unto God, 'If thou *art* about to save
Israel by my hand, as thou hast spoken, 37. behold, I am setting
a fleece of wool on the threshing-floor: if there be dew upon the
fleece alone, and it be dry upon all the ground, then I shall
know that thou wilt save Israel by my hand, as thou hast spoken.'
38. And it was so: he rose up on the morrow, and wrung the
fleece, and squeezed the dew out of the fleece, a bowlful of water.
39. And Gideʿon said unto God, 'Let not thine anger be kindled
against me, and I will speak only this once: let me make proof,
prithee, but this once with the fleece; let it, prithee, be dry
upon the fleece alone, and upon all the ground let there be dew.'
40. And God did so that night: for it was dry upon the fleece
alone, and upon all the ground there was dew.

36. '*If thou* **art** *about to save, etc.*' The emphasis on the '*art*' (*i.e.* '*really* art, etc.') is expressed in Heb. by the use of the substantival form יֶשְׁךָ, with the Participle used as a 'Futurum instans.' Cf. Gen. 24[42] אִם־יֶשְׁךָ־נָּא מַצְלִיחַ דַּרְכִּי 'Prithee, if thou art indeed about to prosper my way, etc.' Where such emphasis is absent, the Participle alone suffices: cf. *ch.* 11[9], אִם מְשִׁיבִים אַתֶּם אוֹתִי וג׳ 'If ye are going to bring me back.'

37. *a fleece of wool.* Heb. *gizzath haṣ-ṣémer* denotes a *shorn* fleece; therefore Cooke's suggestion that it was 'perhaps his sheep-skin cloak with the wool on it' is excluded.

39. '*Let not thine anger, etc.*' On the resemblance of this passage to Gen. 18 [30.32] J, cf. p. 178 *footnote.*

let me make proof, etc. The threshing-floor, in all probability a flat rocky hill-top or prominence, would not collect much dew, and what little there was would soon evaporate; whereas the fleece would naturally collect and hold the moisture. It thus occurs to Gideʿon (*after* his first test) that the phenomenon may after all be nothing in the nature of a portent. The reversed condition of things —a dry fleece upon the wet rock—will be much more unexpected; and therefore more reliable as a sign of supernatural intervention.

pawing the ground, as they stand drawn up in line of battle (Job 39 [21]) is clearly to be regarded as an open plain, like the great Merǵ ibn ʿÂmir.

While, therefore, it may be true that *ʿēmeḳ* (lit. 'depression') 'is a highlander's word for a valley as he looks down upon it,' the further conclusion that the term is 'never applied to any extensive plain away from hills, but always to wide avenues running up into a mountainous country,' is, as the facts quoted above go to show, entirely unwarranted.

7. 1. And Jerubba'al (^{RJE} that is, Gide'on), E and all the people who were with him, rose up early in the morning, and encamped beside the spring of Ḥarod: and the camp of Midian was to the north of him, ⟨beneath⟩ the hill of the Oracle-giver in the vale.

7. 1. *Jerubba'al* (*that is, Gide'on*). The original narrative, E, here employs the name Jerubba'al; while the insertion of the hero's other name is due to the redactor of J and E. Cf. p. 178.

the spring of Ḥarod. Assuming that the description of the position of the two forces is from the same source as 6 ^{33} E, which describes the encampment of Midian in the vale of Jezre'el (or that, if 7 $^{1a\beta b}$ is from J, both narratives describe the same scene of action), then we must look for the spring of Ḥarod upon the southern edge of the vale, and somewhat above it. These conditions are satisfied by the 'Ain Ĝâlûd, which Rob. (*BR.*³ ii. p. 323) describes as 'a very large fountain, flowing out from under a sort of cavern in the wall of conglomerate rock, which here forms the base of Gilboa'. The water is excellent; and issuing from crevices in the rocks, it spreads out at once into a fine limpid pool, forty or fifty feet in diameter. . . . From the reservoir, a stream sufficient to turn a mill flows off eastwards down the valley.' Smith states that the spring 'bursts some fifteen feet broad and two deep from the very foot of Gilboa', and mainly out of it, but fed also by the other two springs, flows [in] a stream considerable enough to work six or seven mills. The deep bed and soft banks of this stream constitute a formidable ditch in front of the position on Gilboa', and render it possible for the defenders of the latter to hold the spring at their feet in face of an enemy on the plain' (*HG.* pp. 397 f.). The name *Ḥărôdh* is susceptible of the interpretation 'trembling'; and there is thus no doubt a play upon the meaning in the narrative which follows: cf. *v.*³, 'Whosoever is fearful and trembling (*ḥārēdh*).'

was to the north . . . in the vale. Reading הָיָה־לוֹ מִצָּפוֹן מִתַּחַת לְגִבְעַת הַמּוֹרֶה בָּעֵמֶק. The text of 𝔐 cannot be original, it being impossible to attach any sense to מִגִּבְעַת הַמּוֹרֶה. R.V. *text*, 'by the hill of Moreh' is an unjustifiable perversion of the sense of מן 'from'; nor does the gratuitous addition of 'onwards' by R.V. *marg.*—'from the hill of Moreh *onwards* in the valley'—commend itself as at all probable. The emendation adopted supposes simply that מִגִּבְעַת is a scribe's error for מִתַּחַת לְגִבְעַת; and the reason for its adoption is connected with the probable site of 'the hill of the Oracle-giver,' on which see below.

Bu. emends הָיָה־לוֹ מִתַּחַת מִצָּפוֹן לְגִבְעַת הַמּוֹרֶה בָּעֵמֶק 'was beneath him, north of the hill of the oracle-giver in the vale' (so Kit., No.). Mo., who supposes that combination with *v.*^{8b} is responsible for the

2. E[2] And Yahweh said unto Gide'on, 'The people who are with thee are too many for me to give Midian into their hand; lest Israel vaunt themselves against me, saying "My hand hath

disorder of the passage, prefers to read הָיָה מִצָּפוֹן לְגִבְעַת הַמּוֹרֶה בָּעֵמֶק 'was north of the hill of the oracle-giver in the vale.' This sense is given by 𝔙 (with omission of בעמק), 'Erant autem castra Madian in valle ad Septentrionalem plagam collis excelsi'; and by 𝔖[P] (with retention of לו) ܘܡܫܪܝܬܐ ܕܡܕܝܢ ܗܘܬ ܠܗ ܡܢ ܓܪܒܝܐ ܕܓܒܥܬܐ ܪܡܬܐ ܒܥܘܡܩܐ 𝔊, 𝔗 offer the same text as 𝔐.

'The hill of the Oracle-giver'* is generally supposed to be the Ǵebel Neby Daḥy or Little Ḥermon, to the north of mount Gilboa' across the vale of Jezre'el. If this location is correct, the name may be connected with the fact that 'En-dor, which in the time of Saul was the seat of a witch or woman with a familiar spirit (1 Sam. 28 [7]), lies in close proximity to the north of Neby Daḥy. Assuming the correctness of the reading either of Bu. or Mo. (as noticed above), an objection to this identification may be found in the fact that we have already been informed in 6 [33] that the Midianites were encamped in the vale of Jezre'el, *i.e.* if the ordinary assumption is correct (cf. *note ad loc.*), in the Nahr Ǵâlûd to the *south* of Ǵebel Neby Daḥy; whereas the present passage would place the encampment to the *north* of the hill, perhaps not far from Nain or 'En-dor. This difficulty is not much helped by Mo.'s alternative emendation of our passage (followed by Cooke), which substitutes בְּגִבְעַת for מִגִּבְעַת and omits בָּעֵמֶק, thus obtaining the reading, 'was on his north, on the hill of the oracle-giver'; since it is clear from *vv.* [8b.12] that the Midianites were not encamped upon a hill, but below the Israelites in the vale. The desiderated sense (making the reference to be to Neby Daḥy *and* placing the encampment of Midian in the Nahr Ǵâlûd) can only be obtained by the emendation offered in our text. Adopting this conclusion, the positions of Gide'on and the Midianites exactly correspond to those of the two hosts in 1 Sam. 28 [4]—Saul's army on Gilboa', and the Philistines at Shunem close under Neby Daḥy.

If, however, the present passage comes from J, it is conceivable, as Mo. points out, that the author of this narrative may have placed the scene of action, not in the vale of Jezre'el, but somewhere in the near neighbourhood of 'Ophrah, *i.e.* not far from Shechem. The name Moreh is elsewhere found only in the neighbourhood of Shechem (Gen. 12 [6], Deut. 11 [30], 'the terebinth *or* sacred tree *or* trees of Moreh'); though this is a point which does not carry great weight, since there were doubtless such 'oracle-givers' in other localities. It is, however,

* *Ham-môrê*='the giver of *tôrā*,' *i.e.* decision or counsel purporting to be dictated by divine or supernatural agency.

wrought deliverance for me." 3. Now, therefore, prithee proclaim in the ears of the people, saying, "Whosoever is fearful and trembling, let him return, and decamp from mount ⌜Galud⌝."'

worthy of note that the introductory narrative of J presupposes (6 [11]) that marauding Midianites were in very close proximity to ʿOphrah (to which, all the same, they may have come up from their main encampment in the vale of Jezreʿel); and that in *ch.* 7 [22] two different accounts of the line of flight appear to be combined, one of which *may* have been down the Wâdy Farʿah from the neighbourhood of Shechem—though, in our ignorance of the localities mentioned, this cannot be affirmed. Cf. *note ad loc.*

3. '*Whosoever is fearful, etc.*' For the terms of the proclamation, cf. Deut. 20 [8].

and decamp from mount Galud. Reading וְיִצְפֹּר מֵהַר הַגָּלוּד. The difficulty connected with 𝔐 וְיִצְפֹּר מֵהַר הַגִּלְעָד is twofold.

In the first place, if וְיִצְפֹּר is original, it stands alone in Heb. as used in the present connexion; and scholars have exhausted their ingenuity in attempting to assign the verb a suitable meaning under some one of the different roots צפר which are known in Semitic. R.V. *text*, 'and depart,' seems to be guided by the rendering of 𝔊 καὶ ἐκχωρείτο. R.V. *marg.* 'go round about' follows the explanation of Abulwalid, Tanchum, Kimchi (second alternative), etc., who connect the verb with the subst. צְפִירָה 'chaplet' or 'fillet' (Isa. 28 [5]), upon the incorrect* assumption that this is so-called as *going round* the head. A.V., 'depart early,' goes back to Rashi, Kimchi (first alternative), and Levi ben-Gershon, who, connecting with the Aram. *ṣaphrā* 'morning,' explain the verb as meaning 'to depart in the early morning.' The only really philological explanation is that offered by Siegfried and Stade (*Hebr. Wörterbuch*, *s.v.*), who make the verb the equivalent of the Ar. *ḍafara*, which may mean 'to go quickly, spring, leap in running'‡ (Lane). This is plausible, and has been adopted in our rendering 'decamp'; since the context seems to offer scope for an unusual word—perhaps a colloquialism which was calculated to cast ridicule upon the cowards (like our 'cut and run'). Failing this explanation, it is possible that וְיִצְפֹּר may be a corruption of וַיַּעֲבֹר 'and pass on' (Grä.): cf. 𝔊 καὶ ἐκχωρείτω, 𝔙 'et recesserunt.'

Secondly, the reference to 'mount Gileʿad' as the spot upon which Gideʿon's army was stationed is quite inexplicable. The name הַגִּלְעָד 'the Gileʿad' is elsewhere confined to the well-known district east of

* The root-meaning of צפירה is seen in the Ar. *ḍafara*='to plait *or* braid.'

‡ ضفر is given as a synonym of عدا and سعى by the Arabic lexicographists.

And there returned of the people twenty and two thousand, and ten thousand were left.

4. And Yahweh said unto Gideʿon, 'The people are still

Jordan; and though it is perhaps too bold to say that the same name *could* not have been applied to a mountain on the western side of the river, yet such a coincidence in nomenclature is at any rate highly improbable. Le Clerc suggests the substitution of מֵהַר הַגִּלְבֹּעַ 'from mount Gilboaʿ'; but against this Stu. (who quotes Dathe) and Mo. argue with some reason that, since Gideʿon's army was actually encamped upon Gilboaʿ, the naming of the mountain by Gideʿon in his command to depart would be extremely superfluous. Michaelis, by vocalizing מַהֵר 'quickly' (cf. *ch.* 2 [17.23]) instead of מֵהַר, and understanding הַגִּלְעָד as an accusative of direction, seeks to obtain the meaning of 'flee quickly to Gileʿad,' *i.e.* escape across the Jordan: but this is directly opposed by *vv.* [7.8] (Mo.), where it is stated that the people were sent back to their own homes.

In face of these difficulties, Mo. proposes to conclude Gideʿon's proclamation with יָשֹׁב, and to emend the words under discussion וַיִּצְרְפֵם גִּדְעוֹן. The passage thus runs '"Whosoever is fearful and trembling, let him return." *So Gideʿon tested them.*' In support of וַיִּצְרְפֵם Mo. compares *v.* [4b], 'Bring them down unto the water, *that I may test them* (וְאֶצְרְפֶנּוּ) for thee there.'* This suggestion is adopted by Bu. (*Comm.*), No., La., Kit., Kent, Gress. Ingenious and attractive as it is, however, it can hardly be accepted as satisfactory. For, firstly, if the name of Gideʿon had originally stood in the sentence, it is incredible that it should have become so illegible as to be mistaken for 'Mount Gileʿad'; and, secondly, though the verb צרף 'test' is appropriate to the method adopted in *vv.* [4ff.], where the men are selected and segregated in accordance with their different methods of drinking, the effect produced by Gideʿon's proclamation can scarcely be termed a 'testing' in the same sense, and it is very doubtful whether the verb צרף could be applied to it.

The close resemblance between הַגִּלְעָד 'the Gileʿad' and the modern Ar. name of the spring of Ḥarod, ʿAin Ǵâlûd, together with the stream which is fed by it—the Nahr Ǵâlûd—can scarcely escape

* It may be noticed that Rabbi Isaiah states that ויצפר is a metathesis of ויצרף (*i.e.* apparently, the Nïph'al וַיִּצָּרֵף 'and so be tested'), just as we get the alternative forms כֶּשֶׂב, כֶּבֶשׂ. The view that the verb is a metathesis appears to explain the rendering of 𝔗, יתבחר.

many: bring them down unto the water, that I may test them for thee there: and it shall be, of whomsoever I shall say unto thee, "This one shall go with thee," the same shall go with thee, and all of whom I shall say unto thee, "This one shall not go with thee," the same shall not go.' 5. So he brought the people down to the water: and Yahweh said unto Gideʿon, 'Everyone who lappeth of the water with his tongue, as the dog lappeth, thou shalt set him apart; and everyone who bendeth down upon

notice; and suggests that Ǵâlûd may be an ancient name, and may have been applied, not only to the spring and stream, but also to the mountain-spur from which the spring issues. If this is so, however, it is natural to inquire into the etymology of the name. According to Smith (*HG.* pp. 397 f. *n* 2), Boha-ed-Din (*Vit. Salad.* ch. xxiv.) gives the name as ʿAin el-Ǵâlût or 'well of Goliath,' with whose slaughter by David the *Jerusalem Itinerary* connects Jezreʿel. This is obviously mere guess-work, and cannot be regarded as a serious explanation.

Now it is worthy of notice that in Bab. the verb *galâdu* means 'to be afraid';* and, in default of other explanation of the Ar. Ǵâlûd, it is by no means improbable that this preserves an old Heb. or Amorite name, the root-meaning of which was identical with the Babylonian. Thus ʿAin Ǵâlûd may have some such meaning as 'the Coward's Spring'; and 'the Spring of Ḥarod *or* Trembling' may have been a variant name with similar meaning. It is not too bold to assume that the mountain-spur from which the spring issues may also have borne the name הַר הַגָּלוּד 'the Coward's Mount,' and that the story may have been woven round this name; an archaic and possibly obsolete root being explained by the learned writer in the sentence מִי־יָרֵא וְחָרֵד 'Whoso is fearful and afraid.' If this is so, it supplies adequate reason for the mention of the name of the mountain, viz. the play upon the meaning of Galud in the terms of the proclamation.

4. *that I may test them.* Heb. וְאֶצְרְפֶנּוּ may be rendered as by Mo., 'and let me separate them.' The verb *ṣāraph* is used of the *smelting* process which separates the fine metals from the dross.

5. At the end of the verse, תַּצִּיג אוֹתוֹ לְבָד 'thou shalt set him apart,' is supplied upon the authority of 𝔊^{AL}, 𝔖^{h} μεταστήσεις αὐτὸν κατ᾽ αὐτόν. So 𝔖^{P}. Cf. also the rendering of 𝔙, 'qui autem curvatis genibus biberint, in altera parte erunt.' The words are necessary to complete the sense of the final sentence, the 'likewise' of R.V., inserted before

* The cognate *galâtu* has a similar meaning.

his knees to drink ⟨thou shalt set him apart⟩.' 6. And the number of those that lapped [] was three hundred men; but all the rest of the people bent down upon their knees to drink water, ⟨putting their hand to their mouth⟩.

'every one that boweth down, etc.,' being unwarranted by the Heb. text.

6. *And the number of those that lapped, etc.* 𝔐 makes 'putting their hand to their mouth' to refer to 'those that lapped'; but since the lapping is stated in the previous verse to have been 'as the dog lappeth,' it is clear that the words are out of place, since the dog laps by putting his tongue to the stream. The words are not found in 𝔊^{AL}, 𝔖^{h}, 𝔏, which read instead בִּלְשׁוֹנָם, 'with their tongue'; and this may be original: cf. *v.*^{5}. Bu. (*RS.* p. 112, *n*^{3}) was the first to point out that the words 'putting their hand, etc.,' are out of place in 𝔐, and should properly apply to those 'who bowed down upon their knees to drink.' He referred them to the end of *v.*^{5}; but Mo. is more probably right in placing them at the end of *v.*^{6}. Very possibly the statement was not part of the original narrative, but a later gloss, written upon the margin of a MS., which crept into 𝔐 in the wrong place.

Stade illustrates the posture adopted by those who lapped water from the spring by a quotation from K. v. d. Steinen: *Unter den Naturvölkern Zentral-Brasiliens*, p. 73. Here the writer remarks, 'It was a comic sight to see how the rising generation and their sisters drank from the Kulisehu: their mouth in the water; supported upon both hands; one leg in the air; not unlike young monkeys' (*ZATW.*, 1896, p. 186). On the other hand, the description given by Moody Stuart (*PEF. Qy. St.*, 1895, p. 345) of the man whom he observed drinking in Madeira, though he terms the method 'lapping' (misled by the misplacement in *v.*^{6} which has just been noticed), really illustrates the method of those who knelt down and scooped up the water in the palm of the hand:—'One afternoon, in riding leisurely out of Funchal, there came toward the town a man in the light garb of a courier from the mountains running at the top of his speed; as he approached me he stopped to quench his thirst at a fountain, in a way that at once suggested the lapping of Gideon's men, and I drew up my pony to observe his action more exactly, but he was already away as on the wings of the wind, leaving me to wonder and admire. With one knee bent before him, and the other limb stretched out in the same attitude as he ran, and with his face upward toward heaven, he threw the water apparently with his fingers in a continuous stream through his open lips, without bringing his hand nearer his mouth than perhaps a foot and a half, and so satisfied his thirst in a few moments.' Cf. further, *Addenda*, pp. xiv ff.

7. And Yahweh said unto Gide'on, 'By the three hundred men who lapped I will deliver you, and will give Midian into thy hand; but let all the people go, every man unto his place.'

7. *By the three hundred . . . I will deliver you.* The grounds upon which the three hundred were retained and the great bulk of the host rejected, have formed a puzzle for interpreters since the time of Josephus. It would be a fruitless task to tabulate the different suggestions which have been offered; but, speaking generally, it may be said that the majority of explanations are vitiated (*a*) by the misplacement in *v.* [6] 𝔐, which has led to a misapprehension of the two forms of drinking; and (*b*) by the presupposition that those chosen must have adopted a method which marked them out as more ready and alert, and therefore more suitable for Gide'on's undertaking.*

Granted, however, that the two forms of drinking are correctly explained in the preceding *note*, it is obvious that (in so far as the test was a test of *attitude*) the main part of the army who knelt to drink, and raised the water in their hands, were the better suited for the enterprise, as adopting a method in the practice of which they were the less likely to be taken by surprise by a lurking foe than

* A striking exception, as regards this latter point, is offered by Josephus, who explains that those who were chosen were marked out by their conduct as the greatest cowards, whom it would have been natural to reject: 'And so, in order that they might learn that the matter was one for His assistance, He advised him to bring his army about noon, in the violence of the heat, to the river, and to esteem those who bent down on their knees, and so drank, to be men of courage, but to esteem all those who drank hastily and tumultuously to be cowards and in dread of the enemy. And when Gide'on had done as God suggested to him, there were found three hundred men who took water in their hands with fear in an agitated manner; and God bade him take these men and attack the enemy' (*Ant.* V. vi. 3). This explanation, in so far as it assumes that God made what was, from the human point of view, an unexpected choice, is in harmony with the explanation which is offered above.

The way in which the two factors (*a* and *b*) noted above have operated in concert in leading an interpreter astray is illustrated by the explanation offered by Smith (*HG.* pp. 398 f.): 'Those Israelites therefore who *bowed themselves down on their knees*, drinking headlong, did not appreciate their position or the foe; whereas those who merely crouched, lapping up the water with one hand, while they held their weapons in the other and kept their face to the enemy, were aware of their danger, and had hearts ready against all surprise. The test in fact was a test of attitude, which, after all, both in physical and moral warfare, has proved of greater value than strength or skill—attitude towards the foe and appreciation of his presence. In this case it was particularly suitable. What Gide'on had in view was a night march and the sudden surprise of a great host. . . . Soldiers who behaved at the water as did the three hundred, showed just the common sense and vigilance to render such tactics successful.' It will be obvious at once that this explanation exactly reverses the methods employed by the three hundred and the main body of the army, as stated in the narrative. Those 'who bowed themselves down on their knees' were not 'drinking headlong'; whereas 'those who merely crouched' obviously could not lap 'as the dog lappeth.'

8. R[JE] And they took ⌜the pitchers⌝ of the people in their hand, and their trumpets; E[2] and all the men of Israel he sent every man to his home, but the three hundred men he retained. And the camp of Midian was beneath him in the vale.

those who rested on their hands or lay prone upon the ground so as to lap like a dog by placing their mouths to the water. But if we take into account the fact that the whole narrative is obviously intended to emphasize the lesson that victory results from Divine assistance and not from the numbers or tactics of the human instruments employed (cf. *v.*[2]), it seems likely that the lapping method, which, from the purely human point of view, might seem to amount to criminal carelessness in presence of the enemy, may have been taken by the narrator as exhibiting trust in the protection and assistance of Yahweh, as opposed to the anxious alertness of those who believed that their hope of success depended upon themselves. If this is so, a commentary on the narrative may be found in 1 Sam. 16[7]: man looks at the outward appearance of fitness; but God looks at the heart.

8. *And they took the pitchers of the people.* Reading וַיִּקְחוּ אֶת־כַּדֵּי הָעָם after Mo. 𝔐 וַיִּקְחוּ אֶת־צֵדָה הָעָם is rendered by R.V., 'So the people took victuals.' If this meaning were intended, however, we should expect וַיִּקְחוּ הָעָם צֵדָה.* 𝔊, 𝔗 offer the rendering 'And they took the victuals of the people' (*i.e.* אֶת־צֵידַת הָעָם or אֶת־צֵיד הָעָם); *i.e.* the three hundred took the victuals of the nine thousand, seven hundred, who were returning home. It is obvious, however, that Gideʿon's little force, which was bent upon a hasty night-attack upon the Midianite camp, would not encumber itself with so large a quantity of useless provisions; and it need not be doubted that Mo.'s suggestion, כַּדֵּי 'pitchers' for צֵדָה, is correct. The statement is due to R[JE], who explains how Gideʿon's army came to have a sufficient number of pitchers (J) and trumpets (E) for the ruse which is to be described in *vv.*[16ff.] Bu. suggests the further emendations וַיִּקַּח 'And he (Gideʿon) took' for וַיִּקְחוּ, in agreement with the sing. שִׁלַּח 'he sent' which follows; and מִיָּדָם 'from their hand' in place of בְּיָדָם.

to his home. Lit. 'to his tents.' Cf. *ch.* 19[9] *note*.

and the camp of Midian, etc. Resumptive of *v.*[1b], after the insertion of the narrative relating the reduction of Gideʿon's army. Cf. p. 180.

* The order *verb, object, subject,* though rare, is occasionally found: cf. cases cited by Driver, *Tenses,* § 208, (4). את צידה, however (את before the indefinite object), cannot be original.

9. E And it came to pass the same night that Yahweh said unto him, 'Arise, go down against the camp; for I have given it into thine hand. 10. But, if thou fearest to go down, go down, thou and Purah thy lad, unto the camp, 11. and hear what they say; and afterward thine hands shall be strengthened, and thou shalt go down against the camp.' So he went down, he and Purah his lad, unto the outskirts of the armed men who were in the camp. 12. And Midian and 'Amaleḳ and all the children of the East were lying along in the vale like locusts for multitude; and their camels were without number, like the sand which is upon the sea-shore for multitude. 13. And when Gide'on came, behold a man was recounting a dream to his comrade: and he said, 'Behold, I dreamed a dream, and, behold, a cake of barley-bread was rolling into the camp of Midian; and when it came to a tent, it smote it so that it fell, and it

10. *But, if thou fearest, etc.* Ros. appositely compares the passage from *Iliad* x. 220 ff. in which Diomedes, in offering to go down to the enemy's camp, says that he will do so with more confidence and boldness if he can have a companion:—

Νέστορ, ἐμ' ὀτρύνει κραδίη καὶ θυμὸς ἀγήνωρ
ἀνδρῶν δυσμενέων δῦναι στρατὸν ἐγγὺς ἐόντα,
Τρώων· ἀλλ' εἴ τίς μοι ἀνὴρ ἅμ' ἕποιτο καὶ ἄλλος·
μᾶλλον θαλπωρὴ καὶ θαρσαλεώτερον ἔσται.

11. *thine hands shall be strengthened. I.e.* 'thou shalt gain courage and confidence': cf. 2 Sam. 2^{7}, 16^{21}, *al.*

the armed men. Heb. *ha-ḥᵃmûšîm* occurs again in Ex. 13^{18} E, Josh. 1^{14}, 4^{12}, R^{D} (Num. 32^{17} 𝔊, 𝔙), and has been restored in *ch.* 5^{8}. The root-meaning of the word is obscure; but Ar. *ḫamîs* 'army' is possibly connected: cf. BDB. *s.v.* Whether the term *ḥᵃmûšîm* refers to the Midianite warriors as a whole, or only to a special class among them, is not clear. Mo. thinks it 'natural to imagine that in such a raid a part of the invaders, better armed and perhaps better disciplined than the rest, lay along the front of the camp to cover it from attack.'

13. *a cake.* The Heb. term, *ṣᵉlûl Kt.*, or *ṣᵉlîl Kᵉrê*, only occurs here, and the precise meaning is uncertain; but the context demands a flat circular cake or round loaf.

was rolling. The Participle *mithhappēkh* describes the action as the speaker sees it going on.

when it came to a tent. Heb. idiom says '*the* tent,' *i.e.* the particular tent which actually appeared to be knocked down, and so is

turned it upside down [].' 14. And his comrade answered and said, 'This is nothing else than [] the men of Israel: God hath given into their hand Midian and all the camp.'

15. And when Gide'on heard the telling of the dream, and its elucidation, he bowed himself down; and he returned unto the camp of Israel, and said, 'Arise! for Yahweh hath given into

vividly marked by the Definite Article. On this idiomatic usage, cf. *NHTK.* on 1 Kgs. 13^{14}; G-K. § 126 *r*; Davidson, *Syntax*, § 21 *e*.

it smote it . . . upside down. At the end of the verse 𝔐 adds וְנָפַל הָאֹהֶל, 'and the tent fell' (R.V. 'and the tent lay along'), which is redundant after the preceding 'so that (*lit.* and) it fell, etc.,' and is marked as a gloss by the false tense (Perfect with *weak* ו). The words are omitted by some MSS. of 𝔊 (cf. Mo., Kit., *BH.*), and apparently by 𝔙, which renders the whole sentence 'percussit illud, atque subvertit (?וַיִּפֹּל), et terrae funditus coaequavit.' So Mo., Bu., No., Kit., Gress. וַיִּפֹּל 'and it fell' might also be dispensed with before ויהפכהו למעלה 'and it turned it upside down,' which is all that sense requires. It is omitted by 𝔊^{L}, Mo., Bu., La., No., Cooke. 𝔖^{P} omits ויכהו as well as ויפל.

14. *the men of Israel.* 𝔐, 'the sword of Gide'on the son of Joash, a man of Israel'; and so all the Versions. It is unlikely, however, that the original narrator would picture the Midianite as knowing the name of the Israelite leader (Mo.); and elsewhere the expression אִישׁ יִשְׂרָאֵל is regularly used in a collective sense, and not of a particular Israelite. The cake of barley-bread clearly represents the Israelite peasantry as a whole, just as the tent denotes the Midianites collectively. חֶרֶב 'the sword of' may have been introduced from *v.*^{20}.

15. *its elucidation.* Heb. *šibhrô*, only here. We may compare Bab. *šabrû*, fem. *šabrâtu*, 'seer' or 'interpreter,' which seems to be formed from *šubrû* 'to cause to see,' the Shaph'el (Causative) modification of *barû* 'to see,' whence *bârû* 'seer.'* So Haupt, *SBOT. ad loc.* Cf. further, *Addenda*, p. xvi.

16-22. The reasons for the detailed analysis of these verses, which divides the narrative between J, E, and R^{JE}, have been fully set forth in the *introd.* pp. 180 f. We here give the narratives of J and E in parallel columns, in order that it may be seen how far each narrative forms an independent whole. Naturally, in the piecing together of

* Kimchi explains שברו from the ordinary Heb. verb שבר 'break' as, literally, 'its breaking,'—'for the dream is like a thing which is sealed and closed up, and the interpretation breaks it and reveals it.' This explanation is adopted by several modern commentators who are unaware of the Bab. parallel.

your hand the camp of Midian.' 16. J And he divided the three hundred men into three bands; and placed in the hand of all of them R^{JE} trumpets and J empty pitchers, and torches inside

two narratives which are nearly parallel throughout, some portions of each may be expected to have been omitted; but it is remarkable how very nearly each narrative, as reconstructed, appears to run continuously, without a break of any importance.

J

16 And he divided the three hundred men into three bands; and placed in the hand of all of them empty pitchers, and torches inside the pitchers. 17a And he said unto them, 'Ye shall see what I do, and shall do likewise. . . .

20 And they brake the pitchers, and held fast the torches in their left hand, and in their right hand the sword; and they cried, 'For Yahweh, and for Gide'on!' 21 And they stood every man in his place round about the camp: and all the camp awoke, and gave a shout, and fled 22bβ toward Ṣeredah, as far as the edge of Abel-meḥolah, by Ṭabbath.

E

17b And behold, when I come into the extremity of the camp, it shall be that, as I do, so shall ye do. 18 When I blow the trumpet, even I and all that are with me, then shall ye also blow the trumpets round about all the camp.' 19a And Gide'on and the hundred men that were with him came into the outskirts of the camp at the beginning of the middle watch; they had only just stationed the guards; 19bα and they blew the trumpets.

22 And the three hundred blew the trumpets; and Yahweh set every man's sword against his comrade throughout all the camp; and the host fled as far as Beth-shiṭṭah.

16. *trumpets.* Heb. *šôphārôth*, properly 'horns.' The *šôphār* seems to have been the curved horn of a cow or ram; while the *ḥ*^{a}*ṣôṣ*^{e}*rā* was a long straight trumpet made of metal. Cf. illustrations of both in Driver, *Amos* (*Camb. Bib.*), p. 145.

R^{JE} has already indicated his view in *v.* 8a as to the source of so large a number of trumpets and pitchers.

pitchers. Heb. *kaddîm*, earthenware-jars used as water-pitchers (Gen. 24 14ff., 1 Kgs. 18 34, Eccles. 12 6), and also for containing meal

the pitchers. 17. And he said unto them, 'Ye shall see what I do, and shall do likewise: E and behold, when I come into the outskirts of the camp, it shall be that, as I do, so shall ye do. 18. When I blow the trumpet, even I and all that are with me, then shall ye also blow the trumpets round about all the camp; R^{JE} and ye shall say, "For Yahweh and for Gideʿon!"'

19. E And Gideʿon and the hundred men that were with him came into the outskirts of the camp at the beginning of the middle watch: they had only just stationed the guards; and

(1 Kgs. 17 [12ff.]). It is possible that each man may have had his jar with him as a receptacle for provisions.

torches inside the pitchers. The pitcher would serve to hide the glowing end of the torch from observation, and at the same time to preserve it from the wind. Lane (*Modern Egyptians*, p. 120) quotes a practice which was in vogue among the police at Cairo about the time at which he wrote (5th edit. 1860), which throws remarkable light on our passage:—'The Ẓábiṭ, or Ágha of the police, used frequently to go about the metropolis at night, often accompanied by the executioner and the "sheạlegee," or bearer of a kind of torch called "sheạleh," which is still in use. This torch burns, soon after it is lighted, without a flame, except when it is waved through the air, when it suddenly blazes forth: it therefore answers the same purpose as our dark lantern. The burning end is sometimes concealed in a small pot or jar, or covered with something else, when not required to give light.'

17. *Ye shall see what I do.* Lit. 'Ye shall see from me,' *i.e.*, as we might say, 'Ye shall take your time from me.'

18. '*For Yahweh and for Gideʿon!*' Nine Codd. (de Rossi) of 𝕳, some MSS. of 𝕲 (cf. Kit., *BH.*), $𝕾^{P}$, 𝕿 read 'A sword for Yahweh, etc.'—doubtless a harmonistic addition in agreement with *v.* [20] as it stands in 𝕳.

19. *the outskirts of the camp.* He reserves for himself and his own contingent the most hazardous task of working across the open plain to the far side of the Midianite encampment (under Neby Daḥy? cf. *note* on *v.* [1]). The object of the whole stratagem was, of course, to make the Midianites believe that their camp was surrounded on all sides by an overwhelming hostile force.

the middle watch. The passage implies that the night was commonly divided into three watches. These watches were probably each of about four hours' duration, throughout the dark hours; and the middle watch would therefore have commenced about 10 P.M. 'The morning-watch' is mentioned in Ex. 14 [24] J, 1 Sam 11 [11]. In Roman times the Jews seem to have adopted the Roman system of

they blew the trumpets, $^{\mathrm{R^{JE}}}$ and dashed in pieces the pitchers that were in their hand. 20. And the three bands blew the trumpets; J and they brake the pitchers; and they held fast the torches in their left hand, and in their right hand $\mathrm{R^{JE}}$ the trumpets to blow; J and they cried $\mathrm{R^{JE}}$ 'A sword J for Yahweh and for Gide῾on!' 21. And they stood every man in his place round about the camp: and all the camp ⌜awoke⌝, and gave a

four watches; cf. Matt. 14^{25} = Mark 6^{48}, 'In the fourth watch of the night he came unto them, walking upon the sea.' This fourfold division is referred to by our Lord in Mark 13^{35}—ὀψέ, μεσονυκτίου, ἀλεκτροφωνίας, πρωΐ. The Talmud (*Berachoth* 3b) discusses the question whether the night should properly be divided into three watches, on the authority of our passage, or into four.

20. *and in their right hand, etc.* The passage has clearly been adapted by $\mathrm{R^{JE}}$ in his endeavour to combine the pitchers of J with the trumpets of E. If, according to J, the men held the pitchers in their left hand, it was natural for $\mathrm{R^{JE}}$ (on the assumption that the two narratives are complementary) to assign the trumpets to the right hand. This he has done without regard to the fact that idiom requires בַּשּׁוֹפָרוֹת after וַיַּחֲזִיקוּ (cf. בַּלַּפִּידִים), and not the accusative הַשּׁוֹפָרוֹת. But granted the inference that the trumpets do not belong to J's account at all, and taking note of the fact that the battle-cry of *v.*^{18b} is simply 'For Yahweh, etc.', and not 'A sword for Yahweh, etc.,' as in the present verse, Bu.'s suggestion seems very plausible that the word חֶרֶב 'a sword' really gives us the clue to the true form of J's original narrative, which may have read בַּחֶרֶב in place of הַשּׁוֹפָרוֹת לִתְקוֹעַ—'and in their right hand *the sword*.' This emendation could not be adopted in our text without essentially modifying the composite narrative of $\mathrm{R^{JE}}$; but has been embodied in the narrative of J as given above in parallelism to that of E (p. 215).

'*A sword for Yahweh, etc.*' Originally, 'For Yahweh and for Gide῾on!' as in *v.*^{18}. The present form of the battle-cry in this verse results from $\mathrm{R^{JE}}$'s attempt to combine the narratives of J and E. Cf. the preceding *note*.

21. *all the camp awoke.* Reading וַיִּיקַץ, as suggested by Mo., in place of וַיָּרָץ 'all the camp *ran*.' The verb רוּץ is not elsewhere used in the sense 'run away'; and is in any case superfluous beside וַיָּנוּסוּ 'and fled' (the regular verb in such a connexion) at the end of the verse. The *order* of 𝔐—ran, shouted, fled—is very strange, and can barely be explained by the supposition that 'ran' means 'rushed

shout, and fled.   22. ᴇ And ⌜the⌝ three hundred blew ⌜t⌝he trumpets ; and Yahweh set every man's sword against his comrade [] throughout all the camp ; and the host fled as far as

hither and thither'—for which there is no justification.   On the other hand, if we adopt Mo.'s emendation, the description of the awakening, followed by a wild cry of alarm and precipitate flight, is very effective. So No., La., Cooke.

and gave a shout and fled.   The shout is rightly explained by Kimchi as a cry of panic.   ᴳ, καὶ ἐσήμαναν appears to understand וַיָּרִיעוּ in the sense 'gave the signal,' or, as we should say, 'sounded the retreat.'   So Rashi תרועת מסע וניסה 'an alarm (outcry) for breaking camp and flight.'   In rendering 'and fled,' we follow *Ḳᵉrê* וַיָּנֻסוּ. Adopting *Kt.* וַיָּנִיסוּ (Hiph'îl), we should have to understand this verb and the preceding in the sense 'and they [the Israelites] raised the battle-cry, and put [them] to flight.'   Cf. R.V.   The Hiph'îl of נום, without expression of object, as here, is used in *ch.* 6¹¹ in a different sense ('*to save* [it] from Midian'); but in the present passage omission of the object is not very natural.   For וַיָּרִיעוּ in the sense 'raised the battle-cry' cf. *note* on 'After thee, Benjamin,' *ch.* 5¹⁴.

22. *And the three hundred blew the trumpets.*   Reading וַיִּתְקְעוּ שְׁלֹשׁ־הַמֵּאוֹת בַּשּׁוֹפָרוֹת, with ᴲ, 'Et nihilominus insistebant trecenti viri buccinis personantes.'   ᴹ, וַיִּתְקְעוּ שְׁלֹשׁ־מֵאוֹת הַשּׁוֹפָרוֹת, can only mean 'And they blew the three hundred trumpets'—though here again (cf. *v.*²⁰ *note*) we note the use of the Accusative after תקע, in place of the customary בְּ : cf. *vv.* 19b.20a.   This בְּ is supplied in the rendering of ᴳᴮ, καὶ ἐσάλπισαν ἐν ταῖς τριακοσίαις κερατίναις, which would seem to suggest וַיִּתְקְעוּ בִּשְׁלֹשׁ וְגֹ ; but may very possibly point to a text וַיִּתְקְעוּ בַּשּׁוֹפָרוֹת שְׁלֹשׁ־הַמֵּאוֹת, in which שְׁלֹשׁ הַמֵּאוֹת was really intended as the subject of the verb, in accordance with our emendation.

and Yahweh set, etc.   This verse, as contrasted with *v.* ²¹ ᵇ, offers perhaps the most obvious mark of divergency between the two narratives.   The camp having fled in a panic (*v.* ²¹ ᵇ), it is clear that *the same narrative* cannot have gone on to state that the Midianites began to fight friend in mistake for foe 'throughout all the camp'; and we are not justified in explaining (with Cooke) that they 'tried to fly,' and then, 'believing themselves to be completely surrounded,' turned their arms against one another prior to the flight becoming general.

throughout all the camp.   Reading בְּכָל־הַמַּחֲנֶה, with omission of the conjunction ו, as in ᴳᴮ, ᴸᴸ, ᴴᶠ.   The ו is probably to be explained

Beth-shiṭṭah J toward Ṣere⌈d⌉ah, as far as the edge of Abel-meḥolah,

(with Mo.) as due to dittography of the last letter of the preceding word ברעהו. A.V. renders ובכל המחנה 'even throughout all the host'; but such an explicative use of ו is highly questionable: cf. ch. 6 25 *footnote* ‡. R.V. 'and against all the host' requires no refutation.

The Heb. term *maḥ^a^né* (from the verb *ḥānā* 'encamp') is used both to denote the camp of an armed host, and also the same body of soldiers in action, which we should designate a *host* or *army*. Thus it is impossible to employ a single uniform rendering for the term; 'camp' being in some connexions the more suitable rendering, and in others 'host.' Cf. the similar usage of the Greek *στρατόπεδον*.

as far as Beth-shiṭṭah, etc. None of the places mentioned can be identified with any certainty. Rob. (*BR.*³ ii. p. 356, *n* ³) was the first to suggest identification of Beth-shiṭṭah with the modern Šaṭṭâ, which lies on the north side of the Nahr Ǵâlûd in the line of flight towards the fords of the Jordan. An objection to this, however, may be found in the fact that (supposing the Midianites to have been encamped south of ed-Daḥy in the neighbourhood of Shunem) Šaṭṭâ is barely seven miles south-east of Shunem, and the nearest fords of the Jordan (east of Bêsân), for which the Midianites may have been making, are some eight miles further east-south-east: whereas the preposition עד can scarcely denote '*in the direction of* Beth-shiṭṭah' (which would suit Šaṭṭâ), but must rather mean '*up to*,' *i.e.* (as rendered above) '*as far as*,' as though Beth-shiṭṭah were in some degree the *destination* of the Midianite host—as it might be considered if it were at or near a ford of the Jordan; or as far as the fugitives got before they were intercepted by the Ephraimites (*v.* 24). The name Beth-shiṭṭah means 'Place of Acacias'; and since the acacia is common in the Jordan valley (cf. the name Shiṭṭim 'Acacias' east of Jordan opposite Jericho, Josh. 2 1, *al.*, and the modern Ǵôr es-Sêsabân 'Vale of the Acacias' in the same locality), there are many sites, east or west of Jordan, to which such a name may have been applied in ancient times.

We read צְרֵדָתָה with 20 MSS. of 𝔐, in place of the common reading צְרֵרָתָה 'toward Ṣerērah.' This further description of the line of flight 'toward Ṣerēdah, as far as etc.,' can scarcely have originally stood beside 'as far as Beth-shiṭṭah'; and is probably to be assigned to the other source. Ṣerēdah, which is mentioned in 2 Chr. 4 17 in connexion with Succoth east of Jordan (*i.e.* probably opposite to it on the western side of the river), is the same as Ṣarĕthan in the parallel passage, 1 Kgs. 7 46. A Ṣarĕthan is named in 1 Kgs. 4 12, which speaks of 'all Beth-she'an which is in proximity to Ṣarĕthan, beneath Jezreʿel'—a position which would suit the line of flight of the Midianite host down the Nahr Ǵâlûd, as we gather it from our narrative. In Josh. 3 16, however, the city of Adam, the name of which is probably preserved in the modern ford ed-Dâmiyyeh, is said to be 'beside Ṣarĕthan'; and ed-Dâmiyyeh is some twenty-seven miles to the south of Beth-she'an—a position which suits the allusion to Ṣerēdah, 2 Chr. 4^{17} = Ṣarĕthan, 1 Kgs. 7^{46}, since evidence seems to indicate that Ṡuccoth must have been close to the Jabboḳ, perhaps a little to the south of it in the Jordan valley: cf. Driver, *Jacob's Route from Ḥaran to Shechem*, in *Expos. Times*, xiii. pp. 457-460; more briefly in *Genesis*, *Westm. Comm.*, pp. 300-302. Indeed, it is likely, as Mo. suggests, that 1 Kgs. 7^{46} originally mentioned the ford ed-Dâmiyyeh; the obscure בְּמַעֲבֵה הָאֲדָמָה (R.V. 'in the clay ground') being probably a corruption of בְּמַעְבְּרַת אֲדָמָה 'at the crossing of Adamah.'

It is questionable whether the Ṣerēdah of 1 Kgs. 11^{26}, which was the native city of the Ephraimite Jeroboʿam, can be the same as the site above discussed. 𝔊 states in 1 Kgs. 11^{43}, 12^{24b} (according to the numeration of Swete's edition), that Jeroboʿam's city was ἐν τῷ ὄρει Εφραιμ; whereas the Ṣerēdah-Ṣarĕthan of the other passages must certainly have been in or near the Jordan valley. Van de Velde's proposed identification of Ṣarĕthan with Ḳarn Ṣarṭabeh (the סרטבא of the Mishna)—on a spur of the hill-country which runs into the Jordan valley south of the Wâdy Farʿah and due west of ed-Dâmiyyeh, forming a prominent landmark—though unsuitable so far as identification of the ancient and modern *names* is concerned, yet suits geographically all allusions to Ṣerēdah-Ṣarĕthan, except that in 1 Kgs. 4^{12}: cf. Cheyne in *EB.* 5383.

Abel-meḥolah (the native city of Elishaʿ, 1 Kgs. 19^{16}) is mentioned in 1 Kgs. 4^{12} as marking one limit of an overseer's district, the other limit being Beth-she'an. It was evidently south of Beth-she'an; and is identified by Eusebius (*OS.* 227^{35}) with Βηθμαιελα, ten miles from Scythopolis (Beth-she'an). This is conjectured by Conder (*SWP. Mem.* ii. p. 231) to be the modern ʿAin el-Ḥelweh in the Wâdy el-Mâliḥ, which is about that distance south of Bêsân.

There is, needless to say, no philological connexion between Ḥelweh and Meḥolah (as Conder seems to suppose*); the ʿAin el-Ḥelweh, 'spring of sweet water,' being so called in contrast to the generality of the springs in the Wâdy el-Mâliḥ, 'wâdy of the salt water,' which are salt or brackish.‡ The only argument which can really be advanced in favour of this site is the very slender one that it suits the distance from Beth-she'an as given by Eusebius. But here the resemblance between -μαιελα and Mâliḥ creates a suspicion that Eusebius may have fallen into error; and that the only ground for his identification was the supposition that some site called Bêth-Mâliḥ in his day, in the Wâdy el-Mâliḥ, preserved the old name Meḥolah.

No theory as to the site of Abel-meḥolah deserves consideration unless it does justice to the striking expression 'the *edge* (lit. 'lip,'

* His words are, 'Ain Helweh, the name of which contains the proper radicals [of Abel Meḥolah].'

‡ Cf. Conder, *Tent Work*, p. 227.

שְׂפַת) of Abel-meḥolah,' which is employed in our passage.* This expression is used elsewhere geographically of the *shore* (lip) of the sea, the *bank* (lip) of a river, and the *edge* (lip) of a wâdy. It is this latter usage which here concerns us. It occurs in Deut. 2 [36], 4 [48]; Josh. 12 [2], 13 [9.16]; Ezek. 47 [6.7]. All these occurrences, except those in Ezek., refer to the site of '‘Aro'er, which is upon the edge (lip) of the wâdy Arnon,' *i.e.* the modern ‘Arâ‘îr, which is described by Tristram (*Moab*, p. 129) as a desolate heap of ruins, on the northern edge of the precipitous ravine.‡ Such a 'lip,' overhanging a wâdy, appears then to be what our writer has in mind in speaking of 'the lip of Abel-meḥolah.' Conder, in advocating the site ‘Ain el-Ḥelweh, makes no mention of any such *lip* or *edge* in its vicinity; and this question, which does not seem to have entered into his consideration, should form a subject for future topographical investigation, if this site is to be maintained.

Another theory as to the site of Abel-meḥolah may be put forward as not unworthy of consideration. We have observed above that 1 Kgs. 4 [12] mentions both Ṣarĕthan (Ṣerēdah) and Abel-meḥolah; and we have also seen that the statement in this passage that Beth-she'an was 'in proximity to Ṣarĕthan' causes great difficulty; since other allusions to Ṣerēdah-Ṣarĕthan seem to place it much further south, in the vicinity of the ford ed-Dâmiyyeh. The supposition that the words 'which is in proximity to Ṣarĕthan' (אֲשֶׁר אֵצֶל צָרְתָנָה) have been accidentally transposed, and should properly follow 'Abel-meḥolah,'§ has the double merit of dissociating Ṣarĕthan from

* The importance of the investigation of this expression was first pointed out to the present writer by Dr. Driver, who, however, advanced no theory as to the site of Abel-meḥolah.

‡ The ravine and its northern edge (in contrast to the southern) are thus described by Tristram. 'The ravine of the Arnon does not show till we are close upon it. . . . The rolling slopes come close down to the precipitous descent, the plain being perfectly level on either side, breaking away in limestone precipices to a great depth. No idea of the rift can be formed till the very edge is reached. As far as we could calculate, the width is about three miles from crest to crest; the depth by our barometers 2150 feet from the south side, which runs for some distance nearly 200 feet higher than the northern edge. . . . We were much struck by the contrast between the two sides, and this impression was confirmed when, next day, we viewed the southern from the northern edge. The protrusion of the basaltic dyke has been subsequent to the formation of the wady, and the continued detaching of its fragments has made the slope less precipitous, giving a variety to the colouring and the vegetation, wanting on the other side. The northern bank, on the contrary, looked an almost unbroken precipice of marly limestone, faintly tinged with the green hue of a very sparse vegetation, and occasionally protruding cliffs and needles, shining pink in the sunbeams' (*op. cit.* pp. 125 f.).

§ Notice that Beth-she'an is already defined as 'beneath Jezre'el.' It is reasonable, therefore, to suppose that the words 'in proximity to Ṣarĕthan,' instead of being a second definition of the position of Beth-she'an, should refer to Abel-meḥolah, the position of which is otherwise unspecified.

Beth-she'an, and bringing it into connexion with Abel-meḥolah, as in Judg. 7 [22]. The verse then runs, 'Ba'ana the son of Aḥilud: Ta'anach and Megiddo, and all Beth-she'an beneath Jezre'el; from Beth-she'an to Abel-meḥolah which is in proximity to Ṣarĕthan; as far as the other side of Joḳme'am.'

Now we have already noticed, in speaking of the site of Ṣerēdah-Ṣarĕthan, that identification with the modern Ḳarn-Ṣarṭabeh would suit all Biblical allusions except that of 1 Kgs. 4 [12] as 𝔐 now stands, where it is brought into connexion with Beth-she'an. This difficulty, as we have seen, is removed, if by our transposition we bring it into connexion with Abel-meḥolah, as in Judg. 7 [22].

Rob. (*BR* [3]. iii. p. 317), in speaking of the view of the northern Ġôr (Jordan valley) from a point east of Jordan near Kefr Abil, above the Wâdy Yâbis, mentions the opening of the Wâdy Far'ah between the ridge of Ḳarn-Ṣarṭabeh to the south, and 'the opposite lower bluff el-Makhrûd' to the north. This el-Makhrûd is the el-Maḫrûḳ of the *SWP. Great Map* and *Name List*: cf. Map III. in this commentary. The term *bluff* seems exactly to answer to what the O.T. writers mean by a *lip* or *edge* above a wâdy.

Looking again at 1 Kgs. 4, which describes the respective spheres of Solomon's twelve commissariat officers, we notice that, in *v.* [8], the hill-country of Ephraim is assigned to Ben-Ḥur. All immediately north of this, bounded on the south by the line along which the territory of Manasseh marched with that of Ephraim, seems to have fallen within the sphere of Ba'ana the son of Aḥilud, whose sphere of action (*v.* [12]) immediately concerns us.

Now P's account of the boundary between Ephraim and Manasseh in Josh. 16, 17 is admittedly obscure: but at any rate it seems clear that the eastern part * of this boundary was practically marked by the great Wâdy Far'ah, which forms an important dividing factor (notice the allusions in 16 [6] to Ta'anath-Shiloh and Janoaḥ—perhaps the modern Ta'na and Yânûn; and the mention in 17 [7] of 'Michmethath which is in front of Shechem'). Ba'ana's district, then, seems to have embraced the hill-country bounded on the north by the plain of Esdraelon (Ta'anach and Megiddo: cf. *ch.* 1 [27] *note*), eastward to and including Beth-she'an where the vale falls to the Jordan valley 'below Jezre'el'; and then southward to Abel-meḥolah, the 'lip' of which, if it corresponded to the south-eastern limit of Manasseh, must have been the 'bluff' of el-Maḫrûḳ.

If then, the 'lip' of Abel-meḥolah is el-Maḫrûḳ (the city itself perhaps lying above this 'lip' to the north, on some part of the headland Râs 'Umm el-Ḫarrûbeh), while Ṣerēdah-Ṣarĕthan is Ḳarn-Ṣarṭabeh—the northern and southern ramparts of the Wâdy Far'ah, where it opens out into the Jordan valley; we then perceive why the

* On the western part of the boundary between the two tribes, cf. *notes* on 'Manasseh' and 'Ephraim,' *ch.* 1 [27, 29].

edge of Abel-meḥolah should be mentioned together with Ṣerēdah in the narrative of the flight of the Midianites: and also why (if our transposition is correct) Abel-meḥolah should be described as 'in proximity to' (אֵצֶל 'beside') Ṣarĕthan in 1 Kgs. 4 [12].

The site of Ṭabbath cannot be conjectured.

It now remains to inquire whether any inference can be drawn from this verse as to the line of flight which is presupposed. It is clear that the Biblical indications noticed above as to the positions of the places mentioned may furnish some guide upon this point, even though the actual sites defy identification.

We have seen that, according to E, the field of action is laid in the vale of Jezreʿel; with Gideʿon's army upon a spur of Mount Gilboaʿ to the south, and the Midianites encamped in the vale—probably below Neby Daḥy (cf. 6 [33], 7 [1] *notes*). As regards J this is not so clear; the conjecture being open that this narrative may have laid the scene of the night-attack near ʿOphrah (close to Shechem), and pictured the flight as taking place down the Wâdy Farʿah towards the ford ed-Dâmiyyeh (cf. the last paragraph to *note* on *v.*[1], 'was to the north . . . in the vale'). Laying aside the allusions to Beth-Shiṭṭah and Ṭabbath (about which we know nothing), we have such information as we have gleaned with regard to Ṣerēdah and Abel-meḥolah to guide our inquiry.

The allusion to Ṣerēdah-Ṣarĕthan in 1 Kgs. 4 [12], as 𝔐 stands, suits the vale of Jezreʿel and excludes the Wâdy Farʿah. On the other hand, 2 Chr. 4 [17] = 1 Kgs. 7 [46], Josh. 3 [16], and 1 Kgs. 4 [12] according to our re-arrangement, imply proximity to ed-Dâmiyyeh, and so may seem to favour the Wâdy Farʿah as the scene of flight. That ed-Dâmiyyeh was, as a matter of fact, used as a crossing by Midian (at least according to J) is almost necessarily to be inferred from *ch.* 7 [24f.], where the Ephraimites are invited by Gideʿon to hold the fords of the Jordan against Midian: since it is clear that Ephraim could scarcely have been summoned to hold a position north of this point; and, had the Midianites been making for the fords due east of Beth-she'an, such a summons would be out of the question, since the foe would have gained and crossed them before Gideʿon's messenger had even reached the Ephraimite territory.

There remains, however, the possibility that E, like J, may have represented the Midianites as making for the ford ed-Dâmiyyeh; *i.e.* as turning southwards down the Jordan valley from the Nahr Ǵâlûd, and so leaving the fords east of Beth-she'an unattempted, either through their haste or through ignorance of them. It is significant that E in *ch.* 8 [4ff.] seems to picture Gideʿon as arriving at Ṡuccoth and Penuel * directly he has crossed the Jordan; and the inference there-

* Reference has been made earlier in this *note* to the site of Ṡuccoth. With regard to Penuel, Driver's conclusion is:—'A site, S. of the Jabboḳ near where

fore is that he crossed at ed-Dâmiyyeh, after which he struck eastward 'in the direction of the track of the tent-dwellers,' east of Jogbehah (Aǵbêhât)—a further fact which lends colour to the same conclusion.

The question then is—supposing the sites of Ṣerēdah and the 'lip' of Abel-meḥolah to have been as we have conjectured (the former at Ḳarn-Ṣarṭabeh, and the latter at el-Maḫrûḳ), does the form in which these sites are referred to give us any clue as to whether the line of flight was down the Wâdy Far'ah from 'Ophrah, or down the Jordan valley from the Nahr Ǵâlûd—in either case with the ford ed-Dâmiyyeh as the goal?

It is probably significant that ה *locale* is used with Ṣerēdah, while the preposition עד is employed in the reference to the 'lip' of Abel-meḥolah; *i.e.* while the line of flight was *in the direction of* Ṣerēdah, it was actually *up to* or *as far as* the 'lip' of Abel-meḥolah that the fugitives reached.* Here is a point which seems to favour the view that this narrative pictures the flight as down the Jordan valley from the Nahr Ǵâlûd; since this would involve taking the direction of Ḳarn-Ṣarṭabeh, but at the same time turning off some miles short of it *at* el-Maḫrûḳ in order to make for the ford ed-Dâmiyyeh.‡ On the other hand, had the course of the fugitives been down the Wâdy Far'ah, it is difficult to see why the distinction should be drawn in the form of reference to the two localities.

Evidence is insufficient to guide us to a decision as to whether the description which we have been considering belongs to J or E. In any case, however, we are probably justified in concluding that the

the Ghôr route crosses the route from es-Salṭ to the ford ed-Dâmiyeh, though it can only be assigned conjecturally, would satisfy the conditions of the Biblical narrative.' Cf. references cited, and *Genesis* (*Westm. Comm.*), p. 296.

* The same distinction in usage between ה *locale* and the prep. עד is to be observed in Gen. 10 [19] J, where it is stated that 'the border of the Cana'anite was from Ṣidon as thou goest *in the direction of* Gerar (גְּרָרָה), *as far as* Ġaza (עַד־עַזָּה); as thou goest *in the direction of* Sodom and Ġomorrah and Admah and Ṣeboiim (סְדֹמָה וגו'), *as far as* Lesha' (עַד־לָשַׁע).' Gerar is some distance south-east of Ġaza; so if Ġaza marks the south-west point of the Cana'anite territory, the distinction indicated by the use of ה *locale* with Gerar—further on beyond the boundary—is perfectly correct. The whole definition is, however, somewhat strange; and, as Skinner remarks (*ICC. ad loc.* p. 217), 'would only be intelligible if Gerar were a better known locality than Ġaza.' Hence some scholars think that עַד־עַזָּה is a later gloss. With regard to the places which are named on the south-east we can draw no conclusions, since we are ignorant of their precise positions.

‡ It is actually *at* el-Maḫrûḳ that the road down the Jordan valley from the north intersects the road which, coming from the hill-country to the west, enters the Wâdy Far'ah and runs down to the ford ed-Dâmiyyeh: cf. *Map* III.; *SWP. Great Map*, sheet XV.; Smith, *HG.* Plate V. The name el-Maḫrûḳ signifies 'the perforated,' *i.e.* a rock-cutting through which a road passes.

by Ṭabbath. 23. And the men of Israel were called to arms Gl? from Naphtali and from Asher, and J from all Manasseh, and they pursued after Midian. 24. And Gide῾on sent messengers throughout all the hill-country of Ephraim, saying, 'Come down to meet Midian, and take ⌜the fords⌝ of the Jordan against them': so all the men of Ephraim were called to arms, and took ⌜the fords⌝ of the Jordan. 25. And they took the two princes of Midian, ῾Oreb and Ze'eb; and they slew ῾Oreb at

variation between the two narratives, as regards topography, was by no means so great as some scholars have assumed.

23. *were called to arms.* Cf. *ch.* 6[34] *note.*

from Naphtali and Asher. Upon the summoning of these tribes, cf. p. 181.

24. *the fords of the Jordan.* Reading אֶת־מַעְבְּרוֹת הַיַּרְדֵּן, as in *ch.* 3[28], 12[5.6], in place of 𝔐 אֶת־הַמַּיִם עַד בֵּית בָּרָה וְאֶת־הַיַּרְדֵּן 'the waters as far as Beth-barah, and the Jordan,' the meaning of which has proved a puzzle to commentators. No such site as Beth-barah is known; and Mo.'s suggestion that 'the waters' are the perennial stream of the Wâdy Far῾ah, between which and the Jordan 'the Midianites would be in a *cul de sac,*' is vitiated by the fact that the lower part of the Wâdy Far῾ah, which is known as the Wâdy eǵ-Ǵôzeleh, flows into the Jordan some five miles south of the ford ed-Dâmiyyeh; and therefore, if the Midianites were aiming at ed-Dâmiyyeh, they would not need to cross the Wâdy Far῾ah stream at all. Even apart, however, from the difficulty of identifying Beth-barah, the whole description is curiously vague and unintelligible. Why are 'waters' mentioned instead of *naḥal*, wâdy (if any particular wâdy is meant); and what is the force of עד 'unto' or 'as far as,' which suggests that the Ephraimites are expected to line 'the waters' for an indefinite distance, as far as the locality specified? Is it, again, possible that 'and the Jordan' can be original, without reference to any particular ford or fords?

Our emendation supposes that the letters הממעדבתברהואת are simply corrupt dittography of מַעְבְּרֹת, which can be recognized once in letters 3 to 7 with transposition of ב and ר and corruption of the latter letter to ד(מעדבת). Letters 2, 8, 9, 13 preserve genuine letters of the doublet; this time with בר in the right order.

25. *῾Oreb and Ze'eb.* The names mean 'Raven' and 'Wolf.' It has been thought that the use of such animal-names presupposes a primitive totemistic stage of society; and evidence quoted from Arabian sources is somewhat striking: cf. Robertson Smith, *Animal worship and animal tribes among the Arabs and in the Old Testa-*

the rock of ʿOreb, and Ze'eb they slew at the wine-vat of Ze'eb; R^{JE} and they pursued ⌈ ⌉ Midian; J and the head⌈s⌉ of ʿOreb and Ze'eb they brought unto Gideʿon R^{JE} beyond the Jordan.

8. 1. J And the men of Ephraim said unto him, 'What is this thing that thou hast done unto us, not to call us when thou didst go to fight with Midian?' and they chode with him

ment; Journal of Philology, ix. pp. 75 ff. Among examples of tribal animal-names collected from Suyûṭî's dictionary of gentile names, we find Ẕîb, 'wolf,' son of 'Amr, a sub-tribe of the Azd; and Ġurâb, 'raven,' a sub-tribe of the Fazâra: cf. *op. cit.* p. 79. On animal-names in the O.T., cf. Gray, *Hebrew Proper Names*, pp. 86 ff.

the rock of ʿOreb . . . the wine-vat of Ze'eb. Conder (*SWP. Mem.* iii. p. 177) tentatively suggests as possible sites the modern 'Ušš el-Ġurâb, 'the nest of the raven,' a sharp conical peak some 2½ miles north of the modern Jericho (Erîḫa); and Tuwêl eẕ-Ẕiyâb, 'the ridge of the wolves' (apparently a clan bearing the name eẕ-Ẕiyâb), nearly 5 miles north-west of the same point. These sites are probably much too far south of the scene of action; and in any case we cannot attach importance to designations embodying animal-names which (at any rate in the case of Ẕîb, plur. Ẕiyâb) appear to be elsewhere in frequent use.*

they pursued Midian. Reading אֶת־מ' in place of אֶל־מ', 𝔐.

the heads. Reading רָאשֵׁי in place of the sing. ראשׁ, 𝔐.

beyond the Jordan. On the manner in which this verse has been glossed by R^{JE} in order to make it fit in with the narrative of 8 $^{4ff.}$, cf. p. 182.

8. 1. *And the men of Ephraim said, etc.* The conduct of the Ephraimites towards Jephthaḥ, ch. 12 $^{1ff.}$, is very similar; and the grounds alleged for the quarrel, viz. failure to summon them to the battle in the first instance, are the same. There is no reason, however, to assume, with some scholars, that one of the narratives is therefore secondary to the other. Cf. Mo. *ad loc.*, who remarks that in the two stories 'the sequel is as different as can be imagined, and in each is in entire conformity with the situation.'

* Other instances of the name 'wolf' in place-names in or near the Jordan valley, as noted in the *SWP. Great Map*, are:—a second Tuwêl eẕ-Ẕiyâb, 5½ miles due north of Râs 'Umm el-Ḫarrûbeh (sheet xii.); Meṭîl eẕ-Ẕîb, 'the peak of the wolf,' in the Jordan valley, 3½ miles south-west from ed-Dâmiyyeh (sheet xv.); Wâdy Unḳûr eẕ-Ẕîb, 'wâdy of the water-holes of the wolf,' running from the hill-country into the Jordan valley about 8 miles south-west of ed-Dâmiyyeh; and Wâdy Meḳûr eẕ-Ẕîb (with the same meaning), 3 miles further south (sheet xv.).

violently. 2. And he said unto them, 'What have I done now in comparison with you? Is not the gleaning of Ephraim better than the vintage of Abi'ezer? 3. Into your hand hath ⌜Yahweh⌝ given the princes of Midian, even 'Oreb and Ze'eb: and what was I able to do in comparison with you?' Then was their anger against him abated, when he had spoken this word.

4. E And Gide'on came to the Jordan, ⌜and he⌝ passed over,

2. *Is not the gleaning, etc.* The Heb. term *'ôlēlôth* is confined to the gleaning of grapes (Mic. 7^{1}, Jer. 49^{9}, Ob. ^{5}, Isa. 24^{13}) and olives (Isa. 17^{6}), and is never used of the gleaning of grain, for which another term, *léḳeṭ*, is employed. The point of Gide'on's words is that, though not called to lend their aid until the rout of Midian was an accomplished fact, yet the Ephraimites might be said actually to have secured the greater honour, through the capture of the two princes of the enemy. The fact has already been noted (p. 182) that Gide'on's allusion to his own small force as 'Abi'ezer' seems to indicate that this narrative (J) pictured the muster as consisting of Abi'ezrites only (*ch.* 6^{34}), and knew nothing of the gathering and subsequent dispersion of a very large force from several tribes (E ^{2}).

3. *Yahweh.* So 𝔊, 𝔙, 𝔗, in place of 𝔐 'God.'

their anger. Lit. 'spirit,' or, as we might say, 'temper.' For this use of Heb. *rûaḥ*, cf. Prov. 16^{32}, 25^{28}, Job 15^{13}, Zech. 6^{8}, Eccles. 10^{4}.

4. *and he passed over.* Reading וַיַּעֲבֹר, which seems to be presupposed by 𝔊, 𝔙, $𝔖^{P}$, with Grä., Bu., Oort, No., La., Cooke; in place of the Participle עֹבֵר in 𝔐.. The use of this latter, though grouped by Driver (*Tenses*, § 161, (2)) under clauses 'with a participial determination of the subject as the secondary predicate,' is difficult to justify syntactically; the Participle here expressing not an action *concomitant with* the action expressed by the main verb (וַיָּבֹא 'And he came'), but resulting from it.* The Imperfect with ו *consecutive* is the regular construction to express such a sense.

* Thus such an instance as Jer. 17^{25} וּבָאוּ . . . רֹכְבִים 'shall enter *riding*' is evidently different, since here the participle describes the *manner of entry*; and Judg. 1^{7}, Isa. 36^{22}, Jer. 2^{27}, *al.*, are similar to this. Perhaps the case most like our passage is Num. 16^{27} יָצְאוּ נִצָּבִים 'they came forth *stationed* (or '*so as to be* stationed,') where נִצָּבִים expresses the *result* of יָצְאוּ: but, in order to make our passage really parallel to this, we should have to alter the *'Athnaḥ* from הַיַּרְדֵּנָה to עֹבֵר—'came to the Jordan, *crossing over*' (*i.e.* '*so as to* cross over'); and then what is to happen to the latter half of the verse which also exhibits its

he and the three hundred men who were with him, exhausted and ⌈famished⌉. 5. And he said to the men of Ṡuccoth, 'Prithee, give loaves of bread to the men who are following me, for they are exhausted; and I am pursuing after Zebaḥ and Ṣalmunnaʿ,

exhausted and famished. Reading וּרְעֵבִים with 𝔊^AL, 𝔖^h, 𝔏^L. So Houb., Bu., Grä., Frankenberg, Kit., Oort, No., La. This correction seems almost to be postulated by *v.* [5], where the request for bread is made of the men of Ṡuccoth. In order to justify the reading of 𝔐, we have to treat the conjunction ו as adversative, as is done by A.V., R.V., 'faint *yet* pursuing.' Possibly the alteration of רְעֵבִים into רֹדְפִים may have been due to the fact that in *v.* [5] כִּי־עֲיֵפִים הֵם, 'for they are exhausted,' is followed by וְאָנֹכִי רֹדֵף, 'and I am pursuing.'

5. *Ṡuccoth.* The actual sites of Ṡuccoth and Penuel have not been discovered; but evidence goes to show that they must have been not far south of the Jabboḳ: cf. *note* on 'as far as Beth-shiṭṭah, etc.,' *ch.* 7 [22].

loaves of bread. Heb. *kikkᵉrôth léḥem* means lit. '*rounds*' or '*circles* of bread,' *i.e.* probably, round, flat cakes.

who are following me. Lit. 'who are at my feet.' Cf. 4 [10] *note.*

Zebaḥ and Ṣalmunnaʿ. The names זֶבַח and צַלְמֻנָּע mean respectively 'sacrifice' ('sacrificial victim') and 'shelter withheld.'* It is obvious that these forms cannot be original, but must be later

participial determination of the subject, עֲיֵפִים וגו׳ 'exhausted, etc.'? We should have to treat it as a circumstantial clause: 'He and the three hundred, etc., were exhausted, etc.' As the verse is accented, however (with break on הַיַּרְדֵּנָה), we can only render, 'he and the three hundred men that were with him *were crossing over*, exhausted and famished'; the use of the Participle עֹבֵר being apparently intended to indicate that, *at the time when they were crossing*, they were in the condition described by עֲיֵפִים וגו׳. This, however, is very unnatural. Mo. suggests that עָבַר, the Perfect, 'he crossed over,' was originally a marginal gloss, which, when transferred to the text, was forced into construction by pronouncing עֹבֵר.

* For צֵל מְמֻנָּע. צֵל 'shadow' occurs in the sense 'shelter' in Jer. 48 [45], Num. 14 [9], Ps. 91 [1], *al.* For the vocalization צַל, cf. בְּצַלְאֵל Bĕṣal'ēl, 'In the shelter of God.' On the Puʿal Participle מֻנָּע, with dropping of preformative מ, cf. G-K. § 52 *s*.

the kings of Midian.' 6. And the officers of Ṡuccoth said ⌜⌝, 'Are the hands of Zebaḥ and Ṣalmunnaʿ now in thine hand, that we should give bread to thy host?' 7. And Gideʿon said, 'Well then, when Yahweh hath given Zebaḥ and Ṣalmunnaʿ into mine hand, I will thresh your flesh together with thorns of the desert and

modifications in jesting allusion to the fate of the kings as related in *vv.* $^{18\,ff.}$ Cf., for similar perversions, *notes* on Adoni-bezeḳ, *ch.* 1^{5}, and Cushan-rishʿathaim, *ch.* 3^{8}. The original forms of the names can hardly be conjectured. It is likely, however, that the first three consonants of Ṣalmunna, צלמ, embody the name of the god Ṣalm, who is known to us through inscriptions from Têma in North Arabia: cf. Nöldeke, *Berichte d. Berl. Akad.*, 1884, pp. 813 ff.; Baethgen, *Beiträge*, pp. 80 f.; *KAT.*^{3} pp. 475 f.; Cooke, *NSI.* pp. 195 ff.; La., *ÉRS.*^{2} pp. 502 f.

6. *And the officers of Ṡuccoth said.* We must, of course, read plur. וַיֹּאמְרוּ instead of the sing. וַיֹּאמֶר in 𝔐.

7. *Well then.* Lit. 'Therefore'; *i.e.* 'Since you choose to adopt such an attitude.'

I will thresh your flesh together with, etc. The Heb. verb *dûš*, which is here used, means *to tread in threshing*; the operation of threshing being performed either by the feet of cattle, or by the threshing-drag (*môrāgh*) shod beneath with stone or basalt (cf. Isa. 41^{15}, Am. 1^{3}), which was weighted and dragged round the threshing-floor by oxen (cf. 2 Sam. 24^{22}, Hos. 10^{11}), thus separating the grain and grinding the straw into chaff.* The equivalent Ar. verb *dâsa* is used generally in the sense *to trample* with the foot (*e.g.* of horses trampling on the slain), and also specifically of *threshing* grain, either by the feet of beasts, or by repeatedly drawing over it the *midwas* or threshing-drag (Lane). Bab. *dâšu* means *to tread down* or *crush.*

The preposition rendered 'together with' is את, which is always used of *accompaniment*, and never of the instrument. So 𝔙 renders correctly 'cum spinis tribulisque deserti'; 𝔖^{P} ܥܠ ܟܘ̈ܒܐ ܕܡܕܒܪܐ ܘܥܠ ܡܘܪ̈ܓܠܐ 'upon thorns of the desert and upon briars'; 𝔗 על כובי מדברא וג׳, *id.*

Thus Gideʿon threatens that he will lay the men of Ṡuccoth 'naked upon a bed of thorns' (Mo.), and treat them as corn is treated in threshing, either by trampling them down or by drawing threshing-wains over them (cf. Am. 1^{3}).

R.V. *text*, in rendering 'I will tear your flesh with the thorns, etc.,' commits the double error of giving to *dûš* a sense which (so far

* For illustration and description of the threshing-board as used at the present day in Syria and Palestine, cf. Driver, *Joel and Amos* (*Camb. Bib.*), pp. 227 f.

thistles.' 8. And he went up thence to Penuel, and spake unto them on this wise; and the men of Penuel answered him as the men of Succoth had answered. 9. And he spake also unto the men of Penuel, saying, 'When I return in safety, I will break down this tower.'

10. Now Zebaḥ and Ṣalmunnaʿ were in Ḳarḳor, and their host was with them, about fifteen thousand men, even all that were left out of all the host of the children of the East: for they that had fallen were an hundred and twenty thousand men who drew sword. 11. And Gideʿon went up ⌜towards⌝ the track of

as we know) it never possesses, either in Heb. or in the cognate languages; and of rendering את 'with' in an instrumental sense, as is done by 𝔊 ἐν ταῖς ἀκάνθαις κ.τ.λ. In *v.* 16, which relates the carrying out of Gideon's threat, the words used are ⌜וידיש⌝ בהם (on the emended verb, cf. *note ad loc.*); and here the ב might have an instrumental sense (𝔊 ἐν αὐτοῖς) if it were possible to explain the verb *dûš* 'thresh' in the sense 'thrash' or 'flog,' the briars and thorns being used in place of a stick or flail. As we have seen, however, this form of threshing is never denoted by *dûš*; the verb which denotes the *beating out* of corn with a stick being *ḥābaṭ*: cf. *ch.* 6 11 *note.* We must explain ב, therefore, as meaning (like את) 'together with,' a sense which this prep. possesses: cf. BDB. *sv.* ב, III. 1. *a.*

thistles. The precise meaning of Heb. *barḳānîm* is unknown; but the close connexion with *ḳôṣê ham-midhbār*, 'thorns of the desert,' demands that the word should denote some kind of prickly plant. The explanation advocated by J. D. Michaelis, Ges., *Thes.*, etc., threshing-sledges shod with *fire*-stones, is simple guess-work, depending upon a supposed connexion of the word with *bārāḳ*, 'lightning.'

10. *Ḳarḳor.* The site is unknown. Eusebius (*OS.* 272 62) identifies with Καρκαρία, one day's journey distant from Petra; but this seems too far to the south. On the other hand, the Ḳarḳar at which Shalmaneṣer III. met and defeated Bir-idri of Damascus and his allies (*KB.* i. pp. 172 f.; Rogers, *CP.* pp. 295 f.) must have been in the neighbourhood of Ḥamath, and would thus be much too far to the north.

they that had fallen, etc. The huge number is clearly the exaggeration of a late writer. The expression *šōlēph ḥérebh*, 'that drew sword,' is a favourite one in the part of the narrative of *ch.* 20 which is due to R^{P}, and where similar high figures are given: cf. *vv.* 2.15.17.35.46. Possibly, as Mo. suggests, the latter part of the verse may have been added by a redactor to harmonize 8 10a with 7 23ff.

11. *towards the track of the tent-dwellers.* Reading דַּרְכָּה שֹׁכְנֵי בָאֳהָלִים, with Bu., in place of 𝔐 דֶּרֶךְ הַשְּׁכוּנֵי בָאֳהָלִים, which offers

the tent-⸢dwellers⸣, east of Nobaḥ and Jogbehah; and he smote the host, whilst the host was careless. 12. And Zebaḥ and Ṣalmunnaʿ fled; and he pursued after them, and captured the two kings of Midian, even Zebaḥ and Ṣalmunnaʿ, but all the host ⸢he devoted to destruction⸣. 13. And Gideʿon the son of Joash

the grammatical solecisms of the Article with the Construct State, and the Passive Participle of the Stative verb which is elsewhere unknown. The track of the tent-dwellers was doubtless the beaten track running north and south by which the nomads were accustomed to travel—much like the modern *ḥaǵǵ*-route which runs from Damascus to Mecca. Gideʿon, guessing that the fugitives would make for this track in order to escape southward, struck south-eastward from the Jordan valley until he reached it.

Nobaḥ. According to Num. 32^{42} J (cf. p. 51), Nobaḥ, a clan of Manasseh, conquered Ḳĕnāth and its dependencies, and called its name Nobaḥ. Eusebius (*OS.* 269^{15}) says of Ḳĕnāth that it is *εἰς ἔτι Καναθα λεγομένη, . . . κεῖται δὲ καὶ ἔτι καὶ νῦν ἐν Τραχῶνι πλησίον Βοστρων.* He refers to the modern el-Ḳanawât in the Ḥaurân; but this seems much too remote to be the site intended in our passage: cf. *note* following.

Jogbehah. The name is preserved in the modern Aǵbêhât, twenty miles east-south-east from the ford ed-Dâmiyyeh at which Gideʿon seems to have crossed the Jordan.

careless. Heb. *béṭaḥ*, lit. 'confidence,' and so 'confident' of safety, the substantive being used, as often, in place of an adjective. Cf. *note* on *Yahweh shālôm*, *ch.* 6^{24}.

12. *he devoted to destruction.* Reading הֶחֱרִים, as conjectured by Scharfenberg (*apud* Mo.), Ewald, etc., for 𝔥 הֶחֱרִיד, which can only mean (as rendered by R.V. *marg.*), 'he terrified,' and in illustration of which 2 Sam. 17^{2}, Ezek. 30^{9}, are cited by Stu., and Zech. 2^{4} by Mo. This, however, is a very weak conclusion to the campaign. The mere throwing into a panic of Israel's mortal foes (for the *second* time in the course of the rout: cf. $7^{21.22}$) cannot have been intended by the narrator: contrast the late narrative of Num. 31^{7} P, where every male of Midian is put to the sword. The corruption of 𝔥 is an ancient one, being found in the Versions: 𝔊^{B} *ἐξέστησεν*, 𝔙 'turbato omni exercitu eorum,' 𝔖^{P} ܙܘܥ, 𝔗 אזיע. 𝔊^{A} *ἐξέτριψεν*, 𝔊^{L} *ἐξέστρεψεν*, and similarly 𝔖^{h} ܗܦܟ, seem to be corrections of the reading of 𝔊^{B} in order to produce a sense more consonant with the context. Jos., however (*Ant.* v. vi. 5), must have read or understood the passage in accordance with our emendation; for his paraphrase is *ἅπαντας διέφθειρε τοὺς πολεμίους.*

The correctness of הֶחֱרִים (rather than הִכְחִיד, Ex. 23^{23}, Ps. 83^{5},

returned from the battle, [] 14. and captured a lad of the men of Ṡuccoth, and questioned him; and he wrote down for him the officers of Ṡuccoth and the elders thereof,' even seventy-seven men. 15. And he came unto the men of Ṡuccoth, and said, 'Behold Zebaḥ and Ṣalmunnaʿ, concerning whom ye did taunt me, saying, "Are the hands of Zebaḥ and Ṣalmunnaʿ now in thy hand, that we should give bread to thy men that are exhausted?" 16. And he took the elders of the city, and thorns of the desert

as suggested by Mo., 'if an emendation is necessary') is attested by the doublet which is noted in *v.*^{13}.

13. *returned from the battle.* 𝔐 adds מִלְמַעֲלֵה הֶחָרֶס, R.V. 'from the ascent of Heres.' These words have formed a puzzle to interpreters in all ages. The Versions treat the allusion either as topographical (𝔊, 𝔖^{P}), or as a note of time, understanding חרס as the rare word for 'sun' (𝔙, 'ante solis ortu'; 𝔗, עד לא מעל שמשא, 'before the sun had set'). Modern commentators suppose that the passage is intended to indicate that Gideʿon returned from battle by a different route; and thus (it is assumed) took the town of Ṡuccoth by surprise.

It is astonishing that no one should have perceived that the words are simply a variant of *v.* $^{12b\beta}$, which has come into the text from the margin. This may at once be seen if we write them below the original form of *v.* $^{12b\beta}$:

וכלהמחנההחרם
מל מעלההחרם

It will be noticed that the last four letters of the doublet, החרם, tend to confirm the emendation הֶחֱרִים which is adopted in *v.* $^{12b\beta}$.

14. *he wrote down for him, etc.* A boy or youth captured by chance, and therefore (we may infer) without any exceptional qualifications as a scholar, writes down the names of the elders of Succoth; probably scratching them with a sharp-pointed implement such as a pin or knife, in the alphabetic (so-called Phoenician) script, upon a fragment of shale or similar material. This may seem to us to be surprising, but need not be regarded as incredible. Cf. further *Additional note*, p. 253. The rendering of R.V. *text*, 'he described for him,' which seems to be intended to obviate the conclusion that the names were *written*, is absolutely unwarranted.

the officers of Ṡuccoth, and the elders thereof. The distinction between the officers, *sārîm* (mentioned alone in *v.* ^{6}), and the elders *zᵉḳēnîm* (mentioned alone in *v.* ^{16}) is somewhat obscure. The *zᵉḳēnîm* were the heads of families in whose authority the government of the city was vested. In distinction from these, the *sārîm* were probably concerned, not with civil government, but with military organization.

and thistles; and ⌜threshed⌝ therewith the men of Succoth. 17. And the tower of Penuel he brake down, and slew the men

16. *and threshed therewith.* Reading וַיָּדָשׁ בָּהֶם, in place of 𝔐 וַיֹּדַע בָּהֶם 'and taught therewith,' a somewhat strange expression in Heb.* The emendation is supported by the parallelism of *v.* 7 וְדַשְׁתִּי 'I will thresh'; and by 𝔊B *καὶ ἠλόησεν* (*v.* 7 *ἀλοήσω*), 𝔊A *καὶ κατέξανεν*, 'and he carded' (*v.* 7 *καταξανῶ*). 𝔙 'et contrivit cum eis, atque comminuit' (*v.* 7 'conteram') may also have read וַיָּדָשׁ; but the double rendering of the verb suggests the possibility of a paraphrastic explanation of the curious וידע of 𝔐. In the same way, 𝔖P ܘܐܦܠܓ ܒܗܘܢ 'and he tortured therewith' (but *v.* 7 ܐܕܘܫ 'I will thresh'); 𝔗 ותבר עליהון 'and upon them he broke' (*var. lect.* וגרר עליהון 'and upon them he dragged') the men, etc. (but *v.* 7 ואדוש 'I will thresh'), may perhaps be paraphrases of 𝔐.

We cannot, however, be sure that by this simple emendation we have arrived at the original form of the verse. 𝔊 offers evidence of another original considerably different from 𝔐. Thus the verse runs in 𝔊L, *καὶ ἔλαβε [τοὺς ἄρχοντας καὶ] τοὺς πρεσβυτέρους τῆς πόλεως καὶ κατεδίωξεν αὐτοὺς ἐν ταῖς ἀκάνθαις τῆς ἐρήμου καὶ ταῖς βαρκηνειμ,* [*καὶ κατεδίωξαν ἐν αὐτοῖς ἄνδρας Σοκχωθ*]. So 𝔊A, with *κατέξανεν* in place of *κατεδίωξεν*. 𝔖h, 𝔏L are similar. Here we have bracketed *τοὺς ἄρχοντας καὶ* as a harmonistic addition (cf. *v* 14), and the last six words as a doublet embodying the 𝔐 tradition. The remainder seems to represent a Heb. original

וַיִּקַּח אֶת־זִקְנֵי הָעִיר וַיְדֻשֵׁם אֶת־קוֹצֵי הַמִּדְבָּר וְאֶת־הַבַּרְקָנִים

'And he took the elders of the city, and threshed them together with thorns of the desert and thistles.' This has strong claims to consideration as the original text. 𝔐, 'And he took the elders of the city, and thorns,' etc., is certainly suspicious; and it is possible that the verb וידשם may have fallen out before את קוצי וג׳, and that *v.* 16b may have been added subsequently as an explanatory gloss.

17. *the tower of Penuel.* It may be inferred that the city was unwalled, and the tower was intended as a refuge in case of danger. Cf. *ch.* 9 46ff. 51ff.

* Perhaps the nearest parallel to the usage of the verb וַיֹּדַע in 𝔐 is 1 Sam. 14 12, where the Philistines, on espying Jonathan and his armour-bearer, say, 'Come up unto us, that we may teach you a thing' (ונודיעה אתכם דבר); if it is legitimate to explain this somewhat obscure expression as used with a touch of irony, 'give you a lesson,' or 'give you something to think about.' Here, however, we have the addition of the object דבר; whereas a similar object is lacking in our passage.

of the city. 18. Then he said unto Zebaḥ and unto Ṣalmunnaʿ, 'Where are the men whom ye slew at Tabor?' And they said, 'As thou art so were they: ⌜e⌝ach resembled the children of a king.' 19. And he said, 'They were my brethren, my mother's sons: as Yahweh liveth, if ye had kept them alive, I would not have slain you.' 20. And he said to Jether his first-born, 'Arise, slay them!' But the lad drew not his sword, for he was afraid, because he was still a lad. 21. And Zebaḥ and Ṣalmunnaʿ said, 'Arise *thou* and fall upon us, for a man hath a man's strength.'

18. '*Where are the men, etc.*' Gideʿon knows that the Midianite kings are responsible for his brothers' death; and he thus challenges them to produce them alive in order to save their own lives (cf. *v.* [19]: so Bu.). The Midianites are aware that they are doomed, and, with the true savage instinct, glory in acknowledging the murders. Question and answer thus do not formally correspond; but 𝔙, 𝔖[P], R.V. 'What manner of men, etc.,' is both impossible as a rendering of 𝔐 אֵיפֹה הָאֲנָשִׁים; and also very much weaker than the legitimate rendering. This latter consideration also tells against the emendation adopted by Mo. (*SBOT.*), La. מִי אֵפוֹא הָאֲנָשִׁים 'Who, then, were the men, etc.'?

in Tabor. Mount Tabor, north of the plain of Esdraelon, is some thirty miles or more to the north of Shechem; near which, as we have seen (cf. *note* on "ʿOphrah,' *ch.* 6 [8]), the clan of Abiʿezer must have been situated. Bu. suggests an original תֵּבֵץ Tebeṣ: cf. *ch.* 9 [50].

each. Reading לְאֶחָד for 𝔐 אֶחָד. Cf. Ex. 22 [22], Num. 15 [12].

20. *he said to Jether, etc.* Robertson Smith (*Religion of the Semites*,[2] p. 417, *n* [3]) cites Nilus as stating that the Saracens charged lads with the execution of their captives.

but the lad drew not his sword, etc. It does not necessarily follow that Jether had taken part in the battle; for it is very probable that the captives were taken back in triumph to ʿOphrah before their execution. The arming of the lad with a sword may have been simply in view of the task assigned to him, which he had not the heart to perform when called upon to act.

21. *Arise* **thou**. The pronoun is emphatic; and the request of the Midianites, like their answer in *v* [18], is a tribute to Gideʿon's prowess and noble bearing.

a man has a man's strength. The rendering of Mo.; lit. 'as the man, (so) his strength.' כֵּן 'so,' or כְּ, is exceptionally omitted. There is no doubt that Gideʿon will slay them at a blow; whereas a mere lad might make a bungling attempt. 𝔊[B] reads ὅτι ὡς ἀνδρὸς ἡ

So Gideʿon arose and slew Zebaḥ and Ṣalmunnaʿ. And he took the crescents which were upon the necks of their camels.

22. E^2 And the men of Israel said unto Gideʿon, 'Rule over us, both thou, and thy son, and thy son's son; for thou hast saved us out of the hand of Midian.' 23. And Gideʿon said unto them, '*I* will not rule over you, neither shall my son rule over you; Yahweh shall rule over you.' 24. E And Gideʿon said unto them, 'Let me make a request of you: give me every man the ear-rings of his spoil.' For they had golden ear-rings, because

δύναμίς σου, *i.e.* כִּי כָאִישׁ גְּבוּרָתֶךָ, which may possibly be original. Bu. emends כִּי אִישׁ גִּבּוֹר אַתָּה 'for thou art a mighty man.' This, though involving no great change of 𝔐, hardly seems necessary.

crescents. Heb. *sah*^{a}*rônîm* occurs once besides (Isa. 3^{18}) in a list of feminine ornaments. On the form, cf. G-K. § 86*g*. In Ar. *šahr* denotes the *new moon*; and Aram. *ṡih*^{a}*rā*, Syr. *ṡahrå* mean *moon*. The crescents were doubtless threaded on necklaces, and worn as amulets. Similar strings of amulets are placed upon Bedawi camels and horses at the present day.

22. *the men of Israel.* The reference is to the tribes of Israel as a whole—or at least the central and northern west-Jordanic tribes, most of whom, according to the later narrative (E^2), had borne a share in the campaign, and were benefited by its outcome. This, however, as we have seen, is not the conception of the old narrative J, which pictures Gideʿon's *coup de main* as carried out with the assistance of his own clan merely, and invests its outcome with a local, rather than a general, importance. It is difficult to picture the haughty Ephraimites of J, *ch.* 8^{1-3}, who turn upon the victor in the hour of his triumph, and whose aggressive indignation has to be calmed by a diplomatic rejoinder, as taking part in a request to Gideʿon to become their king because he had 'saved' them out of the hand of Midian. The older narrative of E seems to have agreed with J in making Gideʿon's influence local rather than general. Cf. *introd.* to the story of Abimelech, p. 267.

23. '***I** will not rule over you, etc.*' The conception of Theocracy here put forward belongs to the later eighth century stage of prophetic thought. Cf. the discussion on pp. 183 f.

24. *ear-rings.* Heb. *nézem* may denote an ear-ring (Gen. 35^{4} E, Ex. $32^{2.3}$ E, Prov. 25^{12}), or a nose-ring (Gen. 24^{47} J, Isa. 3^{21}, Ezek. 16^{12}). Here, as worn by men, the former is the more probable meaning, since (as Mo. notices) nose-rings appear in the O.T. only as the ornaments of women. Pliny (*Hist. Nat.* xi. 50) refers to the wearing of ear-rings by men in the East. The custom does not exist

they were Ishma'elites. 25. And they said, 'We will surely give them.' And they spread out a mantle, and cast therein every man the ear-rings of his spoil. 26. And the weight of the golden ear-rings which he requested was one thousand and seven hundred sheḳels of gold; beside the crescents, and the pendants, and the purple garments which were upon the kings of Midian, and beside the necklaces which were upon the necks of their camels. 27. And Gide'on used it for an Ephod, and

generally among the Bedawin at the present day; though Mackie states that, 'in the case of an only son, the ear-ring is sometimes worn as an amulet in the form of a large silver ring suspended round the outer ear, with discs or balls attached to the lower half of the ring, hanging visible below the lobe of the ear': *DB.* i. p. 633*b*.

they were Ishma'elites. Upon the interchange between the terms 'Midianite' and 'Ishma'elite,' cf. *note* on 'Midian,' *ch.* 6 [1].

25. *they spread out.* 𝔊, 𝔏[L], 'he spread out.' So Kit., No., La., Gress.

26. *one thousand and seven hundred sheḳels of gold.* Taking the weight of the heavy sheḳel at 252.5 grs. troy (cf. G. F. Hill in *EB.* 4444), the total weight of the golden ear-rings would be nearly 75 lbs. If reckoned by the light sheḳel, it would be about half as much.

beside the crescents, etc. Mo. regards the whole of this half-verse as an editorial addition, on the ground that 'this catalogue of things which were not used in making the *ēphōd* is quite superfluous, and only interrupts the narrative.' A similar view is taken by Wellh. and Sta., who, taking $v^{21b\beta}$ as part of the original narrative, find in it the origin of the later addition $v.^{26b}$. On the other hand, Bu. takes the last quarter of the verse, 'beside the necklaces, etc.,' to be genuine, supposing it to be the origin of $v.^{21b\beta}$, which he regards as a later gloss.

It is unsafe to express a definite opinion on such a point. The narrative of E in $vv.^{22\text{-}27}$ has, as we have seen, been worked over by E^2; but it is difficult to divine any *purpose* in such an editorial addition as this (whether by E^2 or some later hand), beyond the desire to glorify Gide'on's exploit, which may equally have been present in the mind of the original narrator. The half-verse may seem to *us* to interrupt the proper sequence between $v.^{26a}$ and $v.^{27}$; but would this fact have counted for much in the mind of a narrator who was fascinated by the richness and variety of the spoil, as reported by tradition?

27. *an Ephod.* As regards the nature of the Ephod, evidence is extremely vague; and it is even doubtful whether it was everywhere and at all times the same thing. The Ephod of the Priestly Code (*i.e.* of post-exilic, though probably also of earlier, times) is described (Ex. 28 P) as a decorated vestment, apparently of the nature of an

apron,* fastened partly by a band at the top round the body (חֵשֶׁב אֲפֻדָּתוֹ אֲשֶׁר עָלָיו 'the band of its attachment which is above it,' ‡ *v.*[8]), and partly by two shoulder-straps (כְּתֵפוֹת, *v.*[7]). These latter were probably intended to keep the band of the Ephod in a position round the wearer's middle well above the loins, and thus to obviate the possibility of its becoming contaminated with sweat.§ The shoulder-straps appear to have been joined to the apron at its two upper corners;|| and their upper ends may have been fastened to the shoulders of the *mᵉʿîl* (see below) by the two onyx-stones in filigree settings (*vv.*[9-12]), which very likely served the purpose of brooches. It is possible, however, that the stones were merely ornamental and symbolical; and, if so, the shoulder-pieces may have

* The older view regarded the Ephod of P as a kind of waistcoat; but this seems to be excluded by the position of the band of its attachment עָלָיו '*above* it' (*v.*[8]), rather than '*upon* it'; and likewise by the position of the pouch *above* (עַל) the band (*v.*[28])—scarcely *upon* it. The position of the rings which fastened the pouch to the Ephod—the two upper ones attached to the shoulder-straps, and the two lower ones above the band of the Ephod—favours the same conclusion.

The view that the Ephod was of the nature of an *apron* rather than a *kilt*, *i.e.* that it covered the front of the trunk below the waist and did not extend round the body and join at the back, depends upon the emendation noticed in *footnote* ||.

‡ This rendering assumes the view that *ḥēšebh* is a metathesis of *ḥēbheš* from *ḥābhaš* 'to bind on'; so, 'band.' Cf. Driver's *note ad loc.* in *Camb. Bib.* The sense 'attachment' given to *'ăphuddā* makes the term a secondary derivative from the denominative verb *'āphadh* 'to attach the Ephod,' which is used in Ex. 29[5], Lev. 8[7] (|| *ḥāghar* 'gird on').

§ The very curiously phrased injunction in Ezek. 44[18b] לֹא יַחְגְּרוּ בַּיָּזַע, *i.e.*, apparently, 'they shall not gird themselves with (*or* in) sweat,' which is understood by R.V. to mean 'with *that which causeth* sweat' (*i.e.* with woollen materials in distinction from linen), was understood by the Jewish interpreters to mean that they were prohibited from girding themselves as high as the arm-pits or as low as the loins—either position being conducive to sweating—but were to adopt an intermediate position. So Rashi and Kimchi. This interpretation is as old as 𝔗J, which paraphrases the passage ולא יזרזון על חרציהון אלהין על לבביהון יסרון 'and they shall not gird themselves about their loins, but shall bind themselves about their hearts.' It may well be doubted whether the passage (the genuineness of which is open to suspicion) is capable of such an explanation; yet it is quite likely that the interpretation depends upon a true tradition as to the ritual position of girding, and the reason by which it was dictated.

|| In Ex. 28[7] we should read plural verbs יְחֻבָּרוּ, יִהְיוּ, referring to the two shoulder-straps, in place of the singulars יְחֻבָּר, יִהְיֶה of 𝔐. Cf. 𝔊 δύο ἐπωμίδες συνέχουσαι ἔσονται αὐτῷ ἑτέρα τὴν ἑτέραν, ἐπὶ τοῖς δυσὶ μέρεσιν ἐξηρτισμέναι. On the use of the masc. form of the 3rd plur. Imperfect, in place of the fem., with reference to a fem. subject preceding, cf. G-K. § 145 *u*.

been joined together at the back of the neck so as to form a yoke ; or else they may have joined the band of the Ephod at the back, and held it up like braces.

The Ephod is mentioned in connexion with the pouch (חֹשֶׁן, A.V., R.V. 'breast-plate,' *v.* 15), which contained the objects known as Urim and Tummim. This latter was fastened by rings at its four corners, the two upper rings to the shoulder-straps (*vv.* 23-25), and the two lower to the band of the Ephod (*vv.* 26-28). The dimensions of the pouch were a span, *i.e.* about nine inches, square (*v.* 16) ; and when the Ephod was in place, the Urim and Tummim within the pouch lay upon the heart of the high priest (*v.* 30)—a fact which makes it clear that the band of the Ephod must have been well above the loins, as has already been indicated.

The material of Ephod, band, and pouch alike, and doubtless also of the shoulder-straps, was of 'blue, and purple, and scarlet, and fine twined linen,' interwoven with gold thread or wire (פְּתִילִים), which was cut from a plate of beaten gold (*ch.* 39 3). The pouch was further adorned by twelve precious stones, set in gold (*vv.* 17-21). The Ephod was girded on over the *meʿîl*, a long garment with sleeves, of blue material (*vv.* 31 ff.).

Probably similar to this Ephod in form, though doubtless of simpler workmanship, and (so far as we know) unconnected with any special means of obtaining an oracle,* was the *'ēphôdh badh* 'Ephod of linen,' ‡ with which the child Samuel was 'girt' (חָגוּר) when he ministered as a temple-servant (1 Sam. 2 18) ; and with which King David was similarly 'girt,' when he danced ceremonially before the Ark, whilst it was being brought up from the house of ʿObed-edom to the sanctuary at Jerusalem (2 Sam. 6 14). On this occasion David excited the outspoken contempt of his wife Michal, for exposing his

* There must, no doubt, have been some ultimate connexion between the *'ēphôdh badh* and the oracular Ephod noticed above in the next paragraph ; and it is possible that the former may have been a kind of 'dummy' Ephod, typical of the relationship in which those who exercised priestly service stood towards the Deity, though actually unequipped with the means of casting lots (Urim and Tummim). Foote recalls the fact that the oracular lots in the temple of Fortuna at Praeneste were mingled and drawn by a child ('quid igitur in his [sortibus] potest esse certi, quae Fortunae monitu pueri manu miscentur atque ducuntur' ; Cicero, *De Divinatione*, ii. 41, 86 : a similar practice is observed in the modern State-lotteries of Italy and France), and thinks that the child Samuel may have been entrusted with a similar office. There is, however, absolutely no evidence of any such practice among the Israelites.

‡ The derivation of *badh* is unknown ; but the view that it denotes the *material* of which the Ephod was made, and that this was some form of *linen*, is probably correct. Foote's theory that *badh* means 'member,' and so *membrum virile*, which the Ephod (the primitive loin-cloth) was designed to cover, is sufficiently refuted by Lev. 16 4, where the word is applied to the various parts of the priestly attire, turban included, and evidently describes their *material*.

person 'like one of the lewd fellows'; and the inference is that he wore nothing but the Ephod, and that this was of scanty dimensions *—perhaps not unlike the apron which the Egyptian priest Pe-nḥēsi is represented as wearing, when performing an act of ceremonial worship; cf. Perrot et Chipiez, *Histoire de l'Art dans l'Antiquité*, i. p. 253.‡ Sellin and Mo. (*EB.* 1306) suppose that the assumption of this scanty attire may have been a return to a primitive costume rendered sacred by its antiquity; much as Mohammedan pilgrims, so soon as they approach Mecca, are obliged to adopt the simple loin-cloth which was the primitive dress of the Arabs. §

More doubt has been expressed as to the precise nature of the Ephod which, in the days of 'Eli, Saul, and David, was regularly employed in the cultus of Yahweh. The priest is never said to *wear* or to *be girt* with this, but always to *bear* it (נָשָׂא; 1 Sam. 2^{28}, 14^{3}, 22^{18}||). Abiathar, when he escapes from the slaughter of the priests at Nob, comes down to David with an Ephod 'in his hand' (1 Sam. 23^{6}). ¶ Here 'in his hand' refers to the carrying of the Ephod when not in use; but the verb 'bear' is clearly used ceremonially, and is most naturally to be explained from the use of the same verb in Ex. 28^{12}, where it is said that Aaron 'shall bear' (וְנָשָׂא א׳) the names of the children of Israel before Yahweh engraved upon the stones of the two shoulder-straps of the Ephod; and similarly (*v.* 29) that he 'shall bear' their names upon the pouch. We learn from 1 Sam. 23^{6} that the Ephod was used in consulting the oracle, or 'enquiring of Yahweh'; and from 1 Sam. 14 it seems, as in later times, to have been employed in connexion with Urim and Tummim (in *v.* 18 $\mathfrak{G}^{BL}$ preserves the true reading 'Ephod' in place of

* The Chronicler (who was evidently somewhat scandalized by the narrative as it stands in 2 Sam.) clothes David in a *m^e'il bûṣ* 'robe of byssus,' in addition to the Ephod of linen, and omits all allusion to the episode in which Michal plays a part (1 Chr. 15^{27}).

‡ It is worthy of note that Pe-nḥēsi's apron is loosely girt well above the loins, being apparently supported in that position by a band from the shoulders.

§ In the description given by the Roman lawyer Gaius (iii. 192-193) of the house-search for stolen articles—'furtum licio et lance conceptum'—the leather apron, 'licium' ('consuti genus quo necessariae partes tegerentur') is explained by Ihering as a relic of antiquity—the usual dress of the ancient Aryans—preserved in a ceremonial institution dating from hoary antiquity. Cf. *The Evolution of the Aryan*, pp. 2 ff.

|| This last passage, as it stands in $\mathfrak{M}$, speaks of 'bearing the Ephod of linen'; but it is not improbable that the word *badh*, which is omitted by $\mathfrak{G}^{B}$, is an erroneous insertion.

¶ The passage is in some slight disorder. As it stands in $\mathfrak{M}$, אֵפוֹד יָרַד בְּיָדוֹ seems to mean 'an Ephod came down in his hand.' $\mathfrak{G}^{B}$, however, after the words 'unto David,' presupposes a text וְהוּא עִם דָּוִד קְעִילָה יָרַד וְאֵפוֹד בְּיָדוֹ 'he went down with David to Ḳe'ilah, having an Ephod in his hand.' This is very possibly the original text: cf. Driver, *NHTS.*² *ad loc.*

𝔐 'Ark of God'). When asked to consult the oracle, the priest is told to *bring it near* (הַגִּישָׁה, 14[18], 23[9], 30[7]); and, when ordered to desist, the command is 'withdraw thine hand' (אֱסֹף יָדֶךָ, 14[19]), which seems to presuppose some form of manipulation in connexion with the sacred lot. The *locus classicus* for the use of this latter (Urim and Tummim) is 1 Sam. 14[41] 𝔊, which has already been noticed under *ch.* 1[1] *note* on 'enquired of Yahweh.' Thus, if we are to explain the Ephod of 1 Sam. by the Ephod of P, it may have been the receptacle in which the sacred lot was preserved—possibly a pouch and apron or girdle combined—the prototype of the later priestly vestment.

The character of Gide'on's Ephod has formed subject for much discussion. It is commonly supposed that the description of *v.* 27 can only be satisfied by the supposition that here the Ephod denotes some kind of *idol*, and not simply a vestment and pouch employed in consulting the oracle. In favour of this view the following points have been alleged.

If the words ויעש אותו ג' לאפוד mean that Gide'on *made* the 1700 shekels of gold *into* an Ephod, it seems to follow that the Ephod must have been something of the character of an idol, or possibly an non-eikonic symbol (ξόανον) of considerable size; since so great a weight of metal cannot have been employed in the manufacture of a mere belt and apron, with pouch attached, even if we suppose these to have been heavily overlaid with gold. The verb ויצג, again, rendered 'and he set it up,' suggests an idol rather than an instrument of divination which, when in use, was girt on to the body of the priest. Further, the strong terms of reprobation employed by the writer—'and all Israel went a whoring after it, etc.'—though appropriate in application to the worship of an idol, seem rather strange if they are to be understood of an object which is mentioned, without a word of blame, as commonly employed in ascertaining the oracle of Yahweh in the days of Samuel and David, and the continued use of which in post-exilic times is specifically provided for in the ritual enactments of the Priestly Code.

Added to the arguments based upon the reference to Gide'on's Ephod, there are other references which have been thought to point in the same direction. The story of Micah and his private sanctuary, Judg. 17.18, is clearly composite in origin; and the Ephod and Teraphim of the one narrative are parallel to the graven image and molten image of the other—or rather to the graven image only, the molten image being a later addition. In 1 Sam. 21[10] the sword of Goliath is preserved in the sanctuary of Nob 'wrapped in a cloth behind the Ephod'—a reference which may be taken to mean that the Ephod stood by itself, clear of the wall, as an image would do. Lastly, the obscure phrase of Isa. 30[22] (probably a late passage), אֲפֻדַּת מַסֵּכַת זְהָבֶךָ, R.V. 'the plating of thy molten images of gold, is parallel to צִפּוּי פְּסִילֵי כַסְפֶּךָ 'the overlaying of thy graven images of silver'; the term *'ăphuddā* (cognate to *'ēphôdh*) being interpreted by R.V. as 'plating' owing to its parallelism with *ṣippûy* 'overlaying' (for which cf. Ex. $38^{17.19}$, Num. $17^{3.4}$). If, then, *'ăphuddā* means the 'plating' of an idol, it is inferred that *'ēphôdh* denotes such a plated idol, *i.e.* a wooden idol overlaid with metal.

Taking these points in order—it should be observed that, while the phrase עשה ל may be used in the sense '*he made into*' (cf. especially Isa. 44^{17} וּשְׁאֵרִיתוֹ לְאֵל עָשָׂה 'and the remnant thereof he *made into* a god'; so *v.*^{19}; cf. also Deut. 9^{14}, Ezek. 4^{9}), it may equally well have the sense '*he used for.*' This is the sense of the phrase in 1 Sam. 8^{16}, 'Your servants, etc., shall he take and *use* them *for* his work'; Ex. 38^{24}, 'All the gold that was *used for* the work'; Ezek. 15^{5}, 'It (the wood of the vine) cannot be *used for* work.' Similarly, in Hos. 2^{8} (𝔐 ^{10}), זָהָב עָשׂוּ לַבָּעַל is more naturally to be rendered 'the gold which they *used for* the Ba'al' (*i.e.* in his service) than 'the gold which they *made into* the Ba'al'; הַבַּעַל by itself being nowhere else used of the *image* of the false god. Thus, the rendering of the phrase which is adopted in our translation is at any rate quite legitimate; the statement being understood to mean that Gide'on used the gold not merely in the manufacture of the Ephod, but also in the provision of such accessories as were necessary for its proper maintenance as a cultus-object, *i.e.* a sanctuary and priestly caretaker, etc.

The verb ויצג, whether rendered 'he set it up,' or, as above, 'he established it' (cf. Am. 5^{15} הַצִּיגוּ בַשַּׁעַר מִשְׁפָּט 'establish judgment in the gate'), need not imply that the Ephod was an image; since, upon the alternative assumption that it was, here as elsewhere, a vestment employed in ascertaining the will of the oracle, it is not clear what other verb could have been more suitably employed to describe the fact that it was kept and used in divination at 'Ophrah. What the writer wishes to express is that it was there that the Ephod-cult was 'established'; and any alternative expression, such as 'he *placed*' or '*kept* it at 'Ophrah,' would scarcely have been possible.

The strong reprobation of the Ephod-cult is explained by the fact that the passage comes from E^2; whereas the passages in 1 Sam. which seem to regard the Ephod as the natural and appropriate means of ascertaining the will of Yahweh, belong to the much older narrative of J. The difference in point of view is no greater here than in the two accounts of the institution of the kingship; where, while J regards the granting of a king as a mark of Yahweh's favour to Israel (1 Sam. $9^{15.16}$), E^2, on the other hand, stigmatizes Israel's demand for a king as a definite act of rejection of Yahweh (1 Sam. 8 7). It is at least probable, if not certain, that the prophetic school represented by E² grouped the Ephod with other conventional forms of divination, and regarded it with disfavour; and Hosea', whose influence is to be traced in E² (cf. *Introd.* p. xlv), makes disparaging reference to Ephod together with Teraphim (Hos. 3 4). It is generally acknowledged that in 1 Sam. 14 18 the original form of the passage is preserved in 𝔊:—*καὶ εἶπεν Σαουλ τῷ Αχειᾳ Προσάγαγε τὸ εφουδ· ὅτι αὐτὸς ἦρεν τὸ εφουδ ἐν τῇ ἡμέρᾳ ἐκείνῃ ἐνώπιον Ισραηλ.* In 𝔐, however, אֲרוֹן הָאֱלֹהִים, 'the Ark of God' has taken the place of 'the Ephod'—an alteration which must have been purposely made, and that most probably in order to avoid reference to the consultation of the will of Yahweh by a form of divination which the corrector of the text regarded with some disfavour. The fact that, in post-exilic times, the Priestly Code lays down detailed regulations for the manufacture and use of the Ephod is not an argument to prove that in late pre-exilic times the school of E² could not have disapproved of its use. Rather, we may argue that, if P had supposed that the term Ephod had at any time been used of a definitely idolatrous symbol, such a term would not have been perpetuated by the Code in reference to a legitimate instrument of divination. The evidence of the Priestly Code, therefore, tells in favour of the inference that the codifiers of this body of legislation were unaware that the term 'Ephod' had been applied in early times to an idol.

The fact that, in Judg. 17.18, one narrative equips Micah's sanctuary with Ephod and Teraphim, while the parallel narrative speaks of a graven image merely, is no argument to prove that the graven image was the same as the Ephod. Nor would the case really be strengthened if the second narrative had originally mentioned (as it does now) both graven image and molten image; since there is no reason whatever for supposing that the two traditions were so absolutely at one that graven image and molten image must denote *the same things* as Ephod and Teraphim. As Mo. has shown, however, the molten image is a late addition to the narrative.

In 1 Sam. 21 10 the statement that the sword of Goliath at the sanctuary of Nob was 'wrapped in a cloth behind the Ephod' may very well mean that both sword and Ephod were hanging on a large peg fixed in the wall (Lotz, Foote, Sellin), the Ephod, as being constantly in use, hanging outermost.

Lastly, the interpretation of אֲפֻדַּת מַסֵּכַת זְהָבֶךָ in Isa. 30 22 is very obscure: but on any interpretation the phrase can scarcely carry much weight in proof that the term Ephod was ever applied to an idol. Foote argues that מַסֵּכָה never means 'molten image' where, as here, it is a genitive. It means a 'casting'; and as a genitive it means that the *nomen regens* is not carved, nor beaten, but cast.

established it in his city, even in ʿOphrah ; E^2 and all Israel went a whoring after it there, and it became a snare to Gideʿon and to his house. 28. R^{E2} So Midian was subdued before the sons of Israel, and they lifted up their head no more. And the land had rest forty years in the days of Gideʿon.

This conclusion is supported by such phrases as עֵגֶל מַסֵּכָה, lit. 'bull of casting,' *i.e.* 'cast *or* molten bull'; אֱלֹהֵי מַסֵּכָה 'gods of casting,' *i.e.* 'molten gods.' Thus, אֲפֻדַּת מַסֵּכַת זְהָבֶךָ might mean 'thy cast band of gold,' lit. 'the band (attachment) of the casting of thy gold.' It may be considered doubtful whether the parallelism of פְּסִילֵי כַסְפֶּךָ 'thy graven images of silver,' does not tell against Foote's conclusion, and compel us to explain מַסֵּכַת זְהָבֶךָ as 'thy molten image of gold.' But even so, it is likely that אֲפֻדָּה has the same meaning here as in Ex. 28^8, viz. 'attachment' or 'band,' and thus refers to the priestly band or vestment which was in this case worn by the idol, and not to an actual part of the idol, such as a metal sheathing—a sense which is purely hypothetical.

We conclude then that, while the reference to Gideʿon's Ephod is involved in considerable difficulty, there is nothing in the statement, nor in other statements which we have noticed, to compel us to believe that it was an idol, or anything else but the ordinary priestly vestment which was employed in obtaining an oracle.

The explanation of the Ephod here adopted follows, in the main, the lines laid down by Lotz, *Realencyklopädie für protestantische Theologie und Kirche*, 1898, v. pp. 402-406; Foote, *JBL.*, 1902, pp. 1-47; Sellin, *Das israelitische Ephod* (*Orient. Studien T. Nöldeke gewidmet*, 1906, pp. 699-717): cf. also the brief summary given by Benzinger, *Hebräische Archäologie*,[2] pp. 347 f.

went a whoring. Cf. *ch.* 2^{17} *note.*

a snare. Heb. *môḳēš.* Cf. *ch.* 2^3 *note.*

28. On the characteristic phraseology of R^{E2}, cf. *Introd.* p. xlviii.

YAHWEH OR YAHU ORIGINALLY AN AMORITE DEITY

(Cf. *note* on 'the Ashera,' *ch.* 6^{25}.)

Sayce was the first to call attention (*ET.* ix. p. 522) to the existence of the name *Ya-u-um-ilu* on a Babylonian text of the First Dynasty period (published in *CT.* iv. 27). This can scarcely mean anything else than 'Ya-u is god'; and is thus identical in form and meaning with the Hebrew יוֹאֵל Jo'el. Sayce's conclusion was accepted by Hommel, who further cited the name *Ḫa-li-pi-um*, *i.e.*, probably, *Ḫa-li-ya-um*,* 'Ya-u is maternal uncle' (Ar. *ḫâl*), as occurring in a document of the same period (*ET.* x. p. 42: the list in which *Ḫa-li-ya-um* occurs is published in *CT.* iv. 27). *Ya-u-um-ilu* was subsequently cited by Delitzsch, together with the two forms *Ya-a'-we-ilu*, *Ya-we-ilu* (which he explained as meaning 'Yahweh is God') in proof of the recognition and worship of the God Yahweh in Babylonia in early times (*Babel und Bibel*, pp. 46 f.). Upon this evidence Delitzsch based much too far-reaching assumptions as to the derivation of Hebrew monotheism from Babylonian sources; and his conclusions excited a keen and voluminous controversy.‡ In particular, his reading of the names *Ya-'a-we-ilu*, *Ya-we-ilu* was hotly disputed, upon the ground that the syllable which he read as WE might be interpreted as PI, and that the first element of the names *Ya-'a-pi* or *Ya-pi* was probably a verbal form. Early Babylonian usage favours the reading WE or WA for the disputed syllable rather than PI; yet, even so, it is by no means certain that the element *Ya-'a-we*, *Ya-we* in the names in question is a divine name and not a verbal form. Thus Ranke, who transcribes *Ya-'aḫ-wi-ilu*, takes the meaning to be '(The) god lives' (assuming an Amorite verb חוה = Heb. חיה 'to live'); while Hilprecht, reading *Ya-'-wi-ilu*, understands as 'God has spoken' (Bab. *awû* or *amû* 'to speak'; but in this case the normal Babylonian form would be *êwi*, *êmi*, not *ya'wi*).§ More recently, the publication by Thureau-Dangin of the First Dynasty tablets preserved in the Louvre|| reveals the existence of the name *Ya-wi* (*we*, *wa*, *pi?*)-(*ilu*)-*Dagan*¶; and association with the name of the deity Dagan greatly strengthens the case for regarding the disputed form as a verb—the only alternative being to suppose that the name identifies a deity *Ya-wi* with the deity *Dagan*: cf. the compounds Hadad-Rimmon, Zech. 12^{11}, and the Moabite 'Ashtar-Chemosh (*Moabite Stone*, l. 17). It is thus evident that the names *Ya-'a-we-ilu*, *Ya-we-ilu* cannot be cited with any probability as instances of compounds containing the divine name Yahweh.

Clay's publication of *Personal Names of the Cassite Period* (1912), *i.e.* the period subsequent to the First Dynasty period, ranging from *cir.* B.C. 1760 to 1185, throws further light upon the use of the divine

* The cuneiform sign-group, which has the syllabic value PI in Assyrian documents of a later period, is commonly used with the value WE, WA, and YA in Babylonian documents of the First Dynasty period, and later still into the period of the T.A. Letters (*cir.* B.C. 1400). For *Ḫa-li-ya-um* with the common sign for YA, cf. p. 245 (from Thureau-Dangin, *op. cit. infra*, p. 22).

‡ For the literature of this controversy, cf. Rogers, *Relig. Bab. and Assyr.* p. 92.

§ Cf. Ranke, *Early Bab. Personal Names of the Hammurabi Dynasty*, 1905.

|| *Lettres et contrats de l'époque de la Première Dynastie Babylonienne*, 1910.

¶ *Op. cit.* p. 23. The occurrence of this name and its bearing on the controversy were first brought to the notice of the present writer by Dr. R. W. Rogers.

name *Ya-u* in Babylonia. He chronicles the forms *Ya-a-u*, *Ya-u-ba-ni*, *Ya-u-gu*, and the apparently feminine forms *Ya-(a-)u-tum*, *Ya-a-i-tum*. *Ya-u-ba-ni* can only mean 'Ya-u is creator,' the form being precisely analogous to *Ilu-ba-ni*, 'The god is creator,' *Ellil-ba-ni*, 'Ellil is creator,' etc. The form *Ya-u-ba-ni* recalls the familiar name of the king of Ḥamath who was contemporary with Sargon (B.C. 721-705), (*ilu*) *Ya-u-bi-ʾ-di* (Winckler, *Sargon*, pp. 102, 178), *Ya-u-bi-ʾ-di* (*id.* p. 170), which alternates with *I-lu-bi-ʾ-di* (*id.* p. 6), just as in Hebrew we find both יְהוֹנָתָן and אֶלְנָתָן. Here *Ya-u* is marked by the determinative prefix *ilu*, 'god,' which proves beyond a doubt that it is a divine name. The element *Ya-u*, as the first element of a proper name, appears in *Ya-u-ḫa-zi*, the Assyr. equivalent of the Heb. Jehoʼaḥaz, *i.e.* the Judaean king ʼAḥaz, in an inscription of Tiglath-pileser IV. (cf. Rost, *Tiglath-pileser*, p. 72). Cf. The form *Ya-u-a* which occurs as the representation of the name of the Israelite king Jehu, in the inscriptions of Shalmaneser III. (cf. *KB.* i. pp. 140, n^1, 150). The shortening of *Ya-u* into *Ya* as the first element of a proper name is seen in *Ya-ma-e-ra-aḫ*, *i.e.* 'Ya indeed is the moon,' *CT.* viii. 17.

In face of this evidence, it is impossible to doubt that *Ya-u* or *Ya-um* (with mîmation) is a divine name, and corresponds to the Heb. —יְהוֹ or —יוֹ, the shorter form of the divine name Yahweh, which regularly occurs as the first element in Israelite proper names. On the form *Ya-u-tum*, cf. p. 248.

We find, moreover, a large class of proper names occurring in Babylonian documents of the First Dynasty and Kaššite periods in which the *second element* of the name is *Ya*, *Ya-u-a* (once), *Ya-tum*, *Ya-u-tum*, *Ya-u-ti*; the names themselves being precisely parallel in form to other names in which the second element is indisputably the name or title of a deity.

Thus, where the relation is that of a genitive following a Construct State, we may notice *A-pil-ya*, *A-pil-ya-tum*, apparently 'son of Ya *or* Yatum,' like *A-pil-i-li-šu*, 'son of his god.'

Ardi-ya, *Ardi-ya-um*, apparently 'servant of Ya *or* Ya-um,' like *Ardi-ilâni*, 'servant of the gods'; *Ardi-(ilu)-Marduk*, 'servant of (god) Marduk'; *Ardi-Šamaš*, 'servant of Šamaš,' etc.

Nûr-ya-u-ti, apparently 'light of Ya-u-tu,' like *Nûr-Ellil*, 'light of Ellil'; *Nûr-Ištar*, *Nûr-Marduk*, etc.

Cases in which the relation to a preceding substantive is predicative, the copula being understood, are :—

A-bi-ya, *A-bi-ya-tum*, *A-bi-ya-u-ti*, apparently 'Ya *or* Ya-tum *or* Ya-u-tu is father,' like *A-bi-ilu*, '(the) god is father'; *A-bi-i-li*, 'my god is father'; *A-bi-i-li-šu*, 'his god is father'; *A-bi-e-ra-aḫ*, 'the moon is father,' etc.

Ḫa-li-ya-um, *Ḫa-li-ya-tum*, apparently 'Ya-um *or* Ya-tum is maternal uncle.'

Be-li-ya, *Be-li-ya-tum*, *Be-li-ya-u-tum*, apparently 'Ya *or* Ya-tum *or* Ya-u-tum is lord,' like *Be-li-a-bi*, 'my father is lord.'

Ṣili-ya, *Ṣili-ya-u-tum*, apparently 'Ya *or* Ya-u-tum is my protection' (lit. 'shadow'; cf. Heb. בְּצַלְאֵל, 'In the shadow of God'), like *Ṣili-Addu*, 'Addu is my protection'; *Ṣili-(ilu)-Amurru*, *Ṣili-(ilu)-Dagan*, *Ṣili-Marduk*, *Ṣili-Šamaš*, *Ṣili-Ištar*, etc.

Tukulti-ya-u-ti, apparently 'Ya-u-tu is my help,' like *Tukulti-Ellil*, 'Ellil is my help,' etc.

It is doubtful whether *A-ḫi-ya*, *A-ḫi-ya-u-a*, *Aḫ-i-ya-tum*, *A-ḫi-ya-u-ti*, like *A-ḫi-ilu* (or *-ili*), should fall into the first or second of these classes. *A-ḫi-ya* might mean 'Ya is brother,' or 'brother of Ya,' just as *A-ḫi-ilu* might mean '(the) god is brother,' or (taking the ideogram for 'god' as the genitive *ili*), 'brother of (the) god.' In favour of the latter supposition we may cite the fem. name *A-ḫa-ti-ya*, presumably 'sister of Ya'; scarcely 'Ya is sister.' Cf. masc. *E-ri-ši-ya*, 'bridegroom of Ya,' beside the fem. names *E-ri-iš-ti-(ilu)-A-a*, 'bride of (god) A-a'; *E-ri-iš-ti-Addu*, 'bride of Addu'; and Phoenician חמלך 'brother of Milk,' אחתמלך 'sister of Milk,' חתמלקרת 'sister of Melḳart.'

A third class, in which the first element of the name is a verbal form, is represented by *I-din-ya*, *I-din-ya-tum*, apparently 'Ya *or* Ya-tum has given,' like *I-din-ili-šu*, 'his god has given'; *I-din-Marduk*, 'Marduk has given'; *I-din-(ilu)-Amurru*, *I-din-Sin*, etc.

It must be admitted that the explanation of *-ya*, *-ya-tum*, etc., as divine names is not generally accepted, some scholars (*e.g.* Ranke and Clay) explaining them as hypocoristic terminations in substitution for some fuller and more definite form (*Ardi-ya* thus conceivably implying *Ardi-(ilu)-Marduk*, or *-(ilu)-Sin*, etc.). Against this view, and in favour of that which is here advocated, the following points may be made :—

(1) In cases in which *Ya-u*, *Ya-u-um* occur as the *first element* in a proper name (as in *Ya-u-ba-ni*, *(ilu) Ya-u-bi-'-di*, *Ya-u-um-ilu* above cited), the hypocoristic explanation breaks down; it being impossible to explain *Ya-u* as anything else than a divine name or title. If, then, as has been shown, names ending in *-ya*, etc., are identical in formation with names containing as their second element the name of a god such as Marduk, Sin, Šamaš, etc., it is reasonable to infer that *-ya* as the second element of these names denotes the same deity as *Ya-u* when occurring as the first element in other names. In fact, as we have seen, the full form *A-ḫi-ya-u-a* occurs side by side with *A-ḫi-ya*. That *Ya-u*, when occurring as the second element in a proper name, should normally be shortened to *-ya* is precisely analogous to the usage of Hebrew proper names containing the divine name —יָה (as well as —יָהוּ) as the second element, answering to —יְהוֹ, —יוֹ as the first element. And further, an

instance of such shortening when *Ya* is the *first* element is seen in *Ya-ma-e-ra-aḫ*, assuming this to mean 'Ya indeed is the moon.'

(2) The forms *A-bi-ya*, *A-ḫi-ya*, *Be-li-ya* are identical in all respects with the Hebrew אֲבִיָּה, אֲחִיָּה, בְּעַלְיָה. אֲבִיָּה, אֲחִיָּה are variations of the fuller forms אֲבִיָּהוּ, אֲחִיָּהוּ; and the fact that in these Hebrew names the element *Ya* or *Yahu* is a divine name corresponding to the fuller form *Yahweh* is generally admitted.* It is difficult, therefore, to believe that the identity in form of the Babylonian names is accidental, and does not involve identity of meaning.

(3) The name *A-ḫi-ya-mi* occurs in a Babylonian letter from Taʿanach of *cir.* B.C. 1450 (cf. Rogers, *CP.* p. 282; *TB.* i. p. 129), borne by the Amorite writer of the letter. Here the element *-mi* is probably not to be understood as equivalent to *-wi*, as has been supposed, *Ya-wi* thus answering to *Yahweh*; but more probably *-mi* is the Babylonian enclitic particle which is regularly employed in letters of this period from Canaʿan in place of the normal enclitic *-ma*. The purpose of the enclitic, thus used, is to predicate a fact with some emphasis. Thus *A-ḫi-ya-mi* would denote 'Ya indeed is brother,' or 'brother of *Ya* (emphatic)'; cf. *Ya-ma-e-ra-aḫ*, 'Ya indeed is the moon' above noticed. *Ilu-ma-ilu*, '(The) god indeed is god'; *I-li-ma-a-bu-um*, 'My god indeed is father'; *I-li-ma-a-ḫi*, 'My god indeed is my brother', and the S. Arabian אֲבִימָאֵל *'Abi-ma-'el* (Gen. 10[28], 1 Chr. 1[22]), 'God is father indeed,' side by side with the normal אֲבִיאֵל *'Abi-'el*, 'God is father.' But, if emphasis is thus thrown upon *Ya*, it seems clear that the sense intended is '*Ya and no one else*'; and it is out of the question that *Ya* thus emphasized should be simply a hypocoristic termination, and not a genuine divine name or title.

A further important fact (noticed by the present writer in *JTS.* ix. p. 341) is that a Babylonian syllabary (*CT.* xii. 4) which gives a large number of equivalents of the star-ideogram which is the ordinary symbol for *ilu*, 'god,' offers as the first of these equivalents the word *Ya-'-u*, a form which would appear in Hebrew as יָהוּ *Yāhû*, the light breathing in Bab. here answering to the Heb. ה. The second equivalent on the list is *Ya-a-ti*, which recalls *Ya-tum* in the names which we have been examining; but which Sayce is perhaps right in regarding as an etymology offered by the Babylonian scribe for the (to him) unintelligible *Ya-'-u*, viz. Bab. *yâti*, 'myself' (*ET.* xviii. p. 27; xix. p. 525).

The relationship of the apparently fem. forms *Ya-tum*, *Ya-u-tum* to *Ya-u* or *Ya-'-u* is obscure. The following attractive explanation

* Cf., however, Jastrow, *JBL.* xiii. (1899), pp. 110 ff., who takes *-ya*, *-yahu* as afformatives.

has been offered by Sayce :—'By the side of the masculine Yaû we have the feminine Yaûtum, corresponding with a Hebrew יהוה. And just as יהוה is used in Hebrew for the masculine, so we find Yaûtum used not only as a feminine but also as a masculine name. That is to say, the absorption of the feminine Yaûtum, יהוה, by the masculine יהו, יה, יו, which is fully carried out in Hebrew, is in process of being carried out in the Babylonian of the Cassite age. How the goddess, who in so many cases possessed after all only a grammatical existence, came to be identified with the god, I have explained in my Lectures on the Religion of the Babylonians ; a well-known example of the fact is the Ashtar-Chemosh of the Moabite Stone. While the Latin races, like the natives of Asia Minor, seemed to have craved for a female divinity, the Semites resembled the Teutonic populations in their tendency to believe only in a male deity' (*ET.* xviii. p. 27). The transformation of an originally female deity into a male deity in the case of the Sabaean ʿAthtar has already been noticed in *note* on 'the ʿAshtarts,' p. 59.*

Babylonian evidence for the worship of the deity *Ya-u*, *Ya-u-tum* (*Ya*, *Ya-tum*) appears, then, to be abundant during the First Dynasty period, and onward into the Kaššite period, though not earlier ‡ ; and this fact lends high probability to the view of Sayce and Hommel that this deity was first introduced into Babylonia by the 'Amorite' immigrants, to whom the foundation of the First Dynasty seems to have been due : cf. *Introd.* pp. lvii ff. §

* Identification of *Ya-u-tum*, *Ya-tum* at one time with a female deity (Ištar) and at another with a male deity (Sin) is perhaps to be seen in *Ištar-ya-ut-tum* (Clay, *op. cit.*), *Sin-ya-tum* (Ranke and Thureau-Dangin, *opp. citt.*).

‡ The view put forward by the present writer in *JTS.* ix. p. 342, that the divine name *Ya-um* is to be found so far back as *cir.* B.C. 2700 in *Lipuš-ʾ-a-um* (or *E-a-um*), the name of the daughter of Narâm-Sin, a priestess of Sin, now appears to him to be too doubtful to be cited as evidence : cf. Rogers, *Religion of Babylonia and Assyria*, p. 94 *n* 1. On Ball's plausible explanation of *Ya-u amêlu* in *Gilgameš-Epic*, Tab. X. Col. iv. l. 17, as 'god-man,' cf. *JTS.* ix. pp. 341 f.

§ It is difficult to escape the impression that the reluctance of some scholars—especially Jewish scholars—to recognize the existence of the divine name Yahu or Yahweh in Babylonian documents of an early period is due to the feeling that such a fact, if true, must tend to derogate from the uniqueness of Israel's privilege as the sole recipient of the revelation implied by the name which has always been regarded as peculiarly the *proper name* of the God of Israel. In view of this tendency, and to guard against the misunderstanding of his own position, the present writer hastens to affirm that the views which he puts forward in this *Addit. note* as regards the use of the name in very early times among the people of Amurru, from whom Israel sprang, and in the following *Addit. note* as to the early identification of Yahweh with the moon-god Sin, do not, in his opinion, derogate in any respect from the *uniquely new significance* in which the name is related in Ex. 3 to have been revealed to Moses at Ḥoreb. That revelation, with its new exposition of the name Yahweh as 'He who will become' (*i.e.* the God of progressive Revelation—'I will become what I will become'; cf. *note* on *ch.* 6 16, 'I will be with thee'), no less than the fulness of moral and spiritual meaning which Israel's prophets and psalmists were inspired to draw from the name in later ages, stands unparalleled in the history of Semitic religions ; and is

EARLY IDENTIFICATION OF YAHWEH WITH THE MOON-GOD

(Cf. *note* on 'the Ashera,' *ch.* 6 [25].)

We have seen, in the preceding *note*, how the name Yahu, Yahweh (*Ya-u* or *Ya-ʾ-u*, *Ya-u-tum*) comes into prominence at the period of the First Babylonian Dynasty; and evidence appeared to indicate that the knowledge and worship of this deity in Babylonia was due to the 'Amorite' immigrants, who may be supposed to have been the founders of the First Dynasty. It is a noteworthy fact that, while proper names compounded with the names of various Babylonian deities such as Šamaš, Marduk, Ištar, etc., are frequent at this period, by far the largest number of such theophoric names are framed in honour of the Moon-god Sin. Among these, we have already noticed *Sin-ya-tum*, which appears to equate or identify Sin with Yatum or Yahweh. The occurrence has also been cited of the name *Ya-ma-e-ra-aḫ*, 'Ya indeed is the moon,' *i.e.* the moon-god Sin.

Now the fact is significant that Gen. 14 makes Abraham, the traditional ancestor of Israel, a contemporary of Ḫammurabi ('Amraphel), the most celebrated king of the First Babylonian Dynasty. Biblical records, again, associate Abraham with Ur, the southern seat of the worship of Sin; and depict him as moving thence to Ḫarran, the northern seat of the worship of the same deity, before his migration westward to the land of Canaʿan. Abraham's movements are represented in the O.T. as dictated by the influence of a higher form of religion than was current at the time in Babylonia. His immediate ancestors are stated to have been polytheists, the worshippers of deities other than Yahweh (Josh. 24 [2] E).

Ḫarran * (Bab. *Ḫarrânu*, 'way *or* road') appears to have been so named as the *road* from east to west, the gateway by which Babylonian trade and culture penetrated into and permeated the coast-land of Syria, including Canaan. It possessed a celebrated temple of Sin, called E. ḪUL. ḪUL, the antiquity of which is vouched for by Nabonidus, when he tells us that 'since ancient days Sin, the great lord, had dwelt therein as the abode of his heart's delight.' ‡ Included

wholly unaffected by the fact that the name itself appears to have been known and used in earlier times, and among a wider circle of peoples. Cf. on this point, Rogers, *Relig. of Bab. and Assyr.*, p. 97; Driver, *Genesis* (*Westm. Comm.*), p. 409, *Exodus* (*Camb. Bib.*), p. li. The document J (as distinct from E) regards the use of the name Yahweh as primeval; since it states, in Gen. 4 [26], that in the days of Enosh, the grandson of Adam, 'men began to call with the name of Yahweh,' *i.e.*. to use the name in invocations. Yet J by no means implies that the name was used in these early times with anything like the fulness of meaning which it attained when it became the covenant-name of Israel's God.

* The Hebrew vocalization חָרָן Ḥārān is due to the objection which was felt, at the time of the creation of the Massoretic vowel-system, to the doubling of ר; but the 𝔊 form Χαρραν makes it certain that, at the time when Hebrew was a spoken language, the Hebrew and Babylonian forms of the name were identical. Cf. *note* on *harrîm*, p. 168.

‡ Cf. *KB.* iii. 2, p. 96; Ball, *Light from the East*, p. 208.

in the pantheon of Ḫarran were Šarratu ('the Queen'), wife of the moon-god Sin, and Malkatu ('the Princess'), a title of the goddess Ištar. The names Šarratu and Malkatu are identical in form with the Hebrew Sarah and Milcah, who are related to have been respectively the wife and sister-in-law of Abraham, and to have joined in the migration from Ur to Ḫarran (Gen. 11 [27 ff.]). *

The two forms Abram, Abraham, point to Babylonian originals, the former to *Abu-râmu*, the latter to *Abu-ra'imu* (the Bab. -ʾ- being represented in Heb. by ה; cf. *Ya-ʾ-u* = יָהוּ). But *râmu*, *ra'imu* are variant participial forms of the verb *râmu* (Heb. *rāḥam*), 'to love *or* show pity.' Abram, Abraham may therefore mean 'loving (merciful) father,' or 'the father is loving (merciful).' ‡ It is at least very probable that the father here originally intended was the moon-god Sin. The attribute of *love* or *mercy* (denoted by this verb) is very characteristic of Sin. We may notice such proper names as *Sin-ra-im-u-ri*, 'Sin loves Ur (?)'; *Sin-ra-im-Uruk* (*KI*), 'Sin loves (the city) Uruk'; *Sin-ra-ʾ-im-zêr*, 'Sin loves the seed (offspring)'; (*ilu*) *Sin-ri-me-ni*, '(the god) Sin, is merciful.' The title 'Father' was especially appropriate to Sin. He was regarded as the father of the gods, the 'merciful, gracious father (*a-bu rîm-nu-u ta-a-a-ru*), in whose hand the life of the whole world rests.' §

Thus, without asserting that the origin of the figure of Israel's great ancestor is to be found in a personification of the Moon-god (which indeed it would be rash to do, in view of the fact that the name was known as a personal name at the period to which Abraham is assigned by the Biblical narrative; cf. *footnote* ‡), it may at least be maintained with some reason that the narrative of the movement which brought the ancestors of the Hebrews from Ur to Ḫarran and finally to Cana'an, appears to be bound up with the worship of Sin; just as it is manifestly bound up with definite adhesion to the worship of Yahweh, involving the repudiation of the 'other gods' which the ancestors of Abraham are traditionally recorded to have worshipped.

* Cf. Jensen, *ZA*. xi. pp. 299 f.; Zimmern, *KAT*.[3] p. 364.

‡ This solution of the meaning of the two forms Abram, Abraham was first suggested to the present writer many years ago by Dr. Ball. More recently Ungnad has discovered the name *Aba-râma*, *Abam-râma* in Bab. contract-tablets from Dilbat of the reign of Ammizaduga (cf. *Beiträge zur Assyr.* vi. 5, 1909, p. 60); and here, since the first element is an Accusative, it is probable that the meaning is 'he loves the father,' the name belonging to a series of Bab. names thus formed: cf. Ranke quoted by Gressmann, *ZATW*. xxx. (1910) pp. 2 f. Thus Ball's conclusion as to the pure Bab. origin of the name Abram, Abraham, and his connexion of the second element with the verb *râmu*, are confirmed; but the possibility (though not the necessity) is opened that the Heb. name may be precisely equivalent to the Bab., and should be so interpreted. Langdon has also noted (on the basis of Ungnad's discovery) that the variants *-rām*, *-rāhām* are explicable through the Bab. variants *râmu*, *ra'imu*: cf. *ET*. xxi. (1909), p. 90.

§ Cf. the hymn to Sin in iv.[2] R. 9, translated by Jastrow, *RBA*. i. pp. 436 f.; Ungnad, *TB*. i. pp. 80 f.; Jensen, *KB*. vi. 2, pp. 90 ff. Rogers, *CP*. pp. 141 ff.

The fact which next calls for notice is the close connexion of Abraham with Be'er-sheba' (Gen. 21 [22-31] E, 21 [32] J, 22 [19] E), a connexion which is continued in the narrative of Isaac, where it is related that Yahweh appeared to Isaac on the night of his arrival at Be'er-sheba', revealing Himself as 'the God of Abraham thy father,' and re-affirming the promises made to Abraham (Gen. 26 [23ff.] J). It is from Be'er-sheba' that Jacob sets out when he leaves his parents in order to go to Paddan-Aram (Gen. 28 [10] J); and when, in much later life, he reaches Be'er-sheba' on his way to Egypt, he offers sacrifice there 'unto the God of his father Isaac,' and is the recipient of a Theophany in which God once more repeats His covenant promises made to Abraham and Isaac (Gen. 46 [1-5] E).

The name Be'er-sheba' means 'Well of number Seven,' שֶׁבַע, 'Seven,' being here identical with the Babylonian (*ilu*) *Sibitti* '(god) number Seven,' who seems to have represented one aspect of the moon-god, the seven-day week as a lunar quarter: cf. *Addit. note* pp. 43 f. The connexion which might naturally be inferred from these facts alone between שֶׁבַע Sheba', 'God Seven,' and Yahweh, is confirmed by the existence of the Israelite proper names אֱלִישֶׁבַע, Elisheba', 'God is number Seven,' and especially יְהוֹשֶׁבַע, Jehosheba', 'Yahu *or* Yahweh is number Seven.' We may recall, in this connexion, how Sabbath (the lunar quarter) and New Moon were observed in later times in connexion with the worship of Yahweh.

Coming now to Moses, we observe that the mountain at which God revealed Himself to him under the name of Yahweh, which is called Ṡinai in the narratives of J and P, must have been so called on account of an ancient connexion with the moon-god Sin, who gives His name to the whole district in which the mountain is situated ('the wilderness of Ṡin'). According to the account of the Theophany preserved by E, Ḥoreb (as the mountain is called in E and D) is already, prior to the revelation made to Moses, known as 'the mount of God' (Ex. 3 [1]), *i.e.* it was invested with sacred associations owing to its connexion with the worship of a particular deity—doubtless the god Sin. Jethro, Moses' father-in-law, who was a Ḳenite, is styled 'the priest of Midian,' *i.e.* the supreme interpreter of the religion of his tribe; and there can be little doubt that the God whom he worshipped was the God Yahweh, and that the central seat of this worship was Mount Ṡinai. No doubt the sacred associations of the place, and very possibly the conversation which Moses may have had with his father-in-law anent the character and worship of the tribal God, in a great measure prepared Moses' mind for the revelation which he was to receive.* It is interesting in this connexion to

* The view here put forward that Moses' mind may thus have been prepared, to some extent, for the Theophany, does not, of course, diminish the extraordinary and providential character of that Theophany, any more than does the fact that St. Paul was doubtless reflecting upon the argument of St. Stephen's speech, and

recall the account of the meeting of Moses with Jethro after the deliverance of the Israelites from Egypt. Moses gave Jethro an account of the course of events, laying stress upon the fact that it was Yahweh who had brought about this great deliverance; and it is recorded that 'Jethro rejoiced for all the goodness which Yahweh had done to Israel, in that he had delivered them out of the hand of the Egyptians. And Jethro said, Blessed be Yahweh, who hath delivered you out of the hand of the Egyptians, and out of the hand of Phara'oh. . . . Now know I that Yahweh is greater than all gods.' Jethro then proceeded to take 'a burnt offering and sacrifices for God: and Aaron came, and all the elders of Israel, to eat bread with Moses' father-in-law before God' (Ex. 18 8ff. JE). Here no doubt we have a sacrificial meal, in token of communion of Israel and the Ḳenite in the worship of Yahweh, the God of Ṡinai (Sin's mountain).

These conclusions, with regard to the religion of the Ḳenites, are strengthened by consideration of the name of the North Arabian tribe Jeraḥme'el, which was closely associated with the Ḳenites, as, subsequently, with the tribe of Judah: cf. *Addit. note*, p. 45. We may infer from 1 Sam. 30 26-31 that the Jeraḥme'elites were worshippers of Yahweh. David is recorded to have sent presents 'of the spoil of the enemies of Yahweh' to the elders of Judah, including 'those who were in the cities of the Jeraḥme'elites and those who were in the cities of the Ḳenites.' 1 Chr. 2, which makes Jeraḥme'el a descendant of Judah, *i.e.* an integral part of the tribe, gives, in *vv.* 25-33, the genealogy of the descendants of Jeraḥme'el, and includes among them Aḥijah and Jonathan, two names which assert allegiance to Yahweh. The name Jeraḥme'el is compounded of *Yeraḥ-ma-'el*, 'the moon indeed is god.'* Cf. for the formation of the name, *'Abi-ma-'el* (noticed p. 247). Thus this tribe of Yahweh-worshippers bore a name which proclaimed their allegiance to the moon-god.

The description of the Theophany on Mount Ṡinai, after the ratification of the Book of the Covenant (Ex. 24 9-11 J) is undoubtedly very ancient, and primitive in conception. It tells us that 'Then went up Moses, and Aaron, Nadab, and Abihu, and seventy of the elders of Israel; and they saw the God of Israel; and there was under his feet as it were a pavement of sapphire, and as the heaven itself for clearness. And upon the nobles of the children of Israel he put not forth his hand: and they beheld God, and did eat and drink.' It is difficult to escape the impression that the imagery is here suggested by the spectacle of the moon, riding at its full in the deep sapphire sky; and it can scarcely be objected that such an explanation involves a more crude and unspiritual conception than that which

the circumstances of the martyr's death, when he received the revelation upon the Damascus road, affect the character of that revelation as an interposition of Divine Providence. Each case illustrates the fact that God works through human agents in order to prepare the way for His signal manifestations in history.

* Cf. Hommel, *Grundriss*, i. p. 95, *n* 3.

seems to be the only possible alternative, viz. that the writer pictured a revelation in human form.

It would be possible to make kindred speculations as to the ultimate meaning of other primitive descriptions of Theophanies—*e.g.* Jacob's ladder (Gen. 28 [12] E), the pillar of fire (Ex. 13 [21f.] J, 14 [24] J), and the revelation to Moses on Sinai (Ex. 33 [17]-34 [7] J). Such speculations, however, would be at the best highly precarious, and are not needed in order to strengthen this argument for the primitive association of Yahweh with the Moon-god. It is sufficient to observe, in conclusion, that the opening words in which Yahweh proclaims His character to Moses in Ex. 34 [6], יהוה יהוה אל רחום וחנון 'Yahweh, Yahweh, a merciful and gracious God,' are identical in conception with the 'Merciful gracious Father' in the hymn to Sin already quoted (p. 250).

THE USE OF WRITING AMONG THE ISRAELITES AT THE TIME OF THE JUDGES.

(Cf. *ch.* 8 [14] *note.*)

The earliest written documents from Cana'an of which we have knowledge are the T.A. Letters written *cir.* 1400 B.C. by the petty rulers of Cana'anite and North Syrian cities to their Egyptian suzerain Amenḥotp III., and, subsequently, to his son and successor Amenḥotp IV. or Aḫnaton (cf. *Introd.* p. lxix). These are written in cuneiform Babylonian upon clay tablets. Similar letters, belonging to the same period, have been unearthed at Lachish and Ta'anach. The earliest known documents written in the West Semitic language (using this term broadly to embrace Cana'anite or Phoenician, Hebrew, Moabitic, and also early Aramaic) are very much later. From Southern Syria we have the Moabite stone, *cir.* B.C. 850; the Gezer agricultural calendar, probably not later than the eighth century B.C.; the Siloam inscription, *cir.* B.C. 700.* To these we may now add the ostraka from Samaria of the time of 'Omri and Aḥab, *i.e.* the earlier part of the ninth century B.C., facsimiles of which have not yet (1918) been published; ‡ and a limited number of inscribed seals and jar-handles, the most important of which is the seal from Megiddo

* These inscriptions may conveniently be consulted in *NHTS.*² pp. vii. ff. where further references are given.

‡ Cf. Driver in *PEF. Qy. St.*, 1911, pp. 79 ff.; and, for a summary account of the excavations at Samaria, based upon the reports in the *Harvard Theol. Journ.*, 1908-1911, Handcock, *The latest light on Bible Lands*, pp. 245 ff.

inscribed 'Belonging to Shama', the servant of Jerobo'am,' *i.e.* very possibly Jerobo'am II., B.C. 783-743.* To Central Syria belongs the Phoenician inscription on fragments of a bronze bowl from the Lebanon, probably of the eighth century B.C.‡ Northern Syria offers the inscriptions of Kalumu (latter half of ninth century B.C.), Panammu, and Bar-rekub (latter half of eighth century B.C.), kings of Sam'al and Ya'di, and an inscription of Zakir, king of Ḥamath and La'ash, *cir.* B.C. 800.§ These are written in the alphabetic script which was the prototype of the later West Semitic (Hebrew, Samaritan, and Syriac) and Central Semitic (Arabic) alphabets, as also of the alphabet of the Greeks.

It thus appears that we possess no direct evidence for the use of the alphabetic script in Syria earlier than the commencement of the ninth century B.C.; though its wide diffusion throughout Syria in the ninth and eighth centuries (as proved by the examples above cited) is a clear indication that its first employment must go back to a very considerably earlier date.

The fact that, in the fourteenth century B.C., the cuneiform script was regularly employed in Cana'an in official correspondence with the kings of Egypt, and even (as exemplified by the Ta'anach Tablets ||) in private correspondence between Cana'anite governors, is not in itself a proof that the alphabetic script was unknown and unused even at this early period. The Cana'anite practice in this respect may very well have been parallel to that which existed among the Ḥittites at about the same periods (as shown by Winckler's discoveries at Boghaz Keui); these latter employing the cuneiform script and Babylonian language together with their own hieroglyphic writing.

The reason why cuneiform Babylonian documents have survived from this early period, whereas no alphabetic West Semitic documents belonging to the same period are known to exist, may possibly be explained by the following facts. The cuneiform method of writing is the direct result of the material employed for written documents by the Babylonians and their imitators—this being normally the clay tablet, upon which, when in a damp condition, the characters were impressed with some form of angular stylus, before the document was baked or sun-dried. Thus, characters which were originally pictographs came to assume the form of conventional combinations of wedges or arrow-heads, the intractability of the writing material being unfavourable to the preservation of the linear

* For the seals generally, cf. *NHTS.*[2] p. iv.; *TB.* ii. pp. 103 ff.; and for the Megiddo seal, *Tell el-Mutesellim*: *Bericht über die . . . Ausgrabungen*, i., 1908, p. 99; Driver, *Schweich Lectures*, p. 91. For the jar-handles, cf. Driver, *op. cit.* pp. 74 f., with references there cited.

‡ Cf. *CIS.* I. i. 1, pp. 22 ff.; Ball, *Light from the East*, p. 238; Cooke, *NSI.* pp. 52 ff.

§ On these North Syrian inscriptions, cf. further pp. 173 f.

|| Cf. Rogers, *CP.* pp. 281 ff.; *TB.* i. pp. 128 f.

pictograph.* On the other hand, the West Semitic alphabetic script, also without doubt originally pictographic, has preserved its linear form because (though capable of being carved, like cuneiform, upon stone) it was never, apparently, written upon clay tablets, ‡ but with a pen and ink upon skin or papyrus. But skin and papyrus necessarily perish in the course of ages when exposed to the damp climate of Syria ; therefore, it is well within the range of possibility that such documents, written in the West Semitic script, may have existed at this early period and subsequently perished, while the cuneiform tablets survived. Indeed, the striking paucity of written documents from ancient Palestine may perhaps be explained by the hypothesis that skin or papyrus were commonly employed for writing purposes ; and, if this was so, we may be sure that the script employed was the West Semitic alphabet, and not cuneiform. §

* The present editor has made experiments in the writing of cuneiform upon soft putty with a wooden penholder cut to a triangular shape, with one very sharp angle, the end of the 'stylus' being cut off flat. This is held through the full of the hand, as the bearded Assyrian scribe is holding his stylus in the bas-relief figured in Plate I. (from Layard, *Monuments of Nineveh*, ii. Pl. 26). These experiments have proved to him that the wedges can only be formed successfully *by impression without drawing*, the variation in form being affected by differentiating the slope at which the stylus is applied to the putty—the short broad wedges being formed mainly by the end of the stylus, while the longer and narrower ones result from impressing the sharp edge of the stylus into the putty at an angle of approximately forty-five degrees, a still more acute angle (flatter application of the stylus) being necessary for the production of a very long wedge. Initial attempts to produce the latter by *drawing* with the stylus resulted in failure, as the surface of the putty tended to crumble, and the characteristic clear-cut impression was lost. The same difficulty would obviously stand in the way of drawing linear pictographs or West Semitic alphabetic characters upon this kind of material.

‡ The only known exceptions are the Aramaic dockets on cuneiform contract-tablets of the late Assyrian, Neo-Babylonian, and Achaemenian periods, written, for the most part, upon the edges of the tablets, so that their contents might be seen at a glance when they were stacked upon a shelf. These have generally a rough appearance, and must have been difficult to draw upon the damp clay. Their existence certainly does not prove that it was *usual* to write the Aramaic script upon clay, but simply that it was *convenient*, in the later stages of the use of cuneiform writing, to have *cuneiform* documents so docketed. For these Aramaic dockets, cf. *CIS.* II. i. Nos. 15 ff.; J. H. Stevenson, *Assyrian and Babylonian Contracts with Aramaic Reference Notes* (*Vanderbilt Oriental Series*, 1902); A. T. Clay, *Babylonian Expedition of the University of Pennsylvania*, Vol. X. (1904), 'Business Documents of Murashû sons of Nippur dated in the reign of Darius II,' pp. 5 ff.; Vol. VIII. (1908), 'Legal and Commercial Transactions dated in the Assyrian, Neo-Babylonian, and Persian Periods,' pp. 14 ff.; A. T. Clay, 'Aramaic Endorsements, etc.', in *Old Testament and Semitic Studies in Memory of William Rainey Harper* (1908), Vol. I. pp. 286 ff.; *University of Pennsylvania Museum, Publications of the Babylonian Section*, Vol. II. No. 1, 'Business Documents, etc.,' by A. T. Clay (1912), Plates 116-123.

§ This latter is very ill-suited for writing with a pen and ink. Layard, *Monuments of Nineveh*, 2nd Series, Plate 54, represents a fragment of coloured

The scribes who wrote the T.A. Letters which came from Cana'an were obviously more at home in using the West Semitic language than in using Babylonian. This fact is proved by their employment of Cana'anite 'glosses' on Babylonian terms, or substitution of Canaanite words when at a loss for the Babylonian equivalent (cf. p. 166). If, however, they were familiarized with the idea of writing through their official correspondence in Babylonian, and could write their own West Semitic language in Babylonian cuneiform syllables, as is proved by the 'glosses,' and were accustomed to express themselves in West Semitic rather than in Babylonian, why has no discovery been made of documents in the West Semitic language, but written in cuneiform upon clay tablets? A reasonable inference is that no such documents existed; the West Semitic tongue, if written at all at this period, being written upon perishable materials such as skin or papyrus, in the alphabetic script.

There is a fact in connexion with the T.A. correspondence which may very possibly indicate that the West Semitic alphabet *was* actually known to, and normally used by, the Cana'anite scribes of this period. It is probable that the secretary at the Egyptian court, whose business it was to read and interpret the Cana'anite correspondence to the king of Egypt, was himself not a native Babylonian, or a specially trained Egyptian, but a Western Semite like those with whose correspondence it was his duty to deal. He was possibly a personal friend of ARAD-Ḫiba of Jerusalem, who regularly concludes his letters to the king with a postscript addressed to the secretary, begging him to impress upon the king's mind the main points with which his letters are concerned. Thus, in one of his letters he writes to him, 'Bring thou in plain words unto the King, my Lord. The King my Lord's entire territory is lost' (Knudtzon, 286). The phrase here rendered 'is lost,' in Babylonian *ḫal-ḳa-at*, occurs, in the same connexion, in another of ARAD-Ḫiba's letters (Knudtzon, 288, l. 52), and is glossed, for the sake of emphasis, by the Cana'anite *a-ba-da-at* (Heb. אָבְדָה). We can scarcely err in interpreting this emphasis as

pottery on which are a few cuneiform characters painted with a brush; but apart from this no instance is known to the present editor of the writing of the script otherwise than with a stylus upon clay or stone. In the bas-relief mentioned in an earlier footnote (cf. Plate I.), which is part of a scene representing a bearded Assyrian scribe taking a memorandum of the spoils of war in cuneiform writing upon a tablet, this figure is accompanied by another who is writing with a pen upon a piece of curling material which obviously represents a scroll of leather or papyrus. The fact that this latter man is beardless marks him as a foreigner (possibly a eunuch); and it may be inferred therefore that he is writing in a non-cuneiform script—very possibly in the alphabetic Aramaic script. The two scribes are thus making a double entry in Assyrian and Aramaic respectively. The relief in question, which is of the seventh century B.C., is to be found in the British Museum, Kouyunjik Gallery, West Wall, Nos. 4-8. Nos. 15-17 in the same gallery evidently contain a continuation of the same series, and here too we have two similar scribes engaged in the same employment.

carrying the implication, 'Do not let there be any mistake: when I say *ḫalḳat*, I mean *abadat*'; and hence the inference is fair that the Egyptian king's secretary, like his correspondent, was more familiar with West Semitic than with Babylonian.

Now among the T.A. correspondence there were found certain fragments of Babylonian legends which had apparently been written as exercises in the writing of the cuneiform script by the secretary of whom we have been speaking, or by some one else holding the same position. These exercises are written in the simplest possible form, ideograms and compound syllables (*i.e.* syllables both beginning and ending with a consonant) being avoided, and the words built up entirely with simple syllables (*i.e.* vocalic syllables or syllables containing one consonant only). In illustration we may quote the first few lines of the story of Nerigal and Ereškigal, which, apart from its occurrence among the T.A. Letters, would be unknown to us:—

i-nu-ma i-lu iš-ku-nu ki-e-ri-e-ta
a-na a-ḫa-ti-šu-nu e-ri-eš-ki-i-ga-a-al
iš-pu-u-ru ma-a-ar ši-i-ip-ri
ni-i-nu u-lu nu-ur-ra-da-ak-ki
u at-ti ul ti-li-in-na-a-ši
šu-u-up-ri-im-ma li-il-gu ku-ru-um-ma-at-ki.

'When the gods prepared a feast,
To their sister Ereškigal
They sent a messenger;
"Even if we should descend to thee,
Thou wouldst not come up to us;
Therefore send and take thy portion."'

A native Babylonian scribe, writing in normal fashion, would have expressed this as follows:—

e-nu-ma DINGIR.MEŠ *iš-ku-nu ki-ri-ta*
a-na a-ḫa-ti-šu-nu (DINGIR) *e-riš-ki-gal*
iš-pu-ru TUR *šip-ri*
ni-nu u-lu nu-ur-ra-dak-ki
u at-ti ul ti-li-in-na-ši
šup-rim-ma lil-ḳu ku-rum-mat-ki.

Here we give the ideograms DINGIR.MEŠ = Bab. *ilâni*, TUR = Bab. *mâr*, in Sumerian form in order more clearly to illustrate the normal Babylonian method of using ideograms.

The use of simple, as distinct from compound, syllables suggests that the scribe was accustomed to an *alphabet* rather than to a syllabary, the simple syllables being for him the equivalents of his own alphabetic signs. We say *the equivalents*, because it is obvious that the West Semitic *alphabet*, which has no signs to denote vowels, and which we are accustomed to regard as wholly consonantal, must really have been regarded—at any rate by its framers and earliest users—as *a simple syllabary*, in which each consonantal sign carried the vowel which was appropriate to the word in which it was used.* In certain cases, *e.g.* in *ga-a-al* for *gal*, *ši-i-ip* for *šip*, the T.A. scribe uses the opportunity afforded him by the Babylonian syllabary of expressing the *vowel* even in a closed syllable in which the vowel is short. He does this because the language is unfamiliar to him, and it is convenient to be able to employ a *phonetic complement*; and, in so doing, he anticipates the history of the development of the written vocalic system in Hebrew, which was simply the invention of a series of phonetic complements when the fact that Hebrew had become comparatively unfamiliar to the Jews necessitated such a course.

Be this as it may, we have definite evidence to prove that by the twelfth century B.C., *i.e.* during the early part of the period covered by the Book of Judges, papyrus was employed in Palestine as a writing material; and therefore, we must infer a form of writing other than cuneiform was known and used. The Egyptian envoy Wenamon (*cir.* B.C. 1114; cf. *Introd.* pp. xcvi ff.) mentions, among the presents shipped from Egypt in payment to Zakar-ba'al, king of Gebal, for timber from the Lebanon, five hundred rolls of papyrus.‡ It is evident, therefore, that this Phoenician king knew and valued a material which could only be employed for writing with pen and ink; and there is no reason to doubt that this writing was the 'Phœnician' alphabetic script. It is interesting to observe that, in the earliest known examples of this script to which we have already referred—the ostraka from Samaria belonging to the early ninth century B.C., the writing is not scratched or otherwise incised upon the sherds, but written in ink with a reed pen, in a free and flowing style. §

The evidence afforded by philological examination of the terms employed in Bib. Heb. in connexion with *writing* is as follows.

The ordinary Heb. verb which means 'to write' is *kāthabh*, the ground-significance of which is uncertain. This verb may be used of engraving upon stone (*e.g.* the two tablets of the ten commandments), or of writing with ink in a book. Other verbs which denote 'to engrave' are *ḥāraš*, *ḥārath*, *ḥāḳaḳ*; but the latter verb, as used in Isa. 30[8] ('inscribe it in a book'), may have come to be applied to writing in ink. It is worthy of note that the ordinary Bab. and Assyr. verb 'to write,' *šaṭâru*, is not so used in Heb.; though the

* Thus, if a Western Semite read דבר, he did not—like modern learners of Hebrew—think of it as a mere series of consonants *d-b-r*, to which the addition of the vowels was a matter of guess-work aided by the context; but he thought of it as *da-ba-rum* if it happened to be the substantive meaning 'word,' or otherwise as the context dictated, the decision as to the precise vowel which the written sign carried being instinctive to a born user of the language, just as the decision as to a cuneiform sign-group, which, *e.g.*, might have the different values *dan*, *kal*, or *rib*, was instinctive from its context to the practised reader of Babylonian.

‡ Cf. Breasted, *AR.* iv. § 582.

§ Cf. Handcock, *The Latest Light on Bible Lands*, p. 255.

participial form *šoṭ^{e}rîm*, which is applied to a class of minor officials who had to do with the civil and military organization of the people, perhaps originally denoted 'scribes' or 'secretaries.'

Heb. *sêpher*, 'missive, document, book,' is probably an ancient loan-word from Bab. *šipru*, 'missive, message,' which is derived from *šapâru*, 'to send'; and this very probably points to the Babylonian origin of the use of written documents among the Western Semites. Bab. *šipru*, however, never seems itself to denote the document or clay tablet on which the message was inscribed; the regular term for this being *duppu*. That the Heb. *sêpher* came, at a relatively early date, to denote a leather or papyrus document written in ink, and therefore in the alphabetic script, is clear from such a passage as Ex. 32^{32} (prob. J) where Moses is pictured as petitioning God, 'Wipe me, prithee, out of thy book which thou hast written' (מְחֵנִי נָא מִסִּפְרְךָ אֲשֶׁר כָּתָבְתָּ), the verb *māḥā* implying the wiping of something written in ink off a roll of papyrus or leather, and not the erasure of cuneiform characters from a clay tablet.

The Heb. *m^{e}gillā*, 'roll,' from *gālal*, 'to roll' (sometimes coupled with *sêpher* in the phrase 'the roll of a book') can, of course, only have been a document of papyrus or leather, written in ink. The term is earliest used of Jeremiah's roll (Jer. $36^{2\,ff.}$), written in the reign of Jehoiakim, *cir.* B.C. 600. This was divided into *d^{e}lāthôth* (lit. 'doors'), *i.e.* perhaps rectangular 'columns,' or, less probably, 'leaves' (*v.*^{23}), and the writing is stated to have been in 'ink' (*d^{e}yô*, *v.*^{18}). Ezekiel's 'roll of a book,' 'written on the face and on the back' (Ezek. 2^{10}) is of nearly the same date. It is probably merely accidental that the term *m^{e}gillā* does not occur at an earlier period.

The regular Heb. term for a *tablet* for writing is *lûaḥ*, which is most commonly applied to the two tablets of stone on which the ten commandments were inscribed. The term is used besides in Isa. 30^{8}—'Now go, write it on a tablet in their presence, and inscribe it in a book, that it may be for a future day, ⌜for a testimony⌝* for ever'; and in Prov. 3^{3}, 7^{3}, Jer. 17^{1}, in the figurative expression, 'the tablets of the heart.' In all these passages the reference is to the making of a permanent memorial: and the inference is that tablets, probably of stone, were used for such a purpose. No mention of the use of *clay* as a writing material occurs in the O.T.

Heb. *ḥéreṭ*, 'stylus,' Isa. 8^{1}, must have been, in the first instance, a graving tool for cutting incised characters upon stone or metal: cf. the use of the same substantive to describe the tool with which Aaron 'fashioned' (וַיָּצַר) the molten bull, Ex. 32^{4} E; and the Aram. verb *ḥ^{a}raṭ*, 'to cut *or* scratch.' The term may, however, have come to denote a pen for writing with ink. The *gillāyôn* upon which the writing is to be done in Isa. 8^{1} may have been a polished metal

* Vocalizing לְעֵד, in place of 𝔐 לָעַד 'for eternity.'

tablet (cf. R.V.), if (as is doubtful) the plur. form *gilyônîm* in Isa. 3[23] denotes tablets of polished metal used as mirrors (from verb *gālā* in the sense 'display, reveal'); but comparison of the Talmudic *gilyôn*, which denotes the *empty margin* of a page or roll (from verb *gālā* in the sense 'be uncovered, *and so*, bare'; cf. Ar. *ǵala*) suggests that Isaiah may have been thinking of the blank page of a book: cf. 𝔊[A] τόμον χαρτοῦ καινοῦ.* Heb. *'ēṭ*, 'pen' or 'stylus,' was probably usually a reed-pen for writing in ink. Jeremiah, who himself, as we have seen, used a 'roll' for the writing of his prophecies, refers to 'the lying pen (*'ēṭ*) of the scribes'; and we may infer that his own pen (or rather, that of Baruch) would have been described as *'ēṭ*. 'The pen of a rapid writer,' Ps. 45[1], 𝔐[2], would naturally be a reed. The *'ēṭ*, however, might also be an iron stylus for incising characters upon stone or metal. Jeremiah, in speaking of the ineradicable character of Israel's sin, says that it 'is written with a pen of iron with diamond point' (Jer. 17[1]): cf. also Job 19[24].‡

So far, then, as Biblical evidence is concerned, we gather that written records in pre-exilic times were in special cases engraved on stone; but more commonly written in ink upon a roll or book of papyrus or leather. The earliest definite reference to the employment in a 'book' of writing which could be wiped off, and was therefore presumably in ink, is Ex. 32[32] (Moses' prayer), which, of course, does not *prove* anything more than that the J writer (if the passage is rightly assigned to him) in the ninth century B.C. supposed that Moses would think of a book written in ink. It is likely, however, that J may be embodying an oral tradition emanating from an indefinitely earlier period. On the other hand, we find no reference whatever to the use of *clay* tablets by the Israelites, and no hint that it is in any way reminiscent of the use of the cuneiform script in early times.

If, as we have seen from the allusion in the story of Wenamon, papyrus was used for writing in Palestine in the twelfth century B.C., it is at any rate very possible that the use of the alphabetic script may

* In either case, the terms are most probably used metaphorically, as is not obscurely hinted by the expression 'stylus of a man,' *i.e.* 'human stylus,' and by *v.*[3] which refers the symbolism to the begetting of a son who is to be named Maher-shalal-ḥash-baz. The *gillāyôn* of *v.*[1] is a metaphor, then, for 'the prophetess' of *v.*[3], who, if described as a blank page, may very possibly have been Isaiah's second wife, and not the mother of She'ar-yashub of *ch.* 7[3]. On his explanation, the want of apparent connexion between the symbolism of *v.*[1] and that of *v.*[3] disappears; and there is no occasion to suppose that the *gillāyôn* was a metal tablet to be set up in some public place, or that the expression *ḥéreṭ 'ěnôš*, 'stylus of a man,' means an *ordinary stylus* which would write 'common characters, intelligible to all' (as strangely explained by BDB. p. 355).

‡ Heb. *'ēṭ* is probably connected with Bab. *ḫaṭṭu*, which usually means 'sceptre,' but also, no doubt, 'stylus' (the ideogram which expresses it may also denote 'scribe'). The cognate verb *ḫaṭâṭu* means 'to cut into.'

have been well diffused throughout the country at the time of the Judges. How far the art of writing was generally understood and practised, or had only been mastered by a class of specially trained scribes, we cannot say. In the Gezer-calendar, however, in which the months of the year are distinguished by the agricultural operations with which they were associated ('The month of ingathering, the month of sowing, etc.'), it is generally recognized that we have the work of a peasant-farmer who was able to write in a fair and legible hand; and if such an accomplishment was possible for a peasant in the eighth century B.C. there is no valid reason for supposing that it would have been impossible for the boy captured by Gide'on some three or four centuries earlier.

The conclusion that the use of the alphabetic script may quite possibly have been well-diffused in Cana'an at the time of the Judges is as much as this note is concerned to argue. The question how far back the script is to be traced is a much wider one, and is bound up with the problem of its origin—a problem which has been much debated, and upon which the paucity of evidence does not at present permit us to speak with any certainty. It can hardly, however, be disputed that there exist a few traces of the use of the West Semitic alphabet at a period far earlier than the earliest of the documents mentioned on pp. 253 f. The alphabetic letters discovered by Schumacher at Megiddo (cf. *Tell el-Mutesellim*, p. 109) are dated by Kit. (*GVI.*[2] i. p. 120) between the sixteenth and thirteenth centuries B.C. Some of the signs on fragments of pottery discovered by Bliss at Tell el-Ḥasy (Lachish) bear a remarkable resemblance to West Semitic letters (cf. *A Mound of Many Cities*, chap. ii.); and it is at least highly doubtful whether they can be dismissed as 'owners' marks' merely. These pot-sherds were, with but one exception, found exclusively in the earliest strata of the mound, dated by Bliss not later than *cir.* 1600 B.C.*

As for the origin of the West Semitic script, few if any scholars at the present day would maintain de Rougé's theory which attempted

* The inscription on an Egyptian statute of Ḥatḥor, discovered by Petrie at Serabit in the Sinai-peninsula (cf. *Researches in Sinai*, pp. 129 ff.), and dated by him *cir.* 1500 B.C., was discussed by Ball in *PSBA.*, 1908, pp. 243 f., who took the writing as an early form of Phoenician, and read the first four characters as עתתר, *'Athtar.* The publication by Gardiner of further inscriptions from the same locality now shows that the characters are badly written Egyptian hieroglyphics: cf. *Journal of Egyptian Archæology*, iii. (1916), pp. 1-21. Gardiner attempts to prove that these signs are the prototypes of an early Semitic alphabet of Egyptian origin, basing his argument upon the supposed occurrence of בעלת, *Ba'alath*, 'Mistress'—the title of the goddess—which recurs in several of the inscriptions (reading from left to right, or from top to bottom); but his theory, though supported by Cowley and Sayce, depends too much upon assumption to carry weight as a plausible solution of the problem of the origin of the alphabet.

to trace it to the Egyptian hieratic character. The theory of an origin from the Babylonian, or rather Sumerio-Akkadian, linear script which was the prototype of the cuneiform syllabary has been maintained by Ball, Hommel, Winckler, and others. In favour of this theory many attractive arguments have been adduced,* though in the present state of our knowledge these cannot be claimed

* Cf. especially Ball, *The Origin of the Phœnician Alphabet*, *PSBA.*, 1893, pp. 392-408; reproduced in revised and abridged form in *Light from the East*, pp. 232-238. Perhaps the most striking instances of close resemblance in *form* and *sound* between the linear Babylonian and West Semitic characters are the following. The Sumerian sign ZI, ZIDA, ZIDE, Bab. *Zîtu* (cf. Heb. *Ṣādē*, Greek Ζῆτα) probably represents a flowering reed. There being no consistent differentiation between *z* and *ṣ* in old Babylonian, the difference between the West Semitic sounds seems to have been effected by taking the upper part (flower) of the reed for ז, and the lower part (a leaf) for צ. The Sumerian sign GAM (meaning, according to Babylonian lexicographers *ḳadâdu* 'to bow down,' and representing some bowed or bent object, conceivably a broken reed) is practically identical in form with the West Semitic *Gîmel*. *Gîmel* corresponds to the Greek Γάμμα, a form of the name which is not to be regarded as a modification of an original Γάμλα (as suggested by Bevan, *EB.* 5360), but rather represents a more primitive form of the name: cf. Ar. *Ǵîm*. But the Sumerian GAM may also have been pronounced GAMMA: cf. DUG, DUGGA; IL, ILLA; etc. The Heb. name *Gîmel* 'camel' may then be taken to be a later modification of the name GAM, due at once to the similarity in sound and to the fancied resemblance of the sign to the head and neck of a camel. If the names Ζῆτα, Γάμμα really find their origin not in West Semitic but in Sumerio-Akkadian, the linear Babylonian theory of the alphabet may well be regarded to be as good as proved.

We can, of course, argue nothing from such names of the alphabet as happen to be Semitic words of known meaning; since these may conceivably have been bestowed at a relatively late date in the history of the alphabet (we have already argued that the name *Gîmel* is probably later than GAM or GAMMA). Thus the fact that ר bears the name *Rêš* 'head,' and not the Cana'anite or Hebrew name *Rôš*, while it suggests the Bab. *rêšu*, is more probably to be explained from the Aram. *rêšā*; the fact being well established that it was the Aramaean development of the alphabet which was the parent of the Hebrew square character—the *kᵉthâbh 'aššûrî* 'Assyrian (*i.e.* Mesopotamian) script'—rather than the Phoenician development which resulted in the Samaritan script. Ῥῶ, the Greek form of *Rêš*, may be compared with Ar. *Râ*, and with Sumerian RU, the name of the triangular character which is practically identical wth the early West Semitic ר *Rêš*. But the Sumerian sign for RU may also bear the value DA, just as ר *Rêš* and ד *Dāleth* are nearly identical in form in early West Semitic—a fact which suggests that ר and ד may have had a common origin, and also that DA (for DAL? cf. Ar. *Dâl*) may have been the original name for the latter letter, this being later on semiticized into the word of known meaning *Dāleth* 'door.'

A point in favour of the linear Babylonian theory which should not be overlooked is the fact that we have actual evidence, in the old Persian cuneiform writing, of the utilization of the cuneiform script for alphabetic purposes. On the manner in which the syllabary may have been gradually adopted so as to form an alphabet, cf. Ball, *op. cit.*, and also the facts which we have noticed above (p. 257) as to the simplification of the syllabary by a Cana'anite scribe *cir.* 1400 B.C.

actually to amount to a demonstration. Most recently Sir Arthur Evans has attempted to prove (*Scripta Minoa*, vol. i. 1909) that the Minoan script discovered by him in his excavations at Knossos in Crete is closely connected with the West Semitic alphabet; and this writer therefore argues for a Mediterranean origin for the alphabet, holding it to have been introduced into Cana'an by the Philistines and other kindred sea-peoples who invaded and settled in Palestine at the end of the thirteenth and beginning of the twelfth centuries B.C. This theory assumes the doubtful position that there is no trace of the use of the alphabetic script in Cana'an prior to the thirteenth century B.C.; and, while ignoring the striking parallels, both in *form* and *sound*, between the linear Babylonian and certain of the West Semitic letters, draws similar parallels between the Minoan and West Semitic scripts based on *form* only, the value of the Minoan characters being at present undetermined.* Evans also fails to take account of the possibility that such resemblances as may be traced between the Mediterranean and West Semitic scripts may conceivably be due to a common dependence, whether direct or indirect, upon linear Babylonian. ‡

8. 29-32. *R^P's introduction to the story of Abimelech.*

This short section forms a necessary introduction to the story of Abimelech contained in *ch.* 9. As is noticed elsewhere (cf. p. 268), *ch.* 9, though derived from the old composite narrative and forming part of R^{JE}'s history of the Judges, must have been cut out of the book by R^{E2}, who substituted the short summary 8 $^{33-35}$ in place of it. We infer therefore that the story of Abimelech, together with *chs.* 16-21, was re-inserted into the book by the final editor R^P; and if this is so, this editor must have been responsible for 8 $^{29-32}$ introducing *ch.* 9, apart from which the information which these verses contain is superfluous to the narrative. The phraseology of 8 $^{29-32}$ points to the influence of P: cf. יֹצְאֵי יְרֵכוֹ 'that came out of his loins,' an expression elsewhere (Gen. 46 ^{26}, Ex. 1 ^{5} †) peculiar to P; בְּשֵׂיבָה טוֹבָה 'in a good old age,' Gen. 15 ^{15} (late editorial interpolation), Gen. 25 ^{8} P, 1 Chr. 29 ^{28} †.

* This criticism applies equally to Petrie's recently published theory of the evolution of the alphabet, by survival, out of a large and widely diffused signary which had, according to him, its origin in prehistoric Egypt, and drew accretions from the whole of the nearer East (*The Formation of the Alphabet*, 1912, published as Vol. III. of *The British School of Archæology in Egypt Study Series*). The theory really shows how deceptive arguments from *form* are when divorced from *value*.

‡ Thus, to take one illustration only, the coincidence (if such it be) is at any rate very remarkable that the Cypriote sign PA, noted by Evans (*op. cit.* p. 1, *n* 3; p. 71, no. 4) and compared by him with the same sign in Minoan, is absolutely identical in form and bears the value PA in Sumerio-Akkadian.

29. R^P (E) And Jerubba'al the son of Joash went and dwelt in his house. 30. And Gide'on had seventy sons, that came out of

Naturally R^P must have been dependent for his *facts* upon the original narrative introductory to the story of Abimelech. This probably belonged, like the main narrative of *ch.* 9, to E; notice the name Jerubba'al in *v.* 29, as in *ch.* 9 1.2.5a.5b.16.19.24.57

8. 29. *went and dwelt, etc.* Logically, we should have expected this fact to have been narrated before the account of the making of the Ephod in *vv.* 24 ff. There is a reason, however, for the order of events. The Israelites (*v.* 22) ask Gide'on to become their king. He refuses this (*v.* 23), but at the same time takes the opportunity (*v.* 24) of asking for the ear-rings of their spoil; and it is natural that this should immediately be followed by the account of the use to which the gold was put, and the abuse which the Ephod became. It is not until these facts have been narrated that the writer gets the opportunity of stating that (instead of accepting the offer of the kingship) the hero retired into private life, which is what the statement of *v.* 29 'he went and dwelt in his home' (or, as suggested by Bu., וַיֵּשֶׁב לְבֵיתוֹ 'and returned to his home') amounts to; and this reference is a natural introduction to the account of his becoming the founder of a large family (*vv.* 30.31). To conclude, therefore, that *v.* 29 'stands singularly out of place' (Mo.), and 'originally closed the narrative in *vv.* 1-3, or that in *vv.* 4-21' (Cooke) entirely misses the point. The verse *might* immediately have followed *v.* 23, but *could not* have preceded it.

30. *seventy sons.* The same number is given for the sons of Aḥab, 2 Kgs. 10 1. The sons and the grandsons of the Judge 'Abdon are said to have been seventy in all, Judg. 12 14. In the inscription on the monument erected by Bar-rekub, king of Ya'di, in honour of his father Panammu (cf. p. 173) it is stated that seventy brethren (or kinsmen) of Panammu's father Bar-ṣur perished in an insurrection. Adoni-ṣedeḳ boasted that he had seventy captive kings picking up crumbs under his table, Judg. 1 7. We can only conclude that in all these cases *seventy* represents a large round number.

that came out of his loins. Heb. *yārēkh* (properly 'hip' or 'thigh') is here used of the seat of procreative power: so also (in addition to the other occurrences of the same phrase, cited above) in the phrase (preparatory to the calling for a specially solemn oath) 'Put thy hand under my *yārēkh*,' Gen. 24 2.9 J, 47 29 J †, where the reference is probably 'to an oath by the genital organs, as emblems of the life-giving power of the deity—a survival of primitive religion': Skinner, *Genesis* (*ICC.*), p. 341. The force of the expression as used in our passage is that these sons belonged to Gide'on's clan *by male descent*, in contrast to Abimelech, mentioned in the next verse, who belonged

his loins: for he had many wives. 31. And his concubine who was in Shechem, she also bare him a son; and he made his name Abimelech. 32. And Gide'on the son of Joash died in a good old age, and was buried in the sepulchre of Joash his father, in 'Ophrah ⌈of⌉ the Abi'ezrites.

by birth *to the clan of his mother*: cf. *note ad loc.* Robertson Smith remarks that the term *faḫiḏ* 'thigh' denotes a *clan* in the Palmyrene inscriptions and elsewhere in Arabic literature, and contrasts it with *baṭn* 'belly' or 'womb' which is similarly used; arguing that 'the "thigh" or clan of male descent, stands over against the "belly" or clan of mother's blood': cf. *Kinship and Marriage in early Arabia*,[2] p. 38.

31. *his concubine, etc.* The connexion was not, according to the custom of the time, an irregular one. It seems to have been a marriage of a type well known among the early Arabians, in which the wife does not become the chattel or property of her husband, but is known as his *ṣadîḳa** or 'female friend,' and remains with her own clan, being visited by her husband from time to time. Samson's marriage with his Philistine wife (*ch.* 14) was very possibly of the same character. In such cases, the children of the marriage belong to the wife's clan—a fact which has an important bearing on the events related in *ch.* 9: cf. *note* on *v.* 2 'your bone, etc.' On *ṣadîḳa*-marriage, cf. Robertson Smith, *op. cit. supra*, pp. 93 ff.

he made his name. Heb. וַיָּשֶׂם אֶת־שְׁמוֹ, lit. 'he set *or* appointed his name.' This somewhat peculiar usage (in place of the normal וַיִּקְרָא 'he called') is seen again in 2 Kgs. 17[34], Neh. 9[7]; cf. Dan. 1[7].

Abimelech. The name, which probably means 'the (divine) king is father' (*sc.* of the bearer of the name) is borne by the king of Gerar in Gen. 20[2 ff.] E, 26[1 ff.] J. Abi-milki (which is identical) is the name of the governor of Tyre who figures in the T.A. Letters *cir.* 1400 B.C., and of a prince of Arvad who was tributary to Ashurbanipal: *KB.* ii. pp. 172 f. On the use of the element *Mélekh* or *Milk* in proper names, cf. *KAT.*[3] pp. 469 ff.; Baethgen, *Beiträge*, pp. 37 ff.; Gray, *Hebrew Proper Names*, pp. 115 ff.; La., *ÉRS.*[2] pp. 101 ff.

32. *in 'Ophrah, etc.* Reading בְּעָפְרַת in place of the Absolute form בְּעָפְרָה 𝔐. It is possible, however, that the original narrative may have read 'in 'Ophrah' simply, and that the definition 'of the Abi'ezrites' was added subsequently as a gloss from *v.* 24, without altering בְּעָפְרָה into the Construct State.

* The form *ṣadāḳa* given by Cooke is unknown in this sense. He seems to be making a confusion with *ṣadâḳ*, which denotes a gift given by the husband to the wife on the occasion of marriage.

33. R[E2] And, when Gide'on was dead, the children of Israel turned back, and went a whoring after the Ba'als, and made Ba'al-berith their god. 34. And the children of Israel did not remember Yahweh their god, who had delivered them out of the hand of all their enemies round about. 35. And they did not show kindness to the house of Jerubba'al (Gide'on), according to all the goodness which he had shown to Israel.

8. 33-35. *R[E2]'s summary in place of the story of Abimelech.*
These verses, which are clearly marked by their phraseology as due to R[E2], give a summary account of Israel's apostasy based upon *ch.* 9 (cf. *vv.* [33b.35a]), and evidently intended to take its place; since, if *ch.* 9 had stood in R[E2]'s book, such a summary would have been superfluous. Cf. further *Introd.* to *ch.* 9.

8. 33. *when Gide'on was dead.* Cf. 2 [6-10] E, 2 [19], 4 [1] R[E2]. According to the main editor's philosophy of history, apostasy regularly follows after the death of a judge.

went a whoring. Cf. 2 [17] *note.*

the Ba'als. Cf. 2 [13] *note.*

Ba'al-berith. Cf. 9 [4]. The title means 'Lord *or* owner of the covenant.' In 9 [46] El-berith, 'God of the covenant,' is used. Whether this deity was thought to preside over a league of Cana'anite cities, or whether the 'covenant' was between him and his worshippers, cannot be determined. Cf. Cheyne, *EB.* 404 for different views.

Ba'al-bĕrîth, according to *ch.* 9, was the local Ba'al of the Cana'anites at Shechem. This narrative, whence R[E2] derives his information, says nothing about a general defection of the *Israelites* after the Ba'al; the fact being quite clear that the inhabitants of Shechem were *Cana'anites*, and that Abimelech obtained and held sway over them in virtue of his *Cana'anite* descent. Cf. p. 267.

35. *did not show kindness, etc.* A summary reference to the facts narrated in 9 [1-21]. Here again R[E2] misses the point of the narrative, and assumes that the execution of Jerubba'al's seventy sons and the appointment of Abimelech as king were due to the Israelites.

Jerubba'al (Gide'on). R[E2] (or possibly some later hand) adds the name Gide'on in order to make the fact clear that the two names refer to one and the same man. Cf. the similar insertion in 7 [1].

9. 1-57. *The story of Abimelech.*

Besides the Commentaries, etc., quoted throughout the book, cf. H. Winckler, *AF.* i. (1893) pp. 59-62.

This ancient narrative is of the highest interest on account of the light which it throws upon the circumstances of the early stages of Israel's occupation of Cana'an. After the death of Gide'on or Jerubba'al, the hegemony which he had exercised over his own clan at 'Ophrah and (as we gather from this narrative) over the neighbouring

Cana'anite city of Shechem, passed in natural course to his family. Thus we see Israelite and Cana'anite living side by side in a relationship of mutual toleration if not of friendship. Both races alike are sufferers from the incursions of the Midianites from without; and, when a deliverer such as Jerubba'al arises, both races thereafter are willing to recognize his right to exercise some form of chieftainship or government. Distinctions of race are, however, by no means obliterated, as subsequent events prove. Abimelech, half-Cana'anite by birth, is wholly Cana'anite by tribal custom: cf. *note* on *v.*[2]. He uses his racial connexions to incite the members of his mother's clan at Shechem in his own favour; and by their aid he wipes out (with one exception) all the other sons of Jerubba'al who by birth were Israelites, and secures a short-lived kingship over Shechem and the neighbouring district. The statement (*v.*[22]) that Abimelech was prince 'over Israel' seems to belong to the point of view which regards Israel at this time as already forming an organic unity, and supposes that the authority exercised by the Judges was general, and not simply local. The fact that Israelites as well as Cana'anites were included under Abimelech's sway is, as Mo. notices, to be inferred from *v.*[55]; but it is clear that the framer of the narrative misses, or at least fails to pay due regard to, the fact that Abimelech was essentially a Cana'anite, who used his Cana'anite connexions in order to secure his local kingship.*

Evidence of the employment of more than one source may be noticed in the middle part of the narrative. As Mo. points out, the growth of hostilities between Abimelech and the men of Shechem is traced to two distinct causes. According to *v.*[23], God sends an evil spirit between Abimelech and the citizens of Shechem, which causes these latter to deal treacherously with their ruler. In *vv.*[26-29], however, a new situation is created by the arrival on the scene of one Ga'al and his family. These new-comers stir up the racial pride of the blue-blooded Shechemites against the half-breed Abimelech, and thus foster a revolt. Clearly this second cause is distinct from, and not cumulative upon, the first. In *v.*[25b] it is stated that Abimelech was informed of the treacherous aggressions of the Shechemites; and the expectation is created that he will immediately take action. Instead of this, however, the narrative of Ga'al intervenes, and is continued down to *v.*[41]; at which point, after Ga'al's defeat by Abimelech and subsequent expulsion from Shechem, he disappears from the narrative, which is now concerned (*vv.*[42 ff.]) with the reprisals taken by Abimelech upon the Shechemites as a whole.

* Cooke misapprehends this point when he states (p. 98) that 'at Shechem the native Canaanites were in the ascendant, and yet there was a sufficiently strong Israelite element in the place to raise Abimelech to the position of ruler.' Yet he rightly recognizes (p. 97) that, in the *ṣadîḳa* marriage, 'the children remained with their mother and belonged to her tribe,' and that 'the narrative seems to imply that the woman was a Canaanite' (p. 97).

It will be noticed that *v.*[42b], 'and they told Abimelech,' repeats *v.*[25b], 'and it was told Abimelech,' with but trifling variation. We may plausibly infer that the main narrative, interrupted after *v.*[25b], is resumed by R^{JE} in *v.*[42b]. Probably *v.*[42a], 'And, on the morrow, the people went out into the field,' represents the redactor's attempt to make what follows read as a continuation of the Ga'al-narrative. It anticipates *v.*[43b], 'the people came forth from the city,'—an event which clearly took place *after* and not *before* Abimelech had laid his ambush as recorded in *v.*[43a].

We conclude, then, with Mo., that the Ga'al-narrative contained in *vv.*[26-41] is derived from a distinct source. The rest of the narrative appears to be homogeneous; and, except for a few later additions (cf. *notes* on *vv.*[16-20], *v.*[22]), may well have been derived, as Mo. supposes, from a single ancient source.*

The source of the main narrative appears to be E: cf. the use of the name Jerubba'al, which elsewhere belongs to E (cf. p. 178); *'ĕlōhîm* 'God,' and not 'Yahweh,' *vv.*[7.23.56.57]; 'with truth and with integrity' (באמת ובתמים) *vv.*[16.19], a phrase which only occurs elsewhere (in reversed order) in Josh. 24[14] E; *'āmā* 'bond-maid' *v.*[18] (J's phrase is *šiphḥā* in the same sense); and, generally, the emphasis laid upon the moral that wickedness is sure to meet with its due punishment. If *vv.*[1-25.43-57] were derived from E, the inference is natural that the Ga'al-fragment, *vv.*[26-41], may have belonged to J; but of this we have no direct evidence, since phrases elsewhere characteristic of J appear altogether to be lacking. It is worthy of notice, however, that the expression of *v.*[33] 'thou shalt do to him as occasion serveth' (lit. 'as thy hand shall find,' כאשר תמצא ידך) occurs again in 1 Sam. 10[7] ('then do as occasion serveth') which belongs to J.

Ch. 9, like *chs.* 16-21, exhibits no trace of the hand of R^{E2}, and clearly did not enter into his pragmatic scheme, as outlined in *ch.* 2[6]-3[6], and worked out in the histories of the 'major' Judges. That R^{E2} had the story before him in the earlier composite narrative which he employed (the work of R^{JE}) is proved, however, by the fact that he knew it, and composed a short summary (*ch.* 8[33-35]) which was intended to take its place. For R^{E2} Abimelech was very far from being a divinely appointed Judge. The narrative relating his reign had no interest in connexion with R^{E2}'s religious philosophy of history, except as illustrating (from his point of view) a period of apostasy which could fitly be summarized in a few sentences. The re-insertion of the story into the Book of Judges must have been due to the last editor (R^{P}; cf. *note* introductory to 8[29-32]), who seems to have reckoned Abimelech among the Judges: cf. the reference in the introduction to the first of the 'minor' Judges, 10[1a], whose insertion in the book appears to have been due to this editor (cf. *note ad loc.*).

* The attempts which have been made by Winckler, Bu., and No. to prove a more detailed analysis are not convincing; any more than is the argument of La. that the whole narrative is derived from a single source.

9. 1. E And Abimelech the son of Jerubba'al went to Shechem unto his mother's brethren, and spake unto them and unto all the clan of the house of his mother's father, saying,

9. 1. *Shechem.* The Roman Flavia Neapolis, and the modern Nâblus,* situated thirty miles north of Jerusalem in the fertile valley which runs east and west between Mt. 'Ebal on the north and Mt. Gerizim on the south, forming an easy pass between the maritime plain and the Jordan valley. Placed at a point at which many important roads converge, the city must always have exercised considerable importance: cf. Smith, *HG.* pp. 332 ff. The name Shechem, denoting *shoulder*, probably refers to the position of the city on the watershed, 1870 feet above the Mediterranean.

The early history of the relations between Israelites and Cana'anites at Shechem is involved in great obscurity. The city was occupied, prior to the arrival of the ancestors of Israel west of Jordan, by the Cana'anite clan of the Bᵉnê-Ḥamor. The natural advantages which it enjoyed rendered it the principal city of Central Palestine, and the earliest Israelite clans (the Patriarchs) gravitated thither on their arrival in Cana'an, and lived on terms of friendship and alliance with the Bᵉnê-Ḥamor (Gen. 12$^{6.7}$ J, 33^{18} P, 33$^{19.20}$ E). These relations were broken by the treacherous aggressions of the Sime'on and Levi clans (Gen. 34 ‡), which seem to have provoked such retaliation on the part of the Cana'anites of the district as decimated and dispersed these Israelite clans, the remnant of them seeking refuge in other parts of the land (Gen. 49$^{5-7}$ J). On the arrival of the Joseph-clans in Cana'an and their settlement under Joshua', Shechem lay within the district which they overspread. North Israelite tradition recorded that the bones of Joseph were brought up from Egypt and buried in a plot of ground at Shechem acquired by purchase from the Bᵉnê-Ḥamor (Gen. 33^{19} E, 50$^{24-26}$ E, Ex. 13^{19} E, Josh. 24^{32} E); and according to a later tradition (Josh. 24^{1} E^{2}) Shechem appears as the rallying-place of 'all the tribes of Israel' on the occasion of Joshua''s farewell charge. Thus we are probably justified in assuming that the early relations between the Joseph-tribes and the Bᵉnê-Ḥamor were of a friendly character. We find, however, that, in the time of the Judges, Shechem is still in possession of the Benê-Ḥamor, the burghers or free-born 'owners of Shechem' (בַּעֲלֵי שְׁכֶם) clearly belonging to this Cana'anite clan: cf. 9^{28} *note.* The services rendered

* With Nâblus as the Arabized form of Neapolis, cf. Yerablus for Hierapolis.

‡ This narrative is clearly a thinly-veiled description of tribal relations between Israelites and Cana'anites, at first friendly, then hostile. The two sources employed in the chapter bear respectively the characteristics of J and P; but there are difficulties in the way of correlating the J narrative with the main document J: cf. Skinner, *Genesis* (*ICC.*), pp. 417 f.

2. 'Prithee speak in the ears of all the citizens of Shechem, "Which is better for you, that seventy men should rule over you, even all the sons of Jerubba'al, or that one man should rule over you? Remember also that I am your bone and your

by Jerubba'al in ridding the country of the Midianite pest benefited Israelite and Cana'anite alike, and the B^e^nê-Ḥamor at Shechem were thereafter willing to acquiesce in Israelite predominance in the district as represented by Jerubba'al and his sons. Abimelech's rise to power was achieved through the stirring up of racial antipathies between Cana'anite and Israelite; but the pure-blooded B^e^nê-Ḥamor were not able for long to acquiesce in the domination of the half-bred upstart ruler, and the friction which ensued resulted in the destruction of Shechem, as related in our narrative.

When next we hear of Shechem, it is an Israelite town in possession of the Joseph-tribes, and still holds the position of importance which was the natural outcome of its physical advantages; so that it appears in 1 Kgs. 12 [1] as the city to which 'all Israel' resorts in order to anoint a successor to Solomon. The tradition in Gen. 48 [22] E—where the aged Israel on his death-bed bequeaths to Joseph one *shoulder* (Heb. Shechem) above his brethren, which he claims to have captured from the hand of the Amorite with his sword and with his bow—may have arisen no earlier than the time of David or Solomon, as a northern Israelite explanation of the way in which the most favoured spot in Cana'an came into the possession of the Joseph-tribes—a special gift made by the common father of the Israelite clans to his most favoured son. The contrast, however, with the other E tradition noticed above—which speaks of rights at Shechem acquired by purchase from the B^e^nê-Ḥamor—is very striking—and indeed inexplicable. Cf. further *Introd.* p cxi.

The fact that Shechem was not easily defensible against an outside foe rendered it unsuitable as the capital of the organized kingdom of Northern Israel; and it was for this reason that 'Omri built Samaria on a site five miles to the north-west which his military eye selected as peculiarly adapted for a fortified capital city.

2. *the citizens of Shechem.* Heb. בַּעֲלֵי ש', lit. the *owners* of Shechem. The same term is used of the citizens of Jericho (Josh. 24 [11] E), of the high places of Arnon (Num. 21 [28] E*), of Gibe'ah (Judg. 20 [5]), of Ḳe'ilah (1 Sam. 23 [11.12]), and of Jabesh of Gile'ad (2 Sam. 21 [12]).

your bone and your flesh. The same expression is used in Gen. 29 [14] J, 2 Sam. 5 [1], 19 [12.13] (𝔐 [13.14]); cf. Gen. 2 [23] J. As belonging to

* Here, however, 𝔐 is almost certainly corrupt. We need a verb in place of בַּעֲלֵי—possibly בָּעֲרָה '*It* (the fire) *hath consumed* the high places, etc.' 𝔊 καὶ κατέπιεν seems to have read בִּלְּעָה or וַתְּבַלַּע.

flesh."' 3. So his mother's brethren spoke concerning him in the ears of all the citizens of Shechem all these words: and their heart inclined after Abimelech, for they said, 'He is our brother.' 4. And they gave him seventy shekels of silver from the temple of Ba'al-berith; and Abimelech hired therewith worthless and reckless men, and they followed him. 5. And he came unto his father's house at 'Ophrah, and slew his brethren the sons of Jerubba'al, even seventy men, upon one stone: but Jotham the youngest son of Jerubba'al was left, because he hid himself.

6. And all the citizens of Shechem and all Beth-millo

his mother's clan and not to his father's (cf. 8[31] *note* on 'his concubine, etc.'), Abimelech could claim that he was of one race with the Shechemites (the Bᵉnê-Ḥamor; cf. *v.*[28]), in contrast to Jerubba'al's other seventy sons who were of Israelite descent (cf. 8[30] *note* on 'that came out of his loins').

4. *from the temple, etc.* The temple, like that at Jerusalem (cf. 1 Kgs. 7[51], 14[26], 15[18], *al.*), contained a treasury in which were accumulated the gifts and fees of worshippers. Possibly also it may have been the repository of public treasure: cf. the ὀπισθόδομος of the Parthenon at Athens, and the *aerarium* of the Temple of Saturn at Rome (cited by Stu.).

Ba'al-berith. Cf. 8[33] *note.*

worthless. Heb. *rêḳîm,* lit. 'empty.' Cf. *ch.* 11[3] *note.*

reckless. Heb. *pōḥᵃzîm*, a participial form, occurs once again in Zeph. 3[4]; a cognate subs. *paḥᵃzûth* is found in Jer. 23[32]†; and subs. *páḥaz* in Gen. 49[4]†. In the latter passage it is said of Re'uben that he is '*páḥaz* ("wantonness," *i.e.* "wanton" or "unbridled") like water.' The cognate root in Ar. means 'to be insolent,' and in Aram. 'to be lascivious'—facts which suggest that the original idea may have been *to overpass bounds, be uncontrolled* (cf. the comparison with *water*). Cf. Hiph'îl *hiphḥîz* in Ecclus. 8[2], 19[2].

5. *upon one stone.* The statement (repeated in *v.*[18]) is striking. Possibly the stone may have been the official place of execution. The great stone used by Saul for the slaughter of cattle in conformity with sacrificial rule (1 Sam. 14[33 f.]) is compared by Mo., who thinks that 'the very conformity to the precautions taken in slaughtering animals in the open field shows that the motive was to dispose of the blood, in which was the life of his victims, in such a way that they should give him no further trouble. It is an instructive instance of the power of animistic superstitions.'

6. *Beth-millo.* Cf. *v.*[20]. A place of this name in the kingdom of Judah is mentioned in 2 Kgs. 12[20], 𝔋[21]. The Millo at Jerusalem

assembled themselves together, and went and made Abimelech king by the terebinth of ⸢the standing-stone⸣ which was in Shechem. 7. And men told Jotham, and he went and stood on the top of Mount Gerizim, and lifted up his voice, and cried, and said to them,

'Hearken unto me, Shechem's citizens,
That so God may hearken unto you.

formed part of the fortifications of the City of David; and if the word is rightly explained as from the causative stem of the verb *mālē* 'to be filled,' it must be understood as meaning something which *fills* or *banks up*, and so possibly an *earthwork*: cf. Talmudic *mûlîthā*, 'filled-up ground'; Bab. *mulû*, 'earthwork.' Probability, however, favours the view that the Jerusalem Millo was more than a simple earthwork—rather, perhaps, a massive fortification on the northern side of the city where such protection was specially needed. If, in our passage, Beth-millo has some such sense as 'House (place) of the fortress,' it may have been identical with 'the Tower of Shechem' (apparently distinct from the city of Shechem) mentioned in *v.* [46].

the standing stone. Reading הַמַּצֵּבָה with most moderns, in place of 𝔐 מֻצָּב which only occurs again in Isa. 29 [3] in the sense of a *palisade* or *entrenchment*. Possibly the *maṣṣēbhā* may have been the stone which tradition stated to have been set up by Joshua (Josh. 24 [26] E).

7. *stood on the top, etc.* Not actually on the summit, which is nearly 1000 feet above Shechem; but on one of the lofty precipices overhanging the city (cf. Thomson, *LB.* p. 473) from which he was able to make himself heard from below, and at the same time to beat a safe retreat after speaking.

8-15. The parable is intended to contrast the position of Jerubba'al and his sons with that of the mere adventurer Abimelech, and to predict that nothing but misfortune can result from the course which has been taken by the Shechemites. The olive, the fig-tree, and the vine, which are invited in succession to accept the kingship, represent men who, like Jerubba'al, possess a status which has been won by service for the public good. These have business more important than the acceptance and exercise of the office of kingship. On the other hand, the buckthorn, a low-growing and worthless shrub, is unequal to the task of affording shelter to the trees; but only too likely to be the cause of a forest-fire which may end in the destruction of all.

The parable is cast into a rhythmical form which is very well marked. After the summons to attend (*v.* [7b]), which forms a couplet of 3-beat stichoi, there follow four strophes, corresponding to the

8. Time was when the trees set out
To anoint o'er themselves a king;
And they said to the olive, "Reign thou over us."

9. But the olive said to them,
"Shall I leave my fatness
⌜whereby⌝ men honour God [],
And go to wave over the trees?"

applications to the four different trees. The first of these contains six stichoi; the second and third, five stichoi; and the fourth, seven stichoi. Most of the stichoi contain 3 beats; but stichos 3 of strophe 1 contains 4 beats, and in each strophe the response of the tree is given in a long stichos which exhibits 5, or $2+3$ beats (in strophe 4 perhaps 6, or $3+3$, beats). The English rendering is intended, as nearly as possible, to reproduce the rhythm of the original.*

8. *Time was . . . set out.* The Heb. says literally 'Going they went,' *i.e.* the action is introduced with some emphasis, much as we might say, '*Once upon a time* the trees went.'

the olive. The olive, the fig, and the vine are the staple products of Palestine, upon which its agricultural wealth and prosperity mainly depend. Cf. G. A. Smith, *Jerusalem*, i. pp. 299 ff.

9. *Shall I leave.* Lit. 'Am I to have left,' the Perfect tense being idiomatically used in Heb. 'to express astonishment at what appears to the speaker in the highest degree improbable': cf. Driver, *Tenses*, § 19.‡

whereby, etc. Reading בּוֹ in place of 𝔐 בִּי with 𝔊 ἐν ᾗ, 𝔙 'quâ,' 𝔗 דמניה 'from which,' and omitting וַאֲנָשִׁים. This latter, which spoils the rhythm by causing one beat too many, has obviously been introduced from *v.*[13a], 'which rejoiceth God and men.' The Imperfect יכבדו is impersonal; and is therefore rendered 'men honour.'

men honour God. The reference is to the use of oil in sacrifice and worship.

to wave. The Heb. *nua'* denotes the *swaying* motion of the

* The scheme adopted above agrees in nearly every detail with that offered by Sievers (*Metrische Studien*, i. pp. 388 f.), though worked out independently. The only difference is that Sievers makes the response of the trees in each case a 6-beat line; in *v.* [9aβ] by accepting 𝔐 as it stands, and in *vv.* [11aβ.13aβ] by inserting אני after החדלתי. Cf. also Rothstein, *ZA.* xxvi (1914), pp. 22 ff.

‡ The form הֶחֳדַלְתִּי is very anomalous. The most probable explanation of it is that חדלתי is the Perfect Ḳal, and that the *Ḳāmeṣ* of the first syllable, falling between the tone and the countertone, is weakened into *ḥāteph Ḳāmeṣ* through loss of emphasis: so G-K. § 63 *k*. The view that the form should be vocalized as a Hiph'il or Hoph'al is less probable.

10. Then said the trees to the fig-tree,
"Come *thou*, reign over us."

11. But the fig-tree said to them,
"Shall I leave my sweetness,
and my goodly produce,
And go to wave over the trees?"

12. Then said the trees to the vine,
"Come *thou*, reign over us."

13. But the vine said to them,
"Shall I leave my must,
which rejoiceth God and men,
And go to wave over the trees?"

branches in the wind; cf. Isa. 7 [2]. This is 'represented as a gesture of authority' (Mo.).

13. *must.* Heb. *tîrôš*, which is frequently coupled with *dāghān*, 'corn,' and *yiṣhār*, 'fresh oil,' as a natural product of the land, seems commonly to denote the grape-juice when first trodden out from the grapes. In Joel 2 [24], Prov. 3 [10] it is mentioned as filling the *vats*; and the term *yéḳebh*, 'vat,' denotes the trough into which the juice flowed after being trodden out in the *gath* or 'wine-press'; cf. *ch.* 6 [11] *note.* The connexion in which *tîrôš* is used in the present passage ('which rejoiceth, etc.') implies that it is regarded as an *exhilarating* beverage; and this suggests that the term may have been used of wine in some degree *fermented*, as it certainly is in Hos. 4 [11], where it is coupled with 'whoredom' and 'wine' (*yáyin*) as something which 'taketh away the heart' (*i.e.* the *intellect*). The fact is well known that the ancients were in the habit of making a light wine by checking the process of fermentation at an early stage; and it may be assumed that *tîrôš* may denote such a light wine, as well as the unfermented juice when first pressed out from the grapes.

The view that *tîrôš* denotes the *vine-fruit* and not a liquid is sufficiently refuted by the passages from Joel and Prov. already quoted. The grapes in their natural state were placed in the *gath*, and it was the *juice only* which flowed into the *yékebh*, the purpose of which was to separate the liquid from the solid matter. Cf. further Driver in *Amos* (*Camb. Bib.*), pp. 79 f.

God and men. Or possibly 'gods and men.' The allusion is to the use of wine in libations at sacrificial feasts, when the god, as well as his worshippers, was thought to be cheered by the beverage.

14. Then said all the trees to the buckthorn,
"Come *thou*, reign over us."

15. And the buckthorn said to the trees,
"If in truth ye wish to anoint
me as a king over you,
Come ye, take refuge in my shadow:
But if not, then come fire from the buckthorn,
And devour the cedars of Lebanon."

16. Now, therefore, if ye have dealt in truth and in integrity, in that ye have made Abimelech king,$^{\mathrm{R^{JE}}?}$ and if ye have dealt well with Jerubba'al and with his house, and if ye have done to him according to his deserts; 17. (in that my father fought for

15. *the buckthorn.* A variety of *Rhamnus* (so 𝔊, 𝔙), probably *Rhamnus palaestina*, a low and straggling bush which is common in the hill-country of Palestine.

Come ye, take refuge, etc. The irony of the parable culminates in the absurdity of the invitation, which the buckthorn issues in all seriousness.

16-20. The application fits somewhat loosely on to the parable; but such lack of strictly logical connexion as exists is a common characteristic of Oriental reasoning. The main point of the parable is that the Shechemites had chosen a king who could not command confidence and respect; but who, if treated otherwise than in good faith (באמת *v.*[15]), was capable of compassing their ruin. The application takes up the theme of the good faith of the Shechemites (באמת *v.*[16]), and points out that this has been markedly absent in their dealings with Jerubba'al, a man who was, in the highest degree, worthy of their confidence and gratitude. *A fortiori*, therefore, it was most unlikely that good relations between them and Abimelech would last for long; and, once they failed, the ruin of both parties was bound quickly to ensue. This moral is emphasized in the narrative which follows: *vv.* [23.24.56.57].

Doorn., Bu., Mo., and others improve the connexion between parable and application by marking *vv.*[16b-19a] as a later addition. The reference of באמת 'in truth' or 'in good faith,' in *v.*[16] is then the same as in *v.*[15], *i.e.* it refers to their good faith *towards Abimelech*: 'If ye have made Abimelech king, intending to act towards him in good faith, I congratulate you; but if not, the parable teaches you what to expect.'

16. *according to his deserts.* Lit. 'according to the dealing of his hands.'

you, and risked his life, and delivered you from the hand of Midian; 18. and *ye* have risen up against my father's house this day, and have slain his sons, even seventy men, upon one stone, and have made Abimelech, the son of his bond-maid, king over the citizens of Shechem, because he is your brother); 19. if ye have acted in truth and in integrity with Jerubba'al and with his house this day,[E] rejoice in Abimelech and let him also rejoice in you. 20. But if not, let fire come forth from Abimelech, and devour the citizens of Shechem and Beth-millo; and let fire come forth from the citizens of Shechem and Beth-millo, and devour Abimelech.' 21. And Jotham ran away and fled, and went to Be'er, and dwelt there, on account of Abimelech his brother.

22. And Abimelech was prince [RJE] over Israel [E] three years. 23. And God sent an evil spirit between Abimelech and the

17. *risked his life.* Lit. 'cast his life *in front*' or '(so as to be) *at a distance*' (cf. the use of מִנֶּגֶד in Deut. 32 [52], 2 Kgs. 2 [15], *al.*); *i.e.* exposed it to the utmost risk, without a thought of personal safety.

19. *his bond-maid.* The Heb. *'āmā* implies a slave-concubine, such as were Hagar to Abraham, and Zilpah and Bilhah to Ja'cob. As we have seen, however, *ch.* 8 [31] implies that Abimelech's mother was a free-woman, dwelling with her clan at Shechem. The misconception involved in the present passage is a point in favour of its later date.

20. *let fire come forth from the citizens, etc.* That the buckthorn, in destroying the other trees, would itself perish, is implied though not stated in the parable.

21. *Be'er.* The place intended may have been el-Bîreh, twenty-two miles south of Shechem and eight miles north of Jerusalem, which has been supposed to be the site of Be'eroth of Josh. 9 [17], *al.* The name, which means 'well,' was, however, doubtless of frequent occurrence in ancient times; just as its modern Ar. equivalent is at the present day.

22. *was prince over Israel.* On this statement, as implying a later conception than that of the original narrative, cf. *Introd.* to chapter, p. 267. The early narrative pictures Abimelech as possessing the authority of a local sheikh over Shechem and the neighbouring district.

23. *God sent an evil spirit.* Cf. the evil spirit sent by God upon Saul, 1 Sam. 16 [14], 18 [10]; and the spirit divinely commissioned to deceive Aḥab, in order that he might go up and fall at Ramoth-Gil'ead, 1 Kgs. 22 [19 ff.]. The view that God, from motives of displeasure,

citizens of Shechem; and the citizens of Shechem dealt treacherously with Abimelech. 24. ⌜To bring⌝ the violence done to the seventy sons of Jerubba'al, and to lay their blood upon Abimelech their brother, who slew them, and upon the citizens of Shechem, who encouraged him to slay his brethren. 25. And the citizens of Shechem set men in ambush upon the hilltops to his hurt, and they robbed all that passed by them on the way: and it was told Abimelech.

may incite men to their own ruin, is frequent in the O.T. Thus He hardens Pharaoh's heart (*hikbīdh*, lit. 'made heavy,' Ex. 10¹ J; *ḥizzēkh*, lit. 'made strong,' Ex. 4²¹, 10²⁰·²⁷ E or R^JE; 9¹², 11¹⁰, 14⁴·⁸·¹⁷ P; *hiḳšā*, lit. 'made hard *or* rigid,' Ex. 7³ P), and similarly He prompts Siḥon, king of the Amorites, to resist Israel in order that He may give him into their hands, Deut. 2³⁰. So too, in 2 Sam. 24¹, He is pictured as inciting David to a pernicious action; in Isa. 19²·¹⁴ He is said to stir up civil strife in Egypt, and to mingle a spirit of perverseness in the midst of her; and in Ezek. 14⁹ He deceives the false prophet to his own destruction.

24. *to bring*. Reading לְהָבִיא after 𝔊 τοῦ ἐπαγαγεῖν, with Grä., Oet., La., in order to avoid the very awkward change of subject in 𝔐 לָבוֹא and the following לָשׂוּם—'that the violence . . . might come, and to lay their blood, etc.' The alternative is to follow Mo., Bu., No., Oort in retaining 𝔐 לָבוֹא and deleting לָשׂוּם as the introduction of a scribe who missed the verb governing דָּמָם—'That the violence done to the seventy sons of Jerubba'al and their blood might come, etc.'

encouraged him. Lit. 'strengthened his hands.'

25. *set men in ambush, etc.* The Shechemites began to set armed bands in the mountains to rob the passing caravans, thus enriching themselves at the cost of Abimelech either by injuring his trade or by interfering with the dues which he was accustomed to exact for the safe conduct of merchandise through his territory. The force of the *Dativus incommodi* לוֹ 'to his hurt' is very idiomatic, and may be compared with the use of the preposition in *ch.* 3²⁸, 7²⁴, 12⁵, 'take the fords of the Jordan *to the detriment of*' (so, *against*) a foe. R.V. renders 'set liers in wait for him' (cf. *ch.* 16² וַיֶּאֶרְבוּ־לוֹ); and this is explained by Cooke, 'They hoped to catch Abimelech, who apparently was non-resident, and failing him, they plundered his friends.' This is very improbable.

and it was told Abimelech. The sequel to this statement follows in *v.*⁴³, after its repetition with slight variation in *v.*⁴²ᵇ, as already

26. J And Ga'al the son of ⌜'Obed⌝ came with his brethren, and they went over into Shechem; and the citizens of Shechem put their trust in him. 27. And they went forth into the field, and cut their vintage, and did the treading, and held a praise-festival,

explained (pp. 267 f.). Otherwise, if we assume the narrative of *vv.* 26 ff. to be of a part with *v.* 25, the information conveyed to Abimelech seems to have produced no result.

26. *Ga'al.* Wellh. vocalizes as גֹּעַל Go'al, comparing Ar. *ǵu'al* 'dung-beetle': *Isr. u. Jüd. Gesch.*[2], p. 44. Mo. (*SBOT.*) notes that (according to Lane) *ǵu'al* in Ar. is 'also applied to a black and ugly and small man, or to a contentious one.' This vocalization is favoured by Jos. Γυάλης (*Ant.* V. vii. 3 f.).

'Obed. Vocalizing עֹבֵד with 𝔙, in place of 𝔐 עֶבֶד. The same form is suggested by 𝔊B Ιωβηλ, which, as Mo. points out, is probably an uncial error ΙΩΒΗΛ for ΩΒΗΔ.* The form Ωβηδ occurs in HP. 30, Ωβιδ HP. 56. 𝔊AL Αβεδ supports 𝔐. The participial form 'Obed, 'server,' *i.e.* 'worshipper' of a deity, is well known as a proper name; whereas the substantive 'Ebed, 'servant,' though used in composition in 'Abdi, 'servant of Yah,' 'Abdiel, 'servant of God,' does not occur elsewhere by itself, and is unlikely to have been so used. A less probable view has been put forward by Kue. (*Ond.* § 19[5]) and others, who regard Ιωβηλ as pointing to an original יוֹבַעַל 'Yahweh is Ba'al'—a name which was offensive to later thought, and was therefore altered in contempt into 'Ebed, 'servant.' With this view is involved the supposition that Ga'al, as the son of a worshipper of Yahweh, must have been an *Israelite*, whose object was to stir up the Israelite population of Shechem against the rule of the Cana'anite Abimelech. This, however, is plainly refuted by the fact that the men whose ear Ga'al succeeds in gaining are 'the citizens of Shechem' (בַּעֲלֵי שׁ', *v.* 26), *i.e.* the same people who, according to *vv.* 2.6, made Abimelech king on the ground that he was their own kinsman ('your bone and your flesh,' *v.* 2).

27. *cut their vintage.* Here the plural of *kérem*, 'vineyard,' is used by metonymy of the *produce* of the vineyard, as is indicated by the fact that it is coupled with the verb *bāṣar*, which is the regular term for *cutting* grapes: cf. Deut. 24[21].

a praise-festival. If rightly connected with *hillēl*, 'to praise,' Heb. *hillûlîm* here seems to denote a festival of thanksgiving to the deity. The term occurs only once besides, in Lev. 19[24] H, in the phrase

* The form Ιωβηδ, for עוֹבֵד Ωβηδ, occurs in 𝔊A in 1 Chr. 2 12(twice).37.38, 11 47 (𝔊B Ιωβηθ), 26 7, 2 Chr. 23 1.

and went into the house of their god, and did eat and drink, and cursed Abimelech. 28. And Ga'al the son of ⌜'Obed⌝ said, 'Who is Abimelech, and who is Shechem, that we should serve him? ⌜should⌝ not the son of Jerubba'al and Zebul his officer ⌜serve⌝ the men of Ḥamor, the father of Shechem? but why

ḳōdeš hillûlîm, 'a holy thing of praise';* the reference here being to the produce of fruit-trees in the fourth year, when it was consecrated to Yahweh in token of thanksgiving. In Aram. *hillûlā* denotes a *marriage-song* (cf. the use of the Hoph'al *hullālû* in Ps. 78 [63]). Ar. *tahlîl* is used of a *shout of praise* (ordinarily applied to the pronouncing of the formula, 'There is no god but God'). This term, however, is connected by Wellh. with *hilâl* 'the new moon,' and is supposed by him to have been associated originally with the festival in honour of the new moon: cf. *Reste arab. Heidenthums*, p. 108.

28. *Who is Abimelech, etc.* Reading Imperfect יַעַבְדוּ in place of 𝔐 Imperative עִבְדוּ.

As the text stands in 𝔐, Ga'al's speech can only be rendered as in R.V.: 'Who is Abimelech and who is Shechem, that we should serve him? is not he the son of Jerubba'al? and Zebul his officer? serve ye the men of Ḥamor the father of Shechem: but why should we serve him?' Here 'Shechem' seems to stand as the rhetorical equivalent of 'Abimelech': cf. 1 Sam. 25 [10], 'Who is David, and who is the son of Jesse?' This is clearly the view adopted by 𝔊, which renders καὶ τίς ἐστιν υἱὸς Συχεμ for וּמִי שְׁכֶם. We can hardly assume, however, that a reading בֶּן־שְׁכֶם lies behind the 𝔊 rendering; since, as Robertson Smith (quoted by Mo.) has rightly pointed out, this expression is never used in the sense *Shechemite*: and that 'Shechem' by itself should be employed as a synonym of 'Abimelech' is incredible. The alternative explanation is to take 'Shechem' as an antithesis to 'Abimelech'—'we Shechemites'; but, *as the text stands*, this is excluded by the fact that there is no similar antithesis in the answer which Ga'al supplies to his own question (we should expect, 'is he not the son of J., etc., *while we are, etc.*'). Further, the Imperative עִבְדוּ 'serve ye' should naturally be followed by the 2nd person plur., 'but why should ye serve him'; and the occurrence of the 1st person, 'but why should we, etc.,' is at least very awkward. And again, in ולמה נעבדנו אנחנו the emphasis on the *subject* of the verb, as indicated by the personal pronoun, is very great—'but why should *we* serve him?' i.e. *we* in implied contrast to some other

* Probably we ought to place the *'athnaḥ* upon *ḳōdeš*, and render, 'And in the fourth year all its fruit shall be holy (lit. a holy thing), a praise-offering to Yahweh.'

should *we* serve him? 29. Oh, would that this people were under my hand! then would I remove Abimelech, ⌜and would say⌝ to Abimelech, "increase thine army, and come out."'

person or persons; whereas, if the earlier part of the sentence is correct as it stands in 𝔐, we should expect the emphasis to be thrown upon the *object* of the verb—'but why should we serve *him*?' (in contrast to 'the men of Ḥamor, etc.').

Adopting our simple emendation, the following explanation is plausible. The speech contrasts the antecedents of Abimelech and Shechem (*i.e.* the *citizens* of Shechem, or free-born Bᵉnê-Ḥamor)—'What is there in Abimelech's antecedents as compared with ours, that we (pure-blooded Bᵉnê-Ḥamor) should serve him (the half-breed)? Ought not the relations to be reversed, and Abimelech and his placeman Zebul to serve the hereditary owners of Shechem?' This is substantially the explanation of Mo., which has been adopted by Bu., La., etc.; except that these scholars read the Perfect עָבְדוּ in place of 𝔐 עִבְדוּ—'Did not the son of J. and Z. his officer serve the men of Ḥ., etc.?' *i.e.* 'he himself was formerly a subject of the old Ḥamorite nobility of Shechem.' It may be urged, however, against this reading that it implies that, prior to the election of Abimelech as king, the ruling class in Shechem had been the Bᵉnê-Ḥamor; whereas, as a matter of fact, *vv.*[1.2] represent the Bᵉnê-Ḥamor as acquiescing in time past in the rule of the Israelite Jerubbaʿal and his sons.

Upon the various other explanations and emendations of the passage which have been offered, cf. Mo. *Comm.*, and especially the same writer's very full note in *SBOT.* pp. 46 f. For the most part they depend upon the mistaken assumption that Gaʿal was an Israelite, and that the rebellion which he was fomenting was an upheaval of the Israelites against the rule of the Shechemite Abimelech. Upon this theory, cf. *note* on "ʿObed,' *v.*[26].

29. *under my hand.* Lit. 'in my hand,' *i.e.* subject to my authority.

and would say. Reading וְאֹמַר with 𝔊 καὶ ἐρῶ and most moderns in place of 𝔐 וַיֹּאמֶר '*And he said* to Abimelech.' It is clear from what follows that Gaʿal's words are merely a boast which was not carried into execution until his hand was forced, as related in *v.*[39].

Bu., however, thinks that, if the words 'and would say to A. "Increase thine army, etc.,"' really formed part of Gaʿal's boast, the *challenge* which they contain would have preceded and not followed its *result* as embodied in the words 'then would I remove A.' He therefore suggests that the words 'Increase thine army, etc.,' originally formed part of Zebul's message to Abimelech, as related in *vv.*[32 f.], and were later on erroneously inserted in their present position, with the introduction 'and he said to A.' This objection can hardly

30. And when Zebul, the governor of the city, heard the words of Ga'al the son of ⌜'Obed⌝; his anger was kindled. 31. And he sent messengers to Abimelech at ⌜Arumah⌝, saying, 'Behold,

be maintained. It is obvious that Ga'al may first have stated the main fact, viz. that he would soon get rid of Abimelech if he had the chance, and then have gone on to boast *how* he would attain this end—by challenging him to pitched battle.

30. *Zebul the governor of the city.* It is clear from the narrative that Abimelech did not *reside* at Shechem, but at the neighbouring city of Arumah: cf. *vv.* 31.41, with *note* on the former verse. Zebul appears to have been his representative at Shechem. Whether he was a Cana'anite or an Israelite cannot be determined.

31. *at Arumah.* Reading בַּאֲרוּמָה (or בָּארוּמָה; cf. *v.* 41) in place of 𝔐 בְּתָרְמָה. R.V.'s rendering of this latter, 'craftily,' is the interpretation of 𝔖P ܒܢܟܠܐ. It presupposes that a ἁπ. λεγ. *tormā*,* from the root *rāmā*, 'to deceive,' is used in place of the normal *mirmā* or *tarmîth* in the sense 'deceit.' A.V., 'privily,' follows the majority of the versions: 𝔊B ἐν κρυφῇ, 𝔙 'clam,' 𝔗 ברז, Ar. سِرًّا. This rendering likewise presupposes derivation from the root *rāmā*, upon the view that an expression properly meaning 'in deceit' is used in the sense 'in secret.' Thus A.V. adds marg. 'Heb. craftily.' So Rashi, Kimchi (first explanation), and the older commentators generally. Granted, however, that *be-tormā* is the equivalent of *be-mirmā*, such a sense as 'privily' is illegitimate; the only possible meaning of the statement being 'that Zebul sent to Abimelech a *deceptive*, and therefore an *erroneous* message' (Stu.). But this is excluded by the context, which makes it clear that the message embodied a true statement of affairs.

Kimchi (second explanation) and Levi ben-Gershon rightly divined that what we should expect is the name of the place at which Abimelech was residing; and observing that Arumah is named as his residence in *v.* 41, supposed that Tormah and Arumah are variant names of the same city. We may follow most moderns in concluding that תרמה represents a simple corruption of the latter name. 𝔊AL, 𝔖h μετὰ δώρων, *i.e.* בִּתְרוּמָה, suggests that the Greek translator may have used a text in which the ו was written as in בארומה, *v.* 41.

* The form תָּרְמָה is strange if derived from √רמה. König (*Lehrgebäude* I. ii. p. 193) groups it with תַּאֲנָה from √אנה Judg. 14 4 תּוּגָה from √יגה Prov. 10 1, 14 13, 17 21, Ps. 119 28.

Gaʿal the son of ⌜ʿObed⌝ and his brethren are come to Shechem, and, behold, ⌜they are stirring up⌝ the city against thee. 32. Now, therefore, arise by night, thou and the people who are with thee, and lie in wait in the field. 33. And in the morning, when the sun is up, thou shalt rise early and make an onset against the city: and, behold, he and the people who are with him will come forth unto thee, and thou shalt do to him as occasion serveth.'

34. And Abimelech arose, and all the people who were with him, by night, and they lay in ambush against Shechem in four bands. 35. And Gaʿal the son of ⌜ʿObed⌝ went out, and stood in the entry of the gate of the city; and Abimelech rose up, and

The site of Arumah is unidentified. The modern el-ʿOrmeh (written with ע and not א*, about five miles south-east of Shechem has been suggested.

are stirring up. Reading מְעִירִים with Frankenberg, Bu., Mo. (*SBOT.*), No., in place of 𝔐 צָרִים, which can only mean 'are besieging,' and is so rendered by the Versions. As Mo. points out, however, the Heb. construction is irregular,‡ and the sense 'are inciting to hostility,' which has been adopted by many commentators, is illegitimate.

33. *make an onset.* The Heb. verb *pāšaṭ*, which occurs again in our narrative in *v.*[44] (twice), expresses (as appears from the context in these and other occurrences) the making of a sudden and unexpected raid or attack. The connexion with Heb. *pāšaṭ* 'strip off' (one's garment) is obscure. The explanation offered by BDB—'*put off* (one's shelter), i.e. *make a dash* (from a sheltered place)'—is very precarious.§

as occasion serveth. Lit. 'as thy hand shall find.'

34. *four bands.* Lit. 'four *heads*': cf. p. 181. So *v.*[37b]. The expression, though most frequent in J, is used in the parallel narrative E in *vv.*[43f].

* Substitution of ע for א is seen in the modern 'Asḳalân for ancient 'Ashḳelon, and in 'Ânâ for 'Ono. The converse change is seen in 'Endûr for 'En-dor.

‡ We should expect צרים על העיר, not צרים את העיר. The only other occurrence of צור followed by את of the city is 1 Chr. 20[1] ויצר את רבה, where ‖ 2 Sam. 11[11] has the normal על.

§ New Heb. *pāšaṭ*, Aram. *pešaṭ*, mean 'to extend,' and also 'to make plain'; while Bab. *pašâṭu* has the sense 'expunge, obliterate,' *sc.*, *writing* by smearing or covering it with clay. The bond of connexion (if such exists) between the various senses of the root requires investigation.

the people who were with him, from the ambuscade. 36. And when Gaʿal saw the people, he said unto Zebul, 'Behold, people are coming down from the tops of the hills.' And Zebul said unto him, 'The shadow of the hills thou seest like men.' 37. And Gaʿal spoke yet again and said, 'Behold, people are coming down from the navel of the land, and one band is coming by way of the soothsayers' terebinth.' 38. And Zebul said unto

36. *The shadow, etc.* A taunt suggesting that 'his fears make him imagine enemies where there are none' (Mo.). Zebul's policy was to force Gaʿal's hand by insinuating that he dared not be as good as his word: cf. *v.*[38].

37. *the navel of the land.* The meaning of Heb. *ṭabbûr* is elucidated by new Heb. *ṭabbûr*, *ṭibbûr*, and Aram. *ṭibbûrā*, 'navel.' So 𝔊 ὀμφαλός, 𝔙 'umbilicus.' The other versions paraphrase: 𝔗 תוקפא 'stronghold,' 𝔖[P] ܐܘܡܢܗ̇ (meaning dubious), Ar. أقصي 'furthest part.' Rashi and Kimchi explain as a hill or elevation forming a stronghold, and R. Isaiah as a central position from which roads diverged. In Ezek. 38[12], the only other occurrence of the term in O.T., it is also used topographically, the inhabitants of the hill-country of Judah being described as 'those dwelling upon the navel of the earth,' *i.e.* (from the Israelite point of view) the most prominent and central part of the Universe (cf. Ezek. 5[5]). In the present passage the expression is obviously a closer definition of 'the tops of the mountains,' *v.*[36], and probably describes some neighbouring *height* (or even *heights*; for *v.*[37b] seems to indicate that the bands are coming from different directions) which was regarded as the central part of the main mountain-range of Canaʿan.

the soothsayers' terebinth. Heb. *'êlôn meʿônenîm*, some well-known tree which was the seat of the practice of divination. Gen. 12[6]J speaks of a tree called *'êlôn môrê*, 'terebinth of the oracle-giver' (cf. for *môrê*, *footnote* p. 206), which was also in the near neighbourhood of Shechem, and may have been identical with the tree mentioned in the present passage.

The form of soothsaying practised by the *meʿônēn* is uncertain. If the Heb. root *ʿānan* is connected with Ar. *ġanna*, 'to omit a hoarse nasal sound,' *meʿônēn* may denote the *murmurer* or *hoarsely humming one.* So Robertson Smith (*Journal of Philology*, xiv. pp. 119 ff.), who states that 'the characteristic utterance of the Arabic soothsayer is the monotonous rhythmical croon called *sağʿ*, properly the cooing of a dove.' According to Wellh., however (*Reste arab. Heidenthums*[2], p. 204), the term is to be explained, from Ar. *ʿanna*, 'to appear,' as meaning *dealer in phenomena.*

him, 'Where is now thy boast, in that thou saidst, "Who is Abimelech, that we should serve him?" Are not these the people whom thou didst despise? Pray, go forth now, and fight with them.' 39. So Gaʿal went forth before the citizens of Shechem, and fought with Abimelech. 40. And Abimelech pursued him, and he fled before him: and there fell down many slain up to the entry of the gate. 41. And Abimelech dwelt in Arumah: and Zebul drove out Gaʿal and his brethren, so that they should not dwell in Shechem.

42. R^JE And on the morrow, the people went out into the field: and men told Abimelech. 43. E And he took the people and divided them into three bands, and lay in ambush in the

38. *thy boast.* Lit. 'thy *mouth*.' The Heb. *pé*, 'mouth,' is used similarly in Ps. 49[13] (𝔐[14]), 'This is the way of them that have self-confidence, and of those who following them approve their speech (*mouth*).' Bab. *pû* 'mouth' frequently has the meaning 'speech.'

Are not these the people, etc. The situation is aptly summed up by Mo.: 'Zebul, by reminding Gaʿal, doubtless in the presence of many bystanders in that public place, of his former boasts, goads him into fighting. He had indeed no choice; if he declined the challenge, his prestige and influence in Shechem were gone.'

41. *And Abimelech dwelt, etc.* Abimelech returned to the city in which he was dwelling (possibly the narrative may originally have run וַיָּשָׁב א׳ וַיֵּשֶׁב בא׳ 'And A. *returned*, and dwelt in A.'), and did not trouble to follow up his victory, feeling no doubt that Zebul was capable of dealing with the situation. Gaʿal's incompetence as a leader having been sufficiently demonstrated by his shameful defeat, Zebul had no difficulty in expelling him from Shechem, together with the other members of his family or clan. Thus the disaffection in the city, of which Gaʿal was the author, comes (at least temporarily) to an end. 'The citizens of Shechem,' who had been persuaded by the impostor to adopt him as their leader, were no longer concerned to support him; and Zebul could scarcely have expelled him from the city without their aid, or, at any rate, without their acquiescence. The continuation of the narrative in *vv.*[42 ff.], which represents 'the people,' *i.e.* the same citizens of Shechem, as still at active hostilities with Abimelech 'on the morrow,' is thus not of a piece with the Gaʿal narrative. As we have seen (cf. *note* on *v.*[25b]), *vv.*[43 ff.] are clearly the proper continuation of the main narrative, which is broken off at *v.*[25], and resumed by the Redactor in *v.*[42].

42. *And on the morrow . . . field.* On this statement, as representing an attempt on the part of R^JE to harmonize his two narratives, cf. p. 268.

field; and he looked, and, behold, the people were coming out from the city; and he rose up against them, and smote them. 44. And Abimelech, and ⌜the band⌝ that was with him, made an onset, and stood in the entry of the gate of the city: and the two bands made an onset upon all who were in the field, and smote them. 45. And Abimelech fought against the city all that day; and he captured the city, and the people who were in it he slew: and he broke down the city, and sowed it with salt.

43. *the people were coming out, etc.* Coming out upon one of the predatory excursions described in *v.* [25].

44. *the band.* Reading sing. הָרֹאשׁ with 𝔙 and some MSS. of 𝔊, in place of 𝔐 plur. הָרָאשִׁים 'the bands.' According to *v.* [43a], Abimelech had divided his available forces into *three* bands, and according to *v.* [44b] *two* bands attacked the Shechemites in the field while Abimelech was seizing the gate of the city with his own contingent.

made an onset. Cf. *v.* [33] *note.*

45. *sowed it with salt.* A symbolic action, apparently intended to indicate that nothing thereafter was to live and flourish there. The turning of a fruitful land into a salt desert as the result of a curse is mentioned in Deut. 29 [23], Ps. 107 [34]; cf. Jer. 17 [6], and the story of the destruction of the cities of the plain in Gen. 19 J. Ros. and commentators after him refer to Pliny, *Hist. Nat.* xxxi. *ch.* 7; Virgil, *Georg.* ii. 238, as mentioning the well-known fact of the infertility of a salt soil. More to the point, in connexion with our passage, is Tiglath-pileser I.'s account of his destruction of the city of Ḫunusa (*Annals*, col. vi. 14): 'The three great walls of their city, which with burnt brick were strongly built, and the whole of the city I laid waste, I destroyed, I turned into heaps and ruins; and salt (?) thereon I sowed';* cf. Budge and King, *Annals of the Kings of Assyria*, i. p. 79; *KB.* i. pp. 36 f. Scheiden, *Das Salz*, p. 95 (quoted in *EB.* 4250) cites the tradition that Padua was sown with salt by Attila, and Milan by Barbarossa.

Robertson Smith (*Religion of the Semites* [2], p. 454, *n* [1]) adopts a

* The word rendered 'salt' is (*abnu*) ṢI. PA; and unfortunately we cannot be sure of the meaning of ṢI. PA (or ṢI. ḪAD), which is most likely the ideographic form in which an otherwise unknown Assyrian word is written; though the rendering above adopted appears to be the most probable. The Determinative Prefix *abnu*, 'stone,' marks the substance as a *mineral*; and there is a variant reading plur. *abnê*, 'stones' (lumps of salt?). The Assyr. *azrû*, 'I sowed (it),' is the same verb as is used in our passage by the Heb., *way-yizra'ĕhā*. The reference in the Annals of Ašurbanipal (col. vi. 79; cf. *KB.* ii. pp. 206 f.) cited in *EB.* 4250 from Gunkel, *Genesis* [2], p. 187, which is supposed by Gunkel to refer to the same ceremony, is of too doubtful significance to be quoted.

46. And when all the citizens of the tower of Shechem heard it, they entered into the crypt of the temple of El-berith. 47. And it was told Abimelech that all the citizens of the tower of Shechem had gathered themselves together. 48. And Abimelech went up to Mount Ṣalmon, he and all the people who were

different explanation, supposing that the salt was used as a symbol that the city was *consecrated* to the deity as a devoted thing (*ḥérem*; cf. *note* on *ch.* 1 17), since the sprinkling with salt has a religious meaning, as a symbol of consecration, in Ezek. 43 24. This parallel, which refers to the sprinkling of a whole burnt-offering with salt, must be deemed of doubtful validity.

46. *the tower of Shechem.* This stood, apparently, apart from the city of Shechem, and was probably (like the tower of Penuel, *ch.* 8 9.17) the stronghold of an unwalled hamlet.

crypt. Heb. *ṣᵉrîaḥ.* The meaning of the term is somewhat obscure. In its only other occurrence in the O.T., 1 Sam. 13 6, it seems to denote an *underground chamber*, natural or artificial;* and this sense is borne out by the use of *ṣᵉrîḥā* in the Nabataean inscriptions to denote a tomb hewn out of the rock: cf. Euting, *Nabatäische Inschriften*, 15 3.4. In Ar. the cognate word *ḍarîḥ* denotes '*a trench*' or *oblong excavation in the middle of a grave*, in distinction from *laḥd* (an excavation in the *side*); or it may denote *the grave altogether*, as in the benediction 'May God illumine his grave!' (*ḍarîḥahu*): cf. Lane *s.v.*

How such a rock-hewn crypt could have been set on fire is not evident. Possibly the door may have been in the side of a rock, with steps descending into the interior; and, the faggots being piled *against* this door, the fire burnt it through and suffocated the refugees. Or, if we explain (as we legitimately may do) that the faggots were placed *upon* (על) the crypt, we may picture a flat trap-door on the top of which the fire was laid, so that the mass of burning material eventually fell upon the people in the crypt beneath.

A.V., R.V., in giving the more general rendering 'hold,' seem to depend upon 𝔊AL ὀχύρωμα, 𝔙 (*v.* 49) 'praesidium.' Abulwalid compared the Ar. *ṣarḥ*, 'a lofty building or chamber *standing apart*' (from *ṣaraḥa* 'to be unmixed, clear,' here used in the sense 'to *stand clear*'); and hence the sense 'citadel' or 'tower' was adopted by many of the mediæval and earlier modern commentators. Most recent scholars adopt the explanation which is given above.

48. *Mount Ṣalmon.* The name Ṣalmon seems to mean 'the shady'

* In this passage *ṣᵉrîḥîm* are coupled with *bôrôth*, 'cisterns,' *i.e.* rock-hewn receptacles for water which, in a disused state, might form effectual hiding-places.

with him; and Abimelech took an axe ⌜⌝ in his hand, and cut a bundle of brushwood, and took it up and placed it on his shoulder; and he said unto the people who were with him, 'What ye have seen me do, make haste, do likewise.' 49. And all the people also cut each his bundle ⌜⌝: and they went after Abimelech, and placed them against the crypt, and set the crypt on fire over them: so all the men of the tower of Shechem died also, about one thousand men and women.

50. And Abimelech went unto Tebeṣ, and encamped against Tebeṣ, and captured it. 51. Now there was a strong tower in the midst of the city, and thither fled all the men and women,

—probably a reference to the woods which (as the context shows) clothed its sides.*

an axe. Reading sing. הַקַּרְדֹּם with 𝔊^AL, 𝔖^h, 𝔙, 𝔖^P, in place of 𝔐 plur. הַקַּרְדֻּמּוֹת 'axes.' The Heb. idiom says '*the* axe,' the Definite Article being so used with familiar objects which are understood elements in the situation: cf. Davidson, *Syntax*, § 21 *d*; G-K. § 126 *s*; *NHTK*. p. 1. The idiom may be illustrated in English by the way in which we speak of 'boiling *the* kettle'—never 'boiling *a* kettle.' The emendation קַרְדֻּמּוֹ 'his axe,' adopted by Mo., Bu., No., Kent, Cooke, is much less idiomatic; apart from the fact that 'his' is not pre-supposed by any of the versions above cited.

49. *his bundle.* Reading fem. שׂוֹכָתוֹ (cf. *v.*[48]) in place of 𝔐 שׂוֹכֹה, which, as vocalized, is intended to convey the same sense, being regarded as a masc. form שׂוֹךְ with suffix of the 3rd masc. sing. (on the suffix-form; cf. G-K. §§ 7*c*, 91*e*). Probably 𝔐 should be vocalized שׂוֹכָה '*a* bundle,' which may be the original text.

against the crypt. Or possibly, '*upon* the crypt'; cf. *note* on *v.*[46].

50. *Tebeṣ.* The modern Ṭûbâs, twelve miles N.E. of Shechem, has been identified by Rob. (*BR.*[3] ii. p. 317) as the site which Eusebius gives as the ancient Tēbēṣ; which is described by him as thirteen Roman miles from Neapolis (Shechem) in the direction of Scythopolis

* That the meaning 'to be dark *or* shady' belongs to the root צלם is clear from the subst. צַלְמוּת (for 𝔐 צַלְמָוֶת) 'deep shade,' and the Bab. root *ṣalâmu*, 'to be dark *or* black.' Probably Heb. צֶלֶם 'image' properly means 'shadow' (so-called as being *black* in a land of strong lights and shades), since an image is the *shadow* or *replica* of that which it represents. Cf. Delitzsch, *Prolegomena*, p. 141; *KAT.*[3] p. 475, *n*[6]. BDB.'s explanation of צֶלֶם as 'something *cut out*,' based on Ar. *ṣalama*, 'to cut off' (properly 'to extirpate by amputation') is very far-fetched.

even all the citizens of the city, and shut themselves in, and went up on to the roof of the tower. 52. And Abimelech came unto the tower, and fought against it, and he drew near to the door of the tower to burn it with fire. 53. And a certain woman cast an upper millstone upon the head of Abimelech, and brake his skull. 54. And he called quickly unto the lad who bore his armour, and said to him, 'Draw thy sword and despatch me, lest they say of me, "A woman slew him."' So his lad thrust him through, and he died. 55. And when the men of Israel saw that Abimelech was dead, they went every man to his place.

(Bethshe'an), *OS.* 262 [44]. This identification is accepted by some modern writers (so, most recently, Cooke); but must, on philological grounds, be deemed highly precarious.*

53. *an upper millstone.* Heb. *pélaḥ rékhebh*, lit. 'cleft (stone) of riding,' so-called as *riding* upon the lower stone (*pélaḥ taḥtîth*, Job 41[24], 𝔐 [16]). The complete mill is termed *rêḥáyim.* The hand-mill still used in Palestine is formed of two flat stones: a peg in the centre of the lower one corresponds to a hole in the upper, which is thus kept in place; and the upper being turned by a wooden handle, the corn which is placed between the two stones is ground. The diameter of the mill is usually about eighteen inches, the upper stone being of smaller diameter than the lower and two or three inches thick. These mills are usually turned by women, the performance of such work by men being regarded as a badge of degradation: Judg. 16[21], Lam. 5[13], Jer. 52[11] (𝔊). Cf. Kennedy in *EB.* 3091 ff.

54. *Draw thy sword, etc.* Similarly, Saul commands his armour-bearer to slay him when he perceives that otherwise he must fall into the hands of the Philistines: 1 Sam. 31 [4].

despatch me. Heb. *môthēth*, the causative and *intensive* form of *mûth*, 'to die,' always has the sense 'to kill outright.' Cf. especially 1 Sam. 14 [13], where it is stated that the Philistines 'fell before Jonathan, and his armour-bearer despatched them (*m^e môthēth*) after him.'

55. *the men of Israel.* Abimelech, in succeeding to the power and influence exercised by Jerubba'al and his seventy Israelite sons, may be supposed to have ruled over Cana'anites and Israelites alike in the district about Shechem. The feelings of the Israelites against the B^e nê-Ḥamor of Shechem and the Cana'anites of the neighbouring

* There is correspondence of one consonant only between Tēbēṣ and Ṭûbâs; and the *û* in the latter name ought naturally to represent ו in Heb. The modern Ar. form would accurately correspond to a Heb. טוּבָשׁ, rather than תֵּבֵץ; cf. Cheyne, *EB.* 5033.

56. Thus God requited the wickedness of Abimelech which he had done to his father, in slaying his seventy brethren: 58. And the wickedness of the men of Shechem did God requite upon their head: and there came upon them the curse of Jotham the son of Jerubbaʽal.

cities must have been intensified by the fact that the assassination of Jerubbaʽal's Israelite sons was a Canaʽanite movement (cf. p. 267); and, hostile at heart as they must have been to Abimelech as the Canaʽanite nominee, they would naturally support him when it came to a conflict with the Canaʽanites: and they probably formed the bulk, if not the whole, of his army. Cf. Mo. *ad loc.*

56. *Thus God requited, etc.* It is characteristic of E to draw a religious moral from the facts of history.

10. 1-5. *The 'Minor' Judges: Tolaʽ and Ja'ir.*

The so-called 'minor' Judges, Tolaʽ and Ja'ir (10 [1-5]), Ibṣan, Elon, and ʽAbdon (12 [8-15]) appear scarcely to stand upon the same level as historical personages with Ehud, Baraḳ, Gideʽon, Abimelech, and Jephthaḥ. Tolaʽ is said to have been 'the son of Pu'ah the son of Dodo, a man of Issachar,' and to have 'dwelt in Shamir in the hill-country of Ephraim.' In Gen. 46 [13] P both Tolaʽ and Pu'ah appear as sons, *i.e.*, doubtless, *clans* of Issachar; and this is also the case in Num. 26 [23] P, 1 Chr. 7 [1ff]. Ja'ir the Gileʽadite, whose thirty sons had thirty towns called Ḥavvoth-Ja'ir, is the same as Ja'ir the son or *clan* of Manasseh who made conquests in Gileʽad which were afterwards known as Ḥavvoth-Ja'ir (*i.e.* 'the tent-villages of Ja'ir'), according to Num. 32 [41] J, Deut. 3 [14], 1 Kgs. 4 [13]. Elon is described as 'the Zebulonite'; and in Gen. 46 [14] P Elon is a son of Zebulun, and, according to Num. 26 [26] P, founder of the *clan* of the Elonites. That Ibṣan and ʽAbdon are also clan-names may be inferred. We know that Ja'ir's thirty sons represent thirty village-settlements: when we read that Ibṣan had thirty sons and thirty daughters, and that ʽAbdon had forty sons and thirty grandsons, it is reasonable to infer that the writer's meaning is the same in these cases also. The statement that Ibṣan made outside-marriages for his daughters, and brought in wives for his sons, doubtless refers to the numerous alliances and connexions with other clans which were formed by branches of the clan of Ibṣan.

It is a further question whether these 'minor' Judges were included in the historical scheme of R^{E2}. In the survey of the course of Israel's history during this period which forms the introduction to his book in *ch.* 2 [11-23] (cf. pp. 52 ff.), R^{E2} traces the periods of oppression by foreign foes to Israel's declension from the service of Yahweh, and regards the raising up of the Judges as deliverers as an act of condescension on Yahweh's part when punishment has been meted out. This view of history is faithfully followed out by the editor in the cases of the 'major' Judges; but in the brief notices of the 'minor' Judges mention of Israel's defection from Yahweh, and the naming of the particular foes into whose power they were delivered, are conspicuously absent. Of Tola' it is simply stated that he 'arose after Abimelech to save Israel'; and of Ja'ir even more briefly that he 'arose after him.' Ibṣan, who is made to succeed Jephthaḥ, is said to have 'judged Israel after him'; and the same formula is used of Elon and 'Abdon. Thus it may be inferred with great probability that the notices of the 'minor' Judges were inserted into the book subsequently to the redaction of R^{E2}. The purpose of the interpolator may have been to raise the number of the Judges to *twelve*, and, so far as possible, to make them representative of the twelve tribes of Israel. Thus we have

'Othniel	Judah.
Ehud	Benjamin.
Baraḳ	Naphtali.
Gide'on	West Manasseh.
Abimelech	
Tola'	Issachar.
Ja'ir	East Manasseh.
Jephthaḥ	Gad.
Ibṣan	?
Elon	Zebulun.
'Abdon	Ephraim.
Samson	Dan.

If the Bethleḥem which is mentioned as the native city of Ibṣan (*ch.* 12 $^{8.10}$) is the Bethleḥem which is assigned to Zebulun in Josh. 19 ^{15} P, *i.e.* the modern Bêt Laḥm seven miles west-north-west of Nazareth, this city seems to have been on the border between Zebulun and Asher; and thus Ibṣan may have been regarded as the representative of Asher. Re'uben and Sime'on are unrepresented, while Abimelech properly gives a second representative to West Manasseh; still, the scheme is sufficiently complete to make it probable that the theory above suggested was in the mind of the editor who added the notices of the 'minor' Judges.

Who this editor was may be inferred from the fact that his book contained the story of Abimelech, and that this usurper was counted by him as one of the Judges: cf. *ch.* 10 ^{1}. He can hardly have been other than the editor who reinserted the narrative of Abimelech into R^{E2}'s book, *i.e.* the late editor whom we have characterized as R^{P}.

For the grounds upon which the notice of Shamgar in *ch.* 3 ^{31} is to be regarded as still later than the work of R^{P}, cf. p. 76.

10. 1. R[P] And after Abimelech there arose to save Israel Tolaʿ the son of Pu'ah, the son of Dodo, a man of Issachar;

10. 1. *Pu'ah.* Heb. פּוּאָה; so 1 Chr. 7 [1]. The form פֻּוָּה Puwwah is given by Gen. 46 [13], Num. 26 [23]. The name is probably the equivalent of Ar. *fuwwah*, which denotes the species of madder called *Rubia tinctorum*, L., from the root of which a red dye is derived* (cf. Lane *s.v.*; Löw, *Pflanzennamen*, p. 251); whereas Tôlaʿ, which means 'worm' in Ex. 16 [20] (more commonly fem. *Tôlá'ath*, cf. Bab. *tultu*), is used in Isa. 1 [18], Lam. 4 [5] to denote the crimson dye called cochineal (properly the *insect* from which the dye is prepared; so, more commonly, fem. *Tôlá'ath*). The coincidence suggests that kindred clans adopted kindred totem-objects.

Dodo. This name occurs again in 2 Sam. 23 [9] *Ḳ*ᵉ*rê* = 1 Chr. 11 [12]; 2 Sam. 23 [24] = 1 Chr. 11 [26]. 2 Sam. 23 [9] *Kt.* gives the form Dodai; and similarly 𝔊[BAL] reads Δωδαι in || 1 Chr. The same form is favoured by the evidence of 𝔊 in 2 Sam. 23 [24] and || 1 Chr. Dodai occurs in 1 Chr. 27 [4], where the reference seems to be to the same man as is named in 1 Chr. 11 [12] (called 'the Aḥoḥite' in both passages). The form Dodo may be paralleled by Dûdu, the name of an official (probably a Canaʿanite) in the service of the Pharaʿoh, which occurs in the T.A. Letters (cf. Knudtzon, Nos. 158, 164); cf. also דדא Dada in Palmyrene (de Vogüé, *La Syrie centrale*, 93; Cooke, *NSI.* p. 301), and the names from cuneiform texts cited in *KAT.*[3] p. 483.

The meaning of the name has been the subject of some discussion. The most probable theory regards both Dodo and Dodai as hypocoristic abbreviations of a fuller form such as Dodiel or Dodiyya (דּוֹדִיָּה; cf. דּוֹדָוָהוּ Dodavahu, 2 Chr. 20 [37]). The element *Dôd* is then the same as the subst. which means 'uncle' on the father's side (used in 1 Sam. 14 [50], 2 Kgs. 24 [17], *al.*), properly, it may be assumed, 'object of *love*' (so in Heb. the word often has the meaning 'beloved,' which is also seen in Bab. *dâdu*). Thus Dodo, Dodai, may mean 'the god is uncle' (i.e. *kinsman* or *patron* of the bearer of the name) ‡; or, conceivably, 'Beloved of the god': cf., for the latter sense, the name יְדִידְיָה Jedidiah, 'Beloved of Yah,' 2 Sam. 12 [25]; and David, *i.e.*, probably, 'Beloved' (by God). Cf. Cheyne, *EB.* 1122; Gray, *Heb. Proper Names*, pp. 60 ff. A passage of interest in this connexion is found in the Inscription of Meshaʿ, where the Moabite king, in relating his success against Israel east of Jordan, says, 'The king of Israel had built ʿAṭaroth for himself: and I fought against the city and took it; and I slew the whole of it, even the people of the city, as a gazing-

* Eusebius explains Puah ἐρυθρά, *OS.* 200 [98]; Jerome, *rubrum*, *ib.* 6 [21].

‡ Cf. the South Arabian name Dâdi-kariba, 'My (divine) kinsman has (*or* is) blessed'; Hommel, *AHT.* p. 86.

and he dwelt in Shamir in the hill-country of Ephraim. 2. And he judged Israel twenty and three years, and died, and was buried in Shamir.

3. And after him there arose Ja'ir the Gile'adite; and he judged Israel twenty and two years. 4. And he had thirty sons who rode on thirty ass-colts; and they had thirty ⌜cities⌝ (they

stock unto Chemosh and unto Moab. And I captured thence the altar-hearth of דודה, and dragged it before Chemosh in Ḳeriyyoth' (*Moabite Stone*, ll. 10-13). Here the word דודה should perhaps be vocalized דּוֹדָהּ 'its (divine) Patron,' *i.e.* the God of the city * (Yahweh? Cf. ll. 17 f., where, after taking the city of Nebo, Mesha' states that he took the vessels of Yahweh, and dragged them before Chemosh). Failing this explanation, דודה must be vocalized *Dôdô*, and regarded as the proper name of a deity, which may (on this hypothesis) perhaps be recognized in the O.T. proper names above discussed: cf. Baethgen, *Beiträge*, p. 234; *KAT.*³ p. 225.

𝔊 υἱὸς πατραδέλφου αὐτοῦ, 𝔙 'patrui Abimelech,' 𝔖ᴾ ܒܪ ܕܕܗ, treat Dodo, not as a proper name, but as the subst. meaning 'uncle' with suffix of the 3rd masc. sing.‡: 'son of his (*i.e.* Abimelech's) uncle.' Such an explanation is excluded by the fact that, while Tola' is expressly described as 'a man of Issachar,' Abimelech, so far as he was Israelite in extraction, belonged to Manasseh. Several minuscules of 𝔊 (grouped by Mo. as 𝔊ᴹ) offer the reading καὶ ἀνέστησεν ὁ Θεὸς . . . τὸν Θωλα υἱὸν Φουα υἱὸν Καριε (or Καρηε) πατραδέλφου αὐτοῦ, omitting the words 'a man of Issachar.' Here Καριε may represent the name קָרֵחַ Ḳareaḥ: cf. 2 Kgs. 25 [23], Jer. 40 [8], *al.* The origin of this text is wholly obscure.

Shamir. The site is unknown. 𝔊ᴬᴸ ἐν Σαμαρείᾳ.

4. *who rode, etc.* A similar statement is made in *ch.* 12 [14] with regard to 'Abdon's descendants. The detail is mentioned as a badge of rank: cf. *ch.* 5 [10a].

cities. Reading עָרִים with all Versions, in place of 𝔐 עֲיָרִים 'ass-colts,' which has arisen from accidental imitation of the same word preceding.

* In the difficult expression in Am. 8 [14] 'as *the way* of Be'ersheba' liveth!' דֶּרֶךְ 'way' is plausibly emended by Winckler (*AF.* i. p. 194 f.) into דֹּדְךָ. This gives the sense 'As thy (divine) patron liveth, O Be'ersheba',' an excellent parallel to 'As thy god liveth, O Dan': cf. 𝔊 ὁ θεός σου in place of דֶּרֶךְ.

‡ This explanation is also offered by 𝔙, 𝔖ᴾ in 2 Sam. 23 [9.24], 1 Chr. 11 [12.26], and by a 𝔊 doublet in 2 Sam. 23 [9.24].

are called Ḥavvoth-Ja'ir unto this day), which are in the land of Gile'ad. 5. And Ja'ir died, and was buried in Ḳamon.

Ḥavvoth-Ja'ir. Probably 'the tent-villages of Ja'ir.' Heb. *ḥawwā* is explained from Ar. *ḥiwâ'*, 'a group of tents near together.' Most likely the Ḥivvites, who are mentioned among the peoples of Cana'an, obtained their name as originally inhabitants of such primitive village-communities.

which are in the land of Gile'ad. So Num. 32^{41}, 1 Kgs. 4^{13}, 1 Chr. 2^{22}. In Deut. 3^{14}, Josh. 13^{30} R^{D} the Ḥavvoth-Ja'ir are incorrectly localized in *Bashan.* On the origin of this error, cf. Driver, *Deuteronomy* (*ICC.*) p. 55.

5. *Ḳamon.* Polybius (v. lxx. 12) mentions a Kamûn east of Jordan as captured by Antiochus the Great:—καὶ προάγων, παρέλαβε Πελλαν, καὶ Καμουν, καὶ Γεφρουν. The name of Ḳamon is very possibly preserved in the modern Ḳumêm, a village six and a half miles west of Irbid. About one mile north-west of Ḳumêm, a ruined site Ḳamm may correspond to the ancient city. It should be noted that the name Γεφρουν, which is coupled with Καμουν, *i.e.* doubtless the Ephron (עֶפְרוֹן) of 1 Macc. 5^{46}, seems to be preserved in the Wâdy el-Ġafr which lies some two miles north of Ḳamm. Cf. Buhl, *Geogr.* p. 256.

10. 6–16. *Further apostasy receives its punishment.*

Besides the Commentaries, etc., cited throughout the book, cf. Stade, *ZATW.*, i. (1881) pp. 341-343; Stanley A. Cook, *Critical Notes on Old Testament History* (1907), pp. 24 ff., 33 ff., 48 f., 127 f.

This is a section which raises interesting questions in connexion with the original composition of the history of the Judges. As it now stands, it was clearly intended by R^{E2} as an introduction both to the narrative of the oppression of the 'Ammonites and the raising up of Jephthaḥ as judge (*ch.* 10^{17}-12^{7}), and to that of the oppression of the Philistines and the raising up of Samson as judge (*chs.* 13 ff.): cf. *v.*^{7}. The ordinary formulæ of the pragmatic scheme of R^{E2} may be traced in full in *v.*^{6} (omitting the specification of 'the gods of' various nations), *vv.*$^{7.10a}$: cf. the type-form given on p. 54. On the face of it, however, it is obvious that the whole section cannot have been *composed by* R^{E2} for the purpose which it now fulfils in his book. There is no reason why, at this particular point in his narrative, he should depart from his ordinary practice of introducing the history of each particular judge singly and in his regular brief form; and, as a matter of fact, the repetition of his ordinary formula at the beginning of the Samson-narrative, *ch.* 13^{1}, renders the mention of Israel's apostasy leading to the oppression of the Philistines ($10^{6a.7b\alpha}$) superfluous in *ch.* 10. Further, it should not escape notice that, if 10^{6-16} was actually composed by R^{E2} as an introduction to the narratives of the oppression of the 'Ammonites and Philistines *in that order*, he would scarcely have employed the opposite order in *v.*^{7b}; 'and he sold them into the hand of the Philistines and into the hand of the children of ʿAmmon.'

Closer examination reveals the fact that the phraseology of the section is in many points identical with that which characterizes the later strata of E; especially as seen in Josh. 24, Judg. 6^{7-10}, 1 Sam. 7^{2-4}, 10^{17-19}, 12. The most striking phrases are 'we have sinned' (חטאנו) *vv.*$^{10.15}$, as in 1 Sam. 7^{6}, 12^{10}; 'oppress' (לחץ) *v.*^{12}, as in Judg. 6^{9}, 1 Sam. 10^{18}; 'foreign gods' (אלהי הנכר) *v.*^{16}, as in Josh. $24^{20.23}$, 1 Sam. 7^{3}; 'put away' (הסיר), in reference to the 'foreign gods,' *v.*^{16}, as in Josh. $24^{20.23}$, 1 Sam. 7^{3} (on these phrases as generally characteristic of E^2, cf. Driver, *LOT.*^{9} p. 177); as well as the retrospect of Israel's past history, especially the deliverance from Egypt, *vv.*$^{11.12}$, as in Josh. $24^{6f.}$, Judg. 6^{8}, 1 Sam. 10^{18}, $12^{6.8}$.

Thus it may be inferred that we have, in 10^{6-16}, a section originally belonging to E's history of the Judges, which was incorporated by R^{JE} into his composite history, and then used by R^{E2} in place of (or it may be, in combination with) his ordinary brief introductory formula. The purpose which this section fulfilled in E's history seems to be indicated by the reference to the Philistines as the oppressors in *v.*^{7b} (so Bu., *RS.* p. 128); the fact that this people is mentioned first probably indicating that the reference to the children of ʿAmmon which follows is a later addition, due to R^{JE}, and intended to make the section serve as an introduction to *ch.* 10^{17}-12^{7} as well as to *chs.* 13 ff.

But, if this is so, this introduction from E to the narrative of a Philistine oppression cannot have referred to the Samson-story as given in Judges, since this is derived wholly from J (cf. p. 336)—apart from the fact that a section in which the religious motive is so fully developed can never have been designed to introduce a story of which the crude and primitive character is almost unrelieved. It is scarcely open to doubt that E's history of the Philistine oppression is that which now forms one strand of the composite narrative in 1 Sam.; and the proper conclusion to this narrative, as it took form under the same hand (E^2), is found in the account of the deliverance from the Philistines as effected by Samuel, which is now contained in 1 Sam. 7 (so Mo., p. 276; S. A. Cook).

It is impossible accurately to determine how far R^{E2} felt it necessary to supplement his source; since, as we have noticed in the *Introduction* (p. xlvi ff.), his phraseology is modelled throughout upon that of E^2, and therefore cannot with certainty be differentiated from it. Probably he was responsible for the summary statement of Israel's apostasy which opens *v.*^{6}; but the remaining formulæ which normally we associate with his pragmatic introductions were most likely already existent in the work of E^2. Thus, for example, *v* ^{7} down to 'Philistines,' which is cast in the well-known formulæ of R^{E2}, must,

6. R^{E2} And the children of Israel again did that which was evil in the sight of Yahweh, E^2 and served the Baʿals, and the ʿAshtarts, R^P and the gods of Aram, and the gods of Ṣidon, and the gods of Moab, and the gods of the children of ʿAmmon, and the gods of the Philistines; E^2 and they forsook Yahweh, and served him not. 7. And the anger of Yahweh was kindled against Israel, and he sold them into the hand of the Philistines, R^{JE} and into the hand of the children of ʿAmmon. 8. E^2 And they brake and crushed the children of Israel in that year, R^{JE} eighteen years, even all the children of Israel who were beyond Jordan in the land of the Amorites, which is in Gileʿad. 9. And

if our theory of the origin of the section be correct, have already existed in E's introduction to the Philistine oppression.

The passages in *vv.*[7-9] which serve to make the section suitable as an introduction to the narrative of the oppression of the ʿ*Ammonites* must be due to the Redactor who placed it before 10[17]-12[7], *i.e.*, we may assume, R^{JE}. The references in *v.*[6] to the gods of various nations, and in *vv.*[11.12] to various nations *besides* Egypt as oppressors (some of them, *e.g.* the Philistines and the ʿAmmonites, out of place in a retrospect of past oppressions *and deliverances*) must be due to a much later hand, to whom the somewhat lengthy record of apostasy and its outcome seemed adapted for the insertion of such detailed lists.

10. 6. *the Baʿals and the ʿAshtarts.* Cf. *ch.* 2[13] *notes.*

8. *they brake.* Heb. *rāʿaṣ* (once again in O.T., Ex. 15[6b]) perhaps = *raḫâṣu* in the T.A. Letters, which Zimmern (*KAT.*[3] p. 653) regards as a Canaʿanism; cf. Kn. 127, l. 33; 141, l. 31, 'and may the bow-troops of the King my lord . . . shatter (*ti-ra-ḫa-aṣ*) the head of his enemies.'

in that year, eighteen years. As Mo. remarks, such a collocation is impossible. The eighteen years probably belongs to R^{E2}'s system of chronology, referring to the duration of the ʿAmmonite oppression; while '*in that year* is more suitable to the verbs at the beginning of the verse which suggest a signal catastrophe rather than a long-continued subjugation and oppression' (Mo.), and probably refer to the first stage of the Philistine aggressions, as narrated by E^2.

even all the children of Israel, etc. The facts related by R^{E2} in this verse and *v.*[9] as to the extent of the ʿAmmonite aggressions were probably derived by him from one of the ancient sources which narrated the story of Jephthaḥ. Cooke's statement that 'the extension of the oppression to *all the children of Israel* on both sides of the Jordan is probably due to the latest editor' is groundless. The writer does not refer to the whole of Israel east and west of Jordan, but to all Israel in Gileʿad east of Jordan, and to certain tribes (Judah, Benjamin, Ephraim) west of Jordan which (he implies) were some-the children of ʿAmmon crossed the Jordan to fight also against Judah, and against Benjamin, and against the house of Ephraim; E^2 and Israel was in sore straits. 10. And the children of Israel cried unto Yahweh, saying, 'We have sinned against thee; [] for we have forsaken ⟨Yahweh⟩ our God, and have served the Baʿals.' 11. And Yahweh said unto the children of Israel, 'Did not [] Egypt, R^P and [] the Amorites, ⌜and⌝ the children of

what harassed by raids, though not oppressed in the same degree as the inhabitants of Gileʿad. That the Ephraimites at any rate were interested parties is proved by the narrative of *ch.* 12 [1ff].

10. *for.* Reading כִּי simply with several MSS. of 𝔐, and 𝔊, 𝔙, $𝔖^P$, in place of 𝔥 וְכִי 'and because,' R.V. 'even because.'

Yahweh our God. The addition of 'Yahweh' is supported by six MSS. of 𝔐, and by $𝔊^A$, $𝔏^L$, 𝔙. The phrase 'Yahweh our God' is characteristic of E^2 (as, subsequently, of D); and the proper name *Yahweh* is desiderated by the contrast with 'the Baʿals.'

11. *Did not Egypt, etc.* Reading

הֲלֹא מִצְרַיִם וְהָאֱמֹרִי וּבְנֵי עַמּוֹן וּפְלִשְׁתִּים

with $𝔊^{AL}$, $𝔖^h$, $𝔏^L$, 𝔙, $𝔖^P$, and taking the list as part of the subject of the verb לָחֲצוּ in *v.*[12]. So Mo. (*SBOT.*), No., Kit., Kent.

𝔥 (supported by $𝔊^B$, 𝔗, Σ.), by reading מִן 'from' before each of the peoples enumerated, offers an impossibly harsh anacoluthon, omitting an indispensable verb, which is supplied by A.V., '*Did* not *I deliver you* from the Egyptians, etc.'; R.V., '*Did* not *I save you* from, etc.' Such a verb, whether הִצַּלְתִּי אֶתְכֶם (A.V.) or הוֹשַׁעְתִּי אֶתְכֶם (R.V.), could not be *understood* in Heb.; though it is conceivable that its omission may be due to an error of transcription. Against such a view, however, is the fact (noted by Mo.) that we should expect either verb to be followed, not by מִן 'from' simply, but by מִיַּד '*from the hand of.*' Thus E^2, with whose work we are dealing, employs this expression exclusively after הִצִּיל 'deliver' both in Judg. and 1 Sam.: cf. Judg. 6 [9], 1 Sam. 7 [3], 10 [18], 12 [10.11]; so Judg. 8 [34] R^{E2}. In the same way הוֹשִׁיעַ 'save' is regularly followed by מִיַּד in Judg.: cf. 2 [16.18], 8 [22], 10 [12], 12 [2], 13 [5]; once by the synonymous מִכַּף, 6 [14].

The emendation above adopted has, as we have seen, the predominant support of the Versions, and offers the simplest solution of the textual difficulty. We cannot, however, exclude the possibility that הֲלֹא מִמִּצְרַיִם of 𝔥 *may* originally have been followed by

ʿAmmon, and [] the Philistines, 12. and the Ṣidonians, and ʿAmaleḳ, and ⸢Midian⸣E² oppress you; and when ye cried unto me, I saved you from their hand? 13. But *ye* have forsaken

הֶעֱלֵיתִי אֶתְכֶם (cf. *ch.* 2 [1] R[P], 6 [8], 1 Sam. 10 [18] E²) or הוֹצֵאתִי אֶתְכֶם (cf. Josh. 24 [5] E²), 'Did not I *bring you up* (or, *bring you out*) from Egypt?' and that the verb was lost through later blundering insertion of the names which follow at the end of the verse (so Bu., La., Cooke). The relationship of *v.*[11] to *v.*[12] will then exactly resemble that of *v.*[8] (the bringing out from Egypt) and *v.*[9] (oppression of surrounding nations) in 1 Sam. 12 E². In this case the reading of the Versions which we have followed represents an attempt to make sense of a text identical with 𝔐.

the Amorites. We find no specific allusion to the Amorites as oppressors; the fact, mentioned in *ch.* 1 [34], of their forcing* the children of Dan from the vale into the hill-country being scarcely of sufficient importance, and also not followed by any signal act of deliverance. Taking 'Amorites' as a general designation for the inhabitants of Canaʿan (as is usual in E; cf. *note* on ch. 1[1] 'against the Canaʿanites'), it is conceivable that the allusion may be to the oppression of Sisera and 'the kings of Canaʿan' related in *chs.* 4, 5. Possibly, however, as suggested by 𝔖[P], הָאֱמֹרִי may be a corruption of הַמֹּאָבִים 'the Moabites' (for the Gentilic form, cf. especially Deut. 2 [11.29]) or מוֹאָב 'Moab,' since it is rather surprising to find no allusion to the oppression of this latter people, as related in *ch.* 3[12ff]. 𝔊[AL], while retaining οἱ Ἀμορραῖοι, adds καὶ Μωαβ after καὶ οἱ υἱοὶ Αμμων.

the children of ʿAmmon. These are named in *ch.* 3 [13] as aiding ʿEglon king of Moab in his oppression of Israel; but such a passing allusion could not have been in the writer's mind—at any rate unless he had previously mentioned Moab (cf. *note* preceding). Probably, like the mention of the Philistines with which it is coupled, the allusion is to the narrative *following*; and since reference to *deliverance* from the ʿAmmonites and Philistines (*v.*[12b]) is historically out of place, we may regard the names as a later careless insertion.

12. *the Ṣidonians.* We know of no occasion on which these people played the rôle of oppressors of Israel. Possibly, as Mo. suggests, their insertion here may be due to the mention of Ṣidon in *v.*[6].

ʿAmaleḳ. Cf. *ch.* 3 [13], 6 [3], where the mentions of ʿAmaleḳ, though very possibly later than the main narratives in which they occur (cf. *notes ad loc.*), are earlier than the present passage.

Midian. So 𝔊[BAL] (𝔊[A] *before* ʿAmaleḳ), and most moderns. Some MSS. of 𝔊, 𝔖[h], Σ., 𝔙 read 'Canaʿan'; while 𝔖[P] reads "ʿAmmon,'

* וילחצו—the same verb as לחצו 'oppressed' in 10 [12].

me, and have served other gods; therefore I will no more save you. 14. Go and cry unto the gods whom ye have chosen; let *them* save you in the time of your distress.'

15. And the children of Israel said unto Yahweh, 'We have sinned; do *thou* to us whatsoever seemeth good in thy sight: only pray deliver us this day.' 16. And they put away the foreign gods from the midst of them and served Yahweh: and his soul was impatient for the misery of Israel.

having omitted the reference to the children of ʿAmmon and the Philistines in *v.*[11]. 𝔐 'Maʿon' is apparently the modern Maʿân some eighteen miles east-south-east of Petra. The Maʿonites (Heb. *Meʿûnîm*) are mentioned in later times as antagonists of Judah (1 Chr. 4[41], 2 Chr. 26[7]; and probably also 2 Chr. 20[1]); but we have no record of any aggressions by them in the time of the Judges. On the other hand, mention of the Midianite oppression (*ch.* 6) is to be expected.

14. *whom ye have chosen.* For the use of the verb 'choose' in this connexion, cf. Josh. 24[15] E[2], 'and if it be evil in your eyes to serve Yahweh, choose ye this day whom ye will serve.'

16. *and served Yahweh.* 𝔊[B] adds μόνῳ, *i.e.* לְבַדּוֹ, as in 1 Sam. 7[4].

his soul was impatient. Lit. 'was *short.*' So elsewhere of Yahweh, Zech. 11[8]; of the Israelites, Num. 21[4b]. With רוּחַ 'spirit' as subject, Mic. 2[7], Job 21[4]. The antithetical idea—'was patient'—is expressed by הֶאֱרִיךְ נַפְשׁוֹ 'he *prolonged* his soul'; cf. Job 6[11].

The rendering of 𝔊[AL] καὶ οὐκ [L]εὐηρέστησε ([A]εὐηρέστησαν ἐν) τῷ λαῷ, καὶ [A]ὠλιγοψύχησεν ([L]ὠλιγοψύχησαν) ἐν τῷ κόπῳ Ισραηλ seems to embody a doublet, the first clause being a rendering of וַתִּקְצַר נַפְשׁוֹ בָּעָם, and the second correctly reproducing the text and meaning of 𝔐.

10. 17–12. 7. *Jephthaḥ.*

Besides the Commentaries, etc., cited throughout the book, cf. R. Smend, *Jeftas Botschaft an den König von Ammon*, *ZATW.* xxii. (1902), pp. 129-137.

The hand of R[E2] is to be seen in 11[33b] (cf. *ch.* 3[30], 4[23], 8[28]). In 12[7a] this editor employs the formula which he probably found already existing in the narrative of R[JE] (cf. *ch.* 15[20], 16[31b], 1 Sam. 4[18b], 7[15]).

Discussion of the ancient source, or sources, of the narrative must take its start with an examination of 11[12-28], which relates the sending by Jephthaḥ of an embassy to the king of ʿAmmon, protesting against his encroachment upon the territory of Israel between the Arnon and the Jabboḳ, and substantiating Israel's claim to hold it by right of conquest from Siḥon, king of the Amorites. It is a difficulty with regard to this argument, as put into the mouth of Jephthaḥ, that, except for the single reference to ʿAmmon at the end of *v.*[15], it refers throughout not to ʿAmmon but to Moab. Thus, *vv.*[17.18] state that

Israel, in approaching Cana'an from the east, was careful not to encroach upon the territory of Moab, *i.e.* the country south of the Arnon; but was content to conquer and settle in the territory of the Amorite Ṣiḥon, north of the Arnon and south of the Jabboḳ. The appeal of *v.* 24 is obviously addressed to Moab: 'Those that Chemosh thy god dispossesseth—wilt thou not possess *them*? etc.' Chemosh was the national god of Moab; while the god who stood in this position to 'Ammon was Milcom. In the same way, reference is made (*v.* 25) to the example of an earlier king of Moab, Balaḳ the son of Ṣippor, who left Israel unmolested in the enjoyment of their newly acquired territory.

As regards the origin of 11 12-28, two possibilities present themselves. Either the section is a late insertion into an otherwise homogeneous narrative, framed in order to establish Israel's claim to the territory between the Arnon and the Jabboḳ—possibly in view of some later encroachment of 'Ammon* (Mo., Cooke, etc.); *or*, the section, referring properly to Israel's relations with *Moab*, is part of a variant tradition, according to which Jephthaḥ appeared as a deliverer of the Israelites in Gile'ad from the aggressions, not of the 'Ammonites, but of the *Moabites*. On this latter hypothesis, we may expect to find the strand which embodies this variant tradition interwoven throughout the narrative as a whole (Holzinger, followed by Bu., Cor., No., Kit., Kent).

The former theory depends upon the fact that Jephthaḥ's speech, as given in *vv.* 15-27, appears to be drawn chiefly from Num. 20.21, exhibiting, here and there, verbal similarities (cf. *notes* on text). We must suppose that the interpolator, finding ready to his hand an ancient narrative which related the way in which Israel, in making their conquest and settlements east of Jordan, were careful to respect the old-established rights of *Moab*, adapted the facts extracted from this narrative so that they might apply equally to 'Ammon by the mere insertion of the words 'and the land of the children of 'Ammon' at the end of *v.* 15. This theory is vitiated by the fact that, while it is quite conceivable that the author of the interpolation may have thought that a narrative which illustrated Israel's care to avoid infringing the rights of the two kindred peoples, Edom and Moab, was applicable by inference to their attitude towards another kindred people ('Ammon), it offers no explanation of the reference to the example of Balaḳ, an earlier king of *Moab*, as a precedent, and (most markedly) it is obliged to assume that the writer is guilty of a gross error in confusing Chemosh, the god of the Moabites, with the god of the 'Ammonites. The fact has also been remarked that there is no evidence to prove that the section is very late in origin. It depends, as we have noticed, to some extent upon Num. 20 14-21, 21 13.21-24a, but by

* Mo. suggests that the occasion of the interpolation may have been the aggressions of the 'Ammonites upon the ancient territory of Israel at the beginning of the sixth century B.C., as mentioned in Jer. 49 1.

no means slavishly so *; and the conception of Chemosh in *v.* ^{24} as a national deity, exercising a potency and influence in relation to his people comparable to that which Yahweh exercises over Israel, may be paralleled by the conception of the same deity's power within his own land which underlies the old narrative of 2 Kgs. $3^{26.27}$. ‡ It is at least unlikely that such a view should have found expression at a period when at any rate in prophetic circles a doctrine of high spiritual monotheism had gained currency.

Rejecting this theory, then, we are thrown back upon the alternative which regards 11^{12-28} as forming part of an originally distinct narrative, in which Jephthaḥ is raised up to meet the aggressions, not of the ʿAmmonites, but of the Moabites. Looking carefully at 10^{17}-12^{7} as a whole, and examining it in detail, we are led to the conclusion that, while evidence that the narrative is composite throughout is by no means so obvious as *e.g.* in the Gideʿon-narrative, yet traces of the combination of two traditions varying in detail really do exist.

Thus we note that, according to 11^{1-11}, Jephthaḥ is an outlaw from Gileʿad, dwelling in the land of Ṭob, and is fetched thence by the elders of Gileʿad in order that he may act as their leader in repelling the ʿAmmonite invasion. According to $11^{30.31.34 \text{ ff.}}$, however, his home is at Miṣpah of Gileʿad; and the fact that he has lived there some time as a person of consequence, possessing a considerable retinue of dependents, seems to be indicated by the terms of his oath—'The comer-forth that cometh forth from the doors of my house to meet me' suggests some range of possibility as to the projected victim; and the idea that this may prove to be his only daughter is sufficiently remote not to have entered into his reckoning. We may also observe (with Frankenberg) that the words of Jephthaḥ's daughter, 11^{36}, 'Forasmuch as Yahweh hath wrought for thee full vengeance upon thine enemies,' clearly indicate that Jephthaḥ had a personal ground of quarrel with the ʿAmmonites; apart from which, indeed, his vow is difficult to explain. This fact, however, is hard to reconcile with the representation of him in 11^{1-11} as an outsider, who undertakes at a price to organize resistance to the enemy.

Further, 10^{17} can scarcely stand in original relationship to 10^{18}, 11^{1-11}. According to 10^{17}, the presence of an invading ʿAmmonite army in Gileʿad has been met by an organized muster of the Israelites at Miṣpah. The double וַיַּחֲנוּ, 'and they encamped,' clearly implies two hostile armies in battle-array: cf. *ch.* 6^{33}, 7^{1}, 1 Sam. 4^{1}, $17^{1.2}$, 28^{4}. From 10^{18}, however, we learn, to our surprise, that the Israelite army is without a leader; and it is only at this stage that the Gileʿadites conclude, after deliberation, that they have no man of their own fit to undertake command, and are obliged to send their elders to

* Cf. Kue. *Ond.* § 13^{13}; § 19^{6}.

‡ Cf. *NHTK. ad loc.*, and the present editor's *Outlines of O.T. Theology*, pp. 34 ff.

the land of Ṭob to fetch back Jephthaḥ. Assuming for the moment that this difficulty is not insuperable, it is very strange that, while according to 10 [17] the ʿAmmonite invasion has already taken place, and the critical conflict is impending, 11 [4] informs us (as though it were a fresh fact) that 'after a while the children of ʿAmmon fought with Israel.' If, however, 10 [17] is not really of a piece with 11 [1-11], this mention of the ʿAmmonite invasion in 11 [4] forms the appropriate prelude to the mission of the Gileʿadite elders to fetch Jephthaḥ, as related in 11 [5-11].

Jephthaḥ's proceedings, again, as related in 11 [29], can only be explained as actuated by the necessity of raising an army before attacking the ʿAmmonites. Yet according to 10 [17], as we have seen, the army is already mustered at Miṣpah.

Thus we seem to have established several points which indicate that 10 [17] has no original relationship to 11 [1-11.29], but belongs to a different narrative. If this be so, 10 [18] can be nothing else than the clumsy attempt of a redactor to fit 10 [17] on to 11 [1 ff]. The statement 'he shall be head, etc.,' is clearly drawn from 11 [8b].*

If, then, 10 [17] is distinct in origin from 11 [1-11], its proper sequel is probably 11 [12-28], a section which we observed at the outset to be also distinct from 11 [1-11], as making Moab, and not ʿAmmon, the aggressor. But 11 [30.31.34-40] has also been argued to be distinct from 11 [1-11], on the ground that Jephthaḥ the influential householder at Miṣpah is distinct from Jephthaḥ the outlaw. On the other hand, we have seen that 11 [29] coheres with 11 [1-11], and not with 10 [17]. The resumption of 11 [29b] may be seen in 11 [32a], where the redactor of the two narratives picks up the thread which has been broken by the insertion of 11 [30.31]. Traces of the fusion of two accounts may perhaps be seen in 11 [33a], since we appear to have a double *terminus ad quem* for the rout—'until thou comest to Minnith,' and 'as far as Abel-ceramim.' Probably 'from ʿAroʿer until thou comest to Minnith' belongs to the Moabite narrative, the ʿAroʿer in question being the frequently mentioned city on the Arnon at the northern boundary of Moab which has been mentioned in *v.* [26]; though this is uncertain (cf. *note ad loc.*). 'As far as Abel-ceramim' may then be supposed to come from the ʿAmmonite

* It is a point worthy of notice that, in the account of the institution of the monarchy in Israel in 1 Sam. 8-12, where two practically complete narratives, from J and E respectively, have been combined, the opening words of R^{JE}'s connective narrative in 11 [12-15] are phrased in precisely the same form as Judg. 10 [18]:—

'And the people said every man to his fellow, Who is the man
'And the people said unto Samuel, Who is he

that shall begin to fight with the children of ʿAmmon?
that said, Shall Saul reign over us?

he shall be head over all the inhabitants of Gileʿad.'
bring forth the men that we may put them to death.'

narrative, unless it be taken as a further definition of the *terminus ad quem*.

Lastly, we observe that the transition from 11^{40} to 12^{1} is somewhat unexpected. The account of the sacrifice of Jephthaḥ's daughter, and the yearly commemoration of this event which was thereafter established, seems naturally to wind up the narrative; and the events related in 12$^{1-6}$ give us the impression of belonging to an originally different source. We may assign 12$^{1-6}$, therefore, to the 'Ammonite narrative 11$^{1-11}$, etc., and we do this with the more confidence through observation of the fact that Jephthaḥ's words in *v.*^{3}, 'and I passed over unto the children of 'Ammon, and Yahweh gave them into mine hand,' are an echo of 11$^{29b.32}$.*

Thus we may reconstruct two distinct narratives, which probably ran originally as follows, square brackets being used where details have now to be supplied by conjecture.

(1) 10^{17}, 11$^{12-28.30.31.33\text{ (in part)}.34-40}$.

[The Moabites oppress the Israelite inhabitants of Gile'ad (some details possibly derived from this narrative by R^{JE} in 10$^{8b.9a}$). Jephthaḥ, an influential citizen of Miṣpah, undertakes the defence of his country. On the rumour, possibly, of warlike preparations among the Gile'adites], a Moabite army is mustered, and encamps in Gile'ad; the Israelite force being brought together in readiness at its leader's native city (11^{17}). Before joining battle, Jephthaḥ has recourse to diplomacy, but without success (11$^{12-28}$). He, therefore, decides to attack the Moabites; and vows that, if Yahweh will grant success to his arms, he will offer up a human sacrifice from among the members of his household (11$^{30.31}$). [The battle results in a decisive victory for Israel, the rout of the Moabites and slaughter of the fugitives extending] over a specified area, and including the destruction of twenty cities (11$^{33\text{ in part}}$). On Jephthaḥ's return in triumph to Miṣpah, his only daughter is designated by fate as the sacrificial victim. Though torn by grief, he is faithful to the terms of his vow; and a yearly commemoration of Jephthaḥ's daughter thereafter becomes an institution among the daughters of Israel (11$^{34-40}$).

In this narrative 'the children of 'Ammon' has been substituted for 'Moab' or 'the Moabites' ‡ in 10^{17}, 11$^{12.13.14.27.28.30.31}$, and additions referring to the children of 'Ammon have been made in *vv.*$^{15.36}$. The object of these changes was, of course, to bring the narrative into

* The threat of the Ephraimites in 12$^{1b\beta}$, 'we will burn thy house over thee with fire,' might be supposed to point to the narrative in which Jephthaḥ is a householder in Gile'ad (11$^{31.34}$) rather than to that in which he is an outlaw. This is a point, however, which need not weigh against the conclusion adopted above; since the first essential of the Gile'adites' compact with their new ruler (11$^{9.10}$) would be the granting him a residence at Miṣpah.

‡ While the expression 'the children of 'Ammon' is regularly used to denote the 'Ammonites, we do not find 'the children of Moab' used of the Moabites; though we know of no reason why such a phrase should have been avoided.

line with the parallel narrative in which Jephthaḥ appeared as deliverer from the ʿAmmonite aggressions; and the author of them was the redactor of the two narratives whom we must assume to have been R^{JE}.

The source from which this narrative is derived is indicated by the fact, already noticed, that $11^{12\text{-}28}$ depends very largely upon Num. $20^{14\text{-}21}$, $21^{13.21\text{-}24a}$. These sections belong mainly, if not wholly, to E; and thus we are justified in inferring that E is the source of the narrative which makes use of them.

(2) $11^{1\text{-}11}$ (except *vv.*$^{1b.2.5a}$, on which see below), $11^{29.32b.33\text{ (in part)}}$, $12^{1\text{-}6}$.

Jephthaḥ, a Gileʿadite without any tribal position owing to the accident of his birth, becomes an outlaw from Israelite territory, and takes up his abode in the land of Ṭob, where he gathers a band of desperadoes like himself, and gains a reputation as a successful freebooter. The ʿAmmonites commence hostilities against the Israelites in Gileʿad; and the elders of Gileʿad [having made an unavailing appeal for help to the tribes on the west of Jordan,* and] having no one among themselves equal to the task of raising and leading an army, are obliged to have recourse to Jephthaḥ in the land of Ṭob, and to entreat his services. He consents upon the understanding that, if successful, he is to become ruler of Gileʿad, and the compact is sealed 'before Yahweh' at Miṣpah ($11^{1\text{-}11}$). After traversing the country of Gileʿad and East Manasseh in order to raise an army, Jephthaḥ advances against the ʿAmmonites (*v.*^{29}) in order to attack them; Yahweh gives them into his hand (*v.*^{32b}), and he smites them with a great slaughter as far as Abel-ceramim (*v.*$^{33\text{ in part}}$). After the battle, an armed force of Ephraimites crosses the Jordan and threatens Jephthaḥ with reprisals, upon the false excuse that he did not summon them to aid him in the battle with the ʿAmmonites. Once more gathering the Gileʿadites to his banner, he puts the Ephraimites to the rout, and seizing the fords of the Jordan, cuts off all fugitives, so that forty-two thousand Ephraimites are slain ($12^{1\text{-}6}$).

Since the other narrative must be assigned to E, the inference is that the present narrative belongs to J; and in favour of this we may remark that the arrogant conduct of the Ephraimites ($12^{1ff.}$) is strikingly similar to their behaviour to Gideʿon as related in the J narrative, *ch.* $8^{1\text{-}3}$. A narrative reflecting discredit upon the Ephraimites, and possibly coloured by tribal antagonism, is more naturally assigned to a Judæan than to an Ephraimite source.

It only remains to notice interpolations in the narrative which appear to be very late in origin.

$11^{1b.2}$. It is clear from 11^{7} that Jephthaḥ's expulsion from Gileʿad was tribal and not family. The 'brethren' of *v.*^{3} are therefore his fellow-

* It is possible, however, that 11^{29} in its original form may have related an ineffectual attempt made *by Jephthaḥ* to gain the assistance of these tribes. Cf. *note ad loc.*

clansmen and not his natural brothers, as seems to be implied by *v.*[2]. Moreover, it is evident from the use of 'Gile'ad' in *vv.*[1b.2], as though it were the name of an individual, that we have here to do with the method of narration which characterizes the late priestly school of writers, in which districts, clans, and cities are spoken of as individuals. Instances of this method are frequent in the genealogies of P and 1 Chr. (cf. for 'Gile'ad' so treated, *note* on 'Machir' *ch.* 5 [14]); and we have already found illustration of it in the accounts of the 'minor' Judges, which, as we saw, emanated from the latest redactor, R^P.

The term וַיּוֹלֶד 'begat,' *v.*[1b], is very characteristic of P. Cf. $CH.^P$ 30.

It is clear, however, that the main narrative 10 [17]-11 [11] is literal and not figurative, and deals actually with the doings of individuals. Possibly the reference in *v.*[2] to Jephthaḥ's expulsion, 'and they drave out Jephthaḥ' may have been derived from the main narrative (so Bu.); cf. *v.*[7a]. On the other hand, it is very possible that *v.*[7a] combined with *v.*[1a] may be the *source* of the allusion in *v.*[2], as it comes from the hand of R^P (so Mo.).

11[5a]. This half-verse is superfluous by the side of *v.*[4], and has the appearance of a late gloss. It is omitted by $\mathfrak{G}^{AL}$; while $\mathfrak{G}^{B}$ appears to include it and to omit *v.*[4].

11 [26aβ]. The reference to Israel's possession of Gile'ad as having lasted undisputed for three hundred years is obtained by computation of the periods of oppression and deliverance (including the periods assigned to the 'minor' Judges) given in the preceding narrative up to the beginning of the 'Ammonite oppression (exactly, three hundred and one years). This date must therefore have been inserted by R^P or by some later hand.

12 [7b]. The record of Jephthaḥ's death and burial is given precisely in the form which recurs in 8 [32], 10 [2b.5], 12 [12.15], and represents the regular formula of R^P.

It has been maintained by some scholars (cf. Sta., *GVI.* i. p. 68; Wellh., *Comp.*[3] p. 224) that the story of Jephthaḥ is altogether without historical basis. Tradition supplies no historical details as to his campaign. The account of his birth (cf. 11 [1b], 'Gile'ad begat Jephthaḥ') and death and burial (cf. 12 [7b] 𝔐, 'and he was buried in the cities of Gile'ad') makes him a shadowy figure who is evidently only the *heros eponymus* of an obscure Gile'adite clan, apparently of mixed origin (cf. 11[1a], 'the son of a harlot'). The story is supposed to have grown up round the yearly festival which was customary in the narrator's time (11 [39.40]), and which was, in origin, a celebration of the death of the virgin-goddess, for the observance of which in Palestine evidence is forthcoming from other sources (cf. *Additional note*, p. 332).

The probability that the women's festival of later times may have been erroneously explained as commemorative of the sacrifice of Jephthaḥ's daughter does not, however, compel us to conclude that

17. R^{JE} And the children of ʿAmmon E were called to arms,

the story of this sacrifice was invented in order to account for the festival. The fact of such a sacrifice is not inherently improbable. There is ample evidence to prove that human sacrifice was not altogether unknown and unpractised among the Israelites in early times (cf. *Additional note*, p. 329); though it seems to have been sufficiently rare to have evoked the feeling of horror which is implicit in the narrative. It is at least as likely that an originally independent tradition of the death of Jephthaḥ's daughter may have come to be associated with a festival the idolatrous origin of which was forgotten, as that the story is a deliberate invention without historical basis. The absence—or rather, the paucity—of details as to Jephthaḥ's campaign is no argument against its historical truth. It might equally be urged, on the other hand, that a mere inventor would have found no difficulty in supplying such details.

These considerations have their weight even upon the assumption that the narrative is derived from a single source. If, however, as has been argued above, we have a combination of two somewhat variant traditions from J and E, the case for an historical basis for the tradition is greatly strengthened; more especially as one of these narratives appears (at any rate in the form in which we know it) to have been independent of the story of the sacrifice with its commemorative festival. The details of 11^{1b}, 12^{7b}, which are cited by Wellh. in support of his theory of a clan-myth, have been shown above to be additions which are due to the post-exilic hand R^P.

10. 17. *the children of ʿAmmon.* This is the ordinary designation of this people; ʿAmmon by itself occurring only twice, viz. 1 Sam. 11^{11} (but 𝔊, $𝔖^P$ 'the children of ʿA.'), and the late (probably Maccabean) Ps. 83^7, 𝔥 ^{8}. The land of the children of ʿAmmon (in Assyr. inscriptions Bît Ammân, or, in short form, Ammân) lay immediately east of the territory captured by the Israelites from Ṡiḥon king of the Amorites, which formed the southern part of Gileʿad, between the Arnon and the Jabboḳ, and from which Ṡiḥon appears previously to have expelled the Moabites (cf. 11^{13} *note*). The boundary between the two territories is given in Num. 21^{24} (𝔊) as Jaʿzer;* a city which Eusebius places ten Roman miles west of Philadelphia and fifteen miles from Ḥeshbon (*OS*. 264^{98}). The site intended seems to be the modern Ḫirbet Ṣâr

* 𝔊 ὅτι Ιαζηρ ὅρια υἱῶν Αμμων ἐστιν. 𝔥 כי עז גבול בני ע׳ 'For the border of the children of A. *was strong*,' gives an unsuitable sense in the context; and 𝔊's reading יעזר (of which עז is a relic) is generally adopted.

Josh. 13^{25} P (probably influenced by David's conquests, as related in 2 Sam. 10. 11) assigns to the tribe of Gad 'half of the land of the children of ʿAmmon as far as ʿAroʿer which is to the east of Rabbah.' In contrast with this, Deut. 2^{19} represents Moses as forbidding the Israelites to encroach upon ʿAmmonite territory.

and encamped in Gile'ad. And the children of Israel

—a name which may possibly preserve a relic of the ancient name, in spite of the difference of sibilant.* The name 'Ammon is preserved in the modern 'Ammân, the site of Rabbah or Rabbath-'Ammon, the chief city of the 'Ammonites, which was rebuilt in the second century B.C. as the Roman city Philadelphia, considerable remains of which still survive.

were called to arms. Cf. 6^{34} *note.*

Gile'ad. The country immediately east of Jordan, when accurately described in the O.T., is divided into three divisions—the Mîshôr or 'Table-land' to the south, Gile'ad (or 'the Gile'ad') in the centre, and the Bashan to the north: cf. Deut. 3^{10}, 4^{43}, Josh. 20^{8}. This division corresponds with the physical characteristics of the country: cf. especially Smith, *HG.* pp. 534 f. The Mîshôr, 'an absolutely treeless plateau,' covers the southern half of the modern el-Belḳâ, extending from the Arnon to a line a little north of Ḥeshbon, 'practically coincident with the Wâdy Ḥesbân' (Smith, *HG.* p. 548). North of this, 'the country is mainly disposed in high ridges' of limestone, 'fully forested,' as far as the Yarmuḳ. This is the ancient Gile'ad, the name of which, if rightly connected with the Ar. *ǵal'ad* 'hard, rough,' is to be understood as referring to the geological characteristics of the mountain-ridges (cf. Conder, in Smith, *DB.*[2] i. 1191*a*). North of the Yarmuḳ lies the Bashan (cf. Ar. *baṯneh* 'soft and smooth ground'), an ancient volcanic region, where 'the soil is rich, red loam resting on beds of ash,' and the rock black basalt.

Gile'ad is divided into halves by the Jabboḳ (cf. Deut. 3^{12}, Josh. $12^{2.5}$, 13^{31}). The southern half, together with the Mîshôr (*i.e.* all the country between the Arnon and the Jabboḳ) was conquered by Israel from Siḥon king of the Amorites (Josh. 12^{2}), and became the territory of the tribes of Gad and Re'uben (Deut. 3^{12}). According to P in Josh., the Mîshôr fell to Re'uben (13^{15-23}), and South Gile'ad to Gad

* Philological purists question, or even categorically deny, the possibility of connexion between the names *Ya'zēr* and *Ṣâr* on the ground of the difference between the sibilants. It is more than doubtful whether such an attitude is justified. That *z* and *ṣ* were very easily confused, both within the Hebrew language itself and among the different Semitic languages, is proved by such variations as Heb. *z'ḳ* and *ṣ'ḳ*, *z'r* and *ṣ'r*, *zrb* and *ṣrb* (where the variation appears to be purely *accidental*, and not to embody any different shade of meaning); Heb. and W. Aram. *ṣdḳ*, but Palmyrene and Syr. *zdḳ*; Heb. *ṣáyidh*, but Ar. *zâd*, Aram. *zᵉwādhā*, Bab. *ṣ(z)îdîtu*. If such interchanges as these are possible, it goes without saying that a place-name preserved for many centuries by means of popular pronunciation merely may quite conceivably have substituted *ṣ* for an original *z*.

If *Ṣâr* really represents *Ya'zēr*, the wearing away of the opening syllable with its weak consonants may be illustrated by Yiblᵉ'ām and Bilᵉ'ām, modern Bel'ameh; Yizrᵉ'el, mod. Zer'in; 'Ayyālôn, mod. Yâlô; Bêth-'ēḳed, mod. Bîtḳâd; 'Aphēḳ, (probably) mod. Fîḳ.

gathered themselves together, and encamped in Miṣpah. 18. R^{JE} And ⌜the people of Israel⌝ said every man to his fellow, 'Who is the man who will begin to fight with the children of ʿAmmon? he shall be head over all the inhabitants of Gileʿad.'

(13 [24-28]). North Gileʿad is assigned, together with the Bashan, to East Manasseh (Deut. 3 [13], Josh. 13 [29-33] P); and was probably conquered by Manassite clans from the west subsequently to the settlement in West Palestine: cf. *note* on 'Machir,' *ch.* 5 [14].

Such is the more accurate application of the term 'Gileʿad'; though it seems at times to have been used with greater elasticity. Thus in Deut. 34 [1] it denotes the whole of the country east of Jordan, as far north as Dan.: cf. also 1 Macc. 5 [20 ff]. Elsewhere, again, 'Gileʿad' is restricted exclusively either to the northern or the southern half of Gileʿad proper. In the present narrative (as in *ch.* 5 [17]; cf. *note*) it denotes the southern half, including probably the Mîshôr, *i.e.* the whole region between the Jabboḳ and the Arnon—the modern el-Belḳâ. For the classified occurrences of the different usages, cf. BDB. *s.v.* The name of Gileʿad survives in the modern Ǵebel Ǵilʿâd, the highest part of the mountain-range south of the Jabboḳ.

Miṣpah. The site is unknown, and the various conjectures which have been put forward are devoid of all foundation. The name means 'place of outlook' (from the root *ṣāphā* 'to look out, watch'); hence we may infer that the city was situated on some eminence or spur of the Gileʿad-range overlooking a wide prospect. The Miṣpah of Gen. 31 [49] J can hardly be the same, since it must have lain *north* of the Jabboḳ on the north-east border of Gileʿad, overlooking Aramaean territory; unless, indeed, the verse is a later gloss upon its context, as there is some reason to suppose: cf. Driver, *Westm. Comm. ad loc.*

18. *the people of Israel.* Reading עַם יִשְׂרָאֵל in place of 𝔐 הָעָם שָׂרֵי גִלְעָד 'the people, the princes of Gileʿad.' Here 'the princes of Gileʿad' is usually regarded as a late gloss, explicative of 'the people,' and intended to connect the verse with 11 [5]. If this is the case, however, why do we not read 'the *elders* of G.,' as in 11 [5.7.8.9.10.11]? The term 'princes' is not used elsewhere in the narrative. Our emendation assumes that ישראל was misread as שרי גל׳; and that עם, coming thus to be regarded as the Absolute, and not the Construct, State, received the addition of the Definite Article.

For the expression עם ישראל, cf. 2 Sam. 18 [7], 19 [40], 𝔐 [41]. In such a connexion עם 'people' has almost the force of 'soldiers' or 'army'; cf. BDB. *s.v.*, **2d**; *NHTK.* on 1 Kgs. 16 [15].

11. 1. J Now Jephthaḥ the Gile'adite was a mighty man of valour, and he was the son of a harlot: R^P and Gile'ad begat Jephthaḥ. 2. And the wife of Gile'ad bare him sons; and when the wife's sons were grown up, they drave out Jephthaḥ, and said to him, 'Thou shalt not inherit in our father's house, for thou art the son of another woman.' 3. J And Jephthaḥ fled from his brethren, and dwelt in the land of Ṭob; and there

11. 1. *Jephthaḥ.* The name means 'He (*i.e.* God) openeth' (*sc.* the womb?). The fuller form Jephthaḥ-el is cited by Halévy as a proper name in Sabaean (*Études Sabéennes*, 148[1]), and occurs as a place-name in Josh. $19^{14.27}$ P. Cf. the proper name Pethaḥiah 'Yah has opened,' 1 Chr. 24^{16}, *al.*

the son of a harlot. The mother may have been a non-Israelite; and seems, at any rate, not to have belonged to the father's clan. Jephthaḥ, as his mother's son, was therefore outside the father's clan also. Cf. *note* on 'his concubine,' *ch.* 8^{31}.

and Gile'ad begat, etc. Here the *district* is personified as father of Jephthaḥ—a mark of late date for *vv.* $^{1b.2}$, which can have formed no part of the original narrative: cf. pp. 303 f. $\mathfrak{G}^B$, ἣ ἐγέννησεν τῷ Γαλααδ, $\mathfrak{G}^{AL}$, $\mathfrak{S}^h$ καὶ ἔτεκεν τῷ Γαλααδ, seem merely to represent attempts to improve the connexion with *v.* ^{1a}, and not an originally different text וַתֵּלֶד לְגִ׳.

3. *the land of Ṭob.* In 2 Sam. $10^{6.8}$ 'the men of Ṭob' are mentioned, together with the Aramaeans of Beth-Reḥob and Zobaḥ and the king of Ma'acah, as allied with the 'Ammonites in their war with David. Τώβιον or Τούβιον east of Jordan, 1 Macc. 5^{13}, the inhabitants of which are called Τουβεινοί or Τουβιανοί in 2 Macc. 12^{17}, is probably the same district. The Jerusalem Talmud makes the land of Ṭob identical with Ṡûsîtha (*Shebiith*, vi. 1, fol. 36*c*), which is identified by Neubauer (*Géographie du Talmud*, p. 239) with Hippos in the Decapolis, *i.e.* probably the modern Sûsiyyeh on the eastern side of the Sea of Galilee. This would seem to suit Sayce's proposed identification (*Records of the Past*,[2] v. p. 45) with Tubi mentioned by Ṭḥutmosi III. in a list of conquered cities a little before Astiratu, *i.e.* Tell 'Aštarah, this latter being twenty miles east-north-east of Sûsiyyeh. Conder (*Heth and Moab*, p. 176) and Smith (*HG.* p. 587) find the name Ṭob in the modern eṭ-Ṭayyibeh, south of the Yarmuḳ and some eight miles a little south of due west of Irbid. Buhl. (*Geogr.*, p. 257, *n* [867]) refers to another eṭ-Ṭayyibeh, some twenty-three miles east of Irbid, between Der'â and Boṣrâ.

worthless men. Lit. '*empty* men,' as in *ch.* 9^4. 'Worthless' is not altogether a satisfactory rendering. Heb. *rêḳîm*, as here used, does not specifically imply moral obliquity; but rather a lack of the qualities which command success in the leading of a regular life

collected themselves worthless men unto Jephthaḥ, and they went out with him.

4. And after a while the children of ʿAmmon fought with Israel. 5. ᴳˡ· And when the children of ʿAmmon fought with Israel,ᒧ the elders of Gileʿad went to fetch Jephthaḥ from the land of Ṭob. 6. And they said to Jephthaḥ, 'Come, and be our ruler, that we may fight with the children of ʿAmmon.' 7. And Jephthaḥ said to the elders of Gileʿad, 'Was it not ye who hated me, and drave me out from my father's house? Why then are ye come unto me now when ye are in straits?' 8. And the elders of Gileʿad said unto Jephthaḥ, 'Therefore have we now returned unto thee; so go with us, and fight with the children of ʿAmmon, and thou shalt be head over us, even over all the inhabitants of Gileʿad.' 9. And Jephthaḥ said unto the elders of Gileʿad, 'If ye bring me back to fight with the children of ʿAmmon, and Yahweh deliver them before me, I shall be head

('ne'er-do-wells'), and possibly also (as suggested by the usage of the adverbial form *rêḳām*, 'with empty hands') a lack of material goods such as property and tribal status. Cf. the description of the men who attached themselves to David when he was leading the life of an outlaw in the cave of ʿAdullam, 1 Sam. 22 [2]. These include unsuccessful, needy, and discontented men, to whom it is not necessary to suppose that any *moral* stigma was attached. In 2 Sam. 6 [20], 2 Chr. 13 [7], *rêḳîm* does seem to denote the absence of specific moral qualities. In post-Biblical Heb. the term comes to denote *intellectual* vacuity (cf. the use of κενός in Jas. 2 [20]); but is also often used as a general term of contempt (so probably Ῥακά = רֵיקָא in Matt. 5 [22]).

went out with him. I.e. engaged in predatory forays.

5. *And when, etc.* Literally rendered, the Heb. runs, 'And it came to pass, when the children of ʿA. fought with Israel, *and* the elders of G., etc.,' it being idiomatic in Hebrew to continue with 'and' after the time-determination, which is really a parenthesis. Thus, if we regard the first half of the verse as a later gloss (cf. p. 304), the 'and' connects *v.*[5b] directly on to *v.*[4]. Cf. the similar *note* on *ch.* 1 [1] 'the children of Israel enquired.'

6. *ruler.* Heb. *ḳāṣîn* is the philol. equivalent of Ar. *ḳâḍy*—properly one who *decides* judicially. On the *n*-termination, cf. Bevan, *ZA.* xxvi. (1912), p. 37.

8. *Therefore, etc.* The words contain a tacit admission that they were in the wrong. At all costs it was necessary to secure Jephthaḥ's aid without further parley. 𝔊^AL οὐχ οὕτως, *i.e.* לֹא כֵן for 𝔐 לָכֵן, is certainly incorrect.

over you?' 10. And the elders of Gileʿad said unto Jephthaḥ, 'Yahweh shall be hearer between us; surely according to thy word so will we do.' 11. So Jephthaḥ went with the elders of Gileʿad, and the people set him over them as head and ruler; and Jephthaḥ spake all his words before Yahweh in Miṣpah.

12. E And Jephthaḥ sent messengers unto the king of R^{JE} the children of ʿAmmon, E saying, 'What hast thou to do with me, that thou art come unto me to fight against my land?' 13. And the king of R^{JE} the children of ʿAmmon E said unto the messengers of Jephthaḥ, 'Israel took away my land when they came up out of Egypt, from Arnon even unto the Jabboḳ, and unto the Jordan: now, therefore, restore ⌜it⌝ peaceably.' 14. And

10. *hearer.* The expression is used in a judicial sense, as in 2 Sam. 15 [3], Deut. 1 [17], *al.* Cf. the manner in which the compact is sealed, as related in *v.*[11b].

11. *and Jephthaḥ spake, etc.* The reference is to the compact of *v.*[10]. Jephthaḥ was not content with a merely casual promise; but took care that it should be solemnly ratified at the local sanctuary of Miṣpah, and therefore in Yahweh's presence as 'hearer.'

12. *unto the king of the children of ʿAmmon.* Upon the reasons which compel us to suppose that the message was addressed to *Moab*, and that, throughout *vv.*[12.28], 'the children of ʿAmmon' has been substituted for 'Moab,' cf. pp. 298 f.

What hast thou to do with me? Lit. 'What to me and to thee?' *i.e.* 'What business have we with each other?' the regular idiom in deprecation of interference: cf. 2 Sam. 16 [10], 19 [22], 𝔐 [23], 1 Kgs. 17 [18], 2 Kgs. 3 [13], 2 Chr. 35 [21], Matt. 8 [29], Mark 5 [7], John 2 [4]. The ordinary rendering 'What have I to do with thee?' obscures the sense.

13. *Israel took away my land, etc.* The excuse had some amount of justification if, as we gather from Num. 21 [26], the territory in question, though captured by Israel from Ṡiḥon king of the Amorites, had previously been wrested by Ṡiḥon from Moab.

from Arnon. The modern Wâdy Môǵib, which runs into the Dead Sea from the east, about twenty-two miles from its northern end. A description of the ravine of the Arnon is given on p. 221.

even unto the Jabboḳ. The modern Wâdy ez-Zerkâ, the principal tributary of the Jordan. The distance from the Arnon to the Jabboḳ is about fifty miles; and the breadth of the strip of territory from the Jordan to Ḫirbet Ṣâr (assuming this to be the site of Jaʿzer; cf. 10 [17] *note*) about sixteen miles.

restore it. Reading sing. אוֹתָהּ (in reference to אַרְצִי 'my land') with some MSS. of 𝔊, 𝔏[L], 𝔙, in place of 𝔐 plur. אֶתְהֶן.

Jephthaḥ sent messengers yet again unto the king of R^JE the children of ʿAmmon, 15. E and said to him, 'Thus saith Jephthaḥ, Israel did not take away the land of Moab, R^JE and the land of the children of ʿAmmon. 16. E But when they came up from Egypt, Israel went through the wilderness unto the Red Sea, and came to Ḳadesh. 17. And Israel sent messengers unto the king of Edom, saying, "Prithee, let me pass through thy land"; but the king of Edom hearkened not: and also unto the king of Moab did he send; but he was unwilling: so Israel dwelt in Ḳadesh. 18. Then he went through the wilderness, and compassed the land of Edom and the land of Moab, and came along the eastern side of the land

15. *and the land of the children of ʿAmmon.* Cf. pp. 299, 302.

16. *went through . . . to Ḳadesh.* Bu., following Wellh. and Holzinger, finds in this passage support for the theory of a more original narrative of the wilderness-journey, direct from the Red Sea to Ḳadesh, which was the scene of the giving of the Law. But, however probable may be the theory which locates Sinai or Ḥoreb in the near neighbourhood of Ḳadesh (cf. pp. 109 ff.), no support can justly be drawn for this or any similar theory from the present passage; since Jephthaḥ's sole concern was to relate the negotiations which took place *from Ḳadesh*, and any allusion to earlier events of the journey, *e.g.* the law-giving at Sinai, would have been wholly out of place. La. remarks justly, 'Surtout Jephté ne peut vraiment pas remonter au déluge; les faits du Sinaï n'avaient rien à faire ici: il mentionne la sortie d'Égypte par la mer Rouge et arrive aussitôt à Cadès, point de départ des négociations.'

17. *And Israel . . . Edom.* Cf. Num. 20^{14} E, 'And Moses sent messengers from Ḳadesh unto the king of Edom.'

Prithee . . . land. Cf. Num. 20^{17} E, 'Prithee let us pass through thy land.'

but the king of Edom hearkened not. A summary of Num. $20^{18\text{-}21}$ E.

and also unto the king of Moab, etc. We find no account of negotiations with Moab in Num. or Deut.

Israel dwelt in Ḳadesh. Cf. Num. $20^{1a\beta}$ E, Deut. 1^{46}.

18. *Then he went . . . Edom.* Cf. Num. $20^{21b\text{-}22a}$, 'So Israel turned aside from him. And they journeyed from Ḳadesh,' Num. 21^{4}, 'by way of the Red Sea to compass the land of Edom.' All that intervenes in Num., from 20^{22} to 21^{4} down to 'Mount Hor,' is derived from sources other than E.

compassed. I.e. 'went round,' so as to avoid encroaching upon it.

and came along . . . Moab. Cf. Num. 21^{11} E, 'and they encamped . . . over against Moab on the eastern side.'

of Moab, and they encamped on the other side of Arnon, and did not come within the border of Moab; for Arnon was the border of Moab. 19. And Israel sent messengers unto Ṡiḥon king of the Amorites, the king of Ḥeshbon, and Israel said to him, "Prithee, let us pass through thy land unto my place." 20. But Ṡiḥon ⌜refused⌝ ⌜to allow⌝ Israel to pass through his

and they encamped, etc. Cf. Num. 21^{13} E, 'and they encamped on the other side (מֵעֵבֶר) of Arnon, which is in the wilderness that cometh forth from the border of the Amorites; for Arnon is the border of Moab, between Moab and the Amorites.'

19. *And Israel sent, etc.* Cf. Num. $21^{21.22}$ E, 'And Israel sent messengers unto Ṡiḥon king of the Amorites, saying, Let me pass through thy land. . . . By the king's highway will we go until we shall have passed thy border'; Deut. $2^{26.27}$, 'And I sent messengers from the wilderness of Ḳedemoth unto Ṡiḥon king of Ḥeshbon with words of peace, saying, Let me pass through thy land: by the highway only will I go; I will neither turn aside to the right hand nor to the left.'

Ḥeshbon. The modern Ḥesbân, sixteen miles east of Jordan and twenty-four miles north of the Arnon.

20. *But Ṣiḥon refused, etc.* Reading וַיְמָאֵן ס׳ תֵּת יִשְׂרָאֵל עֲבֹר וג׳; cf. Num. 20^{21} וַיְמָאֵן אֱדוֹם נְתֹן יִשְׂרָאֵל עֲבֹר בִּגְבֻלוֹ. $\mathfrak{G}^{L}$ καὶ οὐκ ἠθέλησε Σιων τὸν Ἰσραηλ διελθεῖν κτλ, $\mathfrak{G}^{A}$ καὶ οὐκ ἠθέλησεν διελθεῖν τὸν Ισραηλ κτλ, $\mathfrak{S}^{h}$ ܘܠܐ ܨܒܐ ܣܝܚܘܢ ܕܢܫܒܘܩ ܠܐܝܣܪܝܠ, support וימאן for $\mathfrak{H}$ ולא האמין (מֵאֵן = οὐ θέλειν in Gen. 37^{35}, 39^{8}, 48^{19}, Num. 20^{21}, 22^{14}, 2 Sam. 13^{9}, 1 Kgs. 20^{35}, Isa. 1^{20}, Hos. 11^{5}, and frequently in Jer.), but clearly did not read תֵּת 'to allow,' as above adopted, since this would certainly have been represented in translation by δοῦναι; cf. Num. 20^{21} καὶ οὐκ ἠθέλησεν Εδωμ δοῦναι τῷ Ἰσραηλ παρελθεῖν κτλ.

Num. 21^{23} reads וְלֹא־נָתַן ס׳ אֶת־יִשׂ׳ עֲבֹר בִּגְבֻלוֹ 'And Ṡiḥon did not allow Israel to pass through his border'; and it is possible that our author, having this text before him, and intending to substitute וַיְמָאֵן תֵּת for וְלֹא נָתַן, may have accidentally omitted תֵּת; since the construction וימאן את יש׳ עבר 'refused Israel to pass' is quite unparalleled, and cannot have been intentionally written (מֵאֵן is regularly followed by the Infinitive). This hypothesis explains the rendering of $\mathfrak{G}^{AL}$, $\mathfrak{S}^{h}$, and also the corruption of וימאן first into וַיַּאֲמֵן and then into וְלֹא הֶאֱמִין in $\mathfrak{H}$. An alternative hypothesis

border, and Ṡiḥon gathered together all his people, and they pitched in Jahaṣ; and he fought with Israel. 21. And Yahweh the God of Israel gave Ṡiḥon and all his people into the hand of

is to suppose that the את before ישראל is a corruption of תֵּת, which was already existent in the Heb. MS used by 𝕲. 𝕳, as it stands, is rendered by R.V. 'But Ṡiḥon trusted not Israel to pass, etc.'; but the Heb. construction is impossible. Had the writer wished to use the verb האמין in this connexion he would have written some such sentence as וְלֹא הֶאֱמִין ס׳ ביש׳ וְלֹא נָתַן לוֹ עֲבֹר וגו׳ 'But Ṡiḥon did not trust in Israel, nor suffer them to pass, etc.' Deut. 2 [30], וְלֹא אָבָה ס׳ מֶלֶךְ חֶשְׁבּוֹן הַעֲבִרֵנוּ בּוֹ 'But Ṡiḥon king of Ḥeshbon was not willing to let us pass by him.'

and Ṣiḥon gathered . . . Israel. Cf. Num. 21 [23] E, 'and Ṡiḥon gathered together all his people, and went out against Israel to the wilderness, and came to Jahaṣ, and fought with Israel'; Deut. 2 [32] 'and Ṡiḥon came out against us, he and all his people, to battle at Jahaṣ.'

in Jahaṣ. Heb. בְּיָהְצָה 'in Jáhṣah,' with so-called ה *locative* ending. So Jer. 48 [21], 1 Chr. 6 [78], 𝕳 [63]; cf. Num. 21 [23], Deut. 2 [32] (where, however, the ה *loc.* may embody the sense of *direction towards*, after a verb of motion—'to Jahaṣ'). We find the form יַהְצָה Jáhᵃṣah, Josh. 13 [18]. Elsewhere the form is Jáhaṣ; Isa. 15 [4], Jer. 48 [34], *Moabite Stone*, ll. 19, 20. The site is unidentified. Our narrative suggests that the city must have lain on the south-east border of Ṡiḥon's territory, north of the upper reaches of the Arnon, and this view is supported by its mention in 1 Chr. 6 [78] as a Levitical city in Re'uben next before Ḳedemoth: cf. the reference in Deut. 2 [26] to the wilderness of Ḳedemoth (*i.e.* 'eastern regions') as the district outside Ṡiḥon's territory to the east from which Israel sent an embassy to him. Mesha' king of Moab says (*Moabite Stone*, *loc. cit.*), 'And the king of Israel had built Jahaṣ, and abode in it, while he fought against me. But Chemosh drave him out from before me; and I took of Moab two hundred men, even all its chiefs, and I brought them up against Jahaṣ, and took it, to add it unto Dibon.' This suggests proximity to Dibon (the modern D̲îbân), to the east of which the site of Jahaṣ is probably to be sought. Eusebius states (*OS.* 264 [94]) that the site was shown in his day between Medeba and Dibon (if this is intended by Δηβους); but this would place it too far to the west, well into the interior of Siḥon's territory.

21. *And Yahweh . . . smote them.* Cf. Deut. 2 [33], 'And Yahweh our God gave him up before us, and we smote him and his sons and all his people.' Num. 21 [24a] E has simply 'and Israel smote him at the edge of the sword.'

Israel, and they smote them: so Israel possessed all the land of the Amorites, who dwelt in that land. 22. And they possessed all the border of the Amorites, from Arnon even unto the Jabboḳ, and from the wilderness even unto the Jordan. 23. So now, Yahweh the God of Israel hath dispossessed the Amorites from before his people Israel, and shouldest *thou* possess them? 24. Those that Chemosh thy god dispossesseth⌜⌝—wilt thou not

so Israel possessed, etc. Cf. Num. 21 ^{25} E, 'and Israel dwelt in all the cities of the Amorites.'

22. *And they possessed, etc.* Cf. Num. 21^{24b} E, 'and possessed his land from Arnon unto Jabboḳ, unto the children of ʿAmmon; for ⌜Jaʿzer⌝ is the border of the children of ʿAmmon' (on the reading, cf. *note* on 10^{17}). In Deut. 2 $^{36.37}$ the conquered territory is defined as extending from ʿAroʿer on the edge of the Wâdy Arnon as far as Gileʿad, *i.e.* the northern half of Gileʿad, north of the Jabboḳ (on the variations in the use of the term 'Gileʿad,' cf. *note* on 10^{17}); and the fact is carefully noted that no encroachment was made on the territory of ʿAmmon, this latter being defined as 'all the side of the Wâdy Jabboḳ and the cities of the hill country': cf. Josh. 12^2 R^D. Here the reference must be to the *upper course* of the Jabboḳ, which, starting eastwards in the neighbourhood of Ḫirbet Ṣâr (Jaʿzer) takes a northward and then north-westward curve before turning due westward, and thus seems in this passage to be regarded as the (ideal) boundary between Israel and ʿAmmon.*

23. *and shouldest* **thou,** *etc.* The italics, here and in *v.*^{24}, represent great emphasis in the original.

possess them. I.e., of course, 'possess *their territory*.' So in *v.*^{24}.

24. *those that Chemosh, etc.* The speaker assumes just as real an *existence* for Chemosh as for Yahweh. He is no *monotheist* in the proper sense of the term, *i.e.* he does not hold the doctrine that Yahweh is the one and only God of the whole earth, and that the existence of other gods is a delusion. Yahweh is for him, doubtless, the sole object of Israel's allegiance and worship; but the holding of

* In Num. 21 ^{24b} it is doubtful whether 'unto Jabboḳ' defines the northern limit of the territory merely; or, taking a comprehensive survey of the whole course of the wâdy, makes the reference to define the northern *and* eastern borders. On the latter hypothesis, 'unto the children of ʿAmmon' is a *further* definition of this north-east border-line in so far as the upper part of the Jabboḳ-wâdy is identical with the border of ʿAmmon. The fact, however, that in our passage in Judg. 'unto Jabboḳ' clearly defines the *northern* limit of Ṣiḥon's territory, 'from the wilderness' explaining the eastern limit, makes it probable that the expression is used in the same way in Num., the statement meaning—the strip of territory as defined from south to north, of which the eastern limit is the land of ʿAmmon, marching with Ṣiḥon's territory along a line which runs approximately north and south through Jaʿzer. Cf. Gray, *ICC. ad loc.*

possess *them*? so, all that Yahweh our God hath dispossessed from before us—*them* will we possess. 25. Now, then, art

this faith (monolatry) does not hinder him from believing that Chemosh really stands in the same kind of relation to Moab as Yahweh does to his own nation; *i.e.* he thinks of Yahweh as the *national God* of Israel, not as the God of the whole earth. His religious belief thus differs from that of the eighth-century prophets and their successors, who proclaim a doctrine of virtual monotheism—*i.e.* a doctrine which, if not as yet in all respects worked out to its logical conclusion, yet undoubtedly contains all the elements of a full belief in the existence of one God only. Further passages in the O.T. which embody the more primitive conception are noticed and discussed in the editor's *Outlines of O. T. Theology*, pp. 34 ff.

Chemosh. Cf. *Introd.* to the narrative, p. 299. Chemosh is always mentioned elsewhere in the O.T. as the god of the Moabites; Num. 21^{29}, 1 Kgs. $11^{7.33}$, 2 Kgs. 23^{13}, Jer. $48^{7.13.46}$ †. In Num. 21^{29}, Jer. 48^{46} Moab is called 'the people of Chemosh.' In the inscription of the *Moabite Stone* Meshaʿ king of Moab ascribes the oppression of Moab by Israel to the fact that 'Chemosh was angry with his land' (l. 5); and the turn in Moab's fortunes which is marked by successes against Israel is regarded as due to the renewal of the favour of the god (ll. 8 f., 33), who is pictured as directing Meshaʿ's plan of campaign: 'And Chemosh said unto me, Go, take Nebo against Israel' (l. 14); 'Chemosh said unto me, Go down, fight against Ḥoronên' (l. 32). Chemosh is represented as the leader in battle, 'Chemosh drave him (the king of Israel) out (of Jahaṣ) from before me' (l. 19); the population of the city of ʿAṭaroth is utterly devoted to him as a 'gazing-stock' or spectacle over which he may gloat with satisfaction (רית,* l. 12); and the altar-hearth of the divine Patron ‡ of the city is dragged before him at Ḳeriyyoth as a trophy (ll. 12 f.). In this mode of thought, and the phraseology in which it finds expression, we cannot fail to trace close resemblance to the ideas which were current in Israel in early times as to Yahweh's relationship to His people.

Two kings of Moab, as known to us, bear names which are honorific to Chemosh—Chemoshkân,§ *i.e.* '(He whom) Chemosh has established' (cf. כְּנָיָהוּ, יְכָנְיָהוּ, יְהוֹיָכִין, similar forms in honour of Yahweh),

* Probably to be vocalized רַיִת, a contracted form from רְאַיִת from the verb רָאָה. Cf. Halévy, *Revue Sémitique*, xiv. (1906), pp. 180 f.; Grimme, *ZDMG.* lxi. (1907), pp. 81 ff.

‡ Cf. *note* on 'Dodo,' *ch.* 10[1].

§ The second element in the name is doubtful, the letters being nearly illegible. The reading adopted is that of Lidsbarski, as the result of a fresh examination of the stone (cf. *Ephemeris für Semit. Epigr.* i. pp. 3 f.). The old reading, Chemoshmelekh, seems to be excluded by the fact that there is scarcely room for more than two consonants. Clermont-Ganneau has suggested Chemoshgad.

thou at all better than Balaḳ the son of Ṣippor, king of Moab? Did he contend at all with Israel, or did he fight at all against them? 26. When Israel dwelt in Ḥeshbon and its dependencies, and in ʿAr⸢oʿe⸣r and its dependencies, and in all the cities

the father of Meshaʿ (*Moabite Stone*, l. 1), and Kammusunadbi, the Assyr. form of Chemoshnadab, *i.e.* probably 'Chemosh is liberal *or* princely' (cf. יְהוֹנָדָב, אֲבִינָדָב), who is mentioned by Šennacherib as paying tribute in B.C. 701 (*KB.* ii. p. 90). The Bab. form (ilu) Ka-mu-šu-šar-uṣur '(god) Chemosh protect the king' occurs in a business-document of the sixth year of Cambyses (quoted in *KAT.*^{3} p. 472). Two seals of doubtful date and genuineness bear respectively the legends לכמשצדק '(belonging) to Chemoshṣedeḳ,' לכמשיחי '(belonging) to Chemoshyᵉḥî,' in Phoenician characters (cf. Lidsbarski, *Ephemeris für Semit. Epigr.* i. pp. 136 ff.); and each has a representation of the winged solar-disk, possibly, as Baethgen suggests (*Beiträge*, p. 14), connecting Chemosh with the sun.

dispossesseth. Reading יוֹרִישׁ with Mo. in place of 𝔐 יוֹרִישְׁךָ, R.V. 'giveth thee to possess.' The correction seems to be demanded by the parallel clause in the latter half of the verse, and the final ך may very probably have arisen through dittography from the initial letter of כמוש. On the verb *hôrîš*, meaning both 'to cause to possess' and 'to dispossess,' cf. *note* on 1^{19}.

25. *Balaḳ the son of Ṣippor.* The story of Balaḳ and Balaʿam, Num. 22^{2}-24^{25}, is a composite narrative which raises problems of more than ordinary difficulty. Most scholars hold that the sources J and E are here combined: but the characteristics of J are not so well marked as those of E, and the existence of the former source has thus been questioned; whilst the question of the stages by which the narrative attained its present form affords scope for considerable difference of opinion. Cf. Gray's full discussion in *ICC.* pp. 307 ff.

26. *dependencies.* Lit. 'daughters.' Cf. *ch.* 1^{27}. The expression is commonly characteristic of J.

ʿAroʿer. Vocalizing, as normally, עֲרֹעֵר, in place of the anomalous עֲרוֹעֵר of 𝔐. The city is the modern ʿArâʿîr: cf. *note* p. 221. It is commonly mentioned as situated 'on the edge (lip) of the Wâdy Arnon,' and as the southernmost limit of the territory conquered by Israel from Ṣiḥon.

𝔊^{A}, in place of 'in ʿAroʿer' reads ἐν Ἰαζηρ, and in place of 'by the side of Arnon,' 𝔊^{AL} reads παρὰ τὸν Ἰορδάνην, 𝔙 'juxta Jordanem'; and these readings are adopted by Mo. (*SBOT.*, followed by La., Cooke) on the ground that '*Aroer* and the *Arnon* come from *v.*^{18} (cf. Num. $21^{13\,ff}$); while *Jaazer* and the *Jordan*, which are not suggested by anything in the context, are original.' More probably, as Bu.

which are by the side of Arnon,[RP] three hundred years; [E] why, pray, didst ⌜thou⌝ not recover ⌜them⌝ at that time? 27. *I*, therefore, have not sinned against *thee*; but *thou* doest *me* wrong in fighting against me. Let Yahweh, who is Judge this day, judge between the children of Israel and the children of [RJE] ʿAmmon.' 28. E Howbeit, the king of [RJE] the children of ʿAmmon E hearkened not unto the words of Jephthaḥ which he sent unto him.

29. J And the spirit of Yahweh came upon Jephthaḥ, and he

(*Comm.*) suggests, they represent a later attempt to adapt the argument to Israel's relations with ʿ*Ammon*, instead of (as was originally intended; cf. pp. 298 ff.) with *Moab*. On Jaʿzer, as marking the boundary between the territories of Israel and ʿAmmon, cf. *notes* on 10[17], 11[22].

three hundred years. On the source of this figure, cf. p. 304.

why, pray. Lit. '*and* why.' On the idiomatic use of ו *copulative* to give a forcible and sarcastic turn to a question, cf. *NHTK.* on 1 Kgs. 2[22], and *note* on *ch.* 6[13].

didst thou not recover them. Vocalizing הִצַּלְתָּם with 𝔊[B] ἐρρύσω αὐτούς, Stu., Mo., in place of 𝔐 הִצַּלְתֶּם (plural verb with object unexpressed). The sing. verb is in agreement with the context, the subject being, not the particular king of Moab addressed, but the land of Moab personified as an individual. Cf. *v.*[27a], where '*I*' clearly refers, not to Jephthaḥ, but to Israel (cf. *v.*[15]). Strictly speaking, we should expect a fem. suff. in reference to the 'cities' preceding; but such a use of masc. suff. for fem. is not uncommon: cf. G-K. § 135*o*.

27. ***I***, *therefore, etc.* For the form and thought of the sentence, cf. 1 Sam. 24[12b], 'And I have not sinned against thee, but thou art hunting my life to take it.'

who is Judge this day. Connecting הַשֹּׁפֵט closely with הַיּוֹם, as the order of words seems to demand. So Mo. R.V., in agreement with accents (which connect השפט more closely with the preceding יהוה than with the following היום), renders 'The Lord, the Judge, be judge this day,' making הַיּוֹם to refer to the verb יִשְׁפֹּט at the commencement of the sentence. For the invocation of Yahweh as arbiter between two parties, cf. Gen. 16[5] J, 1 Sam. 24[12], 𝔐[13].

29. *And the spirit of Yahweh, etc.* Cf. *ch.* 3[10] *note.*

and he passed, etc. The passage is obscure; but not so obscure as it appears to those scholars who fail to recognize the combination of two sources in the narrative (cf. the remarks of Mo., and the paraphrase of them given by Cooke). Looking at the opening statement of the verse, 'And the spirit of Yahweh came upon Jephthaḥ,' and comparing it with the connexion in which the identical phrase (of ʿOthniel)

passed through Gileʿad and Manasseh, and he passed over ⌈to⌉ Mizpeh of Gileʿad, and from Mizpeh of Gileʿad he passed over ⟨to⟩

stands in 3^{10}, and the similar phrase (of Gideʿon) in 6^{34}, we may justly infer that what follows refers to Jephthaḥ's efforts to raise an army to meet the ʿAmmonites: nor is this inference invalidated by the fact that, according to 10^{17}, an army had already been mustered (Mo., Cooke), since, as we have seen, this verse belongs to a different narrative. Even 11^{11a}, which, according to our analysis, belongs to the *same* source as 11^{29}, cannot be cited to the contrary (as by Mo.), since 'the people' of Gileʿad who made Jephthaḥ their head can hardly have been already a fully organized army. They doubtless formed some part of the material for such an army; but the whole point of the narrative 11^{1-11} is that the Gileʿadites resorted to Jephthaḥ because they possessed no one of sufficient initiative not only to *lead* but also to *raise* an army at all adequate to meet the aggressor. Observing further that the closing statement of *v.*[29] (picked up and expanded in *v.*[32a] after the interposition of a portion of the other source, *vv.*[30.31]) speaks of Jephthaḥ's advance to give battle to the ʿAmmonites, it may be claimed that our inference that the middle part of the verse refers to the mustering of the army becomes a certainty.

Granted, however, that this is the case, it still appears most improbable that the narrative stands in its original form. The phrase ויעבר את גלעד וג׳ can only be intended to mean 'and he *passed through* Gilead, etc.'; but in this sense the construction (עבר followed by the Accusative) is almost, if not quite, without parallel* (the regular construction is עבר ב). As the text stands, 'Gileʿad' is here, as elsewhere in the narrative, the region south of the Jabboḳ (cf. 10^{17} *note*), while 'Manasseh' most probably denotes the region to the north of the wâdy, *i.e.* East Manasseh. We cannot be sure that clans from West Manasseh had by this time crossed the Jordan and made their settlement in the east (they had not done so in the time of Deborah; cf. *note* on 'Machir,' *ch.* 5^{14}); though this is a consideration which need not have weighed with a narrator who may have assumed that what was true of his own age was also true of an earlier period. Still, taking note of Jephthaḥ's claim in 12^{2} to have summoned *Ephraim* to his assistance without success (a statement which seems to presuppose an earlier reference in the narrative from

* Possible instances, *e.g.* Gen. 32^{32} כאשר עבר את פנואל, Josh. 16^{6} ועבר [הגבול] אותו [תאנת שלה], are probably to be understood in the sense *pass by* (cf. with the Accus., Judg. 3^{26}, 2 Kgs. 6^{9}), rather than *pass through*. In any case, these passages deal with *city-sites*, not with widely extended *districts* like Gilead and Manasseh. Notice the carefully marked contrast in Num. 20^{17}, 21^{22} between עבר ב *pass through* or *traverse* a land, fields, vineyards, and עבר with Accus. *pass over* or *cross* the border of a land regarded as a definitely marked line.

to the children of ʿAmmon. 30. E And Jephthaḥ vowed a vow to Yahweh and said, 'If thou wilt indeed give RJE the children of ʿAmmon E into my hand, 31. then the person that cometh forth from the doors of my house to meet me, when I return in peace from RJE the children of ʿAmmon, E shall belong to Yahweh, and I will offer him up as a burnt offering.'

which it is drawn), it is not unlikely (as Holzinger and Bu. suggest) that 'Ephraim' may originally have stood in the present passage in place of 'Gileʿad'; in which case 'Manasseh' will refer to West and not to East Manasseh. Thus (reading אל for את three times after ויעבר) the passage may have run 'and he crossed over (the Jordan) to Ephraim and to Manasseh, and he crossed over (again) to Miṣpeh of Gileʿad.' The double ויעבר, if referring to his crossing and *re*-crossing the Jordan (cf. 6 33), is thus not redundant.

Even so, the passage must have been abbreviated from its original form, as 12 2 certainly presupposes prior mention of the fact that the appeal to Ephraim was fruitless. Probably the narrative was cut down and mutilated when the two sources J and E were pieced together; and this, possibly, in view of the fact that the narrative E in 10 17 pictures the Israelite army as already mustered and encamped at Miṣpah. Such a conclusion at any rate may suffice to account for the obscurity of the verse, which the view that it 'is a somewhat unskilful attempt to fasten the new cloth, *v.* 12-28, into the old garment' (Mo.), or (otherwise expressed) that 'an editorial hand has attempted to pick up the thread of the narrative after the long interpolation, *vv.* 12-28' (Cooke) certainly does not do.

and he passed over to Miṣpeh, etc. Reading אֶל for 𝔐 את, as seems to be demanded by the context. Whatever view be taken as to the precise form of the description of Jephthaḥ's earlier movements (cf. *note* preceding), we can in the present statement scarcely find anything else than the account of his *return* to Miṣpeh after raising his army, and immediately prior to his attack upon the foe. The forms Miṣpeh, Miṣpah appear to be used interchangeably with reference both to this locality and to others of the same name.

to the children of ʿAmmon. Inserting אֶל before בני עמון with twelve MSS. of 𝔐.

31. *then the person that cometh forth, etc.* Lit. 'the comer-forth that cometh forth'—a phrase which implies that from the first a *human* sacrifice is contemplated. Ros., Stu., and others quote the remarkable parallel from Servius on *Aeneid*, iii. 331: 'Idomeneus de semine Deucalionis natus, Cretensium rex, cum post eversam Trojam reverteretur, in tempestate devovit diis sacrificaturum se de re, quae primum occurrisset. Contigit autem, ut filius ejus primus

32. ^{RJE} So Jephthaḥ passed over unto the children of ʿAmmon
J to fight against them, and Yahweh gave them into his hand.
33. And he smote them $^{E?}$ from ʿAroʿer until thou comest to

occurreret : quem cum, ut alii dicunt, immolasset, ut alii, immolare voluisset, et post orta esset pestilentia, a civibus pulsus est regno.' Cheyne (*EB.* 2362) cites an Arabian tradition mentioned by Lyall (*Ancient Arabian Poetry*, Introd. p. xxxviii): 'Al-Mundhir had made a vow that on a certain day in each year he would sacrifice the first person he saw: ʿAbîd [a poet] came in sight on the unlucky day, and was accordingly killed, and the altar smeared with his blood.'

The narrator, though regarding the sequel of the vow—the fact that the victim should prove to be the hero's only child—as a terrible tragedy, yet does not seem to hold that such a vow is contrary to the spirit of Yahweh's religion. It is an extraordinary sacrifice, offered in a great emergency as a supreme bid for the active co-operation of the deity. Cf. the Moabite king's sacrifice of his firstborn son as a last resort (2 Kgs. $3^{26.27}$)—a costly sacrifice which is supposed by the narrator to have been effectual in arousing the god Chemosh, and thus enabling the Moabites to expel the invaders from their land.* On the further evidence for the occurrence of human sacrifice among the Israelites, cf. *Additional note*, p. 329.

33. *from ʿAroʿer.* Besides the frequently mentioned city on the edge of the Wâdy Arnon (cf. *v.*^{26} *note*), there was, according to Josh. 13^{25} P, another city named ʿAroʿer to the east of Rabbath-ʿAmmon, *i.e.* in ʿAmmonite territory. Our ignorance as to the source of the present statement forbids our making a decision as to which ʿAroʿer is here referred to. If (as we conjecturally suppose) the source is E, then the reference will be to ʿAroʿer on the Arnon. If, on the other hand, the passage is an extract from J, the allusion probably is to the ʿAroʿer of Josh. 13^{25}.

Minnith. The site is unknown. Eusebius (*OS.* 280^{44}) identifies it with a village called Μααυιθ, four Roman miles from Ḥeshbon, on the road to Philadelphia; a locality which, according to Buhl (*Geogr.* p. 266), would suit the modern ruins which bear the name Ḫešrûm. Such a position, however, appears unsuitable either to the Moabite (E) or the ʿAmmonite (J) narrative. 'Unto Minnith' marks the extreme limit within which the twenty cities smitten must be pictured as lying; and clearly these can hardly have been *within the invaded territory*, i.e. *Israelite* cities which had previously been captured and occupied by the foe. Indeed, upon either view of the site of ʿAroʿer, such an assumption is impossible, since ʿAroʿer marks the *starting-point* of the conquest, which must be presumed to have extended from

* On this explanation of the somewhat obscure passage in 2 Kgs. 3^{27}, 'And there came great wrath, etc.,' cf. *NHTK. ad loc.*

Minnith, even twenty cities,J as far as Abel-ceramim, with a very great slaughter. R[E2] So the children of ʿAmmon were subdued before the children of Israel.

34. E And Jephthaḥ came to Miṣpah unto his house; and behold his daughter coming forth to meet him with timbrels and with dances: and she was absolutely an only child; he had not beside ⌜her⌝ son or daughter. 35. And when he saw her, he rent his garments, and said, 'Alas, my daughter! thou hast indeed brought me low, and *thou* art become the supreme cause

ʿAroʿer on the Arnon southward into Moabite territory (if the statement comes from E), or from ʿAroʿer to the east of Rabbath-ʿAmmon presumably further eastward (if it comes from J).

Abel-ceramim. The name means 'meadow of vineyards'; and Eusebius (*OS.* 225 [5]) informs us that in his day there was a village named Abel with productive vineyards (κώμη ἀμπελοφόρος) six miles from Philadelphia (Rabbath-ʿAmmon)—though in what direction he does not state. If we may assume that this is a correct identification, the statement 'as far as Abel-ceramim' is naturally to be assigned to J.

34. *and behold his daughter, etc.* So the Israelite women celebrate the triumph of their people in Ex. 15 [20 f.] E (exactly as here, 'with timbrels and with dances'), 1 Sam. 18 [6 f.], Ps. 68 [11] (𝔐 [12]).

she was absolutely an only child. The Heb. is extraordinarily emphatic—lit. 'and she only was an only child.' R.V., by omitting to render the Heb. רַק, misses this emphasis altogether.

beside her. Reading מִמֶּנָּה with fem. suffix, in place of the erroneous מִמֶּנּוּ 'beside him' of 𝔐. So 𝔊[AL], 𝔖[h], 𝔏, 𝔖[P].

35. *brought me low.* Lit. 'bowed me down.' The expression is very forcible.

the supreme cause of my trouble. Heb. בְּעֹכְרָי. Lit. 'as (in the character of) my troublers,' the idiomatic ב *essentiae* (cf. BDB. *sub* ב I. 7) followed by the *plural* denoting *intensity* (the so-called *pluralis excellentiae*). R.V. 'thou art one of them that trouble me' misses the force of the expression altogether, supposing it to mean 'among my troublers.' We find exactly the same idiom in Ps. 54 [4] (𝔐 [6]), 'The Lord is *the great supporter* of my soul' (Heb. בְּסֹמְכֵי, lit. 'in the character of the supporters'); Ps. 118 [7], 'Yahweh is for me *my great helper*' (Heb. בְּעֹזְרָי, lit. 'in the character of my helpers'). In both these passages (as in our passage) the feeble and erroneous rendering of R.V. implies that Yahweh is only one among many helpers!

The Heb. verb *ʿākhar*, for which the only general reading is 'to trouble,' denotes, as its occurrences prove, the causing of poignant

of my trouble; seeing that *I* have opened my mouth unto Yahweh, and cannot go back.' 36. And she said unto him, 'My father, thou hast opened thy mouth unto Yahweh; do to

distress or anxiety. In New Heb. it has the meaning 'to make turbid'; in Ar. *'akira* 'to be turbid.'

The renderings of Jephthah's words in 𝔊[B] ταραχῇ ἐτάραξάς με, καὶ σὺ ἦς ἐν τῷ ταράχῳ μου, 𝔖[P] ܡܣܚܦܘ ܣܚܦܬܝܢܝ ܘܐܢܬܝ ܗܘܝܬܝ ܝܘܡܢܐ ܡܢ ܡܣܚܦܢܝ 'Thou hast utterly overthrown me, and thou art to-day one of my overthrowers,' 𝔙 'decepisti me, et ipsa decepta es,' suggest a Heb. original with the same verb in each clause. This may have been עכר; though in the thirteen other occurrences of this root none of these Versions represent it by the verbs which they use in this passage. 𝔊[L]'s rendering of הכרע הכרעתני, ἐμπεποδοστάτηκάς μοι (so 𝔊[A] in corrupt form, 𝔖[h] ܟܘܒܐ ܥܘܩܬ ܠܝ, 𝔏 'impedisti me') certainly suggests עֲכַרְתַּנִי; cf. the rendering of עוֹכֵר by ὁ ἐμποδοστάτης in 1 Chr. 2[7]. If, however, the first clause had originally run עֲכַרְתִּנִי (עָכֹר), or, as suggested by Houb., Grä., הָעֲכֵר הֶעֱכַרְתִּנִי (no occurrence of Hiph'îl elsewhere), the following clause would be tautological, and we should suspect the existence of a doublet. The rendering of ואת היית בעכרי given by the 𝔊[AL], 𝔖[h], 𝔏 group, εἰς σκῶλον ἐγένου ἐν ὀφθαλμοῖς μου points to מוֹקֵשׁ ,לְמוֹקֵשׁ הָיִית בְּעֵינַי (rendered by σκῶλον Ex. 10[7], Deut. 7[16], Judg. 8[27]) being apparently taken by the translator in the sense of a *thorn* or *sharp-pointed instrument* (cf. its use in Job 40[24]). More probably the Heb. was intended to mean 'Thou art become a snare in my sight,' *i.e.* an almost irresistible temptation to break the vow made to Yahweh, the existence of which he makes known to her in the next clause.

𝔗, 'A., Σ., Θ. support the text of 𝔐, from which there is no good reason to depart.

I have opened my mouth. The Heb. verb *pāṣā* 'to open' is similarly used (with subj. שְׂפָתָי—'which my lips *uttered*') of making vows in Ps. 66[14].

36. *do to me, etc.* Since the father has not actually *mentioned* his vow to the daughter, Bu. (*RS.* p. 126) supposes that the narrative must have undergone abbreviation, the daughter's inquiry as to the cause of her father's distress, and his explanation of it, having fallen out. But Mo. is assuredly correct when he remarks, 'To me it seems, on the contrary, much more in accord with the native art of the story-teller that he lets the situation and a woman's quick presentiment suffice, without this prosaic explanation.'

me according to that which hath gone forth from thy mouth, forasmuch as Yahweh hath wrought for thee full vengeance upon thine enemies, R[JE] even upon the children of ʿAmmon.' 37. E And she said unto her father, 'Let this thing be done for me: let me alone two months, that I may go, ⌜and wander free⌝ upon the mountains, and weep over my maidenhood—I and my

that which hath gone forth, etc. The same expression is used of a vow in Num. 30² (𝔐 ³).

full vengeance. Heb. 'vengeances'—another case of the intensive plural. Cf., for other instances, G-K. § 124*e*.

37. *and wander free.* Reading וְרַדְתִּי with RSm., Kit., Cooke. Cf. the use of the verb *rûdh* in Jer. 2³¹ 'we have wandered at large'; and Ar. *râda* 'to go to and fro.'* 𝔐 וְיָרַדְתִּי 'that I may go *and go down* upon the mountains' is obviously impossible, it being a forced expedient to follow Kimchi, who explains that 'Miṣpah, where Jephthaḥ's house was, was higher than the surrounding mountains; or else the verb is used with reference to the valley which lay between Miṣpah and the mountains.'‡ 𝔙 'circumeam,' 𝔖ᴾ ܘܐܗܠܟ 'walk about,' 𝔗 ואתנגיד 'and wander' (lit. 'extend myself') suggest our emendation ורדתי; but may be simply paraphrasing וירדתי in order to obtain the sense demanded by the context.

The view that וירדתי is out of place, and should properly stand at the end of the verse, either as a gloss (Doorn.) or a genuine part of the text (Bu.), in the sense 'and then I will descend'—*i.e.* return from the mountains to offer myself as a willing victim—has nothing to commend it. If it is unnatural to speak of 'descending' from Miṣpah to the mountains, the converse is equally unnatural; since Miṣpah, as its name implies (10¹⁷ *note*), must have stood on a prominent height.

and weep over my maidenhood. Stanley (*Jewish Church*, I. Lect. xvi.) aptly compares the lament of Antigone (Sophocles, *Ant.* 890), of which

* La. emends והרדתי, the Hiphʿîl of the same verb in a similar sense (Internal Hiphʿîl as in Ps. 55³). This form should surely be vocalized וַהֲרִדֹתִי, and not וַהֲרַדְתִּי, as given by La.; ע״ו forms without separating vowel being rare (cf. G-K. § 72*k*.).

‡ Kimchi actually brings forward the suggestion that וירדתי may be *explained from* the verb *rûdh* which we have adopted in our emendation, and quotes Ps. 55³ in which the Internal Hiphʿîl occurs אריד בשיחי, 'I am restless (*or* toss to and fro) in my murmuring.' He then rejects this in favour of the explanation noticed above. Rashi is perplexed by the verb 'go down,' and explains that it is 'a term denoting lamentation, an example of which is seen in the passage (Isa. 15³) 'on their housetops and in their broad places every one lamenteth, running down (יֹרֵד lit. "going down") in weeping.'

companions.' 38. And he said, 'Go.' So he sent her away two months, and she went—she and her companions, and wept over her maidenhood upon the mountains. 39. And at the end of two months she returned unto her father, and he did to her that which he had vowed, she having never known a man. And it

the maiden's grief is 'the exact anticipation . . . sharpened by the peculiar horror of the Hebrew women at a childless death—descending with no bridal festivity, with no nuptial torches, to the dark chambers of the grave':—

ὦ τύμβος, ὦ νυμφεῖον, ὦ κατασκαφὴς
οἴκησις ἀείφρουρος, οἷ πορεύομαι . . .
καὶ νῦν ἄγει με διὰ χερῶν οὕτω λαβὼν
ἄλεκτρον, ἀνυμέναιον, οὔτε τοῦ γάμου
μέρος λαχοῦσαν, οὔτε παιδείου τροφῆς.

my companions. *Kᵉrê* רֵעוֹתַי has the support of the analogous form רֵעוֹתֶיהָ in *v.*[38]. For the *Kt.* form רֵעְיֹתַי, cf. רַעְיָתִי, Cant. 1 [9.15], 2 [2.10.13], 4 [1.7], 5 [2], 6 [4]†.

39. *and he did to her, etc.* Thus the narrator draws a veil over the final tragedy; but there can be no doubt that he intends to imply that the sacrifice was carried out. On the various explanations which have been offered in order to obviate this conclusion, cf. the very full note given by Mo., pp. 304 f. The earliest Jewish interpreters (*e.g.* 𝔗, Josephus) and the Christian Fathers explained the passage in its natural sense; and it seems not to have been till the Middle Ages that another solution was sought. Thus Kimchi explains that Jephthaḥ built a house for his daughter, in which she was kept in isolation from the world, and so in perpetual virginity; and that annually the daughters of Israel went to visit her and bewail her fate. This explanation, under differently modified forms, gained acceptance after Kimchi both among Jews and Christians. But the literal interpretation was never without its supporters, and is now the generally accepted view.

she having never known, etc. A circumstantial clause, of the form noted in Driver, *Tenses*, § 160. The emphasis laid on the virginity of the sacrificed maiden is perhaps bound up with the mythological motive which very possibly lies at the bottom of the yearly festival. Cf. *Additional note*, p. 332.

and it became a custom. Reading וַתְּהִי לְחֹק with La. The subject of the fem. verb ותהי is neuter; so exactly Ps. 69 [11] וַתְּהִי לַחֲרָפוֹת לִי 'and it became reproaches unto me.' On the use of the fem. in a neuter sense, cf. G-K. § 122*q*. The view of König (*Syntax*, § 323*h*) that the subject is the היא of the preceding sentence—'and she (the

became ⌈⌉ a custom in Israel; 40. yearly the daughters of Israel go to commemorate the daughter of Jephthaḥ, four days in the year.

12. 1. J And the men of Ephraim were called to arms, and

maiden) became a pattern'—is very unlikely. 𝔥 וַתְּהִי חֹק makes the masc. חֹק the subject of the fem. verb—a want of concord which Bu. would remedy by reading וַיְהִי; but this does not give so idiomatic a phrase as that which we adopt.

Since the 'custom' refers to the women's festival mentioned in *v.* 40, it is clear that *vv.* 39-40 are wrongly divided, and that ותהי לחק should stand at the beginning of *v.* 40. As is noted by Le Clerc, Ros, etc., the reason for the division adopted by 𝔐 may be gathered from an addition in 𝔗, according to which חק is explained, not as a 'custom,' but as an 'ordinance' forbidding the sacrifice of son or daughter, which is assumed to have been promulgated in order to obviate the recurrence of such a tragedy: 'It was made an ordinance in Israel in order that no man should offer up his son or his daughter for a burnt-offering, as Jephthaḥ the Gile'adite did because he did not consult Phineḥaś the priest. If, however, he had consulted Phineḥaś the priest, he would have redeemed her at a price.'

40. *yearly.* Heb. מִיָּמִים יָמִימָה, lit. 'from days unto days,' *i.e.* 'from year to year,' in accordance with the idiomatic use of the plural ימים: cf. BDB. *s.v.* יום **6 c.**

the daughters of Israel go. The Imperf. תֵּלַכְנָה describes a frequentative action which still recurs in the writer's time. R.V. 'went,' *i.e.* 'used to go' (as though the annual custom had ceased) is certainly wrong.

to commemorate. On the meaning of the Heb. verb here used, cf. *note* on 'they recount,' *ch.* 5 11. The festival is discussed in *Additional note*, p. 332. Since the commemoration most probably took the form of a ceremonial *wailing*, we might expect some more specific term than לְתַנּוֹת. If the text should be emended, the easiest alteration would be לְאַנּוֹת 'to lament'; cf. the use of the verb in Isa. 3 26, 19 8, and the substantival forms תַּאֲנִיָּה וַאֲנִיָּה 'lamentation and mourning,' in Isa. 29 2, Lam. 2 5. So Ball, privately.

12. 1. *And the men of Ephraim, etc.* On the resemblance between this incident and that recorded in *ch.* 8 1 ff., cf. *note ad loc.*

were called to arms. Cf. *note* on 6 34.

passed over to Ṣaphon; and they said to Jephthaḥ, 'Why didst thou pass over to fight with the children of ʿAmmon without having called *us* to go with thee? We will burn thy house over thee with fire.' 2. And Jephthaḥ said unto them, 'I had a quarrel—even I and my people, and the children of ʿAmmon ⟨oppressed me⟩ sorely; and I ⌜summoned⌝ you, but ye did not save me from their hand. 3. And when I saw that ⌜there was none⌝ to save ⌜I put⌝ my life in my hand, and passed over unto

to Ṣaphon. A city of this name is mentioned in Josh. 13 [27] P, together with Succoth, as lying in the Jordan valley. This is identified by the Jerusalem Talmud (*Shebiith.* ix. 2, *fol.* 38 *d*) with מתו, *i.e.* the Amathus of Eusebius and Jerome, twenty-one Roman miles south of Pella (*OS.* 91 [27], 219 [76]), and the modern ʿAmâteh, situated in the mouth of the Wâdy Râǵib, about seven miles north of the Jabboḳ. But we should have expected the Ephraimites to have crossed the Jordan *south* of the Jabboḳ at the ford ed-Dâmiyyeh in order to reach Miṣpah; and the position of Succoth, with which Ṣaphon is associated in Josh. 13 [27], was probably south of the Jabboḳ: cf. p. 220. 𝔊ᴮ, 'A. Σ., Θ., 𝔙, 𝔖ᴾ render 'northward,' and this is adopted by R.V. text; but the rendering appears to be topographically impossible.

without having called us. Lit. 'and us thou hadst not called'—a circumstantial clause.

we will burn, etc. Cf. *ch.* 14 [15], 15 [6].

2. *I had a quarrel.* Lit. 'I was a man of strife.'

oppressed me. Supplying עִנּוּנִי, as suggested by 𝔊ᴬᴸ ἐταπείνουν με (so 𝔏ᴸ, 𝔖ʰ), with most moderns. This verb 'might easily be omitted by a scribe after עמון' (Mo.), and *some* verb is indispensable, unless (with 𝔙 'contra filios Ammon,' 𝔖ᴾ ܥܡ ܒܢ̈ܝ ܥܡܘܢ, R.V. 'with the children of A.') we treat the ו as '*wāw* of association': cf. cases cited by BDB. *s.v.* ו, 1 g.

and I summoned you. Reading Hiphʿîl וָאַזְעֵק אֶתְכֶם, as in *ch.* 4 [10.13], 2 Sam. 20 [4.5]. 𝔐 *Kal* וָאֶזְעַק should be followed by אֲלֵיכֶם—'and I cried unto you' (cf. 𝔊ᴬᴸ καὶ ἐβόησα πρὸς ὑμᾶς).

The application made by the Gileʿadites to the western tribes of Israel for help against the ʿAmmonites finds a close parallel in 1 Sam. 11, where the inhabitants of Jabesh of Gileʿad seek help in this direction against the aggressions of Naḥash, king of ʿAmmon.

3. *that there was none to save.* Reading כי אין מושיע with 𝔊ᴬᴸ, 𝔖ʰ, 𝔖ᴾ, Bu., Oort., No., La., Kit. For the phrase, cf. Deut. 28 [29.31], 1 Sam. 11 [3], 2 Sam. 22 [42], Ps. 18 [41], 𝔐 [42]. 𝔐 כי אינך מושיע 'that thou wouldest not save.'

I put, etc. Reading *Ḳᵉrê* וָאָשִׂימָה in place of the anomalous *Kt.*

the children of ʿAmmon, and Yahweh gave them into my hand: why then are ye come up unto me this day to fight against me?' 4. Then Jephthaḥ gathered together all the men of Gileʿad, and fought with Ephraim; and the men of Gileʿad smote Ephraim []. 5. And Gileʿad took the fords of the Jordan against Ephraim; and whenever the fugitives of Ephraim said, 'Let me pass over,' the men of Gileʿad said to each, 'Art thou

ואישמה. On the phrase, as expressive of risking one's life, cf. *note* on *ch.* 5 [18], 'that scorned its life, etc.'

4. *and the men of Gilʿead smote Ephraim.* After these words 𝔐 adds כִּי אָֽמְרוּ פְּלִיטֵי אֶפְרַיִם אַתֶּם גִּלְעָד בְּתוֹךְ אֶפְרַיִם בְּתוֹךְ מְנַשֶּׁה 'because they said, "Fugitives of Ephraim are ye Gileʿadites, in the midst of Ephraim, in the midst of Manasseh,"' *i.e.* the Ephraimites taunted the Gileʿadites with being, in origin, renegade members of their own tribe, without territorial status, and existing on sufferance in the territory of Ephraim and Manasseh. But, according to the earlier narrative, the reason why the Gileʿadites smote Ephraim was not on account of any such taunt (however much this may be supposed to have exacerbated the combat), but because the Ephraimites forced battle upon them. It is not clear how the Gileʿadites could, in one breath, be called 'fugitives of Ephraim,' and yet be charged with living 'in the midst of Ephraim'; nor, again, is this latter expression, which seems to suggest that the Ephraimites owned or at any rate claimed territory in Gileʿad east of Jordan, susceptible of any explanation. The term *pᵉlîṭîm*, 'fugitives,' always elsewhere denotes survivors who have escaped from the battlefield,* and is in fact so used in *v.* [5]. It is here that we find the solution of our difficulty. In the Heb. the first four words of the difficult sentence in *v.* [4], כי אמרו פליטי א׳ 'because they said, "Fugitives of Ephraim,"' are, with one slight variation (Perfect אמרו for Imperfect), identical with the words of *v.* [5] rendered 'whenever the fugitives of Ephraim said.' It can hardly be doubted that these words from *v.* [5] have come into *v.* [4] through an error of transcription, and then, on the assumption that the subject of the verb אמרו refers back to 'Ephraim' preceding, and that the words 'fugitives of Ephraim' form the commencement of what the Ephraimites said, the sentence has been conjecturally filled out as we find it in 𝔐. The words are lacking in the 𝔊 MSS. HP. 54, 59, 82, 84, 106, 108, 128, 134, and are marked by an asterisk in 𝔖ʰ.

5. *took the fords, etc.* Cf. *ch.* 3 [28], 7 [24].
whenever . . . said. The Imperfect יאמרו denotes recurrence.

* Heb. *pālaṭ*, 'to escape,' seems properly to mean 'to survive,' and to be identical with Bab. *balâṭu*, 'to live.'

an Ephraimite?' And if he said, 'No,' 6. they said to him, 'Say now *Shibbóleth*,' and he said '*Sibbóleth*,' and ⌜was⌝ not ⌜able⌝ to pronounce aright. Then they laid hold on him and

6. *Say now Shibbóleth.* The word *Shibbóleth*, which may denote either 'stream' (Isa. 27 12, Ps. 69 3.16), or 'ear of corn' (Job. 24 24, Gen. 41 5 ff., *al.*), appears to have been selected at random as an example of a word commencing with the difficult letter שׁ (so Kimchi). We have no means of ascertaining the precise sibilant sound which the narrator represents by ס in the Ephraimite pronunciation. It is possible that it was actually ס (an emphatic *s*), which is the sibilant which represents the *š* of some Babylonian loan-words in Heb. (cf. סֵפֶר = *šipru*, סַרְגּוֹן = *Šargânu*, etc.). Or, bearing in mind the fact that the word meaning 'ear of corn,' which is written with שׁ, *š*, in Heb., Aram., and Bab., is pronounced in Ar. with س, *s* (*sunbul*, *sunbula*), we may conjecture that the Ephraimites may have used the Ar. pronunciation; but since the narrator could not, in unpointed Heb., reproduce the difference between שׁ and שׂ, he was obliged to write ס in place of the latter in order to make his meaning clear. Kimchi states that the people of Ṣarĕphath were unable to pronounce שׁ, *š*, and reproduced it as aspirated ת, *th* (*i.e.* probably ث), and he suggests that the Ephraimite pronunciation may have been similar. Cf. the view of Marquart, *ZATW.*, 1888, pp. 151-155.

Of the parallels for the test cited by commentators, the most striking (quoted by Ber., etc.) is the incident of the Sicilian Vespers, Mar. 31, 1282, when the French were ordered to pronounce *ceci e ciceri*, and those who betrayed their nationality by pronouncing *c* as in French (*sesi e siseri*) were immediately cut down.

was not able. Reading לֹא יָכֹל with 𝔖ᴾ ܠܐ ܡܫܟܚ ܗܘܐ, 𝔗, 𝔙 'non valens,' Grätz, Mo., Bu., Cooke. 𝔐 לֹא יָכִין, lit. 'he could not fix,' must be taken to imply ellipse of some such object as פִּיו 'his mouth,' or שְׂפָתָיו 'his lips.' The view taken by BDB. and some commentators that the assumed object is לֵב 'the heart,' *i.e.* 'the mind' (as in the late passages, Job, 11 13, Ps. 78 8, 1 Chr. 29 18, *al.*), and that the expression means 'he did not give attention,' is less probable. The error in pronunciation was clearly due to dialectical peculiarity and not to inattention; it being most unlikely that the Ephraimites would fail through carelessness if they realized (as they must have done) that it was a matter of life or death whether they satisfied the test or not. Apart, however, from the inelegancy of יכין followed by כן, the use of the simple Imperfect is singular in the midst of a series of Imperfects with ו *consecutive*. Twelve MSS.

slew him at the fords of the Jordan: and at that time there fell of Ephraim forty and two thousand.

7. R^JE And Jephthaḥ judged Israel six years. R^P And Jephthaḥ the Gile'adite died, and was buried in ⌜his city⌝, ⟨in Miṣpeh of⟩ Gile'ad.

of 𝕳 in place of יָכִין read יָבִין 'he *did not understand* how to speak aright.'

Then they laid hold . . . Jordan. At this point Bu. (followed by La.) proposes to insert the words of *v.* [4] כי אמרו פליטי א׳ אתם 'for they said, "Ye are fugitives of Ephraim."' Since, however, the context deals with each individual case, we should have expected פליט א׳ אתה 'Thou art a fugitive of Ephraim.'

7. *in his city, in Miṣpeh of Gile'ad.* Reading בְּעִירוֹ בְּמִצְפֵּה גִלְעָד with Stu., Doorn., Bu., Mo., La., Kent, Cooke. This text has the support of several minuscules of 𝔊 which read ἐν τῇ πόλει αὐτοῦ ἐν Σεφε (or Σεφ) Γαλααδ. Here Σεφε seems to point to a Heb. original in which the מ of מצפה was obliterated. Jos. (*Ant.* V. vii. 12) seems to have used a similar text, for he writes Αὐτὸς δὲ ἄρξας ἓξ ἔτη τελευτᾷ καὶ θάπτεται ἐν τῇ αὐτοῦ πατρίδι Σεβέῃ· τῆς Γαλαδηνῆς δ' ἐστὶν αὕτη. 𝕳 בְּעָרֵי ג׳ 'in the cities of Gile'ad,' is impossible; it being quite illegitimate to render, with A.V., R.V., 'in *one of* the cities.' 𝕿 follows 𝕳. 𝔊^B ἐν τῇ πόλει αὐτοῦ ἐν Γαλααδ. 𝔊^AL, 𝕾^h ἐν τῇ πόλει αὐτοῦ Γαλααδ, 𝕷, 𝖁 'in civitate sua Galaad.' 𝕾^P ܒܡܕܝܢܬܐ ܕܓܠܥܕ 'in a city of Gile'ad.'

HUMAN SACRIFICE AMONG THE ISRAELITES.

(Cf. *ch.* 11[31] *note.*)

Evidence shows that the practice of human sacrifice (especially the sacrifice of the firstborn) was not unknown among the Israelites; though in historical times it seems to have been very exceptional. In pre-Mosaic times it was probably more frequent, if not customary. The Book of the Covenant (Ex. 20[22]-23[33] E), many of the regulations of which probably grew up in Cana'an at a period immensely earlier than the age of Moses,* seems expressly to contemplate that the normal fate of a firstborn son is that he should be sacrificed to

* The standpoint here assumed is that the Book of the Covenant represents very largely the consuetudinary legislation of Cana'an from a period long prior to the entry and settlement under Joshua' of those Israelite tribes (chiefly, if not solely, the Joseph tribes) who had come under the leadership and influence of Moses, and had thereby gained a higher and purer conception of Yahweh and the requirements of his religion. This view seems to explain the close connexion in many points of this early legislation with the Code of Ḫammurabi, which must

Yahweh. The enactment of 22.[29b] says, without qualification, 'The firstborn of thy sons shalt thou give to me'; and this is immediately followed by the enactment with regard to the firstborn of animals, which is couched in precisely similar terms: 'So shalt thou do to thine ox and to thy sheep: seven days it shall be with its mother; on the eighth day thou shalt give it to me' (*v.* [30]). We know of course how the former enactment was interpreted elsewhere, and that in early legislation. The law of J in Ex. 34[20] lays down that 'Every firstborn of thy sons thou shalt redeem'; and this is repeated in Ex. 13[13b] P. Thus it appears probable that an animal-substitute may usually have been provided at an early period in Israel's history. The story of Abraham's projected sacrifice of Isaac in Gen 22 E was probably intended to show that the Father of the Faithful had been ready to make the most costly sacrifice, and God had graciously vouchsafed to be pleased with an animal in its place. Such a tradition (if we are justified in regarding it as ancient) was doubtless not without its influence in determining the interpretation of the old regulation. Mic. 6[1-8], if really the work of the eighth-century prophet, indicates that in the mind of the average Israelite of Micah's day there still lurked the idea that Yahweh might conceivably be propitiated by the sacrifice of a firstborn son as the most costly form of offering; but whether this idea was often, or ever, carried into practice at this period we cannot say. It is quite possible, as many scholars have thought, that the passage may be due to a prophetic teacher

(if not *in toto*, at least as regards a large part of its enactments) have been operative in Syria as well as in Babylonia *cir.* B.C. 2000 (on Ḫammurabi as king of the West as well as of Babylonia, cf. *Introd.* pp. lxi ff.). It explains also the extremely primitive character of many of the enactments of the Book of the Covenant; *e.g.* 21[6], 22[8.9] (𝔐 [7.8]), where *hā-'ĕlōhîm* can scarcely, except on the most forced exegesis, be explained otherwise than as 'the (household) gods'—probably identical with Teraphim. In 21[6] the scene of the ceremony is clearly the master's own house (*not* the local sanctuary), just as it is in Deut. 15[16 f.]; the only difference being that in the later enactment the reference to *hā-'ĕlōhîm* is dropped, doubtless as offensive to the purer form of Yahwism. In 22[8] *hā-'ĕlōhîm* are agents or means of *divination*, just as the Teraphim appears to have been (cf. *note* on *ch.* 17[5]). If this view of the origin of the legislation of the Book of the Covenant is correct, we can understand how a code which was probably from primitive times the property both of the Cana'anites and of such Israelite elements as had not come under the influence of Mosaic Yahwism, may have contained an enactment enjoining the offering of the firstborn, which later on came, under the refining influence of Mosaic Yahwism, to be interpreted as satisfied by the redemption of the firstborn of man by the sacrifice of an animal.

On the view that the history of Israel's religion in early times is the history of a conflict between the high ethical Yahwism which was the outcome of the teaching of Moses, and a much cruder and more naturalistic form of Yahwism practised by Israelite tribes which had never been in Egypt nor come under the influence of the great teacher, cf. an article by the present editor entitled *A Theory of the Development of Israelite Religion in Early Times*, *JTS.*, Apr. 1908, pp. 321-352.

during the idolatrous reaction under Manasseh in the seventh century B.C., when it became the custom to sacrifice children as holocausts to the god Molech (cf. 2 Kgs. 21 [6], Jer. 3 [24], 7 [31], 19 [4-6], 32 [35], Ezek. 16 [20.21], 23 [37-39]). *

The same abuse is stated by the Deuteronomic redactor of Kgs. to have been practised in the reign of Aḥaz (2 Kgs. 16 [3]), and during the closing days of the Northern Kingdom (2 Kgs. 17 [17]); but no allusion to such child-sacrifices is made by Isaiah in his prophecies which seem to belong to Aḥaz's reign, nor by Amos and Hosea' in their indictment of the sins of the Northern Kingdom; and it seems probable, therefore, that R^D in Kgs. may be erroneously attributing the corrupt practice of Manasseh's age to an earlier period. Ps. 106 [37 f.] is not evidence that the custom was general throughout pre-monarchic times; but we may probably infer from Isa. 57 [5 f.] that the seventh-century practice survived into post-exilic times among the degraded remnant of the Judaean population which was left in Palestine during the exile. 2 Kgs. 17 [31] states that it was in vogue among a section of the foreign settlers who were introduced into the Northern Kingdom after the fall of Samaria.

The practice of the rite of child-sacrifice among the Cana'anites is alluded to in Deut. 12 [31], 18 [9.10], and forbidden to Israel (cf. Lev. 18 [21], 20 [2] H). Excavation has brought to light numerous examples of the burial of infants of about a week old in jars in the vicinity of a sanctuary.‡ These are probably evidence for the practice of the sacrifice of the firstborn among the Cana'anites; though it is only rarely that the remains of the infants appear to have been subjected to the action of fire. Another form of human sacrifice which has been attested by excavation is the foundation-sacrifice, in which the victim (infant or adult) has been buried (probably alive) in the foundations of a building. An instance of this form of sacrifice among the Israelites is perhaps to be found in 1 Kgs. 16 [34]; but, if this be so, the mere fact that the event is placed on record seems to indicate that it was very unusual.

* The phrase which is often used in allusion to this form of sacrifice—העביר באש, rendered by A.V., R.V., 'cause to pass through the fire' (sometimes העביר simply)—has been otherwise explained as though it referred to some rite of initiation. But the meaning of the expression is more probably 'make over' ('cause to pass over') to the deity 'by fire' (cf. the use of the verb in Ex. 13 [12]); and the fact that this really denotes a sacrifice in which the victim was first slain and then burnt has been strongly maintained by Mo. (*EB.* 3184) by comparison of passages in which the phrase occurs with parallel passages in which the reference to the slaughter of children is unambiguous. Cf. especially Jer. 32 [35] with 19 [5.6]; Ezek. 23 [37-39] with 16 [20 f].

‡ Cf. Vincent, *Canaan*, pp. 188 ff.; Driver, *Schweich Lectures*, pp. 67 ff.; Stanley A. Cook, *Religion of Ancient Palestine*, pp. 38 ff.; Handcock, *Archæology of the Holy Land*, pp. 368 ff. On the foundation sacrifice generally, cf. Trumbull, *The Threshold Covenant*, pp. 45 ff. A different theory as to the buried infants has been offered by Frazer, *Adonis, Attis, Osiris*, pp. 82 f.

THE WOMEN'S FESTIVAL OF JUDGES, 11. 40.

Whatever be the historical value of the story of the sacrifice of Jephthaḥ's daughter, it is probable that the festival which existed in the narrator's time, and which he explained as commemorative of this traditional event, really had its origin in a cultus which was based upon mythology and not upon history. There is evidence for the practice of a similar ceremonial in Syria in later times. The worship of Κόρη, *i.e.* the heavenly virgin, by the inhabitants of Shechem is attested by Epiphanius (*Adv. haeres.* iii. 2, 1055), who supposed that the ceremonial sacrifice was connected with the commemoration of Jephthaḥ's daughter. Porphyry (*De Abstinentia*, ii. 56) states that at Laodicea on the Syrian coast a virgin was in ancient times offered to Athena, and that the ceremonial still survived, a stag being substituted for the human sacrifice. Pausanias (III. xvi. 8) identifies the goddess who was thus honoured with Artemis, whose image, he tells us, had formerly stood at Brauron, but had been presented to the Laodiceans by Seleucus. Robertson Smith (*Religion of the Semites*,[2] p. 466) argues that the town of Laodicea was of much greater antiquity than its re-christening by Seleucus; and that, if the goddess in question had really been Greek, she would not have been identified with Athena as well as with Artemis. His conclusion is that she must originally have been a form of the native Syrian goddess ʿAshtart (cf. also Frazer's note in his edition of Pausanias, vol. iii. pp. 340 f.). The connexion of this sacrifice with the Iphigenia-legend (as recognized by Pausanias) is clear; especially with that form of the legend in which a hind was substituted by Artemis as a sacrifice, in place of the maiden. It is much more likely that the Greek legend had its source in Western Asia (like many other elements of Greek mythology), than, conversely, that the legend, and the rites in which it was celebrated, penetrated from Greece into the Syrian littoral.

The resemblance between the stories of Iphigenia and Jephthaḥ's daughter has often been remarked: cf., *e.g.*, the series of parallels drawn by Capellus, *De voto Jephthae*, § xii. (*Annotata ad Libros Historicos V.T.*, Tom. ii. 1660, p. 2082). If this resemblance is more than accidental, it goes far to anticipate the objection which might be brought against the validity of the evidence which has already been adduced for the existence in Syria of rites analogous to the women's festival of Judg. 11 ^{40}, viz. that the former is very late in comparison with the latter; since it is clear, from the early date at which the legend of Iphigenia appears in Greek mythology, that, if at all dependent upon Semitic cultus, it must testify to a cultus of very considerable antiquity.

As to the original significance of this cultus we are altogether without definite evidence, and can only make conjecture. Mo. (p. 305) thinks that 'the annual lamentation of the women of Gilead for Jephthaḥ's daughter belongs to a class of ceremonies, the original significance of which, often disguised by the myth, is mourning for the death of a god.' Jeremias (*OTLAE.* ii. pp. 168 f.) would bring the sacrifice into connexion with the Tammuz-Ištar cult.

This latter cult appears to have been inherited by the Babylonians from their Sumerian predecessors, and is consequently of very high antiquity. It was borrowed from the Babylonians by the Phoenicians, among whom Tammuz was venerated under the title *Adon* 'lord'; and from the Phoenicians the Tammuz-Ištar myth spread westwards into Greece, in the well-known form of the story of Adonis and Aphrodite. We may gather from the O.T. some few traces of the cult in Israel, where, as elsewhere, it seems pre-eminently to have been practised among women.* Its central observance was ceremonial mourning for the *death of the god*, who typified the youthful sun of springtime, or, according to a variant conception, the luxuriant vegetation produced by this sun, which is cut off and destroyed by the fierce heat of the sun of midsummer. This mourning took place in the fourth month, which falls at or about the summer-solstice (cf. *OTLAE.* i. pp. 96 ff.), and which bears the name of Tammuz in the Babylonian (as in the later Jewish) calendar.‡

The cult of Ištar, as the earth-goddess of fertility, stands in intimate connexion with that of Tammuz. She appears variously as his virgin-mother, sister, wife, and lover. Sometimes, indeed, Tammuz seems to have been regarded as feminine, and bore titles which properly belong to the goddess.§ The conception seems to vary according as

* Ezek. 8 14 speaks of the women at Jerusalem weeping for Tammuz. In Isa. 17 10 the phrase נטעי נעמנים, which R.V. *text* translates 'pleasant plants,' is more probably to be rendered, as in the *marg.*, 'plantings of Adonis': cf. the Greek Ἀδώνιδος κῆποι, *i.e.* pots or baskets containing quick-growing, and quickly-fading, plants, which were dedicated to Aphrodite as emblems of her lover's beauty and early death (cf. Plato, *Phædrus*, 276 B; Theocritus, 15, 113). Some would find a similar reference in the allusion to 'gardens' in Isa. 1 29.30. In Dan. 11 37 the phrase חמדת נשים 'the desire (desired one) of women,' which the context shows to be the title of a deity, probably refers to Tammuz (cf. the commentaries of Bevan and Driver *ad loc.*). The reference in Zech. 12 11 to 'the mourning of Hadad-Rimmon in the valley of Megiddo' is obscure, and the grounds for associating it with the Tammuz-wailing are highly precarious; while the supposition that an allusion to the ceremonial is to be found in 'the mourning for an only son' Am. 8 10, and that the formulæ of lamentation for the dead mentioned in Jer. 22 18, 34 5 are derived from the cult, is most improbable. Cf. Baudissin, *Adonis und Esmun*, pp. 87-93.

‡ Succinct accounts of the Tammuz-myth and ritual in Babylonia are given by Sayce, *DB.* iv. pp. 676 f.; Cheyne, *EB.* 4893 f.; Zimmern, *KAT.*3 pp. 397 f.; Jastrow, *RBBA.* pp. 343-350, 370 f. For greater detail, cf. Zimmern, *Der babylonische Gott Tamûz* (*Abhandl. der phil.-hist. Klasse der K. Sächs. Gesellsch. der Wissensch.* xxvii., 1909, pp. 701-738); Langdon, *Tammuz and Ishtar*, 1914. For the Phoenician form of the cult, cf. Baudissin, *Adonis und Esmun*, 1911. For the cult in its wider developments, cf. Frazer, *Adonis, Attis, Osiris*3, 1914 (many very questionable assumptions).

§ Cf. Zimmern, *Tamûzlieder*, pp. 211, 213; *Der Bab. Gott Tamûz*, pp. 7 ff.; Hommel, *Grundriss*, pp. 387 f., 395; Jastrow, *op. cit.* pp. 347 f.; Langdon, *op. cit.* pp. 16 ff.

8. R[P] And after him Ibṣan of Bethleḥem judged Israel. 9. And he had thirty sons, and thirty daughters he sent abroad, and thirty daughters he brought in for his sons from abroad: and he judged Israel seven years. 10. And Ibṣan died, and was buried in Bethleḥem.

11. And after him Elon the Zebulonite judged Israel; and he judged Israel ten years. 12. And Elon the Zebulonite died, and was buried in Aijalon in the land of Zebulun.

Ištar is regarded as the spontaneously-productive virgin (or sexless) Mother-Earth, or fertility is conceived as the result of union between Spring-Sun and Earth. When the former conception held force, Tammuz, as the emanation of Mother-Earth, might naturally be regarded as virgin and feminine like herself.

The Greek myth of the abduction of Kore-Persephone (a vegetation-goddess) to the Underworld, and her return to the earth in the spring, is ultimately of Babylonian origin. The relation between Demeter (originally the Earth-goddess) and Kore (the spring-vegetation) represents one form of the Tammuz-Ištar myth, just as the relation between Aphrodite and Adonis represents another form. It is probable that the yearly sinking of Kore (or the feminine Tammuz) to the Underworld may at one time have been marked (at least in Syria) by a virgin-sacrifice, for which in later times another offering (*e.g.* a hind) was substituted. We recall the fact already noticed that the sacrifice of the Shechemites mentioned by Epiphanius, and connected by him with the sacrifice of Jephthaḥ's daughter, was made to Kore. The emphasis on virginity belongs to the basic conception of the Earth-mother herself as virgin or sexless. Cf. further, *Addenda*, pp. xvii ff.

Among the many virgin-sacrifices of early Greek mythology we may compare that of Polyxena, who, as her name implies—'she of the many guests'—is in origin a queen of the Underworld, the wife of Polydector or Polydegmon (*i.e.* Hades, so-called as πολλοὺς δεχόμενος): cf. Murray, *The Rise of the Greek Epic*, pp. 121 f.

12. 8-15. *The 'Minor' Judges, Ibṣan, Elon, and 'Abdon.*
On the 'minor' Judges generally, cf. pp. 289 f.

8. *Bethleḥem.* Jos. (V. vii. 13) takes this city to be Bethleḥem of Judah; and the same view is assumed by Rashi, Kimchi, and Levi ben-Gershon, who preserve a tradition that Ibṣan was the same as Boaz the ancestor of David. There is, however, a northern Bethleḥem mentioned in Josh. 19[15] P which is probably the modern Bêt Laḥm, seven miles west-north-west of Naẓareth, and it is not unlikely that this may be the city intended. Cf. p. 290.

12. *was buried in Aijalon.* Possibly the distinction drawn by 𝔐 between the name of the judge and that of his city is merely artificial.

13. And after him ʿAbdon the son of Hillel the Pirʿathonite judged Israel. 14. And he had forty sons and thirty grandsons, who rode upon seventy ass-colts: and he judged Israel eight years. 15. And ʿAbdon the son of Hillel the Pirʿathonite died, and was buried in Pirʿathon in the land of Ephraim, in the hill-country of the ʿAmalekites.

𝔊[B] reproduces both names as Αιλωμ, *i.e.* אֵילֹן. So Nöldeke (*Untersuchungen zur Kritik des A. T.*, p. 184), Mo., La., Cooke.

13. *the Pirʿathonite.* Pirʿathon corresponds philologically to the modern Farʿatâ, six miles west-south-west of Shechem. The Φαραθων fortified by Bacchides (1 Macc. 9^{50}) appears to have lain further south.

15. *in the land of Ephraim.* Some 𝔊. MSS. here read ἐν ὄρει Εφραιμ ἐν γῇ Σελλημ. This is adopted by Mo. (*SBOT.*) who supposes that ἐν γῇ Σελλημ = בְּאֶרֶץ שַׁעֲלִים, *i.e.* the land of Shaʿalim mentioned in 1 Sam. 9^{4}. In support of this view he adduces the southern position of Pirʿathon, as inferred from 1 Macc. 9^{50}, and the fact that the name ʿAbdon occurs in the genealogical lists in Benjamin, 1 Chr. 8^{23}, $8^{30} = 9^{36}$. That Σελλημ = שַׁעֲלִים (in 1 Sam. 9^{4}, 𝔊[A] Σααλειμ, 𝔊[L] Σεγαλειμ) is, however, a bold assumption; and, since ʿAbdon is not an uncommon name, there is no reason for supposing that the Benjaminite ʿAbdon of 1 Chr. must be identical with the ʿAbdon of the present passage.

in the hill-country of the ʿAmalekites. Cf. p. 132.

13. 1–16. 31. *Samson.*

Besides the Commentaries, etc., cited throughout the book, cf. B. Stade, *Ri.* 14, *ZATW.* iv. (1884), pp. 250-256; W. Böhme, *Die älteste Darstellung in Richt.* $6^{11\text{-}24}$ *und* $13^{2\text{-}24}$ *und ihre Verwandtschaft mit der Jahveurkunde des Pentateuch*, *ZATW.* v. (1885), pp. 251-274; A. van Doorninck, *De Simsonsagen. Kritische Studiën over Richteren* 14-16, *Theol. Tijdschrift*, xxviii. (1894), pp. 14-32.

On the solar-mythological interpretation of the story, cf. (selected bibliography) E. Meier, *Geschichte der poetischen National-Literatur der Hebräer*, 1856, pp. 97-108; G. Roskoff, *Die Simsonsage nach ihrer Entstehung, Form und Bedeutung, und der Heraclesmythus*, 1860; H. Steinthal, *The Legend of Samson* (trans. of an article in *Zeitschrift für Völkerpsychologie*, 1862), in Appendix to J. Goldziher, *Mythology among the Hebrews*, 1877; F. Baethgen, *Beiträge zur semit. Religionsgesch.*, 1888, pp. 161-173; H. Stahn, *Die Simsonsage*, 1908; A. Smythe Palmer, *The Samson-saga, and its place in comparative Religion*, 1913.*

This narrative introduces us to the period of the Philistine oppression, for the history of which the way has been prepared by the account of Israel's apostasy in $10^{6\text{-}16}$; cf. the reference to the

* Meier and Roskoff are selected as good representatives of the earlier writers on the subject, who were mainly concerned with drawing out the parallels between the deeds of Samson and those of Herakles. Steinthal goes much

Philistines in *v.*[7].* It was this oppression which led ultimately to the institution of the kingship in Israel; and, so far as we can gather from the oldest sources, the strong hand of the Philistines was not relaxed to any appreciable extent until some amount of consolidation had been achieved among the Israelites through the establishment of the monarchy. The narrative thus occupies its right chronological position in the Book of Judges, *chs.* 17-21 being of the nature of an appendix (cf. *Introd.* p. xxxvii).

The Samson-narrative, though consisting of a number of semi-independent stories, shows no sign of compilation from parallel and divergent sources; and the generally accepted view is that it has been extracted in its entirety from one of the two main ancient sources of Judg.‡ That this source was J can hardly be doubted. Böhme has proved conclusively that *ch.* 13 must be derived from J. He notes the striking resemblances which it exhibits to the Gide'on-narrative 6 11-24 J—the appearance of the Angel of Yahweh as the bearer of specific injunctions; the offering of a kid upon a rock-altar; the miraculous disappearance of the supernatural visitor, whilst the heavenly fire consumes the offering; the terror of the human actors on realization that they have seen a divine being, and their subsequent reassurance that Yahweh is well-disposed towards them. Especially striking is the verbal identity between *vv.*[5.7] and Gen. 16 11 J in the phrase הנך הרה וילדת בן 'Behold, thou art with child, and shalt bear a son,' and *v.*[18a] and Gen. 32 30 J למה זה תשאל לשמי 'Wherefore, now, askest thou concerning my name?' Other resemblances cited by Böhme are, *v.*[6] ואת שמו לא הגיד לי 'and his name he told me not,' and Gen. 32 30 J הגידה נא שמך 'tell me, prithee, thy name'; *v.*[10] ותרץ ותגד 'and she ran and told,' and Gen. 24 28, 29 12 J, where the same two verbs are similarly coupled; the association of מהר 'hasten' and רוץ 'run' in *v.*[10], as in Gen. 18 6.7, 24 20 J; *v.*[11] ויאמר אני

further than his predecessors in elaborating the solar-mythological theory; and, while laying himself open to grave criticism in many points of detail, he marks a distinct stage in the serious treatment of the subject. A valuable criticism of Steinthal is offered by Baethgen. Stahn is useful as giving a very full bibliography of earlier monographs, with brief summaries of the views of different scholars. Smythe Palmer deals with the subject in a far more detailed and systematic way than has been attempted by earlier scholars, bringing together a large and varied mass of material in support of his thesis. The value of the book would have been greatly enhanced if this material had been more critically sifted. The book is weakest in its Semitic philology, suggestions of a transparently fallacious character being too often accepted and built upon.

* On 10 6-16, as originally intended by the E narrator to introduce, not the judgeship of Samson, but that of Samuel, cf. p. 294.

‡ An attempt to prove compilation from the two main ancient sources of Judg. has been made by E. von Ortenberg, *Beil. z. Jahresber. d. Gymn. zu Verden*, 1887; but has not met with acceptance among scholars. The present editor has not been able to obtain access to this publication.

'and he said, "*I*"' (*i.e.* 'I am he'), as in Gen. 27 [24] J (elsewhere only 1 Kgs. 13 [14]; cf. ויאמר אנכי 2 Sam. 2 [20]). In addition to these, we may note as characteristic J phrases, מלאך יהוה 'the Angel of Yahweh,' *vv.*[3.13.15.16.17.18.20.21] (on מלאך האלהים *vv.*[6 9] cf. *notes*), הנה נא 'Behold, now,' *v.*[3]; עתר 'intreat,' *v.*[8], בי אדני 'Oh, my lord' *v.*[8], למה זה 'Wherefore' *v.*[18]; cf. CH.[J] 4, 9, 48, 56*b*, 89*b*. Finally, the prolonged barrenness of the hero's mother is a trait which characterizes the J narrative; cf. Gen. 11 [30] (Sarai), Gen. 25 [21] (Rebeḳah), Gen. 29 [31] (Rachel), which are the only occurrences of the adjective עקרה 'barren' in *narrative* outside Judg. 13 [2.3].

While, however, *ch.* 13 thus abounds with indications that it is derived from J, the literary characteristics of J are absent from *chs.* 14-16. These latter chapters are entirely *sui generis*, full of the rough vigour and broad humour of the rustic story-teller, but lacking the literary grace and finish which distinguish the finer parts of J and E. It is obvious, moreover, that the religious motive which colours the narrative of *ch.* 13 is altogether absent from *chs.* 14-16. The birth-narrative prepares us for a Gide'on or a Samuel, keenly alive to the fact that he holds a divine commission, and upheld in his performance of it by consciousness of the divine support. Samson, however, proves to have no commission at all, and recognizes no higher guide than his own wayward passions. Again, the fact can hardly be denied that the story-cycle of *chs.* 14-16 contains a mythological element which must be very primitive, and which is, in origin, far removed from the Yahweh-religion of J (cf. *Addit. note*, p. 391).

Yet that *ch.* 13 was written to introduce the narrative of *chs.* 14-16 cannot be questioned. Had it originally prefaced a Samson-narrative more in accordance with its own tone, we cannot imagine why this should have been rejected by a later editor in favour of the present narrative. Moreover, *chs.* 14-16 are not entirely without points of connexion with *ch.* 13. We notice 14 [4a], the allusion to Yahweh's divine purpose working unseen through Samson's wayward inclination; and 16 [17a] 'No razor hath come up upon my head, for a Nazirite of God have I been from my mother's womb'—a statement which presupposes the injunction of 13 [5.7]. These are passages which lie upon the surface of the narrative, and are easily detachable from it without in any way affecting its sequence. The inference which may be drawn is that the J narrator made use of an ancient cycle of folk-tales which were current in his day, incorporating them into his work practically unaltered from their popular form, except for one or two touches such as we find in the passages above noticed.

This is the view of van Doorninck, who, however, is inclined to assign to the later narrator not merely the passages above mentioned, but also Samson's last prayer to Yahweh 16 [28], and the three allusions to his feats of strength as inspired by the sudden inrush of the spirit of Yahweh in 14 [6.19], 15 [14]; whereas on other occasions (*e.g.* 15^8, 16^9, *al.*) he appears to act without any such initiative. So drastic an elimination from the ancient folk-tales of all allusions to Yahweh's influence on the hero (a proceeding which, to be complete, should include $15^{18.19}$ in its present form) can hardly be accepted. However much the stories may, in their origin, have been coloured by the solar-mythological motive, it cannot be doubted that this motive had long been forgotten by the time that the tales were utilized by the J writer for his narrative: and, if this was so, and Samson's feats had come to be related as the actual deeds of an actual member of the tribe of Dan, it is natural that they should have come to be explained, like other events of a phenomenal character, as due to the active co-operation of the Spirit of Yahweh.* Such a presentation marks a stage midway between the purely pagan (non-Yahwistic) conception of the hero, and his adoption by the author of *ch.* 13 as the commissioned agent of Yahweh, of which the most salient feature is the interpretation of his long locks (originally in all probability a solar trait; cf. *Addit. note*, p. 404) as the distinctive badge of dedication to Yahweh, from his birth and even earlier, as a *Nazirite*—a conception which it is difficult to regard as originally inherent in the stories of *chs.* 14-16 (cf. *note* on 13^5).

This view of the growth of the Samson-narrative is indicated in the text by the marking of the old story-cycle as J^1, and the later construction put upon it by the main J narrator (as embodied in *ch.* 13 and in the touches in *chs.* 14-16 above noticed) as J^2. The next stage was the full acceptance of Samson as a member of the series of divinely commissioned *Judges* by R^{JE}, whose hand is seen in 13^{5b}, and in this editor's ordinary formula of conclusion in 16^{31b}. The principal editor of our Book of Judges, R^{E2} (whose regular formula of introduction is seen in 13^1), appears to have laboured under a sense of the moral unsuitability of the hero for inclusion in such a category; and thus to have made extensive excisions from the narrative, including among them the account of Samson's death as a slave of the uncircumcised. Probably he would have been by no means averse from excluding him altogether, but found his figure too firmly enshrined in the popular imagination to allow of the practicability of so drastic a proceeding. R^{E2}'s revised account ended with *ch.* 15, as we may see by the occurrence of the concluding formula as to the length of the judgeship in 15^{20}, which is the formula of R^{JE}, adopted by R^{E2} from 16^{31b} when 16^{1-31a} was cancelled.‡ At a later time the excised

* As a matter of fact, 14^{19a} *is* probably to be regarded as a later addition to the narrative (cf. *note ad loc.*), but not on the ground that it pictures Samson as animated by the Spirit of Yahweh; the particular phrase in which this is described being probably copied from 14^6, where it seems to be an integral part of the narrative.

‡ The considerations which may have influenced R^{E2} in his inclusions and omissions from the story-cycle have been well indicated by Bu.:—'Down to the close of *ch.* 15, Samson is the husband of *one* wife, and love to her, along with

stories were once more inserted, as we have them in *ch.* 16, doubtless by the hand which restored the story of Abimelech and the Appendix, *chs.* 17-21 (R^P; cf. *note* on *ch.* 8 29-32).

The Samson-narratives (*i.e.* the ancient story-cycle, *chs.* 14-16) stand alone in the O.T. as illustrations of a type of story emanating, not from the literary circle of the prophets, but from the popular traditions of the country-folk. As Bu. points out (*DB.* iv. p. 380 *a*), 'the ideal of the country-hero was exactly the same in Israel then as it is at the present day. The lion of a village must be first in success with the female sex, first in bodily strength, courage, and fondness for brawling, and first in mother-wit.' As has been argued elsewhere (cf. *Addit. note*, p. 391), the stories seem to exhibit strongly-marked traces of an ancient solar myth, the original significance of which had doubtless been forgotten when it was drawn upon to enrich the halo of the marvellous with which popular imagination loved to surround the deeds of the tribal hero. When, however, allowance has been made for this element in the narratives, there can be no doubt that they possess unique value as illustrating the village-life of the time, and the relations between Israelites and Philistines living in the border-country. The two villages Ṣorʿah and Eshta'ol, on the edge of the Shẹphelah, appear as the homes of a small cluster of Danite clans. The Danites must have been few in number; and it is very probable that the migration of the main part of the tribe to seek a new home in the extreme north (as related in *ch.* 18 26ff., Josh. 19 47 J) may already have taken place. In any case, the Danites of the south were at this time confined within a very small district; and, together with the neighbouring clans of Judah, were in subjection to the Philistines, and stood in wholesome dread of sharing the responsibility of any action which might excite the animosity of their masters (cf. 15 11).

The question must remain open whether any historical reality is to be attached to the figure of Samson. It can hardly be denied that, given the existence of a cycle of stories relating to a mythical solar hero who had come to be popularly regarded as an historical individual, we have sufficient substratum to account for the whole Samson-tradition; such elements in the story as are originally unconnected with the solar myth belonging quite conceivably to the local colouring which was the work of popular story-tellers. There is, however, an abundance of analogy for the accretion of mythologi-

love to his native land is the motive of all his actions. But in *ch.* 16 he appears as the slave of sensual passion, caught in the toils of a succession of paramours, to the last of whom he even betrays the secret of the divine strength that animated him. If this itself must have appeared to the mind of R^D [our R^{E2}] quite unworthy of a God-called judge (cf. 2 16.18f.), his fate also was an unfitting one, namely that he should end his life as prisoner and slave of the unbelievers' (*DB.* iv. p. 378 *b*).

cal tales round historical persons; and the fact that this is so should warn us against pronouncing a categorical opinion that the figure of Samson is wholly unhistorical.

Such a question is, however, of very slight importance. If we could grant the historical character of the whole Samson-narrative, Samson would still not be the initiator or furtherer of any movement, religious or political, in the history of Israel which would invest his figure with the slightest historical significance. The real value of the narrative lies in its local setting, which bears intrinsic evidence of being very true to life, and in its preservation of a mythical tradition, akin to that of other Semitic races, of the existence of which in Israel we should otherwise be ignorant.

13. 1. R^{E2} And the children of Israel again did that which was evil in the sight of Yahweh; and Yahweh gave them into the hand of the Philistines forty years. 2. J^2 And there was a certain man of Ṣorʿah, of the clan of the Danites, and his name

13. 1. *the Philistines.* On the origin of the Philistines, and their settlement in Canaʿan, cf. *Introd.* pp. xcii ff.

2. *a certain man.* Heb. 'one man'—an indefinite use of אֶחָד 'one' which is usually somewhat characteristic of the North Palestinian dialect; so in E in *ch.* 9[53] אשה אחת 'a certain woman.' For the classified instances of אחד in this sense, cf. *NHTK.* p. 209. This small point cannot, however, weigh against the evidence already adduced (p. 336) in proof that our narrative belongs to J. The whole phrasing of *v.*[2a] closely resembles that of *v.*[1] of 1 Sam. 1—a chapter which, if reliance is to be placed upon striking parallels in diction (cf. 1 Sam. $1^{11b\beta}$ with *v.*$^{5a\alpha}$, 1 Sam. 1^{15a} with *v.*$^{4a\beta}$, 1 Sam. $1^{20a\beta.b\alpha}$, $3^{19a.b\beta}$ with *v.*[24]), should belong to J rather than (as commonly supposed) to E. The details added to the narrative by Jos. (*Ant.* v. viii. 2 f.) are apparently derived from his own imagination.

Ṣorʿah. The modern Ṣarʿah, fourteen miles due east of Jerusalem in the Shephelah, upon an elevation on the northern side of the wâdy eṣ-Ṣarâr (the wâdy of Soreḳ; cf. 16[4]), up which the railway from Jaffa to Jerusalem now travels. Beth-shemesh, *i.e.* 'Temple of the Sun,' the modern ʿAin-šems, stands on a corresponding eminence on the opposite side of the wâdy, and its proximity may help to account for the solar-mythological traits which the story of Samson seems to exhibit (cf. *Addit. note*, p. 391). From the manner in which Ṣorʿah is named with the neighbouring village Eshtaʾol in *v.*[25], *ch.* 16[31], 18[2.8.11] as the home of the Danites, it would appear that they were at this time nearly, if not wholly, confined to these two villages. The latter village, if rightly identified with the modern ʾEšûaʿ (cf. *v.*[25] *note*), is less than two miles off further up the wâdy to the north-east. The Danites must thus have been very few in number; and it is to be

was Manoaḥ; and his wife was barren and had not borne. 3. And the Angel of Yahweh appeared unto the woman, and said unto her, 'Behold, now, thou art barren and hast not borne; Gl. but thou shalt conceive, and bear a son. 4. J² Now,

noted that they are described, both in this narrative, and in *ch.* 18 2.11.19, as a *clan* (*mišpāḥā*; *šebheṭ*, 'tribe,' occurs, however, in 18 1.19.30). Their limitation to this small district on the edge of the hill-country is explained in *ch.* 1 34; cf. further *note ad loc.*

Manoaḥ. The manner in which the Manaḥtites of Ṣorʿah (הַמָּנַחְתִּי הַצָּרְעִי lit. 'the Ṣorʿite Manaḥtites') are mentioned in 1 Chr. 2 54 has suggested to many commentators that Manoaḥ may have been the eponymous ancestor of the clan-division of the Danites inhabiting Ṣorʿah. It seems, however, to be likely that the connexion in form between Manoaḥ and Manaḥtites is merely accidental; the Manaḥtites being a Calibbite clan, a portion of which inhabited the district of Ṣorʿah in *post-exilic* times.* The Calibbites formed an element of the mixed tribe of Judah (cf. *note* on *ch.* 1 12); and we are informed in Neh. 11 29 that Ṣorʿah was one of the cities occupied by the children of Judah after the Exile.

3. *the Angel of Yahweh.* Cf. *ch.* 2 1 *note.*

but thou shalt conceive, etc. The words have the appearance of an

* The composite genealogy of the Calibbites in 1 Chr. 2 42-55 is very problematical; but it seems likely, as Benzinger and Curtis assume (commentaries *ad loc.*; cf. also *EB.* 630) that *vv.* 50-55 have to do with the *post-exilic* Calibbites, who, owing to the occupation of their former territory by the Edomites, were obliged after the Exile to settle further north. Thus we find part of the Manaḥtites at Ṣorʿah (*v.* 54), and another part in the neighbourhood of Ḳiriath-jeʿarim (*v.* 52; read הַמָּנַחְתִּי for הַמְּנֻחוֹת). These two divisions are traced respectively to Salma and Shobal, who are said to have been 'sons,' *i.e. clans* of Caleb. These Manaḥtites can hardly be unconnected with Manaḥath, son of Shobal, who is mentioned in Gen. 36 23 P (cf. 1 Chr. 1 40) in the Ḥorite division of the Edomites. Though Manoaḥ is only mentioned by name in Judg. 13 and 16 31a, and not in the old story-cycle of *chs.* 14-16, the connexion of his name with Samson and Ṣorʿah must be of respectable antiquity (J²); and if he is really only the eponymous ancestor of the Manaḥtites, we must assume that, after the migration of the Danites to the north, the last remnant of the tribe soon disappeared from Ṣorʿah, and that the district was occupied by Manaḥtites at so relatively early a period that the J narrator, in writing his introduction to the Samson-stories, erroneously supposed that this Calibbite clan was Danite in origin. This is most improbable. The only remaining possibility seems to be the assumption that the tribe of Dan owed its origin, wholly or in part, to a Calibbite or related Edomite strain; but, had this been so, should we not expect Dan to be connected by tradition with Leʾah (like Judah) or at least with her handmaid Zilpah, rather than with Bilhah—a relationship which seems to imply early connexion with the Joseph-tribes rather than with Judah?

The name Manoaḥ is identical in form with the wâdy el-Munâḥ which runs into the wâdy Ṣarâr from the direction of Tibneh (Timnah); but this is perhaps a mere coincidence.

therefore, prithee, take heed, and drink neither wine nor strong drink, and eat nothing unclean: 5. for, behold, thou art with child, and shalt bear a son, and a razor shall not come up upon his head; for the lad shall be a Nazirite of God from the womb:

awkward anticipation of the announcement of *v.*[5]. They are probably a gloss (so Bu., Böhme, etc.); and it seems likely that they were absent from the archetype of 𝔊[B]. 𝔊[B] now represents them by καὶ συλλήμψῃ υἱόν, *i.e.* והרית בן—probably an addition from another translation; contrast the rendering of הנך הרה ἰδοὺ σὺ ἐν γαστρὶ ἔχεις, in *vv.*[2.7] (so Mo.).

5. *and shalt bear.* On the Heb. Participial form, here and in *v.*[7], וְיֹלַדְתְּ, cf. G-K. § 80*d.* It occurs again in the parallel passage Gen. 16[11].

a Nazirite. Heb. *nāzîr* means 'dedicated' or 'consecrated' to the service of the Deity. The law regulating the Nazirite vow is given in the Priestly Code, Num. 6[1-21]; but it relates to a vow taken for a limited period only, and not to a lifelong vow like that imposed upon Samson. According to Num. 6 the Nazirite is bound to observe three rules: (1) he must abstain from wine and all other products of the grape, including even the fresh and dried fruit; (2) he must allow the hair of his head to grow, and must not touch it with a razor so long as his vow lasts; (3) he must not come near a dead body, lest he incur defilement; no relaxation of the rule being allowed in the case of the death of father, mother, brother, or sister (wife and child are not mentioned). Failure to observe this rule, such as might be incurred through a sudden and unexpected death in his company, involved the abrogation of his vow. The hair of his head —which was regarded as the outward symbol of his consecration— was considered to be defiled, and he remained unclean until the seventh day, when he shaved his head, and on the eighth day made a specified offering. This being done, his head was once more consecrated by the priest, and he began again to perform the period of his vow; the days which had elapsed before his defilement being considered to be forfeited. The completion of his vow without defilement was signalized by the shaving of his head and the burning of the hair on the altar, with the offering of sacrifices and the observance of due formalities. Such a temporary vow is illustrated by Acts 21[17 ff.]; and that vows of this kind were frequent in post-exilic times is indicated by such allusions as 1 Macc. 3[49], Jos., *Ant.* XIX. vi. 1; *BJ.* II. xv. 1.

The literary setting of the law of Num. 6 is, of course, like the rest of P, post-exilic; but there is no reason to doubt that in substance the law is ancient, like so many other laws which are codified in P. We note the resemblance between the regulation laid on Samson's *mother* with regard to abstaining from all products of the vine (cf. especially *v.*[14]), and the regulation on this point as laid down in Num. 6 [3.4]. Apart from Samson, the only allusion to Nazirites in pre-exilic times is found in Am. 2 [11.12], where they are coupled with the Prophets and spoken of as raised up by Yahweh to their vocation —the inference being that their vow was a lifelong one. This passage shows that the regulation of abstention from wine was fundamental; and this is a trait which connects the Nazirites with the Rechabites (Jer. 35), with whom they were probably also associated in enthusiasm for a purer and simpler form of Yahweh-worship (cf. 2 Kgs. 10 [15 ff.]), as opposed to the accretions (akin to Ba'al-worship) which were the outcome of the settled life in Cana'an.* The fact that Ḥannah, in dedicating her son to Yahweh all the days of his life, vows that a razor shall not come up upon his head (cf. 1 Sam. 1 [11] with Judg. 13 [5]) has been taken by many to imply that Samuel was another instance of a lifelong Nazirite; and this inference is strengthened if the addition of 𝔊 in *v.*[11], *καὶ οἶνον καὶ μέθυσμα οὐ πίεται*, be regarded as a genuine part of the original text; but the probability is rather that the passage has undergone amplification 'with the view of representing Samuel's dedication as more complete' (*NHTS.*[2] *ad loc.*). Samuel is called a Nazirite in Ecclus. 46 [13] (Heb. text).

It is certainly a somewhat remarkable fact that, whereas such references as we have to the Nazirite vow in pre-exilic times seem to regard it as lifelong, the instances which occur in post-exilic times are temporary merely; ‡ but, in view of the scantiness of the evidence which we possess, there is nothing in this to indicate that the two forms of the vow were fundamentally different in conception,§ or did not coexist throughout Israel's history.

* Cf. the present editor in *JTS.* ix. (1908), pp. 330 f., 346 f.

‡ The view that St. John the Baptist was a lifelong Nazirite is plausible, but lacks evidence for its confirmation. The description given by Hegesippus of St. James the Just, the brother of our Lord, represents him as a lifelong ascetic, and uses language which is certainly based on the O.T. description of the Nazirite obligations:—*Οὗτος δὲ ἐκ κοιλίας μητρὸς αὐτοῦ ἅγιος ἦν. Οἶνον καὶ σίκερα οὐκ ἔπιεν, οὐδὲ ἔμψυχον ἔφαγε. Ξυρὸν ἐπὶ τὴν κεφαλὴν αὐτοῦ οὐκ ἀνέβη, ἔλαιον οὐκ ἠλείψατο, καὶ βαλανείῳ οὐκ ἐχρήσατο.* Cf. Eusebius, *HE.* ii. 23.

§ The most striking difference in the two forms of the vow—viz., that the temporary vow found its culmination in the *hair-offering*, whereas in the lifelong vow such an offering was an impossibility—is more apparent than real. The conception involved in this form of offering appears to be that the hair, as a living part of the human organism, represents the man's *personality*, which is equally consecrated to the service of the Deity whether the hair is offered by fire upon the altar at the conclusion of the vow, or remains inviolate upon the Nazirite's head throughout his life. What is essential to the conception is that the head of hair must not pass away from the sphere of consecration and be treated as something profane; and this is secured, in the temporary vow, by ceremonial burning, and, in the lifelong vow, by the death of the Nazirite.

On the conception involved in the hair-offering, cf. Robertson Smith, *Religion of the Semites*,[2] pp. 323 ff.

The failure of Samson to conform to the regulations prescribed to the Nazirite in Num. 6 has led to the assumption that in ancient times there must have been an essential difference in the character of the obligations imposed by the vow. Judging by the narrative of Samson's life, the only obligation which he recognized was the wearing of his hair unshorn (16 [17]). He can scarcely be supposed to have abstained from wine; for at his marriage-festival he gives a feast, the Hebrew term for which (*mišté*, 14 [10.12.17], from *šāthā* 'to drink') means lit. a *drinking-bout*; and that this feast was of the character which its name implies is expressly indicated by the statement that, in so doing, he did as other young men were accustomed to do in like circumstances (14 [10]). It may be inferred also that his slaughter of the Philistines would have involved him in defilement through contact with the dead.* The conclusion of Cooke that 'there was nothing ascetic about the Nazirite in the early days,' and that 'abstinence from wine did not become a mark of this type of devotee till a later time (Am. 2 [12]),' does not, however, solve the difficulty. The Samson-narrative as a whole is not self-consistent on this point. The birth-narrative, *ch.* 13, agrees well enough with Am. 2 [11.12], and even with Num. 6, but cannot be reconciled with *chs.* 14-16. The injunction laid upon Samson's mother to abstain from wine and strong drink and from other products of the vine, and to avoid eating anything unclean, so far from not being binding on the child (as Cooke assumes ‡), is expressly based upon the fact that he is to be 'a

* The question has been raised by Gray (*JTS.* i. pp. 206 f.) whether Samuel, on the assumption that he was a Nazirite, could have been bound by the regulations which forbade the drinking of wine and the touching of a dead body. He 'used to be present on festal occasions when it can scarcely be doubted that wine was drunk, and we are never told that he himself abstained'; and he 'hewed Agag in pieces,' and so 'must have suffered pollution.' It is to be observed, however, that on the three occasions on which Samuel is said to have presided at a festival-meal (1 Sam. 9 [11 ff.], 11 [14 f.], 16 [2 ff.]), the meal was in every case sacrificial, and doubtless very different from Samson's rollicking 'drinking-bout.' If wine was drunk at such sacrificial feasts, there is no reason why Samuel should not have abstained. Was every Nazirite who was bound by the law of Num. 6 thereby debarred from taking part in such sacrificial meals during the period of his vow, or throughout his life if he was a lifelong devotee?

The slaying of Agag was a solemn execution 'before Yahweh' (1 Sam. 15 [33]); and it is at least an open question whether the slaughter of Yahweh's enemies carried defilement like ordinary contact with the dead. When war was 'consecrated' (cf. Jer. 6 [4], Joel 3 [9], 𝔐 4 [9]), *i.e.* a holy war proclaimed, were Yahweh's 'consecrated ones' (Isa. 13 [3]), *i.e.* His warriors, who were under special regulations of purity and taboo (Deut. 23 [10-15], 2 Sam. 11 [11]), defiled by active participation in it? The Ark at any rate did not suffer pollution through going into battle at the head of the army.

It may be admitted, however, that we have not the same ground for assuming the prohibition of contact with the dead to have been characteristic of the early form of the Nazirite vow, as we have with regard to the prohibition of drinking wine.

‡ 'The restrictions are laid upon the mother; nothing is said about the child observing them' (p. 132).

R^{JE} and it is he that shall begin to save Israel from the hand of the Philistines.' 6. J^2 And the woman came and told her husband, saying, 'A man [ ] came unto me, and his appearance was like the appearance of [ ] ⌈a⌉ god, very awful; and I asked him not

Nazirite of God *from the womb.*' If, then, he is bound, through his mother, by this obligation when still unborn, *a fortiori* its stringency is not intended to be relaxed in his after-life. Yet not only, as we have seen, does he apparently drink wine, but he also eats honey which has been taken from the decomposed carcase of a lion; and in all this the narrator of *chs.* 14-16 evinces no consciousness that his hero is infringing the terms of his vocation. The conclusion to which we are led is that of Kue. (*Religion of Israel*, i. p. 308): 'Is it not evident from this that Samson has been *made* a Nazirite, although, with the exception of this one feature [his long locks], his whole history is opposed to this conception?' The author of *ch.* 13 (which, as we have seen, is later than the stories of *chs.* 14-16 which it introduces) seems to have assumed that the long locks with which his hero was endowed marked him as a Nazirite; and so in the birth-narrative he represented him as such—this inference being the easier owing to the fact that his supernatural strength was, according to the old tradition, bound up with the retention of his locks, just as a divine endowment might be granted to a Nazirite on the condition of the faithful performance of the terms of his vow. The difficulty of accepting Samson as a Nazirite is in itself a warrant for investigating the claims of a different explanation of the meaning of his long hair (cf. p. 404).

begin to save. In using this qualified phrase, R^{JE} (cf. p. 338) appears to be influenced partly by the difficulty of regarding Samson as an effective 'judge' (saviour), and partly by the fact that his history was to contain E's narrative of the signal deliverance under the judgeship of Samuel (1 Sam. 7; cf. especially *v.*[13]). Mo. explains 'begin to save' as meaning no more than 'be the first to save' (cf. 10^{18} 'begin to fight,' also R^{JE}); but this is less likely.

6. *a man.* Reading אִישׁ simply, with Bu., No., Kit., Ehr. Cf. *v.*[10], where the woman alludes again to the visitor as 'the man.' 𝔐 אִישׁ הָאֱלֹהִים must be intended to mean '*a* man of God' (an inspired man, or prophet); but this should naturally be אִישׁ אֱלֹהִים (cf. 1 Sam. 2^{27}, 9^{6}, 2 Kgs. 1^{10}, 4^{9}), the use of the Definite Article before אלהים making the whole phrase definite—'*the* man of God,' as in *v.*[8] and very frequently elsewhere. It is probable that, as Bu. assumes, האלהים has been carelessly added from *v.*[8].

a god. Reading אֱלֹהִים, with Böhme, Holzinger, Bu., No., Kit.

whence he was, and his name he told me not. 7. And he said to me, "Behold thou art with child, and shalt bear a son; now, therefore, drink neither wine nor strong drink, and eat not anything unclean; for the lad shall be a Nazirite of God from the womb unto the day of his death."'

8. And Manoaḥ intreated Yahweh, and said, 'Oh, Lord, prithee let the man of God, whom thou didst send, come again unto us, and teach us what we shall do to the child that shall be born.' 9. And ⸢Yahweh⸣ hearkened to the voice of Manoaḥ, and the Angel of ⸢Yahweh⸣ came again unto the woman, as she was sitting in the field; and Manoaḥ her husband was not with her. 10. And the woman made haste, and ran, and told her husband, and said unto him, 'Behold the man hath appeared unto me that came unto me the other day.' 11. And Manoaḥ arose, and went after his wife, and came unto the man, and said to him, 'Art thou the man that spake unto the woman?' And

The sense intended seems to be 'a *supernatural being*'; so probably in *v.*[22]. For this use of *'ĕlōhîm*, cf. 1 Sam. 28[13], where the witch of 'Endor, when she has called up the shade of Samuel (and also, apparently, attendant spirits; cf. *NHTS.*[2] *ad loc.*), says, 'I see *'ĕlōhîm* (supernatural beings) coming up from the earth.' 𝔐 כְּמַלְאַךְ הָאֱלֹהִים 'like the Angel of God'; but the regular expression elsewhere in the narrative (*vv.*[3.13.15.16.17.18.20.21]; on *v.*[9], cf. *note*) is 'the Angel of *Yahweh*'; and it appears to be not till *v.*[21] that Manoaḥ and his wife even suspect the *real* character of their visitor (*v.*[16b]; cf. also *ch.* 6[22]).

9. *And Yahweh . . . and the Angel of Yahweh.* Reading יהוה in both cases for האלהים; in the first case with 𝔏[L], 𝔙, 𝔖[P], and in the second with 𝔏[L], 𝔖[P]. As Mo. remarks, the substitution of האלהים in 𝔐 may have been accidentally due to the proximity of איש האלהים in *v.*[8]

10. *the other day.* Heb. בַּיּוֹם, lit. 'on the day,' *i.e.* the day which was noteworthy on account of the event with which it was connected.*

* The use of the Definite Article is somewhat similar in the phrase ויהי היום וג׳ (1 Sam. 1[4], 14[1], 2 Kgs. 4[8.11.18], Job 1[6.13], 2[1]†), where English idiom renders 'And there came a day when, etc.,' but which literally means 'And *the* day was, etc.,' *day* being defined on account of the events (to be related) which happened on it. Cf. the discussion in *NHTS.*[2] p. 6.

he said, 'I am.' 12. And Manoaḥ said, 'Now, if thy word⌈⌉ come to pass, what shall be the rule for the lad and his work?' 13. And the Angel of Yahweh said unto Manoaḥ, 'Of all that I said unto the woman let her take heed. 14. Of all that cometh of the grape-vine she shall not eat, and wine and strong drink let her not drink, and anything unclean let her not eat: all that I have commanded her let her observe.' 15. And Manoaḥ said unto the Angel of Yahweh, 'Prithee let us detain thee, and make ready before thee a kid of the goats.' 16. And the Angel of Yahweh said unto Manoaḥ, 'Though thou detain

12. *Now, if, etc.* The 'if' is not expressed in Heb., the two clauses being placed side by side so as to form a virtual hypothetical sentence —'Now, let thy word come to pass, what shall be, etc.,' implies '*Assuming that* thy word, etc.' Cf. *ch.* 6 [13], lit. 'And *is* Yahweh with us, why, then, etc.,' *i.e.* 'If Yahweh *is*, etc.': Driver, *Tenses*, § 149. Perles (*Analekten*, p. 35) and La. propose to emend עֵת for עַתָּה—'*At the time when* thy word cometh true, what shall be, etc.' (cf. Ps. 105 [19] עַד־עֵת בֹּוא־דְבָרוֹ 'Until the time when his word came to pass'); but the change is no improvement.

thy word. Reading sing. דְּבָרְךָ with many MSS. and 𝔊, Θ., 𝔏[L], 𝔙, 𝔖[P], in place of 𝔐 plur. דְּבָרֶיךָ.

the rule for the lad. Heb. מִשְׁפַּט הַנַּעַר. Heb. *mišpāṭ* is here used in its common sense of *ordinance* or *rule of life*. That this should be the sense intended seems to be demanded by the Angel's answer, which repeats the injunctions laid upon the woman. So R.V. *marg.* 'ordering.' R.V. *text*, 'What shall be *the manner of the child*?' interprets *mišpāṭ* in the sense which it seems to possess only elsewhere in 2 Kgs. 1 [7], 'What is the manner of the man that came up to meet you?' *i.e.* 'How would you describe him?' Apart, however, from the exceptional character of this use of *mišpāṭ* as the summary of *distinctive characteristics*, such a sense is less suitable to the context than that which we have adopted.

15. *make ready before thee.* As Mo. observes, the expression is a pregnant one, equivalent to 'make ready and set before thee.' La. assumes that לפניך 'before thee' implies something further, and so follows St. Augustine in supposing that Manoaḥ is contemplating a sacrificial meal, which the Angel rejects in favour of a holocaust; but this view is expressly precluded by *v.*[16b], where we are told that Manoaḥ was unaware of the extraordinary character of his guest.

16. *Though thou detain me, etc.* The J narratives Gen. 18 [1ff.],

me, I will not eat of thy bread; but if thou wilt prepare a burnt offering, to Yahweh shalt thou offer it.' For Manoaḥ knew not that he was the Angel of Yahweh. 17. And Manoaḥ said unto the Angel of Yahweh, 'What is thy name? When thy word⌈⌉

Judg. 6 11-24, which have strong points of resemblance to our narrative, differ somewhat as regards the guest's reception of the offer of hospitality. In Gen. 18 the supernatural visitors accept the offer and partake of the meal. In Judg. 6 the Angel of Yahweh, after assenting to Gide'on's proposal, converts the meal into a sacrifice. Here he refuses the meal, but suggests instead the offering of a sacrifice to Yahweh. The three narratives thus seem to mark an advance from a very primitive stage in which Yahweh Himself (cf. Gen. 18 1.13 *) is thought to visit men and accept their hospitality, to later modification of the *naïveté* of the conception by substitution of the Angel of Yahweh for Yahweh Himself (cf. *note* on *ch.* 2 1 at end), and conversion of the meal into a sacrifice offered to Yahweh, who seems in the present passage to be definitely distinguished from His Angel.

17. *What is thy name?* Heb. מִי שְׁמֶךָ, lit. 'Who is thy name?'—perhaps through a sub-consciousness of the equivalence of the question to 'Who art thou?' Elsewhere (Gen. 32 28, Ex. 3 13) מה is used; and it is possible that ה and י, which are very similar in the old character, may have been confused in our passage.

when thy word . . . honour. Heb. כִּי־יָבוֹא דְבָרְךָ וְכִבַּדְנוּךָ. 𝔊AL, 𝔙, 𝔖P, R.V. 'that when thy words come to pass we may do thee honour'; and this rendering is adopted by commentators generally without remark upon the difficulty of justifying it syntactically. The opening 'that' apparently represents the ו of וכבדנוך (so Ros. renders 'si eveniat quod praedixeris, ut honoremus te'), and this would have been the natural interpretation if the order of the sentence had been וכבדנוך כי יבא דברך 'that we may do thee honour when thy word cometh to pass'; but it is more than doubtful whether such a rendering can be extracted from the sentence in its present order. It is perhaps just possible to render כי 'for' and treat what follows as a virtual hypothetical (cf. *note* on *v.* 12, 'Now, if, etc.')—'for, let thy word come to pass, and we will, etc.' (cf. 𝔗), *i.e.* 'for, when (*or* if) thy word . . . we will, etc.'; cf. *v.* 12 *note.* On the whole, however, the rendering adopted above (so Stu.) is the most natural one.

thy word. Reading sing. דְּבָרְךָ with *Ḳ*e*rê*, many MSS. of 𝔐, and 𝔊, 𝔙, 𝔖P, in place of *Kt.* דבריך.

* The confusion in this narrative between the sing. 'Yahweh' (*vv.* 1a.3.10a.13.17.20.22b.ff.) and the plur. 'three men' (*vv.* 2.4,5.8.9a.16.22a) is very obscure. Cf., however, the interesting remarks of Skinner, *ICC.* pp. 302 f.

cometh to pass we will do thee honour.' 18. And the Angel of Yahweh said to him, 'Wherefore, now, askest thou concerning my name, seeing that it is wonderful?' 19. And Manoaḥ took the kid of the goats, Gl. with the meal-offering, J² and offered it up upon the rock to Yahweh.[ ] 20. And, when

18. *wonderful.* The adj. *pil'î* occurs only once again in the fem. *pil'iyyā* Ps. 139 6,* which illustrates the meaning in the present passage:—

> 'Such knowledge is too *wonderful* for me;
> Too high, I cannot attain unto it.'

The root-meaning is *separate* from the ordinary, and so *surpassing* it. For the verbal form in the Niph'al with the sense *surpassing understanding*, cf. Ps. 131 1, Prov. 30 18, Job 42 3.

19. *with the meal-offering.* This use of *minḥā*, which in pre-exilic literature is the ordinary term for *offering* generally, in the specific sense of *meal*-offering, is late, and characterizes the ritual of the Priestly Code. Böhme is therefore probably correct in regarding the reference here and in *v.*23 as a late addition made for the sake of liturgical correctness.

and offered it up, etc. Manoaḥ, we must assume, kindles his sacrifice in the ordinary way. Contrast 6 21. The narrative of Jos. (*Ant.* v. viii. 3) is here strongly coloured by recollection of *ch.* 6 18-21. Manoaḥ regards the offering not as a sacrifice but as a mark of hospitality. It is the Angel who commands him to place 'the loaves and flesh, without the vessels,' on the rock, and who by touching it with the end of his rod converts it into a burnt-offering, then disappearing in the smoke of the sacrifice.

upon the rock. The reference seems to be to a *rock-altar*: cf. *note* on *ch.* 6 20. Such a primitive rock-altar exists at the present day in the neighbourhood of Ṣar'ah: cf. Kittel, *Studien zur hebräischen Archäologie und Religionsgeschichte* (1908), pp. 97-158 (with two plans); *Über primitive Felsaltäre in Palästina*, pp. 243-255 of *Hilprecht Anniversary Volume* (with photographs).

At the end of the verse 𝔐 adds, וּמַפְלִא לַעֲשׂוֹת וּמָנוֹחַ וְאִשְׁתּוֹ רֹאִים, *i.e.* 'and doing wondrously, and Manoaḥ and his wife were looking on.' Here the Participle מפלא is without a subj., and cannot have thus stood originally. 𝔊AL al. τῷ θαυμαστὰ ποιοῦντι (in apposition to preceding τῷ Κυρίῳ), 𝔙 '(Domino,) qui fecit mirabilia,' presuppose

* In these passages *Kt.* should be vocalized פִּלְאִי, פִּלְאִיָּה. *Ḳerê* פֶּלִי, פְּלִיאָה.

the flame went up from off the altar towards heaven, the Angel of Yahweh went up in the flame of the altar : and Manoaḥ and his wife were looking on, and they fell on their faces to the ground. 21. And the Angel of Yahweh appeared no more unto Manoaḥ and his wife. Then Manoaḥ knew that it was the Angel of Yahweh. 22. And Manoaḥ said unto his wife, 'We shall surely die, for it is a god that we have seen.' 23. And his

הַמַּפְלִא לַעֲשׂוֹת 'who doeth (*or* who did) wondrously,' and this is adopted by Mo., La., Kent. Maurer (quoted by Stu.), Oet. suggest וְהוּא מַפְלִא וג' 'He (Yahweh) doing wondrously'; but, as Stu. remarks, it is awkward to have two circumstantial clauses (this and the following וּמָנוֹחַ וג') thus side by side. Oet. gives as an alternative וַיַּפְלִא וג' 'and he did wondrously'; cf. 𝕲ᴮ καὶ διεχώρισεν ποιῆσαι. Houbigant supplies a subj. וַיהוה מַפְלִא וג' 'and Yahweh did wondrously.' R.V. 'and *the angel* did wondrously' could only be justified by the insertion of a subj. הוּא or הַמַּלְאָךְ. Kit. supposes that the words are misplaced, and should properly follow *v.*²⁰ᵃ—'and the Angel of Yahweh ascended in the flame of the altar *in a most wonderful way*.' It is, however, very superfluous to state at this point that the Angel's action was extraordinary.

It can hardly be doubted that the difficult words are really a marginal explanation—'doing wondrously'—of the rare adj. *pilʾî* 'wonderful' in *v.*¹⁸ (*pilʾî*, lit. '*extraordinary*' is explained by the cognate verb *maphlī*, '*making extraordinary* as regards doing,' *i.e.* acting in an extraordinary way). This has crept into the text in the wrong place, together with erroneous repetition of the words 'and Manoaḥ and his wife were looking on' from *v.*²⁰. So Ber., Böhme, Oort, Bu.

20. *the altar. I.e.* 'the rock' of *v.*¹⁹, which was evidently an ancient place of sacrifice (cf. the use of the verb וַיַּעַל 'and he offered it up'), and, as such, may be appropriately described by the term מִזְבֵּחַ. There is no reason for suspecting the originality of the verse (Stu.), or for supposing that 'the altar' has been substituted for 'the rock' by a later hand (Böhme).

went up, etc. The description is more specific than that of 6²¹, where the Angel merely vanishes from Gideʿon's sight.

We shall surely die. Cf. 6²² note.

for it is a god, etc. The order of the Heb., כִּי אֱלֹהִים רָאִינוּ, is very emphatic. R.V. renders *ʾĕlōhîm* 'God'; but had this been intended we should have expected Manoaḥ to have used the name

wife said to him, 'If Yahweh had been pleased to kill us, he would not have received at our hand a burnt offering Gl. and meal-offering, J[2] and would not ⌜have instructed us⌝ [ ] ⌜thus⌝.' [ ]

Yahweh, and not *'ĕlōhîm*: cf. the verse following. On the sense in which *'ĕlōhîm* is probably used, cf. *note* on *v.*[6].

23. *and would not have instructed us thus.* Reading וְלֹא הוֹרָנוּ כָּזֹאת in place of 𝔐 וְלֹא הֶרְאָנוּ אֶת־כָּל־אֵלֶּה וְכָעֵת לֹא הִשְׁמִיעָנוּ כָּזֹאת 'neither would he have shewed us all these things, nor would he at this time have told us such a thing as this.' The difficulty of 𝔐's text is two-fold. (1) The expression כעת 'at this time' (omitted in some 𝔊 MSS., 𝔏, 𝔙) is very rare, occurring again only in *ch.* 21 [22], Num. 23 [23], in both of which passages it causes some little difficulty and its originality is questioned. Granted that it means 'at this time' or 'just now,' its position in the sentence is strange, since, referring as it does very strikingly to לא השמיענו, and not to the preceding לא לקח . . . ולא הראנו, 'it seems to oppose the hearing, as recent, to the seeing and the sacrifice' (Mo.). Mo.'s suggested emendation כִּי עַתָּה 'for now,' is unsuitable apart from omission of all that precedes from לא לקח to אלה and the reading of לא חפץ for לו חפץ— 'Yahweh is not pleased to kill us; for now he would not have told us,' etc.

(2) If ולא הראנו וג', 'neither would he have shewed us all these things,' refers to the sights which they had just witnessed, *i.e.* the appearance of the Angel and his subsequent proceedings, since it was on account of this appearance that Manoaḥ supposed that Yahweh *would* slay them, it is obvious that it could not be adduced as a reason why He *would not* slay them. If, on the other hand, the verb 'shewed' refers to the information with regard to the birth of the child and his future, it is superfluous by the side of לא השמיענו כזאת 'he would not have told us, etc.,' since it says the same thing with but slight variation.

𝔊[AL], 𝔏, 𝔖[h] render ולא הראנו by καὶ οὐκ ἂν ἐφώτισεν ἡμᾶς, which points to an original וְלֹא הוֹרָנוּ 'and would not have instructed us'; cf. their rendering of וְיוֹרֵנוּ *v.*[8] by καὶ φωτισάτω ἡμᾶς.* The fact that לא הורנו and לא השמיענו are synonymous expressions seems to postulate the existence of a doublet. We assume, then, that ולא הורנו כזאת was the original reading (cf. ויורנו *v.*[8]), and

* The rendering is probably due (as Mo., *SBOT.*, observes) to false etymological association of הורה with אור. The verb is similarly rendered in 2 Kgs. 12[2], 17[27,28].

24. And the woman bare a son, and called his name Samson: and the lad grew up, and Yahweh blessed him. 25. And the

לא השמיענו כזאת, a marginal variant or explanatory gloss, was subsequently introduced into the text. Later stages of corruption are represented by the alteration of הורנו to הראנו (thus making reference to seeing *and* hearing in place of the double reference to hearing), the glossing of the first כזאת by את כל אלה, and its subsequent alteration to כעת, and then to וכעת when taken to refer to the words which follow it. The conclusions of Mo. (*SBOT.*) and La. are similar.

24. *Samson.* 𝔐 Šimšôn. The *a*-vowel of the English form, which is found in 𝔊 Σαμψων, 𝔙 'Samson,' represents the primitive vocalization.* Cf. the name Šamšânu cited by Hilprecht, *Business Documents of Murâshu Sons of Nippur*, pp. 27, 70.

The connexion of the name with *Šémeš* 'sun' may be considered certain, and no other proposed explanation is at all plausible ‡; but the precise meaning borne by the name is wholly vague. The view that it is a diminutive form—'little sun'—is not very probable, the only analogous formation that can be cited being *'îšôn* 'pupil of the eye'—apparently 'little man' (reflected in pupil)—formed from *'îš* 'man': cf. G-K. § 86 *g*. More plausible is the suggestion that the termination makes the form adjectival; cf. *ḳadhmôn* 'eastern'; from *ḳédhem* 'east': G-K § 86 *f*. Samson might then mean 'solar one,' just as יְרִיחוֹ 'Jericho' very possibly means 'lunar' (*sc.* city)§; but the precise significance of such a title—whether 'sun-like,' 'solar hero,' or 'protegé of the sun-god'—is obscure. The proximity of Beth-shemesh 'Temple of the Sun' to Samson's birthplace (cf. *note* on 'Ṣorʿah,' *v.*[2]) suggests the likelihood that the hero's name was, in origin, honorific of the sun-god. It is possible, indeed, that the name may be hypocoristic for a fuller Šamši-el, 'Šamaš is God'; cf. ʿAbdon, *ch.* 12 [13.15], *al.*, by the side of ʿAbdi-el, 'Servant of God,' 1 Chr. 5 [15]. Similar South Palestinian names are Shēshai and Shavsha (cf. p. 10), and possibly Shimshai of Ezr. 4 [8.9.17.23].

* Cf. *note* on *baggabbōrīm*, pp. 168 f.

‡ The statement of Jos. (*Ant.* v. viii. 4), καὶ γενόμενον τὸ παιδίον Σαμψῶνα καλοῦσιν, ἰσχυρὸν δ' ἀποσημαίνει τὸ ὄνομα, is probably guesswork, it being unlikely that he connected it with *šāmēn* (Meier) in the sense 'robust': cf. *ch.* 3 [29]. Ewald (*HI.* ii. p. 396) suggests derivation from New Heb. *šimmēš*, Aram. *šammēš* 'to serve,' in the sense 'servant' of God, *i.e.* Nazirite. Other views—*e.g.* that the name stands for *Šamšôm*, a reduplicated form from *šāmēm*, in the sense 'devastator' (cf. Ber.); or that it is to be explained from Ar. *ṣamṣam*, 'vir fortis et audax' (Golius quoted by Ros.)—are philologically impossible.

§ That the denominative termination *-ô*, as seen in יריחו, is probably an abbreviation of *-ôn*, is suggested by the parallel forms *Megiddô*, *Megiddôn*, and the adjectival forms *Shîlônî* from *Shîlô*, *Gîlônî* from *Gîlô*: cf. Stade, *Lehrbuch der heb. Gramm.*, § 296 *e*.

spirit of Yahweh began to impel him in Maḥaneh-Dan, between Ṣorʿah and Eshta'ol.

25. *to impel him.* *I.e.* to stir him up by a sudden access of frenzy in which he was moved to put forth his supernatural strength. The Heb. verb *păʿam* is used elsewhere of the *disquieting* of the human spirit through anxiety or perplexity; Gen. 41^{8}, Dan. 2$^{1.3}$, Ps. 77^{4} (𝔐 ^{5})†.

Maḥaneh-Dan. Possibly a hamlet dependent upon Ṣorʿah which was the home of Manoaḥ; since the same definition of locality—'between Ṣorʿah and Eshta'ol'—is used in 16^{31} of the site of the family-sepulchre. The name, which means 'the camp of Dan,' is explained in *ch.* 18^{12} as owing its origin to an encampment of the Danites to the west of Ḳiriath-Jeʿarim, when they were on the march from Ṣorʿah and Eshta'ol to seek a new home in the north. Ḳiriath-Jeʿarim, if rightly identified with Ḳuryet el-ʿEnab, is nearly eight miles east-north-east of Ṣorʿah. The existence in close proximity of two places bearing the same name Maḥaneh-Dan is very improbable; and since the connexion in which the name occurs in 18^{12} favours its originality in that passage, it is very possible that it may be an erroneous insertion in the present context. S. A. Cook's proposal (*EB.* 2904; *Notes on O.T. History*, p. 88) to emend Manaḥath-Dan in both places, and to find allusion to the two divisions of the Manaḥtites, one in connexion with Ḳiriath-Jeʿarim (1 Chr. 2^{52}) and the other at Ṣorʿah (1 Chr. 2^{54}), is ingenious but not convincing. As we have noticed above (*footnote*, p. 341), the Manaḥtites seem to have been post-exilic Calibbite settlers in these districts, and to have had no connexion with the tribe of Dan.

Eshta'ol. Commonly identified with the modern 'Ešûaʿ, not much more than a mile and a half to the north-east of Ṣorʿah; cf. *note* on Ṣorʿah, *v.*^{2}. On the rare (in Heb.) Iphteʿal form of the name, which is possibly to be derived from the verb *šăʾal* 'ask' in the sense 'ask for one-self,' and so may mean 'place of consulting the oracle' (the site of an ancient sanctuary), cf. the present editor's note in *JTS.* xiii. (1911), p. 83.

14. Doorn. and Sta. (followed by Mo., Bu., and most recent commentators) have rightly perceived that the narrative of this chapter has been extensively worked over, for the purpose of representing Samson, so far as was possible, in the light of a dutiful son. As the story stands, it seems as though Samson's parents, though at first strongly opposed to his wish to marry a Philistine maiden (*v.*^{3}), finally acquiesce and accompany him to Timnah in order to forward his plans (*vv.*$^{5.10}$). There are, however, very obvious difficulties in the way of accepting such a situation. In *v.*^{5}, though Samson is accompanied by his parents, it is he alone who is confronted by the lion; and, when he has slain it, his parents are unaware of the fact (*v.*^{6b}). We can only infer that he must have outstripped his parents on the

way (Kimchi), or turned aside along a bypath in the vineyards; yet of this there is no hint in the narrative. In *vv.*[7.8] the parents disappear altogether; and it is Samson alone who interviews the woman and arranges the preliminaries of the wedding, returning after a time to carry it through. In *v.*[10a] the father appears in a belated way; but it is Samson who makes the marriage-feast (*v.*[10b]), and acts throughout on his own responsibility.

The account of the journeys to and from Timnah is also, as the narrative stands, very confused. After the first visit in company with his father and mother, the return to Ṣorʿah is assumed but not mentioned; and *v.*[8] narrates a second visit to Timnah of Samson by himself in order to get married (לקחתה). On the way down he visits the carcase of the lion and discovers the honey; some of which he gives to his father and his mother. Yet we cannot suppose that he had returned to Ṣorʿah prior to the actual marriage-festival (*vv.*[10ff.]), since it was for the sake of this that he went to Timnah, as recorded in *v.*[8]; nor can we assume that his parents accompanied him again in *v.*[8], and that he gave them the honey on the way down or *at* Timnah, since it is not till *v.*[10] that his father comes down (from Ṣorʿah).

The narrative at once becomes clear if, with Doorn. and Sta., we omit ואביו ואמו and read the sing. ויבא in *v.*[5]; omit *v.*[6b] ולא הגיד to עשה; omit לקחתה *v.*[8]; read שמשון in place of אביהו in *v.*[10a], and omit the name in *v.*[10b]. In face of his parents' opposition to the match, Samson goes *alone* to Timnah, and returns after a few days to his parents' house at Ṣorʿah (*v.*[8]), bringing them some of the honey which he has discovered on his journey home. The simple removal of לקחתה 'to marry her' in *v.*[8] at once solves the difficulty noted above as to the journeys to and fro, by allowing the obvious inference that it was *on his return to Ṣorʿah* that he found the honey, and not, as the interpolator imagined, on going a second time to Timnah, after a return home unrecorded. He would naturally inspect the lion's carcase on the earliest opportunity. His second visit to Timnah, in order to celebrate his marriage, *is* recorded in *v.*[10], which originally ran 'And Samson went down unto the woman, and he made there a feast, etc.'

There is another point which confirms this view of affairs. From Samson's request to his parents in *v.*[2] it is clear that he originally contemplated a marriage of the ordinary kind, when his father would have interviewed the father of the maiden and arranged the *mōhar* (purchase-price), and the bride would have been brought back to the bridegroom's house at Ṣorʿah, where the feast would have been held. In this case the bridegroom's 'companions' who assisted at the function would have been young men from his own clan. According to *v.*[11], however, these 'companions' are not Danites but Philistines; the feast, though provided by Samson, takes place not at Ṣorʿah but at Timnah; and it is there, evidently, that the marriage would have been consummated (*v.*[18], reading הַחֲדָרָה; cf. *note*) if Samson had not left in a rage after the unfair discovery of his riddle. This is still further borne out by *ch.* 15 [1], where, on regaining his good temper, he returns to Timnah with a present for his bride, and expects to enjoy the rights of marriage at her father's house. It is evident, therefore, that after failing to persuade his parents to agree to such a marriage as he had at first contemplated, he arranges, without their consent, a marriage of the *ṣadîḳa* type (cf. *ch.* 8 [31] *note*), in which the custom was that the bride remained with her own people, the children of the marriage belonging to the mother's, and not to the father's clan, and the marriage-contract being frequently for a limited period merely.

This explains the fact that the bridegroom's 'companions' of *v.*[11] are Philistines and not Danites. The only difficulty, as this verse stands, is that they are selected, not by Samson, but by persons undefined who seem to have thought it wise to have a strong body of Philistines on the spot on account of the formidable appearance of the bridegroom. Here the fact that the narrative has been worked over is transparently evident. Probably the verse originally ran, 'And he (*i.e.* Samson) took thirty companions, and they remained with him'; but the policy of representing Samson's conduct in the best possible light, which seems to have dominated the reviser of the narrative, has led to alteration of the text—instead of Samson himself choosing his marriage-companions from among the uncircumcised, they were forced upon him; and a reason for this has to be invented and supplied.

As to when the narrative was thus extensively glossed we have no means of determining. Probably the additions were made in late post-exilic times (so Mo., *SBOT.*), though this is by no means certain. They are marked in the text by the symbol Gl., *i.e.* 'Gloss.'

Further interpolations (*vv.* [14 f.19]) are noticed in their place.

14. 1. J[1] And Samson went down to Timnah, and saw a

1. *Timnah.* The form תמנתה Timnátha with Accusative termination, which is natural in *vv.*[1a.5a] where *direction towards* is implied (ה *locative*; cf. Gen. 38 [12.13.14]), is used without this implication in *vv.*[1b.2.5b], Josh. 19 [43]; cf. *note* on Jahaṣ, *ch.* 11 [20]. תמנה Timnah occurs in Josh. 15 [10.57], 2 Chr. 28 [18]. Timnah is the modern Tibneh, in the Shephelah, some four miles south-west of Ṣorʿah. The elevation of Ṣorʿah is 1171 feet above the Mediterranean, while that of Timnah is 800 feet; hence the use of the verb 'went down' here and in *vv.* [5.7.10], and conversely 'went up,' *vv.* [2.19], of the homeward journey. Timnah, which is here a Philistine city, is assigned to Dan in Josh. 19 [43] P; while in Josh. 15 [10] P it appears as a border-city of Judah. 2 Chr. 28 [18] mentions a Philistine raid on the Shephelah and

woman in Timnah of the daughters of the Philistines. 2. And he went up, and told his father and his mother, and said, 'I have seen a woman in Timnah of the daughters of the Philistines: now, therefore, get her for me to wife.' 3. And his father Gl. and his mother J[1] said to him, 'Is there not a woman among the daughters of thy brethren, or among all my folk, that thou art going to take a wife of the uncircumcised Philistines?' And

the Negeb in the reign of Aḥaz, when Timnah and neighbouring cities were captured from Judah.

a woman. Bu. comments on the uncommon use of *iššā* here and in *vv.* 2a.7.10 instead of *naʿᵃrā* 'maiden,' the ordinary term for an unmarried girl. He suggests that the 'woman' may have been a widow or divorced wife, or else that the term may be used with a shade of contempt. The latter suggestion is the more probable; cf. the application of the term to Delilah in *ch.* 16 4.

2. *get her, etc.* The preliminaries of marriage, such as the settlement of the *mōhar* (cf. p. 354), were a matter of arrangement between the fathers of the suitor and his desired bride: cf. the later version of the story of Gen. 34, especially *vv.*4.6.8.12. Samson addresses both his parents and uses the plur. verb קחו 'get *ye*.' This inclusion of the mother may be due to J[2] in view of her prominence in *ch.* 13, or to a later hand for the same reason; but this is by no means certain. Though the negotiations rested with the father, there is no reason why he should not have been to some extent dependent on his wife's advice. In the following *v.*3a it is probable that ואמו 'and his mother' is an addition in imitation of *v.*2. Notice the sing. suffix of עמי '*my* folk' in the father's speech, and the fact that Samson's response in *v.*3b is addressed to his father only.

3. *among the daughters of thy brethren.* 'Brethren' here = 'fellow-clansmen'; cf. *ch.* 16 31, 9 1.3, 2 Sam. 19 13. 𝔖P presupposes בְּבֵית אָבִיךָ 'in thy father's house,' *i.e.* thy *family* or *clan*; cf. 16 31, and very frequently in P and Chr. (cf. references in BDB. p. 110*a*). This is adopted by Bu., No.; but the change is unnecessary.

my folk. 𝔊L, 𝔖P, Houbigant, Bu., Oort, No., La., עַמְּךָ 'thy folk' is plausible. But 𝔐 עַמִּי is very natural in the father's mouth; and it is likely that the reading of 𝔊L, 𝔖P may have arisen under the influence of the preceding אחיך (so Mo.).

uncircumcised. A term of opprobrium, applied to the Philistines elsewhere in *ch.* 15 18, 1 Sam. 14 6, 17 26.36, 31 4, 1 Chr. 10 4. The Philistines appear to have been the only race known to the Israelites in early times who did not practice circumcision. Upon the diffusion of the custom, cf. articles in *DB.* and *EB.*, and Skinner, *Genesis*, *ICC.*, pp. 296 f.

Samson said unto his father, 'Get *her* for me; for she it is that pleaseth me.' 4. J² And his father and his mother knew not that it was from Yahweh: for he was seeking an occasion against the Philistines. Now at that time the Philistines were ruling over Israel.

5. J¹ And Samson went down, Gl. and his father and his mother, J¹ to Timnah, and Gl. they J¹ came to the vineyards of Timnah: and, behold, a young lion came roaring to meet him. 6. And the spirit of Yahweh rushed upon him, and he rent it

Get **her** *for me.* Heb. אוֹתָהּ קַח־לִי, with very emphatic order of words—*her* and none other. Samson will brook no interference with his wayward inclinations.

pleaseth me. Lit. 'is right in mine eyes.' So *v.*7b.

4. *And his father and his mother, etc.* The whole verse seems to have formed no part of the original narrative. The first half of the verse has a back reference to *ch.* 13, and was added, probably, by the author of that chapter (J²) in explanation of the fact that an inspired Nazirite should have determined to contract such a marriage-alliance (so Doorn.). To the same hand, probably, belongs the reference to the Philistine domination (possibly derived from 15 11), which would be superfluous if due to a *later* hand than R^{E2} in 13 1b, or even than R^{JE} in 13 5b.

an occasion. *I.e.* an opportunity for the provocation of hostilities.

5. *And Samson, etc.* Originally, 'And Samson went down to Timnah, and came, etc.' Failing to gain his father's co-operation, he starts off on his own account to contract a *ṣadîḳa*-marriage. Cf. pp. 354 f.

a young lion. כְּפִיר אֲרָיוֹת, lit. 'a young lion of the lions'; cf. the phrase גְּדִי עִזִּים 'a kid of the goats.' Heb. *kephîr* denotes a lion which has ceased to be a *gûr* or *whelp*, and has come to full growth and attained the power of hunting its own prey: cf. especially Ezek. 19 2.3; also Isa. 5 29, 31 4, Am. 3 4, Mic. 5 7, Ps. 35 17, 104 21.

6. *And the spirit of Yahweh, etc.* Cf. *note* on *ch.* 3 10. The verb *ṣālaḥ*, which is applied to the powerful inrush of the divine impulse upon Samson here and in *v.*19, *ch.* 15 14, is similarly used with reference to Saul in 1 Sam. 10 6.10, 11 6 J.

he rent it. The Heb. verb. *šissa'* is used in Lev. 1 17 P of *tearing open* a bird by its wings, when offered as a whole burnt-offering. This was done 'without dividing it,' *i.e.* without tearing it into two halves. The verb is also employed, together with the cognate substantive, of *cleaving* the *cleft* (*šéša'*) of the hoof, *i.e.* having a cloven hoof—one of the distinctive marks of sacrificially clean animals.

as one might rend a kid; and there was nothing in his hand: Gl. but he told not his father and his mother what he had done. 7. J[1] And he went down, and spoke to the woman; and she pleased Samson. 8. And he returned after a while Gl. to take her, J[1] and he turned aside to see the carcase of the lion: and,

Judging by these usages—especially by Lev. 1 [17]—Samson must have torn the lion down the middle,* and may be supposed to have done this by tearing the hind legs apart, precisely as Gilgameš' companion Engidu is represented as doing (Plate II., fig. 4), and also the colossal figure from Cyprus (perhaps Melḳart-Herakles; Plate VI.).

In the Jerusalem 𝔗 *šašša'* is used as the rendering of 𝔐 וַיְפַשְּׁחֵנִי 'and he hath torn me in pieces' (as a lion rends its prey), Lam. 3 [11].

as one might rend a kid. Lit. 'like the rending of a kid,' *i.e.* as easily as an ordinary man would perform the same action on a kid. Mo. renders 'as a man tears a kid,' and thinks that this, like Lev. 1 [17], may be a reference to some ceremonial act. The whole point of the description lies, however, in the *ease* with which Samson's extraordinary strength enabled him to perform the deed, rather than on the manner in which it was done.

and there was nothing, etc. Cf. the representations of Gilgameš, etc., noticed above. Herakles is related to have strangled the Nemaean lion with his bare hands ‡ (cf. the references collected by Bochart, *Hierozoicon*, i. p. 754); and Pulydamas of Scotusa in Thessaly, moved by desire to emulate the feats of Herakles, is said to have slain a large and powerful lion on Mount Olympus without weapons (Pausanias, vi. 5).

but he told not, etc. An interpolation of the reviser of the narrative, based upon *vv.*[9b.16b], and necessitated by the insertion of the words 'his father and his mother' in *v.*[5]. If Samson's parents were with him on the journey, it would be natural (apart from this statement) to suppose that they would hear of the incident, even if they did not witness it.

8. *and he returned after a while, etc.* Omitting the words 'to take her' as a later addition, the reference naturally is to Samson's return to Ṣor'ah after his visit to Timnah (cf. p. 354). The phrase מִיָּמִים 'after a while' is used in 11 [4], 15 [1] of an indeterminate period, and, as the latter reference proves, can be used of quite a short period as well as of a long one (often, specifically, *a year*; cf. references in BDB. *s.v.* יוֹם, 6c).

* Mo. is not justified in stating that 'he tore the lion limb from limb.' Had he done this, there would not have been much of the carcase left for the bees to build in.

‡ Jos. (*Ant.* v. viii. 5) is possibly influenced by the Herakles-myth when he states that Samson *strangled* the lion (ἄγχει ταῖς χερσί).

behold, there was a swarm of bees in the body of the lion, and

there was a swarm of bees, etc. Bees will not build their combs in putrefying matter; but probably we are to picture the carcase as reduced to little more than a skeleton by jackals, vultures, or ants, and dried by the heat of the sun (cf. Post in *DB.* i. p. 264 *a*); or, as Mo. suggests, 'the body dried up, the skin and shrivelled flesh adhering to the ribs, the belly hollow.' It is true that the few days (presumably) before Samson's return from Timnah would hardly suffice for the building of combs and the gathering of a considerable store of honey; but clearly we cannot press the details of the narrative. Herodotus' story of the head of Onesilus, which, when an empty skull, was occupied by a swarm of bees which filled it with a honeycomb (*Hist.* v. 114) has often been compared by commentators.

An alternative theory is that we have here an instance of the widely spread ancient belief that bees were generated from putrefying animal-matter (cf. references in Bochart, *Hierozoicon*, ii. p. 502; Sachs, *Beiträge zur Sprach- und Alterthumsforschung*, i. p. 154; ii. pp. 92 f.); the origin of which has been supposed to be due to the fact that the drone-fly, *Eristalis tenax*, which is easily mistaken for a bee by those who are not entomologists, may have been observed to spend its larval stage within the carcases of large animals.* This view,

* Cf. especially the monograph of Osten Sacken, *On the oxen-born bees of the Ancients* (1894). The difficulty which seems to lie in the way of regarding *Eristalis* as the supposed 'bee' which was generated from the carcases of cattle is that the larva of this fly is *aquatic*, thriving in all kinds of liquid filth, but not in the solid tissues of a carcase. The body of a dead animal, such as Samson's lion, would speedily become infested with carrion-feeding larvæ, such as those of *Calliphora* (the blue-bottle fly) and *Lucilia* (the green-bottle fly) which bear no resemblance to bees; but only by *Eristalis* if it happened to be lying in a pool of water (as was the case with the sheep, which seems to be the only certified instance known to Sacken in which this fly has actually been observed hovering over, or settling on, a carcase), or if the process of putrefaction had led to liquefaction of the viscera. It is worthy of notice, however, that the directions given by Virgil (*Georg.* iv. 295 ff.) for the production of bees from the carcase of a bullock, according to the Egyptian method—the bruising of the body while the skin remains intact and the apertures of the nose and mouth are carefully stopped—seem to be aimed at producing a fluid condition of the interior ('solvuntur viscera,' l. 302) after the lapse of the period during which the carcase is kept closed up in a narrow chamber; and such a condition would be favourable to the production of *Eristalis*, supposing that the fly could deposit its eggs in such a way that the larva could reach this internal fluid (*e.g.* if the skin of the bullock eventually burst). As a matter of fact, when, as Virgil goes on to relate, Aristaeus, who was the first to learn the secret, used this method—or something like it—to renew his stock of bees, and was successful, we are told (ll. 554 ff.) that

'Hic vero subitum ac dictu mirabile monstrum
Aspiciunt, liquefacta boum per viscera toto
Stridere apes utero et ruptis effervere costis.'

'Bees' thus produced may very well have been *Eristalis*.

honey. 9. And he scraped it out into his palms, and went on, eating as he went. And he came to his father and his mother, and gave to them, and they did eat: but he told them not that it was out of the body of the lion that he had scraped the honey. 10. And Gl. his father J[1] went down unto the woman, and Gl. Samson J[1] made there a feast, for so were the young men

while accounting for the (supposed) bees, would not explain the *honey* in the carcase; yet, once given the existence of such a belief as to the origin of bees, the story that honey was actually derived from such a source might easily follow.* It should be remarked, however, that the ancient theory connected bees specifically with the carcases of *oxen* (whence it is termed βουγονία), just as it traced the origin of wasps to the carcases of horses, etc.; and we nowhere find any suggestion that bees were generated from the bodies of other animals, *e.g.* lions.

On the theory that the story of the lion and the honey has a solar-mythological origin, cf. *Addit. note*, p. 405.

9. *he scraped it out.* The verb *rādhā*, which only occurs in this passage in the O.T., is used in post-Biblical Heb. of *extracting* or *scraping out* bread from an oven (if, for instance, it adheres to the oven in baking).

And he came, etc. According to Jos. he took three honeycombs from the breast of the lion, and gave them, not to his parents, but to the damsel at Timnah, together with the rest of the presents which he had brought for her. This alteration may be due to the difficulty noticed on p. 354, viz. that, as the text stands, he was on his way to *Timnah*, and his parents were not with him.

10. *And his father . . . feast.* Originally, 'And Samson went down unto the woman, and he made there a feast.' Cf. the discussion on p. 354.

a feast. 𝔊, 𝔖[P] 'a seven days' feast' is probably based upon *vv.*[12.17]. Had there been anything unusual about the length of the festivities we should have expected it to have been specified in this verse; but seven days seems to have been the customary period in ancient times (cf. Gen. 29[27] E, Tob. 11[19]), and is still customary at the present day among the Syrian peasantry (cf. Wetzstein, *Zeitschrift für Ethnologie*, 1873, pp. 287 ff.); so the duration of the feast did not call for specification.

for so were the young men, etc. The statement implies that the

* Such a process of legendary accretion is aptly illustrated by Osten Sacken (*op. cit.* pp. 18 f.) by a quotation from Massoudi (died A.D. 955 in Cairo) in his *Golden Meadows* (translated by Barbier de Meynard and Pavet de Courteille, Paris, 1861). Massoudi 'relates a conversation which took place in Arabia, and of which this is a fragment: "Had the bees which produced this honey deposited

wont to do. 11. Gl. And because they ⌜feared⌝ him, they J[1] took thirty companions, and they remained with him. 12. And Samson said to them, 'Prithee let me propound a riddle to you: if ye can tell it me during the seven days of the feast,

narrator is referring to a custom which was obsolete, or at any rate unusual, in his own day. This can hardly refer to the giving of a feast, or to its duration—supposing that to have been originally specified (cf. *note* preceding). What calls for note is the fact that the feast was given 'there,' *i.e.* at the house of the bride's parents, instead of at the bridegroom's house (so Mo.).

11. *because they feared him.* Reading בְּיִרְאָתָם אוֹתוֹ, or 'כִּיר, with 𝕲AL, 𝕷L, 𝕾h, Jos. (*διὰ δέος τῆς ἰσχύος τοῦ νεανίσκου*), and many moderns. יִרְאָה is here, as frequently, Infin. Constr.; cf. G-K. § 45 *d.* 𝕳 כִּרְאוֹתָם אוֹתוֹ 'when they saw him,' is explained by Black, Mo. 'saw what a dangerous-looking fellow he was'; but surely, with all his coming and going to and fro, the Timnites must have been familiar enough with his appearance.

On the reasons for which we assume that *v.*11a is the reviser's addition, and that *v.* 11b originally opened with sing. וַיִּקַּח 'and he (*i.e.* Samson) took,' cf. p. 355.

thirty companions. The *υἱοὶ τοῦ νυμφῶνος*, Matt. 9 15, Mark 2 19, Lu. 5 34. In the modern Syrian peasant-marriage they are termed in Ar. *šabâb al-ʿarîs*, 'the bridegroom's young men,' and their number varies in accordance with the scale of the marriage-festivities, part of the cost of which they commonly defray. Probably the custom of choosing a large number of such companions dates from very early times, when the condition of the country was unsettled, and it was necessary to provide a bodyguard during the marriage-festival. Cf. Wetzstein, *op. cit.* p. 288, *n*2.

12. *a riddle.* Heb. *ḥîdhā*, only in this chapter denoting a trivial conundrum invented to pose ingenuity. The term is used in 1 Kgs. 10 1 of the 'hard questions' with which the Queen of Sheba tested Solomon's wisdom; while in Ps. 49 4 (𝕳 5) 78 2, Prov. 1 6 (R.V. in each case 'dark saying') it denotes a perplexing question of ethics or morals.

it in the body of a large animal?" asked Yiad. The surveyor answered: "Hearing that there was a hive near the sea-coast, I sent people to gather the honey. They told me that they found at that place a heap of bones, more or less rotten, in the cavity of which bees had deposited the honey that they brought with them."' Sacken's comment is: 'This case, as a parallel to Samson's bees, is a remarkable instance of the force of imaginative association in the human brain, and of the sameness of its illogical conclusion under similar circumstances.'

Gl. and find it out, J[1] I will give you thirty linen wrappers and thirty suits of festal apparel. 13. And if ye are not able to tell it me, *ye* shall give *me* thirty linen wrappers and thirty suits of festal apparel.' And they said to him, 'Propound thy riddle, and let us hear it.' 14. And he said to them,

'From the eater there came forth something to eat,
And from something strong came forth something sweet.'

and find it out. Heb. וּמְצָאתֶם, omitted by some MSS. of 𝔊 and by 𝔏[L], and marked by an asterisk in 𝔖[h], stands in 𝔥 in a most awkward position, and must be regarded (with Sta., Mo., etc.) as a gloss from *v.*[18b]. Had the expression formed a genuine part of the text, we should have expected 'If ye can find it out and tell it, etc.'

linen wrappers. Heb. *ṣādhîn* (Greek σινδών) was a large rectangular piece of fine linen, which might be worn either as a garment or as a sleeping wrap (cf. Mark 14 [51 f.]). It is mentioned in Isa. 3 [23] among other articles of female attire; and in Prov. 31 [24] as made by the capable woman, and sold by her to 'the Canaʿanites,' *i.e.* the Phoenician traders—a reference which perhaps gives us a hint as to the origin of the term in Greek. The word is well diffused in the other Semitic languages (Bab., Ar., Syr.), and is used in the Talmud of a curtain, wrapper, or shroud (cf. references given by Mo.; and for the last usage, cf. Matt. 27 [59], Mark 15 [46], Luke 23 [53]).

suits of festal apparel. Heb. *ḥ^a lîphôth b^e ghādhîm*, as in 2 Kgs. 5 [5.22.23]; similarly, *ḥ^a lîphôth s^e mālôth* twice in Gen. 45 [22] E. Here *ḥ^a lîphôth* is probably to be explained as meaning '*changes*' (cf. the use of the word in Job 10 [17], 14 [14], Ps. 55 [19], 𝔥 [20]); 'changes of raiment' denoting the best garments, which were only worn on festal occasions, in distinction from the everyday dress. Cf. the use of the cognate verb of *changing* the raiment in Gen. 35 [2] E, הַחֲלִיפוּ שִׂמְלֹתֵיכֶם. Less probable is connexion (suggested by Delitzsch, *Assyr. Studien*, p. 112) with Assyr. *ḫalâpu* 'to cover,' whence are derived *naḫlapu*, *naḫlaptu*, *naḫluptu*, all meaning *garment* or *covering*; since, on this explanation, we have to regard *b^e ghādhîm* (or *s^e mālôth*) as standing in explanatory apposition to *ḥ^a lîphôth*—a term which, *ex hypothesi*, bears the same meaning.

14. A 3-beat distich:—

mēhā'ōkhḗl yāṣā́ ma'^a khā́l
ûmēʿáz yāṣā́ māthṓḳ.

And from something strong, etc. Heb. עַז and מָתוֹק, both of which are adjectives, are used indefinitely without the Article; hence the rendering adopted above rather than that of R.V., 'and out of the strong came forth sweetness.'

And they were not able to tell the riddle Gl. for ⌜six⌝ days. 15. And on the seventh day J^{1} they said to Samson's wife, 'Beguile thy husband, that he may tell us the riddle, lest we burn thee

עַז has normally the meaning 'strong' or 'fierce.' Bochart, however (*Hierozoicon*, ii. p. 523), remarks that we should expect a paradox in the contrast between עַז and מָתוֹק, just as we have one between הָאֹכֵל 'the eater,' and מַאֲכָל 'something to eat,' in the first line. He thinks that עַז may have a range of meaning similar to the Latin *acer* (which may mean either 'pungent,' or 'fierce'), comparing Ar. *mirra* 'strength,' and *marîr* 'strong,' from the verb *marra*, 'to be bitter' (cf., however, *footnote*, p. 380); and so he renders 'ab acri prodiit dulce,' and in $v.^{18}$, 'Quid dulcius est melle? Et quid acrius est leone?'

The need for such a paradox was felt by $\mathfrak{S}^{P}$, which renders ܘܡܢ ܡܪܝܪܐ ܢܦܩ ܚܠܝܐ 'and from something *bitter*, etc.' It might be brought out in English if we were justified in representing עַז by some such rendering as 'something *biting*,' where the reference would of course really be to the biting (*i.e. ferocious*) lion, but the contrast with 'sweet' would immediately suggest that it referred to something of a biting (*i.e. acrid*) taste: cf. the word-play in *ch.* 15^{16}. The difficulty is that we possess no evidence that עַז was used in the sense *acrid* or *bitter*; yet the question is not set at rest by Mo. when he remarks that there is in reality only one antithesis in the couplet (that between 'eater' and 'something to eat'), and that it is unnecessary therefore to make out a perfect antithesis between the adjectives independently. The rhythmical parallelism of the clauses favours such an antithesis, in sense as well as in form.*

for six days. Reading שֵׁשֶׁת in place of $\mathfrak{M}$ שְׁלֹשֶׁת 'three,' which cannot stand alongside of $v.^{15}$ 'and on the seventh day.' So Doorn., Mo. The alternative correction is to read 'the fourth day' in $v.^{15}$; and this has the support of $\mathfrak{G}^{BA}$, $\mathfrak{L}^{L}$, $\mathfrak{S}^{P}$, and most moderns.

* It is, at any rate, a moot point whether *'az* may not have been used in the sense *harsh* or *acrid*, and applied to a flavour. The adj. *mar* '*bitter*,' which is commonly used of a flavour, denotes a *fierce* disposition in *ch.* 18^{25}, 2 Sam. 17^{8}, Hab. 1^{6}; and, conversely, it may be inferred that *'az*, which is commonly used of a *fierce* disposition, may also have denoted a *bitter* flavour. The Ar. parallel offered by Bochart in illustration of connexion between the meanings *strong* and *bitter* is questionable; yet it seems likely that a similar range of meaning may have been possessed by the Heb. root קָשָׁה. This has the sense 'to be hard, severe, fierce' (so BDB.); and, in the adjectival form *ķāšé*, is used in parallelism to *'az* as a synonym in Isa. 19^{4} ('*harsh* lord . . . *fierce* king'). The root קָשָׁא, from which is derived *ķiššû'îm* 'cucumbers,' was plausibly connected by the Jews with קשה; cf. *Aboda zara*, fol. xi. 1, 'Why are they called *ķiššû'îm*? Because they are as *harsh* (*ķāšîn*) to the human body as a sword.' Similarly, Pliny (*Hist. Nat.* xix. 5) says of cucumbers, 'vivunt hausti in stomacho in posterum diem,

and thy father's house with fire: was it to beggar us that ye invited us ⌜hither⌝?' 16. And Samson's wife wept upon him, and said, 'Thou surely hatest me, and dost not love me: thou

Adopting either emendation, it is impossible, however, to square the note of time with the narrative which follows, according to which, when the Philistines have persuaded Samson's bride to extract the answer of the riddle from her husband, she weeps over him the whole seven days during which the feast lasts (*v.*[17]). Clearly, then, the Philistines can have made no serious attempt to solve the riddle for themselves, but must have had recourse to the woman on the day when Samson propounded it to them. The note of time in *vv.*[14.15] must be due to a later hand, who, overlooking *v.*[17], supposed that the Philistines would have spent at least part of the time in attempting to discover the answer themselves; and we may conclude (with Sta.) that the narrative originally ran 'and they were not able to tell the riddle; and they said to Samson's wife, etc.'

15. *was it to beggar us.* Heb. הֲלְיָרְשֵׁנוּ. For the verb ירשׁ in this sense, cf. the use of the Niph'al in Gen. 45 [11] E, Prov. 20 [13], 23 [21], 30 [9]. On the exceptional retention of י in the Infin. Constr. Ḳal, cf. G-K. § 69 *m*. There is a variant vocalization הֲלְיָרְשֵׁנוּ which apparently treats the form as Pi'el.

hither. Reading הֲלֹם with five Heb. MSS., 𝔗, and moderns. 𝔐 הֲלֹא 'or not' is irregular in construction; אִם לֹא being usual in the second half of a disjunctive question: cf. G-K. § 150 *g*, *n* [1].

16. *surely.* רַק has here an asseverative force, as in Gen. 20 [11],

nec perfici queunt in cibis' (both references cited by Ges., *Thes.* p. 1241 *b*). Both these passages refer to indigestibility rather than to flavour; yet there can be little doubt that there was a close connexion in thought between the indigestibility of the cucumber and its *bitter* or *acrid* taste when eaten with the rind or in an over-ripe state. We may compare the incident related in 2 Kgs. 4 [38-41], where, when wild gourds (probably *Citrullus colocynthis, L.*, allied to the cucumber, the pulp of which is 'intensely bitter,' and forms 'a drastic cathartic, and, in quantities, an irritant poison'; cf. Post in *DB.* ii. p. 250) have been accidentally included in the stew, the fact that 'there is death in the pot' is recognized by the *flavour*.

It may be added that this connexion between the Heb. roots קשׁה and קשׁא is made in full consciousness of the fact that in the former the *š* runs through Heb., Ar., and Aram., whereas in the latter, Heb. *š*=Ar. *ṯ*=Aram. *ṭ* (for *t* after *ḳ*). Such a difference does not imply original diversity of root; but may represent merely a slight differentiation in sound for the sake of marking a variation in the shade of meaning. Cf. the way in which *e.g.* the Heb. *ḳāṣā* appears in Ar. as *ḳaṣa* 'to cut' in the literal sense, but as *ḳaḍa* when denoting a metaphorical 'cutting,' *i.e.* 'deciding.'

hast propounded the riddle to the sons of my people, and thou hast not told it to *me*.' And he said to her, 'Behold, I have not told it to my father or my mother, and should I tell it to *thee*?' 17. And she wept upon him the seven days during which the feast lasted; and on the seventh day he told her, because she pressed him sorely; and she told the riddle to the sons of her people. 18. And the men of the city said to him on the seventh day, before he entered ⌜the bridal chamber⌝,

'What is sweeter than honey?
And what is stronger than a lion?'

Deut. 4^{6}, I Kgs. 21^{25}, Ps. 32^{6}. The restrictive meaning '*only*' is clearly not so suitable.

18. *before he entered the bridal chamber.* Reading הַחַדְרָה as the last word in place of 𝔐 הַחַרְסָה 'before *the sun* went down,' where the word for 'sun' is very uncommon (cf. *ch.* 1^{35} *note*) and of anomalous form (with the old accusative ending). הַחַדְרָה (cf. *ch.* 15^{1a}), first suggested by Sta., has been generally adopted; and is supported by 𝔖ᴾ, in which the inexplicable ܩܘܣܛܢܐ must be an error for ܩܘܛܢܐ 'inner chamber' (חדר is so rendered in *ch.* $16^{9.12}$, I Kgs. 20^{30}, *al*; cf. references in Payne Smith, *Thesaurus Syriacus*, *s.v.* col. 50).* 'The Timnathites waited till the last moment, to heighten their triumph and his discomfiture' (Mo.).

It would appear from this passage that the marriage was not to have been consummated until the end of the seventh day of the festival; and this also seems to follow from *v.*[20], where, after Samson has rushed off in a rage, the bride is at once given in marriage to his 'chief friend,' clearly in order that she may escape the disgrace and ridicule which would have fallen upon her if the marriage had not been completed (cf. her father's words in 15^{2}); but otherwise (we may presume) an unnecessary step to take. Such a custom of deferring the completion of the marriage is, however (apart from this instance), unknown to us. Jacob consummates his marriage with Le'ah upon the first of the seven days (Gen. 29^{21-28} E); and the same practice is observed in the modern Syrian marriage (cf. Wetzstein, *op. cit.*)

What is sweeter, etc. A rhythmical 2-beat distich:—

mam-māthṓḳ middᵉbháš
ûme-'áz mēᵃrî́.

* The editor's attention was called to this point by Prof. Bevan.

And he said to them,

> 'If ye had not plowed with this heifer of mine,
> Ye would not have found out this riddle of mine.'

19. ^{Gl.} And the spirit of Yahweh rushed upon him, and he went down to Ashḳelon, and smote thirty men ⌈from thence⌉, and

If ye had not, etc. The 3-beat distich is rhymed upon the suffix of the 1st pers. sing. :—

> *lûlê ḥᵃraštém bᵉᶜeghlāthî*
> *lô mᵉṣāthém ḥîdāthî.*

The rendering 'of mine' for 'my' attempts to reproduce this in English. Cf. the similar rhyme in *ch.* 16²⁴.

19. *and smote . . . riddle.* Reading מֵשָׁם for מֵהֶם, חֲלִיפוֹתָם for חֲלִיצוֹתָם, and omitting הַחֲלִיפוֹת after וַיִּתֵּן, with 𝔊^{AL}, 𝔖^h, καὶ ἔπαισεν ἐκεῖθεν τριάκοντα ἄνδρας, καὶ ἔλαβε τὰς στόλας αὐτῶν καὶ ἔδωκε τοῖς ἐπαγγείλασι τὸ πρόβλημα. Cf. also 𝔙. 𝔐 מהם 'of them,' *i.e.* of the Ashḳelonites, *as assumed* from the preceding 'he went down to Ashḳelon,' is very awkward ; while חליצותם 'their spoil' (lit. 'what was *stripped off* them' ; cf. 2 Sam. 2²¹) is so similar to חליפותם that it is natural to regard it as a corruption, which has led, in turn, to the addition of החליפות after ויתן ('he gave—not the spoil as a whole, but—the festal attire'). Adopting our emendation, the use of ויתן without expressed object—this being inferred from preceding חליפותם —is very idiomatic ; cf., with the same verb, Gen. 18⁷·⁸, 20¹⁴, 21¹⁴, *al.*

Sta. and Doorn. are probably right in regarding the whole of *v.*¹⁹ᵃ as a later addition to the narrative. We need not press the improbability of Samson's actually rushing off in his frenzy to a seaside town some twenty-three miles distant (cf. *ch.* 16³, where he carries the gates of Gaza to the top of a hill to the east of Ḥebron some thirty-eight miles off), getting exactly what he wanted (the suits of festal attire) from the bodies of the slaughtered Philistines, returning to pay his wager (the same night ?), and then departing, still in angry mood, to his father's house. Nor is the fact that nothing results from his raid on Ashḳelon in the way of reprisal necessarily fatal to the originality of the verse. It is obvious, however, that the statement of *v.*¹⁹ᵇ 'and his anger was kindled, etc.,' is curiously weak and inappropriate when following after *v.*¹⁹ᵃ (the superhuman access of frenzy denoted by ותצלח וג׳ ; cf. *v.*⁶ *note*) ; but, on the rejection of *v.*¹⁹ᵃ, it forms a natural description of his rage at the underhand trick by which the Philistines had discovered the solution of the riddle. We assume, then, that the original story made Samson depart home

took ⌜their suits of festal apparel⌝, and gave them [ ] to the tellers of the riddle. J^1 And his anger was kindled, and he went up to his father's house. 20. And Samson's wife was given to his companion, whom he had made his chief friend.

15. 1. After a time, however, in the days of wheat-harvest, Samson visited his wife with a kid of the goats; and he said, 'I will go in unto my wife into the bridal chamber.' But her father would not suffer him to go in. 2. And her father said, 'I verily thought that thou didst *hate* her, so I gave her to thy companion: is not her younger sister fairer than she? prithee

in anger without paying the wager, which had not been fairly won; and that the addition is due to an interpolator who thought that the story would be improved if he were represented as paying, and at the same time inflicting damage on his foes.

20. *And Samson's wife, etc.* Cf. *note* on *v.*^{18}.

his companion. The φίλος τοῦ νυμφίου (Jo. 3^{29}), or, as we should say, *best man*; called in the modern Syrian wedding *wazîr*, *i.e.* vizier or *chargé d'affaires* (from *wazara* 'to bear a burden') to the *king*, as the bridegroom is termed during the seven days' festival (Wetzstein, *op. cit.*).

15. 1. *in the days of wheat-harvest.* This varies in Palestine in accordance with the elevation, the harvest of the Jordan valley being considerably earlier than that of the hill-country. In the district of Timnah wheat-harvest falls (according to La.) from mid-May to mid-June. The season is mentioned in view of the incident of *vv.*$^{4.5}$.

a kid of the goats. Cf. Gen. $38^{17\,ff}$. The gift seems to have been of the kind which was called *ṣadâḳ* among the ancient Arabians; and was probably made to the *ṣadîḳa*-wife on each occasion of such a visit. Cf. Robertson Smith, *Kinship*,[2] pp. 83, 93.

2. *I verily thought.* Heb. אָמֹר אָמַרְתִּי, lit. 'Saying I said (to myself).' The force of the Infin. Absolute is to emphasize the mental process by which he arrived at his conclusion—much as we might say in colloquial English, 'What I *thought* was, etc.' Cf. Davidson, *Syntax*, § 86 *a*.

that thou didst **hate** *her.* Here the force of the Infin. Absolute in the phrase שָׂנֹא שְׂנֵאתָהּ can only be expressed by italicizing the verb; unless, with Mo., we render 'that thou didst certainly hate her.' R.V. 'that thou hadst utterly hated her' is very erroneous; the emphasis being not on the quality of the feeling denoted by the verb (*bitter* hatred), but upon the *accurate definition* of the feeling (hatred, and not love). A similar error is perpetrated by R.V. in *v.*^{13} (cf. *note*).

let her be thine instead of her.' 3. And Samson said to them, 'I am quits this time with the Philistines; for I am about to do them a mischief.' 4. And Samson went and caught three

3. *said to them.* 𝔊^AL, 𝔖^h, 𝔏^L, 𝔙 read 'said to him.' This, however, is probably an alteration induced by the fact that the woman's father only is speaking in *v.*[2]. In favour of 𝔐 cf. *v.*[7]. As Mo. remarks, 'It is not necessary to suppose that in either case the words were spoken in their hearing; the threat was addressed to them.'

I am quits, etc. נִקֵּיתִי is a Perfect of certitude. As the brilliant idea strikes him which, when put into action, will, he forsees, *wipe off all scores* which he owes to the Philistines, he speaks of it as an accomplished fact. Cf. Driver, *Tenses*, § 13.

The verb *niḳḳā*, as here used, followed by *min*, means *freed from obligation towards* (the obligation in this case being, of course, that of *taking vengeance*); and it would be best expressed by the old phrase '*quit of*,' as used *e.g.* in Shakespeare, *Coriolanus*, IV. v. 89:—

> 'To be full quit of these my banishers,
> Stand I before thee here.'

The phrase is used (of gaining freedom from obligation of *service*) in Num. 32 [22], where Moses, in impressing upon the two and a half tribes that they can only gain the right to the territory conquered by all Israel east of Jordan if they in their turn will cross the Jordan with the other tribes, and help them to conquer the territory to the west, adds that, when this has been accomplished, 'afterward ye shall return, *and shall be quit of Yahweh and of Israel*' (והייתם נקים מיהוה ומישראל).

This sense is expressed by R.V. *marg.* and by La. R.V. *text* follows the Versions, Jewish commentators, and nearly all moderns in rendering, 'This time shall I be blameless in regard of the Philistines, when I do them a mischief'—an interpretation which is bound up with the rendering of כִּי־עֹשֶׂה אֲנִי וגו׳ as a temporal clause, which can scarcely be justified (we should surely expect כִּי עָשִׂיתִי 'when I shall have done,' etc). עֹשֶׂה is to be explained as *Futurum instans*; cf. the rendering given above.

4. *three hundred foxes.* Since the fox is a solitary animal, it has been supposed by many that the reference is to *jackals*, which live together in large packs, and could be caught in numbers without great difficulty. It is, however, a very doubtful expedient to attempt to explain Samson's feats by depriving them of the element of the marvellous.

hundred foxes, and took torches and turned tail to tail, and put a torch between every two tails in the midst. 5. And he set fire to the torches, and turned them loose into ⌜the fields⌝ of the Philistines, and burned both shocks and standing corn and vineyards ⟨and⟩ olives. 6. And the Philistines said, 'Who hath done this?' And they said, 'Samson, the son-in-law of the Timnite; because he took his wife, and gave her to his companion.' Then the Philistines went up, and burned her and her father's ⟨house⟩ with fire. 7. And Samson said to them, 'If ye do after this manner, surely I will be avenged of you, and after that I will cease.' 8. And he smote them leg upon thigh with a

took torches, etc. Commentators generally have noted the remarkable resemblance of the action here ascribed to Samson to the custom which was observed at Rome during the festival of Ceres, when foxes with burning torches attached to their brushes were hunted through the Circus (Ovid, *Fasti*, iv. 679 ff.). This point is discussed in *Addit. note*, pp. 393 f.

5. *into the fields.* Reading בִּשְׂדוֹת with Bu., in place of 𝔐 בְּקָמוֹת 'into the standing corn,' which occurs only here in the plur., and is not very suitable before the following statement 'and burned both shocks and standing corn' (קָמָה sing.).

and vineyards and olives. Reading וְעַד־כֶּרֶם וָזָיִת with 𝔊; 𝔙, in place of 𝔐 וְעַד־כֶּרֶם זָיִת (rendered by R.V. 'and also the oliveyards'; as though כֶּרֶם—elsewhere always *vineyard*—here meant 'yard' or 'plantation' of olives). Vineyards and olives are thus coupled in Ex. 23[11] E, Deut. 6[11], 28[39.40], Josh. 24[13] E, 1 Sam, 8[14], 2 Kgs. 5[26], Neh. 5[11], 9[25]. 𝔖^{P}, 𝔗 וְעַד־כֶּרֶם וְעַד־זַיִת. There is no reason to suppose, with Mo., that the words 'are probably an addition by a later hand, exaggerating the mischief.'

6. *and her father's house.* Reading וְאֶת־בֵּית אָבִיהָ with many MSS. of 𝔐, 𝔊^{AL}, 𝔖^{h}, 𝔖^{P}, Mo., Bu., etc. (cf. *ch.* 14[15]), in place of וְאֶת־אָבִיהָ 'and her father.'

7. *surely I will be avenged of you.* Heb. כִּי אִם־נִקַּמְתִּי בָּכֶם. The particles כי אם are closely connected, with a strong asseverative force, and נקמתי is a Perfect of certitude: cf. the precisely similar construction in 2 Kgs. 5[20] (*note* on construction in *NHTK.*), Jer. 51[14]. כי אם is so used, followed by the *Imperfect*, in 1 Sam. 26[10] (*note* in *NHTS.*[2]), 2 Sam. 15[21] *Kt.*; cf. also 1 Sam. 21[6], Ru. 3[12] *Kt.*

8. *leg upon thigh.* Heb. *šôḳ* denotes the *leg* generally, or specifi-

great slaughter, and went down, and abode in a cleft of the crag ʿEṭam.

9. Then the Philistines went up, and encamped in Judah, and

cally the *shank* from the knee downwards, as distinct from the thigh; while *yārēkh* is used of the *thigh*, or rather, the whole of the upper part of the leg from the hip down to the knee (cf. Ar. *warik* 'hip' or 'buttock'). The only plausible explanation of the difficult expression *šôḳ ʿal yārēkh* is that it is a wrestler's term, akin to the English *cross-buttock*, which is thus described in the *Sporting Magazine*, xxx. (1808), 247 A:—'A cross-buttock in pugilism is, when the party, advancing his right leg and thigh, closes with his antagonist, and catching him with his right arm, or giving a round blow, throws him over his right hip, upon his head.' Cf. D'Urfey, *Collin's Walk* (1690), ii. p. 74:—

> 'When th' hardy Major, skill'd in Wars,
> To make quick end of fight prepares,
> By strength o'er buttock cross to hawl him,
> And with a trip i' th' Inturn maul him.'

Castle (*Lexicon heptaglotton*, 3716) and Le Clerc connected the phrase with wrestling; but supposed that the *leg* (*šôḳ*) of the victor was impacted *against the thigh* (*ʿal yārēkh*) of the vanquished. To Smythe Palmer (p. 225) belongs the credit of connecting the phrase with a cross-buttock, in view of the cylinder-seals in which Gilgameš is figured as wrestling with an antagonist, and throwing him across his own thigh (cf. Plate II., fig. 5).

The Versions were evidently puzzled by the phrase. 𝕲 renders literally κνήμην ἐπὶ μηρόν; 𝖁 'ita ut stupentes suram femori imponerent'; 𝕾ᴾ ܡܢ ܫܩ̈ܝܗܘܢ ܘܥܕܡܐ ܠܚܨ̈ܝܗܘܢ 'from their legs even to their loins'; 𝕿 פרשין עם רגלאין 'horsemen with footmen.'* Other attempted explanations—such as those of Kimchi, 'shank over thigh,' as they fell in precipitate flight (or, as we might say, 'heels over head'), and Ges., *Thes.*, 'in frusta eos concidit ita ut membra eorum, crura et femora, alia super aliis disjecta jacerent'—merely serve to illustrate the lengths to which perverted ingenuity can go.

the crag ʿEṭam. A city of Judah named ʿEṭam is mentioned in 2 Chr. 11^{6} as built by Reḥoboam; and the order in which the name occurs, between Bethleḥem and Teḳoaʿ, favours a site at or near the modern Urṭâs, near which is a spring called ʿAin ʿAṭân: *SWP. Mem.*

* This rendering inverts the order of the phrase, *šôḳ* being interpreted of those who go on foot (cf. Ps. 147^{10}); while the sense attributed to *yārēkh* may be gathered from the Ar. verb *waraka*, which (according to Kazimirski, *Dict. Ar.-Français*) may mean 'Appuyer un côté du corps sur le dos du cheval et voyager ainsi.'

spread themselves abroad in Leḥi. 10. And the men of Judah said, 'Why have ye come up against us?' And they said, 'To bind Samson have we come up, to do to him as he hath done to us.' 11. Then three thousand men from Judah went down

iii. p. 43. This, however, is too far removed from the scene of Samson's exploits. Schick, *ZDPV.* x. (1887), pp. 143 f., and Hanauer, *PEF. Qy. St.*, 1896, pp. 162 ff., have plausibly suggested the rock called ʿArâḳ Ismaʿîn, near Ḫirbet Marmîtâ, some two and a half miles east-south-east of Ṣorʿah, in which there is a cave which exactly suits the description of our narrative. 'The cave is approached by descending through a crack or fissure in the very edge of the cliffs overhanging the chasm of wâdy Ismaʿîn. The crack is scarcely wide enough to allow one person to squeeze through at a time. It leads down to the topmost of a long series of rudimentary steps, or small artificial foot-ledges, cut in the face of the cliff, and descending to a narrow rock terrace running along the front of the cave, and between it and the fragments of massive wall (belonging to an ancient Christian cœnobium)': Hanauer, *op. cit.*, p. 163.

9. *and spread themselves abroad.* Heb. וַיִּנָּטְשׁוּ again in this sense in 2 Sam. 5[18.22].

in Leḥi. As the narrator is about to record the incident from which, according to his tradition, the place obtained its name of *Lĕḥî* 'jawbone,' he uses the name here and in *v.*[14] proleptically. Probably the name was originally given to some hill or ridge on account of its resemblance to a jawbone. Commentators generally compare the Greek Ὄνου γνάθος—the name of a promontory at the southern end of Laconia; cf. Strabo, VIII., v. 1. Schick (*ZDPV.* x. pp. 152 f.) proposes to identify Leḥi with Ḫirbet eṣ-Ṣiyyâġ, a hill with ruins a little south-west of ʿArâḳ Ismaʿîn. Ḫirbet eṣ-Ṣiyyâġ means 'ruin of the goldsmiths'; but such a name is very strange in this locality, and the view is plausible that Ṣiyyâġ really represents the Greek σιαγών, which is the rendering of Leḥi employed by ʿA., Σ., Jos. (*Ant.* V. viii. 8 f.), and by 𝔊 in *vv.*[14ff].

Leḥi is mentioned again in 2 Sam. 23[11] (emended text*) as the scene of an exploit of Shammah, the son of Agee, one of David's heroes, in withstanding and smiting a large number of Philistines single-handed. On the suspicious similarity between the deeds of Samson, Shammah, and Shamgar, cf. p. 75.

11. *three thousand men.* The huge numbers here and in *v.*[15], *ch.*

* Reading 'Now the Philistines were gathered together ⌜to Leḥi⌝' (i.e. לְחָיָה for the very obscure לַחַיָּה of 𝔐, after 𝔊[L] ἐπὶ σιαγόνα). This emendation is generally accepted.

unto the cleft of the crag ʿEṭam, and said to Samson, 'Knowest thou not that the Philistines are ruling over us? What then is this that thou hast done to us?' And he said to them, 'As they did to me, so have I done to them.' 12. And they said to him, 'To bind thee are we come down, to deliver thee into the hand of the Philistines.' And Samson said to them, 'Swear to me that ye will not fall upon me yourselves.' 13. And they spake to him, saying, 'Nay, but we will *bind* thee, and deliver thee into their hand; but we will not *slay* thee.' So they bound him with two new ropes, and brought him up from the crag. 14. As soon as he came unto Leḥi, the Philistines came shouting to meet him: and the spirit of Yahweh rushed upon him, and the ropes that were upon his arms became like flax that hath been burnt with fire, and his bonds melted from off his hands. 15. And he found a fresh jawbone of an ass, and put forth his hand, and took it, and smote therewith a thousand men. 16. And Samson said,

'With the red ass's jawbone ⌜I have reddened them right red⌝;
With the red ass's jawbone I have smitten a thousand men.'

16 [27] are of a piece with the marvellous character of the narrative as a whole.

13. *Nay, but we will* **bind** *thee, etc.* The use of the Infinitive Absolute here—lit. 'binding we will bind thee . . . but slaying we will not slay thee'—is intended to emphasize what they *will* do, in distinction from what they will *not* do; and can only be rightly reproduced in English by the use of italics. R.V. 'we will bind thee fast, etc.,' is erroneous in supposing the emphasis to be on the *security* of the binding. Cf. the similar error in *v.*[2] (*note* on 'that thou didst *hate* her').

14. *melted.* Heb. וַיִּמַּסּוּ, a graphic description of the powerlessness of the bonds as against Samson's strength.

15. *a fresh jawbone.* Heb. טְרִיָּה, lit. 'moist,' explains how the jawbone was suitable for use as a weapon. Had it been old and dry it would have been too brittle.

16. *with the red ass's jawbone, etc.* A 4-beat distich:—

Bilᵉḥí haḥᵃmór ḥāmór ḥimmartîm
Bilᵉḥí haḥᵃmôr hikkéthî ʾeleph-ʾíš.

We vocalize the first stichos בִּלְחִי הַחֲמוֹר חָמוֹר חִמַּרְתִּים. There is a play upon the word for *ass* (*ḥᵃmôr*), which means lit. the *reddish-*

coloured animal, and the verb (*ḥāmar*; in Piʿēl, *ḥimmēr*) applied to the slaughtered Philistines, which is explained from Ar. *ḥamara*, properly 'to be *or* to make red,' used *e.g.* of *skinning* a sheep so as *to make it appear red*, and in Conj. II. (the equivalent of the Heb. Piʿēl) of *dyeing* a thing *red* (so Lane). Cf. the use of the Peʿalʿal in Heb. in Job. 16 16, 'my face is reddened (*ḥomarmerû*) from weeping.' The pun is suggested to Samson by the appearance of the blood-stained corpses.* As an alternative possibility, we might vocalize as Ḳal חֲמַרְתִּים, and regard the verb *ḥāmar* as a denominative from *ḥamôr*, with the meaning 'treat as an ass' (in this case, by *belabouring* them), a sense which is also possessed by *ḥamara* in Ar. Thus, if we were justified in coining (not for the first time ‡) a verb *to ass* in this sense, we might bring out the word-play by rendering:

'With the jawbone of an ass I have thoroughly assed them.'

This explanation is adopted by Levesque (*Revue Biblique*, 1900, pp. 89 ff.), who reproduces the assonance excellently by use of the French *rosse = a sorry jade* and the denominative verb *rosser = to beat* or *belabour violently*, properly, *to treat as a jade* (cf. Littré, *Dict. de la lang. Franç.*, 1761):—

'Avec une mâchoire de rosse, je les ai bien rossés.'

So also La.

𝔐 חֲמוֹר חֲמֹרָתָיִם is rendered by A.V., R.V. 'heaps upon heaps,' with *marg.* Heb. 'an heap, two heaps' (cf. רַחַם רַחֲמָתַיִם *ch.* 5 30), upon the assumption that חֲמוֹר (though identical with the word for 'ass' preceding) has the same meaning as חֹמֶר Hab. 3 15 (text very suspicious), plur. חֳמָרִים Ex. 8 10 J; and this is the sense which was probably intended by the vocalization. 𝔊, however, treats the two words as Infin. Absol. and Finite verbs, ἐξαλείφων ἐξήλειψα αὐτούς; and the other Versions explain חמרתים as a verbal form:—𝔙 'delevi eos,' 𝔖 ܟܡܘܪܐ ܟܡܪܬ ܡܢܗܘܢ, 'I have heaped some of them in heaps,' 𝔗 רמיתנון דגורין, 'I have cast them in heaps.'

The view that we should read Infin. Absol. Ḳal, coupled with a Finite verb, either Ḳal or Piʿēl, is adopted by most moderns; but very various meanings are assigned to the verb. J. D. Michaelis

* This explanation occurred to the present editor, and was adopted by him as given above, before he noticed that he had been anticipated by Zenner, *Zeitschr. für kath. Theol.*, 1888, p. 257, quoted and followed by Cheyne, *EB.*, 2340.

‡ The verb *to ass*, in the sense 'to call an ass,' is quoted by the *New English Dictionary* from G. Harvey, *Pierces Supererogation* (1592), 57:—'He . . . bourdeth, girdeth, asseth the excellentest writers of whatsoever note that tickle not his wanton sense.'

17. And when he had finished speaking, he cast away the jawbone out of his hand; so that place was called Ramath-leḥi. 18. And he was sore athirst, and called unto Yahweh, and said, '*Thou* hast given this great victory by the hand of thy servant; and now, I must die of thirst, and fall into the hand of the uncircumcised.' 19. Then God clave the Mortar that is in Leḥi, and there came water thereout; and when he had drunk, his spirit returned, and he revived: wherefore its name

(quoted by Ros.) connected the 𝔊 rendering with Ar. *ḥamara* in the sense *to skin* or *shave*, and this explanation is adopted by Doorn. (followed by Bu. doubtfully, No., Kit.), 'I have thoroughly flayed *or* shaved them.' Mo. (followed by Bu. doubtfully, Cooke), 'I have heaped them up in heaps'—חמר 'perhaps a casual denominative, invented for the paronomasia'; cf. 𝔖^{P}. It is a defect in these and other explanations, as compared with those given at the beginning of this *note*, that the play upon *ḥ*^{a}*môr* 'ass' is one of *sound* merely, apart from any connexion in *meaning*.

17. *Ramath-leḥi.* Here *Râmath* is explained by וַיַּשְׁלֵךְ 'be cast away,' as though derived from *rāmā* 'to cast *or* throw'—the name being taken to mean 'the throwing of the jawbone.' With such a derivation we should expect the form to be vocalized *R*^{e}*math*. *Râmath* should be derived from the root *rûm* 'to be high'; and there can be no doubt that the name really means 'the height of Leḥi'; cf. the proper names רָמָה or הָרָמָה 'the height,' רָמַת הַמִּצְפֶּה 'the height of the outlook-point,' etc. The story is based upon an unphilological interpretation of the name.

19. *Then God clave, etc.* The story probably embodies a trace of solar mythology: cf. *Addit. note*, p. 406.

the Mortar. Heb. *ham-makhtēš*—doubtless a circular depression in the rock or soil, of the appearance of a mortar, from the side of which the spring issued. There was a place called 'the Mortar' at Jerusalem: Zeph. 1^{11}.

that is in Leḥi. Leḥi is here, of course, the *place*, as is proved by the statement at the end of the verse that the spring was in existence in the narrator's own day. The rendering of 𝔙, 𝔖^{P}, A.V., R.V. *marg.* suggests that the spring issued from a 'hollow place' in the actual *jawbone.*

his spirit returned. Heb. וַתָּשָׁב רוּחוֹ. So exactly in 1 Sam. 30^{12} of the return of *animation* and *vigour* after faintness. Heb. *rûaḥ* is the essential principle of life, the removal of which from the body results in death (cf. Ps. 104^{29}).

he revived. Lit. 'he lived.'

was called 'Ên-haḳ-ḳōrē, which is in Leḥi, unto this day. 20. R^{E2} And he judged Israel in the days of the Philistines twenty years.

16. 1. J^1 And Samson went to Ġaza, and saw there a harlot,

'Ên-haḳ-ḳōrē. The name means 'the spring of the caller,' and is explained by the narrator as referring to Samson; cf. the statement of *v.* [18] 'and he called (*way-yiḳrā*) unto Yahweh.' *Haḳ-ḳōrē*, however, is the Heb. term for the *partridge* in 1 Sam. 26 [20], Jer. 17 [11], referring to its call-note, which is a familiar sound in the hill-country of Palestine; and modern commentators (following J. D. Michaelis) consider that the name of the spring was *the Partridge-spring*, and that the explanation given by the narrator, like that of Ramath-leḥi, represents a later adaptation of the meaning. It is tempting to suppose that, if *haḳ-ḳōrē* really here refers to a bird, 'the caller' may in this case be, not the partridge, but its near relative the *quail* (elsewhere called *s^elāw*), which is likewise distinguished by a very clear and resonant call-note.* Bochart (*Hierozoicon*, ii. p. 99) quotes from Athenaeus (ix. 47) the myth that Herakles, when slain by Typhon, was restored to life by smelling a quail—whence arose the proverb among the Greeks,

Ὄρτυξ ἔσωσεν Ἡρακλῆν τὸν καρτερόν.

According to Eudoxus (Athenaeus, *loc. cit.*), the Phoenicians annually sacrificed a quail in commemoration of the resurrection of Herakles in the month Peritius (Feb.-Mar.), at the season when the quail returns to Palestine in great numbers (cf. Robertson Smith, *Religion of the Semites*,[2] p. 449)—a ceremony which is almost certainly to be brought into connexion with the solar myth: cf. *Addit. note*, p. 406. If the quail was thus sacred to Herakles-Melḳart, the possibility is opened that the bird may have played a part in the story which related the revival of Samson's vital powers (ותשב רוחו); though, if this was so, the original connexion was so remote from (*or* so explained away by) the narrator that 'the caller' became, not the bird, but the hero himself.

20. *And he judged, etc.* On this notice as the conclusion of the Samson-narrative in R^{E2}'s book, cf. p. 338.

16. 1. *Ġaza.* Heb. עַזָּה. The English form of the name is from 𝔊 Γαζα, in which the Γ reproduces the harder form of ע—a consonant which, when Heb. was a spoken language, must have repre-

* Cf. Tristram, *Nat. Hist.* p. 232:—'A few remain there [in Palestine] throughout the winter, but their numbers are suddenly reinforced at the end of March, when every patch of grass resounds with their well-known peculiar call-note.'

and went in unto her. 2. ⟨And it was told⟩ to the Ġazathites, saying, 'Samson hath come hither.' And they came round about, and laid wait for him all ⌜day⌝ in the gate of the city; and they kept quiet all night, saying, 'when the morning dawns we will

sented two distinct sounds, akin respectively to ع and غ in Ar.: cf. G-K. § 6 *e*. The modern Ar. name is Ġazzeh (identical with the Heb. form); and the city, which in ancient times was of considerable importance as a trade-centre on the caravan-routes to Egypt and Arabia, still possesses a considerable population: cf. Smith, *HG*. pp. 181 ff. Ġaza is some thirty-six miles south-east of Ṣorʿah.

2. *And it was told.* Supplying וַיֻּגַּד with 𝔊^{B} καὶ ἀνηγγέλη, 𝔊^{AL} καὶ ἀπηγγέλη, 𝔖^{P} ܘܐܬܬܚܘܝ, 𝔗 אתחוה, and all moderns. 𝔙 reads, 'quod cum audissent Philisthiim.' 𝔐 is untranslatable without a verb.

all day. Reading כָּל־הַיּוֹם with Kit., in place of כָּל־הַלַּיְלָה 'all night,' erroneously copied from the latter half of the verse. The point of the statement 'and they kept quiet all night, saying, etc.,' must be that during the night they were off their guard, relying upon the supposition that, *so long as the city-gates were closed*, Samson could not escape. It was thus—as they imagined—unnecessary for them to be back at their post till dawn; but Samson baffled them by rising in the middle of the night and removing the gates. It must therefore have been not *all night* that they laid wait for him in the gate of the city; but so much of the preceding *day* during which, after Samson's arrival, the gates remained open, and it was necessary to guard them. We may safely rule out any such explanation of 𝔐 as that they kept watch all night, but fell asleep at their post (unawakened even by the noise of the tearing up of the gates!), or that Samson overawed or otherwise quelled their attack—since such details, had they been presupposed, would certainly have been mentioned in the narrative. Stu. (who was the first to put forward the explanation above adopted) simply omits the first כל הלילה; and is followed by Sta., Doorn., La. Mo. conjectures that the whole sentence, 'and they came round about . . . gate of the city,' is a later addition 'intended to make Samson's escape the more wonderful by exaggerating the precautions which the Philistines took to prevent it.' So No.

When the morning dawns. Heb. עַד־אוֹר הַבֹּקֶר may perhaps mean 'Till the morning dawns': with ellipse of 'Wait,' which is supplied in translation by 𝔊^{AL} Ἕως φωτὸς πρωὶ μείνωμεν. Cf. *note* on 'at morning,' *ch.* 6[31]. It is unnecessary to follow Mo. (*SBOT.*) in supplying נֶחֱבֶּה (cf. 2 Kgs. 7[9]).

slay him.' 3. And Samson lay until midnight, and arose at midnight, and laid hold of the doors of the city-gate, and the two posts, and plucked them up together with the bar, and put them upon his shoulders, and carried them up to the top of the hill that is in front of Ḥebron.

4. Now afterwards he loved a woman in the wâdy of Soreḳ, whose name was Delilah. 5. And the lords of the Philistines came up unto her, and said unto her, 'Beguile him, and see by what means his strength is great, and by what means we may

3. *and laid hold, etc.* Cf. the description of the probable construction of the gates given by Mo. The bar let into the two posts, and stretching across the gates, would keep the latter firmly locked in position, and enable Samson to carry off the whole, when plucked up, 'in one piece.'

in front of Ḥebron. I.e. to the east of it—the sense which is always possessed by עַל־פְּנֵי, except when following the verb נִשְׁקַף ('look out *over*'); cf. the instances collected by Mo. and by BDB. p. 818 *b*. The distance from Ġaza to Ḥebron is some thirty-eight miles; but this is a mere detail to the narrator. The connexion of Samson with a point so far removed from the scene of most of his exploits is obscure, unless we are justified in suspecting a solar *motif*: cf. *Addit. note*, pp. 406 f.

4. *the wâdy of Soreḳ.* The modern wâdy eṣ-Ṣarâr on the northern edge of which Ṣorʿah is situated (cf. *note* on *ch.* 13[2]). The name Soreḳ (which is the name of a choice kind of grape-vine) is preserved in Ḫirbet Sûrîḳ,* two miles west of Ṣorʿah.

Delilah. We are not told whether the woman was a Philistine, or an Israelite in the pay of the Philistines, though the general trend of Samson's inclinations favours the former supposition. Her name is Semitic in *form*; but this affords no indication as to her nationality, since Semitic names appear to have been largely used among the Philistines (cf. Ṣidḳâ, Ṣilbêl, etc.). On the probable meaning of the name, and its importance in relation to the mythological element in the story, cf. p. 407.

5. *the lords of the Philistines.* Cf. *note* on *ch.* 3[31].

by what means his strength is great. Heb. בַּמֶּה כֹּחוֹ גָדוֹל. A.V., R.V. render 'wherein his great strength lieth,' with 𝕲, 𝖁; but

* The law which governs the interchange of sibilants in Heb. and Ar. would lead us to expect Šûriḳ. The use of *s* in the Ar. form is perhaps an indication that the later Heb. pronunciation of the name substituted ס for שׂ (the two consonants are often interchanged in Heb.).

prevail over him and bind him, so as to reduce him; and we ourselves will each give thee eleven hundred sheḳels of silver.' 6. And Delilah said unto Samson, 'Prithee tell me by what means thy strength is great, and by what means thou mayest be bound so as to reduce thee.' 7. And Samson said unto her, 'If they bind me with seven fresh bowstrings which have not been dried,

such a rendering would only be legitimate if הַגָּדוֹל were read.* גָּדוֹל without the Definite Article can only be predicate. 'By what means' suggests the supposition that his strength depended upon some magic charm (so Le Clerc, Mo., etc.).

to reduce him. I.e. to reduce *or* overcome his strength; Heb. לְעַנּוֹתוֹ. This seems to be the meaning rather than A.V., R.V. *text* 'to afflict him,' *marg.* 'to humble him'; Mo., La. 'to torment him.' Cf. *note* on *v.*^{19}.

will each give thee. 'Each' probably refers to the *five* lords of the principal Philistine cities. Cf. *ch.* 3^{3}.

eleven hundred sheḳels of silver. Why this particular sum is fixed, rather than what we should term a *round* sum, cannot be said. Commentators display a singular unanimity in repeating Reuss' suggestion that the meaning is *a full thousand*, or *over a thousand.* If this is so, we can only say that they allowed a substantial margin. The sum mentioned in *ch.* 17^{2} happens to be the same.

The value of the Heb. silver sheḳel, as calculated by Kennedy (*DB.* iii. 420 *a*) was about 2s. 9d.; so the sum promised by each of the princes would have amounted to something like £151 in our money. Money at this period was not coined; but the value of the metal was determined by weight. The verb *šāḳal* 'to weigh' (from which the subs. sheḳel is derived) is commonly employed in descriptions of money-transactions: cf. Gen. 23^{16} P, Ex. 22^{16} E, 1 Kgs. 20^{39}, *al.*

7. *seven fresh bowstrings.* For Heb. *yéther* in this sense, cf. Ps. 11^{2}, and the usage of the Ar. *watar*, Syr. *yathrâ*. The bowstrings were, no doubt, of twisted gut which was still *moist* (the lit. meaning of לַחִים), and therefore less likely to fray or break. The rendering of A.V., R.V. *text* 'green withs (withes)'—cf. Jos. κλήμασιν . . . ἀμπέλου—is improbable in itself and without support in usage. The number *seven* was probably considered to have a magical virtue.

* Maurer (*apud* Ros.) cites אֲחִיכֶם אַחֵר 'your other brother,' Gen. 43^{14}, as an instance of an adj. without the Article qualifying a subs. made definite by a pronominal suffix. This single instance, however (which may be due to textual corruption) does not prove the possibility of such a usage in the present passage.

then shall I become weak, and shall be like any other man.' 8. Then the lords of the Philistines brought up to her seven fresh bowstrings which had not been dried, and she bound him with them. 9. Now she had liers-in-wait abiding in the inner chamber. And she said unto him, 'The Philistines are upon thee, Samson!' And he snapped the bowstrings just as a strand of tow is snapped when it feeleth fire. So his strength was not known. 10. And Delilah said unto Samson, 'Behold, thou hast mocked me, and told me lies: now, prithee, tell me by what means thou mayest be bound.' 11. And he said unto her, 'If they only bind me with new ropes wherewith no work hath been done, then shall I become weak, and shall be like any other man.' 12. So Delilah took new ropes, and bound him with them, and said unto him, 'The Philistines are upon thee, Samson!' Now the liers-in-wait were abiding in the inner chamber. And he snapped them from off his arms like a thread. 13. And Delilah said unto Samson, 'Hitherto thou hast deceived me, and told me lies: tell me by what means thou mayest be bound.' And he said unto her, 'If thou weave the seven locks of my head along with the web, ⟨and beat up with

like any other man. Heb. כְּאַחַד הָאָדָם, lit. 'like one of mankind.'

9. *The Philistines, etc.* The alarm is given, not to call out the ambush, but to test the success of the experiment. When this proves a failure, the Philistines must, of course, be supposed to remain in hiding, so that Samson is unaware of their presence, and thinks that Delilah is merely playing with him in order to gratify her own curiosity.

when it feeleth the fire. Lit. 'when it *smelleth* the fire,' *i.e.* without actual contact. For the simile, cf. *ch.* 15^{14b}.

11. *with new ropes.* Cf. *ch.* 15^{13}.

13. *the seven locks, etc.* The precise sense in which Heb. *maḥl^ephôth* is used—whether of natural *curls* or *plaits*—is uncertain, the etymology of the word being obscure.* 𝔊 *σειρὰς* or *βοστρύχους*, 𝔙 'crines,' 𝔖^P ܟܘ̈ܣܦܬܐ 'plaits,' 𝔗 גדילת *id.* We are reminded of the way in which Gilgameš is represented on seal-cylinders, with hair divided into curling locks; though these are always *six* in number (not *seven*, as stated by Jeremias, Cooke, and Smythe Palmer), three falling on

* The explanation given by BDB. for the sense '*plaits*,' 'so called from *intertwining, passing through* each other, of the strands,' is based on the fact that the verb *ḥālaph*, which commonly means 'to pass on *or* away,' seems in two passages

the pin, then shall I become weak, and shall be like any other man. 14. So, when he slept, Delilah took the seven locks of his head, and wove them along with the web,〉 and beat up with the pin, and said unto him, 'The Philistines are upon thee,

each side of his face: cf. Plate II., figs. 3, 4, 5; Plate III., figs. 1, 2. On the probable solar significance of this characteristic, cf. *Addit. note*, *p.* 404.

13, 14. *and beat up . . . the web.* Adding וְתָקַעַתְּ בַּיָּתֵד וְחָלִיתִי וְהָיִיתִי כְּאַחַד הָאָדָם׃ וַיְהִי בְּשָׁכְבוֹ וַתִּקַּח דְּלִילָה אֶת־שֶׁבַע מַחְלְפוֹת רֹאשׁוֹ וַתַּאֲרֹג עִם־הַמַּסֶּכֶת. The words are necessary to complete both Samson's directions and also the account of the way in which Delilah exactly carried them out: cf. the correspondence between his words and her actions in *vv.*[7.8], [11.12], [17b.19]. They have fallen out of 𝔐 through homœoteleuton; the scribe's eye passing from the first occurrence of עם המסכת 'along with the web' to the second. The missing words occur, with variations, in MSS. of 𝔊, and in 𝔏[I], 𝔖[h]. We follow the reading of 𝔊[B], according to which *vv.*[13b.14aα] run *καὶ εἶπεν πρὸς αὐτήν, Ἐὰν ὑφάνῃς τὰς ἑπτὰ σειρὰς τῆς κεφαλῆς μου σὺν τῷ διάσματι καὶ ἐνκρούσῃς τῷ πασσάλῳ εἰς τὸν τοῖχον, καὶ ἔσομαι ὡς εἷς τῶν*

to have the sense 'to pass through (cf. *ch.* 5[26] *note*); but the connexion in idea which is here assumed appears somewhat uncertain (unless—as privately suggested by Prof. Margoliouth—we may justify such a transition in meaning by the analogy of the Ar. root *marra*, 'to pass by *or* beyond, pass along,' from which are derived *marîr* 'a rope that is slender and long, and *strongly twisted*,' *'amarru* 'more *or* most tightly twisted'—an elative form). The comparison of Ges., *Thes.*, with Ar. *ḫalîf*, 'contortus, convolutus,' is derived from Golius; but this meaning is not given by modern Ar. lexicons. There is an Ar. word *ḫalîf* which means 'a woman who lets her hair fall down her back behind' (Ar. *ḫalafa* meaning 'to come after, succeed' temporally, and also 'to come behind *or* at the back' locally); and *ḫalf* denotes 'the location *or* quarter which is behind' (Lane), and is used *e.g.* of joining the hands *behind the back* (Dozy). This suggests the possibility that *maḥalāphôth* may properly denote *locks which fall down the back.* Cf. the description given of Gilgameš when, after his conquest of Ḫumbaba, he washed and polished his arms, put on fine raiment, and 'caused his long hair to fall down upon his back' (*unaššik kimmatsu eli ṣirišu*; Tab. VI., l. 2. The passage is one which unmistakeably embodies a solar *motif*: cf. *Addit. note*, pp. 396 f.). It is worthy of notice that *maḥalāphā* is, in *form*, the exact equivalent of Bab. *naḫlaptu*, which denotes something which *covers* or *clothes*. Possibly the word may have existed in Heb. in the sense of *trapping* or *adornment*, and may have been applied to a curl. More probable, however, than any of these suggestions is connexion with Heb. *ḥālaph* in the sense *to sprout*: cf. Ps. 90[4.5] (Ḳal), Job 14[7] (Hiph'îl)—a meaning which, though explained by BDB. as derived from the idea *to shew newness*, is rather to be associated with Bab. *elêpu*, *to sprout*, applied to a tree (*ša iṣi*), or *to be long*. מחלפות ראשי would then properly denote 'the sproutings (long tresses) of my head': cf. the use of the verb צמח 'to sprout' in *v.*[22] of the fresh growth of the hero's hair after it had been cut off.

ἀνθρώπων ἀσθενής. καὶ ἐγένετο ἐν τῷ κοιμᾶσθαι αὐτὸν καὶ ἔλαβεν Δαλειδα τὰς ἑπτὰ σειρὰς τῆς κεφαλῆς αὐτοῦ καὶ ὕφανεν ἐν τῷ διάσματι κτλ. Here εἰς τὸν τοῖχον appears to be an explanatory gloss, due to misunderstanding of the meaning of ותקעת ביתד (see below); but the rest of the passage presupposes a clear and self-consistent original.* So. Mo. The text of 𝔊^AL offers a conflation between that of 𝔊^B and a variant text which is preserved most nearly in the group of MSS. cited by Mo. as 𝔊^Lp (cf. *SBOT.*). In this latter text the most noteworthy variation is in the commencement of *v.*14, καὶ ἐκοίμισεν αὐτὸν Δαλιδα, καὶ κατέκρουσεν κτλ. Hence Bu. reads ׳וַתְּיַשְּׁנֵהוּ וַתַּאֲרֹג וג (cf. *v.*19).

The precise nature of the test which is thus described has been elucidated by Mo. (*Proceedings of the American Oriental Society*, 1889, pp. clxxvi ff.; cf. also Comm. and *SBOT.* So, previously, Braun, *De Vestitu Sacerdotum Hebraeorum*, Amstel., 1698, p. 252, who is followed by Stu.). Mo. seems, however, to be incorrect in assuming that the loom was of the upright kind: cf. Kennedy, article 'Weaving' in *EB.*, who points out that, in the ancient Egyptian representations, which are given by him (col. 5279), and by Mo., *SBOT. Eng. trans.*, p. 86, the looms are really horizontal; though absence of perspective makes them appear at first sight to be upright. We should probably picture a horizontal loom of the simplest sort, in which two pairs of posts firmly fixed in the ground hold the yarn-beam and the cloth-beam respectively. A piece of unfinished stuff (the *maššēkheth* 'web') is standing in the loom; and Delilah, having manœuvred so as to get Samson to sleep with his head on her knees beside the loom, weaves his long hair into the warp with her fingers, and beats it up tightly into the web by means of the *yāthēdh*, *i.e.* the 'pin' or 'batten' (a flat piece of wood with a thin edge), so that his hair actually becomes part of the finished material.‡ When aroused

* בשכבו is adopted as the original of ἐν τῷ κοιμᾶσθαι αὐτόν because שכב, properly 'to lie down to rest,' is regularly rendered by κοιμᾶν in 𝔊 (151 cases cited in Hatch and Redpath's *Concordance*); whereas only one passage (Isa. 5 27) is cited in which ישן is so rendered.

‡ Cf. the description of a modern Bedawin loom given by Palmer (*Desert of the Exodus*, i. p. 125), who, in referring to his visits paid to Bedawin encampments, tells us that 'On one of these occasions I noticed an old woman weaving at the tent door. Her loom was a primitive one, consisting only of a few upright sticks upon which the threads were stretched: the transverse threads were inserted laboriously by the fingers, without the assistance of a shuttle, and the whole fabric was pressed close together with a piece of wood. Beside her stood a younger female spinning goats' hair to supply the old lady with the material necessary for her task.' So, too, Rob. (*BR.*3 i. 169) relates that 'Just before setting off [from 'Aḳabah], we saw in one corner the process of manufacturing the goats' hair cloth of which the common Arab cloaks are made. A woman had laid her warp along the ground for the length of several yards, and sat at one end of it under a small shed, with a curtain before her to ward off the eyes of passers-by. She wove by passing the woof through with her hand, and then driving it up with a flat piece of board having a thin edge.'

Samson!' And he awoke from his sleep, and plucked up [ ] the loom and the web. 15. And she said unto him, 'How canst thou say, "I love thee," when thy heart is not with me? three times already thou hast deceived me, and hast not told me by what means thy strength is great.' 16. And when she

by the alarm, Samson leaps up; and, as he raises his head, he pulls the four posts of the loom out of the ground, and carries off web and loom together attached to his hair.

The 𝔊 addition εἰς τὸν τοῖχον, noticed above, assumes erroneously that *yāthēdh* (as in *ch.* 4[21.22], 5[26]) denotes a *peg* which Delilah *hammered into the wall* (καὶ ἐνκρούσῃς τῷ πασσάλῳ κτλ., καὶ ἔπηξεν τῷ πασσάλῳ κτλ.; cf. 𝔙 'et clavum his circumligatum terrae fixeris') in order to secure the web; and a similar error is probably responsible for the insertion of היתד in *v.*[14b] 𝔐 (cf. *note*). That *yāthēdh*, however, can be used in other senses is proved by Deut. 23[14], where it denotes an implement for digging. 𝔖ᴾ renders ܢܘܠܐ, *i.e.* the 'cross-beam' of the loom to which the warp is attached; so 𝔗 אכסן in *v.*[14b], but in *v.*[14a] סכתא 'peg.' The meaning of Heb. *maśśékheth* 'web,' from *nāśakh* 'to weave' (cf. Ar. *nasaǵa*), may be illustrated by the usage of the nearly identical form *maśśēkhā*, which occurs in Isa. 25[7] ('the web that is woven over all nations'), 30[1] ('to weave a web'), and in Isa. 28[20] in the sense of '(woven) bed-spread.' Kennedy (*EB.* 5282) supposes that *maśśékheth* and *maśśēkhā* primarily denote the 'warp,' and then by metonymy the 'web,' on the ground that the post-Bib. Heb. verb *hēśēkh* is used of *setting the warp* in the loom. This view, however, is opposed by the relation of Heb. *nāśakh* to Ar. *nasaǵa*, which certainly means 'to interweave.'

14. *the loom.* 𝔐 הַיְתַד הָאֶרֶג is intended to mean 'the peg of the loom.' הַיְתַד (which is condemned as an insertion by the anomalous use of the Article with the Construct State) must have been originally a marginal addition made by a scribe who, taking יתד in *v.*[14a] to mean the *peg* with which Delilah *fastened* the web to the wall or ground, desiderated a reference to Samson's plucking this out when he freed himself. As we have seen, however (preceding *note*) יתד has quite a different meaning, and it was the loom itself which Samson pulled up.

15. *How canst thou say, etc.* Cf. *ch.* 14[16].

when thy heart, etc. Mo. brings out the sense by rendering, somewhat paraphrastically, 'seeing that thou dost not confide in me.' 'Heart,' as he points out, is used not of the *affections*, but of 'the inner man with its secret thoughts.' Cf. *v.*[17], 'he told her all his heart.'

pressed him sore with her words continually, and urged him, his soul was impatient unto death. 17. And he told her all his heart, and said to her, J² No razor hath come up upon my head, for a Nazirite of God have I been from my mother's womb: J¹ if I be shaven, then my strength will depart from me, and I shall become weak, and shall be like all other men.' 18. And when Delilah saw that he had told her all his heart, she sent and called the lords of the Philistines, saying, 'Come up this once, for he hath told ⌜me⌝ all his heart.' And the lords of the Philistines ⌜came up⌝ unto her, and brought up the money in their hand. 19. And she made him sleep upon her knees, and called for a man, and ⌜he⌝ shaved off the seven locks of his head; and ⌜he⌝ began ⌜to be reduced⌝, and his strength departed from him. 20. And she said, 'The Philistines are upon thee, Samson!' And he awoke out of his sleep, and said, 'I will go out as at

17. *no razor . . . womb.* As to the grounds upon which this passage is to be regarded as an addition to the old story by the author of *ch.* 13, cf. pp. 337 f. Its excision from the narrative causes Samson's answer ('If I be shaven, etc.') to commence in precisely the same form as in *vv.*[7.11.13].

18. *hath told me.* Reading לִי for *Kt.* לה, with *Kᵉrê*, many MSS. of 𝕳, and all Versions.

came up. Reading וַיַּעֲלוּ, the regular tense form in narration, with many MSS. of 𝕳, in place of the irregular וְעָלוּ.

19. *and he shaved off.* Reading וַיְגַלַּח. 𝕳 וַתְּגַלַּח 'and she shaved off'; but, if Delilah did this herself, it is not clear why the man should have been needed.

and he began to be reduced. Reading וַיָּחֶל לֶעֱנוֹת (or לְעַנּוֹת) with 𝕲[AL] καὶ ἤρξατο ταπεινοῦσθαι, 𝕾[h] ܘܫܪܝ ܠܡܬܡܟܟܘ. The reference is to the gradual ebbing away of his strength as he is shorn of his locks. Cf. *v.*[5] *note*, and the use of עִנָּה in Ps. 102[23] (𝕳 [24]), 'He *weakened* my strength in the way.' 𝕳 וַתָּחֶל לְעַנּוֹתוֹ 'and she began to afflict him,' has the support of 𝕲[B], 𝕾[P], 𝕿, and is paraphrased by 𝖁 'et coepit abigere eum, et a se repellere.' Whatever meaning, however, be read into the statement, it involves (coming as it does before 'and his strength departed from him') something of a *hysteron-proteron*; since it would be only *after* his loss of strength that Delilah would venture to treat him with contumely.

other times, and shake myself free'; not knowing that Yahweh had departed from him. 21. And the Philistines laid hold on him, and bored out his eyes; and they brought him down to Gaza, and bound him with bronze fetters; and he did grind in the prison-house. 22. But the hair of his head began to grow when he had been shaved.

23. And the lords of the Philistines gathered themselves together to sacrifice a great sacrifice unto Dagon their God, and

20. *and shake myself free.* The expression suggests that Delilah had bound him (cf. *v.*[6]), in addition to causing his locks to be shaved off; and Mo. may be right in his conjecture that a statement to this effect has been accidentally omitted.

not knowing, etc. Heb. וְהוּא לֹא יָדַע וגו׳, a circumstantial clause.

that Yahweh, etc. Doorn. supposes that כֹּחוֹ 'his strength' originally stood in place of 'Yahweh'; cf. *v.*[19bβ]. Cf., however, the remarks on pp. 337 f.

21. *and he did grind.* The Heb. וַיְהִי טוֹחֵן implies that this was his constant occupation. On grinding as a badge of degraded servitude, cf. *note* on *ch.* 9[53]. It is probable, however, that the reference in Samson's case is not to a mere handmill, but to a heavy mill such as would usually be turned by an ox or an ass. The reference may very possibly embody a solar *motif*: cf. *Addit. note*, p. 408.

22. *But the hair of his head, etc.* This statement carries the mind of the sympathetic reader beyond the immediate blackness of the hero's fate, by hinting at the *dénouement* in which Samson will perform his greatest feat of all.

23. *Dagon.* A Philistine deity who had a temple not only at Gaza, but also at Ashdod (1 Sam. 5[1], 1 Macc. 10[83 f.]; 11[4]), and (if the text of 1 Chr. 10[10] is to be trusted) at Beth-she'an. Beth-Dagon ('Temple of D.') was the name of a city in the Shephelah which is assigned to Judah in Josh. 15[41] P; and the same name was borne by a city on the border of Asher, apparently east of Carmel and not far from the border of Zebulun; Josh. 19[27] P. The former of these names may show Philistine influence in the Shephelah; while the latter conceivably indicates the presence of the kindred people called Ṯakkara, whom we know to have settled at Dor, a little south of Carmel (cf. *Introd.* p. xcvi). Among modern Ar. place-names, we find Bêt-Deǵân *

* Whether this is the same as the Beth-Dagon of Josh. 15[41] is doubtful. It is so identified by Eusebius (*OS.* 235[14]), Βηθ Δαγων. *φυλῆς* Ιουδα. *καὶ ἔστι νῦν κώμη μεγίστη* Καφαρ *Δαγων μεταξὺ* Διοσπόλεως *καὶ* Ιαμνίας. The site lies outside the Shephelah properly so called (cf. *note* on *ch.* 1[9]); but the list of cities in Josh. in which the name occurs is so confused that we can draw no certain conclusion.

five and a half miles south-east of Jaffa, with a ruined site Dağûn a little further south. One of these, no doubt, is the Bît-Daganna mentioned before Joppa by Ṡennacherib in his Prism-inscription: cf. *KB.* ii. p. 92.

It seems probable, however, that Dagon was not a foreign deity introduced from the west by the sea-peoples in their influx into Cana'an, but rather a native Semitic deity, adopted (like Ba'al-zebul,* the god of 'Eḳron, 2 Kgs. 1 2 f.) after their settlement in the land. There is another Bêt-Değân some seven miles east of Nâblus (Shechem), whither we have no reason for supposing that Philistine influence ever extended. It can hardly be doubted that Dagon is identical with the god Dagan, who is known to us from the cuneiform inscriptions. Dagan is sometimes connected with the god Anu (*e.g.* by the Assyrian kings Šamši-Adad vii., *KB.* i. p. 174, and Ṡargon, *KB.* ii. p. 38), occupying in relation to Anu the position which is commonly filled by Enlil, to whom there is reason for assuming that he was regarded as the equivalent.‡ Among the T.A. Letters there are two from a Cana'anite vassal of the king of Egypt named Dagan-takala (Winckler, *KB.* v. Nos. 215 f.; Knudtzon, Nos. 317 f.); and the name of the deity is especially frequent as an element in proper names of the Babylonian First Dynasty period, several of which (*e.g.* Yašub-(ilu)-Dagan, Yašmaḫ-(ilu)-Dagan, etc.§) appear, from the verbal forms which they embody, to have been borne by Western Semites (men of Amurru; cf. *Introd.* p. lix); cf. the way in which Ḫammurabi, in the introduction to his Code (iv. 27), speaks of Dagan as *his creator* (*bânišu*). We first meet with Dagan in the theophoric names of two successive rulers of the city-state of Nîsin, Idin-Dagan and Išme-Dagan, dated by King *cir.* B.C. 2250 (*Sumer and Akkad, Appendix II.*). These rulers, though members of a dynasty which used the Sumerian language|| and adopted Sumerian customs, yet bear Semitic names (meaning respectively 'Dagan has given' and 'Dagan has heard'); and there is thus some ground for the conjecture of Meyer (*GA.*[2] I. ii. pp. 501 f.) that the dynasty of Nîsin may have been of Amorite origin, and may have brought the worship of Dagan with them from the west.¶

The view that Dagon was represented as half man and half *fish* is based upon supposed connexion of the name with Heb. *dāgh* 'fish,'

* On this form of the name, as original rather than Baal-zebub of 𝔐, cf. p. 5.

‡ Cf. the full discussion of Jensen, *Kosmologie*, pp. 449 ff.

§ Cf. the lists given by Thureau-Dangin, *Lettres et contrats de l'époque de la Première Dynastie Babylonienne.*

|| Cf. the inscriptions given by Thureau-Dangin, *Die Sumerischen und Akkadischen Königsinschriften*, pp. 204-207.

¶ Cf. also for this view, Zimmern, *KAT.*[3] p. 358; Jastrow, *RBA.* i. pp. 219 ff. King, who formerly maintained the Sumerian origin of the dynasty of Nîsin (*Sum. and Akk.*, pp. 284, 303), now holds it to have been Semitic (*Bab.* pp. 131 ff.).

and first appears in the commentaries of Rashi and Kimchi on 1 Sam. 5;* but, apart from this assumed etymology, it can claim no external support. The Assyr. representations of a deity part man and part fish, figured in Riehm, *HWB.*[2] i. p. 290, in the article 'Dagon,' represent Ea-Oannes‡ (cf. the quotations from Eusebius and Helladius given in *OTLAE.* i. p. 48), whom we have no reason to associate with Dagon. More plausible is the association of the name with Heb. *dāghān* 'corn,' put forward by Philo of Byblos, who states that Dagon was the inventor of corn and the plough, and was known as Ζεὺς ἀρότριος. Granted this connexion, we may either suppose, with Sayce (cf. *HCM.* p. 326), that the worship of an originally Sumerian deity travelled westward to Cana'an, and a native etymology having been found for his name, he 'became a god of corn, an agricultural deity who watched over the growth and ripening of the crops'; or (as seems more probable), that the name of an originally Amorite corn-deity came to be used to denote *corn*, much as the Romans derived *cerealia* from *Ceres*, and used the term to denote 'cereal crops.' It is worth noticing, in this connexion, that among the Babylonian First Dynasty names there occurs Izraḫ-(ilu)-Dagan, *i.e.* 'Dagan sows,'§ a name in which the thought may have been that the god of sowing sows the seed of a man. Cf. the

* The difficult passage 1 Sam. 5[4] states that, after the image of the deity had lost its head and hands, רַק דָּגוֹן נִשְׁאַר עָלָיו 'only Dagon was left upon him' (*i.e.*, apparently, 'belonging to him' *or* 'of him'). It is upon this passage that Kimchi bases his statement that Dagon was fish from the navel downwards, and human above—a view which he cites as a generally received opinion ('They say, etc.'). Wellh.'s emendation דָּגוֹ for דָּגוֹן 'only *his fishy part* was left' (*TBS. ad loc.*), supports this view, but has not gained general acceptance. We seem to need some word meaning 'stump' or 'trunk,' such as is suggested by the 𝔊 rendering πλὴν ἡ ῥάχις Δαγων ὑπελείφθη. Cf. *NHTS.*[2] *ad loc.*

‡ Cf. also *TB.* ii. p. 60, figs. 99 and 100; and Jastrow, *Bildermappe zur Religion Bab. und Assyr.*, figs. 70a and 95, who takes the figure clad in a fish-skin to represent, not the god himself, but his priest.

§ *Izraḫ* probably stands for יזרע, *ḫ* in early cuneiform representations of Amorite words standing for the weaker as well as the stronger form of ע. Cf. *Yašmaḫ-(ilu)-Dagan* already cited=ישמעדגן, *Yadîḫ-ilu*=ידיעאל (as in 1 Chr. 7[6,10,11], 11[45], 26[2]), and cases cited in *Introd.* p. lxxv, *footnote*. It may be admitted, however, that there is not the same certainty that *Izraḫ* is an Amorite Imperfect as exists in the case of the first elements in such First Dynasty names as *Yašmaḫ-(ilu)-Dagan*, *Yašub-(ilu)-Dagan*, *Yamlik-ilu*, *Yakun-(ilu)-Adad*, etc., where the verbal forms are clearly not Babylonian, and, in *Yašmaḫ*, we have the original *a* of the preformative syllable of the Imperf. Ḳal preserved as in Ar. (cf. *yazkur*=יזכר among the T.A. glosses; p. 169 *note*). If, as assumed, *Izraḫ*=יזרע, we must suppose that in this case the thinning process from *a* to *i* has already taken place. It is possible, however, that the form may be præterite of the Bab. verb *zarâḫu* 'to shine,'=Heb. זרח.

to rejoice: and they said, 'Our god hath given into our hand Samson our enemy.' 25. And when their hearts were merry they said, 'Call Samson, that he may make sport for us.' So they called Samson from the prison-house, and he made sport

place-name יִזְרְעֶאל Jezreʿel, *i.e.* 'the god sows,' which, if (as is doubtless the case) it goes back to Canaʿanite times, may represent a dedication to Dagon.*

25.24. The change in order of verses follows the suggestion of Bu. (so No., Kit., Cooke). 'And when the people saw him' ($v.^{24}$) is out of place until Samson has been fetched and brought in to the festival ($v.^{25}$); but, with the transposition, the reference of $v.^{24}$ is most appropriate, and the narrative runs smoothly. La. retains the order of 𝔐 on the view that the Object in 'when they saw him' is the god Dagon, whose image was carried in procession or otherwise exhibited; but this is most improbable.

25. *when their hearts were merry.* *Kt.* כִּי טוֹב (Perfect) and *Kerê* כְּטוֹב (Infin. Constr.) are equally idiomatic. The Massoretes substitute the construction which is found in 2 Sam. 13 28, Hos. 10 1, Est. 1 10, possibly failing to recognize טוב of *Kt.* as a Perfect. The occurrences of this Perfect form are often difficult to distinguish from the Adjective; but the real existence of such a form (verb middle *o*, like בּוֹשׁ) is proved by the occurrence of the plur. טֹבוּ, Num. 24 5, Song 4 10.

that he may make sport for us. Whether the reference is to minor exhibitions of strength and dexterity, or to the exercise of his jesting proclivities, is not clear. $\mathfrak{S}^{P}$, Ar. suppose that he was to *dance* before them.

and he made sport. Here 𝔐 somewhat strangely varies the spelling

* It is very possible that the passage in the Sarcophagus-inscription of Eshmunʿazar, king of Ṣidon, ll. 18 f., should be rendered, 'And, moreover, the Lord of kings gave us Dor and Joppa, the excellent land of Dagon, which is in the field of Sharon' (so Schlottmann, Movers, and Blau, as cited in *CIS.* 1. i. p. 18). The phrase ארצת דגן האדרת is taken, however, by most scholars to mean 'the excellent corn-land.' On this view, the passage seems to illustrate the fact that the region inhabited by the worshippers of Dagon was principally noted for its *dāghān* 'corn' (as is still the case in modern times)—a fact which has its importance in relation to the view above discussed that Dagon was a corn-deity.

Sayce (*HCM.* p. 327) cites a seal preserved in the Ashmolean Museum as bearing the inscription Baʿal-Dagon in Phoenician letters, together with the representation (among other symbols) of an ear of corn. The reading is, however, very doubtful. Lidzbarski (*Ephemeris für Nordsemit. Epigr.*, i. p. 12) thinks that it should more probably be read Baʿal-regem; whilst the ear of corn requires considerable ingenuity for its detection.

before them: and they made him stand between the pillars. 24. And when the people saw him, they praised their god, ⌜and⌝ said,

'Our god hath given
Our enemy into our hand,
And him who laid waste our land,
And who multiplied our slain.'

of the verb, using the form צחק which is found elsewhere only in the Pentateuch (so invariably; thirteen times) and in Ezek. 23[32], whereas in *vv.*[25a.27] we have the ordinary form שׂחק. Very possibly the variation may be due merely to a copyist. It is noteworthy, however, that in place of 𝔐 וַיְצַחֵק לִפְנֵיהֶם, 𝔊^AL, 𝔖^h read καὶ ἐνέπαιζον αὐτῷ, *i.e.* probably וַיִּתְעַלְּלוּ־בוֹ (cf. the 𝔊 renderings of this verb in *ch.* 19[25], 1 Sam. 31[4], *al.*), 'and they made sport of him,' *i.e. insulted* him. This text appears to lie at the back of the doublet of 𝔊^B καὶ ἐράπιζον αὐτόν (perhaps a corruption of the reading of 𝔊^AL) which follows after καὶ ἔπαιζεν ἐνώπιον αὐτῶν—an accurate rendering of the text of 𝔐. Jos. (*Ant.* v. viii. 12) seems to support the reading of 𝔊^AL when he states that the Philistines sent for Samson ὅπως ἐνυβρίσωσιν αὐτῷ παρὰ τόν πότον. It is conceivable that 𝔊^AL may represent the original text, and that the variation of spelling in 𝔐 may be due to the fact that the text has been altered by a later hand.

24. *and said.* Reading וַיֹּאמְרוּ with 𝔊^A καὶ εἶπαν, in place of 𝔐 כִּי אָמְרוּ 'for they said.' So Bu., No. Clearly the words which follow embody the expression of praise, and not simply the reason for it. כ and ו were frequently confused in the older form of writing: cf. instances collected in *NHTK.* p. 177.

Our god, etc. The words fall into a rough rhythm, with recurrent rhyme upon the suffix *-ēnû* 'our':—

Nāthán 'elōhḗnū
beyādhḗnū 'eth 'ōyebhḗnū
we'eth maḥarībh 'arṣḗnū
wa'ašer hirbhā́ 'eth ḥalālênū.

Such rhymes are by no means infrequent, especially in short poetical pieces or proverbial sayings preserved by story-tellers in their narratives. In longer poems they are occasional; but not used systematically or extensively. Cf. Gen. 4[23], 27[29a], 49[6a.11.25aα], Ex. 15[2.9], Num.

26. And Samson said unto the lad that held his hand, 'Suffer me that I may feel the pillars ᴳˡ· whereon the house is supported, J¹ and may lean upon them.' 27. Now the house was full of men and women; and all the lords of the Philistines were there, and upon the roof were about three thousand men

$21^{18a.28}$,* $23^{9a.21b.23}$, $24^{7b.21b.22}$, Deut. $32^{2a.6b.9.25b.30b.35.41a}$, $33^{3.8.10b.18.25}$, Judg. 14^{18b}, 1 Sam. 18^{7b}, 2 Sam. 1^{20b}. Occasional instances may be found in the Psalms; *e.g.* $2^{3.6.11}$, 6^{2}, $18^{12a.15.19.20.21.23.29.37.45.47.49.51}$, *al.* The most frequent and approximately systematic use of rhyme is in the Song of Songs: cf. the present editor's note in *JTS.* x. pp. 584 ff.

26. *that I may feel.* *Ḳᵉrê* וַהֲמִישֵׁנִי from מוש (cf. Ps. 115^{7}; Ḳal Gen. 27^{21} †), *Kt.* וְהֵימִשֵׁנִי from ימשׁ (otherwise unknown). Since משׁשׁ is the verb ordinarily used in the sense required, it is probable that we should read וַהֲמִשֵּׁנִי.

whereon the house is supported. Doorn. is probably right in regarding these words as a gloss from *v.*^{29}. Samson would hardly have risked betraying his purpose by using them.

27. *Now the house, etc.* Apparently we are to picture a banqueting hall with one side open to a courtyard, the roof on this side being supported by a pair of central pillars. Samson makes sport in the courtyard where he can be seen both by those inside the building and by those on the roof. Having thus exhibited his powers, he is brought forward and placed between the pillars—possibly in order that the lords of the Philistines and the other more important people *within* the hall may obtain a closer view of him.

Doorn. regards the latter half of the verse (from 'and upon the roof, etc.') as a gloss in exaggeration of the foregoing; while Mo. (followed by Bu., etc.) would delete the middle part ('and all the lords . . . men and women'), upon the ground that the Article with the Participle הראים then refers naturally to האנשים והנשים. It is difficult to believe, however, in view of the great emphasis in *v.*^{30b} upon the huge number slain, that the verse as thus attenuated is more

* Here we observe the scheme of rhyming lines 1, 2, and 4, with non-rhyming 3, as in Arabic poetry:—

kī éš yāṣᵉ'ā́ mēḤešbṓn
lehābhā́ mikḳiryáth Ṡîḥṓn
'ā́khᵉlā 'Ár Mṓ'ā́bh
ba'ᵃlé bāmṓth 'Arnṓn.

Cf. Num. $24^{21b.22}$, and the instances cited from the Song of Songs in *JTS. loc. cit.* p. 586.

and women, looking on while Samson made sport. 28. And Samson cried unto Yahweh, and said, 'Lord Yahweh, prithee remember me, and prithee strengthen me only this once, O God, that I may avenge myself upon the Philistines in one vengeanc⌜e⌝ ⌜for⌝ my two eyes.' 29. And Samson grasped the two middle pillars whereon the house rested, and leaned upon them, one with his right hand, and the other with his left. 30. And Samson said, 'Let my soul die with the Philistines!' And he bowed himself mightily; and the house fell upon the lords, and upon all the people who were therein. So the dead that

original in form. On the use of the Def. Art. in הראים, cf. G-K. § 126 *x*.

28. *this once.* Heb. הַפַּעַם הַזֶּה. We should expect הַפַּעַם הַזֹּאת or הַפַּעַם simply (cf. *ch.* 6^{39}, Gen. 18^{32}, Ex. 10^{17}).

in one vengeance for my two eyes. Reading נְקָמָה אַחַת בִּשְׁתֵּי עֵינַי for 𝔐 נְקַם אַחַת מִשְּׁתֵי עֵינַי. He prays that at one stroke he may exact an adequate vengeance for his grievous loss. So $\mathfrak{G}^{BA}$, 𝔙. This meaning is adopted by R.V. *text*, but cannot be extracted from 𝔐 as it stands. 𝔐 can only mean 'a vengeance for (*lit.* of) one of my two eyes'; and this rendering is adopted by R.V. *marg.*, Kimchi, Rashi, and most moderns. But, jester as Samson was, the dignity and pathos of the context seem to forbid the idea that he is here facing death with a jest on his lips.

30. *Let my soul die.* The use of נַפְשִׁי 'my soul' as a choice synonym for 'me' is frequent in Heb., especially in poetry. The *néphes̆* (properly, that which *breathes*) is the principle of life which animates the *bāsār* 'flesh,' and the exit of which results in death. It is not 'soul' in the sense in which we use the term, *i.e.* of the immortal *ego*.

he bowed himself. Probably we are to picture Samson as grasping the pillars with either arm, and then bending forward so as to force them out of the perpendicular. Mo., who renders וַיִּסָּמֵךְ עֲלֵיהֶם in *v.*^{29}, 'and he braced himself against them,' explains וַיֵּט here as meaning 'he thrust,' supposing that 'standing between the two columns, he pushed them apart by extending his arms.' Such a sense attached to נטה may perhaps be justified by its use to denote the *stretching forth* of the hand (Ex. 8^{1}, Isa. 5^{25}, *al.*), though it is not very natural without expression of the object ('his hands *or* arms'); nor is it easy, on this interpretation, to justify וַיִּלְפֹּת, *v.*^{29}. If he pushed the pillars apart, he would hardly have *grasped* them.

he did to death at his death were more than those that he did to death in his life. 31. And his brethren and all his father's house went down, and took him, and brought him up, and buried him between Ṣorʿah and Eshta'ol, in the grave of Manoaḥ his father. R[JE] And he judged Israel twenty years.

he did to death. This rendering of הֵמִית (which would ordinarily be translated 'he slew') is adopted in order to bring out the paradoxical word-play which is intended in the original.

31. *went down.* Cf. *note* on 'Timnah,' *ch.* 14^{1}.
between Ṣorʿah, etc. Cf. *ch.* 13^{25} *note.*

THE MYTHICAL ELEMENT IN THE STORY OF SAMSON

The view has frequently been put forward that the story of Samson contains many legendary elements derived from the solar mythology which seems to have been the common property, not merely of the Semitic peoples, but of other races widely distinct from them. In this respect, it has been argued, the Hebrew Samson is analogous to the Phoenician Melḳart and to the Babylonian Gilgameš among the Semites, as well as to the Greek hero Herakles, the main features of whose portrait may well have been derived from Semitic sources.*

The subject is one which lends itself very readily to theorizing; and there can be no doubt that the arguments which have been adduced to prove that the whole, or the major part, of Samson's exploits are based upon a solar myth are insufficiently attested. When this has been said, it must be affirmed, on the other hand, that there *are* certain elements in the story which seem to have been drawn ultimately from solar mythology; and the evidence that this is so can hardly be ignored.

The *name* Samson or Šimšon, connected as it doubtless is with Heb. *Šémeš* 'sun' (cf. *note* on *ch.* 13^{24}), has of course been adduced as an argument for the theory of the solar myth. Bu. (*DB.* iv. p. 381 *a*) maintains on the contrary that the derivation 'tells rather against than in favour of this view, for it is not the way with a nature-

* The comparison of the deeds of Samson with those of Herakles is as old as Eusebius (*Chron.*, ed. Schoene, p. 54), Philastrius (*de Haeres. c.* viii), and Augustine (*de Civ. Dei*, xviii. 19). That Herakles represents the sun is maintained by Macrobius (*Saturnal.* I. xx) upon etymological grounds:—'Et re vera Herculem solem esse vel ex nomine claret. Ἡρακλῆς enim quid aliud est nisi Ἥρας id est aeris κλέος? quae porro alia aeris gloria est, nisi solis illuminatio?'

myth to borrow or even to derive the name of its hero from the cosmical object which it describes.' Be this as it may, it can hardly be denied that the name must have been in origin *honorific* of the sun, and so must indicate the existence of sun-worship in the locality —a fact which is indeed attested by the place-name Beth-shemesh, 'Temple of the Sun,' in the immediate neighbourhood of the scene of the hero's exploits.

We are probably justified in going further, and in associating this sun-worship, not with an alien Cana'anite clan inhabiting the district, but with the tribe (or rather *clan*) of Dan itself. As is well known, the Heb. *Dân* means 'Judge,' and is so explained in Gen. 30^{6} J or E, 49^{16} J. The tribe of Dan is one of the four Israelite tribes whose descent is traced, not from a wife of Jacob, but from a handmaid—a tradition which is probably to be interpreted as meaning that these tribes were regarded as not belonging to Israel by full-blooded descent, but as occupying in some way or other an inferior position among the tribes. Very possibly they were settled in Cana'an prior to the entry of the Joseph-tribes under Joshua', and were only incorporated into the Israelite confederation at a later period (cf. *Introd.* pp. cvi f.).

As regards Dan, we may gain support for this view from the old poem of Gen. 49. The statement of *v.*^{16},

> 'Dan shall judge his people
> As one of the tribes of Israel,'

is scarcely satisfied by the jejune explanation that he shall maintain his independence as successfully as any other tribe (so, many commentators). It undoubtedly implies that he will vindicate his claim to be reckoned as an Israelite tribe, *i.e.* will raise himself out of a position in which he was looked down upon as outside the full blood-brotherhood.

Now in the case of two of the handmaid-tribes, Gad and Asher, it seems clear that the tribal names were originally the names or titles of deities (cf. the remarks on pp. 197 f.). It is not, therefore, unlikely that the name *Dân* referred originally to a divine *Judge* who was regarded as the patron of the clan. The god of the Babylonian Pantheon who was pictured as *the* Judge *par excellence* was Šamaš the Sun-god, whose common title among the Babylonians and Assyrians was *Dân* (i.e. *Daian*) *šamê u irṣiti*, 'Judge of heaven and earth': cf. the numerous references under the heading 'Šamaš, Richter (Gott der Gerechtigkeit)' in Jastrow, *RBA*. ii. 2, p. 1098; and the citations under *dânu* 2 in Muss-Arnolt, *Dict.* i. p. 258. If, then, we may assume that the ancient patron-deity of the tribe of Dan was the Sun-god under his aspect of divine Judge, we shall not be surprised if we find relics of solar mythology surviving in a euhemerized form among the folk-traditions of the tribe.

Can we, however, lay our finger upon any such mythological elements in the story of Samson with reasonable probability? The one incident which must *certainly* be interpreted as the product of folk-mythology is the fox-story of *ch.* 15 [3-5]. It is impossible to suppose that this can be unconnected with the ceremonial hunting of foxes with blazing torches attached to their brushes which took place annually in the Circus at Rome during the Cerealia, April 19, as stated by Ovid (*Fasti*, iv. 679 ff.). Ovid cites, in explanation of this custom, a tale which he had heard from an old countryman of Carseoli. A twelve-year-old farmer's son, having caught a vixen-fox which had repeatedly robbed his father's hen-roosts, wrapped it in straw and hay, to which he then proceeded to set fire. The fox, escaping, rushed through the fields of corn and set them in a blaze; hence a law was formulated at Carseoli dealing with the fate of captured foxes.* Clearly this story is nothing more than a popular invention in explanation of an ancient rite, the origin and significance of which had passed into oblivion. Preller (*Römische Mythologie*,[3] ii. pp. 43 f.) brings the ceremony into connexion with the Robigalia, which were celebrated at the same time of year (April 25), when (as he states) young puppies of a red colour were sacrificed in the grove of Robigus, the spirit who was supposed to work in the *robigo*, *i.e.* the red rust or mildew which was so apt to attack the corn when approaching maturity. Here he seems to be not quite accurate. The sacrifice of red sucking whelps (*rutilae canes*), together with an augury made from their *exta* (*augurium canarium*), took place outside the Porta Catularia at Rome, and appears to have been a moveable festival, distinct, at least in origin, from the offering of the *exta* of a sheep and a dog at the grove of Robigus, which was situated at the fifth milestone on the Via Claudia: cf. Ovid's description, *Fasti*, iv. 901 ff. Yet the two rites were doubtless closely connected, if not (at any rate in later times) identified: cf. Warde Fowler, *Roman Festivals*, pp. 88 ff.; Pauly-Wissowa, *Real-Encyc. der class. Altertumswiss.*, iii. col. 1981 (*s.v. Cerealia*); Wissowa, *Religion und Cultus der Römer*, p. 163. The resemblance in colour between the sacrificed puppies and the foxes is not likely to be accidental; and it is probable, as Preller supposes, that both the red puppies which were deemed an appropriate sacrifice to Robigus, and also the red foxes which

* Precisely what this fate was to be escapes us owing to a corruption of the text. The best MSS. read:—

> 'Factum abiit, monimenta manent: nam dicere certam
> Nunc quoque lex volpem Carseolana vetat.'

Here 'nam dicere certam' yields no sense; and has been corrected into 'nam vivere captam,' which is found in some inferior MSS. Other suggestions which have been offered are 'namque icere captam,' 'namque ire repertam,' 'namque urere captam,' 'incendere captam,' etc. Cf. Warde Fowler, *Roman Festivals*, p. 78; Postgate, *Corp. Pt. Lat.* i. p. 519.

were hunted at the festival of the corn-goddess Ceres, were typical of the red-coloured blight with its destructive burning properties,* which in the one case it was hoped might be averted by the sacrifice,‡ and in the other was supposed, by a kind of sympathetic magic, to be chased away so that it might not do damage to the crops.

Now the ancient theory as to the origin of rust was that it was due to the action of the *hot sun* upon the corn-stalks when left damp by the dew.§ The view of Steinthal and Smythe Palmer is thus highly plausible that, in the incident of Judg. 15 [3-5], Samson plays the part of the Sun-god with his fiery heat, letting loose the destructive plague of rust which burns up the standing corn of the Philistines. That the Roman custom is to be traced ultimately to a Semitic source (whence it was derived, possibly, as Bochart, *Hierozoicon*, i. p. 857, supposed, through the Phoenicians) may be inferred from the fact that it took place in the latter part of April—the period when, in Syria, the corn is approaching maturity and the danger of rust is to be apprehended, but some considerable time before the crop reaches such a stage in Italy.|| It may well have been, therefore, 'that the rite was transferred bodily to Latin soil without any rectification of season to make it significant' (Smythe Palmer, p. 105).

* *Robigo* is also termed *uredo* in Lat., as *burning up* the crops, just as rust is dialectically termed *brand* in Norfolk, Suffolk, and Devon for the same reason (cf. Wright, *Dialect Dict.* i. 376). Smythe Palmer (pp. 101 ff.) cites the Greek λάμπουρις 'torch-tail' applied to the fox, and compares the German *Brand-Fuchs* (occurring dialectically in Eng. as *brant-fox*), a term which associates the fox with *burning* on account of its red colour.

‡ Ovid versifies the prayer which he heard the Flamen Quirinalis utter when offering the *exta* at the grove of Robigus:

'Aspera Robigo, parcas Cerealibus herbis,
Et tremat in summa leve cacumen humo.
Tu sata sideribus caeli nutrita secundi
Crescere, dum fiant falcibus apta, sinas.
. . . . .
Parce, precor, scabrasque manus a messibus aufer,
Neve noce cultis; posse nocere sat est, etc.'

§ Cf. Ovid, *Fasti*, iv. 917 ff.:

'Nec venti tantum Cereri nocuere, nec imbres,
Nec sic marmoreo pallet adusta gelu,
Quantum si culmos Titan incalficit udos:
Tunc locus est irae, diva timenda, tuae.'

Pliny (18, 68, 10) mentions this as the commonly accepted view, but contradicts it: 'Plerique dixere, rorem inustum sole acri frugibus rubiginis causam esse et carbunculi vitibus: quod ex parte falsum arbitror, omnemque uredinem frigore tantum constare, sole innoxio.' Columella (*Arbor.* 13), Palladius (i. 55), and Servius (*ad.* 1 *Georg.* 131) supposed the cause to be 'malae nebulae.'

|| 'The corn harvest in middle Italy took place in the latter half of June and in July.'—Warde Fowler, *op. cit.* p. 154.

We have dealt at length with this single incident, because it may be claimed that it proves decisively the real existence of a mythological element in the story of Samson; and, further, suggests very strongly that this element is solar in character—an inference which, when taken in connexion with the known existence of sun-worship in the locality in which the hero's exploits are laid, and the solar significance of his name (cf. pp. 352, 392), may fairly be claimed to be raised to a reasonable certainty. The gaining of such a vantage-ground provides justification for further advance, in the confidence that, however speculative in detail such investigations may be, the theory with which they are bound up is not in itself illusory, but possesses a solid basis in fact.

In the *notes* on the text, comparison has more than once been drawn between the exploits or characteristics of Samson and those of the Babylonian hero Gilgameš. The fact that Gilgameš is a solar hero is well established. As he is known to us from the famous Epic,* he is not identical with Šamaš, for he is represented as under the protection and patronage of that deity. 'Šamaš loves him' (Tab. I. col. v. l. 21); he figures as patron to him and to his friend Engidu (II. iii. 27 ff.; VI. 171 ff.); the mother of Gilgameš makes an offering to Šamaš before her son's expedition against the giant Ḫumbaba, and asks why the god has placed in her son a heart which sleeps not, and so dominates him that he incites him to the most dangerous exploits (III. ii. 8 ff.). Yet there can be no doubt that the hero is a *double* of the Sun-god; and the fact that his exploits find their ultimate explanation in the passage of the sun through the heavens is transparently obvious.

Thus, for example, *he follows the course of the sun, and goes where no one but the sun has been.* Most important, in this connexion, is the account of the journey which he undertakes, after the death of Engidu, in search of the secret of immortality (IX., X.). We find him arriving at the mountain of Mâšu,‡ where scorpion-men guard the entrance and exit of the sun. In spite of the terrible and death-dealing aspect of these warders, he prevails upon them to admit him through the gate; and he journeys for twelve double-hours along a route where the darkness is dense, until he emerges once more into the light of day. Here he finds himself in a garden in which grows the tree of the gods, the branches of which, formed of

* The cuneiform text of the Epic has been edited by Haupt, *Das babylonische Nimrod-Epos.* Transliteration and translation with notes by Jensen in *KB.* vi. pp. 116 ff.; Dhorme, *Choix des textes religieux assyr.-bab.*, pp. 182 ff., 100 ff. Translation and discussion by Ungnad and Gressmann, *Das Gilgamesch-Epos.* More or less detailed outlines by Jeremias, *Izdubar-Nimrod*; Zimmern, *KAT.*[3] pp. 566 ff.; Ungnad, *TB.* i. pp. 39 ff.; La., *ERS.*[2] pp. 342 ff.; Rogers, *CP.* pp. 80 ff.

‡ *Mâšu*='twin.' The mountain thus appears to be the twin- (double-peaked) mountain which appears in representations of the God Šamaš emerging through the gates of sunrise, which attendants throw open to him: cf. Pl. III., fig. 3.

precious stones, produce rare fruits. The custodian of this garden is the maiden Siduri-Sabîtu, who sits on a throne by the shore of the ocean. Gilgameš' aim is to cross this ocean, in order to reach the abode of his ancestor, Uta-napištim (the Babylonian Noaḥ), who, after surviving the Flood, has, with his wife, been raised to immortality by the gods, and dwells beyond the ocean. He at least may be expected to possess the secret by which death may be escaped. In answer to the hero's inquiries as to the possibility of a crossing, Sabîtu replies :—

'O Gilgameš, there hath never been a passage,
And no one, from all eternity, hath crossed the ocean.
The warrior Šamaš hath crossed the ocean ;
But save for Šamaš, who shall cross ?
Difficult is the passage, laborious its course,
And deep are the waters of death which bar its access.
Why then, O Gilgameš, wilt thou cross the ocean ?
When thou arrivest at the waters of death, what wilt thou do ?'

The ocean, then, is the western ocean which is regularly crossed by the Sun in his journey towards the region of sunset. The narrative goes on to relate how, by the aid of Uta-napištim's mariner, Ur-Šanabi, Gilgameš succeeds in making the passage, and safely reaches the abode of his ancestor, from whom he learns the narrative of the Flood—with which in the present connexion we are not concerned.

Moreover, Gilgameš not only traverses the sun's path, but *he undergoes changes which indubitably illustrate the phases through which the sun passes during its yearly course.* In illustration of this we may quote first a most important passage at the commencement of Tab. VI., following immediately after the victory over Ḫumbaba, of which only a fragmentary account survives in Tab. V.

'He washed his weapons, he furbished his weapons,
He caused his long hair to fall down upon his back.
He doffed his soiled raiment, he donned his clean raiment,
With . . . ? he clothed himself, and bound on a doublet ;
Yea, Gilgameš decked himself with his diadem, and bound on a doublet.
To the beauty of Gilgameš majestic Ištar raised the eyes ;
"Come, Gilgameš, be thou my spouse !
Thy fruit to me, I pray thee, yield !
Be thou my husband ; let me be thy wife !
Let me yoke for thee a chariot of lapis lazuli and gold,
With wheels of gold, with horns of diamond ;
Thou shalt yoke daily the great steeds.
Into our house enter thou mid the perfume of cedar.

Into our house when thou enterest,
⟨They that sit on⟩ thrones shall kiss thy feet;
Beneath thee shall prostrate themselves kings, lords, and nobles;
The . . . ? of the mountain and land shall bring thee tribute."'

Gilgameš rejects Ištar's advances, reminding her of the sad fate of former lovers whom she has quickly spurned and made the victims of various misfortunes through which their vital force is lost. As Jastrow (*RBBA.* pp. 127 f.) remarks, 'The tale is clearly a form of the general nature-myth of the union of sun and earth, which, after a short time, results in the decline of the sun's force. Tammuz, an ancient personification of the sun of the springtime, is named as the first of Ištar's lovers; he becomes her consort and is then slain by the goddess and consigned to the nether world, the abode of the dead. The promise made by Ištar to Gilgameš to present him with a chariot of lapis lazuli, and to shelter him in a palace of plenty, unmistakably points to the triumph of the sun when vegetation is at its height. Tammuz and Ištar, like Gilgameš and Ištar, thus represent the combination of the two principles which bring about life; and upon their separation follow decay and death.'*

In revenge for this rebuff, Ištar persuades her father Anu to send a heavenly bull to destroy Gilgameš; but the beast is slain by the hero and his friend Engidu (cf. Pl. III. fig. 2). Gilgameš dedicates the horns to his god Lugal-banda, and returns in triumph to his city of Erech. Tabs. VII. and VIII. are unfortunately very fragmentary; but enough remains for us to gather that Engidu is suddenly afflicted with some fell disease, and, after taking to his bed, dies at the end of twelve days. The cause of his malady does not appear from the text as it now stands; but we are probably right in inferring that it was due to the curse of Ištar, following upon the failure of her first attempt to punish Gilgameš (cf. the account of Engidu's deliberate insult offered to the goddess, Tab. VII. ll. 178 ff.). Gilgameš' grief at the death of his friend is vividly portrayed at the end of Tab. VII.; and from the beginning of Tab. VIII. we learn that its poignancy is increased by the thought that the same fate must ultimately overtake him also:

'Gilgameš for Engidu his friend
Bitterly weepeth and wandereth through the desert:
"Must not I too die like Engidu?
Grief hath pierced mine inward part;
I fear death, and I wander through the desert."'

* The description of the chariot is (as Dhorme notes) strikingly similar to Ovid's description (*Metam.* ii. ll. 107 ff.) of the chariot of the Sun:—

'Aureus axis erat, temo aureus, aurea summae
Curvatura rotae, radiorum argenteus ordo,
Per juga chrysolithi positaeque ex ordine gemmae
Clara repercusso reddebant lumina Phoebo.'

It is at this point that he forms the resolution to seek out his ancestor Uta-napištim, who by some means (as yet unknown to him) has gained immortality, and who may possibly be able to hand on the secret to him. He at once, therefore, sets out upon the journey which we have already outlined.

In the course of this journey, as indeed prior to it, those whom he encounters comment in identical terms upon the shocking spectacle which he presents: *

> 'Why is thy strength consumed, thy face bowed down?
> Thy heart is in evil case, thy features are perished,
> And there is sadness in thine inward part;
> Thy face is like that of one that hath journeyed far;
> . . . distress and grief enflame thy face,
> . . . . . . and thou wanderest through the desert.'

To each of these inquiries he replies by asking why he should not appear thus, seeing that he has just lost so close a friend. It seems, however, to be clear that he is afflicted by something more than grief, and that in all probability the disease which has destroyed Engidu has fastened its hold upon him also. At any rate, when he reaches Uta-napištim, he is in a terrible condition, as appears from the words of his ancestor in which he directs the sailor, Ur-Šanabi, to take him to a washing-place where he may bathe and restore his health (xi. 251 ff.):—

> 'The man before whom thou didst walk,
> Whose body is covered with boils,
> The beauty of whose flesh is marred with scales—
> Take him, Ur-Šanabi, to the washing-place bring him;
> His boils in water let him wash (white) as snow;
> Let him cast off his scales, and let the sea bear (them) away;
> Fair let his body appear;
> Let the turban of his head be renewed;
> With a robe let him be clothed, his garment of modesty;
> Until he come to his city,
> Until he come to his own way,
> Let the garment not become threadbare,‡ but let it be new—
> be new!'

Uta-napištim's directions are followed, and Gilgameš is able to make the return-voyage, reaching Erech in perfect health, and clad in fair attire. The account of his actually finding, and then through

* So, some one whose name has disappeared, VIII. v. 7 ff.; Ur-Šanabi, X. iii. 1 ff.; Uta-napištim, X. iv. 42 ff. There is every reason to suppose that the same inquiry should be restored and put into the mouth of Siduri in X. i. 33 ff.

‡ Lit. 'throw off grey hair,' *i.e.* perhaps, its surface-wool, or, as we might say, *lose its nap.* A different explanation is given by Haupt, *AJSL.* xxvi. (1909), p. 16.

an accident losing, the magic herb by means of which he might have secured immortality, does not concern our present purpose.

Here, then, we have, in a parable the inner meaning of which is transparently obvious, an account of the sun's triumph in springtime, followed by its gradual decline in force as it starts on its long journey towards the waters of death. This culminates in the last stage of disease when it reaches its goal, where it undergoes a process of lustration, so that, when it appears once more in the east, it possesses its original beauty and glory. The meaning of the story of Engidu, who actually dies as the result of Ištar's malice, may perhaps not be affirmed with equal certainty; but the whole trend of evidence goes to suggest that he is a chthonic deity, typifying the reproductive vigour of animal-nature in the springtime, which dies away as the year passes onward on its course.*

Were it necessary to add anything in support of this clear evidence that Gilgameš is a solar hero, it might be found in the material which

* This is suggested by the description of his early life as a companion of the beasts of the field, and by the satyr-like form—half man and half bull—in which he is represented upon early seal-cylinders: cf. Pl. II. fig. 5; Pl. III. fig. 2. He is described in I. iv. 6 as *lulâ amêlu* 'the man of animal-desire.'

It is a hopeless task to attempt to construct a wholly satisfactory and consistent explanation of the cosmology of the Gilgameš-epic; Cf., on this subject, Jeremias, *Izdubar-Nimrod*, pp. 66 ff.; Jensen, *Das Gilgamesch-Epos*, pp. 77 ff.; Zimmern, *KAT.*[3] pp. 566 ff.; Dhorme, *Choix des textes religieux assyr.-bab.*, pp. 271 f., 278 f.; Ungnad and Gressmann, *Das Gilgamesch-Epos*, pp. 154 ff. The view that the twelve tablets present us with the sun's doings during the twelve months of the year, and that each of these is associated with its appropriate zodiacal sign, seems to be improbable. It may be worked out in a few instances, but breaks down in the majority. Thus, Tab. III., which relates the beginning of the adventures of Gilgameš and Engidu, might stand for *Gemini* (though the cementing of the friendship between the two heroes takes place as early as the end of Tab. I.); Tab. VI. which contains the Ištar-incident might stand for *Virgo*; and, most strikingly, Tab. XI., the Flood-narrative, for *Aquarius*. If, however, the creation of Engidu, who, as we have already remarked, is figured as half bull, represents *Taurus*, we should expect to find the account of this in Tab. II. and not in Tab. I.; and the Scorpion-men of the mountain of Mâšu (*Scorpio*) should appear in Tab. VIII. rather than in Tab. IX., unless indeed they stand also for *Sagittarius*: cf. the representation of a scorpion-man as an archer on an ancient boundary-stone (v. R. 57; *OTLAE.* i., fig. 2, p. 11), and also on the seal-cylinders figured by Delaporte, *Cylindres orientaux*, Pl. XXI. figs. 313, 316. Probably the truth is that some of the incidents in the Epic do represent the course of the sun through the zodiacal stations, but not (at least in the form in which the Epic has come down to us) in any consistent order, or, at any rate, in an order which is marked by the twelve tablets into which the poem is divided.

Again, it seems probable that the incidents of the poem typify not merely the *yearly* course of the sun, but that there is a combination of the yearly and daily courses which it is difficult or impossible to unravel. Gilgameš' adventure at the mountain of Mâšu, where he starts a journey of twelve double-hours over the route of the sun—*ḫarran* (*ilu*) *Šamši*—is most naturally to be understood of the daily circuit of twenty-four hours; though, in view of the fact that all the way the darkness is dense, and it is only at the end of the journey that he emerges into the

is supplied by the ancient seal-cylinders of Babylonia. On these we not infrequently find the figures of Gilgameš and the Sun-god used interchangeably in precisely similar settings. One such series is illustrated on Pl. II. Here in figs. 1 and 2 we have a figure described in pictographic writing as *ilu Šamaš*, who contends with antelopes and lions. In fig. 3 Gilgameš likewise contends with the same animals, the arrangement of the figures being identical with that of figs. 1 and 2. That the central figure in fig. 3 is intended for Gilgameš is indicated by his full-face representation (peculiar to figures of Gilgameš and Engidu), and by the arrangement of his hair in six locks; cf. the Gilgameš-figures on Pl. III. figs. 1, 2. There are similar series which are no less significant.*

light 'before the sun,' we should expect the reference to be to the *nocturnal* course of the sun from west to east, which should rather occupy six double-hours or twelve hours. His journey across the ocean with Ur-Šanabi occupies one month and fifteen days before he comes to the waters of death. Since the condition in which we find him at this point, in the last stage of disease, can hardly denote anything else than the winter-ṣolstice, when the power of the sun is at its lowest ebb, it may be that this voyage represents the half of the winter-quarter; the corresponding half being occupied by the return of the sun after purification in a condition to renew once more his yearly course.

It is impossible, again, to attain any degree of certainty in attempting to define the conception of the Epic as to the earthly counterpart of the heavenly course of the sun. Jensen places the cedar-mountain where the hero and his friend conquer the giant Ḫumbaba among the mountains of Elam to the east of Babylonia, over which the sun rises. Thence Gilgameš reaches his city of Erech where he is at the climax of his glory. From this point Jensen would make him pursue his course due west across the Syrian desert to the Lebanon and Anti-Lebanon, which he regards as the twin-mountain of Mâšu, and over the whole length of the Mediterranean Sea to the waters of death—the Atlantic. This view is adopted by Zimmern; though it is difficult to see how the Atlantic can have come within the Babylonian horizon. Of course Jensen and Zimmern have the Pillars of Hercules in their minds; but the Phoenicians must surely have been the earliest Semitic traders to get so far west. Other scholars find the name Mâšu in the Syro-Arabian desert, which Ašurbanipal calls the land of Maš, and describes as 'a place of thirst and languor, wherein no bird of heaven flies, nor do wild asses and gazelles graze there': cf. *KB.* ii. p. 220; Delitzsch, *Paradies*, pp. 242 f. Across this they would make Gilgameš travel not due west but south-west, till he reaches South Arabia, where dwells Siduri who is termed Sabîtu, *i.e.* on this interpretation 'the Sabaean': cf. Hommel, *AHT.* pp. 35 f. This perhaps agrees better with the sun's course as viewed from the northern hemisphere—not due west across the zenith, but south-west. Yet the theory of a very early date for the origin of the Sabaean kingdom is now not regarded as probable.

* Cf., in Delaporte, *Catalogue des Cylindres orientaux . . . de la Bibliothèque Nationale*, Pl. IV. fig. 41, a figure described as *ilu Šamaš* in conflict with a human-headed bull; Pl. V. fig. 43, a similar figure unspecified contending with the same human-headed bull, in company with Engidu contending with a lion; fig. 45, Gilgameš with the human-headed bull (duplicated), and Engidu with the lion; fig. 44, Gilgameš with the human-headed bull *together with* a figure like that of fig. 43 contending with another bull of the same kind, and Engidu with the lion. We may notice also, in Hayes Ward, *Cylinders . . . in*

The adventures of Gilgameš and Engidu form favourite subjects for representation on seal-cylinders in the Sumerian and early Semitic Babylonian period, as well as in later times. The heroes are most commonly depicted in conflict with beasts—either Gilgameš attacks a wild bull or water-buffalo while Engidu is similarly engaged with a lion, or Gilgameš by himself is seen in conflict with the latter beast: cf. Pl. II. fig. 4; Pl. III. figs. 1, 2. In spite of the fragmentary condition of parts of the Epic, it affords us ample evidence that the two heroes were mighty hunters.*

The space which we have devoted to the Gilgameš-epic may seem to be out of all proportion to its importance in relation to the story of Samson; but this is not really so. In the first place, it has enabled us to establish the fact of the existence of a Semitic solar myth in a form of which the significance is incontrovertible, and the widespread influence of which in countries adjacent to Babylonia can easily be demonstrated. In Pl. IV. we have Gilgameš as pictured by the Assyrians; Pl. V. illustrates the fact that the hero and his companion were familiar to the Ḥittites of Carchemish; Pl. VI. exhibits the movement of the same myth westward to Cyprus, the colossal figure clearly exhibiting Assyrio-Babylonian influence in the treatment of the beard and hair (cf. p. 498), and in the manner in which he is rending the lion.‡ This last figure is probably rightly identified with the Phoenician Melḳart, whose influence on the Greek myth of

the Library of J. Pierpont Morgan, Pl. V. fig. 22, a figure marked *ilu Šamaš* attacking a lion by seizing its tail and one hind leg and placing a foot on the back of its neck; Delaporte, *op. cit.*, Pl. III. fig. 22, Gilgameš attacking a lion in precisely the same way (duplicated); cf. also Pl. II. fig. 21.

* Sayce, *ET.* xxiv. (1912) p. 39, in endeavouring to identify the hero of the seal-cylinder representations with a supposed Namra-Uddu (*i.e.* the Biblical Nimrod) and *not* with Gilgameš, makes the assertion, 'Gilgameš was not a hunter, and he never struggled with lions or held slaughtered animals in his hands.' This statement strangely overlooks the words which are addressed to Gilgameš in VIII. v. 5,

'<In the passes> of the mountain thou didst slay lions,'

as well as the refrain of the hero's lament over Engidu (cf. X. v. 11),

'<My friend who with me> slew the lions, etc.'

Cf. also, in Gilgameš' description to Uta-napištim of the difficulties of his journey (X. v. 31 f.),

'The *kâsu*-bird, the *buṣu*-bird, the lion, the panther, the jackal(?), the stag, the ibex, the wild bull,

Their <flesh> I eat, and with their skins I <clothe myself>.'

It is highly probable that one of the Tabs. III., IV., or V., which are very fragmentary, originally contained an account of a lion-combat, possibly corresponding to the zodiacal station *Leo*.

‡ Cf. the representation of Engidu and the lion in Pl. II. fig. 4.

Herakles in many of its details can scarcely be gainsaid.* The proved existence of such a solar myth is the most weighty fact which can influence our decision as to whether solar elements do or do not enter into the Samson-tradition. In comparing Samson with Gilgameš in our search for solar traits, we are not bolstering up the merely hypothetical interpretation of one series of traditions by the scarcely less hypothetical interpretation of another series ; but we are testing the former series by that which, in the latter, may be regarded as a well-ascertained conclusion.

In the second place, for a right estimation of the character of the Samson-narrative, it is as important to notice the *contrast* which it offers to the Gilgameš-epic as it is to register the points of resemblance between the two stories. The Gilgameš-epic as a whole (and this is also true of the Herakles-saga) moves in a plane which is wholly mythical. Gods and goddesses take their part in the sequence of events like ordinary mortals. The hero and his friend are distinguished as semi-divine by the use of the determinative prefix *ilu* 'god,' before their names. Indeed, the fact that Gilgameš possesses a divine strain in his blood is more than once emphasized in the Epic (I. ii. 1 ; IX. ii. 16) by the statement

'Two-thirds of him are god, and his third part is human.'

* Wilamowitz-Moellendorf, in his edition of Euripides, *Herakles*, i. p. 276 (1st ed., 1889), dismisses the theory of the derivation of the Greek Herakles from old Babylonian sources with great contempt, having clearly never taken the trouble to investigate and appreciate the evidence which can be advanced in its favour. Later on (pp. 290 ff.) he goes on to enumerate the earliest elements in the Herakles-myth as follows :—(1) the descent of the hero from the highest gods ; (2) the conflict with the lion ; (3) the conflict with giants ; (4) the journey to the Underworld, and the conquest of death ; (5) the journey to the garden of the gods. As a matter of fact, as Jeremias (*Izdubar-Nimrod*, pp. 70 ff.) points out, these are the very incidents which can be most strikingly paralleled from the Gilgameš-epic. In his 2nd edition (1895) Wilamowitz-Moellendorf makes grudging concession to Jeremias that 'the resemblance of Herakles to "Izdubar-Nimrod" is of course remarkable in the highest degree (allerdings höchst merkwürdig). Naturally this also struck the ancients, and necessarily led to identification, as *e.g.* the Cyprian representation of the Geryones-adventure demonstrates : *Journ. of Hell. Stud.*, xliii. 74.' It may be observed that this concession does not touch Jeremias' point that the *earliest* elements in the Herakles-myth (*teste* W.-M.) are those which find closest parallel in the Babylonian-myth.

Jeremias further remarks that it is reasonable to hold that, just as we have the series Ištar—'Ashtart—Aphrodite, so we also have the series Gilgameš—Samson —Herakles ; a conclusion which may be accepted with substitution of the Phoenician Melḳart for the Israelite Samson, the conception of whom can hardly have had any direct influence on Greek mythology. The line of transference was probably Babylonian—Phoenician—Greek ; while Samson, as is argued above, seems to represent a lateral development of the myth in a very diluted form. Herodotus (ii. 44) states that he visited the temple of Herakles at Tyre ; and that this was of very great antiquity, being said to be contemporary with the foundation of the city, which he places at 2300 years before his time. That this Herakles was the god Melḳart (*i.e.* 'King of the city') admits of no doubt.

The world in which events are enacted is not our world; or at any rate it is ours only in a very remote and symbolical sense.* The Samson-narrative (and here we are referring to *chs.* 14-16, apart from the later-added *ch.* 13) is markedly different. Samson indeed performs prodigies of strength which are incredibly marvellous; but the *whole setting* of the narrative, so far from being artificial, is as fresh and true to life as almost anything contained in the O.T. It leaves us no doubt that we are breathing the natural atmosphere of the border-country between the Israelites and Philistines, and are witnessing scenes of social intercourse such as must have been of everyday occurrence at the period with which the narrator deals.‡

Again, the author of the Gilgameš-epic was an educated man of great literary ability.§ He had evidently reflected much on the problems of life and death; and, had we had occasion to refer to his speculations as to human mortality, we might have quoted passages of wonderful beauty and pathos. He seems to have been versed in the astronomical knowledge of his day. The *technique* of the poem is highly developed, and its descriptive power (as witnessed *e.g.* by the Flood-story) of a very high order. In contrast, the charm of the Samson-narrative lies in its artlessness, and in the fact that it comes straight from the lips of the rustic story-teller, whose sole equipment consisted in a retentive memory, a sense of humour, and a native power of description. Whether it be possible or not to explain every detail of the Gilgameš-epic as an integral part of the solar myth, there can be no question that this method, if applied to the Samson-narrative, goes very widely astray. The whole narrative is so intimately bound up with the occurrences of everyday life, and quite possibly with the actual doings of an historical individual, that the fallaciousness of such a method is self-evident.

Thus it is clear that the difficulty of distinguishing the solar traits in the Samson-narrative is very considerable. A particular incident may bear resemblance more or less close to a characteristic *motif* in the stories of other solar heroes; but unless it is impossible to regard it as an actual incident which may have occurred in real life, its interpretation as a solar trait must remain extremely precarious. To take a single example: Samson slew a lion single-handed, and so did Herakles, and Gilgameš very possibly slew several; but, again, similar incidents are recorded of David (1 Sam. 17 [34 f.]) and Benaiah (2 Sam. 23 [20]); and we have, in these latter instances, no ground for regarding the feat as other than historical, because it is the kind of feat that a strong and brave man might reasonably accomplish.

Bearing these considerations in mind, we may proceed to notice

* Cf. the last paragraph of the first *footnote*, p. 400.

‡ Cf. the remarks on p. 339.

§ In speaking of the author, in the singular, it is not intended to express any opinion as to the unity, or composite character, of the Epic. All that is affirmed is true of the Epic as a whole, whether it be the work of one or more authors.

certain points in the Samson-narrative which may very well owe their origin to solar mythology.

Among these the most striking is the conception that the strength of the hero lies in his long hair, and that when this has been shaved off he becomes powerless; just as the sun when adorned with his rays (which are pictured as hair in the literature of all nations *) is endowed with great strength, but sinks into weakness when he loses these in the winter-season. We have noticed how Gilgameš, when he figures as the glorious sun of springtime, is said to wear his long hair falling down his back; and this hair is prominent in early seal-cylinder representations of the Babylonian hero, arranged in six curling locks which fall on either side of his head (cf. Pl. II. figs. 3, 4, 5; Pl. III. figs. 1, 2), with which we may compare the six rays which are depicted as issuing from the shoulders of the Sun-god (Pl. III. fig. 3). Samson's hair was also arrayed in locks, though these were seven and not six.‡ We are not definitely told that Gilgameš loses his long locks when his strength fails him and he becomes the victim of disease, § though, since they are so prominently mentioned as a mark of his beauty when at the height of his youthful power, it is perhaps not an unfair inference that he is to be pictured as deprived of them in his affliction (cf. the remarks as to his changed appearance quoted on p. 398). When he is washed clean and free from disease 'the turban of his head' || is renewed; but no mention is made of his locks, which, if they were lost, must be pictured as gradually growing again. The sun does not arrive at its full strength and glory at the turn of the year. Samson's hair began to grow again after it was cut off, but some time elapsed before he was able to put forth his pristine strength. In the *note* on *ch.* 13[5] we have observed how ill the conception of the author of this chapter that Samson was a Nazirite fits in with the portrait of him which is to be gathered from the older *chs.* 14-16, and have concluded that the view that he was under such a vow must probably be regarded as a later interpretation of the meaning of his long locks. If we are right in explaining them as an ancient solar trait, we can now understand why the author of *ch.* 13, who endeavours to view Samson and his

* Cf. the admirably full body of evidence collected by Smythe Palmer in *ch.* iv.

‡ We have noticed above (*note* on *ch.* 16[13]) that the statement that Gilgameš wore his hair in *seven* locks, which seems to emanate from Jeremias (cf. *OTLAE.* ii. p. 172), is incorrect. For the possible meaning of Samson's *seven* locks, cf. the conjectures put forward by Smythe Palmer, *ch.* v., who cites instances of the Sun-god depicted as adorned with *seven rays,* the most striking of which is perhaps the Pompeian wall-painting figured by Roscher, *Lexikon der griech. u. rom. Mythol.*, 2003.

§ Smythe Palmer's statement (p. 221) that when Gilgameš 'begins to fail and fall ill' he 'loses his hair in which lay his strength,' unfortunately goes beyond his facts as they may be gathered from the Epic. It is an inference merely.

|| Bab. *parsigu ša ḳaḳḳadišu.* The term *parsigu* is used elsewhere of a *bandage.*

doings from the standpoint of a pious Yahweh-worshipper (cf. p. 338), should have read a different meaning into this characteristic.

Much more doubtfully significant as a solar trait is Samson's slaying of the lion, though greatly emphasized as such by many writers; because, as we have already remarked, it is the kind of deed which might naturally have been performed by a strong man, or might naturally be ascribed to him, without the involving of any symbolical meaning. The term which is used to describe the hero's *rending* of the lion *does* seem, however, to suggest connexion with the Gilgameš-myth: cf. *notes* on *ch.* 14[6]. A similar connexion may possibly be traced in the fact that the incident occurs early in Samson's career and immediately prior to his being ensnared by the charms of Philistine womankind, which leads to his ultimate undoing. Gilgameš' lion-slaying feats must, as we have noticed,* have occurred a little before the Ištar-incident which marks the beginning of the hero's misfortunes.‡

A much clearer trace of solar mythology is to be found in the story of the bursting forth of the spring at Ramath-leḥi to satisfy

* Cf. *footnote* *, p. 401.

‡ The present writer can attach no weight at all to Steinthal's theory that the story of the honey in the lion's carcass belongs to the solar myth with the symbolical meaning that, when the sun is in the zodiacal sign *Leo* (*i.e.* in July), honey is most plentiful. This theory is built up upon a series of assumptions, any one of which is open to question. It is assumed that no other explanation of bees building in a carcass is satisfactory; whereas, as we have seen (cf. *note* on 14[8]), this may be explained either by the supposition that the carcass was hollow and sun-dried, or by the *βουγονία*-theory. Again, the claim that this explanation offers the Philistines a possibility of solving the riddle, which is otherwise insoluble apart from a knowledge of the facts, can hardly carry weight. Samson's wit was not of so high a class that he must be deemed incapable of a very bad, and so, unfair riddle; especially as the story makes it clear that he was confident that he would win the wager. And lastly, the assumption that July is the month when honey is most plentiful seems to be based upon experience of the habits of bees in the temperate regions of Europe where flowers abound throughout the summer, and to overlook the fact that in the sub-tropical climate of Palestine the flowering season ceases and herbaceous vegetation is burnt up by about the middle of May, after which (presumably) the bees are living on their store of honey, and the supply is gradually *decreasing*.

Steinthal's further conjecture that Samson's slaying of the lion typifies the milder sun of autumn extinguishing his own burning rays (the lion representing the fierce heat of midsummer) is in itself so incredible that it requires no refutation. It may be noticed, however, that it seems to involve a kind of *hysteron-proteron*; for the autumnal sun stifles the heat of midsummer *before* the bees—which typify the fact that honey is plentiful in midsummer—establish themselves in the carcass.

At the same time, the fact is undoubted that in Babylonian mythology the lion is closely associated with the god Nergal, who typifies the hot sun of midsummer; the choice of this animal being no doubt dictated by its fierce and destructive disposition, its tawny colour, and its shaggy mane which suggests not remotely the rays of the sun.

Samson's need. Abundant evidence exists in proof that springs—and especially hot springs—were associated with the sun or with solar heroes.* Athenaeus (xii. 512) states that all hot springs which break forth from the earth are sacred to Herakles: cf. also Diod. Sic., iv. 23, v. 3; Strabo, pp. 60, 172, 425, 428; Livy, xxii. 1; *al.* The original idea seems to have been that such springs are warmed by the sun during his nocturnal course under the earth. Cf. especially the account given by Herodotus (iv. 181) and Lucretius (*De Rerum Natura*, vi. 848 f.) of the spring of the sun in the oasis of Ammonium (Siweh) in the Libyan desert, which is cold by day but boiling hot at night. The point is interesting as definitely connecting Herakles with the sun. In some cases at any rate (cf. Diod. Sic. *loc. cit.*) the traditional connexion with the solar hero was that the springs had been caused to burst forth in order that he might bathe in them when weary.

That cold springs were also associated with the sun by the Semites is proved by the occurrence of the name 'En-shemesh 'the spring of the sun,' Josh. 15[7], 18[17]—the modern 'Ain el-Ḥôd 'the Apostle's spring,' a little east of Bethany on the road to Jericho; and 'Ain-šems, the modern Ar. name of Beth-shemesh. Whether the hero bathes in the warm spring, as does Herakles, or drinks from the cool spring, as does Samson, the effect is the same, viz. the restoration of his vitality which through weariness or faintness has reached a low ebb. The conception seems to be bound up with the restoration of the sun's power in the springtime: cf. the way in which Gilgameš has to bathe in order to free himself from his disease and renew his beauty—a figure which, as we have seen (pp. 398 f.), typifies the renewal of the sun's powers after he has reached his lowest ebb at the winter-solstice.

If any weight may be attached to our suggestion (*ch.* 15[19] *note*) that, in the name 'Ên-hak-ḳōrē given to the spring of Leḥi, *ḳōrē* originally denoted not the partridge but the *quail*, we seem here to trace the combination of a kindred mythical conception as to the return of the sun in springtime. The reason why the quail was sacrificed by the Phoenicians to Herakles-Melḳart in the early spring, and the reason why Herakles was thought to have been restored to life by smelling this particular bird, was that the quail was the bird which—as its Greek name ὄρτυξ, Sanskrit *Vartikâ* 'the returning one,' denotes—was *par excellence* the migrant whose reappearance heralded the return of the sun in the spring. Hence, according to Max Müller (*Science of Language*, ii. p. 506) is derived Ortygia (the name of the island which was otherwise called Delos 'the bright'), which was regarded as the birthplace of Apollo, the young Sun-god of springtime.

The incident of Samson's removal of the gates of Ġaza, and his

* Cf. the evidence brought together by Smythe Palmer, *ch.* xi.

setting them up on a hill to the east of Ḥebron, is probably connected with the conception that the sun, in rising, issues through a door with double gates on the extremity of the eastern horizon. Cf. the representation of the Sun-god Šamaš passing through such gates, which are held open for him by attendants: Pl. III. fig. 3. The subject is one which is frequently figured on Babylonian seals. Samson removes the gates after spending the night in company with his paramour—a conception which reminds us of the description of the sun at his rising in Ps. 19[5] (𝔐[6]):

> 'And he is like a bridegroom issuing from his bridal chamber;
> He rejoiceth like a mighty man to run the course.'

It is rash to look for any symbolical meaning in the names Ġaza and Ḥebron, these particular cities being probably merely part of the local setting of the story. It is possible, however, that some particular hill to the east of Ḥebron may have acquired a name as the hill over which, from the Shephelah, the sun was regularly observed to rise.

The name of Samson's paramour, Delîlah, is of some importance as exhibiting almost certainly the influence of Babylonian thought upon the story. Comparison with the Bab. proper names *Dalil-(ilu)-Ištar*, *Dilîl-(ilu)-Ištar*,* 'worshipper of Ištar,' though (so far as the present writer knows) it has not before been made, is obvious. Delîlah, 'worshipper' or 'devotee,' may be assumed to be a hypocoristic for the full form Delîlat-Ištar (*or* ʿAštart).‡ As applied to a woman, the connotation of this name (at least according to the original form of the tale) can hardly be mistaken. Delîlah must have been a sacred prostitute devoted to the service of the goddess (Heb. *ḳᵉdhēšā*, Bab. *ḳadištu*, *ḫarimtu*, *šamḫatu*, or *kazratu*). The close connexion of these consecrated female worshippers with Ištar in her relations with Gilgameš is illustrated by the Epic in the narrative of Tab. VI. 184 ff. We may compare also Tab. I. iii. 1 ff., where Engidu, whilst living the life of a wild man among the beasts of the field, is decoyed away by the attractions of such a *ḫarimtu* and adopts a life of civilization. It is Samson's relations with Delîlah which prove the cause of his undoing, just as it is through Ištar that Gilgameš' misfortunes are brought about. We may compare the way

* Cf. T. N. Strassmaier, *Alphabetisches Verzeichniss der Assyrischen und Akkadischen Wörter*, 1835 and 1975.

‡ Such a contraction is, of course, common in Heb. proper names: *e.g.* Nathan for Nᵉthan'ēl, or Baruch, 'Blessed' (*sc.* of Yahweh).

In *Dalil-(ilu)-Ištar*, *Dalil* is an active participle, while *Dilîl* in the cognate form appears to be a substantive 'worship' for 'worshipper.' Heb. *Delîlā* might appear at first sight to be a passive form; but this is not necessarily so, since, as G-K. § 84[al] points out, the form *ḳātîl* may result from an original active *ḳăṭīl* as well as from a passive *ḳāṭîl*. At the same time it is likely that the intransitive or passive meaning of the word (Bab. *dalâlu* properly = 'to submit oneself') would favour the development of such a formation.

in which the hatred of Hera is the prime cause of the labours and sufferings of Herakles.

Possibly, though not certainly (since the incident is one which might very well have happened in real life; cf. p. 403), the story of Samson as a blinded captive grinding in the prison-house may have a solar significance, based on the fact that the sun, powerful as he is, yet covers the same beaten track day after day, and so may be conceived to be the victim of some external compulsion, which obliges him to perform the same allotted task daily without variation. If, as seems probable, the mill at which Samson grinds is to be pictured, not as a small hand-mill, but as a large mill which is ordinarily turned by an ox or ass which travels round and round in an unvarying track, the analogy is the more striking. Probably the same idea lies at the root of the story that Herakles was under compulsion to perform his labours at the bidding of the weak and tyrannical Eurystheus.

Finally, the account of Samson's death can hardly be dissociated from the solar myth. The point has been so thoroughly illustrated by Smythe Palmer (*ch.* xv.) that it is needless to treat it at length. By pulling down the western pillars which were thought to support the vault of heaven * (Job 26 [11]), the sun overwhelms himself and the world with the darkness of night. The idea is aptly illustrated by Homer's description of sunset (*Il.* viii. 485 f.):

ἐν δ' ἔπεσ' Ὠκεανῷ λαμπρὸν φάος ἠελίοιο,
ἕλκον νύκτα μέλαιναν ἐπὶ ζείδωρον ἄρουραν.

The red glow of sunset probably suggested the idea of a great carnage wrought by the downfall of the sky-temple; just as, in the Herakles-myth, it suggested the conception of the hero's glowing funeral-pyre on Mount Oeta. In the words of Smythe Palmer—'We may suppose, then, that some such thoughts as these were present to the primaeval gazer on the changing drama of sunset. See! the mighty sun has fallen! His enemies were too strong for him! In dying, he has dragged down the bright sky after him! The pillars of heaven are broken and darkness comes crashing down! But see! the place where he fell is red with the carnage of his foes! The clouds which obstructed him and exulted over him are ensanguined—involved with him in a common ruin!' (*op. cit.* p. 180).

17. 1–18. 31. *The story of Micah and the Danites.*

The fact that this narrative is composite is very evident; and it can hardly be doubted that we have to do with two originally independent parallel narratives (so Vatke,‡ Ber., Bu., Mo., etc.), rather

* We may compare the pillars set up by Hercules at Gades, the westernmost point of the then-known world.

‡ To Vatke (*Die biblische Theologie*, 1835, p. 268) belongs the credit of first

than with a single narrative which has undergone extensive interpolation (Wellh.,* Kue., La., Gress.). It is not, however, always easy to disentangle the strands with any certainty, probably because the two versions of the story were originally closely similar in detail.

According to $17^{1\text{-}4}$, Micay^{e}hu (מיכיהו) restores the stolen silver, which is then made into a graven image (and a molten image). The idol (or idols) is placed in Micay^{e}hu's own house. In 17^{5}, however, we are told that the man Micah (מיכה a shorter form of מיכיהו) already possessed a temple (בית אלהים), for which he made an Ephod and Teraphim, and installed one of his sons as priest. Here we note that the graven image and molten image of $17^{3.4}$ stand over against the Ephod and Teraphim of 17^{5}; and the inference that the one pair may be peculiar to the first narrative (which we may term A), while the other pair is peculiar to the second narrative (provisionally called B), is confirmed, rather than the reverse, by the curious way in which all four are mentioned together in $18^{14.17.18}$, and three of them in 18^{20}—passages which have all the appearance of having been filled out by a redactor. In $18^{30.31}$ the graven image is mentioned by itself, just as it occurs without the molten image in 18^{20}; and this fact, taken in connexion with the fact that the verb ויהי 'and it was' in 17^{4} seems clearly to refer to *a single idol*, and not to two (graven image *and* molten image), suggests (as perceived by Mo.) that the narrative A originally referred to a graven image only, and that the molten image is a late interpolation, possibly made in view of the fact that the silver was handed over to a 'smelter' (צורף).

Further, it can hardly be doubted that $17^{7\text{-}13}$ combines two accounts of the appearance of the Levite on the scene. In 17^{7} he is introduced as 'a youth' (נער) who was a Levite, who happened to be sojourning 'there'—*i.e.*, obviously, in Micah's village or the near neighbourhood of it. In 17^{8}, however, where he is termed 'the man' (האיש), he sets forth from Bethleḥem of Judah to sojourn where he may find employment, and chancing to arrive at Micah's home, he is hired by him as priest (*vv.*$^{8\text{-}11a}$). The terms in which Micah, in *v.*^{10}, invites the Levite to become to him '*a father* and a priest' appear absurdly inappropriate if the latter was very young, as is implied by the term *ná'ar* used in *v.*^{7}, which denotes little more than a mere boy.

perceiving that our story, as it stands, contains repetitions and discrepancies which are only to be explained by the hypothesis of the combination of two parallel narratives. He correctly perceived that the *sacra* are differently described in the two narratives, though erring in the supposition that the wandering Levite appears in one narrative only, his place in the other being taken by Micah's son (*ch.* 17^{5}), who is the Jonathan of *ch.* 18^{30} of the *tribe* of Manasseh. The general outline of the two stories is briefly indicated by Vatke, and not worked out in detail. Mo. (*Comm.* pp. 367 f.) gives a convenient summary of the analyses adopted by different scholars.

* In an appendix to *Comp.*^{3} (pp. 363 ff.) Wellh. adopts the theory of two parallel narratives.

As a matter of fact, in *v.*^{11b}, where the term *nă'ar* is next used, it is stated that 'the youth' became to Micah 'like one of his sons.' We have here, then, a clear mark of differentiation. According to 17$^{7.11b.12a}$, a youthful Levite of the clan of Judah [is adopted or hired by Micah] and becomes like one of his own sons, being installed as priest. According to 17$^{8\text{-}11a.12b.13}$, a Levite from Bethleḥem of Judah, of mature age, is travelling in search of employment when he receives an offer from Micah which he accepts (*v.*^{11a}), and takes up his abode in his house (*v.*^{12b}).* Micah then congratulates himself (*v.*^{13}) on having obtained the services of a *Levite*—clearly as opposed to those of his own non-Levitical son (*v.*^{5}). This last point indicates that 17$^{8\text{-}11a.12b.13}$ belongs to the narrative B, to which we have assigned *v.*^{5}; hence 17$^{7.11b.12a}$ is to be assigned to A, to which it is quite suitable.‡

We have thus accounted for the whole of *ch.* 17 except *v.*^{6}—a statement which, repeated as it is, in whole or in part, in 18^{1a}, 19^{1a}, 21^{25}, is clearly editorial, inserted for the purpose of explaining a condition of religion and morality which, from the editor's own standpoint, was a very low one. Whether this editor is the pre-exilic redactor of the old narratives (R^{JE}), or the post-exilic redactor who added the Appendix (*chs.* 17-18, 19-21) to Judg., may be considered an open question. In the view of some scholars (*e.g.* Kue., Bu., Cor., Driver, *LOT.*^{9}, Cooke) the form of expression used by the editor implies without a doubt that when he wrote there *was* a king in Israel, and that therefore his standpoint is earlier at any rate than the close of the Judaean monarchy. Such a conclusion is questionable. It is obvious that an exilic or post-exilic editor, surveying the course of Israel's past history, may equally well have drawn a distinction between premonarchic and monarchic times, regarding the former in comparison with the latter as an unsettled and disorganized period. Further, the occurrence of the statement in 17^{6} is clearly called forth by the (from the editor's point of view) irregularities of cultus which the old narrative relates—the use of images, etc., in Yahweh-worship and the appointment of a non-Levitical priest. Is it likely that R^{JE}, living, as we must assume, at or about the time of the idolatrous reign of King Manasseh, would have explained such irregularities by the fact that the kingship had not yet been established, regarding the kingship as a moderating and restraining influence, favouring a relative

* The reason why this half verse is referred to this narrative rather than to the other is that we are told in 18^{15a} that the youthful Levite had a house of his own.

‡ It is possible that *v.*$^{12a\alpha}$ may belong to B, leaving only the words 'and the youth became his priest' to A. This is a point which it is impossible to settle decisively. The words 'from Bethleḥem of Judah' in *vv.*$^{7.8}$ belong to B; cf. *v.*^{9b}. A's description of the Levite's native place is given more vaguely in the words 'of the clan of Judah,' *v.*^{7}. We may infer, then, that the second occurrence of 'from Bethleḥem of Judah' (*v.*^{8}) is redactional, in order to explain the reference 'from the city,' after the intervening words in *v.*^{7} from A.

purity of cultus? Such a view is surely more closely allied to the constitutional and priestly aspect of religion which we see *e.g.* in a post-exilic writer like the Chronicler, than to the highly spiritualized aspect which characterizes prophetic thought in the seventh century B.C. Again, the position occupied by the statement in 21^{25}, rounding off a composite narrative which admittedly contains a large post-exilic element, suggests that it, like other redactional matter in the narrative, is due to R^{P}.

The explanatory note in $18^{1b\beta}$ ('for there had not fallen, etc.') has the appearance of a late addition. $18^{1b\alpha}$ is naturally continued by 18^{2}. In 18^{2a}, however, the description of the spies who are sent out by the Danites is somewhat unwieldy, and may well be composite. Comparison of 18^{11a} suggests that the words 'from their whole number, men of valour' are alien to the rest of the description; for by their excision this latter tallies exactly with the description of the band of warriors in *v.*^{11a}. In continuation, the words 'to spy out the land and to explore it' seem to be redundant by the side of the following 'and they said unto them, "Go, explore the land"'; and in view of the established fact that we are dealing with two parallel narratives, we may suspect that these are parallel passages from the two sources. The main strand of 18^{2a} is marked as B by its parallelism with 18^{11a}; and by the fact that it seems properly to be continued by 18^{2b}, which belongs to that source. Thus the two insertions, 'from their whole . . . valour,' 'to spy out . . . explore it,' are left by inference to A, to which the phrase 'to spy out, etc.' seems to belong in *vv.*$^{14a.17a}$.

In 18^{2b} the spies arrive at Micah's house and spend the night there; but in 18^{3} it is when they are *near* the house of Micah (עם בית מ') that they happen to recognize the voice of the youthful Levite, and this causes them to *turn aside* thither (ויסורו שם), *i.e.* arrests them on their journey, and turns them out of the way. Clearly, then, 18^{2b} and 18^{3} are from different sources; and it is interesting to observe that the former is connected with B by the rather curious use of the prep. עד in the phrase 'as far as (lit. *up to*) the house of Micah,' exactly as in 17^{8}, 18^{13b}; and the latter with A by its reference to 'the youth, the Levite'; cf. $17^{7.11b.12a\beta}$, 18^{15}.

The dialogue in $18^{3b\text{-}6}$ may be suspected of containing elements from both narratives. In *v.*^{3b} the final question 'and what is thy business here?' is perhaps redundant after the question preceding. If, as there is no reason to doubt, the first two questions connect with *v.*^{3a}, and are addressed to the youthful Levite, they belong to A. The last question may then be assigned to B, from which, in continuation, *vv.*$^{4\text{-}6}$ seem to be drawn: notice in *v.*^{4} the reference to the agreement under which the Levite was hired to become priest, which recalls $17^{10.13}$ (the phrase היה לכהן is common to $17^{10.13}$, 18^{4b}); and the reference in *v.*^{6a} to 'the priest,' whereas in A the regular phrase is 'the youth, the Levite.'

In the description of Laish and its inhabitants in 18[7], the words 'dwelling in security after the manner of the Ṣidonians' are marked as alien to the preceding by the use of the fem. יושבת, which cannot refer to העם 'the people,' but must presuppose a reference in its own source to העיר 'the city' (fem.). It is also clear that the phrase 'dwelling in security' is superfluous by the side of 'quiet and secure' which follows. This latter phrase (שקט ובטח) refers naturally to 'the people' (העם masc.) of the early part of the verse; cf. על עם שקט ובטח 'unto a people quiet and secure,' *v.*[27]—a passage which, as we shall see, belongs to B. The remaining statements in the verse appear to belong to the same narrative; cf. *vv.*[10b.28aα]. We may thus assign the whole of *v.*[7] to B, except the intrusive passage 'dwelling . . . Ṣidonians,' which is presumably derived from A.

18[8-10] presents something of a problem. Most likely 'to Ṣorʿah, etc,' in *v.*[8] belongs to a different source from 'unto their brethren.' The question 'What news have ye?' in *v.*[8b] seems to demand as answer, not the exhortation of *v.*[9aα], but the statement of fact 'We have seen the land, etc.,' *v.*[9aβb]. The proper continuation of *v.*[9aα] seems to be found in *v.*[10aα], which gives a reason for the hortatory form in which it is couched; but *v.*[10aβ], 'for God hath given it, etc.,' which connects most lamely on to *v.*[10aα], is admirably fitted as the continuation of *v.*[9b], 'be not slothful to go to enter in to possess the land.' On removal of this statement, *v.*[10b], 'a place, etc.,' falls naturally into apposition with 'the land is broad,' which, no doubt, it immediately followed in the original source. This division of sources yields us two narratives, each of which is practically complete in itself; as we may see by placing them side by side.

A

[8] And they came unto their brethren, and their brethren said to them, 'What news have ye?' [9] [And they said,] 'We have seen the land, and, behold, it is very good: and will ye be still? be not slothful to go in to possess the land, [10] for God hath given it into your hand.'

B

[8] [And they came] to Ṣorʿah and Eshta'ol, [9] and said, 'Arise! and let us go up against Laish, for [10] when ye come [thither] ye shall come unto a people secure, and the land is broad—a place where there is no lack of anything that is in the earth.'

Our decision as to the sources is based upon the parallelism of the one narrative with *v.*[27a], which undoubtedly belongs to B.

18[11-13] read as a single narrative; and this is marked as B by the recurrence of the phrase 'and they came as far as (עד) the house of Micah,' as in 17[8b], 18[2b]. At the end of *v.*[12] the words 'behold, etc.,' which define more precisely the position of Maḥaneh-Dan in relation to Ḳiriath-jeʿarim, are probably a gloss.

In 18 [14-19] we have a combination of two accounts of the theft from Micah's sanctuary. These seem naturally to divide themselves as follows :—

A

[14] Then answered the five men that went to spy out the land, and said unto their brethren, 'Do ye know that there is in these houses a graven image? Now therefore consider what ye will do.' [15] And they turned aside thither, and came unto the house of the youth the Levite, and asked him of his welfare. [16] And the six hundred men girt with their weapons of war were standing at the entrance of the gate : [17a] and the five men that went to spy out the land went up ; they went in thither, they took the graven image.

B

[17b] And while the priest was standing at the entrance of the gate, with the six hundred men that were girt with the weapons of war, [18] these others went into the house of Micah, and took the Ephod and Teraphim. And the priest said unto them, 'What do ye?' [19] And they said to him, 'Hold thy peace, lay thy hand upon thy mouth, and go with us, and be to *us* a father and a priest : is it better for thee to be a priest to the house of one man, or to be priest to a tribe and to a clan in Israel?'

Here we notice that *v.*[14a] and *v.*[17a] are connected by the phrase 'to spy out the land' (לְרַגֵּל אֶת־הָאָרֶץ), which also occurs in *v.*[2a], belonging apparently to the A narrative. Other marks of this narrative are 'their brethren' *v.*[14], as in *v.*[8] ; 'they turned aside thither' *v.*[15], as in *v.*[3b] ; 'the youth the Levite' *v.*[15], as in *v.*[3a] ; cf. 17 [7a.11b.12aβ]. The characteristic marks of B are 'the priest' *vv.*[17b.18], as in *v.*[6a] ; 'and be to *us* a father and a priest' *v.*[19], as in 17 [10].

Further, it is not unnatural to assume that in *v.*[17] the first object mentioned, viz. הפסל 'the graven image,' is original, and that the others are redactors' additions ; whereas, in the curious phrase of *v.*[18] את פסל האפוד, which as it stands can only mean 'the graven image of the Ephod,' it is probable that פסל has been carelessly inserted by the redactor, and that the original narrator wrote ויקחו את האפוד ואת התרפים. This conclusion, which has been adopted in the distribution of sources given above, thus apportions a description of the theft to each of the two narratives.

Besides the conflate allusions to the *sacra* in these verses and in *v.*[14], we have assigned to the redactor 'Laish' in the curious expression 'the land Laish' in *v.*[14] (Laish of *vv.*[7.27.29] is a *city* and not a land ; and, had the name been assigned to the surrounding district, the phrase would have been ארץ ליש 'the land *of* Laish.' In A the spies explore 'the land' unnamed—cf. *vv.*$^{9a\beta b.17a}$; the city Laish belongs to B); 'the house of Micah' *v.*^{15a}, explicative (from the redactor's point of view) of 'the house of the youth, the Levite'; 'that were of the children of Dan' *v.*^{16b}—awkward in position and redundant.

On the removal of these redactional additions, the whole remaining text can be made, as we have seen, to fall into two narratives which read connectedly; yet there are difficulties in the apportionment of *vv.*$^{16.17}$ which appear to be insuperable. Closely parallel as the two narratives doubtless were, it is scarcely credible that the phrase 'six hundred . . . weapons of war' occurred in that form in *each* (*vv.*$^{16a.17b\beta}$); nor, again, that the phrase 'standing at the entrance of the gate' is common to both, referring in the one (*v.*^{16a}) to the six hundred, and in the other (*v.*$^{17b\alpha}$) to the priest. In *v.*^{17a} the asyndeton באו שמה לקחו 'they went in thither, they took, etc.,' is extraordinarily harsh in the Heb., and can scarcely be original; while in *v.*^{17b} the construction והכהן נצב . . . ושש וג׳ 'and the priest was standing . . . with (lit. *and*) the six hundred, etc.,' though it is possible to justify it syntactically (cf. *note ad loc.*), yet imparts to the sentence an unnatural appearance.

We must conclude, therefore, that these two verses have undergone such an amount of alteration—probably owing to textual corruption and the introduction of marginal glosses—that it is impossible to ascertain their original form.*

18$^{20-29}$ shows no trace of the combination of two narratives. It is clearly the direct continuation of *v.*^{19}, which, as we have seen, belongs to B. Notice, as a mark of this narrative, the repeated reference to 'the priest,' *vv.*$^{20.24.27}$. Redactional additions are—the introduction of 'and the graven image' in *v.*^{20a}; the topographical note in *v.*$^{28a\beta}$; and, probably, *v.*^{29} from 'after the name of Dan' to the end. The final statement, *v.*^{29b}, is framed precisely in the form of Gen. 28^{19b}.

The two verses 18$^{30.31}$ have occasioned considerable discussion. Clearly, they cannot be the work of a single writer; since, while *v.*^{30}, according to 𝔐, speaks of the worship of the graven image as existing at Dan 'unto the day of the captivity of the land'—*i.e.*, we must sup-

* It is possible, of course, by cutting out portions of *vv.*^{16,17} as marginal doublets, to reduce the narrative of the theft to a single account, which is then to be assigned to the source B. Such a measure is suggested by 𝔊^{B}, in which *vv.*$^{17.18}$ run as follows:—*καὶ ἀνέβησαν οἱ πέντε ἄνδρες οἱ πορευθέντες κατασκέψασθαι τὴν γῆν, καὶ εἰσῆλθον ἐκεῖ εἰς οἶκον Μειχαια, καὶ ὁ ἱερεὺς ἑστώς· καὶ ἔλαβον τὸ γλυπτὸν καὶ τὸ εφωδ καὶ τὸ θεραφειν καὶ τὸ χωνευτόν. καὶ εἶπεν πρὸς αὐτοὺς ὁ ἱερεύς, κτλ.* On the basis of this it is open to conjecture that B's account may have run ויעלו חמשת האנשים ויבאו בית מיכה והכהן נצב שמה ויקחו את האפוד ואת התרפים ויאמר אליהם הכהן וג׳. Such a process of selection and rejection is, however, too arbitrary to be accepted as a *conclusion*. 𝔊^{L} offers a single account by omission of *vv.*$^{17b.18a}$; but this may be due to homœoteleuton *καὶ τὸ χωνευτόν*—cf. 𝔊^{A} which offers the full text of 𝔐.

pose, until B.C. 734, when Tiglath-Pileser IV. overran Northern Israel and deported the inhabitants (2 Kgs. 15 [29]; cf. Rost, *Keilschrifttexte Tiglat-Pilesers*, pp. 78 ff; Rogers, *CP.* pp. 320 f.), *v.*[31] refers it simply to the period during which the house of God was at Shiloh—*i.e.* down to the capture of the Ark by the Philistines and the death of ʿEli, as related in 1 Sam. 4; after which we hear no more of the sanctuary of Shiloh, and are probably justified in inferring that it had suffered destruction (cf. Jer. 7 [12.14], 26 [6.9], Ps. 78 [60 ff.]). Mo. refers *v.*[31] to the narrative which we distinguish as A, and supposes that *v.*[30] belongs to the other narrative, B, 'the graven image' having been substituted by an editor for 'the Ephod,' and the reference to the captivity of the land being also a late alteration (cf. *SBOT.*). If, however, 'the Ephod' had originally been mentioned, it would hardly have been cut out of the narrative; the redactional practice in regard to the *sacra* being that of conflation, and not substitution.

The probable explanation of the origin of the duplication in the two verses is suggested by Kimchi's conjecture that 'the captivity of the land' refers to the capture of the Ark and its sequel, upon the basis of which Houbigant substitutes הָאָרוֹן 'the Ark' for הָאָרֶץ 'the land.' 'All the time that the house of God was in Shiloh' has been glossed by the explanation 'up to the day when the Ark went into captivity,' with reference to the narrative of 1 Sam. 4: cf., for the use of גלה 'go into captivity' in this connexion, 1 Sam. 4 [21.22], 'glory hath gone captive from Israel.'* If this is so, it is further probable that *v.*[31a] is a marginal gloss on *v.*[30], offering the variant וישימו 'set up' for ויקימו 'reared up,' and explaining הפסל as the image made by Micah. The mention of the name of the priest—'Jonathan, the son of Gershom, the son of Moses'—is undoubtedly ancient, and must emanate from one of the old narratives—presumably from the narrative to which 'the graven image' of *v.*[30a] belongs, *i.e.* A; but it is difficult to suppose that a fact of so much interest (the grandson of *Moses*) originally found mention at the close of the narrative for the first time. We should expect the Levite's name to have been mentioned at the point at which he is first introduced; and very possibly a trace of it may survive in the final words of *ch.* 17 [7] (cf. *note ad loc.*).

We may then regard *v.*[30] down to 'Danites' and *v.*[31b] as belonging to the narrative A.

Assuming the existence of a double strand of narrative in the story of Micah to be proved, the presumption is that the two narratives were derived, like other double narratives in Judg., from J and E respectively: yet, owing to the lack of phrases which might guide us

* Kimchi compares Ps. 78 [61],

'And He delivered into captivity (לשבי) His strength,
And His glory into the hand of the adversary.'

in assigning either narrative to one or other of these sources, it is difficult or impossible to pass any decisive verdict. The only really characteristic phrase in either narrative seems to be רִגֵּל 'to spy out,' which occurs in $18^{2.14.17}$—passages which we have assigned to our narrative A. This phrase is characteristic of E in the Hexateuch; cf. Gen. $42^{9.11.14.16.30.31.34}$, Josh. 2^{1}, $6^{22.23}$, to which we may perhaps add Num. 21^{32} (E ?). The verb is only found in J in Josh. 7^{2}. It occurs again in Deut. 1^{24}, Josh. 6^{25} (R^{JE}), 14^{7} (R^{D}). Another point which favours the assigning of this narrative to E is the fact that the description of the circumstances which led to the making of the idol in 17^{2-4} is almost certainly intended to cast contempt and ridicule upon it: cf. *notes ad loc.* A similar motive dominates E's narrative of the theft of Laban's Teraphim in Gen. 31; cf. *vv.*$^{34.35}$, where Rachel conceals the idols from her father by sitting upon them. E's opposition to idolatry is well-marked: cf. the references to the putting away of 'strange gods' in Gen. 35^{2-4}, Josh. 24^{14-25}, 1 Sam. $7^{3.4}$.

As an indication that our narrative B is derived from J, we may notice the way in which Ṣorʿah and Eshta'ol figure in this narrative as the home of the Danite clans in $18^{2.8.11}$, as in the Samson-narrative, 13^{25}, 16^{31}. The phrasing of 18^{11} ממשפחת הדני מצרעה ומאשתאל is closely similar to 13^{2a} איש אחד מצרעה ממשפחת הדני.

If the foregoing analysis is approximately correct, the story of Micah and the Danites presents a combination of two ancient narratives from J and E which were, in all essentials, strikingly similar. The whole complexion of the story, in both traditions, is naïve and archaic. With the exception of E's account of the origin of the graven image in 17^{2-4}, there is nothing in either narrative which suggests disapproval of Micah's proceedings in establishing a private sanctuary for the practice of an idolatrous form of Yahweh-cultus; and this fact, together with the picture of the wandering Levite seeking a livelihood as best he could, and of the movements of the Danites in search of a new home in the north when (as stated in *ch.* 1^{34} J; cf. *note*) the pressure of alien foes rendered their earlier home too constricted for them, bears upon its face the unmistakeable stamp of historical truth, unmodified by the thought of a later age. The story, then, may take rank with the history of Abimelech, *ch.* 9, as one of the most ancient and valuable historical sources which we possess dealing with the conditions of life in Canaʿan during the period of the Judges.

If, as there seems to be no reason to doubt, the tradition which makes the Levite a grandson of Moses is historical, and if, again, the reference means that he was Moses' grandson in the literal sense, and not simply a more remote descendant ('son of Gershom' being used in the wider sense of *descendant*), then the narrative must obviously relate to events which took place very early in the period covered by the Book of Judges. That this is so is favoured by the allusion to the tribe of Dan in the Song of Deborah, where it seems to be pictured as settled in its northern home in security, and so wrapped up in seafaring interests as to ignore the call to united tribal action issued by Deborah: cf. *ch.* 5[17] *note.* The Danites of Ṣorʿah and Eshta'ol, as they appear in the story of Samson, were probably a small remnant left behind in the ancient home after the migration of the main body of the tribe had taken place (cf. p. 339).

17. 1. E Now there was a man of the hill-country of Ephraim, whose name was Micayᵉhu. 2. And he said to his mother, 'The eleven hundred sheḳels of silver which were taken from

17. 1. *Micayᵉhu.* Heb. מִיכָיְהוּ here and in *v.*[4]. The form, of which מִיכָה Micah is an abbreviation, was perhaps originally used throughout the E narrative. Another form of the name is מִיכָיָה, which occurs in Jer. 26[18] *Kt.* with reference to the prophet מִיכָה.

2-4. The text of these verses in 𝔐 is clearly disarranged; the disarrangement being as old as the Versions. In *v.*[2a] the words spoken by the mother have fallen out (וגם אמרת באזני can only mean 'and didst also say in mine ears,' אמר being regularly followed by the words spoken.* R.V. 'and didst also speak it in mine ears' is an illegitimate rendering: had this sense been intended, we should have expected דִּבַּרְתְּ for אָמַרְתְּ). In *v.*[3a] Micayᵉhu returns the money to his mother; in *v.*[3bβ] she declares her intention of returning it to him; and in *v.*[4a] he returns it to her once more in order that she may hand it over to the silversmith. Bu. was the first to observe that the words of *v.*[3bβ] 'and now I will restore it to thee' must be part of Micah's speech in *v.*[2a]. He places *vv.*[3bβ.4a] after *v.*[2a], and excises *v.*[3a] as a repetition of *v.*[4a] (in *Comm.* excising also the two words ותאמר אמו in *v.*[4b]). The reconstruction proposed by Mo. seems to be superior to this, and has been adopted above. Mo. holds that the missing words of the mother's adjuration in *v.*[2a]—which Bu. supposes to have been suppressed owing to the terrible character of the curse (but cf. *note* on 'didst take an oath')—are the words of *v.*[3bα], which have been misplaced in the general dislocation of the text, and are there introduced by the gloss ותאמר אמו. He agrees with Bu. in placing *v.*[3bβ] after *v.*[2a], and in regarding *v.*[3a] as a repetition of *v.*[4a]; but he leaves *v.*[4a] in the position

* Ex. 19[25] J וירד משה אל העם ויאמר אלהם is a very curious exception; and it seems probable that the words spoken by Moses have disappeared in the piecing together of the sources. In Gen. 4[8] J ויאמר קין אל הבל אחיו, the words spoken by Cain, which are missing in 𝔐, are found in the Versions.

thee, concerning which thou didst take an oath, and also didst say in mine ears, ⟨3ba. "I do surely consecrate the silver to

in which it stands in 𝔐, the fact that, by the removal of *v.*3bα to *v.*2a, the whole of *v.*3 is accounted for, rendering the position of *v.*4a before *v.*4b highly suitable.

2. *concerning which thou didst, etc.* Lit. 'and thou didst, etc.' The Personal Pronoun of the 2nd fem. sing. preserves the more primitive form, *Kt.* אַתִּי, which occurs elsewhere sporadically in O.T., and seems to be specially characteristic of the North Palestinian (Ephraimitic) dialect. Cf. *NHTK.* p. 208.

didst take an oath. Heb. אָלִית. The oath was the solemn promise to devote the silver to Yahweh's service. Such an oath brought a curse upon the person who violated it, whether this were the maker of the oath, or any one else who misappropriated the consecrated thing. It was, no doubt, the fear of this curse which caused Micah to confess to the theft and to make restitution; and very possibly his mother may have suspected his guilt when she made the adjuration in his hearing. The verb *'ālā* invariably means 'to take an oath' before God (1 Kgs. 8 31 = 2 Chr. 6 22, Hos. 4 2, 10 4; Hiph'îl, 'cause to take such an oath,' 1 Sam. 14 24, 1 Kgs. 8 31 = 2 Chr. 6 22 †), and *does not* mean 'utter a curse' (R.V. *text*, Bu.*), *i.e.* 'curse the thief' (Mo. *Comm.*,‡ Cooke). Had such a sense been intended, it would have been expressed by another verb (*ḳillēl* or *'ārar*). The subst. *'ālā*, which means 'oath' before Yahweh, may be used in the sense 'curse'; but only of a curse which results *from the violation of such an oath* (different therefore from *ḳelālā*, which is used *e.g.* of the curse of Jotham, *ch.* 9 57, and of Shime'i's cursing David, 1 Kgs. 2 8).

I do surely consecrate. Heb. הַקְדֵּשׁ הִקְדַּשְׁתִּי. The Perfect appears to be used in accordance with the idiom noted by Driver, *Tenses*, § 10, 'to describe the immediate past, being generally best translated by the present.' As the words pass her lips, she *has effected* the consecration. Cf. Gen. 14 22, 'lift up (הֲרִמֹתִי) my hand to heaven'; 1 Sam. 17 10, 'I reproach (חֵרַפְתִּי) the armies of Israel this day.' It is of course possible to render as an Aorist, 'I did surely consecrate,' *i.e.* in time past, prior to the theft; but it is more likely that the idea

* Bu. so far misunderstands the meaning of the verb as to suggest that the form may originally have carried an Accusative suffix אֲלִיתִיו 'didst curse *him*' (!)

‡ In *SBOT.* Mo. brings out the correct sense by rendering 'didst make a solemn declaration'; though this is not so forcible as 'didst take an oath,' since it does not so clearly imply that a penalty was attached to its violation.

Yahweh from my hand ⌜alone⌝, to make a graven image R^P and a molten image"⟩—E behold, the silver is with me; it was I that took it; ⟨$3^{b\beta}$. and now I will restore it to thee.'⟩ And his mother said, 'Blessed of Yahweh be my son!' 3. [] 4. So he

of making the silver sacred to Yahweh occurred to her owing to its loss. If it was not found, *she* was under no further obligation, whereas the thief (as noticed above) would bring himself under a curse.

from my hand alone. Reading לְבַדִּי in place of 𝔐 לִבְנִי with $𝔊^{AL}$ $𝔖^h$, $𝔏^L$, Mo., La. Mo. seems rightly to explain the point of the restriction implied by the words:—'No one else can fulfil the vow of consecration, and, by having an image made, lift the taboo from the rest of the silver.' In the phrase יָדִי לְבַדִּי, the speaker says lit. 'the hand of me, in my separateness'—an idiom which is exactly paralleled by Ps. 71[16] צִדְקָתְךָ לְבַדֶּךָ 'thy righteousness alone.' Bu.'s stricture that 'my hand alone' should be יָדִי לְבַדָּהּ is therefore unwarranted.

𝔐 לבני means 'for my son,' *i.e. on his behalf*, in order that he may benefit by the piety of the action. Assuming לבני to be a corruption of לבדי, the reading can only have arisen subsequently to the dislocation of the text by which the mother's words appeared to be spoken *after* Micah's confession of the theft. The dedication is made in expiation of his guilt.

a graven image and a molten image. Etymologically *pěsel* denotes an idol *carved* or *hewn* out of wood or stone, while *maššēkhā* denotes one which is *cast* of metal in a mould. In spite of its etymology, however, *pěsel* may also denote a cast-metal idol (probably sometimes an idol with a core of wood or base metal overlaid with precious metal), as is proved by such passages as Isa. 40[19], 44[10] (where it is connected with the verb *nāsakh* 'to cast'), Jer. 10[14], 51[17] (connected with *ṣōrēph* 'smelter,' the term rendered 'silversmith' in *v.*[4] of our narrative). As has been shown above (p. 409), the original E narrative seems to have mentioned a single idol only, termed *pěsel*, which was *cast* by the *ṣōrēph* out of the silver; but a later hand, taking *pěsel* etymologically as a *graven* image, added *û-maššēkhā* on the ground that the context demanded mention of a *cast* or *molten* idol.

with me. *I.e.* 'in my possession'—an idiomatic usage of the prep. 'with'; cf. cases cited by BDB. *s.v.* את, 3a.

it was I, etc. Heb. אני לקחתיו. Emphasis is expressed by the use of the separate Personal Pronoun before the verb.

Blessed of Yahweh, etc. The mother's blessing neutralizes the curse which would have resulted from misappropriation of the consecrated silver.

restored the silver to his mother. Then his mother took two hundred sheḳels of silver, and gave them to the silversmith, and he made thereof a graven image $^{R^P}$ and a molten image: ^{E} and it was in the house of Micayᵉhu. 5. J And the man Micah had a sanctuary; and he made an Ephod and Teraphim, and

4. *two hundred sheḳels.* We are not told what became of the remaining nine hundred sheḳels. Kimchi supposes that the two hundred sheḳels were merely the payment made to the silversmith for making the idol out of the rest of the silver; while Ros., Stu., Ber., etc., assume that the nine hundred sheḳels were devoted to the building and furnishing of the sanctuary. Mo. thinks that the woman was under no obligation to devote the whole of the silver to Yahweh—'The intention of the dedication (*v.* ³) was not to devote the whole of the treasure to the making of an image, but to compel the thief to restore it by putting the whole under a taboo until she herself had made, from this silver, an image of Yahweh.' This view is accepted by Bu., La. There is, however, much to be said for the view first put forward by Auberlen (*Studien und Kritiken*, 1860, p. 548), and adopted by Kue., that, after the woman had got back the silver through the expedient of consecrating it to Yahweh, her avarice caused her to seek to fulfil the vow by devoting merely an insignificant portion of it, and keeping back the major part. Cf. the parallel offered by the action of Ananias and Sapphira, Acts 5. Both mother and son are thus represented in an odious light; and it is wholly in the manner of the E narrator to make his point allusively (cf. Gen. 31 ³⁴·³⁵), and not to labour it in a heavy-handed manner.

5. *a sanctuary.* Heb. בית אלהים 'a house of God (*or* gods).' Whether this is to be pictured as a small shrine within, or attached to, Micah's own house (cf. the parallel narrative in *v.*⁴ᵇᵝ), or as a separate building, is not clear.

an Ephod. Cf. the full discussion in *note* on *ch.* 8 ²⁷. Reference to the present passage occurs on pp. 240, 242.

Teraphim. The nature of the object, or objects, denoted by this term is highly obscure. That some kind of idol is intended appears from Gen. 31 ³⁰·³² E, where Laban accuses Jacob of having stolen his 'gods' (*'ĕlōhîm*); and that this was an image in human form seems to be clear from 1 Sam. 19 ¹³ᶠᶠ·, where Michal is related to have placed the Teraphim in David's bed in order to simulate him, and thus to facilitate his escape from Saul's emissaries. If the Teraphim of this passage was a complete human figure, we must infer that it was life-size; but the life-sized image of a human head or bust might have served Michal's purpose almost equally well. Laban's Teraphim, which Rachel hid by placing them under a camel's saddle and sitting upon them (Gen. 31 ³⁴ E), must, if they were complete human figures, have been much smaller. Like the plural *'ĕlōhîm*, the plural Tera-

installed one of his sons, and he became his priest. 6. R[P] In

phim may denote one image (1 Sam. *loc. cit.*) or more than one (Gen. *loc. cit.*; cf. the plural suffixes עליהם . . . ותשמם in *v.*[34]).

It is clear that Teraphim were employed as oracle-givers. In Hos. 3[4], as in our narrative, they are mentioned together with the oracular Ephod; and in 1 Sam. 15[23], Zech. 10[2], Ezek. 21[21.22], 𝔓[26.27] with the form of divination called *ḳésem*, *i.e.*, as we know from the passage in Ezek. and the use of the root in Ar., a method of casting lots by shaking headless arrows out of a quiver. It is possible that the association of Teraphim with familiar spirits and wizards in 2 Kgs. 23[24] may connect them with the practice of necromancy. The view that they were a form of household-god is based upon their occurrence as the property of private individuals (Laban, Micah, David); and many scholars suppose that their cult was connected with ancestor-worship: cf. Schwally, *Das Leben nach dem Tode*, p. 36; Stade, *GVI.*[2] i. p. 467; Nowack, *Hebr. Archäologie*, ii. p. 23. Very possibly they were identical with the *'ĕlōhîm* mentioned in the Book of the Covenant, Ex. 21[6], 22[8.9], on which cf. *Footnote*, p. 330.*

The derivation of the word *t[e]rāphîm* is obscure. A plausible suggestion connects it with *r[e]phā'îm* 'ghosts' or 'shades' of the dead. If this is so, the root of both is probably to be seen in Bab. *rabû* or *rapû*, which is used of the *sinking* of the heavenly bodies into the Underworld: cf. the use of Heb. רפה in this sense in *ch.* 19[9]. *T[e]rāphîm*, then, like *r[e]phā'îm*, will denote, not the *weak* or *flaccid ones* (as the latter term is commonly explained), but *those who have sunk down to* or *disappeared* in the Underworld: cf. the use of the Iphte'al of *rabû* in iv.[2] R. 30, No. 2, Obv. 24, 25, (*ilu*) *Šamaš irtabî* ŠU *ana irṣitim mîtûti*, 'The Sun-god sinketh, the Sun-god sinketh, into the Land of the Dead.'‡ So Ball, *Proc. Brit. Acad.*, vii. p. 16.

installed. The Heb. phrase *millē yadh*, lit. 'filled the hand of,' is the technical expression for installation in the priestly office: cf. (besides *v.*[19]) Ex. 28[41], 29[9.29.33.35], Lev. 8[33] (all P), Lev. 16[32], 21[10]

* The curious explanation of Teraphim which is found in the Jerusalem 𝔗 and in Pirḳê d[e] Rabbi Eli'ezer (early ninth century A.D.), identifying the object with the head of a sacrificed first-born son, pickled in salt and oil, upon the tongue of which was laid a charm written upon a thin plate of gold, and which was then hung upon the wall, and worshipped and consulted as an oracle-giver (cf. references in Buxtorf, *Lexicon Chald. Talm. et Rabbin.*, *s.v.* תרפים), closely corresponds with the description of the rites of the pseudo-Ṣābians of Ḫarrân, as known to us at the period of the Mohammedan expansion (cf. discussion and authorities cited in Chwolson, *Die Ssabier*, ii. pp. 19 ff., 150 ff., 388 ff.), and the two cannot be independent: but whether the Ṣābian rites were of remote antiquity, and, if so, whether they had any connexion with the Teraphim-cult, is wholly unknown to us.

‡ Here ŠU=*šanîtu*='repetition' (Br. 10840), indicating that the preceding words are to be repeated, as in the Sumerian text of this bilingual fragment.

those days there was no king in Israel: every man was used to do that which was right in his own eyes.

7. E Now there was a youth J from Bethleḥem of Judah, E of the clan of Judah, and he was a Levite, and he sojourned there. 8. J And the man departed from the city, R^{JE} from Bethleḥem of Judah, J to sojourn where he might chance: and he came to the hill-country of Ephraim, as far as the house of Micah, in

(both H), Num. 3 [3] P, 1 Kgs. 13 [33], 1 Chr. 29 [5], 2 Chr. 13 [9], 29 [31], and metaphorically of the consecration of an altar, Ezek. 43 [26] †. The expression is usually supposed to refer to the ceremony of filling the hands of the person to be consecrated with the choice portions of the sacrifice for a waive-offering: cf. Ex. 29 [22-25], Lev. 8 [25-28] (both P). These portions are called *millû'îm* in Ex. 29 [34], Lev. 8 [28].

In Bab. and Assyr. inscriptions, however, the same phrase *umalli ḳâta* is used more generally in the sense of *entrusting authority to* any one, usually with some one of the gods as subject. Thus, *e.g.* it is said of Adadnirari IV. *ša (ilu) Ašur malkut lâ šanân umallû ḳâtuššu* 'whose hand (the god) Ašur filled with an unrivalled kingdom' (*KB.* i. pp. 188, 190): cf. Muss-Arnolt, *Dict.* i. p. 542, where other examples are cited.

6. *In those days, etc.* On this statement as the work of the latest redactor, R^P, cf. p. 410. The statement is no doubt called forth here to explain the (from the late priestly standpoint) grave irregularity of the appointment of a non-Levitical person to exercise priestly functions.

7. *Bethleḥem of Judah.* The modern Bêt-Laḥm, five miles south of Jerusalem. The definition 'of Judah' is perhaps intended to distinguish the city from the northern Bethleḥem of Zebulun, on which cf. *ch.* 12 [8] *note.*

of the clan of Judah. The difficulty raised by this statement that the Levite was a Judaean by birth is discussed in *Addit. note*, p. 436.

and he sojourned there. Heb. וְהוּא גָר־שָׁם. The statement implies that he was enjoying the rights of protection extended to an alien *gēr* or sojourner by the clan with which he dwelt. Cf. the parallel narrative in *v.*[8] לָגוּר בַּאֲשֶׁר יִמְצָא. Considering, however, that in the present passage the words גר שם contain the identical letters of the name גֵּרְשֹׁם Gershom (cf. the explanation which is offered of the meaning of the name in Ex. 2 [22] J), and also that the mention of the Levite's name at the end of the narrative (*ch.* 18 [30]) and not at the beginning is very strange, it is possible that והוא גר שם may be a relic of an original וּשְׁמוֹ יְהוֹנָתָן בֶּן־גֵּרְשֹׁם 'and his name was Jonathan, the son of Gershom.' Cf. *Addenda*, p. xx.

order to accomplish his errand. 9. And Micah said to him, 'Whence comest thou?' And he said unto him, 'I am a Levite from Bethleḥem of Judah; and I am going to sojourn where I may chance.' 10. And Micah said to him, 'Abide with me, and be to me a father and a priest, and *I* will give thee ten

8. *in order to accomplish his errand.* Heb. לַעֲשׂוֹת דַּרְכּוֹ, lit. 'to make (*or* do) his way.' Cf. Isa. 58^{13} מֵעֲשׂוֹת דְּרָכֶיךָ 'not doing thy ways' (*i.e.* 'thy wonted *pursuits*'—less specific, but yet parallel). Heb. *dérekh*, which is frequently used in the sense of *journey* (cf. cases cited by BDB. *s.v.* דֶּרֶךְ 2), here seems to be used of *the object of the journey*, just as it is in *ch.* $18^{5.6}$ (noted by Mo.) and, more generally, in Deut. 28^{29}, Josh. 1^{8}, 1 Sam. 18^{14}, *al.* The point of the statement is, of course, not that the Levite came to Micah's house with the specific expectation of finding work there and nowhere else, but that up to arriving at that point he had not as yet accomplished the object of his journey, and so had it in view. The rendering here adopted is favoured by Mo. (*Comm.*), Ehr.

R.V. renders 'as he journeyed,' and so Mo. (*SBOT.*) 'in the course of his journey,' and this explanation is generally adopted: but it is opposed (if not precluded) by the facts that such a use of an Infin. with ל appears to be unparalleled,* and that the phrase 'make a journey,' though natural enough in English, is not found elsewhere in Heb.

10. *a father.* For the title as a term of respect, cf. BDB. *s.v.* אב, 8.

The 𝔐 addition at the end of the verse, וַיֵּלֶךְ הַלֵּוִי, is clearly a corrupt duplication of וַיּוֹאֶל הַלֵּוִי at the commencement of *v.*^{11} (so most moderns); being marked as such by the repeated הלוי, and

* No. objects (against Mo., *Comm.*) to the explanation which we have adopted, and renders (in accordance with R.V., etc.) 'auf seine Reise,' asserting that לעשות is a gerundial usage of the Infin. with ל, and should fall among the cases cited in G-K. § 114 *o*. In the very miscellaneous list of cases embodied in this section, the uses of the Infin. with ל may be classified as follows:—*Purpose* ('in order to'), Lev. 8^{15}, 1 Sam. 20^{36}, Ps. 63^{3}, 101^{8}, $104^{14 f.}$, Prov. 2^{8}; *Reference* or *closer definition* ('as regards' or 'through'), Gen. 3^{22}, 18^{19}, $34^{7.15}$, Num. 14^{36}, 1 Sam, 12^{17}, 14^{33}, 19^{5}, 2 Sam. 3^{10}, 1 Kgs. $2^{3 f.}$, 14^{8}, Jer. $44^{7 f.}$, Ps. 78^{18}, 103^{20}, 111^{6}, Prov. 8^{34}, Neh. 13^{18}; *Consequence* ('so as to'), Ex. 23^{2}, Lev. $5^{4.22.26}$, Prov. 18^{5}. If, however, לעשות דרכו really means 'in making his journey,' such a usage of ל is *circumstantial*, and cannot be brought under any of the preceding categories. Such a rendering makes לעשות the equivalent of כעשות or בעשות (or, more properly, of כעשותו or בעשותו).

shekels of silver a year, and a suit of apparel, and thy living.' [] 11. And the Levite consented to dwell with the man; E and the youth became to him like one of his sons. 12. And Micah installed the Levite, and the youth became his priest, J and was in the house of Micah. 13. Then said Micah, 'Now I know that Yahweh will do me good, seeing that the Levite hath become my priest.'

18. 1. R^P In those days there was no king in Israel; J and in those days the tribe of the Danites were seeking them an inheritance to dwell in; R^P for there had not fallen unto them unto that day ⟨a land⟩ for an inheritance among the tribes of Israel. 2. J And the children of Dan sent from their clan five

---

by the unsuitability of the verb to the context. The words could only mean 'and the Levite *went*,' *i.e.* 'departed' (cf. Gen. 18 [33], 34 [17], 1 Sam. 14 [3], 15 [27], *al.*). R.V. 'went *in*' (*sc.* to Micah's house) would require וַיָּבֹא at least. The words are omitted by 𝔙.

11. *consented.* On the usage of the Heb. verb *hô'îl*, cf. ch. 1 [27], *note* on 'persisted.'

13. *Now I know, etc.* A Levite as priest is regarded as highly desirable, but not as vitally necessary.

18. 1. *In those days . . . Israel.* Mo. refers R^P's statement here to the close of the preceding part of the narrative, in reference to the (from the later point of view) ritual irregularities which are there related. His view is that 'Jerome erroneously joined the words to the following: "In diebus illis non erat rex in Israel, et tribus Dan quaerebat possessionem sibi, etc."; and was naturally followed in the division of the chapters which was introduced in the Latin Bible in the thirteenth century, and from it into the printed Hebrew Bible.' This conclusion is adopted by No., La., Cooke. It may be observed, however, that, while the full form of the comment concludes a narrative-section in 17 [6] and 21 [25], the shorter form (as in this passage) *opens* the narrative of *ch.* 19. It is not clear why the statement should not be intended to explain the independent and lawless action of the Danites as related in *ch.* 18.

for there had not fallen, etc. The subject of the verb is missing in 𝔥. We must supply אֶרֶץ 'a land' with Stu.: for the constr. נפלה ארץ בנחלה cf. Num. 34 [2], Josh. 13 [6.7]. 𝔊 ὅτι οὐκ ἐνέπεσεν αὐτῇ . . . κληρονομία possibly presupposes a text in which נחלה stood as subject in place of 𝔥 בנחלה.

men E from their whole number, men of valour, J from Ṣorʿah, and from Eshtaʾol, E to spy out the land and to explore it; J and they said unto them, 'Go, explore the land': and they came to the hill-country of Ephraim, as far as the house of Micah, and spent the night there. 3. E When they were by the house of Micah, they recognized the voice of the youth, the Levite: and they turned aside thither, and said to him, 'Who brought thee hither? and what doest thou in this place? J and what is thy business here?' 4. And he said unto them, 'Thus and thus hath Micah done for me, and he hath hired me, and I am become his priest.' 5. And they said to him, 'Prithee enquire

2. *from their whole number. I.e.* representatives of the whole clan (its several branches). Heb. *ḳᵉṣôthām* means lit. 'their *extremities*'—a 'condensed term for what is included within extremities = the whole' (BDB. *s.v.* קצה). The idiom is well elucidated by Num. 22 [41], 'and he saw from thence *the uttermost part of* the people' (קְצֵה הָעָם), *i.e.* by implied inclusion, *the whole of them.* Cf. *NHTK.* on 1 Kgs. 12 [31].

from Ṣorʿah and from Eshtaʾol. Cf. *notes* on 13 [1.25].

to spy out. Heb. *riggēl* is a denominative from *réghel* 'foot,' like Lat. *vestigare* from *vestigium.* On the usage of the verb as characteristic of E cf. p. 416.

3. *When they were by . . . they recognized.* Heb. המה עם בית מיכה והמה הכירו, lit. '*They* were by the house of Micah, and *they* recognized.' The great emphasis upon the Personal Pronoun in each clause throws the two clauses into vivid antithesis, the object being to emphasize the circumstances in which the fact narrated in the second clause took place. This usage is very idiomatic: cf. Driver, *Tenses*, §§ 168, 169.

by the house. Heb. עם בית, lit. '*with* the house,' *i.e. close to* it. For this idiomatic use of the preposition, cf. *ch.* 19 [11] ('*near* Jebus'), Gen. 35 [4], Josh. 7 [2], 2 Sam. 20 [8], 1 Kgs. 1 [9], *al.*

they recognized the voice. The view put forward by Stu. that Heb. *ḳôl*, 'voice,' here means *dialect*, by which the Danites recognized the Levite as a Judaean and not an Ephraimite, is most improbable. The obvious meaning is that they happened to have known him personally before, when he was living in Judah. Cf. for the closeness of local association between the tribes of Dan and Judah, *ch.* 15 [9 ff].

and what is thy business here? Heb. ומה לך פה, lit. 'and what to thee here?'

5. *Enquire of God.* Cf. *note* on *ch.* 1 [1]. We note the fact that, while the Danites' request is 'Enquire of *'ĕlōhîm*,' the response (*v.* [6])

of God, that we may know whether our journey on which we are going shall be prosperous.' 6. And the priest said to them, 'Go in peace: before Yahweh is your journey whereon ye go.'

is 'Before *Yahweh* is your journey, etc.' Here, though the ordinarily unquestioned conclusion is that *'ĕlōhîm* denotes '*God*,' and is synonymous with 'Yahweh,' the possibility presents itself that the two terms, as they stand, may embody a distinction with a difference. The reference of *'ĕlōhîm* may be to the *Teraphim*, regarded as the *medium* rather than the source of the divine response: cf. the use of *hā-'ĕlōhîm* in Ex. 21 [6], 22 [8.9] (noted on p. 330), and Micah's reference to 'my gods,' *v.* [24] (cf. Gen. 31 [30.32] E), as well as *Bêth-'ĕlōhîm*, *ch.* 17 [5], if this means properly 'house of *gods*.' If this be so, the force of the prep. ב may very possibly be '*by*' or '*through*': cf. Num. 27 [21] P, 'He (Joshua') shall stand before Ele'azar the priest, who *shall enquire* for him *by* the judgment of the Urim before Yahweh' (ושאל לו במשפט האורים לפני יהוה); Ezek. 21 [21] (𝔐 [26]), 'He (the king of Babylon) *enquired through* the Teraphim' (שאל בתרפים; here it is of course possible to render 'he enquired *of* the Teraphim'); 1 Sam. 28 [8], where Saul says to the witch of 'Endor, 'Prithee divine for me *through* the familiar spirit' (קסומי נא לי באוב), and, with reference to the same incident, 1 Chr. 10 [13], 'and also, for that he (Saul) *enquired through* the familiar spirit' (וגם לשאול באוב).* Upon this explanation, the Danites say, 'Enquire *through 'ĕlōhîm*' (or, vocalizing בָּאֱלֹהִים '*through the 'ĕlōhîm*'), and the Teraphim, when thus interrogated, returns the answer, 'Before Yahweh is your journey whereon ye go.' Even with retention of the ordinary sense of *šā'al bᵉ*, 'enquire *of*,' the primary meaning may be, 'Enquire of *the oracle*'—a sense which likewise implies that *'ĕlōhîm* is not identical with Yahweh, but simply voices His attitude towards the project of the Danites.

A distinction in phraseology, identical with that of our passage, is drawn in *ch.* 20 [18], 'They enquired of (*or* through) *'ĕlōhîm* . . . and *Yahweh* said'; cf. also 1 Sam. 14 [37], 2 Sam. 16 [23].

our journey. I.e. the *object* of it, '*our errand*': cf. *note* on *ch.* 17 [8].

6. *before Yahweh.* Heb. *nōkhaḥ*, rendered 'before,' means lit. 'in front of' or 'opposite.' So Mo., 'under the eye of Yahweh.'

* Here, whatever be the precise meaning of *'ôbh*, rendered 'familiar spirit' (on which cf. *NHTK.* p. 354; Driver, *Deuteronomy, ICC.*, p. 226; T. W. Davies in *EB.* 1120 f.), it is clear that the enquiry is made *through* and not *of* the *'ôbh*. The response comes from the spirit of Samuel, and the *'ôbh* acts merely as intermediary.

7. So the five men went, and came to Laish, and saw the people that were therein, E dwelling in security, after the manner of the Ṣidonians, J quiet and secure, and there was no ⌜want of any⌝-

7. *Laish*. Heb. לַיִשׁ means 'lion.' In Josh. 19 [47] J the name is given as לֶשֶׁם Leshem—a variant form which ought probably (as suggested by Wellh., *De gentibus et familiis Judaeis*, p. 37) to be vocalized לֵשָׁם, *i.e.*, לֵישָׁם *Lêshām*, the same name as לַיִשׁ with formative termination: cf. עֵיטָם *'Eṭām* from עַיִט *'ayiṭ* 'bird of prey' (so Gray, *Heb. Proper Names*, p. 93).

Eusebius and Jerome locate Laish or Dan four Roman miles from Paneas (the modern Bânyâs) on the way to Tyre (*OS*. 114 [26], 249 [32]), and state that it is here that the Jordan breaks forth (*OS*. 136 [11], 275 [33]). The site intended is no doubt the modern Tell el-Ḳâḍy, an oblong mound, from the western side of which there issues a copious stream which forms one of the sources of the Jordan.* Jos. (*BJ*. IV. i. 1) knows this site as Daphne, and states that its springs, beneath the temple of the golden bull, supply water to the little Jordan, which flows into the great Jordan. This identification is accepted by Rob. (*BR*.[3] iii. pp. 390 ff.) and most modern writers. The Ar. name Ḳâḍy, which like Heb. Dan means 'judge,' may possibly offer a point of connexion. Smith (*HG*. pp. 473, 480) prefers to find the site of Laish-Dan at Bânyâs,‡ on the ground that the meadows and springs of the upper Jordan could not be held against an enemy without also holding Bânyâs and its castle; but, as Cheyne not unjustly remarks (*EB*. 997), 'From Judg. 18 we do not gather that Laish was a place of exceptional natural strength; its inhabitants were a peaceful folk, who trusted not in their fortress but in their remoteness from troublesome people like the Danites.'

dwelling. On the fem. form יוֹשֶׁבֶת, as implying a fem. antecedent הָעִיר 'the city,' in the source from which the extract is derived, cf. p. 412.

in security. *I.e.* without apprehension of danger from outside. Heb. לָבֶטַח.

and there was no want . . . earth. Reading וְאֵין מַחְסוֹר כָּל־דָּבָר אֲשֶׁר בָּאָרֶץ as in *v*.[10], with Ber., Bu., Mo. (*SBOT*.), No., La., Kit.,

* This stream has not been indicated in Map I.

‡ Theodoret (on Jer. 4 [15]) and Jerome (on Ezek. 48 [18], and Am. 8 [14]) speak of Paneas as occupying the site of Dan.

Why Smith (p. 473) should say that Bânyâs is 'scarcely an hour *to the north*' of Tell el-Ḳâḍy is not clear. His own maps, like the *SWP. Great Map*, locate it nearly due east.

thing ⟨that is⟩ in the earth, [] and they were far from the Ṣidonians, and had no dealings with ⌜Aram⌝. 8. E And they came unto their brethren J to Ṣor'ah and Eshta'ol: E and their brethren said to them, 'What news ⌜have ye⌝?' 9. J And they

Cooke, Gress., in place of 𝔐 וְאֵין־מַכְלִים דָּבָר בָּאָרֶץ. Here the curious מכלים דבר, which can only be understood as 'one insulting (*or* humiliating) in a matter,' very early caused difficulty, and was glossed by יוֹרֵשׁ עֶצֶר 'one usurping coercive power'* (omitted by 𝔊^A) which has crept into the text of 𝔐. This explanation of the latter phrase as a gloss is simpler and more natural than the view of Bu. (based on 𝔊^L κληρονόμος θησαυροῦ, 𝔙 'magnarumque opum') that it is an integral part of the text, meaning 'possessing *riches*,' *i.e.* either אוֹצָר or עֹשֶׁר of which two readings 𝔐 עצר represents an amalgamation.

far from the Ṣidonians . . . Aram. Lying at the southern mouth of the valley which runs between the Lebanon and Ḥermon ranges, Laish was isolated from Ṣidon by the Lebanon range to the north-west, and from Aram-Damascus ‡ by the Ḥermon range to the north-east. The reading אֲרָם 'Aram,' which is offered by 𝔊^AL, 𝔖^h, 𝔏^L, Σ., is adopted by Bu., La., Kit., Gress., and is undoubtedly superior to 𝔐 אָדָם—'had no dealings with *mankind*.' The reference to Ṣidon requires a more definite antithesis.

8. *What news have ye?* Reading מָה אִתְּכֶם, lit. 'what is with you?' with Wellh. (*Comp.*^{3} p. 365), No., Kit., in place of 𝔐 מָה אַתֶּם which offers an incomplete sentence, 'What ye?' For the use of את '*with*,' cf. 2 Kgs. 3 ^{12}, Jer 27 ^{18}, where the word of Yahweh is said to be *with* a prophet, *i.e.* revealed to him; and the employment of the preposition in the sense '*known to*' in Job 12 ^{3}, 14 ^{5}.

𝔊^B, making the words part of the speech of *the spies*, renders καὶ εἶπον τοῖς ἀδελφοῖς αὐτῶν Τί ὑμεῖς κάθησθε; *i.e.* וַיֹּאמְרוּ לַאֲחֵיהֶם מָה אַתֶּם יֹשְׁבִים. Such an inquiry, however, is redundant by the side of וְאַתֶּם מַחְשִׁים 'and will ye be still?' in *v.*^{9}, apart from the fact that we should expect לָמָּה rather than מָה. 𝔊^AL, though agreeing with

* The subs. עֶצֶר is a ἅπαξ λεγόμενον, but the sense implied appears to be sufficiently guaranteed by the usage of the verb עָצַר.

‡ It seems probable that the narrator is thinking of the kingdom of Damascus rather than of the small Aramaean states in the immediate neighbourhood (Beth-reḥob and Ma'achah) to which Mo. alludes.

said, 'Arise! and let us go up ⌜to Laish⌝: for E we have seen the land, and, behold, it is very good: and will ye be still? be not slothful to go to enter in to possess the land. 10. J When ye come, ye will come unto a people secure, and the land is broad: E for God hath given it into your hand; J a place where there is no want of anything that is in the earth.'

11. Then there set forth from thence of the clan of the Danites, from Ṣorʿah and from Eshtaʾol, six hundred men girt with weapons of war. 12. And they went up, and encamped in

𝔐 in making the words an address *to* the spies, yet, like 𝔊[B], has the reading *κάθησθε*; and Mo. deduces from this the possibility that ישבים may be the corruption of an original מְשִׁיבִים—'What (news) are ye *bringing back*?' Bu.'s suggestions מָה [רְ]אִתֶם 'What have ye seen?' or מַה־[מְּצָ]אתֶם 'What have ye found?' are improbable.

9. *Arise!* The sing. קוּמָה is used as a stereotyped interjection in place of the plur. (which appears in several Codd., probably as a correction). Cf. הָבָה 'Come!'—originally 'Give!' or 'Permit!'—addressed to a plurality of persons, Gen. 11[3.4.7]; לְכָה 'Come!' addressed to a woman, Gen. 19[32]; רְאֵה 'Behold!' addressed to Israel in the plural, Deut. 1[8].

let us go up. On the use of the verb *ʿālā* 'go up,' in the general sense of making a military expedition, cf. *ch.* 1[1] *note.*

to Laish. Reading לַיְשָׁה with No., in place of 𝔐 עֲלֵיהֶם 'against them,' the suffix of which has no antecedent. 𝔊[A] *ἐπ αὐτήν*, *i.e.* עָלֶיהָ, may represent the first stage in the corruption.

It is worthy of notice, however, that there exists a doublet in 𝔊[AL al.], 𝔖[h] (marked by obelus) which may possibly contain the original text. This runs in 𝔊[L] as follows: *εἰσήλθαμεν καὶ ἐμπεριεπατήσαμεν τὴν γῆν ἕως εἰς Λαισα, καὶ εἴδομεν τὸν λαὸν τὸν κατοικοῦντα ἐν αὐτῇ ἐπ' ἐλπίδι κατὰ τὸ σύγκριμα τῶν Σιδωνίων καὶ μακρὰν ἀπέχοντας ἐκ Σιδῶνος, καὶ λόγος οὐκ ἦν αὐτοῖς μετὰ Συρίας· ἀλλὰ ἀνάστητε καὶ ἀναβῶμεν ἐπ' αὐτούς, ὅτι κτλ.* This is accepted as original by La. in the following form: בָּאנוּ וַנִּתְהַלֵּךְ בָּאָרֶץ עַד־לַיִשׁ וַנִּרְאֶה אֶת־הָעָם אֲשֶׁר בְּקִרְבָּהּ יוֹשֵׁב לָבֶטַח כְּמִשְׁפַּט צִידֹנִים וּרְחוֹקִים הֵמָּה מִצִּידֹנִים וְדָבָר אֵין־לָהֶם עִם־אֲרָם קוּמוּ, in place of 𝔐 קוּמָה. This provides us with the necessary antecedent to עֲלֵיהֶם; but the passage is somewhat unnecessarily tautological after *v.*[7], and may have been constructed in imitation of that verse.

Ḳiriath-je'arim, in Judah: wherefore that place was called

12. *Ḳiriath-je'arim.* The name means 'woodland-town.' Eusebius places the city nine (*OS.* 271 [40]) or ten (*OS.* 234 [94]) Roman miles from Jerusalem on the road to Diospolis (Lydda). The site intended has been identified, since Rob. (*BR.*[3] ii. pp. 11 f.), with Ḳuryet el-'Enab ('town of grapes'), or el-Ḳuryeh,* and the position suits the connexion in which Ḳiriath-je'arim is mentioned in Josh. 9[17] among the Gibe'onite cities Gibe'on, Kephirah, and Be'eroth; and also the description of the northern boundary-line of Judah as described in Josh. 15[8ff.] P, where, after running just south of Jerusalem to the hill to the west of the valley of Ḥinnom and north of the vale of Repha'im, it continues in a north-westerly direction to the spring of the waters of Nephtoaḥ (probably Liftâ ‡), Mount 'Ephron (unidentified), and Ḳiriath-je'arim (Ḳuryet el-'Enab), where it takes a turn (ונסב *v.*[10]) south-westward to Mount Se'ir, and passing along the northern shoulder of Mount Je'arim § where Chesalon (Keslâ) is situated, it descends to Beth-shemesh ('Ain-šems) and passes on to Timnah (Tibneh). Cf. also the description of the southern boundary of Benjamin in Josh. 18[14ff.] P.

* The village is often called Abû Ġôš after a celebrated family of bandits which resided there during the earlier half of the nineteenth century.

‡ The interchange between *n* and *l*, as seen in Nephtoaḥ, Liftâ, may be illustrated by Heb. *niškā* and *liškā* 'chamber,' Heb. *nāḥaš* (root of *nāḥāš* 'serpent') and *lāḥaš* 'to hiss,' Bab. *nêšu* and Heb. *láyiš* 'lion,' New Heb. *nāḳaṭ* and Bib. Heb. *lāḳaṭ*, Aram. *neḳaṭ* and *leḳaṭ*, 'to pick up,' Heb. *nāthan* and Aram. *nethan* and *nethal* 'to give,' Heb. *'almānā* and Aram *'armelā* 'widow,' etc. The interchange is not confined to Semitic: thus the English *Lincoln* appears in Northern French as *Nicole*; *level* is from Old French *livel*, which has become *niveau* in modern French; *lilac* comes ultimately from the Persian *lilak*, a variation of *nilak* 'blue'; etc.

If, as seems likely, the *n* in Nephtoaḥ is formative, and the root is *pāthaḥ* 'to open,' in the sense of *an opening in the rock for the exit of water* (cf. the use of the verb in Isa. 41[18], Ps. 105[41]), the disappearance of the final guttural *ḥ* in Liftâ may be illustrated by the fact that both *pāthaḥ* and *pāthā* occur in Heb. in the sense of *opening*. Liftâ possesses 'a large spring and the stones of some very ancient buildings at the E. entrance to the village' (Baedeker, *Palestine*,[3] p. 18).

§ הר שעיר 'the hairy, *i.e. scrubby*, mountain' (cf. Ar. *ša'âr*, 'tangled, *or*, abundant and dense, trees') and הר יערים 'the woodland-mountain' appear respectively to denote the hill on which Sarîs stands to the north of the wâdy el-Ḥamâr, and the hill on which Keslâ stands, south of the same wâdy. Both hills are still covered by scrub and the remains of old woods: cf. *SWP. Great Map*, xvii., and Buhl, *Geogr.* p. 91. Baedeker, *Palestine*,[3] p. 16, in describing the road from Jaffa to Jerusalem in the neighbourhood of Sarîs, says: 'The hills are overgrown with underwood; besides the wild olives the carob-tree is frequently observed.' Similarly, Macmillan's *Guide to Palestine*,[5] p. 15: 'On either side of the road are rocky heights, with olive-trees occupying every point of vantage, and amongst them may be seen many carob-trees, conspicuous by their handsome dark green foliage. There are also several fine oak and terebinth trees.'

Maḥaneh-Dan, unto this day: R^P behold, it is to the west of Ḳiriath-je'arim. 13. J And they passed on thence to the hill-country of Ephraim; and they came as far as the house of Micah. 14. E Then answered the five men that went to spy out the land R^JE Laish, E and said unto their brethren, 'Do ye know

The rival identification (proposed by Henderson and Conder, *SWP. Mem.* iii. pp. 43 ff.) is the ruined site 'Ermâ, on the southern side of the wâdy Ṣarâr about four miles east of 'Ain-Šems. This suits the proximity to Beth-Shemesh, which is suggested by 1 Sam. 6 [20.21],* but is irreconcilable with the description of the boundary of Judah as noticed above,‡ and (as Cheyne points out, *EB.* 2680) is too near Ṣor'ah and Eshta'ol to suit the present narrative.

Maḥaneh-Dan. Cf. *note* on *ch.* 13 [25].

to the west of. Lit. '*behind.*' Cf. the phrase 'behind (*i.e.* to the west of) the wilderness' in Ex. 3 [1] E, and contrast the phrase '*in front of* Ḥebron,' *ch.* 16 [3] *note.*

14. *the land Laish.* On Laish (the *city*) as a gloss inserted by the redactor of the two narratives, cf. p. 413.

Now therefore consider, etc. *Verbum sap.* For the phrase, cf. 1 Sam. 25 [17].

15-18. The two accounts, which are here interwoven, seem to have been further confused by later glossing (cf. p. 414), but the general situation is surely not so obscure as Mo. (who is closely followed by Cooke) makes out. Some difficulty is caused by the repeated reference (*vv.*[16.17]) to 'the entrance of the gate.' The term *šá'ar* 'gate' is never applied to the door of a house; yet it is clear from *vv.*[14.22] that Micah's house was one among a few others forming a small village, certainly not surrounded by a massive wall with a gate. Mo., while rightly remarking, upon *v.*[14], that 'Micah evidently lived in an open village,' yet explains *v.*[16] as meaning that 'the main body [of Danites] halted without the village,' and speaks later on of 'the armed men at the entrance of the village'—an expression

* The statement of Jos. (*Ant.* VI. i. 4) that Ḳiriath-Je'arim was in the neighbourhood of Beth-shemesh is probably based merely upon this narrative.

‡ Leaving out of account the plausible identification of Nephtoaḥ with Liftâ, the mere fact that Ḳiriath-je'arim occupies a position on the boundary-line *between* the valley of Ḥinnom (Josh. 15 [8]) and Chesalon (*v.*[10]) seems absolutely to exclude the site 'Ermâ. How could the line run from Ḥinnom to 'Ermâ (presumably along the upper course of the Wâdy Sarâr), strike north-east to Chesalon (Keslâ) at an acute angle, and then return south-west at a still more acute angle, over the shoulder of the hill on which Chesalon is situated, so as to reach Beth-shemesh? As a matter of fact, we are told in *v.* [10] that, after reaching Ḳiriath-je'arim, the boundary (so far from striking north-eastward) turned *westward* (ימה 'towards the sea') to Mount Se'ir and Chesalon.

that there is in these houses ^{RJE} an Ephod, and Teraphim, ^{E} and a graven image ^{RP} and a molten image? ^{E} Now therefore consider what ye will do.' 15. And they turned aside thither, and came unto the house of the youth the Levite, ^{RJE} the house of Micah, ^{E} and asked him of his welfare. 16. $^{E?+Gl.}$ And ⌈the⌉ six hundred men, girt with their weapons of war, that were of the children of Dan, were standing at the entrance of the gate: 17. and the five men that went to spy out the land went up; they went in thither, they took the graven image, ^{RJE} and the

adopted *verbatim* by Cooke. Neither of these scholars explains what kind of 'entrance' he pictures an unwalled village as possessing; yet it is clear that the phrase 'the entrance of the gate' must postulate a *real gate* *; and the natural inference seems to be that Micah, as a man of some position, had a house surrounded by a courtyard,‡ and that it was at the gate of this courtyard, and not outside the village, that the men at arms were standing whilst their companions slipped inside (cf. La.). If this was so, the difficulty does not seem very great. The Danites might endeavour to distract the priest's attention by parleying at the gate, yet it would still be possible for him to observe the movements of the five spies, and to intervene with his feeble protest as recorded in *v.*[18].

16. *the six hundred men, etc.* We must read הָאִישׁ as in *v.*[17], in place of 𝔐 אִישׁ indefinite.

17. *went up.* The precise significance with which the verb is used is obscure. Ros. and Stu. assume from it that Micah's sanctuary was an *'ăliyyā* or upper chamber on the roof of his house, to which the ascent would have been by an external staircase; but such an inference is precarious. It is not impossible that *'ālā* may be used simply of an aggressive entry, in much the same way as it is frequently employed of making a hostile expedition (cf. *ch.* 1[1] *note*), without implication of an actual *ascent.*

they went in thither, they took, etc. The asyndeton is very harsh in the Heb., and can hardly be the work of the original narrator. Wellh.§ (in Bleek, *Einleitung*[4], p. 198) and Bu. suggest that the two Perfects should be vocalized as Imperatives (בֹּאוּ שָׁמָּה לְקָחוּ), and

* Whether the statement of Ex. 32[26] J that Moses 'stood in the gate of the camp' implies that the camp of Israel was surrounded with a *zarîba* or barricade with an actual gate is not clear; but in any case 'gate' by itself has not the same definiteness as פתח השער, lit. 'opening of the gate,' in our narrative.

‡ Cf. Warren in *DB.* ii. p. 432*a*: 'In the villages there is usually a court attached to the house, in which the cattle, sheep, and goats are penned.'

§ Wellh. retracts this suggestion in *Comp.*[3] p. 366.

Ephod, and the Teraphim, R^P and the molten image. J+Gl. And while the priest was standing at the entrance of the gate, with the six hundred men that were girt with the weapons of war, 18. J these others went into the house of Micah, and took R^{JE} the graven image, J the Ephod, and the Teraphim, R^P and the molten image. J And the priest said unto them, 'What do ye?' 19. And they said to him, 'Hold thy peace, lay thy hand upon thy mouth, and go with us; and be to *us* a father and a priest: is it better for thee to be priest to the house of one man, or to be priest to a tribe and to a clan in Israel?' 20. And the priest's heart was glad, and he took the Ephod, and the Teraphim, R^{JE} and the graven image, J and went in the midst of the people. 21. So they turned and departed, and put the little ones and the cattle and the goods before them. 22. When they were a good way from the house of Micah, the men that were in the houses which were near to Micah's house were called to arms, and followed hard after the children of Dan. 23. And they cried unto the children of Dan. And they turned their faces, and said to Micah, 'What aileth thee, that thou art up in arms?' 24. And he said, 'My gods that I made ye have

that the words originally formed the continuation of the spies' advice in *v.*[14]—'Now, therefore, consider what ye will do: go in thither, take the idol, etc.' This destroys the terse suggestiveness of *v.*[14] as it stands in 𝔐. We might parallel the asyndeton in narrative by *ch.* 20[31] (הנתקו), 20[43] (כתרו . . . הרדיפהו); but here again the originality of the text may be questioned.

And while the priest, etc. Lit. 'And the priest was standing . . . and these went in, etc.' For the construction, cf. Driver, *Tenses*, § 169.

with the six hundred, etc. Lit. '*and* the six hundred.' The construction may be justified as an instance of '*wāw* of association' (cf. BDB. p. 253*a*); yet it is not very natural, and tends to accent our suspicions as to the state of the text.

19. *lay thy hand, etc.* For the expression, cf. Mic. 7[16], Job 21[5], 29[9], 40[4], Prov. 30[32].

21. *the goods.* Heb. כְּבוּדָּה only here; but cf. the usage of the masc. כָּבוֹד in Gen. 31[1], Isa. 10[3], *al.*

22. *when they were, etc.* Lit. '*They* were a good way from . . . and the men that were, etc.'—a circumstantial construction similar to that noticed in *v.*[3].

were called to arms. Cf. *note* on *ch.* 6[34].

23. *art up in arms.* Lit. 'art called to arms' as in *v.*[22]. The

taken away, and the priest, and are departed, and what have I more? and how then say ye unto me, "What aileth thee?"' 25. And the children of Dan said unto him, 'Let not thy voice be heard near us, lest hot-tempered men fall upon you, and thou lose thy life and the life of thy household.' 26. And the children of Dan went their way: and when Micah saw that they were stronger than he, he turned and went back unto his house. 27. And *they* took that which Micah had made, and the priest that had belonged to him, and came unto Laish, unto a people quiet and secure, and smote them at the edge of the sword, and the city they burned with fire. 28. And there was no deliverer, because it was far from Ṣidon, and they had no dealings with ⌜Aram⌝; R^P and it is in the vale which belongeth to Beth-reḥob. J And they built the city, and dwelt therein. 29. And they called the name of the city Dan, R^P after the name of Dan their father: howbeit Laish was the name of the city at the first. 30. E And the children of Dan reared up for themselves the graven image: and Jonathan, the son of Gershom, the son of Mo⌜⌝ses, he and his sons became priests to the tribe of the

passive verb, which seems inappropriate as addressed to Micah who was the *musterer*, of course contemplates the whole company as *mustered*.

25. *hot-tempered men.* Heb. אנשים מרי נפש, lit. 'men bitter of soul,' *i.e.* of *fierce* (or *acrid*, Mo.) *temper*, and so, easily roused. On this use of the adjective *mar*, cf. *footnote*, p. 363.

27. *that which Micah had made.* Heb. את אשר עשה מיכה without expressed antecedent. The reference of course is to the Ephod and Teraphim of the J source; and Mo. is perhaps right in his suggestion that these originally stood in the narrative, but were omitted by the redactor of the two sources in order to make the statement more general (including the graven image).

28. *Aram.* For the emendation, cf. *v.*[7] *note.*

Beth-reḥob. Cf. *note* on Reḥob, *ch.* 1 [31]. 'The vale' (Heb. *hā-'ēmeḳ*) in which the city was situated is the broad plain of el-Buḳâ' between the two Lebanon ranges.

30. *Moses.* 𝔐 מְנַשֶּׁה 'Manasseh,' with *Nûn teluyā* ('suspended') —a rabbinic device intended to spare the reputation of Moses by not stating openly that he was the grandfather of a priest who practised idolatry. The fact that the reference is really to Moses was, however, acknowledged by early Jewish scholars: cf. *e.g.* the words of Rashi: 'Because of the honour of Moses was the *Nûn* written so as to alter

Danites Gl. up to the day when ⌈the Ark⌉ went into captivity. 31. And they set them up the graven image of Micah which he had made, E all the time that the house of God was in Shiloh.

the name. The *Nûn*, however, is suspended to tell thee that it was not Manasseh but Moses.' The name Manasseh was explained as referring, not to the ancestor of the tribe bearing that name, but to the idolatrous king of Judah of the 7th century B.C., on the ground of likeness of character between him and Micah's priest: cf. Kimchi's remarks on *ch.* 17 [7]. Three other cases of a 'suspended' letter occur in the Heb. Bible, viz. Ps. 80 [14], Job 38 [13.15]. In many Heb. MSS. and early editions מנשה is written without *Nûn tᵉlûyā*. Cf., for a full conspectus of Rabbinic discussion on the subject, Ginsburg, *Introduction to the Massoretico-critical edition of the Hebrew Bible*, pp. 334 ff.

'Moses' is the reading of some 𝔊MSS., 𝔏L, 𝔙, and appears in the conflate text of 𝔊MSS., 𝔖h. 'Manasseh' appears in 𝔊BAL, 𝔖P, 𝔗.

the Ark. Reading הָאָרוֹן in place of 𝔐 הָאָרֶץ 'the land.' The grounds upon which this emendation is adopted are explained on p. 415.

31. *all the time . . . in Shiloh.* Shiloh is the modern Sêlûn in the hill-country of Ephraim, some nineteen miles north of Jerusalem and twelve miles south of Shechem. It appears in 1 Sam. 1-4 as the site of 'the House of Yahweh' (1 Sam. 1 [7.24], 3 [15]), which was apparently not a mere tent but a solid structure (called *hêkāl* 'temple' in 1 Sam. 1 [9], 3 [3]) with doors (1 Sam. 3 [15]) and door-post (1 Sam. 1 [9]).* This sanctuary had the custody of the Ark of Yahweh (1 Sam. 3 [3], 4 [3ff.]), having apparently succeeded Bethel in this capacity (cf. *note* on 'unto Bethel,' *ch.* 2 [1]). After the defeat of Israel and the capture of the Ark by the Philistines (1 Sam. 4 [10ff.]) we hear no more of the sanctuary of Shiloh; and though the narrative of 1 Sam. draws a veil over its fate, the assumption that it was destroyed by the Philistines seems to be justified, both from the allusions in Jer. 7 [12.14], 26 [6.9],‡ Ps. 78 [60ff.], and from the fact that the Ark, when restored by the Philistines, did not return thither but remained in private custody at Ḳiriath-jeʿarim (1 Sam. 6 [20.21], 7 [1]) until brought up by David to Jerusalem (2 Sam. 6), and that the principal centre of Yahweh-cultus in Saul's reign was not at Shiloh but at Nob (1 Sam. 21.22).

* The passage in 1 Sam. 2 [22] which refers to the sanctuary as 'the Tent of Meeting' is not found in 𝔊, and is generally regarded by scholars as an interpolation: cf. *NHTS.*[2] *ad loc.*

‡ The view which has been advanced by some scholars that Jer. 7 [12.14], 26 [6.9] does not refer to the destruction of the sanctuary at Shiloh in ʿEli's time, but to a disaster (otherwise unmentioned) which was recent and still fresh in men's minds when Jeremiah wrote, is purely gratuitous. The deep and lasting impression which was made by the tragedy of 1 Sam. 4 is sufficiently illustrated by Ps. 78 [60ff.].

The meaning of the note of time 'all the time that, etc.' is very obscure. We can scarcely be intended to infer a coincidence between the *cessation* of the Dan-cultus and that of the Shiloh-cultus. The view of Ber. that the allusion is to the rough correspondence in time between the supersession of Shiloh by Jerusalem as the principal seat of Yahweh-cultus, and the supersession of Micah's image by Jeroboʿam's costly golden bull and the merging of the particular cultus of the Danites into that of the northern half of Jeroboʿam's kingdom, does not commend itself as at all likely.* More probably the reference is not to the *cessation* of either cultus, but to the fact that the establishment of the sanctuary at Dan was *of the same antiquity as* the establishment of the house of God at Shiloh.

THE ORIGIN OF THE LEVITES

(Cf. *ch.* 17 [7] *note*)

The terms in which the Levite is introduced in the story of Micah raise, in its most acute form, a difficulty with regard to the tribe of Levi which appears, on present evidence, to be almost insuperable. If Levi was, as is generally assumed throughout the O.T., in origin an independent Israelite tribe, possessing full tribal rights (the third son of Le'ah ; Gen. 29 [34] J), how can the Levite of our narrative be spoken of as having clan-connexions with the tribe of Judah (מִמִּשְׁפַּחַת יְהוּדָה) ? The distinction between the Levite's position in Judah and in Ephraim is well marked ; for it is stated that, whereas he belonged to the clan of Judah, he *was sojourning* merely in Ephraim, *i.e.* he was a *gēr* or stranger enjoying certain rights of protection whilst living with a tribe of alien origin to himself : cf. the similar allusion to the Levite of *ch.* 19 [1] (sojourning in the hill-country of Ephraim). Hence it has been supposed by many that the Levites were in origin not members of a separate tribe, but a *priestly caste* marked out by a special ritual training handed down from father to son. This view is thought to gain support from Ex. 4 [14] R^{JE}, where Yahweh, in addressing Moses, speaks of 'thy brother Aaron the Levite.' Driver (*Camb. Bib. ad loc.*) remarks, 'As Moses, equally with Aaron, belonged to the tribe of Levi (Ex. 2 [1]), the term, as applied distinctively to the latter, must denote, not ancestry, but pro-

* Even if we assume the very doubtful conclusion that the establishment of Yahweh's seat at Jerusalem marks the close of the Shiloh-period, there still, according to Biblical chronology (cf. 2 Sam. 5 [5], 1 Kgs. 2 [11], 11 [42]) remains a difference of at least seventy years between David's bringing up of the Ark to Jerusalem and the establishment by Jeroboʿam of the bull-worship at Dan ; or, if we suppose that the Jerusalem-period dates from the completion of the Temple in the seventh year of Solomon, a difference of at least thirty-three years.

fession.' He thinks (citing MacNeile, *West. Comm. ad loc.*) that 'there must have been a period in the history of the "Levites" when the term was "the official title of one who had received the training of a priest, regardless of the tribe of which he was a member by birth."' According to this view the name *Lēwî* is rightly connected in Gen. 29^{34} J with the verb *lāwā* 'to be joined' or 'to attach oneself'; but originally in the sense of those who have attached themselves to distinctively priestly functions, *i.e.*, as we might say, *clerics* as distinct from laymen: cf. the use of the verb in Num. 18$^{2.4}$ P, where they are spoken of as *attached* to Aaron for the service of the Tabernacle (וְיִלָּווּ, וְנִלְווּ), and in Isa. 56^{6} which alludes to the strangers *who are attached* (הַנִּלְוִים) to Yahweh to minister to him. The theory gains greatly in plausibility if we may assume a connexion between *Lēwî* and the term *lawi'u* (fem. *lawi'at*) which, according to Hommel (*AHT.* p. 278), is used in Minaean inscriptions to denote priests and priestesses of the god Wadd.*

The outstanding objection to this theory, which has never been met, lies in the fact that in the (in the main) very early poem ‡ which is known as the 'Blessing of Ja'cob,' Gen. 49, Levi appears as a purely secular tribe, and, together with Sime'on, is censured for some act of aggression and violence which is regarded as having brought a curse upon them resulting in their dispersion among the other tribes (*vv.*$^{5-7}$). The event to which allusion is here made is naturally to be found in the treachery practised by Sime'on and Levi upon the Shechemites, as related in Gen. 34 (J and P combined), which may very well have led to such reprisals as decimated the two Israelite tribes and forced their remnants to seek a new home in other parts of the land. As a matter of fact, we know from Judg. 1$^{3.16.17}$ that, at a somewhat later—but still, very early—period, Sime'on is found seeking a settlement in the Negeb in the midst of Judah, with which tribe it seems ultimately to have become merged (cf. *note* on *ch.* 1^{3}). It is by no means improbable that the remnant of Levi may in like manner have sought a home in this region; and such an hypothesis would sufficiently

* Professor Margoliouth suggests (privately) the comparison of *Lēwî* with Ar. *wely*, the ordinary Mohammedan term for a *saint*—properly one who *is near to* God, *i.e.* in intimate association with Him, from the root *wala* 'to follow after, be near to.' For connexion of *wala* with לוה, cf. Ar. *waṣa*, Heb. צוה, both in Pi'ēl with sense 'to enjoin'; Ar. *waḥa*, Heb. חוה, both 'to declare *or* reveal.'

‡ According to Skinner (*Genesis, ICC.*, pp. 510 f.), 'the Blessing' is a composite production, the earliest portions (on Re'uben, Sime'on and Levi) referring to events in the remote past, and probably composed before the Song of Deborah; those on Issachar, Dan, and Benjamin at any rate earlier than the establishment of the monarchy; while that on Judah presupposes the existence of the Davidic monarchy. The Joseph-section may be, in whole or in part, still later; but this is a very disputed question.

explain the fact that a Levite could be spoken of as 'of the clan of Judah,' much as the clan of Caleb came to be regarded as belonging to the tribe of Judah, though in origin distinct from it (cf. *note* on *ch.* 1 [12]).

In 'the Blessing of Moses,' Deut. 33, belonging probably to the period of the divided monarchy,* Levi is regarded (in contrast to Gen. 49 [5-7]) as entrusted with priestly functions; but still figures none the less as a *tribe*, and on a par in this respect with the other tribes of Israel. There seems no good reason to doubt that there may be truth in the constant Israelite tradition that a tribe originally secular came at a particular period to be invested with such functions, though the tradition as to the circumstances which led to this may very well have fluctuated.‡ The one basic fact probably is that the Levites inherited the privilege *from Moses*, who, according to Ex. 2 [1] E, was himself a member of the tribe, and who, in the only early account which we possess of the Tent of Meeting (Ex. 33 [7-11] E), appears as the sole intermediary between Yahweh and Israel.

What, however, are we to infer as to the relative periods to which these events in the history of the tribe belong? To assume, as some scholars have done, that the Shechem-incident of Gen. 34, though placed by the narrator in Patriarchal times, properly refers to the period of the Judges, is surely very wide of the mark. In the first place, there is a sharp contrast between the antique tone of Gen. 34, in which tribes figure symbolically in the guise of individuals, and the vivid realism of the story of Abimelech in Judg. 9, which, while it also centres round Shechem, is as true to the life as any historical portion of the O.T. Again, while Gen. 34 brings Sime'on and Levi into connexion with Shechem, the Book of Judges has nothing in this connexion to tell us of these tribes, but pictures *Manassite* clans as occupying the district—*i.e.* elements of the Joseph-tribes concerning which tradition is strong that they invaded Cana'an from the east under Joshua' at some period subsequent to the Exodus from Egypt. Sime'on, however, is pictured, at the same period or earlier, as already settled with Judah in the south (Judg. 1 [3.17] J); and a similar inference with regard to Levi may be drawn (as we have seen) from the genuinely old story of Judg. 17, 18, according to which the Levite was a native of Bethleḥem in Judah, but a *gēr* merely in Ephraim. Lastly, the whole tone of Gen. 49 [5-7], which has nothing but a curse for Levi as a predatory secular tribe which, with Sime'on, is regarded

* Cf. the allusion to Judah in *v.* [7], with Driver's note, *ICC. ad loc.*

‡ On the one hand, we have the tradition of Ex. 32 [25ff.] (J and E combined), where the zeal of the Levites on Moses' side as against the bull-worshippers appears as the cause of their selection; on the other hand the allusion of 'the Blessing' in Deut. 33 [8] seems to point to a tradition which related the testing of the fidelity of the tribe at Maššah and Meribah (an explanation of the origin of these names different from that which is given in Ex. 17 [7] JE combined, Num. 20 [13] P). Deut. 10 [8] alludes to the selection of the tribe by Yahweh for the performance of priestly functions without specifying the circumstances.

as a disgrace to its kindred, stands, as we have noticed, in striking antithesis to Deut. $33^{8\text{-}11}$; and as surely as the latter reflects the work and personality of Moses and the priestly privileges conferred by him on his tribe, so does the former point to an age when the name and reputation of Israel's great religious leader lay as yet in the bosom of the future.

If, where all is vague and uncertain, it be possible to bridge the gulf between the secular and sacred tribe of Levi by a structure of which the outlines appear to offer an approximation to reality, we may picture the Joseph-tribes as already settled in Egypt, possibly for a considerable period, while the Le'ah-clans of Sime'on and Levi —which, after expulsion from central Cana'an, have, together with clans of Judah, settled in the far south, in close contact, and on amicable terms, with their North Arabian neighbours—move across the Egyptian frontier in time of drought and famine with that ease with which we gather from Egyptian inscriptions that Semitic Bedawin tribes were admitted even after the fall of the Hyksos and under the restored Theban aristocracy of the Eighteenth and Nineteenth Dynasties.* This would account for the birth of Moses of Levitical parents in Egypt, and the subsequent events through which he escapes from Egypt as a political refugee and settles in Midian,‡ receives a revelation at Sinai, leads the tribes out of Egypt, and conducts them to the scene of the Theophany, which lay probably in the neighbourhood of Ḳadesh-Barnea', south of the Negeb, which seems to

* Cf. the two Egyptian inscriptions given by Breasted, *AR.* iii. §§ 10 ff., 636 ff. The first of these is attached to a mutilated relief depicting officials receiving instruction as to the reception of Asiatic refugees who, in time of distress, petition for a home in the domain of Phara'oh 'after the manner of your fathers' fathers since the beginning.' This, according to the inscription, is granted by Phara'oh. This inscription belongs to the reign of Ḥaremḥeb, the first king of the Nineteenth dynasty; or possibly, as Breasted prefers to think, to one of the later kings of the Eighteenth dynasty under whom Ḥaremḥeb held the position of general. The second inscription, which belongs to the reign of Mineptaḥ of the Nineteenth dynasty (the assumed Phara'oh of the Exodus: cf. *Introd.* p. civ), is a letter from a frontier-official in which he informs his superior that certain Edomite Bedawin have been allowed to pass the frontier and pasture their flocks in the Wâdy Ṭûmîlât close to Pithom, *i.e.* in the district of Goshen.

That Sime'on at any rate joined the Joseph-tribes at a subsequent period is perhaps to be inferred from the tradition embodied in Gen. $42^{24,36}$ E.

‡ The story of Moses' escape to Midian, where he marries the daughter of a Midianite chieftain and settles down for a time, is remarkably paralleled by the Egyptian tale of Sinuhe, who was a political exile in the reign of Sesostris I. of the Twelfth dynasty, some 700 years earlier. Sinuhe escapes from Egypt to a region in or near Cana'an, and is hospitably received by the local sheikh, whose daughter he eventually marries and becomes himself a sheikh of the tribe for some years, after which he returns, like Moses, to Egypt. Cf. Breasted, *AR.* i. §§ 486 ff.; Maspero, *Popular Stories of Ancient Egypt*, pp. 68 ff.; Alan Gardiner, *Notes on the Story of Sinuhe* (translation pp. 168 ff.). The parallel shows how well within the range of historical probability the Biblical story lies.

have formed their headquarters during the wilderness-period (cf. pp. 109 ff.).

Here we find him, according to the oldest tradition (cf. especially Ex. 18 $^{14ff.}$, 33 $^{7-11}$ E) occupying the position of supreme, or rather *sole*, exponent of religion as intermediary between Yahweh and Israel. Nothing, according to this tradition, is said of any participation by Aaron in these priestly functions—still less of his occupying the supreme position in the priesthood. In the only instance, indeed, in which Aaron is brought into connexion with the Tent of Meeting in the old narrative, he goes there with Miriam to receive a sentence of condemnation and rebuke for having ventured to speak against Moses, who is specified as God's servant with whom He is accustomed to speak mouth to mouth (Num. 12 E). In view of these facts, it at once becomes obvious that, in the expression 'thy brother Aaron the Levite' of Ex. 4 ^{14} J, which came under discussion at the beginning of this *note*, either the specification 'the Levite' does *not* distinctively denote priestly profession, or if (as seems more likely) it *does* do so, it must represent *the later point of view*, according to which Aaron and not Moses was the priest *par excellence*, and so is without value as regards any bearing upon the question of the *origin* of the Levites.

It seems not unlikely that, after a period spent in the neighbourhood of Ḳadesh-Barneaʿ (the wilderness-sojourn), while the Joseph-tribes eventually broke off from this centre, and travelled round the land of Edom in order to enter Canaʿan from the east of Jordan, bearing with them the Ark of Yahweh with its priestly (Levitical) caretakers, the main part of the tribe of Levi, which, *ex hypothesi*, had even prior to the Exodus possessed associations with the North Arabian clans (subsequent elements of the tribe of Judah) inhabiting the region south of the Negeb, preferred to throw in its lot with these Judaean clans, and so moved up northward with them at their conquests in the Negeb and the hill-country beyond it, which came later on to be known as the heritage of the tribe of Judah (cf. *Addit. note*, p. 44).

This theory appears satisfactorily to account for the tribal connexion of the Levites with Judah, as found *e.g.* in Judg. 17 $^{7ff.}$, 19 ^{1}. It also offers an explanation of the story of the golden bull in Ex. 32, in which (at any rate in the form of the narrative which has come down to us) Aaron appears in an unfavourable light as the maker of the image, and the Levites in a favourable light as uncompromising adherents to the pure form of Yahweh-worship. The inference lies near to hand that the narrative, in its present form, was intended as a polemic against the bull-worship of the Northern kingdom.* The

* The narrative of Ex. 32 is composite, *vv.* $^{1-6.15-24.35}$ being assigned to E, and *vv.* $^{25-34}$ (in which the Levites figure as champions on Moses' side against the idolatry) to J; while *vv.* $^{9-14}$ exhibit marks of a later hand, and are usually attributed to the redactor R^{JE}. Both J and E (written from the standpoint of the

words, 'These be thy gods, O Israel, which brought thee up out of the land of Egypt' (Ex. 32 [4]) are identically the same as are put into the mouth of Jerobo'am in 1 Kgs. 12 [28], in the account of this king's institution of the bull-worship at Bethel and Dan. As spoken by Jerobo'am, the plural 'gods' naturally refers to the two images of Bethel and Dan: but in the Exodus-narrative it is difficult, if not impossible, to justify the plural as applied to the single image. If, then, at the period at which the story of Ex. 32 took shape, 'Aaron' stands as the representative of the bull-worship of the Northern kingdom, we may infer that 'the sons of Levi' are the priestly families of the kingdom of Judah, who are the champions of a purer form of cultus.* It seems to follow that, while the 'sons of Aaron' were connected with the early sanctuaries of the Joseph-tribes, Bethel, Shiloh, and Nob, the main Levite stock supplied the priestly needs of Judah in the days when this tribe lived in comparative isolation from the central and northern Israelite tribes; ‡ though single Levites might wander northward in search of a livelihood, through exercise of the priestly functions which they were fitted to discharge by birth as well as by training.§

prophetic schools of the two kingdoms) are keenly antipathetic to the bull-worship. It is possible, however, 'that—although Jerobo'am himself appointed non-Levitical priests (1 Kgs. 12 [31])—there may have been among the priests of the calves some who traced their ancestry to Aaron, and claimed him as the founder of the calf-worship in Israel. If this were the case, it would make Aaron's condemnation the more pointed' (Driver, *Camb. Bib. ad loc.*).

* Jerobo'am's appointment of non-Levitical priests to his newly equipped sanctuaries (1 Kgs. 12 [31]) may have been dictated by political motives, owing to the close association of the Levites with the tribe of Judah.

‡ It is worthy of notice that, though Samuel, who was an Ephraimite, held a position at the sanctuary at Shiloh which we might have expected a Levite to fill, he *is nowhere termed a Levite*; and this is surely a very surprising fact upon the assumption that the term 'Levite' denotes official and not tribal status. His example goes to prove that in northern Israel at that period it was not deemed *necessary* that a priestly official should be a Levite by birth, rather than that a man trained for the priesthood, whatever his tribe, *ipso facto* became a Levite by profession.

§ If, as we have assumed, the remnant of the tribe of Levi found in early times a home among the North Arabian (Judaean) clans to the south of the Negeb; and if, again, members of this tribe came to adopt a wandering life in search of a livelihood as priests; is it beyond the range of possibility that some of them may have migrated southward into Arabia, and may thus account for the use of the term *lawi'u* to denote a priest, which we have noticed as occurring in the Minaean inscriptions from el-'Olâ?

19. 1—**21.** 25. *The outrage at Gibeʿah, with its consequences.*

Besides the Commentaries, etc., cited throughout the book, cf. Güdemann, *Tendenz und Abfassungzeit der letzten Capitel des Buches der Richter, Monatschrift für Gesch. u. Wissenschaft d. Judenthums*, xviii. (1869), pp. 357-368; W. Böhme, *Richter c.* 21, *ZATW*. v. (1885), pp. 30-36.

In *ch.* 19 signs of duplication in the narrative are evident in *vv.*$^{1-15}$—most strikingly in the speech of *v.*^{9b}, where repetition of statement is combined with variation in number, the speaker using the plural in one set of clauses and the singular in the other: 'Behold, prithee, the day hath waned toward evening; prithee stay ye the night; and ye shall arise early to-morrow for your journey' (לינו . . . והשכמתם לדרככם); 'Behold the day hath closed in; stay thou the night here, and let thy heart be merry . . . and thou shalt depart to thy home' (לין . . . לבבך . . . והלכת לאהלך). In *vv.*$^{4a.9b}$ the expression 'his father-in-law, the damsel's father,' is inelegantly redundant; and we observe that, while the former designation stands alone in *v.*^{7b}, the latter so stands in *vv.*$^{3b.5b.6b.8}$. The expression 'the damsel's father' (predicating no position of relationship to the husband on the father's part) is suitable to the damsel's position as concubine merely and not a full wife; whereas the term *ḥōthēn* 'father-in-law' seems (at any rate to us) somewhat surprising in such a connexion, and it is reasonable to infer that it may belong to a version of the story in which the girl held the full status of a wife. Possibly a trace of this may be found in the statement of *v.*^{1b}, 'he took to him a wife, a concubine,' where אשה may be derived from one narrative, and פילגש from the other.* Further, the father's offers of hospitality are couched in two different phrases, each of which occurs twice—'Strengthen thine heart,' *vv.*$^{5b.8a\beta}$ (in each case put into the mouth of 'the damsel's father'); 'Let thine heart be merry,' *vv.*$^{6b\beta.9b\alpha}$. We may notice also *v.*^{2b} 'some time, four months'—a double (indefinite *and* definite) note of time (cf. *note ad loc.*); *v.*^{4a}, 'he abode with him three days,' but *v.*^{4b}, 'and they stayed the night there'—*i.e.* apparently, the *first* night; 'they (he) arose early in the morning,' *vv.*$^{5a\beta.8a\alpha}$ (cf. *v.*$^{9b\beta}$), beside 'the man (he) rose up to depart,' *vv.*$^{5a\beta.7a.9a\alpha}$; 'he came over against Jebuṡ,' *v.*$^{10a\beta}$, but 'they were near Jebuṡ,' *v.*$^{11a\alpha}$, as though the proximity to this city were now mentioned for the first time; in *v.*^{12b} the man specifies Gibeʿah as the place at which they will spend the night, but in *v.*^{13} he again speaks (without any intervening response from his lad), and proposes Gibeʿah *or* Ramah (here it is clear that, while the response to *v.*^{11} is contained in *v.*^{12}, *v.*^{13}—alien to this account—is continued by *v.*^{14}, the question 'Gibeʿah or Ramah'?

* This inference is of course precarious. אשה פילגש may be a compound term 'concubine-wife' (or simply 'concubine-woman,' like אשה נביאה 'prophetess-woman, *ch.* 4^{4}): cf. נשים פלגשים 2 Sam. 15^{16}, 20^{3}.

being settled by the sun's disappearance whilst they are 'alongside of' the former city).

On the basis of these facts, we may make (somewhat tentatively) the following distribution. To the main narrative may be assigned *v.*^{1b} (omitting אשה 'wife'); *vv.*$^{2.3}$ (omitting 'four months' in *v.*^{2b}); 'the damsel's father' in *v.*^{4a}; *v.*^{4b}; 'and they arose early in the morning' in *v.*^{5a}; *v.*^{5b} (*except* 'unto his son-in-law'); *v.*^{6} (*except* 'and let thine heart be merry';) *v.*$^{7b\beta}$; *v.*^{8} (*except* 'on the fifth day'); *v.*$^{9a\beta}$; in *v.*^{9b} 'the damsel's father,' and the portions of the speech which are addressed to a plurality of persons (as noted above); *vv.*$^{10b.11.12.15}$. This narrative, which runs almost continuously, seems to bear clear indications that it is derived from J. We may notice the use of לקראת 'to meet' in *v.*^{3b} of going to welcome a guest, as in the J passages Gen. 18^{2}, 19^{1}, 29^{13}; סעד לבך פת לחם 'strengthen thine heart with a morsel of bread,' *v.*^{5} (so *v.*^{8} without פת לחם), which closely resembles Gen. 18^{5} J, ואקחה פת לחם וסעדו לבכם 'and let me take a morsel of bread, and strengthen ye your hearts'; the immediately following ואחר תלכו 'and afterward ye shall depart,' compared with אחר תעברו 'afterward ye shall pass on' which immediately follows in Gen. 18^{5} (cf. also אחר תלך Gen. 24^{55} J); the use of התמהמה 'tarry' or 'delay,' *v.*^{8}, as in Gen. 19^{16}, 43^{10}, Ex. 12^{39}, all J; והשכמתם מחר לדרככם 'and ye shall arise early to-morrow for your journey,' *v.*^{9}, as in Gen. 19^{2} J, והשכמתם והלכתם לדרככם 'and ye shall arise early, and shall depart for your journey.' The phrase of *v.*^{1b} בירכתי הר אפרים 'in the *furthermost parts* (lit. *sides* or *flanks*) of the hill-country of Ephraim' (so also in *v.*^{18}) is most easily explicable from a Judaean point of view.

This J narrative is continued by the remainder of the chapter, which reads as a single continuous narrative. Points which connect *vv.*$^{16-21}$ with J are as follows: וישא עיניו וירא 'and he lifted up his eyes and saw,' *v.*^{17}, as in Gen. 13^{10}, 18^{2}, 24^{63}, 33^{1}, 43^{29}, Josh. 5^{13}, all J, as against Gen. 22$^{4.13}$ E; אנה תלך 'whither goest thou?' *v.*^{17}, as in Gen. 16^{8}, 32^{17} (𝔐 ^{18}) J; מאין תבוא 'whence comest thou?' as in *ch.* 17^{9} J, cf. Gen. 29^{4}, 42^{7} J (Josh. 9^{8} doubtful, but assigned to J by Holzinger); גם תבן גם מספוא 'both straw and provender,' *v.*^{19}, exactly as in Gen. 24^{25} J, whilst the two substantives are similarly coupled in Gen. 24^{32} J, and the remaining occurrences of מספוא 'provender' (Gen. 42^{27}, 43^{24}) are confined to this document; use of גם . . . גם 'both . . . and,' *v.*^{19}, cf. CH.^{J} No. 11; use of יש 'there is,' *v.*^{19} twice, cf. CH.^{J} No. 84; אין מחסור כל דבר 'there is no want of anything,' *v.*^{19}, as in *ch.* 18$^{7.10}$ J; רק ברחוב אל תלן 'only do not spend the night in the market-place,' *v.*^{20}, cf. Gen. 19^{2} J, ברחוב נלין 'we will spend the night in the market-place'; וירחצו רגליהם 'and they washed their feet,' *v.*^{21}, cf. Gen. 18^{4}, 19^{2}, 24^{32}, 43^{24} (all J).* The account of the outrage, *vv.*$^{22ff.}$, is parallel phrase by phrase with Gen. $19^{4ff.}$ J in so remarkable a manner as to compel the conclusion that one narrative must have been deliberately modelled on the other. The action taken by the Levite after his return home is strikingly paralleled by Saul's action when summoning the tribes to the assistance of Jabesh of Gile'ad, 1 Sam. 11 J. The closeness of verbal coincidence is exhibited in the comparison which follows :—

Judg. 19.^{22} They were making merry, when behold the men of the
Gen. 19.^{4} They had not yet lain down, when the men of the

Judg. 19. city, base fellows, surrounded the house (נסבו את הבית)
Gen. 19. city, the men of Sodom, surrounded the house (נסבו על הבית)

Judg. 19. . . .
Gen. 19. . . .^{5} 'Where are the men who came unto thee to-night?

Judg. 19. 'Bring forth the man who came unto thine house, that we
Gen. 19. 'Bring them forth unto us that we

Judg. 19. may know him.' ^{23a} And the man, the owner of the house,
Gen. 19. may know them.' ^{6} And Lot

Judg. 19. went forth unto them, and said unto them, 'Nay, my
Gen. 19. went forth unto them, . . .^{7} and said, 'Nay, my

Judg. 19. brethren, do not act wickedly, I pray you. ^{24} Behold,
Gen. 19. brethren, do not, I pray you, act wickedly. ^{8} Behold, now,

Judg. 19. my daughter, who is a virgin, and his
Gen. 19. I have two daughters who have not known a man ;

Judg. 19. concubine ; let me, pray, bring them forth and humble
Gen. 19. let me, pray, bring them forth unto you,

Judg. 19. ye them, and do to them that which is good in
Gen. 19. and do to them according to that which is good in

Judg. 19. your sight ; but to this man ye shall not do a thing of this
Gen. 19. your sight ; only to these men do not do a thing

Judg. 19. wantonness, ^{23b} inasmuch as this man hath entered into my
Gen. 19. forasmuch as they have entered into the

Judg. 19. house.' . . .
Gen. 19. shadow of my roof.' . . .

* One characteristic E phrase, אמתך 'thy handmaid,' is to be noted in *v.*^{19}. J's ordinary expression in this sense is שפחה.

Judg. 19.^{29} And he entered into his house, and took a knife, and took
I Sam. 11.^{7} And he took a yoke of oxen,

Judg. 19. hold of his concubine, and cut her up (וינתחה), limb by limb,
I Sam. 11. and cut them up (וינתחהו),

Judg. 19. into twelve pieces, and sent her throughout all the border of
I Sam. 11. and sent them throughout all the border of

Judg. 19. Israel. 20^{1} And all the children of Israel came out
I Sam. 11. Israel. . . . And they came out

Judg. 19. (*or* were called to arms) . . . like one man.
I Sam. 11. (*or* were called to arms) like one man.

The second narrative in *vv.* $^{1-15}$ is fragmentary, and seems to have been used merely as a supplement. It may be traced in the use of אשה 'wife,' *v.*^{1b}; 'four months,' *v.*^{2b}; *v.*^{4a} (*except* 'the damsel's father'); *v.*^{5a} (*except* 'and they arose early in the morning'); 'and let thine heart be merry' in *v.*$^{6b\beta}$; *v.*$^{7ab\alpha}$; *v.*$^{9a\alpha}$, and the parts of the speech in *v.*^{9b} in which the man is addressed in the singular (as noted above); *vv.*$^{10a.13.14}$. Since the other narrative has been identified as J, it is natural to infer that the present narrative may be derived from E, though there occur no characteristic E phrases to substantiate this view. It may be noted, however, that Hosea', in alluding (9^{9}, 10^{9}) to 'the days of Gibe'ah' as marking the depth of depravity to which Israel was capable of sinking, appears to have this narrative in mind,* and also to assume that so allusive a reference will be sufficient to recall it to those for whom he is writing; and, if this is so, we must conclude that the story formed part of the historical tradition of the Northern Kingdom, whether in written (E) or oral form.

Redactional links, supplied by R^{JE}, are probably to be seen in the words 'unto his son-in-law,' *v.*^{5}, an explicative addition to J suggested by חתנו 'his father-in-law' of E; 'on the fifth day,' *v.*^{8}, with back-reference to *v.*^{5a}. Lastly, *v.*^{1a} is obviously from the same hand as 17^{6}, 18$^{1a\beta}$, 21^{25}, viz. R^{P}.

Passing on to *chs.* 20, 21, we are confronted by a far more intricate problem. In *ch.* 19 the story, as we have it from J and (so far as we can judge from its fragmentary remains) in the parallel source which we have assigned to E, bears at least a superficial appearance of

* This is the only natural explanation of the allusion: cf. Cheyne's note (*Camb. Bib. ad loc.*): 'The prophet's language is correct from his own point of view. True, Israel as a people took summary vengeance on the Benjaminites for the outrage of Gibe'ah. But the seed of wickedness remained, and developed into evil practices worthy only of the Gibe'ah of old.' The interpretation of 𝕿 on Hos. 10^{9} finds reference to the election of Saul as king; and this explanation has been revived by Wellh., *Comp.*^{3} p. 233, *n*^{1}; Stade, *GVI.* i. p. 580; Nowack, *Handkommentar, ad loc.*; but it cannot be regarded as at all plausible. Cf. the discussion by Mo., *Comm.* pp. 405 f.

antiquity, and might, for ought that tells to the contrary, be assumed to embody a genuinely historical tradition. In *chs.* 20, 21, the whole atmosphere of the story is different. The tribes of Israel, when in receipt of the Levite's gruesome summons, assemble 'as one man' (20$^{1.8.11}$) and form themselves into *hā-'ēdhā* 'the congregation' (20^{1}, 21$^{10.13.16}$)—a term which, in this connotation, is elsewhere characteristic of P in the Hexateuch.* Their assembling is expressed by the verb *niḳhal* (20^{1}), *i.e.* 'assembled themselves as a *ḳāhāl*,' this substantive being the term employed in 21$^{5.8}$, and in the phrase 'the assembly of the people of God,' 20^{2}—expressions which are nearly confined to D and P.

Moreover, from this point onwards, a large part of the detail of the story is manifestly unhistorical. Considering that the old narratives of Judg. as a whole exhibit the tribes of Israel as for the most part disunited and struggling to maintain their bare existence against alien races, fighting each for its own hand, and only at the best attaining a very limited measure of cohesion when it was a matter of life or death in face of a common foe, it is impossible to entertain the credibility of the picture of a judicially constituted assembly of all Israel, mustered at short notice to sit in judgment upon Gibe'ah for an outrage (however heinous) committed against a single individual. Such an appeal as that made by the Levite may no doubt have aroused a large measure of support (cf. 1 Sam. 11 J), and resulted in reprisals upon the guilty city, if not upon the tribe of Benjamin to which it belonged, which may, as related, have rallied to its support; but this can surely not have happened in the form and on the scale pictured in the narrative as it now stands. The huge numbers of the narrative are certainly unhistorical. 25,000 Benjaminites + 700 men of Gibe'ah are mustered to oppose 400,000 men of Israel (20$^{15.17}$). On the first day's battle the Benjaminites slay 22,000 Israelites, apparently without themselves suffering a single casualty (20$^{19-21}$). On the second day the Israelites lose 18,000, while the Benjaminites come off with the same immunity as before (20$^{24.25}$). On the third day as the result of Israel's ruse the tables are turned, and the Benjaminites lose 25,100 men (20^{35}; cf. *v.*$^{44-46}$), the whole tribe being exterminated with the exception of a bare 600 (20^{47}). Contrast with these figures the statement of the Song of Deborah, which puts the whole fighting force of Israel at 40,000 (5^{8b}). Again, if the fact that

* העדה 'the congregation' occurs 77 times in Ex., Lev., Num., and Josh.; עדה without def. art. once; עדת (בני) ישראל 'the congregation of (the children of) Israel' 37 times; עדת יהוה 'the congregation of Yahweh' 4 times. All these occurrences belong to P, the expression being wholly absent from J, E, and D. Outside the Hexateuch the only occurrences of העדה are 1 Kgs. 8^{5} R^P=2 Chr. 5^{6}, 1 Kgs. 12^{20}, and the four instances in Judg. 20, 21 noticed above. These calculations are based on Davidson's *Hebrew Concordance* (with addition of עדת בני יש׳ Num. 13^{26}, omitted by Davidson).

Saul, a member of the tribe of Benjamin, was elected the first king of Israel, does not necessarily cast doubt upon the story of the disgrace of the tribe, and its reduction to the verge of extinction at some date not very long previous,* yet the account of the total destruction of the inhabitants of Jabesh of Gileʿad is at any rate rendered somewhat improbable by the fact that the city appears as a fortified city of some strength in the narrative of 1 Sam. 11. Indeed, the conjecture lies near to hand that the whole story of Judg. 19-21 may have taken its rise out of antipathy to the memory of Saul—his native city Gibeʿah, his tribe Benjamin, and the men of Jabesh of Gileʿad who owed him a debt of gratitude (1 Sam. 11) which they were not forgetful to repay to the best of their ability (1 Sam. 31 [11ff.]) being in turn held up to execration by the narrator.‡

Close examination of *chs.* 20, 21 reveals the presence of a mass of discrepancies, repetitions, and dislocations which sufficiently proves that the narrative in its present form must have resulted from a very complicated process of combination and later working over. The following points may be noted :—

According to 20 [1] the Israelites gather *unto Yahweh* at *Miṣpah.* Miṣpah may be assumed therefore to have been the site of an important sanctuary : cf. 20 [3a], 21 [1.5b.8a]. In spite of this, however, they have, according to 20 [18.26], 21 [2], to go up to *Bethel* to consult the oracle of Yahweh.

20 [3a], the mention of the fact that the Benjaminites heard of the mustering of the Israelites, interrupts the sequence of the narrative in the midst of which it stands, and does not receive its natural continuation until *v.*[14].

The gathering of all the men of Israel against Gibeʿah in 20 [11] refers, as it stands, not to mobilization (already mentioned in *v.*[1]), but to the beginning of active hostilities. We should expect the negotiations

* On the assumption of the substantially historical character of the narrative of Judg. 19-21, it is of course possible that the events narrated may have occurred early in the period of the Judges, and so perhaps some two hundred years before the days of Saul. Saul speaks of the tribe of Benjamin as 'the smallest of the tribes of Israel' (1 Sam. 9 [21] J), and the smallness of the tribe might be explained by the circumstances narrated in Judg. 20 [35.47ff.]; but it should be remarked that the fact of the smallness of Benjamin is inherent in the whole tradition that he was Jacob's youngest son. The narrative of Judg. 20 does *not* suggest that the tribe was *originally* a small one, but rather the contrary; 25,700 fighting men as against 400,000 men mustered from the rest of Israel pictures Benjamin as not markedly smaller than the average of the other tribes. It is possible therefore (in view of the suggestion put forward above that the story is coloured by antipathy to Saul and his tribe) that, so far from the smallness of the tribe in subsequent times being due to the disaster which it suffered in the days of the Judges, the story of the disaster may be a spiteful invention suggested by its smallness in the narrator's day (in face of the genuinely old tradition which implies that the tribe was small from the first, and not that it *became* small after having previously been normal in size).

‡ Cf. Güdemann, *op. cit.*; Wellh., *Comp.*[3] p. 232 f.; Kue. *Ond.* § 20 [9].

of *vv.*[12.13] to have *preceded*, and not to have followed, so extreme a measure, and to have taken place whilst the Israelites were still assembled at Miṣpah, and prior to the investment of Gibeʿah.

The consulting of the oracle at Bethel, 20 [18], as to which of the tribes shall begin the attack, results in the specification of Judah; but there is no allusion to this in what follows. It is Israel as a whole, and not Judah simply, which offers battle to Benjamin and meets with disaster on the first day (*vv.*[19-21]); and there is no mention of the separate action of other tribes on the second and third days, nor, on the other hand, of a change in the strategy resulting in the combination of all the tribes as a *new* measure.

20 [22], where the Israelites, in spite of the first day's disaster, take courage and again join battle, should follow and not precede *v.*[23] in which they are overwhelmed by the disaster (of the first day) and consult the oracle as to whether they are to resume hostilities on the second day (*v.*[24]).

20 [27a] must originally have been directly continued by לאמר 'saying' of *v.*[28], and cannot, as at present, have been separated from it by the lengthy and awkward parenthesis.

20 [35] relates the smiting of 25,100 Benjaminites, *i.e.* the whole of their force except the 600 survivors of *v.*[47], and in *v.*[36a] it is stated that the remnant of the Benjaminites realized that they were defeated; yet in *v.*[36b] we find the Israelites still giving ground to Benjamin with the object of drawing them off from Gibeʿah, and it is not till *v.*[41] that the Israelites, at the appointed signal, face about and confront the Benjaminites.

The account of the smiting of the 25,100 Benjaminites (20 [35]) is repeated at a later stage in the narrative, *vv.*[44-46] (here in a round number 25,000).

20 [45aα] —the flight of the survivors to the crag of Rimmon—is repeated in *v.*[47a], obviously as a resumption of the narrative after the insertion of an interpolation. The purpose of this interpolation is plain, viz., to square the 18,000 of *v.*[44a] with the 25,100 of *v.*[35a] by the addition of 5000 + 2000 in *v.*[45], resulting in the total given in *v.*[46].

The remorse of 'the people' at the practical extinction of one tribe from Israel having been described with some detail in 21 [2-4], it is at least strange that it should be mentioned again, as though it were a fresh piece of information, in *v.*[6].

The inquiry of 21 [5] anticipates that of *v.*[8]. While *v.*[8] is clearly in place, offering itself as it does as a possible solution of the question put forward in *v.* [7], 'How shall we do for wives for them?' etc., *v.*[5] as clearly comes too early in the narrative.

21 [9] is redundant after *v.*[8b]; and though it might be just possible to refer both to the same narrator by explaining that *v.*[8b] states that as a matter of fact Jabesh of Gileʿad was unrepresented in the army, and that this was then *found out* by the numbering of *v.*[9], yet this

repetition is most inelegant, and it is clear that, for the purpose of the narrative, either *v.*[8b] or *v.*[9] by itself is amply sufficient.

The question of 21[17], 'How shall a remnant be left to Benjamin, etc.,' is strange if steps had already been taken to provide wives for the major part of the surviving Benjaminites; and the inference at once suggests itself that the sparing of the maidens of Jabesh and the rape of the maidens of Shiloh may have belonged to two different accounts of the manner in which wives were obtained for the Benjaminites, and that these accounts have been harmonized in *vv.*[13-16] by the explanation that the former were not sufficient, and therefore some further source of supply had to be found.

In spite of this complication, there exists a clue, the following of which seems to lead us far in the process of unravelling the different sources of the narrative. The Israelites are described by three distinct phrases. Thus we have (A) 'the children of Israel,' answering to 'the children of Benjamin,' both terms naturally construed with a plural verb; (B) 'the men of Israel,' a collective term (איש ישראל), corresponding to 'Benjamin' as a description of the Benjaminites; both of these terms are usually construed with a singular verb; (C) 'the people,' a term which appears to be used exclusively in passages which are marked by phraseology and standpoint as belonging to the latest hand of all, and in short insertions of the character of glosses in their context.*

Using this criterion, we may construct two parallel and self-consistent narratives A and B. A is practically continuous, except for omission of the account of the setting of the ambuscade (after *v.*[28]), and the ruse by which it captured the city (after *v.*[34a]); while B, which has been drawn upon for an account of these facts, lacks the account of Israel's defeat on the first (after *v.*[20]) and second (after *v.*[25a]) days, of the earlier stage of the battle on the third day (after *v.*[33a]), and of the escape of the surviving Benjaminites—details which are sufficiently supplied by the narrative of A.‡

* It is of course not implied that there is anything in the ordinary Heb. usage of העם 'the people' which favours the view that it is a late usage, since the fact is evident that the contrary is the case. Our postulate merely is that, *as used in the present narrative*, its occurrences happen to stand either as manifest glosses or in close association with phrases and ideas which manifestly belong to the latest stratum.

‡ The division of the sources allows, in places, room for a small amount of ambiguity. Is 20[37b] superfluous after 20[37a]? Probably not. While the first half of the verse mentions the onset of the ambuscade, the second half describes the *manner* in which it was made (viz. by deployment), and its result. The manner in which allocation is made of 20[45aα,47] depends upon the assumption that both A and B probably mentioned the escape of the surviving Benjaminites to the crag of Rimmon, and upon the possibility that the difference סלע הרמון *vv.*[45aα,47a], סלע רמון *v.*[47b], 21[13] may mark the different sources. It is of course

A

1 Then all the children of Israel were called to arms as one man unto Yahweh at Miṣpah. 3a And the children of Benjamin heard that the children of Israel had gone up to Miṣpah; 14 and the children of Benjamin were gathered together out of the cities unto Gibeʿah, to go out to battle with the children of Israel. 19 And the children of Israel arose in the morning, and encamped against Gibeʿah. 21 And the children of Benjamin came out from Gibeʿah, and felled of Israel to the ground in that day two and twenty thousand men. 23 And the children of Israel went up, and wept before Yahweh until the evening; and they enquired of Yahweh, saying, 'Shall I again approach to battle with the children of Benjamin my brother?' And Yahweh said, 'Go up against him.'

24 So the children of Israel drew near against the children of Benjamin on the second day; 25 and [the children of Benjamin] again felled to the ground of the children of Israel eighteen thousand men. 26 Then all the children of Israel went up . . . and wept, and sat down there before Yahweh until the evening. 27a And the children of Israel enquired of Yahweh, 28 saying,

B

11 Then all the men of Israel were gathered together against the city as one man in confederacy.

20 And the men of Israel went out to battle with Benjamin; and the men of Israel set the battle in array against them at Gibeʿah . . .

22 And the men of Israel took courage, and again set the battle in array in the place where they had set it in array on the first day. 25a And Benjamin went out to meet them from Gibeʿah on the second day . . .

impossible to regard *v.* 45aα and *v.* 47a as being parallel accounts of the escape to the crag from the two sources for the reason already given, p. 448), where it is shown that *v.* 47a represents the redactor's resumption of *v.* 45aα after his interpolation. The B narrative as allocated contains two references to 'the children of Benjamin,' in place of the ordinary 'Benjamin' or 'the men of Benjamin,' viz. 20^{48}, 21^{13}; but both these are rather different from the ordinary allusions, referring, not to the army in the field, but in the first case to those who remained at home (old men, women, and children), and in the other to the survivors specified as being on the crag of Rimmon.

'Shall I again go out to battle with the children of Benjamin my brother, or shall I forbear?' And Yahweh said, 'Go up; for to-morrow I will deliver him into thine hand' . . .

30 And the children of Israel went up against the children of Benjamin on the third day, and set themselves in array against Gibeʿah as aforetime. 31 And the children of Benjamin went out to meet them, and were drawn away from the city; and they began to smite and kill as afore-time in the field about thirty men of Israel. 32 And the children of Benjamin said, 'They are smitten down before us as at the first': but the children of Israel said, 'Let us flee; and draw them away from the city into the highways.' 33b And the ambuscade of Israel burst forth from its place on the west of Gebaʿ, 34a and they came in front of Gibeʿah, even ten thousand chosen men out of all Israel. . . . And the battle was sore, 35 and Yahweh smote Benjamin before Israel: and the children of Israel felled of Benjamin on that day twenty-five thousand, one hundred men. 36a And the children of Benjamin saw that they were smitten; 45aα and they turned and fled toward the wilderness unto the crag of Rimmon, 47aβ even six hundred men. . . .

29 And Israel set an ambuscade against Gibeʿah round about. 33a And all the men of Israel rose up from their place, and set themselves in array at Baʿal-tamar . . .

34b but *they* knew not that evil was closing upon them. 36b And the men of Israel gave place to Benjamin, for they trusted in the ambuscade which they had set against Gibeʿah. 37 And the ambuscade hasted and made an onset against Gibʿeah: and the ambuscade opened out, and smote all the city at the edge of the sword. 38 Now the appointment between the men of Israel and the ambuscade was, that when they should make a beacon of smoke to rise up out of the city, 39 the men of Israel should face about in the battle. And Benjamin began to smite and kill among the men of Israel about thirty men; and they said, 'Surely they are utterly smitten before us as in the first battle!' 40 Then the beacon began to ascend from the city in a column of smoke; and when Benjamin looked back, behold, the holocaust of the city rose up toward heaven. 41 And the men of Israel faced about; and the men of

Benjamin were dismayed, for they saw that evil had closed upon them. [42] So they turned before the men of Israel unto the way to the wilderness; but the battle overtook them, and they that were from the city were destroying them in the midst, [43] and they beat down Benjamin, and pursued him from Noḥah as far as over against Geba' towards the east. [44] And there fell of Benjamin eighteen thousand men . . . [47b] And they abode on the crag of Rimmon four months. [48] And the men of Israel turned back unto the children of Benjamin, and smote them at the edge of the sword, both inhabited city, and cattle, and everything that there was; moreover all the cities that there were they set on fire.

21.[6] And the children of Israel were moved to pity for Benjamin their brother, and said, 'One tribe is cut off to-day from Israel.' [17] And they said, 'How shall a remnant be left to Benjamin, that a tribe be not blotted out from Israel, [18] seeing that *we* are not able to give them wives of our daughters?' for the children of Israel had sworn, saying, 'Cursed be he that giveth a wife to Benjamin.' [19] And they said, 'Behold, there is the feast of Yahweh in Shiloh yearly.' [20] And they commanded the children of Benjamin, saying, 'Go, and lie in wait in the vineyards; [21] and see, and, behold, if the daughters of Shiloh come forth to dance in the dances, then come ye forth from the vineyards, and snatch ye every man his wife from the daughters of Shiloh, and go to the

21.[1] Now the men of Israel had sworn in Miṣpah, saying, 'There shall not any of us give his daughter to Benjamin to wife.' . . . [7] 'How shall we do for wives for them, seeing *we* have sworn by Yahweh not to give them of our daughters to wives?' [8] And they said, 'What one is there of the tribes of Israel that came not up unto Yahweh to Miṣpah? And, behold, there had come no man to the camp from Jabesh of Gile'ad. [10] So they sent thither twelve thousand men of the most valiant, and commanded them, saying, 'Go, and smite the inhabitants of Jabesh of Gile'ad at the edge of the sword, with the women and the little ones; [11] but the virgins ye shall save alive.' And they did so. [12] And they found of the inhabitants of Jabesh of Gile'ad four hundred

land of Benjamin. [22] And when their fathers or their brothers come to complain unto you, ye shall say, 'Grant them graciously to us; for we took not every man his wife in battle: for if *ye* had given them to us, ye would now be guilty.' [23] And the children of Benjamin did so, and took wives according to their number of the dancers that they had forcibly carried off: and they went and returned unto their inheritance, and built the cities, and dwelt in them. [24a] And the children of Israel departed thence at that time, every man to his tribe and to his clan.

virgin girls, that had not known a man; and they brought them unto the camp. [13] Then they sent, and spake unto the children of Benjamin that were on the crag of Rimmon, and proclaimed peace to them. [14] And Benjamin returned at that time, and they gave them the women that they had saved alive of the women of Jabesh of Gileʿad. . . . [24b] And they went out thence every man to his inheritance.

The occurrences of phrase (C) 'the people' are 20 [2a.8a.10a.16.22a.26a.31b.*], 21 [2.4.9.15]. The fact that this phrase is an editorial gloss in 20 [22a.26a] is obvious; whilst in 20 [2a] it is associated with the phrase 'the assembly of the people of God' (קהל עם א׳) which is of a piece with the late priestly conception of Israel as 'the congregation' (העדה) in *v.*[1]; and in 20 [26], 21 [2-4] with the going up to *Bethel* and the offering of sacrifices. Here Bethel is doubtless regarded, from the post-exilic standpoint, as the single sanctuary for sacrifice at this time, legalized as such by the presence of the Ark and the ministration of Phineḥas as Aaron's lineal descendant: cf. *ch.* 2 [1-5]. The writer accepts the allusion to Miṣpah in the two older narratives as the *place of muster*, but does not recognize it as a *sanctuary*, in spite of the fact that the expression 'unto Yahweh' and the allusion to the oath taken there seem to imply that it was such. It is probable that in 20 [26] mention of Miṣpah as the place to which 'the children of Israel went up' was cut out by him when he inserted 'and all the people, and came to Bethel'; and a similar excision may have been made in 20 [23].

The conception of all Israel acting together as a politico-ecclesiastical body (*ʿēdhā*) seems to be based upon the expression 'as one man,' which, if our analysis is correct, occurs both in A (20 [1]) and in B (20 [11]). This latter expression, while not in itself a mark of post-exilic date (see below), was admirably fitted to form the text of the post-exilic writer's expansion. The *ʿēdhā* is naturally conceived as acting in accordance with a strictly judicial procedure, as appears

* The occurrence in 20 [31a] 𝔐 לקראת העם disappears under our emendation לקראתם. Cf. *note ad loc.*

in 20^{3b-13}; and it should not be doubted that this passage (though the section *vv.* $^{3b-8}$ is commonly assigned by scholars to the oldest narrative) belongs, at least in its present form, to the latest hand. The fact that it breaks the connexion which must once have existed between *v.*^{3a} and *v.*^{14} favours the view that it is an interpolation. Besides the two occurrences of 'the people' (*vv.* $^{8a.10a}$), we may notice, as marks of this hand, the use of זמה 'lewdness' in *v.*^{6} (in this sense a characteristic phrase of H and Ezek.), 'the country of the inheritance of Israel' in *v.*^{6}, and the phrase בער הרע 'extirpate the wickedness,' *v.* ^{13} (D and later). The details of the outrage as described by the Levite are naturally drawn by the late hand from the old narrative of *ch.* 19; but the statement of *v.*^{5b} 'me they thought to have slain' is a softening down of the grossness of 19^{22b}, which possibly marks the superior refinement of a later age.

The account of the numbering of the two rival armies in *vv.*$^{15-17}$ has been assigned, in its present form, to the late hand, the main determining factor being the combination of the phrases 'the children of Benjamin' (*v.*^{15}), 'this people' (*v.*^{16}), 'the men of Israel' (*v.*^{17}). Both the narratives A and B, however, deal with large numbers in their account of the battle, and may therefore be conjectured to have made mention of the original numbers of the two hosts; and fragments of their accounts may well have been incorporated by the late hand. There is an obvious connexion between the 25,000 Benjaminites + 700 men of Gibeʿah, and A's account of the 25,100 who fell in battle, leaving 600 survivors. The verb התפקד, where used again in the narrative (21^{9}) undoubtedly belongs to the late hand.

The account in *v.*^{18} of the consulting of the oracle at Bethel as to which tribe shall open the attack, and the designation of Judah—a proceeding which, as we have already noticed (p. 448), seems to have no effect whatever upon the subsequent course of action—is of great interest. Clearly it has been taken straight from the J narrative *ch.* 1$^{1.2}$, without regard for its appropriateness; and since it was R^{P} who added the Introduction *ch.* 1^{1}-2^{5} to Judg., it is fair to assume that the extract is due to this redactor, and that it is his handiwork which we have been discussing as 'the late hand,' and not some originally distinct and independent *source*. We have already observed that the designation of Bethel as Israel's proper sanctuary goes back to *ch.* 2$^{1-5}$.

In 21^{11} ידעת משכב זכר and in *v.*^{12} the addition למשכב זכר seem to be derived directly from Num. 31$^{17.18.35}$ P. For the older narrative the phrase אשר לא ידעה איש suffices; cf. *ch.* 11^{39}.

The remaining passages assigned to R^{P} fall into the following groups:—passages governed by the conceptions of the *ʿēdhā* and of Bethel as the sacrificial centre, and by reference to 'the people,' 20$^{26 \text{ in part}.27b.28a \text{ in part}}$, 21$^{2-5.9.(10.13. \text{ in part}) 15.16}$; harmonistic links, 20$^{45a\beta b.46.47a\alpha}$,

21 [14b]; statistical notes introduced by כל אלה, 20 [25b.35b.44b] (so *v.*[46b]; cf. כל זה *v.*[16b], and for שלף חרב *vv.*[2b.15a.17a.46b], *ch.* 8 [10]); topographical notes, 20 [31b in part], 21 [12bβ.19 in part] (cf. *ch.* 18 [12bβ.28aβ]; and for the descriptive phrase 'which is in the land of Cana'an,' 21 [12bβ], cf. Josh. 22 [9.10] P); 21 [25], cf. 17 [6], 18 [1a], 19 [1aβ].

There still remains the question of identification of the sources A and B. As regards B this seems sufficiently clear. The phrase 'the men of Israel' occurs in 19 [30] as restored after 𝕲, and this passage is the continuation of the preceding J narrative in that chapter, and may well have been the antecedent to our narrative B. The account of the ruse by which the city of Gibe'ah was ambushed and burnt, and the panic-stricken Benjaminites caught between two forces of Israel, which has been assigned to B, bears close resemblance to the ruse by which 'Ai was captured and destroyed, as related in Josh. 8 which is mainly from J. Cf. especially *v.*[34b], 'but *they* did not know (והם לא ידעו) that evil was closing upon them,' with Josh. 8 [14b], 'but *he* did not know (והוא לא ידע) that there was an ambush against him behind the city'; *v.*[40b] 'and Benjamin looked back, and, behold, the holocaust of the city rose up toward heaven,' with Josh. 8 [20aα] 'and the men of 'Ai looked back and saw, and, behold, the smoke of the city rose up toward heaven'; *v.*[42aα] 'so they turned . . . unto the way to the wilderness,' with Josh. 8 [15] 'and they fled by the way to the wilderness'; *v.* [42aβb] 'but the battle overtook them, and they that were from the city were destroying them in the midst' (בתוך), with Josh. 8 [21b.22], 'then they turned again and smote the men of 'Ai. And the others came forth out of the city against them; so they were in the midst of Israel (ויהיו לישראל בתוך), some on this side, and some on that side; and they smote them, etc.'; *v.*[48] 'and the men of Israel turned back unto the children of Benjamin, and smote them at the edge of the sword,' with Josh. 8 [24b], 'and all Israel turned back unto 'Ai, and smote it at the edge of the sword.' The description of the muster of the men of Israel 'as one man' (20 [11]) and the large number of Benjaminites slain (18,000 according to 20 [44]), cannot be said to be inconsistent with J's authorship. In the narrative of 1 Sam. 11, part of J's account of the circumstances which led to Saul's election to the kingship, which is of acknowledged antiquity as compared with the parallel narrative from E, and which, in 11 [7], shows close affinity to the J narrative in Judg. 19 (cf. p. 445), it is stated that, on the receipt of Saul's summons, the Israelites were called to arms 'as one man,' and the muster produces the incredible numbers of 300,000 Israelites and 30,000 men of Judah. There is no ground whatever for the assumption that exaggeration of numbers is peculiar to post-exilic narrative. Any narrative, whether pre- or post-exilic, if committed to writing long after the events which it narrates, seems to have been liable to this failing. We have already noticed (cf. p. 120) that, in contrast to the modest assessment of 40,000 able-bodied men of Israel given by the contemporary Song of Deborah, the narrative of J in Ex. 12 ^{37b}, Num. 11 ^{21} estimates the men who came out of Egypt as 600,000. The very fact that our narrative in 19 ^{29} states that the Levite divided his concubine into *twelve* pieces, and sent her throughout all the border of Israel, pictures Israel as already a federated entity of twelve tribes, and paves the way for the description of a unanimous response (contrast the *historical* account of the merely partial response to Deborah's summons), and for an incredibly high estimate of the muster. While, however, we assign the narrative B to J, the fact cannot be overlooked that this narrative, in *ch.* 19 as in *chs.* 20, 21, must belong to the latest stratum of J. The fact that it exhibits throughout so close a verbal connexion with various other parts of J (Gen. 19 $^{1-8}$, 1 Sam. 11 ^{7}, Josh. 8), proves that the dependence is on its side and not *vice-versâ*, and therefore that it has been constructed by a process of selective imitation, and must be much later than the old narratives which it has employed, and, in its present form at least, almost certainly unhistorical. On the other hand, the fact that the author has employed J, and J only, as his model, and that his phraseology is uncoloured by the influence of later literature,*

* Exception will doubtless be taken to our inclusion of 21 $^{7.8.10.12-14a}$ (in the main) as part of J, this being a narrative which many critics (*e.g.* Mo.) regard as the latest part of the narrative, on the ground that it is based on Num. 31 $^{1ff.}$—the carrying out of the *ḥérem* or ban upon Midian—a story which is assigned with good reason to a secondary stratum of P. The striking points of connexion between the two narratives which are adduced are (1) the fact that the number of warriors sent to execute the *ḥérem* is the same in each narrative, viz. 12,000, and (2) the phrase which occurs in Judg. 21 $^{11.12}$ to mark the distinction between the married and unmarried women (ידעת משכב זכר, לא ידעה איש למשכב זכר), as compared with Num. 31 $^{17.18.35}$. It should be recollected, however, that the custom of the *ḥérem* was very ancient; and that, when this was practised, the saving of the unmarried girls as slave-concubines must have been frequent, if not regular (cf. Deut. 21 $^{10-14}$). The phrase noted under (2) *does* seem to have been derived from the narrative of Num., as remarked above. On the other hand, we should not overlook such distinctions between the two narratives as the regular and exclusive use of הרג 'kill' in Num. (*vv.* $^{7.8 bis.17 bis.19}$) as contrasted with הכה לפי חרב 'smite at the edge of the sword' in Judg. 21 ^{10}, החרים 'ban *or* devote to destruction' *v.* ^{11}; הטף בנשים 'the young among the women' in Num. 31 ^{18}, but נערה בתולה 'virgin-girls' in Judg. 21 ^{12}. The identity in number, 12,000, is, it may be admitted, somewhat striking; but, if on this score we are to infer connexion between the two narratives, the dependence is quite as likely to be on the side of the late narrative in Num. as *vice-versâ*. The involving of Jabesh of Gile'ad in the odium which falls upon Gibe'ah and upon the whole tribe of Benjamin fits in so well with the theory that the story as a whole makes an attack upon the memory of Saul (cf. p. 447) that it is difficult to suppose that the whole Jabesh-narrative was only inserted as a very late afterthought.

seems to indicate that we are right in regarding him as pre- and not post-exilic.*

The origin of the narrative A is far more dubious. If B is rightly identified with J, it is natural to look for indications of the hand of E in the companion-narrative, more especially as the second source in 19^{1-15} has been conjecturally assigned to E; and since the use of high numbers in $20^{21.25.35}$ does not (as we have just noticed) necessarily imply a post-exilic point of view, there is no *primâ facie* reason why this narrative should not date from pre-exilic times. No signs of E's phraseology are, however, apparent in the narrative; while, on the other hand, there are several indications that it, like B, was acquainted with J's account of the attack on ʿAi in Josh. 7, 8: cf. *ch.* $20^{23.26}$, 'they wept before Yahweh until the evening,' with Josh. 7^{6}, 'he fell on his face to the earth before the Ark of Yahweh until the evening'; 20^{31a} 'they were drawn away (הנתקו) from the city,' *v.*^{32b}, 'Let us flee and draw them away (ונתקנוהו) from the city,' with Josh. $8^{5b\beta.6a\alpha}$, 'and we will flee before them . . . until we have drawn them away (עד התיקנו אותם) from the city,' $8^{16b\beta}$ 'and they were drawn away (וינתקו) from the city'; *ch.* 20^{32} 'And the children of Benjamin said, "They are smitten down before us as at the first" (כבראשנה); but the children of Israel said, "Let us flee, etc.,"' with Josh. 8^{6} 'for they will say, "They are fleeing before us as at the first" (כאשר בראשנה); so we will flee before them'; *ch.* 20^{34a} 'and they came over against (מנגד ל) Gibeʿah,' with Josh. 8^{11}, 'and they came over against (נגד) the city.' These facts, together with the artificial appearance of the narrative of the three days' battle (which, however, is scarcely more marked than in E^{2}'s narrative in *ch.* 7^{2-8}), and, especially, the fact that the *combination* of A and B appears to have been effected, not by a pre-exilic redactor (such as R^{JE}), but by R^{P} himself (cf. especially the redactional link 21^{14b-16}), seem to favour the conclusion that we have in A a post-exilic narrative of unknown provenance, possibly containing some independent and relatively ancient elements (*e.g.* the story of the rape of the maidens of Shiloh ‡), but otherwise perhaps ultimately based upon the older J narrative with which it was eventually com-

* It may be noted that the J writer is characterized, in the account of the battle, by an unusual fondness for placing the subj. before the verb when the subj. changes in the sequence of the narrative:—cf. 20^{33a} וכל איש ישראל קמו, 20^{37a} והארב החישו, 20^{38a} והמועד היה, 20^{39b} ובנימין החל, 20^{40} והמשאת החלה, 20^{41a} ואיש ישראל הפך, 20^{48a} ואיש ישראל שבו, 21^{1a} ואיש ישראל נשבע.

‡ The fact that this story is probably ancient has been generally recognized. Unlike other parts of the narrative which have the superficial appearance of antiquity, but are really based on other narratives (cf. the foregoing discussion of the J narrative), it appears, so far as we can judge, to be independent; and it may well be that, if any part of *chs.* 19-21 is historical as it now stands, such an historical element may be contained in this story. It seems not impossible that it may have been derived ultimately from the E source.

bined by R^P. The narrative A, as of unknown source, has been marked in the text by the symbol X.*

* The foregoing analysis was worked out independently by the present editor prior to consultation of the attempted analyses of other scholars, and differs very widely from them. Chapters 20 and 21 have not unnaturally given scope for great divergency of opinion among commentators in the past; but, speaking generally, it may be said that in the main some agreement in the guiding principle of analysis has been reached by the most recent writers, as represented, *e.g.*, by Mo. (*Comm.* and *SBOT.*), Bu. (*Comm.*), No., Driver (*LOT.*[9], p. 170), Kent. This principle appears to be that, since *ch.* 19 'is old in style and representation,' its continuation in *chs.* 20, 21 must have been similar, the assumption being that such similarity should be found in absence of the element of exaggeration and incredibility. Thus, drastic elimination is made, not merely of the passages which picture Israel as organized as an *'ēdhā* (assigned by us to R^P), but (in spite of 1 Sam. $11^{7.8}$ J) of all passages which speak of Israel as acting 'as one man,' and which deal with incredibly large numbers. Mo. (*SBOT.*) assigns to J $20^{1a\alpha.1b\beta.3-8.14.19.29.36.37a.38.39}$ (om. 'as in the first battle') $^{40.41.44a.47}$, $21^{1.15.16b-19a\alpha.20b.21.22a\alpha.22b.23}$, and regards the rest of the narrative as a post-exilic Midrash, $20^{11.18.23.24.27b.28a\alpha.37b}$, $21^{4.5.8\ \text{end}}$ ('unto the assembly') ^{19} (from 'which is north,' etc.) being redactional. Driver (on the basis, mainly, of the analyses of Bu. and No.) assigns to the earlier source (except a few words here and there) $20^{1a\alpha.1b\beta.3-8.14.19.29.31-34.36b.37a.38.40-42.44a.47}$, $21^{1.6-8.10-12}$ (in briefer form) $^{13-14}$ (with 'they' for 'the whole congregation') $^{15.17-25}$. These analyses give us, as the oldest (presumably historical) narrative, the account of the outrage as given in *ch.* 19, with the Levite's summons to Israel; the assembling at Miṣpah and an enquiry into the circumstances of the crime, followed by a *one day's* battle in which by aid of an ambuscade the Benjaminites are defeated and almost exterminated; and, lastly, provision of wives for the survivors [by saving the unmarried maidens of Jabesh, and] by capture of the maidens of Shiloh.

The fallaciousness of an analysis which is based on the view that the older narrative can be recovered by elimination of all that is patently unhistorical has been sufficiently demonstrated by the foregoing discussion. The antiquity of *ch.* 19 is (as Wellh. rightly recognizes) more apparent than real, since, as we have seen, this narrative (at least in part) is framed in close imitation of older J stories—a fact which leads us with some reason to question its historical value. Why, *e.g.*, should we accept the account of the Levite's method of appeal to the tribes of Israel, which is manifestly connected with 1 Sam. 11^{7}, and at the same time reject both the allusion to the Israelites' assembling 'as one man' (though this identical phrase occurs in the same verse of 1 Sam. 11), and also the use of high numbers (though this is paralleled by 1 Sam. 11^{8})? Again, if, as cannot be denied, the account of the ambushing of Gibe'ah (generally accepted as ancient) depends on Josh. 8, why should not the account of success attained by this ruse have been preceded by a narrative of two days' failure, on the analogy of Joshua's first failure against 'Ai, as related by the J narrative in Josh. 7? Lastly, what ground exists for the supposition that a narrative which bears strongly the stamp of J phraseology, and is obviously modelled on earlier J elements, was continued by the story of the rape of the Shilonite maidens, which contains no J phrases and is independent of any earlier similar narrative?

On the other hand, the merit of the criterion for analysis which we have adopted (cf. p. 449) rests in the fact that, without any sleight of hand, it immediately resolves the confusion of the narrative as it now stands, and offers us two parallel and nearly continuous narratives, together with the additions of a later redactor, the object of which can easily be divined. The distinction in the usage

19. 1. R[P] Now in those days, when there was no king in Israel, J there was a certain Levite sojourning in the furthermost parts of the hill-country of Ephraim, who took to him E a wife, J a concubine out of Bethleḥem of Judah. 2. And his concubine ⌜was vexed⌝ with him, and went away from him unto

19. 1. *in those days.* *I.e.* in the days of the Judges, rather than (as Mo. thinks) 'loosely dating the following story in the period of the Danite migration.'

When there was no king, etc. Cf. p. 410.

a certain Levite. Lit. 'a man, a Levite'; so *ch.* 20[4] 'the man, the Levite,' *ch.* 18[3.15] 'the youth, the Levite.' The man is only twice described as a Levite, being elsewhere mentioned merely as 'the man': hence Bu. supposes that the words לוי גר 'a Levite sojourning' are a late insertion under the influence of the preceding narrative—but this hypothesis has little to support it.*

the furthermost parts. Heb. *yarkethê*, lit. 'sides' or 'flanks,' is used of the *innermost recesses* of a cave, 1 Sam. 24[4], a house, Am. 6[10], a ship, Jon. 1[5], the pit (*i.e.* She'ol), Isa. 14[15], or of the *remote parts* of the north, Isa. 14[13], *al.*, or, of the earth, Jer. 6[22], *al.* Hence the expression as here used is taken by Mo., Cooke to refer to the most northerly parts of Ephraim, from the Judaean point of view. More probably the reference is to the actual flanks of the hill-country, whether to the east or west, which, lying away from the main route from south to north (which then, as now, must have run along the centre of the range) might, especially from the Judaean standpoint, be viewed as somewhat remote.

2. *was vexed with him.* Reading וַתִּזְעַף עָלָיו with Böttcher, Houb., Grätz, Mo. (*SBOT.*), Kit. Cf. 𝔊[AL], 𝔖[h], 𝔏 *καὶ ὠργίσθη αὐτῷ* (the root זעף is rendered by *ὀργίζειν* in 2 Chr. 16[10]). For זעף followed by על, cf. Prov. 19[3]. 𝔐 וַתִּזְנֶה עָלָיו, R.V. 'played the harlot against him,' can hardly be original; for (1) the context

of the phrases 'the men of Israel' and 'the 'children of Israel' was observed by Ber. as one of his criteria; though he does not work it out consistently, and also fails to distinguish the redactional passages from the sources. His analysis is as follows:—A 20 [1.2b-10,14.(18).19.24-28.29-36a.47], 21 [5-14.24]; B 20 [2a.11-13.15-17.20-23.36b-44.45.46.48], 21 [1-4.15-23].

* Bu. finds fault with the constr. וַיְהִי אִישׁ לֵוִי גָּר וגו׳ on the ground that we should expect וְהוּא גָר; but it is difficult to see any essential difference between the participial usage in our passage and, *e.g.*, Gen. 25[27] וְיַעֲקֹב אִישׁ תָּם יֹשֵׁב אֹהָלִים 'and Ja'cob was a simple man, dwelling in tents.'

her father's house, unto Bethlehem of Judah, and was there some time, E four months. 3. J And her husband arose, and

demands that the cause of estrangement should be a passing tiff and not an act of unfaithfulness, and (2) the constr. זנה followed by על of the person against whom the offence is committed is unparalleled (the verb is regularly in this sense followed by מן 'away from,' by itself or in combination with another prep., מעל, מאחרי, מתחת).

𝔖ᴾ ܘܢܓܠܝ ܥܠܘܗܝ reproduces 𝔐; and it is probable that 𝔊ᴮ *καὶ ἐπορεύθη ἀπ' αὐτοῦ*, 𝔙 'quae reliquit eum,' Jos. (*Ant.* v. ii. 8) *καταλιποῦσα τὸν ἄνδρα*, are merely paraphrases of the same reading: cf. the comment of Levi ben-Gershon, who explains that the verb must be taken to mean simply that the woman forsook him, and not in its ordinary sense, otherwise it would have been unlawful for the Levite to fetch her back. 𝔗 ובסרת עלוהי, 'despised him,' may also be a paraphrase, unless ובסרת represents וַתִּבְזֶה (Dathe); but here again the following עליו forms a difficulty (only found in the late passage, Neh. 2 [19]). The same objection is valid against the easy emendation וַתִּזְנַח, adopted by Michaelis, Ewald (*HI.* ii. p. 352), Stu., Wellh. (*Comp.*[3] p. 230), etc.; this verb being ordinarily (if not exclusively*) transitive and followed by an accusative in the sense *cast off* or *spurn* a personal or impersonal object. Mo. suggests, as another possibility, that the original of *καὶ ὠργίσθη αὐτῷ* was וַתֶּאֱנַף עָלָיו, that this verb was corrupted into וַתִּנְאַף ('she committed adultery'), which, again, was later on corrected into וַתִּזְנֶה upon the ground that the woman was not a wedded wife. This suggestion (favoured by Bu., No., La.) is almost too ingenious; and, as Mo. himself observes, the prep. ב (and not על) is regularly used after the verb אנף.

some time, four months. Heb. יָמִים אַרְבָּעָה חֳדָשִׁים. Here ימים (as in *ch.* 14[8], 15[1]) seems to refer to a period of *indefinite length*, which is then accurately defined by ארבעה חדשים; ‡ and the natural inference is that the latter definition is a gloss upon the former, or rather (as assumed in our analysis) that it is derived from the parallel source (cf. the precision of this source in *vv.*[4.5], 'three days,' etc.). The appositional relation between ימים and ארבעה חדשים is hardly

* It may, however, be possible that זנח, when used absolutely (cf. *e.g.* Ps. 74[1], 77[8], Lam. 3[31]) may possess the sense 'to be angry,' which regularly belongs to the Bab. equivalent *zinû*. If this be so, it is not inconceivable that the verb might be construed with על 'was angry *against*,' much as the Bab. verb is construed with *itti*, 'be angry *with*' (cf. the illustration cited p. 59).

‡ ימים וארבעה חדשים, 1 Sam. 27[7], is of course different; this meaning 'days (*i.e.*, by usage, *a year*) *and* four months.'

went after her, to speak kindly to her, to bring ⌜her⌝ back again, having his lad with him, and a couple of asses, and ⌜he came⌝ to her father's house: and when the damsel's father saw him, he came joyfully to meet him. 4. E And his father-in-law, J the damsel's father, E detained him; and he abode with him three days: J and they did eat and drink, and stayed the night there. 5. E And on the fourth day J they arose early in the morning, E and he rose up to depart: J and the damsel's father said R^{JE} unto his son-in-law, J 'Strengthen thine heart with a morsel of bread, and afterward ye shall depart.' 6. So they sat down, and did eat, both of them together, and drank: and the damsel's father said unto the man, 'Prithee consent, and stay the night, E and let thine heart be merry.' 7. And the man rose up to depart: but his father-in-law urged him, J and he stayed the night there again. 8. And he arose early in the morning R^{JE} on the fifth day J to depart: and the damsel's father said, 'Prithee strengthen thine heart'; so they tarr⌜ied⌝ till the day declined, and did eat,

identical with the very idiomatic usage of ימים when it pleonastically *follows* the statement of a definite period, as *e.g.* in חֹדֶשׁ יָמִים 'a month of time' (lit. 'a month, days'). Cf., on this latter usage, the discussion in Ges., *Thes.* 585*b*, where the analogous usage of *zamân* 'time,' in Ar. is cited.

3. *to speak kindly to her.* Lit. 'to speak to her heart.' Cf., for this idiom, Gen. 34[3], 50[21], 2 Sam. 19[7], 𝔐[8], Isa. 40[2], Hos. 2[14], 𝔐[16], Ru. 2[13], 2 Chr. 30[22], 32[6] †.

to bring her back again. Reading *Kᵉrê* לַהֲשִׁיבָהּ, in place of *Kt.* להשיבו.

and he came. Reading וַיָּבֹא with 𝔊[AL], 𝔖[h], and moderns, in place of 𝔐 וַתְּבִיאֵהוּ. Mo. plausibly suggests that the readings of 𝔐 here and in the preceding להשיבו—which he renders 'that she might win him back'—are early alterations based upon the corruption ותזנה in *v.*[2], on the view that, since the man was the injured party, it was for the woman to make the advances towards reconciliation.

5. *Strengthen thine heart.* Heb. סְעָד לִבְּךָ. Here the Imperative is to be pronounced *sᵉʿŏdh* (not *sᵉʿādh*) the conjunctive accent *Darga* which it bears being used as a substitute for *Methegh*: cf. G-K. § 64*c*, *n*[2].

8. *So they tarried.* Reading וַיִּתְמַהְמְהוּ with La., in place of 𝔐 וְהִתְמַהְמְהוּ which can only be an Imperative (so all Versions). Since, however, in *v.*[9] the father uses the fact that the day has declined as

bŏth of them. 9. E And the man rose up to depart, J he and his concubine and his lad; E and his father-in-law, J the damsel's father, E said to him, J 'Behold, prithee, the day hath waned to setting, prithee stay ye the night: E behold, the day hath closed in; stay thou the night here, and let thy heart be merry; J and ye shall arise early to-morrow for your journey, E and thou shalt

a reason why they should stay the night, and leave (presumably in good time) on the morrow, he would scarcely in the first place have urged them to tarry till the decline of day before starting on their return. Mo. notes the fact that certain groups of 𝔊 MSS. (cited by him as 𝔊[MN]) offer (in place of והתמהמהו, which is rendered by 𝔊[AL] *καὶ στρατεύθητι*, 𝔊[B] *καὶ στράτευσον**) the reading *διεπλάνα αὐτόν* or *διεπλάτυνε αὐτόν* (cf. Field, *Hex.*, *ad loc.*), *i.e.* וַיְפַתֵּהוּ; whence he conjectures that the original text may have run וַיְפַתֵּהוּ וַיִּתְמַהְמַהּ, 'and he persuaded him, and he lingered,' etc. This gives an excellent sequence, and is accepted by Bu., No., Kit., with the modification וַיִּתְמַהְמְהוּ; but the method of constructing a composite text from two variant readings must be deemed somewhat questionable.

and did eat. 𝔊[AL] adds *καὶ ἔπιον* (so 𝔖[h] with obelus); cf. *vv.*[4.6].

9. *the day hath waned to setting.* Heb. רָפָה הַיּוֹם לַעֲרוֹב, lit. 'the day hath sunk down so as to set.' 'Day' is here used by metonymy for 'sun,' as sometimes in English: cf. passages cited in the Oxford *New Eng. Dict. s.v.* 'set' II. 9 b. The use of *rāphā* may be paralleled by Bab. *rabû* or *rapû* which is used of the *sinking* of the sun to the Underworld: cf. Muss-Arnolt, *Dict.* p. 949, and *note* on 'Teraphim,' p. 421. There is no ground for substituting נטה for רפה with Mo. *SBOT.* 𝔊 *εἰς (τὴν) ἑσπέραν* reads לָעֶרֶב for לַעֲרוֹב, which may be original.

behold, the day hath closed in. Heb. הִנֵּה חֲנוֹת הַיּוֹם, lit. 'behold, the closing (declining) of day.' Heb. *ḥānā*, which is elsewhere used in the special sense of *encamping*, is here a synonym of *nāṭā* (cf. *v.*[8]) in the sense *bend down* or *decline*, which, as is shown by the cognate languages (Ar., Syr.) is the original meaning of the root.

𝔊[B], 𝔖[P] omit לינו נא הנה חנות היום, thus removing the duplication in the invitation which probably marks the different sources (cf. p. 442). 𝔊[AL] *κατάλυσον* ([L]*δή*) *ὧδε ἔτι σήμερον* seems to have arisen through combination with the preceding לינו נא and the reading of הִנֵּה as

* Mo. notices that the original 𝔊 reading is clearly *στραγεύθητι* (for *στραγγεύθητι*) which is found in the HP. codd. 15, 18, 64, 65; 𝔖[h] ܘܐܬܠܠܗܐ. This has become *στρατεύθητι* through the not uncommon confusion between Γ and T in uncial writing; and *στράτευσον* represents a grammatical correction.

depart to thy home.' 10. And the man would not stay the night; but he rose up and departed, and came over against Jebuṡ Rᴾ (that is Jerusalem): J and with him were a couple of asses saddled; his concubine was with him also. 11. When they were near Jebuṡ, the day ⌜was far spent⌝; and the lad said unto his master, 'Prithee come, and let us turn aside into this city of the Jebuṡites, and stay the night in it.' 12. And his master said unto him, 'We will not turn aside into the city

הֵנָּה (apparently לִֽינִ־נָא הֵנָּה עוֹד הַיּוֹם); but we are not justified in looking to this 𝔊 rendering for the original text (as does Mo., followed by Cooke), since לִין should be followed by הלילה 'to-night,' and not by היום 'to-day.'

to thy home. Lit. 'to thy tents': cf. for this usage *ch.* 7^{8}, 20^{8}, Deut. 16^{7}, Josh. $22^{4.6.7.8}$, 1 Sam. 13^{2}, 2 Sam. 19^{9}, $20^{1.22}$, 1 Kgs. 8^{66}, 12^{16}. According to Driver (on Deut. *loc. cit.*), 'the expression is a survival from the time when Israel was a nomadic people and actually lived in tents; it remained in use long after the "tents" had given place to permanent "houses."' Since, however, Heb. *'ŏhel* is the philological equivalent of Ar. *'ahl* 'community of settlers,' Bab. *âlu* 'city,' originally 'settlement,' it is perhaps truer to say that we have in this Heb. usage a survival of the wider and more primitive usage of the term.

10. *Jebuṡ.* Apart from the present narrative, this name is only applied to Jerusalem in 1 Chr. $11^{4.5}$ (a narrative expanded from 2 Sam. $5^{6\,ff.}$ in which the name Jebuṡ does not appear). The manner in which it is explained here by the editorial addition 'that is Jerusalem' seems to suggest that it was the more ancient name; but that this cannot be so is proved by the occurrence of the latter name in the form Urusalim in the T.A. Letters of the fourteenth century B.C. (cf. Knudtzon, Nos. 287, 289, 290 = Winckler, Nos. 180, 182 + 185, 183).

his concubine, etc. The addition καὶ ὁ παῖς αὐτοῦ, found in some MSS. of 𝔊, is probably due to a precisionist.

11. *was far spent.* Reading יָרַד (lit. 'had gone down') in place of the inexplicable רַד of 𝔐. יָרַד, however, does not occur elsewhere of the decline of day,* the nearest parallel being 2 Kgs. 20^{11}, where it is used of the decline of the shadow on the step-clock of Aḥaz.

12. *the city of foreigners who, etc.* Reading plur. נָכְרִים for sing. נָכְרִי, and masc. הֵמָּה for fem. הֵנָּה with several MSS. of 𝔐.

* Why Mo. (*SBOT.*) should cite 1 Kgs. 1^{25} as a parallel is inexplicable.

of foreigner⸢s⸣, ⸢who⸣ are not of the children of Israel, but we will pass on as far as Gibeʿah.' 13. E And he said to his lad,

Gibeʿah. The name occurs elsewhere, as here, without the Def. Art. גבעה; and also, as in *vv.*13.14.15.*al.*, with the Def. Art. הגבעה '*the* Hill' *par excellence* as being גבעת האלהים 'the Hill of God,' *i.e.* the site of an ancient sacred place, 1 Sam. 10 5.* The city is sometimes defined as 'Gibeʿah of Benjamin' (1 Sam. 13 15, 14 16; 'G. of the children of B.,' 2 Sam. 23 29; cf. 'G. which belongeth unto B.' in *v.*14 of our narrative), or 'Gibeʿah of Saul' (1 Sam. 11 4, 15 34, Isa. 10 29). Some confusion has arisen here and there in the O.T. between Gibeʿah and Gebaʿ (a masc. form also meaning 'hill'); but that the two sites are distinct is proved by Isa. 10 28-32, where both are mentioned. The site of Gebaʿ has been certainly identified in the modern Ǵebaʿ south of the wâdy Suwênîṭ, five and a half miles north-north-east of Jerusalem. We must read Gebaʿ for Gibeʿah in *ch.* 20 43, 1 Sam. 13 2, 14 2 (cf. 13 16, 14 5); and, conversely, Gibeʿah for Gebaʿ in *ch.* 20 10, 1 Sam. 13 3 (cf. 10 5.10).

The present narrative makes it clear that Gibeʿah lay close to the road which runs north from Jerusalem to Nâblus, and was reached from Jerusalem rather sooner than Ramah (cf. *v.*13); and, further (*ch.* 20 31), that not far off from it the road divided, one branch going to Bethel—*i.e.* the main northern road, and the other to Gibeʿon (on the reading, cf. *note ad loc.*)—*i.e.* the road by the two Bethḥorons to Joppa. Further evidence is furnished by the statement of Jos. (*BJ.* V. ii. 1) that Titus, when advancing against Jerusalem from Gophna (Ǵifnâ) on the road from Samaria, pitched his camp in the Valley of Thorns, near a village called Gibeʿah of Saul, about thirty stadia (*i.e.* rather over three miles) from Jerusalem, in order to await reinforcements coming from Emmaus (Nicopolis), *i.e.* ʿAmwâs, which would naturally arrive by the Bethḥoron road. Similarly, Jerome ‡ describes how Paula journeyed from Nicopolis by the ascent to Upper and

* That גבעת האלהים is identical with הגבעה, which was Saul's native city, is evident from the narrative of 1 Sam. 10 5.10-16. When Saul is seized with the prophetic ecstasy, 'those who knew him before time' (*v.*11), who, according to this narrative, give rise to the proverb, 'Is Saul among the prophets?' are clearly his fellow-townsmen; and when he ceases to prophesy (*v.*13), we find him (*vv.*14ff.) at home among his relatives without further travelling (read probably in *v.*13b הביתה 'he came *home*'—as in 1 Kgs. 13 7.15, *al.*—for 𝔐 הבמה '*to the high-place*,' with which we should expect ויעל 'he went up'—not ויבא: so Wellh., Driver, Kennedy, H. P. Smith, etc.). The identification of גבעת האלהים proposed by Smith, *HG.* p. 250, with Râm-Allah (meaning in Ar. 'the Hill of God') a mile west of Bîreh is therefore out of the question, since it is impossible that Gibeʿah of Saul can have lain so far to the north.

‡ 'The Pilgrimage of the holy Paula' (translated in *Palestine Pilgrims' Text Society*, i. (cf. § 6).

THE DISTRIC

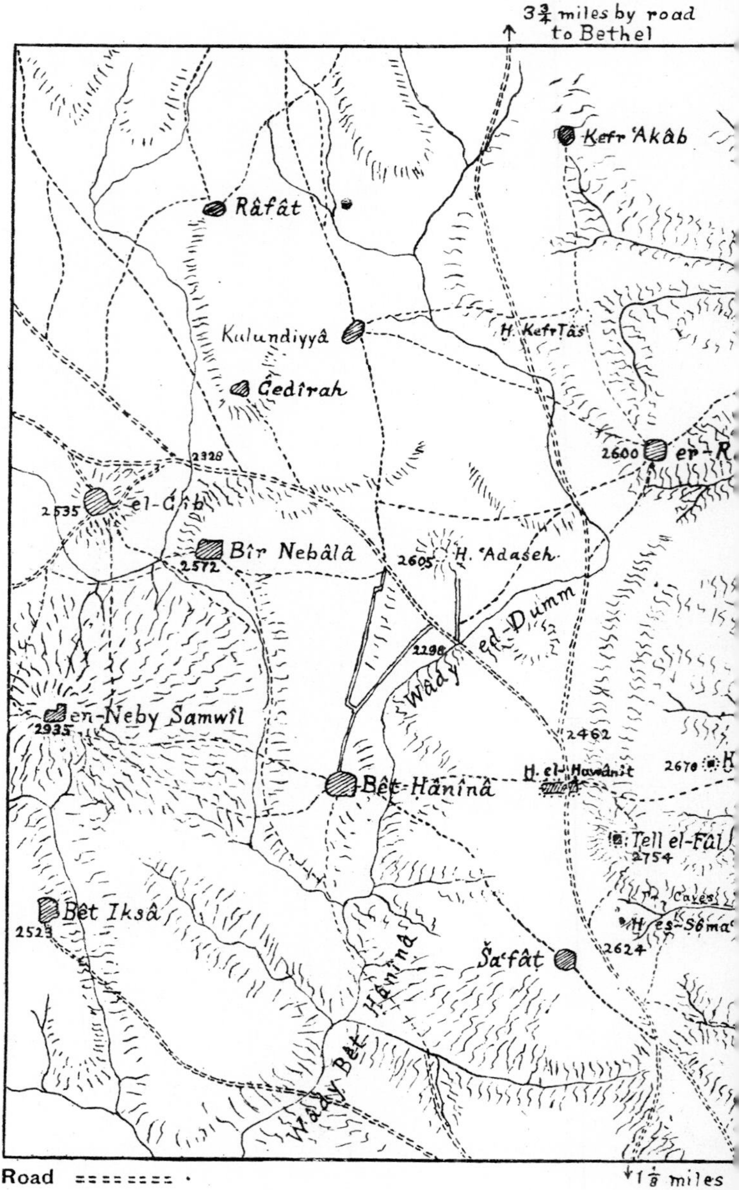

Road ========

Track --------

Heights in English feet

(Based on Survey

OUND GIBE'AH

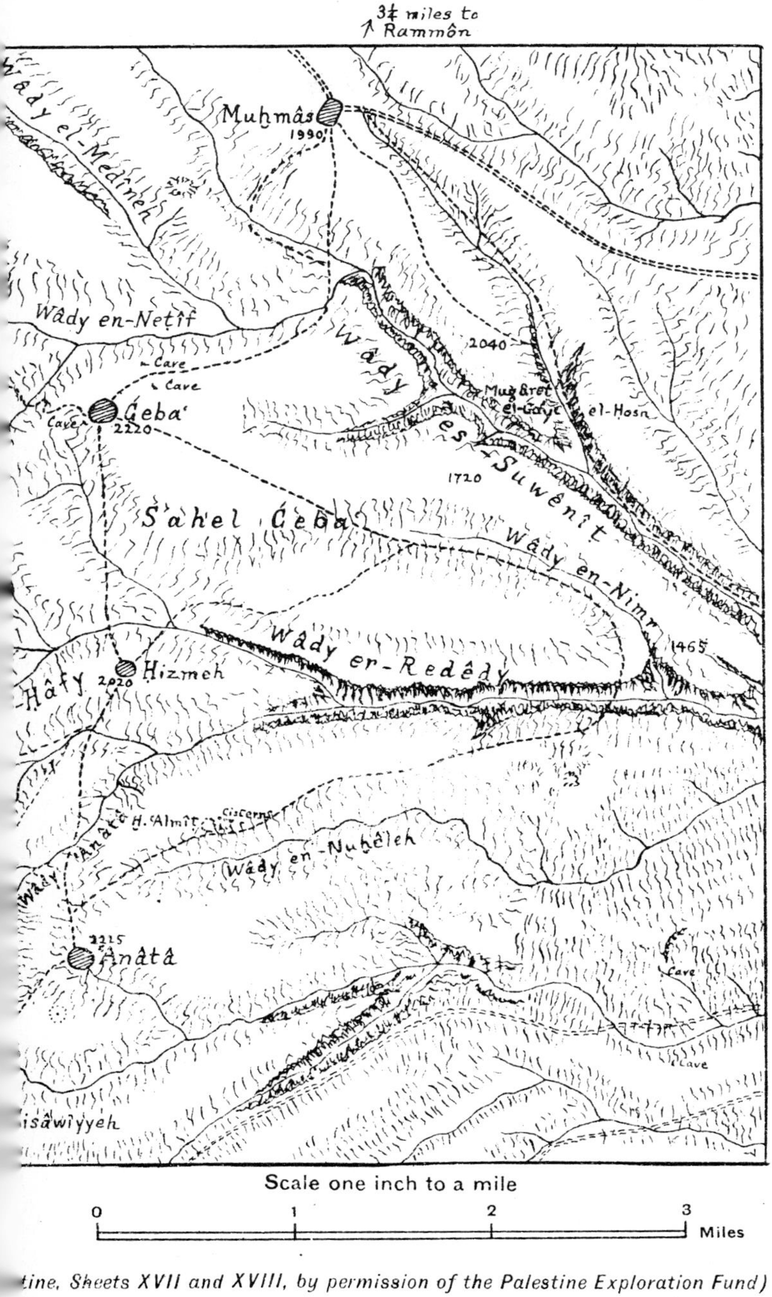

tine, Sheets XVII and XVIII, by permission of the Palestine Exploration Fund)

Lower Bethḥoron, beholding on her right Aijalon and Gibe'on, and resting awhile at Gibe'ah before continuing her journey to Jerusalem.

It is clear from these facts that Gibe'ah must have lain close to the junction of the two roads, and south rather than north of this junction; and adding the fact (derived from Jos.) that the distance of the city from Jerusalem was not less than three miles, the possibilities of site are confined within narrow limits.

The site proposed by Rob. (*BR.*[3] i. pp. 577-579), following a suggestion made by Gross (*Theol. Stud. u. Kritiken*, 1843, p. 1082) is Tell (*or* Tulêl) el-Fûl, a high Tell crowned by the remains of a fortress some three hundred or four hundred yards to the east of the north road, about three miles due north of Jerusalem and two miles due south of Ramah (er-Râm). This has been accepted by many moderns. Objection is raised to the identification by Féderlin (*Revue Biblique*, 1906, p. 271) and Hagemeyer (*ZDPV.* xxxii., 1909, pp. 1 ff.) on the ground that there exist no traces of an ancient village, such *e.g.* as the rock-hewn cisterns which must necessarily have existed on such a site. Féderlin favours Ḫirbet eṣ-Ṣôma', on a small eminence about six hundred yards south of Tell el-Fûl, where there are considerable remains, among which are to be found about fifteen cisterns. This is probably too far south of the junction of the two roads, and too close to Jerusalem, unless we accept the variant statement of Jos. in his account of the Judges-episode (*Ant.* v. ii. 8) where he gives the distance as twenty stadia only (this, however, has not the same appearance of comparative accuracy as the statement in *BJ.*). Hagemeyer proposes the ruins called Ḫirbet el-Ḥawânît, five hundred yards north-west of Tell el-Fûl, and actually *on* the main road. Here there are the remains of massive walls, and ancient cisterns, and the upper part of the wâdy Bêt Ḥannîna to the west may represent the Valley of Thorns. This identification, however, seems to be excluded (1) by the fact that it is unconnected with a hill, and so could scarcely have borne the name הגבעה, and (2) by the fact that it is actually *on* the road, whereas the verb ויסרו in *v.*[15] of our narrative implies that the Levite's party had to 'turn aside' from the road for some little way before reaching the city.

All things considered, the ruined site Ḫirbet Râs eṭ-Ṭawîl, about half a mile north-east of Tell el-Fûl and three-quarters of a mile nearly due east of the junction of the two roads, and also a little south of the wâdy el-Ḥâfy (which may have been the Valley of Thorns *), merits

* It is worthy of notice that the wâdy el-Ḥâfy joins the wâdy es-Suwênîṭ a few miles east of Ḫirbet Râs eṭ-Tawîl. Ar. es-Suwênîṭ means 'the little acacias,' *i.e.* thorny trees of the Mimosa tribe (of course distinct from the American tree called acacia in England): cf. the name Šeneh 'thorn-bush' applied to the 'tooth of rock' on one side of the wâdy in 1 Sam. 14[4]. Ἄκανθα denotes the acacia in Herod. ii. 96, and is used by Θ. as the rendering of Heb. *šiṭṭā* 'acacia.' The supposition is therefore plausible that in the time of Jos. the name 'Valley of Thorns' (Ἀκανθῶν αὐλών) may have been applied to *both* branches of the wâdy—the wâdy el-Ḥâfy as well as the wâdy es-Suwênîṭ.

'Com⌜e⌝, and let us draw near to one of the places, and stay the
night in Gibeʿah or in Ramah.' 14. So they passed on and
went their way; and the sun went down upon them close to
Gibeʿah, which belongeth to Benjamin. 15. J And they turned
aside there to go in to stay the night in Gibeʿah; and he went
in, and sat down in the market-place of the city; and there was
no man that took them into his house to pass the night. 16.
And, behold, an old man came in from his work, from the field,
at evening: and the man was from the hill-country of Ephraim,
and was sojourning in Gibeʿah; but the men of the place were
Benjaminites. 17. And he lifted up his eyes, and saw the wayfaring man in the market-place of the city; and the old man
said, 'Whither goest thou? and whence comest thou?' 18.
And he said unto him, 'We are passing from Bethleḥem of
Judah unto the furthermost parts of the hill-country of Ephraim:
from thence am I, and I went as far as Bethleḥem of Judah;
and I am going ⌜unto my home⌝; and there is no man that

further investigation as a possible site. This site is mentioned as an alternative to Tell el-Fûl by Sir C. Wilson (Smith *DB.*^{2}, *s.v.* 'Gibeʿah') and by Mo. It is marked by ancient remains: cf. *SWP. Mem.* iii. p. 124.

13. *Come.* *Ḳᵉrê* לְכָה for *Kt.* לְךְ.

Ramah. Cf. *ch.* 4^{5} *note.*

14. *which belongeth to Benjamin.* In distinction from other sites bearing the same name, *e.g.* the Gibeʿah of Judah (Josh. 15^{57}), and the Gibeʿah of Phineḥaṣ in the hill-country of Ephraim (Josh. 24^{33}).

15. *market-place.* Heb. *rᵉḥôbh*, lit. 'broad place,' was an open space in the city, usually near the gate, which served as a meeting-place for business or social purposes. Cf. especially Job 29^{7}, 2 Chr. 32^{6}, Neh. $8^{1.3.16}$.

16. *and the man was, etc.* The fact that the old man was merely a sojourner in Gibeʿah is emphasized in order that his conduct may by contrast bring the inhospitality of the Gibeʿathites into bolder relief. On the sacred duty of hospitality in the East, cf. Cheyne, *EB.* 2128.

18. *unto my home.* Reading אֶל בֵּיתִי with 𝕲 εἰς τὸν οἶκόν μου (cf. *v.*^{29}), in place of 𝔐 אֶת־בֵּית יְהוָה, which has no doubt arisen through a copyist's mistake of ביתי for an abbreviated בית י׳, to which the fact that the man was a Levite may have been a contributory cause. Cf. the errors of 𝕲 in rendering τὸν θυμόν μου (חמתי) for

taketh me into his house. 19. Yet there is both straw and provender for our asses, and there is bread and wine also for me, and for thine handmaid, and for the lad with thy servants: there is no want of anything.' 20. And the old man said, 'Peace be to thee; howsoever let all thy wants lie upon me; only do not pass the night in the market-place.' 21. So he brought him into his house, and foraged for the asses; and they washed their feet, and did eat and drink. 22. They were making merry, when, behold, the men of the city, men that were sons of Belial, surrounded the house, beating on the door, and spake unto the master

חמת יהוה in Jer. 6[11], θυμοῦ μου (אפי) for אף יהוה in Jer. 25[37]. Cf. *NHTS.*[2] p. lxix, *n* [2].

21. *foraged.* Heb. *bālal*, only used here, is a Denominative verb from subs. *b^e lîl* 'fodder' (properly *moistened* or *mixed* fodder), with the meaning 'to give fodder.' Thus the relation between the verb and subs. is exactly reproduced by the English use of 'forage' as subs. and (hence) as verb.

22. *men that were sons of Belial.* Heb. אַנְשֵׁי בְנֵי־בְלִיַּעַל 'men, sons of B.', with Suspended Construct State: cf. G-K. § 130 *e.**

The meaning of Belial, or rather, *b^e liyyá'al*, is highly obscure. The form, as vocalized, is evidently a compound, the first element of which is the negative *b^e lî.* It is in connexion with the second element that difficulty arises. If we put aside the Talmudic explanation (*Sanhedrin*, 111 *b*, 'sons who have broken the yoke of Heaven from off their necks') which implies a different vocalization from 𝔐, *b^e lî* + *'ōl*, 'without yoke'—adopted by Jerome in the present passage, 'filii Belial (id est, absque jugo)'—the explanations in debate at the present day are two. (1) The second element *yá'al* is taken as a subs. meaning 'worth,' which, though otherwise unknown in Heb. or any other Semitic language, is *assumed* from the existence of the verbal form in the Hiph'îl modification, *hô'îl*, with the meaning 'to be profitable.' *B^e liyá'al* is thus supposed to mean '*worthlessness*'; and this is the generally accepted modern explanation, adopted *e.g.* by BDB., and appearing in R.V. *marg.* (2) The explanation of *yá'al* as an apocopated Imperfect from *ya'^a lé* '(that which) comes up' is as old as Kimchi, who supposes that 'not coming up' has the sense 'not prospering,' *i.e.* '*ne'er-do-well.*' So Hupfeld among moderns.

The objection that the context in which the term is regularly used requires something much stronger than a merely negative term, *e.g.*

* Perhaps, however, we ought to read אנשים for אנשי, as in *ch.* 20[13], Deut. 13[14], 1 Kgs. 21[10].

of the house, the old man, saying, 'Bring forth the man who came unto thy house, that we may know him.' 23. And the man, the master of the house, went out unto them and said unto them, 'Nay, my brethren, do not wickedly, I pray you: seeing

malignity or *dangerous wickedness* may perhaps be met by the parallels offered by other languages in which terms originally negative have come to assume a very definite positive meaning—*e.g.* ἀσεβής, German 'Unheil,' Old Eng. 'naughty' (cf *NHTK.* p. 245). A real objection is, however, advanced by Cheyne (cf. *EB.* 525 f., and articles in *ET.* there cited) when he points out that neither explanation suits the occurrence of the word in 2 Sam. 22 [5.6] = Ps. 18 [4.5] (𝔐 [5.6]) which must be deemed crucial for its interpretation. This passage runs—

'Billows of Death encompassed me;
Torrents of *B^e^liyyá'al* o'erwhelmed me;
Toils of She'ol surrounded me;
Snares of Death * confronted me.'

Here *B^e^liyyá'al* is parallel to Death and She'ol, and Cheyne with great plausibility suggests that it denotes the Abyss as '(the place from which) one comes not up'; cf. the Bab. *mât la târi* 'the Land of No-return,' a title of the Underworld. That there was, in Heb. thought, a definite connexion between the ideas of the Abyss and abysmal wickedness is proved by the use of the term *hawwā*, or more frequently the intensive plur. *hawwôth*, as that which characterizes the wicked man's 'inward part' (Ps. 5 [9], 𝔐 [10]), or, which he plots or meditates (Ps. 38 [12], 𝔐 [13], 52 [2.7], 𝔐 [4.9], 55 [11], 𝔐 [12], *al.*). *Hawwā* corresponds to Ar. *hâwiya*, 'a deep pit, hell,' Syr. *hawthå*, 'gulf, chasm' (cf. BDB. p. 217 *b*), and its only satisfactory rendering as used in the cases noted is Cheyne's 'engulfing ruin' (now generally adopted). On this analogy it is reasonable to assume that *b^e^liyyá'al*, as the Abyss from which there is no ascent, came to be applied to wickedness of an appalling and catastrophic character. Lagarde has acutely pointed out (*Prophetae Chaldaice*, p. xlvii) that in Ps. 41 [8] (𝔐 [9]) the derivation of *b^e^liyyá'al*, as understood by the poet, seems to be given. If we vocalize דֶּבֶר for דְּבַר, the passage runs—

'A plague of *b^e^liyyá'al* is poured out upon him;
And now that he hath lain down he shall arise no more.'

Here stichos *b* indicates that *débher b^e^liyyá'al* in stichos *a* is to be understood as 'a plague of not rising up' (*i.e.* 'from which one does not arise'), or, as we should say, 'a mortal sickness.'

* The repeated מות is suspicious. Possibly we should emend צַלְמוּת 'deep darkness' with Cheyne, *Book of Psalms*[2], *ad loc.*, who rendered the four terms 'Deathland . . . Ruinland . . . She'ol . . . Gloomland.'

that this man hath come into my house, do not this wantonness. 24. Behold my daughter, who is a virgin, and his concubine, let me, pray, bring them out, and humble ye them, and do to them that which is good in your sight; but to this man ye shall not do any such wantonness.' 25. But the men would not hearken to him: so the man laid hold on his concubine, and brought her out unto them outside; and they knew her, and abused her all the night until the morning, and let her go when the dawn arose. 26. Then came the woman at the approach of day, and fell down at the doorway of the man's house where her lord was, till daylight. 27. And her lord arose

In 2 Cor. 6^{15} Βελιαλ or Βελιάρ is used, as often in Apocalyptic literature (cf. references in *EB.* 525), as a name of Satan.

23. *wantonness.* Heb. *n^ebhālā.* The term denotes the action of a person (called *nābhāl*) who is morally insensible of the claims of either God or man. In the present passage *n^ebhālā* is used, as most often, of *immorality* viewed as a callous disregard of the rights of other people. Cf. Driver's notes in *Parallel Psalter*, Glossary, p. 457; *NHTS.*[2] p. 200.

A.V., R.V., in rendering *nābhāl* 'fool,' *n^ebhālā* 'foolishness,' are not only inadequate but misleading. Driver renders 'senseless,' 'senselessness'; but an objection to this rendering is that the English terms would not naturally be understood (apart from explanation) to convey the meaning of *moral and religious insensibility.* There seems to be no English rendering of *nābhāl* which suits all occurrences. Perhaps the best general rendering is 'impious,' if we may use this adj. to denote one who lacks *pietas* in the full and wide sense in which the term is employed in Latin. When, however, the term *nābhāl* expressly contemplates a man's attitude towards his fellowmen, the rendering 'churl' may be more appropriate. Cf. Abigail's summary of the character of her husband in 1 Sam. 25^{25}— '*Churl* (*Nābhāl*) is his name, and *churlishness* (*n^ebhālā*) is with him.' The character of the *nābhāl* is summarized in Isa. $32^{5f.}$ (A.V., R.V. here 'vile person'; *n^ebhālā v.*^{6} 'villainy').

24. *Behold my daughter, etc.* The view of Ber. that this verse is a later interpolation from Gen. 19^{8} is improbable in view of the fact that the whole narrative is closely modelled on Gen. $19^{2\,ff.}$ in the first place (cf. p. 444).*

* The abnormal suffix-form פילגשהו is doubtless an error for פילגשו; cf. *vv.*$^{2.25.27.29}$ (G-K. § 91*d*). For the masc. plur. suffixes אותם (twice), להם, we should of course expect the fem.; but such a use of masc. for fem. is frequent (cf. instances collected by König, *Syntax*, § 14).

in the morning, and opened the doors of the house, and went
out to go on his way, and, behold, the woman his concubine
was fallen down at the doorway of the house, with her hands on
the threshold. 28. And he said unto her, 'Up, and let us be
going'; but there was none that answered: then he took her
up upon the ass; and the man arose, and went to his place.
29. And he entered into his house, and took his knife, and laid
hold on his concubine, and divided her, limb by limb, into
twelve pieces, and sent her throughout all the border of Israel.
30. []<And he commanded the men that he sent, saying, 'Thus

28. *but there was none that answered.* The addition of 𝔊^MSS. ὅτι ἦν νεκρά adds an unnecessary explanation, and is clearly a gloss.

30. *And he commanded... and speak.* Reading וַיְצַו אֶת־הָאֲנָשִׁים אֲשֶׁר שָׁלַח לֵאמֹר כֹּה תֹאמְרוּ לְכָל־אִישׁ יִשְׂרָאֵל הֲנִהְיְתָה כַּדָּבָר הַזֶּה לְמִיּוֹם עֲלוֹת בְּנֵי יִשְׂרָאֵל מִמִּצְרַיִם עַד הַיּוֹם הַזֶּה שִׂימוּ לָכֶם עָלֶיהָ עֵצָה וְדַבֵּרוּ. This text follows 𝔊^A, *al.*, which, after a text corresponding to 𝔐 in *v.*[30a], offers the doublet καὶ ἐνετείλατο τοῖς ἀνδράσιν οἷς ἐξαπέστειλεν λέγων Τάδε ἐρεῖτε πρὸς πάντα ἄνδρα Ισραηλ Εἰ γέγονεν κατὰ τὸ ῥῆμα τοῦτο ἀπὸ τῆς ἡμέρας ἀναβάσεως υἱῶν Ισραηλ ἐξ Αἰγύπτου ἕως τῆς ἡμέρας ταύτης; θέσθε δὴ ἑαυτοῖς βουλὴν περὶ αὐτῆς καὶ λαλήσατε. That this rendering has a genuine Hebrew text behind it is proved by the mistranslation πρὸς πάντα ἄνδρα Ισραηλ, which clearly represents the collective expression לכל איש ישראל (cf. *ch.* 20[11], *al.*). It is to be expected that the Levite should have entrusted his envoys with a verbal message; and the exhortation 'Take ye counsel,' etc., comes more naturally from him than from those to whom the messengers are sent. In 𝔐 והיה כל הראה ואמר וג׳ the tenses are difficult, and, if part of the original narrative, can only be taken as frequentatives—'And it kept happening that everyone that saw would say,' etc.; but such a use of the frequentative is hardly natural. Assuming the text which we adopt to represent the original, the corruption in 𝔐 may have arisen as follows. The words 'And he commanded . . . men of Israel' were omitted through homoeoteleuton, the preceding *v.*[29] ending with 'Israel.' The speech 'Hath there been,' etc. being thus disconnected, and the spokesman undefined, attempt was made to solve the difficulty by insertion of 'And it was so, that everyone that saw it said,' the fact that this is a late gloss being indicated by the tenses והיה . . . ואמר, which are to be regarded as Perfects with *weak* ו, not ו *consecutive.* The substitution of לא for ה interrogative at the beginning of the speech may have arisen through dittography of the final ל of ישראל.

shall ye say to all the men of Israel〉, "⌜Hath⌝ there been ⌜such a deed as this⌝ since the day that the children of Israel came up from [] Egypt unto this day? Take ye ⌜counsel⌝ concerning it, and speak."'

20. 1. X Then all the children of Israel ⌜were called to arms⌝ R^P and the congregation was assembled X as one man, R^P from

Bu., Mo. (*SBOT.*), No., La., Kit. *BH.*, Cooke prefer to construct a text from 𝔊^A *v.*^{30a}, 𝔊^A, 𝔐 *v.*^{30b}, 𝔐 *v.*^{30a}; *i.e.* after receiving the Levite's message, the spectators respond by echoing it in substance. Such repetition is, however, from the literary point of view, almost intolerable; and it is difficult to justify the conflate text. We certainly cannot explain the omission of the injunction to the messengers in 𝔐 through homoeoteleuton ('unto this day' in the words of the messengers and in the response of the spectators) as is done by Mo. and Cooke, since such homoeoteleuton would naturally result in omission of the response of the spectators and not *vice versâ*, the scribe's eye passing from the first עד היום הזה to the second and omitting all that came between. How could it pass from the second to the first and omit all that came before the first? On the other hand, the text of 𝔊^A (*i.e.* the second reading which we take to be original) *might* have omitted 𝔐 *v.*^{30a} by homoeoteleuton; but in this case we should expect omission also of 𝔊^A, 𝔐 *v.*^{30b} which, as forming part of the Levite's message, must *ex hypothesi* have preceded 𝔐 *v.*^{30a}.

take ye counsel, etc. The expression שִׂימוּ עֵצָה, 'Apply (*lit.* set) counsel,' does not occur elsewhere: cf., however, *ch.* 20^{7b} הָבוּ לָכֶם עֵצָה וְדָבָר הֲלֹם, 'Give here your advice and counsel,' with the same Ethic Dative לכם (it is possible that we should read וְדָבָר for וְדַבְּרוּ as in 20^{7b}). 𝔐 שִׂימוּ־לָכֶם עָלֶיהָ עֻצוּ וְדַבֵּרוּ, 'set [your mind] upon it, take counsel, and speak,' implies an ellipse of לְבַבְכֶם after שִׂימוּ, as in Isa. 41^{20}. Houb., Stu., etc., read לְבַבְכֶם for לָכֶם. The verb עוץ 'take counsel' (for the normal יעץ) occurs once again in Isa. 8^{10}.

20. 1. *were called to arms.* Reading וַיִּצָּעֲקוּ with Bu. in place of 𝔐 וַיֵּצְאוּ 'came out,' etc., to battle (Mo.). The emended verb is more natural in connexion with the words following 'unto Yahweh at Miṣpah.' The same emendation is probably to be made in the parallel passage 1 Sam. 11^{7} on the authority of 𝔊: cf. *NHTS.*^{2} *ad loc.*

the congregation. Cf. p. 446.

Dan even to Be'er-sheba', and the land of Gile'ad, X unto Yahweh at Miṣpah. 2. R^P And the chiefs of all the people, ⟨out of⟩ all the tribes of Israel, took their stand in the assembly of the people of God, even four hundred thousand footmen that drew sword. 3. X And the children of Benjamin heard that the children of Israel had gone up to Miṣpah. R^P And the children of Israel said, 'Tell how this wickedness was brought to pass.' 4. And the Levite, the husband of the murdered woman, answered and said, 'To Gibe'ah which belongeth to Benjamin I came, even I and my concubine, to spend the night. 5. And the citizens of Gibe'ah rose up against me, and surrounded the house against me by night; me they thought to have slain, and my concubine they humbled so that

from Dan, etc. So (defining the northern and southern limits of the land of Israel) 1 Sam. 3 [20], 2 Sam. 3 [10], 17 [11], 24 [2.15], 1 Kgs. 4 [25] (𝔐 5 [5]).† With inverted order, 1 Chr. 21 [2], 2 Chr. 30 [5].†

the land of Gile'ad. Gile'ad is used here in its widest sense of all the Israelite territory east of Jordan. Cf. *note* on ch. 10 [17].

unto Yahweh. According to this narrative, Miṣpah seems to be regarded as the site of an important sanctuary. Cf. the remarks on pp. 447, 453.

Miṣpah. The accepted site is the modern Neby Samwîl on a lofty eminence (2935 feet) five miles north-west of Jerusalem, appropriately named 'place of outlook' (cf. *note* on the eastern Miṣpah, *ch.* 10 [17]) as commanding the country round for a great distance. Neby Samwîl is about three and a half miles nearly due west of Ḫirbet Râs eṭ-Ṭawîl, and a little north of due west of Tell el-Fûl (cf. *note* on Gibe'ah, *ch.* 19 [12]). Cf. Map, p. 465.

2. *the chiefs.* Heb. *pinnôth* (1 Sam. 14 [38], Isa. 19 [13], Zech. 10 [4]) is explained as a figurative usage of the word meaning 'corner' (*i.e.* 'corner-stone') of a building. Cf. the usage of the Ar. *ruḳn* 'corner-stone,' and then 'noble.'

out of all the tribes, etc. Reading מִכֹּל־שִׁבְטֵי with Grä., in place of 𝔐 כֹּל־שִׁבְטֵי '(even) all the tribes,' which, as it stands, is awkwardly explicative of הָעָם 'the people.' 𝔊^A, 𝔙 render '*and* all the tribes.' The מ which we insert may easily have fallen out through haplography after העם.

four hundred thousand footmen. On the huge numbers, cf. pp. 446.

me they thought to have slain. On this statement as compared with 19 [22b], cf. p. 454.

5. *they humbled.* 𝔊^{AL}, 𝔏, 𝔖^h add *καὶ ἐνέπαιξαν αὐτῇ*, *i.e.* וַיִּתְעַלְּלוּ־בָהּ as in *ch.* 19 [25].

she died. 6. Then I took hold of my concubine, and divided her, and sent her throughout all the country of the inheritance of Israel, because they had committed lewdness and wantonness in Israel. 7. Here ye all are, ye children of Israel; give here your advice and counsel.' 8. And all the people arose as one man, saying, 'We will not any of us go to his home, neither will we any of us turn unto his house: 9. but now this is the thing which we will do to Gibe'ah; ⟨we will go up⟩ against it by lot, 10. and will take ten men of an hundred of all the tribes of Israel, and an hundred of a thousand, and a thousand of ten thousand, to fetch victual for the people, that they may do [] to Gibe⸢ah⸣ of Benjamin according to all the wantonness that

6. *lewdness.* Heb. *zimmā*, as applied to sins of unchastity, is characteristic of H—Lev. 18 17, 19 29, 20 14 *bis*, and of Ezek. where it is used metaphorically of idolatry under the figure of whoredom and adultery—Ezek. 16 27.43.58, 22 9, 23 21.27.29.35 44.48 *bis*.49, 24 13; so also in Jer. 13 27. Elsewhere of adultery, Job 31 11. Scholars who hold that *vv.* 3b-8 belong to the oldest narrative are forced by these facts to suppose that *zimmā* is a later insertion, the original narrative running simply 'because they had committed wantonness in Israel.'

8. *to his home.* Lit. 'to his tent.' On the usage of the phrase, cf. *ch.* 19 9 *note.* Perhaps we ought here to read the plur. לְאֹהָלָיו, as is usual, rather than the sing. לְאָהֳלוֹ.

9. *we will go up, etc.* Inserting נַעֲלֶה with 𝔊 ἀναβησόμεθα ἐπ' αὐτὴν ἐν κλήρῳ. So Ros., Stu., Mo., etc. This verb may easily have fallen out before עליה. 𝔐 reads simply 'against it by lot,' which clearly cannot be original. 𝔗 נתמני עלה בעדבא 'we will apportion ourselves against it by lot,' 𝔖P ܢܪܡܐ ܥܠܝܗ ܦܣ̈ܐ 'we will cast lots against it,' represent different attempts to fill the lacuna. Bu.'s נַפִּילָה גוֹרָל is less probable than the emendations adopted. The reference of the casting of lots appear to be to *v.* 18, where Judah is selected to begin the attack, a statement which, as we have seen (p. 448), seems to stand out of relation to the main narrative in which all the tribes take part simultaneously in the battle.

10. *that they may do to Gibe'ah, etc.* Omitting לָבוֹאָם, which is intruded in 𝔐 between לעשות and לגבע. R.V. renders 𝔐, 'that they may do, when they come to Gibe'ah of Benjamin, according to all

⌜they⌝ have done in Israel.' 11. J Then all the men of Israel were gathered together against the city as one man, in confederacy. 12. R[P] And the tribes of Israel sent men through all the tribe⌜⌝ of Benjamin, saying, 'What is this wickedness that is brought to pass among you? Now therefore deliver up the men, the sons of Belial, that are in Gibeʿah, that we may put them to death, and extirpate ⌜the⌝ wickedness from Israel.' But ⟨the children of⟩ Benjamin were not willing to hearken to the voice of their brethren the children of Israel. 14. X And the

etc.'; but, apart from the extreme awkwardness of the position of לבואם, the use of the prep. ל in a temporal sense (in place of כ or ב) is unparalleled. לבואם is possibly a corruption of לגבעת which has come in from the margin, where it was noted as a correction of לגבע. 𝔊^A, reading לַבָּאִים for לְבוֹאָם, and placing it before לעשות, renders τοῖς εἰσπορευομένοις ἐπιτελέσαι τῇ Γαβαα, κτλ. This yields a tolerable sense; but may be suspected of being a correction of the text of 𝔊^L, 𝔖^h, where we have the order of 𝔐—ἐπιτελέσαι τοῖς εἰσπορευομένοις Γαβαα, κτλ.

to Gibeʿah. Reading לְגִבְעַת in place of 𝔐 לְגֶבַע, which is an obvious error: cf. *note* on *ch.* 19[12].

they have done. Reading plur. עָשׂוּ with 𝔊^A, 𝔖^h, 𝔖^P, in place of 𝔐 sing. masc. עָשָׂה. Had the city been individualized, we should have expected the fem. sing.: cf. G-K. § 122 *h*.

12. *tribe of Benjamin.* Reading שֵׁבֶט with the Versions for plur. שִׁבְטֵי of 𝔐, which probably arose through unintentional imitation of שִׁבְטֵי יִשְׂרָאֵל at the beginning of the verse. The same error is found in 1 Sam. 9[21]. The Jewish commentators explain the plur. by the assumption that 'tribes' is here equivalent to 'clans' (מִשְׁפָּחוֹת), Kimchi referring to the term Benjaminite clans enumerated in Gen. 46[21]; but such a usage is very improbable.

sons of Belial. Cf. 19[22] *note.*

the wickedness. The Def. Art. is necessary before רעה. Its omission in 𝔐 is due to erroneous division of the words—ונבערה רעה for ונבער הרעה—or to haplography.

the children of Benjamin. So *Ḳ^e^rê*, many MSS. of 𝔐, 𝔊, 𝔖^P, 𝔗. *Kt.* 'Benjamin' simply.

children of Benjamin were gathered together out of the cities unto Gibeʿah, to go out to battle with the children of Israel. 15. R^P And the children of Benjamin were mustered in that day from the cities twenty and ⌜five⌝ thousand men that drew sword, not including the inhabitants of Gibeʿah, [] even seven hundred

14. *out of the cities.* 𝔊, 𝔖^P presuppose מֵעָרֵיהֶם 'out of their cities.'

15. *twenty and five thousand.* So 𝔊^AL, 𝔖^h, 𝔙, in place of 𝔐, 'twenty and six thousand.' The correction is necessary in view of the statement that after 25,100 had fallen (*v.*[35]) the survivors numbered 600 (*v.*[47]). The narrator is very precise in the matter of numbers, and we are hardly justified in following Kimchi, who suggests that the 1000 who are unaccounted for in comparison of the 26,700 of 𝔐 with the numbers given in *vv.*[35.47] combined may have fallen in the battles of the first two days. According to the parallel account (J) 18,000 Benjaminites fell in battle (*v.*[44]), and the redactor is content (*vv.*[45f.]) to raise this number to a round total of 25,000, ignoring the odd 100.

15b.16. *not including, etc.* The text adopted follows 𝔙, 'praeter habitatores Gabaa, qui septingenti erant viri fortissimi, ita sinistrâ ut dextrâ proeliantes, etc.' This differs from 𝔐 in omitting התפקדו in *v.*[15b], and מכל העם הזה שבע מאות איש בחור in *v.*[16a]. So 𝔊, 𝔖^P, except that in *v.*[15b] they retain התפקדו, which they treat as a relative sentence (𝔊^B οἳ ἐπεσκέπησαν, 𝔊^AL οὗτοι ἐπεσκέπησαν, 𝔖^P ܕܐܬܦܩܕܘ), a course which is followed by A.V., R.V.; but illegitimately, since such a rendering demands the insertion of אֲשֶׁר before the verb, or (as Bu. suggests), of הֵמָּה. As 𝔐 stands, the meaning of לבד מישבי הגבעה התפקדו can only be 'not including the inhabitants of Gibeʿah were they (the Benjaminites) numbered.' It is obvious, however, that the inclusion of התפקדו in the text destroys the balanced contrast between the openings of *vv.*[16.17], ויתפקדו בני בנימין . . . ואיש ישראל התפקדו, lit. 'and were numbered the children of Benjamin . . . and the men of Israel were numbered'—a variation of order which is very idiomatic in Heb. (called by Driver, *Tenses*, § 160, *Obs.*, 'the Hebrew equivalent of μὲν . . . δὲ of the Greeks'). As for *v.*[16a]$_{\alpha}$, omitted by 𝔙, 𝔊, 𝔖^P—it is true that such omission *might* be due to homoeoteleuton (איש בחור); yet it seems in the highest degree unlikely that both the inhabitants of Gibeʿah and the left-handed warriors should have been described originally by identically the same phrase, '700 chosen men.' An alternative emendation of the text, favoured by some scholars, is to end *v.*[15]

chosen men 16. [] that were left-handed; all of these were used to sling a stone at a hair and not let it miss. 17. And the men of Israel were mustered, not including Benjamin, four hundred thousand men that drew sword; all of these were men of war. 18. And they arose, and went up to Bethel, and enquired of God, and the children of Israel said, 'Who shall go up for us first to battle with the children of Benjamin?' and Yahweh said, 'Judah first.' 19. X And the children of Israel arose in the morning, and encamped against Gibeʿah. 20. J And the men of Israel went out to battle with Benjamin; and the men of Israel set the battle in array against them at Gibeʿah. 21. X And the children of Benjamin came out from Gibeʿah, and felled of Israel to the ground in that day two and

with התפקדו, making its subj. to be the children of Benjamin, and to retain *v.*[16] as it stands in 𝔐, thus taking the genuine mention of the 700 chosen men to be to the experts with the sling. The objection to such a text (which has no support from the Versions) is that it leaves us in ignorance of the number of the Gibeʿathites—an omission which, in a tale which is so exact in its numbers, is very unlikely.

Adopting our text, it is the Gibeʿathites who form the corps of left-handed slingers; and it is worthy of notice that the warriors who, according to 1 Chr. 12[1ff.], joined David at Ṣiḳlag, and who 'were armed with bows, and could use both the right hand and the left* in slinging stones and in shooting arrows from the bow,' were 'of Saul's brethren of Benjamin,' and their leaders are stated to have been Gibeʿathites.

15. *chosen men.* Heb. *'îš bāḥûr*, *i.e.* young warriors in the prime of manhood.

18. *went up to Bethel.* On the site of Bethel, cf. *ch.* 1[22] note. It lies eight miles to the north-east of Miṣpah (Neby Samwîl). On the introduction of the sanctuary at Bethel, here and in *v.*[26], 21[2], as alien to the conception of the narrative which pictures the tribes as assembling 'unto Yahweh' at *Miṣpah*, cf. pp. 447, 453 𝔙 takes Bethel to refer to 'the house of God' at *Shiloh*, on the assumption that the Ark was at Shiloh from the days of Joshuaʿ (Josh. 18[10]) to those of ʿEli (cf. Mo. on *vv.*[27.28]).

enquired of God. Cf. *note* on *ch.* 1[1]. On the incident recorded in this verse as modelled directly upon *ch.* 1[1.2], cf. pp. 448, 454.

21. *felled . . . to the ground.* Heb. וַיַּשְׁחִיתוּ . . . אַרְצָה. The rendering of A.V., R.V., 'destroyed down to the ground,' accords

* Cf. the explanation of the phrase אטר יד ימינו given by 𝔊, 𝔙—not simply 'left-handed,' but 'ambidextrous.'

twenty thousand men. 22. J And R[P] the people, J the men of Israel, took courage, and again set the battle in array in the place where they had set it in array on the first day. 23. X And the children of Israel went up, and wept before Yahweh until the evening; and they enquired of Yahweh, saying, 'Shall I again approach to battle with the children of Benjamin my brother?' And Yahweh said, 'Go up against him.' 24. So the children of Israel drew near against the children of Benjamin on the second day. 25. J And Benjamin went out to meet them from Gibeʿah on the second day, X and again felled to the ground of the children of Israel eighteen thousand men: R[P] all these drew sword. 26. X Then all the children of Israel, R[P] and all the people, X went up, R[P] and came to Bethel X and wept, and sat down there before Yahweh, R[P] and fasted that day X until the evening, R[P] and offered burnt offerings and peace-offerings before Yahweh. 27. X And the children of Israel enquired of Yahweh, R[P](for the Ark of the covenant of

with the conventional rendering of *hišḥīth*, but offers an unnatural expression in English. Ball points out (verbally) that in the present use of *hišḥīth* we have a preservation of the original meaning of the verb as seen in the Bab. *šaḫâtu* of the T.A. Letters, which means 'to fall,' and would therefore in the causative stem (Hiphʿîl) naturally signify 'to fell.' So *vv.* [25.35] (in the last case with om. of ארצה, 'to the ground'). Cf. for the sense 'cause to fall' in Piʿēl, Gen. 38 [9].

23. *And the children of Israel went up.* We expect the place to which they went up to be mentioned. Probably this was originally specified as Miṣpah by the X narrator, and this name was cut out by R[P] so as not to conflict with his own conception of Bethel as the central sanctuary. Cf. *v.*[26], where the words 'and came to Bethel' have been inserted by R[P].

26. *burnt offerings and peace-offerings.* The burnt offering (wholly consumed by fire on the altar) is here a *piaculum*, and is followed by the peace-offering as a communion-feast shared by Yahweh and His worshippers with the purpose of ratifying and strengthening the covenant-bond. On the origin and conception of these two forms of sacrifice, cf. the present writer's *Outlines of O.T. Theology*, pp. 55 ff. The precise meaning of *šélem*, conventionally rendered 'peace-offering,' is somewhat obscure. For different views, cf. BDB. p. 1023.

27. *the Ark of the covenant of God.* This form of allusion to the Ark ('of the covenant, etc.') is due in the first place to Deuteronomic influence. In ancient narratives it is called 'the Ark' simply, or 'the Ark of Yahweh' (*or* 'of God'). Cf. the conspectus of allusions in *NHTK.* pp. 31 f.

God was there in those days, 28. and Phineḥaš, the son of Ele'azar, the son of Aaron, stood before it in those days,) X saying, 'Shall I again go out to battle with the children of Benjamin my brother, or shall I forbear?' And Yahweh said, 'Go up; for to-morrow I will deliver him into thine hand.' 29. J And Israel set an ambuscade against Gibe'ah round about. 30. X And the children of Israel went up against the children of Benjamin on the third day, and set themselves in array against Gibe'ah, as aforetime. 31. And the children of Benjamin went

28. *Phineḥaš.* There seems to be no doubt that the name is the Eg. *Pe-nḥēsi*, 'the negro,' *i.e.* 'child of dark complexion'; cf. Lauth, *ZDMG.* xxv. (1871), p. 139; W. M. Müller in *EB.* 3728, and, for the general usage of the term *nḥēsi*, *AE.* p. 112. The Eg. origin of the name is an important point in favour of the historical existence of its bearer*; and this is strengthened by the fact that the name reappears as the name of a descendant ‡—the second son of 'Eli (1 Sam. 1 3, *al.*).

stood before it. The phrase, which is here employed of the *service* of the Ark as the typical embodiment of Yahweh's manifestation, is used elsewhere of the Levites' ministrations 'before Yahweh' (Deut. 10 8, 18 7, Ezek. 44 15), and in the mouths of the prophets to illustrate their conception of their relation to Yahweh (1 Kgs. 17 1, 18 15, 2 Kgs. 3 14, 5 16). *Standing in the presence* of a master is the natural attitude of a servant who is ready to execute his behests (cf. 1 Kgs. 1 2, 12 6, Jer. 52 12, *al.*).

31. *to meet them.* Reading לִקְרָאתָם conjecturally in place of 𝔐 לִקְרַאת הָעָם 'to meet the people,' on the ground (argued above, pp. 449, 453) that the use of הָעָם is elsewhere in the narrative characteristic of the redactor R^P, and that the change which we here presuppose is a very easy one.

* In the same way, the identity (generally accepted) of the name Moses (Heb. *Môšé*) with the Egyptian *Mosi*, which appears as an element in theophorous proper names, *e.g.* Aḥmosi, Ṭhutmosi, and also as a name by itself, is historically important. Had Moses been merely a legendary national hero, Israelite historians would hardly have invested him with an Egyptian name.

‡ That the family of 'Eli represented the ancient legitimate priestly line—therefore the line of descent from Ele'azar—seems to follow from 1 Sam. 2 27 ff. The theory of the Chronicler (1 Chr. 24 3) that Ṣadoḳ was a descendant of Aaron's firstborn son Ele'azar, and Abiathar ('Eli's great-great-grandson) a descendant of his youngest (fourth) son Ithamar, is clearly a device intended to legitimitize the claim of Ṣadoḳ's family to the highpriesthood. We note, however, that, according to the earlier theory of 1 Sam. 2 35, Ṣadoḳ (who is clearly hinted at: cf. 1 Kgs. 2 27) is to be raised up on account of his superior moral claims as representing the mind of Yahweh, and nothing is said about his prior claim by birth, the contrary being in fact implied by *vv.* 27.28. Of Ṣadoḳ's antecedents prior to his appointment by David we really know nothing. Cf. Wellh., *Prolegomena*, pp. 126, 138 f.

out to meet ⌈them⌉, ⌈and⌉ were drawn away from the city; and they began to smite and kill R^P of the people, X as aforetime, R^P in the highways, of which the one goeth up to Bethel and the other to Gibe⌈ʿon⌉, X in the field, about thirty men of Israel. 32. And the children of Benjamin said, 'They are smitten down before us, as at the first': but the children of Israel said, 'Let us flee, and draw them away from the city into the highways.' 33. J And all the men of Israel rose up⌈⌉ from their

and were drawn away. Reading וַיִּנָּתְקוּ with Ehr. in place of 𝔐 הִנְּתְּקוּ, which is anomalous in form (we should expect הֻתְּקוּ) and also awkward as an asyndeton. As Ehr. remarks, the ה may easily have arisen through a misreading of וי.

in the highways . . . Gibeʿon. Reading גִּבְעֹנָה in place of 𝔐 גִּבְעָתָה 'to Gibeʿah,' with Bu., No., La., Kit., Cooke.

Heb. *mᵉsillā* denotes, not a mere beaten track, but a properly 'made' highroad. Whatever view be taken as to the precise site of Gibeʿah (cf. 19 [12] *note*), there is no doubt that it was on (*i.e.* just off) the main northern road which led to Bethel: therefore, on the reading of 𝔐, the distinction here so clearly drawn between the *two* highroads is hardly explicable. Half a mile north-west of Tell el-Fûl and nearly due west of Ḫirbet Râs eṭ-Ṭawîl the northern road forks, one branch running north-west, and reaching Gibeʿon (el-Ǵîb) after three miles. Both roads 'go up' on the whole. The elevation at the fork is 2462 feet. The Bethel-road reaches Bîreh (2824 feet) in some five miles, and then makes a further continuous rise to Bethel (2890 feet), which it reaches two miles further on. The Gibeʿon-road falls at first in crossing the wâdy ed-Dumm (2298 feet) at three-quarters of a mile, and then makes a steady rise to Gibeʿon (2535 feet) some two miles further. A line drawn from Miṣpah (Neby Samwîl) to Ḫirbet Râs eṭ-Ṭawîl actually crosses the fork of the road: consequently a hostile army approaching Gibeʿah (assumed to have been at the latter site), and feigning a disordered retreat in order to draw the Gibeʿathites away from their city, would naturally be spread out over the two roads. Cf. Map, p. 465.

in the field. According to our analysis of the sources, this is not a description of the site of Gibeʿon or Gibeʿah, but the direct continuation of 'began to smite and kill as aforetime,' in the narrative of X. The object of the Israelites' feint of retreat was to draw the Benjaminites away from the city-precincts into the *open country* (cf. Josh. 8 [24a]), and thus to facilitate the capture of the city by the ambush.

33. *And all the men of Israel rose up, etc.* Here we have in J the direct continuation of *v.*[29]. Having laid the ambush, the main army makes a move to begin the attack. The *order* of the sentence,

place, and set themselves in array at Baʿal-tamar: X and the ambuscade of Israel burst forth from its place ⌜on the west of⌝

וכל איש ישראל קמו, with the subj. brought into prominence by being placed first, offers an intentional antithesis to *v.*[29] (the ambush was laid thus, *but* the main army, etc.).*

The construction of 𝔐, קָמוּ מִמְּקֹמוֹ, is hardly tolerable. We must read sing. קָם in agreement with the collective איש ישראל, the narrative then continuing with the plur. verb ויערכו as in *vv.*[20.22]; or, accepting the plur. verb with the collective sing. subj., as in *vv.*[36b.37.48], adopt the plur. suffix מִמְּקוֹמָם.

Baʿal-tamar. Unidentified. Eusebius (*OS.* 238 [75]) states that in his day there still existed a Beth-tamar near Gibeʿah.

burst forth. Heb. מֵגִיחַ. The verb *gîaḥ* is only used elsewhere in the O.T. of water bursting forth, Job. 38 [8], 40 [23], Ezek. 32 [2] (doubtful) —cf. *Gîḥôn*, 'the Gusher,' the name of the spring outside Jerusalem; or, of a child bursting forth from the womb, Mic. 4 [10], Ps. 22 [10] (doubtful), cf. Job. 38 [8] already cited. The verb is frequent in Aram. in the Aphʿēl, followed by the accus. קְרָב 'battle,' in the sense 'movere bellum.' The emendation מַשְׁגִּיחַ 'looked forth' (cf. 𝔖[P] ܡܢ ܕܚܙܐ ܗܘܐ), proposed by Grä., is much inferior to 𝔐.

on the west of Gebaʿ. Reading מִמַּעֲרַב לַ with 𝔊[AL], 𝔖[h], 𝔙, and most moderns, in place of 𝔐 מִמַּעֲרֵה. *Maʿaré* (treated by R.V. *text* as a proper name: cf. 𝔊[B] ἀπὸ Μαρααγαβε) is rendered 'meadow' by R.V. *marg.* (A.V. 'meadows'), on the assumption that it means a *bare, naked place*‡ (*i.e.* devoid of trees?): cf. the rendering of 𝔗 מישר 'plain.'§ Such a bare open space would obviously be the last place which an ambush would choose for concealment. 𝔖[P] ܡܢ ܡܥܪܬܐ ܕܒܓܒܥܐ 'from the cave (מְמְּעָרַת) which is in Gebaʿ),

* The hopeless difficulty in which this half-verse has involved commentators, upon the ordinary assumption that it is a continuation of the narrative immediately preceding, is well set forth by Mo. Mo. himself hesitates upon the verge of the conclusion which we have adopted:—'It might be suspected that the half-verse came from the older narrative, in which it would have a passable sense and connexion after *v.*[29], but the construction is so negligent, not to say ungrammatical, that the conjecture is hardly to be entertained.' Cf., however, the remarks on the construction made above. With the slight emendation there advocated it is perfectly idiomatic.

‡ עָרוֹת 'bare places' (?) in Isa. 19 [7], rendered by R.V. '*the meadows* by the Nile,' is itself too dubious to be quoted in support.

§ According to *SWP. Great Map*, xvii., there actually exists a Sahel Ǵebaʿ, *i.e.* 'plain of Ǵebaʿ,' south-east of the village of Ǵebaʿ, but this appears too remote from the scene of action. Cf. Map, p. 465.

Geba‘, 34. and they came in front of Gibe‘ah, even ten thousand

and this is improved upon by Ar., the half-verse being rendered, ‘and the ambuscades were in the caves of Geba‘, looking forth (מְשַׁגִּיחַ) from their positions,’ the plur. ‘caves’ being substituted for the sing. probably on the ground that *one* cave would not suffice for such a force (Ros.). *

Geba‘ is nearly two and a half miles north-north-east of Ḫirbet Râs eṭ-Ṭawîl, and three miles from Tell el-Fûl; so that, if ‘to the west of Geba‘’ is literally interpreted, the ambuscade must have been placed at a considerable distance from the city. Not improbably, however, we may think of it as concealed in the valley which runs from the western side of Ǵeba‘ down to Ḥizmeh (so La.), from which it could rapidly proceed up the wâdy el-Ḥâfy to Râs eṭ-Ṭawîl. Cf. Map, p. 465.

Mo. effects a complete agreement with the Versions upon which we base our emendation by reading ‘west of *Gibe‘ah*’ (𝔊^{AL} ἀπὸ δυσμῶν τῆς Γαβαα, 𝔙 ‘ab occidentali urbis parte’); but this surely cannot be correct, since west of Gibe‘ah was the very direction in which the Benjaminites were advancing to the attack of the Israelite host. The whole account of the stratagem seems to indicate that the ambush attacked Gibe‘ah from the east or north-east, while the Benjaminites were being drawn off to the west.

34. *in front of Gibe‘ah.* Heb. מִנֶּגֶד לַגִּבְעָה. The sense of מנגד is somewhat obscure. It may be supposed that it denotes something more definite than ‘in view of,’ and is intended to describe the quarter from which the city was approached; and, if this is so, we may conjecture that it has the sense often possessed by the analogous expression לִפְנֵי ‘before,’ viz. ‘*eastward of*’: cf. BDB. *s.v.* פנים, 7a (*d*). This is the quarter from which the city could be approached unobserved, and from which it would naturally be approached from the south-west of Geba‘. Such a meaning suits the use of נֶגֶד in the similar description of the capture of ‘Ai in Josh. 8. Here the ambuscade is west of ‘Ai (*v.*[9]), and the main army of Israel, advancing from the Jordan valley, would naturally come ‘in front of the city’ (*i.e.* eastward of it) before encamping on the north of it (*v.*[11]). La. takes a different view, holding that ‘in front of’ means that the ambuscade placed itself between the Benjaminites and Gibe‘ah so as to cut off retreat—therefore, *to the west of* it. A different reading offered by twenty-seven MSS. of 𝔐 and presupposed by 𝔗 (מדרום) is מִנֶּגֶב ‘to the south of.’ This might describe the position of a force coming up the wâdy Zimry to attack Râs eṭ-Ṭawîl; yet the reading is hardly to be preferred to that of 𝔐.

* Three caves are marked at Ǵeba‘ in the *SWP. Great Map*, xvii.

chosen men out of all Israel, and the battle was sore; J but *they* knew not that evil was closing upon them. 35. X And Yahweh smote Benjamin before Israel: and the children of Israel felled of Benjamin on that day twenty-five thousand one hundred men: R^P all these drew sword. 36. X And the children of Benjamin saw that they were smitten: J and the men of Israel gave place to Benjamin, for they trusted in the ambuscade which they had set against Gibeʿah. 37. And the ambuscade hasted, and made an onset against Gibeʿah: and the ambuscade opened out, and smote all the city at the edge of the sword. 38. Now the appointment between the men of Israel and the ambuscade was [] that when they should make a beacon of smoke to rise up

even ten thousand, etc. The reference is to the ambuscade.

but **they** *knew not, etc.* The subj. is clearly the Benjaminites who are the victims of the ruse; and the fact that they are not mentioned in the earlier half of the verse is an indication that we are dealing in this latter half with the other source (J). The antecedent statement in J must have described how the Benjaminites sallied forth to meet Israel at Baʿal-tamar (*v.*[33a]); cf. Josh. 8 [14], where the latter half of the verse bears a marked resemblance to the present passage.

35. *felled.* Cf. note on *v.*[21].

twenty-five thousand one hundred men. I.e. all but the 600 survivors mentioned in *v.*[47]. Cf. *note* on *v.*[15].

37. *opened out. I.e.* deployed. Heb. וַיִּמְשֹׁךְ. Cf. *ch.* 4 [6] *note.*

38. *appointment.* Heb. *môʿēdh*, lit. (here) 'appointed time' (as very frequently; cf. BDB. *s.v.* **1a**). The signal of the smoke-beacon indicated the *môʿēdh* for Israel's *volte-face*, but was not itself the *môʿēdh* (we have no parallel for *môʿēdh* = 'appointed signal').

was, that when, etc. Omitting the *vox nihili* הֶרֶב before לְהַעֲלוֹתָם with some MSS. of 𝔊, 𝔖^P, 𝔙, and all recent commentators, as corrupt dittography of the immediately preceding הָאֹרֵב 'the ambuscade.' 𝔗 דייסגון לאסקא, lit. 'that they should *make great* to send up,' is followed by R.V., 'that they should make a *great* cloud of smoke, etc.' (A.V. is similar.) This rendering apparently regards הֶרֶב as apocopated Imperat. Hiphʿîl of רבה—a view which would be just possible if the injunction were couched in the *oratio recta* (הֶרֶב לְהַעֲלוֹת 'make great to send up,' *i.e.* 'send up as much as you can!'), but is of course out of the question when it is expressed obliquely with the suffix form לְהַעֲלוֹתָם. Some MSS. of 𝔥 read חֶרֶב 'sword,' which appears in 𝔊^{AL} μάχαιρα thrown into the sentence without any intelligible

out of the city, 39. the men of Israel ⌜should⌝ face about in the battle. And Benjamin began to smite and kill among the men of Israel about thirty men; ⌜and⌝ they said, 'Surely they are utterly smitten before us, as in the first battle.' 40. Then the beacon began to ascend from the city in a column of smoke; and when Benjamin looked back, behold, the holocaust of the city rose up toward heaven. 41. And the men of Israel faced about; and the men of Benjamin were dismayed, for they saw that evil had closed upon them. 42. So they turned⌜⌝ before

connexion. 𝕲^B τῆς μάχης (connecting with preceding μετὰ τοῦ ἐνέδρου) appears to represent an attempt to make sense of this.

a beacon. Heb. *mas'ēth*, lit. 'an uplifting.'

39. *the men of Israel should face about.* Reading וְהָפַךְ after the happy suggestion of Mo. (adopted by Driver, *ET.* xviii. p. 332, and Cooke). The Perf. with ו *consecutive* (idiomatically continuing the Infinitive construction: cf. Driver, *Tenses*, § 118) states the other side of the pact. 𝕳 וַיַּהֲפֹךְ 'and the men of Israel *faced about*,' anticipates *v.*[41a], and makes the Israelites *anticipate the appointed signal* which is not given till *v.*[40]. The attempt of some scholars (*e.g.* Kit., La.) to explain the verb as meaning here 'faced about in flight' (which they had already done in *v.*[36b]), and in *v.*[41a] 'faced about to make a stand,' is obviously futile.

and they said. Reading וַיֹּאמְרוּ in place of 𝕳 כִּי אָמְרוּ 'for they said.' Obviously the conclusion drawn by the Benjaminites was the *result* of their preliminary success in smiting Israel. The text of 𝕳 can only be explained as meaning that they began to be successful because they supposed that the same result was bound to ensue as on the preceding days. This, however, is clearly not the intention of the narrative. The confusion of ו and כ is not uncommon: cf. *ch.* 16[24], 1 Sam. 2[21] כי פקד for ויפקד (𝕲 καὶ ἐπεσκέψατο), Jer. 37[16] כי בא for ויבא (𝕲 καὶ ἦλθεν); conversely 1 Kgs. 22[37] וימת for כי מת (𝕲 ὅτι τέθνηκεν), Isa. 39[1] וישמע for כי שמע (𝕲 ἤκουσεν γάρ, and so 𝕳 in 2 Kgs. 20[12]).

40. *The holocaust of the city.* Heb. כְּלִיל הָעִיר. The rendering adopted is that of Mo., who points to Deut. 13[17] for a similar use of *kālîl* in allusion to the destruction of a city by fire: 'And thou shalt burn with fire the city and all its spoil as a holocaust to Yahweh thy God.' R.V., rendering 'the whole of the city,' has to supply the words '*in smoke*' after 'went up.' The similar passage in Josh. 8[20] has 'the smoke of the city went up toward heaven.'

42. *they turned.* Reading וַיִּפֶן in agreement with the singulars

the men of Israel unto the way to the wilderness ; but the battle overtook them, and they that were from ⌜the city⌝ were destroying them in the midst⌜⌝, 43. ⌜and they beat down⌝ Benjamin,

ויבהל, עליו proceeding, and the sing. suffix of הדביקתהו following, in place of 𝔐 plur. וַיִּפְנוּ. So Bu., No., Kit. *BH.*

from the city. Reading מֵהָעִיר with 𝔙 ('sed et hi qui urbem succenderant'), some MSS. of 𝔊, Mo. The reference is, of course, to Gibe'ah. The ambuscade, having burned the city, now joined in the attack of the Benjaminites in the field. Cf. Josh. 8 22. 𝔐 מֵהֶעָרִים, 'from the cities,' must have arisen through dittography of the initial מ of משחיתים immediately following.

in the midst. Reading בַּתָּוֶךְ with Mo., No., La. (cf. 𝔙 'ex utraque parte,' 𝔖ᴾ ܡܟܐ ܘܡܟܐ, 𝔗 מכא ומכא), as in Josh. 8 22, 'And these others [the ambuscade who had just burned the city] came out of the city against them ; so they were in the midst of Israel [lit. they were, as regards Israel, in the midst,' בַּתָּוֶךְ], some on this side, and some on that side : and they smote them,' etc. The meaning of the phrase is the same in our passage, viz. that the Benjaminites were 'in the midst' of the Israelite forces, caught between the main army and the ambuscade which has issued from the city. In 𝔐 בְּתוֹכוֹ, R.V. 'in the midst thereof,' the reference of the suffix is obscure, and we may regard the וֹ as properly the ו *consecutive* belonging to the verb which opens the next verse. Cf. *note* following.

43. *and they beat down . . . Geba'.* Reading וַיַּכְּתוּ אֶת־בִּנְיָמִין וַיִּרְדְּפֻהוּ מְנוּחָה עַד נֹכַח גֶּבַע, in place of 𝔐 כִּתְּרוּ אֶת־בִּנְיָמִן הִרְדִיפֻהוּ מְנוּחָה הִדְרִיכֻהוּ עַד נֹכַח הַגִּבְעָה, rendered by R.V. 'They enclosed the Benjamites about, [and] chased them, [and] trode them down at [their] resting-place, as far as over against Gibeah.' The text of 𝔐 is undoubtedly very corrupt. כתרו, 'they surrounded,' is strange in the description of a *pursuit*; and if the verb is preserved uncorrupted it seems almost necessary to regard the statement 'they surrounded Benjamin' as a marginal gloss upon בתוכו in the preceding verse. Our emendation וַיַּכְּתוּ (so Ehr.) is based on 𝔊ᴮ καὶ κατέκοπτον, 𝔊ᴬᴸ καὶ ἔκοψαν ; cf. the use of the verb in a similar connexion in Num. 14 45 (𝔊 καὶ κατέκοψαν αὐτούς), Deut. 1 44. The disappearance of ו *consecutive* before the verb may be due to the fact that it has been taken as the suffix of the preceding בתוכו, which should be בתוך (cf. *note* preceding). The suggested emendations כִּתְּתוּ or כָּרְתוּ have not the same support in usage.

⌜and⌝ pursued him ⌜from Noḥah⌝ [] as far as over against ⌜⌝Geba‘⌜⌝ towards the east. 44. And there fell of Benjamin

הרדיפהו, הדריכהו are suspicious as being asyndeta. The Hiph‘îl of רדף is otherwise unknown. The Hiph‘îl הדריך can hardly mean 'trod down,' the sense which is assigned to it by A.V., R.V. (we should expect Ḳal; cf. Isa. 63[3]); but probably (as noted by Ros.) the meaning intended is 'overtook,' as in the Ar. Conjugation iv. and Syr. Aph‘ēl of the verb. The close similarity between the two verbs marks them as doublets; and one of them at least must be deleted from the text.* We read וַיִּרְדְּפֻהוּ with La., Ehr. on the assumption that יו has been misread ה (cf. *note* on 'and were drawn away,' *v.*[31]), and delete הדריכהו as a doublet.

מְנוּחָה, 'rest' or 'resting-place,' is treated by R.V., Ber., Ke., Oet. as an Accus. of place; but such a usage would be quite without parallel even if the subs. had the Def. Art. prefixed. The sense in which the word is used in its context has proved a crux to the Versions. 𝔊[AL], καταπαῦσαι αὐτὸν κατάπαυσιν, treats it as a second Accus. after the preceding verb. 𝔖[P] (connecting with following verb) regards מנוחה as an adverbial Accus., ܘܒܢܝܚܐ ܩܛܠܘܗܝ, 'and quietly (easily?) slew him'—hence A.V. 'trode them down with ease,' and similarly Ros., and Böttcher in Winer's *Zeitschr.* II. i. p. 62; but this is a misuse of the meaning of מנוחה. 𝔙, 𝔗, 𝔊[B] treat the initial מ of מנוחה as the particle מן: so 𝔙 somewhat paraphrastically, 'nec erat ulla requies morientium,' *i.e.* מן *of separation*, 'apart from rest'; 𝔗 (connecting with preceding verb) רדופונון מבית ניחהון, 'they chased them from their resting-place'; 𝔊[B] καὶ ἐδίωξαν αὐτὸν ἀπὸ Νουα, treating נוחה as a place-name with מן as the *terminus a quo*. This last explanation, adopted by Houb., is favoured by Mo., who cites Noḥah named in 1 Chr. 8[2] as the fourth 'son,' *i.e. clan* of Benjamin, and so possibly the name of a Benjaminite city or village. This we have adopted in our text (with La., and Driver in *ET.* xviii. p. 332) in default of a better solution; though, since it cannot be maintained with Mo. (*SBOT.*) that the *terminus ad quem* 'as far as over against Geba‘' *requires* a *terminus a quo* (there is none *e.g.* in Num. 14[45], Deut. 1[44]), it must be admitted that the emendation is extremely precarious.‡ The only alternative seems to be to follow Bu. (with No., Kit., Cooke) in omitting מנוחה as due to dittography, on the view that a scribe accidentally duplicated the words בנימין הרדיפהו and the duplication eventually became מנוחה הדריכהו.

* It is conceivable that both may be marginal variants of הדביקתהו in the preceding verse.

‡ Luther and Stu. treat מנוחה as a place-name defining the *terminus ad quem*, 'unto Menuḥah,' this being further defined by 'as far as, etc.' Cf. for this *ch.* 7[22], 'toward Ṣeredah, as far as the edge of Abel-meḥolah.'

eighteen thousand men: R^P all these were men of valour. 45. X And they turned and fled toward the wilderness unto the crag of Rimmon. R^P And they gleaned of him in the highways five thousand men, and they followed hard after him as far as ⌜Geba'⌝, and they smote of him two thousand men. 46. So all

In 𝔐 'as far as over against Gibeʿah to the east,' 'Gibeʿah' is certainly an error, since, as Mo. remarks, 'the Israelites clearly did not desist from pursuit in the immediate vicinity of Gibeʿah, that is, at the very start.' Since the fugitives had as their objective the crag of Rimmon to the north-east (cf. *note* on *v.*[45] for the site), it is natural to suppose that we should read 'Gebaʿ,' the two names (as noted on p. 464) being often confused. So Mo., Bu., La., Kit., Driver (*ET.* xviii. p. 332), Cooke. Why the pursuit ended at the point indicated hardly calls for solution, the reasonable inference being that the ultimate survivors had at this stage succeeded in getting clear away. Mo. remarks that 'Geba (Ǵebaʿ) lies in the line of flight from Gibeah (Tell el-Fūl) toward Rammōn, and the great wady es-Suweinit, with its difficult passage between Ǵebaʿ and Makhmās, would naturally check the pursuit.' Similarly, Cooke—'Jebaʿ lies on the way to Rammon; but before the fugitives could reach their place of refuge (Rimmon, *v.*[45]) the narrow defile of the Wadi Suwēnīt (1 Sam. 14[4 ff.]), between Jebaʿ and Machmās would stop further pursuit.' The present writer can, however, state, from personal inspection of the wâdy, that at any point at which it would naturally be encountered in a flight from Tell el-Fûl or Râs eṭ-Ṭawîl to Rammôn it could be crossed without much difficulty. Only if the fugitives had gone out of their way towards the east, and then struck off northward at an angle, would they have found the wâdy a formidable obstacle. Cf. Map, p. 465.

44. *all these, etc.* Heb. אֶת־כָּל־אֵלֶּה אַנְשֵׁי חָיִל here and in *v.*[46], with את introducing the Nominative with some emphasis—a mark of late and inferior style: cf. G-K. § 117 *m.*

45. *the crag of Rimmon.* Eusebius and Jerome (*OS.* 146[5], 287[98]) mention a village named Rimmon fifteen Roman miles north of Jerusalem. The identification by Rob. (*BR.*[3] i. p. 440) with the modern Rammôn, three and a half miles east of Bethel, 'situated on and around the summit of a conical chalky hill, and visible in all directions,' is generally accepted. Cf., however, *Addenda*, p. xxi, where the claims of a rival identification are discussed.

as far as Gebaʿ. Reading עַד־גֶּבַע with Mo. (*Γαβαα*, *Γαβα* is the reading of the group of 𝔊 MSS. cited by Mo. as 𝔊[N]), in place of 𝔐, עַד־גִּדְעֹם which, as vocalized, can only be regarded as a proper

that fell of Benjamin were twenty and five thousand men that drew sword in that day: all these were men of valour. 47. But there turned and fled towards the wilderness unto the crag of Rimmon X six hundred men; J and they abode on the crag of Rimmon four months. 48. And the men of Israel turned back unto the children of Benjamin, and smote them at the edge

name 'unto Gidʿom'—a locality which is otherwise quite unknown to us.

There should be no doubt that the emendation adopted is correct. The reference occurs in the redactor's interpolation, *vv.*[45aβb.46], the sole object of which is, not to supply *fresh* topographical information, but (cf. p. 448) to cure the discrepancy between the figure 18,000 in *v.*[44] (J), as compared with 25,100 in *v.*[35] (X). As a means of accomplishing this, he had in his sources *two scenes of action* to which the slaughter of further Benjaminites (making up, in round numbers, 25,000, *v.*[46]) might be assigned: (*a*) the battlefield, which, as we learn from *vv.*[31.32], extended over the *meṣillôth*, 'highways,' west and north-west of Gibeʿah (cf. *note* on *v.*[31]); (*b*) the line of flight, which is described in *v.*[43] as extending (from the battlefield) 'as far as over against Gebaʿ.' Thus, on the view that the 18,000 fell on the battlefield before the flight (a deduction implied by the placing of *v.*[44] *before v.*[45aα]), he assigns (*a*) an additional 5000 as the result of a grape-gleaning (for the use of the verb *ʿôlēl*, cf. the subs. *ôlēlôth* in *ch.* 8 [2] *note*), *i.e.* a careful going over the *meṣillôth* a second time to wipe out stragglers; and (*b*) 2000 more as overtaken in the pursuit before it was abandoned on reaching 'as far as Gebaʿ.'

A casual suggestion thrown out (though not adopted) by Mo. in a footnote in his *Comm.* (p. 444) is that we might vocalize the word in 𝔐 as an Infinitive, עַד־גָּדְעָם 'till they cut them off': cf. the use of the verb in *ch.* 21 [6], 'One tribe is cut off (נִגְדַּע) to-day from Israel.' This has been adopted by succeeding commentators (so Bu., No., La., Kit., Cooke). Clearly the syntax will not admit of such a reading. Considering that Benjamin is referred to in the sing. both immediately before (אחריו) and immediately after (ממנו), the writer's choice, had he meant to use such an Infinitive, would have lain between עַד־גִּדְעוֹ (cf. 1 Kgs. 22 [11], Ps. 18 [38]), and, preferably, עַד־גָּדְעָם אֹתוֹ (cf. Jer. 9 [15], 49 [37], Deut. 7 [24], 28 [48], *al.*).

The reading of 𝔖ᴾ, 'Gibeʿon,' is adopted by Grä.; but this city lay in the wrong direction.

48. *turned back unto the children of Benjamin.* The reference is to the non-combatants (old men, women, and children) whom they found at home in the cities and villages.

of the sword, both ⸢inhabited⸣ city, and cattle, and everything that there was; moreover all the cities that there were they set on fire.

21. 1. Now the men of Israel had sworn in Miṣpah, saying, 'There shall not any of us give his daughter to Benjamin to wife.' 2. R^P And the people came to Bethel, and sat there until the evening before God, and lifted up their voice, and wept sore. 3. And they said, 'Wherefore, O Yahweh, God of Israel, hath this come to pass in Israel, that there should be missing to-day one tribe from Israel?' 4. And on the morrow the people rose up early, and built there an altar, and offered burnt offerings and peace-offerings. 5. And the children of Israel, said, 'Who

both inhabited city. Vocalizing מֵעִיר מְתִם, lit. 'both city of men,' as in Deut. 2^{34}, 3^{6}, Job 24^{12}, with several Heb. MSS., Stu., Wellh., Mo., etc., in place of 𝔐 מֵעִיר מְתֹם, which, if genuine, would seem to mean 'both city of *entirety*,' whence R.V. 'both entire city.' The subs. מְתֹם only occurs again in Isa. 1^{6}, Ps. $38^{3.7}$ (𝔋 $^{4.8}$) in a different connexion ('soundness' of body). Even with our emendation the sequence (lit.) 'from city of men unto cattle, unto everything, etc.' is rather strange. 𝔖^P reads ܡܢ ܡܕ̈ܝܢܬܐ ܐܢܫܐ ܘܥܕܡܐ ܠܒܥܝܪܐ, which, if not merely a paraphrase, presupposes מֵאָדָם וְעַד־בְּהֵמָה וג׳ 'from mankind to cattle, etc.': cf. Gen. 6^{7}, 7^{23}, Ex. 9^{25}, 12^{12}, Lev. 27^{28}, Num. 3^{13}, Jer. 50^{3}, 51^{62}, Ps. 135^{8}. This reading, which is adopted by Grä., is certainly easier. Kit. מִמְּתִם 'from men,' omitting עִיר.

21, 4. *and built there an altar.* The statement is difficult to explain in view of $20^{26\text{-}28a}$, according to which Bethel was the scene of the priestly ministrations of Phineḥaš, and the Israelites had already offered there the same forms of sacrifice as are mentioned in the present passage—clearly (it is implied) on the ancient altar pertaining to the sanctuary. Mo. and Bu. regard the statement relating to the new altar as a gloss; but, considering that the Bethel-passages, here and in *ch.* 20, appear to emanate from the late redactor R^P, it is difficult to conjecture what purpose a still later interpolator could have in view in making a fresh altar take the place of the old and orthodox altar as pictured by the priestly writer. May we conjecture that certain elements from one of the sources underlie R^P's work in *vv.*$^{2\text{-}5}$, and that among these there was an allusion to the building of an altar at *Miṣpah*?

is there from among all the tribes of Israel that came not up in the assembly unto Yahweh?' For the great oath had been pronounced concerning him that came not up unto Yahweh to Miṣpah, saying, 'He shall surely be put to death.' 6. X And the children of Israel were moved to pity for Benjamin their brother, and said, 'One tribe is cut off to-day from Israel. 7. J How shall we do for wives for them, R^P for the survivors, J seeing *we* have sworn by Yahweh not to give them of our daughters to wives?' 8. And they said, 'What one is there of the tribes of Israel that came not up unto Yahweh to Miṣpah?' And, behold, there had come no man to the camp from Jabesh of Gileʿad R^P unto the assembly. 9. And the people were mustered, and, behold, there was not there a man of the inhabitants of Jabesh of Gileʿad. 10. J So R^P the congregation

5. *for the great oath, etc.* The definite form in which the reference is couched seems to point to a recognized formula, the provisions of which were well understood (Mo. compares 1 Sam. 14$^{24.26.28}$). Failing this explanation of the Def. Art., we must infer that it points back to an earlier mention of the oath—in which case it is probable that here again we have an element from one of the sources. R.V. 'for they had made a great oath, etc.,' does not bring out the force of the Heb.

6. *is cut off.* Lit. 'is hewn *or* lopped off,' like a branch from a tree (so Mo., who compares Isa. 10^{33}, 14^{12}). In place of נִגְדַּע some MSS. read נִגְרַע 'is withdrawn *or* subtracted,' which, though possible, is not so forcible as the accepted text.

7. *for them, for the survivors.* Here 'for them' originally found its reference in a part of J's narrative which has been omitted by R^P. Thus, to make the allusion clear, R^P has added 'for the survivors' (cf. *v.*^{16a}).

8. *Jabesh of Gileʿad.* The name is preserved in the wâdy Yâbis, which runs into the Jordan from the east about nineteen miles north of the mouth of the Jabboḳ; but the site of the city has not been identified. Eusebius (*OS.* 225^{98}, 268^{81}) describes it as lying 'on the mountain' (table-land) beyond Jordan six Roman miles from Pella on the road to Gerasa. Rob. (*BR.*^{3} iii. p. 319) proposes the ruined site ed-Dêr on the southern edge of wâdy Yâbis, six miles from the Jordan; but this site, though the right distance from Pella (Ḫ. Faḥil), is off the road to Ǵeraš, and, according to Merrill, unmarked by really ancient remains. Merrill (*DB.* ii. p. 524) favours the ancient site Meryamîn on the northern side of wâdy Yâbis; but this, though stated by him to be 'about seven miles from Pella,'

J sent thither twelve thousand men of the most valiant, and commanded them, saying, 'Go, and smite the inhabitants of Jabesh of Gile'ad at the edge of the sword, with the women and the little ones. 11. R^P And this is the thing that ye shall do; every male, and every woman that knoweth cohabitation with a male ye shall devote to destruction, J⟨but the virgins ye shall save alive.' And they did so.⟩ 12. And they found of the inhabitants of Jabesh of Gile'ad four hundred virgin girls, that had not known a man R^P in respect of cohabitation with a male;

appears, as measured on the map, to be not more than two or three miles distant.*

Jabesh is mentioned elsewhere in the O.T. solely in connexion with the history of Saul. It was the rescue of the city from Naḥash the 'Ammonite which (according to the J narrative 1 Sam. 11) gave Saul the opportunity of proving his ability as a leader and led to his election to the kingship; and in grateful memory of this rescue the inhabitants of Jabesh, after the death of Saul at the battle of Mount Gilboa', recovered his body from the wall of Beth-she'an where it had been hung by the Philistines, and buried it, together with the bodies of his sons, in or near their city (1 Sam. 31 8-13). David, on his succession to the kingship at Ḥebron, sent a message of thanks to the Jabeshites for this action (2 Sam. 2 4ff.), and eventually brought back the bones of Saul and his sons from Jabesh and buried them in the ancestral tomb of Ḳish in the land of Benjamin (2 Sam. 21 12ff.). The selection of this city—so friendly and faithful to Saul—for a shameful part in a narrative which deals with an atrocious deed committed by Gibe'ah, Saul's native city, suggests with some reason that the leading motive in the story may have been deep antipathy to the memory of Saul and his adherents. Cf. p. 447.

11. *but the virgins . . . did so.* Adding וְאֶת־הַבְּתוּלוֹת תְּחַיּוּ וַיַּעֲשׂוּ כֵּן after 𝔊^B τὰς δὲ παρθένους περιποιήσεσθε. καὶ ἐποίησαν οὕτως. Cf. 𝔙 'virgines autem reservate.' The addition is indispensable in view of the fact that the saving of the virgin girls was the prime purpose of the expedition.

12. *four hundred virgin girls.* It is not unlikely that, according to J, there were only four hundred surviving Benjaminites to be provided with wives.

[a] There is a discrepancy in the position of Meryamîn as given by the Smith-Bartholomew map and the *EB.* map, the former placing it barely two miles south-east of Ḫ. Faḥil and three and a quarter miles north-west of deir Halāweh (ed-Dêr), while the latter places it nearer the wâdy Yâbis, three and a half miles south-east of Ḫ. Faḥil and two and a half miles north-west of ed-Dêr. Smith's Map VI. in *HG.* agrees more nearly with *EB.*

J and they brought them unto the camp R^P to Shiloh, which is in the land of Canaʿan.

13. J Then R^P the whole congregation J sent, and spake unto the children of Benjamin that were on the crag of Rimmon, and proclaimed peace to them. 14. And Benjamin returned at that time, and they gave them the women that they had saved alive of the women of Jabesh of Gileʿad; R^P and yet so they did not find enough for them. 15. And the people were moved to pity for Benjamin, because that Yahweh had made a breach in the tribes of Israel. 16. And the elders of the congregation said, ‘How shall we do for wives for the survivors, seeing that women have been destroyed out of Benjamin?’ 17. X And they said, ‘⌜How shall⌝ a remnant ⌜be left⌝ to Benjamin, that a tribe be not blotted out from Israel, 18. seeing that *we* are not

to Shiloh. Why the camp should be represented as transferred from Miṣpah (or Bethel) to Shiloh cannot be divined. Mo. thinks that the editor may be already shifting the scene to prepare for the narrative of *vv.* 19 ff., though, as he adds, ‘that story is really quite incompatible with the presence of the Israelite encampment at Shiloh.’

which is in the land of Canaʿan. The same curious definition is found in Josh. 21 2, 22 9, with reference to Shiloh, both passages belonging to the Priestly source. The second passage, which relates how the two and a half tribes leave Shiloh to return to Gileʿad, east of Jordan, suggests that ‘in the land of Canaʿan’ may be the equivalent of ‘west of Jordan,’ as distinct from east of it (cf. Josh. 22 10); but in any case, the fact that the site of Shiloh has to be defined at all indicates a very late date for the comment. Cf. the exact description of the site in *v.* 19.

15. *Yahweh had made a breach.* For the phrase, cf. 2 Sam. 6 8. Similarly (verb פרץ) 2 Sam. 5 20, Ex. 19 22.24.

17. *How shall a remnant be left.* Reading אֵיךְ תִּשָּׁאֵר פְּלֵיטָה as suggested by some MSS. of 𝔊 πῶς ἔσται κλῆρος διασωζόμενος κτλ., with Mo. (who offers the alternative verb תִּוָּשֵׁעַ), La., Kit., Driver (*ET.* xviii. p. 332), Cooke. 𝔐 יְרֻשַּׁת פְּלֵיטָה לְב׳ ‘An inheritance of a remnant for (*or* pertaining to) Benjamin,’ is freely expanded by A.V., R.V. into ‘There must be an inheritance for them that be escaped of Benjamin’; but even if we grant the legitimacy of this rendering, there still remains the difficulty that the question deals with the *territory* of Benjamin, whereas the context makes it clear that the immediate concern was to secure that *the tribe itself* should not be

able to give them wives of our daughters?' for the children of Israel had sworn, saying, 'Cursed be he that giveth a wife to Benjamin.' 19. And they said, 'Behold, there is the feast of Yahweh in Shiloh yearly,' R^P which is on the north of Bethel, on the east of ⌈the⌉ highway which goeth up from Bethel to Shechem, and on the south of Lebonah. 20. X And ⌈they⌉ commanded the children of Benjamin, saying, 'Go and lie in wait in the vineyards; 21. and see, and, behold, if the daughters of Shiloh come forth to dance in the dances, then come ye forth from the vineyards, and snatch ye every man his wife from the daughters of Shiloh, and go to the land of Benjamin. 22. And

blotted out. Oort reads תִּשָּׁאֵר 'let there be left, etc.,' following 𝔖^P ܘܐܫܬܪܘ ܦܠܝܛܘܬܐ ܦܪܝܢ ܠܒܢܝܡܝܢ; while Bu., No., prefer נַשְׁאִירָה 'let us leave, etc.'

19. *Behold there is, etc.* Bu. is doubtless right in regarding these words as addressed to the Benjaminites, and as directly continued by *v.* 20b in the original narrative. The insertion of the topographical note in v. 19 has necessitated the resumption, 'And they commanded, etc.'

the feast of Yahweh. The Heb. term *ḥag* properly means 'a pilgrimage' (cf. Ar. *ḥaǵǵ*); and though the description of the festival suggests that it was local in character, it may have been attended by pilgrims from the country round. Cf. the description of the position occupied by Shiloh as the religious centre for festival-pilgrimages in 1 Sam. 1, 2.

which is on the north, etc. The modern Sêlûn (cf. *ch.* 18 31 *note*) is, as described, nearly ten miles north-north-east of Bêtîn (Bethel), two miles east of the high road to Nâblus (Shechem), and three miles east-south-east of el-Lubbân (Lebonah).*

of the highway. Vocalizing לַמְסִלָּה with the Def. Art., in place of 𝔐 לִמְסִלָּה.

20. *And they commanded.* *Ḳ^erê* וַיְצַוּוּ, in place of Kt. וַיְצַו.

21. *if the daughters of Shiloh come out.* On the plur. masc. predicate before a plur. fem. subj., cf. G-K. § 145 *p*.

* In the phrase מִצְּפוֹנָה לְ cf., for the Construct State before the prep., G-K. § 130 *a*, *n* 3, and, for the ה *locative* with the Construct State, G-K. § 90 *c*. The normal phrase is מִצְּפוֹן לְ, cf. *ch.* 2 9, *al.*

when thei⌜r⌝ fathers or thei⌜r⌝ brothers come to complain unto ⌜you⌝, ⌜ye⌝ shall say, 'Grant the⌜m⌝ graciously to us; for we took not every man his wife in battle: for ⌜if⌝ *ye* had given them to ⌜us⌝, ye would now be guilty.' 23. And the children of

22. *their fathers or their brothers.* Reading fem. suffixes אֲבוֹתָן, אֲחֵיהֶן, in place of the erroneous masc. suffixes of 𝔐. Similarly we must read אֶתְהֶן or אֹתָן (Ezek. 16[54]) for אוֹתָם in the request 'Grant them graciously, etc.' With the mention of the *brothers* as likely to be prominent in demanding satisfaction, cf. Gen. 34[7ff.], 2 Sam. 13[20ff.].

To complain. On *Kt.* לָרוּב, cf. *ch.* 6[32] *note.* *Ḳ*ᵉ*rê* substitutes the normal לָרִיב.

unto you. Reading אֲלֵיכֶם with 𝔊[BA], 𝔖[h], 𝔙, in place of 𝔐 אֵלֵינוּ 'unto us.' The aggrieved Shilonites would naturally complain directly to the captors, rather than to Israel at large.

ye shall say. Reading וַאֲמַרְתֶּם in place of 𝔐 וְאָמַרְנוּ 'we will say.' The emendation is necessitated by that immediately preceding, and by the words of the speech which follow ('to us,' 'for we took not every man his wife, etc.').* The retention of וְאָמַרְנוּ involves emendation of the speech: cf. *notes* following.

Grant them graciously . . . be guilty. Reading לֻא for לֹא (as suggested by Stu.) and לָנוּ for לָהֶם. The Benjaminites are to appeal to the complaisance of the Shilonites, adducing two reasons: (1) that the Shilonites were not bound to a vendetta on account of the rape, since the maidens had not been captured in *battle*; (2) nor, on the other hand, had they *given* their daughters to the Benjaminites, and so they were not guilty of infringing the oath (*v.*[18]). The measure adopted by the Benjaminites had in fact steered a middle course between capture with bloodshed, which must have forced a quarrel on the Shilonites, and request for the maidens as a voluntary gift, which, if granted by the Shilonites, would have brought them under the curse. The double Accus. in חנונו אתן is exactly paralleled by Ps. 119[29] תּוֹרָתְךָ חָנֵּנִי, 'Graciously grant me Thy law.' The Def. Art. in בַּמִּלְחָמָה does not necessarily refer to any specific battle (cf. 1 Sam. 26[10], 30[24], 2 Sam. 19[4]), though it is possible to find in it an allusion to the great battle of *ch.* 20.

* The renderings of A.V., 'because we reserved not to each man his wife, etc.' R.V., 'because we took not for each man [of them] his wife etc.' stand in daring disregard of the meaning of the common Heb. idiom.

Benjamin did so, and took wives according to their number, of the dancers that they had forcibly carried off: and they went and returned unto their inheritance, and built the cities, and dwelt in them. 24. And the children of Israel departed thence at that time, every man to his tribe and to his clan, J and they went out thence every man to his inheritance. 25. R^P In those days there was no king in Israel: every man was used to do that which was right in his own eyes.

A different text is represented by some MSS. of 𝔊, and by $𝔖^h$, *ἐλεήσατε αὐτούς, ὅτι οὐκ ἔλαβεν* (*or ἔλαβον*) *ἀνὴρ γυναῖκα αὐτοῦ ἐν τῷ πολεμῷ* (similarly $𝔊^L$ with omission of *οὐκ*), $𝔖^P$ ܪ̈ܚܡܘ ܥܠܝܗܘܢ، ܡܛܠ ܕܠܐ ܢܣܒܘ ܓܒܪ ܐܢܬܬܗ ܒܩܪܒܐ, cf. 𝔙 'miseremini eorum: non enim rapuerunt eas jure bellantium atque victorum'; *i.e.* (retaining ואמרנו and putting the speech into the mouth of the *Israelites*) חָנּוּ אוֹתָם כִּי לֹא לָקְחוּ אִישׁ אִשְׁתּוֹ בַּמִּלְחָמָה 'Regard them favourably, for they did not receive each his wife in the war.' This text is adopted (with variations in the rendering of חנו אותם) by Mo., Driver (*ET.* xviii. p. 332), Cooke. Here 'in the war' is taken to refer to the raid on Jabesh, which had not sufficed to provide wives for the Benjaminites in question. Since, however, the narrative of Jabesh belongs (on our theory of the sources) to the other source, we must (if we accept this text) trace in the verse the hand of R^P, harmonizing and connecting the two narratives—and this not simply (with Mo.) as regards the words 'for they did not . . . in the war,' but as regards the whole verse, since the conception of the carrying of the grievance 'unto us' surely involves the Priestly theory of a central judicial authority. Bu. regards the text of 𝔐 as due to variation in the *sources*, according to one of which the Shilonites bring their complaint to Israel (אלינו ואמרנו חנו אותם כי לא לקחו וג'), but, according to the other, bring it directly to the Benjaminites (אליכם ואמרתם חנונו כי לא לקחנו וג').

23. *took wives, etc.* Ros. and other commentators compare the Roman legend of the rape of the Sabine women in order to provide wives for the followers of Romulus (Livy, *Hist.* i. 9).

25. *in those days, etc.* Cf. p. 410.

DESCRIPTION OF THE PLATES

PLATE I.

TWO scribes taking note of spoils after an Assyrian victory. The bearded man is writing Assyrian in cuneiform upon a clay tablet, using an angular stylus which is held through the full of the hand to impress the characters upon the soft clay. The other man, who is marked by his shaven face as a foreigner, is writing with a pen upon a roll of leather or papyrus, and employing, no doubt, the West Semitic alphabetic script, to make his entry in a language which we may conjecture to be Aramaic. It is interesting in this connexion to note that a general list of titles and offices contained in ii. R. 31, 64b-65b mentions together A.BA *mât Aššur-a-a* and A.BA *mât Ar-ma-a-a*, *i.e.*, perhaps, 'an Assyrian secretary' and 'an Aramaean secretary' (the honorific title A.BA = 'elder' is here thought to correspond to *dupšarru* 'tablet-writer,'* the Heb. *ṭiphsar* of Nah. 3 [17], Jer. 51 [27]). The representation is part of a large relief from Kouyunjik (Nineveh) figured in Layard, *Monuments of Nineveh*, *2nd Series*, Pl. 26, and is now in the British Museum, Kouyunjik gallery, west wall, series Nos. 4-8. It dates from the seventh century B.C. Similar pairs of scribes are figured in Layard, *op. cit.*, Plates 26, upper tier, 19, 29 (both with scrolls), 35, 37, 50. Cf. the remarks on this Plate on pp. 255 f. of the Commentary.

PLATE II.

Figs. 1 *and* 2. A figure described in pictographic writing as *ilu Šamaš* (the Sun-god) contends with antelopes and lions.

Fig. 3. Gilgameš contends with antelopes and lions. The arrangement of the figures is identical with that of figs. 1 and 2, the only difference being that Gilgameš takes the place of *ilu Šamaš*. That the figure on this seal is Gilgameš is indicated by his full-face representation, and the arrangement of his hair in six locks: cf. Plate III. figs. 1 and 2. Cf. p. 400.

* Cf. Delitzsch, *Paradies*, p. 258; *Beiträge zur Assyriologie*, i. p. 218; *Sumerisches Glossar*, p. 4.

Fig. 4. Gilgameš and Engidu struggling with a bull and lion respectively. On the manner in which Engidu is tearing asunder the hind legs of the lion, cf. *note* on Judg. 14[6].

Fig. 5. Three Gilgameš-figures wrestling with similar figures. The vanquished figure appears to have been thrown by impact of the victor's thigh against his leg—a form of throw which may perhaps be intended by the obscure phrase שוק על ירך 'leg upon thigh' in Judg. 15[8] (cf. *note ad loc.*). Cf. also the seal figured by Hayes Ward, *The Seal Cylinders of Western Asia* (1910), fig. 199.

The five figures included in this Plate are reproduced by permission from Delaporte's *Catalogue des Cylindres orientaux . . . de la Bibliothèque Nationale.*

Plate III.

Fig. 1. Gilgameš struggling with a lion. He appears to be throwing it by impact of his knee against its back, or by turning it across his thigh (cf. description Plate II. fig. 5), possibly in order to break its back (cf. Hayes Ward, *op. cit.*, fig. 157). This is the finest figure of Gilgameš in existence. Note especially the characteristic arrangement of his hair in six locks. The seven locks or plaits (מחלפות) of Samson may perhaps be analogous. Cf. pp. 379 f., 404.

Fig. 2. On the left, Gilgameš and his friend Engidu contend with the heavenly bull (the bull of Anu). On the right, Gilgameš is represented in contest with a lion. This seal illustrates very clearly the fact that, in this and similar representations, we really have to do with scenes from the Gilgameš-epic (against the view of Sayce, as quoted, p. 401, *footnote*). The description of the contest with the heavenly bull (sent against Gilgameš by the god Anu at the request of Ištar, in revenge for the hero's rejection of her advances : cf. p. 397 of the Commentary) exists in a fragmentary state on Tab. VI. ll. 92 ff. of the Epic. Engidu is described as taking the bull 'by the root (thick part) of its tail' (*ina kubur zibbatišu*, l. 147) and 'by its horns' (ll. 134 f.), exactly as he is doing on the cylinder-representation. Engidu is always figured with the face and torso of a man, but with the hind legs, tail, horns, and ears of a bull. When first introduced in the Epic he is described as human, but dwelling among the beasts of the field and sharing their characteristics (Tab. I. col. ii. ll. 35 ff.). Having been enticed away from their society, he becomes the inseparable companion of Gilgameš, and the sharer of his adventures.

Fig. 3. The Sun-god (*ilu Šamaš*) issuing through the gates of sunrise, which are held back by attendants, and stepping on to a double-peaked mountain—probably the mountain of *Mâšu* ('twin-mountain') mentioned in the Gilgameš-epic as standing at the gates of sunrise. Cf. pp. 395, 399 f., 406 f.

The three figures in this Plate are reproduced by permission of the Trustees of the British Museum from wax-impressions specially made for the writer through the kindness of Dr. L. W. King.

All the figures in Plates II. and III. are examples of Sumerian or early Semitic Babylonian art not later than the third millennium B.C.

Plate IV.

Gilgameš with the lion as represented in Assyrian art. The relief is from the palace of Sargon (reigned B.C. 722-705) at Khorsabad (Dûr-Šarrukîn), and is now in the Louvre. From a photograph by Braun et Cie.

Plate V.

Two reliefs from Carchemish, illustrating the spread of the Gilgameš-myth to the Ḥittites.

Fig. 1. Two identical full-faced figures like Engidu as represented on Babylonian seals, with hind quarters, tail, horns, and ears of a bull, but human face and torso, holding spear and advancing left and right. Two lion-headed human figures behind, wearing short tunics. One threatens Engidu with a weapon.

Fig. 2. A figure full-faced like Gilgameš, but with Ḥittite cap, kilt, and boots, holds a lion or lioness by the hind legs with his right hand and a bull by the horns with his left hand. A stag and two lion-cubs (?) are in the field. These figures of Gilgameš and Engidu are the only full-faced figures among the representations from Carchemish.

Dr. D. G. Hogarth, who dates the reliefs about the ninth century B.C., points out that, while Babylonian or Assyrian influence is manifest, the technique is characteristically Ḥittite, the relief returning quite steeply to the bed of the plane. Contrast the Assyrian figure of Gilgameš in Plate IV.

The figures are reproduced, by permission of the Trustees of the British Museum, from *Carchemish: Report on Excavations*, 1914, ed. D. G. Hogarth.

Plate VI.

A colossal figure from Amathus in Cyprus : height 4 m., 20, breadth of shoulders 2 m. The art is Phoenician ; and the figure, which doubtless represents Herakles-Melḳart, illustrates the spread of the

Gilgameš-myth westward. M. Al. Sorlin-Dorigny, who describes the figure in the *Gazette Archéologique*, 1879, pp. 230-236, states that it originally had an ornament on the top of the head, inserted a little behind the horns, in a hole measuring four centimetres in diameter and twelve centimetres in depth. From the edge of this hole all the locks of hair diverge, some, short and wavy, falling over the forehead, others, long and smooth, forming six tresses ('ondulations') in the Assyrian manner, then dividing themselves into three great bunches of curls which rest on the neck and shoulders. The two horns are imperfect. Assyrian influence is very marked in the treatment of the beard.

It will be observed that, while the figure generally suggests Gilgameš, especially as regards hair and beard, there is more than a suggestion of Engidu in the horns and in the manner in which he is rending the lion by tearing its hind legs asunder (cf. Plate II. fig. 4).

The figure is reproduced from Perrot et Chipiez, *Histoire de l'art dans l'antiquité*, iii., fig. 386, by arrangement with Messrs. Chapman and Hall, Ltd., who own the rights of reproduction in England.

On Plates IV.-VI., as illustrating the widespread influence of the Gilgameš-myth, cf. p. 401 of the Commentary.

NOTE ON THE MAPS OF PALESTINE

The Maps of Palestine at the end of this volume have been prepared by Messrs. Bartholomew, who are responsible for the coloured contours and all other physical features. The site-identifications have been carefully weighed by the present editor, whose aim has been to admit no identification which does not seem to him to be reasonably assured upon historical and philological grounds.

The editor is indebted, in the first place, to the Map of Western Palestine, in twenty-six sheets, from surveys conducted under the auspices of the *PEF.* (scale one inch to the mile: cited in the Commentary as *SWP. Great Map*), and to the Arabic Name List prepared for the Survey by Prof. Palmer: for the modern names in Map V. he is chiefly indebted to the map of the Negeb in *EB.*, and to Prof. Guthe's *Bibelatlas* (1911), as well as to the excellent map by Dr. Hans Fischer in *ZDPV.* xxxiii (1910).

The identification of ancient sites depends upon the labours of a number of investigators in the past, among whose works mention may be made of Dr. Robinson's *Biblical Researches in Palestine* (a work which, though based upon travels undertaken so far back as 1838 and 1852, still possesses very considerable value), the *Memoirs* of the Survey of Western Palestine published by the *PEF.*, Sir G. A. Smith's *Historical Geography of the Holy Land* (first published in 1894), and Prof. F. Buhl's *Geographie des alten Palästina* (1896).

The only British *maps* of Palestine marking ancient sites which are thoroughly trustworthy are those contained in *EB.*; and the help afforded by these was usefully supplemented by Prof. Guthe's *Bibelatlas* already mentioned. Other British maps depend chiefly upon the site-identifications contained in the *SWP. Mem.*, and embodied in the maps published by the *PEF.* which mark ancient sites; and these, while offering much that is valuable, are unfortunately vitiated by many identifications which are highly dubious, and by some which are positively misleading.* This stricture extends, unfortunately, in some degree even to the folding map (scale four miles to one inch) published under the direction of Mr. J. G. Bartholomew and edited by Dr. G. A. Smith, which is in many respects the most useful general map which can be employed.‡

As occasion arose in the Commentary, the attempt has been made to note and illustrate the modifications which ancient Biblical names

* Dr. Driver's warning (*NHTS.*[2] p. xcv) may well be reiterated:—'The identification of a modern with an ancient site depends mostly, it must be remembered, in cases in which the ancient name itself has not been unambiguously preserved, partly upon historical, but very largely upon philological considerations: and men who are admirable surveyors, and who can write valuable descriptions of the physical features, topography, or antiquities of a country, are not necessarily good philologists.'

‡ Since the maps for the present Commentary were printed, there has appeared (1915) the long-expected *Atlas of the Historical Geography of the Holy Land*, edited by G. A. Smith and J. G. Bartholomew. This is a work which takes first rank among Biblical Atlases for beauty of execution, and which contains much that is of first importance to the student—notably the valuable maps of Jerusalem at different periods, and modern Jerusalem illustrating recent discoveries, which have already appeared in G. A. Smith's *Jerusalem* (1907), and the sectional maps of Palestine on the scale of one inch to four miles which represent a revision of the folding map to which allusion has been made above. These latter maps will naturally be the most consulted of all that are contained in the Atlas; and it is therefore to be noted with regret that they have not undergone the thorough revision which was anticipated by Dr. Driver when he expressed the conviction (*NHTS.*[2], p. xcv) that the forthcoming Atlas was 'likely to prove in all respects adequate and trustworthy.' To take some points which strike the eye—sect. iii. still contains the preposterous identification of Betsaanim with Sahel el-Aḥmâ which depends (cf. *note* on *ch.* 4^{11}) upon A.V.'s erroneous rendering of *'êlôn* 'terebinth' as 'plain.' In the Orographical map 11-12 the 'plain of Zaanaim' still stands; and here and in sect. map vii. we have the 'plain of Mamre' (A.V.'s error for *terebinths* of Mamre). In sect. vi. Gibeʻah is identified with Gebaʻ and both with the modern Jebaʻ (Gebaʻ), in face of the cogent Biblical evidence noted on *ch.* 19^{12} that Gibeʻah is distinct from Gebaʻ, and of Dr. Smith's own adoption (*Jerusalem*, ii. p. 92, *n* 3) of the commonly received identification of the former with Tell el-Fûl. Other impossible, or highly improbable, identifications (hardly palliated by the fact that they are marked with a query) are 'Ain-Ḥelweh = Abel Meḥolah (cf. *ch.* 7^{22} *note*), 'Osh el-Ghurâb = Rock ʻOreb (*ch.* 7^{25} *note*), Kh. ʻErmâ = Ḳiriath-Jeʻarim (*ch.* 18^{12} *note*), Tell Deir-ʻAllah, north of the Jabboḳ = Succoth (surely, in spite of the Talmudic identification with Darʻala, to be looked for *south* of the Jabboḳ: cf. p. 220). The identifications of Kefr Ḥasan with Ashnah, and of Ta'lat Heisa with the Ascent of Luḥith, which are now (as contrasted with

have undergone in their reproduction in modern Arabic form.* This is a subject which needs, and would repay, more detailed and systematic study than it has as yet received, at any rate in this country. The only scientific attempt to grapple with the subject (so far as the present writer is aware) is that by G. Kampffmeyer in his articles entitled *Alte Namen in heutigen Palästina und Syrien* in *ZDPV.* xv. (1892), pp. 1-33, 65-116; xvi. pp. 1-71, which well repay careful study. Even a superficial examination of the site-identifications which have so far been fixed or proposed suggests that, while, on the one hand, we have to be on our guard against conclusions which have been drawn in ignorance of philology, yet, on the other hand, there is danger lest we should be limited by too strict a regard for the philological laws, as ordinarily understood, which govern correspondence between Hebrew and Arabic forms. When, as must have happened in a multitude of cases, ancient names have been preserved for centuries merely by oral transmission among ignorant peasants, it is surely inevitable that they should sometimes have assumed a form which, as compared with the original, would seem to be incapable of being brought under the laws of correct philological interchange. Further, there is evidence which indicates that, in some few cases at least, the modern name as transmitted has assumed a form which possesses no sort of philological connexion with the ancient name, and has been suggested merely by a rough assonance with its original. Such a case has been noted in the modern name of the Ḳishon, Nahr el-Muḳaṭṭaʿ, *i.e.* 'river of the ford,' which has almost certainly arisen through assonance with the ancient city-name Megiddo of unknown meaning in the near vicinity.‡ Other instances are probably to be seen in the modern name ʿAid el-Mâ, 'the feast of water,' or, in a variant form, ʿAid el-Miyyeh, 'the feast of the one hundred,' which has been plausibly suggested as the modern equivalent of ʿAdullam,

the folding map) marked with a query in deference to Dr. Driver's strictures in *ET.* xxi. pp. 495, 563 f., should surely have been omitted altogether. We also find, without so much as a query, the very questionable identifications el-Lejjûn =Megiddo, instead of (as now established) Tell el-Mutesellim nearly a mile to the north (cf. *ch.* 1 27 *note*), Ṭûbâs=Thebez (cf. *ch.* 9 50 *note*), Tell esh-Sheriʿah =Sharuḥen, edh-Dhaherîyeh=Debir (an identification which, though generally accepted, is really based upon a wholly false etymological conclusion drawn by Conder, and is therefore at best nothing more than a guess at the site, apart from any connexion in name: cf. *ch.* 1 11 *note*). On the other hand, the identification of Liftâ with Nephtoaḥ, which is philologically sound and also suitable to the description of Josh. 15 9, 18 15 (and which the present writer would have included in his own map without a query, if he had made the investigation embodied under *ch.* 18 12 before the completion of the map) is not noticed at all; and Ḳuryet el-ʿEnab, which strong probability marks as the site of Ḳiriath-Jeʿarim (cf. *ch.* 18 12 *note*) is simply marked (with a query) as the site of the obscure Ḳiriath of Josh. 18 28 (where the text is very possibly at fault).

* Cf. the *footnotes* pp. 21, 23, 24, 27, 29, 282, 306, 377, 430.

‡ Cf. *note* on 'the rills of Megiddo,' *ch.* 5 19.

and in ʿAin Ṣârah for the well (or cistern) of Ṡirah (2 Sam. 3^{26}). Doubtless a number of such cases might be collected.

Even when we find a satisfactory correspondence between a modern and an ancient name, this in itself by no means settles the problem of identification. It is clear that there has occurred a certain amount of drifting of ancient place-names, the names being now attached to modern villages or to remains which cannot go back so far as O.T. times. Instances of this may be seen in Erîḥâ (=Jericho, Heb. *Yᵉrîḥô*) which is now the site of a modern village one and a half miles south-east of the mound called Tell es-Sulṭân which undoubtedly represents the site of ancient Jericho; Umm Lâḳis, which probably preserves the ancient name of Lachish,* though the ancient site of this city is fixed with high probability at Tell el-Ḥasy, three miles to the south-east; Zerʿîn, which corresponds accurately with Jezreʿel, though, as Prof. Macalister has recently pointed out (cf. *ch.* 6^{33} *note*), the modern site contains no remains of an antiquity approaching the O.T. period.

To be ideally complete, the evidence for identification of an ancient site should be threefold:—(*a*) The philological equivalence between the ancient and modern names should be satisfactory. (*b*) The site should be attested by the evidence afforded by Biblical and extra-Biblical historians. (*c*) Examination *in situ* should be able to prove the existence of remains of a sufficient antiquity.

The meaning of the geographical terms which occur in Arabic in the maps is as follows:—

ʿAin (plur. *ʿAyûn*) = spring.
Bîr or *Bîreh* = well.
Ǵeb. = *Ǵebel* = mountain.
Ǵisr = bridge.
Ḫ. = *Ḫirbet* = ruin (ruined site).
Kefr = village.
Nahr = river.
Râs = head (headland).
Sahel = plain.
Taʿlat = ascent.
Tell = mound (usually formed by débris of ruined city).
W. = *Wâdy* = watercourse (cf. p. 88).

* The interchange between *k* and *ḳ* which is involved has been thought to constitute a difficulty. Cf., however, the converse interchange in the modern Kânah as compared with the ancient Ḳanah (cf. p. 24).

The following orthographical corrections of names in the maps should be noted :—

Map II.

For Hapharaim read Ḥapharaim.
„ Gilboa „ Gilboaʿ.

Map III.

For Wâdy Ḳanâh (*W. Ḳânah*) read Wâdy Ḳanah (*W. Kânah*).
„ *Kefr Ânâ* read *Kefr ʿÂnâ.*
„ *Mukmâs* „ *Muḫmâs.*
„ Ebal „ ʿEbal.
„ Ẓorʿah „ Ṣorʿah.
„ Miẓpeh „ Miṣpeh.
„ *er-Rummâneh* read *Rammôn.*
Before *Liftâ* add Nephtoaḥ.
„ Ḫ. *Ṣâr* add Jaʿzer ?

Map IV.

For *Ḫ. Gâlâ* read *Ḫ. Ǵâlâ.*
„ Ziḳlag „ Ṣiḳlag.
„ Beth-ẓur „ Beth-ṣur.
„ Nezib (*Bêt Nasîb*) read Neṣib (*Bet Naṣîb*).

Map V.

For Boẓrah read Boṣrah.

INDICES

I. GENERAL INDEX

Aaron, 436, 440 f.
Abd-Aširta, lxxii, lxxvi, lxxviii, lxxx, xcii, 196.
'Abdi, 'Abdiel, 278.
Abdi-Tirši, cxvii.
'Abdon, ciii, 289 f., 335.
Abel-ceramim, 321.
Abel-meḥolah, 220 ff.
Abiathar, lii, 239, 478.
Abi-eshu', lix.
Abi'ezer, 134, 179, 187, 227.
Abimelech, xxxvii, xlix, cii, ciii, 76, 263, 265, 266 ff., 290.
Abi-milki, 265.
Abishua', lix.
Abram, Abraham, lxxiv, lxxx, lxxxv, cix, cx, cxi, cxiv f., 9; meaning of name, 250.
Acacia, 465.
'Acco, 28.
'Achšah, 13.
Achzib, xiii, 29.
Acre, 28.
Adad-Nirari I., lxxix.
Adad-šum-naṣir, ci.
Adam, city of, xiii, 219.
Adoni in compound names, 4.
Adoni-bezeḳ, 4.
Adoni-ṣedeḳ, lxxxvi, cxvii, 5 f., 41, 81, 264.
Adonis. See 'Tammuz.'
'Adullam, 500.
Aegean pottery, xciv.
Aeginetans, 6.
Afḳâ, 29.
Agag, execution of, 344.
Aǵbêhât, 231.
Agum-Kakrime, lxiv.
Aḥab, liii, xcviii.
Aḥaziah of Israel, liii.
Aḫetaton, lxx.
Aḥijah, lii.
Aḥiman, 9 f.
Aḥimelech, lii.
Aḥiṭub, lii.
Aḥlab, 28.
Aḫlamu, lxxix, lxxxiii.
Aḥmosi I., lxvi, lxvii, cxii, cxv, cxvi.
Aḫnaton, lxx, lxxii, lxxiii, lxxix, lxxxvii, lxxxviii, cxii, cxiv, 253. See also 'Amenḥotp IV.'
'Ai, cviii, 21.
'Aid el-Ma, 'Aid el-Miyyeh, 500.
Aijalon, 8, 32, 334.
'Ain 'Aṭân, 370.
'Ain Dilbeh, 14.
'Ain es-Sulṭân, 15.
'Ain Ǵâlûd, 205, 208 f.
'Ain Ǵidî, 16.
'Ain Heǵireh, 14.
'Ain el-Ḥelweh, 220.
'Ain el-Ḥôd, 406.
'Ain Ḳudês, 34, 110.
'Ain Mâhil, 27.
'Ain Ṣârah, 501.
'Ain-šems, xciv, cvii, 340, 406, 430.
'Aḳaywaša, xcii.
Akiya, lxx, lxxxvi.
'Akkâ, 28.
Akkad, lxii; Semitic dynasty of, lv f., lx.
'Aḳrabbim, ascent of, 33 f.
Alasa, xcviii.
Aleppo, lxii.
Alphabet, names of letters in Greek and Hebrew, 262. See also 'Writing.'
Alphabetic script, xcvii, 254 ff., 495.
Altar, primitive rock-, 192, 349, 350; built of stones, 192, 199; at Bethel, 488.
'Amaleḳ, 'Amaleḳites, li, lxxix, 17, 68, 110, 132, 185, 297.
Amarna Tablets. See 'Tell el-Amarna.'
Amathus, 'Amâteh, 326,.
Amenḥotp I., lxvii.
Amenḥotp II., lxix, cxii, cxv, cxvi.
Amenḥotp III., lxix, lxx, lxxii, lxxiii, lxxxiii, cxiii, cxvi, 253.

Amenḥotp IV., lxix, lxx. See also 'Aḫnaton.'
Amḳaruna, 19.
Ammiditana, lviii, lxii, lxxxi.
Ammizaduga, lviii.
'Ammon, children of ('Ammonites), liii, cx, 297, 298 ff.; land of, 305.
Ammonium, oasis of, 406.
Ammu or *Ammi* in proper names, lviii.
Amon, priesthood of, lxxxvii, lxxxviii, xcvi; temple of, lxvii, xcix; barge of, xcvi, xcvii; 'Amon-of-the-Way,' xcvi.
Amor. See 'Amurru.'
Amorite, Amorites, lviii ff., lxiii, lxxxvii, cviii, 3, 30, 41, 297, 385.
'Amos, xxxviii.
Amraphel, lxii, cx.
Amurru, Amor, lvi, lix, lxi, lxii, lxiv, lxvi, lxxiii, lxxix, lxxx, lxxxi, lxxxv, lxxxvii, xc, xcv, cxiv, 41, 196; language of, lxi, 166. See also 'West Semitic language.'
'Amwâs, 464.
'Anaḳites, 9, 10, 20, 46.
'Anâtâ, 30.
'Anath, 30, 76.
'Anath-bethel, 30.
'Anath-el, lxvi.
'Anath-yahu, 30.
'Anathoth, 30.
Anatolian strain in Assyrians, c.
Anatum, Antum, consort of Anu, 30; hypocoristic form, 76.
Angel of Yahweh (of God), 35 f., 89, 151, 186, 192, 341, 346.
Antigone, 323 f.
Anu, 30, 76, 385, 397, 496.
Anum-pî-Sin, lxxxiii.
Aphiḳ, 29.
Aphrodite, 333, 402.
Apil-Sin, lviii.
Apollo, 406.
'*Apuriu*, '*Apriu*, cxiv.
Aquarius, 399.
Arabia, central, early common home of Semites, lvi, lx; north, cviii, 9, 10, 439, 441; south, lix, lxi, 400.
Arabic language, exhibiting primitive formations, lx.
'Arad, 16, 44 f.
ARAD-Ḫiba, lxxiii, lxxiv, lxxv, lxxvii, lxxviii, lxxxi, lxxxii, lxxxiv, lxxxvi, cxvii, 256; nationality of, lxxxvi.
'Arâḳ Isma'în, 371.
Aram-Damascus, 428.
Aram-naharaim, lxxx, 66.
Aramaeans, lxxix f., cx f.
Aramaic language, influence of environment upon, lx; a dialectical form of the language of Amurru, lxi, 175; dockets in, on cuneiform tablets, 255.
Aramäisms, 129, 172 ff.
Arami the son of Gus, cii.
Arandaš, lxxxvi, lxxxix.
Arawna (Araunah), Aranya, lxxxvi, 20.
Arbela, 43.
Arethusa, xiii, c.
Arik-dên-ili, lxxix.
Arioch, lxii.
Ark of God (of Yahweh), 3, 37, 242, 344, 415, 435, 440, 477.
Armenians, lxxi.
Arnon, 221, 305, 306, 312, 314.
Arnuanta, lxxxvi, xcix.
'Aro'er, 'Arâ'îr (by Arnon), 221, 316, 320; (in 'Ammonite territory), 320.
Artakhšatrâ (Artaxerxes), lxxxiv.
Artamanya, lxxxiv, lxxxvi.
Artaššumara, lxxii, lxxxvi.
Artatama, lxix, lxxxvi; (grandson), lxxii, lxxiii.
Artemis, 85, 332.
Arumah, 281.
Arvad, lxviii, xci, ci.
Aryans in Western Asia, lxxxiv f.
Arzawa, letters, lxxi, lxxxiii f.; sons of, lxxxii, lxxxiii f.
Asher, lxxxix, civ, cvi, cvii, 27 f., 29, 143, 197 f.
'Ashera, cvii, 195 ff.
Ashḳelon, lxxiii f., xc, xcii, 19, 282, 366.
'Ashtar-Chemosh, 30, 59, 244, 248.
'Ashtart, 'Ashtarts, xxxv, cxxi, 58 f., 332, 402, 407.
'Ashtoreth. See ''Ashtart.'
Asiatic refugees in Egypt, 439.
Ašîra, 196.
Aširtu, Ašratu, 196.
'Asḳalân, 19, 282.
Ass, 124, 292.
Aššur, lxii.
Assyria, Assyrians, lxvi, lxviii, lxix, lxx, lxxix, xcv, xcviii, xcix, c f.; chronology, liii; Biblical names in Annals of, 99.

Ašurbanipal, 285, 400.
Ašur-dân I., ci.
Ašur-uballiṭ, lxx, lxxix.
Athena, 332.
'Athtar, 59, 261.
Aṯirat, 196.
Atlantic, 400.
'Attar, 59.
Attila, 285.
Avaris, lxv f.
Awan, lv.
Ay, lxxxvii, lxxxviii.
Aziru, lxxiii, lxxvi, lxxviii, lxxxvii.

Ba'al, Ba'als, xxxv, cxx, cxxi, 57 f.
Ba'al a title of Yahweh, 201.
Ba'al-berith, 266.
Ba'al-Gad, xcix, 63.
Ba'al-ḥanan, 202.
Ba'al-Ḥermon, xcix, 63.
Ba'al-tamar, 480.
Ba'al-ya, 202.
Ba'al-yadha', 201.
Ba'al-zebul, 5, 385.
'*Babel und Bibel*' controversy, 244.
Babylonia, Babylon, Semites in, lv f., lvii ff.; First Dynasty of, lviii ff., lxi, lxiii, lxiv, lxxxv, 43, 76, 99, 196, 197, 243 ff.; Second Dynasty of, lviii, lxiv; Third Dynasty of, lviii, lxv, lxxxii, ci (see also 'Kaššites'); struggle with Assyria, c f.; names of kings of First Dynasty, lviii f.; chronology, lvi, lviii, cxvi; language (Semitic) in inscriptions of early rulers of Akkad, lvii; prevalence and persistency of Semitic Bab. language in Babylonia, lx; influence of language upon Hebrew, lxii f.; influence of civilization of, upon Cana'an, lxiv; theory of origin of alphabet from linear script of, 262; rhythm of poetry of, 97.
Badyra, Bod'el, xcvi.
Bai-ti-tu-pa-ïra, 12.
Balaḳ, 299, 316.
Bânyâs, 63, 427.
Baraḳ, xxxvi, cii, 78 ff., 85, 87.
Barbarossa, 285.
Bar-Gus, cii.
Barley-bread, 119.
Bar-rekub, inscriptions of, 173 f., 254, 264.
Bar-ṣur, 264.
Baṣ'annim, 82, 90.
Bashan, 306.
Bayawa, lxxviii.
Be'er, 276.
Be'er-sheba', cx, 43, 251.
Bees in carcase of lion, 359, 405.
Be'eshtĕrā, 58.
Belial, xl, 467 f.
Bêlit-UR.MAḪ.MEŠ, lxxvii.
el-Belḳâ, 306.
Benaiah, 403.
Bᵉnê-Ḥamor, 269 f., 271, 280.
Ben-Hadad II., liii, cii.
Ben-Hadad III., cii.
Benjamin, 20, 21, 133 f.; smallness of tribe of, 447.
Berossus, lv.
Bêsân, 23, 219.
Beṣṣûm, 82, 90.
Bêt-Degân, 384, 385.
Bêt-Ǵibrîn, 8.
Beth-'anath, xc, cvii, 30.
Beth-Arbel, 43.
Beth-barah, 225.
Beth-Dagon, 384.
Bethel, xx, cviii, 21, 37, 441, 447, 448, 453, 476, 477, 479, 488.
Beth-ḥoron, cviii.
Bethleḥem, of Zebulon, 290, 334; of Judah, 422.
Beth-millo, 271 f.
Beth-reḥob, 29, 428, 434.
Beth-she'an, xciii, 23, 24, 219, 220, 222, 223, 490.
Beth-shemesh (in the north?), cvii, 30; (in the south), cvii, 10, 340, 392, 406, 430.
Beth-shiṭṭah, 219.
Bethuel, lxxx.
Bêtîn, 21.
Bêt-Laḥm, 290, 334, 422.
Bezeḳ, 4.
Bezḳeh, Ḫirbet, 5.
Biblical sites, identification of, 499 ff.
Bilhah-tribes, cvii, cx.
Bîreh, 276, 479.
Biridašwa, lxxxiv, lxxxvi.
Biridiya, lxxvii, lxxxii, lxxxiv, lxxxvi.
Bir-idri, liii, cii.
Bît-Daganna, 385.
'Blessing of Ja'cob,' cvi, 437.
'Blessing of Moses,' 4, 438.
Blood-feud, 199.
Bochim, 37.

Boghaz Keui, documents from, lxix, lxxi, lxxii, lxxvi, lxxx, lxxxiv, lxxxvi, xci, xcix, 41, 84, 254.
'Book of the Wars of Yahweh,' xl, 106.
Boundary-stones, 71.
Brand-Fuchs, 394.
Brant-fox, 394.
Buckthorn, 275.
el-Buḳâ', xcix, c, 62, 434.
Bull of Anu, 397, 496; human-headed, 400.
Burnaburiaš, lxx.
Burnt offering, 477.

Caesura, in Hebrew poetry, 160; in Babylonian, 161.
Cain, 14.
Caleb, Calibbites, xl, 8, 9, 10, 12 f., 46, 341.
Cana'an, earliest settlement of Semites in, lv f.; neolithic inhabitants of, lvii; language of, lxi; influence of Babylonian civilization upon, lxi ff.; events leading to invasion and conquest of, by Egypt, lxv ff.; at period of T.A. Letters, lxxiii ff.; non-Semitic element in, lxxxiii ff.; settlement of Philistines in, xcii ff.; decline of Egyptian authority in, xcv ff.; period of freedom in, from external interference of any great power, xcviii ff.; Israel's settlement in, xxxiv f., lxxiv, lxxx f., ciii ff., 1 ff.; partition of, 3; 'seven nations' of, 63; kings of, lxx, lxxiv, 144; king of, 84, 145.
Cana'anite, Cana'anites, lviii, lxxiii, 3, 30, 41, 297.
Cana'anite 'glosses' in T.A. Letters, lxi, 99, 166, 167, 168, 169.
Canon, Hebrew, xxxiv, cxxi.
Caphtor. See 'Kaphtôr.'
Carchemish, lxxix, lxxxii, xcix, ci, cii; bas-reliefs from, 401, 497.
Caria, Carians, xciv f.
Carmel, in Judah, 16; Mount, xciii, 28.
Carseoli, 393.
Cassites. See 'Kaššites.'
Ceres, Festival of, 369, 393.
Chaboras, 66.
Chariots, 20, 151.
Chedorla'omer, lxii.
Chemosh, 299, 314 ff., 320.
Chemoshkân, 315.
Chemoshnadab, 316.
Chemoshṣedeḳ, 316.
Chemoshy^{e}ḥi, 316.
Chesalon, 430.
Chronology, of Judges, l ff.; Biblical, from Abraham to entry into Cana'an, cxii, cxv ff.; early Babylonian, lvi, lviii, cxvi.
Cilicians, xc.
Circumcision, 356.
Clay tablets, use of, in Cana'an, lxix f., 253.
Cochineal, 291.
Coleridge's *Christabel*, rhythm of, 96.
Commagene, xcix.
Concubinage, 265.
'Congregation' of Israel, 446.
Corn, rust in, 393 f.; harvest in Syria and in Italy, 394.
Cosmology of Gilgameš-epic, 399 f.
Covenant, 60; Book of the, 252, 329 f.
'Crag, the,' 34.
Creation-epic, Babylonian, lxiii, 161.
Crete, Cretans, xciv f.
Cross-buttock, 370.
Crypt, 286.
Cubit, 70.
Cuneiform script, in Syria and Cana'an, lxiv, lxix, 253 ff.; in Asia Minor, lxix.
Cup-marks, 192.
Cushan-rish'athaim, 64 ff.
Cybele, 85.
Cyprus, xcviii; Cypriote script, 263.

Daberath, 81.
Dâdi-kariba, 291.
Dagan, lxii, 244, 385 f.
Dagan-takala, lxxvii, lxxix.
Dagon, 384 ff.
Daǵun, 385.
Dalil-(ilu)-Ištar, Dilil-(ilu)-Ištar, 407.
ed-Dâmiyyeh, 219 f., 221, 223 f., 231, 326.
Dan, Danites, xx, xcix, cvi f., 31, 142 f., 339, 340, 341, 392, 411, 417, 436.
Danauna, xciii, xcv.
Danonim, xcv.
Daphne, 427.
Dapur, xc.
Dardanians, xc.
Daroma, cviii.
David, xx, xciv, 68, 403; name, 291; northern limit of kingdom of, xcix f.

Death of Samson, 408.
Debir, conquest of, 8; site of, 10 f.
Deborah, xxxvi, xxxvii, cii, cvi, cvii, 78 ff., 85; Song of, xl, ciii, cxx, 29, 47, 78, 417; compared with Prose-narrative, 78 ff.; literature on, xiv, 94 f.; metrical form of, 96 ff., 158 ff.; strophic arrangement of, 101 f.; corrupt condition of text of, 102; translation of, 103 ff.; discussion of, 105 ff.; ascription of authorship to prophetess, 116; climactic parallelism of, 169 f.; language of, 171 ff.
Debûriyyeh, 81, 88.
Delilah, 377, 407.
Delos, 406.
Delphi, xviii, 85.
Demeter, xvii ff., 85, 334.
'Deploy,' 87.
ed-Dêr, 489 f.
Descent, through father, 264; through mother, 265.
Deuteronomic editor (R^D), in Joshua', xliii ff., cv, 1; in Kings, xlv.
Deuteronomic hand, (D^2) in Judges, xlix, 55, 61.
Deuteronomic school, xli, xliii ff.
Deuteronomy (D), origin and promulgation of, xlv f.
Dibon, Ḏîbân, 313.
Disarmament of Israelites, 119.
Dodo, Dodai, etc., 289, 291 f.
Dor, xcv, xcvi, 23 f., 384.
Drinking, different methods of, xiv f., 210 ff.
Drone-fly, 359.
Dudḫâlia, lxii.
Dûdu, cxiii, 291.

Ea, 30.
Ea-Oannes, 386.
Ear-rings, 235.
East, children of the, 68, 185.
'Ebal, Mount, 269.
Edom, Edomites, cx, 33, 34, 109, 110, 311, 341.
'Eglon, 67 ff., 297.
Egypt, domination of, by Hyksos, lxv, cxii; expulsion of Hyksos from, lxvi, cxv, cxvi; invasion and conquest of Palestine and Syria by kings of the Eighteenth dynasty of, lxvii ff.; correspondence discovered at Tell el-Amarna in, lxix; relations of, with Mitanni, lxviii, lxix; intrigues of Ḥittites against, lxxi f., lxxxvii; relations of the Amorites Abd-Aširta and Aziru with, lxxiii, lxxx; Ḫabiru and SA. GAZ undermine authority of, in Cana'an and Syria, lxxiii ff.; loss of hold on Asiatic dominions by later kings of Eighteenth dynasty, lxxxvii f.; restoration of Asiatic empire by kings of Nineteenth dynasty, lxxxviii ff.; collision of, with Philistines and other sea-peoples, xcii f.; Exodus of Israelites from, liii, civ, cv, cvi; loss of Asiatic empire by kings of Twentieth dynasty of, xcv ff.; connexion of Joseph-tribes with, cviii f.; influx of Semites into, during Empire-period, cxiii f.
Egyptian, Semitic names in, lxviii, xc, cxiv; hieratic character, theory of origin of alphabet from, 261 f.
Ehud, xxxvi, xxxvii, cii, 67 ff.
'Eḳron, 19.
Elam, Elamites, lxi, lxii, lxxxi, ci.
Elders surviving Joshua', xxxv, xxxviii, li, 56.
Ele'azar, 478.
Elephantiné, Jewish garrison at, 30.
Eleutheropolis, cviii, 8.
'Eli, xxxvi, xlix, lii, 415; family of, lii, 478.
Elisha''s fountain, 15.
Elōhîm, preference of E narrative for use of, xxxviii, 178. See also 'God,' and Index of Hebrew terms, *s.v.*
Elohistic document. See 'Ephraimitic document.'
Elon, Elonites, ciii, 289 f., 334.
Emmaus, 464.
Emutbal, lxi.
'En-gedi, 16.
Engidu, 107, 358, 395, 397, 398, 399, 400, 401, 407, 496, 497, 498.
'Ên-haḳ-ḳōrē, 375, 406.
Eniel, cii.
Enlîl, lv, 30, 385.
Enlil-kudur-uṣur, ci.
Ephah, 192.
Ephod, lii, 3, 236 ff., 409, 415.
Ephraim, cvii, 25, 132, 222, 226, 327.
Ephraimitic document (E), xxxvii ff., xlii ff., cxxi, 3, 46, 52 ff., 67 f., 83, 177, 178, 179, 180, 181, 182, 183, 184, 186, 235, 241, 268, 289, 294, 303, 316, 415 f., 440, 445, 457.

'Ephron, 293.
Erech, lv, 397, 398, 400.
Ereškigal, xix, 257.
Eridu, lxii.
Eriḥâ, 15, 501.
'Ermâ, 431.
Esagila, lxiv.
Esdraelon, 203.
Esh-ba'al, 201.
Eshmun'azar, Sarcophagus-inscription of, cxiii, 153, 387.
Eshta'ol, 339, 340, 353, 416.
Ešûa', 340, 353.
'Eṭam, 370.
Euphrates, 66.
Eurystheus, 408.
Evil spirit sent by God, 276 f.
Exodus, the. See 'Israel.'

Far'ah, 187. See also 'Wâdy Far'ah.'
Fârân, Ǵebel, 109.
Far'atâ, 187, 335.
Fig, 273.
Fire, supernatural, 192.
First-born, sacrifice of, 329 f.
Flamen Quirinalis, 394.
Flavia Neapolis, 269.
Flood-narrative, xl, 396, 399, 403.
Fortuna, temple of, 238.
Foundation-sacrifice, 331.
Four, as divine title, 9, 43 f.
Foxes, 368; Samson's, 393 f.

Ga'al, 267, 278.
Ga'ash, Mount, 57.
Gad, cvii, 142, 197, 306.
Gades, 408.
Galilee, 30; Sea of, cviii.
Gâlûd, Mount, 207 ff.
Ġaza, Ġazzeh, 19, 185, 375 f.
Ge, xix.
Geba', Ǵeba', xxi, 464, 480 f., 486.
Gebal, xcvi. See also 'Rib-Adda.'
Gebalites, xcix, 63.
Gemini, 399.
Gera, 69.
Gerizim, Mount, 269, 272.
Gershom, xx, 415, 416, 422.
Geshur, 10.
Gezer, lxxiii f., xcii, xciv, xcviii, 25 f.; agricultural calendar from, 253, 261.
el-Ǵîb, 479.
Gibe'ah, xxi, xxxvii, ciii, 442 f., 464 ff., 479, 481, 486.
Gibe'on, 464, 465, 479.
Gide'on, xxxvi, xxxvii, cii, ciii, 176 ff.
Ǵifnâ, 464.
Ǵil'âd, Ǵebel, 307.
Gilboa', Mount, 205, 206, 208.
Gile'ad, cv, 142, 207 f., 306 f., 318, 472.
Gilgal, xxxiv, cv, 2, 36 f.
Gilgameš, 358, 379, 391, 395 ff., 495, 496, 497, 498; Epic of, 97, 107, 161, 248, 380, 395-407, 496, 497.
Gilu-Ḫipa, lxxii, lxxxvi.
God, moral government of, cxxi; not to be seen by human eyes, 193; inciting men to their own ruin, 276 f.; (*'elōhîm*) as title of supernatural being, 36, 346, 350; as title of judges, 117. See also 'Yahweh.'
Golden bull, 440 f.
Gophna, 464.
Goshen, cix, 439.
Graven image, 409, 415, 419.
Greek alphabet. See 'Alphabet.'
Grinding, possible significance of Samson's, 408.

Ḫabiraean (*Ḫabirâ*), lxxxi, lxxxiii.
Ḫabiru, identity of, lxxiii ff.; identification of, with Hebrews, lxxiv, lxxx f., lxxxiii, cxi.; philological equivalence of name, with *'ibhrî*, lxxiv f.; connexion of, with SA.GAZ, lxxv ff.; 'Ḫabiru-gods,' lxxvi, lxxvii; addition of KI to name, lxxviii, lxxxiii; aggressions of, in Cana'an, lxxiii, lxxvii, lxxx f., lxxxii, civ, cxi, cxvi ff.; connexion of, with Sutû, lxxix; Aramaean nomads, lxxx; early mention of, in Babylonia, lxxxi, cx; called Šasu by the Egyptians, lxxxviii; proposed identification of, with Kaššites, lxxxi f.; proposed identification of, with Ḥittites, lxxxii f.; literature dealing with, lxxxiii.
Ḥabor, 66.
Hadad-Rimmon, mourning of, 333.
el-Ḥaḍîreh, 84.
Hair, worn long, 107 f.; –offering, 343; of Samson and of Gilgameš, 404, 495, 496, 498.
Ḥamath, cii, 63; Entry of, xcix f., 63.
Ḫammurabi, lviii, lxi, lxii, lxiv, lxxxi, lxxxiii, lxxxv, cx, cxv, 42, 196, 197, 330, 385; Code of, lxii, lxiii, 329, 385.
Ḥamor. See 'Beně-Ḥamor.'

Ḫana, Ḫanî (kingdom), lxiii, lxiv, lxxxv.
Handmaid-tribes, cvi f., cviii, 392.
Ḫani (deity), lxiii f.
Ḥaran, Ḫarran, ci, cx, cxv, 249, 250.
Ḫarbišiḫu, lxxxi.
Ḥaremḥeb, lxxxviii, cxii, 439.
Har-ḥereś, 32.
el-Ḥârithiyyeh, 78, 84.
Ḥarod, spring of, 205.
Ḥarosheth, 78, 84.
Ḫarri, lvii, lxxxiv.
Ḫaru, lvii, lxxxviii, xcii.
Ḥaṣor, cxvii, 78, 84.
Ḥatḥor, 197, 261.
Ḥatšepsut, lxvii.
Ḫatti (city), lxix, lxxi.
Ḫattušili I., lxxii.
Ḫattušili II., lxxix, lxxxvi, lxxxviii, xci, 84.
Ḥaurân, lxxxviii, xci, 231.
Ḥavvoth-Ja'ir, 289, 293.
el-Ḥawânît, Ḫirbet, 465.
Ḫayân, 174. See also 'Ḫyân.'
'Heart,' as seat of intellect, 125, 274, 382.
Hebrew language, origin and connexions of, lxi; influence of Babylonian on, lxii f.; words elucidated from other Semitic languages, 171; original pronunciation of, 99, 159; alphabet. See 'Alphabet.'
Hebrew manuscripts, early, abbreviation in, 124, 149, 466; transposition in copying, cxxiii, 124, 210, 417; marginal glosses and doublets incorporated into the text of, cxxiii f., 113, 130, 232; confusion of letters in, cxxiii, 123, 149, 225, 348; dittography in, cxxiii, 225, 423.
Hebrew poetry, rhythm of, 96 ff., 158 ff., 272 f., 365, 366, 372, 388; rhyme in, 388 f.; Climactic parallelism in, 169 f.
Hebrews, identification of, with Ḫabiru, lxxiv, lxxx f., lxxxiii, cxi; movements of, westward, cii, cix f.; supposed identity of *'Apuriu* (*'Apriu*) with, cxiv. See also 'Israel.'
Ḥebron, site, 9; elevation of, 7, 11; Hittites at, lxxxv f.; conquest of, by Judah (Caleb), cv, 8; in Samson-narrative, 377.
Ḥelbah, 28.
Heliopolis, 32.
Hera, 408.
Herakles compared with Samson, 335, 358, 375, 391, 402, 403, 406, 408; Herakles-Melḳart, 497.
Ḥermon, 428; Little, 206.
Ḥeshbon, Ḥesbân, 306, 312.
Ḫešrum, 320.
'Hexameter,' term applied to Hebrew poetry by Josephus, 98.
Hexateuch, xxxviii, xxxix, xl, xli, xlix.
Ḫipa, Ḫepa, lxxxvi.
Ḥittites, invasion of Babylonia by, lxiv, lxxxiv; Anatolian origin of, lxiv, lxxi; oldest references to, lxiv; racial connexions of, lxxi; language of, lxxi; foundation of empire of, lxxii; excavation of capital city of, lxxi; movements of, in Syria, lxxi f., lxxxvii ff.; relations of, with Egypt, lxviii, lxxxix ff.; relations of, with Mitanni, lxxii, lxxxvii; fall of empire of, xcix; a racial element in Syria-Palestine, lxxxiii ff.; one of 'the seven races' of Cana'an, lxxxv f., 63; connexion of Jebušites with, lxxxvi f.; at Ḥebron, lxxxv f.; proposed connexion of Ḫabiru with, lxxxii f.; principalities of, in Syria, xcix f., ci, 23; southern frontier of, in Syria, xcix f., 23, 62 f.; relations of, with Aramaeans, ci f.; allusions to, in Judges, 23, 62, 63; in the Lebanon, xiii, 62 f.; Ḥittite names in Judges, 76, 84, 113; Gilgameš pictured by, 401, 497; literature dealing with, lxxi f.
Ḥivvites, 6, 62, 293.
Ḥizmeh, 481.
Ḥobab, 14 f.
Ḥoms, xcix, c.
Ḥoreb. See 'Sinai.'
Ḥorim, lvii.
Ḥormah, 18, 44, 45.
Horse, Sumerian name for, lxv; introduced into Babylonia by Kaššites, lxv; introduced into Egypt by Hyksos, lxvi; in ancient warfare, 151; gallop of, reproduced in rhythm, 151.
Hosea', religious standpoint and influence of, xlv, 184, 242.
Ḥriḥor, xcvi, 23.
Ḥûleh, Lake, 78.
Ḫumbaba, 380, 395, 400.

Ḫunusa, 285.
Ḫusham, 65.
Ḥyân, lxv, lxvi.
Hyksos, domination of Egypt by, lxv; meaning of name, lxv; racial character of, lxv f.; expulsion of, from Egypt, lxvi; royal names of, lxvi; chronology of, lxvi f.; supposed connexion of Israel in Egypt with, cxii, cxv, cxvi.

Ible'am, 23.
Ibṣan, ciii, 289 f., 334.
Ibziḳ, Ḫirbet, 5.
Idin-Dagan, 385.
Idomeneus, 319.
Î'ezer, 134.
Ilu-bi'di, cii, 245.
Indra, lxxxiv.
Iphigenia, 332.
Irḫulêni, cii.
Isaac, lxxx, cx; story of Abraham's projected sacrifice of, 330.
Ish-ba'al, 201.
Israel, migration of ancestors of, to Cana'an, cix ff.; settlement of tribes in Cana'an, lxxiv, lxxx f., cv ff., 1 ff., 44 ff., 47 ff., 439 f.; name displaces earlier name Ja'cob, cx, cxi; handmaid-tribes of, cvi f., cviii, 392; tribes of, personified as individuals, cix; entry of tribes into Egypt, cxi ff.; duration of sojourn of tribes of, in Egypt, cxii; Exodus of, from Egypt, xl, l, li, liii, civ, cv, cvi, cviii, cxv, cxvi, cxviii, 439; wilderness-wanderings of, l f., cix, 439 f.; external allusions to tribes of, ciii f., cx f., cxv; mention of, by Mineptaḥ, xcii, civ, cv, cxi, cxviii; influence of Babylonian civilization upon, lxiv; conception of tribes as political unity in early times, xxxvi, l, cvi, 235, 267, 446, 453; ideal northern limit of kingdom of, xcix f.; Divine Inspiration guiding religious evolution of, cxix. See also 'Hebrews,' and names of separate tribes.
Išme-Dagan, 385.
Issachar, cviii, 136, 289 f.
Ištar, 58 f., 396, 397, 399, 402, 405, 407.
Itakama, lxxii.
Ithamar, 478.

Jabboḳ, 305, 306, 314.
Jabesh of Gile'ad, 447, 489 f.
Jabin, cxvii, 78, 80 f., 84.
Ja'cob, lxxx, cx f.
Ja'cob-el (personal name), lxvi, ciii, cxv; (place-name), lxviii, civ, cxi.
Ja'el, 79 f., 92 f., 113.
Jahaṣ, 313.
Ja'ir, ciii, 51, 135, 289 f., 292 f.
James the Just, St., 343.
Ja'zer, 305 f., 314.
Jebuš, 7, 463.
Jebušites, lxxxvi f., 7, 20, 21.
Jehoshaphaṭ, xxxviii.
Jehovistic document. See 'Judaean document.'
Jephthaḥ, xxxvi, xxxvii, xlix, cii, 226, 293, 295, 298 ff.; daughter of, 321 ff., 332 ff.
Jeraḥme'el, Jeraḥme'elites, cviii, 9, 12, 45, 136, 252; meaning of name, 252.
Jeremiah, xliii.
Jericho, xxxiv, cv, cviii, 3, 15, 69.
Jerobo'am I., liii, 4.
Jerobo'am II., xxxviii, xcix, 4.
Jerubba'al, 178, 201 f., 264.
Jerusalem, in time of T.A. Letters, lxxiii, lxxviii, cxvii; antiquity of name, 463; racial character of Jebušite inhabitants, lxxxvi f.; capture of, 6 f.; elevation of, 7; Temple at, xx.
Jethro, 14 f., 251 f.
Jezre'el, 202, 387; Vale of, 202 f.
Jogbehah, 231.
John the Baptist, St., 343.
Jonathan the priest, 415, 422, 434.
Jordon, fords of, 75, 225, 327.
Jošeph, story of, cix, cxiii; Jošeph-tribes, cviii f., cxviii, 21, 49 f., 392, 439 f.; in Egypt, cviii ff.
Jošeph-el?, lxviii, civ, cxv.
Joshua', xxxv, xxxviii, li, lxxiv, civ ff., cxvi ff., 1, 2, 22, 56, 438; Farewell-address of, xlii f., xlv.
Jotham's parable, 272 ff.
Judaean document (J), xxxviii ff., cv, cvi, cvii, cviii, 1, 46, 47 ff., 55, 67 f., 83, 176, 177, 178, 180, 181, 182, 183, 184, 235, 268, 303, 316, 336 f., 415 f., 440, 443 ff., 454, 455 ff., 458.
Judah, cviii f., 45 ff.; northern boundary of, 430; southern boundary of, 33 ff., Wilderness of, 15 f.
Judges, Book of, title, xxxiii; period

covered by, xxxiii, cxx; place of, in Hebrew Canon, xxxiv, cxxi; structure of, xxxiv ff.; first introduction to (R^P), xxxiv f., 1 ff.; second introduction to (R^{E2}), xxxv, xxxvii, xxxviii f., 52 ff.; appendix to, xxxvii; religious pragmatism of, xxxv f., cxxi, 54; J & E in, xxxvii ff.; continuation of in 1 Sam., xxxviii; editors of, xli ff. (see also 'Redactors of Judges'); date of redaction of, l; chronology of, l ff., civ, cxviii; permanent religious value of, cxviii ff.; Hebrew Text of, cxxii ff.; Versions of, cxxiv ff.

Judges of Israel, place of, in history, xxxiii f.; raised up by Yahweh, xxxv; local character of influence of, xxxvi, liii f.; historical character of, cii f.; achievements of, wrought by divine strength, cxxii; meaning and use of Hebrew term 'Judge,' xxxiii, 59, 66, 85.

Kadašman-Enlil II., lxxix.
Kadašman-Ḫarbe I., lxxix.
Ḳadesh on the Orontes, lxvii, lxviii, lxxii, lxxxix, xc, xcv, xcix, c, 23, 63.
Ḳadesh-Barneaʿ, xl, cv, cviii, cix, 18, 34, 44, 68, 110, 311, 439 f.
Ḳadîš, 82.
Kalumu, Inscription of, lxvi, xcv, 174, 254.
Ḳamm, 293.
Kammusunadbi, 316.
Ḳamon, 293.
Kamušu-šar-uṣur, 316,
Kaphtor, xciii f.
Kara-indaš I., lxxxii.
Karduniaš, lxix, lxxix, lxxx, lxxxii.
Kârî, xcv.
Ḳarḳar, battle of, liii, cii, 230.
Ḳarḳor, 230.
Ḳarn Ṣarṭabeh, 220, 222, 224.
Karnak, lxvii, xci, xcix.
Kashsha-rishat, 64.
Kaši, lxxxii.
Kaššites (Cassites), lxv, lxvi, lxxix, lxxxi ff., lxxxv, c, 64, 244.
Kaššu, lxxx, lxxxii.
Kataonians, xc.
Katna, xci.
Ḳaṭṭath, 27.
Ḳedesh of Issachar, 82.
Ḳedesh of Naphtali, 78, 80 ff., 89.
Kefr Ḥâris, 57.
Kefr Išûaʿ, 56.
Keftiu, Keftians, xciv.
Ḳeʿilah, lxxxiv.
Ḳenaz, Ḳenizzites, 12 f.
Ḳenites, cviii, cix, 14, 45, 251 f.
Kᵉrêthî, xciv.
Keslâ, 430.
Ḳĕtînîth, Kĕtônîth, 27.
Ḳeṭurah, cix, 184.
Key, 74.
Kinaḫḫi, 41.
Kinship, 265, 267, 270 f.
Ḳinza, Kidša, lxxii.
Ḳiriath-arbaʿ, conquest of, 8; meaning of name, 9, 43 f.
Ḳiriath-jeʿarim, 341, 430, 431.
Ḳiriath-sepher, 11 f.
Kiš, lv.
Ki-šavaš, 10.
Ḳishon, 78, 79, 88, 147, 500.
Ḳiṭron, 27.
Knossos, excavations at, xciv, 263.
Ḳoaʿ, lxxix.
Kore, worship of, xvii ff., 332, 334.
Kudur-Mabuk, lxi, lxxxi.
Kudurra, lxxxi, lxxxiii.
Kumanî, ci.
Ḳumêm, 293.
Kummuḫ, xcix.
el-Kurmul, 16.
Ḳuryet el-ʿEnab, el-Ḳuryeh, 430.
Kuš, 64.
Kuššar, lxxii.
Ḳuteineh, Ḫirbet, 27.
Ḳutû, lxxix.

Laban, lxxx, cx, cxi, 416.
Labaya, lxxvii, lxxxiv; sons of, lxxiii, lxxxii, lxxxiii.
Lachish, cxvii, 501; cuneiform tablet from, 253; signs on potsherds from, 261.
Lagamal, lxii.
Laish, 412, 413, 427, 428.
Laodicea, sacrifice at, 332.
Lappidoth, 85.
Larsa, lxi, lxii, lxxxi, lxxxiii.
Le'ah-tribes, cx.
Leather as writing-material. See 'Skin.'
Lebanon, Lebanons, xiii, lxviii, lxxii, lxxx, lxxxiv, lxxxvii, lxxxix, xc,

xcvi, xcix f., ci, cv, 62 f., 428; as 'twin-mountain' (Mâšû), 400; inscription from, 254.
Left-handed, 69 f., 476.
'Leg upon thigh,' 369 f., 496.
Leḥi, 371, 406.
Leo, 401, 405.
Lêshăm, 427.
Levi, Levite, Levites, cix, 269, 409, 416, 459; origin of, 436 ff.
Libyans, xcii, xcv.
Liftâ, xx, 430, 500.
Liḥḥyan, 10.
Lion, slain by Samson, xix, 357 f., 405; slain by Gilgameš, 401, 495, 496, 497, 498; associated with Nergal, 405.
'Lip' as a topographical term, 220 f.
Loins, 264.
Loom, 381 f.
Loṭ, cx.
Lugal-banda, 397.
Luka. See 'Lycians.'
Lunar worship, among early Hebrews, cx. See also 'Moon-god' and 'Yahweh.'
Luz, 23.
Lycia, Lycians, xc, xcii, xciv.

Ma'achah, Ma'achathites, 135, 428.
Ma'ân, 298.
Machir, cvi, 134 f.
Maḫalliba, 28.
Maḥaneh-Dan, 353, 431.
Maher-shalal-ḥash-baz, 260.
Mahlûl, 27.
el-Maḫrûḳ (Makhrûd), 222, 224.
el-Maḳrah, Ǵebel, 110.
Malkatu, 250.
Malki-ṣedeḳ (Melchizedek), lxxxvii.
Ma'lûl, 27.
Manaḫtites, 341.
Manasseh, cv f., 24, 50, 134 f., 222, 318; substitution of, for Moses, 434 f.
Manetho, lxv, lxvi.
Manoaḥ, 341.
Manôthû, 10.
Manya, lxxxiv.
Ma'on, 16.
Ma'onites, 298.
Maps of Palestine, 498 ff.
Marduk, lxiv.
Marmîtâ, Ḫirbet, 371.
Marriage-customs, 265, 354 f., 356, 360 f., 365.
Maš, 400.
Mašawaša, xcv.
Maššah, 438.
Massoretic Text, vocalization of, 159.
Mâšu, 395, 399 f., 497.
Mattiuaza, lxxxiv, lxxxvii.
Meal-offering, 349.
Mediterranean, 400; Mediterranean origin of alphabet, theory of, 263.
Megiddo, lxvii, lxxviii, lxxxiv, 23, 78, 82, 145, 203, 500; alphabetic letters from, 261.
Melḳart, 358, 391, 401, 402, 406, 497.
Mĕnî, 10.
Merǵ 'Ayyûn, xcix.
Merǵ ibn 'Âmir, 202, 204.
Meribah, 110, 438.
Merib-ba'al, 201.
Merom, 78.
Meroz, 151.
Meryamin, 489 f.
Mesha', lxi, 18. See also '*Moabite Stone.*'
Meshech, xcix.
Mesopotamia, 66.
Micah, xx, xxxvii, xlix, cii, ciii, cvii, 240, 408 ff.
Micayᵉhu, 417.
Midian, cix, 110, 184, 297.
Mikmash = Muḫmâs, xiii.
Milcah, 250.
Milcom, 299.
el-Milḥ, 16.
Milkili, lxxiii, lxxvii, lxxxii.
Mill, millstone, 288.
Millo, 271 f.
Minaean language, lix; inscriptions, 437, 441.
Mineptaḥ, liii, xci f., civ, cv, cxi, cxii, cxviii, 26, 439.
Minnith, 320.
Minoans, xciv; Minoan script, 263.
Minor Judges, the, xxxvi, 289 ff., 334 f.
Minos, xciv.
Miriam, 440.
Mîshôr, 306, 307.
Miṣpah, in Gile'ad, cx, 307, 319; in Benjamin, 447, 453, 472, 477, 479, 488; Land of, 62.
Mitanni, Mitannians, lxviii, lxix, lxx, lxxii, lxxiii, lxxx, lxxxiv f., lxxxvii,

cii; language of, lxxxv; kingdom of, lxxxv.
Mitra, lxxxiv.
Moab, cx, 68, 298 ff.; Moabites spoke Hebrew, lxi.
Moabite Stone (inscription of Mesha'), lxi, lxiii, 18, 30, 59, 155, 174, 253, 291, 313, 315, 316.
Molech, child-sacrifice to, 331.
Molten image, 409.
Money, primitive, 145, 378.
Monolatry, 314 f.
Moon-god, cvii, 9, 44, 196 f., 249 ff.
Moreh, 206.
Mortar, the, 374.
Moses, name of, cix, 478; connexion of, with Levites, cix, 438 ff.; at Midian, 439; father-in-law of, 15, 251; Theophany made to, 189, 248 f.; leads tribes out of Egypt, cvi, cviii; connexion of, with Joshua', cxvi; religious influence of, cvii, cix, cxx f., 329 f.; as typical intercessor, xliii; Blessing of, 4, 438; descendant of, 415, 416, 434 f.
Muġâret el-Ǵa'y, xxi.
Muraṣṣaṣ, 151.
Muršili, lxxxix, xci, 84.
Mûsâ, Ǵebel, 110.
Muškaya, xcix.
Must, 274.
Muwattalli, lxxxix, xc, xci.
Mylitta, 59, 198.
Mysians, xc.

Nabaṭaeans, 34.
Nâblus, 269.
Nabonidus, lvi.
Nahalol, 27.
Naharîn, lxvii, lxviii, lxix, lxxii, lxxviii, lxxxv, lxxxix, xci, 66.
Naḥor, lxxx.
Nahr el-'Auġa, 24.
Nahr Ǵâlûd, 206.
Nahr el-Kelb, lxxxix.
Nahr el-Muḳaṭṭa', 145, 500.
Naḫrima, Narima, lxxviii, 66.
Namyawaza, lxxvii, lxxix, lxxxiv.
Nāphath (Nāphôth) Dor, 24.
Naphtali, cvii, 29, 79, 81, 137.
Narâm-Sin, lvi.
Nâsatya-twins, lxxxiv.
'Navel' as a topographical term, 283.
Nazirite, 337, 338, 342 ff., 404.
Neby Daḥy, Ǵebel, 206.
Neby Samwîl, 472, 479.
Nebuchadneṣṣar, xlvi.
Necromancy, 421.
Nefertiti, lxxii.
Negeb, cviii, 7, 16, 439; conquest of, xl, cv, 44 ff.
Nemaean lion, 358, 403.
Neolithic inhabitants of Palestine, lvii.
Nephtoaḥ, xx, 430, 500.
Nergal, 405.
Nerigal and Ereškigal, story of, 257.
Nesubenebded, xcv ff.
Nicopolis, 464.
Nimrod, 401.
Nineveh, lxii.
Ninib-tukulti-Ašur, lxxxi.
Nisaba, lxiii.
Nîsin, lv, 385.
Nob, 441.
Nobaḥ, 51, 135, 231.
Nubia, lxxxvii f.
Number, exaggeration of, 120, 446, 455 f., 458.

Oath, 418, 489.
'Obed, 278.
Oeta, Mount, 408.
el-'Olâ, 10, 441.
Old Testament, religious value of, cxviii ff.
Olive, 273.
Onesilus, 359.
'Ophrah, 187.
'Oreb, 225 f.
Origen, transliterations of, from Hebrew, 166, 167, 168.
el-'Ormeh, 282.
Ortygia, 406.
'Othniel, xxxvi, ciii, 12 f., 64 ff.
Ox-goad, 77.

Paddan-Aram, lxxx.
Palms, city of, xxxiv, 15, 69.
Panammu, inscription of, 173 f., 254.
Paneas, 63, 427.
Papyrus, use of, as writing material, xcvii, 255, 258, 259, 260.
Papyrus Anastasi I., xci.
Papyrus Golénischeff, xcvi.
Parallelism, Climactic, 169 ff.
Paran, 109.
Partridge, 375.
Paula, pilgrimage of, 464.

Peace-offerings, 477.
Peg, 93, 152.
Pe-nḥesi, xcii, 41.
Pe-nḥēsi, 239, 478.
Pentameter, term applied to Hebrew poetry by Josephus, 98.
Penuel, 223 f., 228, 233.
Perizzites, 6.
Persephone, xviii, xix, 334.
Persian, old, cuneiform writing of, 262.
Perversion of proper names, 5, 58, 64, 65 f., 228 f., 434.
Petra, 34.
Phaestos disk, xciv.
Philadelphia, 306.
Philistines, invasion of Cana'an by, xcii f.; origin of, xciii f.; connexion of, with Minoans of Crete, xciv; head-dress of, xciv; connexion of, with Lycians and Carians, xciv f.; 'Lords of,' 62; Dagon, deity of, 384 ff.; theory of introduction of alphabetic script to Cana'an by, 263; oppression of Israelites by, lii, liii, 295 ff., 335 f.; Samson's relations with, 335 ff.; uncircumcised, 356.
Phineḥaš, lii, 325, 478.
Phoenicia, Phoenicians, lxviii, lxxiii, lxxv, lxxviii, lxxxii, lxxxviii, lxxxix, xciii, xcvi ff., 28, 143, 400; inscriptions, lxi, 254.
Pictographic script, 255.
Piers Ploughman, rhythm of, xiv.
Pig, relation of, to Tammuz, xvii f.
Pillars of Hercules, 400, 408.
Piping to flocks, 141.
Pir'athon, 335.
Pithom, civ, cxvi.
Poetry, Hebrew. See 'Hebrew poetry.'
Polydector, Polydegmon, 334.
Polyxena, 334.
Porta Catularia, 393.
Priestly redactor. See 'Redactors.'
Promontorium album, 28.
Prophets, teaching and spiritual appeal of, cxviii f., cxxi; Prophetical schools, xxxiv, xl, xli ff.
Ptolemais, 28.
Pu'ah, 289, 291.
Pudu-Ḫipa, lxxxvi.
Pulasati. See 'Philistines.'
Pulydamas of Scotusa, 358.
Puppies, sacrificed, 393.

Quail, sacred to Herakles, 375, 406.

Ra'amšeš (store-city), civ, cxvi.
Rabbah, Rabbath-'Ammon, 306.
Rabbinic exegesis, 73.
Rachel, cx, 416.
Ramah, er-Râm, 86, 465.
Ramath-leḥi, 75, 374, 405.
Ra'messe I., lxxxviii.
Ra'messe II., liii, lxxxix ff., civ, cxii, cxiv, cxv, cxvi, cxviii, 27.
Ra'messe III., xcii ff., xcviii.
Ra'messe IX., xcviii.
Ra'messe XII., xcv.
Rammôn, xxi, 486.
Râs el-Abyaḍ, 28.
Râs eṭ-Tawîl, Ḫirbet, 465, 472, 479, 481, 486.
Râs 'Umm el-Ḫarrubeh, 222.
Rebeḳah, lxxx, cx.
Rechabites, 343.
Redactors of Judges:—
  R^{JE}, xli, xlix f., 55, 63, 181, 182, 194, 226, 268, 294, 295, 298, 301, 303, 338, 345, 410, 445.
  R^{E2}, xxxiii, xli ff., 52 ff., 59, 61, 176, 184, 266, 268, 293 f., 295, 298, 338.
  R^{P}, l, 1, 2, 55, 76, 263, 268, 290, 304, 339, 410 f., 424, 454, 457, 458.
Reed-pen, 258, 260.
Reḥob, 29.
Reḥobo'am, liii, xcviii.
Rephidim, li, 68.
er-Restân, xiii, xc, c, cii.
Retenu, Upper, lxvii, xciv.
Re'uben, cviii, 306.
Re'uel, 15.
Revelation of Yahweh, progressive, 189.
Revised Version, criticism of renderings of, 25, 75, 86, 90, 106, 108, 116, 117, 123, 139, 147, 148 f., 157, 189, 190, 205, 212, 229 f., 234, 321 *bis*, 325, 347, 348, 350 *bis*, 367, 368, 372, 377, 378, 418, 423, 476, 485, 493; *margin*, 93, 148 f., 205, 207, 390, 480.
Rhyme. See 'Hebrew poetry.'
Rhythm. See 'Hebrew poetry.'
Rib-Adda, lxxiii, lxxv, lxxviii, lxxix, lxxx, lxxxii.
Riblah, c.
Righteous acts of Yahweh, 129.
Rimmon, xxi, 448, 486.
Rîm-Sin, lxi, lxxxi, lxxxiii, cx.
Robigalia, Robigus, 393 f.

Rock-altar. See 'Altar.'
Romulus, 494.
Roof-chamber, 71.
Rosse, rosser, 373.
Ruḫizzi, lxxxiv.
Ruṣmanya, lxxxiv.
Rust in corn, 393 f.

Sabaean kingdom, 400; language, lix.
Sabbath, 251.
Ṣābians, pseudo-, 421.
Sabine women, rape of, 494.
Sacrifice, 191, 477; human, 320, 329 ff.; of firstborn, 329 f.; child-sacrifice to Moloch, 331; foundation-, 331; virgin-, 332 ff.; of red puppies, 393; of pigs, xviii.
Ṣadoḳ, 478.
eṣ-Ṣafâ, naḳb, 17, 33, 35.
eṣ-Ṣâfiyyeh, 35.
Safrâneh, c.
Sagalassos, xcii.
SA. GAZ (people), lxxv ff., lxxxviii, cxi, cxvii f., 26.
Sagittarius, 399.
Ṣaida, 28.
Šakaluša, xcii, xciii.
Sakere, lxxxvii.
Salitis, lxv.
Ṣalm, 229.
Salma, 341.
Ṣalmon, Mount, 286.
Ṣalmunna', 228.
Salt, City of, 16; covenant of, 42; symbolical use of, 285.
Salt Sea, 34.
Sam'al, cii, 173.
Samaria, capture of, by Sargon, xlvi; ostraka from, 253, 258.
Šamaš. See 'Sun-god.'
Šamšânu, 352.
Šamši-Adad VII., 385.
Samson, xxxvi, xxxvii, xl, xlix, lii, liv, cii, 10, 75, 293, 294, 335 ff.; meaning of name, 352, 391; solar-mythological element in story of, xix, 337, 338, 377, 380, 384, 391 ff.
Samsu-ditana, lxiv.
Samsu-iluna, lix, lxiv.
Samuel, judge, xxxvi, xlix; last address of, xlii f., xlv; as typical intercessor, xliii; length of judgeship of, li f.; a Nazirite (?), 343, 344; not a Levite, 441.
Sangara, 76.
Ṣaphon, 326.
Ṣâr, Ḫirbet, 305 f., 310, 314.
Sarah, 250.
Ṣar'ah, xix, 340, 349.
Šardina, Sardis, Sardinia, xcii, xciii.
Sarĕthan, 219 ff.
Šar-Gani-šarri, lv, lvi.
Sargon of Akkad, lv f., lx.
Sargon of Assyria, xlvi, 385.
Saris, 430.
Ṣarpanitum, lxiv.
Šarratu, 250.
Šarru-kin, Sarru-ukin. See 'Sargon.'
Šasu, lxv, lxxix f., lxxxviii.
Šaṭṭâ, 219.
Saul, lii, lxxix, ciii, 444, 447, 455, 490.
Scorpio, 399.
Scorpion-men, 395, 399.
Scribes, Assyrian and West Semitic, 256, 495.
Sea-country, people of, lxiv.
Seafaring life adopted by Israelite tribes, 143.
Seals, Hebrew inscribed, 253.
Sebaita, xiii, 17.
Ṣedad, c.
Ṣedeḳ, 41 ff.
Ṣeffûriyyeh, 27.
Šêḫ Sa'd, xci.
Seil ed-Dilbeh, 14.
Se'ir, lvii, cxx, 109; in Judah, 430.
Se'irah, 74.
Šela', 34.
Semites, early movements of, lv ff.; early common home of, lvi.
Semitic languages, development of, from a common original, lx; influence of environment upon, lx; primitive connexion with Sumerian, lvii.
Šeneh, 465.
Šennacherib, Prism-inscription of, 28, 385.
Ṣephath, xiii, 17, 45.
Serabit, inscription from, 261.
Ṣerbal, Ǵebel, 111.
Šerdanu (*amêlu Šerdani*), lxxix, xcii.
Ṣerēdah, 219 ff.
Serpent, relation of, to Earth-goddess, xix.
Servant of Yahweh, the, 56.
Sety I., lxxxviii f., civ, cvi, cxviii, 27.
Seven as divine title, 9, 43 f., 251.
Seventy, as large round number, 264.

Sha'albim, 33.
Shalmaneser III., xcviii, cii, 71, 230.
'Shameful thing' substituted in text for Ba'al, 5, 58, 202.
Shamgar, xxxvii, ciii, 75 ff., 113, 290.
Shamir, 292.
Shammah, 75, 77.
Sharon, lxxxiv.
Sharuhen, lxvi.
Shavsha, 10, 352.
She'ar-yashub, 260.
Shechem, xxxv, lxxiii, lxxviii, lxxx, lxxxi, cviii, cix, cxi, 4, 56, 134, 269 f., 437 f.
Shekel, 236, 378.
Shephelah, 7 f., 20.
Shēshai, 9 f., 352.
Shibbóleth, 328.
Shiloh, 37, 415, 435 f., 441, 476, 491, 492.
Shin'ar, lxii, lxviii.
Shisha, 10.
Shishak, xcviii.
Shobal, 341.
Sibitti, 43 f., 251.
Sicilians, xciii.
Ṣidkâ, 377.
Ṣidon, 28; Ṣidonians, 297, 428.
Siduri-Sabîtu, 396, 398, 400.
Śihon, 306, 310, 312 f.
Ṣiklag, 68.
Ṣilbêl, 377.
Siloam-inscription, 253.
Sime'on, lxxv, civ, cviii f., 4, 46, 269, 437 ff.
Simyra, lxviii.
Sin. See 'Moon-god.'
Sin-muballiṭ, lviii, lxi.
Śinai, cxx, 68, 109 ff., 112, 251, 311.
Singar, Ǵebel, lxviii.
Singara, lxviii.
Sinuhe, tale of, 439.
Ṣippôri, 27.
Śirah, well of, 501.
Śiśera, lxvii, 78 ff., 84.
Siweh, 406.
eṣ-Ṣiyyâǵ, 371.
Skin, use of, as writing material, 255, 259.
Ṣobah, c.
Solomon, date of accession of, liii, cxv; kingdom of, xcix.
eṣ-Ṣôma', Ḫirbet, 465.
Soothsayer, 283.
Ṣor'ah, xix, 339, 340, 416.
Sorek, Wâdy of, 340, 377.
'Soul,' as principle of life in man, 390.
Spirit of Yahweh. See 'Yahweh.'
Springs, in solar mythology, 405 f.
'Stand before,' 478.
Stone, as place of execution, 271; standing-, 272.
Stylus, for writing cuneiform, xvii, 254 f.; Hebrew terms for, 259 f.
Šubandu, lxxxiv.
Šubbiluliuma, lxxii, lxxxvii, lxxxviii, xci.
Śuccoth, 220, 228.
Sudanese mercenaries, lxxxii.
Sumer, Sumerians, lvi, lxii, lxiv, c, 385, 386; deities of, lvii; influence of civilization of, lxiii f.; language, ultimate connexion of Semitic biliterals with, lvii; legal code of, lxiii.
Sumu-la-ilu, lix.
Sun, supposed effect of, on corn, 394; course of, in the heavens, 395 f., 399 f., yearly phases of, 396 f., 399; chariot of, 397.
Sun-god, cvii, 42, 333, 392, 395, 396, 400, 406, 407, 421, 495, 496.
Sûrik, Ḫirbet, 377.
Śûśitha, 308.
Sûsiyyeh, 308.
Šutarna, lxxxiv.
Šutatarra, lxxii.
Sutû, Šutû, lxxvii, lxxix f., lxxxiii, cxi.
Šuwardata, lxxvii, lxxxiv.
Synchronistic History of Babylonia and Assyria, c.
Syria, Semites in, lvi, lviii; inclusion of, under name Amurru, lix; connexion of Hyksos with, lxvi; influx of Ḥittites into, lxvi, lxxi; invasion and conquest of, by Egyptian kings, lxvii ff.; sons of chieftains of, educated in Egypt, lxviii; condition of, at period of T.A. Letters, lxx ff.; caravan-service through, lxx; non-Semitic element in population of, lxxxiii ff.; struggle of Egypt with Ḥittites in, lxxxix ff.; Ḥittite principalities in, xcix; Aramaeans in, ci f.; Syrian desert, lxxix f. See also 'Cana'an.'

Ta'anach, Ta'annuk, 23, 79, 82, 131.
Ṭab'al, Tab'ēl, 66.

Ṭabbath, 223.
Tablet for writing, 259.
Tabor, xc, 79 f., 87, 234.
Ṯakkara, xcii ff., xcvi, xcviii, 24, 384.
Talmai, 9 f.
Tammuz, xvii ff., 333 f., 397.
Ṭanṭurah, 24.
Tarḫulara, 84.
Tarḫundaraba, lxxxiii.
Tadu-Ḫipa, lxxii, lxxxvi.
eṭ-Ṭayyibeh, 308.
Tebeṣ, 234, 287.
Tell Abû Ḳudîs, 82.
Tell el-Amarna Letters, lxi, lxix ff., lxxxviii, ci, cxi, cxii, cxiii, cxvi, cxvii, cxviii, 20, 26, 41, 66, 76, 99, 144, 253, 256 ff., 265, 463, 477.
Tell 'Arâd, 16.
Tell (Tulêl) el-Fûl, 465, 472, 479, 481, 486.
Tell Ǵezer, 25.
Tell el-Ḥasy, 501.
Tell el-Ḳâḍy, xcix, 427.
Tell Ma'în, 16.
Tell el-Masḫûṭa, civ.
Tell el-Mutesellim, 23, 82.
Tell eṣ-Ṣâfiyyeh, xciv.
Tell eš-Šihâb, lxxxviii.
Tell es-Sulṭân, 15.
Tell el-Yahudiyyeh, lxv.
Tell Zîf, 16.
Temple, building of, by Solomon, l.
Tentamon, xcvi, xcvii.
Tent of Meeting, 440.
Tent-peg. See 'Peg.'
'Tents' = 'home,' 463.
Teraphim, 117, 409, 416, 420 f., 426.
Terebinth, 187.
Teuwatti, lxxxiv.
Thebes, lxx, lxxxvii, xcvi.
Theocracy, conception of, 183.
Thesmophoria, xviii f.
Thirty, as title of Moon-god, 44.
Threshing-board, 229.
Threshing-floor, 204.
Ṭhutmosi I., lxvii, lxxxv.
Ṭhutmosi II., lxvii.
Ṭhutmosi III., lxvii f., lxxxv, lxxxix, cxii, cxiv, 26.
Ṭhutmosi IV., lxix, lxxii.
Tibneh (N.W. of Bethel), 56; (in Shephelah), 355, 430.
Tid'al, lxii.
Tiglath-Pileser I., lxxix, xcix, ci, 285.
Tiglath-Pileser IV., cii, 415.
Tii, lxxii.
Timnah (N.W. of Bethel), 56; (in Shephelah), 355, 430.
Timnath-ḫereś, Timnath-śeraḥ, 56.
Titus, 464.
Ṭob, land of, 308.
To'i, To'u, cii.
Tola', ciii, 289 f.
Torches in pitchers, 216.
Totemism, xviii, 225, 291.
Tribal names transferred to places or districts, cxi.
Trumpet, 215.
Ṭûbâs, 287.
Tubi, 308.
Tuḫi, cii.
Tukulti-Ninib I., ci.
Tunip, lxxxv, xci.
Turuša, xcii.
Tušratta, lxxii, lxxxvii.
Tut'anhaton (Tut'anḫamon), lxxxvii.
Tuwêl eẕ-Ẕiyâb, 226.
Tyre, xcvi, 402.
Tyrrhenians, xcii.

Umman Manda, lxii.
Ur, lv, lxxxiii, cx, 249, 250.
Urim and Tummim, 3, 239 f.
Ur-Šanabi, 396, 398, 400.
Urṭâs, 370.
Urukagina, lxiii.
Urusalim, 20, 463.
'Ušš el-Ġurâb, 226.
Uta-napištim, 396, 398, 401.

Vale, the, 19, 203 f.
'Valley of Thorns,' 464, 465.
Vandalian Church, 77.
Vartikâ, 406.
Varuna, lxxxiv.
Vine, 273.
Virgin-sacrifice, 332 ff.
Virgo, 399.

Wadd, 437.
Wâdy el-'Ariš, 34.
Wâdy Bel'ameh, 23.
Wâdy Bît Ḥannîna, 465.
Wâdy ed-Dumm, 479.
Wâdy Far'ah, 207, 220, 222, 223, 224, 225.
Wâdy el-Fiḳrah, 33 f.
Wâdy eǵ-Ǵôzeleh, 225.

Wâdy el-Ḥâfy, 465, 481.
Wâdy Ḥesbân, 306.
Wâdy of Jezre'el, 185.
Wâdy Ḳâna, 24.
Wâdy el-Ḳelt, 15, 88.
Wâdy el-Mâliḥ, 220.
Wâdy Môǵib, 310.
Wâdy el-Munâḫ, 341.
Wâdy Râǵib, 326.
Wâdy eṣ-Ṣarâr, 340.
Wâdy Šerrâr, 185.
Wâdy eṣ-Ṣuwênîṭ, xxi, 465, 486.
Wâdy Ṭûmîlât, lxv, civ, cix, 439.
Wâdy Yâbis, 222, 489.
Wâdy ez-Zerkâ, 310.
Wâdy Zimry, 481.
Warad-Sin, lxi, lxii.
Wašaša, xciii.
Watches, night-, 216.
Weaving, 381.
Wenamon, narrative of, xcv, xcvi ff., 23, 24, 258.
West Semitic language (language-group), 253; Arabian affinities in, lviii f., lx; alphabet, 254 ff.
Wheat-harvest in Palestine, 367, 394.
Whistling, effect of, on animals, 141 f.
Wilderness-journey, Israel's, 311.
Wine, new. See 'Must.'
Wine-press, 187, 274.
Witch of 'Endor, 426.
Writing, reference to, in Judges, 232; use of cuneiform in Cana'an, lxix f., 253; earliest known documents in West Semitic language, 253 f.; development of cuneiform from pictographs, 254; cuneiform script and alphabetic script possibly co-existent in Cana'an in early times, 254 f.; explanation of paucity of written documents from Palestine, 255; method of writing cuneiform, xvii, 255, 495; Aramaic dockets on cuneiform tablets, 255; T.A. Letters written by West Semitic scribes, 256; use of alphabetic script in Assyria, 256, 495; exercises in writing cuneiform script, 257; West Semitic alphabet really a syllabary, 258; early use of papyrus in Cana'an, xcvii, 258; terms used in O.T. in connexion with writing, 258 ff.; earliest traces of West Semitic alphabet, 261; theories as to origin of West Semitic alphabet, 261 ff. See also 'Alphabet,' 'Papyrus,' 'Stylus,' 'Cana'anite glosses,' 'Hebrew MSS.'

X, unknown source, 458.

Yabni-el, cxvii.
Ya'di, lxvi, xcv, 173 ff.
Yahweh, predilection of J narrative for use of name, xxxviii; Yahweh Ṣebhā'ôth, xl; Śinai, ancient seat of, cxx, 109, 251; Mosaic Yahwism in conflict with naturalistic Yahwism, cxx, 330; covenant of, cxxi, 60; spirit of, inciting men to action, cxx, cxxii, 66, 203, 317, 337 f., 357, 372; Israel's leader in battle, cxx, cxxii, 91, 109; consultation of oracle of, 3, 239 f., 425 f., 476 f.; sacred ban of, 18, 231, 456; mentioned on Moabite Stone, 18; Angel of, 35 f., 89, 151, 192, 346; title 'Servant of,' 56; strengthening Israel's foes, 68; connexion of, with phenomena of the storm, 91; 'arm of,' 129; 'righteous acts of,' 129; as King of His people, 183; name as denoting progressive revelation, 189; *Yahweh shālôm*, 193; relation of Ashera-cult to worship of, 196 f.; Asher possibly a surname of, cvii, 198; title 'Ba'al' applied to, 201 f.; originally an Amorite deity, 243 ff.; name revealed to Moses with uniquely new significance, 248 f.; early identification of, with Moon-god, 249 ff.; as national God (in restricted sense), 314 f.; human sacrifice to, 319 f., 329 f.; Teraphim in connexion with worship of, 330, 426. See also 'God.'
Yâlô, 32.
Yanḫamu, lxxviii, cxiii.
Yapaḫi, lxxix, cxvii, 26.
Yaphia', cxvii.
Yarimuta, cxiii.
Yarmuḳ, 306.
Yarmuth, cxiii.
Yašdata, lxxxiv.
Ya-u, Ya-u-tum, etc., in proper names, 243 ff.
Ya'u-bi'di, cii, 245, 246.
el-Yemen, naḳb, 33.

Yeno'am, xcii.
Yerîmôth, cxiii.

Zabum, lix.
eẕ-Ẕâhariyyeh, 10 f.
Zakar-ba'al, xcvi ff., 258.
Zakir, Inscription of, lxiii, cii, 173 f., 254.
Zamama-šum-iddin, ci.
Zebaḥ, 228.
Zebul, 279 f., 281, 284.
Zebulun, cviii, 26, 79, 81, 289.
Ze'eb, 225 f.
ez-Zîb, xiii, 29.
Zilpah-tribes, cx.
Zimrida, cxvii.
Ziph, 16.
Ziphron (Zifrân), c.
Zirdamyašda, lxxxiv.
Zodiac, 399.

II. INDEX OF GRAMMATICAL AND PHILOLOGICAL OBSERVATIONS

(*The reference is to Hebrew unless otherwise specified*)

Accusative, adverbial, 149.

Arabic Place names, modern, 499 ff.; modification of consonants in, xx, 24, 27, 29, 282, 306, 500, 501; modification of final *-ēl* to *-în* in, 21; dropping of final syllable in, 23; dropping of preformative י in, 23, 306; formation of, by assonance with ancient names, 85, 145, 500.

Article, Definite, idiomatic usages of, 213, 287, 346, 489; with Construct State, 231; omission of, with Adjective, 378.

Asyndeton, 432.

Babylonian Permansive compared with Hebrew Perfect, lxiii.

Babylonian Praeterite compared with Hebrew Imperfect with *Wāw consecutive*, lxiii.

Biliteral roots, xiii, xvi, 40, 69, 92.

Case-endings, 167.

Circumstantial clause, 324, 326, 384, 425, 433.

Construct State, before Preposition, 136; Suspended, 150.

Darga, as substitute for *Methegh*, 461.

Dativus incommodi, 67, 277.

Diminutives, 27, 352.

Egyptian expression of Semitic Dual-ending, 66.

Egyptian *r* representing *l* in another language, 84; cf. lxxxviii, lxxxix *bis*, xci, xcii, xciii.

Emphasis, expression of, 321, 357, 367, 372, 419, 425.

Hypocoristic affixes in Babylonian, 76, 246.

Hypothetical sentence, virtual, 347.

Imperative, original form of, in Ḳal, 166; 2nd pers. sing. masc. as Interjection, 429.

Imperfect, anomalous use of, 38; in pictorial description, 148; describing recurrence, 176, 185, 325, 327; emphatic form of, 152 f.; masc. form of 2nd pers. plur. referring to fem. subject preceding, 129, 237.

Infinitive Absolute, usage of, 73 f., 367; misunderstood by R.V., 25, 367, 372.

Infinitive Construct with ב, 105 f.; with ל, 423.

Interchange of Consonants in Semitic languages, 111, 174, 430.

Ipht^{e}'al in Hebrew, 353.

Jussive in place of Imperative, 149.

Modus energicus in Arabic, 152, 169.

Nûn t^{e}lûyā, 434.

Order of Sentence, 212, 457, 475, 479.

Participle, usage of, 213, 227, 368, 384; Active Ḳal, original form of, 166; Pu'al, dropping of preformative מ in, 228.

Pasḳā in 𝔐, 38.

Pausal forms, antiquity of, 168.

Perfect, idiomatic usages of, 368, 369, 418; with *Wāw consecutive* after Infinitive, 483; with weak *Wāw*, 73, 214, 470; 2nd pers. fem. sing. of, with archaic termination, 116.

Permansive. See 'Babylonian.'

Phonetic Complement in cuneiform, lxxvi.

Pi'el, final vowel of, 167.

Pluralis excellentiae (intensive plural), 321, 323.

Pronoun, Personal, 2nd pers. fem. sing., 418.

Segholate Nouns, original pronunciation of, 167.

Sibilants, interchange of, in Semitic, 111, 306, 328, 377.

Substantive in place of Adjective, 193, 231.

Substantives ending in *-ûth*, 153.

Tenses, sequence of, 176, 328.

Tone in Arabic, 159.

Transposition of Consonants in Semitic Roots, xv, 437.
Triliteral Roots, modification in, 69, 116.
Verb ע doubled, weakened forms of, 112.
Vocalization, original form of, in Hebrew, 166 ff.
Wāw consecutive, usage of, 93, 227, 483.
Wāw explicative, 194.
Wāw introducing sentences with sarcastic turn, 187, 317.
Wāw of association, 326, 433.
את introducing Nominative, 486.
ב, usage of, 230, 321.
ה locative, 72, 224.
יש, usage of, 204.
כי introducing direct narration, 190.
ל of norm, 7.
ע, harder form of, represented by Γ in Greek, xix, 376; softer form of, represented by ḫ in cuneiform, lxxv, 386.
עד, usage of, 200, 224, 225.
עם, usage of, 425.
ר originally doubled in Hebrew, 168.
שׁ preformative in verbal forms, xvi.

III. INDEX OF FOREIGN TERMS

(*The order of the English alphabet is followed*)

HEBREW (INCLUDING CANA'ANITE 'GLOSSES' FROM THE T.A. LETTERS)

'abbîr, 151.
ābhar, 318.
ākhar, 321.
'ālā, 418.
'ālā, 3, 429, 432.
'ăliyyā, 71, 432.
'allā, *'allôn*, 86.
'āmā, 276.
'āmāl, 153.
'ămēlîm, 153.
'ănāḳ, 20.
ānan, 283.
'ăphuddā, 237, 241.
'ārah, 114.
'ārakh, 198 f.
'ăšterôth ṣônékhā, 58.
'az, 363.
badiu, 166.
bālal, *belîl*, 467.
barḳānîm, 230.
bāsār, 390.
bāṣar, 278.
baṭnu, 167.
beliyá'al, 467 f.
béṣa', 145.
béṭaḥ, 231.
biḳ'ā, 62, 203.
bōšeth, 5, 58, 202.
dāgh, 385.
dāghān, 386.
Dāleth, 262.
dārôm, cvii f.
delāthôth, 259.
dorbhān, *dorbhōnā*, 77.
dûš, 229 f.
'ēdhā, 446, 453.
'ehyeh, 189.
'ēlā, *'ēlôn*, *'ēlîm*, 86, 90, 187.
'éleph, 189.
'ĕlōhîm, 36, 117, 346, 350, 421, 425 f.
'ēmeḳ, 19, 112, 144, 202, 203 f.
'ēphôdh badh, 238.
'ešnābh, 155.
'ēṭ, 260.
gālal, *galgal*, 37.
gāraph, 146.
gath, 187, 274.
gedhērôthāyim, 141.
Gelîl hag-gôyîm, 29.
gēr, 422, 436, 438.
gîaḥ, 480.
gillāyôn, 259 f.
gilyôn, 260.
Gîmel, 262.
gómedh, 70.
gullath, 13.
gûr, 357.
ḥābhaṭ, 187.
ḥag, 492.
ḥāḳaḳ, 258.
ḥālaph, 154, 379 f.
ḥalîphôth beghādhîm, 362.
halmûth, 153.
ḥamôr, *ḥāmar*, 372 f.
ḥamûšîm, 213.
ḥāram, *heḥerîm*, 17 f., 144.
ḥāraš, 258.
ḥārath, 258.
ḫarri, 168.
hāš, 71.
ḥaṣôṣerā, 215.
ḥāthān, 15.
ḥawwā, *ḥawwôth*, 468.
he'ebhîr bā'ēš, 331.
ḥem'ā, 93.
ḥérem, 18, 44, 286, 456.
ḥērēph, 143.
ḥéreṭ, 259; *ḥéreṭ 'ĕnôš*, 260.
ḥēšebh, 237.
hēšēkh, 382.
ḥîdhā, 361.
hillûlîm, 278.
hiphḥîz, 271.
hišḥîth, 477.
hithnaddēbh, 106, 109.
ḥizzeḳ, 68.

hô'īl, 25, 424.
ḥômer, 192.
ḥôreš, 84.
ḥôrīš, xliv, 19, 316.
ḥôšīa', *môšīa'*, xxxiii, 59.
ḥōthēn, 15.
'īšôn, 352.
'iššā, 356.
'iṭṭēr, 69.
kaddîm, 215.
ḳadhmôn, 352.
ḳāhāl, *niḳhal*, 446.
kālîl, 483.
kāra', xiv f.
ḳāṣîn, 309.
kāthabh, 258.
ḳédhem, *ḳiddēm*, 147.
ḳedhēšîm, *ḳedhēšôth*, 58, 407.
ḳedhûmîm, 147.
kên, 137.
kephîr, 357.
kérem, 278.
ḳésem, 421.
ḳeṣôthām, 425.
kethâbh 'aššûrî, 262.
kikkerôth léḥem, 228.
ḳiššû'îm, 363.
ḳôl, 425.
léḳeṭ, 227.
Lēwî, *lāwā*, 437.
limmēdh, 77.
lûaḥ, 259.
ma'arākhā, 198 f.
maddîm, 70.
madh, *middîn*, 122.
māḥā, 259.
māḥaḳ, 154.
maḥalāphā, 379 f.
maḥané, 219.
maḫṣu, 168.
makhtēš, 374.
malmēdh, 77.
mā'ôz, 198.
maš, 25.
maš'abbîm, 129.
māšak, 87, 136.
mas'ēth, 483.
maṣṣēbhā, *maṣṣēbhóth*, 197, 272.
maššēkhā, 'graven image,' 242, 419.
maššékheth, *maššēkhā*, 'web,' 381 f.
mazzālôth, 146.
me'ārā, xix.
mebhô, 22.
megillā, 259.
meḥôḳeḳîm, 122, 136.
me'îl, 238.
mélekh, 265.
me'ônēn, 283.
mêšār, 42.
mesillā, 479.
millē yadh, 421.
millû'îm, 422.
mîma, *mêma*, 168.
minḥā, 70, 191, 349.
minhārôth, 185.
miphrāṣ, 143.
mišderônā, 73.
mîšôr, 203, 306, 307.
mišpāḥa, 189.
mišpāṭ, 347.
mišpetháyim, 141.
mišté, 344.
mô'ēdh, 482.
môhar, 354, 356.
môḳēš, 39 f.
môrāgh, 229.
môthēth, 288.
mûlîthā, 272.
nā, 190.
nā'ar, li.
na'arā, 356.
náḥal, xiii, 88.
nāḳaš, 40.
naḳṣapu, *naḳṣapti*, 169.
nāšakh, 'weave,' 382.
nāšakh, 'cast,' 419.
nāzîr, 342.
nebhālā, *nābhāl*, 469.
népheš, 122, 390.
nézem, 235.
niḳḳā, 368.
nôḳaḥ, 426.
nûa', 273.
'ôbh, 425.
'ôhel, 463.
'ôlēlôth, *'ôlēl*, 227, 487.
'ōreḥā, 114.
pā'am, 353.
pa'amê, 155.
paḥ, 39 f.
pāra', *péra'*, 107 f.
pāraš, 116.
paršedhônā, 72.
pāṣā, 322.
pāšaṭ, 282.
pé, 284.
pelaggôth, *peluggôth*, 139.
pélaḥ rékhebh, 288.

p^{e}lîṭîm, *pālaṭ*, 327.
p^{e}rāzî, 6.
p^{e}rāzôn, 115.
p^{e}rāzôth, 115.
pésel, 419.
p^{e}sîlîm, 71.
pil'î, 349, 350.
pinnôth, 472.
pōḥ^{a}zîm, *paḥ^{a}zûth*, *paḥaz*, 271.
rā'aṣ, 295.
ráḥam, 155.
rāmā, 374.
rāphā, xx, 462.
rêḥayim, 288.
r^{e}ḥôbh, 466.
rêḳîm, *rêḳām*, 308 f.
r^{e}phāîm, 421.
Rêš, 262.
rîbh, 201.
rōz^{e}nîm, 109.
rûaḥ, 227, 374.
rûdh, 323.
rušunu, 169.
šā'al b^e, 426.
šā'ar, 431.
Ṣādē, 262.
šādhar, 73.
sādhé, 111 f., 144.
šādhîn, 362.
šādhûdh, 154.
sah^{a}rônîm, 235.
šaḫri, 167.
šāḳal, 378.
ṣālaḥ, 66, 357.
ṣālam, 287.
ṣāphā, 307.
šāphaṭ, 59, 85; *šōphēṭ*, *šōph^{e}ṭîm*, xxxiii, l.
šāraḳ, 142.
ṣāraph, 208.
sārîm, 232.
šāsā, lxxix.
šatê, 167.
šébher, xvi, 214.
šēbheṭ, 136.
ṣ^{e}ḥôrôth, 124.
š^{e}lûl, *š^{e}lîl*, 213.
s^{e}mîkhā, 92.
šéphel, 152.
sépher, 259.
séren, 62.
ṣ^{e}rîaḥ, 286.
š^{e}rîkôth 'ădhārîm, 141 f.
sîaḥ, 125.
šiššá', *šéšá'*, 357.
ṣippûy, 241.
šiṭṭā, 465.
šôḳ, 369.
šôphār, 215.
šôṭ^{e}rîm, 259.
ṣu'ru, 167.
t^{e}rāphîm, xx, 421.
ṭibbûr, *ṭabbûr*, 283.
tinnā, 129, 325.
ṭiphsar, 495.
tîrôš, 274.
tôlá'ath, 291.
tômer, 86.
tôrā, 206.
tormā, 281.
tûr, 22.
'ûgābh, 142.
yāḳaš, 40.
yārēkh, 264, 370.
yark^{e}thê, 459.
yāšabh, 86, 123.
yāthēdh, 80, 381 f.
yazkur, 169, 386.
yéḳebh, 187, 274.
yéther, 378.
yibbēbh, 154.
yukabid, 168.
zānaḥ, 460.
z^{e}ḳēnîm, 232.
zimmā, 473.
zuruḫ, 168.

BABYLONIAN AND ASSYRIAN (INCLUDING SUMERIAN).

A.BA, 495.
ADDA, lxi.
âlu, 463.
AMA.UŠUMGAL.ANNA, xix.
amêlu, lxxiv.
ANŠU.KURRA, lxv.
Arba'ilu (*âlu*), 43.
balâṭu, 327.
BAR, PAR, xvi.
bêlit taḫâzi, 59.

DA, 262.
dâdu, 291.
dânu, 392.
dâšu, 229.
DUMU.ZI, *Du'ûzu*, *Dûzu*, xvii.
duppu, 259.
dupšarru, 495.
elêpu, 380.
galâdu, 209.
GAM, 262.
GAR.ZA, 116.
ḫabbatum, *ḫabâtu*, lxxvi.
ḫalâpu, *naḫlaptu*, 362.
ḫarimtu, 58, 407.
Ḫarrânu, 249.
ḫaṭṭu, *ḫaṭâṭu*, 260.
ḥazan(n)u, *ḥazianu*, lxxiv.
ḫuršu, *ḫursu*, 85.
ibru, lxxxiii.
ištarâti, 59.
ḳadâdu, 262.
KA.DI, xix.
ḳadištu, 58, 407.
kapâru, *kuppuru*, xvi.
ḳarittu, 59.
kazratu, 407.
kênu, 137.
kettu, 42.
KI, lxxviii.
Kimta rapaštum, lviii.
Kimtum kettum, lix.
KIRRUD.DA, 72,
KIŠ, lv.
ḳudmu, 147.
KUR, 112.
lulâ amêlu, 399.
manzazu, *manzaltu*, 146.
MAR.TU, lix, 41.
MAR.ZA, 116.
mât la târi, 468.
mâtu, 112.
MEŠ, lxxvi.
mêšâru, 42.
mi, *ma*, 247.
muallidat, 59, 199.
mulû, 272.
nîmelu, 154.
PA, 263.
parašdinnu, 72.
parâsu, 116.
parsigu, 404.
parṣu, 116.
pašâṭu, 282.
pirisṭu, 116.
pirtu, 107.
pû, 284.
puluggu, *pulukku*, 139.
rabû, *rapû*, xx, 421, 462.
raḫâṣu, 295.
rêšu, 262.
RU, 262.
ruṣṣunu, 109.
šabrû, *šabrâtu*, xvi, 214.
ṣaddu, 39.
šadû, 112.
šagâšu, lxxvi.
SA.GAZ, lxxv ff., 26.
šaḫâtu, 477.
ṣalâmu, 287.
šamḫatu, 407.
šâpiṭu, xxxiii.
šâru, 133.
šaššu, 10.
šatâru, 258.
seseru, *sisseru*, 84.
SI.PA, (*abnu*), 285.
šipru, *šapâru*, 259, 328.
sîsû, lxv.
ŠU, 421.
talîmu, 10.
tultu, 291.
umalli kâta, 422.
urudû, 152.
urzunu, 109.
zarâḫu, 386.
ZI, ZIDA, ZIDE, 262.
zinû, 460.

Aramaic (including Syriac).

abbûbhā, 142.
'ămal, 154.
biṣṣua', 145.
bizḳā, *bezḳā*, 5.
g^{e}*raph*, 146.
ḥ^{a}*raṭ*, 259.
ḥarrēph, 143.
hawthā, 468.
hillûlā, 279.
îlānā, 86.

kîn, 137.
māthā, 112.
p^{e}*ra'*, 107.
p^{e}*šaṭ*, 282.
pulågå, 140.
rêšā, 262.
ṣaphrā, 207.
šašša', 358.
ṣ^{e}*rîḥā*, 286.
ših^{a}*rā*, *šahrå*, 235.
tannî, 129.
t^{e}*lîm*, 10.
ṭibbûrā, 283.
yabbēbh, 154.
yathrå, 378.

Arabic.

'ahl, 463.
'ahlu-lwabar, 152.
'aḳdama, 147.
'amila, *'amal*, *'amil*, 153 f.
'amm, lviii.
'anna, 283.
baḍ'a, 145.
baṭn, 265.
baṯneh, 306.
ḍafara, 207.
Dâl, 262.
ḍarîḥ, 286.
faḫ, 40.
faḫiḍ, 265.
far', 107.
far'a, 107, 108.
furḍah, *firâḍ*, *faraḍa*, 143.
fuwwah, 291.
ǵala, 260.
ǵal'ad, 306.
ġanna, 283.
ǵarafa, 146.
Ǵîm, 262.
ǵu'al, 278.
ḥaǵǵ, 492.
ḫalafa, *ḫalf*, 380.
ḫalîf, 380.
ḥamara, 373.
ḫamîs, 213.
ḥaruma, 18.
ḥaṣṣa, *ḥiṣṣah*, 126.
ḫâtin, 15.
hâwiya, 468.
ḥiḳḳ, 139.
hilâl, 279.
ḳadûm, 148.
ḳâḍy, 309.
kanna, 138.
kara'a, xiv. f.
laḥd, 286.
lawî'u, *lawî'at*, 437, 441.
leben, 93.
madda, 123.
maḥaḳa, 154.
manzil, *al-manâzil*, 146.
marra, 363, 380.
masaka, 136.
minhara, *minhar*, 185.
muǵâra, xix.
nasaǵa, 382.
râda, 323.
raka'a, xv.
rukn, 472.
šabâb al-'arîs, 361.
ṣadâḳ, 265, 367.
ṣadîḳa, 265, 355, 367.
saǵ', 283.
sahel, 90.
šahr, 235.
ṣaḥûr, *ṣuḥra*, 124.
ṣalama, 287.
sâra, 133.
ṣarḥ, *saraḥa*, 286.
sunbul, *sunbula*, 328.
tahlîl, 279.
ṯanna, 129.
'ulliya, *'illiya*, 71.
wâdy, 88.
waḥa, 437.
walaǵa, xiv.
warik, *waraka*, 370.
waṣa, 437.
watar, 378.
wazîr, 367.
wely, *wala*, 437.
zamân, 461.

Greek.

Ἀδώνιδος κῆποι, 333.
ἄκανθα, 465.
ἀντλητρίαι, xviii.
ἀσεβής, 468.
ἈχαιϜοί, xcii.
Βεελζεβουλ, 5.
Βελιαλ, Βελιαρ, 469.
βουγονία, xix, 360.
Γάμμα, 262.
Δαναοί, xciii.
Ϝαξός, Ὀαξός, Ἀξός, xciii.
Ζῆτα, 262.
Ἡλιοδῶρος, lxxxiv.
κενός, 309.
Κόρη, 332.
λάμπουρις, 394.
μέγαρον, xviii.
Μέλισσα, 85.
μητρόπολις, 9.
Μισωρ, 42.
Μόσχοι, xcix.
Μυλιττα, 59, 198.
Ὄνου γνάθος, 371.
ὀπισθόδομος, 271.
ὄρτυξ, 406.
πεδινή, 8.
πεδίον, 8.
πυγμή, 70.
Ῥακά, 309.
Ῥῶ, 262.
σινδών, 362.
στρατόπεδον, 219.
Συδυκ, 42.
σῦριγξ, 142.
Τευκροί, xciii.
τύραννος, 62.
Τυρσηνοί, xcii.
υἱοὶ τοῦ νυμφῶνος, 361.
φίλος τοῦ νυμφίου, 367.
Ζεὺς ἀρότριος, 386.

Latin.

acer, 363.
Achivi, xcii.
aerarium, 271.
augurium canarium, 393.
cerealia, 386.
Citrullus colocynthis, 364.
dividere, 127.
Eristalis tenax, 359.
furtum licio et lance conceptum, 239.
pietas, 469.
Pistacia terebinthus, 187.
Rhamnus palaestina, 275.
robigo, 393 f.
Rubia tinctorum, 291.
sibila, 141.
uredo, 394.

IV. INDEX OF PASSAGES FROM OTHER BOOKS DISCUSSED

Gen. 4 8 . . . . 417.
Gen. 10 19 . . . . 224.
Gen. 14 . . . . lxi f.
Gen. 16 13 . . . . 193.
Gen. 18 1 ff. . . . . 348.
Gen. 23 . . . . lxxxv f.
Gen. 24 2 . . . . 264.
Gen. 30 11 . . . . 197 f.
Gen. 34 . . . . 438.
Gen. 43 14 . . . . 378.
Gen. 47 29 . . . . 264.
Gen. 48 21.22 . . . . cxi, 270.
Gen. 49 5-7 . . . . 437.
Gen. 49 16 . . . . 392.
Ex. 3 12 . . . . 189.
Ex. 3 14 . . . . 189 f., 248 f.
Ex. 12 40 . . . . cxii.
Ex. 18 8 ff. . . . . 252.
Ex. 19 25 . . . . 417.
Ex. 21 6 . . . . 117, 330.
Ex. 22 8.9 . . . . 117, 330.
Ex. 24 9-11 . . . . 252 f.

Ex. 28 . . . . 236 ff.
Ex. 32 . . . . 440 f.
Ex. 32^{32} 259
Ex. 33^{19} . . . . 189 f.
Ex. 34^{6} . . . . 253.
Num. 6^{1-21} . . . . 342.
Num. 14^{40-45} . . . . 44 f.
Num. 21^{1-3} . . . . 18, 44 f.
Num. 21^{24} . . . . 305, 314.
Num. 21^{28} . . . . 270, 389.
Num. 22^{2}-24^{25} . . . 316.
Num. $26^{29 \text{ ff.}}$ . . . 134.
Num. $31^{1 \text{ ff.}}$ . . . . 456.
Num. 32^{22} . . . . 368.
Num. 32^{39} . . . . 50.
Num. $34^{3.5}$ . . . . 34.
Deut. 1^{41-46} . . . . 44.
Deut. 32^{8} . . . . 37.
Deut. 32^{42} . . . . 107 f.
Deut. 33^{2} . . . . 109 f.
Deut. 33^{6b} . . . . 4.
Deut. 33^{23} . . . . cvii f.
Deut. 33^{29} . . . . 198.
Josh. 1^{5} . . . . 189.
Josh. 7, 8 . . . . 455, 457.
Josh. 8^{17} . . . . 21.
Josh. 11^{3} . . . . 62.
Josh. 13^{13} . . . . 51.
Josh. 14^{15} . . . . 9.
Josh. 15^{1-4} . . . . 34.
Josh. $15^{8 \text{ ff.}}$ . . . . 430, 431.
Josh. 15^{14-19} . . . . 8.
Josh. 15^{63} . . . . 6, 20.
Josh. 16^{10b} . . . . 26.
Josh. $17^{1b.2}$ . . . . 134 f.
Josh. 17^{14-18} . . . . 49 f.
Josh. $18^{14 \text{ ff.}}$ . . . . 430.
Josh. 19^{15} . . . . 27.
Josh. 19^{29} . . . . 28.
Josh. 19^{47} . . . . 31, 51.
Josh. 19^{50} . . . . 32.
Josh. 23 . . . . xliii f.
Josh. 24 . . . . xlii f.
Josh. 24^{28-31} . . . . 52 f.
Josh. 24^{30} . . . . 32.
1 Sam. 1^{22} . . . . 200.
1 Sam. 2^{22} . . . . 435.
1 Sam. 5^{4} . . . . 386.
1 Sam. $8^{6.7}$ . . . . 183.
1 Sam. 11^{12-15} . . . 301.
1 Sam. 12 . . . . xlii f.
1 Sam. 13^{1} . . . . lii.
1 Sam. 13^{5} . . . . 20.
1 Sam. 14^{12} . . . . 233.
1 Sam. 14^{18} . . . . 3, 239, 242.
1 Sam. 14^{41} . . . . 3, 240.
1 Sam. 23^{6} . . . . 239.
2 Sam. 1^{21a} . . . . 112.
2 Sam. 23^{11} . . . . 371.
2 Sam. 24^{6} . . . . xcix, 23.
1 Kgs. 4^{12} . . . . xvii, 221 f.
1 Kgs. $5^{3(17)}$ . . . . 115.
1 Kgs. $12^{28.31}$ . . . . 441.
2 Kgs. 1^{7} . . . . 347.
2 Kgs. $3^{26.27}$ . . . . 320.
Isa. 8^{1} . . . . 259 f.
Isa. 17^{10} . . . . 333.
Isa. 19^{18} . . . . 32.
Isa. 30^{8} . . . . 259.
Isa. 30^{22} . . . . 242 f.
Isa. 57^{9} . . . . 133.
Isa. 63^{9} . . . . 36.
Jer. $7^{12.14}$ . . . . 435.
Jer. $26^{6.9}$ . . . . 435.
Ezek. 13^{20} . . . . 149.
Ezek. $16^{3.45}$ . . . . lxxxvii.
Ezek. 44^{18b} . . . . 237.
Ḥos. $2^{8(10)}$ . . . . 241.
Hos. 5^{8} . . . . 133.
Hos. 8^{10} . . . . 184.
Hos. 9^{10}, 10^{9} . . . . 445.
Am. $2^{11.12}$ . . . . 343.
Am. 3^{5} . . . . 40.
Am. 8^{14} . . . . 292.
Mic. 6^{1-8} . . . . 330.
Zech. 12^{11} . . . . 333.
Ps. $35^{5.6.7}$ . . . . 124.
Ps. $54^{5(6)}$ . . . . 321.
Ps. $69^{31(32)}$ . . . . 194.
Ps. 118^{7} . . . . 321.
Job 6^{19} . . . . 114.
Job 31^{32} . . . . 114.
Dan. 11^{37} . . . . 333.
1 Chr. 2^{42-55} . . . . 341.
1 Chr. 7^{14-16} . . . . 135.
Ecclus. $50^{12 \text{ ff.}}$ . . . 199.

LAUS DEO

NORTHER

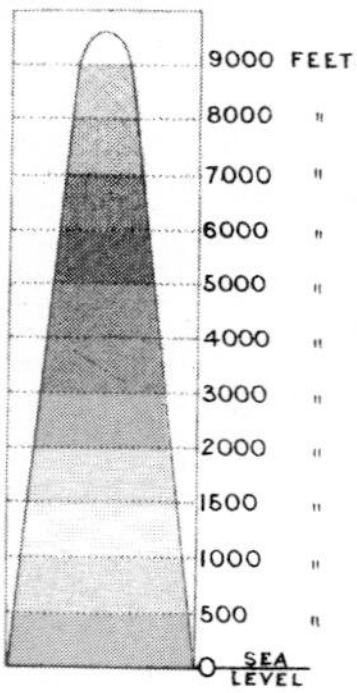

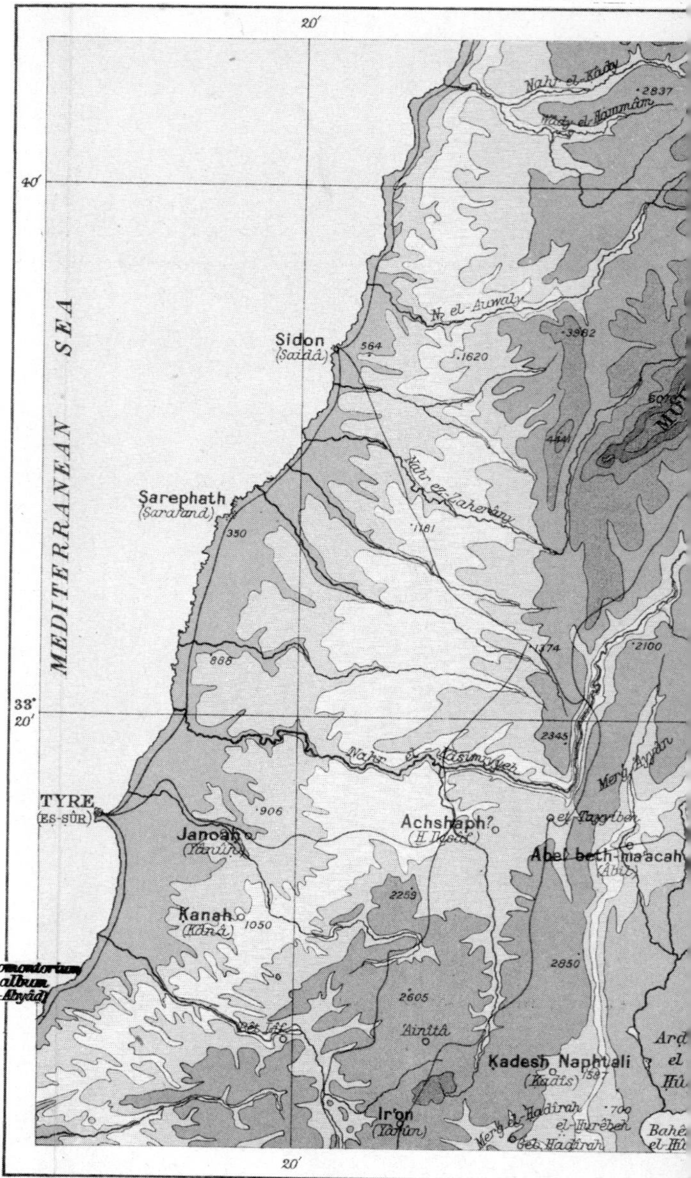

The Edinburgh Geographical Institute

LESTINE

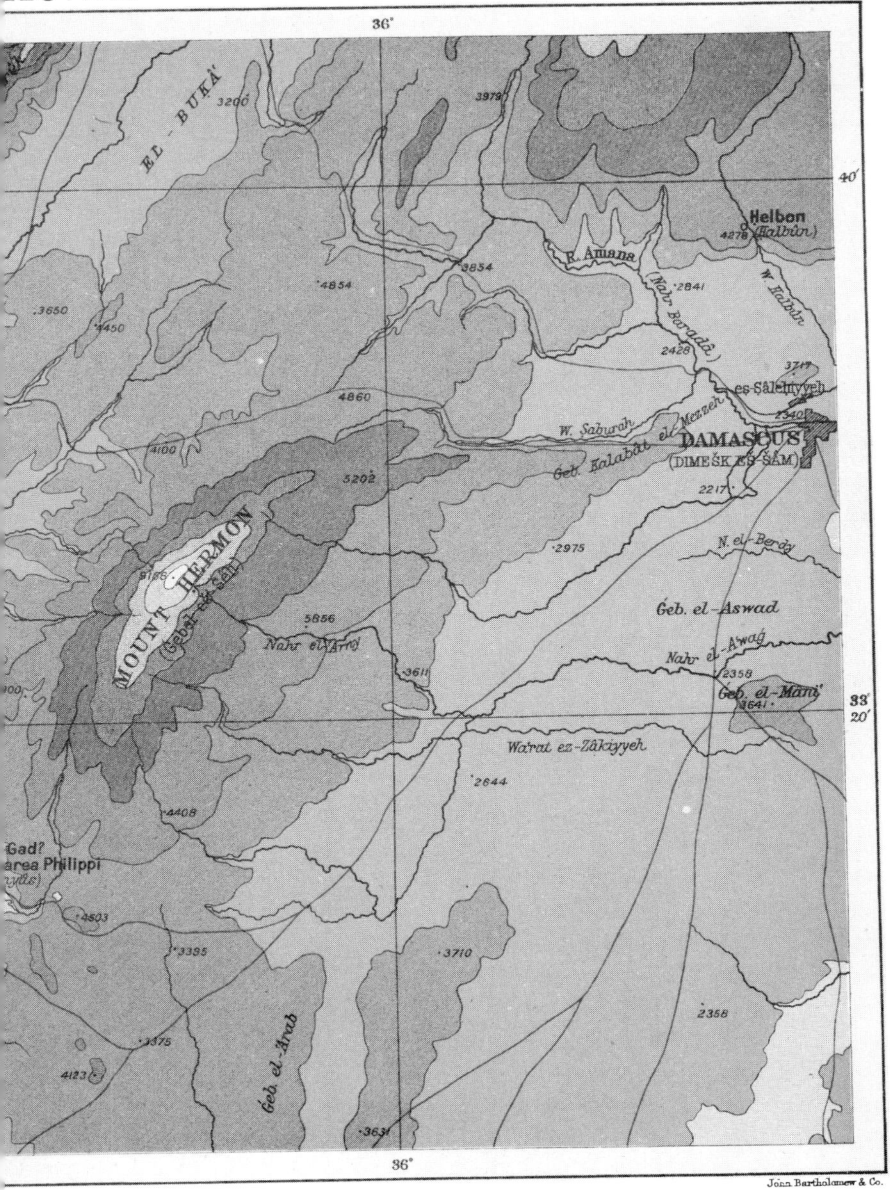

John Bartholomew & Co.

Miles to an Inch
8 10 12 14 16

Roads ————————

CENTRAL PAL

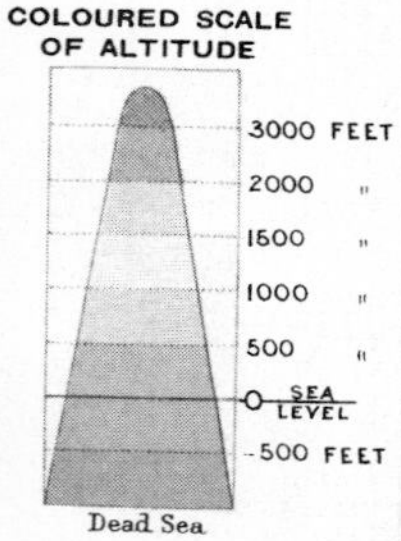

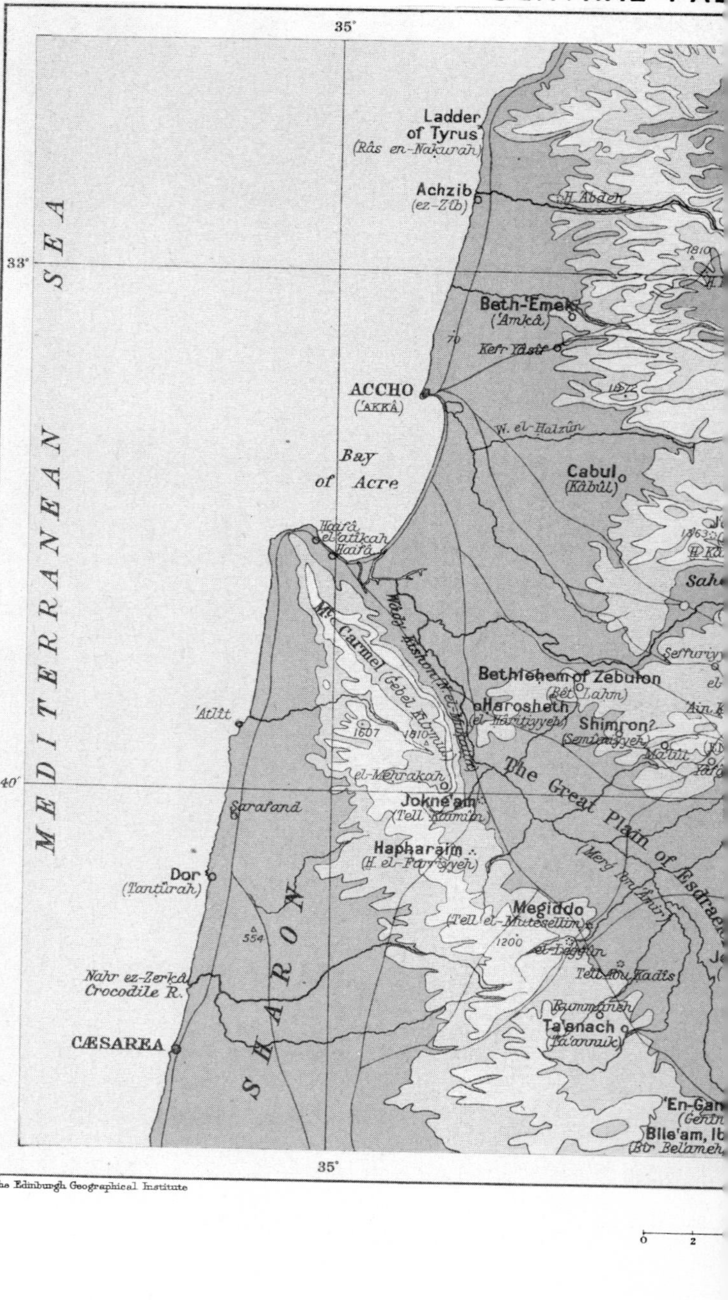

The Edinburgh Geographical Institute

(NORTHERN PORTION)

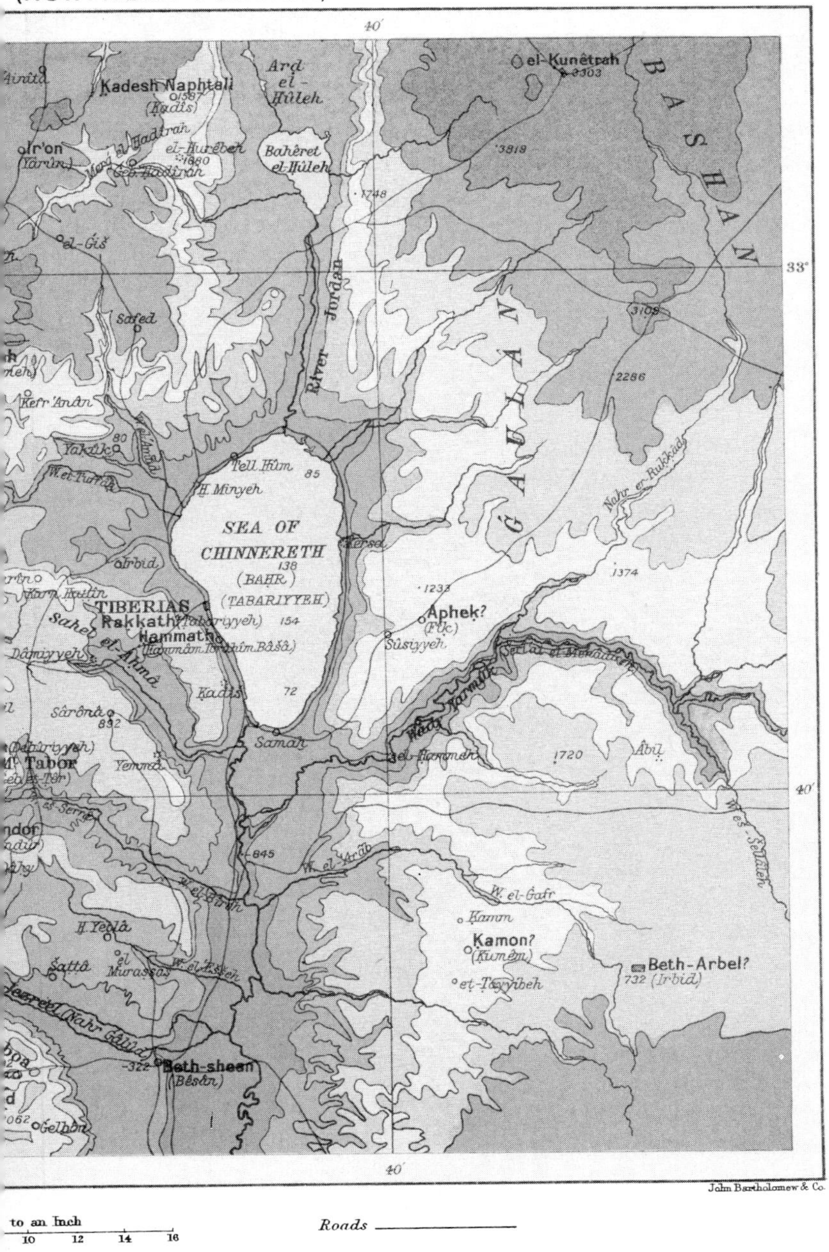

CENTRAL

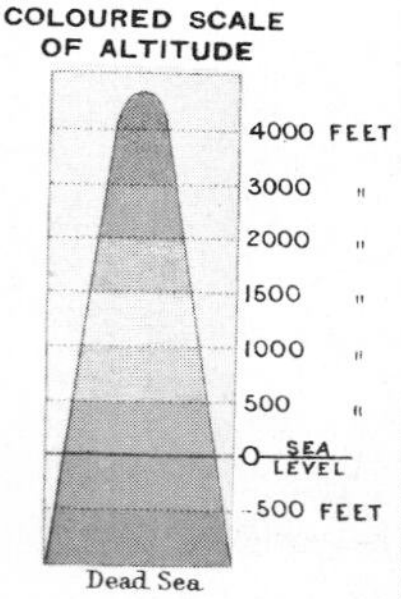

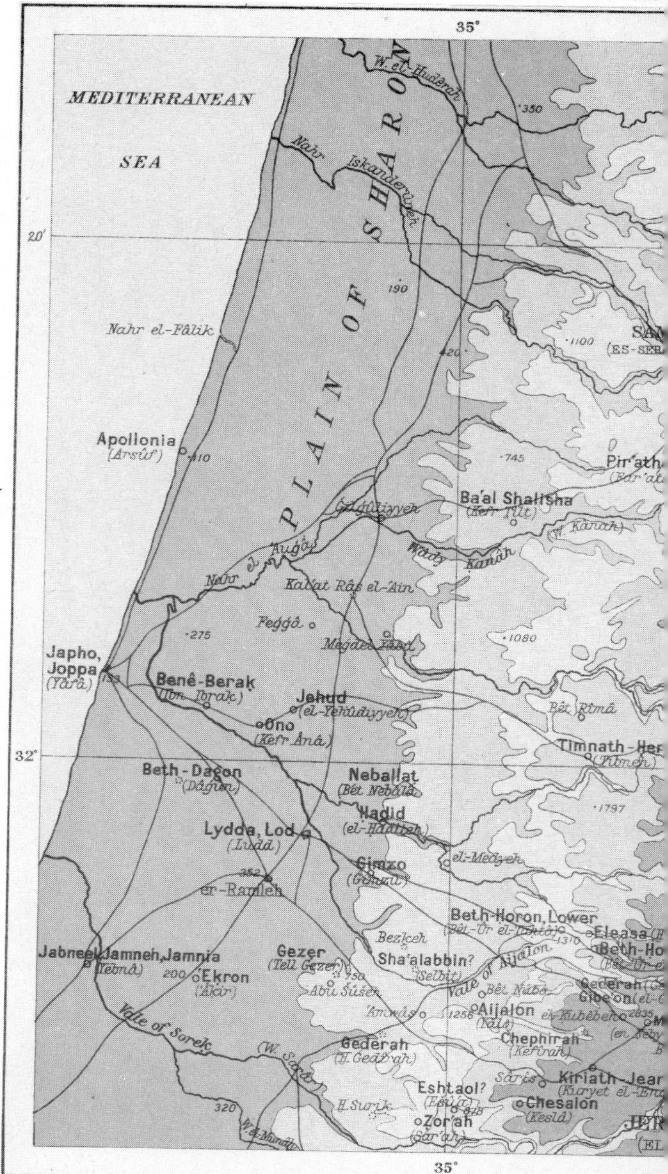

The Edinburgh Geographical Institute

INE (SOUTHERN PORTION)

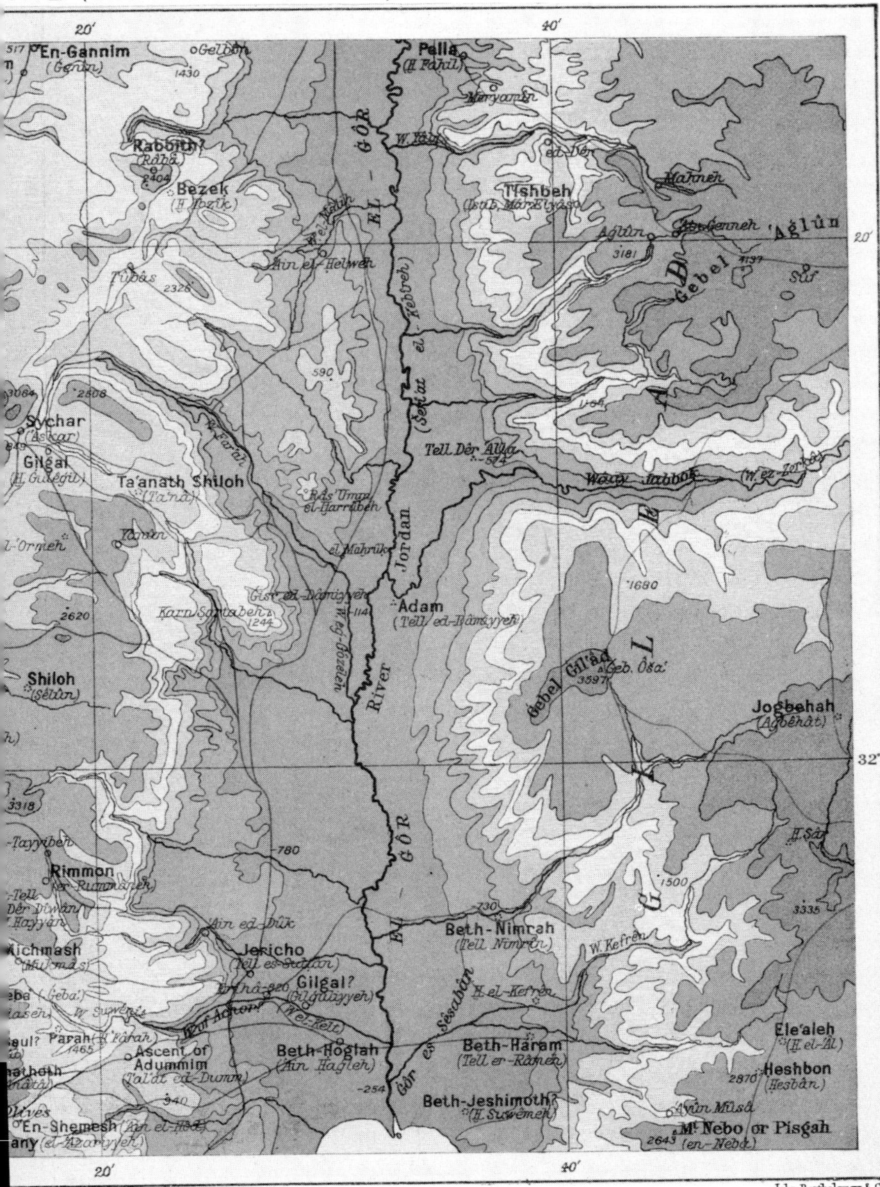

John Bartholomew & Co.

Miles to an Inch
8 10 12 14 16

Roads ————————

COLOURED SCALE OF ALTITUDE

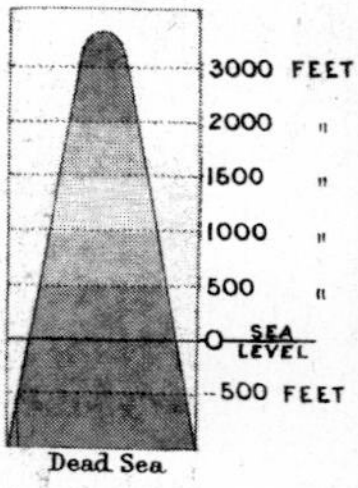

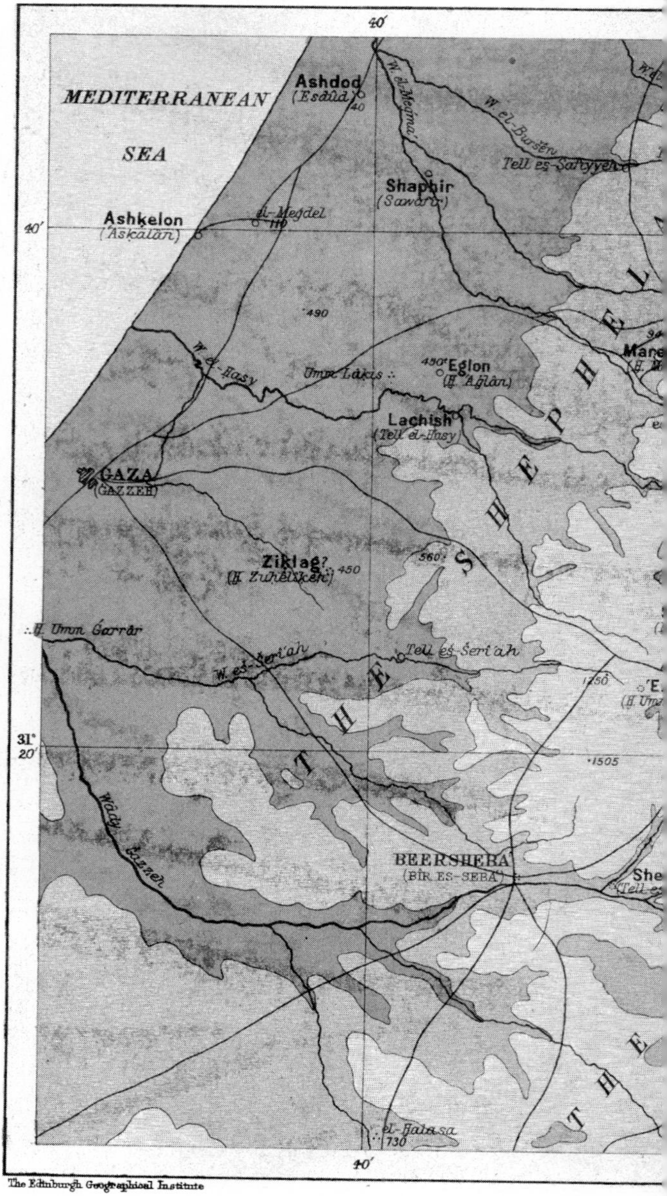

The Edinburgh Geographical Institute

ERN PALESTINE

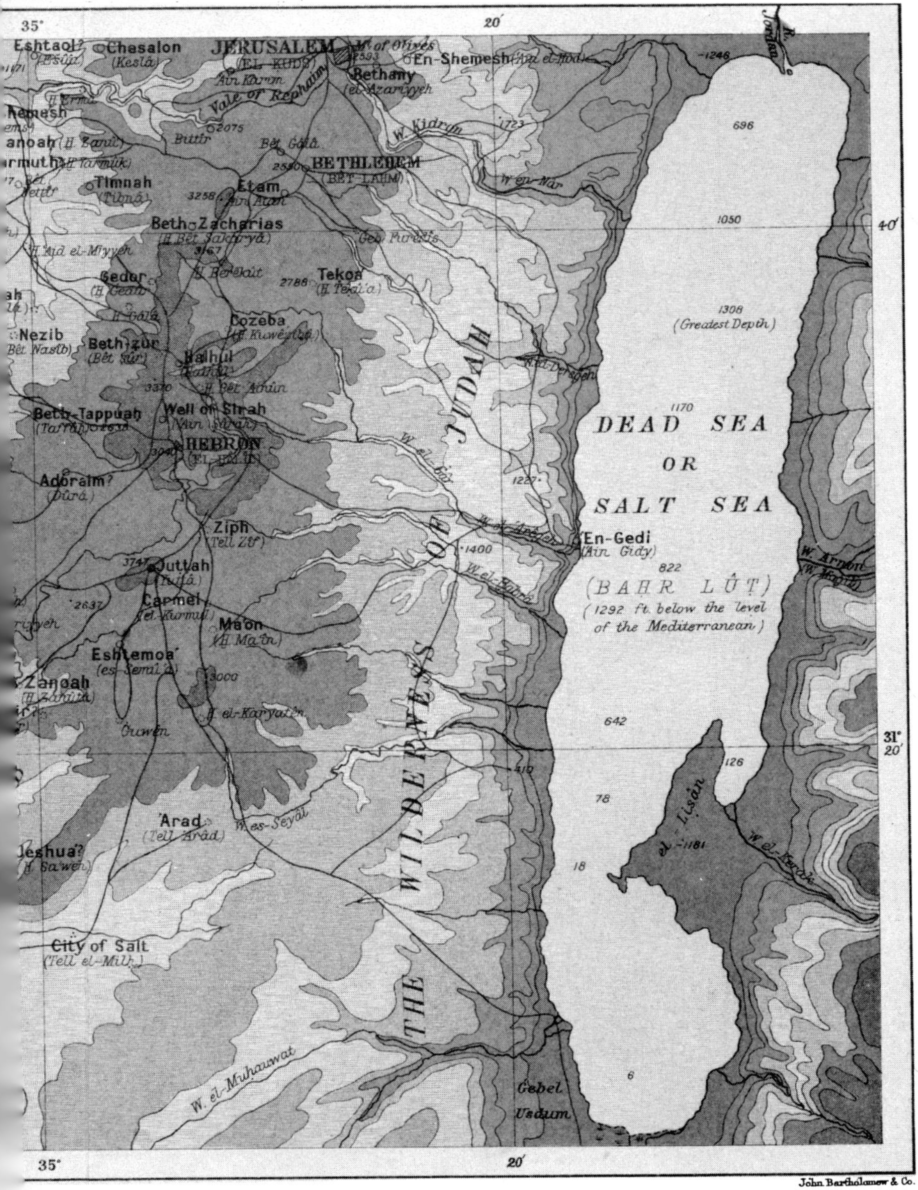

8 Miles to an Inch
8 10 12 14 16

Roads ———————

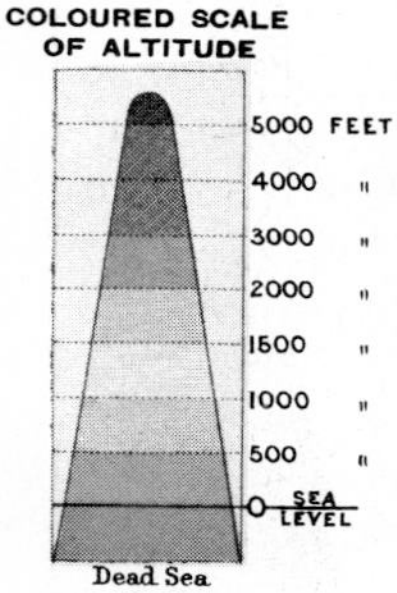

MAP OF

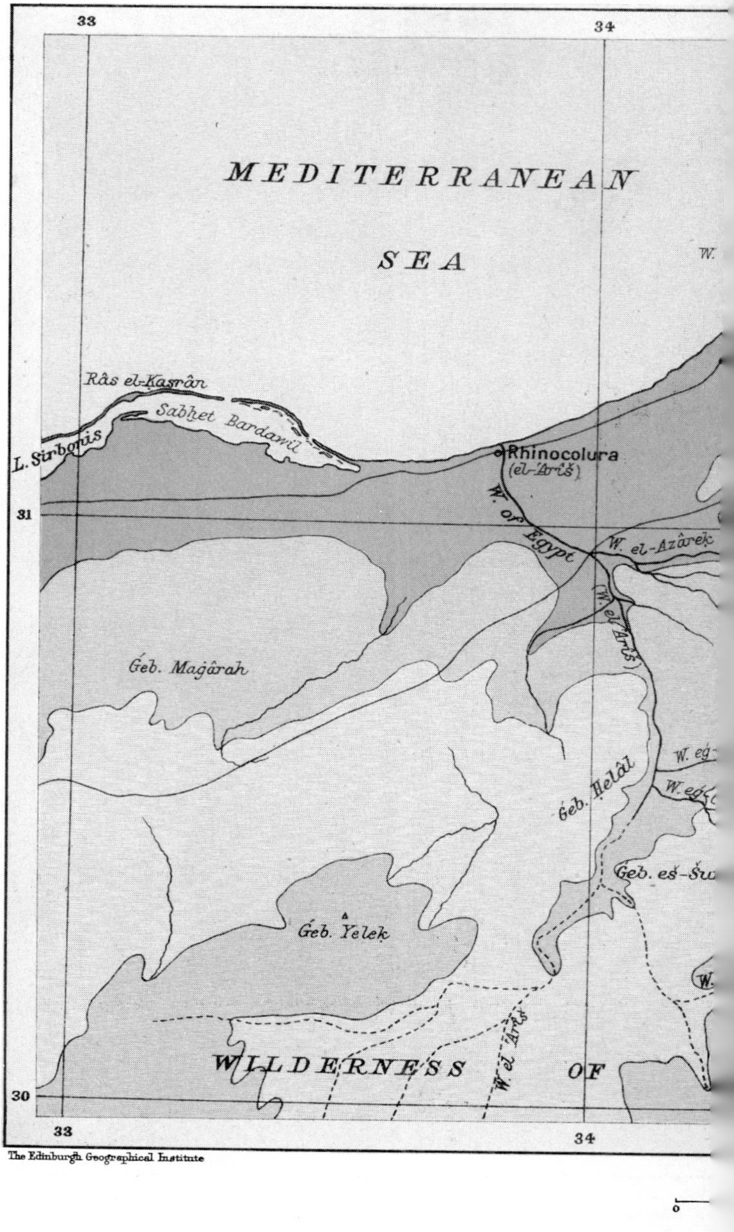

The Edinburgh Geographical Institute

HE NEGEB, ETC.

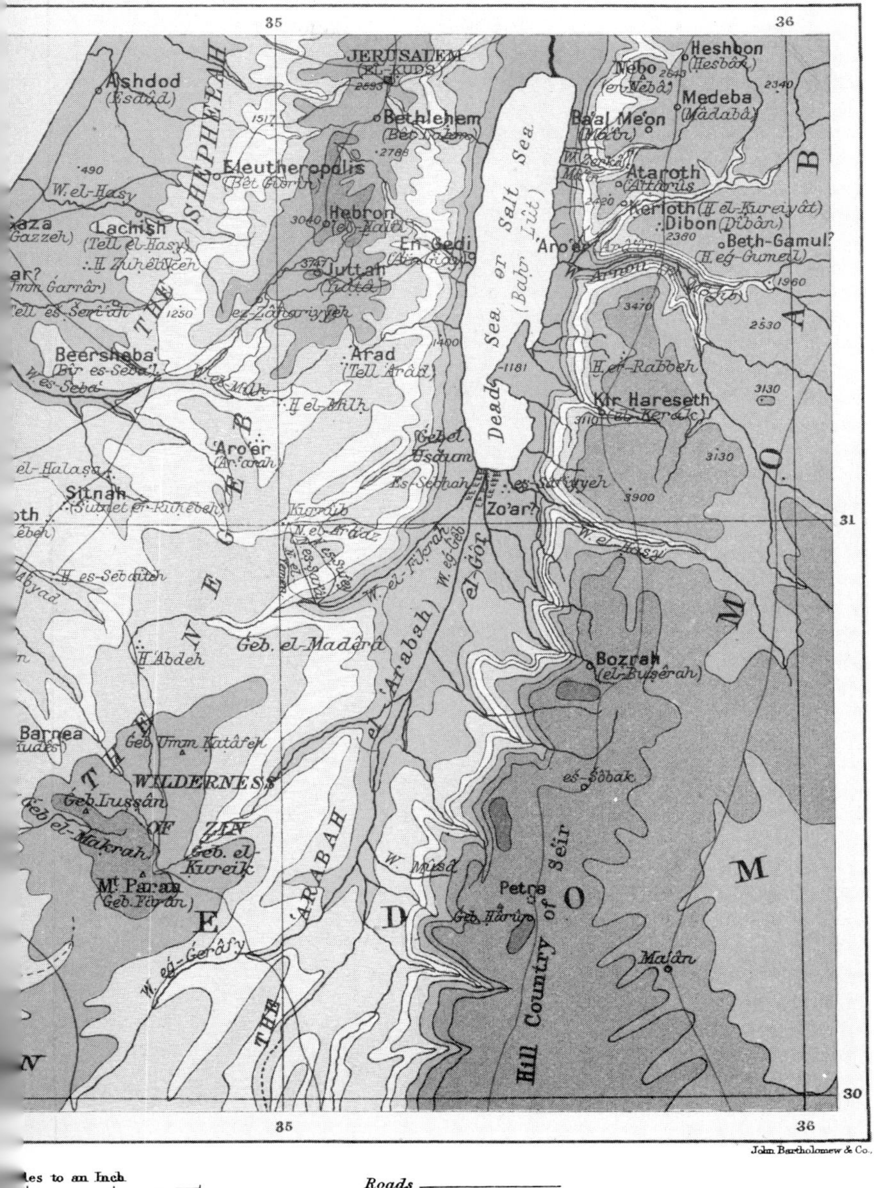
35
36
JERUSALEM
(EL-KUDS)
Ashdod
(Esdûd)
Bethlehem
Eleutheropolis
(Bêt Gibrin)
Hebron
(el-Halîl)
En-Gedi
Juttah
(Yutta)
Lachish
(Tell el-Hasy)
Gazza
(Gazzeh)
THE SHEPHELAH
Beersheba
(Bîr es-Seba')
W. es-Seba'
Arad
(Tell Arâd)
Aro'er
(Ar'arah)
Sitnah
Dead Sea or Salt Sea
(Bahr Lût)
Heshbon
(Hesbân)
Nebo
(en-Nebâ)
Medeba
(Mâdabâ)
Baal Meon
Ataroth
(Attarûs)
Kerioth
Dibon
(Dîbân)
Beth-Gamul?
Aro'er
W. Arnon
Kir Hareseth
(el-Kerak)
Gebel Usdum
Zo'ar?
W. el-Hasy
Bozrah
(el-Buṣêrah)
es-Šôbak
Geb. el-Madêrâ
H. 'Abdeh
W. el-'Arabah
el-Gôr
THE NEGEB
Barnea
THE WILDERNESS OF ZIN
Geb. Lussân
Geb. el-Makrah
Geb. el-Kureik
Mt Paran
(Geb. Fârân)
W. eg-Gerâfy
THE 'ARABAH
W. Mûsâ
Petra
Geb. Hârûn
Hill Country of Seir
EDOM
MOAB
Ma'ân
31
30
John Bartholomew & Co.
Miles to an Inch
20
30
40
Roads

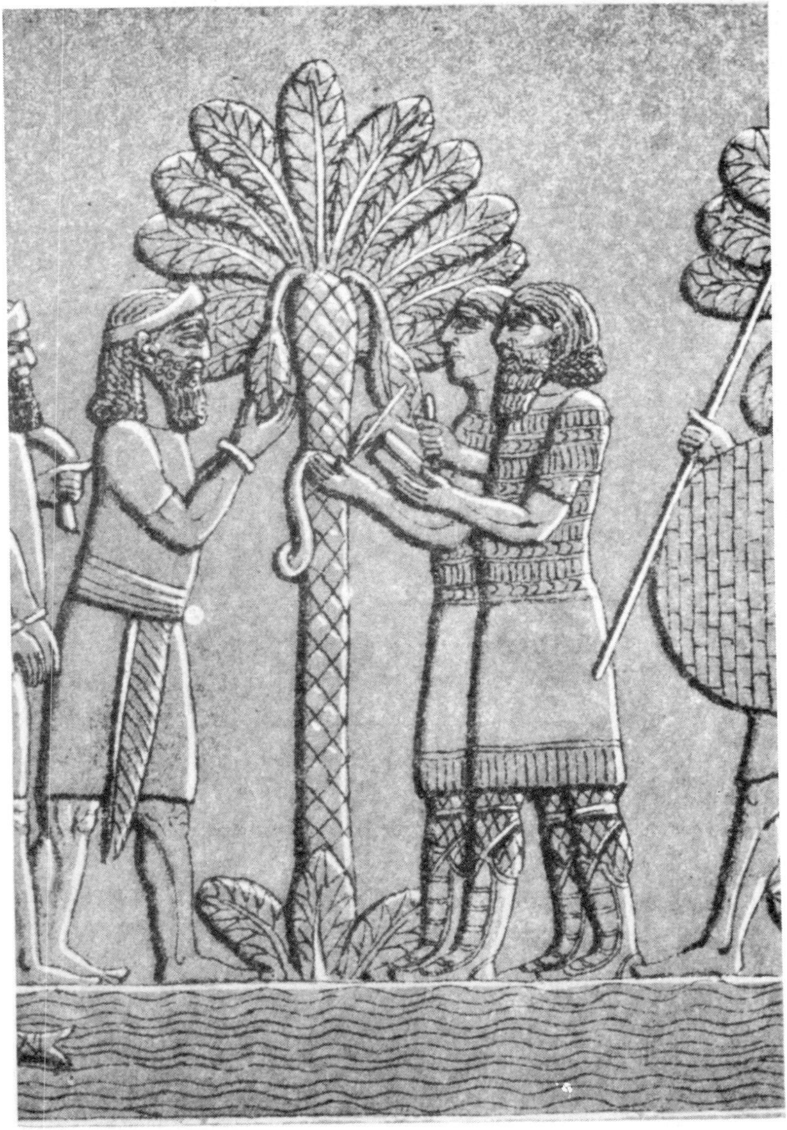

Fig. 1

Fig. 2

Fig. 3

Fig. 4

Fig. 5

PLATE III

Fig. 1

Fig. 2

Fig. 3

PLATE IV

Photo: Braun & Cei.

Fig. 1

Fig. 2

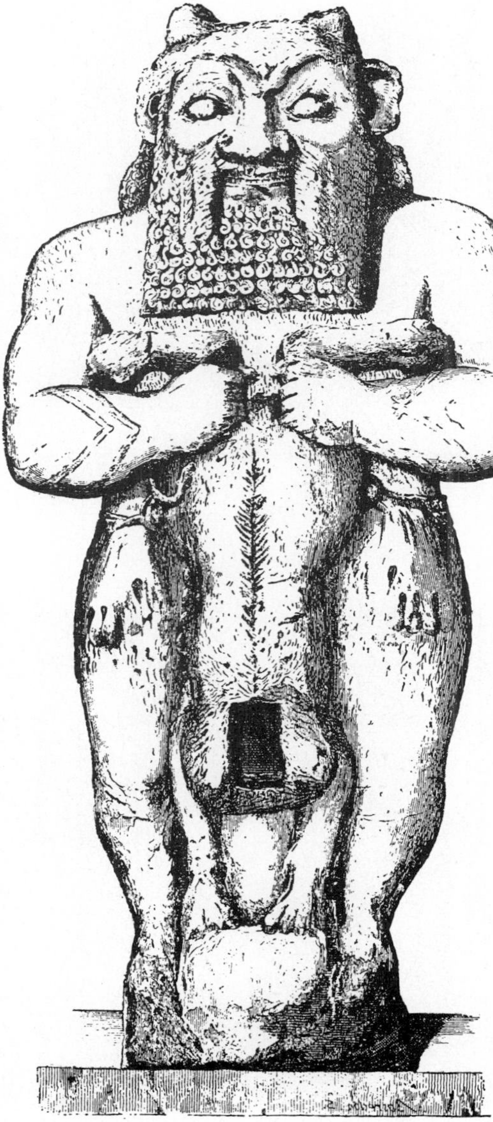

NOTES

ON

THE HEBREW TEXT

OF THE

BOOKS OF KINGS

WITH AN INTRODUCTION AND APPENDIX

BY THE

REV. C. F. BURNEY, M.A.

FELLOW AND LECTURER IN HEBREW OF S. JOHN BAPTIST'S COLLEGE, OXFORD

FIRST PUBLISHED 1903

CONTENTS

Page

INTRODUCTION :—

§ 1. *Structure of Kings* ix

§ 2. *Characteristics of the Chief Ancient Versions of Kings* xx

§ 3. *The Synchronisms of the Compiler* xli

LIST OF ABBREVIATIONS xlv

NOTES ON 1 KINGS 1

NOTES ON 2 KINGS 260

APPENDIX :—

1. *Inscription of Mesha', king of Moab* 371
2. *The Siloam Inscription* 374
3. *Inscription of the Monolith of Shalmaneser II*, ll. 78–102 375
4. *Fragment of the Annals of Shalmaneser II* . . 376
   Descriptive Inscription from the Obelisk of Shalmaneser 377
5. *Narrative of Sennacherib's Third Campaign* (B.C. 701), *from the Taylor Cylinder*, Col. II. l. 34–Col. III. l. 41 377

ADDITIONS 380

INDEX 381

PLATES.

1. Bronze Stand from Larnaka . . . . *to face* p. 91
2. Bronze Stand from Enkomi . . . . *to face* p. 92

PREFACE

THE aim of the present work is to provide a critical and grammatical commentary upon the Hebrew text of Kings, after the model of Dr. Driver's *Notes on the Hebrew Text of the Books of Samuel.* In writing the Notes, the needs of beginners in the study of the Hebrew language have been prominent in my mind, and so I have endeavoured to deal with some fulness with questions of grammar, while at the same time making reference to the best authorities upon the subject. For the purposes of textual criticism it has seemed worth while to utilize as largely as might be the evidence of the Versions. Thus, as far as possible, all variants and additions of the Versions have been cited, where it may reasonably be supposed that these form original elements of the text from which the Version in question was made; upon the view that such readings are worthy of record, even where no definite verdict can be passed as to their value in relation to the Massoretic text. The structure of Kings, and the characteristics of the various sources of the work, have also been dealt with in brief. The Appendix contains the more important contemporary inscriptions which throw light upon the narrative of Kings.

In making use of the work of my predecessors in the same field, I trust that I have in every case made acknowledgement of my obligations. I feel, however, that special acknowledgement is due to Prof. B. Stade for the debt which these Notes owe to his valuable articles on the text of Kings which have appeared from time to time in the *Zeitschrift* of which he is the editor. Lest it should be thought that in places I have drawn too largely upon his arguments and results, it must be pleaded that in such cases my aim has been to place these results within the reach of English students, for whom too often, through ignorance of German, they are inaccessible.

It is a special pleasure to me to express my gratitude to Dr. Driver. To his teaching and example is due most of what may be of value in this book; and I have never been without his kindly encouragement and ready suggestion upon points of difficulty.

In conclusion, my thanks are due to Mr. J. C. Pembrey, M.A., Oriental Reader at the University Press, for the great pains which he has taken in revising and passing the sheets for the press.

C. F. B.

S. John's College, Oxford,
November, 1902.

INTRODUCTION

§ 1. *Structure of Kings.*

THE fact that Kings, like the other historical books of the Old Testament, is based upon pre-existing written sources is universally recognized; and the evidence upon which this elementary proposition is based need not here be set forth[1]. That the main editor or compiler of these sources was a Deuteronomist, i. e. that his work was inspired by the religious revival which took place in the eighteenth year of Josiah (B.C. 621) under the influence of the newly discovered book of Deuteronomy, appears both from his religious standpoint and from his phraseology. This editor is therefore hereinafter cited under the symbol R^D (Deuteronomic Redactor).

To R^D is due the stereotyped form into which the introduction and conclusion of a reign is thrown, and which constitutes, as it were, the framework upon which the narrative as a whole is built. The regularity of the method of R^D in the construction of this framework is worthy of special notice. The form in which the account of a reign is introduced is as follows. *For kings of Judah:*—1. A synchronism of the year of accession with the corresponding reigning year of the contemporary king of Israel, probably calculated by R^D himself. This, commencing with Abijah, naturally ceases with Ḥezekiah, upon the fall of the kingdom of Israel. 2. Age of the king at accession. 3. Length of his reign. 4. Name of the queen-mother. This, together with 2, 3, is drawn from the *Annals* (ספר דברי הימים) which are so constantly cited by R^D. 5. A brief verdict upon the king's character, framed in accordance with the Deuteronomic standard. *For kings of Israel:*—1. A synchronism of the year of accession

---

[1] Cf. the writer's article in Hastings, *BD.* pp. 857 *f.*

with the corresponding reigning year of the contemporary king of Judah. 2. Length of the king's reign, drawn from the *Annals*. 3. A brief verdict as to his character, always unfavourable, and generally consisting of two parts: *a.* Statement of the general fact that he did evil in the sight of Yahwe; *b.* More special mention of his following the sins of Jeroboam [1]. The conclusion of the account of a reign takes the following form:—1. An indication of the principal source employed by R^D, containing further details as to the king in question. Usually we read [2]:—

ויתר דברי פ׳ וכל אשר עשה הלא הם (המה) כתובים על ספר	דברי שלמה דברי הימים למלכי יהודה דברי הימים למלכי ישראל

---

[1] The usual formula is as follows:—

He did not depart from *He walked after* (*in*) *He clave to*	*the sins of J.*	*which he caused Israel to sin.*
He walked in the way of J. and in his sin (*sins*)		

So I. 15. 26 (Nadab), *v.* 34 (Ba'asha), 16. 26 (Omri), II. 3. 3 (Jehoram), 10. 31, cf. *v.* 29 (Jehu), 13. 2 (Jehoaḥaz), *v.* 11 (Jehoash), 14. 24 (Jeroboam II), 15. 9 (Zechariah), *v.* 18 (Menaḥem), *v.* 24 (Pekaḥiah), *v.* 28 (Pekaḥ). In all these cases the antecedent of the relative אשר החטיא is not ירבעם, but חטאות יר׳; cf. II. 17. 21. I. 16. 30 (Aḥab), II. 17. 22 חטאות יר׳ without אשר החטיא וג׳; I. 22. 53 (Aḥaziah), II. 23. 15 אשר החטיא את ישראל, referring not to חטאות (omitted), but to ירבעם; 'J. who made Israel to sin.' In I. 16. 13 the sins of Ba'asha and Elah, and in II. 21. 11 of Manasseh (אשר החטיא את יהודה) are spoken of in the same terms.

[2] When further details, general or special, are mentioned as existing in the source, these usually stand immediately after וכל אשר עשה; e.g. I. 11. 41 וחכמתו. An exception is I. 15. 23 (Asa), where וכל גבורתו precedes.

Slight variations of the stereotyped form are:—

1. ויתר כל דברי וג׳ I. 15. 23 (Asa).

2. Total omission of וכל אשר עשה; without further details five times, viz. I. 14. 19 (Jeroboam), 16. 20 (Zimri), II. 14. 18 (Amaziah), 15. 11 (Zechariah), 15. 15 (Shallum); with further details, II. 20. 20 (Ḥezekiah).

Reading אשר עשה five times, viz. I. 16. 27 (Omri), II. 1. 18 (Aḥaziah of Israel), 14. 15 (Jehoash of Israel), 16. 19 (Aḥaz), 21. 25 (Amon); ואשר עשה I. 16. 5 (Ba'asha); וגבורתו אשר עשה twice, I. 16. 27 (Omri), 22. 46 (Jehoshaphat).

3. הנם in place of הלא הם five times, viz. I. 14. 19 (Jeroboam), II. 15. 11, 15, 26, 31 (Zechariah Shallum, Pekaḥiah, Pekaḥ).

2. Mention of the king's (*a*) death and (*b*) burial[1]:—

וישכב פ׳ עם אבתיו { וַיִּקָּבֵר / ויקברו אתו } (עם אבתיו) ב׳

3. Notice of the due succession of the king's son:—

וימלך פ׳ בנו תחתיו

The following table exhibits the regularity with which this system is carried out. When any fact above mentioned as belonging to the introduction is omitted in that position, but added subsequently in the narrative of the reign or in the summary, this is indicated by the sign + :—

Introduction.			*Conclusion.*	
		David	1 2 *a b*	I. 2. 10
I. 3. 3, 11. 4–6, 42		Solomon		
		Kings of Judah.		
14. 21, 22, 31	2 3 4 (5) + 4	Reḥoboam	1 2 *a b* 3	14. 29, 31
15. 1–3	1 3 4 5	Abijah	1 2 *a b* 3	15. 7ª, 8
15. 9–11	1 3 4 5	Asa	1 2 *a b* 3	15. 23ª, 24
22. 41–44	1 2 3 4 5	Jehoshaphat	1 2 *a b* 3	22. 45, 50
II. 8. 16, 17	1 2 3 5	Jehoram	1 2 *a b* 3	II. 8. 23, 24
8. 25–27, 9. 29	1 2 3 4 5 + 1	Aḥaziah	2 *b*	9. 28ᵇ
11. 3	+ 3	Athaliah	...	...
12. 1–4	2 1 3 4 5	Jehoash	1 2 *b* 3	12. 20, 22
14. 1–4	1 2 3 4 5	Amaziah	1 2 *b* (*a*)	14. 18, 20ᵇ (22ᵇ)
15. 1–4	1 2 3 4 5	Azariah	1 2 *a b* 3	15. 6, 7
15. 32–35	1 2 3 4 5	Jotham	1 2 *a b* 3	15. 36, 38
16. 1–4	1 2 3 5	Aḥaz	1 2 *a b* 3	16. 19, 20
18. 1–3	1 2 3 4 5	Ḥezekiah	1 2 *a* 3	20. 20, 21
21. 1, 2	2 3 4 5	Manasseh	1 2 *a b* 3	21. 17, 18
21. 19–22	2 3 4 5	Amon	1 2 *b* 3	21. 25, 26
22. 1, 2	2 3 4 5	Josiah	1 2 *b* (3)	23. 29, 30
23. 31, 32	2 3 4 5	Jehoaḥaz	...	...
23. 36, 37	2 3 4 5	Jehoiakim	1 2 *a* 3	24. 5, 6
24. 8, 9	2 3 4 5	Jehoiachin	...	...
24. 18, 19	2 3 4 5	Zedekiah	...	...

[1] Once with singular active verb used impersonally: וַיִּקְבֹּר אֹתוֹ 'And (one) buried him,' II. 21. 26 (Amon).

Introduction.		*Kings of Israel.*		*Conclusion.*
I. 13. 33*f.*, 14. 20^{a}	+ 3 *b* 2	Jeroboam	1 2 *a* 3	I. 14. 19, 20
15. 25, 26	1 2 3 *a b*	Nadab	1	15. 31
15. 33, 34	1 2 3 *a b*	Ba'asha	1 2 *a b* 3	16. 5, 6
16. 8, 13	1 2 + 3	Elah	1	16. 14
16. 15^{a}, 19	1 2 + 3 *a b*	Zimri	1	16. 20
16. 23, 25, 26	1 2 3 *a b*	Omri	1 2 *a b* 3	16. 27, 28
16. 29–31^{a}	1 2 3 *a b*	Aḥab	1 2 *a* 3	22. 39, 40
22. 51, 52	1 2 3 *a b*	Aḥaziah	(3) 1	II. 1. 17, 18
II. 3. 1–3	1 2 3 *a b*	Jehoram	. . .	. . .
10. 29, 31, 36	+ 3 *b b* 2	Jehu	1 2 *a b* 3	10. 34, 35
13. 1, 2	1 2 3 *a b*	Jehoaḥaz	1 2 *a b* 3	13. 8, 9
13. 10, 11	1 2 3 *a b*	Jehoash	1 2 *a* (3) 2 *b* 1 2 *a b* 3	13. 12*f.*, 14. 15*f.*
14. 23, 24	1 2 3 *a b*	Jeroboam II	1 2 *a* 3	14. 28, 29
15. 8, 9	1 2 3 *a b*	Zechariah	1	15. 11
15. 13	1 2	Shallum	1	15. 15
15. 17, 18	1 2 3 *a b*	Menaḥem	1 2 *a* 3	15. 21, 22
15. 23, 24	1 2 3 *a b*	Pekaḥiah	1	15. 26
15. 27, 28	1 2 3 *a b*	Pekaḥ	1	15. 31
17. 1, 2	1 2 3 *a*	Hoshea	. . .	. . .

In the body of the narrative there are certain formulae which are employed for the introduction of a historical notice to indicate that it is more or less contemporaneous with the events of the narrative immediately preceding. The frequency with which these formulae occur, especially in the brief citation of facts from the *Annals*, renders the inference fair that they are due to the hand of R^{D}, and represent his method of piecing together the extracts derived from his sources. Of such formulae the most frequent is אז; but we also find the expressions בימים ההם, בימיו, בעת ההיא. Cf. *note*, p. 35.

Besides the construction of the framework of the book and the welding of the material, R^{D} is also responsible for a number of passages of varied length which point and enforce the religious purpose of his composition. These passages generally take the form of a commentary upon the causes which were operative in bringing about the developments of history, framed in accordance with the Deuteronomic model. Very frequently, also, R^{D} allows himself considerable latitude in the expansion and adaptation of the *speeches* contained in the narrative, in illustration of the same standpoint. In passages of this character the hand of R^D may readily be distinguished. They exhibit a constant recurrence of strongly marked phrases, to be found elsewhere for the most part only in Deuteronomy or in the books which exhibit the influence of Deuteronomy, and therefore presumably derived from that source. Other expressions stand alongside of these Deuteronomic expressions, and are of a piece with the thoughts to which they give voice; and these possess an individuality of their own, and are peculiar (or nearly so) to Kings.

The phrases characteristic of R^D receive comment in the *Notes* as they occur. For convenience of reference, however, a list is here given.

Deuteronomic phrases:—

1. שמר משמרת י׳, p. 14.
2. הלך בדרכי י׳, p. 14.
3. שמר חקתיו וג׳, p. 14.
4. למען תשכיל את כל אשר תעשה, p. 14.
5. למען יקים וג׳, p. 14; cf. I. 12. 15.
6. בכל לב (לבבו, לבבם) ובכל נפש (נפשו, נפשם), pp. 14, 125.
7. שמר הברית והחסד ל׳, pp. 30, 116.
8. ביום הזה, p. 30.
9. עמך אשר בחרת, p. 31.
10. הניח י׳ אלהי לי מסביב, p. 53.
11. בחר of Yahwe's *choosing* Jerusalem, p. 115.
12. י׳ אלהי ישראל אין כמוך . . . מתחת, p. 116.
13. אשר נתת (נתן, נתתי) לאבותם, p. 119.
14. באחד שעריו, p. 121.
15. כל הימים . . . האדמה, p. 122.
16. ידך החזקה וזרעך הנטויה, p. 122.
17. כל עמי הארץ, p. 122.
18. נתן לפני, p. 124.
19. השיב אל לב, p. 124.
20. ושבו אליך . . . ובכל נפשם, p. 125.

21. כי עמך ונחלתך . . . ממצרים, p. 125.
22. כור הברזל, p. 125.
23. נתן מנוחה לעמו, p. 126.
24. לא נפל דבר אחד, p. 126.
25. י׳ אלהינו (—ך, —כם), p. 126.
26. למען דעת וג׳, p. 127.
27. כי י׳ הוא האלהים אין עוד, p. 127.
28. לשום שמי שם, p. 130.
29. כל הימים used absolutely; 'for ever,' p. 130.
30. והלכתם . . . להם, p. 131.
31. למשל ולשנינה, p. 132.
32. דבק ב, p. 152.
33. הלך אחרי, p. 152.
34. עשה הרע בעיני י׳, p. 152.
35. עשה הישר בעיני י׳, p. 170.
36. מלא אחרי י׳, p. 153.
37. התאנף, p. 153.
38. והיה אם תשמע, p. 171.
39. השמיד מעל פני האדמה, p. 185.
40. הכעים, p. 186.
41. מעל האדמה הטובה הזאת, p. 187.
42. על כל גבעה גבהה וג׳, p. 192.
43. ככל התועבת . . . ישראל, p. 192.
44. הוריש, p. 192.
45. גלולים, p. 196.
46. כל נשמה, p. 200.
47. הבלים, p. 200.
48. לא אבה (ל)השחית, p. 295.
49. למחות את שם וג׳, p. 320.
50. ויקשו את ערפם, p. 332.
51. שמר לעשות, p. 353.

The following phrases, though not derived directly from Deuteronomy, belong to R^D in common with Jeremiah, whose writings exhibit strong Deuteronomic affinities:—

52. כי שמך נקרא על הבית הזה, p. 123.
53. אשלח מעל פני, p. 132.
54. כל עבר עליו וג׳, p. 133.
55. לא שב . . . מדרכו הרעה, p. 184.
56. הנני מביא רעה אל (על), p. 186.
57. עבדי (עבדיו) הנביאים, p. 330[1].

Phrases and modes of expression wholly or nearly peculiar to R^D are as follow:—

58. כאשר הלך דויד, and similar references, p. 31.
59. למען דוד אביך (עבדי), p. 153.
60. למען היות ניר וג׳, p. 170.
61. לא יכרת לך וג׳, p. 15.
62. בנה בית לשם י׳, p. 28.
63. אשר כמוך וג׳, p. 31.
64. להיות שמי שם, p. 115.
65. לבב שלם עם י׳, p. 128.
66. הרע (לעשות) מכל אשר (היו) לפניו, p. 186.
67. משתין בקיר, p. 186.
68. עצור ועזוב, p. 186.
69. ובערתי אחרי, p. 187.
70. המת וג׳, p. 187.
71. התמכר לעשות הרע וג׳, p. 249.
72. לא סר מן, p. 268.
73. רק הבמות לא סרו וג׳, p. 27.

As Kings now stands, the earliest possible *terminus a quo* for the composition of the book is the date of the latest event related, viz. Jehoiachin's release from prison in the thirty-seventh year of his captivity, i.e. B.C. 561, some twenty-five years after the fall of Jerusalem. As, however, the writer states that the privileges granted by Evil-Merodach to Jehoiachin were continued 'all the days of his life' (II. 25. 30), the strong presumption is created that the words were not penned so early as B.C. 561, but some time later, viz.

[1] Cf. also the phrases noticed by Dri. *LOT.*[6] 203, in the later *chh.* of 2 Kings.

subsequently to Jehoiachin's death, whenever that may have occurred. Agreeable to such an exilic date as is implied by the last two chapters of 2 Kings are certain passages in the body of the work which seem to presuppose the captivity of Judah. These are I. 11. 39; II. 17. 19, 20; 23. 26, 27, and perhaps, though not so clearly, I. 9. 7–9; II. 20. 17, 18; 21. 10–15; 22. 15–20; cf. *notes ad loc.* To these we may add the reference in I. 5. 4 to Solomon's dominion as extending over all the kings 'beyond the River,' a statement which, as referring to the country west of the Euphrates, implies that the writer is living in Babylon on the east side of the river (cf. *note* on עבר הנהר, p. 49).

On the other hand, there are certain indications which show that the main editing of Kings by R^D must have taken place prior to the decay and fall of the Judaean monarchy. Chief among these is the use of the phrase 'unto this day' (עד היום הזה) in the statement that the condition of affairs which the writer is describing continues to exist up to the time of writing. If this phrase always or most frequently occurred in the course of lengthy narratives excerpted by R^D from his sources, there might be room for the theory that a statement which was true as it stood in the old pre-exilic narratives had, through oversight on the part of an exilic editor, been allowed to stand after, through changed conditions, it had lost its force, or rather had become untrue and misleading. But, as a matter of fact, the expression is employed in connexion with terse statements of facts derived from the *Annals*, and in such cases can be due to no other hand than that of R^D himself, who, in using the phrase, either formulates his own statement, or intelligently admits a statement which he is able to verify. The cases of the use of 'unto this day' which should be noticed as implying the continued existence of the kingdom of Judah are the following:—I. 8. 8 (the ends of the staves of the ark still to be seen projecting from the Adytum into the Holy Place); 9. 21 (the Canaanites still subjected by Israel to forced labour, as they had been under Solomon); 12. 19 (the division between the ten tribes and the house of David still in existence); II. 8. 22 (Edom still successful in shaking off the yoke of Judah); 16. 6 (the Edomites still hold Elath, from which the Judaeans were expelled by Rezin, king of Aram). For other occurrences of 'unto this day,' not necessarily presupposing a pre-exilic date, but illustrating the frequency of the formula as employed by R^D, cf. *note* on p. 107.

Again, it seems to be clear that, at the time when R^D is writing, the Davidic dynasty still possesses a monarch reigning at Jerusalem. David has, and is still to have, a *lamp* before Yahwe at Jerusalem continually; cf. No. 60 of the phrases of R^D above noticed. The expression 'before Yahwe at Jerusalem' (I. 11. 36) implies further that the Temple is still standing intact, a point which is also assumed in the dedication prayer of I. 8. 15–53, which owes its present form to R^D (cf. pp. 112 *ff.*). Throughout this prayer the leading petition is that supplication made *in* or *towards Yahwe's Temple built by Solomon* may meet with a favourable answer; cf. *vv.* 29, 30, 31 *f.*, 33, 35, 38, 42, 44, 48. We may notice also I. 9. 3, which likewise occurs in a section in which the hand of R^D is prominent:—'I have hallowed this house which thou hast built to put my name there for ever; and mine eyes and my heart shall be there perpetually.' Upon these grounds it may be concluded that the main editing of Kings (viz. that by R^D) must have taken place prior to the destruction of the Judaean kingdom, and that such sections of the book as imply an exilic standpoint are therefore of the nature of later redactional additions and interpolations.

For the work of R^D, influenced, as we have seen him to be, by the spirit and language of Deuteronomy, the *terminus a quo* is the discovery of Deuteronomy in the year B.C. 621, the *terminus ad quem* the destruction of Jerusalem B.C. 586. And since the writer's standpoint seems to indicate that he wrote before the glamour of Josiah's reformation had wholly or nearly faded during the latter days of the Judaean monarchy, the assumption is fair that he undertook and completed his book not later than B.C. 600 [1].

[1] So Kue. *Ond.* § 26; Wellh. *C.* pp. 298 *ff.*, &c. König, on the contrary, holds that the editor of Kings compiled his work not earlier than B.C. 588, i.e. during the Exile (*Einleitung*, § 53. 3).

From the preceding examination and conclusion as to the date of the main redaction of Kings, it is clear that the pre-exilic book must have received certain additions at the hand of a later editor or editors before it attained the form in which we now possess it. The chief of these additions is the appendix, which carries the history down to the year B.C. 561. To this appendix belongs certainly II. 24. 10—25. 30, and, presumably, 23. 31—24. 9. The conclusion of the pre-exilic book has, however, probably been worked over by the second editor, and so adapted to receive his addition that it is now impossible exactly to discover its position. Any of the *vv.* 25, 28, 30 of *ch.* 23 might have formed a conclusion scarcely more abrupt than the present conclusion, *ch.* 25. 30. *Ch.* 23. 29^a, if not intentionally imitated in style in *ch.* 24. 1^a, must be by the same hand, i.e. presumably the hand of the second editor. But again, it is unlikely that R^D should have appended the usual summary of a reign in *v.* 28 without mentioning the manner of the king's death. The statement of *v.* 25^b seems at first sight to presuppose the writer's acquaintance with the characters of all the succeeding kings of Judah, but may be a later insertion, as *vv.* 26, 27 certainly are. On the whole, the most suitable ending to the pre-exilic book would be *vv.* 29, 30, 28 of *ch.* 23, in that order.

It is noticeable that, apart from the difference of standpoint involved in the destruction of the Judaean kingdom and the Exile, the mould of mind of the author of the appendix and of the passages above noticed (p. xvi) which presuppose the captivity of Judah is essentially the same as that of R^D. Thus it is reasonable to employ the symbol R^{D2} in referring to a later redactor of the same school of thought. It must not, however, be supposed that R^{D2} is in every case necessarily one and the same writer, since it is obvious that more than one Deuteronomist may have had a hand in the revision of Kings. In point of fact it can be argued with high probability that such was the case. For the Deuteronomic passage II. 17. 34^b–40 almost certainly refers to the Samaritans of *post-exilic* times (cf. *note ad loc.*); yet it may fairly be assumed that if the author of the appendix had written in post-exilic times he would have given some account of the restoration from exile.

Kings, as it stands in the Hebrew Bible, has, again, undergone still later revision than that of $R^{D\,2}$. This is clear from certain variations in form and order between the MT. and the recension of the text which is represented by the LXX. While in some cases the condition of the LXX text is greatly inferior to that of MT., yet, on the other hand, it is clear that in a number of sections LXX preserves a superior arrangement in order, or a simpler form, of narrative, which points to the fact that MT. has suffered dislocation and interpolation at the hands of a reviser or revisers of a date later than the separation of the two recensions. As instances of this we may notice I. 4. 20—5. 14; 5. 15—7 in the main, 8. 1–13, 11. 1–13 (cf. *notes ad loc.*), and the position of MT. I. 21 after 19, so that 22 succeeds 20 without a break in the narrative. It is noticeable in certain cases that the additions which are found in MT. are just those passages which are coloured by the influence of the Priestly Code (P) in the Hexateuch. Cf. *notes* on I. 6. 11–14; 8. 1–11. Supposing, therefore, for the sake of simplicity that the author of the interpolations and changes in order as seen in MT. was one and the same redactor, he may conveniently be represented by the symbol R^{P} (Priestly Redactor).

Thus the pedigree of our Books of Kings may be represented as follows:—

ORIGINAL SOURCES:—Book of the Acts of Solomon, Chronicles of the Kings of Judah, Chronicles of the Kings of Israel, &c. &c.

Pre-exilic Redactor
influenced by Deut. [R^{D}]

|

Exilic and post-exilic Editors
influenced by Deut. [$R^{D\,2}$]

|

Post-exilic Editor
influenced by Priestly Code [R^{P}]

|

MASSORETIC TEXT.

Hebrew original
of
LXX TEXT.

§ 2. *Characteristics of the Chief Ancient Versions of Kings.*

For the general characteristics of the Ancient Versions of the Old Testament, and a just estimate of their value for the purposes of textual criticism, the reader is referred to Dr. Driver's Excursus in the Introduction to his *Notes on the Hebrew Text of the Books of Samuel*, § 3, pp. xxxvi–lv. All that is here attempted is a brief account of the Versions of Kings, framed upon the lines laid down by Dr. Driver in dealing with Samuel in § 4 of the same Introduction.

1. The Septuagint.

A. Before a Version can be used to good purpose for the criticism of the MT., it is important to recognize the fact that *all* variations from this latter are not due either to paraphrase or to a different reading in the Hebrew original from which the translation was made. The texts of the Versions, like the MT., were liable to *corruption*, and we find as a matter of fact that corrupt readings do exist in LXX, to a greater or less extent in different books.

But this corruption of single words or sentences is not the only feature in the Greek text which appears to belong to the vicissitudes of transmission. We also not infrequently meet with *conflate* or *double renderings* which are apparently due to the addition of a second translation of a passage, made by some scribe in the margin of the MS., probably because he considered that the first rendering did not adequately represent the sense of the original. This second translation came later on to be incorporated by another scribe in the text itself.

(*a*) Instances of corruptions in the Greek text. These are far more numerous in Cod. B than in Luc.:—

I. 1. 9. אבן Ἀιθή for *λίθου*. Luc. Ἀ., Σ., Θ. read *λίθον*.

ib. אנשי *ἀδρούς* for *ἄνδρας* (read by Luc.).

1. 49. ויחרדו ויקמו *καὶ ἐξανέστησαν*. This represents the latter word. The translation of the former, *καὶ ἐξέστησαν* (*al. exempl.*), has fallen out owing to the resemblance between the two Greek words.

2. 6. לא תורד σὺ κατάξεις for οὐ κατάξεις. The opposite change, οὐ for σύ, perhaps occurs in *v.* 9 (supposing, with Luc., Vulg., the original to have been ואתה, not ועתה).

4. 10. The whole *v.* corrupt in Luc. (cf. *note ad loc.*).

4. 11. ἀνὰ Δάν for 'Αβινάδαβ. ἀνὰ φαθεί for Ναφάθ.

4. 20 (MT. 5. 7). האלה οὕτως for οὗτοι (read by Luc.).

5. 4 (MT. 5. 18). פגע ἁμάρτημα probably for ἀπάντημα (read by Luc., Cod. A).

5. 5 (MT. 5. 19). לבנות οἰκοδομήσω for οἰκοδομῆσαι (read by Luc.).

5. 6 (MT. 5. 20). ידע ἰδίως for εἰδώς (Luc.).

7. 3 (MT. 7. 15). τὸ αἰλάμ for τῷ αἰλάμ (Luc.), apparently representing an original לאולם (cf. *note* on 7. 15).

ib. Luc. καὶ οὗτος for καὶ οὕτως (LXX), representing an original וְכֵן (cf. *note*).

7. 9 (MT. 7. 20). לעבר τῷ πήχει for τῷ πάχει (Luc.), i. e. לְעָבְיוֹ.

7. 10 (MT. 7. 23). שפתו τείχους for χείλους (Luc.).

7. 45 (MT. 7. 8). אשר ישב שם ἐν οἴκῳ καθήσεται ἐκεῖ for ἐν ᾧ κ. ε. (Luc.).

8. 16. להיות μεῖναι for εἶναι (Luc.). Initial μ by dittography from preceding 'Ιερουσαλήμ.

8. 39. ונתת Luc. καὶ δικαιώσεις for καὶ δώσεις (LXX).

8. 59. ביומו ἐν ἡμέρᾳ ἐνιαυτοῦ for ἐν ἡμ. αὐτοῦ (Luc.).

9. 28. אופירה εἰς Σωφηρά for εἰς 'Ωφηρά. So 16. 28 *f.*

11. 36. ניר Luc. θέλησις for θέσις (LXX).

15. 27. ויכהו ἐχάραξεν αὐτόν perhaps for ἐπάταξεν αὐτόν (Cod. A). Luc. ἐχαράκωσεν αὐτόν appears to be an attempt to improve the first reading.

16. 15. גבתון Γαβαών for Γαβαθών, *v.* 17.

16. 16b, 17 *ff.* עמרי Ζαμβρεί for 'Αμβρεί.

16. 17. מגבתון ἐν Γαβαθών for ἐκ Γ. (Luc.).

18. 5. בהמה σκηνῶν for κτηνῶν (Cod. A. Cf. Luc.).

18. 10. והשביע καὶ ἐνέπρησεν according to Klo., for καὶ ἐνέπλησεν, i. e. וְהִשְׂבִּיעַ.

18. 32. תעלה θάλασσαν probably an alteration of the transliteration θααλά (Luc.). So *v.* 38.

18. 45. וירכב καὶ ἔκλαεν for καὶ ἐξέλαεν or ἔλαεν. Luc. has further altered LXX into καὶ ἔκλαιε.

19. 3. γῆν for τῆς (τήν Cod. A).

21. 14 *ff.* (MT. 20. 14 *ff.*). המדינות τῶν χορῶν for τῶν χωρῶν (Luc.).

21. 33 (MT. 20. 33). וימהרו καὶ ἐσπείσαντο for καὶ ἔσπευσαν (Luc.).

22. 13. פה אחד ἐν στόματι ἐπί for ἐν στ. ἑνί (Luc.).

22. 16. עד כמה פעמים πεντάκις for ποσάκις (Luc.).

22. 26. אל אמן πρὸς Σεμήρ for πρὸς Ἐμήρ.

II. 3. 21. ומעלה καὶ εἶπον Ὦ for καὶ ἐπάνω (Luc.), an alteration due to the preceding καὶ ἀνεβόησαν, i.e. וַיֹּאמְרוּ for וַיִּצָּעֲקוּ.

5. 17. משא γομόρ for γόμος (Luc.).

6. 5. שאול κεκρυμμένον for κεχρημένον (Luc., Ἀ., Σ., Θ.).

10. 6. את גדלי וג׳ Luc. οὓς οἱ ἁδροί for οὗτοι ἁδροί of LXX, where את is taken as sign of accusative.

10. 26. מצבות στολήν for στήλην (Luc.).

11. 12. ויכו כף καὶ ἐκράτησαν τῇ χειρί for καὶ ἐκρότησαν τ. χ. (Luc.).

12. 1 (MT. 12. 2). מבאר שבע ἐκ γῆς Βηρσάβεε for ἐκ τῆς Β.

12. 8 (MT. 12. 9). בדק βδέλυγμα for βέδεκ (Luc.).

12. 15 (MT. 12. 16). הם αὐτῶν for αὐτοί (Luc.).

14. 7. בגי מלח ἐν Ῥεμέλε for ἐν Γεμέλε (Luc. Γαιμέλεχ, Cod. A. Γαιμέλα).

14. 11. אשר ליהודה γῇ τοῦ Ἰούδα for τῇ τοῦ Ἰ.

15. 20. שם Luc. ἔτι for ἐκεῖ (LXX).

15. 25. בארמון ἐναντίον probably for ἐν ἄντρῳ. Cf. I. 16. 18 where אל ארמון is translated εἰς ἄντρον.

17. 6. וערי מדי Luc. ἐν ὁρίοις Μήδων, an alteration of καὶ Ὀρὴ Μ. (LXX). Cf. also 18. 11.

18. 20. אמרת Luc. σὺ καὶ πᾶς for Σὺ εἶπας (cf. *note ad loc.*).

19. 12. אשר שחתו οὐ διέφθειραν for οὓς δ. (Luc.).

22. 20. את המלך οἱ βασιλεῖς for τῷ βασιλεῖ (Luc.).

23. 5. והשבית καὶ κατέκαυσεν for καὶ κατέπαυσεν. So *v.* 11.

23. 6. לעפר Luc. ὡς χοῦν for εἰς χ. (LXX).

23. 36. מן רומה ἐκ Κρουμά for ἐκ Ῥουμά.

25. 17. שבכה ורמנים σακαχαρθαί for σαβὰχ καὶ ῥοαί (Cod. A).

(*b*) Instances of double renderings are more frequent in Luc. than in Cod. B :—

I. 1. 36. כן יאמר י׳ אלהי אדני המלך = Luc. πιστώσαι ὁ θεὸς τοὺς λόγους τοῦ κυρίου μου τοῦ βασιλέως· οὕτως εἶπε κύριος ὁ θεός σου, κύριε μου βασιλεῦ.

1. 40. מחללים בחללים ושמחים שמחה גדולה = Luc. ἐχόρευον ἐν χοροῖς καὶ εὐφραινόμενοι εὐφροσύνῃ μεγάλῃ ηὔλουν ἐν αὐλοῖς καὶ ἔχαιρον χαρᾷ μεγάλῃ.

1. 47. וגם באו עבדי = Luc. καί γε ἦλθον οἱ δοῦλοι . . . καὶ εἰσεληλύθασι μόνοι (לְבַדָּם for עבדי in second rendering).

2. 5. בחגרתו = Luc. ἐν τῇ ζωῇ μου καὶ ἐπὶ τῇ ζώνῃ . . . μου.

4. 6. ואחישר על הבית = καὶ Ἀχεὶ ἦν οἰκονόμος, καὶ Ἐλιὰκ ὁ οἰκονόμος, καὶ Ἐλιὰβ υἱὸς Σὰφ ἐπὶ τῆς πατριᾶς, apparently a triple rendering (cf. *note ad loc.*).

6. 15. עד קירות = ἕως τῶν δοκῶν καὶ ἕως τῶν τοίχων. δοκῶν = קוֹרוֹת.

6. 34 (MT. 7. 12^{b}). κυκλόθεν . . . καταπέτασμα probably represents an original מְסָבִיב (מֵסַב) read a second time as מָסָךְ (cf. *note ad loc.*).

7. 3 (MT. 7. 15). חוט = Luc. περίμετρον . . . σπαρτίον.

7. 6 (MT. 7. 18). καὶ ἔργον κρεμαστόν, δύο στίχοι . . . ἔργον κρεμαστόν, στίχος ἐπὶ στίχον, representing ומעשה ? שני טורים (cf. *note ad loc.*).

7. 9 (MT. 7. 20). ἐπίθεμα τὸ μελάθρον representing כתרת repeated from beginning in place of הבטן אשר. Luc. also repeats ἐπ' ἀμφοτέρων τῶν στύλων.

7. 22 (MT. 7. 36). וליות = κατὰ πρόσωπον ἔσω, read as לפנימה and doubly rendered.

7. 32 (MT. 7. 47). [אשר עשה] מרב מאד מאד = Luc. οὗ ἐποίησεν ἄρδην . . . ἃ ἐποίησε ταῦτα ἐκ τοῦ πλήθους σφόδρα (cf. *note ad loc.*).

8. 28. לפניך = ἐνώπιόν σου πρὸς σέ.

8. 60. הוא האלהים = ὁ θεός, αὐτὸς θεός.

8. 66. ויברכו את המלך = Luc. καὶ εὐλόγησεν αὐτόν. καὶ εὐλόγησαν καὶ αὐτοὶ τὸν βασιλέα (cf. *note ad loc.*).

11. 43. εἰς τὴν γῆν Σαρειρά for εἰς τὴν Σ. (Luc.), representing an original אל הצררה (cf. *note ad loc.*).

15. 15. ויבא . . . בית י׳ = Luc. καὶ εἰσήνεγκεν 'Ασὰ εἰς τὸν οἶκον κυρίου . . . καὶ εἰσήνεγκεν εἰς τὸν οἶκ. κ.

16. 33. τοῦ ἐξολοθρευθῆναι . . . ἐκακοποίησεν apparently represents a doublet לְהַשְׁחִית הִשְׁחִית.

18. 38. ואת המים אשר בתעלה = Luc. καὶ τὸ ὕδωρ τὸ ἐπ' αὐτῶν, καὶ τὸ ὕδωρ τὸ ἐν τῇ θααλά.

18. 43^b. שב שבע פעמים. Cf. *note ad loc.*

18. 44. מים = Luc. ὕδωρ ἀπὸ θαλάσσης.

20. 4 (MT. 21. 4). ויבא אחאב אל ביתו סר וזעף = Luc. καὶ ἦλθεν 'Α. πρὸς οἶκον αὐτοῦ συγκεχυμένος καὶ ἐκλελυμένος . . . καὶ ἐγένετο τὸ πνεῦμα 'Α. τεταραγμένον.

20. 25 (MT. 21. 25). רק = πλὴν ματαίως, the word being repeated as ריק (רֵיקָם).

21. 1 (MT. 20. 1). ויעל ויצר על שמרון = καὶ ἀνέβη καὶ περιεκάθισεν ἐπὶ Σαμάρειαν . . . καὶ ἀνέβησαν καὶ περιεκάθισαν ἐπὶ Σ. (Luc. ἐπ' αὐτήν).

21. 16 (MT. 20. 16). מלך עזר אתו = Luc. (*v.* 15) καὶ ὁ βασιλεὺς 'Εζὲρ μετ' αὐτοῦ . . . (*v.* 16) βασιλεῖς οἱ συμβοηθοὶ μετ' αὐτοῦ.

22. 17. לא אדנים לאלה = οὐ Κύριος τούτοις θεός; לָאֵלֶּה read a second time as לֵאלֹהִים.

22. 20. ויאמר זה בכה וזה אמר בכה = Luc. καὶ εἶπεν οὗτος οὕτως καὶ οὗτος οὕτως. καὶ εἶπεν Οὐ δυνήσει. καὶ εἶπεν 'Εν σοί (בְּךָ for בכה).

22. 35. ויצק דם המכה אל חיק הרכב = καὶ ἀπεχύννετο αἷμα ἐκ τῆς πληγῆς εἰς τὸν κόλπον τοῦ ἅρματος . . . καὶ ἐξεπορεύετο τὸ αἷμα τῆς τροπῆς ἕως τοῦ κόλπου τοῦ ἅρματος.

II. 1. 2 *ff.* אלהי עקרון = Luc. προσόχθισμα θεὸν 'Ακκαρών.

1. 4, 6. לכן = Luc. οὐχ οὕτως. διὰ τοῦτο.

3. 21. ויצעקו מכל חגר חגורה ומעלה = Luc. καὶ παρήγγειλαν παντὶ περιζωννυμένῳ παραζώνην καὶ παρατείνοντι, καὶ ἐβόησαν ἐκ παντὸς παραζωννυμένου παραζώνην καὶ ἐπ' ἄνω.

3. 23. החרב = Luc. ῥομφαίας· ἐρίσαντες γάρ.

4. 34. ויגהר עליו = Luc. καὶ συνέκαμψεν ἐπ' αὐτὸν καὶ ἰγαὰδ ἐπ' αὐτόν.

4. 35. ויגהר וג׳ apparently triply rendered in Luc. Cf. *note ad loc.*

6. 8. פלני אלמני = τόνδε τινὰ ἐλιμωνί (unless τόνδε τινά = פלני simply).

7. 2. השליש = Luc. ὁ τριστάτης ὁ ἀπεσταλμένος (? הַשָּׁלוּחַ).

7. 5. בנשף = Luc. ἐν τῷ σκότει ἤδη διαυγάζοντος. So *v.* 7, ἐν τ. σκ. ἤδη διαφώσκοντος.

7.7. 10. ויקראו אל שער העיר = Luc. καὶ ἐβόησαν εἰς τὴν πύλην τῆς πόλεως καὶ ἐκάλεσαν τοὺς στρατηγοὺς τῆς πόλεως.

8. 1. ונם בא אל הארץ שבע שנים = Luc. καὶ παρέσται ἐπὶ τὴν γῆν ἑπτὰ ἔτη· καί γε ἦλθεν κ.τ.λ. (בא rendered (1) as participle, (2) as perfect.)

9. 17. שפעת = Luc. τὸν κονιορτὸν τοῦ ὄχλου.

10. 29. לא סר יהוא מאחריהם = Luc. οὐκ ἀπέστη ἀπ' αὐτῶν Ἰού· ὀπίσω αὐτῶν ἐπορεύετο.

11. 2. אחזיה = Luc. Ὀχοζίου τοῦ ἀδελφοῦ αὐτῆς (אָחִיהָ).

11. 9. הכהן = Luc. ὁ συνετὸς ἱερεύς (firstly הֶחָכָם).

11. 14. והשרים = Luc. καὶ οἱ ᾠδοὶ . . . καὶ οἱ στρατηγοί.

11. 15. הוציאו אתה אל מבית לשדרת = Luc. Ἐξαγάγετε αὐτὴν ἔσωθεν τῶν σαδηρώθ, καὶ εἰσαγάγετε αὐτὴν ὀπίσωθεν οἴκου τῶν στρατηγῶν (השרים for השדרת).

14. 10. הכבד = Luc. ἡ βαρεῖα· ἐνδοξάσθητι.

14. 14. התערבות = Luc. τῶν συμμίξεων τῶν βδελυγμάτων (הַתַּעֲבוֹת).

14. 26. מרה מאד = Luc. πικρὰν σφόδρα, δι' ὅτι ἐλεπτύνθη.

16. 18. השבת = Luc. τῆς καθέδρας τῶν σαββάτων.

17. 5. בכל הארץ = Luc. ἐπὶ πᾶσαν τὴν γῆν . . . καὶ εἰς πᾶσαν τὴν γῆν αὐτῆς.

17. 32. Cf. *note ad loc.*

18. 17. בתעלת = Luc. ἐν τῇ ἀναβάσει ἐν τῷ ὑδραγωγῷ.

19. 3. ותוכחה = Luc. καὶ ὀνειδισμοῦ καὶ ἐλεγμοῦ.

19. 28. ושאננך = Luc. καὶ τὸ στρῆνός σου καὶ τὰ ἐνθυμήματά σου.

20. 13. נכתה = Luc. τῆς ὑπάρξεως αὐτοῦ καὶ τοῦ νεχωθά.

21. 6. הרבה = Luc. ἐπλήθυνε, καὶ ἐπλήθυνε.

21. 23. ויקשרו . . . עליו = Luc. καὶ συνεστράφησαν . . . ἐπ' αὐτὸν καὶ ἐπεβούλευσαν αὐτῷ.

23. 6. האשרה = Luc. τὸ ἄλσος τῆς Ἀσηρώθ.

23. 12. וירץ משם = Luc. καὶ καθεῖλεν αὐτὰ ἐκεῖθεν καὶ ἐξήνεγκεν αὐτὰ καὶ συνέτριψε, apparently a triple rendering.

23. 16. ויפן = Luc. καὶ ἀπέστρεψεν . . . καὶ ἐξένευσε.

B. There are also characteristics of the Version which appear to be due to the translator. The more important of these may now be noticed, with a few illustrations.

(1) Paraphrase.

(*a*) This usually takes place for the sake of making clear the sense of some Hebrew word or phrase which would be liable to be misunderstood in the Greek if literally translated :—

I. 2. 32. את דמו *τὸ αἷμα τῆς ἀδικίας αὐτοῦ.*

4. 20 (MT. 5. 7). כל הקרב *πάντα διαγγέλματα.*

4. 22 (MT. 5. 2). לחם *τὰ δέοντα.*

8. 56. לא נפל דבר *οὐ διεφώνησεν λόγος.*

9. 27. ידעי הים *ἐλαύνειν εἰδότας θάλασσαν.*

15. 4. ניר *κατάλειμμα.*

19. 18. נשק לו *προσεκύνησεν αὐτῷ.*

21. 12 (MT. 20. 12). שימו וישימו *Οἰκοδομήσατε χάρακα· καὶ ἔθεντο χάρακα.*

22. 34. לתמו *εὐστόχως.*

(*b*) At other times paraphrase appears to be used for no apparent reason, merely at the whim of the translator :—

I. 3. 17. ואלד עמה *καὶ ἐτέκομεν.*

5. 12 (MT. 5. 26). שניהם *ἀνὰ μέσον ἑαυτῶν.*

9. 5. מעל כסא ישראל *ἡγούμενος ἐν Ἰσραήλ.*

17. 13. אל תיראי *θάρσει.*

(*c*) Somewhat different are the cases in which phrases are arbitrarily altered by the translator, because it seemed to him that some better expression could be substituted :—

I. 2. 29. אצל המזבח *κατέχει τῶν κεράτων τοῦ θυσιαστηρίου.*

2. 38. ימים רבים *τρία ἔτη* (from *v.* 39).

9. 6. נתתי *ἔδωκεν Μωυσῆς.*

10. 5. לא היה בה עוד רוח *ἐξ ἑαυτῆς ἐγένετο.*

(*d*) Or again, paraphrase may take place when the expression used in the original was somewhat offensive in the eyes of the translator. Under this head comes, e. g., the removal of anthropomorphic expressions applied to God :—

I. 3. 10. בעיני אדני *ἐνώπιον Κυρίου.*

II. 2. 11. השמים *ὡς εἰς τὸν οὐρανόν* (of the translation of Elijah).

24. 3. על פי י׳ *ἐπὶ τὸν θυμὸν Κυρίου.*

(*e*) The last form of paraphrase to be noticed is the translation of a word or phrase by *guess*, the context being taken as a guide to the sense:—

I. 10. 11. אלמגים *πελεκητά.*

17. 21. ויתמדד *καὶ ἐνεφύσησεν.*

18. 21. על שתי הסעפים *ἐπ' ἀμφοτέραις ταῖς ἰγνύαις*, guided by the preceding פסחים.

21. 11 (MT. 20. 11). מפתח *ὁ ὀρθός*, guided by חֹגֵר rendered *ὁ κυρτός* from Talmudic חִגֵּר.

(2) In striking contrast to the paraphrastic tendency, we find renderings in which extreme literality appears to have been the aim of the translator.

(*a*) Thus at times attempts are made to represent in Greek the Hebrew constructions, or to preserve the fancied force of Hebrew words, and the result is a rendering which is often grotesque.

Examples of Hebraisms from I. 1. 2 are the following:—

1. 7. ויעזרו אחרי *καὶ ἐβοήθουν ὀπίσω* (contrast Luc. *καὶ ἀντελαμβάνοντο αὐτοῦ*).

1. 12. איעצך נא עצה *συμβουλεύσω σοι δὴ συμβουλίαν.*

1. 13. לכי . . . ואמרת *εἴσελθε . . . καὶ ἐρεῖς.*

1. 14. עודך מדברת . . . ואני אבוא *ἔτι λαλούσης σου . . . καὶ ἐγὼ εἰσελεύσομαι.*

1. 17. אתה נשבעת בי׳ אלהיך *σὺ ὤμοσας ἐν τῷ θεῷ σου* (but Luc. *κατὰ τοῦ κ. τοῦ θ.*).

1. 51. ויגד . . . לאמר *ἀνηγγέλη . . . λέγοντες* (but Luc. *καὶ ἀπήγγειλαν . . . λέγοντες*).

2. 2. אנכי הלך *ἐγώ εἰμι πορεύομαι.* Cf. II. 4. 13; 10. 9; 22. 20.

2. 37. והיה ביום צאתך ועברת *καὶ ἔσται ἐν τῇ ἡμέρᾳ τῆς ἐξόδου σου καὶ διαβήσῃ* (but Luc. *ἐν τῇ ἡμ. τῆς ἐξ. σου ᾗ διαβήσῃ*).

2. 42. ידע תדע כי מות תמות *γινώσκων γνώσῃ ὅτι θανάτῳ ἀποθανῇ.*

(*b*) Sometimes difficult words, instead of being guessed at, are interpreted very literally according to the sense of the root:—

I. 6. 20. סגור *συνκεκλεισμένῳ.*

7. 28. מסגרות *συνκλειστόν.*

16. 20. קשרו אשר קשר *τὰς συνάψεις αὐτοῦ ἃς συνῆψεν.*

II. 10. 19. בעקבה *ἐν πτερνισμῷ.*

12. 3. הורהו *ἐφώτισεν αὐτόν*, apparently connecting the Hebrew word with אור.

12. 21. ויקשרו קשר *καὶ ἔδησαν πάντα δεσμόν.*

14. 14. התערבות *τῶν συμμίξεων.*

14. 19. ויקשרו עליו קשר *καὶ συνεστράφησαν ἐπ᾽ αὐτὸν σύστρεμμα.* Cf. 15. 8, 30.

(*c*) Another device in the case of a hard word was simply to transliterate it into Greek letters. Such transliterations are very characteristic of Kings, particularly of the second book:—

I. 4. 19. נְצִיב *νασέφ*, Luc. Νασείβ.

5. 11 (MT. 5. 25). מַכֹּלֶת *μαχείρ* (*al. exempl. μαχάλ*).

ib. כֹּר *κόρους.*

ib. כֹּר (correctly בַּת) *βαίθ.*

6. 7; *al.* (MT. 6. 3). אוּלָם *αἰλάμ.*

6. 10; *al.* (MT. 6. 5). דְּבִיר *δαβείρ.*

6. 22; *al.* (MT. 6. 23). כְּרוּבִים *χερουβείν.*

7. 14; *al.* (MT. 7. 27). מְכֹנוֹת *μεχωνώθ.*

11. 14. שָׂטָן *σατάν.*

14. 28. תָּא *θεέ*, Luc. *θεκουέ.*

18. 32, 38. תְּעָלָה Luc. *θααλά.*

19. 4. רֹתֶם Ῥαθμέν, Luc. *ῥαθαμείν.*

II. 2. 14. אַף־הוּא *ἀφφώ.*

3. 4. נֹקֵד *νωκήθ.*

4. 34. וַיִּגְהַר Luc. *καὶ ἰγαάδ.*

4. 39. אוֹרֹת *ἀριώθ.*

4. 42. בְּצִקְלֹנוֹ Cod. A *βακελλέθ* (but cf. *note ad loc.*).

5. 19. כִּבְרַת *δεβραθά*, Luc. *χαβραθά.*

6. 8. פְּלֹנִי אַלְמֹנִי *ἐλιμωνί*, Luc. *φελμουνί.*

6. 25. קַב *κάβου.*
8. 8, 9. מִנְחָה *μαανά,* Luc. *μαναά.*
8. 15. מַכְבֵּר *χαββά.*
9. 13. גֶּרֶם *γαρέμ.*
10. 10. אֶפּוֹא *ἀφφώ.*
10. 22. הַמֶּלְתָּחָה *τοῦ οἴκου μεσθαάλ.*
11. 4. לַכָּרִי וְלָרָצִים *τὸν Χορρεὶ καὶ τὸν Ῥασείν.*
11. 6. מַסָּח Luc. Μεσσαέ.
11. 8. שְׂדֵרוֹת *ἀηδώθ,* Luc. *σαδηρώθ.*
11. 12. הַנֵּזֶר *ἰέζερ.*
12. 6; *al.* בֶּדֶק *βέδεκ.*
12. 10. הַמִּזְבֵּחַ *ἰαμειβείν.* Cod. A *ἀμμασβή.*
14. 7. בְּגֵי־הַמֶּלַח *ἐν Ῥεμέλε,* Luc. *ἐν Γαιμελέχ.*
15. 5. הַחָפְשִׁית *ἀφφουσώθ.*
17. 6. עָרֵי Ὀρή. So 18. 11.
20. 12. מִנְחָה *μαναάν.*
20. 13. נְכֹתֹה *νεχωθά.*
22. 14. מִשְׁנֶה *μασενά.*
23. 4. שַׁדְמוֹת *σαλημώθ.*
23. 5. כְּמָרִים *χωμαρείμ.*
ib. מַזָּלוֹת *μαζουρώθ.*
23. 7. קְדֵשִׁים *καδησείμ,* Luc. *καδησείν.*
ib. בָּתִּים *χεττιείν* (cf. *note ad loc.*).
23. 10. תֹּפֶת *τάφεθ,* Luc. *Θαφφέθ.*
23. 11. פַּרְוָרִים *φαρουρείμ.*
23. 13. הַמַּשְׁחִית *τοῦ Μοσοάθ,* Luc. Ἀμεσσώθ.
23. 24. תְּרָפִים *θεραφείν.*
25. 5. עַרְבוֹת *ἀραβώθ.*
25. 12. גבים *ταβείν.*
25. 14. יָעִים *ἰαμείν.*
25. 17. כֹּתֶרֶת *χωθάρ.*
ib. שְׂבָכָה *γαβαχά.* Cod. A *σαβαχά.*

(3) Another characteristic is the insertion of additional words and sentences by the translator.

(*a*) Such additions are frequently made to fill out the sense, and to make the meaning more clear. Very frequently the subject of a verb is added when the reference seems to be ambiguous:—

I. 2. 22. ὁ ἀρχιστράτηγος ἑταῖρος[1].

2. 32. τὸ αἷμα αὐτῶν, added as obj. of לא ידע.

2. 35. εἰς ἱερέα πρῶτον.

3. 9. ἐν δικαιοσύνῃ, explaining the force of לשפט.

3. 15. κατὰ πρόσωπον τοῦ θυσιαστηρίου τοῦ[1].

3. 27. τῇ εἰπούσῃ Δότε αὐτῇ αὐτό, added to remove the seeming ambiguity of the king's command[1].

4. 21 (MT. 5. 8). ὁ βασιλεύς, subj. of אשר יהיה שם.

8. 53 (MT. 8. 12). ὑπὲρ τοῦ οἴκου ὡς συνετέλεσεν τοῦ οἰκοδομῆσαι αὐτόν[1].

15. 19. διάθου, before ברית[1].

18. 24. ὃ ἐλάλησας, after הדבר.

19. 19. ἐν βουσίν, after והוא חרש.

(*b*) Additions are also very frequently made for the sake of bringing one passage into strict conformity with another:—

I. 2. 26. τῆς διαθήκης, ארון הברית being the usual (Deuteronomic) phrase.

2. 29. καὶ θάψον αὐτόν, to agree with *v.* 31.

2. 37. καὶ ὥρκισεν αὐτὸν ὁ βασιλεὺς ἐν τῇ ἡμέρᾳ ἐκείνῃ, in agreement with *v.* 42.

9. 20. καὶ τοῦ Χαναναίου . . . καὶ τοῦ Γεργασαίου, added to make up the number of the *seven* heathen nations of Palestine.

12. 20. καὶ Βενιαμείν, to agree with *vv.* 21, 23.

21. 23. καὶ οὐ θεὸς κοιλάδος, to agree with *v.* 28.

The relationship of the recension of Lucian to that of Cod. B[2] cannot here be discussed; but it is clear that the author had access to sources which preserved unimpaired original readings of which

---

[1] Discussed in the *notes* on the text.

[2] The origin of the text of Codd. A and B in 3 Kings has been discussed at length by S. Silberstein in *ZATW.*, 1893–4.

we should otherwise have remained in ignorance[1]. Instances of such readings in the text of Kings will be found in the *notes*. Cf. I. 1. 28; 2. 5; 11. 8[b]; 13. 11; 18. 5. II. 3. 25; 5. 1; 7. 7; 10. 11; 12. 5; 15. 10; 17. 2, 7, 27; 18. 34; 24. 13; 25. 4.

2. The Targum.

The chief characteristics of this version may be noticed very briefly.

(*a*) A very marked tendency to do away with anthropomorphic or otherwise seemingly unworthy expressions used with reference to God:—

I. 1. 17. ביהוה אלהיך, Targ. במימרא דיהוה אלהך. So constantly.

3. 10. בעיני אדני, Targ. קדם יהוה.

8. 15. בפיו, Targ. במימריה.

8. 24. ותדבר בפיך, Targ. וגזרתא במימרך.

8. 29. להיות עיניך פתחת, Targ. למיהוי רעיא קדמך. So *v.* 52.

8. 33. ושבו אליך, Targ. ויתובון לפולחנך.

9. 6. מאחרי, Targ. מבתר פולחני.

9. 9. עזבו את יהוה, Targ. שבקו ית פולחנא דיהוה.

ib. אלהים אחרים, Targ. טעות עממיא, to avoid applying the name אלהים to false gods.

(*b*) A general tendency to paraphrase:—

I. 1. 33. גחון, Targ. שילוחא. So *vv.* 38, 45.

1. 38. והכרתי והפלתי, Targ. וקשתיא וקלעיא. So *v.* 44.

1. 42. איש חיל, Targ. גבר דחיל חטאין. So several times.

2. 7. קרבו אלי, Targ. סופיקו צורכיי.

2. 24. אשר עשה לי בית, Targ. דקיים לי מלכו.

3. 16. זנות, Targ. פונדקאן, πανδοκεύτριαι, a softening down of the original.

3. 18. אין זר, Targ. זכאין.

6. 4. חלוני שקפים אטמים, Targ. כוין פתיחן מלגיו וסתימן מלברא.

---

[1] Cf. Dri. *Sam.* p. lii. The value of Luc. for the emendation of the MT. of Kings has been noticed by I. Hooykaas, *Iets over de grieksche vertaling van het Oude Testament* (Rotterdam, 1888).

6. 10. ויאחז, Targ. וטליל.

7. 2. בית יער הלבנון, Targ. בית מקרת מלכיא.

8. 16. להיות שמי, Targ. לאשראה שכינתי.

8. 19. היצא מחלציך, Targ. דתוליד.

8. 27. האמנם, Targ. ארי מן סבר ומן דמי בקושטא.

8. 39. מכון שבתך, Targ. אתר בית שכינתך.

(*c*) A tendency to make explanatory insertions, without any equivalent in the original:—

I. 1. 24. מלכותא in the phrase כורסי מלכותא = כִּסֵּא. So constantly.

5. 13. ואיתנבי על מלכי בית דוד דעתידין למשלט בעלמא הדין ובעלמא דמשיחא; perhaps a haggadic explanation of וידבר על העצים . . . בקיר.

6. 6. למיהוי רישי שריתא ניחין על זיזיא.

8. 2. בירחא דעתיקיא קרן ליה ירחא קדמאה. MT. simply בירח האתנים.

8. 9. דעליהון כתיבין עשרה פיתגמי קימא. Cf. also *v.* 21.

8. 65. חנוכת ביתא . . . חגא. So MT. in 2 Chr. 7. 9.

As a whole this version represents a recension much nearer to MT. than that of any other ancient version.

3. The Peshiṭto.

This translation appears to have been made from a Hebrew text similar in many respects to that presupposed by LXX, though more nearly related to MT. than the LXX original[1]. Instances of the agreement in readings between Pesh., LXX, and Luc. will be found in the *notes*. Cf. I. 2. 26, 29; 6. 9; 7. 10, 15[b]; 8. 37; 10. 8. II. 6. 2. As has been noticed by Dri. in the case of Samuel, the original of Pesh. seems to have been related to that of Luc.: cf. I. 1. 40; 4. 34; 18. 29. II. 2. 14; 10. 14; 14. 29; 19. 15. Affinities with the Vulg. may also be noticed: cf. I. 7. 7, 42;

[1] A conspectus of the variations between Pesh. and MT. in 1 Kings has been given by J. Berlinger, *Die Peschitta zum 1. (3.) Buch der Könige und ihr Verhältniss zu MT., LXX. und Trg.* (Berlin, 1897).

9. 18. Cases in which Pesh. agrees with LXX, Luc., Vulg. against MT. are frequent.

The general characteristics of the Version are those of a close and accurate, though not too servile, representation of the original. Paraphrase is occasionally employed—most frequently in the case of words or phrases which appeared to the translator to need elucidation, and here and there slight additions have been made to the text for the same reason. The following instances may be noticed.

(*a*) Paraphrase:—

I. 1. 36. כן יאמר ܗܟܢܐ ܢܥܒܕ 'So may (Yahwe) *do.*'

1. 50. ויחזק בקרנות המזבח ܘܐܙܠ ܓܘܣܐ ܒܩܪ̈ܢܬܐ ܕܡܕܒܚܐ 'and *took refuge at* the horns of the altar.'

2. 42. ביום צאתך והלכת אנה ואנה ܒܝܘܡܐ ܕܬܦܘܩ ܡܢ ܐܘܪܫܠܡ ܘܬܥܒܪ ܢܚܠܐ ܕܩܕܪܘܢ 'In the day that thou goest forth *from Jerusalem and crossest the brook Kidron.*'

3. 16. ותעמדנה לפניו אל המלך ܠܡܕܢ ܕܝܢ ܩܕܡ ܡܠܟܐ ܫܠܝܡܘܢ '*to plead their case before king Solomon.*'

3. 18. ויהי ביום השלישי ܘܡܢ ܒܬܪ ܬܠܬܐ ܝܘ̈ܡܝܢ 'and *after three days.*'

8. 26. אשר דברת ܕܝܡܝܬ 'which thou didst *swear.*'

12. 32*f.* בחמשה עשר יום לחדש ܒܡܠܝܐ 'on the *full moon.*'

14. 10. כאשר יבער הגלל ܐܝܟ ܕܡܬܠܩܛܝܢ ܥܢܒ̈ܘܗܝ ܕܟܪܡܐ ܡܐ ܕܫܠܡ ܩܛܦܐ '*as the grapes of a vineyard* are swept away *when the vintage is finished.*'

20. 33. ויעלהו ܘܐܘܬܒܗ ܥܡܗ 'and he *caused him to sit with him.*'

21. 11. הישבים בעירו ܕܝܬܒܝܢ ܒܡܕܝܢܬܐ ܥܡ ܢܒܘܬ 'who dwelt in *the* city *with Naboth.*'

II. 2. 10. הקשית לשאול ܐܥܫܢܬ ܫܐܠܬܟ 'thou hast made a *large* request.'

3. 7. כמוני כמוך ܣܠܩ ܐܢܐ ܐܟܘܬܟ '*I will go up* like thee.'

4. 42. מבעל שלשה ܡܢ ܡܕܝܢܬ ܓܢܒܪ̈ܐ 'from *the city of the mighty men.*'

5. 11. ואסף המצרע ܘܐܬܐܣܐ ܡܢ ܓܪܒܐ 'and *I should be healed of leprosy.*'

7. 2, 17, 19. השליש ܓܒܪܐ 'the *man.*'

9. 11. שיחו ܫܛܝܘܬܗ 'his *folly.*'

23. 11. וישבת ܘܩܛܠ 'and he *slew.*'

23. 29. על מלך אשור ܥܠ ܡܒܘܓ 'against *Mabbogh.*'

(*b*) Additions:—

I. 1. 10. ܒܪ ܝܗܘܝܕܥ 'son of Jehoiada,' after בניהו; ܕܕܘܝܕ 'of David,' after הגבורים.

1. 11. ܢܒܝܐ 'the prophet,' after נתן.

1. 21. ܒܫܠܡܐ 'in peace,' after עם אבתיו.

1. 39. ܘܢܬܢ ܢܒܝܐ 'and Nathan the prophet,' after צדוק הכהן.

8. 22. ܘܨܠܝ 'and prayed,' after ויפרש כפיו השמים.

11. 18. ܬܒ ܠܘܬܝ 'Dwell with me,' after אמר לו (cf. *note ad loc.*).

19. 1. ܢܒ̈ܝܐ ܕܒܥܠܐ ܘܕܣܘ̈ܟܠܐ 'the prophets of Ba'al and of the sanctuaries,' for simple הנביאים.

II. 4. 13. ܫܦܝܪ 'prosperously,' before בתוך וג׳.

6. 12. ܠܐ ܗܘܐ ܡܢ ܕܝܠܢ 'It is none of us,' for simple לוא.

10. 15. ܘܐܡܪ ܠܗ 'And he said to him,' before תנה את ידך.

11. 14. ܐܝܟ ܢܡܘܣܐ ܕܡܠܟ̈ܐ 'according to the custom of kings,' for simple כמשפט.

14. 27. ܒܪ ܝܗܘܐܚܙ 'son of Jehoaḥaz,' after בן יואש.

15. 29. ܘܠܐܒܠ ܡܚܘܠܐ ܘܠܟܠܗ ܒܝܬ ܡܥܟܐ 'and Abel-Meḥolah and all Beth-Ma'achah,' for ואת אבל בית מעכה.

18. 27. Insertion of negative: ܕܠܐ ܢܐܟܠܘܢ . . . ܘܠܐ ܢܫܬܘܢ for לאכל . . . ולשתות.

19. 35. ܘܚܙܝܢ 'and beheld,' after וישכימו בבקר.

In certain cases the renderings of Pesh. seem to exhibit connection with Targ.; cf. I. 1. 33, 38, 45 גחון, Pesh. ܫܝܠܘܚܐ, Targ. שילוחא; 1. 38 הכרתי והפלתי, Pesh. ܘܩܫ̈ܬܐ ܘܕܪܩܝܢ ܒܩܠܥܐ, Targ. וקשתיא וקלעיא; 2. 5 וישם . . . ברגליו, Pesh. ܘܫܕܐ ܐܢܘܢ ܐܝܟ ܕܒܩܪܒܐ ܘܐܬܒ ܕܡܗܘܢ ܒܫܠܡܐ ܕܚܪ̈ܨܘܗܝ ܘܕܫ ܒܡܣܐܢܐ ܕܪ̈ܓܠܘܗܝ, Targ. ודמי דתחשיב דמהון עלוהי כדם תבירי קרבא ויתיב להון בכמנת שלמא ואשד דמהון באיספניקי בבחרציה ודש בטלריתא

דברגלוהי ; 5. 32 והגבלים, Pesh. ܘܓܒ̈ܠܝܐ, Targ. וארגובליא ; 18. 21 אתם פסחים על שתי הסעפים, Pesh. ܦܠܓܝܢ ܐܢܬܘܢ ܠܬܪܬܝܢ ܦܠܓܘ̈ܬܐ, Targ. אתון פליגין לתרין פלגון ; 22. 34 משך בקשת לתמו, Pesh. ܫܕܐ ܗܘܐ ܩܫܬܐ ܠܬܡܝܡܘܬܗ, Targ. נגד בקשתא לקיבליה. A few cases of agreement in rendering with Vulg. may also be noticed: I. 6. 1 ויבן, Pesh. ܫܪܝ ܠܡܒܢܝܘ, Vulg. *aedificari coepit;* 18. 45 ויהי עד כה ועד כה, Pesh. ܘܟܕ ܗܘ ܡܬܦܢܐ ܠܗܪܟܐ ܘܠܗܪܟܐ, Vulg. *cumque se verteret huc atque illuc;* 22. 48 ומלך וג׳, Pesh. ܘܡܠܟܐ ܠܝܬ ܒܐܕܘܡ ܕܩܐܡ, Vulg. *nec erat tunc rex constitutus in Edom;* II. 4. 35 ויזורר, Pesh. ܘܐܬܦܫܓ, Vulg. *et oscitavit.*

Cases of corruption in the text of Pesh. are not numerous, and are nearly confined to confusion or transposition of letters in proper names: I. 4. 10 שכה, Pesh. ܣܘܟܬ ; 4. 12 יקמעם, Pesh. ܝܩܡܥܡ ; 5. 4 תפסח, Pesh. ܬܦܣܝܣ ; 22. 10 בגרן, Pesh. ܒܕܪܐ for ܒܐܕܪܐ ; II. 2. 25 שב, Pesh. ܬܘܒ for ܬܒ ; 4. 23 שלום, Pesh. ܫܠܡܘܬܐ for ܫܠܡ ; 4. 28 תשלה, Pesh. ܬܫܠܐ ; 9. 2 נמשי, Pesh. ܢܡܫܝ ; 9. 27 יבלעם, Pesh. ܝܒܠܥܡ ; 14. 7 יקתאל, Pesh. ܝܩܬܐܝܠ ; 15. 16 *ff.* מנחם, Pesh. ܡܢܚܝܡ ; 17. 31 נבחז, Pesh. ܢܒܚܙ ; 18. 2 אבי, Pesh. ܐܒܝ ; 21. 1 חפצי בה, Pesh. ܚܦܨܝܒܗ ; 21. 18, 26 עזא, Pesh. ܥܙܐ. Cases of double renderings may be found in I. 20. 33 והאנשים ינחשו וימהרו ܘܓܒܪܐ ܢܚܫܐ ܗܘܘ ܕܝܢ ܗܘܘ ܘܓܒܪܐ ܢܚܫܘ ܘܐܬܚܦܛܘ ܒܗ ; 22. 34 לתמו ܠܬܡܝܡܘܬܗ ܠܡܫܡܠܝܘܬܗ ; II. 19. 4 ונשאת תפלה ܘܬܨܠܐ ܘܬܬܠ ; 19. 28 יען התרגזך אלי ܚܠܦ ܕܐܬܪܓܙܬ ܘܐܬܚܡܬ ܥܠܝ.

4. The Latin Versions.

(*a*) The Old Latin Version[1] is known to us only in a fragmentary form. For Kings we possess the fragments collected by Sabatier (chiefly from the Fathers), and published in 1743 in his *Bibliorum Sacrorum Antiquae Versiones Latinae*, vol. i; extracts from the margin of a Gothic MS. (tenth century) at Leon in Spain[2],

[1] The question whether the Old Latin represents one version or several distinct translations is discussed by H. A. A. Kennedy in Hastings, *BD.* iii. p. 48.

[2] It should be noticed, however, that F. C. Burkitt (*The Old Latin and the Itala*, p. 9, in the Cambridge *Texts and Studies*, vol. iv) regards it as 'by no

published by Vercellone in 1864 in *Variae Lectiones Vulgatae Latinae editionis*, vol. ii; *Palimpsestus Vindobonensis*, published by J. Belsheim in 1885, containing I. 11. 41—12. 11; 13. 19–29; 14. 6–15; 15. 34—16. 28; 18. 23–29; II. 6. 6–15; 10. 5–13; 10. 24–30; 13. 14–22; 15. 32–38; 17. 1–6, 15–20; *Ein neues Fragment des Quedlinburger Itala-Codex*, published by A. Düning in 1888, containing I. 5. 9 (MT. 5. 23)—6. 11. To these may be added the quotations in Augustine's *Speculum* (i.e. the *Liber de diuinis scripturis siue Speculum*, which in the N. T. is quoted amongst O. L. MSS. as *m*)[1], not included by Sabatier in his work; and the edition of Lucifer by Hartel (*Corp. Script. Eccles.*, Vienna, 1886) may be used to advantage to check the quotations of Sabatier from this writer. The Version, as based upon the Greek text, possesses a secondary value for the purposes of textual criticism. The fragments of Kings which have survived, especially those from the margin of the Gothic MS., testify to a close connexion of the original Greek with the MSS. which were in later times employed by Lucian in the formation of his recension of the LXX. As might have been expected, the text of the Old Latin is not identical with Luc., many of the doublets and other glosses which are found in Luc. having presumably crept into the Greek text subsequently to the formation of the Latin translation; but, on the whole, the testimony of the Old Latin points to a high antiquity for the type of Greek text preserved by Luc. The following points of connexion between Old Latin and Luc. may be noticed:—

I. 1. 40. Goth. *et populus cantabat canticis et melodiis, et gaudebant gaudio magno; organizantes in organis, et iucundabantur in iucunditate magna; et resonabat omnis terra in voce eorum.*	Luc. *καὶ πᾶς ὁ λαὸς ἐχόρευον ἐν χοροῖς καὶ εὐφραινόμενοι εὐφροσύνῃ μεγάλῃ* ηὔλουν ἐν αὐλοῖς καὶ ἔχαιρον χαρᾷ μεγάλῃ, *καὶ ἤχησεν ἡ γῆ ἐν τῇ φωνῇ αὐτῶν.*

means certain that this interesting document does not represent readings extracted and translated from some Greek codex, so that it may have no connexion with the Old Latin properly so called.'

[1] Cf. edit. by F. Weihrich, Vienna, 1887 (*Corp. Script. Eccles.*).

2. 5. Goth. *et uindicavit sanguinem belli in pace; et dedit sanguinem innocentium in uita mea, et zona mea, quae erat circa lumbos meos, &c.*	Luc. καὶ ἐξεδίκησεν αἷμα πολέμου ἐν εἰρήνῃ καὶ ἔδωκεν αἷμα ἀθῷον (so Cod. A) ἐν τῇ ζωῇ μου καὶ ἐπὶ τῇ ζώνῃ τῆς ὀσφύος μου κ.τ.λ.
3. 18. Sab. *peperit etiam haec mulier filium.*	Luc. ἔτεκε καὶ ἡ γυνὴ αὕτη υἱόν.
3. 24. Goth. *Accipite mihi machaeram.*	Luc. Λάβετέ μοι μάχαιραν. So Cod. A.
8. 53. Goth. *Solem statuit in caelo Dominus, et dixit, &c.*	Luc. Ἥλιον ἔστησεν ἐν οὐρανῷ Κύριος καὶ εἶπε κ.τ.λ.
9. 8. Goth. *et domus haec altissima.*	Luc. καὶ ὁ οἶκος οὗτος ὁ ὑψηλός.
10. 11. Goth. *trabes multas valde non dolatas.*	Luc. ξύλα πολλὰ σφόδρα ἀπελέκητα.
10. 26. Goth. *Et erant Salomoni* XL *millia equarum in quadrigis foetantium.*	Luc. καὶ ἦσαν τῷ Σολομῶντι τεσσαράκοντα (so Cod. A[1]) χιλιάδες ἵππων θηλειῶν εἰς ἅρματα τοῦ τίκτειν.
10. 28. Goth. *et ex Thecua et ex Damasco erant negotiatores regis.*	Luc. καὶ ἐκ Θεκοῦε καὶ ἐκ Δαμασκοῦ. καὶ οἱ ἔμποροι τοῦ βασιλέως, κ.τ.λ.
13. 11. Goth. *et pseudo-propheta alius senior.* Sab. *et propheta alius.*	Luc. καὶ προφήτης ἄλλος πρεσβύτης.
14. 27. Goth. *ianuam domus Domini.*	Luc. τὸν πυλῶνα οἴκου κυρίου.
15. 19. Goth. *Testamentum esto inter me et inter te.*	Luc. Διαθήκη ἔστω ἀνὰ μέσον ἐμοῦ καὶ ἀνὰ μέσον σοῦ.
16. 24 *ff.* Vind. *Ambri.*	Luc. Ἀμβρί. Cod. B. Ζαμβρεί.
16. 29. Vind. *gasiba.*	Luc. Γαζουβά. Cod. B. Γαβουζά (עֲזוּבָה MT. 22. 42).
18. 21. Goth. *Usquequo claudicamini utrisque femoribus vestris?*	Luc. Ἕως πότε ὑμεῖς χωλανεῖτε ἐπ' ἀμφοτέραις ταῖς ἰγνύαις ὑμῶν;
18. 44. Goth. *Adducens aquam de mari.*	Luc. ἀνάγουσα ὕδωρ ἀπὸ θαλάσσης.
18. 45. Sab. *Et plorabat, et ibat Achab in Iezrael.*	Luc. καὶ ἔκλαιε (so Cod. A) καὶ ἐπορεύετο Ἀχαὰβ εἰς Ἰεζραήλ.
II. 1. 2. Goth. *Et ascendit Ochozias, &c.*	Luc. καὶ ἀνέβη Ὀχοζίας κ.τ.λ.
1. 7. Goth. *Qualis est hominis iustitia qui ascendit obviam vobis?*	Luc. Τί τὸ δικαίωμα τοῦ ἀνδρὸς τοῦ ἀναβάντος εἰς συνάντησιν ὑμῖν;
2. 14. Goth. *et transiit per siccum in eremum.*	Luc. καὶ διῆλθε διὰ ξηρᾶς.
2. 23. Goth. *et lapidabant eum.*	Luc. καὶ ἐλίθαζον αὐτόν.
3. 10. Goth. *vocavit Dominus hos tres reges tradere in manu Moab.*	Luc. κέκληκε κύριος τοὺς τρεῖς βασιλεῖς τούτους παραδοῦναι ἡμᾶς εἰς χεῖρας Μωάβ.
3. 20. Goth. *ecce aquae veniebant de via eremi Sur ex Edom.*	Luc. ἰδοὺ ὕδατα ἤρχετο ἐξ ὁδοῦ τῆς ἐρήμου Σοὺδ ἐξ Ἐδώμ.
4. 16. Goth. *Noli, domine, homo Dei, deridere ancillam tuam.*	Luc. Μή, κύριε ἄνθρωπε τοῦ Θεοῦ (so Cod. A), μὴ ἐκγελάσῃ τὴν δούλην σου.
4. 19. Goth. *Caput doleo.*	Luc. Τὴν κεφαλήν μου ἀλγῶ.

4. 28. Goth. *Si poposci filium a domino, non sic poposci sicut tu fecisti.*	Luc. Μὴ ᾐτησάμην υἱὸν παρὰ τοῦ κυρίου μου; **οὐχὶ** σὺ **πεποίηκας;**
4. 35. Goth. *et inspiravit in eum.*	Luc. **καὶ** ἐνέπνευσεν ἐπ' αὐτόν.
5. 19. Goth. *chabratha terra.*	Luc. **χαβραθὰ τὴν γῆν.**
5. 23. Goth. *Et dixit Naaman instantius: Accipe &c.*	Luc. καὶ **εἶπε** Νεεμὰν **ἐπιεικῶς** Λαβὲ κ.τ.λ.
6. 8. Goth. *In locum phalmunum obsessionem faciamus.*	Luc. Εἰς τὸν τόπον **τὸν φελμουνὶ** ποιήσωμεν **ἔνεδρον.**
9. 17. Goth. *pulverem populi Hieu.*	Luc. τὸν κονιορτὸν **τοῦ ὄχλου** Ἰού.
10. 6. Vind. *accipiat unusquisque nutritorum caput eius quae nutrivit ex filis regis.*	Luc. **λαβέτω ἕκαστος** τὴν κεφαλὴν **τοῦ υἱοῦ** τοῦ κυρίου αὐτοῦ.
10. 11. Goth. *omnes cognatos eius.* Vind. *proximos eius.*	Luc. πάντας τοὺς **ἀγχιστεύοντας** αὐτοῦ.
10. 29. Vind. *set a peccatis Hieroboam fili Nabat qui peccare fecit Israel non discessit Ieu rex set abit post uaccas peccati quae erant in Bethel et in Dan.* Goth. *non recessit Hieu, sequens observantiam uaccarum peccati.*	Luc. πλὴν ἀπὸ ἁμαρτιῶν Ἰεροβοὰμ υἱοῦ Ναβάτ, ὃς ἐξήμαρτε τὸν Ἰσραήλ, οὐκ ἀπέστη ἀπ' αὐτῶν Ἰού· **ὀπίσω αὐτῶν ἐπορεύετο,** τῶν δαμάλεων **τῆς ἁμαρτίας** τῶν χρυσῶν τῶν ἐν Βαιθὴλ καὶ ἐν **Δάν.**
10. 36. Goth. + *Et erat annus (secundus) Gotholiae cum regnare coepisset Hieu filius Namesse, &c.*	Luc. + **ἐν ἔτει δευτέρῳ τῆς Γοθολίας βασιλεύει κύριος τὸν Ἰοὺ υἱὸν Ναμεσί, κ.τ.λ.** (cf. *note ad loc.*).
11. 12. Goth. *dedit super eum sanctificationem.*	Luc. ἔδωκεν ἐπ' αὐτὸν **τὸ ἁγίασμα.**
11. 14. Goth. *et scidit Gotholia vestimentum suum.*	Luc. καὶ διέρρηξε **τὸ ἱματισμὸν αὐτῆς** Γοθολία.
13. 15. Goth. *Accipe sagittam et bolidas.*	Luc. Λαβὲ τόξον καὶ **βολίδας.**
13. 17. Vind. *et sagitta salutis in Israel.*	Luc. καὶ βέλος σωτηρίας ἐν **Ἰσραήλ.**
16. 18. Goth. *mesech sabbathorum.*	Luc. τὸν θεμέλιον τῆς καθέδρας **τῶν σαββάτων.**
17. 2. Goth. *Et fecit malignum in conspectu Domini prae omnibus qui fuerunt ante eum.*	Luc. καὶ ἐποίησε τὸ πονηρὸν ἐνώπιον κυρίου **παρὰ πάντας τοὺς γενομένους** ἔμπροσθεν αὐτοῦ.
17. 4. Goth. *Et invenit rex Assyriorum in Osee cogitationem adversus eum, et misit nuntios Adramelec Aegyptium inhabitantem in Aegypto, et erat ferens munera regi Assyriorum ab anno in annum.* Vind. *et misit nuntios at Adramelec Ethiopem habitantem in Aegypto, et offerebat Osee munera regi Assyriorum ab anno in annum.*	Luc. καὶ εὗρεν ὁ βασιλεὺς **Ἀσσυρίων** ἐν Ὡσῆε **ἐπιβουλήν,** δι' ὅτι ἀπέστειλεν ἀγγέλους πρὸς **Ἀδραμελὲχ τὸν Αἰθίοπα τὸν κατοικοῦντα** ἐν **Αἰγύπτῳ, καὶ ἦν** Ὡσῆε **φέρων δῶρα τῷ βασιλεῖ** Ἀσσυρίων **ἐνιαυτὸν κατ' ἐνιαυτόν.**

17. 4. Vind. *et iniuriam fecit ei rex Assyriorum.*	Luc. καὶ ὕβρισε τὸν Ὠσῆε ὁ βασιλεὺς Ἀσσυρίων.
18. 34. Goth. + *Ubi sunt dii terrae Samariae?*	Luc. + καὶ ποῦ εἰσὶν οἱ θεοὶ τῆς χώρας Σαμαρείας;
19. 7. Goth. *auditionem malignam.*	Luc. ἀγγελίαν πονηράν.
23. 11. Lucifer + *in domo domus, quam aedificauerunt reges Israel excelso illi Babal et omni militiae caeli.*	Luc. + ἐν τῷ οἴκῳ ᾧ ᾠκοδόμησαν βασιλεῖς Ἰσραὴλ ὑψηλὸν τῷ Βάαλ καὶ πάσῃ τῇ στρατιᾷ τοῦ οὐρανοῦ.

(*b*) The general characteristics of the Vulgate of the Old Testament have been dealt with by Nowack, *Die Bedeutung des Hieronymus für die alttestamentliche Textkritik* (Göttingen, 1875). Cf. also H. J. White in Hastings, *BD.* iv. pp. 883*f.* Jerome describes his method of translation in the introduction to his commentary on Ecclesiastes. He claims for his version a certain independence, as a direct translation from the original Hebrew; but states at the same time that he has kept fairly closely to the LXX where there is no great discrepancy between this version and the Hebrew, and confesses to having had before him and made use of the versions of Aquila, Symmachus, and Theodotion[1]. Instances from Kings of Jerome's employment of these later Greek versions may be noticed; and it will be seen that here, as in other books, the version of Symmachus seems to have been most frequently used as a model:—

I. 4. 13. לו חבל ארגב Σ. καὶ αὐτὸς εἶχε τὸ περίμετρον τοῦ Ἀργάβ, Vulg. *ipse praeerat in omni regione Argob.*

6. 8. בלולים Ἀ. (καὶ ἐν) κοχλίαις, Vulg. *per cochleam.*

9. 18. במדבר בארץ Ἀ., Σ. τὴν ἐν τῇ γῇ τῆς ἐρήμου, Vulg. *in terra solitudinis.*

10. 28. ומקוה Ἄλλος· καὶ ἐκ Κωά, Vulg. *et de Coa.*

[1] '. . ., hoc breuiter admonens, quod nullius auctoritatem secutus sum; sed de Hebraeo transferens, magis me Septuaginta interpretum consuetudini coaptaui: in his dumtaxat quae non multum ab Hebraicis discrepabant. Interdum Aquilae quoque et Symmachi et Theodotionis recordatus sum, ut nec nouitate nimia lectoris studium deterrerem, nec rursum contra conscientiam meam, fonte ueritatis omisso, opinionum riuulos consectarer.'

11. 36. למען היות ניר Σ. ὑπὲρ τοῦ διαμένειν λύχνον, Vulg. *ut remaneat lucerna.*

12. 7. ועניתם 'Α., Σ. καὶ εἴξεις αὐτοῖς, Vulg. *et petitioni eorum cesseris.*

16. 3. מבעיר אחרי בעשא Σ. τρυγήσω τὰ ὀπίσω (Βαασά), Vulg. *demetam posteriora Baasa.*

20. 12. בסכות 'Α. ἐν συσκιασμοῖς, Vulg. *in umbraculis.* Similarly in *v.* 16.

20. 38. באפר 'Α. ἐν σποδῷ, Σ. σποδῷ, Vulg. *aspersione pulveris.*

20. 40. כן משפטך אתה חרצת "Αλλος· τοῦτο τὸ κρίμα ὃ σὺ ἔτεμες, Vulg. *Hoc est iudicium tuum, quod ipse decreuisti.*

II. 3. 4. היה נקד Σ. ἦν τρέφων βοσκήματα, Vulg. *nutriebat pecora multa.*

4. 7. ושלמי את נשיכי Σ. καὶ ἀπόδος τῷ δανειστῇ σου, Vulg. *et redde creditori tuo.*

9. 11. ואת שיחו 'Α., Σ. καὶ τὴν ὁμιλίαν αὐτοῦ, Vulg. *et quid locutus est.*

11. 10. השלטים Σ. τὴν πανοπλίαν, Vulg. *arma.*

12. 6. והם יחזקו את בדק הבית לכל אשר ימצא שם בדק Σ. καὶ αὐτοὶ ἐπισκευασάτωσαν τὰ δέοντα τοῦ οἴκου, ὅπου ἂν εὑρεθῇ δεόμενον ἐπισκευῆς, Vulg. *et instaurent sarta tecta domus, si quid necessarium viderint instauratione.*

23. 12. וירץ משם 'Α. καὶ ἐδρόμωσεν ἀπὸ ἐκεῖθεν, Vulg. *et cucurrit inde.*

23. 24. הגללים 'Α. τὰ μορφώματα, Vulg. *figuras idolorum.*

The Hebrew text employed by Jerome seems to have been very similar to, though not identical with, MT.[1] His version possesses the characteristics of a good translation, and aims at giving the sense of the original rather than at extreme literality of rendering. Phrases and sentences are sometimes filled out in order to make their meaning clearer; cf. I. 2. 40 וילך שמעי ויבא את עבדיו מגת *ivitque ad Achis in Geth ad requirendum servos suos, et adduxit eos de Gath;* 3. 5 שאל מה אתן לך *Postula quod vis ut dem tibi;* 3. 13

[1] Cf. Nowack, *op. cit.* p. 55.

כל ימיך *cunctis retro diebus;* 6. 27 וכנפיהם *alae autem alterae;* 8. 24. כיום הזה *ut haec dies probat.* Occasionally, though not often, the translator goes astray in his desire for lucidity; cf. I. 1. 41[b] ויאמר מדוע קול קריה הומה *sed et Ioab, audita voce tubae, ait; 'Quid sibi &c.';* 16. 7 ועל אשר הכה אתו *ob hanc causam occidit eum, hoc est, Iehu filium Hanani, prophetam.*

§ 3. *The Synchronisms of the Compiler.*

The table on the following page exhibits a scheme of the synchronisms of R^D, as they appear in MT., LXX, and Luc. The upward pointing arrow ↑ indicates a discrepancy with a preceding calculation, the downward pointing arrow ↓ a discrepancy with a calculation following; while the double-headed arrow ↕ points to disagreement both with the preceding and following.

Examination of the three columns makes the fact plain that Luc. exhibits a different scheme of synchronism to MT. from Omri of Israel (I. 16. 23) down to Jehoram of Israel (I. 1. 17). This scheme conflicts with the synchronisms which go before and follow after, and which belong to the system of MT.; but, so far as it goes, is self-consistent, and is the cause of the placing of the narrative of Jehoshaphat's reign (MT. I. 22. 41 *ff.*) before that of Aḥab at the close of I. 16 in both Luc. and LXX, and of the substitution of Ὀχοζίας for יהושפט in the narrative of II. 3 in Luc. On the other hand, LXX, which agrees partly with Luc. and partly with MT., is clearly a patchwork of the two schemes. Two traces of the scheme of Luc. have crept into MT.; viz. in I. 16. 23, where the synchronism according to MT. scheme should be the 27th or 28th year of Asa; and in II. 1. 17, where the Lucianic synchronism co-exists with that of MT. in II. 3. 1. The other inconsistencies of MT. are probably for the most part due to textual corruption. Thus in II. 13. 10 the reading of 39th for 37th brings about agreement both with the preceding and following synchronisms; in II. 15. 1 the substitution of 14th for 27th removes

			MT.		LXX.		Luc.	
	Kingdom.	*King.*	*Length of reign.*	*Synchronism.*	*Length of reign.*	*Synchronism.*	*Length of reign.*	*Synchronism.*
I. 14. 20	I	Jeroboam	22	—	↓22	—	↓22	—
I. 14. 21	J	Reḥoboam	17	—	17	—	17	—
I. 15. 1	J	Abijah	3	18th of Jeroboam	6	18th of Jeroboam	6	18th of Jeroboam
I. 15. 9	J	Asa	41	20th of Jeroboam	41	↑24th of Jeroboam	41	↑24th of Jeroboam
I. 15. 25	I	Nadab	2	2nd of Asa	2	2nd of Asa	2	2nd of Asa
I. 15. 33	I	Baʿasha	24	3rd of Asa	24	3rd of Asa	24	3rd of Asa
I. 16. 8	I	Elah	2	26th of Asa	2	↑20th of Asa (*v.* 6)	2	↑20th of Asa (*v.* 6)
I. 16. 15	I	Zimri	—	27th of Asa	7	wanting	—	22nd of Asa
I. 16. 23	I	Omri	12	↕31st of Asa	12	↑31st of Asa	12	↑31st of Asa
I. 16. 29	I	Aḥab	22	38th of Asa	22	2nd of Jehoshaphat	22	2nd of Jehoshaphat
I. 22. 41	J	Jehoshaphat	25	4th of Aḥab	25	↓11th of Omri (16. 28 *f.*)	25	11th of Omri (16. 28 *f.*)
					25	4th of Aḥab		
I. 22. 52	I	Aḥaziah	2	17th of Jehoshaphat	2	17th of Jehoshaphat	2	24th of Jehoshaphat
II. 1. 17	I	Jehoram		↑2nd of Jehoram J	12	18th of Jehoshaphat	12	↓2nd of Jehoram J
II. 3. 1	”	”	12	18th of Jehoshaphat	12	18th of Jehoshaphat	12	
II. 8. 16	J	Jehoram	8	5th of Jehoram I	↓40	5th of Jehoram I	8	↑5th of Jehoram I
II. 8. 25	J	Aḥaziah	1	12th of Jehoram I	1	12th of Jehoram I	1	11th of Jehoram I
II. 9. 29	”	”		11th of Jehoram I		11th of Jehoram I	1	11th of Jehoram I
II. 10. 35	I	Jehu	28	—	28	—	28	—

II. 11. 3	J	Athaliah	6	—	6	—	6	—
II. 12. 2	J	Jehoash	40	7th of Jehu	40	7th of Jehu	40	7th of Jehu
II. 13. 1	I	Jehoaḥaz	17	23rd of Jehoash J	17	23rd of Jehoash J	17	23rd of Jehoash J
II. 13. 10	I	Jehoash	16	↕37th of Jehoash J	16	↕37th of Jehoash J	16	↕37th of Jehoash J
II. 14. 1	J	Amaziah	29	2nd of Jehoash I	29	2nd of Jehoash I	29	2nd of Jehoash I
II. 14. 23	I	Jeroboam	41	15th of Amaziah	41	15th of Amaziah	41	15th of Amaziah
II. 15. 1	J	Azariah	52	↕27th of Jeroboam	52	↕27th of Jeroboam	52	↕27th of Jeroboam
II. 15. 8	I	Zechariah	$\frac{1}{2}$	38th of Azariah	$\frac{1}{2}$	38th of Azariah	$\frac{1}{2}$	38th of Azariah
II. 15. 13	I	Shallum	$\frac{1}{12}$	39th of Azariah	—	39th of Azariah	$\frac{1}{12}$	39th of Azariah
II. 15. 17	I	Menaḥem	10	39th of Azariah	10	39th of Azariah	10	39th of Azariah
II. 15. 23	I	Pekaḥiah	2	50th of Azariah	2	50th of Azariah	↓10	50th of Azariah
II. 15. 27	I	Pekaḥ	20	52nd of Azariah	20	52nd of Azariah	20	52nd of Azariah
II. 15. 32	J	Jotham	16	2nd of Pekaḥ	16	2nd of Pekaḥ	16	2nd of Pekaḥ
II. 16. 1	J	Aḥaz	16	17th of Pekaḥ	16	17th of Pekaḥ	16	17th of Pekaḥ
II. 17. 1	I	Hoshea	9	↑12th of Aḥaz	9	↑12th of Aḥaz	9	↑12th of Aḥaz
II. 18. 1	J.	Ḥezekiah	29	3rd of Hoshea	29	3rd of Hoshea	29	3rd of Hoshea
II. 21. 1	J	Manasseh	55	—	55	—	55	—
II. 22. 1	J	Josiah	31	—	31	—	31	—
II. 23. 31	J	Jehoaḥaz	$\frac{1}{4}$	—	$\frac{1}{4}$	—	$\frac{1}{4}$	—
II. 23. 36	J	Jehoiakim	11	—	11	—	11	—
II. 24. 8	J	Jehoiachin	$\frac{1}{4}$	—	$\frac{1}{4}$	—	$\frac{1}{4}$	—
II. 24. 18	J	Zedekiah	11	—	11	—	11	—

the double inconsistency, if we make R^D assign 51 years to the reign of Jeroboam II in place of the 41 years of II. 14. 23. The 12th year of Aḥaz in II. 17. 1, which disagrees with preceding synchronisms, is in agreement with the ten years assigned to Pekaḥiah in Luc. II. 15. 23 in place of the two years of MT.; and thus may belong to a different scheme.

The inconsistencies of R^D's system of chronology, as compared with the chronology of the period as known to us from the Assyrian inscriptions, are conveniently stated in G. W. Wade's *Old Testament History*, pp. 319 *ff*.

LIST OF PRINCIPAL ABBREVIATIONS EMPLOYED.

'A. = Aquila's Greek Version, as cited in Field, *Origenis Hexaplorum quae supersunt*, and in F. C. Burkitt, *Fragments of the Books of Kings according to the translation of Aquila* (3 Kgs. 21 (20 MT.) 7–17; 4 Kgs. 23. 12–27), 1897.

AV. = Authorized Version.

Baed. = K. Baedeker, *Palestine and Syria*, 3rd edit., 1898.

Benz. = I. Benzinger, *Die Bücher der Könige*, 1899.

Ber. = E. Bertheau, *Die Bücher der Chronik*, 2e Aufl., 1873.

Bö. = F. Böttcher, *Neue exegetisch-kritische Aehrenlese zum A. T.* 2e *Abtheilung*, 1864.

Buhl, *Geogr.* = F. Buhl, *Geographie des alten Palästina*, 1896.

CIG. = *Corpus Inscriptionum Graecarum.*

CIS. = *Corpus Inscriptionum Semiticarum.*

Cod. A. = *Codex Alexandrinus* of the Septuagint.

COT. = E. Schrader, *The Cuneiform Inscriptions and the O. T.* (trans. from the 2nd German edit.), 1885.

D^2 = The Deuteronomic editor (in citations from Joshua and Judges).

DB.[2] or *BD.*[2] = *Dictionary of the Bible*, ed. by W. Smith, 2nd edit. of vol. i, 1893.

Dri. = S. R. Driver.

Authority = *Authority and Archaeology Sacred and Profane*, 1899.

Deut. = *A Critical and Exegetical Commentary on Deuteronomy* (Internat. Crit. Series), 1895.

LOT[6] = *An Introduction to the Literature of the O. T.*, 6th edit., 1897.

Sam. = *Notes on the Hebrew Text of the Books of Samuel*, 1890.

Tenses = *A Treatise on the Use of the Tenses in Hebrew*, 3rd edit., 1892.

E = The Elohistic document in the Hexateuch.

Encyc. Bibl. = *Encyclopaedia Biblica*, ed. by T. K. Cheyne and J. Sutherland Black, 1899 *ff.*

Ew. = H. Ewald, *History of Israel*, vols. iii and iv, 1871.

Ew. § = H. Ewald, *Syntax of the Hebrew Language of the O. T.* (trans. from the 8th German edit.), 1881.

Field=F. Field, *Origenis Hexaplorum quae supersunt; sive veterum interpretum Graecorum in totum V. T. fragmenta*, 1875.

Ges. or Ges. *Thes.* = W. Gesenius, *Thesaurus linguae Hebraeae*, 1829.

Ges.-Buhl = *W. Gesenius' Heb. und Aram. Handwörterbuch über das A. T.*, bearbeitet von F. Buhl, 13e Aufl., 1899.

G-K. = *Gesenius' Hebrew Grammar, as edited and enlarged by E. Kautzsch* (trans. from the 26th German edit. by A. E. Cowley, 1898).

Grä. = H. Grätz, *Geschichte der Israeliten*, 1875.

H = The code known as 'the Law of Holiness' in Leviticus.

Hastings, *BD.* = *Dictionary of the Bible*, ed. by J. Hastings, 1898–1902.

Heb. Lex. Oxf. = *A Heb. and Eng. Lexicon of the O. T., based on the Lexicon of Gesenius as translated by E. Robinson*, ed. by F. Brown, S. R. Driver, and C. A. Briggs, Oxford, 1892 *ff.*

Hoo. = I. Hooykaas, *Iets over de grieksche vertaling van het Oude Testament*, 1888.

J = The Jahvistic document in the Hexateuch.

JE = The work of the compiler of the documents J and E in the Hexateuch.

Jos. = *Flavii Iosephi Opera*, recognovit B. Niese, 1888.

Kamp. = A. Kamphausen, *Die Bücher der Könige*, in E. Kautzsch's *Die Heilige Schrift des A. T.*, 1894.

*KAT.*³ = *Die Keilinschriften und das A. T.*, von E. Schrader, 3e Aufl. neu bearbeitet von H. Zimmern und H. Winckler, 1e Hälfte, 1902.

Kau. = E. Kautzsch, *Abriss der Geschichte des alttest. Schrifttums*, in *Die Heilige Schrift des A. T.*, 1894.

KB. = *Keilinschriftliche Bibliothek*, Bde 1, 2, 1889–1890.

Ke. = C. F. Keil, *Die Bücher der Könige*, 2e Aufl., 1876.
Kit. = R. Kittel, *Die Bücher der Könige*, 1900.
Kit. *Hist.* = R. Kittel, *A History of the Hebrews*, vol. ii, trans., 1896.
Klo. = A. Klostermann, *Die Bücher Samuelis und der Könige*, 1887.
Kö. = F. E. König.

Lehrg. = *Hist.-krit. Lehrgebäude der Heb. Sprache:* 1e Hälfte, 1881; 2e Hälfte, 1er Theil, 1895.

Syntax = *Hist.-compar. Syntax der Heb. Sprache*, 1897.

Kue. = A. Kuenen.

Ond. = *Hist.-krit. Onderzoek*, 2nd edit., 1887 (German trans., 1890).

Hex. = *The Origin and Composition of the Hexateuch* (trans. of part 1 of the preceding), 1886.

Luc. = Lucian's recension of the Septuagint as edited by P. Lagarde (*Librorum V. T. canonicorum pars prior*, 1883).
LXX = Cod. B of the Septuagint according to the text of H. B. Swete (*The O. T. in Greek according to the Septuagint*, vol. i, 1887).
Maspero = G. Maspero, *Histoire ancienne des peuples de l'Orient classique*, 3 vols., 1895–1899.
MT. = Massoretic Text (D. Ginsburg, 1894; Baer and Delitzsch, 1895).
Oort = *Textus Hebraici emendationes quibus in V. T. neerlandice vertendo usi sunt A. Kuenen, I. Hooykaas, W. H. Kosters, H. Oort*, edidit H. Oort, 1900.
P = The Priestly Code in the Hexateuch.
PEF. = *Palestine Exploration Fund.*

Mem. = *Memoirs.*

Qy. St. = *Quarterly Statement.*

Pesh. = Peshiṭto (ed. Lee).
R^D = The Deuteronomic Redactor of Kings (cf. pp. ix *ff.*).
R^{D2} = Later Deuteronomic Editors of Kings (cf. p. xviii).
R^P = The Priestly Redactor (or Redactors) of Kings (cf. p. xix).
Rob. *BR.* = E. Robinson, *Biblical Researches in Palestine and the adjacent Regions*, 3rd edit., 3 vols., 1867.

Rost = P. Rost, *Die Keilschrifttexte Tiglat-Pilesers III*, 1893.

R. Sm. = W. Robertson Smith.

OTJC^2 = *The Old Testament in the Jewish Church*, 2nd edit., 1892.

Rel. Sem.^{2} = *The Religion of the Semites*, 2nd edit., 1894.

RV. = Revised Version.

Σ. = Symmachus' Greek Version, as cited in Field, *Origenis Hexaplorum quae supersunt.*

Sieg. u. Sta. = C. Siegfried und B. Stade, *Hebräisches Wörterbuch zum A. T.*, 1893.

Smith, *Hist. Geogr.* = G. A. Smith, *The Historical Geography of the Holy Land*, 1894.

Sta. = B. Stade, various articles on the text of Kings in *ZATW.*

Sta. § = B. Stade, *Lehrbuch der Hebräischen Grammatik*, 1er Theil, 1875.

Stanley, *SP.* = A. P. Stanley, *Sinai and Palestine in Connection with their History*, new edit., 1883.

Θ. = Theodotion's Greek version, as cited in Field, *Origenis Hexaplorum quae supersunt.*

Targ. = The Targum of Jonathan (ed. Lagarde).

Th. = O. Thenius, *Die Bücher der Könige*, 2^e Aufl., 1873.

Vet. Lat. = The Old Latin Version.

Vulg. = The Vulgate.

Wellh. *C.* = J. Wellhausen, *Die Composition des Hexateuchs und der historischen Bücher des A. T.*, 1889.

ZA. = *Zeitschrift für Assyriologie.*

ZATW. = *Zeitschrift für die alttest. Wissenschaft.*

al. = *et aliter*, ‘and elsewhere.’

וג׳ = וְגוֹמֵר = ‘&c.’

פ׳ = פְּלֹנִי = ‘such a one (unnamed).’

† indicates that all occurrences in O. T. of a particular word or phrase have been cited.

NOTES

ON

THE BOOKS OF KINGS

I. 1. 1–2. 46. *Close of the history of David. Establishment of Solomon as his successor*[1].

1. 1. בא בימים] A regular idiom. Lit. '*entered into days*,' just as we should say, *advanced in years*. So Gen. 18. 11; 24. 1; Josh. 13. 1; 23. 1, 2 †.

בַּבְּגָדִים] 'With *the* clothes,' which are immediately suggested to the reader by the previous ויכסהו. This use of the article with well-known objects is very common in Heb., and imparts a peculiar vividness to the narrative. Cf. *v.* 39 בַּשּׁוֹפָר, אֶת־קֶרֶן הַשֶּׁמֶן; *ch.* 17. 10 בַּכְּלִי 'in *the* vessel,' almost, 'in *your* vessel,' *v.* 12 בַּכַּד 'in *the* jar,' used in every household for the purpose specified; II. 8. 15; 1 Sam. 10. 25; 18. 10; *al.* Da. § 21[d].

ולא יחם לו] The imperfect expresses the habitual character of the king's condition: 'he *was not*,' or, '*used not to be* warm.' This usage is somewhat rare in prose: cf. *ch.* 8. 8 וְלֹא יֵרָאוּ הַחוּצָה; Gen. 2. 25 וְלֹא יִתְבֹּשָׁשׁוּ; 1 Sam. 1. 7[b] וְלֹא תֹאכַל; 2. 25[b] וְלֹא יִשְׁמְעוּ. Dri. *Tenses*, §§ 30, 42 β, 85 *Obs.*

2. אדני המלך] A ceremonious form of address which is almost constant. המלך אדני 2 Sam. 14. 15† (cf. המ׳ אדניך 1 Sam. 26. 15†). המלך alone is comparatively rare.

---

[1] This section forms the continuation of 2 Sam. *chh.* 9–20, and is probably by the same author. See Dri. *LOT.* 179, and especially Wellh. *C.* 260.

נערה בתולה] A common form of apposition, the second substantive defining more closely the meaning of the first. Cf. *ch.* 3. 16 נָשִׁים זֹנוֹת; *ch.* 7. 14 אִשָּׁה אַלְמָנָה; Deut. 22. 28; Gen. 21. 20 רֹבֶה קַשָּׁת; Isa. 23. 12 הַמְעֻשָּׁקָה בְּתוּלַת וגו׳; *al.* G-K. § 131, 2[a]; Ew. § 287[e] ([b]): Da. § 29[b].

ועמדה] 'And let her stand.' Imperf. with ו *consec.* the continuation of the cohortative יבקשו. Dri. *Tenses,* § 113, 2; Da. § 55[a] The phrase עמד לפני is used idiomatically of those who were in constant attendance upon a superior: cf. *ch.* 10. 8; 12. 8 (|| 2 Chr. 10. 6); Jer. 52. 12; Deut. 1. 38. Of the service of יהוה, *ch.* 17. 1; Ezek. 44. 15; Judg. 20. 28; *al.*

סכנת] 'Attendant,' 'care-taker'; in the masc. סֹכֵן Isa. 22. 15 as a title of Shebna the superintendent of the palace, and also, it seems, in a Phoenician inscription from Lebanon belonging probably to the eighth century B.C., of a guardian or governor of a city, סכן קרתחדשת עבד חרם מלך צדנם 'Soken of the New City, servant of Ḥiram, king of the Sidonians,' *CIS.* I. i. 5.

The word—unless Cheyne is right in connecting it (*Isaiah.* ii. 153) with the Assyrian *šaknu,* 'a high officer,' from *šakin,* 'to set up, place'—will be derived from סכן which in the Hiph'il means to *deal familiarly with;* Num. 22. 30 הַהַסְכֵּן הִסְכַּנְתִּי לַעֲשׂוֹת 'Did I ever deal familiarly to do?' i.e. 'was I ever wont to do?' Ps. 139. 3 כָּל־דְּרָכַי הִסְכַּנְתָּה 'With all my ways thou art familiar'; Job 22. 21 הַסְכֶּן־נָא עִמּוֹ 'Become familiar with him.'

Pesh. ܡܫܡܫܢܝܬܐ 'serving'; LXX, Vulg. more freely θάλπουσα, foveat; Targ. קריבא '*near* to him.'

בחיקך] So Pesh., Θ., 'Ο 'Εβραῖος (Syro-Hex. ܥ. ܠ. ܒܥܘܒܟܝ), Targ. (לותך); בחיקו LXX, Luc., Vulg. There is no reason for doubting the originality of MT. Such a change from 3rd to 2nd pers. is quite in accordance with Hebrew usage in cases in which a superior is addressed. Cf. 1 Sam. 25. 28 כִּי־מִלְחֲמוֹת יְהוָה אֲדֹנִי נִלְחָם וְרָעָה לֹא־תִמָּצֵא בְךָ מִיָּמֶיךָ; 22. 15; *al.*

3. השונמית] Vulg. *Sunamitidem,* Targ. דמן שונם, LXX, Luc. Σωμανῖτιν, Pesh. ܫܠܘܡܝܬܐ. The title השונמית is also applied (II. 4. 12, &c.) to Elisha's hostess at Shunem. הַשּׁוּלַמִּית, Song 7. 1,

is usually thought to be a variation; cf. rendering of Pesh., and modern name of the village.

שׁוּנֵם was one of the cities assigned to the tribe of Issachar, Josh. 19. 18; 1 Sam. 28. 4 it is mentioned as the place where the Philistines encamped, near to the Israelite encampment at גִּלְבֹּעַ, and also to עֵין דּוֹר *v.* 7; II. 4. 8†, a city visited by Elisha, not very far from Mt. Carmel, *v.* 25. The site appears to have been that of the modern *Solam*, a village on the south-west slope of the *Jebel Nebi Dahi* (called 'little Hermon'), about five miles north of *Jebel Fuk'ua* (Mt. Gilboa), and three miles north of *Zer'in* (Jezreel). Cf. Rob. *BR.* ii. 324; Stanley, *SP.* 344; Baed. 243.

4. יפה] So LXX, Vulg., Targ.; יְפַת מַרְאֶה Luc., Pesh. Though יְפַת תֹּאַר, יְפַת מַרְאֶה are common expressions, yet יפה used absolutely is still more frequent. MT. may therefore be retained.

5. מתנשא] The participle expresses the *continuous* development of Adonijah's plans, Dri. *Tenses*, § 135, 1. A single event of brief duration, such as the open declaration of his claims, would have been represented by the perf., or by the imperf. with ו *consec.*

ויעש] 'He made,' i.e. '*instituted.*' For this use of עשה, cf. 2 Sam. 15. 1 וַיַּעַשׂ לוֹ אַבְשָׁלוֹם מֶרְכָּבָה וג׳.

רצים לפניו] The usual bodyguard of a king. Cf 1 Sam. 22. 17; *ch.* 14. 28; II. 11. 4; *al.*

6. ולא עצבו] 'Had not *grieved* him.' עצב means *to hurt*, either bodily, Eccl. 10. 9 מַסִּיעַ אֲבָנִים יֵעָצֵב בָּהֶם, or mentally, Isa. 54. 6 עֲצוּבַת רוּחַ; 2 Sam. 19. 3, such mental pain sometimes culminating in *anger*, as seems to be the case here and in 1 Sam. 20. 3, 34; Gen. 34. 7. LXX καὶ οὐκ ἀπεκώλυσεν αὐτόν seems to presuppose וְלֹא עֲצָרוֹ 'had not *held him back*'; cf. 18. 44. So Klo. Against this reading is the following עשית which, as used of a past event, is opposed to the notion of holding back *before* an action. The other Verss. give the sense 'reprove,' and seem to be guessing from the context; Luc. καὶ οὐκ ἐπετίμησεν αὐτῷ, Vulg. *nec corripuit eum*, Pesh. ܘܠܐ ܟܐܐ ܒܗ, Targ. ולא אכלימה.

מימיו] '*Out of* his days'; i.e. at any time during the whole course of his life. An idiomatic expression; cf. 1 Sam. 25. 28

B 2

וְרָעָה לֹא־תִמָּצֵא בְךָ מִיָּמֶיךָ; Job 38. 12† הֲמִיָּמֶיךָ צִוִּיתָ בֹּקֶר[1]. '*Ever,*' as used in English, will be found to fit each of these cases.

ואתו ילדה אחרי אבשלום] The object, as being the interesting member of the sentence, is brought to the beginning and receives a slight emphasis. This is not uncommon. Cf. 1 Sam. 15. 1 אתי שלח יהוה; 25. 43; *ch.* 14. 11; *al.* Dri. *Tenses*, § 208, 1.

ילדה] '*One* bore.' A semi-impersonal use of the verb; *sc.* הַיֹּלֶדֶת. RV., by accommodation to Eng. idiom, substitutes a pass.; '*He was born.*' Cf. *ch.* 14. 10 כַּאֲשֶׁר יְבַעֵר הַגָּלָל 'as *one* sweeps away dung,' or, 'as dung is swept away'; *ch.* 22. 38 וַיִּשְׁטֹף; *al.* The assumed cognate participle as subj. is sometimes actually expressed; Deut. 22. 8; Isa. 28. 4. Ew. § 294^b, Da. § 108, *Rem.* 1. Klo.'s emendation וְאִשְׁתּוֹ יָלְדָה אֲחוֹת אַבְשָׁלוֹם is quite unnecessary.

7. ויהיו דבריו עם יואב] 'And his words (i.e. *negotiations*) were with Joab.' The idiom is similar to 2 Sam. 3. 17 ודבר אבנר היה עם זקני ישראל; cf. Judg. 18. 7, 28 ודבר אין להם עם אדם.

ויעזרו אחרי אדניה] A pregnant construction; RV. 'and they following Adonijah helped him.' Cf. Deut. 12. 30 השמר לך פן תנקש אחריהם; 1 Sam. 7. 2 וַיִּנָּהוּ אחרי י׳ 'went mourning after'; Ruth 2. 3 ותלקט אחרי; *ch.* 14. 10 ובערתי אחרי; 16. 3 מבעיר אחרי; Jer. 50. 21 החרם אחרי; Lev. 26. 33 והריקתי אחריכם חרב; Ezek. 5. 2, 12; 12. 14; Deut. 1. 36, *al.* מִלֵּא אחרי.

8. שמעי ורעי] These persons are not mentioned elsewhere as holding positions of importance about the court of David or Solomon. Neither שמעי, one of the twelve officers who provided victuals for Solomon's household (*ch.* 4. 18), nor שמעי the Benjamite of Gera seems to have been of sufficient importance to satisfy the mention in this passage; and the name רעי occurs nowhere else. Hence, the text is probably corrupt. Among suggested emendations, the most worthy of notice is that of Klo. who follows Luc. *καὶ Σαμαίας καὶ οἱ ἑταῖροι αὐτοῦ*, i.e. ושמעיה וְרֵעָיו, so far as regards the

[1] Job 27. 6 לֹא־יֶחֱרַף לְבָבִי מִיָּמָי is similar if with RV. we supply an object '*me*' to יחרף; 'my heart shall never reproach me.' But more obviously the object is found in מימי; 'my heart shall not reproach *any one of* my days.'

second word, and emends the first וּשלמה. This suggestion וּשְׁלֹמֹה וְרֵעָיו is to some extent supported by the enumeration in *v.* 10, and would imply that the other princes *did* side with Adonijah, as seems to have been the case from *v.* 19 ויקרא לכל בני המלך. Th.'s emendation וְחוּשַׁי רֵעֶה דָוִד, derived partly from Jos.'s explanation of ורעי as ὁ Δαυίδου φίλος, is plausible. LXX, Vulg., Pesh., Targ. agree with MT.

הגבורים] David's army of picked warriors; 2 Sam. 10. 7; 16. 6; 20. 7; 1 Chr. 19. 8; 28. 1; 29. 24; Song 4. 4. The names of the principal men among them are given in 2 Sam. 23. 8–39; || 1 Chr. 11. 11–47.

אשר לדוד] This construction takes the place of the *stat. constr.* because הַגִּבּוֹרִים (with the article) was the regular title for the army mentioned, and is regarded almost as a proper name, Da. § 28, *Rem.* 5[3]. Such a method of avoiding the *stat. constr.* is especially frequent with proper names; Judg. 18. 28; 19. 14 הַגִּבְעָה אֲשֶׁר לְבִנְיָמִן; *ch.* 15. 27; 17. 9; *al.*

9. עם אבן הזחלת] An idiomatic use of עם; '*by*' or '*close to.*' Cf. Gen. 35. 4 האלה אשר עם שכם; Josh. 7. 2; Judg. 18. 3; 19. 11; 2 Sam. 20. 8; *al.*

הזחלת] 'The serpent'; so called from *crawling;* Deut. 32. 24 זֹחֲלֵי עָפָר; Mic. 7. 17†. This root corresponds to Ar. زحل *to withdraw, lag behind,* and is quite distinct from זחלתי Job 32. 6 = Ar. ذحل = Aram. ܕܚܠ *to fear.* Wellh. (*Reste Arab. Heidentums*, 2e Ausg. 146) compares הזחלת with the Ar. name of Saturn, *Zuḥal*, i.e. (Lane, *Lex.*, 1220) *he who withdraws*, the planet being so named because it is remote, and said to be in the Seventh Heaven.

עין רגל] Pesh. ܥܝܢ ܩܨܪܐ, Targ. עין קצרא, i.e. *spring of the fuller*, רגל being used of *treading* linen with the feet. Mentioned as one of the landmarks upon the boundary line between Judah, Josh. 15. 7, and Benjamin, Josh. 18. 16; during Absalom's rebellion the hiding-place of Jonathan and Ahimaaz whilst awaiting news from Jerusalem, 2 Sam. 17. 17†. The spring has with great probability been identified with the modern 'Fountain of the Virgin,' called '*Ain Umm ed-Deraj*, i.e. 'spring of the mother of steps,' the source which supplies the pool of Siloam. Opposite the fountain there is a rough flight of stone steps leading up the rock to the village of Siloam, and called by the fellahîn *Ez-Zehweileh*, i.e. זחלת. See *PEF. Qy. St.*, 1869–70, p. 253; *DB*². i. 943 *f.*

11. ויאמר נתן . . . לאמר] Luc. *καὶ ἦλθε Ναθὰν πρὸς Βηρσάβεε μητέρα Σολομῶντος καὶ εἶπεν*, i.e. וַיֵּלֶךְ נָתָן . . . וַיֹּאמַר. This is rather preferable to MT., as being less abrupt. So Klo.

12. איעצך . . . ומלטי] 'Let me counsel thee . . . and save thou,' equivalent to 'Let me counsel thee . . . *that thou mayest save*.' The Imperative with ו, ומלטי, stands in place of the usual cohortative with weak ו, expressing with greater force the *purpose* of the action described by the previous verb. Cf. Gen. 12. 2 אעשך לגוי גדול . . . וֶהְיֵה ברכה; 20. 7; 2 Sam. 21. 3; II. 5. 10; *al.* See Dri. *Tenses*, § 65; Ew. § 347ᵃ; G-K. § 110, 2ᵇ; Da. § 65ᵈ.

13. כי] Like *ὅτι recitativum*, introducing the direct narration. Cf. *ch.* 11. 22 ויאמר לו פרעה כי מה אתה חסר עמי; 20. 5; 21. 6; II. 8. 13; Gen. 29. 32, 33; 1 Sam. 2. 16; 10. 19; *al.* Inverted commas are the equivalent in English. RV. rendering 'assuredly,' is not to be followed. Cases like Gen. 18. 20 זעקת סדם ועמרה כי רבה 'the cry on account of Sodom and Gomorrah is *verily* great'; Ps. 118. 10, 11, 12 בשם יהוה כי אמילם 'in the name of Yahweh I will *surely* cut them off,' where כי is joined closely to the verb, are quite different.

14. עודך מדברת . . . ואני אבוא] The two clauses are placed in parallelism, and thus their co-ordination in time is marked with as great vividness as is possible. Cf. *vv.* 22, 42; II. 6. 33 עודנו מדבר עמם והנה המלאך ירד אליו; Gen. 29. 9; *al.* Without עוד in the first clause, *ch.* 14. 17; II. 2. 23; 4. 5; *al.* Dri. *Tenses*, §§ 166–169; G-K. § 116, 5, *Rem.* 4; Da. § 141.

ומלאתי את דבריך] Lit. 'I will *fill up* thy words,' i.e. give them the confirmation of my testimony; so, 'I will *confirm* thy words.' Elsewhere, מלא דבר means to *fulfil a prediction* by subsequent actions; *ch.* 2. 27; 2 Chr. 26. 21.

15. מְשָׁרַת] A contraction or corruption of מְשָׁרֶתֶת.

18. ועתה אדני המלך וג׳] Read וְאַתָּה for ועתה with LXX, Luc., Vulg., Pesh., Targ., and some 200 Codd. So Th., Klo., Kamp.

The pronoun is necessary to mark and emphasize the change of subject in clause *b*, in contrast to the subject of clause *a*, אדניה.

20. ואתה אדני המלך] So LXX, Pesh.; but read וְעַתָּה for ואתה with Targ. and many Codd. So Th. ועתה is employed to summarize the conclusion of all that has gone before. Bathsheba draws together the threads of her speech, and explains why she has brought the state of affairs under the king's notice. This use of ועתה is very common. Cf. e.g. 1 Sam. 25. 26, 27; Gen. 3. 22; *ch.* 2. 9; 8. 25. Klo.'s violent emendation is quite unnecessary.

עיני ... עליך] Expressing concentration of attention. Cf. 2 Chr. 20. 12 כי עליך עינינו; Jer. 22. 17 כי אין עיניך ולבך כי אם על בצעך.

22. עודנה וג׳] Cf. *v.* 14 *note.*

24. אתה אמרת וג׳] The interrogation is indicated by the tone in which the words are spoken. Cf. *ch.* 21. 7 אתה עתה תעשה מלוכה על ישראל; II. 5. 26; 9. 19; 1 Sam. 11. 12; 21. 16; 22. 7; Gen. 27. 24; *al.* G-K. § 150, 1; Da. § 121.

25. ולשרי הצבא] So LXX, Vulg., Pesh., Targ.; but Luc. *καὶ τὸν ἀρχιστράτηγον* 'Ιωάβ, i.e. וּלְיוֹאָב שַׂר הַצָּבָא (as in *v.* 19; cf. *v.* 7; *ch.* 2. 22), is to be followed. So Hoo. Against MT. it is improbable (i) that Nathan should have omitted express mention of Joab, and (ii) that he should have made an assertion, ולשרי הצבא, which would at the moment seem to implicate Benaiah, who next to Joab was one of David's principal generals.

26. לי אני] For the re-enforcement of the suffix pronoun by the personal pronoun, cf. 1 Sam. 19. 23 עליו גם הוא; 25. 24 בי אני אדני העון; Hag. 1. 4 העת לכם אתם לשבת וג׳. G-K. § 135, 2c; Ew. § 311a; Da. § 1.

עבדך] Luc. *τὸν υἱόν σου*, i.e. בִּנְךָ. So Klo., Hoo., correctly. MT. seems to have been altered after *v.* 19. As Klo. notices, the title of submission, appropriate in the mouth of Bathsheba when speaking of her son, is out of place as coming from Nathan.

27. אם] Infrequent in single direct questions. When so employed it is usually equivalent to *num?* Judg. 5. 8 מָגֵן אִם־יֵרָאֶה וָרֹמַח; Am. 3. 6; Isa. 29. 16; Jer. 48. 27; Job 6. 12; 39. 13. In Gen. 38. 17 אִם־תִּתֵּן עֵרָבוֹן עַד שָׁלְחֶךָ it represents *An?* Da. § 112 *end.*

מֵאֵת] *From proximity with*, used to express *origin from;* a more idiomatic expression than the simple מן. מאת is very usual when יהוה is the source named. See instances cited on 2. 15.

נהיה] 'Has been brought about.' Cf. 12. 24; ‖ 2 Chr. 11. 4 כי מאתי נהיה הדבר הזה.

28. קראו לי] לי *Dativus commodi*. Cf. II. 4. 24 אַל־תַּעֲצָר־לִי לִרְכֹּב; 2 Sam. 18. 5 לְאַט־לִי; Judg. 16. 9.

ותבא לפני המלך ותעמד לפני המלך] So Targ. LXX, Vulg. presuppose ותבא לפני המלך ותעמד לפניו; Pesh. ותבא לפניו ותעמד לפני המלך; Luc. ותבא ותעמד לפני המלך. The unnaturalness of Pesh., לפניו preceding לפני המלך instead of *vice versâ*, and its disagreement with LXX, Vulg., point to the probability of all three being attempts to mend the tautology of MT. This repetition is no doubt due to a mistake of the scribe's eye, ותעמד being first omitted, and then added at the end with a repetition of the words which properly followed it. Thus we may, with Klo., Hoo., adopt the reading of Luc. Th. favours that of LXX, Vulg.

29. אשר פדה וג׳] So exactly 2 Sam. 4. 9.

30. כי כאשר . . . כי כן] The first כי introduces the subject of the oath; cf. 2. 24; 18. 15; *al.;* the second כי resumes the first כי after the long intervening clause. Cf. 1 Sam. 14. 39 חי יהוה . . . כי אם ישנו ביונתן בני כי מות ימות; 25. 34; 2 Sam. 3. 9; Jer. 22. 24; Gen. 22. 16, 17.

33. הפרדה אשר לי] '*Mine own* mule'; more emphatic than פִּרְדָּתִי. Cf. 1 Sam. 25. 7 הרעים אשר לך '*thy* shepherds,' emphasized in view of the claim which follows; 2 Sam. 14. 31 את החלקה אשר לי '*my* field,' in contrast to the suffix of עבדיך. Da. § 28, *Rem.* 5[5]. Notice the difference between this class of examples of the construction אשר ל, and that noticed upon *v.* 8. While *here* the emphasis is upon the possessive pronoun, *there* it falls upon the strict definition of the substantive.

אל גחון] Some MSS. כתיב על, קרי אל. See *v.* 38.

גחון] Pesh. ܫܠܘܚܐ, Targ. שילוחא (here and in *vv.* 38, 45) identify with the pool of Shiloaḥ or Siloam; and this is favoured by 2 Chr. 33. 14, where it is stated that Manasseh built an outer wall to the city of David on the west side of *Giḥon in the ravine*, the נחל referred to being probably that of the קִדְרוֹן. The topography of מוצא מימי גיחון העליון is a much disputed subject. See *DB*². i. 1186.

35. נגיד] Lit. *one placed in the fore front*, so '*leader*.' The word in early Hebrew is characteristic of the more elevated style, and is frequent in Sam., Ki., especially in prophetical utterances. 1 Sam. 9. 16; 10. 1; 13. 14; 25. 30; 2 Sam. 5. 2; 6. 21; 7. 8; *ch.* 14. 7; 16. 2; II. 20. 5.

36. אמן כן יאמר י׳ וג׳] So Vulg., 'A., Σ., and substantially Targ. אמן כן תהי רעוא מן קדם יי. Pesh. ܐܡܝܢ ܘܗܟܢܐ ܢܥܒܕ ܡܪܝܐ ܐܠܗܟ; 2 Codd. Kennicott and 1 de Rossi כֵּן יַעֲשֶׂה. Cf. Jer. 28. 6. LXX Γένοιτο οὕτως· πιστώσαι ὁ Θεὸς τοῦ κυρίου μου τοῦ βασιλέως. Luc. Γένοιτο οὕτως· πιστώσαι ὁ Θεὸς τοὺς λόγους τοῦ κυρίου μου τοῦ βασιλέως· οὕτως εἶπε Κύριος ὁ Θεός σου, κύριέ μου βασιλεῦ. A double rendering. Pesh. ܢܥܒܕ is almost certainly a paraphrase of the somewhat harsh expression of MT. LXX, Luc. must have read יַאֲמֵן for יאמר, and then probably added the necessary object את דברי. Klo. follows this, emending אָמֵן כֵּן יַאֲמֵן יְהוָה אֱלֹהֶיךָ אֶת־דִּבְרֵי אֲדֹנִי הַמֶּלֶךְ; and so Hoo. But to say אמן '*true*,' i.e. '*may it come true*,' and then to continue כן יאמן וג׳, is mere tautology. There is no reason for the rejection of MT.

37. יִהְיֶ] Read יהי Kt. with LXX, Vulg.

38. הכרתי והפלתי] David's bodyguard, doubtless composed of foreigners, mentioned only during his reign; *v.* 44; 2 Sam. 8. 18 (‖ 1 Chr. 18. 17); 15. 18; 20. 7, 23 (Q're). The names are *gentilic* in formation; G-K. § 86, 2, *Rem.* 5. In 1 Sam. 30 הכרתי are connected with the Philistines; cf. *v.* 14 with *v.* 16; and this is also the case with כְּרֵתִים which occurs Ezek. 25. 16; Zeph. 2. 5†. This latter is rendered Κρῆτες by LXX, and hence it is thought that כַּפְתּוֹר, from which the Philistines are said (Am. 9. 7; Deut. 2. 23; cf. Jer. 47. 4) to have emigrated, denotes Crete[1]. פלתי has been

[1] Sayce, following Ebers, formerly identified כפתור with the Egyptian *Kaft-ur* or 'greater Phoenicia,' i.e. the coast-land of the Delta (*The Higher Criticism*, 136), but has now abandoned this view (*Academy*, April 14, 1894, p. 314).

supposed, though without ground from analogy, to be a contraction of פלשתי. Th.'s objection to the view that the כרתי ופלתי were foreigners, on the score that David, who was so patriotic and devoted to the worship of the only God, would not have surrounded himself with a foreign bodyguard, will not hold good, in view of the important positions occupied by Uriah the Hittite 2 Sam. 11. 15, and by Ittai the Gittite 2 Sam. 18. 2.

על גחון] In *v.* 33 the better reading is אל גחון. There are many scattered instances of על used in place of אל after a verb of motion; *ch.* 20. 43 (21. 4 אל); 22. 6 (|| 2 Chr. 18. 5 אל); 1 Sam. 2. 11; 2 Sam. 15. 20; Mic. 4. 1 (|| Isa. 2. 2 אל); Isa. 22. 15 (אל . . . על); 66. 20 (56. 7 אל); Ezek. 1. 20 (*v.* 12 אל); 44. 13 (אל . . . על . . . אל); Jer. 1. 7; 31. 11 (אל . . . על); 36. 12; *al.*

40. מְחַלְּלִים בַּחֲלִלִים] So Vulg., and second rendering of Luc.; (Vet. Lat. second rendering *organizantes in organis;* Pesh. ܘܢܩܫܝܢ ܒܨܠܨܠܐ 'were striking sistra'). LXX, and first rendering of Luc. *ἐχόρευον ἐν χορεῖς*. So perhaps Targ. משבחין בחנגיא[1]. Vet. Lat. first rendering *cantabat canticis et melodiis*. Ew., following LXX, reads מְחֹלְלִים בִּחִילִים on the ground that it is unlikely that 'all the people' would be able to play flutes. But, as Th. remarks, the form חילים never occurs (always מְחֹלוֹת), and *round dances*, which would be denoted by חלל, would be unsuitable in a hasty procession. To this we may add the consideration that the stress seems to be laid upon the *noise* which was made; ותבקע הארץ בקולם. Klo.'s emendation הֹלְכִים בַּחֲלִלִים (cf. Isa. 30. 29) is unnecessary. A denom. חִלֵּל = 'to play the flute' may well be formed from חָלִיל.

ותבקע וג׳] The sound of the shouting is compared to the deep rumbling produced by the splitting of the ground during an earthquake. In Num. 16. 31 the phrase וַתִּבָּקַע הָאֲדָמָה is used of an earthquake phenomenon. Th.'s objection to MT. is insufficient.

---

[1] But חנגא *may* have the meaning 'musical instrument'; *Pesachim* 111[b] תלו חנגא בגויה 'they hung a harp in the hollow of the tree'; Targ. Jerus. on Ex. 32. 19 וחנגין בידיהון דרש׳ 'and harp in the hands of the sinners'; Targ. Ps. 5. 1 לשבחא על חננין = Heb. למנצח אל הנחילות. See Levy or Jastrow, s. v. *Studia Biblica*, ii. p. 34.

41. והם כלו וג׳] ‘They *having finished* eating’; a circumstantial clause with the personal pronoun standing as subject. So very frequently; II. 5. 18 והוא נשען על ידי ‘he leaning on my hand’; Gen. 15. 2; 18. 8; *al.* Dri. *Tenses*, § 160.

מדוע קול הקריה הומה] ‘Wherefore is there the sound of the city in tumult?’ So Vulg., excellently, *Quid sibi vult clamor civitatis tumultuantis?* הומה is properly an accus. of *state*, and forms a kind of secondary predicate. Cf. *ch.* 14. 6 קוֹל רַגְלֶיהָ בָּאָה בַפֶּתַח (באה of course referring to the suffix of רגליה); Song 5. 2 קול דודי דופק; Gen. 3. 8. See Dri. *Tenses*, § 161, *Obs.* 2.

For the use of the word המה, cf. Isa. 22. 2; Jer. 6. 23; Ps. 46. 7.

42. עודנו וג׳] Cf. *v.* 14 *note.*

איש חיל] Not ‘a man of *valour*,’ but ‘a man of *worth*’; as also in the expression בן חיל *v.* 52. That חיל can have this meaning is shown by its application to a woman; Ruth 3. 11; Prov. 31. 10; cf. *v.* 29. Targ., here and in *v.* 52; *ch.* 2. 2 (see *note*); 2 Sam. 23. 20, seeks to reproduce this special sense by גבר דחיל חטאין ‘a man who fears sin.’

43. אבל] With a slight adversative force, ‘*Nay but*,’ in repudiation of Adonijah’s suggestion that he is the bearer of good tidings. In late Heb. this adversative signification is strongly marked, ‘*howbeit*’; Dan. 10. 7, 21; Ezra 10. 13; 2 Chr. 1. 4; 19. 3; 33. 17. In classical Heb., though weaker, it is never really absent: Gen. 17. 19 אבל שרה אשתך ילדת לך בן ‘*Nay but* Sara thy wife shall bear thee a son,’ in response to Abraham’s wish that Ishmael might be his representative; 42. 21 אבל אשמים אנחנו על אחינו *however much we may try to repudiate it*, our guilt has found us out; 2 Sam. 14. 5 אבל אשה אלמנה אני the woman *anticipates any refusal* of the king to take up her cause by pleading that she is a widow; II. 4. 14† אבל בן אין לה Gehazi points out that the woman would like, *not* the offers of *v.* 13, *but* the bestowal of a son. Thus ‘verily’ or ‘of a truth,’ the translation of RV. in all these five passages except Gen. 17, is insufficient.

45. ותהם הקריה] 1 Sam. 4. 5 ותהם הארץ; Ruth 1. 19 ותהם כל העיר.

47. Luc. inserts καὶ εἰσεληλύθασι μόνοι after τὸν κύριον ἡμῶν τὸν

βασιλέα Δαυίδ. This seems to point to a Hebrew original in which וגם באו עבדי, at the beginning of the verse, had been by mistake written a second time after אדנינו המלך דוד, and then, making no sense in that position, had been altered into וגם באו לְבַדָּם. Klo. sees in *μόνοι* לְבַדָּם a variant of לברך.

אלהיך] Kt., Pesh.; אלהים Q're, LXX, Vulg., Luc., Targ. The latter should have the preference.

48. אשר נתן היום ישב וג׳] Insert מִזַּרְעִי after היום upon the authority of LXX, Luc. *ἐκ τοῦ σπέρματός μου.* So Th., Klo. The happiness of the event consisted not in the fact that David was to have a successor, which was only natural, but that this successor was to be one of his own family—his son. Pesh., Targ. insert ܒܪܐ, בר. They probably translated from a text in which, like MT., מזרעי had fallen out, and thus felt the necessity for some such insertion.

ועיני ראות] 'Mine eyes beholding it'; a circumstantial clause. The idiom occurs again Deut. 28. 32; 2 Sam. 24. 3; Jer. 20. 4.

50. קרנות המזבח] The four corners of the brazen altar, made of one piece with it (Ex. 27. 2 ועשית קרנתיו על ארבע פנתיו ממנו תהיין קרנתיו), and apparently projecting, for they could be grasped (here, and *v.* 51; 2. 28), and also broken off (cf. Amos 3. 14 ונגדעו קרנות המזבח).

51. ויגד לש׳ לאמר] See *note, ad fin.* on *ch.* 16. 16 וישמע וג׳.

כיום] Properly 'to-day' (כ having a temporal force, as e.g. in 1 Sam. 5. 10 ויהי כבוא ארון וג׳), so 'now,' and then acquiring the special sense *'first of all'*: Gen. 25. 31 מכרה כיום את בכרתך לי; 1 Sam. 2. 16 קטר יקטירון כיום החלב.

אם ימית] 'That he will not slay.' The oath which is implied would take some such form as כה יעשה לו אלהים וכה יוסיף (cf. II. 6. 31; 1 Sam. 3. 17; 25. 22), and thus by the suppression of the apodosis אם 'if' of the protasis, gains the sense of an emphatic negative. This is very common; cf. *ch.* 2. 8; II. 2. 2; 3. 14; 1 Sam. 3. 14; *al.* Da. § 120; Ew. § 356[a].

52. לא יפל משערתו וג׳] 'There shall not fall *even a single hair of him* to the ground.' The fem. שערה is a *nomen unitatis*; cf. Judg. 20. 16 כָּל־זֶה קֹלֵעַ בָּאֶבֶן אֶל־הַשַּׂעֲרָה וְלֹא יַחֲטִא; G-K. § 122, 4[d]. משערתו

properly means '*starting from* one of his hairs'; cf. Deut. 15. 7 אֶבְיוֹן מֵאַחַד אַחֶיךָ 'a poor man, even (*starting from*) one of thy brethren.' This use of מִן, called مِنْ ٱلزَّائِدَةُ (من *otiose*), is very frequent in Ar. when a negation, prohibition, or interrogation with هل precedes; Qor. 6. 38 مَا فَرَّطْنَا فِى ٱلْكِتَابِ مِنْ شَىْءٍ 'We have neglected nothing whatsoever (lit. *starting from* anything) in the Book'; 67. 3 مَا تَرَى فِى خَلْقِ ٱلرَّحْمَٰنِ مِنْ تَفَاوُتٍ 'Thou canst see *no sort of* diversity in God's creation'; *ibid.* هَلْ تَرَى مِنْ فُطُورٍ 'Seest thou *any* gap?' The other occurrences of the proverbial phrase are 1 Sam. 14. 45 אם יפל משערת ראשו ארצה; 2 Sam. 14. 11† אם יפל משערת בנך ארצה.

53. מעל המזבח] 'From *upon* the altar': cf. *ch.* 2. 34 ויעל. The verb עלה also occurs in the sense of *going up upon* an altar, *ch.* 12. 32, 33; II. 16. 12; 23. 9; 1 Sam. 2. 28; and conversely ירד is used of *descent from* the altar here and in Lev. 9. 22. In Ex. 20. 26 *steps* to the altar are expressly forbidden, and hence it has been thought that the ascent was by an *inclined plane*, leading up to a *ledge* (perhaps the כַּרְכֹּב of Ex. 27. 5) which ran round the altar. Solomon's altar, according to 2 Chr. 4. 1, was ten cubits high, and therefore must have been approached by an incline, or by steps; and the altar described by Ezekiel is pictured as having steps leading up to it (43. 17 וּמַעֲלֹתֵהוּ פְּנוֹת קָדִים). Jos. (*Wars*, v. 5, § 6) states that in Herod's Temple the ascent to the altar was by an inclined plane.

2. 1. ויקרבו וג׳] So Gen. 47. 29.

ויצו] צוה is used of a man's last commands; cf. especially 2 Sam. 17. 23 ויצו אל ביתו; II. 20. 1; || Isa. 38. 1 צו לביתך; cf. also Gen. 50. 12, 16; Deut. 31. 23, 25. In New Heb. צַוָּאָה = *a will; Baba bathra* 147[a].

2. אנכי הלך וג׳] Cf. Josh. 23. 14.

וחזקת] RV. 'Be thou strong therefore.' The perf. with ו *consec.* is used as a mild imperative; cf. *v.* 6 ועשית; *ch.* 3. 9 ונתת; 8. 28; *al.* See Dri. *Tenses*, § 119 δ; G-K. § 112, 4[b].

והיית לאיש] Cf. 1 Sam. 4. 9 היו לאנשים. So LXX, Vulg., Pesh., and substantially Σ. (καὶ ἔσο ἀνδρεῖος). Luc. καὶ ἔσει εἰς ἄνδρα δυνάμεως,

Targ. ותהא לגבר דחיל חטאין (cf. *ch.* 1. 42, *note*), and several Codd. Vulg. *esto vir fortis* seem to presuppose והיית לאיש חיל. The regular phrase, however, is היה לבן חיל, cf. *ch.* 1. 52; 1 Sam. 18. 17; 2 Sam. 2. 7; *al.;* and Luc. accordingly in all these passages keeps υἱόν. This makes it probable that δυνάμεως here is only a paraphrastic addition.

3, 4. This passage, in its present form, is due to the pre-exilic Deuteronomic compiler (R^D)[1]. Notice especially the phrases ושמרת את משמרת י׳ Deut. 11. 1; י׳ אלהיך cf. *ch.* 8. 58 *note;* ללכת בדרכיו Deut. 8. 6; 10. 12; 11. 22; *al.;* לשמר חקתיו וג׳ Deut. constantly; למען תשכיל וג׳ Deut. 29. 8; למען יקים וג׳ Deut. 9. 5; בכל לבבך ובכל נפשך Deut. 4. 29; 6. 5; *al.*

3. תשכיל] 'Understand' (so as to *manage successfully*). For השכיל with accus., cf. Ps. 64. 10; 106. 7; Deut. 32. 29; and with the special *nuance* of our passage, Deut. 29. 8 למען תשכילו את כל אשר תעשון. In the application of the word to clause *b*, את כל אשר תפנה שם, there is a slight zeugma.

תפנה] The use of the word is illustrated by Prov. 17. 8 אל כל אשר יפנה ישכיל; 1 Sam. 14. 47 (emend יִוָּשֵׁעַ) בכל אשר יפנה ירשיע.

4. את דברו] The promise referred to is the substance of 2 Sam. 7. 12–16 (Nathan's prophecy).

ללכת לפני] The phrase הלך לפני י׳ is peculiar to Kings; *ch.* 3. 6 (as here, followed by באמת); 8. 23, 25 (|| 2 Chr. 6. 14, 16); 9. 4 (|| 2 Chr. 7. 17)†. Elsewhere the phrase is התהלך לפני י׳; II. 20. 3 || Isa. 38. 3 (followed by באמת); 1 Sam. 2. 30; Gen. 17. 1; 24. 40; 48. 15; Ps. 56. 14; 116. 9†.

לאמר אם ישמרו . . . לאמר] The second לאמר introduces the express words of the promise after a brief summary of the conditions; '*Said he.*' Such cases of resumption after an intervening sentence are not uncommon in Heb.; cf. *ch.* 1. 30 כי כאשר . . . כי כן; 8. 30 ושמעת . . . ושמעת וסלחת; 8. 41, 42 ובא . . . ובא; 13. 11 ויספר[ו] . . . ויספרום; 1 Sam. 29. 10 השכם . . . והשכמתם; Lev. 17. 5 למען אשר יביאו . . . והביאֻם; *al.* The second לאמר is omitted by Cod. Kennicott 170, Th., Kamp., and not expressed by Luc., Vulg.

[1] See *Introduction.*

לא יכרת וג׳] Cf. *ch.* 8. 25 (|| 2 Chr. 6. 16); 9. 5 (|| 2 Chr. 7. 18); Jer. 33. 17. לך is dat. of reference, 'pertaining unto thee.'

מעל] Lit. 'from (sitting) upon,' so '*off.*' A regular idiom; cf. the phrases מֵעַל הַחֲמוֹר 1 Sam. 25. 23; מֵעַל הַגָּמָל Gen. 24. 64; מֵעַל הַמִּזְבֵּחַ *ch.* 1. 53; מֵעַל רֹאשִׁי Gen. 40. 17; מֵעַל הָאֲדָמָה Deut. 28. 21; *al.*

5. ויהרגם] '*How that* he slew them.' The ו is epexegetical of the somewhat vague preceding expression את אשר עשה וג׳. Other instances of the Imperf. with ו *consec.*, '*how that*' or '*in that*,' used to explain a preceding עשה, are *ch.* 18. 13 את אשר עשיתי . . . ואחבא; 1 Sam. 8. 8; Gen. 31. 26. See Dri. *Tenses*, § 76ᵃ; Da. § 47 *end.*

וישם דמי מלחמה בשלם] A very unnatural expression. (i) As it stands it can only mean, (*α*) 'He placed the blood of war upon peace,' or (*β*) taking וישם absolutely, 'He set (i.e. paraph. *shed*) the blood of war during time of peace.' But such an absolute use of שים, followed neither by ב or על of that upon which the object is placed, nor by a second accus. or by ל expressing the result of the action denoted by the verb, is extremely improbable. (ii) Why is the blood of Abner and Amasa called דמי מלחמה? This is inexplicable. Doubtless we ought, with Klo., Hoo., to emend וישם after Luc. καὶ ἐξεδίκησεν, Vet. Lat. *et vindicavit,* i.e. וַיִּקֹּם דמי מלחמה בשלם, the only change being the substitution of ק for שׁ. Joab's crime consisted in having *avenged* in time of peace, blood shed in war—the blood of Asahel justifiably shed by Abner in self-defence. Thus דמי מלחמה is fully explained, and forms an admirable antithesis to בשלם. For the use of נקם דמים cf. Deut. 32. 43 דם עבדיו יקוֹם. LXX καὶ ἔταξεν seems to have had MT. reading; while Vulg. *et effudit,* Targ. ודמי דתחשיב דמהון עלוהי כדם תבירי קרבא, Pesh. ܘܣܡ ܐܢܘܢ ܐܝܟ ܕܒܩܪܒܐ are probably paraphrastic explanations of the same.

ויתן דמי מלחמה בחגרתו] Here we have the same difficulty as to the application of דמי מלחמה. The reading of Cod. A, Luc. αἷμα ἀθῷον is favoured by the fact that Luc. preserves the correct text just before. Accordingly, Bö. suggests דָּמִים לְחִנָּם; Th. דָּם נָקִי; Klo. דְּמֵי חִנָּם or דָּמִים לְחִנָּם. The last expression is the best; cf. *v.* 31

והסירת דמי חנם אשר שפך יואב. Doubtless, as Th. suggests, the corruption arose through the previous דמי מלחמה standing directly above דמי חנם in the MS. from which the copy was made. Targ. דמיהון, Pesh. ܕܡܝܗܘܢ, presuppose דמיהם, which may well have arisen from דמי חנם.

6. ולא תוֹרֵד] The employment of the jussive form with לא is rare. Other instances are, Gen. 24. 8; 1 Sam. 14. 36; 2 Sam. 17. 12; Ezek. 48. 14; Gen. 4. 12; Deut. 13. 1; Joel 2. 2. See G-K. § 109, 1[b]; Dri. *Tenses*, § 174 *Obs.* For the expression הוריד שיבת פ׳ שאול(ה) cf. *v.* 9; Gen. 42. 38; 44. 29, 31.

7. והיו באכלי] 'Let them be *among*, &c.' Cf. Am. 1. 1 עמוס אשר היה בנקדים; Prov. 23. 20 אל תהי בסבאי יין.

כי כן קרבו אלי] 'For *so* did they draw near to me,' i.e. 'with such kindness as thou art to show to them'; Th. So LXX *οὕτως*. If we adopt this explanation, it is unnecessary to suppose, with Hitzig, that כי כן stands for כי על כן, as is suggested by Pesh. ܡܛܠ ܕ; cf. Targ. ארי, Vulg. *enim*. Luc. *οὗτος* is a corruption of *οὕτως*.

קרבו אלי] Klo., following Luc. *οὗτος παρέστη ἐνώπιόν μου*, emends קִדְּמוּ אֹתִי; cf. Deut. 23. 5 לא קדמו אתכם בלחם. This is an unnecessary change. LXX *ἤγγισαν*, Vulg. *occurrerunt* agree with MT.; Targ. סופיקו צורכיי, Pesh. ܣܝܥܘܢܝ ܟܕ ܥܪܩܬ paraphrase.

8. בן הֿימיני] '*The* Benjamite.' So Judg. 3. 15; 2 Sam. 16. 11; 19. 17 †. Cf. בֵּית הַלַּחְמִי 1 Sam. 16. 18; בֵּית־הַשִּׁמְשִׁי 1 Sam. 6. 14; בֵּית הָאֱלִי *ch.* 16. 34; אֲבִי הָעֶזְרִי Judg. 6. 11. In 1 Chr. 27. 12 Kt. לבנימיני (i. e. לַבִּנְיָמִינִי, the origin being forgotten, and the word treated as a single one. Cf. הָאִיעֶזְרִי Num. 26. 30); Q're anomalously לְבֶן יְמִינִי. Cf. Kö. *Syntax*, § 302[d].

נמרצת] Niph'al again in Mic. 2. 10; Job 6. 25; Hiph'il, Job 16. 3 †. The word may be connected with Ar. مَرِضَ *to be sick*,—'a curse *made sick*,' and so '*a sore* or *severe curse*.' Cf. with similar use of a passive participle, מַכָּה נַחְלָה Jer. 14. 17.

9. ועתה] So Targ., Pesh. LXX omits. Luc., Vulg. וְאַתָּה; so Th., Klo., Kamp. MT. should be retained; see *note* on *ch.* 1. 20.

10, 11. This short mention of David's death and burial, and the statement of the length of his reign, is in its present form the work of R^D, whose method of introducing and summarizing the account of a reign is noticed at length in *Introd.*

10. עיר דוד] The ancient city of Jerusalem taken by David from the Jebusites[1], called מְצֻדַת צִיּוֹן 2 Sam. 5. 7; ‖ 1 Chr. 11. 5; צִיּוֹן *ch.* 8. 1. Zion is expressly named in 1 Macc. 4. 37 *f.*; 7. 33 as the hill upon which the Temple stood, and this is further borne out by such expressions as י׳ צבאות השכן בהר צ׳ Isa. 8. 18; צ׳ קדוש ישראל Isa. 60. 14; ציון הר קדשי Ps. 2. 6; הר ציון זה שכנת בו Ps. 74. 2; *al.* In 2 Chr. 33. 14 it is said of Manasseh that 'he built an outer wall to the city of David, on the west side of Giḥon in the ravine (*note* on *ch.* 1. 33), even to the entering in at the fish gate; and he compassed about the Ophel, &c.'

Thus it seems clear that the site of עיר דוד was upon the somewhat low south-east hill of Jerusalem (הָעֹפֶל), the Temple being on the north, and Solomon's palace upon the south, closely adjoining the Temple[2]. The tradition which places Zion upon the south-*west* hill appears to be no earlier than the fourth century A.D.; and the modern maps which so locate it are certainly incorrect. See Sta. *Ges.* i. 315 *f.*; *Encyc. Brit.* ed. 9, Art. *Jerusalem* (Pt. II); Baed. 21 *f.*

13. ויבא . . . אם שלמה] LXX, Luc. add καὶ προσεκύνησεν αὐτῇ, i.e. וַיִּשְׁתַּחוּ לָהּ; possibly genuine, and accepted by Klo. Th. is doubtful, remarking that it is quite as likely to have been inserted by a copyist from *v.* 19, on the consideration that Adonijah would not have acted with less deference than king Solomon.

---

[1] The name יְבוּס applied to the city, Judg. 19. 10, 11; 1 Chr. 11. 4, 5† (cf. Josh. 15. 8; 18. 16, 28 P), is probably no real archaism, but a literary derivative from the name of the ancient inhabitants. Cf. Moore (*Judges*, p. 413), who quotes Judg. 1. 7, 21; Josh. 15. 63 (JE), as showing that the city was called Jerusalem before the time of David, and concludes that 'the question has been set at rest by the Amarna tablets (about 1400 B.C., before the Israelite invasion) in which the name *Urusalim* repeatedly occurs, while there is no trace of a name corresponding to Jebus.'

[2] This agrees with the statement of Ezek. 43. 7^b, 8^a; 'And the house of Israel shall no more defile my holy name, neither they nor their kings, . . . in their setting of their threshold by my threshold, and their doorpost beside my doorpost, and there was but the wall between me and them.'

השלום באך] So 1 Sam. 16. 4. Lit. 'Is thy coming peace?' the abstract substantive being used instead of an adjective. So very frequently with this word; Gen. 43. 27 הֲשָׁלוֹם אֲבִיכֶם; Judg. 6. 24 ויקרא לו יהוה שלום 'he called it, Yahwe is *peace*'; 1 Sam. 25. 6; 2 Sam. 17. 3; Isa. 60. 17; Mic. 5. 4; Ps. 120. 7; 147. 14; Prov. 3. 17; Job 5. 24; 21. 9†; cf. also Num. 25. 12 בריתי שלום 'my covenant—peace,' i.e. 'my peaceful covenant.' With other words; Ex. 17. 12 ויהי ידיו אמונה 'and his hands were *firmness*'; Ps. 110. 3 עמך נדבת 'thy people is *freewillingness*'; &c. See Dri. *Tenses*, § 189, 2.

14. דבר לי אליך] II. 9. 5; Judg. 3. 19, 20.

ותאמר] LXX, Luc., Pesh., Vulg., some Codd. add לו.

15. לי היתה המ׳] '*Mine* was the kingdom.' לי is greatly emphasized by position: cf. Job 15. 19 להם לבדם נתנה הארץ; Hag. 2. 8 לי הכסף ולי הזהב.

עלי שמו . . . פניהם] Expressing attention concentrated in expectancy; cf. the phrase עין על *ch.* 1. 20. In its other occurrences, Ezek. 29. 2; 35. 2† (a variation of שים פנים אל), the expression is used with a hostile *nuance*. שים פנים followed by an infin. with ל describes a purpose at the point of time at which it is about to be put into execution. II. 12. 18 וישם חזאל פניו לעלות על ירושלם; Jer. 42. 15, 17; 44. 12; Dan. 11. 17.

לִמְלֹךְ] Klo. compares II. 12. 18; but this is not quite parallel, the subject of the infin. לעלות being, as in the other passages above cited, the same as that of וישם, while the subject of לִמְלֹךְ is different from that of שמו. Two Codd. De Rossi and all Verss. presuppose the easier reading לְמֶלֶךְ.

מיהוה] The ordering of events in a manner opposed to human calculations is, as Klo. notices, specially spoken of as a divine interposition. Judg. 14. 4 ואביו ואמו לא ידעו כי מיהוה היא; cf. Prov. 16. 1. There is a similar use of מֵאֵת יהוה; *ch.* 12. 24; II. 6. 33; Josh. 11. 20; Ps. 118. 23; *al.*

16. אנכי שאל] The participle used of the immediate future as it merges into the present; the *futurum instans*. 'I am about to ask,' almost equivalent to the simple present 'I ask.' Cf. *v.* 20.

אל תשבי את פני] So Vulg., Pesh., Targ.; but LXX, Luc. τὸ πρόσωπόν σου, i.e. את פניך; and in *vv.* 17, 20 LXX reads οὐκ ἀποστρέψει τὸ πρόσωπον αὐτοῦ ἀπὸ σοῦ for לא ישיב את פניך, and μὴ ἀποστρέψῃς τὸ πρόσωπόν σου for אל תשב את פני. On the contrary, לא אשיב את פניך at the end of *v.* 20 is rendered οὐκ ἀποστρέψω σε. In all these cases, Luc., Targ., Vulg. (paraph. in *v.* 17, *neque enim negare tibi quidquam potest*), Pesh. (ܐܦܝ for פניך in *v.* 17) agree in supporting the reading of MT.

The usage of the expression השיב פנים is as follows. It occurs, as in the LXX text of these passages, of *turning one's own face away from anything*, only in Ezek. 14. 6 שובו והשיבו מעל גלוליכם ומעל כל תועבתיכם השיבו פניכם; cf. Ezek. 18. 30 where there is probably an ellipse of פנים. השיב פנים ל *to turn one's own face towards*, Dan. 11. 18, 19. On the other hand, the expression is used as here in *vv.* 16, 17, 20 of MT., of turning away *the face of another* in *repulse*, in II. 18. 24; || Isa. 36. 9 ואיך תשיב את פני פחת אחד וגו׳, and Ps. 132. 10; || 2 Chr. 6. 42 אל תשב פני משיחך. So also in the opposite expression of *the acceptance of an overture*, נשא פנים, it is always the face of *another person* which is raised.

Thus evidence is all in favour of the retention of MT. text in *vv.* 16, 17, 20.

18. טוב] A formula of assent; cf. 1 Sam. 20. 7; 2 Sam. 3. 13.

19. וישתחו לה] So Vulg., Pesh., Targ. LXX, Luc. καὶ (LXX κατ-) ἐφίλησεν αὐτήν presuppose וַיִּשַּׁק לָהּ or וַיִּשָּׁקֶהָ. Bö. prefers MT., supposing that LXX reading points to an alteration on the part of the Alexandrian Jews, who thought that such an act of obeisance was unworthy of king Solomon. Th. also points out that the ceremonial which follows—the placing of a throne for the queen-mother and her sitting at the king's right hand—is in favour of MT.

The importance of the position of the queen-mother הַגְּבִירָה is attested by *ch.* 15. 13; ||2 Chr. 15. 16 (cf. II. 10. 13; Jer. 13. 18; 29. 2), and by the frequent special mention of her name; *ch.* 14. 21, 31; 15. 2, 10; 22. 42; II. 8. 26; 12. 2; *al.* Thus, as far as can be judged, there would be nothing incongruous in the king's bowing to her.

Klo. adopts LXX reading, describing the action denoted by MT. as 'gegen alle Etiquette'; but as a matter of fact we know too little about the customs of ancient eastern monarchs to be able to dogmatize upon what might fittingly have taken place, and what not so.

20. אַל־תֵּשֶׁב] Here the close connexion of אל to the jussive by means of *Maqqef* causes a retraction of the tone, just as in the case of the Imperf. with ו *consec.* Cf. 1 Sam. 9. 20 אַל־תָּשֶׂם; 2 Sam. 17. 16 אַל־תָּלֶן; *al.*

21. יֻתַּן את אבישג] The passive verb is impersonal, and the object of the action denoted by it follows in the accus.; 'Let there be giving as regards Abishag,' so, 'Let one give,' or, 'Let her be given.' So with the same verb Num. 32. 5 יֻתַּן את הארץ הזאת לעבדיך; cf. also *ch.* 18. 13 הלא הֻגַּד לאדני את אשר עשיתי; 2 Sam. 21. 11; Gen. 27. 42; *al.* See G-K. § 121, 1; Ew. 295[b]; Da. § 79.

22. ולמה] '*And* why?' 'why then?' The ו is very forcible, and here gives a sarcastic turn to the sentence. Cf. II. 7. 19 והנה י׳ עשה ארבות בשמים היהיה כדבר הזה '*Pray*, if Yahwe were to make windows in heaven, could this thing come to pass?' Other instances of the ו with למה are Num. 14. 3; 20. 4; Judg. 6. 13; 12. 3. See Dri. *Tenses*, § 119 *γ*, *n.* 1.

לָמָה] With accent *Milra'* before the following את, instead of לָמָּה. This accentuation is always adopted before words beginning with א, ע, or ה, for the sake of avoidance of *hiatus*. See Sta. § 372[a].

ולו ולאביתר . . . צרויה] RV. 'Ask for him the kingdom ... *even for him, and for Abiathar* &c.' A somewhat dubious rendering. As the text stands ולו can scarcely be correct, and must be omitted as dittography from the first two letters of the following word.

All Verss., however, LXX, Luc., Vulg., Pesh., and probably Targ. (paraph. הלא בעיצא הוו הוא ואביתר), presuppose ולו אביתר הכהן ולו יואב וג׳ '*And on his side* are Abiathar the priest, and Joab &c.' As Th. says, it is natural that a second reason for asking the kingdom for Adonijah should be mentioned. So Bö. For this sense of לו, cf. Ex. 32. 26 מי ליהוה אלי; Josh. 5. 13 הלנו אתה אם לצרינו.

The addition of LXX, Luc., after Joab's name, ὁ ἀρχιστράτηγος ἑταῖρος, appears to be merely a gloss, ὁ ἀρχ. being Joab's usual title, and ἑταῖρος explaining the reference of לוֹ, 'To him Joab . . . *is an ally.*'

Klo., starting from the addition of ἑταῖρος in LXX, Luc., and comparing the Targ. paraphrase הלא בעיצא הוו וג׳, supposes that a word has fallen out at the end of the sentence in MT., and accordingly would supply חֶבֶר; 'To him and to Abiathar . . . *there is an alliance.*' But against this it is to be noticed that the word which is constantly used in the historical books to denote a *conspiracy* or *alliance* is never חֶבֶר but always קֶשֶׁר (cf. II. 11. 14; 12. 21; *al.*), and again, it seems very doubtful whether Targ., if it had had חבר at the end of the sentence, would have represented it by בעיצא at the beginning.

23. כה יעשה וג׳] II. 6. 31; 1 Sam. 3. 17; 14. 44; 20. 13; 25. 22; 2 Sam. 3. 9, 35; 19. 14; Ruth 1. 17. In the mouths of heathen a *plural* verb is used; *ch.* 19. 2; 20. 10†.

כי] If the substance of the oath be a *negation*, it is usual to introduce it by אם '*if*'; *ch.* 20. 10 כה . . . יוספו אם ישפק עפר שמרון לשעלים וג׳ 'So may the gods do to me, and more also, *if* the dust of Samaria suffice for handfuls &c.'; II. 6. 31 כה . . . יוסף אם יעמד ראש אלישע בן שפט עליו היום; 1 Sam. 3. 17; 25. 22. In analogy with this we should expect אם לא if the substance be an *assertion;* and this occurs once; 2 Sam. 19. 14. It is usual, however, to break off after the oath, and introduce its subject by כי, the break in connexion being represented in English by a dash. So in our passage; 'God do so to me and more also—Adonijah hath spoken this word against his life'; *ch.* 19. 2 כה . . . יוספון כי כעת מחר אשים את נפשך כנפש אחד מהם 'So do the gods, &c.—to-morrow I will make &c.'; 1 Sam. 14. 44; 20. 13; 2 Sam. 3. 9; Ruth 1. 17.

כי is thus very frequently used to introduce an *assertion* after the oath חַי יהוה, *and with a suppression of* כה יעשה וג׳; cf. *v.* 24; *ch.* 1. 30; 18. 15; 1 Sam. 14. 39; 20. 3, 21; 25. 34; *al.* (about nineteen times in all). In such a case אם לא occurs only once,

Num. 14. 28, outside of Ezekiel where it is characteristic and uniformly takes the place of the usual construction with כי; 5. 11; 17. 16, 19; 20. 33; 33. 27; 34. 8; 35. 6† (this last a gloss according to Cornill)[1].

If the oath introduced by חי י׳ with a suppressed כה יעשה וג׳ have a *negative* substance, אם occurs constantly.

בנפשו] '*At the cost of* his life'; *Beth pretii.* Cf. 2 Sam. 23. 17 ההלכים בנפשתם 'who went *at peril of* their lives'; Prov. 7. 23; Lam. 5. 9. So *ch.* 16. 34; Josh. 6. 26 בבכרו . . . ובצעירו; 1 Chr. 12. 19 בראשינו; *al.*

24. עשה לי בית] Used idiomatically of Yahwe's assurance to Solomon of *a posterity*. So 2 Sam. 7. 11 והגיד לך י׳ כי בית יעשה לך י׳; cf. Exod. 1. 21. The more usual phrase is בָּנָה בית; 1 Sam. 2. 35; 2 Sam. 7. 27; (|| 1 Chr. 17. 10, 25); *ch.* 11. 38.

25. וימת] LXX, Luc. presuppose the addition אֲדֹנִיָּהוּ בַּיּוֹם הַהוּא 'and A. died that same day.' So Th., and Klo. with om. of name.

26. ענתת] A city of Benjamin, Isa. 10. 30; assigned to the priests, Josh. 21. 18; 1 Chr. 6. 45; the home of Jeremiah, Jer. 1. 1. The modern name is *Anâta*, 2½ miles north-north-east of Jerusalem. This agrees with the statements of Jos. (*Ant.* x. 7, § 3), who places it at twenty stadia from the city, Eusebius (*Onom.*) three miles, Jerome (*ad Jerem.* cap. 1) three miles '*contra septentrionem Jerusalem.*' Rob. *BR.*, i. 437 *f.*; Baed. 118.

על שדיך] על used in place of אל; cf. 1. 38 *note.*

ארון] So all Verss. The occasion to which reference is made seems naturally to be that described in 2 Sam. 6. 12 *ff.* Th., Klo. emend אֵפוֹד, finding an allusion (as is the case in the following וכי התענית וג׳) to the days of David's outlawry, when Abiathar, fleeing from the slaughter of the priests at Nob, carried with him to David the *Ephod* which was used in obtaining the oracle of Yahwe; 1 Sam. 23. 6, 9. But neither אפוד (אדני) יהוה nor אפוד אלהים (Klo.) occurs elsewhere, and, if any correction of the text be deemed desirable, הָאֵפוֹד simply is alone in accordance with usage.

[1] With omission both of apodosis and of formal oath אם לא is by no means infrequent. Cf. *ch.* 20. 23 *note.*

אדני יהוה] אדני, not found in LXX, Luc., Pesh., is probably a mistaken repetition of ארון.

LXX, Luc. insert *διαθήκης*, i.e. ברית, after *κιβωτόν*. This is a gloss derived from the expression ארון ברית י׳ which is frequent elsewhere (see 3. 15 *note*). Other instances of this same insertion are Josh. 3. 13, 15 (twice); 4. 10, 11; 6. 12, 13; 1 Sam. 6. 3, 18; 7. 1 (twice); 2 Sam. 6. 10.

לפני דוד] 'In the presence of,' suggesting the idea of '*at the direction of* David.' So Num. 8. 22 לעבד את עבדתם באהל מועד לפני אהרן ולפני בניו; 1 Chr. 24. 6 ויכתבם . . . לפני המלך.

27. למלא וג׳] 1 Sam. 2. 27–36.

28. ואחרי אבשלום לא נטה] So LXX, Targ.; but Luc., Vulg., Pesh. presuppose וְאַחֲרֵי שְׁלֹמֹה, adopted by Jos. (*Ant.* viii. 1, § 4 *φίλος γὰρ ἦν αὐτῷ ['Αδωνίᾳ] μᾶλλον ἢ τῷ βασιλεῖ Σολομῶνι*), and also by Th., Ew., Grä.

This emendation makes the sentence a little diffuse, since its statement is already contained by implication in the previous words כי יואב נטה אחרי אדניה. On the other hand, a back reference to the position taken by Joab *in the other rebellion of David's reign* is very natural.

29. והנה] Without a specific suffix or pronoun following, the reference being unmistakable. Cf. Gen. 24. 30 ויבא אל האיש והנה עֹמֵד על הגמלים; 37. 15; 18. 9; 16. 14.

אצל המזבח] LXX, Luc., Pesh. אֹחֵז בְּקַרְנוֹת הַמִּזְבֵּחַ. Hence Th. thinks that בקרנות has fallen out of MT., and אחז then become corrupted into אצל. But the use of אצל is very natural here (used frequently in connexion with מזבח; Lev. 1. 16; 6. 3; 10. 12; *al.*), and forms an appropriate variation to the phrase used in *v.* 28. It is much more probable that the alteration of the above-mentioned Verss. is merely due to that desire for the strict uniformity of parallel passages which is so characteristic, e. g. of the LXX translators. *Ch.* 1. 51 appears to have suggested the change. So Klo.

וישלח שלמה] After שלמה LXX, Luc. add *πρὸς 'Ιωὰβ λέγων, Τί γέγονέν σοι ὅτι πέφευγας εἰς* (Luc. *πέφευγες ἐπὶ*) *τὸ θυσιαστήριον; καὶ εἶπεν 'Ιωάβ "Οτι ἐφοβήθην ἀπὸ προσώπου σου, καὶ ἔφυγον πρὸς* (*τὸν*) *Κύριον. καὶ ἀπέστειλεν ὁ Σαλωμών*. This is translated by Th. אֶל־יוֹאָב לֵאמֹר מֶה הָיָה לְּךָ כִּי נַסְתָּ אֶל־הַמִּזְבֵּחַ וַיֹּאמֶר יוֹאָב כִּי יָרֵאתִי מִפָּנֶיךָ וָאָנוּס אֶל־יְהוָֹה וַיִּשְׁלַח שְׁלֹמֹה, and adopted by him as genuine on the ground that a scribe's eye might very well have passed by mistake from the first וישלח שלמה to the second. So Bö., Klo. The words exhibit no attempt to justify the action of Solomon, nor does there seem to be any other reason for their addition by a later hand; a consideration which favours their genuineness.

פגע בו] LXX, Luc. add *καὶ θάψον αὐτόν*, through desire, as Th. remarks, for conformity with *v*. 31.

Klo. would emend וְהוֹצִיאֵהוּ for פגע בו. This is unsupported by any Vers., and though it may seem at first sight to be required by the words of *v*. 30 כה אמר המלך צא, yet this is not really the case. The king, in issuing the command פגע בו, supposed that Joab could be brought away from the altar and executed, but Benaiah, meeting with his refusal to leave the asylum, returned to the king for further instructions.

31. וקברתו] Added out of consideration for the dignity of his position. Cf. II. 9. 34, and contrast II. 9. 10; Jer. 22. 19; Isa. 14. 19; Ps. 79. 3, where the loss of burial is mentioned as a mark of deep dishonour.

וַהֲסִירֹתָ] It is very rare to find the tone not thrown forward with ו *consec*. in 1st and 2nd sing. of verbs ע״ו (or ע״ע). This and וַהֲצֵרֹתִי Jer. 10. 18; וַהֲשִׁיבוֹתִי Am. 1. 8, are probably all the cases which exist. Dri. *Tenses*, § 110, 5, *Obs*.

מעלי] 'From *upon* me'; the blood being regarded as resting upon the head of the guilty person; so *vv*. 33, 37; 2 Sam. 3. 29. Cf. Jon. 1. 14 אל תתן עלינו דם נקיא; 2 Sam. 16. 8; S. Matt. 27. 25.

32. והשיב י׳ . . . על ראשו] 1 Sam. 25. 39; Judg. 9. 57.

את דמו] LXX, Luc. *τὸ αἷμα τῆς ἀδικίας αὐτοῦ*, a paraphrase based upon the supposition that דמו refers, not to Joab's own blood, but to the blood unjustly shed by him.

33. מעם י׳] So *ch*. 12. 15; Ruth 2. 12; Ps. 121. 2; *al*. Cf. the analogous use of מאת י׳ *ch*. 1. 27 *note*.

34. ויעל] 'Went *up*'; in accordance with the expression מעל המזבח *ch.* 1. 53 *note.*

בביתו] So LXX, Vulg., Targ.; Th., Klo. Cf. 2 Chr. 33. 20 ויקברהו ביתו. Luc., Pesh. presuppose בְּקִבְרוֹ, and this is favoured by Kamp. who thinks it extremely unlikely that Joab should have had a *house* in the wilderness.

במדבר] Kamp. suggests בְּמִדְבַּר יְהוּדָה; Judg. 1. 16; Ps. 63. 1.

35. After על הצבא LXX, Luc. insert *καὶ ἡ βασιλεία κατορθοῦτο ἐν Ἰερουσαλήμ.* These words are those of *v.* 46^b of MT. והממלכה נכונה ביד שלמה, בידשלמה being read as בירשלם.

The correct position of the sentence seems to be at the end of *v.* 35 from which in MT. it was separated by the insertion of the Shimei section. Solomon's establishment in the kingdom resulted from the death of his powerful adversaries Adonijah and Joab, and could not have been much enhanced by the death of Shimei some three years later. The fact that in LXX, Luc. these words precede the sentence which relates the elevation of Zadok to the high-priesthood, seems to suggest that this latter is an addition of a later editor, suggested by the detail which refers to Benaiah's succession to Joab.

36. לשמעי] Luc. adds *υἱὸν Γηρά*, i.e. בֶּן־גֵּרָא as in *v.* 8, adopted by Klo., and by Hoo. as coming appropriately at the beginning of the narrative.

37. ועברת] The Perf. with ו *consec.* used in continuation of an Infin. describing a hypothetical event. So in *v.* 42 ביום צאתך והלכת; 8. 33 בהנגף עמך . . . ושבו; *al.* Dri. *Tenses*, §§ 117, 118; Da. § 55^c.

At the end of the verse LXX, Luc. add *καὶ ὥρκισεν αὐτὸν ὁ βασιλεὺς ἐν τῇ ἡμέρᾳ ἐκείνῃ*, i.e. וַיַּשְׁבִּיעֵהוּ הַמֶּלֶךְ בַּיּוֹם הַהוּא. Th., following Bö., regards these words as genuine, on the ground that if they had been an insertion from *v.* 42 (הלוא השבעתיך ביהוה), ביהוה would have been read and ביום ההוא would not have occurred. So Klo., who remarks that since violation of the oath of Yahwe was the ground of Shimei's execution, the swearing of the oath must be mentioned in the previous narrative. These reasons, however, are hardly consistent. Had the passage been genuine, it ought to have followed *v.* 38^a; after Shimei has expressed his assent to the king's decision in general terms, the king then proceeds to take an oath of him. But if Shimei had *at first* taken the oath, he would not have then gone on to use the words of *v.* 38ᵃ. The swearing of the oath of Yahwe may well be *implied* in the account of *vv.* 37, 38ᵃ.

38. ימים רבים] LXX, Luc. *τρία ἔτη* derived from the beginning of the next verse. This is another instance of the harmonizing tendency of the LXX translator, tending to support the judgement expressed above on the LXX passage in *v.* 37.

39. שני עבדים לשמעי] The circumscription of the genitive is employed for greater indefiniteness. שְׁנֵי עַבְדֵי שׁ׳ might have meant '*the* two servants of Shimei.' Cf. *ch.* 5. 15 אֹהֵב היה חירם לדוד, not 'David's friend,' but 'a friend of David'; 1 Sam. 16. 18 בן לישי 'one of Jesse's sons.' Da. § 28, *Rem.* 5[1].

40. וילך שמעי] Luc. adds *ἐξ Ἰερουσαλήμ*. If genuine, the words call special attention to the fact that Shimei passed beyond the limits of his parole; though this seems to be clearly enough implied in the preceding וילך גתה. Klo. supposes Luc.'s reading to be an error for *εἰς Ἰερ.*, and so adopts וילך שמעי ירושלימה. But in this case we should surely expect וַיָּשָׁב and not וילך.

41. וישב] LXX, Luc. *καὶ ἀπέστρεψεν* (Luc. *ἐπέστρεψε*) *τοὺς δούλους αὐτοῦ*, i.e. וַיָּשֶׁב אֶת־עֲבָדָיו; doubtless a mere gloss. Solomon was informed of Shimei's having left Jerusalem, and, as Klo. points out, it was of no importance to tell him whether on his return he was accompanied by his runaway slaves or not.

42. ואעד בך] 'I solemnly admonished thee,' lit. '*protested against*,' the ב following the verb pointing to the person *against* whom the admonition is directed. Cf. Gen. 43. 3 העד הֵעִד בנו האיש; II. 17. 13; 1 Sam. 8. 9; *al.*

טוב הדבר שמעתי] 'Good is the matter; I have heard it,' i.e. I intend to obey it. So Klo., who compares השתחויתי in 2 Sam. 16. 4. טוב הדבר is thus used absolutely as a formula of assent in *v.* 38; *ch.* 18. 24; cf. Deut. 1. 14; 1 Sam. 9. 10 (דברך). This sense is given by Pesh. ܫܦܝܪ ܦܬܓܡܐ: ܗܘܐ ܐܠܟܝ, and apparently by Targ. תקין פיתגמא שמעית. Vulg., Luc. take שמעתי as a relative sentence; *quem audivi; ὃ ἤκουσα*; and this is the sense which is given by RV. Such an omission of the relative is, however, very rare in Heb. *prose*. LXX om. through oversight.

43. שבעת י׳] Ex. 22. 10; 2 Sam. 21. 7†. The meaning of the phrase is elucidated by 1 Sam. 20. 42 אשר נשבענו שנינו אנחנו בשם י׳.

44. והשיב] LXX, Luc., Vulg., Pesh. presuppose a past tense וַיָּשֶׁב 'he hath requited'; probably correctly. The fact that Shimei by his act of perjury had brought the death penalty upon himself was Yahwe's requital for his wickedness towards David. MT. may perhaps be a correction to accord with *v.* 32, where, however, the case is different; והשיב את דמו.

3. 1—**11.** 43. *History of the reign of Solomon.*

The kernel of the narrative is *chh.* 5. 15—7. 51, the description of Solomon's building operations, with its sequel, *ch.* 8. Around this are grouped (*chh.* 4. 1—**5.** 14; *chh.* 9, 10) a series of notices, for the most part brief, illustrative of the king's wisdom, magnificence, and prosperity.

Ch. 3 forms an introduction to the whole, detailing Solomon's request for wisdom, with a signal instance of its exercise: *ch.* 11, as a conclusion, gives a description of the circumstances which paved the way for the disruption of the kingdom.

3. 3–15. *The vision at Gibeon. Solomon's request for wisdom.*

Ch. 3. 4–15=2 Chr. 1. 3–13.

3. 1. There can be little doubt that this verse, together with *ch.* 9. 16, 17ᵃ, originally formed part of the document embodied in the early part of *ch.* 5 (see *note* on *chh.* 4. 20—5. 14).

2, 3. The disapprobation of במה worship is based upon the law of Deuteronomy, which restricts sacrifice to the central sanctuary; see 12. 4–18, esp. *vv.* 13, 14. Similar notices are found in *ch.* 15. 14 (Asa); 22. 44 (Jehoshaphat); II. 12. 4 (Jehoash); 14. 4 (Amaziah); 15. 4 (Azariah); *v.* 35ᵃ (Jotham). In every case the formula is nearly identical, and follows upon a general commendation of the king's conduct; ויעש [*ch.* 22. 43 לעשות] הישר בעיני יהוה. Cf. also the condemnation of Rehoboam's worship, *ch.* 14.

22, 23 (but this may have been mixed with definite idolatry; cf. *v.* 24 וגם קדש היה בארץ), and the wholesale reprobation of the calf-worship of the Northern kingdom as summarized in II. 17. 7–23.

The old narrative treats במה worship as a matter of course; so here in *v.* 4, and in 1 Sam. 9. 12, 14; 7. 9, 17; 10. 8; *al.* Upon this subject, see R. Sm. *OTJC.*, Lect. viii; *DB*², Art. *Deuteronomy*, § 15; Dri. *Deut.* xlix. *ff.* Thus *vv.* 2, 3 both exhibit the influence of Deuteronomy. It is obvious, however, that they cannot be assigned to one author. In *v.* 3 the subject, as in *vv.* 1, 4, is Solomon, while in *v.* 2 *the people* are specified. Verse 3 simply places two facts side by side without any attempt at correlation;—Solomon loved Yahwe, only he sacrificed and burned incense on the high-places: *v.* 2 supplies an explanation;—This במה worship was a popular custom, due to the fact that the house of Yahwe was not yet built. Hence *v.* 3 is the work of R^D^, and opens the account of Solomon's reign by introducing the narrative of the vision at Gibeon; *v.* 2 proceeds from an exilic or post-exilic editor who, with a view to explaining Solomon's conduct, inserted the phrase which he found to be frequent elsewhere רק העם מזבחים בבמות, together with the explanation which follows כי לא נבנה בית וגו׳, and, in order to illustrate this latter, probably moved *v.* 1, which mentions the fact of the house of Yahwe being not yet built, from the position which it properly occupies in *ch.* 5 LXX (*note*). In LXX of this *ch.* *v.* 1 is wanting and *v.* 2 fragmentary.

2. לשם י׳] So *ch.* 5. 17, 19; 8. 17, 20, 44, 48. The original is 2 Sam. 7. 13 הוא יבנה בית לשמי quoted in *ch.* 5. 19; 8. 19.

3. ויאהב . . . ללכת] A distinctively D phrase. Deut. 10. 12; 11. 22; 19. 9; 30. 16. Cf. also 7. 9; 11. 1, 13; 13. 4; 30. 6, 20.

vv. 4–15. This section shows clear traces of the hand of R^D^. In 2 Chr. 1. 3–13 the story appears in a shorter form, and apparently without the additions of the Compiler. That Chr., however, does not exhibit the narrative in its original simplicity is proved by the details of *vv.* 3–6 and *v.* 13 מלפני אהל מועד (cf. *ch.* 8. 4^a^ *note*); by the late words מדע *vv.* 10, 12; נכסים *v.* 12; and the unclassical expression נתון לך *v.* 12.

	1 Kings 3.	2 Chr. 1.	
4	וילך המלך גבענה לזבח שם	Much expanded by the	3–6
	כי היא הבמה הגדולה אלף	Chronicler.	
	עלות יעלה שלמה על המזבח		
5	ההוא: בגבעון נראה	בלילה ההוא נראה אלהים	7
	יהוה אל שלמה בחלום	לשלמה	
	הלילה ויאמר אלהים שאל	ויאמר לו שאל	
6	מה אתן לך: ויאמר שלמה	מה אתן לך: ויאמר שלמה	8
	אתה עשית עם עבדך דוד	לאלהים אתה עשית עם דויד	
	אבי חסד גדול כאשר הלך	אבי חסד גדול	
	לפניך באמת ובצדקה ובישרת		
	לבב עמך ותשמר לו את		
	החסד הגדול הזה ותתן לו	והמלכתני	
	בן ישב על כסאו כיום הזה:	תחתיו:	
7	ועתה יהוה אלהי אתה	עתה יהוה אלהים יאמן	9
	המלכת את עבדך תחת דוד	דברך עם דויד אבי כי אתה	
	אבי ואנכי נער קטן לא אדע	המלכתני	
8	צאת ובא: ועבדך בתוך עמך		
	אשר בחרת עם רב אשר לא	על עם רב כעפר	
9	ימנה ולא יספר מרב: ונתת	הארץ: עתה	10
	לעבדך לב שמע לשפט את	חכמה ומדע תן לי ואצאה	
	עמך להבין בין טוב לרע כי	לפני העם הזה ואבואה כי	
	מי יוכל לשפט את עמך	מי ישפט את עמך	
10	הכבד הזה: וייטב הדבר	הזה הגדול:	
	בעיני אדני כי שאל שלמה		
11	את הדבר הזה: ויאמר	ויאמר	11
	אלהים אליו יען אשר שאלת	אלהים לשלמה יען אשר	
	את הדבר הזה ולא שאלת	היתה זאת עם לבבך ולא	
	לך ימים רבים ולא שאלת	שאלת עשר נכסים וכבוד	
	לך עשר ולא שאלת נפש	ואת נפש שנאיך וגם	
	איביך ושאלת לך הבין	ימים רבים לא שאלת	
12	לשמע משפט: הנה	ותשאל לך חכמה ומדע	

1 Kings 3.	2 Chr. 1.
עשיתי כדברך הנה	אשר תשפוט את עמי אשר
נתתי לך לב חכם ונבון	המלכתיך עליו: החכמה 12
אשר כמוך לא היה לפניך	והמדע נתון לך
ואחריך לא יקום כמוך:	
13 וגם אשר לא שאלת נתתי	
לך גם עשר גם כבוד	ועשר ונכסים וכבוד אתן
אשר לא היה כמוך איש	לך אשר לא היה כן למלכים
14 במלכים כל ימיך: ואם	אשר לפניך ואחריך לא
תלך בדרכי לשמר חקי	יהיה כן:
ומצותי כאשר הלך דויד	
אביך והארכתי את ימיך:	
15 ויקץ שלמה והנה חלום	
ויבוא ירושלם ויעמד לפני	ויבא שלמה לבמה אשר 13
ארון ברית יהוה ויעל	בגבעון ירושלם מלפני
עלות ויעש שלמים ויעש	אהל מועד וימלך על
משתה לכל עבדיו:	ישראל:

The words overlined are the work of R^D; those marked by the dotted line may possibly be due to him. Probably the original form of the narrative was very near to that of Kings, with omission of the insertions of R^D.

The work of R^D may first be considered:—

6. הלך לפניך] See *note* on *ch.* 2. 4.

ובצדקה וג׳] Deut. 9. 5 בצדקתך ובישֶׁר לבבך, the only place where the two words are joined. ישרת *fem.* only here.

ותשמר לו את החסד] Deut. 7. 9, 12 ושמר י׳ אלהיך לך... ואת החסד. Cf. also *ch.* 8. 23; ‖ 2 Chr. 6. 14; Neh. 1. 5; 9. 32; Ps. 89. 29 †.

ותתן לו וג׳] A reminiscence of *ch.* 1. 48^b.

כיום הזה] So again in *ch.* 8. 24, 61 (R^D). The phrase calls attention to the fulfilment of a promise or threat, and is frequent in Deut. and in books which show the influence of Deut. Deut. 2. 30; 4. 20, 38; 8. 18; 10. 15; 29. 27; Jer. 11. 5; 25. 18; 32. 20; 44. 6, 23; 1 Chr. 28. 7; 2 Chr. 6. 15; (‖ 1 Ki. 8); Dan. 9. 7, 15. כְּהַיּוֹם הַזֶּה Deut. 6. 24; Jer. 44. 22; Ezr. 9. 7, 15; Neh. 9. 10. Elsewhere the phrase occurs only in Gen. 50. 20 (E); 1 Sam. 22. 8, 13†. Gen. 39. 11 is different.

8. עמך אשר בחרת] Deut. 7. 6 כי עם קדוש אתה לי׳ אלהיך בך בחר י׳ אלהיך להיות לו לעם סגלה; 14. 2; cf. 4. 37.

10. וייטב הדבר וג׳] Cf. Deut. 1. 23 וייטב בעיני הדבר; Gen. 41. 37 (JE); Josh. 22. 33 (P).

12. לב חכם ונבון] The two adjectives are so coupled in Deut. 1. 13; 4. 6.

אשר כמוך . . . כמוך] Cf. II. 23. 25 וכמהו לא היה לפניו מלך אשר שב אל י׳ בכל לבבו ובכל נפשו ובכל מאדו ככל תורת משה ואחריו לא קם כמהו, a passage clearly marked as belonging to R^D^ by the quotation from Deut. 6. 4. So also II. 18. 5.

14. אם תלך בדרכי לשמר חקי וג׳] See *ch.* 2. 3, 4 *note.*

כאשר הלך דויד] R^D^ constantly refers to David as the standard of piety; *vv.* 3, 6; *ch.* 9. 4; 11. 4, 6, 33, 38; 14. 8; 15. 3, 5, 11; II. 14. 3; 16. 2; 18. 3; 22. 2. Cf. *note* on *ch.* 11. 12.

והארכתי את ימיך] With י׳ as subject only in this passage. There are two more usual constructions:—(1) *Prolong one's own days*, as in Deut. 4. 26 לא תאריכֻן ימים עליה; (2) *Days grow long*, ימים being subject and האריך intransitive (*internal* Hiph.; G-K. § 53, 2); Ex. 20. 12 למען יארכון ימיך.

15. If according to *v.* 4 '*the* great high-place' was at Gibeon, it is difficult to understand why Solomon should have returned to Jerusalem to offer sacrifice, except from the Deuteronomic standpoint. Hence the whole verse, at least in its present form, may be due to R^D^.

ארון ברית י׳] Mainly a D expression. *Ch.* 6. 19; 8. 1, 6; Deut. 10. 8; 31. 9, 25, 26; Josh. 3. 3; 8. 33 (sections belonging to the Deuteronomic editor, marked as D^2; see Dri. *LOT.* 97); Jer. 3. 16; ארון הברית Josh. 3. 6 bis, 8; 6. 6† (all D^2).

Elsewhere ארון ברית י׳ occurs Num. 10. 33; 14. 44; Josh. 4. 7, 18; 6. 8 (all JE); 1 Sam. 4. 3, 4, 5 (LXX om. ברית), and several times in Chr. ארון הברית Josh. 4. 9 JE: ארון ברית האלהים 1 Sam. 4. 4 (LXX om. ברית); 2 Sam. 15. 24; 1 Chr. 16. 6; Judg. 20. 27†. In the curious expressions of Josh. 3. 11, 14, 17 (JE) ארון הברית אדון כל הארץ, הארון הברית, הארון ברית יהוה, הברית is doubtless an interpolation[1].

4. וילך] LXX, Luc. καὶ ἀνέστη καὶ ἐπορεύθη, i.e. וַיָּקָם וַיֵּלֶךְ, adopted by Klo. on the ground that it more appropriately introduces the festive occasion which, as the Chronicler, II. *ch.* 1, shows, was the inaugural action of the young king's reign.

המלך] LXX om.; Luc. Σολομῶν.

כי היא הבמה הגדולה] 'For it was *the* great high-place,' i.e. *the greatest* high-place; an idiomatic method of expressing the superlative degree. The article with the adjective implies that the subject is pre-eminently characterized by the quality described. Gen. 44. 12 בַּגָּדוֹל החל ובקטן כלה 'he began with *the eldest* and finished with *the youngest*.' Da. § 34; G-K. § 133, 3.

יעלה] Probably frequentative; '*used to offer*.' אלף thus need not denote the number of victims slaughtered upon this single occasion, but may be a round number describing the many sacrifices which the king offered from time to time.

על המזבח ההוא: בגבעון נראה] LXX, Luc., Vulg., Pesh. presuppose עַל הַמִּזְבֵּחַ הַהוּא בְּגִבְעוֹן: וַיֵּרָא; a reading scarcely to be preferred, since the omission of the relative אשר before בגבעון is contrary to usage, and ההוא would in such a case be redundant. The reference of ההוא must be to הבמה הגדולה, which of course connotes the presence of an altar. Th. thinks that the Verss. read על המזבח הוא בגבעון which he renders 'upon the altar which is in Gibeon,' a strange use of הוא which can scarcely be paralleled even by Gen. 38. 21 איה הקדשה הוא בעינים.

---

[1] In *pre*-Deut. writings the phrases in use are הָאָרוֹן, אֲרוֹן יהוה in JE in the Hexateuch (only Josh.); הָאָרוֹן, אֲרוֹן יהוה, אֲרוֹן אֱלֹהִים (הָאֱלֹהִים) in the old narratives of Sam. and Kings. The latest expression of all is אֲרוֹן הָעֵדוּת P.

Klo.'s suggestion על מזבח הנחשת אשר בגבעון (cf. 2 Chr. 1. 6) is quite unnecessary.

5. בחלום הלילה] Gen. 20. 3; 31. 24†. Cf. Job 33. 15 בחלום חזיון לילה.

מה] Used as relative without antecedent; 'ask *what* I shall give thee.' So exactly *ch.* 14. 3 הוא יגיד לך מה יהיה לנער 'he shall tell thee what shall happen to the child'; cf. Judg. 9. 48; Eccl. 11. 2. Correctly speaking מה is really the indefinite antecedent ('*anything*,' as in 2 Sam. 18. 22; *al.*), and the relative אשר is omitted. This can be seen from Num. 23. 3 וּדְבַר מַה־יַּרְאֵנִי, lit. 'and word of anything (which) he shall show me.' In the late Heb. of Ecclesiastes we find the relative expressed after מה, מַה־שֶּׁ; 1. 9; 3. 15; 6. 10; *al.* Ew. § 331[b].

6. עמך] The phrase הלך עִם י׳ is very unusual. The only other occurrence appears to be Mic. 6. 8 והצנע לכת עם אלהיך. Cf. the expression התהלך את האלהים Gen. 5. 22, 24; 6. 9†. The common phrase is הלך לפני י׳ which occurs just before.

7. צאת ובא] An idiom expressing the discharge of duties pertaining to a particular position; 1 Sam. 18. 16; Deut. 31. 2.

8. אשר לא ימנה וג׳] *ch.* 8. 5 (|| 2 Chr. 5. 6). Cf. Gen. 16. 10; 32. 13. For the *nuance* of the Imperf. '*cannot* be numbered,' cf. Dri. *Tenses*, § 37[a].

9. לב שמע] Not merely a heart *attentive* to the directions of Yahwe, but expressing further the result of such attention—'an *understanding* heart.' For this sense of שמע, cf. *v.* 11 לשמע משפט; Gen. 41. 15 תשמע חלום לפתר אתו. More commonly it is employed with a negative to express the non-understanding of a foreign tongue; Gen. 11. 7; Deut. 28. 49; *al.*

בין טוב לרע] Lev. 27. 33; 2 Sam. 19. 36†.

לשפט את עמך הכבד הזה] Pesh. ܠܡܕܢܘ ܠܥܡܟ ܥܡܐ ܗܢܐ ܪܒܐ suggests לשפט את עמך העם הכבד הזה, while Vulg. *judicare populum istum, populum tuum hunc multum*, perhaps points to the same reading with a transposition of עמך and העם in translation. MT. is, however, confirmed by 2 Chr. 1. 10 את עמך הזה הגדול.

11. שאלת לך] 'Hast asked for *thyself*.' So only in || 2 Chr.

1. 11; II. 4. 3; 1 Sam. 12. 17, 19; Isa. 7. 11. This *Dativus commodi* is employed far more frequently in the sense, 'ask for some one else'; most commonly in the phrase שאל לפ׳ לשלום; 1 Sam. 17. 22; Gen. 43. 27; *al.*

ושאלת] '*But* hast asked.' The ו connects two *contrasted* ideas, and, by aid of the tautology ולא שאלת, ושאלת, gains a rather strong adversative sense, '*but.*' Somewhat similar, but not so marked, are *ch.* 2. 26 איש מות אתה וביום הזה לא אמיתך 'worthy of death art thou, *but* to-day I will not kill thee'; *ch.* 11. 33, 34 (ולא אקח); *al.* This use of ו is common in Prov.; cf. *ch.* 10 throughout.

The ו *simplex* places the idea in strict co-ordination with the preceding, thus preserving the assonance which would have been destroyed by וַתִּשְׁאַל.

הבין] So Isa. 56. 11 לא ידעו הבין; Ps. 32. 9.

12. עשיתי . . . נתתי] Perfects of certitude used here, as frequently, in a divine promise; Gen. 15. 18; Josh. 6. 2; Judg. 1. 2; *al.* The action determined upon by the will of the speaker is regarded as already accomplished. Dri. *Tenses*, § 13; Da. § 41.

לא היה] 'Shall not have been,' future perfect; or more strictly, '*was not* (*ever*),' upon any occasion that can be specified.

13. אשר לא היה . . . כל ימיך] 'So that there shall not have been any like thee among kings [all thy days].' Here כל ימיך makes no sense, and the sentence is quite complete without it. Vulg. attempts to explain, *cunctis retro diebus*, but doubtless LXX, Luc. are right in their omission of the phrase. It arose probably from an erroneous repetition of כָּמוֹךָ.

15. ויבוא] LXX *καὶ ἀνέστη καὶ παραγίνεται εἰς*, Luc. *καὶ ἀνέστη καὶ εἰσῆλθεν*, i. e. וַיָּקָם ויבא; possibly genuine.

לפני ארון] LXX, Luc. *κατὰ πρόσωπον τοῦ θυσιαστηρίου τοῦ κατὰ πρόσωπον (τῆς) κιβωτοῦ*, i. e. לִפְנֵי הַמִּזְבֵּחַ אֲשֶׁר לפני ארון וג׳. Th., Klo. think that this represents the original text, and that the recurrence of לפני occasioned the omission in MT. More probably the additional words are an insertion of the translator who wished to remove the impression that Solomon passed into the immediate presence of the Ark.

3. 16–28. *A notable example of Solomon's exercise of wisdom.*

16. אז תבאנה] The use of אז to introduce a fresh detail or narrative is very frequent in Kings. The other instances are *ch.* 8. 1, 12; 9. 11^b, 24^b; 11. 7; 16. 21; 22. 50; II. 8. 22^b; 12. 18; 14. 8; 15. 16; 16. 5†. Doubtless this was one of the methods by which R^D pieced together his various sources, and was employed when he wished to show that an event was more or less contemporaneous with the preceding narrative. When greater definiteness seemed desirable, he employed the phrases בימים ההם II. 10. 32; בימיו *ch.* 16. 34; בעת ההיא *ch.* 14. 1 (see *note* on each passage).

תבאנה] The use of the Imperf. after אז introducing a past event is very usual. So in nine of the cases enumerated above, and also Ex. 15. 1; Num. 21. 17; *al.* The event is pictured as *growing out of* the previous circumstances indicated by אז; a form of idea which has become stereotyped in the ordinary construction of the Imperf. with ו *consec.* See Dri. *Tenses*, §§ 67, 68. Probably in Kings R^D sometimes substituted אז with Imperf. for an Imperf. with ו *consec.* standing in his source; cf. *ch.* 8. 1 where we actually meet with a shortened form of the Imperf., אָז יַקְהֵל. When, as in *ch.* 8. 12; 9. 24^b; *al.*, the *Perfect* is employed with אז, the mere occurrence of the *fact* seems to be dwelt upon, without special stress upon its time relationship. G-K. § 107, 1, *Rem.* 1.

17. בי] Properly '*supplication*,' and then '*oh*' or '*pray*.' The word seems to be from √בוי, Ar. بَىَّ 'to supplicate.' Others derive from בעה = Aram. בְּעָא 'to ask,' and make the word a contraction of בְּעִי; like בֵּל for בְּעֵל, רוּת for רְעוּת. Cf. Targ. rendering בבעו, Pesh. ܒܒܥܘ ܐܢܐ ܡܢܟ, here and elsewhere.

עמה] '*With* her,' i. e. 'in her company'; Lev. 25. 39 כי ימוך אחיך עמך 'if thy brother be waxen poor *near* thee'; Ex. 22. 24; Gen. 31. 38. When used of proximity to several persons '*among*' is a fair equivalent; Judg. 18. 25 אל תשמע קולך עמנו 'make not thy voice to be heard among us.' This use of עם with *persons* is closely similar to that with *places* noticed on *ch.* 1. 9.

18. ללדתי] ל with back reference to the point of departure, '*after* my deliverance.' Cf. Gen. 7. 10 ויהי לשבעת הימים 'and it came to pass *after* seven days'; 2 Sam. 13. 23.

זולתי] Not 'except,' as usually (*ch.* 12. 20; Deut. 1. 36; *al.*), but, with a looser connexion with what precedes, '*but only.*' So Deut. 4. 12† תמונה אינכם ראים זולתי קול. Cf. the occasional *nuance* of εἰ μή, ἐὰν μή in N.T.; Gal. 2. 16 εἰδότες δὲ ὅτι οὐ δικαιοῦται ἄνθρωπος ἐξ ἔργων νόμου, ἐὰν μὴ διὰ πίστεως Ἰησοῦ Χριστοῦ. S. Luke 4. 25–27.

19. אשר] '*Because*'; *ch.* 8. 33 אשר יחטאו לך; 15. 5; Gen. 30. 18; 31. 49; *al.* More precise are עַל אֲשֶׁר 2 Sam. 12. 6; מִפְּנֵי אֲשֶׁר Ex. 19. 18; כַּאֲשֶׁר 1 Sam. 28. 18; מֵאֲשֶׁר &c.

21. ואתבונן אל] 'I looked carefully *at.*' So Isa. 14. 16† אליך יתבוננו.

22. אמרת] The participle lends pictorial effect; '*was saying.*'

23. זאת אמרת] LXX, Luc. σὺ λέγεις, i.e. אַתְּ אָמַרְתְּ; scarcely so good as MT., where the participle nearly represents the true English present; 'this one *says,*' 2 Sam. 18. 27. Dri. *Tenses,* § 135, 2 *end.*

זאת . . . וזאת] '*This one . . . and the other*'; *ch.* 22. 20 ויאמר זה בכה וזה אמר בכה 'and one said on this wise and another on that.' Da. § 5.

25. גזרו] 'Cut *in twain.*' So with the substantive, Ps. 136. 13 לגזר ים סוף לגזרים 'into *two* parts'; Gen. 15. 17.

At end of verse Luc. adds καὶ τὸ τεθνηκὸς ὁμοίως διέλετε, καὶ δότε ἀμφοτέραις. So Jos. This appears to be a translator's addition, derived, as Klo. notices, from the law in Ex. 21. 35.

26. נכמרו] So Gen. 43. 30; Hos. 11. 8 (with נִחוּמָי as subject). The ground idea is 'to be *hot*'; cf. Lam. 5. 10 עורנו כתנור נכמרו.

רחמיה] Here, as elsewhere, constantly in the plural, representing the seat of compassion or affection.

על בנה] '*Over* her son,' applied appropriately to the infant, but in Gen. 43 אל '*towards,*' with reference to grown men.

הַיִּלּוֹד] So *v.* 27; 1 Chr. 14. 4 הַיִּלּוֹדִים; but elsewhere only in the expression ילוד אשה three times in Job. In Syr. ܝܰܠܽܘܕܳܐ is a common form.

27. תנו לה את הילוד החי] Since the woman who spoke last was the one who desired the division of the child, we must suppose that the king, in uttering the words תנו לה, made a gesture to indicate that he referred to the other woman. Luc. (so LXX, omitting τὸ ζῶν, τῇ γυναικί) removes the ambiguity by reading Δότε τὸ παιδίον τὸ ζῶν τῇ γυναικὶ τῇ εἰπούσῃ Δότε αὐτῇ αὐτό; a mere exegetical paraphrase. Th., following Bö., supposes that the original may have been תְּנוּ אֹתוֹ לָאֹמֶרֶת תְּנוּ לָהּ אֶת־הַיָּלוּד הַחַי, and that thus אתו לאמרת תנו may have fallen out by homoioteleuton. But if the LXX translator had had these words before him, why should he have transposed אתו and הילוד החי?

28. חכמת אלהים] Wisdom *sent by* or *proceeding from* God. Cf. חִתַּת א׳ Gen. 35. 5; פַּחַד א׳ 2 Chr. 20. 29.

חכמה is here used in the special sense of *shrewdness* and *keen insight into human nature.* Cf. the bearing of the term *wise* as applied to the woman of Tekoa 2 Sam. 14. 2 *ff.;* and the woman of Abel-Meholah 2 Sam. 20. 16. Upon the later development of the term as seen in the '*Ḥokhma* literature' of the Old Testament, cf. Dri. *LOT.*, pp. 368 *ff.*

4. 1—5. 14. *Solomon's officers of state. His prosperity and wisdom.*

Ch. 5. 1^{a} = 2 Chr. 9. 26. *Ch.* 5. 6 = 2 Chr. 9. 25^{a}.

4. 2. השרים אשר לו] The circumlocution has the effect of retaining the greater definiteness which would have been sacrificed if שָׂרָיו had been written. Cf. *note* on *ch.* 1. 8, and Da. § 28, *Rem.* 5^{2}.

עזריהו בן צדוק הכהן] הכהן must refer to עזריהו and not to צדוק, just as elsewhere in the list, the title of the office refers to the man first specified, and not to his father. Hence Vulg., *filius Sadoc sacerdotis*, interprets wrongly. LXX, Luc. omit הכהן, as also כהן in *v.* 5, apparently under the impression that its usage is not to be reconciled with *v.* 4 צדוק ואביתר כהנים. Pesh., Targ. follow MT. The Chronicler, I. 5. 36, mentions an Azariah as הוא אשר כִּהֵן בבית אשר בנה שלמה בירושלם, a statement apparently misplaced from *v.* 35 (see Bertheau, *ad loc.*), where it will refer to our Azariah who is mentioned as son of Ahimaaz son of Zadok. Probably Azariah succeeded to Zadok, and exercised the office of high-priest at the consecration of the new Temple at Jerusalem, and during far the longer portion of Solomon's reign. We know that the statement of *v.* 4^b, as regards Abiathar, only holds good for a very short period during this reign (*ch.* 2. 26 *f.*), and very possibly this is also true of Zadok, whose son Ahimaaz was a man of some experience at the time of Absalom's rebellion (2 Sam. 15. 35, 36), and who therefore must have been well advanced in years at the time of Solomon's accession.

3. אליחרף] The only occurrence of this name. LXX Ἐλιάφ, Luc. Ἐλιάβ seem to substitute the more ordinary אֱלִיאָב.

שישא] LXX Σαβά, Luc. Σαφάτ. In 1 Chr. 18. 16 the same man is called שַׁוְשָׁא, LXX Ἰησοῦς, Luc. Σουσά.

In 2 Sam. 8. 17 apparently the same person appears as שְׂרָיָה, LXX Ἀσά, Luc. Σαραίας; 2 Sam. 20. 25 Kt. שיא, Q're שְׁוָא, LXX Ἰησοῦς, Luc. Σουσά.

Hence—(i) The form שריה has only weak attestation. It is supported by Luc. once, by LXX never[1].

(ii) The form Ἰησοῦς occurring twice in LXX cannot be original, since it is most improbable that so ordinary a name as יהושוע should have suffered corruption. On the other hand, it is very likely that Σουσά has become corrupted into the well-known Ἰησοῦς.

(iii) The form שושא is supported—

(*a*) By שישא in 1 Ki. 4. 3, the interchange of י and ו being of constant occurrence.

(*β*) By Σουσά twice in Luc.

---

[1] It is true that this is the form adopted in three places by Pesh., and in two by Vulg.; but in the case of proper names we cannot attach much importance to the testimony of Vulg., Pesh., Targ., since either the lists in the Heb. texts used by these translators appeared in a later form resembling that of MT., or else some sort of arbitrary uniformity with MT. has been produced by later hands. In the cases to which allusion is here made, correction for the sake of uniformity with 2 Sam. 8. 17 appears to have taken place.

(γ) In some degree by 'Ἰησοῦς twice in LXX, and, as regards the second שׁ, by 'Ασά in a third passage.

Hence שַׁוְשָׁא has by far the best attestation, and may be adopted.

4. ובניהו . . . הצבא] LXX om. through oversight.

וצדוק ואביתר כהנים] No part of the register in its original form as an official state document. This naturally headed the list with the name of the high-priest of the time, עזריהו בן צדוק. The insertion was made by R^D or by some one still earlier who wished, as a matter of historical interest, to notice that Zadok and Abiathar were priests at the commencement of the reign.

5. עזריהו] LXX 'Ορνειά, Luc. 'Ορνιά seem to presuppose אֲדֹנִיָּהוּ with corruption of ר into ד. This officer is apparently not elsewhere mentioned under either name.

זבוד] Only here. Luc. Ζαχούρ, i. e. probably זַכּוּר, a name of frequent occurrence. Pesh. ܙܟܘܪ in part supports this reading.

כהן] A peculiar use of the term to denote some high official whose functions we cannot precisely determine. Cf. 2 Sam. 8. 18 ובני דוד כהנים היו, paraphrased by the Chronicler, I. 18. 17 הראשנים ליד המלך. Dri. (*Sam., ad loc.*) argues from the uniform use of כהן in Heb. that the office, if possibly semi-secular and at times extended to non-priestly men of good family, must have belonged in the first place to the priestly class.

רֵעֶה המלך] This anomalous punctuation of the *st. constr.* is found again in 2 Sam. 15. 37 רֵעֶה דָוִד, and, according to Norzi, in 16. 16 in the best MSS. Klo. omits, as an exegetical gloss to explain the difficult כהן; but all Verss. reproduce the word.

6. ואחישר על הבית] This is the only important official named, *vv.* 2–7, whose father is not mentioned[1]. Hence there is probably some corruption of text.

LXX seem to have a triple, and Luc. a double rendering.

LXX	καὶ 'Αχεὶ ἦν οἰκονόμος	i. e.	ואחי [שׂר] על הבית
	καὶ 'Ελιὰκ ὁ οἰκονόμος	„	ואליאך [שׂר] על הבית
	καὶ 'Ελιὰβ υἱὸς Σὰφ ἐπὶ τῆς πατριᾶς	„	ואליאב בן שף על ?

[1] Verse 4^b is no exception: see *note*.

Luc. καὶ Ἀχιὴλ οἰκονόμος i. e. ואחיאל [שׂר] על הבית
καὶ Ἐλιὰβ υἱὸς Ἰωὰβ „ ואליאב בן יואב על ?
ἐπὶ τῆς στρατιᾶς

The name אֱלִיאָב which occurs in three renderings (ך is a mistake for ב in אליאך) appears to be the genuine form. Probably also the two letters שׁר, which appear to occur in LXX 1, 2, Luc. 1, and in LXX 3 under the form Σάφ, are a remnant of the father's name. Hence we may conjecture

וֶאֱלִיאָב בֶּן־שָׁךְ[יָה] עַל־הַבָּיִת

Th. supposes that LXX 3 (Luc. 2) are a translation of some words which have fallen out of MT., and hence after ואחישר על הבית he would restore וֶאֱלִיאָב בֶּן־שָׁפָט עַל־הַמִּשְׁמַעַת, supposing that LXX πατριᾶς read מִשְׁפָּחָה for משמעת. So Ew.

על הבית] Prefect of the palace, discharging the king's domestic affairs. This office existed subsequently both in the Northern (*ch.* 16. 9; 18. 3; II. 10. 5) and Southern (II. 18. 18; *al.*) kingdoms, and was a position of the highest dignity, being held by Jotham the heir to the throne of Judah after his father Azariah had been smitten with leprosy II. 15. 5; cf. also the exalted language used of Eliakim upon his promotion Isa. 22. 21, 22. The palace prefect was also called סֹכֵן Isa. 22. 15; see *note* on *ch.* 1. 2.

אדנירם] So LXX, Luc. This form of the name, which occurs also in *ch.* 5. 28, is doubtless correct. The form אֲדֹרָם (2 Sam. 20. 24; *ch.* 12. 18; ‖ 2 Chr. 10. 18 הֲדֹרָם) is either a contraction or a corruption.

המס] The forced labour exacted by Solomon for his building operations, according to *ch.* 9. 15–22 only from the Canaanite nations, but according to *ch.* 5. 27 from all Israel. That the latter statement is correct is proved by the unpopularity of Adoniram, who was stoned by men of the ten tribes; *ch.* 12. 18. The מס is mentioned as existing at the end of David's reign, 2 Sam. 20. 24, and is also spoken of as enforced upon the Canaanites at the conquest of the land; Jos. 17. 13 (JE); Judg. 1. 28; *al.*

7. יהיה על] 'It was *incumbent upon*': Ezek. 45. 17 ועל הנשיא

יהיה העולות וג׳; without היה Ezra 10. 4, 12; 2 Sam. 18. 11; *al.* The Imperf. expresses the *periodical* nature of the duty.

על אחד] Read עַל־הָאֶחָד with Q're; LXX, Luc. ἐπὶ τὸν ἕνα. The article is necessary to express the idea of distribution.

8. בן חור] Correct. LXX, Luc. Βαιώρ, a corruption. All twelve officers are mentioned either by their patronymic only, or by their particular name with the addition of the patronymic, which is in no case omitted.

9. בן דקר] LXX υἱὸς Ῥῆχας, Luc. υἱὸς Ῥῆχαβ. The name occurs nowhere else, unless בִּדְקַר II. 9. 25 represents a contraction of it. Luc.'s בֶּן־רֵכָב is at least as probable.

מקץ] Not elsewhere mentioned. LXX Μακεμάς, i. e. apparently מִכְמָשׂ (cf. 1 Sam. 13. 2, 5; 14. 31 Μαχεμάς), cannot be right, since it is clear that the place must have lain, with the others belonging to the same officer, in or about the district originally assigned to Dan, and in the west borders of Judah. Luc. Μαγχάς, and other Verss. support MT.

שעלבים] Judg. 1. 35†. שַׁעַלַבִּין Josh. 19. 42†. One of David's heroes is described in 2 Sam. 23. 32 as הַשַּׁעַלְבֹנִי.

בית שמש] The modern *'Ain Shems*, a village about four miles west-south-west of Jerusalem. Rob. *BR.* ii. 223 *f.*

ואלן בית חנן] LXX καὶ Ἐλὼμ ἕως Βηθλαμάν, Luc. καὶ Αἰλὼν ἕως Βαιθναάμ, read as the names of *two* places, doubtless correctly. In Josh. 19. 43 אילון is mentioned as a town of Dan, and בית חנן appears to have been discovered under the modern name *Beit-Ḥanûn*, a short distance east-north-east of Gaza. Rob. *BR.* ii. 35; Baed. 154. We may, therefore, read וְאֵלוֹן עַד בֵּית־חָנָן; cf. *v.* 12 עד אבל מחולה. So Klo., Kamp.

10. בן חסד . . . חפר] LXX υἱὸς Ἔσωθ, Βηρναμαλουσαμηνχὰ καὶ Ῥησφαραχείν. This, when transliterated, upon the whole supports MT.

MT. בן חסד בארבת לו סכה וכל ארץ חפר
LXX בן חסד בארנם לו ס[מ]נח ו ריץ פרח

The place ארבות is not mentioned elsewhere, but may possibly be the same as אֲרָב Josh. 15. 52, a city near Hebron. The נם of

LXX may easily be a corruption of בת of MT., and ארנם certainly does not point to any known place of a different name. Since יַרְמוּת (probably the modern *Yarmûk*) is mentioned with סכה in Josh. 15. 35, it has been thought, with some plausibility, that this place lies concealed under ארבות. So Th.

The correctness of סכה, which has been identified with *Shuweikeh* close to *Beit Nettîf*, is not to be doubted. Rob. *BR*. ii. 16, 21; Baed. 161. LXX reads נ for כ, ח for ה, and inserts מ, perhaps a corruption of ס erroneously repeated. LXX, פרח is merely a transposition of חפר, which latter seems to be correct, Josh. 12. 17.

Luc. Μαχεὶ υἱὸς Ἐχωβὴρ Βηθναμαλουζὰ καὶ Ἀμηχὰ καὶ τῆς Φαραχιναναδάβ is clearly a further corruption of LXX through an attempt to resolve it into sense. Εσωθ Βηρ- has become Εχωβηρ, then Βηρ- is repeated under the form Βηθ-, -σαμηνχα is divided into -ζα (και) Αμηχα, Ρησ- becomes της, and finally -φαραχειν with the אבינדב of the next *verse* appears as Φαραχιναναδάβ.

11. בן א׳ כל נפת דאר] 'Ben-Abinadab—all the high country of Dor'; correct. For נפת דאר, cf. Josh. 12. 23 נָפַת דּוֹר; 11. 2 נָפוֹת דּוֹר.

The meaning of the root נוף is illustrated by Ps. 48. 3 יְפֵה נוֹף 'beautiful *in elevation*,' of Mount Zion.

LXX ἀνὰ Δάν is a corruption of Ἀβιναδάβ, and ἀνὰ Φαθεί of Ναφάθ. The words ἀνὴρ Ταβληθεί represent דאר טפת read as נאר טבלת. Probably נאר was at first attached to נפת by the translator, the whole being transliterated Ναφαθανηρ, which afterwards came to be divided.

טָפַת] With the old f. termination. So with other personal names, both f.:—בָּשְׂמַת *v*. 15; Gen. 26. 34; מַחֲלַת Gen. 28. 9; 2 Chr. 11. 18; or, more strangely, m.:—גְּנֻבַת *ch*. 11. 20; גִּינַת *ch*. 16. 21; בְּכוֹרַת 1 Sam. 9. 1; גָּלְיַת 1 Sam. 17. 4 *ff*.; אֲחֻזַּת Gen. 26. 26. It is noticeable that most of these names are non-Israelitish: גלית, אחזת Philistine; גנבת probably Edomite or a Semiticized Egyptian name like אָסְנַת Gen. 41. 45; מחלת Ishmaelite; and טפת, בשמת, if daughters of Solomon's foreign wives, probably Canaanite; בשמת Gen. 26. 34 being specified as Hittite. עֲנָת, mentioned Judg. 3. 31; 5. 6 as the parent of שַׁמְגַּר, is the name of the Canaanite goddess, traces of whose cult appears in the localities בֵּית־עֲנָת Judg. 1. 33; בֵּית־עֲנוֹת Josh. 15. 59; עֲנָתוֹת Jer. 1. 1; *al.*

Similarly, we find a number of place-names with this termination, these being clearly Canaanite in origin:—מֵפַּעַת (perhaps a segholate termination) Josh. 13. 18; מַעֲרָת Josh. 15. 59; בָּצְקַת Josh. 15. 39; II. 22. 1; הַמִּכְמְתָת Josh. 16. 6; גִּבְעַת (? text obscure) Josh. 18. 28; הַדָּבְרַת Josh. 19. 12; דָּבְרַת Josh. 21. 28; קַטָּת Josh. 19. 15; חֶלְקַת Josh. 19. 25; חֶלְקָת Josh. 21. 31; שִׁיחוֹר לִבְנָת Josh. 19. 26; חַמַּת, רַקַּת Josh. 19. 35; בַּעֲלָת Josh. 19. 44; *ch.* 9. 18; צְפַת Judg. 1. 17; טַבָּת Judg. 7. 22; צָרְפַת Ob. 20; *ch.* 17. 9, 10; and perhaps נָוַית 1 Sam. 19. 18 (on vocalization, cf. Dri. *ad loc.*)[1]. Outside Palestine we have אֵילַת Deut. 2. 8; *al.*; and מחרת in Moab, Mesha, *l.* 14.

Comparing the inscriptions of neighbouring countries, it may be noticed that both Phoenician and Aramaic afford many examples of f. proper names in *-ath,* this being the regular f. termination in Phoen. as in Moabitic: Phoen. (*CIS.*) כבדת *Kabdath,* 372, *al.*; ארשת *'Arishath,* 307, *al.*; עלשת *'Elishath,* 481, *al.,* &c.;—Aram. Nabathean (Euting, *Nabatäische Inschriften*) בנית *Bunayyath,* 13; גזיאת *Guzai'ath,* 15; הינת *Hînath,* 26, &c.; while Aramaic alone yields instances of m. names with this termination;—Nabathean (Euting) חרתת *Ḥaritath* (Aretas); בגרת *Bagrath,* 8; מרת *Murrath,* 18; חמלת *Ḥamlath,* 7; מנעת *Mun'ath,* 6, 19; עבידת *'Obaidath,* 23, 24; עמירת *'Amirath,* 19;—Palmyrene (De Vogüé, *Syrie Centrale*) אדינת *'Odainath,* 21, *al.*;—Babylon (*CIS.*) אמדת *'Ummadath,* 66;—Assyria, ארתדת *'Artadath,* 100. Phoenician, on the other hand, only exhibits m. names in *-ath* compounded with the f. name of the goddess מלכת *Milkath,* just as Aramaic abounds in m. compounds of the f. אלת *'Allath.*

12. תענך ומגדו] Mentioned together as the scene of the great battle of Deborah and Barak with the Canaanites; Judg. 5. 19. תענך now appears as *Ta'annûk*, not far to the south-west of *Zer'în*, i. e. יזרעאל. מגדו is conjectured by Rob. to be the modern *Lejjûn*,

---

[1] No attempt has been made to include or classify proper names in Chr.

the Legio of Jos. and Eusebius, said by them to be three or four Roman miles from Taanach. This place lies north-west of *Ta'annûk*, and due west of *Zer'în*. *BR.* ii. 316, 328; Baed. 227; Smith, *Hist. Geogr.* 386 *f.*

בית שאן] Also בֵּית שָׁן 1 Sam. 31. 10, 12; or בֵּית־שַׁן 2 Sam. 21. 12; the Scythopolis of later times, and now, by a rather strange contraction, *Beisân* to the west of the other cities, and near the Jordan. Baed. 222; Smith, *Hist. Geogr.* 357 *ff.*

צרתנה] *Ch.* 7. 46 mentioned with סֻכּוֹת (see *note*); Josh. 3. 16 said to be near אָדָם, i. e. probably the modern ford of *ed-Dâmieh* close to *Qarn Ṣarṭabeh*, with which, however, צרתן cannot be identified (Van de Velde, &c.) without violence to philology. 2 Chr. 4. 17 reads צְרֵדָתָה for צָרְתָן of *ch.* 7. 46; צְרֵדָה being mentioned, *ch.* 11. 26, as the home of Jeroboam in the hill-country of Ephraim. The identification of the two places seems, however, to be doubtful.

עד מעבר] 'As far as *the other side of*'; not as RV. marg. 'as far as *over against*,' i. e. *on this side of*. The former is the universal sense of the phrase used from the point of view of the speaker or writer. Thus בְּעֵבֶר הַיַּרְדֵּן, מֵעֵבֶר לַיַּרְדֵּן can denote either the country to the east of Jordan, Num. 22. 1; Deut. 1. 1; Josh. 17. 5; or that to the west of Jordan, Deut. 3. 20, 25; 11. 30; Josh. 5. 1; 9. 1; 12. 7; according to the position or point of view of the user of the phrase. In Num. 32. 19 the double מעבר does not violate the rule, but is employed by way of *contrast*, the first being spoken from the actual position of the speaker east of Jordan, and the second from the new point of view pictured by the calling up before the mind of the country west of Jordan. So in Josh. 22. 7, the phrase is used with reference to the position of the *other* half-tribe on the east. See Dri. *Deut.* xlii. *f.*

יקמעם] A place of this name is mentioned, 1 Chr. 6. 53†, as a Levitical city in the hill-country of Ephraim. In Josh. 21. 22 (|| 1 Chr.) the name is given as קִבְצַיִם, identified by Col. Conder (*Handbook*, 417) with *Tel el-Kabûs* near Bethel. This locality is much too far south of the cities previously named to suit the present mention, and, besides this, the הר אפרים has already been assigned (*v.* 8) to בן חור. This יקמעם therefore cannot be the יקמעם of 1 Chr., unless Conder's identification is wrong, and the city lay quite in the north of the הר אפרים. Rob. *BR.* iii. 115 follows AV. in regarding the name as a corruption of יָקְנְעָם, Josh. 21. 34, *al.*, which he finds as *Tell Qaimûn*, south-east of Carmel. Baed. 228.

13. ברמת גלעד] Cf. *note* on *ch.* 22. 3.

After the first לו, LXX, Luc. omit לו . . . חות by homoioteleuton.

חות] 'the tent-villages'; Ar. حَوَى *collect together*, حِوَاءٌ *a group of tents near together*.

חות יאיר . . . בגלעד] So Num. 32. 40, 41; Judg. 10. 4, rightly. Deut. 3. 14; Josh. 13. 30 (D^2) locate the villages in Bashan. See Dri. *Deut.*, *ad loc.*, who explains the origin of the mistake.

חבל ארגב] Targ. פלך טרכונא 'the region of Trachonitis,' i. e. the modern *El-Leja*, a district to the south of Damascus, forming a great lava-bed of about 350 square miles in extent. This identification seems, however, to be improbable. See Dri. on Deut. 3. 4, 5; and in *DB. Edinb. s. v.* Argob.

ערים גדלות וג׳] 'Great cities . . . walls and bars of bronze'; or, as we should say, '*with* walls, &c.' The extension חומה וג׳, in loose apposition to ערים גדלות, serves in part to describe the cities, in part to characterize their greatness. Cf. Deut. 3. 5; 2 Chr. 8. 5. Dri. *Tenses*, § 188, 1.

14. מחנימה] LXX Μααναιεῖον, Luc. ἐν Μαχειλάμ, perhaps read מַחֲנַיִם; but, as Klo. says, the ה *loc.* can be justified by supposing the implication of some such expression as '*appointed* to M.'

15. לאשה] LXX, Luc. om. through oversight.

16. באשר] LXX, Luc. om.; but allusion to this district follows naturally after נפתלי in previous verse.

וּבְעָלוֹת] No such place as עָלוֹת is mentioned elsewhere, and בַּעֲלָת of *ch.* 9. 18 is apparently the same as the בעלת of Josh. 19. 44 mentioned among the cities assigned to Dan, and so unsuitable, since this district has already been dealt with in *v.* 9. LXX ἐν τῇ Μααλά, Cod. A καὶ ἐν Μααλώτ. This suggests וּמַעֲלוֹת or וּבְמַעֲלוֹת, and accordingly Th. thinks that the country round about Accho and Achzib may have been known as 'the steps' or 'ascents,' even if the original reading of the Heb. text was not מַעֲלֵה צוֹר; cf. Josh. 10. 10 מעלה בית חורן. Against this, we have no trace elsewhere of the use of the term in this district. Luc. ἐν τῇ Γαλαάδ seems to be merely an alteration of LXX. Gilead is dealt with in *vv.* 13, 19. Klo. suggests וּזְבֻלוּן, and since this tribe would naturally be mentioned in connexion with אשר, נפתלי, and יששכר, the emendation is probably correct.

19. בארץ גלעד] LXX, Luc. ἐν τῇ γῇ Γάδ. Probably a mistake. The land of Gad is rather too precise, part of the kingdoms of Sihon and Og having been assigned to Reuben and the half-tribe of Manasseh; Josh. 13. 21, 30 *f.* On the other hand, from the wider term ארץ גלעד we conclude that Geber ben-Uri had supervision of all the country east of Jordan not assigned in *v.* 13.

ונציב אחד אשר בארץ] RV. 'and he was the only officer which was in the land.' This is usually interpreted thus: As the district was a very large one, more than one officer might have been expected to superintend it; but as a matter of fact this was not the case, probably because the country was rugged and thinly populated. But this translation, together with its explanation, would at least require וְהוּא הַנְּצִיב הָאֶחָד אֲשֶׁר בָּאָרֶץ הַהִיא, and there are no signs of the text ever having existed in this form. LXX καὶ νασὲφ εἷς ἐν γῇ 'Ιούδα, Luc. Νασεὶβ ἐν τῇ γῇ 'Ιούδα make the reference to be to yet one more officer who has supervision over Judah, thus restoring the number *twelve* which these Verss. would otherwise have lost through the corrupt rendering in *v.* 11[a]. But it is strange that this officer should be thus vaguely mentioned without record of his name, nor does Luc. appear to be correct in viewing נציב as a proper name; and besides this, having adopted the obviously original בן אבינדב of *v.* 11[a], we have now *thirteen* officers in contradiction to the statement of *v.* 7.

Klo. ingeniously suggests וְנָצִיב אֶחָד עַל כָּל־הַנִּצָּבִים אֲשֶׁר בָּאָרֶץ '*and one officer was over all the officers who were in the land,*' the allusion being to עזריהו בן נתן who is mentioned in *v.* 5 as על הנצבים. Such a second passing notice of this official at the end of the list would be most appropriate. The emendation is to some extent supported by Vulg., *super omnia quae erant in illa terra*, and may be worthily adopted [1].

Verse 20—*chapter* 5. 14.

This section appears in LXX, Luc. in a form somewhat different to MT. 4. 20; 5. 1, 5, 6, and part of *v.* 4 (מתפסח . . . הנהר) do not appear, but are to be found in the addition at the end of *ch.* 2. 46. At the close of *v.* 19 of *ch.* 4 the text continues with *ch.* 5 in the following order: *vv.* 7, 8, 2–4, 9–14, after which follow *ch.* 3. 1; *ch.* 9. 16, 17ª. Thus the commencement of *v.* 7 וכלכלו הנצבים האלה וג׳ hinges directly on to the section *ch.* 4. 7–19 which enumerates the נצבים and their respective districts. This explains הָאֵלֶּה of *ch.* 5. 7, which is otherwise anomalous. There can be no question that the text of the section, as preserved by LXX, is complete in itself, and bears the stamp of originality rather than the somewhat confused account of MT. The disturbing factors in MT. appear to have been 4. 20; 5. 1, 5 [2]. These, which contain no very precise information, were added probably not from a written source but from oral tradition, by an exilic or post-exilic [3] scribe, who desired reference to the happy times under Solomon's golden age. The insertion led to the dislocation of *vv.* 7, 8, causing them to be placed after *vv.* 2, 3, 4. Probably the same hand excerpted the notice about Pharaoh's daughter and her dowry from its true position after *v.* 14, dividing it and placing part at the beginning of *ch.* 3 (for the reason given on 3. 2, 3 *note ad fin.*) and part as a sequel to the mention of גזר in *ch.* 9. 15.

20. כחול וג׳] A common simile for a very large multitude; so exactly 2 Sam. 17. 11; cf. 1 Sam. 13. 5; Josh. 11. 4; Judg. 7. 12.

5. 1. היה מושל] The participle with the substantive verb em-

---

[1] Cf. Jos. (*Ant.* viii. 2, § 3) ἐπὶ δὲ τούτων εἷς πάλιν ἄρχων ἀποδέδεικτο.

[2] Verse 6 belongs properly to *ch.* 10 where it occurs in LXX, Luc. in connexion with *v.* 26.

[3] Necessarily so; for exilic hands had already been at work upon *ch.* 5. 4 (*note*) in the part which is common both to LXX and MT.

phasizing the idea of *duration—'was ruling'*; so *v.* 24 'was giving,' continuously for some long period; *ch.* 12. 6; *al.* Dri. *Tenses*, § 135, 5.

מן הנהר וג׳] The ideal limits of Israel's dominion; cf. Gen. 15. 18; Ex. 23. 31; Deut. 1. 7; 11. 24; Josh. 1. 4. הנהר '*the* river' always denotes נְהַר פְּרָת, the Euphrates; hence Vulg. *a flumine terrae Ph.*, Pesh. ܡܢ ܢܗܪܐ ܕܐܪܥܐ ܕܦܠܫܬܝܐ, which make ארץ פ׳ an accus. of place, are quite wrong. ארץ פ׳ is an accus. of *motion towards*, 'to the land of the Ph.'; cf. Gen. 45. 25 ויבאו ארץ כנען. Da. § 69b. 2 Chr. 9. 26 reads ועד ארץ פ׳.

ועד גבול מ׳] '*Even to* the boundary of Egypt.' The גבול מצרים seems to be the *Wady el-Arîsh,* which bounded the southern extremity of Philistia, and is mentioned elsewhere as the southern boundary of Palestine; *ch.* 8. 65; Num. 34. 5; Josh. 15. 4, 47; Isa. 27. 12.

מגשים...ועבדים] 'They brought &c.'; impersonal. Cf. Gen. 39. 22 את כל אשר עשים שם הוא היה עשה 'whatsoever was done (*lit.* they did) there, he was the doer of it.' This use of the participle with the indefinite subject unexpressed is somewhat uncommon. Cf. Dri. *Tenses*, § 135, 6.

מנחה] '*Tribute*'; so II. 17. 3; Judg. 3. 15, 17; 2 Sam. 8. 2, 6. Elsewhere the word has the more general sense of *a present* brought voluntarily to gain favour in the eyes of the recipient; II. 8. 8; 20. 12; Gen. 32. 14. As a sacrificial term the word in P denotes *the meal-offering*. Cf. further, *ch.* 18. 29 *note*.

3. רעי] 'Pasture'; a ἅπαξ λεγ. The common word is מִרְעֶה. According to the vocalization of בָּקָר *st. abs.*, רְעִי stands in apposition, defining the class under which these cattle fall; '*meadow-fed cattle*.' Dri. *Tenses*, § 188, 1.

ויחמור] LXX, Luc. om.

ברברים אבוסים] ב׳ is a ἅπαξ λεγ. The root אבס is seen again in Prov. 15. 17, שור אבוס 'a stalled ox,' the substantives אֵבוּס 'stall,' Isa. 1. 3; Prov. 14. 4; Job 39. 9; and מַאֲבוּס 'granary,' Jer. 50. 26†. All Verss. give the sense of fatted or selected *fowls*, without specifying the kind; Kimḥi *capons*, Ges. *geese* (from ברר,

to be pure or white), Th. *guinea-fowls* (an onomatop. from the cry of these birds).

4. עבר הנהר] '*The other side of* the river'; referring to Solomon's dominions to the west of the Euphrates. The phrase, as in Ezra 4. 10, 11, 16, 17, 20; 5. 3, 6; 6. 6, 8, 13; 7. 21, 25; 8. 36; Neh. 2. 7, 9; 3. 7, implies an *exilic* standpoint. The passage, therefore, is an insertion later than the redaction of the book by the pre-exilic R^D; but not so late as the dislocation caused by the insertion of 4. 20; &c. See *note ad loc.* On the other hand, the phrase as used in *ch.* 14. 15 (R^D); Josh. 24. 2, 3, 14, 15; 2 Sam. 10. 16; ‖ 1 Chr. 19. 16†; cf. Isa. 7. 20 (בְּעֶבְרֵי נָהָר) denotes the country *east* of Euphrates, from a *western* standpoint.

מתפסח . . . הנהר] The omission in LXX, Luc., though perhaps marking the words as an insertion later than the main part of the *v.*, and by the same hand as 4. 20; &c., may, on the other hand, be merely due to homoioteleuton, the scribe's eye passing from the first עבר הנהר to the second.

מכל עבריו] 'Upon all *sides* of him.' So Jer. 49. 32 מכל עבריו אביא את אידם; cf. Ex. 32. 15 לֻחֹת כְּתֻבִים משני עבריהם. The text of Van der Hooght reads עבדיו, a scriptural error unconfirmed by any Cod. or Vers.

5. תחת גפנו וגו׳] An idiom expressive of pastoral prosperity; Mic. 4. 4†; cf. Zech. 3. 10; II. 18. 31.

מדן ועד באר שבע] The standing phrase to express all the territory of Israel between the north and south limits; Judg. 20. 1; 1 Sam. 3. 20; 2 Sam. 3. 10; 17. 11; 24. 2, 15†. מבאר שבע ועד דן occurs in 1 Chr. 21. 2; 2 Chr. 30. 5†.

6. ארבעים אלף] So Vulg., Pesh., Targ.; and Luc. in 10. 26. LXX in 10. 26 τέσσαρες χιλιάδες, and so 2 Chr. 9. 25 ארבעת אלפים. The smaller number is adopted by Ew., Th., and others, and is perhaps more likely to be correct.

ארות] אֻרְיוֹת ‖ 2 Chr. 9. 25; אֻרָוֹת לכל בהמה ובהמה 2 Chr. 32. 28†. 'Stalls'; Ar. إِرِيّ and آرِيّ; Aram. ܐܘܪܝܐ, corresponding e.g. to אֵבוּס Isa. 1. 3; and to φάτνη S. Luke 2. 7.

7. יְעַדְּרוּ] 'Omitted'; Pi'el only here. Elsewhere Niph'al, 'be

missing,' six times. In Ar. غَدَرَ is used of a sheep lagging behind the rest of the flock.

8. והשערים ... שם] 'And the barley, &c., they used to bring unto the place to which it might pertain.' The subject of יהיה is השערים והתבן, naturally thought of collectively. Each officer had in his month to supply the different עָרֵי הָרֶכֶב, to which allusion is made in *ch.* 10. 26. So Klo., RV. *marg.* 2; &c. LXX, Luc., Vulg. supply הַמֶּלֶךְ as subject of יהיה, and this is followed by RV. *marg.* 1. It seems clear, however, that the word supplied is merely a wrong explanatory gloss on the part of the translator. The business of the נצבים can scarcely have been to follow the king from place to place with fodder for the limited number of horses which he might have with him.

For the *nuance* of the imperf. יהיה cf. Dri. *Tenses*, § 38 β.

רכש] RV. 'swift steeds.' From the contrast to סוסים the word seems to denote some special kind of horse, whether used for riding, Est. 8. 10, 14, or for chariots, Mic. 1. 13†. In Pesh. ܪ̈ܟܫܐ is the constant equivalent of סוס when used as a collective sing., or in the pl.

9. רחב לב] 'Breadth of heart.' לב is here used as the seat of the intellect; cf. Job 12. 3 גם לי לבב כמוכם לא נפל אנכי מכם, and 24; Jer. 4. 9; the expression חֲסַר לֵב 'devoid of intelligence,' peculiar to Prov., where it occurs eleven times, 7. 7; *al.* (חֲסַר תְּבוּנוֹת once as a variation 28. 16); and the common phrase חֲכַם־לֵב Ex. 31. 6; *al.*

With our phrase cf. Ps. 119. 32 דרך מצותיך ארוץ כי תרחיב לבי.

כחול וג׳] Here the figure is suggested not, as in *ch.* 4. 20, by the innumerable grains, but by the vastness of the level expanse.

10. בני קדם] In Gen. 29. 1 this expression is used of Mesopotamia, but elsewhere, Judg. 6. 3, 33; 7. 12 (coupled with מדין ועמלק); Isa. 11. 14; Jer. 49. 28 (‖ קֵדָר); Ezek. 25. 4, 10 (טירותיהם 'their *tents*,' mentioned *v.* 4); Job 1. 3†, the phrase denotes the Arabian tribes to the east of Israel, and spreading as far as the Euphrates. So also, while הררי קדם Num. 23. 7 (‖ אֲרָם) are the mountains of Mesopotamia, ארץ קדם Gen. 25. 6 is the land into which Abraham sent the בְּנֵי הַפִּילַגְשִׁים previously enumerated as *Arab*

tribes, and הר הקדם Gen. 10. 30 seems to be the Arabian hill-country called *en-Nejd* stretching eastward from *Ḥaḍramaut.* Thus Solomon's wisdom seems to be compared, not with the wisdom of the Chaldeans, who were chiefly known as astrologers, but with that of the Arabs, whose country, as Ke. points out, is the fatherland of proverbial wisdom. Agreeable to this is the mention, *ch.* 10, of the visit of the queen of Sheba in south-west Arabia, who came to test Solomon's wisdom with hard enigmas. So Ke., Ew., Th.

חכמת מצרים] The wisdom of the חַרְטֻמִּים, men of the priestly class who employed themselves in the study of hieroglyphics, astronomy, and magic; Gen. 41. 8; Ex. 8. 3, 14; *al.* Ebers, *Aegypten,* p. 344 *f.* Cf. also Isa. 19. 11; Acts 7. 22.

11. איתן האזרחי וג׳] The four (דָּרַע for דרדע; but Codd., Luc., Pesh., Targ. agree with Kings) are mentioned with זמרי 1 Chr. 2. 6 as sons of זֶרַח the son of Judah by Tamar, Gen. 38. 30. So Targ. interprets האזרחי as בר זרח. In 1 Chr. 15. 17, 19 a Heman and an Ethan appear with Asaph as appointed by the Levites to be precentors in the temple, the three representing the families of Kohath (1 Chr. 6. 18), Merari (1 Chr. 6. 29), and Gershom (6. 24–28) respectively. In 1 Chr. 25. 1 הימן and יְדוּתוּן (cf. 1 Chr. 16. 41, 42; 2 Chr. 5. 12; 35. 15; apparently the same as איתן) are mentioned as הַנִּבְּאִים בְּכִנֹּרוֹת וג׳, and in *v.* 5 הימן is called חֹזֵה המלך בדברי האלהים. Ps. 88 is ascribed in the title to הימן האזרחי, Ps. 89 to איתן האזרחי, Pss. 39, 62, 77 to ידותון. Hence the chronicler distinguishes Ethan and Heman, the sages of the tribe of Judah, from Ethan and Heman the musicians, who were Levites; and further, his statement that they were sons of Zeraḥ need not conflict with that of Kings, 'sons of Maḥol,' since Zeraḥ, as is suggested by the title האזרחי, may have been the remoter ancestor, Maḥol the immediate father. On the other hand, the author of the Psalm titles, in naming his men Ezraḥites, seems to be introducing a confusion between the Levites and the Judaeans.

שמו] 'His name,' i.e. his *fame;* cf. the phrases עָשָׂה שֵׁם לְ 2 Sam. 7. 9; *al.;* הָיָה לְשֵׁם Isa. 55. 13; אַנְשֵׁי הַשֵּׁם Gen. 6. 4; cf. Num. 16. 2; בְּנֵי בְלִי שֵׁם Job 30. 8.

12. שירו] שיר is never elsewhere used as a collective. Hence Klo. reads וַיִּהְיוּ שִׁירָיו, supposing that the scribe's eye was caught by the similar ויהי שמו in the previous line.

חמשה ואלף] LXX, Luc., several Codd. Vulg. presuppose חֲמִשָּׁה אֲלָפִים. This latter, as a *round* number, seems preferable.

13. העצים] As a general rule the sing. collective denotes growing trees, the pl. pieces of wood, logs, or timber, as e.g. in *v.* 22; *ch.* 15. 22. When in classical Hebrew the pl. is used of living trees, there seems to be some emphasis, however slight, upon the *different varieties*. So here, Judg. 9. 8 *ff.* (Jotham's parable), and perhaps Isa. 7. 2[1].

Elsewhere the pl. use appears to be late or poetical; Isa. 44. 14; Ezek. eight times; Joel 1. 12, 19; Song of Sol. 2. 3; 4. 14; Ps. 96. 12; || 1 Chr. 16. 33; Ps. 104. 16†.

14. מאת כל מלכי וג׳] '*Deputed by* all the kings, &c.'; so exactly 2 Sam. 15. 3 ושמע אין לך מאת המלך RV. 'there is no man deputed of the king to hear thee.' Ew. makes מאת וג׳ a closer definition of מכל העמים 'specially *some from among* all kings, &c.' For this sense it would be more natural to read מן simply without את[2], and even so the expression would be rather strange.

Luc. inserts καὶ ἐλάμβανε δῶρα before מאת, and similarly Pesh. ܘܡܩܒܠ ܗܘܐ ܡܘܗܒܬܐ, i.e. וַיִּקַּח מִנְחָה adopted by Klo., Hoo., and very probably correct. The reception of rich presents would be one mark of the prosperity of an ideal eastern monarch; cf. e.g. Ps. 72. 10.

5. 15—7. 51. *Solomon's building operations; chiefly, the construction of the Temple and its furniture.*

Chh. 5. 15—7. 51 supply the basis of 2 Chr. 1. 18—5. 1.

15. חירם] The name is contracted from אֲחִירָם 'brother of the

---

[1] Josh. 10. 26, 27 ויתלם על חמשה עצים וג׳ is probably no exception. The meaning seems to be 'five *gibbets*,' and, in addition, the numeral influences the use of the pl.

[2] מאת '*from proximity with*' (see *Heb. Lex.*, Oxf., p. 86) is too closely specific of locality to be used in such a sense as this.

lofty One,' a form which occurs as a Heb. name, Num. 26. 38. The same contraction in Phoenician is seen in the names חמלכת *Ḥimilcat*, for אחמלכת 'brother of Milcat'; חתמלכת *Ḥothmilcat*, for אחתמלכת 'sister of Milcat.' So in Heb. חִיאֵל for אֲחִיאֵל *ch.* 16. 34. The form חוּרָם occurs in 2 Chr. 2. 2, 10, 11; *al.*: cf. the variants אֲבִינַיִל 1 Sam. 25. 3, *al.*, אֲבוּגַיִל Kt. *v.* 18; חֲמִיטַל Kt., חֲמוּטַל Q're II. 23. 31, 24. 18; פְּנִיאֵל Gen. 32. 31, פְּנוּאֵל *v.* 32; אֲבִירָם *ch.* 16. 34, Assyr. *Abu-ra-mu*, *COT.* ii. 479.

אל שלמה . . . למלך] LXX (Luc. τοῦ) χρίσαι τὸν Σ. merely represents a corruption of MT., which latter is supported by other Verss.

אתו] Emphatic by position: 'they had anointed *him*'; perhaps with reference to the events of *ch.* 1.

תחת אביהו] LXX, Luc. ἀντὶ Δαυεὶδ τοῦ πατρὸς αὐτοῦ, correct, as being more circumstantial. The immediate mention of the name דוד in the next sentence favours its inclusion here also.

אהב . . . לדוד] Cf. *ch.* 2. 39 *note*.

כל הימים] 'All the days,' with the implication 'all *his* days.' So very frequently in preference to the use of the suffix כָּל־יָמַי, כָּל־יָמָיו, &c.; *ch.* 12. 7; 14. 30; II. 13. 3; Gen. 43. 9; 44. 32; 2 Sam. 13. 37[b]; *al.* In 1 Sam. 1. 28 we have the expanded phrase כל הימים אשר היה. Upon the phrase כל הימים used absolutely (Deuteronomic) in the sense 'continually,' cf. *ch.* 9. 3 *note*.

16–19. These verses have, in their present form, been amplified by R[D] upon the lines of 2 Sam. 7. On *v.* 17 לבנות בית לשם י' cf. *ch.* 3. 2 *note*; *v.* 19 הוא יבנה הבית לשמי 2 Sam. 7. 13; *v.* 18 ועתה הניח י' אלהי לי מסביב 2 Sam. 7. 1, 11; cf. Deut. 12. 10; 25. 19; Josh. 21. 42; 23. 1 (D[2]), and also Deut. 3. 20; Josh. 1. 13, 15; 22. 4 (both D[2]).

17. אלהיו] LXX, Luc. τοῦ θεός μου, an error.

המלחמה אשר סבבהו וג'] The speaker, in using המלחמה *the state of warfare*, has implicit in his mind הָאֹיְבִים *the enemiës*, who were its cause, and so immediately passes into the pl. סְבָבֻהוּ, and is able to continue עד תת י' אֹתָם. Cf. Judg. 5. 7 חדלו פרזון (*government* for *governors*). This manner of thought is illustrated by the less extreme case Isa. 25. 3 קִרְיַת גוים עריצים ייראוך (where the thought of the sing. קרית is lost in the idea of the גוים who inhabit it), and by the common use of a sing. collective for a pl. Cf. Ew. § 317^{b}; Da. § 17.

LXX, Vulg., Pesh. render המלחמה by a pl. '*wars*'; Luc. τῶν πολεμίων, Targ. עבדי קרבא paraphrase 'enemies.' From this latter Klo. would emend אַנְשֵׁי מִלְחָמָה; but this is unnecessary, and also out of accord with Heb. idiom, the phrase always denoting members of Israel's[1] standing army, never their foes. The expression איש מלחמות תעי 2 Sam. 8. 10 (|| 1 Chr. 18. 10) is different.

תחת כפות רגלו] Cf. Mal. 3. 21.

18. שטן] Illustrated by *ch.* 11. 14, 23, 25; 1 Sam. 29. 4.

פגע רע] 'Evil chance'; Eccl. 9. 11† עת ופגע יקרה את כלם 'time and *chance* encounters all of them.' פֶּגַע is something which *meets* one; cf. the use of the verb, 1 Sam. 10. 5 ופגעת חבל נבאים; Am. 5. 19; *al.*

19. אמר לבנות] 'I *purpose to* build.' So Ex. 2. 14 הלהרגני אתה אמר; 1 Sam. 30. 6; 2 Sam. 21. 16; Ezr. 20. 8; Ps. 106. 23. Similarly in the sense '*promise to*,' *ch.* 8. 12 אמר לשכן; II. 8. 19.

With the meaning '*command to*' the phrase occurs 2 Sam. 1. 18; 2. 26; and very frequently in late Heb., 1 Chr. 13. 4; 15. 16; Est. 1. 10; Dan. 1. 3, 18; 2. 2; *al.*; and in the Aramaic of Dan. 2. 12, 46; 3. 13, 19; 5. 2.

20. צוה ויכרתו] 'Command and let them hew,' i. e. 'command *that they hew*'; the voluntative with weak ו expressing regularly the *purpose* of the previous act. Dri. *Tenses*, § 62.

ארזים] LXX, Luc. ξύλα, i. e. עֵצִים, probably a correction in view of the fact that (*v.* 22) Ḥiram supplied Solomon not merely with עצי ארזים but also with עצי ברושים. Cedar wood, as the most important necessity, may very well be specially mentioned.

21. יהוה] Luc. κύριος ὁ θεὸς τοῦ Ἰσραήλ. So || 2 Chr. 2. 11; Klo., Hoo. As Klo. remarks, the expression יהוה אלהי ישראל is more

---

[1] Joel 4. 9 is the only passage where the phrase is used of foreign armies; and here too the אנשי המ׳ are spoken of, not as Israel's foes, but from the point of view of the גוים themselves.

appropriate in the mouth of Ḥiram than יהוה only. Vulg. *Dominus Deus* preserves part of the original text.

22. אעשה את כל חפצך] So *v.* 23; and of doing one's own pleasure, Isa. 46. 10; 48. 14; 58. 13†.

23. דברות] ἅπαξ λεγ. LXX, Luc. σχεδίας, Pesh. ܡܫܘܛܐ, Targ. תורגסין; '*rafts*' or '*floats*.' This meaning agrees with the following ונפצתים 'I will break them up'; cf. Ps. 2. 9; Jer. 48. 12. Vulg. *in ratibus* is a guess from the context.

In || 2 Chr. 2. 15 רַפְסֹדוֹת, a ἅπαξ λεγ. of doubtful derivation, is used.

24. ויהי חירום נתן] Cf. *v.* 1 *note.*

25. ושלמה נתן וג׳] The subject is intentionally emphasized so as to throw the sentence into antithesis with *v.* 24 ויהי חירום נתן. Cf. *ch.* 10. 10, 13 ותתן למלך . . . והמלך שלמה נתן; 12. 29 וישם את האחד בבית אל ואת האחד נתן בדן; 18. 42 ויעלה אחאב . . . ואליהו עלה; 22. 20b ויאמר זה בכה וזה אמר בכה; Gen. 4. 2, 3, 4; 36. 4. See Dri. *Tenses*, § 160, *Obs.*, who calls this variation in order, 'the Hebrew equivalent to μὲν . . . δὲ of the Greeks.'

מַכֹּלֶת] For מַאֲכֹלֶת Isa. 9. 4, 18†, with assimilation of the weak cons. א. Sta. § 112, 1, *Rem.* 2 quotes as parallels בְּסַאסְּאָה for בְּסַאסְאָה Isa. 27. 8; אֶדַּדֶּה for אתדאדה from דאה (or a redup. of the syll. דא) Isa. 38. 15; שִׁשֵּׁאתִיךָ for שִׁאֲשֵׁאתִיךָ Ezek. 39. 2. More frequent is the dropping of the quiescent א with a lengthening of the preceding vowel; so מָסֹרֶת for מַאֲסֹרֶת Ezek. 20. 37; אָזִין for אַאֲזִין Job 32. 11; *al.* G-K. § 24, 3; § 68, 2, *Rem.* 1; Sta. 112, 1.

עשרים כר שמן] The כר was a dry measure, and the quantity specified is much too small. We must follow LXX, Luc. (and Pesh. for the numeral), and read עֶשְׂרִים אֶלֶף בַּת שֶׁמֶן; cf. 2 Chr. 2. 9. So Jos., Th., Klo., Kamp.

שמן כתית] '*Beaten* oil,' obtained by the pounding of the olives in a mortar. This is specified for the lamp of the Tabernacle, Ex. 27. 20; Lev. 24. 2; and to form part of the מנחת בקר and מנחת ערב, Ex. 29. 40; Num. 28. 5†.

שנה בשנה] So Lev. 25. 53; Deut. 15. 20; *al.* 'Year by year,' properly, 'year *for* year,' the meaning being that what was done in one year exactly corresponded to that which was done in others.

Cf. *ch.* 10. 25 דְּבַר שנה בשנה. *Heb. Lex.*, Oxf., p. 90[a], compares יוֹם בְּיוֹם in very late Heb., Neh. 8. 18; 1 Chr. 12. 23; *al.;* כְּיוֹם בְּיוֹם 1 Sam. 18. 10†; כְּפַעַם בְּפַעַם Num. 24. 1; Judg. 16. 20; *al.;* חֹדֶשׁ בְּחֹדֶשׁ 1 Chr. 27. 1†.

26. כאשר דבר לו] Cf. *ch.* 8. 20 כאשר דבר י׳; *v.* 56 ככל אשר דבר; *v.* 53. The idea and phrase are those of D; cf. Deut. 1. 21; 6. 3; 9. 3; *al.;* Dri. *Deut.* lxxxi, who cites from D fifteen occurrences of כאשר דבר י׳ (ל), besides instances from the compiler of Judg., Josh. Thus the whole of *v.* 26[a] must be assigned to R[D]; and this is confirmed by the fact that the back-reference seems to be not so much to the original narrative of the vision at Gibeon, where Solomon's request is not for חכמה precisely but for לב שמע לשפט את עמך להבין וג׳ (*ch.* 3. 9; cf. *v.* 11), as to R[D]'s own addition (*v.* 12) which states Yahwe's definite promise of a לב חכם ונבון.

27. ויעל] 'Brought up' or '*raised*' a forced levy. So *ch.* 9. 15 המס אשר העלה; cf. *v.* 21 ויעלם . . . למס עֹבֵד.

28. וישלחם . . . חליפות] 'He sent them *in* relays.' ח׳ is an accus. of manner or condition, a usage very common in Heb., whether the accus. be a substantive, adjective, or participle. Such an accus. may determine either the *object*, as here; *ch.* 20. 18 תפשום חיים 'take them alive' (*as* living ones); or the *subject;* II. 5. 2 וארם יצאו גדודים 'and Aram went forth *in* bands'; 18. 37 קרועי בגדים. Da. § 70; Dri. *Tenses*, § 161, 2, 3. Instances of this accus. of state referring to a *genitive* are noticed *ch.* 1. 41.

חליפות] For the meaning cf. Job 10. 17 חליפות וצבא 'a host in *detachments* or *relays*.' Similar is Job 14. 14 כל ימי צבאי איחל עד בוא חליפתי 'all the days of my warfare would I wait, until *my relief* should come,' the figure being that of a soldier at his post.

בביתו] We should expect אִישׁ בְּבֵיתוֹ as in Ezek. 8. 12; *al.* Hence we must suppose either that איש has fallen out, or, with Th., that it is implicit in בביתו. Klo.'s בְּבֵיתָם, which he restores from the free rendering of LXX, Luc. ἐν τοῖς οἴκοις αὐτῶν, is an impossibility in good Heb. style.

29. נשא סַבָּל] Lit. 'bearing as porters,' or 'bearers, porters,' סַבָּל being in apposition to נשא. LXX, Luc., Vulg., Pesh. read

נֹשֵׂא סַבָּל 'bearing *burdens.*' 2 Chr. 2. 1, 17, based upon this verse, omits נשא and reads אִישׁ סַבָּל, סַבָּל.

The relationship of this 70,000 + 80,000 to the 30,000 of *vv.* 27, 28, is obscure. According to 2 Chr. 2. 16, 17 the former consisted of 'the strangers that were in the land of Israel.' Probably *vv.* 29–32 are from a different source to *vv.* 27, 28. So Ew., Sta.; the latter noticing that הלבנון of *v.* 28 is in *v.* 29 called ההר.

30. שלשת אלפים ושלש מאות] LXX τρεῖς χιλιάδες καὶ ἑξακόσιοι, in agreement with 2 Chr. 2. 1, 17, and probably genuine. So Th., Klo. Th.'s attempt to divide the 3,600 into the 70,000 + 80,000 = 150,000 of *v.* 29, + 30,000 of *v.* 28 = 180,000, thus assigning fifty workmen to each overseer, seems to be unlawful; since it places the 30,000 Israelites upon the same footing as the 150,000 strangers, and, in supposing that the overseers had charge of the work of the former, is neither consonant with the statement of 2 Chr. 2, nor with the view that *v.* 28, *vv.* 29 *ff.* are portions of different documents.

Luc. for the second number gives ἑπτακόσιοι, *Cod.* A πεντακόσιοι.

31. ויצו המלך] LXX om., probably owing to the transposition noticed below. Luc. καὶ ἐνετείλατο ὁ βασιλεὺς τοῖς ἄρχουσιν, i.e. לַנִּצָּבִים, scarcely improves MT., and is probably merely an exegetical addition.

In LXX, Luc. *vv.* 31, 32ᵃ are placed after *v.* 32ᵇ, *ch.* 6. 1. Sta. points out that this gives a bad succession, because the command to prepare the stone in the fourth year follows the statement in 5. 17 (LXX) that the hewing of stones and timber had been going on for three years. He also notices that in *vv.* 31, 32ᵃ, 32ᵇ MT. הסיע, פסל, הכין naturally follow one another in appropriate order.

32. וְהַגִּבְלִים] Difficult. As the word stands it has been taken in two senses—

(i) '*The stone-squarers.*' So apparently Targ. וארגובליא, Pesh. ܘܐܪܓܘܒܠܐ[1], and hence AV. However, the word is not used else-

[1] The derivation is doubtful. Levy thinks the word a transposition from the Gk. ἐργολάβος, while Jensen, *ZA.* vii. 218, explains by the Assyr. *bargulu.*

where in Heb. with such a meaning, and if it be adopted we must suppose that the ו is employed for closer specification, '*namely*,' which is improbable.

(ii) '*The Gebalites*.' So Vulg. *Giblii*, RV., Ges., Ke., Ew., Kamp. The ו must then mean '*and especially*,' the men of Gebal being particularly singled out from among the servants of Ḥiram. But, as Th. remarks, no one has as yet succeeded in explaining why they should receive such special notice.

Hence it seems probable that we have here a corruption, and that we must look for some *verb* following upon the preceding ויפסלו. So LXX καὶ ἔβαλαν αὐτούς, Luc. καὶ ἐνέβαλον αὐτούς. Th. restores וַיַּגְבִּלוּם '*and they bordered them with grooved edges*,' and so substantially Klo. וְהִגְבִּילוּם. Th.'s emendation is favoured by *Sieg. u. Sta.; Heb. Lex.*, Oxf., and may be adopted.

לבנות הבית] LXX omits and reads instead τρία ἔτη. Luc. τρισὶν ἔτεσιν εἰς τὴν οἰκοδομὴν τοῦ οἴκου. This addition is favoured by Tḥ., who thinks that without it *v.* 32^b is pointless, and supposes that three years' preparation of stone and timber preceded the commencement of the building, *ch.* 6. 1, in order that the work might go on without interruption. On the other hand, Sta., Klo. regard the words as a false inference from 6. 1. The former points out that even supposing that a very short time elapsed between the commencement of Solomon's reign and his intercourse with Ḥiram, yet, notwithstanding, a longer time than three years is needed for the hewing of the timber in Lebanon and its conveyance to Jerusalem. Sta. thinks also that the long duration of the work of building is not to be understood, if at the commencement stone and timber were already prepared. On these grounds MT. seems to be preferable.

6. 1. As has been noticed above, LXX inserts this verse before *vv.* 31, 32^a of *ch.* 5. In its place we now have *ch.* 6. *vv.* 37, 38^a which give the dates of laying the foundation of the Temple and of its completion. Wellh. (*C.* 267) remarks that these latter verses in MT. break the continuity between 6. 36 and 7. 1–12, while in the position which they occupy in LXX they completely supersede *v.* 1 MT. which holds the 'very unfortunate position' above mentioned. Hence he concludes that *v.* 1 is the work of a later editor who relegated *vv.* 37, 38[a] to their present place in MT. to make room for his addition, and that LXX represents the original text[1]. This will account for the position of *v.* 1 in LXX, the late addition having been first written in the margin of a MS., and afterwards incorporated in the text as best it could be. As a mark of the different authorship of *v.* 1 Wellh. notices that it uses חדש where *vv.* 37, 38[a] have ירח ; בחדש זו הוא החדש השני standing in place of בירח זו הוא החדש השני.

Another consideration favours the lateness of this verse. The number 480 appears to be not strictly historical, but to be a *round* number obtained, as recognized by Bertheau and Nöldeke, from 40 × 12, forty years being regarded as the approximate length of a generation[2], and frequently occurring in Judges in descriptions of the duration of periods of peace or oppression[3]. Attempts have been made so to arrange previous chronological notices that they may together correspond to this given period[4]; but no scheme has been entirely successful.

Now it is at least conceivable that the author of our verse may have been influenced by that fondness for the construction of artificial periods of similar length exhibited by the chrono-

---

[1] Sta. agrees with Wellh. that *v.* 1 is a late insertion, but refuses to regard the position of *vv.* 37, 38[a] in LXX as original, on the ground that a notice as to the completion of the building is out of place at the commencement, the expressions לכל דבריו ולכל משפטו pointing backward to a previous description. This argument scarcely seems to carry conviction.

[2] So in S. Matt. 1. 17 *ἀπὸ τῆς μετοικεσίας Βαβυλῶνος ἕως τοῦ Χριστοῦ γενεαὶ δεκατέσσαρες*, 40 × 14 = 560, approximates very fairly to the real length of the period—586 years.

[3] So of the peace enjoyed after the victories of Othniel (3. 11), Deborah (5. 31), Gideon (8. 28), Ehud (3. 30) eighty years, i.e. 40 × 2; and of the Philistine oppression (13. 1). Samson's judgeship (16. 31) twenty years, is half a generation. Cf. the periods assigned for Eli's judgeship (1 Sam. 4. 18), and for the reigns of David (2 Sam. 5. 4) and Solomon (1 Ki. 11. 42).

[4] Cf. Wellh. *Prolegomena*, 230 *f.* Jos. states the number of years to have been 492.

logist in S. Matt. 1. 17, and may thus have purposely approximated the length of the little-known period from the Exodus to the building of the Temple to the chronology of some subsequent period for the knowledge of which he possessed available sources.

If then we start from the commencement of Solomon's Temple, and add together the years of the reigns of the kings of Judah as given by R^D, we obtain the following result:—

Solomon (40 – 3 years before the commencement of the Temple)	37	I. 11. 42.
Rehoboam	17	14. 21.
Abijam	3	15. 2.
Asa	41	15. 10.
Jehoshaphat	25	22. 42.
Jehoram	8	II. 8. 17.
Ahaziah	1	8. 26.
Athaliah	6	11. 3.
Jehoash	40	12. 2.
Amaziah	29	14. 2.
Azariah	52	15. 2.
Jotham	16	15. 33.
Ahaz	16	16. 2.
Hezekiah	29	18. 2.
Manasseh	55	21. 1.
Amon	2	21. 19.
Josiah	31	22. 1.
Jehoahaz	—	23. 31.
Jehoiakim	11	23. 36.
Jehoiachin	—	24. 8.
Zedekiah	11	24. 18.
Total	430	

To this 430 add the fifty years of the Babylonian exile, and we have from the commencement of the Temple down to the

return from Babylon a second period of 480 years[1] which may be fairly considered as having determined the duration assigned to the former period. Thus *v.* 1 appears to be the work of a *post*-exilic editor, the same no doubt as will later on come into prominence through the insertions made by him under the influence of the Priestly Code[2].

The reading of LXX, *ἐν τῷ τεσσαρακοστῷ καὶ τετρακοσιοστῷ ἔτει*, is a mistake, but cannot be explained with Th., following Winer, ii. 327, *note* 2, as arising from a confusion of פ = 80 with מ = 40. In ancient Hebrew writing the method of expressing numeration, in cases where the number was not fully written in words, was most probably a system of strokes and similar signs, such as we find in Phoenician inscriptions. We have not the slightest evidence to prove that the comparatively late system of expressing numbers by means of letters was ever adopted in Hebrew MSS. of OT.

Luc. agrees with LXX as to the position assigned to *vv.* 37, 38ᵃ in place of *v.* 1, but continues *καὶ ᾠκοδόμησεν αὐτὸν ἐν ἑπτὰ ἔτεσιν, καὶ ᾠκοδόμει τὸν οἶκον τῷ κυρίῳ*, i.e. *vv.* 38ᵇ, 1ᵇ. This has obviously been added to Luc. by a later hand, both sentences in MT. belonging to the author of *v.* 1ᵃ.

2. ששים אמה ארכו] So Vulg., Pesh., Targ., and 2 Chr. 3. 3 (MT. and all Verss.). LXX, Luc. *τεσσαράκοντα μῆκος αὐτοῦ*, the translator apparently fancying erroneously that the reference is to the היכל or Holy Place, exclusive of the דביר, and so altering the text from *v.* 17.

ועשרים] Read ועשרים אמה with LXX, Luc., Vulg., Pesh.

שלשים אמה קומתו] So Vulg., Pesh., Targ.; but LXX, Luc. *καὶ πέντε καὶ εἴκοσι ἐν πήχει τὸ ὕψος αὐτοῦ.* In 2 Chr. 3. 3, and in the description of the dimensions of Ezekiel's Temple (41. 2), there is no record of the height.

3. על פני רחב] 'Upon the face of the breadth,' i.e. *corresponding to it;* but על פני הבית means simply '*before* the house.'

---

[1] This has been already noticed by Sta., *Ges.* i. 88 *ff.;* Kau., *Abriss,* 172.

[2] And therefore elsewhere cited as R^P.

עשר באמה רחבו] LXX omits through oversight.

After *v.* 3, LXX, Luc. insert *v.* 14 **καὶ ᾠκοδόμησεν τὸν οἶκον καὶ συνετέλεσεν αὐτόν.** In spite of what Klo. says to the contrary, it seems to be clearly inconsistent to mention the completion of the house before the details as to its roofing, side-chambers, &c. LXX order is therefore to be rejected.

4. חַלּוֹנֵי שְׁקֻפִים אֲטֻמִים] שקפים (only again in 7. 4[1]) probably means '*frames*,' the reference being to the beams or stones which were fitted together to form the outline of the window. רְבֻעִים שָׁקֶף (7. 5†) doubtless signifies 'square *in framework*'; שקף denoting the beams or stones which formed the sides and lintel of the doorway; מַשְׁקוֹף (Ex. 12. 7, 22, 23†) is the lintel or portal; and the Talmudic שְׁקוֹף has the same meaning 'lintel.' Ar. سَقَّفَ means *to roof a building with a vaulted roof*, سَقْفٌ *an arched or vaulted roof*, the original signification probably being that assigned by Ges., to bend down, incline[2], then, to place upon, especially applied to beams, and so, to joist or construct with beams. אטם is again applied to windows Ezek. 40. 16; 41. 16, 26; and is used in the expression אֹטֵם אָזְנוֹ 'stopping his ear,' Prov. 21. 13; Isa. 33. 15: Ar. أَطَمَ I. *to cover*, *hide*, *be contracted*, IV. *to close* (*a door*): Syr. ܐܬܛܝ̈ܡ *compressed*, *contracted*, then, *thick*, *solid*, and even *hard*, *stubborn* (of a disposition and of anger).

Thus our phrase may be rendered either (i) '*Windows with frames closed in*,' possibly by gratings (this being implied merely and *not* stated), or more probably (ii) '*Windows with narrowed frames*,' i. e. wide on the inner side of the thick wall, and gradually sloping so as to form a mere slit on the outer side, like the windows of ancient western fortresses. So probably Vulg. *fenestras obliquas*, and certainly Pesh. ܟܘ̈ܐ ܡܨܛܠܝ̈ܢܬܐ ܘܐܬܛܝ̈ܡܬܐ 'windows oblique and narrowed' (cf. Ezek. 40. 16 ܘܟܘ̈ܐ ܕܡܨܛܠܝ̈ܢ ܡܢ ܠܓܘ ܘܡܬܛܝ̈ܡܢ ܠܒܪ 'windows oblique within and small without'); Targ. כוין פתיחן מלגיו

[1] שקופים is restored by Cornill in Ezek. 41. 16 חלוני שקופים אטומות.

[2] In Ar. the term أُسْقُفٌّ is used of the *flexible* neck of the ostrich. Lane, *Lex.* 1383.

וסתימן מלברא 'windows opened within and closed without'[1]; Jesu bar-Ali who explains that ܟܘ̈ܐ ܐܛܝ̈ܡܬܐ are ܟܘ̈ܐ ܕܠܐ ܠܘܩܒܠ ܒܪ̈ܝܢ. ܐܠܐ ܡܬܩܦܣܝܢ ܡܢ ܚܕ ܓܒܐ ܠܣܡܠܐܝܬ. 'windows which are not cut through straightly (i. e. squarely), but narrowed upon one side obliquely'; Kamp.; and Cornill on Ezekiel, so far as regards אטמים,—'schräg einfallende Fenster.'

The Greek Verss. generally connect שקפים with השקיף 'to look or lean out of a window':—LXX θυρίδας παρακυπτομένας κρυπτάς, *al. exempl.* διακυπτομένας κρυπτάς, and so Θ.; Σ. θυρίδας καὶ ἐκθέτας ἐπισκέποντας; 'A. ἀποβλέπουσας βεβυσμένας; Luc. θυρίδας δεδικτυωμένας κρυπτάς. Perhaps LXX, Θ., 'A. mean 'with prospects obstructed,' whether by grating or otherwise. So Vet. Lat. *prospicientes absconsas*. Luc. δεδικτ. is probably a corruption of διακυπτ. in view of the explanation noticed below.

RV., Ke., Th., Ew., Sta., Kamp. (and Cornill in Ezek. 41. 16) give to שקפים the sense of *lattices*, *gratings*, or *transverse beams;* but this seems to rest upon pure conjecture; and, besides bearing no resemblance to the meaning of other Hebrew words from the same root, is unsuitable to the use of the same word by the same writer in 7. 4 (see *note*). The rendering of אטמים by RV., Ke., Th., Sta. '*fixed*,' '*festgemachte*,' appears to be an accommodation to the meaning given to שקפים, and fails of justification.

5. ויבן] LXX ἔδωκεν, i. e. וַיִּתֵּן; possible (cf. נתן, *v.* 6), but not superior to MT. Luc. καὶ ἐποίησεν, i.e. וַיַּעַשׂ, is influenced by the recurrence of this word in *vv.* 4, 5^b.

יצוע] The meaning seems to be something spread upon or applied to the wall of a house, so '*side-buildings*' or '*wings*.' So approximately Pesh. ܣܘܚܪ̈ܐ lit. 'surroundings,' Targ. זיזא probably 'projecting buildings.' The word denotes the whole wing, not the single stories: see *notes* on the other occurrences *vv.* 6, 10†. Hence LXX, Luc. μέλαθρα, Vulg. *tabulata*, whence RV. 'stories,' are not quite correct.

---

[1] These Verss., however, appear to derive their rendering 'open (oblique), closed (narrowed)' from the whole phrase שקפים אטמים; and so apparently RV. marg.

Q're יָצִיעַ probably aims at distinction from יָצוּעַ 'bed,' Gen. 49. 4; *al.*

סביב את קירות הבית] LXX, Luc. om. As Sta. points out, the words appear to be merely a gloss upon סביב להיכל ולדביר. So Kamp. The strange accentuation, which places the zaqef in each case upon סביב, cannot be correct.

ויעש צלעות סביב] LXX om., but merely through oversight. The words are found in Luc. and the other Verss., and are, as Sta. remarks, indispensable. צלע, properly a *rib*, is thought to be used distinctively of a *side*-chamber here and in the description of Ezekiel's Temple, but seems to be employed of chambers more generally in 7. 3. Cf. *note* on 7. 2 *ad fin.*

6. היצוע התחתנה] יצוע (the *whole* wing, *v.* 5) is here unsuitable, and is also a masc. word. LXX, Luc. ἡ πλευρά, Targ. מחיצתא point to הַצֵּלָע as the original reading, doubtless correctly. Cf. *v.* 8 הצלע התיכנה. So Th., Sta.; and Klo. doubtfully.

מגרעות] 'Rebatements'; ἅπαξ λεγ. The meaning is clear from the context, and from the common sense of גרע 'take away' or 'diminish.' So perhaps LXX, Luc. διάστημα. Pesh., Targ., guessing from context, ܢܦܩܬܐ, נפקתא 'ledges'; Vulg. *trabes*.

לבלתי אחז בקירות הבית] 'That (the beams) should not have hold in the walls of the house.' The absence of the subject, not previously mentioned, is very harsh; and we may reasonably suppose that הַקּוֹרוֹת has fallen out before בקירות, owing to the similarity of the two words. Cf. the confusion of these words in *v.* 15. Targ. rightly supplies a subject רישי שריתא 'the ends of the beams.'

7. This verse intrudes itself very awkwardly into the midst of the account of the construction of the side-chambers, and, if forming a part of the original description, must at any rate be out of place. Kamp. assigns the notice to R[D], and Sta., following Ew., regards it as a gloss from the margin, and so presumably by a later hand,—perhaps the post-exilic author of *v.* 1, &c. The tradition of the building of the Temple without the use of tools and of previously prepared material is doubtless

derived from or connected with the command of Ex. 20. 25 (J); Deut. 27. 5, 6 (cf. especially the phrase אבנים שלמות) with regard to an altar of stone, and so *can* have been written by the pre-exilic R^D, as is suggested by the occurrence of the verse in the same position in LXX, Luc.

On the other hand, the notice is not in the spirit of R^D—whose insertions, as a rule, subserve a definitely *religious* purpose—and rather answers to the desire for curious details characteristic of a later (post-exilic) age; while the awkward position of the verse is strange to the really skilful handling by R^D of his materials, and more nearly resembles the work of the later editor who has complicated the descriptions of *chh.* 6, 7 throughout.

We may therefore assign the insertion to the post-exilic editor (R^P), and suppose that in LXX the verse was added by a copyist from a Hebrew MS.

אבן שלמה מסע] 'Stone rough-hewn *in* (*as regards*) quarrying.' מסע, in loose apposition (Dri. *Tenses*, § 188, 1; Da. § 29^c), defines the sense in which the stone could be described as שלמה.

שלמה] 'Whole,' as hewn from the quarry, without any further preparation by sawing or otherwise. The term, as employed of the stones of an altar, Deut. 27. 6; Josh. 8. 31, probably denotes stones in their natural condition. מַסָּע, in this sense a ἅπαξ λεγ., is the 'action of removal,' from Hiph'il הִסִּיעַ 'pluck up,' used of moving stones from the quarry in 5. 31. The whole expression אבן וג׳ is an accus. of material; and with an active verb בָּנָה את הבית אבן וג׳ would have formed the second or remoter accus., as in Deut. 27. 6; 7. 15. Dri. *Tenses*, § 195. Cf. Ew. § 284^c; Da. § 80.

כל כלי] For כל at the close of a category *asyndetos* summarizing all possibilities of the class cf. *ch.* 8. 37 כל נגע כל מחלה.

נשמע] The verb agreeing, not with the whole list, but with the nearest subs. כל כלי in sing. Cf. Deut. 8. 13 כסף וזהב ירבה לך; Hos. 4. 11 זנות ויין ותירוש יקח לב; Da. § 114^a.

8. התיכנה] LXX, Luc. τῆς ὑποκάτωθεν, Targ. ארעיתא presuppose הַתַּחְתֹּנָה, which is doubtless correct. So Th., Ew., Sta., Klo., Kamp., Benz., Kit.

לולים] A *ἅπαξ λεγ.*, the meaning of which is not quite clear. RV. 'winding stairs' is derived from LXX, Luc. *ἑλικτὴ* (*εἱλικτὴ*) *ἀνάβασις*, 'A. (*καὶ ἐν*) *κοχλίαις*, Vulg. *cochlea*, Targ. מסבתא; so Ke., Th., Ew., Klo., Kamp. Pesh., however, renders ܒܡܥܠܬܐ 'through *a trap-door*,' and Sta. thinks that this is nearly correct. In Rabb. Hebrew[1] לול can mean a falling shaft covered by a trap-door; *Middoth* 4, 5 לולין היו פתוחין בעליה לבית קדש הקדשים שבהן היו משלשלין את האומנין בתיבות כדי שלא יזונו עיניהן מבית קדשי הקדשים 'There were *lûlîn* in the loft opening into the Holy of Holies through which they used to let down the workmen in boxes that they might not feast their eyes within the most Holy Place.' We also have the word used to denote a hollow room covered above; *Pesachim* 34ᵃ, 77ᵃ, *al.*; and afterwards it comes to mean a hen-roost; *Shabbath* 102ᵇ, 122ᵇ, *al.* Hence Sta. understands by לולים hollow chambers covered above with trap-doors, through which one might ascend by means of a ladder or steps like those of hen-roosts.

Adopting this explanation we may render '*trap-door covered ascents.*'

9. This verse is obviously out of place, breaking the connexion between *vv.* 8 and 10; and, accordingly, with Sta. it shares the fate of *v.* 7 as being a late gloss. Against this it should be noticed (i) that the verse contains the only allusion to the roofing of the house, a detail not likely to be omitted; and (ii) that mention of the completion of the house ought fitly to come into a description of the building, and may reasonably do so immediately after the details as to the construction of the house proper, and before those which concern its inward embellishments[2]. Thus we may regard the verse as original, excepting the words גבים ושדרת not found in LXX, Luc., and place it after *v.* 10, from which position it has been transposed by a very early error of transcription[3].

---

[1] Cf. Levy, *s. v.*

[2] Verse 15 immediately continues with a description of את קירות הבית מביתה.

[3] This conclusion is confirmed by the repetition (*v.* 14) of 9ᵃ by the author of the interpolation *vv.* 11–14. See *note*.

Thus the sequence in description—walls, porch, windows, wings, roofing—is perfect, the last detail aptly rounding off the account of the outside building of the house.

גבים ושדרת בארזים] A rather strange expression. If we adopt RV. 'beams and planks of cedar,' we must suppose that the ב is a variety of the ב *essentiae*; '*consisting of* cedar.' LXX, Luc. *καὶ ἐκοιλοστάθμησεν τὸν οἶκον ἐν κέδροις*, Pesh. ܘܐܘܣܦܗ̇ ܠܒܝܬܐ ܒܩܘܪ̈ܝܐ ܕܐܪ̈ܙܐ seem to have read simply ויספן את הבית בארזים, which was probably the original form of the sentence. The words גבים ושדרת are then a later gloss added to explain more precisely the use to which the cedar beams were put.

גבים ושדרת] גבים elsewhere means 'pits' or 'cisterns'; II. 3. 16; *al.*; while שדרות in its other occurrences, II. 11. 8, 15; || 2 Chr. 23. 14†, denotes 'ranks' of men. Ew., taking גבים to mean lit. 'cavities,' explains that the roof consisted 'of an ornamental ceiling in squares, with small pieces of cedar wood as dividing beams.' This agrees with LXX insertion ※ *φατνώμασιν καὶ διατάξεσιν* ⁴ *κέδροις*, 'panels and cedar boards in rows[1],' Vulg. *laquearibus*, 'with panelled roofs.' Adopting this explanation we may render, '*panels and parallel beams*.' Targ. explains וטליל ית ביתא בהנתוכין ועילא מינהון סידרא דריכפת רישי שרית ארזיא 'And he roofed the house with rafters, and above them were a series of cedar boards joined together.' Lagarde (*Armenische Studien*, § 499; *Mittheil.* i. 211) for גבים reads גְּבָדִים, which he connects with Persian گنبد, Armen. *γμβεθ*, 'vaulted roofs.'

10. Somewhat obscure. MT. is adopted by Ke., Th., Kamp., Klo.; the last explaining:—'He built it (each story) evenly against the wall of the whole house, until it was five cubits high, and then the connexion with the house and the roof of the side-chambers was formed by the cedar beams and planks, which rested upon the rebatements of the house.' Of course this process is conceived to have taken place three times, so that the three stories when

[1] But not, as stated by Ew., with LXX *ἐκοιλοστάθμησεν*, 'made with vaulted roof,' which, as above noticed, is a translation of ויספן merely. Cf. Hag. 1. 4 בְּבָתֵּיכֶם סְפוּנִים, *ἐν οἴκοις ὑμῶν κοιλοστάθμοις*.

built and roofed must have had a height of fifteen cubits. Against this it should be noticed that יצוע in *v.* 5 denotes not a single story (called הַצֵּלָע *v.* 8), but the whole wing consisting of three stories; hence Sta. is probably correct in reading חֲמֵשׁ עֶשְׂרֵה אַמָּה for חמש אמות of MT. So Kit.

The subject of ויאחז, rightly divined by RV., Ke., Sta., Klo., Benz., is היצוע; 'It rested on the house with beams of cedar.' Sta. compares לבלתי אחז of *v.* 6. On the contrary, Verss., RV. marg., Th., Kamp., Kit. make the subject to be the same as that of ויבן; Vulg. *operuit domum*, Targ. וטליל ית ביתא 'he roofed the house,' giving a wrong sense to ויאחז. LXX καὶ συνέσχεν τὸν σύνδεσμον (Luc. τοὺς συνδέσμους) appear to have read ויאחז את היצוע. This reading is favoured by Ew., but is probably merely a mistranslation, due to the mistake in the subject of ויאחז noticed above.

11–14. Omitted by LXX, Luc. Verses 11–13 are assigned by Kue., Wellh., Kamp., Benz., Kit. to R^D; but this is certainly incorrect. The section, it is true, contains some D phrases, such as could and did pass from D into P; but other expressions belong solely to P or to H, and thus mark the verses as the work of R^P. This conclusion is rendered certain by the LXX omission. Verse 14 is by the same hand as *vv.* 11–13; *v.* 9^a being repeated in order to round off the interpolation and attach it to the preceding narrative.

The following are marks of authorship which require notice:—

12. אם תלך בחקתי] This phrase, which never occurs in Deut., is found twice in Jer. 44. 10, 23. On the other hand, it is distinctively characteristic of H, occurring Lev. 26. 3 (cf. 18. 4), and constantly in Ezekiel, whose connexion with P, and especially with H, is well ascertained[1]; 5. 6, 7; 11. 20; 18. 9, 17; 20. 13, 16, 19, 21†. Cf. the phrase הָלַךְ בְּחֻקּוֹת הַגּוֹיִם Lev. 18. 3; 20. 23 (H).

ואת משפטי תעשה] The exact phrase (with יהוה as spokesman; מִשְׁפָּטַי) belongs to H; Lev. 18. 4; Ezek. 5. 7; 11. 12; 18. 17; 20. 24; 1 Chr. 28. 7. In *ch.* 11. 33 לעשות הישר בעיני

[1] Cf. Dri. *LOT.*, pp. 45 *ff.*

וחקתי ומשפטי כדוד אביו, the passage belongs to R^D, but the words וח׳ ומ׳ are an insertion by R^P, as is shown by their omission in LXX, Luc.

Even with הַמִּשְׁפָּטִים, מִשְׁפָּטָיו the phrase is not specially characteristic of Deut.[1]; 26. 16; 33. 21 (Blessing of Moses in Appendix). Elsewhere, Neh. 10. 30.

Similar H phrases are (שָׁמַר) מִשְׁפָּטִים אֲשֶׁר יַעֲשֶׂה אֹתָם הָאָדָם וָחַי בָּהֶם Lev. 18. 5; Ezek. 20. 11, 13, 21†; יִשְׁמֹר מִשְׁפָּטִים וְעָשָׂה אֹתָם Lev. 19. 37; 20. 22; 25. 18; Ezek. 11. 20; 20. 19; 36. 27.

ושמרת את כל מצותי] The phrase appears first in Ex. 20. 6 (E); Deut. 5. 10 לְשֹׁמְרֵי מִצְוֹתַי, and is then very frequent in Deut.; passing on to R^D in Kings, I. 2. 3; 9. 6; 11. 34; *al.*; and to P, which shows several occurrences.

ללכת בהם] So exactly only in Lev. 18. 4 (H) את משפטי תעשו ואת חקתי תשמרו ללכת בהם. D's phrase is ללכת בדרכי י׳; cf. *ch.* 2. 3.

והקמתי את דברי אתך] The expression הקים דבר with יהוה as subj. is found once in Deut. 9. 5, and twice in R^D, *ch.* 2. 4; 12. 15; ‖ 2 Chr. 10. 15; but is also more general; 1 Sam. 1. 23; Jer. 33. 14; Dan. 9. 12; cf. Isa. 44. 26.

אשר דברתי אל דוד] Referring, like R^D in 2. 4, to Nathan's prophecy, 2 Sam. 7. 12–16.

13. ושכנתי בתוך בני ישראל] Very distinctive of P; Ex. 25. 8; 29. 45; Num. 5. 3; 35. 34; Ezek. 43. 9. No occurrences in D.

With the whole verse cf. Lev. 26. 11, 12 (H) ונתתי משכני בתוככם ולא תגעל נפשי אתכם׃ והתהלכתי בתוככם והייתי לכם לאלהים ואתם תהיו לי לעם׃.

12. הבית . . . בנה] A *casus pendens*, 'As for this house,' &c., imperfectly reinforced, after the long protasis, by ושכנתי בתוך בני ישראל (*v.* 13), where we should strictly expect בְּתוֹכוֹ. Cf. Dri. *Tenses*, § 197, *Obs.* 2. Thus we need not, with Kamp., Benz.,

[1] D's usual phrases are שמר משפטים לעשות 'observe judgements to do them'; 5. 1; 7. 11; 11. 32; 12. 1; 2 Ki. 17. 37; Ezek. 20. 21 (cf. 18. 9): לִמֵּד משפטים לעשות 'teach (some one else) judgements to do them'; 4. 1, 5, 14; 6. 1.

suppose that before הבית some words have fallen out, such as עֵינַי יִהְיוּ פְתוּחוֹת אֶל־ 'mine eyes shall be open toward,' as in *ch.* 8. 29.

15. מביתה] Omitted by LXX, Luc.; but scarcely to be dispensed with.

קִירוֹת הַסִּפֻּן] Read קוֹרוֹת הַסִּפֻּן 'the *rafters* of the ceiling,' with the former part of the doublet in LXX, Luc. ἕως τῶν δοκῶν, Vulg. *laquearia*, Pesh. ܩܪ̈ܝܬܗܘܢ. So Bö., Th., Sta., Klo., Kamp., Benz., Kit.

צפה עץ מבית] Rejected by Sta. as a summary of the contents of the verse which has come into the text from the margin, and by Klo., Benz., Kit. as a later gloss added to guard the expression ויבן . . . בְּ against misunderstanding. The words, however, appear in all Verss., and may very well form with the previous מקרקע וג׳ a circumstantial clause; 'And he built the walls of the house within with boards of cedar, *overlaying* with wood within from the floor of the house to the rafters of the ceiling.' Cf. Dri. *Tenses*, § 163, who quotes *ch.* 7. 51 ויבא . . . את הכלים נתן וג׳ 'and he brought in the vessels . . ., *placing* them,' &c.

16. ויבן וג׳] 'And he built off the twenty cubits from the innermost part of the house with boards of cedar.' ירכתי means 'the furthest extremity,' and may be applied to the most secret recesses of a house or cave employed as a place of hiding, Am. 6. 10; 1 Sam. 24. 4; or as women's apartments, Ps. 128. 3; or again in the phrase ירכתי ארץ, to the most inaccessible limits of the earth, Jer. 31. 7; *al.*; cf. ירכתי צפון Ezek. 38. 6; *al.*; ירכתי בור Ezek. 32. 23. מן of מירכתי denotes the point of departure in measurement, as e. g. 1 Sam. 20. 37 ממך והלאה 'on beyond thee.'

הקירות] Read הַקּוֹרוֹת with LXX, Luc. ἕως τῶν δοκῶν, Vulg. *superiora*, Pesh. ܩܪ̈ܝܬܗܘܢ. So the authorities cited for the same emendation in *v.* 15.

16b. ויבן] וַיַּעַשׂ is the reading of 1 Cod., LXX, Luc., Θ., Vulg. So Th.

לו] *Dativus commodi*, as in 1. 28; lit. 'he built for himself'; so Kamp. 'baute er sich's.' Th., RV. 'he even built (them) for it,' i. e. for the house, are incorrect.

לִדְבִר] 'For an adytum.' The word דביר, which only occurs

in this section of Kings, *chs.* 6–8, in the parallel account in 2 Chr. 3–5, and in Ps. 28. 2 [1], is connected with Ar. دَبَرَ *to be behind*, whence دُبْرٌ, دُبُرٌ *hindmost* or *back part*, and so doubtless denotes the *back* or *innermost* room of the Temple. 'A., Σ. *χρηματιστηρίον*, Vulg. *oraculi*, whence AV., RV. 'oracle,' connect דביר incorrectly with דִּבֶּר 'to speak.'

לקדש הקדשים] So *ch.* 7. 50; 8. 6. The phrase occurs four times in P of the innermost sanctuary, Ex. 26. 33, 34; Num. 4. 4, 19; in Num. 18. 9, 10 it refers to the offerings of the b'nê Israel כל מנחתם וג׳; קדשי הקדשים Lev. 21. 22 is the portion of the sons of Aaron; קדש קדשים, seventeen times in P, is applied to the brazen altar, the altar of incense, the twelve cakes of shew-bread, and the portions of various sacrifices which fell to the priests.

These are all occurrences of the phrase in P. Elsewhere it is found only in late books influenced by P; Ezek., Chr., Ezra, Neh., Dan.; and in the three passages noticed in Kings. Thus the phrase in Kings is clearly a gloss made by a post-exilic interpolator under the influence of P, to explain the possibly obsolete term דביר in 6. 16; 8. 6; and בית הפנימי in 7. 50.

The inclusion of the phrase in LXX, Luc. in each passage suggests that it is not due to the post-exilic editor R^P, whose glosses and changes are usually absent from the Greek Vers., or obviously inserted later from the margin, but to earlier post-exilic interpolators upon a smaller scale [2].

17–20[a]. וארבעים . . . . קומתו] The passage as it stands is remarkably involved, and appears to exhibit a double stratum of glosses. LXX reads *καὶ τεσσαράκοντα πηχῶν ἦν ὁ ναὸς κατὰ πρόσωπον τοῦ δαβεὶρ ἐν μέσῳ τοῦ οἴκου ἔσωθεν, δοῦναι ἐκεῖ τὴν κιβωτὸν διαθήκης Κυρίου. εἴκοσι πήχεις μῆκος, καὶ εἴκοσι πήχεις πλάτος, καὶ εἴκοσι πήχεις τὸ ὕψος αὐτοῦ*, i. e. וְאַרְבָּעִים בָּאַמָּה הָיָה הַבַּיִת לִפְנֵי (*v.* 17) הַדְּבִיר בְּתוֹךְ הַבַּיִת מִפְּנִימָה לָתֵת שָׁם אֶת־אֲרוֹן בְּרִית יְהוָה׃ (*v.* 19)

[1] The word should probably be restored in II. 10. 25; see *note*.

[2] These seem to have been mere *scribes* or copyists, not to be dignified by the title 'editor,' working under the influence of P, and thus their small insertions may be cited as belonging to SS^P.

עֶשְׂרִים אַמָּה אֹרֶךְ וְעֶשְׂרִים אַמָּה רֹחַב וְעֶשְׂרִים אַמָּה קוֹמָתוֹ (*v.* 20). So substantially Luc.

Here we notice the omission of הוא ההיכל, also lacking in Vulg., explanatory of הבית in *v.* 17; and the entire absence of *v.* 18, which contains details of the wood-carving of the house. These are clearly insertions made by R^P. By their removal the monstrous לִפְנָי at the close of *v.* 17, together with ולפני הדביר at the commencement of *v.* 20, is explained as arising out of the original לפני הדביר at the close of *v.* 17, through the confusion incident upon the introduction of *v.* 18.

But the account, even as simplified by LXX, cannot stand in its original form. The mention (*v.* 19) of the situation of the דביר is superfluous after *v.* 16, and the expression את ארון ברית יהוה belongs to D; see *note* on 3. 15. Thus *v.* 19 is also an insertion, though of earlier date than those first noticed, and possibly even due to R^D. The description originally ran as follows: (*v.* 17) וְאַרְבָּעִים בָּאַמָּה הָיָה הַבַּיִת לִפְנֵי הַדְּבִיר׃ (*v.* 20) וְהַדְּבִיר עֶשְׂרִים אַמָּה אֹרֶךְ וְעֶשְׂרִים אַמָּה רֹחַב וְעֶשְׂרִים אַמָּה קוֹמָתוֹ׃ 'And forty cubits was the house before the adytum. And the adytum was twenty cubits long, and twenty cubits broad, and twenty cubits high.' So Sta., except for the retention of הוא ההיכל (*v.* 17), against LXX, Luc., Vulg.

18. אל הבית] The preposition אל is not used in a loose way for על, RV. '*on* the house,' i. e. on its walls; but rather expresses presence *in* or *at* the building as pictured from a distance; '*in* the house.' Cf. II. 10. 14 וישחטום אל בור בית עקד 'They slew them *at* the pit of Beth-'Eqed'; Ezek. 31. 7 ושרשו אל מים רבים 'its root was *by* many waters'; 47. 7 הנה אל שפת הנחל עץ רב 'behold, *at* the edge of the ravine there were many trees.'

מקלעת] 'Carving'; only again *vv.* 29, 32; *ch.* 7. 31; while the verb קלע *vv.* 29, 32, 35† is also peculiar to this one interpolator.

פקעים] 'Gourds'; 7. 24†. פַּקֻּעֹת II. 4. 39† means wild gourds gathered from a גֶּפֶן שָׂדֶה. According to Tristram, *DB.*[2] 1244, the *Colocynthis agri* is denoted.

פטורי צצים] 'Open flowers'; *vv.* 29, 32, 35†.

19. לתתן] This anomalous form of the infin. constr. occurs once again, *ch.* 17. 14 Kt., where Q're is תֵּת. König's view (*Lehrg.* I. i. p. 305) that the double occurrence precludes the theory of textual corruption, and that the final ן is a parasitical addition due to the fact that vulgarly the recollection of the connexion of תֵּת with נתן was totally obliterated, is very forced and unnatural.

20. ויצפהו זהב סגור] Sta. argues at length against the originality of all passages which speak of the use of gold plating in Solomon's Temple, making in brief the following points:—

(i) If for the manufacture of brazen vessels a Syrian workman had to be imported (7. 13 *ff.*), it is highly improbable that sufficiently skilful workers in gold were to be found among the men of Israel.

(ii) Later notices in Kings which mention the treasures of the Temple make no allusion to the gold-plating. Thus, 14. 26, Shishak carries off only the אוצרות בית יהוה such as would presumably be stored in the side-chambers, and the golden shields of Solomon; II. 14. 14, Joash king of Israel makes booty of the gold and silver vessels found בית יהוה ובאוצרות בית המלך; II. 16. 17, Ahaz in his need uses merely the great *bronze* vessels found in the Temple; II. 18. 16, Hezekiah overlays the doors of the היכל יהוה with gold-plating, but afterwards cuts it off and sends it to the king of Assyria.

(iii) Verses 21 *f.*, 30 stand in wrong position; *v.* 21, so far as it refers to the gold-plating of the house, is wanting in LXX; and *vv.* 22, 30 are otherwise rendered suspicious by their contents.

(iv) Ezekiel, in his description of the future Temple, knows of no such gold-plating.

Thus in this connexion *vv.* 20^b (in part, ויצפהו זהב סגור), 21 (all but לפני הדביר), 22, 28, 30, 32^b are omitted by Sta.

These arguments, though weighty, are not entirely convincing. צפה may denote not necessarily a heavy gold-plating as in II. 18. 16, but a thin gilding with *liquid* gold[1], such as called for no very

[1] In Prov. 26. 23 כֶּסֶף סִיגִים מְצֻפֶּה עַל־חָרֶשׂ one thinks of a potsherd silvered over, not coated with *plates* of silver.

special skill in preparation and application to the wood, and also need not imply so prodigious a supply of the metal, nor have been calculated to attract the cupidity of a foreign foe bent upon hastily pillaging the treasures of the Temple. Again, the fact that certain notices are absent from LXX rather favours than otherwise the originality of the remainder. Quite probably the narrative has here, as elsewhere, been subject to later glosses; but the total denial to the original account of all references to the employment of gold in Solomon's Temple must be deemed extremely precarious.

זהב סגור] Apparently '*choice*' or '*precious* gold' (cf. the alternative זהב טוב of 2 Chr. 3. 8); though how the word gains this sense is quite uncertain. A subs. סְגוֹר occurs Job 28. 15.

ויצף מזבח ארז] But if the altar was merely overlaid with cedar boards, what was its inner material? As Sta. remarks, an altar if of stone or earth could scarcely be covered outside with boards. LXX, Luc. *καὶ ἐποίησεν θυσιαστήριον*, i. e. וַיַּעַשׂ מִזְבֵּחַ, is doubtless correct as regards the verb, but the mention of the material אֶרֶז is indispensable, and must have fallen out through oversight. So Bö., Th., Sta., Klo., Kamp., Benz., Kit.

21. LXX, Luc. have only the last four words of this verse which they refer to the altar. This seems to be correct. The remainder of the verse is a gloss inserted later, and breaking the connexion. The whole sentence ought to run וַיַּעַשׂ מִזְבֵּחַ אֶרֶז לִפְנֵי הַדְּבִיר וַיְצַפֵּהוּ זָהָב.

וַיְעַבֵּר בְּרַתּיקוֹת זָהָב] This can only mean 'he drew golden chains across,' lit. '*he made a crossing with*,' &c.; but this is very harsh.

In 2 Chr. 3. 14 mention is made of הַפָּרֹכֶת the *veil*; and, in accordance with Th.'s suggestion, it is at least conceivable that in our passage R^P may have written, or intended to write, וַיְעַבֵּר אֶת־הַפָּרֹכֶת וגו׳ 'and he drew the veil across with chains of gold.' עבר Pi'el is only so used in this passage. The sing. רַתּוֹק occurs in Ezek. 7. 23 (but disappears under Cornill's emendation), and a pl. רְתֻקוֹת Isa. 40. 19†. Klo. makes the very conjectural emendation וְאַרְבַּע קַרְנֹתָיו זָהָב 'and its four horns were of gold,' referring to the altar.

22^b^. וכל המזבח וג׳] But we have already been informed about the overlaying of the altar with gold in the previous verse. This passage, omitted by LXX, Luc., is doubtless a gloss, and owes its existence to the gloss in the previous *v.* 21 ויצף . . . ברתיקות זהב which, by breaking the connexion, destroyed the original statement with reference to the gold-plating of the altar, and so caused the necessity for an additional clause to that effect.

23. עצי שמן] So Vulg., Targ. LXX omits. Luc. *ἐκ ξύλων κυπαρισσίνων*, Pesh. ܕܩܝܣܐ ܕܡܫܚܐ. MT. correct.

קומתו] As the verse stands the reference of the suffix is obscure. RV. 'each' is an unsatisfactory escape from the difficulty, and no real translation. LXX, Luc. *μέγεθος ἐσταθμωμένον*, for which Th. suggests קוֹמָה מְתֻכֶּנֶת; but Sta. points out that this cannot mean 'upright stature,' since תִּכֵּן only signifies 'to adjust.' *ἐσταθ.* appears to be merely a translator's flourish. Sta. most cleverly removes all difficulty by placing *v.* 26 between *v.* 23^a^ and *v.* 23^b^. This is doubtless correct. The suffix of קומתו is satisfied by reference to הכרוב השני in *v.* 26^b^, and the account of the measurements of the כרובים closes very appropriately with the summary *v.* 25^b^ מדה אחת וקצב אחד לשני הכרבים.

All Verss. follow the wrong order of MT.

27. ויתן את הכרובים] LXX, Luc. *καὶ ἀμφότερα χερουβεὶν*, i. e. וּשְׁנֵי הַכְּרוּבִים. So Klo., who notices that the fact that the כרובים were brought into the דביר has already been stated in *v.* 23^a^ ויעש בדביר וג׳. Th., Sta. adopt שני as more precise, but retain ויתן את of MT. This latter, as introducing the statement that when so placed their wings touched the wall on either side, can scarcely be considered redundant.

ויפרשו] One MS. ויפרש; so Pesh. ܘܦܪܣ. Possible, but not preferable to MT.

את כנפי הכרבים] LXX, Luc. *τὰς πτέρυγας αὐτῶν*, i. e. אֶת־כַּנְפֵיהֶם, doubtless correct. So Bö., Th., Sta., Klo., Kamp., Benz., Kit.

ותגע וג׳] LXX seems to convey the idea that *each* כרוב had four wings:—*καὶ ἥπτετο πτέρυξ μία τοῦ τοίχου, καὶ πτέρυξ ἥπτετο τοῦ τοίχου τοῦ δευτέρου· καὶ αἱ πτέρυγες αὐτοῦ αἱ ἐν μέσῳ τοῦ οἴκου ἥπτοντο πτέρυξ πτέρυγος.* This is very inferior to the plain statement of MT. supported by Luc. and the other Verss.

29, 30. These verses, though both appearing in LXX, Luc., appear to form no part of the original account. Verse 29 is obviously by the same hand as *v.* 18, assigned to R[P], and *v.* 30 is redundant after *v.* 22[a], and also out of place.

29. מֵסַב] Probably to be emended מִסָּבִיב with Klo.

מלפנים ולחיצון] The reference of 'within and without' is rather ambiguous, a remark which also applies to the similar words in *v.* 30. Klo.'s emendation, לַפְּנִימִי וְלַחִיצוֹן 'both of the inner and of the outer house,' is probably correct; cf. Ezek. 41. 17. The expression הַבַּיִת הַפְּנִימִי is used of the דביר *v.* 27; *ch.* 7. 50.

31. ואת פתח] LXX, Luc., Pesh., Targ. seem to presuppose וּלְפֶתַח; and so Klo. This *may* be original, but is quite as likely to be a paraphrase of the somewhat difficult MT. The latter, as Sta. notices, is quite possible, and may be paralleled; cf. Ex. 26. 1 וְאֶת־הַמִּשְׁכָּן תַּעֲשֶׂה עֶשֶׂר יְרִיעֹת; Dri. *Tenses*, § 195, 1. Th., in retaining MT., cites Ew. § 284[a] for the usage.

Vulg. *et in ingressu oraculi*, takes את פתח הדביר to be an accus. of place as in *ch.* 7. 40 בית יהוה *in templo domini.*

האיל] Of doubtful meaning. Neither Sta. 'door-opening,' nor RV., &c. 'lintel,' seems to be correct; for according to either of these renderings the breadth of the איל ought to be commensurate with that of the doorway, whereas in Ezek. 41. 3 the former is said to be two cubits (broad), the latter six cubits; cf. Ezek. 40. 9—the porch eight cubits, the איל two cubits. Again, the איל is spoken of as something standing in equal proportions upon either side of an entrance or porch; Ezek. 40. 48[a] וַיָּמָד אֵל אֻלָם חָמֵשׁ אַמּוֹת מִפֹּה וְחָמֵשׁ אַמּוֹת מִפֹּה (on 48[b] see Cornill's emendation); cf. 41. 1. Thus the explanation of Bö. (*Proben alttest. Schriftklärung*. 302 *ff.*), *pilasters* or projections in a wall upon either side of an entrance, appears to be near to the truth. So Pesh. ܦ̈ܘܣܠܕܘܗܝ 'its *παραστάδες*[1],' Cornill 'Wandpfeiler,' Kit. 'Einfassung,' and apparently RV. marg. 'posts.' Somewhat similar is the suggestion '*crepidines*,' of Ges., who quotes the passages where the word occurs, and the ancient interpretations.

חֲמִשִּׁית] So Baer. Less accurate texts חֲמִשִׁית. Upon the analogy of 7. 5 וְהַמְּזוּזוֹת רְבֻעִים שָׁקֶף, and the necessary and obvious emendation at the close of *v.* 33 מְזוּזוֹת רְבֻעוֹת, חמשית ought to mean '*a pentagonal*' . So Vulg. *postesque angulorum quinque*, Bö., Th., Sta., Kamp., Benz., Kit. Pesh. ܡܚܡ̈ܫܝܢ suggests the possibility of an original חֲמִשּׁוֹת exactly analogous to רְבֻעִים of 7. 5. The explanation '*a fifth part*' of the entire wall, adopted by Ges., Ke., Klo., is alien to the context, the breadth of the wall not having been mentioned since *v.* 20.

האיל מזוזות חמשית] It is impossible to regard האיל מזוזות as a case of apposition, 'the pilasters *were* doorposts,' &c., because איל is not identical with מזוזות. Hence it is best to adopt Sta.'s emendation הָאַיִל וְהַמְּזוּזוֹת ח׳, rendering 'the pilasters and doorposts were (i. e. formed) a pentagonal.' It is, however, conceivable that the text may have originally read האיל חמשית, and that מזוזות is a gloss from the margin as an (incorrect) explanation of the difficult איל.

32, 35. By the same hand as *vv.* 18, 29.

32. ושתי דלתות וג׳] A *casus pendens*; 'as for the two doors,' &c.

וְקָלַע] The perf. with weak ו here and in *v.* 35, if part of the original text, would be 'an isolated irregularity' (Dri. *Tenses*, § 133, 2), but the construction marks the style of the post-exilic interpolator. Klo. וְקִלַּע; but this, if possible in *v.* 32, is scarcely so in *v.* 35.

וַיָּרֶד] From רדד; 'and he *spread out* the gold upon the cherubim,' &c. The word is that which is used in Targ. Onk. as an equivalent of רִקַּע; Ex. 39. 3; Num. 17. 4; and its use thus forms another

[1] Unless this represent *προστάς*, 'vestibule.' The other Verss. give no help; Targ. אילהי 'but' misunderstands; LXX, Luc., Vulg. omit.

post-exilic indication. Luc. *καὶ κατέβαινεν*, i. e. וַיֵּרֶד; Pesh. ܘܐܚܬ, i.e. וַיֵּרֶב; Targ. ונסיך, apparently וַיָּרֶק or וַיֹּרֶד; Vulg. *et operuit*, a guess. Klo.'s reading וַיֹּרֶד is unnecessary.

33. מאת רבעית] LXX *στοαὶ* (Luc. *στοὰς*) *τετραπλῶς*, i. e. מְזוּזוֹת רְבֻעוֹת 'doorposts standing foursquare,' is doubtless correct. Cf. *ch.* 7. 5. So Th., Sta., Kamp., Benz., Kit. The verse, all but the last two words, is with *v.* 32 omitted by LXX through homoioteleuton with the end of *v.* 31.

34[b]. קלעים] All Verss. rightly presuppose צלעים as in *v.* 34[a]. So Th., Sta., Klo., Kamp.

גלילים] 'Revolving,' or 'turning on hinges,' so '*folding*.' Thus only here. In Ezek. 41. 24 the doors are called שְׁתַּיִם מוּסַבּוֹת דְּלָתוֹת.

35. וצפה] Cf. *v.* 32 *note* on וקלע.

מְיֻשָּׁר עַל־הַמְּחֻקֶּה] 'Applied evenly to the carving.' ישר Pu'al only here; Pi'el 'make straight or even,' of a way, &c.

36. החצר הפנימית] Surrounding the Temple, and *innermost* as contrasted with the חצר האחרת 7. 8, containing the King's palace, both courts lying inside the חצר הגדולה which enclosed the whole group of buildings. See *note* on 7. 12[b], and plan in Sta. *Ges.* i. 314.

At the end of this verse LXX, Luc. continue with the words *κυκλόθεν, καὶ ᾠκοδόμησε κ.τ.λ.* This seems to represent MT. *ch.* 7. 12[b], where it receives discussion.

7. 1–12[a] appear in LXX, Luc. at the close of the *ch.*, being apparently so placed by some scribe who thought it better to give the account of the Temple furniture in immediate sequence to that of the Temple itself, and not separated by the description of Solomon's other buildings. This is shown to be a late dislocation by the fact that *v.* 12[b] has been accidentally left behind in making the alteration, and now follows immediately after the close of *ch.* 6, instead of after *v.* 12[a] to which it clearly belongs. MT., which describes all the buildings first and then the furniture of the Temple, is correct.

2. ארבעה] LXX, Luc. *τριῶν*. Hence Sta. adopts שלשה as in agreement with the statement in *v.* 3 ארבעים וחמשה חמשה עשר הטור.

This, he contends, must refer to the עמודים, and not to the צלעות (Th.) a fem. noun; Ezek. 41. 8. So Kamp., Benz., Kit.

Sta. takes the following view of the construction of the house:—'It was a house of which the back and sides upon the ground-floor were formed of walls, while the front of the bottom story was formed by the fifteen pillars of the first row. The pillars of the second and third rows stood within the building, exactly corresponding to the pillars of the first row. The second story was formed by a number of chambers lying in three rows or flights' (*ZATW.* 1883, p. 150). A further description, together with excellent plans of the building, may be seen in *Ges.* i. 318 *ff.* It may be doubted, however, whether Sta. is correct in his arrangement of the chambers which he assigns to one single story above the pillars. The expressions of *vv.* 4, 5 שקפים שלשה טורים . . . שלש פעמים seem to suggest *three stories* of chambers (so Kit.), and this is agreeable to the height of the building, thirty cubits, even supposing these stories to have been higher than those of the Temple wings (6. 6)—perhaps six cubits each, with the pillars below the first floor of some twelve cubits in height. The house seems to have obtained its name from the fact that the pillars, open to view from the outside, gave to the spectator the idea of a forest of trees. The rooms, if in three stories, may have run right through the breadth of the building, having a window or windows at either end, i.e. at the front and back of the house. This explains *v.* 4 ומחזה אל מחזה שלש פעמים 'and window was over against window three times.' The doors, on the other hand, opening from one room into another, ran lengthways down the centre of the building. Thus each room had two doors opposite to one another and communicating directly with the rooms on either side. This seems to satisfy the expression ומול פתח אל פתח שלש פעמים 'and door was over against door three times,' which we shall adopt in *v.* 5 at the suggestion of LXX, Luc.

We have no information as to staircase or number of chambers. The kind of rooms above described are not strictly the same as those described in 6. 5 *ff.*, supposing the term צלעות to really denote '*side*-chambers.' But the use of צלע '*a rib*,' to describe a chamber is very obscure, and we can scarcely say for certain what sort of room could be so called, and what not. צלעות may perhaps refer to the main beams [1], which, resting on the pillars and running from wall to wall, formed the basis of the partitions between the different chambers, and were, so to speak, the ribs of the building.

כרתות] 'Beams,' as *cut* or *sawn* into the required dimensions. LXX, Luc. ὠμίαι, i. e. כְּתֵפוֹת 'shoulder-pieces' at the top of the pillars, forming a support for the beams. Cf. the use of the word in *v.* 30. This is adopted by Klo., Benz., Kit., but is scarcely superior to MT.

3. After על העמודים LXX, Luc. insert καὶ ἀριθμὸς τῶν στύλων, i. e. וּמִסְפַּר הָעַמּוּדִים. By this addition the verse is relieved, and the precise reference of the number made perfectly clear.

4. שקפים] Explained by Th., Sta., Klo., Kamp., Benz. as the main beams supporting the floors and ceilings of the chambers; a meaning possibly agreeable to the Ar. سَقْفٌ quoted on 6. 4. It should be noticed, however, that *v.* 4b ומחזה אל מחזה וג׳ seems obviously to refer back to the preceding statement, as though מחזה and שקפים were closely connected in meaning. Hence it seems preferable to assign to שקפים, here as in 6. 4, the meaning '*window-frames*.' So RV. 'prospects.' Kit. 'Fenster (?).'

5. והמזוזות] Read וְהַמֶּחֱזוֹת with LXX, Luc. καὶ αἱ χῶραι. So Th., Sta., Klo., Kamp., Benz., Kit.

רבעים שקף] Cf. 6. 4 *note*.

ומול מחזה אל מחזה שלש פעמים] LXX καὶ ἀπὸ τοῦ θυρώματος (Luc. ἀπὸ θύρας) ἐπὶ θύραν τρισσῶς, i. e. וּמִפֶּתַח אֶל־פֶּתַח שָׁלֹשׁ פְּעָמִים, probably standing for וּמוּל פֶּתַח אֶל־פֶּתַח וג׳, which may be adopted. Sta. reads פתח אל פתח, regarding מול as a gloss arising from a marginal note פתח מול פתח.

6. שלשים] LXX πεντήκοντα. But Luc., Vulg., Pesh., Targ. support MT.

---

[1] Cf. the use of the term to denote the *beams* or *boards* which went to form the inner walls of the house, and the partition-wall of the adytum; *ch.* 6. 15, 16a.

After רחבו and before ואולם LXX inserts ἐζυγωμένα, Luc. ἐζυγωμένη. This appears to be a mere gloss by which it was sought to explain the relationship between the second אולם and the אולם העמודים. Or possibly the word may form a doublet of רחבו, the letters being transposed and read as some part of חבר, perhaps מְחֻבָּר.

עב] The meaning is very obscure, and can only be guessed. LXX, Luc. render lit. πάχος, Vulg. *epistylia*, 'cross-beams,' Pesh. ܦܪܘܙܐ 'entrance hall,' Targ. סקופתא 'threshold.' The word occurs again Ezek. 41. 25 וְעָב עֵץ אֶל־פְּנֵי הָאוּלָם מֵהַחוּץ. Here Cornill hazards 'Vordach,' and this is perhaps what is intended by Vulg. in Kings—the front part of the roof of the porch, possibly forming a kind of projecting *cornice*. *Sieg. u. Sta.* also suggests 'Vordach, Schutzdach.' Th., Sta., Klo., Kamp. doubtfully follow the suggestion of Targ., and suppose the word to mean an entrance with steps.

7. אשר ישפט שם] 'Where he *should* or *might* judge'; Dri. *Tenses*, § 39 β.

וְסָפֻן] The usual construction would be אלם משפט עשה סָפֻן בארז 'he made the porch covered,' &c.; cf. Dri. *Tenses*, § 161. 2. It is rare for the participle to be preceded by וְ when thus introducing a subordinate idea as a secondary predicate. See instances under *Obs.* 1 of Dri. § cited.

עד הקרקע] Vulg. *usque ad summitatem*, Pesh. ܘܥܕܡܐ ܠܟܫܘܪܘܗܝ read עַד־הַקּוֹרוֹת, which is to be adopted. So Ew., Th., Sta., Kamp., Benz.; and Klo. doubtfully. Kit. retains MT. The second half of the verse has fallen out in LXX, Luc.; but, according to Field, *Hex.*, the Complutensian reads ἀπὸ ἐδάφους ἕως ὑπερῴου.

8. אשר ישב שם] The same *nuance* as in *v.* 7 ישפט.

חצר האחרת] Also called חֲצַר אֻלָם הַבַּיִת; see *notes* on *v.* 12^b^; *ch.* 6. 36.

It is unusual in classical Hebrew (though customary in post-biblical Hebrew) to omit the article with a subs. when its adj. is so defined according to rule. Cf. חָצֵר הַגְּדוֹלָה *v.* 12. Dri. (*Tenses*, § 209. 1) collects instances of the usage which 'appears to have arisen in connexion with familiar words, which were felt to be sufficiently definite in themselves without the addition of the article.'

מבית לאולם] LXX renders curiously *ἐξ ἐλισσομένης τούτοις*, Luc. *ἐξελισσομένη τούτοις*, apparently a misreading לְאֵלֶּה . . . מ, the former word being some Puʿal or Hophʿal participle. MT. correct.

יעשה] The tense is quite anomalous, and cannot be explained, the perfect alone being suitable to describe a single fact in so prosaic a connexion[1]. It is at least possible that some scribe, intending to copy וּבַיִת עָשָׂה, wrote by mistake וביתו עשה through confusion with וביתו at the beginning of the verse, and that this וביתועשה was subsequently interpreted as ובית יעשה. The omission of יעשה in LXX suggests as a second hypothesis that the word may be a later gloss carelessly inserted.

9. כמדות] 'According to measurements,' i.e. of regular dimensions, and not of various sizes. So *v.* 11.

מְגֹרָרוֹת] 'Sawn'; only here. A *dĕnom.* from מְגֵרָה which is derived from גרר 'drag.' Both subs. מגרה and *denom.* verb in Qal and Niphʿal occur in post-biblical Hebrew.

מַסַּד] 'Foundation'; a *ἅπαξ λεγ.* from יסד, the י being assimilated according to the small class of contracted verbs פ״י; G-K. § 71. Other contracted forms from this root are מוּסָּד Isa. 28. 16; לִיסּוֹד 2 Chr. 31. 7.

עד הטפחות] RV. 'unto the coping'; so LXX, Luc. *ἕως τῶν γείσων* (with a Schol. *στεφανωμάτων ἢ ἄκρων*), and approximately Σ. (*ἕως*) *τῶν ἀπαρτισμάτων*, Vulg. *usque ad summitatem parietum*, Pesh. ܘܟܦܝܦܐ ܕܛܠܠܐ; Th., Klo., *Sieg. u. Sta.* Sta., Kamp., Kit. follow Ges. in rendering *mutules* or projecting stones (Kragsteine) upon which the ends of the beams rested. The word, which occurs only here in this sense, elsewhere means a 'handbreadth'; *v.* 26; *al.* So Targ. בפושכיא, 'A. (*ἕως*) *τῶν παλαιστωμάτων*.

The first וּמִחוּץ, which is indispensable, has fallen out in LXX,

[1] Kö., however (*Lehrg.* I. ii. § 368 *k*), classes the use with *ch.* 20. 33ᵃ ינחשו as an *Inchoative*.

Luc. through oversight. The second וּמִחוּץ is very difficult. As Sta. remarks, it forms no contrast to החצר הגדולה. Sta.'s emendation ומבית יהוה is, however, not quite correct. We ought rather to read וּמֵחֲצַ[ר בֵּית יְהוָֹה], a correction which accords with *v.* 12, and accounts for the letters* ומחצ in MT.

10. ומיסד] LXX, Luc. τὴν τεθεμελιωμένην, Pesh. ܕܡܫܬܐܣܐ, apply this specially to the great court. It seems better to regard it as having a vague general application to כל אלה at the beginning of *v.* 9; all the buildings. Sta. 'und fundamentirt (war alles).' So Th., Kamp., Benz.

12b. ולחצר . . . הבית] As has before been noticed, LXX, Luc. at the close of *ch.* 6. 36 contain the words κυκλόθεν· καὶ ᾠκοδόμησε τὸ καταπέτασμα τῆς αὐλῆς τοῦ αἰλὰμ τοῦ οἴκου τοῦ κατὰ πρόσωπον τοῦ ναοῦ, i.e. probably מִסָּבִיב וַיִּבֶן מָסָךְ לַחֲצַר אֻלָם הַבַּיִת אֲשֶׁר עַל־פְּנֵי הַהֵיכָל. This seems to represent MT. *ch.* 7. 12b ולחצר בית יהוה הפנימית ולאלם הבית. מסך certainly cannot be original, the phrase ויבן מסך being absurd. The word is probably therefore a corruption of מִסָּבִיב repeated from the preceding, and καὶ ᾠκοδόμησε is clearly a gloss formed through repetition of ויבן 6. 36a, to explain the connexion of καταπέτασμα with the previous sentence. The first מִסָּבִיב is genuine, and should be restored before לַחֲצַר in place of the ו of MT. LXX is also correct in reading וְלַחֲצַר אֻלָם הַבַּיִת (this referring to חצר האחרת of *v.* 8), but has omitted לחצר בית יהוה הפנימית through the homoioteleuton לחצר. Possibly, as Sta. thinks, הפנימית is a gloss from 6. 36, and redundant after בית יהוה. Finally, the sentence אשר על פני ההיכל appears to be a gloss derived from 6. 3, והאולם על פני היכל הבית, through a wrong identification of the אולם here mentioned.

We may therefore read *v.* 12b מִסָּבִיב לַחֲצַר בֵּית־יְהוָֹה (הַפְּנִימִית) וְלַחֲצַר אֻלָם הַבַּיִת 'round about the (inner) court of the House of Yahwe, and the court of the porch of the palace.'

13, 14. In 2 Chr. 2. 12, 13 the workman is called חוּרָם אָבִי, and he is בֶּן־אִשָּׁה מִן־בְּנוֹת דָּן. According to Giesebrecht (*ZATW.* i. 239 *ff.*) the text of Chr. is the more original, the name חורם אבי (misunderstood as by LXX in Chr.) having undergone correction in Kings, and אלמנה being an insertion to suggest that this builder of Solomon's Temple was purely Israelitish, and not half Phoenician.

15–22. This very mutilated and obscure account may be compared with the summary in *vv.* 41, 42; ‖ 2 Chr. 4. 12, 13, and with the description in II. 25. 17, of which a better and fuller form exists in Jer. 52. 21–23.

15[a]. ויצר] LXX, Luc. *καὶ ἐχώνευσε*, i.e. וַיִּצֹק; probably correct. So Th., Sta., Klo., Kamp., Benz., Kit.

את שני העמודים נחשת] LXX omits by oversight. Luc. reads all but נחשת, which is scarcely necessary after the precise statement of *v.* 14 לעשות כל מלאכה בנחשת, and so *may* be a gloss, but on comparison with *vv.* 16, 27, 30, 38 is more likely to be original[1], נחשת being an accus. of material. At this point Luc. adds *τῷ αἰλὰμ τοῦ οἴκου*, and so also LXX with *τό* by mistake for *τῷ*, i.e. לְאוּלָם הַבָּיִת. This is accepted by Sta. on the ground that the expression שני העמודים '*the* two pillars,' requires some such specification of their destined position to justify the use of the article. So Th., Klo., Kamp., Kit.

15[b]. שמנה . . . השני] LXX *ὀκτὼ καὶ δέκα πήχεις ὕψος τοῦ στύλου· καὶ περίμετρον τέσσαρες καὶ δέκα πήχεις ἐκύκλου αὐτόν, τὸ πάχος τοῦ στύλου· τεσσάρων δακτύλων τὰ κοιλώματα· καὶ οὕτως στύλος ὁ δεύτερος*, i.e. שְׁמֹנֶה עֶשְׂרֵה אַמָּה קוֹמַת הָעַמּוּד וְחוּט שְׁתֵּים־עֶשְׂרֵה אַמָּה יָסֹב אֹתוֹ עֳבִי הָעַמּוּד אַרְבַּע אֶצְבָּעוֹת נָבוּב וְכֵן הָעַמּוּד הַשֵּׁנִי 'eighteen cubits was the height of the (one) pillar, and a thread of twelve cubits compassed it about; the thickness of the pillar was four fingers; it was hollow: and the second pillar was similar.' This description corresponds accurately with that which is given in Jer. 52. 21, and is doubtless correct, except that הָאֶחָד is to be retained with MT. after the first העמוד. LXX text is confirmed substantially by Luc., and in part by Pesh. ܘܪܘܡܗ ܕܥܡܘܕܐ ܚܕ ܬܡܢܥܣܪܐ ܐܡܝ̈ܢ. ܘܚܘܛܐ ܕܬܪܬܥܣܪܐ ܐܡܝ̈ܢ ܚܕܪ ܠܗ. ܘܗܟܢܐ ܠܥܡܘܕܐ ܐܚܪܢܐ 'the height of the one pillar was eighteen cubits, and a thread of twelve cubits compassed

[1] On the other hand, *v.* 23 omits נחשת in MT. and Verss.

it about; and the second pillar was similar.' So Ew., Th.[1], Sta., Klo., Kamp., Benz.[1], Kit.[1]

יסב] '*Could* or *might* encompass'; so *v.* 23 יסב, *v.* 26 יכיל '*could* contain' (or in this instance perhaps '*contained*,' as a customary state). Dri. *Tenses*, § 37 β. Da. (§ 44, *Rem.* 2) is scarcely correct when he renders 'encompassed' or 'ran round,' 'in describing the course of an ornamentation,' as if this חוט or the קו of *v.* 23 were *part of the ornamentation*, and not rather an imaginary line of measurement.

נבוב, adopted in the emendation, occurs, besides the passage cited in Jer., Ex. 27. 8; 38. 7 נְבוּב לֻחֹת 'hollow, with boarded sides,' of the altar of burnt offering, and figuratively Job 11. 12† 'a *hollow*' or '*empty-headed* man.'

16. כתרות] 'Chapiters'; only used in the description of these pillars, here and in II. 25, 2 Chr., Jer. Connected with the root כתר 'surround,' Piʿel, Judg. 20. 43; Ps. 22. 13, from which comes the late word כֶּתֶר 'diadem,' three times in Est.†, and in new Hebrew.

מצק נחשת] 'A casting of brass,' so 'of cast or molten brass.' מוצק as in *vv.* 23, 33, 37; cf. Job 38. 38 'a congealed mass.' נחשת has fallen out of LXX, but is found in Luc. and the other Verss., and, as in the previous verse, is to be retained. LXX is also wrong in its omission of וחמש . . . השנית.

17. שבכים . . . שרשרות] LXX, Luc. καὶ ἐποίησε δύο δίκτυα, i.e. וַיַּעַשׂ שְׁתֵּי שְׂבָכִים, are correct, the words מעשה . . . שרשרות being certainly a gloss. שבכים (הַשְּׂבָכָה, הַשְּׂבָכוֹת) occurs in all the other descriptions, but the expressions מעשה שבכה, גדלים, שרשרות are not so found[2]. LXX is followed by Th., Sta., Kamp., Benz., Kit.; and Klo. as regards the addition of ויעש שתי.

שבכים] With pl. ־ים— only here; elsewhere שְׂבָכוֹת from sing. שְׂבָכָה. The word is derived from Ar. شَبَكَ *interweave*, whence شَبَكَة

[1] Th. presupposes הַנְּבוּבִים instead of נָבוּב, but otherwise agrees with the text as given above. Benz. וְעָבְיוֹ, Kit. וְעָבְיוֹ (omitting הָעַמּוּד).

[2] The statement in 2 Chr. 3. 16 is doubtless derived from the gloss in our passage.

net (for catching fish, birds, &c.), and in biblical Hebrew, outside the description of these pillars, it occurs only in II. 1. 2 of the *lattice* of a window, and in Job 18. 8, where the parallel word is הָרֶשֶׁת 'the net[1].' Thus the meaning in this description is clearly '*network*' or '*trellis*.'

גְּדִלִים] 'Festoons'; Deut. 22. 12 of the *fringes* of a garment. Ar. جَدِيل *a bridle of plaited thongs*. Syr. ܓܕܠ very commonly means *to plait* or *interweave;* e.g. S. Matt. 27. 29, of plaiting the crown of thorns.

שרשרות] 'Chains'; 2 Chr. 3. 5, 16; so in Ex. 28. 14; 39. 15†, of the ornaments or fastenings of the breastplate. שַׁרְשֹׁת Ex. 28. 22 is a corruption of the same. The word is a Pilpel (intensive) form from שרר 'twist.'

לכתרת אשר על ראש העמודים] LXX περικαλύψαι τὸ ἐπίθεμα τῶν στύλων, Luc. ἐπικαλύψαι τὰ ἐπιθέματα τῶν στύλων, i.e. לְכַסּוֹת אֶת־כֹּתֶרֶת הָעַמּוּדִים (כֹּתֶרֶת). In *v.* 18 we meet with a sentence which is very like a combination of these readings of MT. and LXX, viz. לְכַסּוֹת אֶת־הַכֹּתָרֹת אֲשֶׁר עַל־רֹאשׁ הָרִמֹּנִים. Here הָרִמֹּנִים is quite incomprehensible, and we may follow Pesh. ܕܥܡܘܕ̈ܐ and emend העמודים agreeably to *v.* 41b. This sentence of *v.* 18 is not to be found in LXX, Luc., and thus Th., Sta. are doubtless correct in supposing that, after having fallen out of *v.* 17 in MT., it was first written in again on the margin, and then inserted in the text in a wrong position, viz. in *v.* 18. So Kamp., Benz., Kit.

שבעה . . . ושבעה] LXX, Luc. δίκτυον . . . καὶ δίκτυον, i. e. שְׂבָכָה . . . וּשְׂבָכָה; doubtless correct. So Bö., Th., Sta., Klo., Kamp., Benz., Kit.

Thus *v.* 17, as restored, will run:—וַיַּעַשׂ שְׁתֵּי שְׂבָכִים לְכַסּוֹת אֶת־הַכֹּתָרוֹת אֲשֶׁר עַל־רֹאשׁ הָעַמּוּדִים שְׂבָכָה לַכֹּתֶרֶת הָאֶחָת וּשְׂבָכָה לַכֹּתֶרֶת הַשֵּׁנִית׃ 'And he made two trellises to cover the chapiters which were upon the top of the pillars; a trellis for the one chapiter, and a trellis for the second chapiter.'

---

[1] The root סבך, which ought properly to be שׂבך, occurs Nah. 1. 10; Job 8. 17 with the meaning 'intertwine.' Hence come סְבָךְ, סֹבֶךְ 'thicket.'

18. העמודים] Obviously incorrect. At this stage of the description the statement 'he made the pillars' is out of place. Two MSS. read הָרִמֹּנִים 'the pomegranates,' and this is to be adopted with Bö., Th., Sta., Klo., Kamp., Benz., Kit. Vulg., Pesh., Targ. follow MT.; LXX, Luc. *καὶ ἔργον κρεμαστόν*, i. e. ? . . . וּמַעֲשֵׂה[1] a misreading of ויעש הרמנים.

וישני טורים סביב על השבכה] LXX, Luc. *δύο στίχοι ῥοῶν χαλκῶν δεδικτυωμένοι*, i. e. [הָאֶחָת] וּשְׁנֵי טוּרֵי רִמֹּנִים נְחֹשֶׁת עַל־הַשְּׂבָכָה. *δεδικτ.* is thought by Klo. to be a corruption of *δικτύῳ ἐνί*, which is possible (cf. *v.* 42 *τῷ δικτύῳ τῷ ἐνί*), but not really necessary. LXX reading is correct, and is adopted by Sta., Kamp. So Th., with addition of סביב.

LXX, Luc. continue with *ἔργον κρεμαστόν, στίχος ἐπὶ στίχον.* This appears to be merely a doublet of the previous *καὶ ἔργον κρεμαστόν, δύο στίχοι.*

The sentence לכסות וג׳ having been adopted into its proper position in *v.* 17, *v.* 18 now ends abruptly with וכן עשה לכתרת השנית, no special reference being previously made to הכתרת האחת. Th. therefore inserts, before the closing sentence, *v.* 20[b] in the form in which it appears in Pesh. ܘܪ̈ܘܡܢܐ ܡܐܬܝܢ ܬܪ̈ܝܢ ܣ̈ܕܪܝܢ ܚܕܪ ܚܕܪ ܠܟܘܫܒܬܐ ܚܕܐ, i.e. וְהָרִמֹּנִים מָאתַיִם שְׁנֵי טוּרִים סָבִיב עַל־הַכֹּתֶרֶת הָאֶחָת, MT. being improved by the addition of שני, and the emendation האחת for השנית. This is satisfactory; and it is worthy of notice that Pesh. continues this sentence with ܘܗܟܢܐ ܠܟܘܫܒܬܐ ܐܚܪܬܐ, precisely the same words with which it is finished off when placed in *v.* 18. The transposition is adopted by Sta., Benz. with omission of the words שני טורים on the ground that they have already occurred in the earlier part of the verse—a scarcely justifiable belief in the writer's extreme precision in avoiding even the smallest repetition. Kamp., Kit. also follow Th., reading טורים as in MT. for שני טורים; and Klo., while taking *v.* 20[b] into *v.* 18,

---

[1] This can scarcely represent ומעשה שבכה, since שבכים is correctly rendered *δίκτυα* in the preceding verse; nor can it well translate ומעשה שרשרות, this being elsewhere suitably rendered *ἔργον πλοκῆς*, Ex. 28. 14; *ἔργον ἁλυσιδωτοῦ*, *v.* 22; *ἔργον ἐμπλοκίου*, 39. 15; and *χαλαστά*, 2 Chr. 3. 5, 16.

expands and alters the whole verse thus formed to a quite unnecessary extent.

Thus the probably original form of *v.* 18 is:—וַיַּעַשׂ אֶת־הָרִמֹּנִים וּשְׁנֵי טוּרֵי רִמֹּנִים נְחֹשֶׁת עַל־הַשְּׂבָכָה הָאֶחָת וְהָרִמֹּנִים מָאתַיִם שְׁנֵי טוּרִים סָבִיב עַל־הַכֹּתֶרֶת הָאֶחָת וְכֵן עָשָׂה לַכֹּתֶרֶת הַשֵּׁנִית׃ 'And he made the pomegranates; and two rows of pomegranates in brass were upon the one trellis, and the pomegranates were two hundred[1], two rows round about upon the one chapiter; and so did he to the second chapiter.'

19, 20ᵃ, 22. The *vv.* 19, 20 appear in LXX, Luc. *after v.* 21, while *v.* 22 is altogether missing. Now *v.* 21, which relates the erection and naming of the pillars, ought obviously to come at the close of the description; and this consideration, together with the state of LXX text, goes, as Sta. has seen, to point to the probability of *vv.* 19, 20ᵃ, 22 being merely a gloss.

This is still further borne out if we compare the contents of these verses with the description of the chapiters given in the original text. In *vv.* 16–18 all that we gather with regard to the chapiters relates to their size, and to the trellises and pomegranates with which they were ornamented. The description of their appearance seems to come naturally to an end with the sentence וכן עשה לכתרת השנית at the close of *v.* 18, and then *v.* 21, containing the account of their erection in their destined position, might fitly be expected to follow as the conclusion of the reference. But instead of this we have fresh details with regard to the מַעֲשֵׂה שׁוֹשַׁן, i.e. apparently the lily-like form of the chapiters, and the chapiters properly so called seem to be distinguished from a part of the pillar immediately beneath them which is known as הַבֶּטֶן. Now it is reasonable to suppose that in a consistent description the account of the *actual form and appearance* of the chapiters would *precede* rather than follow the reference to such

---

[1] In view of the precise statement of the number of the pomegranates as 100 in Jer. 52. 23, it may be questioned whether we ought not in this passage also to read מֵאָה for מאתים.

appendages as the pomegranates and trellises. But, assuming for the moment that the additional details are genuine, let us turn to *vv.* 41, 42, where a summary of Ḥiram's work at the pillars is given. Here we have mention of the עַמֻּדִים themselves, the גֻּלֹּת הַכֹּתָרוֹת which surmounted them, the שְׂבָכוֹת, and the רִמֹּנִים; but there is not the slightest reference to any מַעֲשֵׂה שׁוּשַׁן of the chapiters, nor to a part called הַבֶּטֶן connected with them. Hence we may confidently regard *vv.* 19, 20[a], 22 as a gloss added to the text by a later hand. The interpolator's idea of the form of the chapiters appears to have resembled the accompanying illustration. Judging from the ex-

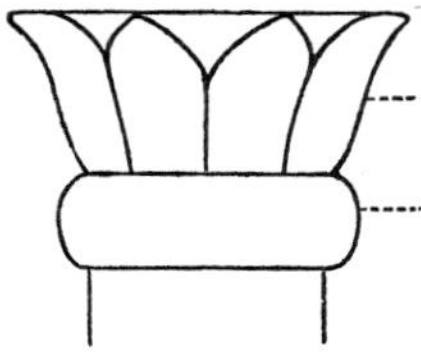

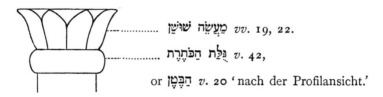

מַעֲשֵׂה שׁוּשַׁן *vv.* 19, 22.

גֻּלַּת הַכֹּתֶרֶת *v.* 42,

or הַבֶּטֶן *v.* 20 'nach der Profilansicht.'

pression גֻּלֹּת הַכֹּתָרוֹת in *v.* 42, he supposed the existence of a bowl-shaped portion of the pillar underneath the actual chapiter, which looked at, as Th. says, 'nach der Profilansicht,' might be described as הַבֶּטֶן. This led him to add the account of the shape of the actual chapiters, which he describes as מַעֲשֵׂה שׁוּשַׁן. The original narrator, however, in speaking of גֻּלֹּת הַכֹּתָרוֹת, appears to mean the actual chapiters, which from their rounded form might be thus described.

19. באולם] So Vulg., Pesh., Targ. Probably correct, and an awkward intimation of the position occupied by the pillars 'in the porch.' Cf. the notice which we derive from Luc. in *v.* 15 לאולם הבית, and *v.* 21. LXX, Luc. κατὰ τὸ αἰλάμ, i.e. כָּאוּלָם, seems to be an easy correction of this, and scarcely increases the lucidity of the expression.

20. מלעמת] 'In connexion with': cf. Ex. 25. 27 לְעֻמַּת הַמִּסְגֶּרֶת תִּהְיֶיןָ הַטַּבָּעֹת; 28. 27; *al.* לְעֻמַּת in the Hexateuch is peculiar to P. With מן only in this passage. LXX τῶν πλευρῶν points to a misreading לְצַלְעֹת. For the other peculiarities of this verse in LXX cf. *notes* on corruptions and doublets in *Introduction*.

לְעֵבֶר] ‘Over against’ or ‘at the side of’; RV. ‘beside.’ Cf. the use of עבר illustrated 5. 4 *note.*

23. מוצק] LXX om. through oversight. Luc. χυτήν.

שלשים] LXX τρεῖς (Luc. τριῶν) καὶ τριάκοντα through a mistaken repetition of שלשים as שלש. The measure given is the circumference answering to the diameter עשר באמה משפתו עד שפתו.

קוה] Q're קָו is the usual word. Kt. קָוֶה only occurs elsewhere Jer. 31. 38; Zech. 1. 16, with Q're קָו in each place. וְקָו שְׁלֹשִׁים בָּאַמָּה is a case of apposition; ‘a line—thirty cubits.’ So Ex. 27. 16 מָסָךְ עֶשְׂרִים אַמָּה; Dri. *Tenses*, § 192. 1.

יסב] See *v.* 15 *note.*

24. עשר באמה] This can only be translated as it is by Vulg., Pesh., Targ. ‘for ten cubits.’ The rendering of RV. marg. ‘ten (sc. פקעים) in a cubit,’ besides supposing, as Sta. remarks, the mistake of עשר for עשרה, is quite contrary to the universal usage of the expression. We find the same words occurring in || 2 Chr. 4. 3, and the most obvious explanation is to suppose that an early scribe, perhaps R^D himself, through lapse of memory confused the circumference of the sea with its diameter, when all the while he was intending to write שְׁלֹשִׁים בָּאַמָּה. Sta. omits.

מקפים את הים סביב] Omitted by LXX, but contained in Luc., Vulg., Pesh., Targ. Sta. regards the sentence as a gloss on the ground that the author never elsewhere uses the word הִקִּיף, and has already said סביב סבבים אתו. So Kamp., Benz., Kit.

שני טורים . . . ביצקתו] LXX, Luc. om., probably through oversight. Th., Sta., Klo., Kamp., Benz., Kit. retain as original.

26. This verse in LXX, Luc. precedes *v.* 25, an emended order which is certainly to be adopted. It is only natural that the remaining details with regard to the sea—its thickness, the formation of its brim, and its interior capacity—should precede the account of the oxen upon which it was placed. So Sta., Kamp., Benz., Kit.

אלפים בת יכיל] Not found in LXX, Luc.; but the similar reference to the contents of the lavers in *v.* 38, ארבעים בת יכיל, speaks for the genuineness of the notice in this case also. On the tense יכיל, cf. *v.* 15 *note* on יסב.

Fig. 1.

BRONZE STAND FROM LARNAKA.

27–37. This difficult section, which was formerly regarded as involved in almost hopeless obscurity, has received considerable elucidation through recent discoveries in Cyprus. Two bronze stands of late Mycenaean workmanship[1] have been unearthed, the one from Larnaka and the other from Enkomi. The light which these bronzes were capable of throwing upon the ten מכונות of Solomon's Temple was first noticed by A. S. Murray with reference to the stand from Enkomi: *Journal of Royal Inst. of Brit. Architects*, 1899, vii. pp. 20 *ff.* The subject was worked out at length by A. Furtwängler in an article in the *Sitzungsberichte der philos.-philol. und der histor. Classe der kgl. bayer. Akademie der Wissenschaften zu München*, 1899, Bd. 2, Heft 3. This was followed by a detailed examination by Stade of the section in Kings in the light of the new discoveries (*ZATW.* 1901, pp. 145 *ff.*), in which he largely modified his earlier views upon the subject, as expressed in the article on Solomon's buildings (*ZATW.* 1883), and illustrated by a figure in his *Ges.* i. p. 341. Figures of the Cyprus bronzes are here given[2]. That from Larnaka measures 39 cm. in height, 23 cm. in width of side, 12 cm. in diameter of wheels; that from Enkomi is 16 cm. in height, and about 13 cm. in width.

It is clear that we have two divergent accounts of the מכונות combined in *vv.* 27–37. This was first noticed by Klo., who distinguished *vv.* 34–36 as belonging to a second account. His view was accepted in the main by Benz. Furtwängler regards *vv.* 32–36 as the remains of an ancient doublet; while Sta. supposes that the two accounts have been not simply placed side by side, but to a large extent interwoven. Sta. notices the following double descriptions:—1. Decoration of the מכונה

---

[1] Furtwängler places the date of the Necropolis at Enkomi *cir.* B.C. 1200–1000. Cf. *Antike Gemmen*, Bd. iii. 440.

[2] The upper figure in Plate 1 I have been kindly allowed by Dr. Furtwängler to reproduce from his article; the under figure I owe to Mr. J. L. Myres, of Christ Church, Oxford, who obtained the photograph for me through the British Commissioner at Cyprus. The two reproductions in Plate 2 are from photographs taken by the University Press.

with figures in *v.* 29 and *v.* 36. The two verses exhibit discrepancies (*a*) in description of the figures—*v.* 29 mentions lions, oxen, and cherubim, *v.* 36 cherubim, lions, and palm trees; (*b*) in naming the part of the מכונה so decorated—*v.* 29 מסגרות and שלבים, *v.* 36 לחות. 2. The Wheels. These are described briefly in *v.* 30[a], and in detail in *vv.* 32, 33. 3. The כתפות of the corner pillars in *v.* 30 and *v.* 34. Obviously the indefinite וארבע כתפות of *v.* 34 belongs to an account in which the parts so named have not been previously mentioned. 4. The part at the top of the מכונה which held the laver. This is called פיהו in *v.* 31, while in *v.* 35 the name has fallen out. 5. The double statement that the ידות of the wheels were of one part with the מכונה; *v.* 32 and *v.* 35.

While, however, it is certain that *vv.* 34–36 cannot, from their contents, belong to the preceding account, this is not necessarily the case with *vv.* 33, 34, since there is nothing in the contents of these verses to prevent us from regarding them as a description of the wheels in detail, after their brief mention in *v.* 30[a].

27. LXX, Luc. give the length of the bases as five cubits, the breadth as four cubits, and the height as six cubits. Sta. remarks that from this difference between length and breadth the inference might be drawn that the lavers standing upon the מכונות were not round but elliptical; but that this is opposed to *v.* 28, where the 'four cubits' can only be taken as the diameter of a round laver. The מכונות of Figs. 1 and 2 are square, and have round cylinders to hold the lavers. Thus the measurements of MT., four × four, are to be accepted. It seems not improbable that the six cubits of LXX, Luc. represent the *total height* of the מכונה three cubits + the אופנים $1\frac{1}{2}$ cubits (*v.* 32) + the פה $1\frac{1}{2}$ cubits (*v.* 31).

28. מסגרת] The question as to whether this word means 'borders' (RV.) or 'panels' (RV. marg.) is not at all elucidated by the Verss. LXX, Luc. *συγκλειστόν* translate according to the sense of the root, and perhaps vocalize מְסֻגֶּרֶת; Vulg. *interrasile* + *sculpturae* appears to be merely guessing; Pesh., Targ. ܓܕ̈ܢܦܐ, גדנפין is the word used by Pesh. to translate מגרעות in *ch.* 6. 6, with the meaning 'ledges.' The only other connexion in which מסגרת

Fig. 2.

BRONZE STAND FROM ENKOMI.

in a similar sense occurs, viz. as a part of the table of shewbread, Ex. 25. 25, 27; 37. 12, 14, is greatly in favour of the meaning 'border' (i.e. what we now call the *frame* of the table), whether immediately below the top of the table, as in our modern tables, or connecting the ends of the legs; cf. especially מִסְגֶּרֶת טֹפַח 'a border of a handbreadth,' scarcely 'a panel of a handbreadth.'

שלבים] Only in this description of the bases. The Puʿal participle of a verb שלב occurs Ex. 26. 17; 36. 22† שְׁתֵּי יָדוֹת לַקֶּרֶשׁ הָאֶחָד מְשֻׁלָּבֹת אִשָּׁה אֶל־אֲחֹתָהּ 'there shall be two tenons to each board, *morticed* one to another.' In Talmudic שליבה denotes *the rung of a ladder;* so *Maccoth* 7b היה עולה בסלם ונשמטה שליבה מתחתיו 'he was mounting a ladder when a rung gave way beneath him.' Hence we may understand by שלבים the corner uprights of the מכונה, and possibly also uprights at regular intervals between the corners (cf. Fig. 2). The מסגרות then ran horizontally בין השלבים, forming a connexion or framework to the corner uprights. Cf. the four horizontal bars in Fig. 2. Perhaps the best rendering of שלבים is '*supports*.' Vulg., Pesh. seem to approximate to the right meaning with their renderings *juncturas*, ܣܢ̈ܝܦܐ 'connexions'; Targ. שְׁלִיבַיָּא, LXX, Luc. ἐξεχομένων.

מסגרות להם ומסגרת בין השלבים] Are the second מִסְגְּרֹת different from the first? i.e. ought we to render ומסגרת 'and *also* border-frames'? or, if the two are identical, why do we not read וְהַמִּסְגְּרֹת 'and *the* border-frames,' already mentioned? Again, why הַשְּׁלַבִּים '*the* supports,' when these have *not* been previously mentioned? Klo., observing these difficulties, emends מִסְגְּרֹת לָהֶם וּשְׁלַבִּים לָהֶם וְהַמִּסְגְּרֹת בֵּין הַשְּׁלַבִּים 'they had border-frames and supports, and the border-frames were between the supports.' It is preferable to suppose that the first מסגרות has been written by mistake for שלבים which would naturally be first mentioned; שְׁלַבִּים לָהֶם וּמִסְגְּרֹת בֵּין הַשְּׁלַבִּים '*they had supports, and there were border-frames between the supports.*'

29. אריות וג׳] Cf. the winged figures of Fig. 1, and the lions (?) of Fig. 2.

ועל השלבים כן] 'And upon the supports *likewise*.' The rendering of Furtwängler, 'And upon the supports *there was a pedestal*,'

is unsuitable, because this part of the מכונה is described below in
v. 31 not as a כֵּן but as a פֶּה.

מִמַּעַל] Follow LXX, Luc. וּמִמַּעַל ' *and* above and below &c.'

לֹיוֹת] Doubtless a corruption of וְלַכְּרוּבִים, which is desiderated after
לַאֲרָיוֹת וְלַבָּקָר. The corruption is due to the influence of *v.* 30 end.

מַעֲשֵׂה מוּרָד] LXX, Luc. appear to explain rightly ἔργον καταβάσεως, ' step-work,' or, as we should say, '*bevelled work*'; i.e. probably
the edges of the מִסְגֶּרֶת were bevelled in the form of steps :—

or a section viewed from the end would have appeared thus :—

The ornamental borders in Fig. 1, above and below the winged
figures, have something of this character.

30. סְרְנֵי] A ἅπαξ λεγ.; but in Syr. ܣܰܪܢܳܐ ' axle ' is common.
Probably the axles were similar in form to those of Fig. 1.

וְאַרְבָּעָה פַעֲמֹתָיו וג'] RV. ' and the four feet thereof had undersetters.' If כְּתֵפֹת (lit. ' shoulders ') could mean ' undersetters,' we
might identify them with the diagonal stays which strengthen the
legs in Figs. 1 and 2. But these stays would scarcely be described
as ' shoulder-pieces,' and in fact they seem to be denoted by
a more suitable term יָדוֹת in *v.* 32. Moreover, they could scarcely
be described as מִתַּחַת לַכִּיֹּר, i. e. immediately under the laver. The
position of these כְּתֵפֹת should rather be that of the four birds
(doves?), at the four upper corners of the מכונה in Fig. 1, which
might aptly be described as ' *shoulder-pieces*.' So Hommel,
Furtwängler, Sta. But then ארבעה פעמתיו (rather אַרְבַּע פַּעֲמֹתֶיהָ,
with reference to the מכונה), ' its four feet,' can scarcely be correct ;
for we cannot, with Sta., force the interpretation and suppose that
' the corner pillars with reference to their lower ends could very
well be described as the פַעֲמוֹת of the מכונה.' When we are speaking
of the shoulder-pieces we are thinking of the *upper* ends of the

corner pillars, and besides, these corner pillars or supports have already been described as שלבים. In the second account, *v.* 34, four כְּתֵפוֹת are said to have been אֶל אַרְבַּע פִּנּוֹת הַמְּכֹנָה 'at the four *corners* of the base.' A more suitable term to describe the position of the shoulder-pieces could not be selected, and we may follow Kamp. in emending וְאַרְבַּע פִּנּוֹתֶיהָ '*and its four corners had shoulder-pieces.*' LXX, Luc. μέρη αὐτῶν appears to be an alteration of the difficult פעמתיו into פֵּאֹתָן; cf. Ex. 25. 26, where עַל אַרְבַּע הַפֵּאֹת is rendered ἐπὶ τὰ τέσσαρα μέρη.

מעבר איש ליות] ליות (לְוָיֹת) appears to denote 'wreaths' or 'spiral work,' such as forms the principal ornamentation in Fig. 2, and appears round the cylinder in Fig. 1. מעבר איש is properly '*beyond* or *at the side of each.*' Cf. the phrase מכל עבריו '*at* all *sides* of him,' *ch.* 5. 4 *note*. We may render '*with spirals at the side of each.*' The spirals may have run between the shoulder-pieces along the top edges of the מכונה.

31. ופיהו] Read וּפִיהָ '*and its mouth,*' the suffix referring to the מכונה. The פה is clearly the mouth or opening of the cylinder, seen in Figs. 1 and 2, to contain the laver. So Furtwängler, Sta.

מבית לכתרת] R.V. 'within the chapiter.' But כֹּתֶרֶת, elsewhere always the *crown* or *chapiter* of a column, scarcely seems a suitable term to describe the part of the מכונה which contained the פה; and the fact that the word is defined by the article rather indicates that it refers to something already mentioned. We may therefore follow Ew.'s emendation (adopted by Klo., Sta., and others), and read מִבֵּית לַכְּתֵפֹת '*within the shoulder-pieces,*' just described.

ומעלה באמה] A number must have fallen out before באמה, and this was probably אֶחָד (Kamp., Sta.). But ומעלה, which qualifies the statement as to the height, ought naturally to follow after it. We may therefore read אֶחָד בָּאַמָּה וָמַעְלָה '*was one cubit and upwards.*' The statement which comes later in the verse, אמה וחצי האמה, is merely a repetition of the same fact in more exact terms, and ought probably, therefore (with Sta.), to be regarded as a marginal gloss.

מעשה כן] '*After the structure* (*form*) *of a pedestal.*' כן is used of the pedestal of the כִּיּוֹר in Ex. 30. 28; 31. 9; *al.*

ומסגרתיהם וג׳] If this sentence is in place, the statement ought naturally to refer to the פֶּה. But then we should expect וּמִסְגְּרֹתָיו, i.e., in contrast to the round opening itself, '*its borders were foursquare, not round*,' thus forming a pedestal which corresponded in shape to the square מכונה beneath. If this be the meaning of the passage, the pedestal differed from those in Figs. 1 and 2, which are round outside as well as inside. Sta. considers the statement to be out of place, and, reading מִסְגְּרֹתֶיהָ, refers it to the border-frames of the מכונה proper.

32. וידות האופנים במכונה] '*And the stays of the wheels were in the base*'; i.e. of one casting with it. ידות seems to denote the diagonal stays, which are seen under the מכונות in Figs. 1 and 2.

33. גביהם] 'Their felloes'; i.e. the rounded portion of the wheel, from גבב 'to be curved.' So, in this sense, Ezek. 1. 18†.

וחשקיהם וחשריהם] Both ἅπαξ λεγγ. Ges. connects the former word with חשק 'cleave to' or 'join,' so חֲשׁוּקִים 'those which join' sc. the felloe to the nave, i.e. the *spokes*; but his derivation of the latter word from Ar. حشر *congregavit*, so חִשּׁוּר 'place in which the spokes *come together*,' i.e. the *box* or *nave*, seems more than doubtful, since, apart from the dubious meaning, a wrong interchange of consonants is implied.

34. מן המכנה כתפיה] '*Of one casting with* the base were its shoulder-pieces.' The same meaning is to be attached to ממנה in *v.* 35. Cf. Ex. 27. 2. Sta. regards *v.* 34ᵇ as a gloss, mainly on the ground of the masc. pl. form כתפיה in place of כתפותיה.

35. ובראש המכונה וג׳] The subject of the sentence has fallen out. In accordance with *v.* 31 it should be פֶּה, or some similar term.

חצי האמה] אמה וחצי האמה must have been read, if this account originally agreed with that of *v.* 31.

ידתיה ומסגרתיה] The ידות on the top of the מכנה cannot be identified; the מסגרות are probably those described in *v.* 31ᵇ.

36. ויפתח] 'He carved.' The subject is Ḥiram.

הלחת] 'The panels' are peculiar to this second account. Judging by the reference to the figures carved upon them, we may suppose that they answer to the מסגרות of *vv.* 28, 29.

ידתיה ועל ומסגרתיה] To be rejected as an erroneous dittography from the preceding verse. ועל was probably added later as an attempt to give sense to the words as they stand. So Kamp., Sta.

ותמרת] Palm trees take the place of the oxen of *v.* 29. Cf. the palms (?) in Fig. 1 between the winged figures.

כמער וג׳] Read מעבר איש ליות סביב, in accordance with *v.* 30.

37. קצב אחד] LXX, Luc. omit.

לְכֻלָּהֵנָה] The suffix occurs once again, בְּתוֹכֲהֵנָה Ezek. 16. 53, also in pause. Cf. G-K. § 91 *f;* Sta. § 352 *b.* Klo. emends לְכֹל הֵנָּה.

39[a]. LXX *καὶ ἔθετο τὰς πέντε μεχωνὼθ ἀπὸ τῆς ὠμίας τοῦ οἴκου ἐξ ἀριστερῶν* omits הבית מימין וחמש על כתף through homoioteleuton. Luc. further omits *πέντε*, thus making it appear that *all* the bases were placed on the left; but this is clearly an emendation of LXX text.

40. הכירות] LXX, Luc. *τοὺς λέβητας*, Vulg. *lebetes*, i.e. הַסִּירוֹת 'the pots.' Pesh. ܩܕ̈ܪܐ ܘܩܣ̈ܛܐ, i.e. הכירות והסירות. הסירות is doubtless correct. It occurs ||2 Chr. 4. 11; in the summary *v.* 45 (|| 2 Chr. 4. 16); and in II. 25. 14; Jer. 52. 18, where the allusion is apparently to the same vessels. So Th., Sta., Klo., Kamp., Benz., Kit.

סיר is usually a cooking pot in which flesh (Ex. 16. 3) or broth (II. 4. 38 *ff.*) is boiled; but as a sacrificial implement it is mentioned in connexion with the brazen altar; Ex. 27. 3 וְעָשִׂיתָ סִירֹתָיו לְדַשְּׁנוֹ 'and thou shalt make its pots *to take away its ashes.*'

היעים] 'The shovels'; included (Ex. 27. 3; 38. 3; Num. 4. 14) among the כְּלֵי הַמִּזְבֵּחַ, and employed for transferring the ashes into the סירות; cf. Kimḥi's explanation:—שהיו מסירים בהם הדשן כתרגומו במגרפיתא שהיה גורף בהם הדשן מהמזבח. A verb יעה occurs Isa. 28. 17† ויעה ברד מחסה כזב, probably 'and hail shall *sweep away* the refuge of lies'; Ar. وَعَى I. 'collect into one place.'

המזרקות] 'The bowls,' which were used for *tossing* or dashing the blood *in a volume* against the altar. Cf. the use of the verb זרק in e.g. Ex. 24. 6 וחצי הדם זרק על המזבח. The action denoted is constantly distinct from that expressed by הִזָּה 'sprinkle with the fingers'; Lev. 4. 6; *al.* מזרק is always sacrificial, except in Am. 6. 6 השתים במזרקי יין 'who drink in (i.e. *out of*) bowls of wine.'

בית יהוה] Accus. of place as in Gen. 18. 1, 10; *al.* Da. § 69.

† H

41. גלת הכתרת] Cf. *note* on *vv.* 19, 20ª, 22.

42. שני טורים רמנים] 'Two rows—pomegranates'; cf. Dri. *Tenses*, § 194. It would be more natural to read either שְׁנֵי טוּרֵי רִמֹּנִים as in *v.* 18ª above emended, or else רִמֹּנִים שְׁנֵי טוּרִים 'pomegranates *in* two rows,' שני ט׳ being then an accus. of manner: Da. § 70.

על פני העמודים] Certainly wrong. LXX, Luc. are probably correct in reading עַל־שְׁנֵי הָעַמּוּדִים. So Th., Sta., Klo. Vulg., Pesh. presuppose על ראש העמודים as in *v.* 41. So Kamp., Benz., Kit.

45. האהל] Q're הָאֵלֶּה certainly correct. Thus Targ. translates האלין, and then, apparently with reference to Kt., adds the gloss כעובד מני משכנא דעבד משה 'according to the structure of the vessels of the Tabernacle which Moses made.' LXX, Luc., Vulg. omit the word. Pesh. ܕܠܡܫܟܢܐ, probably a paraphrase of Kt. הָאֹהֶל. Sta., in adopting Q're, points out that the וְ before את כל הכלים האלה must (as in Vulg.) be omitted, since otherwise האלה is unnecessary.

After the sentence אשר עשה חירם למלך ש׳ בית י׳, LXX, Luc. add *καὶ οἱ στύλοι τεσσαράκοντα καὶ ὀκτὼ τοῦ οἴκου τοῦ βασιλέως καὶ τοῦ οἴκου Κυρίου· πάντα τὰ ἔργα τοῦ βασιλέως ἐποίησεν Χειράμ* . . . , i.e. וְהָעַמּוּדִים אַרְבָּעִים וּשְׁמֹנָה לְבֵית הַמֶּלֶךְ וּלְבֵית יְהוָֹה אֶת־כָּל־מְלֶאכֶת הַמֶּלֶךְ עָשָׂה חִירָם. It is to be noticed that *vv.* 41–45ª sum up the work of Ḥiram, which is described in detail in *vv.* 15–40; *vv.* 41, 42 corresponding to *vv.* 15–22, *v.* 43 to *vv.* 27–39, *v.* 44 to *vv.* 23–26, and *v.* 45ª to *v.* 40. If, however, the LXX addition be regarded as genuine, we have here a matter of great importance mentioned for the first time in the summary without previous detailed description of any kind. And not only so, but a work so considerable as the casting of these forty-eight pillars is mentioned last of all, even subsequently to the notice of the making of articles so comparatively unimportant as the brazen pots, &c. We may therefore regard the passage as a gloss, of uncertain source. So Sta.; but Bö., Th., Benz., and to some extent Klo., adopt as genuine.

נחשת ממרט] '*Burnished* brass.' The verb מרט is used again in the participle Puʿal מֹרָטָה for מְמֹרָטָה Ezek. 21. 15, 16, and Qal passive מְרוּטָה Ezek. 21. 14, 33, of a *burnished* sword; and in Isa. 18. 2, 7 מוֹרָט (for מְמֹרָט) describes the *polished* appearance of the skin of the Ethiopians. Elsewhere the word is used of plucking out hair, and this is the first meaning in Ar. and Syr. The Verss. merely guess at the sense of ממרט. Targ. נחש טב, Vulg. *de aurichalco*, Pesh. ܕܢܚܫܐ ܡܦܘܪܛܠܐ, LXX *χαλκᾶ ἄρδην*[1], Luc. simply *χαλκᾶ ἦν*.

46–50. This section as it stands can scarcely exhibit its original form.

(i) וינח . . . מאד] *v.* 47 is very obscure and awkward. It can only mean, 'And Solomon *left* all the vessels because of their very great number.' This we have to interpret, 'He *left them unweighed*,' a forced and unparalleled explanation.

(ii) It is unnatural to say that the brass could not be weighed because the vessels were so *numerous*. We have just had a description of the great vessels, &c., which were made by Ḥiram, the sea, the bases and lavers, and the two pillars, the casting of which must have taken an enormous quantity of brass; and in comparison with this the brass used for the pots, shovels, &c., however numerous they may have been, must have been comparatively trivial in quantity. Hence, the reason why the brass went unweighed was not *the number* of the vessels, most of which were small, but the *great quantity* of brass which was used, chiefly for the comparatively few large vessels.

(iii) After the very lengthy description of the brazen vessels made by Ḥiram, it is surely strange that so short a summary (*vv.* 48–50) of the golden vessels, &c., should be given, without any account of their appearance or mention of their maker. We are justified in regarding an allusion of such brevity, in the midst of a document which seems to aim at peculiar minuteness in description, as the work of a later hand who desiderated some reference to the *golden* vessels of the Temple[2].

---

[1] This is simply a paraphrase derived from the context, and cannot represent בְּמְאֹד of Th.; still less Klo.'s נְחֹשֶׁת חֵרֶם or מְחֻרָם, supposed to mean 'consecrated (?) brass,' according to the (free) rendering of Mal. 3. 24 פֶּן־אָבוֹא וְהִכֵּיתִי אֶת־הָאָרֶץ חֵרֶם, *μὴ ἔλθω καὶ πατάξω τὴν γῆν ἄρδην*.

[2] These verses are omitted by Sta., together with *v.* 47.

Turning to the Verss., we find that LXX, Luc. presuppose a considerably divergent text. In both *v.* 47 precedes *v.* 46, and *vv.* 47, 48ᵃ exhibit striking variation from MT.

LXX, *v.* 47, *οὐκ ἦν σταθμὸς τοῦ χαλκοῦ οὗ ἐποίησεν πάντα τὰ ἔργα ταῦτα ἐκ πλήθους σφόδρα· οὐκ ἦν τέρμα τῶν σταθμῶν τοῦ χαλκοῦ.*

v. 46. As in MT., omitting המלך.

v. 48ᵃ. *καὶ ἔλαβεν ὁ βασιλεὺς Σαλωμὼν τὰ σκεύη ἃ ἐποίησεν ἐν οἴκῳ.*

vv. 48ᵇ–50. Substantially as in MT.

This may be re-translated :—

v. 47. אֵין מִשְׁקָל לַנְּחֹשֶׁת אֲשֶׁר עָשָׂה אֶת־כָּל־הַכֵּלִים [?] הָאֵלֶּה מֵרֹב מְאֹד מְאֹד לֹא נֶחְקַר מִשְׁקַל הַנְּחֹשֶׁת׃.

v. 46. As in MT., omitting המלך.

v. 48ᵃ. וַיִּקַּח הַמֶּלֶךְ שְׁלֹמֹה אֶת־הַכֵּלִים אֲשֶׁר עָשָׂה בֵּית [יְהוָֹה].

Luc. is slightly different :—

v. 47. *οὐκ ἦν σταθμὸς τοῦ χαλκοῦ οὗ ἐποίησεν ἄρδην· πάντα τὰ σκεύη ἃ ἐποίησε, ταῦτα ἐκ τοῦ πλήθους σφόδρα· οὐκ ἦν τέρμα τῷ σταθμῷ τοῦ χαλκοῦ.*

v. 46. As in MT., omitting המלך.

v. 48ᵃ. *καὶ ἔδωκε Σολομῶν ὁ βασιλεὺς τὰ σκεύη ἃ ἐποίησεν ἐν τῷ οἴκῳ κυρίου.*

vv. 48ᵇ–50. Substantially as in MT.

Translate :—

v. 47. אֵין מִשְׁקָל לַנְּחֹשֶׁת אֲשֶׁר עָשָׂה בִּמְאֹד [?] כָּל־הַכֵּלִים הָאֵלֶּה אֲשֶׁר עָשָׂה מֵרֹב מְאֹד מְאֹד לֹא נֶחְקַר מִשְׁקַל הַנְּחֹשֶׁת׃.

v. 46. As in MT., omitting המלך.

v. 48ᵃ. וַיַּנַּח הַמֶּלֶךְ שְׁלֹמֹה אֶת־הַכֵּלִים אֲשֶׁר עָשָׂה בֵּית יְהוָֹה.

In *v.* 47 Luc.'s rendering can scarcely be original. The repetition of אשר עשה, and the construction of כל הכלים in apposition to לנחשת, are very awkward. On the other hand, LXX text is here very clear and good, completely disposing of difficulty (i) by the substitution of אין משקל וג׳ for וינח שלמה, and of (ii) by the reference of מרב מאד מאד back to אין משקל לנחשת instead of to את כל הכלים. Luc.'s text of this verse probably arose through the insertion of *ἄρδην* as a doublet of מרב מאד מאד, this breaking the sentence and causing the repetition of *ἃ ἐποίησε*.

By the transposition of *v.* 47 and *v.* 46 we gain a better sequence, the great quantity of brass being naturally mentioned before the locality in which the vessels, &c., were cast.

In *v.* 48ᵃ Luc. is to be preferred to LXX. The וינח שלמה of the commencement of *v.* 47 MT. is here referred to its proper place, and its position in MT. is perhaps explained by the transposition of *vv.* 46 and 47. The writer, having wrongly written *v.* 46 first, was proceeding to write *v.* 48 which properly followed it, when he noticed that he had omitted *v.* 47, and so added it then and there. Thus the first two words of *v.* 48 came to be placed at the beginning of *v.* 47.

According to Luc., *v.* 48ᵃ describes the destination of the golden vessels; it ought, however, properly to refer to the brazen vessels, and to conclude the account of them. This should naturally lead the way to *v.* 51, the conclusion of the whole notice. The alteration of *v.* 48ᵃ in MT. ויעש for וינח, and in LXX καὶ ἔλαβεν for καὶ ἔδωκε, is most probably due to the gloss *vv.* 48ᵇ–50 which mentions the golden vessels.

Upon these grounds the following may plausibly be considered the original text of these *vv.* 46–51:—

v. 47. אֵין מִשְׁקָל לַנְּחֹשֶׁת אֲשֶׁר עָשָׂה אֶת־כָּל־הַכֵּלִים הָאֵלֶּה מֵרֹב מְאֹד מְאֹד לֹא נֶחְקַר מִשְׁקַל הַנְּחֹשֶׁת׃

v. 46. As in MT., omitting המלך.

v. 48. וַיַּנַּח [הַמֶּלֶךְ] שְׁלֹמֹה אֶת־הַכֵּלִים אֲשֶׁר עָשָׂה בֵּית יְהוָה׃

v. 51. As in MT.

v. 47. 'There was no weight to the brass wherewith he made all these vessels, because it was exceeding much; the weight of the brass was not found out. *v.* 46. In the plain of Jordan did he cast them, in the clay ground between Succoth and Zarethan. *v.* 48. And [King] Solomon placed the vessels in the house of Yahwe.

v. 51. 'Thus all the work that king Solomon wrought in the house of Yahwe was finished. And Solomon brought in the things which David his father had dedicated, even the silver and the gold and the vessels, placing them in the treasuries of the house of Yahwe.'

46. ככר הירדן] 'The *circle* of the Jordan'; ‖ 2 Chr. 4. 17; Gen. 13. 10, 11†; called also הַכִּכָּר '*the* circle,' Gen. 13. 12; 19. 17; Deut. 34. 3; 2 Sam. 18. 23; *al.* The term, a Pilpel form (כִּרְכָּר) from כרר 'move in a circle,' is used of the depressed region which forms the lower stage of the Jordan valley by which the river flows into the Dead Sea; but may in the earliest times have been exclusively applied to the fertile region occupied by the circle of cities forming the עָרֵי הַכִּכָּר; Gen. 13. 12; 19. 29. See Stanley, *SP*. 284.

במעבה האדמה] RV. 'In the *clay* ground'; so Vulg. *in terra argillosa*. מעבה, root עבה 'to be thick, dense' (*ch*. 12. 10), only occurs here, ‖ 2 Chr. 4. 17 having בַּעֲבִי הָאֲדָמָה. Moore (on Judg. 7. 22) emends במעברת [ה]אדמה 'at the crossing (ford) of Adamah,' regarding Adamah as identical with אָדָם of Josh. 3. 16 (*ed-Damieh*) which is there said to be near צרתן.

סכות] The identification of Rob. (*BR*., iii. 309 *ff*.) with *Sâkût* (*'Ain es-Sâqâṭ*) on the west bank of Jordan some nine miles south of Beisan, though suiting the connexion with צרתן which is mentioned (*ch*. 4. 12) together with בית שאן, is improbable as being philologically unsound. Moore, in accordance with his emendation above noticed, thinks סכות to be the place named in Genesis and Joshua *east* of Jordan. This, according to the Talmud (*Shebiith* ix. 2, *Gemara*), was in later times called דרעלה Dar'ala, i.e. probably 'the present *Tell Deir 'Alla*, a high mound in the Jordan valley, about one mile north of the Jabbok.' G. A. Smith, *Historical Geography*, 585; Buhl, *Geogr*. 259 *f*.

51^b^. נתן] The perf. *asyndetos* as a circumstantial clause; 'he placed,' &c., so '*placing*,' &c. Cf. *ch*. 13. 18 כחש לו; Dri. *Tenses*, § 163.

13–51. Wellh. comments upon the absence of any allusion to the making of the *brazen altar* in this description of the Temple furniture, assuming that, in accordance with the mention of an altar in *ch.* 8. 64; II. 16. 14, 15, such a reference must have originally existed, and has therefore been purposely removed by the post-exilic editor, upon the supposition that the brazen altar of Moses mentioned by P was, like the Ark, still in existence. Now, as we have seen, the glosses of R^P are for the most part either absent in LXX, Luc., or can at any rate be easily detected and separated from the original text into which they have come from the margin; and the method of treating the LXX text as representing upon the whole a recension untouched by R^P has, through the results, justified itself as reasonable. Thus, if mention of the casting of the brazen altar had existed in the original description, some trace of it would certainly have remained in LXX; but this is not the case. And not only so, but there are no other traces of the rejection by R^P of the statements of the original[1], such a proceeding being quite contrary to his method, which was to interpolate without excision.

Again, as will be seen, the section *ch.* 8. 1–11 has been largely interpolated by R^P, and in *v.* 4 there is mention of the carrying up to the Temple of the ארון יהוה ואת אהל מועד ואת כל כלי הקדש אשר באהל. If, therefore, this editor had only just previously excised from *ch.* 7 the mention of the making of the brazen altar for the reason above noticed, he would surely have expressly named it in *ch.* 8. 4 among the furniture of the אהל מועד which was taken up to the Temple.

Thus we may confidently conclude that mention of the brazen altar was, for whatever reasons, *not* contained in the original recension of 7. 13–51. The allusion in 2 Chr. 4. 1 ויעש מזבח נחשת עשרים אמה ארכו ועשרים אמה רחבו ועשר אמות קומתו is marked as a late addition by the absence of all detail in the description.

[1] The addition of LXX, Luc. in *v.* 45, with reference to the forty-eight pillars, is to be regarded as a gloss, for reasons above given.

8. *Dedication of Solomon's Temple.*

Ch. 8=2 Chr. 5. 2—7. 10.

8. 1. אז יקהל שלמה וג׳] LXX prefaces these words with the sentence καὶ ἐγένετο ὡς συνετέλεσεν Σαλωμὼν τοῦ οἰκοδομῆσαι τὸν οἶκον Κυρίου καὶ τὸν οἶκον ἑαυτοῦ μετὰ εἴκοσι ἔτη. So Luc., with the variation ἐν τῷ συντελέσαι Σολομῶντα. This is regarded by Bö., Th. as part of the original text. But more probably the words are an addition of the translator, who objected to the use of אז without 'any definite point of attachment in the preceding narrative.' This peculiar use of the particle is, however, characteristic of R^D (see collected instances in 3. 16 *note;* and cf. Dri. *LOT.* 192), and it is very noticeable that in no single case does אז occur as introduction to the apodosis of a sentence, after the protasis has contained a definite notice of the point of departure. In such a case the usual construction would certainly be וַיְהִי . . . וְ (cf. 9. 1, 2), and there is no reason why this should have been relinquished in favour of וַיְהִי . . . אָז. The form of the gloss was determined by 9. 1, and the time-notice μετὰ εἴκοσι ἔτη derived from the addition of שבע שנים 6. 38, and שלש עשרה שנה 7. 1.

1–11. This section has clearly received considerable interpolation by post-exilic hands under the influence of P. In LXX *vv.* 1–5 appear in a considerably shorter form, which reads smoothly and without trace of abridgement:—τότε ἐξεκκλησίασεν ὁ βασιλεὺς Σαλωμὼν πάντας τοὺς πρεσβυτέρους Ἰσραὴλ ἐν Σειὼν τοῦ ἐνεγκεῖν τὴν κιβωτὸν διαθήκης Κυρίου ἐκ πόλεως Δαυείδ, αὕτη ἐστὶν Σειών, (2) ἐν μηνὶ Ἀθαμείν. (3) καὶ ἦραν οἱ ἱερεῖς τὴν κιβωτὸν (4) καὶ τὸ σκήνωμα τοῦ μαρτυρίου καὶ τὰ σκεύη τὰ ἅγια τὰ ἐν τῷ σκηνώματι τοῦ μαρτυρίου· (5) καὶ ὁ βασιλεὺς καὶ πᾶς Ἰσραὴλ ἔμπροσθεν τῆς κιβωτοῦ θύοντες πρόβατα, βόας, ἀναρίθμητα. So substantially Luc. Here we notice the following omissions:—

1. ואת כל ראשי המטות נשיאי האבות לבני ישראל אל המלך שלמה] Here ראשי . . . האבות belongs distinctively to P. Cf. ראשי המטות ‖ 2 Chr. 5. 2; Num. 30. 2†. ראשי אבות המטות Num. 32. 28; Josh. 14. 1†. ראשי האבות למטות Josh. 19. 51†. ראשי אבות [האבות] Ex. 6. 25; Num. 31. 26; 36. 1; Josh.

21. 1, and very frequently in Chr., Ezra, Neh. (34 times)†. [ראשי בית אבות [האבות, אֲבֹתָם Ex. 6. 14; Num. 7. 2, and four times in Chr.† נשיא in the Hexateuch occurs but once outside P, Ex. 22. 27 (J); in P 82 times, Ezek. 37 times, Chr. six times†.

ירושלם] Probably original. The reading of LXX, Luc. seems to be a scriptural error due to the occurrence of ציון at the end of the verse.

2. ויקהלו אל המלך שלמה כל איש ישראל] An addition rendered almost necessary to introduce the date after the weighting of the previous verse with the long insertion above noticed. Niph. נקהל occurs most often in P, Lev. 8. 4; Num. 16. 3; 17. 7; 20. 2; Josh. 18. 1; 22. 12, and in books influenced by P (Ezek. 38. 7; Chr., Ezra, seven times); though not unknown in earlier writings, Ex. 32. 1 (JE), Judg. 20. 1; 2 Sam. 20. 14; Jer. 26. 9†. Notice the phrase המלך שלמה here and in the additions of *vv.* 1, 5 contrasted with שלמה *vv.* 1, 12, or המלך *v.* 5, of the original narrative.

בחג הוא החדש השביעי] The reference בֶּחָג being drawn from *v.* 65 ויעש שלמה בעת ההיא את החג, the editor plausibly assumes from the mention of its duration שבעת ימים[1] that this was *the* Feast, i.e. the Feast of Tabernacles, and so adds the statement הוא החדש השביעי as in Lev. 23. 34 (H). In Dt. 16. 13 the date is more vaguely defined as בְּאָסְפְּךָ מִגָּרְנְךָ וּמִיִּקְבֶךָ.

3. ויבאו כל זקני ישראל] A resumption from *v.* 1ª, due to the number of additions intervening.

4. ויעלו את ארון יהוה] In *vv.* 3, 5, 7 (twice), 9 simply הָאָרוֹן.

ויעלו אתם הכהנים והלוים] The distinction drawn between priests and Levites implies the standpoint of P. Cf. Dri. *Deut.* 219:—'The term Levite, it must always be remembered, has in Deuteronomy a different meaning from "Levite" in P. In P it denotes the members of the tribe,

[1] On the rejection of ושבעת ימים ארבעה עשר יום, cf. *note ad loc.*

exclusive of the priests, the descendants of Aaron; in Deuteronomy it denotes *all* members of the tribe, without distinction. The "Levites" of P are inferior members of the tribe, who are assigned various subordinate duties in connexion with the Tabernacle (Num. 3–4; 18. 1–7), but are peremptorily forbidden to intrude upon the office of priest. In Deuteronomy this sharp distinction between priests and the common Levites is not recognized; it is implied (18. 1ª) that *all* members of the tribe are qualified to exercise priestly functions; 18. 1ᵇ, 2ᵇ assign to the whole tribe the altar-dues reserved in Num. 18. 20 for the priests alone; and 18. 6–8, relating to the "Levite" coming from the country to reside at the central sanctuary, describes his services there in terms which elsewhere, when used in ritual connexion, denote regular priestly duties.'

In contrast to this distinction of *v.* 4ᵇ, cf. *vv.* 3, 6, 10, 11 where הַכֹּהֲנִים alone are mentioned; and *ch.* 12. 31 where *all* Levites seem to be regarded as fit to exercise priestly functions:—ויעש כהנים מקצות העם אשר לא היו מבני לוי.

5. שלמה] Inserted for the sake of accordance with the title used in *vv.* 1ᵇ, 2.

עדת] The phrase עֲדַת יִשְׂרָאֵל is of constant occurrence in P, outside which it never occurs but here and in ‖ 2 Chr. 5. 6.

הנועדים עליו אתו] יעד means to *appoint* or *define* a place or time, and Niph'al נועד has the sense *set oneself at the appointed place.* This latter occurs very constantly in a ceremonial connexion, and so used is characteristic of P; ‖ 2 Chr. 5. 6; הנועדים עלי [על י'] Num. 14. 35; 16. 11; 27. 3; ונועדו אליך Num. 10. 3, 4; and, with י' as subject, ונועדתי (אועד)ל Ex. 25. 22; 29. 42, 43; 30. 6, 36; Num. 17. 19. Cf. the phrase אֹהֶל מוֹעֵד (see below) 'the tent of *meeting*,' i.e. of Yahwe and His people in the person of their representative. Elsewhere Niph'al נועד is only used without ceremonial connotation; Josh. 11. 5 (JE); Am. 3. 3; Ps. 48. 5; Job 2. 11; Neh. 6. 2, 10†.

ולא ימנו מרב] LXX, Luc. ἀναρίθμητα for the whole אשר לא יספרו ולא ימנו מרב appears at first sight to omit the last three words. But a comparison of *ch.* 3. 8, where the same phrase is rendered by LXX ὃς οὐκ ἀριθμηθήσεται, suggests that the translator's single word is intended to satisfy the whole expression in the Hebrew.

Further omissions of LXX in this section (*vv.* 1–11) are:—

6. ברית יהוה] Omitted by LXX only, but contained in Luc. The phrase is properly Deuteronomic (cf. 3. 14 *note*).

8. ויהיו שם עד היום הזה] Quite different in character from the other omissions. The phrase implies a *pre-exilic* standpoint, and is thus original, and has been removed by the LXX translator (or by a later copyist) because in his time its purport had ceased to be true. עד היום הזה occurs again 9. 13, 21; 10. 12; 12. 19; II. 2. 22; 8. 22; 10. 27 (עד היום); 14. 7; 16. 6; 17. 23, 34, 41. The phrase is in most cases the addition of R^D, and thus has important bearing upon the date of compilation of Kings. See *Introduction.*

10, 11. בית יהוה] LXX omits יהוה and reads הַבַּיִת. Luc. in both cases τὸν οἶκον Κυρίου.

Thus it is clear that the omissions in LXX (*vv.* 1–5) are later additions to the text from the hand of R^P. But beyond these additions, in the text which is common to LXX and MT. there are a few phrases which exhibit unmistakeably the influence of P. These must be prior to the separation of the recensions represented by MT. and LXX, and therefore prior also to R^P; and are to be assigned to late exilic or early post-exilic scribes influenced by P, mentioned above (*ch.* 6. 16) under the symbol SS^P. The phrases in question are as follow:—

4ª. אהל מועד] This phrase occurs a few times in JE; Ex. 33. 7; Num. 11. 16; 12. 4; Deut. 31. 14; but is chiefly characteristic of P, in which it occurs some 132 times. Outside the Hexateuch, it is found only in 1 Sam. 2. 22; *ch.* 8. 4ª; and in Chr. In 1 Sam. the last member of the verse, containing the expression, is wanting in LXX, and seems to be of the character of an interpolation. So Wellh., Kamp., Budde. Probably also in our passage אהל מועד (the tent of Moses) has been substituted for an original הָאֹהֶל (the tent of David; *ch.* 1. 39). LXX, Luc. τοῦ μαρτυρίου after באהל in this verse is probably added for the sake of uniformity with the previous אהל מועד.

6. אל קדש הקדשים] Cf. *ch.* 6. 16 *note*.

8, 10. מן הקדש] הקדש is 'the holy place,' i.e. the outer room of the Temple, called הַהֵיכָל in 6. 17, 33; 7. 21. The term is obviously used in relation to the name given to the inner room קדש הקדשים, as is the case in Ex. 26. 33 והבדילה הפרכת לכם בין הקדש ובין קדש הקדשים.

8. ולא יראו החוצה] Probably added by the same hand as מן הק׳, to guard against the supposition that the staves were exposed to the public gaze.

Thus the original form of the section *vv.* 1–11, as it left the hand of R^D^, was probably as follows:—

1 אז יקהל שלמה את כל זקני ישראל ירושלם להעלות את ארון ברית
2, 3 יהוה מעיר דוד היא ציון : בירח האתנים : וישאו הכהנים את הארון :
4, 5 ואת האהל ואת כל כלי הקדש אשר באהל : והמלך וכל ישראל לפני
6 הארון מזבחים צאן ובקר אשר לא יספרו ולא ימנו מרב : ויביאו
הכהנים את ארון ברית יהוה אל מקומו אל דביר הבית אל תחת
7 כנפי הכרובים : כי הכרובים פרשים כנפים אל מקום הארון ויסכו
8 הכרבים על הארון ועל בדיו מלמעלה : ויארכו הבדים ויראו ראשי
9 הבדים על פני הדביר ויהיו שם עד היום הזה : אין בארון רק שני
לחות האבנים אשר הניח שם משה בחרב אשר כרת יהוה עם בני ישראל
10 בצאתם מארץ מצרים : ויהי בצאת הכהנים והענן מלא את הבית :
11 ולא יכלו הכהנים לעמד לשרת מפני הענן כי מלא כבוד יהוה
את הבית :

The words overlined are the work of R^D^; those marked by the dotted line may perhaps be due to him.

1, 6. ארון ברית יהוה] Cf. 3. 15 *note*. Probably הארון stood in the original narrative, as in *vv.* 3, 5, 7, 9.

8. ויהיו שם וג׳] Discussed above.

9. אשר כרת י׳ עם בני ישראל] The idea of the covenant between Yahwe and Israel appears first in JE; Ex. 19. 5; 24. 7, 8; 34. 10, 27; but is brought into special prominence through the emphasis laid upon it in Deuteronomy; cf. 5. 2 *f.* יהוה אלהינו כרת עמנו ברית בחרב; 4. 23; *al.* The supposition that this sentence is the work of R^D explains its imperfect connexion with the preceding, the only antecedent to אשר כרת being שני לחות האבנים. Doubtless R^D was thinking of the idea of the covenant (הברית) implied by these לחות, and so made his insertion in its existing form. So vague a relationship of relative to antecedent would scarcely be possible if the whole verse were by one hand. LXX, Luc. insert after לחות האבנים, πλάκες τῆς διαθήκης, i.e. לֻחוֹת הַבְּרִית, an addition which brings the sentence into close accord with Deut. 9. 9 לקחת לוחת האבנים לוחת הברית אשר כרת יהוה עמכם. Probably this is a gloss inserted to smooth away the roughness in connexion. The explanation of אשר כרת י׳ '*where* Yahwe made,' &c., with an ellipse of ברית as in 1 Sam. 20. 16; 22. 8, is possible but scarcely necessary.

Possibly בצאתם מארץ מצרים may also belong to R^D, in continuation of the preceding. If, however, it belong to the first narrative, it probably originally ran בצאת בני ישראל וג׳.

12. אז אמר. See *ch.* 3. 16 *note.*

אמר לשכן] 'Hath *promised to* dwell'; RV. 'Hath said that He will dwell'; 1 Chr. 27. 23 אמר י׳ להרבות את ישראל; 2 Chr. 21. 7; Est. 4. 7. With ל of the person to whom the promise is made, II. 8. 19. Cf. *ch.* 5. 19 *note.*

בערפל] ערפל is frequently mentioned as the sign of Yahwe's theophany:—‖ 2 Chr. 6. 1; Ex. 20. 21; Dt. 4. 11; 5. 19; 2 Sam. 22. 10; ‖ Ps. 18. 10; Ps. 97. 2; Job 22. 13. The word is connected seven times with עָנָן, twice with חֹשֶׁךְ, once with צַלְמוּת, and once with עָבִים. ערפל had the appearance of the dark lowering storm-cloud, as is clear from 2 Sam. 22. 10 *ff.* and Ex. 20. 21; cf. 19. 16.

13. בית זבל] Possibly 'a house of *elevation*,' or '*lofty* house.' For the meaning of זְבוּל 'elevation' or 'height,' Schrader (*COT.* i. 175) quotes Assyr. *bît zabal* = בית זבל; Cheyne (*Isa.* ii. 172 *f.*) cites M. Stanislas Guyard as stating that Assyr. possesses the root *zabâlu* = *nasû* (נשא) in the sense of 'bearing,' and hence (but by *inference* merely) of 'elevating.' This interpretation suits all the Biblical occurrences of זבול as well as, or better than, the old unphilological explanation 'habitation'; ‖ 2 Chr. 6. 2; Isa. 63. 15; Hab. 3. 11; Ps. 49. 15 (Cheyne מִזְּבֻל)†. The verb occurs once, Gen. 30. 20 הפעם יזבלני אישי 'This time will my husband *extol* me.' In New Heb. זבול = 'temple'; *Berachoth* ix. 13ᵇ אותן שפשטו ידיהן בזבול 'those (heathen) who stretched out their hands against the temple.'

מכון לשבתך] So Ex. 15. 17 מכון לשבתך פעלת יהוה. מְכוֹן שִׁבְתְּךָ *vv.* 39, 43, 49, cf. Ps. 33. 14. מכון gives prominence to the idea of the *fixed security* of Yahwe's dwelling-place. So מְכוֹן כִּסְאֶךָ Ps. 89. 15; מְכוֹן כִּסְאוֹ Ps. 97. 2; מְכוֹנִי Isa. 18. 4.

עולמים] Used adverbially, 'for ever,' in place of the more prosaic לְעוֹלָם. So only ‖ 1 Chr. 6. 2; Ps. 61. 5 אגורה באהלך עולמים.

The two *vv.* 12, 13 occur in LXX *after* the section *vv.* 14–53, and exhibit considerable divergence from MT. Τότε ἐλάλησεν Σαλωμὼν ὑπὲρ τοῦ οἴκου ὡς συνετέλεσεν τοῦ οἰκοδομῆσαι αὐτόν

Ἥλιον ἐγνώρισεν ἐν οὐρανῷ Κύριος·
εἶπεν τοῦ κατοικεῖν ἐκ γνόφου.
Οἰκοδόμησον οἶκόν μου, οἶκον ἐκπρεπῆ σαυτῷ,
τοῦ κατοικεῖν ἐπὶ καινότητος.

οὐκ ἰδοὺ αὕτη γέγραπται ἐν βιβλίῳ τῆς ᾠδῆς; So Luc. with the variations ἔστησεν for ἐγνώρισεν, καὶ εἶπε for εἶπεν, ἐν γνόφῳ for ἐκ γνόφου, εὐπρεπῆ for ἐκπρεπῆ, ἐπὶ βιβλίου for ἐν βιβλίῳ. Here the words ὑπὲρ . . . αὐτόν are clearly a gloss, due to the fact that when the section *vv.* 14–53 is made to precede *v.* 12 the reference of Solomon's words in this latter verse is not immediately obvious. The remainder, however, as is shown by Wellh. (*C.* 271), presupposes, after the easy correction of a few translator's errors, a text substantially superior to MT. ἐγνώρισεν perhaps represents הֵבִין[1] an error for הֵכִין which Luc. renders rightly ἔστησεν, σαυτῷ לוֹ for לִי, ἐπὶ καινότητος עֲלוּמִים for עוֹלָמִים, τῆς ᾠδῆς הַשִּׁיר for הַיָּשָׁר. We thus may retranslate:—

אָז אָמַר שְׁלֹמֹה
שֶׁמֶשׁ הֵכִין בַּשָּׁמַיִם יְהוָה
אָמַר לִשְׁכֹּן בָּעֲרָפֶל׃
בְּנֵה בֵיתִי בֵּית נָוֶה לִי
לָשֶׁבֶת עוֹלָמִים
הֲלֹא הִיא כְתוּבָה עַל־סֵפֶר הַיָּשָׁר׃

'Then said Solomon,
The sun hath Yahwe set in the heavens,
But hath promised to dwell in thick darkness;
—Build my house, a house of habitation for me,
That I may dwell therein for ever.
Is it not written in the Book of the Upright[2]?'

Here in *v.* 12, in place of the single clause of MT., we have two antithetically parallel distichs, setting in pointed contrast the sun brightly shining in the sky above and the thick black cloud which fills and overhangs the House of Yahwe. The substance of Yahwe's command and promise is appropriately introduced in *v.* 13[a b], while *v.* 13[c], as in Josh. 10. 13 (Joshua at the battle of Beth-ḥoron), 2 Sam. 1. 18 (David's lament over Saul and Jonathan), bears the stamp of genuineness and ensures the antiquity of the short extract. Klo. follows LXX in *v.* 12, supposing that ἐγνώρισεν translates יֹּדֵעַ, a mistaken reading of יֻוָּדַע—'The sun *is manifest* in the heavens.' In *v.* 13[a b], however, he abides by MT.[3], with

[1] But הֵבִין is never elsewhere in LXX rendered by γνωρίζω.

[2] So Kamp. Wellh. reads עֲרָפֶל for בָּעֲרָפֶל, בְּסֵפֶר for עַל־סֵפֶר, but in both cases Luc. indicates the more accurate reading.

[3] But more probably the expressions זְבֻל, מָכוֹן exhibit traces of a later phase of thought as to Yahwe's dwelling-place. See above as to usage and occurrence of these phrases.

the small alteration וַאֲנִי בָּנִיתִי for בנה בניתי from ‖ 2 Chr. 6. 2, while *v.* 13c LXX is bracketed as doubtful. Jos.'s somewhat lengthy reproduction of Solomon's words (*Ant.* viii. 4, § 2) depends upon a combination of Kings and Chronicles freely wrought up and expanded. Thus καὶ ἐξ ὧν σαυτῷ εἰργάσω γεγονότα τὸν οὐρανὸν οἴδαμεν κ.τ.λ. represents Ἥλιον ἐγνώρισεν ἐν οὐρανῷ Κύριος of 1 Kings, while Τοῦτον δέ σοι κατεσκεύασα τὸν ναὸν ἐπώνυμον is drawn from καὶ ἐγὼ οἰκοδόμηκα οἶκον τῷ ὀνόματί σου, 2 Chr. 6. 2.

Vulg. agrees closely with MT. Pesh. ܡܪܝܐ ܐܢܬ ܐܡܪܬ ܠܡܥܡܪ ܒܥܪܦܠܐ 'Lord, *thou hast* promised to dwell in thick darkness,' is probably an arbitrary alteration from 3rd to 2nd pers. in view of the use of the 2nd pers. in the following verse. Targ. יהוה אתרעי לאשראה שכינתיה בירושלם 'Yahwe hath been pleased to establish his *Shechinah* in Jerusalem' is obviously a paraphrase in the translator's usual style. Nevertheless, Th., finding difficulty in the use of ערפל '*black* darkness' to describe the appearance of the כבוד י׳ or שכינה, by inference a *bright* cloud, obtains by combination of Pesh. and Targ. the emendation יְהוָה אַתָּה אָמַרְתָּ לִשְׁכֹּן בִּירוּשָׁלַםִ 'Yahwe, thou hast promised to dwell in Jerusalem,' a somewhat prosaic statement which is partially anticipated by Bö.'s suggestion יְהוָה הָאֹמֵר לִשְׁכֹּן בְּיִשְׂרָאֵל.

14–66. This long section, containing Solomon's address to the people (*vv.* 14–21), the dedication prayer (*vv.* 22–53), the blessing (*vv.* 54–61), and the short account of the festival (*vv.* 62–66), presents throughout clear indications that it owes its present form to the hand of R^D^. The final portion (*vv.* 62–66) may perhaps exhibit an older narrative into which Deuteronomic additions have been incorporated, but the remainder, and especially the central prayer of dedication, has been so thoroughly amplified by the editor that it is impossible to discover any older kernel upon which he may have based his work. The choice of subjects in the successive divisions of the prayer seems for the most part to have been suggested by the catalogue of curses contained in Deut. 28. 15–68.

	1 Kings 8.		Deut. 28.
31	את אשר יחטא איש לרעהו וג׳		
33	בהנגף עמך ישראל לפני אויב	25	יתנך י׳ נגף לפני איביך
35	בהעצר שמים ולא יהיה מטר	23, 24	והיו שמיך אשר על ראשך נחשת וג׳
37	דבר כי יהיה	21	ידבק י׳ בך את הדבר וג׳
	שדפון ירקון	22	יככה י׳ . . . בשדפון ובירקון
	ארבה חסיל	38	ומעט תאסף כי יחסלנו הארבה
			Cf. also *vv.* 39, 42.
	כי יצר לו איבו וג׳	52	והצר לך בכל שעריך
			Cf. *vv.* 49 *ff.*
	כל נגע כל מחלה		*vv.* 22, 27, 35, 59–61.
41	וגם אל הנכרי		
44	כי יצא עמך למלחמה		
46	אשר יחטאו לך . . . ונתתם לפני אויב ושבום וג׳		*vv.* 36, 37, 64–68.

Deuteronomic phraseology is noticed below verse by verse.

It is more difficult to decide whether the section has suffered interpolation at the hands of later Redactors.

(i) The division of the prayer *vv.* 46–49, which brings forward the possibility of a general captivity of Israel in punishment for sins, is considered by Wellh. (*C.* 270), Sta. (*Ges.* i. 74), Kamp., Benz., Kit. to be marked by its contents as not earlier than the Exile, and therefore later than R^{D}[1].

Against this view may justly be cited the vagueness of the terms of *v.* 46 ושבום שביהם אל ארץ האויב רחוקה או קרובה, and the fact that the writer (*v.* 48) appears to regard the Temple as still standing during the period of the Exile, . . . והתפללו אליך דרך ארצם והבית אשר בנית לשמך. But the chief argument for the pre-exilic date of the passage is to be derived from comparison of Deut. 28, which, as we have seen above, forms to some extent the model of the dedication prayer. This *ch.* 28 is regarded by all critics as

[1] Wellh., Sta. seem to regard these verses as determining the exilic date of the whole section *vv.* 14–66. Kamp. assigns *vv.* 44–53 to D^2; Benz., Kit. *vv.* 44–51.

being, if not an integral portion of D (*chs.* 5–26)[1], at least closely akin to D in standpoint and date, and thus certainly pre-exilic; yet notwithstanding, *vv.* 36, 37, 64–68 threaten a captivity of the nation in language decidedly more definite than that of the passage of the prayer which has been called in question. We may therefore be content to regard these verses as containing nothing necessarily opposed to the supposition of a pre-exilic authorship, and so, as of one piece with the whole, *vv.* 22–53[2].

(ii) Sta. (*Ges.* ii. 248 *note*) regards אל השמים *v.* 30, and the local accusative השמים *vv.* 32, 34, 36, 39, 43, 45, 49 as later insertions made upon the view that Yahwe's habitation was not the Temple, as is suggested by the old narrative, *vv.* 11–13, but the heavens, out of which he exercised a supervision over the Temple. Accordingly, portions of *vv.* 22, 54 ויפרש כפיו השמים ; וכפיו פרשות השמים, and *v.* 27 which questions the possibility of God's dwelling upon the earth, are also assigned to the same hand.

This opinion of Sta. is decidedly favoured by syntactical considerations. The local accusative השמים '*in* heaven,' following upon ואתה תשמע, *v.* 32 *al.*, can scarcely be paralleled. Th. compares חצר האחרת *ch.* 7. 8. Da. § 69, *Rem.* 1 places it among words subordinated in the accusative more freely 'in elevated speech and poetry[3].' ופנית, again, at the commencement of *v.* 28 hinges very imperfectly on to the end of *v.* 27, and much more readily follows upon *v.* 26.

If this view be adopted, אל מקום שבתך *v.* 30 will refer originally not to the heavens but to the Temple, agreeably to the idea not only of the old narrative, but of the framer of the prayer (R^D); cf. *v.* 38 ופרש כפיו אל הבית הזה, where *the House* seems to be regarded as Yahwe's abode; *vv.* 35, 42, *al.* So also מכון שבתך *vv.* 39, 43, 49, where, upon the removal of השמים, מִמְּכוֹן שבתך must be restored.

---

[1] Kue. *Hex.* § 7, 21; Dri. *Deuteronomy*, 303 *f.*

[2] Cf. Kue. *Ond.* § 26, 5.

[3] ‖ 2 Chr. 6. 21, 23, 25, 30, 33, 35, 39 reads מן השמים, but in *v.* 27 השמים as in Kings.

The view that heaven, not the Temple, is Yahwe's proper abode, belongs to exilic times, and doubtless owed its origin to the destruction of the first Temple. Cf. Isa. 66. 1 כה אמר י׳ השמים כסאי והארץ הדם רגלי אי זה בית אשר תבנו לי. On the other hand, according to Ezekiel the newly constructed Temple and city are to be specially dignified by Yahwe's Presence, though doubtless according to a more heightened and spiritual conception; 48. 35 ושם העיר מיום יהוה שמה.

15. י׳ אלהי ישראל] A phrase very characteristic of R^D. Cf. *vv.* 17, 20, 23, 25, (26 om. י׳); 11. 9, 31; 14. 7, 13; 15. 30; 16. 13, 26, 33; 22. 54; II. 10. 31; 14. 25; 21. 12; 22. 15, 18. Elsewhere in Kings the phrase is found only in I. 1. 30, 48; II. 9. 6; 19. 15, 20, and in I. 17. 1, 14 where the text is doubtful (see *note*).

After אלהי ישראל LXX, Luc. insert σήμερον, i. e. הַיּוֹם. This is natural, and probably original; cf. *ch.* 5. 21 ויאמר ברוך יהוה היום.

אשר דבר . . . מלא] So *v.* 24; Jer. 44. 25. The special reference of אשר דבר וג׳ is to 2 Sam. 7. 5 *ff.*: cf. *v.* 16[a] with 2 Sam. 7. 6[a]; *v.* 16[b] with 2 Sam. 7. 8–11; *v.* 19 with 2 Sam. 7. 13[a].

16. לא בחרתי בעיר וג׳] Cf. Deut. 12. 5, 11, 18, 21, 26; *al.* So in *vv.* 44, 48; 11. 13, 32, 36; 14. 21; II. 21. 7; 23. 27; all R^D or R^D2.

להיות שמי שם] So *v.* 29; II. 23. 27. Cf. לָשׂוּם שמי שם *ch.* 9. 3 *note.*

17. ויהי עם לבב] 'It was *at* the heart' (*apud cor,* lit. *with* the heart). This idiomatic use of עם is of fair frequency; *v.* 18; ‖ 2 Chr. 6. 7, 8; *ch.* 10. 2; ‖ 2 Chr. 9. 1; 1 Chr. 22. 6; 28. 2; 2 Chr. 1. 11; 24. 4; 29. 10; Deut. 8. 5; 15. 9; Josh. 14. 7†.

לשם י׳] *Ch.* 3. 2 *note.*

19. היצא מחלציך] Only ‖ 2 Chr. 6. 9; Gen. 35. 11 ומלכים מחלציך יצאו.

20. ויקם י׳ את דברו] 2 Sam. 7. 25.

כאשר דבר י׳] *Ch.* 5. 26 *note.* LXX om. יהוה.

21. ברית י׳ אשר כרת וג׳] *Ver.* 9 *note.* Luc. διαθήκη Θεοῦ, but ברית אלהים seems only to occur Lev. 2. 13; 2 Chr. 34. 32; Ps. 78. 10; Prov. 2. 17, and in the very rare expression ארון ברית אלהים upon which see *ch.* 3. 15 *note.* כרת LXX, Luc. διέθετο Κύριος.

23. מתחת . . . אין כמוך] Deut. 4. 39 יהוה הוא האלהים בשמים ממעל ועל הארץ מתחת אין עוד; Josh. 2. 11[b] (D[2]).

שמר הברית והחסד] Deut. 7. 9; Neh. 1. 5; 9. 32; Dan. 9. 4. Cf. Deut. 7. 12; Ps. 89. 29.

לעבדיך וג׳] Owing to the influence of the following verse this has become altered in LXX into *τῷ δούλῳ σου τῷ πορευομένῳ ἐνώπιόν σου ἐν ὅλῃ τῇ καρδίᾳ αὐτοῦ*, while in Luc. we have further the paraphrase *τῷ πατρί μου* for *τῷ δούλῳ σου*. Doubtless MT. is correct. The verse enunciates Yahwe's character as shown in His dealings with His servants *in general*.

ההלכים לפניך] *Ch.* 2. 4 *note*.

בכל לבם] *Ch.* 2. 3, 4 *note*.

24. לו . . . אשר שמרת] LXX *ἃ ἐφύλαξας τῷ δούλῳ σου Δαυεὶδ τῷ πατρί μου*, making אשר refer not to יהוה of the previous verse, but to הברית והחסד, and omitting the then redundant את אשר דברת לו. This interpretation depends upon the reading of עַבְדְּךָ for עֲבָדֶיךָ in the previous verse, since אֲשֶׁר שָׁמַרְתָּ לְעַבְדְּךָ, שֹׁמֵר . . . לְעַבְדְּךָ are simply tautologous if יהוה be regarded as the antecedent of אשר.

כיום הזה] *Ch.* 3. 6 *note*.

25. לא יכרת וג׳] *Ch.* 2. 4 *note*.

רק אם ישמרו וג׳] *Ch.* 2. 4 *note*.

כאשר הלכת לפני] *Ch.* 3. 14 *note*.

26. יֵאָמֶן נא דבריך] As in Gen. 42. 20 וְיֵאָמְנוּ דִבְרֵיכֶם; 2 Chr. 1. 9.

דְּבָרֶיךָ] LXX, Luc., Pesh. confirm Q're דברך.

27. הַאֻמְנָם] Elsewhere only ‖ 2 Chr. 6. 18; Num. 22. 37 (JE); Ps. 58. 2; הַאַף אֻמְנָם Gen. 18. 13 (J).

אֻמְנָם serves to point the question very forcibly, '*Is it indeed the case that*.' On the other hand, the form אָמְנָם, which occurs nine times, seems, with the single possible exception Job 19. 5, to be reserved for *non*-interrogative asseverations.

יֵשֵׁב] '*Can* God dwell.' So לא יכלכלוך '*cannot* contain Thee;' Dri. *Tenses*, § 37. *a*.

על הארץ] ‖ 2 Chr. 6. 18 אֶת־הָאָדָם עַל־הָאָרֶץ. So LXX, Luc. here add *μετὰ ἀνθρώπων*, Targ. בנו בני אינשא. This is probably genuine, and is adopted as such by Th., Klo., Benz.

השמים ושמי השמים] Deut. 10. 14; 2 Chr. 2. 5. שמים ושמי השמים || 2 Chr. 6. 18. שמי השמים Ps. 148. 4.

אף כי] Lit. *Indeed* (or strictly, *adding*) *that* this house (cannot contain Thee); so, with reference to the preceding sentence, '*how much less* this house.' Cf. 2 Chr. 32. 15; Prov. 17. 7; Job 4. 19 (without כי); 9. 14; 15. 16; 25. 6, where, as here, the preceding sentence states a negation. When preceded by a positive statement אף כי naturally gains the sense '*how much more*'; so Deut. 31. 27; 2 Sam. 16. 11; Prov. 11. 31; *al.*

28. ופנית] '*So* turn Thou'; so ושמעת *v.* 30. Cf. *note* on וחזקת *ch.* 2. 2.

אל תפלת עבדך ואל תחנתו] LXX, Luc. ἐπὶ τὴν δέησίν μου appear to have passed, through oversight, from תפלת to תחנתו, and then not unnaturally to have read י the suffix of 1st pers. instead of ו.

אלהי] LXX, Luc. ὁ Θεὸς Ἰσραήλ. The more personal reference of MT. agrees better with the preceding עבדך. Possibly LXX Ἰσραήλ arose from a mistaken repetition of the last letter of אלהי and the first of לשמע, יל being regarded as a contraction of ישראל.

ואל התפלה] LXX omits. The words are, however, found in Luc. and the other Verss., and are demanded by the following מתפלל which cannot refer merely to הָרִנָּה.

29. להיות עינך פתֻחת] || 2 Chr. 6. 20; *v.* 52; 2 Chr. 6. 40; 7. 15; Neh. 1. 6.

לילה ויום] So Vulg., Targ.; but LXX, Luc., Pesh., || 2 Chr. 6. 20 יומם ולילה, probably an arbitrary alteration to the more usual order. At the close of the verse LXX, Luc. add ἡμέρας καὶ νυκτός.

30. אל מקום שבתך אל השמים] '*At* Thy dwelling-place, even *at* heaven.' Cf. *ch.* 6. 18 *note.*

30b. ושמעת] LXX, Luc. καὶ ποιήσεις, i.e. וְעָשִׂיתָ. This, though adopted by Klo., appears to be merely a correction of the translator, who took offence at the repetition of the verb שמע, and so made the alteration in order to produce an outward harmony with *vv.* 32, 43. But these two cases are different from our passage. It is only appropriate that ועשית should be used of punishing the wicked and vindicating the righteous (*v.* 32), or of bringing about the request of the stranger (*v.* 43), but here, where the question is simply of *forgiveness* which would not need to be manifested in any outward action, וְעָשִׂיתָ would be less apposite.   On the other hand, וְשָׁמַעְתָּ, as a resumption from the commencement of the verse after the lengthy intervening sentence, is quite in accordance with Hebrew usage.   Cf. *ch.* 2. 4 *note.*

31. אֵת אֲשֶׁר יֶחֱטָא] Rather difficult.   אֵת אֲשֶׁר seems to be used in the same way as אֲשֶׁר alone, which occurs here and there in the sense '*in case*' or *when;* cf. *v.* 33 אֲשֶׁר יֶחֶטְאוּ לָךְ; Lev. 4. 22 אֲשֶׁר נָשִׂיא יֶחֱטָא וְעָשָׂה וְגֹ'; Deut. 11. 27; 18. 22; Josh. 4. 21; Isa. 31. 4. Just possibly אֵת אֲשֶׁר was intended in the first instance for a kind of *accusativus pendens* which should have owed subordination to וְאַתָּה תִּשְׁמַע *v.* 32, 'That which &c. . . . do thou hear,' but owing to the length of the intervening sentence the connexion was imperfectly effected.   LXX, Luc. ὅσα ἂν ἁμάρτῃ, Vulg. *Si peccaverit,* Pesh. ܣ̈ܒ̈ paraphrase slightly to overcome the difficulty; Targ. יַת דִּיהוֹב literal. || 2 Chr. 6. 22 אִם יֶחֱטָא.   So Lev. 4. 3, 13, 27 compared with *v.* 22 above cited.

לְרֵעֵהוּ] 'Against,' or strictly, '*with reference to* his neighbour.' So most commonly; Gen. 20. 6; 40. 1; 1 Sam. 7. 6; *al.*

וְנָשָׁא בוֹ אָלָה] The phrase only here and || 2 Chr. 6. 22.   נָשָׂא 'take up,' i. e. עַל־פֶּה Ps. 50. 16, or עַל־שְׂפָתַיִם Ps. 16. 4.

וּבָא אָלָה] Scarcely correct.   If the sense intended were 'and the oath come,' we should expect וּבָאָה הָאָלָה.   LXX, Luc. καὶ ἐξαγορεύσῃ, Pesh. ܘܝܐܡܐ, Targ. וְיוֹמֵינֵיהּ all presuppose וְאָלָה, and Vulg. *et venerit propter juramentum* seems to be a slightly paraphrastic rendering of the same text.   Thus, with Klo., Kamp., Benz., we may emend וּבָא וְאָלָה 'and he come and swear,' in preference to the suggestion of Bö., followed by Th., וּבָא אָלֹה 'and he come swearing,' and the alternative of Kamp., adopted by Kit., וּבָא בְאָלָה 'and he enter into an oath' (cf. Neh. 10. 30).

32. וְעָשִׂיתָ] 'And shalt do.'   An absolute use of עשׂה, the implied object being 'that which is meet to be done,' as is shown by the following וְשָׁפַטְתָּ וְגֹ'.   Such a pregnant use of this verb with יהוה as subject is not infrequent in lofty or poetic style; Ps. 119. 126

עת לעשות לי׳; 22. 32; 37. 5; 52. 11; Isa. 44. 23; 64. 3; Jer. 14. 7; Ezek. 20. 9, 14, 22; Dan. 9. 19. With another subject cf. 1 Sam. 26. 25; Isa. 10. 13; Dan. 8. 12, 24; 11. 28, 30, 32; 2 Chr. 31. 21.

להרשיע] '*In respect of* condemning,' or, '*so as to* condemn.' ל of reference explains the action described by ושפטת.

לתת דרכו בראשו] ‖ 2 Chr. 6. 23. Elsewhere only in Ezek. 9. 10; 11. 21; 16. 43; 22. 31†. Cf. 17. 19, and the kindred phrase והשיב י׳ את רעתך בראשך *ch.* 2. 44.

33. בהנגף . . . לפני אויב] Luc. καὶ ἐν τῷ πταῖσαι τὸν λαόν σου Ἰσραὴλ ἐνώπιόν σου καὶ πεσεῖν ἐνώπιον ἐχθρῶν αὐτῶν, i.e. בְּהִנָּגֵף עַמְּךָ יִשְׂרָאֵל לְפָנֶיךָ וְנָפְלוּ לִפְנֵי אוֹיֵב. Very probably correct, the scribe's eye passing from לפניך to לפני. The idea that Yahwe smites Israel by the hand of a foreign nation is found in 1 Sam. 4. 3 למה נגפנו י׳ היום לפני פלשתים; cf. Judg. 20. 35. So Deut. 28. 25 יתנך י׳ נִגָּף לפני איביך.

אשר יחטאו לך] 'In case they shall sin against thee'; scarcely as RV. here and in *v.* 35, 'because *they have sinned* against thee.' Cf. *v.* 31 *note*.

ושבו אליך והודו] LXX, Luc. agree with ‖ 2 Chr. 6. 24 in omitting אליך, the meaning then being, 'and shall once more confess'; cf. *v.* 47 ושבו והתחננו. But the phrase שוב אל י׳ is very frequent; cf. *v.* 48; Deut. 30. 10; Hos. 5. 4; 7. 10; 14. 3; 1 Sam. 7. 3; Isa. 44. 22; *al.*; and ought not here to be rejected. A kindred phrase is שוב עַד־י׳; Deut. 4. 30; 30. 2; Hos. 14. 2; *al.*

והתחננו אליך] Here also אליך is omitted by LXX, Luc. General usage favours MT.; *v.* 47 (LXX, Luc. δεηθῶσίν σου); Deut. 3. 23; Job 8. 5; Ps. 30. 9; 142. 2; Gen. 42. 21; II. 1. 13. ‖ 2 Chr. 6. 24 לפניך; cf. *v.* 59; *ch.* 9. 3. התחנן is elsewhere followed by לְ, but appears to be never used absolutely.

34. עמך] So Luc., Vulg., Targ.; but LXX τοῦ δούλου σου, i.e. עַבְדְּךָ, Pesh. ܕܥܒܕܝܟ ܘܕܥܡܟ either a doublet or in conformity with *v.* 36. MT., which is agreeable to the phrase in *v.* 33, is to be retained.

אשר נתת לאבותם] So *vv.* 40, 48; cf. *ch.* 14. 15; II. 21. 8 (R^D); Deut. 26. 15 and the common phrase of Deut. אשר יהוה אלהינו

נָתַן לנו (לך), referring to the land or to portions of it; Deut. 1. 20, 25; 2. 29; 3. 20; 4. 40; 5. 16; *al.*

35. יָשׁוּבוּן] The form of the 3rd and 2nd pers. pl. of the imperf. with the so-called *Nûn paragogicum* is not uncommon in Hebrew. Cf. this same verb, Isa. 35. 10; 51. 11; Jer. 44. 28; *al.*; תְּמֻתוּן Gen. 3. 3, 4; יְקוּמוּן Deut. 33. 11; 2 Sam. 22. 39; *al.* This form is usual in Aram. and in class. Ar.; יִקְטְלוּן, ܢܶܩܛܠܽܘܢ *neqtᵉlûn*, يَقْتُلُونَ *yaqtulûna.* See Wright, *Compar. Sem. Gramm.* pp. 184, 145, for the origin of the termination. In Hebrew the form is rather an affected than a real archaism, and is most common in elevated poetical style, or in pause as being heavier and more impressive.

כִּי תַעֲנֵם] According to vocalization the only possible rendering is 'when thou shalt answer them,' Pesh. ܡܳܐ ܕܰܥܢܺܝܬ ܐܶܢܽܘܢ, Targ. ארי תקביל צלותהון; but this is unsuitable. Hence it is better to follow LXX, Luc. ὅταν ταπεινώσῃς αὐτούς, Vulg. *propter afflictionem suam*, and to vocalize כִּי תְעַנֵּם 'when thou shalt humble them.' So Th., Kamp., Benz., Kit. Klo.'s emendation כִּי תַכְנִעֵם, after 2 Chr. 7. 14, is unnecessary.

36. אשר ילכו בה] 'In which they *are to* walk' or '*should* walk.' For this *nuance* of the imperf. cf. Ex. 10. 26 לא נדע מה נעבד את י׳ עד באנו שמה 'We do not know how we *are to* serve Yahwe until we come thither.' Dri. *Tenses*, § 39 *a*.

נתתה...לנחלה] 'Gavest...*for an inheritance*'; so ‖ 2 Chr. 6. 27; Deut. 29. 7; Josh. 11. 23 (D²); 14. 13 (E recast by D²); Ps. 136. 21; Num. 18. 21, 24 (P; in these verses the reference is to *tithe*, not to *the land*)†. So היה לנחלה Josh. 14. 9, 14 (E recast by D²); 24. 32 (E); Ezek. 36. 12; 44. 28†. The usual phrase of Deuteronomy is נתן נחלה; Deut. 4. 21; 15. 4; 19. 10; 20. 16; 21. 23; 24. 4; 25. 19; 26. 1; Ps. 135. 12†. נתן בנחלה occurs Num. 36. 2 (P)†; חִלֵּק בנחלה Num. 26. 53 (P); Josh. 13. 7 (D²); נפל בנחלה (הפיל) Josh. 13. 6; 23. 4 (D²); Num. 34. 2 (P); Judg. 18. 1; Ezek. 45. 1; 47. 14, 22†.

37. רעב כי יהיה] This order—subject, conjunction, verb—serving to give slight emphasis to the subject, is common in P; Lev. 1. 2;

2. 1; 4. 2; 5. 1, 4, 15, 21; 7. 21; *al.;* Num. 5. 12; cf. Ezek. 3. 19; 14. 9, 13; 18. 5, 18, 21; 33. 6. So Isa. 28. 18; Mic. 5. 4; Ps. 62. 11.

חסיל] A kind of locust; ‖ 2 Chr. 6. 28; Ps. 78. 46; Joel 1. 4; 2. 25; Isa. 33. 4†. This and the other words used to denote the locust, חָגָב, גֵּבִים, גָּזָם, יֶלֶק, and the ordinary אַרְבֶּה, cannot with any degree of certainty be distinguished as describing different species or stages of growth. A verb חסל occurs once; יַחְסְלֶנּוּ הָאַרְבֶּה 'the locusts *shall consume* it,' Deut. 28. 38. In Aram. חסל means 'bring to an end'; so Targ., Jer. וחסיל כספא = Heb. וַיִּתֹּם הַכֶּסֶף; but most frequently, as in Syr., has gained the more special secondary sense 'wean.' LXX, Luc., connecting ארבה חסיל as one expression, render ἐρυσίβη 'red blight.'

בארץ שעריו] So ‖ 2 Chr. 6. 28. The expression is very forced and unnatural, even if it can be regarded as giving any sense at all. LXX, Luc. ἐν μιᾷ τῶν πόλεων αὐτοῦ, Pesh. ܚܕܐ ܡܢ ܡܕܝܢ̈ܬܗܘܢ furnish the correct text, בְּאַחַד שְׁעָרָיו '*in any of* his gates,' a regular phrase of D; Deut. 15. 7; 16. 5; 17. 2; 23. 17; cf. 18. 6†. So Klo., Kamp., Benz., Kit., Oort. Th. emends בְּאַחַת עָרָיו; but this is not the usual phrase, nor is it postulated by the renderings of LXX, Luc., Pesh. which very commonly represent שערים by πόλεις, ܡܕ̈ܝܢܬܐ; cf. Deut. 12. 17, 18, 21; 15. 7; 17. 2; *al.*

כל נגע וג׳] Cf. כל כלי וג׳ *ch.* 6. 7 *note.*

38. כל תפלה וג׳] The construction is somewhat involved, since כל תפלה כל תחנה can scarcely be regarded as part of the category formed by the plagues mentioned in *v.* 37. Thus *v.* 37 must be regarded as breaking off with an aposiopesis, and the apodosis ואתה תשמע וג׳ as answering to the protasis formed by the second and different category כל תפלה וג׳; 'Whatsoever prayer, &c., there be, *or*, If there be any prayer, &c. . . . , then hear thou,' &c.

לכל עמך ישראל] LXX, Luc. omit correctly. The words are a gloss upon לכל האדם, to explain that this refers to Israel in contrast to הנכרי of *v.* 41. So Klo., Kamp., Benz., Kit.

ידעון] So *v.* 43. Cf. *v.* 35 *note.*

נגע לבבו] A rather obscure expression. The idea seems to be that each man will recognize in the case of his *particular* plague, be it famine, pestilence, or some other above enumerated, that it is sent by God as a punishment for his sin. So ‖ 2 Chr. 6. 29 נגעו ומכאבו. Klo., however, interprets נגע, not as 'plague,' but as 'Berührung,' '*the touching* of his heart';—'Because God will through the misfortune awaken the humiliating consciousness of sin.' So apparently LXX, Luc. *ἁφὴν καρδίας αὐτοῦ*. Cf. 1 Sam. 10. 26.

39. ונתת לאיש ככל דרכיו] ‖ 2 Chr. 6. 30; Jer. 17. 10; 32. 19; Ezek. 7. 9.

40. כל הימים . . . האדמה] ‖ 2 Chr. 6. 31; Deut. 4. 10; 12. 1; 31. 13†. Cf. *note* on כל הימים *ch.* 9. 3.

אשר נתת וג׳] *Note* on *v.* 34.

41. אל הנכרי] Dependent upon אתה תשמע, *v.* 43, as is noticed by Th. So apparently LXX, Luc. *καὶ τῷ ἀλλοτρίῳ . . . καὶ σὺ εἰσακούσῃ*.

Vulg. *et alienigena*, Targ. מן בר עממין seem to take the expression as a kind of *casus pendens*, 'as for the stranger,' a use of אל scarcely to be justified. Pesh. ܥܠ ܢܘܟܪܝܐ seems to mean 'on behalf of the stranger,' and supposes the ellipse of some such expression as ܒܥܝܢܐ 'I pray.'

LXX, Luc. in ‖ 2 Chr. 6. 32 read *πᾶς ἀλλότριος*, and Klo. accordingly emends כָּל־הַנָּכְרִי 'jeder Fremdling.'

ובא וג׳] Deut. 29. 21 הנכרי אשר יבא מארץ רחוקה.

41, 42. ובא . . . הנטויה] These fifteen words have fallen out in LXX, Luc. through homoioteleuton. For the second ובא reinforcing the first after the intervening words cf. *ch.* 2. 4 *note*.

42. את ידך החזקה וזרעך הנטויה] The two phrases occur in combination ‖ 2 Chr. 6. 32; Deut. 4. 34; 5. 15; 7. 19; 11. 2; 26. 8; Jer. 21. 5 (different order); 32. 21 (אֶזְרוֹעַ); Ezek. 20. 33, 34; Ps. 136. 12†. יד חזקה alone, Deut. 3. 24; 6. 21; 7. 8; 9. 26; 34. 12; Ex. 3. 19; 6. 1; 32. 11 (all JE); 13. 9 (E); Num. 20. 20 (JE; referring to Edom); Neh. 1. 10; Dan. 9. 15†. Cf. Josh. 4. 24 (D^2). זרוע נטויה alone, Deut. 9. 29; II. 17. 36; Jer. 27. 5; 32. 17; Ex. 6. 6 (P)†.

43. כל עמי הארץ] ‖ 2 Chr. 6. 33; *vv.* 53, 60; Deut. 28. 10; Josh.

4. 24 (D^2); Ezek. 31. 12; Zeph. 3. 20 are the only occurrences of the exact phrase. LXX, Luc. omit הארץ.

לְיִרְאָה] ‖ 2 Chr. 6. 33. A common phrase in Deut.; 4. 10; 5. 26; 6. 24; 8. 6; 10. 12; 14. 23; 17. 19; 28. 58; 31. 13; Jer. 32. 39; Neh. 1. 11; Ps. 86. 11†.

כי שמך נקרא על הבית הזה] 'That thy name is called over this house,' i. e. in token of *ownership*. The phrase is most clearly elucidated by 2 Sam. 12. 27, 28, where Joab, having taken Rabbath-Ammon, sends to David that he may come and complete the capture, פן אלכד אני את העיר ונקרא שמי עליה 'lest *I* take the city, and my name be called over it,' as having the credit of its conquest.

The phrase occurs besides:—as here, of the Temple ‖ 2 Chr. 6. 33; Jer. 7. 10, 11, 14, 30; 32. 34; 34. 15; of the chosen people Deut. 28. 10; Jer. 14. 9; Isa. 63. 19; 2 Chr. 7. 14; of Jerusalem Jer. 25. 29; of Jerusalem and the chosen people Dan. 9. 18, 19; of Jeremiah Jer. 15. 16; of the nations Am. 9. 12†.

44. אל יהוה] So Targ. קדם יהוה. The other Verss. are different; LXX, Luc. *ἐν ὀνόματι Κυρίου*, Vulg. *te*, Pesh. ܩܕܡܝܟ ܡܪܝܐ; ‖ 2 Chr. 6. 34 (MT. and Verss.) אֵלֶיךָ. Probably אֵלֶיךָ is original, and the MT. reading due to this having been read אל יה׳. LXX seems to have had the reading of MT., and to have paraphrased in order to explain the transition from the second to the third person.

דרך העיר] '*In the direction of* the city.' So *v.* 48; ‖ 2 Chr. 6. 34, 38; *ch.* 18. 43 הבט דרך ים 'look *toward* the sea,' Ezek. 8. 5; 41. 12; *al.*

העיר אשר בחרת בה] *Note* on *v.* 16.

והבית וג׳] *Ch.* 3. 2 *note.*

45. ועשית משפטם] 'And wilt execute their right.' The exact phrase (עשה משפט פ׳, with יהוה as subject) occurs only besides in *v.* 49; ‖ 2 Chr. 6. 35, 39; *v.* 59; Deut. 10. 18; Mic. 7. 9; Ps. 9. 5†.

46. כי אין וג׳] Cf. Eccl. 7. 20 כי אדם אין צדיק בארץ אשר יעשה טוב ולא יחטא.

ואנפת בם] LXX rather curiously *καὶ ἐπάξεις αὐτούς*, Luc. *καὶ ἐὰν ἐπαγάγῃς ἐπ' αὐτούς*. This latter may perhaps be explained by supposing an ellipse of *ὀργήν*. Cf. Ps. 7. 12, where זֹעֵם is rendered ὀργὴν ἐπάγων, Isa. 26. 21 ἐπάγει τὴν ὀργήν for לִפְקֹד עָוֹן. Similarly LXX may be a corruption of ἐπάξεις αὐτοῖς, the alteration being due to some one who supposed the sense intended by the Greek to be '*lead them away* and deliver them up,' &c. In LXX of ‖ 2 Chr. 6. 36 there is a further alteration—καὶ πατάξεις αὐτούς. Luc., however, renders καὶ ἐὰν θυμωθῇς ἐπ' αὐτούς.

ונתתם לפני אויב] 'And thou *set them before* the foe,' i. e. deliver them over to his power and disposal. The other occurrences of the phrase in this sense are ‖ 2 Chr. 6. 36; Deut. 1. 8, 21; 2. 31, 33, 36; 7. 2, 23; 23. 15; 28. 7, 25; 31. 5; Josh. 10. 12; 11. 6 (both D[2]); Judg. 11. 9; Isa. 41. 2†.

47. והשיבו אל לבם] 'And shall bring back to their heart,' or as we should say, 'their mind.' So RV. 'shall bethink themselves.' ‖ 2 Chr. 6. 37; Deut. 4. 39; 30. 1; Isa. 44. 19; 46. 8 (עַל־לֵב); Lam. 3. 21†. The verse is a reminiscence of Deut. 30. 1 *ff*.

בארץ שביהם] LXX ἐν γῇ μετοικίας αὐτῶν, Luc. ἐν τῇ γῇ τῆς μετοικεσίας αὐτῶν agree with ‖ 2 Chr. 6. 37 in reading בְּאֶרֶץ שִׁבְיָם, which is probably correct. Cf. Jer. 30. 10; 46. 27.

חטאנו וג׳] Cf. Ps. 106. 6; Dan. 9. 15, both reminiscences of this passage.

חטאנו וְהעוינו] Weak ו co-ordinating two synonymous ideas. Cf. Isa. 1. 2 בָּנִים גִּדַּלְתִּי וְרוֹמַמְתִּי; 1 Sam. 12. 2; Deut. 2. 30; *al.*; Dri. *Tenses*, §§ 131, 132. חטא, like ἁμαρτάνειν, means literally to *miss the mark*; so Job 5. 24 ופקדת נוך ולא תחטא 'And thou shalt visit thy pasture and shalt miss nothing'; and in Hiph'il, Judg. 20. 16. עוה = Ar. عَوَى *bend*; so Hiph. העוה *make crooked* (with obj. דַּרְכָּם Jer. 3. 21), i.e. *act perversely*. רשע, a more general word, *act wickedly*, perhaps has its origin in the notion of *raising a tumult*; Job 34. 29 והוא ישקט ומי ירשע; cf. Job 3. 17. רשענו *asyndetos* after the two previous verbs connected by ו is a little harsh, and, following the suggestion of Ps. 106. 6, it seems preferable to reject the ו before העוינו, and to read חטאנו העוינו רשענו. So LXX, Vulg., Targ. Pesh., on the other hand, inserts ܘ before the last verb, ܚܛܝܢ ܘܐܣܟܠܢ ܘܐܪܫܥܢ. Luc., omitting והעוינו, Ἡμάρτομεν, ἠνομήσαμεν. ‖ 2 Chr. 6. 37 חטאנו העוינו ורשענו.

48. ושבו אליך . . . ובכל נפשם] Deut. 30. 10; II. 23. 25; cf. Jer. 3. 10. On שוב אל י׳ cf. *v.* 33 *note;* on בכל לבבם וג׳ cf. *ch.* 2. 3, 4 *note.*

אשר שבו אתם] LXX, Luc. οὗ μετήγαγες αὐτούς possibly read אשר שְׁבִיתָם, but more probably render somewhat freely, as is the case with Vulg. *ad quam captivi ducti fuerint.*

דרך ארצם] *Note* on *v.* 44.

אשר נתתה] *Note* on *v.* 34.

העיר אשר בחרת] *Note* on *v.* 16.

והבית וג׳] *Note* on *ch.* 3. 2.

49. את תפלתם . . . משפטם] LXX, Luc. omit. The words are very probably a gloss from *v.* 45. In this former verse the phrase ועשית משפטם, of vindicating Israel's *right* against the encroachments of their foes, is highly appropriate; but in *v.* 49, where the captivity is regarded as a just penalty for sins committed, the force of the expression is scarcely so immediately apparent, the idea of *a right* and of *concession granted through forgiveness* (וסלחת *v.* 50) being somewhat incompatible.

50. לעמך . . . לך ו] LXX, Luc. omit. The following words ולכל פשעיהם down to the close of *v.* 51 are not found in ‖ 2 Chr. 6. 39.

ונתתם לרחמים] Neh. 1. 11; Ps. 106. 46; the latter being probably a reminiscence of our passage: cf. *v.* 47 *note* on חטאנו וג׳.

51. כי עמך ונחלתך . . . ממצרים] Deut. 9. 26, 29. In application to the chosen people עַם and נַחֲלָה appear as parallel terms;—Deut. 32. 9; Isa. 47. 6; Joel 2. 17; 4. 2; Ps. 28. 9; 78. 62, 71; 94. 5, 14; 106. 4, 5, 40. Cf. Mic. 7. 14.

כור הברזל] Deut. 4. 20; Jer. 11. 4†. The meaning of the phrase may be illustrated by Isa. 48. 10, בחרתיך בכור עני 'I have tested thee in the furnace of affliction.'

52. להיות וג׳] *Note* on *v.* 29. ‖ 2 Chr. 6. 40 עתה אלהי יהיו נא עיניך פתחות ואזניך קשבות לתפלת המקום הזה. Similarly LXX, Luc. in our passage insert καὶ τὰ ὦτά σου, i.e. וְאָזְנֶיךָ, after עיניך. This is probably a gloss due to the idea of the unsuitability of *eyes only* being open to a supplication. The words of 2 Chr. are probably no older than the Chronicler, if we may judge by the use of קַשֻּׁב

which appears to be a late form; 2 Chr. 7. 15; Ps. 130. 2†; קַשֶּׁבֶת Neh. 1. 6, 11†.

בכל קראם אליך] Deut. 4. 7† בְּכָל־קָרְאֵנוּ אֵלָיו. For the constr. cf. Gen. 30. 41 בְּכָל־יַחֵם הַצֹּאן; 1 Chr. 23. 31 לְכֹל הַעֲלוֹת עֹלוֹת.

53. כי אתה הבדלתם וג׳] Cf. Lev. 20. 24, 26 (H) אני יהוה אלהיכם ואבדיל אתכם מן העמים להיות לי; אשר הבדלתי אתכם מן העמים.

לנחלה] Cf. Deut. 4. 20 להיות לו לעם נחלה. Israel is styled Yahwe's נחלה also in II. 21. 14 (R^{D2}); Jer. 12. 7, 8, 9; Mic. 7. 18; Isa. 19. 25: see further the cases given on *v.* 51. חֶבֶל נחלתו Deut. 32. 9; שֵׁבֶט נחלתו Jer. 10. 16; 51. 19; Ps. 74. 2 (ש׳ נחלתך); Isa. 63. 17 (שִׁבְטֵי נחלתך). The *land* of Israel is named the נחלה of Yahwe in Jer. 2. 7; 16. 18; 50. 11; Ps. 68. 10; 79. 1; cf. 2 Sam. 20. 19; 21. 3; Ex. 15. 17 (הר נחלתך; E).

מכל עמי הארץ] *Note* on *v.* 43.

כאשר דברת] *Ch.* 5. 26 *note.*

ביד משה] 'By the *hand* of Moses,' i. e. by *his agency*. The idiom is very frequent of a word of Yahwe delivered through the agency of a prophet;—*ch.* 12. 15; 14. 18; 15. 29; 16. 7, 12, 34; 17. 16; II. 9. 36; 10. 10; 14. 25; 17. 13, 23; 21. 10; 24. 2; 1 Sam. 28. 15, 17; *al.*

54. וכפיו וג׳] 'With his hands spread forth &c.'; a circumstantial clause, giving further detail as to Solomon's attitude whilst kneeling. Cf. *v.* 22.

55. קול גדול] Accus. of closer specification, defining the *manner* of the action described by ויברך. Cf. Ps. 3. 5 קולי אל י׳ אקרא; 142. 2. Ew. § 279[d].

56. אשר נתן מנוחה לעמו] Cf. Deut. 12. 9 לא באתם עד עתה אל המנוחה; Ps. 95. 11 אם יבאון אל מנוחתי.

ככל אשר דבר] *Ch.* 5. 26 *note.*

לא נפל דבר אחד] So Josh. 21. 43; 23. 14 (both D^2); cf. II. 10. 10. The use of the Hiph'il is similar: '*suffer to fall*' (though not of *Yahwe's* words) 1 Sam. 3. 19; Est. 6. 10.

57. יהוה אלהינו] So *vv.* 59, 61, 65; II. 18. 22; 19. 19; י׳ אלהיך *ch.* 1. 17; 2. 3 (R^D); 10. 9; 13. 6, 21; 17. 12; 18. 10; י׳ אלהיכם II. 17. 39; 23. 21 (both R^D). The phrases י׳ אלהינו ,י׳ אלהיך (most

frequent), י׳ אלהיכם are very characteristic of Deuteronomy, occurring more than three hundred times. In D² of Joshua there are four occurrences of י׳ אלהיך, twenty-seven occurrences of י׳ אלהיכם. Elsewhere in Hexateuch:—J, E, JE י׳ אלהינו nine times, viz. Ex. 3. 18; 5. 3; 8. 22, 23; 10. 25, 26; Josh. 18. 6; 24. 17, 24; י׳ אלהיך twelve times, viz. Gen. 27. 20; Ex. 15. 26 (D?); 20. 2, 5, 7, 10, 12; 23. 19; 32. 4, 8; 34. 24, 26; י׳ אלהיכם six times, viz. Ex. 8. 24; 10. 8, 16, 17; 23. 25; Josh. 4. 5: P י׳ אלהינו three times, viz. Ex. 8. 6; Josh. 22. 19, 29; י׳ אלהיכם seven times, viz. Num. 10. 9, and in the phrase אני י׳ אלהיכם Ex. 6. 7; 16. 12; Lev. 11. 44; Num. 10. 10; 15. 41 (twice): H י׳ אלהיכם twice, viz. Lev. 23. 28, 40; אני י׳ אלהיכם twenty-one times, viz. Lev. 18. 2, 4, 30; 19. 2, 3, 4, 10, 25, 31, 34, 36; 20. 7, 24; 23. 22, 43; 24. 22; 25. 17, 38, 55; 26. 1, 13. In other books the phrases occur here and there, but not 120 times in all. Cf. Dri. *Deut.* lxxix.

58. להטות לבבנו אליו] Cf. Josh. 24. 23ᵇ (perhaps added to E by D²).

ללכת בכל דרכיו ולשמר וג׳] *Ch.* 2. 3, 4 *note.*

ומשפטיו] LXX, Luc. omit, probably through oversight. With MT. cf. Deut. 26. 17; 30. 16, where precisely the same enumeration is made.

59. ויהיו דברי . . . קרבים] Contrast Ps. 22. 2 רחוק מישועתי דברי שאגתי.

ומשפט עמו] So Luc., Vulg., Pesh., Targ. LXX omits through oversight.

דבר יום ביומו] Lit. 'matter of a day in its day'; so RV. 'as every day shall require.' The idiom is not infrequent, being used e.g. of the daily allowance of Jehoiachin at the court of the king of Babylon, II. 25. 30 (|| Jer. 52. 34); and of that of Daniel and his friends, Dan. 1. 5; of the manna gathered by the people, Ex. 16. 4; or again of the daily burden imposed by the Egyptian task-masters, Ex. 5. 13, 19.

60. למען דעת וג׳] Cf. Josh. 4. 24 (D²). On כל עמי הארץ cf. *v.* 43 *note.*

כי י׳ הוא האלהים אין עוד] Deut. 4. 35, 39. Cf. also the exclamation of the populace upon the issue of the trial between Elijah and the false prophets, *ch.* 18. 39.

61. והיה לבבכם שלם וג׳] Cf. *ch.* 11. 4; 15. 3, 14 (all R^D). LXX, Luc., Vulg. suggest לְבָבֵינוּ for לבבכם; probably an alteration suggested by the following אלהינו.

י׳ אלהינו] *Note* on *v.* 57.

ללכת וג׳] *Ch.* 2. 3, 4 *note.*

כיום הזה] *Ch.* 3. 6 *note.*

62. לפני יהוה] Luc. ἐνώπιον Κυρίου τοῦ Θεοῦ, perhaps under the influence of י׳ אלהינו *v.* 57.

63. וצאן . . . אלף] LXX omits.

64. את חלבי השלמים] 'The fat *or* choice portions of the peace-offerings.' So Lev. 6. 5; 2 Chr. 29. 35; cf. Gen. 4. 4 מבכרות צאנו ומחלבהן 'of the firstlings of his flock and of their *fat pieces*.' The slight variations of LXX, Luc. in the enumeration of the sacrifices are due to error in transmission of the Greek text.

65. בעת ההיא] The phrase is that of R^D. Cf. *ch.* 14. 1 *note.* In Deuteronomy בעת הַהִוא is of frequent occurrence in the retrospects, when events more or less contemporaneous are co-ordinated by the writer; 1. 9, 16, 18; 2. 34; 3. 4, 8, 12, 18, 21, 23; 4. 14; 5. 5; 9. 20; 10. 1, 8. Possibly also ביום ההוא *v.* 64[a] may mark the hand of R^D, though this phrase is not so characteristic. In *ch.* 13. 3; 16. 16; 22. 35; II. 3. 6 the expression is quite as likely to be part of the old narrative. On בימים ההם R^D cf. II. 10. 32.

הֶחָג] '*The* Feast'; i.e. probably the Feast of Tabernacles as the most important festival of the year; cf. Neh. 8. 14; *v.* 2 *note.*

מלבוא חמת וג׳] The whole kingdom from extreme north to extreme south. Jeroboam II is said to have restored the kingdom of Israel מלבוא חמת עד ים הערבה II. 14. 25; cf. Am. 6. 14. לבוא lit. '*at the entry of*'; לבוא חמת Num. 13. 21; 34. 8; Josh. 13. 5; Judg. 3. 3; 1 Chr. 13. 5; Ezek. 47. 20; 48. 1; לבוא מִדְבָּרָה 1 Chr. 5. 9; לבוא מצרים 2 Chr. 26. 8; לבוא צְדָדָה Ezek. 47. 15. On נחל מצרים, the *Wady el-Arîsh*, cf. *ch.* 5. 1 *note.*

י׳ אלהינו] *Note* on *v.* 57. After this LXX, Luc. have the words ἐν τῷ οἴκῳ ᾧ ᾠκοδόμησεν, ἐσθίων καὶ πίνων καὶ εὐφραινόμενος (Luc. adds *καὶ αἰνῶν*) *ἐνώπιον κυρίου θεοῦ ἡμῶν*, i.e. according to Klo. בַּבַּיִת אֲשֶׁר בָּנָה אֹכֵל וְשֹׁתֶה וְשָׂמֵחַ וּמְהַלֵּל לִפְנֵי י׳ אֱלֹהֵינוּ; so substantially Th., Benz., Oort. These words have the ring of genuineness, and may easily have been omitted in MT. through homoioteleuton.

שבעת . . . יום] LXX has here simply *ἑπτὰ ἡμέρας*, i.e. שִׁבְעַת יָמִים, the remaining words ושבעת . . . יום being omitted. The manner in which the next verse continues, ביום השמיני וג׳, LXX, Luc. *καὶ ἐν τῇ ἡμέρᾳ κ.τ.λ.*, establishes the genuineness of the shorter שבעת ימים, and points to the conclusion that the remainder of the sentence is an insertion in accordance with 2 Chr. 7. 9, probably due to R^P^. So Th., Klo., Kamp., Benz., Kit., Oort.

66. ביום] LXX, Luc., Pesh., Vulg. correctly presuppose וּבַיּוֹם. The omission of the ו was made when the gloss was added at the end of the previous verse.

ויברכו את המלך] LXX *καὶ εὐλόγησεν αὐτόν*, 'and they blessed him,' i.e. *the king*, as in MT. The plural verb with הָעָם as subj. is rendered in LXX by sing., as e.g. in *ch.* 1. 39, 40; 12. 30; *al.* Luc., however, taking *καὶ εὐλόγησεν αὐτόν* in the sense 'and he blessed *it*,' i.e. *the people*, makes the addition *καὶ εὐλόγησαν καὶ αὐτοὶ τὸν βασιλέα*, and thus exhibits a double rendering.

שמחים וטובי לב] So Est. 5. 9. טובי לב has the meaning *cheerful* or *merry;* Prov. 15. 15 טוב לב משתה תמיד 'the merry-hearted has a continual feast.' Cf. Judg. 16. 25 Q're ויהי כְּטוֹב לבם; Eccl. 9. 7 שתה בלב טוב יינך; and the verbal phrase יטב לב פ׳ 'one's heart is cheerful,' *ch.* 21. 7; Judg. 18. 20; 19. 6, 9; Ruth 3. 7. טוּב לבב (לב) 'cheerfulness of heart,' Deut. 28. 47; Isa. 65. 14.

9. 1–9. *Solomon's Second Vision.*

Ch. 9. 1–9 = 2 Chr. 7. 12–22.

1–9. This account is coloured throughout by the spirit of Deuteronomy, and, owing to the terms in which it speaks of the exile of Israel and the destruction of the Temple (*vv.* 7–9; cf. emendation in *v.* 8), is regarded by Kue., Wellh., Sta., Kamp., Benz., Kit. as the work of R^D2^ in exilic times.

Such a conclusion, however, is by no means inevitable. The

expression of *v.* 3 לשום שמי שם עד עולם וג׳ goes quite as far to prove a pre-exilic position, as do the words of *vv.* 6–9 to argue a post-exilic point of view; nor are the terms of these latter verses so definite as to forbid the opinion that they were penned by R^D in the reign of Josiah; cf. *note* on *ch.* 8. 46–49 under *vv.* 14–66 *note.* If *vv.* 7–9 *do* imply an exilic standpoint, *vv.* 6–9 (and not the whole section) will belong to R^{D2}, *vv.* 1–5 to R^D.

1. את כל חשק ש׳ אשר חפץ וג׳] 'All the pleasure of Solomon which he wished to do.' The substantive חֵשֶׁק only occurs again Isa. 21. 4 נֶשֶׁף חִשְׁקִי 'the twilight of my pleasure,' and in *v.* 19, ‖ 2 Chr. 8. 6, with the cognate verb, את חֵשֶׁק ש׳ אשר חָשַׁק לבנות וג׳. Pesh., Targ., which render in *v.* 1 ܘܟܠܗ ܨܒܝܢܗ ܕܫܠܝܡܘܢ ܕܨܒܐ ܠܡܥܒܕ, וית כל רעות שלמה דאיתרעי למעבד, and similarly in *v.* 19, appear therefore in the former verse, as in the latter, to have read חָשַׁק for חָפֵץ, probably correctly. LXX, Luc. *καὶ πᾶσαν τὴν πραγματείαν Σ. ὅσα ἠθέλησεν ποιῆσαι*; Vulg. paraphrastically, *et omne quod optaverat et voluerat facere.*

3. את תפלתך ואת תחנתך וג׳] The expressions of R^D in *ch.* 8; cf. *vv.* 33, 38, 54; *al.* LXX *τῆς φωνῆς τῆς προσευχῆς σου κ.τ.λ.*, i.e. אֶת־קול תפלתך וג׳; but Luc., Vulg., Pesh., Targ. as MT.

After התחננתה לפני LXX, Luc. add (Luc. *ἰδοὺ*) *πεποίηκα* (LXX *σοι*) *κατὰ πᾶσαν τὴν προσευχήν σου*, i.e. הִנֵּה עָשִׂיתִי כְּכָל־תְּפִלָּתְךָ; so Th., Klo., Oort. The words are probably genuine; cf. *ch.* 3. 12 הנה עשיתי כדבריך.

הקדשתי] *'I have hallowed,'* referring to the previous manifestation of Yahwe's glory in the house, *ch.* 8. 10; or else a perfect of certitude referring to time really future, as in English we might say 'I hallow.' For this latter explanation cf. Dri. *Tenses*, § 13.

לשום שמי שם] So *ch.* 11. 36; 14. 21; II. 21. 4, 7 (referring to I. 9. 3) all R^D. Cf. להיות שמי שם *ch.* 8. 16 *note.* In Deuteronomy the ordinary phrase is לְשַׁכֵּן שמו שם 'to cause his name to dwell there'; 12. 11; 14. 23; 16. 2, 6, 11; 26. 2. לשום שמו שם only in 12. 5, 21; 14. 24.

והיו עיני ולבי שם] In response to *ch.* 8. 29, 52.

כל הימים] 'All the days,' i.e. 'continually,' as a parallel to

עד עולם. So *ch.* 11. 36, 39; II. 8. 19; 17. 37 (all R^D). The phrase is very characteristic of Deut., occurring 4. 40; 5. 26; 6. 24; 11. 1; 14. 23; 18. 5; 19. 9; 28. 29, 33; cf. also Josh. 4. 24 (D^2); 1 Sam. 2. 32, 35 (Deut. redactor); Jer. 31. 35; 32. 39; 33. 18; 35. 19. Thus the expression *used absolutely* appears to be purely Deuteronomic. In Deut. 4. 10; 12. 1; 31. 13; *ch.* 8. 40 it is defined and to some extent limited by the added words אשר אתם (הם) חיים על האדמה. Upon כל הימים used in a strictly limited sense of the lifetime of an individual (non-Deut.) cf. *ch.* 5. 15 *note.*

4. אם תלך לפני] *Ch.* 2. 4 *note.*

כאשר הלך דוד] *Ch.* 3. 14 *note.*

בתם לבב] Gen. 20. 5, 6 (E); Ps. 78. 72; 101. 2†.

צויתיך] LXX, Luc. ἐνετειλάμην αὐτῷ, referring the clause to David. Probably a later correction.

חקי] LXX, Luc., Vulg., Pesh., || 2 Chr. 7. 17 read וְחֻקַּי correctly. So Th., Klo., Kamp., Benz., Kit.

חקי ומשפטי תשמר] *Ch.* 2. 3, 4 *note.*

5. כסא ממלכתך] Deut. 17. 18; 2 Sam. 7. 13 (Deut. redactor); 2 Chr. 23. 20†; cf. Hag. 2. 22. Elsewhere כסא הַמְּלוּכָה (once; *ch.* 1. 46), כסא מַלְכוּת, כסא הַמְּלָכִים (מְלָכִים).

כאשר דברתי על דוד] 'As I spake *concerning* David.' So *ch.* 2. 4 אשר דבר עלי. Several Codd., however, read אל דוד '*unto* David,' and this is also suggested by LXX, Luc., Vulg., Pesh., Targ.

לא יכרת וג׳] *Ch.* 2. 4 *note.*

6. אם שוב תשבון . . . מאחרי] Cf. Num. 14. 43; 32. 15 (both JE); Josh. 22. 16, 18, 23, 29 (P?); 1 Sam. 15. 11; Jer. 3. 19.

ולא תשמרו מצותי וג׳] *Ch.* 2. 3, 4 *note.*

אשר נתתי לפניכם] Cf. Jer. 9. 12; 26. 4 (referring to תורתי); 44. 10 (בתורתי ובחקתי).

והלכתם . . . להם] So exactly || 2 Chr. 7. 19; Josh. 23. 16 (D^2); cf. Deut. 11. 16; 17. 3. The phrase עבד אלהים אחרים occurs also Deut. 7. 4; 13. 7, 14; 28. 36, 64; Jer. 16. 13; Judg. 10. 13 (Deut. compiler); Josh. 24. 2, 16 (E); 1 Sam. 8. 8; 26. 19; cf. Jer. 44. 3. אלהים אחרים with עבד, not preceding as governing verb, but closely following with suffix in reference, is found *v.* 9 (|| 2 Chr. 7. 22);

II. 17. 35; Deut. 8. 19; 13. 3; 28. 14; 30. 17; 31. 20; Jer. 11. 10; 13. 10; 16. 11; 22. 9; 25. 6; 35. 15; Judg. 2. 19 (Deut. compiler). אלהים אחרים without עבד:—*ch.* 11. 4, 10; 14. 9; II. 17. 7, 37, 38; 22. 17 (|| 2 Chr. 34. 25) all R^D; II. 5. 17; Deut. 5. 7; 6. 14; 11. 28; 18. 20; 31. 18; Jer. 1. 16; 7. 6, 9, 18; 19. 4, 13; 32. 29; 44. 5, 8, 15; Judg. 2. 12, 17 (Deut. compiler); Ex. 20. 3 (E); 23. 13 (J); Hos. 3. 1; 2 Chr. 28. 25†.

7. אשר נתתי להם] Cf. *note* on *ch.* 8. 34.

אשלח מעל פני] Cf. Jer. 15. 1 שַׁלַּח מֵעַל־פָּנַי וְיֵצֵאוּ (reference to הָעָם הַזֶּה).

למשל ולשנינה] So || 2 Chr. 7. 20; Deut. 28. 37; Jer. 24. 9, these being all the occurrences of שנינה. משל thus used denotes a *proverb* or *byword* used in mockery, שנינה a *pointed, witty,* or *spiteful saying*, the speech and its object being in both cases identified. משל alone in this sense Ps. 44. 15; 69. 12; Ezek. 14. 8 (לִמְשָׁלִים).

8. והבית הזה יהיה עליון] This can only mean 'And this house shall be most high,' and we cannot, with RV., force the language and render 'And though this house be so high.' || 2 Chr. 7. 21 והבית הזה אשר היה עליון is an obvious correction. LXX supports MT. καὶ ὁ οἶκος οὗτος ἔσται ὁ ὑψηλός, and this in Luc., for the sake of gaining some sort of sense, has been altered into καὶ ὁ οἶκος οὗτος ὁ ὑψηλός, ἔσται κ.τ.λ.

Pesh., however, in reading ܚܪܒ 'desolate' in place of עליון, suggests an original והבית הזה יהיה עִיִּים 'And this house shall be *ruinous heaps.*' This, as giving excellent sense and supposing merely a small corruption in the MT., may reasonably be regarded as the true text: cf. Mic. 3. 12 וירושלַם עיין תהיה (עיין for assonance with ציון), || Jer. 26. 18 (עיים); Ps. 79. 1 (לעיים). Targ. וביתא הדין דהוה עיליי יהי חריב appears to embody a double rendering; but Th., Klo., Kamp. suppose that it represents the original text:—וְהַבַּיִת הַזֶּה אֲשֶׁר הָיָה עֶלְיוֹן יִהְיֶה לְעִיִּין. Such a text, however, would imply that the Chronicler copied אשר היה עליון from Kings before textual corruption set in; and in this case, why did he not also transcribe יהיה לעיין which must have existed in his MS. of Kings? Or are we to suppose that he *did* copy these words, and that subsequently through coincidence this reference to עיין disappeared both from Kings and Chronicles?

Vulg. *Et domus haec erit in exemplum* is a paraphrase of which it is impossible to determine the precise original.

כל עבר עליו וג׳] Cf. Jer. 18. 16 (reference to the land of Israel); 19. 8 (Jerusalem); 49. 17 (Edom); 50. 13 (Babylon); Zeph. 2. 15 (Nineveh). Similar also is Lam. 2. 15.

ואמרו וג׳] For this question put by the heathen from outside, together with its answer in *v.* 9, cf. Deut. 29. 23–27; Jer. 22. 8 *f.*

9. ויחזיקו באלהים אחרים] The phrase occurs only here and in ‖ 2 Chr. 7. 22. Deut. above quoted has וילכו ויעבדו אלהים אחרים וישתחוו להם; Jer. וישתחוו לאלהים אחרים ויעבדום.

9. 10—10. 29. *Further details of Solomon's magnificence and wisdom.*

Chh. 9. 10—10. 29=2 Chr. 8. 1—9. 24, 27, 28. 2 Chr. 1. 14–17.

Mainly a series of short notices drawn from the same sources as *chh.* 4—5. 14. The originals appear to have been cut up and pieced together with no great skill; but whether the arrangement throughout is due to R[D], or later hands have employed themselves in altering the sequence of the account, it is impossible to determine. In LXX, Luc. the arrangement is somewhat different, but scarcely superior, to that of MT.; *v.* 24[a] (אָז for אך; add בַּיָּמִים הָהֵם after לה), *vv.* 10–14 (om. ויהי מקצה *v.* 10[a]), *vv.* 26–28 (*v.* 26[a] being connected on to *v.* 14 by addition of the words ὑπὲρ οὗ after καὶ ναῦν—a later device), *ch.* 10. 1–22; *ch.* 9. 15, 17[b]–22; *ch.* 10. 23–25; *v.* 26 combined with *ch.* 5. 6; *ch.* 5. 1[a]; *ch.* 10. 27–29.

One single original document appears to be represented by *ch.* 9. 10, 17, 18, 19, 15, 20, 21, 22, 23, and these verses may very well have originally taken this order, the completion of Solomon's building operations being first narrated, and then followed by an account of the forced levy raised to carry out these works. After *v.* 23 there probably followed in the original a list of the *names* of the שרי הנצבים. The statement of *v.* 24[b], connected by R[D] to *v.* 24[a] by אז (*ch.* 3. 16 *note*), is probably from the same document.

Next to the account of the king's building activity—his most important work, there would naturally follow mention of his achievement next in importance—the provision of an efficient shipping for the increase of his wealth from external sources. This succeeds in *ch.* 9. 26–28; *ch.* 10. 11. But reference to the ships naturally leads up to mention of the imports introduced by their means, as we see in *ch.* 9. 28; *ch.* 10. 11, and the use to which these rare and valuable materials were put. Thus there follows *ch.* 10. 12, 14–22. The general subject of imports suggests allusion to a specially important item—horses from Egypt (or Muṣri), apparently first introduced into the kingdom of Solomon in any considerable numbers:—*ch.* 10. 26 (with *ch.* 5. 6; see *note* on 4. 20—5. 14), 28, 29.

Thus the disturbing factors introduced into this main account are seen to be *ch.* 9. 11–13, 14, 16, 24ª, 25; *ch.* 10. 1–10, 13, 23–25, 27. Notice in *ch.* 9. 11, 16, 24 the awkward pluperfects pointed by the order—subj., verb, obj., פרעה מלך ,חירם מלך צר נשא את ש׳ אך בת פרעה עלתה וג׳ ,מצרים עלה וג׳, and marking the passages as mere *excerpts* from sources which in describing a regular sequence of events must have read וַתַּעַל בת ,וַיַּעַל פרעה ,וַיִּנַּשֵּׂא חירם פרעה. In *v.* 11ᵇ אז יתן וג׳ cannot represent the apodosis of *v.* 10, since אז used in this connexion in place of ו *consec.* would be quite without analogy (cf. *ch.* 8. 1 *note*). Moreover, even if *v.* 11ᵇ *could* form the apodosis, the parenthesis *v.* 11ª would come in with very great awkwardness. Verse 16 has already been discussed (*note* on 4. 20—5. 14), and together with *ch.* 3. 1 has been seen to fall into its proper position after *v.* 14 of *ch.* 5. From the same source would seem to be derived *v.* 24ª, while *v.* 25, though clearly alien to its immediate context, cannot definitely be assigned to any special source. *Ch.* 10. 1–10, 13 is an ancient narrative introduced at this point to illustrate Solomon's wealth and wisdom, much in the same way as *ch.* 3. 16–28 serves to depict his discernment in judgement; and the two stories may very possibly be derived from the same source. Finally, *vv.* 23–25, 27 of *ch.* 10, couched in vague and generalizing statement, are probably relatively late in origin, and are here introduced to give the finishing touch to the picture of Solomon's prosperity.

11. נִשָּׂא] For נִשֵּׂא 2 Sam. 5. 12. On the confusion of verbs ל״א and ל״ה cf. *note* on *ch.* 17. 14.

אז יתן וג׳] On the use of אז as employed by R^D cf. *ch.* 3. 16 *note*. In place of this notice we find in the parallel account 2 Chr. 8. 1, 2 the statement that Ḥiram gave Solomon certain cities, and that Solomon built these and settled Israelite inhabitants in them; an explanation of the transaction probably grounded upon objection to the idea that Solomon parted with any portion of his territory. Jos. (*Ant.* viii. 5, § 3) states that when Ḥiram had inspected the cities and found them displeasing, he sent word to Solomon that he did not need them.

ארץ הגליל] 'Land of *the circuit*' or '*district*,' the title applied to a region in Naphtali on the north border of the kingdom of Israel, and adjoining Ḥiram's dominions. Cf. Josh. 20. 7; 21. 32; 1 Chr. 6. 61, where קֶדֶשׁ is mentioned as belonging to this district. In Isa. 8. 23 the phrase גְּלִיל הַגּוֹיִם 'district of the nations' is applied to the land of Zebulon and Naphtali, and would seem to imply that the population was for the most part non-Israelitish. הַגְּלִילָה Ezek. 47. 8†; גְּלִילוֹת Josh. 13. 2 (ג׳ הפלשתים); 18. 17; 22. 10, 11 (ג׳ הירדן); Joel 4. 4†, are used more generally as geographical terms.

13. ארץ כבול] The name is obviously regarded as employed to express Ḥiram's dissatisfaction with the cities. Thus Ew.'s explanation is probably correct, that the name is connected with כ + בַּל '*like nothing*,' so 'good for nothing,' 'worthless.' This does not embody a true etymology, but is intended for a witty play of words suggested by similarity of sound; cf. Gen. 11. 9 בָּבֶל connected with בלל as if for בַּלְבֶּל; Mic. 1. 10–15 בְּגַת אַל־תַּגִּידוּ play upon גת — נגד, בְּבֵית לְעַפְרָה עָפָר הִתְפַּלָּשְׁתִּי, לָרֶכֶשׁ — לָכִישׁ, הַיֹּרֵשׁ — מָרֵשָׁה, אַכְזִיב — אַכְזָב; *al.* Jos. (*Ant.* viii. 5, § 3) explains μεθερμηνευόμενον γὰρ τὸ Χαβαλὼν κατὰ Φοινίκων γλῶτταν, 'οὐκ ἀρέσκον' σημαίνει, a statement which seems to have no further foundation than the inference to be drawn from *v.* 12^b. LXX, Luc. in interpreting Ὅριον, must have read גְּבוּל. Talm., *Shabbath*, 54^b,

gives the fanciful derivation שהיו בה בני אדם שמכובלין בכסף ובזהב '(A land) in which men dwelt who were *bound* with silver and gold (fetters).' No modern interpretation commends itself.

כבול is mentioned, Josh. 19. 37, as one of the towns assigned to Asher; and Jos. (*Vit.* 42–44) speaks of Χαβωλώ in the district of Ptolemais forty stadia west of Jotaparta. The town is identified by Rob. (*BR.* iii. 88) with the modern *Kabûl.* Thus it may be supposed that the name of one of the twenty cities was given by Ḥiram to the whole district.

עד היום הזה] Cf. *ch.* 8. 8 *note.*

15. המס אשר העלה] *Ch.* 5. 27 *note.*

המלוא] Part of the fortifications of the city of David, existing in the old Jebusite city (2 Sam. 5. 9; ‖ 1 Chr. 11. 8), and mentioned, as here, in connexion with the walling up of the breaches of the city (*ch.* 11. 27), and the repair of the wall and towers by Hezekiah (2 Chr. 32. 5). Joash is said to have been murdered at בֵּית מִלֹּא (II. 12. 21), but it is not clear whether this was at Jerusalem; and in Judg. 9. 6, 20 a בית מלוא is mentioned in connexion with the city of Shechem.

The word is usually connected with the root מלא *be filled,* and interpreted as meaning *something which fills or banks up* (a Pi'el form causat. of Qal), and thus *an earthwork.* So Targ. renders מיליתא, this word being elsewhere used to translate Hebrew סֹלְלָה; 2 Sam. 20. 15 וישפכו סללה אל העיר=וצברו מיליתא על קרתא; II. 19. 32; Jer. 32. 24; *al.* Cf. also Talm. מוליא 'filled-up ground *or* mound,' *Baba bathra,* 54[a] שקיל מוליא ושדי בנוציא 'If one takes *earth from the mound* and throws it on the low ground.' This derivation cannot, however, be regarded as certain. The word may, as Moore (*Judg.* 9. 6) suggests, be Canaanite in origin; and it seems reasonable to suppose that the Millo was not a simple earthwork, but rather a massive fortress or tower built into that part of the city wall where such a protection was specially needed. So LXX, Luc. render ἡ ἄκρα. מגדל שכם, Judg. 9. 46, may thus perhaps be identical with בית מלוא of 9. 6, 20.

חצר] A chief city of North Canaan belonging to King Jabin, and captured and burnt by Joshua (Josh. 11. 1, 10; *al.*). The city was not far from the waters of Merom, the modern lake of *Hûleh* (Josh. 11. 5), and was afterwards assigned to the tribe of Naphtali (Josh. 19. 36). In Judg. 4 a second Jabin king of Ḥazor is mentioned as oppressing Israel, and as conquered by Deborah and Barak. The site is not well ascertained. Buhl (*Geogr.* 236) finds the name preserved in the modern name of the valley *Merj-el-Ḥaḍîre*, S.S.W. of *Ḳedes* (קֶדֶשׁ Josh. 19. 37), on the N. side of the *Wadi 'Auba* which runs into the lake of *Hûleh*. Cf. also Baed. 297.

מגדו] *Ch.* 4. 12 *note.*

גזר] A town on the border of Ephraim assigned by Joshua as a Levitical city (Josh. 16. 3; 21. 21). Horam king of Gezer came to the assistance of Lachish against Joshua, but was defeated and his army utterly destroyed by the Israelites (Josh. 10. 33). The city of Gezer, however, held out against the invader, and seems to have remained in the hands of its Canaanite (and Perizzite, LXX) inhabitants until the days of Solomon (Josh. 16. 10). The site of Gezer has been discovered by M. Clermont-Ganneau in the modern *Tell-Jezer* about eighteen miles W.N.W. of Jerusalem. On this and on the inscription תחמגזר, i. e. probably 'the boundary of Gezer,' which confirms the authenticity of the site, cf. *PEF.* 1873, 78*f.*; 1875, 74*f.*; Hastings, *BD. s.v.*; Smith, *Hist. Geogr.* 215 *ff.*

16. שִׁלֻּחִים] 'A dowry' given when the wife is 'sent away' from the home of her parents; cf. Mic. 1. 14, and the use of the verb שִׁלַּח Gen. 24. 59.

17. בית חרן תחתון] Also בית חורון הַתַּחְתּוֹן || 2 Chr. 8. 5; so called in distinction from (עליון) בית חורון הָעֶלְיוֹן 1 Chr. 7. 24; *al.* בית חורן without closer specification also occurs: Josh. 10. 10, 11; 18. 14; *al.* In Josh. 10. 10, 11, LXX reads 'Ωρωνείν i.e. חֹרֹנַיִם 'the two Ḥorons'; so 2 Sam. 13. 34 ἐκ τῆς ὁδοῦ τῆς 'Ωρωνήν stands in place of the corrupt מדרך אחריו, and is adopted by Wellh., Dri., Budde. Elsewhere (Isa. 15. 5; *al.*) חרנים is a Moabite city. The two Beth-ḥorons were upon the boundary line of Ephraim (Josh. 16. 3, 5), and the pass running between them was the scene of Joshua's pursuit of

the five Amorite kings who made a combined attack upon Gibeon (Josh. 10. 10, 11). In modern times they have been with certainty identified, the lower with *Beit 'Ûr et-tahta*, the upper with *Beit 'Ûr el-fôqa*, the former being about one mile north-west of the latter, which is some three or four miles north-west of Gibeon,—*el-Jîb*. See Rob. *BR*. iii. 250 *f*., *PEF. Mem*. iii. 86.

18. בעלת] ‖ 2 Chr. 8. 6. Mentioned Josh. 19. 44† as a city assigned to Dan. The conjectural site is *Bel'aîn* about two and a-half miles north of *Beit 'Ûr et-tahta*. *PEF. Mem*. ii. 296.

תַּ֯מֹר] Q're תַּדְמֹר, i. e. Palmyra the modern *Tudmur*, is supported by all Verss.[1], and by ‖ 2 Chr. 8. 4 (so all Verss.). The other towns, however, mentioned *vv*. 17, 18 are all in South Palestine, and in Ezek. 47. 19; 48. 28 we have a תָּמָר cited as being in the extreme south of the land—פְּאַת נֶגֶב תֵּימָנָה. Thus in spite of ‖ 2 Chr., which connects Solomon's building of Tadmor with a successful campaign against Ḥamath-zobah, Kt. in our passage seems to deserve the preference. So Bö., Th., Kamp., Benz., Kit.; Smith, *Hist. Geogr*. 270 *note* 2, 580 *note* 2.

במדבר בארץ] 'In the wilderness in the land'; a vague and pointless statement. בארץ cannot be intended to distinguish the city from another of the same name outside the land, for in such a case a closer definition of the locality would be expected. Vulg. *in terra solitudinis*, Pesh. ܒܐܪܥܐ ܕܡܕܒܪܐ suggest בְּאֶרֶץ הַמִּדְבָּר 'in the desert country.' The phrase בארץ מדבר occurs only in the poetical passage Deut. 32. 10 and in Prov. 21. 19, but might reasonably be used in plain prose. Targ. follows MT., while LXX, Luc. (*ch*. 10. 23) omit. Very probably בארץ is the corruption of some place-name. So Bö. בְּמִדְבַּר פָּארָן; plausible, but rather far towards the south. Kit. בַּמִּדְבָּר בְּאֶרֶץ יְהוּדָה. Perles (*Analekten zur Textkritik des A.T.*, 22), following Eichhorn, regards בארץ as a contraction of באר׳ צ׳ בַּאֲרַם צוֹבָה, upon the view that Q're תדמר is correct, and comparing 2 Chr. 8. 3, 4.

19. ואת חשק וג׳] Cf. *v*. 1 *note*.

[1] LXX Ἰεθερμάθ, i. e. את הרמר, ד being misread ר. The passage in LXX occurs *ch*. 10. 23.

20, 21. כל העם . . . בניהם] This form of *casus pendens*, where a substantive is reinforced by the pronominal suffix of a following substantive, is idiomatic and frequent. 1 Sam. 2. 10 יהוה יֵחַתּוּ מְרִיבָו; Gen. 17. 15 שרי אשתך . . . את שְׁמָהּ; 34. 8 שכם . . . נפשו. Cf. other instances in Dri. *Tenses*, § 197, 2.

21. בניהם אשר נתרו . . . ויעלם] The predicate introduced by ו *consecutive* after the preceding *accusativus pendens* בניהם; a rather uncommon construction. Cf. *ch.* 12. 17 ובני ישראל הישבים בערי יהודה וימלך עליהם רחבעם; *ch.* 15. 13 וגם את מעכה אמו ויסרה מגבירה; II. 16. 14; Dri. *Tenses*, § 127 *a*.

מַס־עֹבֵד] 'A forced levy of bondmen.' עבד is sing. collective. So Gen. 49. 15; Josh. 16. 10†.

עד היום הזה] Cf. *ch.* 8. 8 *note*.

22. ומבני ישראל וג׳] But cf. the statement of *ch.* 5. 27, and see *ch.* 4. 6 *note*.

שלישיו] A word of unknown meaning and derivation. LXX which here omits (*Cod.* A, Luc. τρισσοί) elsewhere usually renders τριστάτης, a term to which Origen on Ex. 14. 7 gives as one explanation among others the meaning, *one of three warriors in a chariot;* Εἰς τὰς χρείας τῶν πολέμων ἅρματα ἐποίουν μεγάλα, ὡς καὶ τρεῖς χωρεῖν· ἵν' ὁ μὲν εἷς ἡνιοχῇ, οἱ δὲ δύο πολεμῶσιν. So Greg. Nyss.; cf. the more precise rendering of LXX in Ex. 15. 4 ἀναβάτας τριστάτας. This explanation, which appears to depend upon the context of Ex. 14. 7, has been adopted by some moderns, but is purely conjectural, and is rightly opposed by Dillmann, who points out that the ancient chariot as figured on the monuments has usually but two occupants—the driver and the fighting man, and that only kings and the highest officers would have had in addition a third man as shield-bearer. It may be added that in accordance with Ex. 14. 7 וְשָׁלִשִׁם עַל־כֻּלּוֹ *third man* could not describe a spare man acting as armour-bearer, but would denote the most important occupant of the chariot, viz. the combatant. This meaning, however, is opposed to the use of the word of an officer immediately attendant upon a king, whether in a chariot (II. 9. 25) or elsewhere (II. 7. 2, 17, 19; 15. 25).

Derivation thus failing, the most that can be said is that, judging from the context of our passage ('ש next to שרי רכבו) II. 9. 25; 10. 25 (שלישים coupled with רצים 'foot-runners' as though in contradistinction); Ex. 14. 7, שלישים may have been a class of warriors usually connected with chariots; but it is with wisdom that AV., RV. 'captains' agree with Vulg. *duces*, Pesh. ܓܢܒܪܘܗܝ, Targ. גיברוהי in rendering by a very general term.

23. חמשים וחמש מאות] LXX (section following *ch.* 2. 35) gives the number as τρεῖς χιλιάδες καὶ ἑξακόσιοι, Luc. τρεῖς χιλιάδες καὶ ἑπτακόσιοι—probably an arbitrary alteration of the translator with the view of bringing the number into correspondence with that of *ch.* 5. 30 with which our verse is closely parallel in wording. The other Verss. support MT. 550.

Possibly after the completion of the Temple and Palace the number of the שרי הנצבים may have been greatly diminished, and in any case it is easier to believe that the exact parallelism of the Greek translator is a change for the sake of conformity, than that *vice versâ* the alteration was made in MT. for no apparent reason. ‖ 2 Chr. 8. 10 gives the number as חמשים ומאתים, a variation explained by Kennicott as a misreading רנ for דנ; but such a method of notation in early OT. MSS. is highly improbable. Cf. *ch.* 6. 1 *note*.

24. אך] Very difficult. Th. explains '*As soon as* . . . then he built, &c.' אך has here a restrictive sense *only* or *scarcely*, and the meaning *as soon as* is determined by the following אז which marks the point of time immediately following that denoted by אך עלתה. But the case is scarcely parallel to the only two examples which can be compared, Gen. 27. 30 אך יצא יצא יעקב . . . ועשו אחיו בא, and Judg. 7. 19 אך הקם הקימו את השמרים ויתקעו בשופרות, for in both these passages great stress is laid upon the very immediate sequence in time of the two events described, and to suppose the existence of a similar stress in our passage would be absurd. Moreover, the back reference of אז to אך is opposed to the characteristic usage of this former particle in Kings—its employment with merely vague reference to the period which is being described, and without

distinct attachment to any definite point of time (*ch.* 3. 16 *note*). And further, the change of subject implied in בנה, without mention of the new subject שלמה, is very strange. Thus some slight corruption of the text may reasonably be supposed.

Vulg., Pesh., Targ. seem to agree with MT., except for the addition of שלמה after בנה in Vulg., Pesh.—probably a translator's addition made for the sake of lucidity. LXX, Luc. offer two renderings—the first in the insertion following *ch.* 2. 35, the second in immediate sequence to *ch.* 9. 9. The former translation exactly follows MT., except for reading *οὕτως*, i. e. probably כֵּן, in place of אך. The latter rendering is somewhat different:—*Τότε ἀνήγαγεν Σαλωμὼν τὴν θυγατέρα Φαραὼ ἐκ πόλεως Δαυεὶδ εἰς οἶκον αὐτοῦ ὃν ᾠκοδόμησεν αὐτῷ ἐν ταῖς ἡμέραις ἐκείναις.* This agrees closely with the MT. of ‖ 2 Chr. 8. 11; and supposing the LXX translator to have inserted *τότε* upon his own responsibility or through a misreading אָז for וְאֵת, and also to have read בֵּיתֹה, לֹה for בֵּיתָהּ, לָהּ, we may believe the original text of our passage to have been וְאֶת־בַּת פַּרְעֹה הֶעֱלָה שְׁלֹמֹה מֵעִיר דָּוִד אֶל־בֵּיתָהּ אֲשֶׁר בָּנָה לָהּ בַּיָּמִים הָהֵם. This emendation removes all difficulties above noticed. The אך of MT. will thus be a scribe's error for ואת due to the occurrence of the same two letters in במלאכה the word immediately preceding; and further, it is possible that פרעהעלה may have been copied by mistake for פרעההעלה, and that later on a second scribe, perceiving that עלה must thus refer to בת פרעה, may have altered it into the feminine עלתה.

25. והעלה] 'Used to offer;' frequentative.

והקטיר אתו אשר לפני י׳] Scarcely original. The curious אִתּוֹ cannot be used in place of עָלָיו and refer to the altar (Pesh., Targ., Ges.), nor can we believe (Ew., Th.) that it refers to Solomon;—'He would offer incense *by himself*' (without the intervention of another)[1]. LXX, Luc. (after *ch.* 2. 35) altogether omit the words אתו אשר, and seem simply to have read והקטיר לפני יהוה. So Oort.

---

[1] Th. cites Gen. 39. 6; Isa. 44. 24 for this use of אִתּוֹ, and regards אשׁר as a mistaken insertion.

Klo. ingeniously suggests וְהִקְטִיר אֶת־אִשּׁוֹ לִפְנֵי י׳ 'and would burn *his fire-offering* before Yahwe'—a very plausible emendation.

ושלם את הבית] RV. 'So he finished the house,' and so all Verss.;—LXX, Luc. καὶ συνετέλεσεν τὸν οἶκον, Vulg. *perfectumque est templum*, Pesh. ܘܫܠܡܗ ܠܒܝܬܐ, Targ. ושלם ית ביתא. It is impossible, however, to explain why the perfect with ו *consecutive* should be thus used, as though the fact narrated were in due sequence to the preceding frequentatives והעלה . . . והקטיר; and moreover such a statement is out of place in this connexion, where events are being recorded which must have taken place only *after* the completion and consecration of the building. Hence Ew. renders 'and he would *take leave of* (*say farewell to*) the house'; Th. 'and he would *completely furnish* the house,' i. e. provide upon each occasion of his visits that all the requirements of the Temple and its services should be fully met. Neither of these translations can be justified by analogy; and it seems not improbable that the letters ושלם are a mistaken repetition of ושלמים in the earlier part of the verse, and את הבית a later addition to form a complete sentence intended to convey the meaning given by the Verss.

26. אשר את אלות] 'Which is *near* Eloth'; an idiomatic use of the preposition in definition of locality. Cf. II. 9. 27 במעלה גור אשר את יבלעם; Judg. 3. 19; 4. 11; Ezek. 43. 8. For the similar use of עִם see *ch.* 1. 9 *note*.

28. ארבע מאות ועשרים] LXX ἑκατὸν εἴκοσι is unsupported by Luc. and the other Verss., all of which agree with MT.

10. 1. לשם יהוה] 'Through the name of Yahwe'; lit. '*at* the name.' The meaning is that the fame of Yahwe's name led to the diffusion of a report concerning the wise and prosperous king who enjoyed His favour and protection; and this is in full accordance with the prominence which the queen in this story assigns to Yahwe as the chooser and supporter of Solomon (*v.* 9). The phrase לשם י׳ occurs elsewhere Josh. 9. 9; Isa. 60. 9; Jer. 3. 17†, and the *nuance* of the preposition is closely similar to that in the expression לקול '*at* the sound of'; Jer. 10. 13 לקול תתו המון מים בשמים; 11. 16; 51. 16; Ezek. 27. 28; Hab. 3. 16; Ps. 42. 8; Job 21. 12. Cf. also

Ps. 18. 45 לִשְׁמֹעַ אֹזֶן יִשָּׁמְעוּ לִי '*At* the hearing of the ear they shall obey me'; Job 42. 5.

There is thus no need to have recourse to the emendation of Klo., Kamp., Benz., Kit., וְאֶת־שֵׁמַע הַבַּיִת אֲשֶׁר בָּנָה לְשֵׁם יהוה 'and the report of the house which he had built to the name of Yahwe.' LXX, Luc. καὶ τὸ ὄνομα Κυρίου, Pesh. ܘܫܡܗ ܕܡܪܝܐ are probably merely loose renderings, and do not presuppose וְשֵׁם, in place of which, as Th. points out, we should rightly expect וְאֶת־שֵׁם.

חִידוֹת] RV. '*hard questions*' is perhaps the best rendering; cf. Prov. 1. 6 דִּבְרֵי חֲכָמִים וְחִידֹתָם. The word here denotes something less trivial than the mere *riddle* of Samson, Judg. 14. 12 *ff.*, but, on the other hand, has not advanced to the later sense of a perplexing question of ethics or morals, Ps. 49. 5; 78. 2.

2. עִם לְבָבָה] *Ch.* 8. 17 *note.*

5. מוֹשַׁב עֲבָדָיו וּמַעֲמַד מְשָׁרְתָיו] 'The *sitting* of his servants and the *attendance* of his ministers.' For מַעֲמַד in this sense cf. the phrase עָמַד לִפְנֵי used of *service; ch.* 1. 2 *note.* This explanation alone suits the context. The whole of *v.* 5 down to וּמַשְׁקָיו refers to Solomon's magnificent *display at his banquets.* עֲבָדָיו are his courtiers and מְשָׁרְתָיו his waiters, and naturally in this connexion מַלְבּוּשֵׁיהֶם their gorgeous robes call for special notice. On the other hand, Th.'s explanation of מוֹשַׁב, מַעֲמַד as substantives of *place,* denoting the *dwellings* or *quarters* of Solomon's servants, is quite alien to the context. It is impossible to think that the mere *dwellings* of the king's servants should be singled out either for their magnificence or number as exciting the queen's admiration, while no special mention is made of the impression left upon her by the sight of the Palace, the Temple, and the Lebanon house. The mention also of the garments and the cup-bearers is upon this interpretation deprived of significance.

There is no difficulty in assigning to these substantives with מ preformative a signification other than that of *place.* The Arabic nouns of this form (*nomina vasis*) are used of *place* or *time*, and e. g. مَجْلِس '*the place where,* or *time when, several persons sit, room, assembly, party*' (Wright, i. 221) may aptly be quoted in this special connexion. So in Hebrew we may cf. e.g. מִשְׁפָּט, מוֹצָא, where, as with מושב, מעמד, the idea of *time* or *place of action* seems to have passed further into definition of the *action* itself.

ומשקיו] Pesh. adds ܘܠܒܘܫܝ̈ܗܘܢ i.e. a repetition of the previous ומלבשיהם; an unnecessary redundancy.

ועלתו אשר יעלה בית יהוה] 'And his burnt-offering which he used to offer at the house of Yahwe.' Here it is still the large scale of the king's *doings*, rather than his buildings, which forms the writer's theme. So all Verss. both here and in ‖ 2 Chr. 9. 4, RV. marg., Th., Klo., Kamp., Kit. ‖ 2 Chr. reads עֲלִיָּתוֹ, doubtless intending to convey the sense 'the ascent by which he used to go up to the house of Yahwe'; and this rendering is adopted by RV., Ke., Ew.

לא היה בה עוד רוח] 'There was no more *spirit* in her'; i.e. Solomon's display of wisdom and magnificence deprived her of all *courage* to attempt further to compete with him. The *nuance* of רוח is like that in the English expression 'a woman of *spirit*,' and may be partly paralleled by the use of the term in *ch.* 21. 5; Gen. 45. 27 and the phrases עֲצוּבַת רוּחַ Isa. 54. 6, דַּכְּאֵי רוּחַ Ps. 34. 19. The common explanation following LXX, Luc. καὶ ἐξ ἑαυτῆς ἐγένετο, 'she was beside herself (with *astonishment*),' misses the precise meaning.

6. אמת היה הדבר] '*Truth* was the saying.' The abstract substantive used in place of an adjective; cf. *ch.* 2. 13 *note*, and Dri. *Tenses*, § 189, 2. The *order* of words is highly emphatic; *Tenses*, § 208.

7. לא הגד לי החצי] LXX οὐκ εἰσὶν (Luc. ἔστι κατὰ) τὸ ἥμισυ καθὼς ἀπήγγειλάν μοι, merely a somewhat paraphrastic rendering of the same text. In place of החצי ‖ 2 Chr. 9. 6 has חֲצִי מַרְבִּית חָכְמָתֶךָ.

הוספת וג׳] LXX, Luc. προστέθεικας ἀγαθὰ πρὸς (LXX αὐτὰ ἐπὶ) πᾶσαν τὴν ἀκοὴν ἣν ἤκουσα ἐν τῇ γῇ μου, i.e. הוֹסַפְתָּ טוֹב אֶל־כָּל־הַשְּׁמוּעָה אֲשֶׁר שָׁמַעְתִּי בְּאַרְצִי. Probably correct.

חכמה seems to be the addition of a later precisionist, and is really covered by טוב which includes everything which makes for *prosperity*. The repetition of בארצי (from *v.* 6) is not out of place.

LXX πρὸς αὐτὰ ἐπὶ πᾶσαν κ.τ.λ. probably arises from repetition of אל read first as אֲלֵיהֶם. || 2 Chr. יספת אל השמועה אשר שמעתי.

8. אנשיך] LXX, Luc., Pesh. presuppose נָשֶׁיךָ 'thy *wives*'; so in || 2 Chr. 9. 7 Luc. (Pesh. omits). Adopted by Bö., Klo., Kamp., Benz., Kit., Oort. correctly. אנשיך by the side of עבדיך is redundant, and, as Klo. suggests, may be a later alteration in view of the facts of *ch.* 11. 1-3.

9. לעלם] LXX στῆσαι εἰς τὸν αἰῶνα, Luc. τοῦ στῆσαι αὐτὸν εἰς τὸν αἰῶνα agree with || 2 Chr. 9. 8 לְהַעֲמִידוֹ לְעוֹלָם. This addition, which is almost indispensable, may be adopted. Klo.'s emendation מִכָּל־הָעַמִּים is not to be preferred.

11. עצי אלמגים] So *v.* 12†. עצי אלגומים 2 Chr. 2. 7; 9. 10, 11†. The tree is usually thought to be the red sandal-wood (*Pterocarpus santalinus*) which is very heavy, fine grained, and of a brilliant red colour, and is said still to be highly esteemed in the east for the construction of lyres and other musical instruments. The meaning and derivation of the word are, however, quite uncertain: Hastings, *BD.* i. 63; Tristram, 332[1]. LXX ξύλα πελεκητά (Luc. ἀπελέκητα), Vulg. *ligna thyina*, Pesh. ܩܝܣܐ ܕܡܫܟܘܬܐ (explained by lexx. as a scented and variegated wood, sandal-wood), Targ. אעי אלמוגיא.

12. מסעד] 'A support' or 'supports,' i.e. upon the easiest interpretation, *pilasters* or *light buttresses;* so LXX, Luc. ὑποστηρίγματα, Vulg. *fulcra*. The substantive only occurs here, and || 2 Chr. 9. 11 reads מְסִלּוֹת, perhaps 'terraces' or 'verandahs,' an explanation which Th. seeks to fit also to מסעד. This rendering, however, like that of Pesh. ܬܨܒܝܬܐ 'ornamentation,' Ke., Ew. 'balusters' or 'balustrade,' Bö., Klo. 'furniture,' depends merely upon conjecture.

לא בא כן וג׳] 'There came not *thus* (i.e. in such quantity and of such excellence) almug trees,' and so, by accommodation to Eng. idiom, 'there came not *such* almug trees.' Cf. Ex. 10. 14 לפניו לא היה כן ארבה כמוהו 'before them there were no such locusts as they.'

---

[1] The latest discussion is that by Cheyne (*Expository Times*, July, 1898, pp. 470 *ff.*), who cites Assyr. *êlammâku*, a tree used by Sennacherib in building his palaces.

After אלמגים in *v.* 12b LXX, Luc. add ἐπὶ τῆς γῆς, i. e. עַל־הָאָרֶץ, perhaps correctly. Cf. ‖ 2 Chr. 9. 11 ולא נראו כהם לפנים בארץ יהודה.

עד היום הזה] *Ch.* 8. 8 *note.*

13. והמלך שלמה נתן] Upon the emphatic position of the subject, in antithesis to *v.* 10a [1], cf. *ch.* 5. 25 *note.*

כיד המלך] 'According to the king's *hand*,' i. e. his '*bounty*.' So Est. 1. 7; 2. 18†. ‖ 2 Chr. 9. 12 reads מלבד אשר הֵבִיאָה אל המלך for which Ber. emends מלבד אשר הֵבִיא לָהּ המלך.

15. לבד מאנשי התרים] Very difficult. Supposing אנשי התרים to denote 'men of the merchants' (though תור *spy out, investigate* has nowhere else the sense of *trading*, and the phrase אנשי הת׳ is peculiar), we still seek allusion, not to the traders themselves, but to the *revenue* which they produced. Thus RV., going further than MT. warrants, renders 'Beside *that which* the chapmen *brought*'; LXX, Luc. χωρὶς τῶν φόρων τῶν ὑποτεταγμένων, Targ. בר מאגר אומניא suggest ? . . . לְבַד מֵעֹנֶשׁ 'beside the *duties* &c.[2]'; cf. II. 23. 33 where עֹנֶשׁ is rendered φόρον by Luc.; 2 Chr. 36. 3 וַיַּעֲנֹשׁ LXX, Luc. καὶ ἀπέβαλεν φόρον. So Bö. לְבַד מֵעַנְשֵׁי הַתָּרִים, Th. לְבַד מֵעָנְשֵׁי הָרְדוּיִם; but הרדוים 'the subject people' is not to be paralleled. The best and easiest emendation, though independent of any Vers., is that suggested by Kamp. for the whole half-verse לְבַד מֵאֲשֶׁר בָּא מִסַּחַר הָרֹכְלִים 'beside that which came from the traffic of the merchants.'

כל מלכי הערב] RV. 'all the kings of *the mingled people*.' LXX, Luc. πάντων τῶν βασιλέων τοῦ (Luc. τῶν ἐν τῷ) πέραν, i. e. כל מלכי הָעֵבֶר; Vulg. *omnes reges Arabiae;* Pesh. ܘܟܠܗܘܢ ܡܠܟܐ ܕܥܪܒܝܐ, so ‖ 2 Chr. 9. 14 וְכָל־מַלְכֵי עֲרָב; Targ. וכל מלכי סומכוותא 'and all the kings of the allied peoples.' These מַלְכֵי הָעֶרֶב are mentioned Jer. 25. 24 as הַשֹּׁכְנִים בַּמִּדְבָּר, and in connexion with כָּל־מַלְכֵי עֲרָב 'all the kings of Arabia.' In Jer. 25. 20 כָּל־הָעֶרֶב are cited together with כָּל־מַלְכֵי אֶרֶץ הָעוּץ, and in Ezek. 30. 5 כּוּשׁ וּפוּט וְלוּד וְכָל־הָעֶרֶב וְכוּב.

[1] Verse 12 must have originally followed immediately upon *v.* 10; cf. *note* on *ch.* 9. 10—*ch.* 10. 29.

[2] Perhaps Vulg. is a paraphrase of the same: Excepto eo, quod afferebant viri, *qui super vectigalia erant.*

In Jer. 50. 37 they appear as the mercenaries of the king of Babylon. Hence it may be inferred that these were kings or sheiks of the mixed nomad tribes of SE. Arabia who came more or less under Solomon's power and so were subject to tribute.

In Ex. 12. 38 עֵרֶב רַב 'a great mixed multitude' is mentioned as coming up out of Egypt with Israel, and in Neh. 13. 3 כָּל־עֵרֶב 'all the mixed multitude' is separated from the returned exiles by Nehemiah; but the connexion of these with הָעֶרֶב is not clear.

ופחות הארץ] פחות 'viceroys' or 'governors.' The view that these are identical with the נצבים of *ch.* 4. 7–19 (Th.; Ber. on ‖ 2 Chr. 9. 14) is opposed by the close connexion with the *foreign* מלכי הערב. More probably the reference is to petty *vassal-princes* who were allowed to retain a nominal suzerainty at the price of an annual tribute: cf. the inscription (l. 12) in which Panammu is termed פחי ואחי יאדי 'viceroy and neighbour-king of Ya'di,' appointed by 'his lord the king of Asshur' (Lidzbarski, *Nordsemit. Epigr.* 443). Elsewhere in OT. the title is used of military commanders under the Aramaean Hadadezer *ch.* 20. 24 *note*, and the Assyrian Sennacherib II. 18. 24 *note*, ‖ Isa. 36. 9, of governors under the Babylonian king, Jer. 51. 23, 57, the king of Media, Jer. 51. 28, and the Assyrian (and Chaldean) Ezek. 23. 6, 12, 23; but with far the greatest frequency of governors of provinces appointed by the Persian monarchs, e.g. of Zerubbabel, Hag. 1. 1, 14; 2. 2, 21; Nehemiah, Neh. 5. 14, 18; 12. 26; the governors generally 'beyond the River,' Neh. 2. 7, 9, &c.

Many critics, regarding פחה as a Persian word connected with Sanskrit *paksha* or *pakkha*, *friend* or *ally*, are obliged therefore to consider the occurrences in Kings as late interpolations (cf. especially Giesebrecht, *ZATW*. i. 233). Against this Schrader argues with force, citing the use of the term in Assyr. *paḫat*, pl. *paḫâti*, *viceroy*, and abstract *piḫat*, *satrapy* in the Khorsabad inscription of the time of Sargon (B.C. 722–705), two centuries before the Persian era, and maintaining the purely Semitic character of the word: *COT.* i. 175 *f.*

The feminine termination of פֶּחָה pl. פַּחוֹת is perhaps to be explained as used with a term denoting *office*, as in Ar. خَلِيفَةٌ 'viceroy,' خَالِقَةٌ 'creator,' *al.;* cf. G-K. § 122 *r*[1].

16. מאתים צנה זהב שחוט] 'Two hundred targets—beaten gold,' זהב standing in explanatory apposition to צנה, and defining the *class* to which it belongs. So in *v.* 17 ושלש מאות מגנים זהב שחוט, שלשת מנים זהב. Cf. Dri. *Tenses*, §§ 186–188.

זהב שחוט] Only in this connexion; *v.* 17 ‖ 2 Chr. 9. 15, 16†[2]. '*Beaten* gold,' RV., Bö., Ke., Th., Ber., Klo., Kamp., שחט meaning *strike* or *beat down.* So LXX, Luc. χρυσᾶ ἐλατά. The other Verss. give the sense '*fine* or *pure* gold';—Vulg. *de auro purissimo*, Pesh. ܕܕܗܒܐ ܛܒܐ, Targ. דדהבא טבא. The explanation '*alloyed* gold,' Ges., Winer, obtained from Ar. شَحَطَ *dilute wine with water*, cannot be maintained.

יעלה על] Lit. '*went up upon*,' describing the laying of the gold plating upon the (wooden) framework or foundation. The Imperf. describes the *norm* which *characterized* each shield of the class.

18. זהב מופז] Probably, as RV., *al.* '*finest* or *purest* gold.' So LXX, Luc. χρυσίῳ δοκίμῳ, Targ. דהבא טבא, ‖ 2 Chr. 9. 17 זהב טהור. The verb occurs only here, but the substantive פָּז nine times. Identification with Ar. فَضَّ *break, separate*, on the view that this may be used of separating the gold from the ore (Ges.), seems to be precarious. Pesh., Arab. presuppose זהב מֵאוֹפִיר 'gold from Ophir'; so Pesh., Targ. in Jer. 10. 9 זהב מֵאוּפָז, and many moderns in Dan. 10. 5 כתם אוּפָז. Vulg. *auro fulvo nimis.*

21. משקה] 'Drink'; so Lev. 11. 34.

סגור] *Ch.* 6. 20 *note.*

אין כסף לא נחשב] Scarcely, as the accents suggest, and as rendered by LXX, Luc., Vulg. 'There was no silver, it was not accounted of'; but rather a negation strengthened by duplication of the negative, 'silver was *not* accounted of *at all*.' Such a duplication is found in Zeph. 2. 2 בטרם לא יבוא עליכם 'before there

[1] The meaning and use of the term קֹהֶלֶת is too uncertain to permit of its being cited as a parallel.

[2] In Jer. 9. 7 Kt. חֵץ שׁוֹחֵט 'a *destroying* arrow' is to be preferred; see Graf, *ad loc.*

come upon you,' and in the phrase הַמְקַבְּלֵי אֵין, II. 1. 3, 6, 16 המבלי אין אלהים בישראל; Ex. 14. 11. Cf. Ew. § 323. Pesh. ܘܡܟܡܐ ܠܐ ܡܬܚܫܒ ܗܘܐ omits one negative, thus agreeing with || 2 Chr. 9. 20 which is without לא.

22. אני תרשיש] 'A fleet of Tarshish'; i.e. a fleet consisting of ships such as were used by the Phoenicians for communication with their distant colony at Tartessus in Spain. || 2 Chr. 9. 21 makes Tarshish the destination of the ships, כי אניות למלך הלכות תרשיש עם עבדי חורם (so 2 Chr. 20. 36, 37), but that this is incorrect is shown by mention of the cargo of the ships—products of the *East*, and by the reference in *ch.* 22. 49 to Jehoshaphat's fleet or ship (see *note ad loc.*) of Tarshish which was stationed at Ezion Geber on the Aelanitic gulf in order to go to Ophir. Cf. *ch.* 9. 26–28 where the allusion is doubtless to one and the same fleet of Solomon[1].

שנהבים] Cod. A[2], Vulg., Targ., and in || 2 Chr. 9. 21, LXX, Luc. render '*elephants' teeth*'; Pesh. in both places ܦܝܠܐ 'elephants'; Vulg. in Chr. *ebur*. Elsewhere 'ivory' is always שֵׁן alone, or with the generic art. הַשֵּׁן; and it is generally thought that some foreign word meaning 'elephants' is here represented by הַבִּים. So Ges., Ber. regard the word as a contraction of הָאִבִּים, and compare Sanskrit *ibha* = 'elephant.' Or הבים is thought to be a corruption of הַפִּיל, *pîl* being the Persian name for the elephant which has thence passed into Ar. and Aram. Assyr. *šin-ni pi-ri* denotes 'teeth of elephants.' In Ezek. 27. 15 there is mention of קרנות שן וְהָבְנִים 'horns of ivory and *ebony*' (הָבְנִים = Egypt. *heben*, Gk. ἔβενος, Lat. *hebenum*), and Bö., Th., following Rödiger and reading in our passage שֵׁן הַבִּים as two words, explain '*ivory* (*and*) *ebony*,' regarding הבים as a contraction or corruption of הבנים.

קופים] Pesh., Targ. transliterate; Cod. A, and in 2 Chr. LXX, Luc. πιθήκων, Vulg. *simias*. The word is doubtless foreign, and the rendering '*apes*' is generally adopted, upon comparison of

---

1 Sayce (*Expository Times*, Jan. 1902, p. 179) argues for identification of תרשיש with Tarsus in Cilicia.

2 The rendering of LXX, Luc. λίθων τορευτῶν καὶ πελεκητῶν (Luc. ἀπελεκήτων), for the whole שנהבים וקפים ותכיים, is obscure.

Sanskrit and Malabar *kapi*, from whence comes the Greek κῆβος, κεῖβος, κῆπος, a species of long-tailed monkey.

תכיים] Cod. A ταώνων, Vulg. *pavos*, Pesh. ܛܘܣܐ, Targ. טווסין, i. e. '*peacocks*'; ‖ 2 Chr. Luc. τεχείμ, LXX omits. Another foreign word. The Tamil or Malabar name for the peacock is *tôgai* or *thôgai*, and תכי may represent this, with interchange of the back-palatals *g*, *k*. So most moderns.

23. מלכי הארץ] LXX omits הארץ. With MT. cf. *ch.* 5. 14.

24. וכל הארץ] LXX, Luc., Pesh. presuppose וכל מלכי הארץ; so ‖ 2 Chr. 9. 23 probably rightly.

25. כלי כסף] LXX, Luc. omit, perhaps in view of *v.* 21b.

נשק] Elsewhere (eight times) the word always denotes '*arms*' or '*armour*,' and this is the meaning here given by Vulg., Pesh., Targ. So RV., Bö., Th., Klo., Kamp., Kit. The mention of armour follows not inappropriately after שלמות 'raiment.' LXX, Luc. render στακτήν, 'oil of myrrh or cinnamon,' and this is favoured by Ew., Ber. who compare Ar. نَشِقَ 'breathe in an odour through the nostrils.' For this, however, regular interchange of consonants would require נשׂק. Possibly LXX was influenced in its rendering by the following בשמים ἡδύσματα.

26. ויהי לו . . . רכב] In place of this statement LXX reads καὶ ἦσαν τῷ Σαλωμὼν τέσσαρες χιλιάδες θήλειαι ἵπποι εἰς ἅρματα, Luc. καὶ ἦσαν τῷ Σολομῶντι τεσσαράκοντα χιλιάδες ἵππων θηλειῶν εἰς ἅρματα τοῦ τίκτειν, i. e. *ch.* 5. 6a with mistaken rendering of the rare word ארות. The following words of *ch.* 10. 26 and *ch.* 5. 6b are identical; ושנים עשר אלף פרשים. 2 Chr. 9. 25a = *ch.* 5. 6; 2 Chr. 1. 14a = *ch.* 10. 36a; 2 Chr. 9. 25b = 2 Chr. 1. 14b = *ch.* 10. 26b. Thus (as is testified by the partial combination of the two Kings' passages in LXX, Luc., and 2 Chr. 9. 25) the original account, which was properly incorporated in *ch.* 10 (see *note* on *ch.* 9. 10–*ch.* 10. 29), probably ran as follows:—וַיֶּאֱסֹף שְׁלֹמֹה רֶכֶב וּפָרָשִׁים וַיְהִי לִשְׁלֹמֹה אַרְבַּעַת אֲלָפִים אֻרְוֹת סוּסִים לְמֶרְכָּבוֹ וַיְהִי־לוֹ אֶלֶף וְאַרְבַּע־מֵאוֹת רֶכֶב וּשְׁנֵים עָשָׂר אֶלֶף פָּרָשִׁים וַיַּנְחֵם בְּעָרֵי הָרֶכֶב וְעִם הַמֶּלֶךְ בִּירוּשָׁלִָם׃. Here the smaller number 4,000 is adopted in accordance with LXX and ‖ 2 Chr. 9. 25. The mention of the number of chariots is not found in LXX, Luc.,

but is agreeable to the reference to the ערי הרכב which follows. וַיַּנִּיחֵם of ‖ 2 Chr. in place of וַיַּנְחֵם has the support of all Verss.

27. את הכסף] Before these words LXX, Luc. insert τὸ χρυσίον καί—a later and unwarranted insertion.

בשפלה] Always (except Josh. 11. 16 שְׁפֵלָתֹה with suff.) with def. art. '*the* Lowland,' i.e. the tract of low hills or 'downs' lying between the maritime plain of Philistia and the mountain-country of Judah, and separated from the latter 'by a series of valleys, both wide and narrow, which run all the way from Ajalon to Beer-sheba.' Cf. Smith, *Geogr.* ch. x.

28. ומוצא וג׳] It may be regarded as certain that a place-name underlies the obscure מקוה. So LXX, Luc. ἐκ Θεκουε, for which Field cites a variant ἐκ Κωά. Eusebius (*Onom.*) Κώδ, πλησίον Αἰγύπτου is rendered by Jerome *Coa, quae est juxta Aegyptum*, and so Vulg. translates מקוה *de Coa.* Lenormant (*Les origines de l'histoire*, iii. 9) was the first to make identification with *Kuë*, i.e. the plain of Cilicia. The same discovery was independently arrived at by Winckler (*Alttest. Untersuchungen*, 168 *ff.*; cf. *Altoriental. Forschungen*, i. 28) together with its complement, viz. that מצרים does not in our passage denote Egypt, but the North Syrian land of *Muṣri*, south of the Taurus, which often figures in Assyrian inscriptions. The horse, which was unknown in Egypt before B.C. 1700–1500, can scarcely ever have been bred in sufficient numbers for wholesale exportation, while the pastures of N. Syria and Cilicia must have been eminently suited for breeding upon a large scale. With this agrees the statement of Ezek. 27. 14 that Israel derived horses, chargers, and mules not from Egypt but from *Togarmah*, i.e. N. Syria and Asia Minor. We may therefore render: 'And Solomon's import of horses was from Muṣri (perhaps מִמִּצְרִי or מִמֻּצָר) and from Kuë (וּמִקְּוֵה); the king's traders received them from Kuë at a price.' So Hommel (*Gesch. Babyl.* 610), Benz., Kit. On Muṣri see further, II. 7. 6. König (*Fünf neue arab. Landschaftsnamen im A. T.* 25) agrees as to Kuë, but thinks that the fact that Solomon supplied horses for the Hittites and Aramaeans is inexplicable if they were obtained

from North Syria, but natural if they came from Egypt. It must be noticed also that Deut. 17. 16 connects the supply of horses with Egypt. Cf. Isa. 31. 1.

‖ 2 Chr. 9. 28 ומוציאים סוסים ממצרים לשלמה ומכל הארצות. 2 Chr. 1. 16 as in Kings, but with מקוא (i. e. perhaps מִקְּוֹא) for מקוה.

29. בשש מאות . . . בחמשים ומאה] LXX, Luc. ἀντὶ ἑκατὸν . . . ἀντὶ πεντήκοντα. In ‖ 2 Chr. 1. 17 LXX, Luc. agree with MT.

לכל מלכי החתים] Cf. II. 7. 6 *note*.

בידם יצאו] LXX, Luc. κατὰ θάλασσαν ἐξεπορεύοντο, i. e. בַּיָּם יֵצְאוּ, inferior to M. T.

11. 1–13. *Solomon's foreign wives, and his idolatry.*

This section in its present form is coloured by the hand of R^D. His phrases are as follow:—

2. אשר אמר וג׳] The reference is to Deut. 7. 1–4; Ex. 34. 12–16 (J). Cf. Josh. 23. 7 (D^2).

בהם דבק] The same phrase is used with reference to the חטאות ירבעם II. 3. 3 (R^D). With reference to Yahwe it occurs in Deut. 4. 4 (adj. הַדְּבֵקִים); 10. 20; 11. 22; 13. 5; 30. 20; Josh. 22. 5; 23. 8 (both D^2); II. 18. 6 (R^D).

4. אלהים אחרים] Cf. *ch.* 9. 6 *note*.

ולא היה לבבו שלם וג׳] Cf. *ch.* 8. 61 *note*.

כלבב דויד אביו] Cf. *ch.* 3. 14 *note* on כאשר הלך דויד.

5. וילך ש׳ אחרי] So, of following a false god, *v.* 10; *ch.* 21. 26; II. 17. 15 (all R^D); *ch.* 18. 18, 21; Deut. 4. 3; 6. 14; 8. 19; 11. 28; 13. 3; 28. 14; Judg. 2. 12, 19 (Deut. compiler); Jer. 2. 5, 23; 7. 9; 11. 10; 13. 10; 16. 11; 25. 6; 35. 15; Ezek. 20. 16; cf. Hos. 2. 7, 15†. Of following Yahwe *ch.* 14. 8 (R^D); 18. 21; Deut. 13. 5; 2 Chr. 34. 31; Hos. 11. 10†.

6. ויעש ש׳ הרע בעיני י׳] So *ch.* 14. 22; 15. 26, 34; 16. 19, 25, 30; 21. 20, 25; 22. 53; II. 3. 2; 8. 18, 27; 13. 2, 11; 14. 24; 15. 9, 18, 24, 28; 17. 2, 17; 21. 2, 6, 15, 16, 20; 23. 32, 37; 24. 9, 19 (all R^D or R^{D2}); 2 Chr. 21. 6; 22. 4; 29. 6; 33. 2, 6, 22; 36. 5, 9, 12; Num. 32. 13 (JE); Deut. 4. 25; 9. 18; 17. 2; 31. 29; Judg. 2. 11; 3. 7, 12; 4. 1; 6. 1; 10. 6; 13. 1 (all Deut. compiler); 1 Sam. 15. 19; Jer. 52. 2†. Cf. 2 Sam. 12. 9; Isa. 65. 12; 66. 4; Jer. 32. 30; Ps. 51. 6.

ולא מלא אחרי י׳] Deut. 1. 36; Josh. 14. 8, 9, 14 (JE recast by D^2); Num. 32. 11, 12 (JE)†.

9. ויתאנף] II. 17. 18 (R^D); Deut. 1. 37; 4. 21; 9. 8, 20†.
י׳ אלהי ישראל] Cf. *ch.* 8. 15 *note.*

11. ולא שמרת . . . חקתי] Cf. *ch.* 2. 3 *note.*

12. למען דוד אביך] Cf. *v.* 13 למען דוד עבדי; so *vv.* 32, 34; 15. 4; II. 8. 19; 19. 34; 20. 6 (all R^D)†.

13. למען ירושלם אשר בחרתי] Cf. *ch.* 8. 16 *note.*

The view that the latter portion of this section is not earlier than the exile (R^{D2}; so Kue. *vv.* 9–13, Kamp., Benz., Kit. *vv.* 9, 10) is based upon the words of *v.* 9 הנראה אליו פעמים, and presupposes that the narrative of the second vision, *ch.* 9. 1–9, comes from the hand of R^{D2}; but upon this opinion see *note ad loc.* On the other hand, the fact that *vv.* 11–13 speak of a division of the kingdom but make no mention of an exile, favours their pre-exilic authorship.

1–8. LXX, Luc. arrange differently. After the first four words of *v.* 1 והמלך ש׳ אהב נשים there follows *v.* 3^a; then the remainder of *v.* 1 in the form וַיִּקַּח נשים נכריות וג׳, and with the addition Σύρας אֲרַמִּיּוֹת after עמוניות, καὶ Ἀμορραίας וַאֱמֹרִיּוֹת after חתית, and omission of צדנית; *v.* 2; *v.* $4^{a\alpha}$ ויהי לעת זקנת ש׳ followed by *v.* 4^b ולא היה לבבו וג׳; *vv.* 3^b, $4^{a\beta}$ represented by וַיַּטּוּ נָשָׁיו הַנָּכְרִיּוֹת אֶת־לְבָבוֹ אַחֲרֵי אֱלֹהֵיהֶן; *v.* 7 with εἰδώλῳ, i.e. אֱלֹהֵי, for שקץ in both cases and omitting בהר אשר על פני ירושלם, followed by *v.* 5^a in the form וּלְעַשְׁתֹּרֶת תּוֹעֲבַת צִדֹנִים; *v.* 8 where for מקטירות וג׳, LXX ἐθυμίων καὶ ἔθυον κ.τ.λ., Luc. reads ἐθυμία καὶ ἔθυε κ.τ.λ., i.e. מַקְטִיר וּמְזַבֵּחַ וג׳; *v.* 6.

This arrangement is, in the main, correct. The general allusion to Solomon's love of women leads on to the fact that many of his wives belonged to the neighbouring nations with whom intercourse was strictly forbidden, and that these wives turned away his heart after their strange gods. After mention in some detail of the concessions which the king made to their religious rites, the writer sums up by saying that Solomon did evil in the sight of Yahwe, and did not walk after Yahwe like David his father. This forms a natural and appropriate transition to *v.* 9 ויתאנף וג׳.

The following points call for special notice:—

The mention of the number of wives and concubines *v.* 3^{a} is no part of the original account, but is an addition from the margin which has come into MT. and LXX in a different position, and thus to some extent accounts for their variation in arrangement.

The words ויקח נשים of *v.* 1 have been omitted in MT. through homoioteleuton.

ואת בת פרעה '*and* the daughter of Pharaoh,' i. e. '*and also*,' or, as RV. marg., '*beside*.' Pharaoh's daughter is introduced not as a crowning instance, but rather as *not* falling under the count which is brought against Solomon, since she was not מן הגוים אשר אמר וג׳, i. e. the neighbouring nations whose territory fell within Solomon's dominions. Probably, however, the words are a later interpolation suggested by the mention of foreign wives and referring back to *ch.* 3. 1.

In the category of foreign wives *v.* 1^{b}, LXX Σύρας ארמית is merely a doublet of אדמית. Καὶ Ἀμορραίας ואמריות *may* be original, since there is no special reason for its insertion unless it be a third representation of אדמית. צדנית is omitted through oversight. *Vv.* 3^{b}, $4^{a\beta}$ are a repetition of the same fact accounted for by the insertion at this point in MT. of *v.* 3^{a} from the margin.

LXX is correct in making the apodosis of the sentence ולא היה וג׳ after the time-determination ויהי לעת וג׳, and in then continuing with ויטו. The reading אלהיהן (from *v.* 2^{a}) is, however, inferior to אלהים אחרים of MT.

בהר אשר על פני ירושלם *v.* 7 is a detail added by a later hand. LXX in reading אלהי for שקץ in this verse is more original, but the opposite change in *v.* 5, תּוֹעֲבַת (שקוץ) for אלהי, is probably a later alteration; cf. *note* on *v.* 33.

In *v.* 8^{b} Luc. supplies the original text. *Solomon himself* burnt incense and offered sacrifice to the strange gods, but this fact has been toned down by some later hand into the statement of MT. Syntax, however, has suffered in the process (we should expect at least הַמַּקְטִירוֹת וְהַמְזַבְּחוֹת). On the other hand, the original מקטיר וג׳,

determining the subject of עשה, is perfectly regular in construction; cf. e.g. Jer. 2. 26, 27; 17. 25.

Accordingly, the original narrative of R^D probably ran as follows:—

וְהַמֶּלֶךְ שְׁלֹמֹה אֹהֵב נָשִׁים וַיִּקַּח נָשִׁים נָכְרִיּוֹת רַבּוֹת מֹאֲבִיּוֹת עַמּוֹנִיּוֹת
אֲדֹמִיֹּת צִדֹנִיֹּת חִתִּיֹּת [וַאֲמֹרִיּוֹת]. מִן־הַגּוֹיִם אֲשֶׁר אָמַר י׳ אֶל־בְּנֵי יִשְׂרָאֵל
לֹא־תָבֹאוּ בָהֶם וְהֵם לֹא־יָבֹאוּ בָכֶם אָכֵן יַטּוּ אֶת־לְבַבְכֶם אַחֲרֵי אֱלֹהֵיהֶם בָּהֶם
דָּבַק שְׁלֹמֹה לְאַהֲבָה. וַיְהִי לְעֵת זִקְנַת שְׁלֹמֹה וְלֹא־הָיָה לְבָבוֹ שָׁלֵם עִם־י׳
אֱלֹהָיו כִּלְבַב דָּוִד אָבִיו וַיַּטּוּ נָשָׁיו אֶת־לְבָבוֹ אַחֲרֵי אֱלֹהִים אֲחֵרִים. אָז
יִבְנֶה שְׁלֹמֹה בָּמָה לִכְמוֹשׁ אֱלֹהֵי מוֹאָב וּלְמִלְכֹּם אֱלֹהֵי בְּנֵי עַמּוֹן וּלְעַשְׁתֹּרֶת
אֱלֹהֵי צִדֹנִים. וְכֵן עָשָׂה לְכָל־נָשָׁיו מַקְטִיר וּמְזַבֵּחַ לֵאלֹהֵיהֶן. וַיַּעַשׂ שְׁלֹמֹה
הָרַע בְּעֵינֵי י׳ וְלֹא מִלֵּא אַחֲרֵי י׳ כְּדָוִד אָבִיו.

'Now King Solomon was a lover of women; and he took many strange wives, Moabites, Ammonites, Edomites, Zidonians, Hittites [and Amorites]; of the nations whereof Yahwe said unto the children of Israel, Ye shall not go among them, neither shall they come among you; for surely they will turn away your heart after their gods: Solomon clave unto these in love. And it came to pass, when Solomon was old, that his heart was not perfect with Yahwe his God like the heart of David his father; but his wives turned away his heart after other gods. Then did Solomon build a high place for Chemosh the god of Moab, and for Milcom the god of the children of Ammon, and for Ashtoreth the goddess of the Zidonians. And so did he for all his wives, burning incense and offering sacrifice to their gods. And Solomon did that which was evil in the sight of Yahwe, and went not fully after Yahwe, as did David his father.'

1. צֵדְנִיֹּת] From masc. sing. צִדוֹנִי Ezek. 32. 30; Judg. 3. 3, pl. צִדוֹנִים *v.* 5; *al.*, would naturally be formed fem. sing. צִדוֹנִית, pl. צִדוֹנִיּוֹת; and doubtless this last was the original pronunciation in our passage. For the Massoretic punctuation cf. Q're in Neh. 13. 23 אַשְׁדֳּדִיּוֹת עַמֳּנִיּוֹת, where Kt. is אַשְׁדּוֹדִיּוֹת עַמּוֹנִיּוֹת.

2. אכן] A strong asseveration, '*Surely*.' LXX, Luc. *μή*, Pesh. ܕܠܡܐ, Targ. דילמא suggest פֶּן־ (so Klo.), but this rendering is

merely an accommodation to the context, and weakens the force of the statement.

לאהבה] ל of reference defining the manner of the verb דבק. אהבה is the substantive, not the Infinitive construct.

3. ויהי לו נשים] The verb coming at the beginning of the sentence takes the 3rd masc. sing. as the simplest form, although really predicate to the pl. fem. subj. נשים. This constr. is not infrequent; cf. Gen. 1. 14 יְהִי מְאֹרֹת, but following the subj. once named וְהָיוּ וגו׳. So in *v.* 3[b] ויטו נשיו masc. pl. predicate precedes fem. pl. subj. Cf. Ew. § 316[a]; Da. § 113[b].

5. עשתרת אלהי צדנים] So *v.* 33. For this application of the term אלהים to a *goddess* cf. Phoen. לאלי עשתרת '*deo suo Astartae*' *CIS.* I. i. 4; Baethgen, *Semit. Relig.* p. 71.

7. אז יבנה] Cf. *ch.* 3. 16 *note.*

9. הַנִּרְאָה] Intended by the punctuators to represent a 3rd sing. *perfect* Niph. with the article used with relatival force; cf. Isa. 56. 3 הַנִּלְוָה. This construction of art. with perf. is well known in late Hebrew; e.g. 1 Chr. 26. 28 הַהִקְדִּישׁ; 29. 17 הַנִּמְצְאוּ; *al.;* but it is very noticeable that in classical Hebrew the only occurrences depend *upon the vocalization or accentuation*, and if this be altered we obtain the common construction of the participle with the article. So here הַנִּרְאֶה (as in Gen. 12. 7; 35. 1), Isa. 56. 3 הַנִּלְוֶה; and with forms of ע״ו verbs accented as 3rd fem. perf., Gen. 18. 21; 46. 27 הַבָּאָה, Isa. 51. 10 הַשָּׂמָה, *al.*, where change of accentuation gives הַבָּאָה, הַשָּׂמָה, 3rd fem. participle with article. We never meet with pl. forms הַנִּרְאוּ, הַבָּאוּ, where the constr. depends *upon the consonants*, except in the single instance Josh. 10. 24 הֶהָלְכוּא which may well be a corruption of הַהֹלְכִים. Hence it is reasonable to think that this construction of perf. with art. was unknown to early Hebrew, and that all supposed occurrences rest merely upon a theory of the punctuators.

The solitary instance of the article used as relative with a *preposition*, הֶעָלֶיהָ 'that which was on it,' 1 Sam. 9. 24, is probably a textual error. See Da. § 22 *Rem.* 4; Ew. § 331[b], 1; and especially Dri. *Sam.* I. 9. 24.

10. וצוה] The use of the perfect with waw *simplex* is an irregularity which cannot here be justified. In view of the vocalization of הַנִּרְאָה the participle in the previous verse as a perfect (see *note*), it seems possible that here also a change to the perfect may have been effected later, and that we should restore וּמְצַוֶּה in continuation of הַנִּרְאָה. So Klo.

ולא שמר] LXX *καὶ φυλάξασθαι ποιῆσαι*, Luc. *καὶ φυλάξαι καὶ ποιῆσαι*, i. e. וְלִשְׁמֹר לַעֲשׂוֹת—correct; cf. II. 17. 37; 21. 8. MT. is an easy alteration under the influence of ולא שמרת *v.* 11.

צוה] LXX, Luc., Vulg., Pesh. appear to presuppose צִוָּהוּ 'had commanded *him*,' but the addition of the suffix pronoun is not really necessary, and may be regarded as a natural translator's addition.

LXX, Luc. add to the end of the verse *οὐδ'* (Luc. *οὐκ*) *ἦν ἡ καρδία αὐτοῦ τελεία μετὰ Κυρίου κατὰ τὴν καρδίαν Δαυεὶδ τοῦ πατρὸς αὐτοῦ*, a gloss from *v.* 4.

11. עמך] '*With* thee,' i. e. 'in thy *thought*,' or, more fully, as referring to an action carried into effect, 'to be taken into reckoning in estimating thy *character*.' Cf. Job 10. 13 ידעתי כי זאת עמך parallel to ואלה צפנת בלבך; 23. 14; 27. 11; cf. Num. 14. 24.

בריתי וחקתי] LXX, Luc. *τὰς ἐντολάς μου καὶ τὰ προστάγματά μου*, i. e. מִצְוֹתַי וְחֻקֹּתַי; Cod. A. *τὰ προστάγματά μου καὶ τὰς ἐντολάς μου*, Pesh. ܡܠܬܝ ܘܢܡܘܣܝ ܘܦܘܩܕܢ̈ܝ, i. e., supposing ܡܠܬܝ to be an error for ܩܝܡܝ, בריתי וחקתי ומצותי. These variations in order seem to indicate that מצותי is a later addition made first upon the margin as being a word often coupled with חקתי.

12. אקרענה] LXX, Luc. *λήμψομαι αὐτήν*, i. e. אֶקָּחֶנָּה; so *v.* 13 אקרע LXX, Luc. *λάβω*, Vulg. *auferam*, i. e. אֶקַּח. This reading, as agreeing better with the phrase מיד בנך *v.* 12 (*v.* 11 קרע מעליך . . . אקרע), and according with *vv.* 34, 35, is to be adopted.

11. 14–25. *Solomon's adversaries; Hadad the Edomite and Rezon the Syrian.*

14–22. The narrative in its present form seems to be somewhat confused. Hadad, though but 'a little lad' at the time of his flight into Egypt, at once finds favour with Pharaoh, and receives from him a house, an allowance, and land. He then, in spite of his extreme youth, marries the sister of Pharaoh's queen Tahpenes, and his son Genubath is brought up in the palace together with Pharaoh's sons. The form אדד *v.* 17, as a variation of הדד, creates further suspicion as to the integrity of the narrative.

Winckler (*Alttest. Untersuchungen*, 1 *ff.*) believes that two accounts have here been interwoven, and attempts the task of unravelling the skein by the aid of a discriminating use of LXX. Winckler's two narratives run as follows:—

14 ויקם יהוה שטן לשלמה
את הדד האדמי מזרע
15 a^{α}, b^{β} המלוכה באדום. ויהי
בהכרית דוד את אדום
17 *b* ויך כל זכר באדום והדד
נער קטן. [ויקחהו אחד
17 a^{β} מעבדי אביו [ויביאהו
מצרימה אל פרעה.]
19 וימצא הדד חן בעיני פרעה
מאד ויתנהו לתחפנים
20 a^{β} אשתו הגבירה ותגדלהו
20 b^{β} בתוך בית פרעה בתוך
21 בני פרעה. וישמע הדד
במצרים כי שכב דוד עם
אבתיו ויאמר אל פרעה
שלחני ואלך אל ארצי.
22 ויאמר לו פרעה כי מה
אתה חסר עמי והנך
מבקש ללכת אל ארצך
ויאמר לו כי שלח תשלחני
וישב הדד אל ארצו.

ויהי בעלות יואב שר 15 a^{β}
הצבא לקבר את החללים
כי ששת חדשים ישב שם 16 *a*
יואב וכל ישראל [ויכו
את כל אדום עַד־כַּלֵּה.]
ויברח אדד הוא ואנשים 17 a^{α}
אדמיים אתו לבוא מצרים. 17 a^{γ}
ויקמו ממדין ויבאו פארן 18
ויקחו אנשים עמם מפארן
ויבאו מצרים אל פרעה
ויתן לו בית ולחם אמר
לו וארץ נתן לו. ויתן 19 *b*
לו אשה את אנות אחות
תחפנים. ותלד לו את 20 a^{α}*
גנבת בנו ויהי גנבת בית 20 b^{α}
פרעה.

'And Yahwe raised up an adversary unto Solomon, Hadad the Edomite, of the royal seed in Edom. And it came to pass, when David cut off Edom, and smote every male in Edom, that Hadad was a little lad. [And one] of his father's servants [took him, and brought him into Egypt unto Pharaoh]. And Hadad found great favour in the sight of Pharaoh, and he gave him to Tahpenes his chief wife, and she brought him up in Pharaoh's house among the sons of Pharaoh. And Hadad heard in Egypt that David slept with his fathers, and he said to Pharaoh, Let me depart, that I may go to my own country. And Pharaoh said to him, What hast thou lacked with me, that, behold, thou seekest to go to thine own country? And he said to him, Let me in any wise depart. So Hadad returned to his own land.'

'And it came to pass, when Joab the captain of the host was gone up to bury the slain, that he remained there six months, even Joab and all Israel, [and they smote all Edom until they had utterly destroyed them]. And Adad fled, he and certain Edomites with him, to go into Egypt. And they arose out of Midian, and came to Paran; and they took men with them out of Paran, and they came to Egypt, unto Pharaoh. And he gave him a house, and appointed him victuals, and gave him land. And he gave him to wife Anoth the sister of Tahpenes. And she bare him Genubath his son; and Genubath lived in the house of Pharaoh.'

In the first narrative the *Edomite* Hadad is carried into Egypt by his father's servant, and brought up by Pharaoh's queen. The second account seems to make Adad a *Midianite* prince, who flees with his adherents into Egypt, taking with him certain Edomites[1]

[1] אנשים ארמיים. Had Adad and his followers been Edomites, such a specification would here have been unnecessary.

from Paran, and is well received by Pharaoh, who gives him for wife Anoth the sister of his queen. A son, Genubath, is born to him, but of his fate we are not informed. Winckler conjectures that just as the two accounts exhibit similarity in their commencement with David's campaign against Edom and in the allied names Hadad, Adad, so the conclusion of the second may have resembled that of the first in relating the journeying of Genubath from Egypt into Midian the land of his father, and his there establishing himself as an adversary to Solomon.

In the two accounts the following portions of MT. are rejected as glosses:—

(i.) *v.* $20^{a\beta}$ תחפנים, *v.* 21^{a} וכי מת יואב שר הצבא (introduced in accordance with *v.* 15 by the welder of the two narratives), *v.* 21^{b} הדד.

(ii.) *v.* 18^{b} מלך מצרים.

The sentences enclosed in square brackets are supplied by conjecture.

Words overlined are emendations dependent upon LXX, as follow:—

v. 14. מלך הוא] LXX τῆς βασιλείας = הַמְּלוּכָה. So Klo., Benz.

v. 15. בהיות] LXX ἐν τῷ ἐξολοθρεύειν = בְּהַכְּרִית. So Klo., Kamp. Pesh. ܒܡܚܬ = בְּהַכּוֹת adopted by Bö., Th., Benz., Oort.

v. 20^{a}. ותגמלהו] LXX καὶ ἐξέθρεψεν αὐτόν = וַתְּגַדְּלֵהוּ. So Klo., Benz.

v. 22 end] LXX adds καὶ ἀνέστρεψεν Ἀδὲρ εἰς τὴν γῆν αὐτοῦ = וַיָּשָׁב הֲדַד אֶל־אַרְצוֹ.

v. 19^{b}. ויתן לו וג׳] Here ויתנהו לתחפנים is restored by conjecture in (i.). The name אנות in (ii.) is derived from LXX, Luc. *ch.* 12. 24^{e} καὶ Σουσακεὶμ ἔδωκεν τῷ Ἰεροβοὰμ τὴν Ἀνὼ ἀδελφὴν Θεκεμείνας τὴν πρεσβυτέραν (Luc. adds ἀδελφὴν) τῆς γυναικὸς αὐτοῦ εἰς γυναῖκα· (Luc. καὶ) αὕτη ἦν μεγάλη ἐν μέσῳ τῶν θυγατέρων τοῦ βασιλέως, καὶ ἔτεκεν τῷ Ἰεροβοὰμ τὸν Ἀβιὰ υἱὸν αὐτοῦ, a statement which occurs in the midst of the account of Jeroboam. Winckler considers the question whether this passage (obviously correspondent to MT.

ch. 11. 19[b], 20[a 1]) belongs properly to the Hadad or to the Jeroboam narrative, and concludes that the recurrence of the name Ἀνώ in *ch.* 12. 24 [g, k, l] (=MT. *ch.* 14. 2, 8, 9) makes for the latter view, but may be due to interpolation in accordance with *ch.* 12. 24[e]; while, on the other hand, the obviously incorrect position[2] of the account in LXX, and the supposition that Pharaoh would more reasonably have given his queen's sister as wife to a Midianite *prince* than to an Israelite *rebel,* are conclusively in favour of the former.

14. שטן] Cf. *ch.* 5. 18 *note.*

16. עד הִכרית] Cf. II. 3. 25 *note* on עד הִשאיר.

18. ולחם אמר לו] '*Assigned* or *appointed* him an allowance.' So exactly 2 Chr. 29. 24 כי לכל ישראל אמר המלך העולה והחטאת 'because for all Israel had the king appointed the burnt-offering and the sin-offering.' The same construction is common in Ar., where, however, the object is always connected with ب, which is said to strengthen the government of the verb, acting as an emphatic representation of the accusative; e.g. أَمَرَ لَهُ بِدِرْهَمٍ 'He assigned him a *dirhem* (piece of money).' Pesh., mistaking this *nuance* of אמר, connects ולחם closely with the previous ויתן לו בית, and supplies after אמר לו the words which Pharaoh is supposed to have spoken:—ܘܝܗܒ ܠܗ ܒܝܬܐ ܘܡܣܝܒܪܢܘܬܐ. ܘܐܡܪ ܠܗ. ܬܒ ܠܘܬܝ 'and he gave him a house and an allowance, and said to him, Dwell with me!'

19. הגבירה] Here '*the queen.*' In *ch.* 15. 13; ‖ 2 Chr. 15. 16 גבירה is used of the *queen-mother.* The other occurrences of the word are II. 10. 13; Jer. 13. 18; 29. 2†, where it is not clear whether the reference is to the queen or to the queen-mother. גבירה properly denotes the '*chief lady*' of the harem, and Bö. is

---

[1] *αὕτη ἦν μεγάλη κ.τ.λ.* answers to *v.* 20[a] read as וַתִּגְדַּל הִיא בְּתוֹךְ בְּנוֹת הַמֶּלֶךְ וַתֵּלֶד וג׳.

[2] Jeroboam hears of Solomon's death, and asks leave to return to Ephraim (*v.* 34 or 24[d]); but Pharaoh, instead of granting his request, marries him to Anoth, by whom he has a son (*vv.* 35–37 or 24[d, e]). After this Jeroboam makes a fresh effort to depart, and, in spite of the delay, returns in time to be created king of Israel at the rebellion upon Rehoboam's accession.

probably correct in assuming that this position would be usually occupied by the queen-mother, but, in the event of her death or removal, by the chief wife or queen. Cf. also Benz. There is no reason for thinking, with Klo., Kamp., Kit., that גבירה must always mean 'queen-mother,' and therefore emending הַבְּכִירָה after LXX, Luc. *ch.* 12. 24[e] τὴν πρεσβυτέραν. In *ch.* 11. 19, LXX τῆς μείζω, Luc. τὴν μείζω, i. e. הַגְּדוֹלָה, is also inferior to MT.

20. גנבת] On the form of the name cf. *note* on טפת *ch.* 4. 11.

21. כי שכב וג׳] So Gen. 47. 30; 2 Sam. 7. 12. Elsewhere (23 times in Kings and 10 times in ‖ 2 Chr.) the phrase forms part of the formula of R^D in concluding his notice of a reign.

22. כי מה אתה וג׳] Not as RV. '*But* what hast thou lacked,' &c. כי, as in the second half of the verse כי שלח תשלחני, simply introduces the direct oration. See *ch.* 1. 13 *note*.

לא] Read Q're לוֹ. לא cannot mean 'nothing,' RV., and '*Nay* but,' &c., is inappropriate as an answer to the question.

23–25. LXX, Luc. omit *vv.* 23–25$^{a\,\alpha}$ (down to שלמה), and then, in place of the impossible MT., continue αὕτη ἡ κακία ἣν ἐποίησεν 'Αδέρ· καὶ ἐβαρυθύμησεν (Luc. ἐβαρύνθη ἐπὶ) 'Ισραήλ, καὶ ἐβασίλευσεν ἐν τῇ (Luc. γῇ) 'Εδώμ, i. e. זֹאת הָרָעָה אֲשֶׁר עָשָׂה הֲדַד וַיָּקָץ בְּיִשְׂרָאֵל וַיִּמְלֹךְ עַל־אֱדֹם 'This is the evil which Hadad did; and he abhorred Israel, and reigned over Edom[1].' This is correct both in reading and position, referring as it does the latter part of *v.* 25 to Hadad, and adding the necessary summary as to his relationship to Solomon. So Klo., Benz., Kit., Oort. The definiteness of the statement זאת הרעה suggests that in the original narrative some explicit account of Hadad's aggressions must have intervened after *v.* 22.

The short reference to Rezon, thus omitted by LXX, Luc., has been inserted between *vv.* 14[a] and 14[b], but clearly by a later hand. So placed, it breaks the connexion of the Hadad story, and necessitates the resumption καὶ 'Αδὲρ ὁ 'Ιδουμαῖος 14[b], repeated

---

[1] Vulg. agrees with LXX in reading *et hoc est malum Adad*, but with MT. in the position of the notice concerning Rezon, and in reading אֲרָם for אֱדֹם.

from 14[a]. The notice is ancient and genuine[1], but its original position cannot now be accurately determined.

23. רזון] See note on חֶזְיוֹן *ch.* 15. 18.

24. גדוד] Generally a *marauding band;* II. 5. 2; 6. 23; 13. 20, 21; 24. 2; 1 Sam. 30. 8, 15, 23; *al.* So, of the *foray* made by such a band, 2 Sam. 3. 22. The word is perhaps used of more regular detachments of an army 2 Sam. 4. 2; but this use seems generally to be late—1 Chr. 7. 4; 2 Chr. 25. 9, 10, 13; 26. 11.

בהרג דוד אתם] LXX, Luc. omit. The statement is probably a gloss from the margin, referring to *v.* 23[b]. So Klo., Winckler (*Alttest. Untersuchungen*, p. 60), Benz. In place of אתם read אֲרָם with Klo., Benz.

25. ויקץ] So, of racial hostility, Ex. 1. 12; Num. 22. 3, followed in both places by מִפְּנֵי, expressing dislike.

11. 26—14. 20. *History of Jeroboam.*

Ch. 11. 26–43 properly belongs to the section of 1 Kings, *chh.* 3. 1—11. 43, which deals with the reign of Solomon. See summary at head of *ch.* 3. Since, however, the history of Jeroboam commences with *v.* 26, it is convenient at this point to consider the structure of the narrative. The arrangement of events in LXX, Luc. presents a striking variation from that of MT., as may be best seen by a parallel summary of the two accounts.

MT.	LXX.
11. 26. Jeroboam, an Ephraimite of Zeredah, son of a widow, comes into prominence in connexion with Solomon's building operations at Jerusalem.	
11. 29. He is marked out as future king of the ten tribes by the prophet Aḥijah.	
11. 40. Solomon seeks to kill Jeroboam, who takes flight into Egypt, where he stays until the death of Solomon.	
11. 41. Death and burial of Solomon.	

[1] A notice so straightforward and unembellished can scarcely be thought (Kit. *Hist. Heb.* ii. 53) merely to have grown up out of the *lapsus calami* אֲרָם for אֱדֹם.

<table>
<tr><th>MT.</th><th>LXX.</th></tr>
<tr><td></td><td>11. 43. Jeroboam returns so soon as he hears of Solomon's death, and settles in Zeredah.
Repeated notice of Solomon's death. Reḥoboam succeeds him.</td></tr>
<tr><td colspan="2">12. 1. Reḥoboam goes to Shechem to be crowned by all Israel.</td></tr>
<tr><td>12. 2. Jeroboam returns from Egypt upon the news of Reḥoboam's accession.</td><td></td></tr>
<tr><td>12. 3. The people of Israel summon him, and he and all Israel come and lay their grievances before Reḥoboam.</td><td>12. 3. The people (without Jeroboam) come and lay their grievances before Reḥoboam.</td></tr>
<tr><td colspan="2">12. 5. Reḥoboam, after asking a delay of three days, decides to answer the people harshly and to add to their burdens.</td></tr>
<tr><td>12. 12. Jeroboam and all the people come to Reḥoboam upon the third day to receive his answer.</td><td>12. 12. All Israel (without Jeroboam) come to Reḥoboam upon the third day to receive his answer.</td></tr>
<tr><td colspan="2">12. 13. Reḥoboam's answer results in the revolt of all Israel except the tribe of Judah</td></tr>
<tr><td></td><td>and Benjamin.</td></tr>
<tr><td colspan="2">12. 20. All Israel, when they hear of Jeroboam's return, send for him and make him their king.</td></tr>
<tr><td colspan="2">12. 21. Reḥoboam goes to Jerusalem, and assembles all Judah and Benjamin to fight against Jeroboam, but is restrained by the word of God through the prophet Shemaiah.</td></tr>
<tr><td></td><td>12. 24[a]. Repeated notice of Solomon's death and of Reḥoboam's accession. His age at accession, length of his reign, and his mother's name. Verdict as to his character.</td></tr>
<tr><td></td><td>12. 24[b]. Repeated introduction to Jeroboam;—an Ephraimite, son of a harlot. Solomon advances him.</td></tr>
</table>

MT.

LXX.

12. 24[b]. Notice of Solomon's building operations, and of his chariots.

12. 24[c]. Solomon seeks to kill Jeroboam, who flees into Egypt, where he remains until the death of Solomon.

12. 24[d]. Jeroboam hears of Solomon's death, and asks leave of Pharaoh to return to his own country. Pharaoh, instead of granting the request, gives him his daughter Anoth as wife. She bears him Abijah.

12. 24[f]. Jeroboam renews his request to return to Ephraim, and leaving Egypt arrives at Zeredah, where he gathers all the tribes of Ephraim, and builds a fort.

12. 24[g]. Jeroboam's son falls sick at Zeredah. He sends his wife to inquire as to the issue of the sickness. Aḥijah prophecies the death of the child and the utter extirpation of Jeroboam's posterity (but without assigning any cause).

12. 24[n]. Jeroboam goes to Shechem, and gathers the tribes of Israel against the arrival of Reḥoboam.

12. 24[o]. Shemaiah the prophet marks out Jeroboam as future king of the ten tribes.

12. 24[p]. The people lay their grievances before Reḥoboam, who, after asking a delay of three days, decides to answer the people roughly and to add to their burdens.

12. 24[t]. Revolt of all Israel except the tribes of Judah and Benjamin.

12. 24[x]. Reḥoboam assembles all Judah and Benjamin to fight against Jeroboam, but is restrained by the

MT. | LXX.

word of Yahwe through the prophet Shemaiah.

12. 25. Jeroboam builds Shechem and Penuel.

12. 26. His calf-worship at Bethel and Dan a measure to prevent the return of Israel to the house of David.

13. 1. The narrative concerning the prophet who came from Judah to rebuke Jeroboam.

13. 33. In spite of this Jeroboam maintains his worship, and thus seals the doom of his house.

14. 1. Jeroboam's son falls sick at Tirzah. He causes his wife to disguise herself, and sends her to inquire of Aḥijah as to the issue of the sickness. She is at once recognized by Aḥijah, who prophecies the death of the child and the utter extirpation of Jeroboam's posterity, because of 'the sins of Jeroboam,' i. e. his idolatrous calf-worship.

14. 19. Death of Jeroboam; record of the length of his reign, and mention of his successor.

Here the following points are to be noticed:

1. The superiority of LXX to MT. in 11. 43—12. 24. Jeroboam would naturally return from Egypt upon the news of the death of Solomon (LXX), and would scarcely delay until he had received information of Reḥoboam's accession (MT.; read in 12. 2^b וַיָּשָׁב יָרָבְעָם מִמִּצְרָיִם with ∥ 2 Chr. 10. 2). This point, however, cannot be pressed, since MT. may not be intended to represent the logical order of events. The variations in *vv.* 3^a, 12^a are more important. From *v.* 20 in both MT. and LXX it is certainly to be gathered that Jeroboam had taken no part in the previous negotiations, but that news of his return first reached the people when they were looking around for a new leader after their rejection of the house

of David. This agrees with the previous narrative in LXX, but conflicts with the statements of MT. in *vv.* 3^a, 12^a. LXX is therefore to be preferred.

2. The inconsistency of LXX 12. 24^{a-z} with LXX 11. 43—12. 24, and its inferiority to MT.

(*a*) The section is inconsistent with the previous section in LXX. Many of its notices are mere duplications of what has been previously recorded in 11. 43—12. 24. Thus the notice of Solomon's death and Reḥoboam's accession, 12. 24^a, repeats 11. 41, 43; the introduction to Jeroboam, 12. 24^b, is superfluous after 11. 26; Solomon's attempt to kill Jeroboam is a repetition of 11. 40, and comes in very awkwardly without any narrative preceding to explain the king's action; 12. 24° is merely a variation of the story of 11. 29 *ff.*, and cannot exist side by side with it; 12. 24^{p-z} answers to 12. 3–24, while the whole account in its second form is inconsistent with the first account, in representing Jeroboam as having gathered the tribes to Shechem to meet Reḥoboam 12. 24^n, and so presumably as present during the negotiations, and taking part in them.

(*b*) The section is inferior to the narrative of MT. On LXX 12. 24^{d-f} as compared with MT. 11. 19^b *ff.* see *note* on *ch.* 11. 14–22. The relative value of the two forms of the story of the sickness of Jeroboam's son admits of some difference of opinion. See, for LXX, Winckler, *Alttest. Untersuchungen*, 12 *ff.*; for MT. Kit. *Hist.* ii. 206 *f.* The variation between the two narratives is clearly too considerable to admit of the supposition that the one was derived from the other; and it seems necessary to suppose that each was drawn independently from some earlier source. Thus regarded, LXX may represent the more original form of the story, since it is easier to believe that *vv.* 7–9, 14–16 MT.[1] are a later addition than that in LXX they were purposely cut out in order to place the story at the commencement of Jeroboam's career (Kit.). It is

[1] The work of R^D. His hand, however, is also to be traced in *v.* 10, which appears in LXX. See *notes ad loc.*

certain, however, that *from the point of view of* R^D the story in MT. occupies the right position, and, as intended to exemplify God's visitation upon Jeroboam on account of the idolatry of his calf-worship, aptly closes the history of his life, and is followed, *vv.* 19, 20, by the short notice as to his death. In LXX all reference to the death of Jeroboam is lacking, a point which further argues the inferiority of the section.

The inference to be drawn from the foregoing points is that the history of Jeroboam, as it left the hand of R^D, is represented, as nearly as can be determined, by MT., LXX 11. 26–42; LXX 11. 43—12. 24; MT. 12. 25—14. 20. LXX 12. $24^{a\text{-}z}$, as both inconsistent with the previous section in LXX and inferior to MT., must be considered to be a history of Jeroboam which came independently into the hands of some copyist of the LXX, and was inserted after *ch.* 12. 24 at the expense of the omission of the original text.

The origin of the section LXX 12. $24^{a\text{-}z}$ is not clear. It may have been, and probably was, drawn in part from our Book of Kings (the recension of R^D). But, as has been noticed above, the story 12. $24^{g\text{-}n}$ appears to come from some independent source; and 12. $24^{a\text{-}f}$, composed, like the LXX insertions in *ch.* 2 after *vv.* 35, 46, of fragments which in the main can be paralleled in MT., contains a few independent statements. Thus *v.* 24^b καὶ ᾠκοδόμησεν Σαλωμὼν (Luc. Ἱεροβοὰμ τῷ Σολομῶντι) τὴν Σαρειρὰ τὴν ἐν ὄρει Ἐφράιμ, καὶ ἦσαν αὐτῷ ἅρματα τριακόσια ἵππων, and καὶ ἦν ἐπαιρόμενος ἐπὶ τὴν βασιλείαν, *v.* 24^f καὶ ἐξῆλθεν Ἱεροβοὰμ ἐξ Αἰγύπτου, καὶ ἦλθεν εἰς γῆν Σαρειρὰ τὴν ἐν ὄρει Ἐφράιμ· καὶ ᾠκοδόμησεν Ἱεροβοὰμ ἐκεῖ χάρακα. Further, the narrative of *vv.* $24^{d\text{-}f}$, though ultimately identical with MT. 11. 19 *ff.* (see *note*), must certainly have been derived from some other source than Kings.

The view of Kue. (*Ond.* § 26. 10) is that we have in this section a version of the history of Jeroboam undertaken in his interest, and thus representing him as marrying the daughter of Pharaoh, and purposely omitting a large portion of Aḥijah's prophecy against him. But, as Kit. points out, the fact that his mother is represented as a harlot, and the revolt laid at his door, is entirely alien to such a purpose[1].

11. 26–43. *Jeroboam's early career.*

11. 26. הצרדה] Only here in MT. LXX, Luc. Σαρειρά, here and in *v.* 43; 12. 24[b, f, k, l, n]. In 11. 43; 12. 24[b] Σαρειρά is said to be ἐν τῷ ὄρει Ἐφράιμ, perhaps an inference from *v.* 26. The view that צרדה is the same as צרתן (*ch.* 4. 12 *note;* 7. 46, where ‖ 2 Chr. 4. 17 has צְרֵדָתָה) is by no means certain.

In Judg. 7. 22 צְרֵרָתָה (with ה *loc.*) mentioned as the scene of the flight of the Midianites, is usually thought to be miswritten for צְרֵדָתָה, but nothing definite as to locality can be gathered from this passage, which seems to embody a confusion of sources (see Moore, *ad loc.*). Conder suggests as the site of צרדה *Ṣurda*, a small village four kilometres north-west of Bethel; *Memoirs*, ii. 295.

ושם אמו צרועה] LXX, Luc. omit, probably owing to the translator's eye passing from הצרדה to צרועה.

וירם] The ו *consec.* is here employed to introduce the predicate with some little emphasis after the words intervening between it and the subject: 'And Jeroboam, &c., *he* lifted up &c.' Cf. Gen. 30. 30 כי מעט אשר היה לך לפני ויפרץ לרב; 1 Sam. 14. 19; Dri. *Tenses*, § 127 *a*. These words are omitted in LXX, Luc. through confusion with *v.* 27[a].

27. וזה הדבר אשר] 'And this is the reason why &c.' So Josh. 5. 4 וזה הדבר אשר מל יהושע וג׳.

המלוא] *Ch.* 9. 15 *note.*

עיר דוד] *Ch.* 2. 10 *note.*

28. גבור חיל] 'A mighty man of *skill*,' i. e. 'a man of great ability.' So 1 Chr. 9. 13; cf. 1 Chr. 26. 8. So in Ruth 2. 1 (and perhaps 1 Sam. 9. 1) the phrase is used not in the special sense of great valour in battle, but of marked moral or material *worth*. Cf. *note* on חיל *ch.* 1. 42.

---

[1] Ranke takes the view that LXX 12. 24[a-z] is of superior historical value to the previous section in LXX, and to MT.; see *Weltgeschichte*, iii. 2, pp. 4–12.

29. וימצא אתו . . . בדרך] LXX, Luc. add *καὶ ἀπέστησεν αὐτὸν ἐκ τῆς ὁδοῦ*, i.e. וַיְסִירֵהוּ מִן־הַדֶּרֶךְ. The words, which are necessary in view of the following statement ושניהם לבדם בשדה, have fallen out of MT. through homoioteleuton. The motive of the action, to insure privacy, may be compared with 1 Sam. 9. 27, where Samuel causes Saul's servant to pass on before, and with II. 9. 2, where the young prophet is directed to take Jehu into חדר בחדר.

השילני] Cf. *ch.* 14. 1 *note.*

והוא] LXX, Luc., Pesh. וַאֲחִיָּה, probably original. In any case the reference is to Aḥijah (Th., Klo.) and not to Jeroboam (Ew.), the garment being assumed for the special purpose described in *v.* 30; cf. Jer. 13. 1 *ff.*; Isa. 20. 2.

ושניהם לבדם בשדה] LXX omits לבדם; Luc. reads *ἐν τῇ ὁδῷ* for בשדה. MT. correct.

31–39. Aḥijah's speech has taken its present form at the hands of R^{D}. Notice the following phrases:—

31. י׳ אלהי צבאות] Cf. *ch.* 8. 15 *note.*

32. למען דוד עבדי] So *v.* 34; cf. *v.* 12 *note.*

ירושלם העיר אשר בחרתי] So *v.* 36; cf. *ch.* 8. 16 *note.*

33. ולא הלכו בדרכי] So *v.* 38; cf. *ch.* 2. 3 *note.*

לעשות הישר בעיני] So *v.* 38; 14. 8; 15. 5, 11; 22. 43 (‖ 2 Chr. 20. 32); II. 10. 30; 12. 3 (‖ 2 Chr. 24. 2); 14. 3 (‖ 2 Chr. 25. 2); 15. 3, 34 (‖ 2 Chr. 26. 4; 27. 2); 16. 2 (‖ 2 Chr. 28. 1); 18. 3 (‖ 2 Chr. 29. 2); 22. 2 (‖ 2 Chr. 34. 2). Deut. 12. 25; 13. 19; 21. 9; and, with addition of הטוב, 6. 18; 12. 28. Elsewhere only Ex. 15. 26 (JE or D?); Jer. 34. 15. For the contrary phrase of R^{D} עשה הָרַע בעיני י׳ cf. *v.* 6 *note.*

כדוד אביו] Cf. *ch.* 3. 14 *note* on כאשר הלך דוד.

34. אשר בחרתי אתו] Cf. Deut. 17. 15 שום תשים עליך מלך אשר יבחר י׳ אלהיך בו.

36. למען היות ניר לדויד עבדי] So 15. 4; II. 8. 19 (‖ 2 Chr. 21. 7); cf. Ps. 132. 17. The figure of the unquenched lamp represents a lasting posterity; cf. Prov. 13. 9; Job 18. 6.

כל הימים] So *v.* 39; cf. *ch.* 9. 3 *note.*

לשום שמי שם] Cf. *ch.* 9. 3 *note.*

28. והיה אם תשמע] So Deut. 28. 1, 15; with pl. 11. 13; cf. 15. 5; 11. 28. In the same way (obedience the condition of a promise) כי תשמע Deut. 13. 19; 28. 2, 13; 30. 10; אשר תשמעו 11. 27.

לשמר וג׳] Cf. *ch.* 2. 3 *note.*

כאשר עשה דוד] Cf. *ch.* 3. 14 *note.*

ובניתי לך וג׳] Cf. the promise in 2 Sam. 7. 11, 16, 27 Nathan's prophecy referred to elsewhere by R^D;—*ch.* 2. 4; 5. 16–19. For the phrase cf. 1 Sam. 2. 35 and (עשה for בנה) 25. 28.

Not improbably the speech has received some few later additions. In *v.* 33 וחקתי ומשפטי is wanting in LXX, and the use of these terms after לעשות rather than לשמר being characteristic of P or H (see *ch.* 6. 12 *note*), the two words may reasonably be suspected as an insertion due to R^P. LXX also omits אשר שמר מצותי וחקתי at the end of *v.* 34, and though the phrase is Deuteronomic, yet the repeated אשר has something of the awkward ring of an insertion, and the words may be due to the same interpolator. The omission of the close of the speech by LXX ונתתי לך את ישראל: ואענה את זרע דוד למען זאת אך לא כל הימים, taken in connexion with the reference of *v.* 39—the affliction of the seed of David, but not for ever—suggests that this also may be an addition of exilic or post-exilic times; though, as Kue. points out, the statement of *v.* 39 *need* not imply an exilic standpoint: cf. 2 Sam. 7. 14ᵇ. The use of the imperf. with weak ו, ואענה, for the perf. with ו *consec.*, seems to be another mark of the late hand: cf. *ch.* 6. 32 *note* on וְקָלַע.

32. והשבט האחד] LXX, Luc. καὶ δύο σκῆπτρα, an alteration in view of *v.* 30ᵇ; *ch.* 12. 23. So *v.* 36. Cf. the addition καὶ Βενιαμείν in *ch.* 12. 20. The inconsistency in MT. between the '12 pieces' of *v.* 30 and the 10 + 1 of *vv.* 31, 32 perhaps points to a modification of the original narrative only partially effected.

33. יען אשר עזבוני] LXX, Luc., Vulg., Pesh. presuppose the sing. verb throughout the verse; עֲזָבַנִי וַיִּשְׁתַּחוּ . . . וְלֹא הָלַךְ. This, as agreeing with the sing. שלמה of *vv.* 31, 32, and the sing. מִיָּדוֹ of *v.* 34, is to be adopted.

לעשתרת אלהי צדנין וג׳] LXX, Luc. τῇ Ἀστάρτῃ βδελύγματι Σιδωνίων καὶ τῷ Χαμὼς καὶ ἐν τοῖς εἰδώλοις (Luc. εἰδώλῳ) Μωὰβ καὶ τῷ βασιλεῖ αὐτῶν (Luc. τῷ Μελχὸμ) προσοχθίσματι υἱῶν Ἀμμών, i.e. לעשתרת תּוֹעֲבַת צדנין ולכמוש אלהי מואב ולמלכם שִׁקּוּץ בני עמון[1]. MT., in reading אלהי in each case, is more original. The expressions תועבת, שקוץ represent alterations to avoid applying the term אלהים to heathen gods, in accordance with the feeling of a later time. Cf. the variations in *vv.* 5, 7 MT. and LXX.

צדנין] The plural termination ִין—, used in Aramaic and upon the Moabite stone, occurs in Hebrew some twenty-five times, chiefly in late Books. In earlier Books the form, if not dialectical (so perhaps Judg. 5. 10), is due to error in transcription under the influence of Aramaic. For the occurrences cf. G-K. § 87 *e;* Sta. § 323ᵃ.

34. נשיא אשתנו] LXX, Luc. ἀντιτασσόμενος ἀντιτάξομαι αὐτῷ appear to have read נָשֹׂא אֶשָּׂאֶנּוּ, or better נָשֹׂא אֶשָּׂא לוֹ, interpreting נשא incorrectly in a reflexive sense 'lift myself up against'; cf. LXX rendering of Hos. 1. 6 כִּי נָשֹׂא אֶשָּׂא לָהֶם. Given the text of LXX, we might render 'for I will surely *forgive* him during his life-time &c.'; but this is inferior to MT.

37. ומלכת . . . נפשך] So exactly 2 Sam. 3. 21. Cf. Deut. 14. 26; 1 Sam. 2. 16. אִוָּה Pi'el and subs. אַוָּה are used almost exclusively in connexion with נֶפֶשׁ.

40. שישק] LXX Σουσακίμ, Luc. Σουσακείμ. Identified with Sheshonk I, first king of the twenty-second dynasty of Manetho. Cf. *ch.* 14. 25 *f. note.*

41 *ff.* ויתר וג׳] For this summarizing formula of R^D see *Introd.*

וחכמתו] LXX, Luc. וְכָל־חָכְמָתוֹ, adopted by Th. upon the ground that *ch.* 5. 9–14 merely gives a summary account of this wisdom.

על ספר דברי ש׳] Luc. ἐν βιβλίῳ λόγων ἡμερῶν Σ., Vulg. *in libro verborum dierum S.*, i.e. על ספר דברי הימים לש׳, probably a correction in accordance with the phrase used in the records of the

[1] In LXX προσόχθισμα usually = תועבה, but never = שקץ; βδέλυγμα often = שֶׁקֶץ, שִׁקּוּץ, but more than twice as frequently = תועבה. In Deut. 7. 26 we get the two words in juxtaposition, שַׁקֵּץ תְּשַׁקְּצֶנּוּ וְתַעֵב תְּתַעֲבֶנּוּ, προσοχθίσματι προσοχθιεῖς καὶ βδελύγματι βδελύξῃ.

kings of Israel and Judah. 2 Chr. 9. 29 ושאר דברי ש׳ הראשנים והאחרונים הלא הם כתובים על דברי נתן הנביא ועל נבואת אחיה השילוני ובחזות יֶעְדּוֹ החזה על ירבעם בן נבט.

43. The notice with reference to the return of Jeroboam from Egypt, inserted correctly (see *note* on 11. 26—14. 20) by LXX, Luc. between *v.* 43[a] and *v.* 43[b], must have run in the original:— וַיְהִי כִּשְׁמֹעַ יָרָבְעָם בֶּן־נְבָט וְהוּא עוֹדֶנּוּ בְמִצְרַיִם אֲשֶׁר בָּרַח מִפְּנֵי שְׁלֹמֹה וַיֵּשֶׁב בְּמִצְרַיִם וַיָּשָׁב וַיֵּלֶךְ אֶל־עִירוֹ אֶל־הַצְּרֵדָה אֲשֶׁר בְּהַר אֶפְרַיִם וַיִּשְׁכַּב הַמֶּלֶךְ שְׁלֹמֹה עִם־אֲבֹתָיו. LXX *κατευθύνειν*, Luc. more correctly *καὶ κατευθύνει* represents וַיָּשָׁב read as וַיִּשַׁר; cf. 1 Sam. 6. 12 וַיִּשַּׁרְנָה *καὶ κατεύθυναν.* In LXX *τὴν γῆν Σαρειρά* the word *γῆν* appears to be a corrupt repetition of *τήν*: cf. LXX *ch.* 12. 24[f], where LXX *γῆν* = Luc. *τήν*.

12. 1–24. *Reḥoboam's accession and the defection of the ten tribes.*

Ch. 12. 1–24 = 2 Chr. 10. 1—11. 4.

In this narrative *vv.* 15, 17, 21–24 appear to be additions of a later hand. *v.* 15, with its reference to the prediction of Aḥijah, probably presupposes *ch.* 11. 31 *ff.* in its present form, and must in this case be due to R[D]. *vv.* 21–24, standing in close connexion with *v.* 15 (cf. *v.* 15 כי היתה סבה מעם י׳; *v.* 24 כי מאתי נהיה הדבר הזה), give a Judaic turn to the originally impartial narrative of *vv.* 1–20, and are scarcely consistent with the statement of *ch.* 14. 30 ומלחמה היתה בין רחבעם ובין ירבעם כל הימים, a genuine excerpt from the ancient annals. Notice further that, while *v.* 20 speaks only of the tribe of Judah, *vv.* 21, 23 are careful to make reference also to the tribe of Benjamin. *v.* 17, which stands in an awkward position, and is absent from LXX, is probably a later gloss, though not by the same hand as *vv.* 15, 21–24, since it makes no reference to Benjamin.

1. שכם] The Roman *Flavia Neapolis* and modern *Nâbulus*, lying under the north-east base of Mount Gerizim. See Rob. *BR.* ii. 275, 287 *ff.;* Baed. 252 *ff.*

2. וישב וג׳] Vulg., ‖ 2 Chr. 10. 2 וַיָּשָׁב יָרָבְעָם מִמִּצְרָיִם, correctly. Cf. *note* on *ch.* 11. 43 LXX.

3. See, on LXX, Luc., *note* on *chh.* 11. 26—14. 20. Pesh. omits קהל.

4. עלנו] עֹל as a figure of *hard bondage* is very frequent, though always elsewhere of that imposed by a foreign nation:—Gen. 27. 40 (Israel's subjection of Edom); Lev. 26. 13; Hos. 11. 4; Jer. 2. 20 (Egypt); Isa. 9. 3; 10. 27; 14. 25 (Assyria); Jer. 27. 8, 11, 12; 28. 2, 4, 11, 14; 30. 8; Isa. 47. 6; Ezek. 34. 27 (Babylon); Deut. 28. 48 (general); of the moral restraints of religion Jer. 5. 5, cf. Lam. 3. 27; of the bonds of sin (late) Lam. 1. 14.

5. עֹד] LXX, Luc., Vulg., Pesh., Targ. presuppose עַד 'Depart *until* three days (sc. have elapsed),' i. e. 'until the third day.' This is doubtless correct. עֹד of MT. would rather suggest that a *previous* postponement had taken place.

העם] LXX, Luc. omit. Pesh. ܟܠܗ ܥܡܐ, i. e. כָּל־הָעָם.

6. וַיִּוָּעַץ] So with *pathaḥ* always in this form (11 times). According to König, *Lehrg.* I. i. 419, the emphatic pronunciation of the צ is better served by the broader '*Pathaḥ gadol* in place of *Pathaḥ qaton*' (=*Seghol*).

7. דברים טובים] 'Favourable words'; Zech. 1. 13.

כל הימים] Cf. *ch.* 5. 15 *note*.

8. אשר העמדים לפניו] 'Who were those who stood before him'; but this is harsh unless we read אשר הֵם העמדים וג׳. ‖ 2 Chr. 10. 8, omitting אשר, gives the simple sense 'who stood before him,' and is doubtless correct.

10. ואתה] LXX, Luc. *καὶ σὺ νῦν*, i. e. ואתה עתה in conformity with *v.* 4.

קָטָנִּי] From *st. abs.* קֹטֶן. For vocalization cf. קָבְלוֹ Ezek. 26. 9. Doubtless the original and correct form was קָטְנִי, like אָהֳלִי, פָּעֳלוֹ, with half-open syllable, and a later stage of pronunciation first raised the *ḥatef qameç* to the position of a full short vowel, and then proceeded in consequence to place it in a closed syllable by doubling the ל. So ‖ 2 Chr. 10. 10 קָטָנִּי.

קטני, only here and in ‖ 2 Chr.,='my littleness,' so, no doubt rightly, 'my little finger,' Vulg., Pesh. LXX, Luc. *ἡ μικρότης μου.* Targ. paraphrases חלשותי 'my weakness.'

11. עקרבים] Explained by Pesh. ܡܪ̈ܓܢܐ, Targ. מרגנין, i.e. *μάραγναι*, 'scourges,' probably so named from being loaded with metal or

stones to produce keener *sting*. For the use of the article in בְּעקרבים, בַּשּׁוטים cf. *note* on בַּבגדים *ch.* 1. 1.

12. ויבו] Read Q're וַיָּבוֹא. The sing. verb agrees, as is frequently the case, with the nearest member of the compound subject. Cf. Da. § 114[b]. On this verse in LXX, Luc. cf. *note* on *chh.* 11. 26—14. 20.

13. ויען וג׳] 'And the king returned the people *a harsh response*.' For קָשָׁה '*something harsh*' cf. || 2 Chr. 10. 13; 1 Sam. 20. 10; *ch.* 14. 6; Ps. 60. 5; plur. קָשׁוֹת Gen. 42. 7, 30†.

15. סבה] A ἅπαξ λεγ.; something *turning* or bringing about, 'fate' or 'providence.' So LXX, Luc. *μεταστροφή*, Pesh. ܡܥܒܪܢܘܬܐ 'instigation'; Targ. פלונתא, passive, 'fated lot,' so || 2 Chr. 10. 15 נְסִבָּה *ἅπαξ λεγ.* The verb appears to be used with a similar sense in 1 Sam. 22. 22 אנכי סַבֹּתִי בכל נפש בית אביך 'I have brought about (sc. death) upon every member of thy father's house.' This, however, with ellipse of the direct object מָוֶת, is extremely harsh, and Th., Wellh., Dri., Budde emend חַבְתִּי '*I am guilty* in respect of &c.' In late Rabbinic Hebrew סִבָּה='cause.'

ביד אחיה] Cf. *ch.* 8. 53 *note*.

16. כל ישראל] Luc. *πᾶς ὁ λαός*, Vulg. *populus*.

לאמר וג׳] The words of Sheba son of Bichri are nearly identical; 2 Sam. 20. 1.

מה לנו חלק] 'There is *not* a portion to us'; practically equivalent to אֵין לנו חלק 2 Sam. 20. 1, but מה, originally interrogative=*num?* gives more emphatic point to the negation. This use of מה, though very usual in Arabic, is rare in Hebrew; Cant. 8. 4 מה תעירו ומה תעררו את האהבה answers to 2. 7; 3. 5 אם תעירו וג׳; cf. also Job 31. 1 ומה אתבונן על בתולה 'and how shall I gaze &c.'='and I will *not* gaze'; 9. 2; 16. 6; Prov. 20. 24. Ew. § 325[b].

לְאֹהָלֶיךָ] With full long vowel in the antepenult upon which there dwells a *countertone*, thus facilitating the due pronunciation of the two weak letters אה. So אֹהָלָיו, אֹהָלִים. Cf. Sta. § 109.

ראה ביתך] The point of the taunt appears to be in the suffix of ביתך 'look to *thy* house' (so Th.), emphasizing the old division (2 Sam. 2. 4, 8–11) and jealous hostility (2 Sam. 2. 16; 19. 42–44) existing between the tribe of Judah and the northern tribes. For the nuance of ראה 'look after' cf. Gen. 39. 23. LXX, Luc. *βόσκε τὸν οἶκόν σου*, i. e. רְעֵה ביתך.

17. ובני ישראל] Luc. *καὶ οἱ υἱοὶ Ἰούδα καὶ οἱ υἱοὶ Ἰσραήλ*. The additional words represent a marginal correction afterwards inserted in the text.

ובני ישראל . . . וימלך עליהם] Cf. *ch.* 9. 21 *note*.

18. After וישלח המלך ר׳ Pesh. adds ܠܘܬ ܟܠܗ ܐܝܣܪܝܠ, i. e. אֶל־כָּל־יִשְׂרָאֵל.

אדרם] Luc., Pesh. read אֲדֹנִירָם; cf. *ch.* 4. 6 *note*.

המס] Cf. *ch.* 4. 6 *note*.

וירגמו . . . בו אבן] So with ב of person stoned ‖ 2 Chr. 10. 18; Lev. 24. 16†. Elsewhere once with עַל of person Ezek. 23. 47, but most generally with accusative Lev. 24. 14; *al.* (11 times). With ב of instrument בָּאבן, בָּאבנים Lev. 20. 2; Num. 14. 10; *al.*

19. עד היום הזה] Cf. *ch.* 8. 8 *note*.

20. שבט יהודה] LXX, Luc. add *καὶ Βενιαμείν*, for conformity with *v.* 23. Cf. *ch.* 11. 32, 36.

21. מאה ושמנים אלף] LXX, Luc. *ἑκατὸν καὶ εἴκοσι χιλιάδες* (*-δας* Luc.).

24. כי מאתי וג׳] Cf. *ch.* 1. 27.

12. 26–33. *Jeroboam's institution of the calf-worship.*

Judging by the stress which R^D constantly lays upon Jeroboam's cult as the cause of all subsequent deflexion of Israel from the pure worship of Yahwe (cf. *Introduction*), it is probable that this narrative has obtained its present *casting* at his hands, though there is no reason hence to infer that any detail of *fact* is underived from the older source. Kue. (*Ond.* § 25. 4) observes justly, 'Jeroboam's measures with reference to the worship must already have been related in older narratives, but it is only natural that the redactor, when dealing with a matter which so specially excited his interest, should not fail to set before us his own construction and his own verdict.' *vv.* 32, 33 serve to introduce the story of *ch.* 13. No special phrases of R^D are to be noticed.

28. רב לכם מעלות] Not, as RV. text, 'It is *too much for you* to go up' (this would be רַב מִכֶּם; cf. *ch.* 19. 7), but, as marg., 'Ye have gone up *long enough*.' The מן before עלות is logically redundant, as in Ezek. 44. 6 רַב־לָכֶם מִכָּל־תּוֹעֲבוֹתֵיכֶם 'Enough of all your abominations,' and the normal construction is that of Deut. 1. 6 רַב־לָכֶם שֶׁבֶת וגו׳; 2. 3. Cf. the similar use of מן after הֲנָקֵל; Ezek. 8. 17 הֲנָקֵל לְבֵית יְהוּדָה מֵעֲשׂוֹת וגו׳; but *ch.* 16. 31 הֲנָקֵל לֶכְתּוֹ.

הנה אלהיך וג׳] Cf. Ex. 32. 4, 8 (E).

29. וישם את האחד . . . ואת האחד נתן] For contrasted order of words cf. *ch.* 5. 25 *note.*

בית אל] The modern *Beitîn*, a short distance to the north of Michmash (*Mukhmâs*) of Benjamin, and so upon the southern frontier of Jeroboam's kingdom. For the substitution of Ar. *-în* for Heb. אֵל cf. *Zer'în*=יזרעאל. See Rob. *BR.* i. 448 *ff.*; Baed. 249.

30. לחטאת] Luc. adds τῷ 'Ισραήλ, לישראל, which, as more definite and agreeing with the frequent phrase of R^D אשר החטיא את ישראל, may be deemed correct.

וילכו וג׳] Obviously incomplete in making mention only of the worship at Dan. We should probably restore כִּי יֵלְכוּ הָעָם לִפְנֵי הָאֶחָד אֶל־בֵּית־אֵל וְלִפְנֵי הָאֶחָד עַד־דָּן 'for the people used to go before the one to Bethel and before the other unto Dan.' The words supplied may be thought to have fallen out through homoioteleuton, and in וילכו for כי ילכו we have a case of the confusion between כ and ו seen elsewhere in *ch.* 22. 37 וימת, LXX ὅτι τέθνηκεν, i.e. כִּי מֵת; Isa. 39. 1 וישמע for כי שמע; Jer. 37. 16 כי בא for ויבא; 1 Sam. 2. 21 כי פקד for ויפקד. Luc., which adds καὶ πρὸ προσώπου τῆς ἄλλης εἰς Βαιθήλ *after* the reference to Dan, probably exhibits a later restoration of the text, since, if this be regarded as the original order, it is not clear why the words should have fallen out. Vulg. *ibat enim populus ad adorandum vitulum usque in Dan* paraphrases in order to overcome the difficulty of the single האחד. LXX, Pesh., Targ. as MT.

31. ויעש את בית במות] Read, with Luc., ויעש ירבעם בית במות

'And Jeroboam made houses of high places,' i.e. temples erected upon the high places. בית is collective, as in II. 17. 29, 32 בְּבֵית הַבָּמוֹת of the temples of the various cults at Samaria. *Ch.* 13. 32; II. 23. 19, plur. בָּתֵּי הַבָּמוֹת. The use of את before the indefinite בית במות is anomalous; the case being different to *ch.* 16. 18 וישרף עליו את בית מלך 'and he burnt the king's house over him,' where בית מלך, like מקדש מלך, בית ממלכה Am. 7. 13, is really definite; cf. Da. § 22, *Rem.* 3; Ew. § 277[c]. Cases like 1 Sam. 24. 6 (cf. LXX); 2 Sam. 5. 24[1] (cf. || 1 Chr. 14. 15); 18. 18, where את appears to be used before an indefinite object, are probably textual errors.

מקצות העם] '*From among the whole of* the people'; lit. 'from the end of.' So *ch.* 13. 33; II. 17. 32; Gen. 19. 4 כל העם מִקָּצֶה 'all the people, *one and all*'; Jer. 51. 31 נלכדה עירו מִקָּצֶה 'his city is taken *throughout*'; Isa. 56. 11 כלם לדרכם פנו איש לבצעו מִקָּצֵהוּ 'all of them have turned to their own way, each to his gain, *one and all*'; Ezek. 25. 9 מעריו מִקָּצֵהוּ 'from his cities *in every quarter*'; 33. 2 איש אחד מִקְּצֵיהֶם 'one man *from among the whole of them*.' The phrase may be illustrated e.g. by Num. 22. 41 וירא משם קְצֵה העם 'and he saw thence *the uttermost part of* the people,' and so, by implied inclusion, *the whole of them*.

32. בחמשה עשר יום] Pesh. ܒܟܣܐ here and in *v.* 33, i.e. 'upon the full moon'; cf. Heb. בַּכֶּסֶה Ps. 81. 4.

כֶּחָג] 'Like *the* feast,' i.e. the feast of Tabernacles; cf. *ch.* 8. 2, 65. This, however, was on the fifteenth day of the *seventh* month, Lev. 23. 34; hence the statement of *v.* 33[aβ].

ויעל על המזבח] Cf. *ch.* 1. 53 *note*.

כן עשה . . . אשר עשה] There can be little doubt that this latter portion of *v.* 32, together with the first three words of *v.* 33 ויעל על המזבח repeated from the previous verse, represents a very early gloss inserted on account of the omission in *v.* 30. After the loss of the words to be supplied in this latter verse, לפני האחד אל ביתאל ו, it is clear that the reference to the institution of the priests and the

[1] Da.'s explanation of את קול צעדה as 'a *known* kind of divine rustling' is inadequate; § 72, *Rem.* 4.

festival, *vv.* 31, $32^{a\alpha}$, might be taken to refer only to the sanctuary at Dan, and so give rise to this explanatory insertion. Notice the awkwardness of כן עשה *asyndetos*, and והעמיד perf. with weak ו.

33. ויעל . . . השמיני] Pesh. omits.

אשר בדא מִלִּבֹּד] 'Which he had invented out of his own heart.' בדא occurs only once beside in OT.; Neh. 6. 8 מִלִּבְּךָ אַתָּה בוֹדָאם 'out of thine own heart art thou inventing them' (for בּוֹדְאָם). In Rabbinic Hebrew and Aramaic the verb has the same meaning, always with a bad *nuance*. Q're מִלִּבּוֹ, with the sense 'at his own initiative,' is correct; cf. Num. 16. 28; 24. 13; Ezek. 13. 2, 17.

13. 1–32. *The prophecy against the altar at Bethel.*

The style of the language shows traces of decadence:—cf. וְנָתַן perf. with weak ו *v.* 3, דבר אלי, צוה אתי apparently first written as דְּבַר אֵלַי, צִוֵּיתִי *vv.* 9, 17, לנביא אשר השיבו *v.* 23 (but cf. *note ad loc.*), and perhaps מתת *v.* 7—and this fact, together with the anachronism בערי שמרון *v.* 32 (cf. II. 17. 24, 26; 23. 19), and the non-mention of the names of the principal actors, marks the narrative as being of comparatively late origin. It may be thought to have been a story previously current in the form of oral tradition, and to have assumed a literary form very shortly after the event predicted—the destruction of the altar at Bethel—had come about. Notice the precision of the statement יאשיהו שמו *v.* 2. The style is about contemporary with that of the annals of Josiah's reformation, II. 23. 1–15, 19–24, where the perf. with weak ו is used with some frequency:—*vv.* 4, 5, 8, 10, 12, 14, 15. It is, however, by no means to be hence inferred that the story is of the character of a *vaticinium post eventum*. Such a view presupposes that it, together with the notice of II. 23. 16–18, was inserted into Kings subsequently to the redaction of R^D (Wellh. *C.* 280; Kue. *Ond.* § 25. 4); whereas on the contrary *ch.* 12. 26 *ff.* appears to have been carefully edited by R^D so as to lead up to the story, and the resumption of the main narrative in *ch.* 13. 33, 34, forming the link to *ch.* 14. 1–20, constructs of the history a harmonious whole. If the story be merely a very late Judaean fiction, the point of the details as to the disobedience and punishment of the *Judaean* prophet seems to be quite inexplicable.

1. בדבר י׳] So *vv.* 2, 5, 9, 17, 18, 32. Elsewhere in this sense *ch.* 20. 35; 1 Sam. 3. 21; 2 Chr. 30. 12†. בִּדְבְרֵי י׳ 2 Chr. 29. 15†.

עמד על המזבח] Cf. *ch.* 1. 53 *note.*

2. כה אמר] Pesh. prefixes ܫܡܥܘ ܦܬܓܡܗ ܕܡܪܝܐ 'Hear the word of the Lord.'

ישרפו] Impers. 'shall they burn,' so 'shall be burnt.' LXX, Luc., Vulg., Pesh. presuppose יִשְׂרֹף.

3. מופת] 'A wonder' or 'miracle,' as a proof of the divine commission; so Ex. 4. 21; 7. 9; 2 Chr. 32. 24, 31; cf. Deut. 13. 2, 3.

6. חל נא את פני י׳] 'Entreat the favour of Yahwe'; lit. '*Make sweet the face* &c.' Ar. حَلَا, حَلِيَ, Aram. חֲלִי, ܚܠܐ = *to be sweet* or *pleasant.*

כבראשנה] Judg. 20. 32; Isa. 1. 26; Jer. 33. 7, 11†. More loosely כְּבָרִאשֹׁנָה Deut. 9. 18; Dan. 11. 29†.

7. וּסְעָדָה] So וּצְעָקִי Jer. 22. 20, וּסְאָה II. 7. 18. Elsewhere we find *ḥatef-pathaḥ* with a sibilant after the *ū*-sound:—וּשְׁבַע *ch.* 14. 21, וּשְׁלַח II. 9. 17, וּשְׁמַע II. 19. 16[a], וּזֲהַב Gen. 2. 12, וּשְׁקָה 27. 26, וּשְׂדֵה Lev. 25. 34, וּשְׁבֵה Judg. 5. 12, Dan. 9. 18. According to G-K. (§ 10 *g*) the *ḥatef-qameç* in the former cases arises under the influence both of the preceding *ū and* the following guttural; but probably König (*Lehrg.* I. i. 262) is correct in regarding the slightly fuller sound of this half-vowel as due to the more emphatic sibilants ס, צ.

מתת] Ezek. 46. 5. 11; Prov. 25. 14; Eccl. 3. 13; 5. 18†. A bye-form of the more usual מַתָּנָה, contracted from מַתֶּנֶת.

8. אם תתן וג׳] Cf. the words of Balaam, Num. 22. 18; 24. 13 (JE). On the form of the conditional sentence, expressing the merest (hyperbolical) possibility, cf. Dri. *Tenses,* § 143.

9. כי כן צוה אתי] 'For so one commanded me,' the implied subject being the voice of Yahwe, or, as in *v.* 18, the divine messenger. For other instances of this semi-impersonal construction, employed where the intervention of divine agency (or agencies) is implied,

cf. Zech. 9. 12 מגיד; and in plur. Job 7. 3 מִנּוּ־לִי; Ezek. 32. 25 נתנו. So in Aramaic Dan. 4. 22 טרדין; 4. 28 אמרין; *al.* It seems, however, to be not improbable that צוה אתי represents the alteration of an original צֻוֵּיתִי 'I was commanded.' Cf. Wellh. *C.* 280; Klo., Kamp., Benz., Kit. See on דבר לי *v.* 17.

11. נביא אחד זקן] '*A certain* old prophet.' For this use of אחד, mainly characteristic of northern Palestinian narrative and of the later style, cf. instances cited p. 209. The usage is common in Rabbinic Hebrew. Luc. προφήτης ἄλλος, i. e. נביא אַחֵר; 'and *another* prophet, an old man, was dwelling in Bethel.' אחר, where the name of neither prophet is mentioned, is most apposite, and may well be original.

ויבא בנו וג׳] LXX, Luc., Vulg., Pesh. presuppose וַיָּבֹאוּ בָנָיו וַיְסַפְּרוּ rightly, in accordance with plur. ויספרום *v.* 11ᵇ, אלהם *v.* 12.

היום] '*That* day.' So only here. The writer seems to lapse into the point of view of the sons, to whom it was היום '*to-day*.' Luc. ἐν τῇ ἡμέρᾳ ἐκείνῃ suggests the more usual בַּיּוֹם ההוא, but is more likely to be an alteration of LXX ἐν τῇ ἡμέρᾳ.

ויספרום וג׳] Resuming the previous ויספרו; cf. *ch.* 2. 4 *note.* LXX, Luc. strangely καὶ ἐπέστρεψαν τὸ πρόσωπον τοῦ πατρὸς αὐτῶν, apparently reading through corruption ויסרפנם לאביהם, i. e. וַיָּסִירוּ פָנִים לַאֲבִיהֶם; ἐπέστρεψαν an alteration of ἀπέστρεψαν.

12. וידבר אלהם אביהם] LXX, Luc. add λέγων; so Klo. לֵאמֹר. But the word is similarly absent in MT., and supplied by LXX, Luc. in *vv.* 17, 22.

אי זה הדרך] 'Where is the way?' so 'Which way?' So II. 3. 8; 2 Chr. 18. 23; Job 38. 19, 24, always, as here, with omission of relative אשר before the following verb. On the enclitic זה, strongly pointing the question, cf. *note* on למה זה *ch.* 14. 6.

וַיִּרְאוּ וג׳] 'Now his sons *had seen* &c.' LXX, Luc., Vulg., Pesh. are greatly superior in presupposing וַיַּרְאוּ 'and his sons *showed* (him).' So Benz., Kit. וַיַּרְאֻהוּ, Klo., Kamp. וַיֹּרֻהוּ; cf. Ex. 15. 25.

14. האלה] '*The* terebinth,' which the writer's vivid imagination pictures as the tree under which the prophet was sitting. So *ch.* 18. 4 ויחביאם . . . בַּמערה 'and hid them in *the cave*,' marked

as having thus afforded an asylum; 2 Sam. 17. 17 והלכה השפחה 'and *a wench* used to go &c.,' pictured by the writer as '*the* wench' simply as being the agent thus employed; 1 Sam. 9. 9 כה אמר האיש 'thus spake *the man*,' who, as a matter of fact, did so speak; but according to English idiom, 'thus spake *a man*'; 2 Sam. 15. 13; Gen. 14. 13; *al.* This method of thought may be most clearly understood in such a case as 1 Sam. 17. 34 ובא הארי 'and if *a lion* came,' where the speaker has had *active experience* of the coming of the lions which he thus recalls to his mind. Cf. Da. § 21 ε. This use of the article is a very idiomatic extension of the usage noticed in *ch.* 1. 1.

16. ולבוא אתך] LXX, Luc. omit. Pesh. ܘܠܡܥܠ ܠܒܝܬܟ, i. e. ולבוא בֵּיתֶךָ 'and to enter thy house,' is preferable to MT.

ולא אשתה אתך] LXX, Luc., Vulg., Pesh. omit אתך, but Pesh. supplies the word after the previous ולא אכל.

17. כי דָבָר אלי] LXX, Luc., Pesh., Targ. suggest כי דֻבַּר אלי 'for *it was said* unto me.' So Wellh., Klo., Kamp., Benz., Kit. Cf. *note* on *v.* 9.

18. מלאך] As in *ch.* 19. 5; Zech. 1. 9, 14; *al.* מלאך יהוה *ch.* 19. 7; II. 1. 3, 15; Gen. 16. 7; 22. 11; Ex. 3. 2; *al.*

כחש לו] The perfect thus used *asyndetos* forms a circumstantial clause,—'*lying unto him*'; cf. *ch.* 7. 51 נתן; 18. 6 אחאב הלך וג׳ 'Aḥab going one way &c.' Dri. *Tenses*, § 163.

19. וַיָּשָׁב אִתּוֹ] LXX, Luc. καὶ ἐπέστρεψεν αὐτόν, i. e. וַיָּשֶׁב אֹתוֹ.

20. ויהי הם ישבים . . . ויהי וג׳] 'And it came to pass—they were sitting at the table—and there came &c.'; so, 'And it came to pass, *as they were sitting* at the table, that there came &c.' The circumstantial clause הם ישבים אל השלחן, elevated to so striking a position *in advance of* the principal sentence, lays great stress upon the moment of time at which the event described by the latter took place. Cf. II. 2. 11 ויהי המה הלכים הלוך ודבר והנה רכב אש וג׳ 'And it came to pass, *while they were going on and talking as they went*, that behold a chariot of fire &c.'; II. 8. 5. Cf. Dri. *Tenses*, § 165, who terms the participle thus used *the participle absolute*.

אל השלחן] '*At* the table'; cf. *ch.* 6. 18 *note* for this use of אל.

In Neh. 5. 17 we have על שלחני, lit. '*above* or *over* my table'; 1 Sam. 20. 34 Jonathan gets up מעם השלחן '*from proximity with* the table.' When the idea of *eating* at the table is prominent, it is natural and accurate to use על '*upon*'; so 2 Sam. 9. 7, 10, 13, cf. Ezek. 39. 20. In *ch.* 2. 7; 18. 19; 2 Sam. 19. 29, however, we have the simple *st. constr.* employed;—אֹכְלֵי שלחן.

21. יען כי] So *ch.* 21. 29; Num. 11. 20; Isa. 3. 16; 7. 5; 8. 6; 29. 13. The more usual expression is יַעַן אֲשֶׁר; *ch.* 3. 11; 8. 18; *al.* יַעַן appears to be originally a substantive = '*response*,' contracted from יַעֲנֶה from verb ענה. So with מַעַן in the phrase לְמַעַן 'on account of,' 'in order (that).' Cf. עֵקֶב 'recompense' used in the sense 'in return for,' 'because'; Deut. 7. 12; *al.*

מרית פי י׳] So *v.* 26; 1 Sam. 12. 15; Num. 20. 24; 27. 14; Lam. 1. 18†; and with Hiph'îl Deut. 1. 26, 43; 9. 23; Josh. 1. 18; 1 Sam. 12. 14†.

22. לא תבא וג׳] Illustrated by the dying injunction of Jacob, Gen. 47. 30, and of Joseph, 50. 25.

23. שתותו] LXX, Luc., Pesh. add מַיִם in accordance with *vv.* 8, 16, 18, 19.

לנביא אשר השיבו] Very awkward. The sentence would most obviously mean 'for the prophet who had brought him back' (cf. *vv.* 20, 26), but in accordance with the context can only be rendered 'for the prophet whom he had brought back,' the suffix of השיבו referring back to the antecedent נביא, as in Aram.; cf. Duval, *Gramm. Syr.* § 399 *b*. LXX, Luc., in place of these words and the וילך of *v.* 24[a], read *καὶ ἐπέστρεψεν καὶ ἀπῆλθεν*, i. e. וַיָּשָׁב וַיֵּלַךְ: '*and he once more departed*'; probably the original text. Pesh. ܠܢܒܝܐ ܕܐܠܗܐ: ܘܗܦܟ ܘܐܙܠ., i. e. לְנָבִיא אֱלֹהִים וַיָּשָׁב וַיֵּלַךְ, suggests that MT. arose from the incorporation into the text of the words לנביא אלהים, a marginal note explanatory of the previous לו.

24. ותהי . . . משלכת] Cf. *ch.* 5. 1 *note* on היה משל.

26[b], 27. LXX omits.

26. כדבר וג׳] The phrase כדבר י׳ אשר דבר occurs frequently in Kings to call attention to the fulfilment of a prophecy. So *ch.* 22. 38. Most often mention of the prophetic agent is added in the form

בְּיַד פ׳;—*ch.* 14. 18; 15. 29; 16. 12, 34; 17. 16; II. 14. 25; 24. 2. Cf. also II. 10. 17; 4. 44; 7. 16; 9. 26; 1. 17; 23. 16; 2. 22.

28ª. וחמור והאריה] Emend וְהַחֲמוֹר והאריה. Klo. וַחֲמוֹרוֹ וג׳.

28ᵇ. את הנבלה] LXX τὸ σῶμα τοῦ ἀνθρώπου τοῦ θεοῦ, to harmonize with *v.* 29.

29. אל החמור] אל for על; cf. *ch.* 16. 13; 18. 46; II. 5. 11; 9. 3, 12; Josh. 5. 14; 1 Sam. 13. 13; *al.* For the converse change, after a verb of motion, cf. *ch.* 1. 38 *note.*

וישיבהו . . . לקברו] LXX, Luc. run more smoothly and naturally:— καὶ ἐπέστρεψεν αὐτὸν (Luc. αὐτὸ) εἰς τὴν πόλιν ὁ προφήτης, τοῦ θάψαι αὐτόν, i. e. וַיְשִׁיבֵהוּ הַנָּבִיא אֶל־הָעִיר לְקָבְרוֹ. LXX, however, is incorrect in omitting וינח את נבלתו of *v.* 30 and joining בְּקִבְרוֹ on to לקברו of *v.* 29.

30. ויספדו] Luc., Pesh. presuppose sing. וַיִּסְפֹּד.

הוי אחי] Cf. Jer. 22. 18.

31. אחרי קברו אתו] LXX, Luc. μετὰ τὸ κόψασθαι αὐτόν, Vulg. *cumque planxissent eum*, presuppose אחרי סָפְדוֹ עָלָיו.

במותי וקברתם אתי] 'When I die, then bury me.' For the ו *consec.* with perf. after the very terse time determination cf. Ezek. 24. 24 בבואה וידעתם 'When it (the sign) come to pass, ye shall know &c.' Dri. *Tenses*, § 123 β, Da. § 56.

32. בתי הבמות] Cf. *ch.* 12. 31 *note.*

בערי שמרון] Cf. *note* on *vv.* 1–32.

13. 33, 34. *A brief resumption by* Rᴰ *of the main thread of the history from the end of chapter* 12.

33. אחר הדבר הזה] 'After this *event.*' The phrase occurs only here, the more usual (and less precise) expression being אחר הדברים האלה *ch.* 17. 17; 21. 1; Gen. 15. 1; 22. 1; 40. 1; Ezr. 7. 1; Est. 2. 1; 3. 1†; אחרי הדברים האלה Gen. 22. 20; 48. 1; Josh. 24. 29; 2 Chr. 32. 1†.

לא שב . . . מדרכו הרעה] Jer. 18. 11; 25. 5; 26. 3; 35. 15; 36. 3, 7; Jon. 3. 8, 10; Ezek. 13. 22 (מדרכו הָרָע)†; and with pl.

II. 17. 13 (R^D); 2 Chr. 7. 14; Zech. 1. 4†. Cf. Jer. 23. 22; Ezek. 3. 19; 33. 11.

מקצות העם] Cf. *ch.* 12. 31 *note.*

ימלא את ידו] 'He used to fill his hand,' i. e. 'he would *install him*' as priest. The expression seems to be derived from the ceremony of filling the hands of the person to be consecrated with the choice portions of the sacrifice for a waive-offering Ex. 29. 22–25; Lev. 8. 25–28, these being called מִלֻּאִים Lev. 8. 28. The phrase is used of the consecration of the priest at Micah's sanctuary Judg. 17. 5, 12, but is elsewhere characteristic of P and of later Books.

ויהי כהני במות] Impossible. LXX, Luc., Vulg., Pesh. וַיְהִי כֹּהֵן לַבָּמוֹת 'and he became priest to the high-places'; so Kamp. Klo. prefers to follow Targ. and emend וְהָיוּ כֹּהֲנֵי בָמוֹת.

34. לחטאת וג׳] Read, with LXX, Luc., Pesh. לְחַטָּאת לְבֵית יר׳. Cf. *ch.* 12. 30[a].

להשמיד מעל פני האדמה] So Deut. 6. 15; Am. 9. 8†; cf. Josh. 23. 15 (D^2). השמיד, pass. נשמד is very frequent in Deut. (27 times); cf. Dri. *Deut.* 1. 27.

14. 1–18. *The sickness and death of Jeroboam's son Abijah.*

Upon the LXX Version of this narrative in its relationship to MT. see *note* on *chh.* 11. 26—14. 20. The story exhibits very clear traces of the hand of R^D in Aḥijah's prophecy *vv.* 7–16, with which should be compared the prophecies of Jehu son of Ḥanani against Ba'asha *ch.* 16. 1–4, of Elijah against Aḥab *ch.* 21. 20–24, and of the young prophet against the house of Aḥab II. 9. 6–10. The following phrases are to be noticed:—

7. י׳ אלהי ישראל] So *v.* 13. Cf. *ch.* 8. 15 *note.*

יען וג׳] So exactly *ch.* 16. 2[a].

8. ולא היית כעבדי דוד] Cf. *ch.* 3. 14 *note* on כאשר הלך דוד.

אשר שמר מצותי] Cf. *ch.* 2. 3 *note.*

הלך אחרי] Cf. *ch.* 11. 5 *note.*

בכל לבבו] Cf. *ch.* 2. 4 *note.*

לעשות וג׳] Cf. *ch.* 11. 33 *note.*

9. ותרע . . . לפניך] Cf. *ch.* 16. 25, 30, 33; II. 17. 2; II. 21. 11. As used of Jeroboam the expression מכל אשר היו לפניך is somewhat mechanical.

אלהים אחרים] Cf. *ch.* 9. 6 *note.*

להכעיסני] Not, as RV., 'to provoke me to anger,' but, 'to *vex* me' by treatment wholly undeserved. So subs. כַּעַס='*vexation*' or '*chagrin*,' the rendering 'grief' being too general, and 'anger' incorrect; cf. Ps. 10. 14; 1 Sam. 1. 16; Job 6. 2. The verb (Hiph'îl) is very characteristic of R^D:—*v.* 15; 15. 30; 16. 2, 7, 13, 26, 33; 21. 22; 22. 54; II. 17. 11, 17; 21. 6 (‖ 2 Chr. 33. 6), 15; 22. 17 (‖ 2 Chr. 34. 25); 23. 19, 26; cf. 2 Chr. 28. 25; Deut. 4. 25; 9. 18; 31. 29; 32. 16; Jer. 7. 18, 19; 8. 19; 11. 17; 25. 6, 7; 32. 29, 30, 32; 44. 3, 8. Elsewhere, with יהוה as obj., only six times. Pi'el, Deut. 32. 21.

10. הנני מביא רעה אל] Cf. *ch.* 21. 21; II. 22. 16 (‖ 2 Chr. 34. 24 על; cf. *v.* 20 ‖ 2 Chr. 34. 28) both R^D; Jer. 6. 19; 11. 11 (cf. *v.* 23); cf. 19. 15; 35. 17. With על II. 21. 12 R^D; Jer. 19. 3; 45. 5; cf. Jer. 17. 18; 23. 12; 36. 31; 49. 37; 51. 64.

משתין בקיר] *Ch.* 16. 11; 21. 21; II. 9. 8 R^D. Only besides 1 Sam. 25. 22, 34†.

עצור ועזוב] *Ch.* 21. 21; II. 9. 8; 14. 26 (all R^D); Deut. 32. 36†. The phrase means '*restrained and let loose*' (עזב as in Ex. 23. 5 'release'; Job 10. 1), i.e. '*all*,' every one being supposed to fall under one of the two categories. Cf. the expressions of Deut. 29. 18 הרוה את הצמאה; Isa. 2. 9 וישח אדם וישפל איש 'mean man . . . great man'; Ps. 49. 3; Job 12. 16; Eccl. 9. 2; and for examples from Ar. cf. *Thes.* 1008, 1362. The precise application of the phrase is obscure. The most plausible explanation is that of Ew. *Antiquities*, 170, '*kept in* (by legal defilement) *and at large*.' For this sense of עצור cf. Jer. 36. 5 אני עצור לא אוכל לבוא בית י׳; 1 Sam. 21. 8 נעצר לפני י׳. So R. Sm. *Rel. Sem.*[2] 456;

Dri. *Deut.* 32. 36. Other suggestions are:—'*bond and free*,' Ges.; cf. עצר II. 17. 4; Jer. 33. 1; *al.*: '*married and celibate*,' De Dieu, Ke.; Ar. عَزِيبٌ '*azîb* = 'celibate,' أَعْصَرُ '*a'ṣaru*, explained wrongly (cf. Roediger, *Thes.* Append. 104) as 'paterfamilias': '*under and over age*,' Th., Kamp., following Schmidt, 'puer, qui domi adhuc *detinetur*, et qui *emancipatus* est.' For the alliteration of the phrase Dri. (*loc. cit.*) cites נִין וָנֶכֶד Isa. 14. 22; Gen. 21. 23; Job 18. 19; עֵר וְעֹנֶה Mal. 2. 12; שֹׁד וָשֶׁבֶר Isa. 59. 7; 60. 18; Jer. 48. 3; Ecclus. 40. 9; שָׁמִיר וָשַׁיִת Isa. 5. 6; *al.* (7 times). Add נָע וָנָד Gen. 4. 12, 14; הֶגֶה וָהִי Ezek. 2. 10; צָנִיף וְצִיץ Ecclus. 40. 4; חַרְחֻר וָחֹרֶב Deut. 28. 22; Ecclus. 40. 9[1]; דֶּבֶר וָדָם Ezek. 5. 17; cf. 38. 22.

ובערתי אחרי] Cf. *ch.* 21. 21†; מבעיר אחרי *ch.* 16. 3†; both R^D^.

11. המת וג׳] *Ch.* 16. 4; 21. 24† R^D^; cf. II. 9. 10, 36; *ch.* 21. 19, 23; 22. 38.

15. מעל האדמה הטובה הזאת] So exactly Josh. 23. 13, 15 (D²) †. The usual phrase in Deut. of the land of Canaan is הארץ הטובה; cf. Dri. *Deut.* lxxxi.

אשר נתן לאבותיהם] Cf. *ch.* 8. 34 *note.*

16. בגלל חטאות וג׳] Cf. *ch.* 15. 30. Reference to the sins of Jeroboam in these terms is very constant in R^D^. See *Introd.*

1. בעת ההיא] A phrase employed by R^D^ in synchronizing events narrated in different sources; II. 16. 6; 18. 16; 20. 12; 24. 10. Cf. *ch.* 8. 65; 11. 29; II. 8. 22. For similar expressions thus used cf. *note* on אז *ch.* 3. 16.

2. והשתנית] *Hithpa'el* only here: 'and thou shalt *change thyself*,' i. e. 'change thy clothes,' 'disguise thyself.' So in Syr. ܐܶܫܬܰܢܝ for ܐܶܬܫܰܢܝ Ethpe'el of ܫܢܳܐ, here and in *ch.* 22. 30; 1 Sam. 10. 6; *al.*

ולא ידעו] Impers., 'that (men) may not know,' so RV. 'that thou be not known.'

---

1 The vocalization חֹרֶב 'drought,' in preference to חֶרֶב, is adopted by most moderns. Cf. Dri. *Deuteronomy*, *ad loc.*

אתי] Kt. אַתִּי as in II. 4. 16, 23; 8. 1; Judg. 17. 2; Jer. 4. 30; Ezek. 36. 13†; Q're always אַתְּ. אַתִּי is the more ancient form of the pron. 2nd pers. fem. sing., and appears to be a dialectical survival. Cf. Ar. أَنْتِ, Eth. አንቲ: *anti;* Assyr. *atti-e;* Syr. ܐܢܬܝ *att,* where ܝ, though written, is not pronounced.

שִׁלֹה] Also written שִׁלוֹ, שִׁילוֹ; probably originally שִׁלוֹן, and so גִּלֹה Josh. 15. 51; 2 Sam. 15. 12 originally גִּלוֹן, as forming adjectives שִׁילֹנִי *ch.* 11. 29; *al.;* גִּלוֹנִי 2 Sam. 15. 12; 23. 34. Wright, however (*Compar. Gramm.* 138 *f.*), suggests the possibility of an original *Shailâ'u, Gailâ'u* with termination like Ar. ٰاءُ—. The site of Shiloh is described in Judg. 21. 19 as 'N. of Beth-el, E. of the highway which goes up from Beth-el to Shechem, S. of Lebonah,' and this accurately corresponds to the modern *Seilûn;* cf. Rob. *BR.* ii. 268 *ff.;* Baed. 250.

הוא דבר עלי למלך] 'He spoke of me *as* (lit. *for*) king,' i.e. predicted that I should be king; a use of ל common in such phrases as נתן ל, שים ל, עשה ל, פקד ל, but somewhat strange after דבר. Cod. A τοῦ βασιλεῦσαι, Vulg. *quod regnaturus essem,* Pesh. ܕܐܡܠܟ, Targ. למהוי מלכא suggest לִמְלֹךְ '*that I should reign,*' probably correctly. So Th., Klo., Kamp., Benz., Kit.

3. נקדים] Only elsewhere Josh. 9. 5, 12, where the word denotes dry fragments of old bread. Here probably some kind of *cakes* or dry *biscuits;* so LXX, Luc. κολλύρια, Vulg. *crustulam,* Pesh. ܩܠܘܪܐ, Targ. כיסנין (cf. Levy *s.v.*).

5. ויהוה אמר] 'Now Yahwe *had* said'; pluperfect. The writer, wishing to narrate an event *anterior* to that described in the previous verse ותבוא וג׳, cuts the thread of continuous narrative formed by the succession of imperfects with ו *consec.* by interposing the subject between the conjunction and the verb, and thus starts afresh from a new standpoint. Cf. *ch.* 22. 31 ומלך ארם צוה '*had* commanded,' prior to the commencement of the battle; II. 7. 17; 9. 16b; Gen. 31. 34; *al.;* Dri. § 76 γ *Obs.*

לדרש דבר] 'To seek an oracle.'† Cf. II. 1. 16 לדרש בדברו. The more usual phrase is לדרש את יהוה 'To seek, or inquire of Yahwe'; *ch.* 22. 8; II. 22. 18; Gen. 25. 22; *al.*

כָּזֹה וְכָזֶה] So Judg. 18. 4; 2 Sam. 11. 25. On זֹה cf. II. 6. 19 *note*.

ויהי כבאה וג׳] Read, with Cod. A, Vulg. וַיְהִי כבאה וג׳ 'And it came to pass that, as she came in, she was dissembling herself.' The sentence belongs to the narrator's description, and not, as the MT. vocalization is intended to indicate, to the words of Yahwe. מתנכרה lit. 'making herself strange' here and in *v.* 6; elsewhere in this sense only in Gen. 42. 7, of Joseph's conduct to his brethren.

6. את קול רגליה באה] 'The sound of her feet as she came in.' The participle באה agrees with the suffix of רגליה. So, if vocalization be correct, Ps. 69. 4 כָּלוּ עֵינַי מְיַחֵל וג׳ 'mine eyes consume as I wait &c.' Cf. *note* on *ch.* 1. 41.

למה זה] 'Why, now?' or, with emphasis, '*Why?*' The enclitic זה, with something of adverbial force, gives point and colour to the query. So often:—Gen. 18. 13; 25. 22; *al.* Cf. מַה־זֶּה *ch.* 21. 5; *al.*; מִי־זֶה 1 Sam. 17. 55, 56; *al.*; אֵי־זֶה *ch.* 13. 12 *note*; with ה interr. הַאַתָּה זֶה *ch.* 18. 7 *note*; הִנֵּה־זֶה *ch.* 19. 5 *note*; עַתָּה־זֶה *ch.* 17. 24; II. 5. 22. In Ar. ذَا is used in the same way:—لِمَاذَا, مَاذَا, مَنْ ذَا; cf. Fleischer, *Kleinere Schriften*, i. 355 *f.*

ואנכי שלוח אליך קשה] 'Seeing that I am sent unto thee with something harsh.' קשה is direct accusative after שלוח,—'given in commission something harsh,' and with an active verb would form the remoter accusative,—שְׁלָחַנִי קָשָׁה 'he has commissioned me (with) something harsh.' For this use of שלח with double accusative cf. Ex. 4. 28 כל דברי י׳ אשר שְׁלָחוֹ; so with צִוָּה, 1 Sam. 21. 3 המלך צוני דבר; Ex. 34. 32; *al.* For קשה cf. *ch.* 12. 13 *note*.

7. נגיד] Cf. *ch.* 1. 35 *note*.

9. ואתי השלכת וג׳] So Ezek. 23. 35; Neh. 9. 26. Of Yahwe's remission of sins, Isa. 38. 17†. Cf. Ps. 50. 17.

10. עצור וג׳] See *note* on *vv.* 1 *ff.*

כאשר יבער הגלל] Cf. *ch.* 1. 6 *note*.

12. בבאה] If not an error for בְּבֹא, an isolated instance of the feminine termination with infin. constr. of a verb ע״ו. The explanation of Ew. § 309[c], that the termination is suff. 3 fem. sing. (with omission of *Mappiq* from ה as in II. 8. 6; *al.*), and refers by anticipation to הָעִירָה, is very unnatural.

13. דבר טוב] ‘Something good.’

14. זה היום] ‘*To-day!*’ or ‘this very day!’ If the text be correct (cf. *note* following), זה is used δεικτικῶς, and adds point to היום which in English can scarcely be brought out but by emphasis in pronunciation. Occurrences of the pronoun thus preceding the subs. to which it is in apposition are rare and in most cases poetical. Cf., however, II. 6. 33 זֹאת הָרָעָה; Isa. 23. 13 זֶה הָעָם; Josh. 9. 12 זֶה לַחְמֵנוּ.

ומה גם עתה] Most obscure, and probably corrupt. The only possible rendering seems to be ‘But what? (*sc.* do I say?’ מה used *asyndetos* as in Prov. 31. 2), so with emphasis ‘*Nay*, even *now!*’ The words thus form a climax to זה היום, as though this expression did not sufficiently depict the instant imminence of the destruction of Jeroboam’s house.

15. אשריהם] ‘Their Asherim.’ The אֲשֵׁרָה was made of wood Judg. 6. 26, probably in most cases of a whole tree-trunk, Deut. 16. 21 (אֲשֵׁרָה כָּל־עֵץ in appos. ‘an Ashera—any kind of tree’), and was planted (נטע Deut. *l.c.*) or set on end (העמיד 2 Chr. 33. 19) in the ground. When destroyed it is said to be cut down (כרת Judg. 6. 25; II. 18. 4; 23. 14), chopped down (גדע Deut. 7. 5; 2 Chr. 14. 2; 31. 1), plucked up (נתש Mic. 5. 13), pulled down (נתץ 2 Chr. 34. 7), or burnt (Deut. 12. 3; II. 23. 15)[1]. Thus אשרה is thought to designate a pole set up as a symbol or substitute for the sacred tree venerated by the ancient Semites as the abode of the deity. This pole appears to have usually stood beside the altar at the Bāmōth of the Canaanites, and to have been adopted from them by the Israelites in their perverted worship of Yahwe, or definitely extraneous worship; cf. Deut. 16. 21; Judg. 6. 25 *ff.* See R. Sm. *Rel. Sem.*[2] 187 *ff.*[2]

---

[1] שבר והדק ‘broke in pieces and beat small,’ 2 Chr. 34. 4, probably applies chiefly to the graven and molten images, and only by zeugma to the (wooden) Asherim. LXX, Luc., making a different division of the verse, read *καὶ* (Luc. ἐξ)ἔκοψε τὰ ἄλση, i.e. וַיְגַדַּע הָאֲשֵׁרִים.

[2] F. B. Jevons, *Introduction to History of Religion*, pp. 134 *f.*, collects instances of the use of symbolic poles among non-Semitic races:—‘This *ashera* appears again amongst people which differ as widely as possible from one another in race and place and time: it is presupposed by the ξόανα of the

It is a moot question whether the name Ashera is also used to designate a particular Canaanite *goddess*. Mention is made of an *image* of the Ashera placed by Manasseh in the Temple, II. 21. 7, cf. *ch.* 15. 13 *note;* II. 23. 7 perhaps speaks of the making of 'shrines' for the Ashera (cf. *note ad loc.*); and the Baʿal and the Ashera are coupled together as the objects of idolatrous worship, *ch.* 18. 19 (but see *note*); II. 23. 4; cf. Judg. 3. 7. In the Tell-el-Amarna inscriptions we find a name *Abd-Ašratu* = 'servant of Ashera' (cf. Schrader, *ZA.* iii. 363 *f.; KAT.*[3] i. 276), and the name occurs twice with doubtful significance in Phoenician inscriptions. Cf. Dri. *Deut.* pp. 201 *ff.*

Verss.:—LXX always ἄλσος, pl. ἄλση, except 2 Chr. 15. 16 τῇ Ἀστάρτῃ (so Luc.); 24. 18 ταῖς Ἀστάρταις (Luc. τῇ Ἀστάρτῃ); Isa. 17. 8; 27. 9 τὰ δένδρα; Luc. in II. 23. 4 τῇ Ἀσηρώθ. Vulg. always *lucus*, except Judg. 6. 25, 26, 30 *nemus*, 3. 7 *Astaroth*. Pesh. 19 times ܕܚܠܬܐ, pl. ܕܚ̈ܠܬܐ 'object of reverence'; Judg. 3. 7; 6. 25, 26, 28, 30 ܐܣܛܪܐ, pl. ܐܣܛܪ̈ܬܐ 'Astarte'; Deut. 16. 21; Mic. 5. 13 ܡܛ̈ܠܠܬܐ 'trees'; Deut. 7. 5; 12. 4 ܡܣܟ̈ܠܬܐ 'molten images' (?); 2 Chr. 15. 6; 24. 18 ܙܕܡܐ, pl. ܙܕ̈ܡܐ 'image'; 2 Chr. 34. 3; Isa. 17. 8 ܦܬܟ̈ܪܐ 'idols'; 2 Chr. 14. 2 ܐܢܕܪ̈ܝܛܐ ἀνδριάντας; 2 Chr. 17. 6 ܢܟ̈ܠܘܬܐ 'high-places'; 1 Chr. 31. 1; 33. 3; 34. 3 ܢܨܒ̈ܐ 'nemora' (?) Targ. transliterates.

מכעיסים] The participle determines the subject, forming the secondary predicate; 'because they have made &c., *vexing* Yahwe.' Cf. Dri. *Tenses*, § 161, 2.

16. ויתן] 'Shall *give up*.' Cf. the phrase נתן לפני אויב *ch.* 8. 46 *note.*

17. היא באה וג׳] Cf. *ch.* 1. 14 *note.*

Greeks; it is found among the Ainos; the gods of the Brazilian tribes were represented by poles stuck upright in the ground, at the foot of which offerings were laid; the Hurd Islanders "in their houses had several stocks or small pillars of wood, four or five feet high, as the representatives of household gods, and on these they poured oil [which takes the place of fat or blood], and laid before them offerings of cocoa-nuts and fish"; the Kureks at irregular times slaughter a reindeer or a dog, put its head on a pole facing east, and mentioning no name, say, "This for thee: grant me a blessing."'

14. 19, 20. *Summary of Jeroboam's reign.*

R^D. Cf. *Introduction.*

19. דברי הימים] 'Acts of the days,' i. e. 'daily record of events,' and so 'annals.'

14. 21–31. *Reḥoboam, king of Judah.*

Ch. 14. 26–28, 31 = 2 Chr. 12. 9–11, 16.

Beside the introductory and summarizing formulae *vv.* 21, 22[a], 29–31 (see *Introd.*), the hand of R^D is to be noticed in *vv.* 22–24:—

21. בירושלם העיר וג׳] Cf. *ch.* 8. 16 *note.*

22. ויקנאו אתו] 'And they moved him to jealousy'; cf. Deut. 32. 21 המה קנאוני בלא אל. Cf. the phrase of the decalogue אֵל קַנָּא 'a jealous God,' Ex. 20. 5 (E); ‖ Deut. 5. 9, so Deut. 4. 24; 6. 15†. אֵל־קַנּוֹא Josh. 24. 19 (E); Nah. 1. 2†.

23. על כל . . . רענן] So exactly II. 17. 10 (R^D); Jer. 2. 20; cf. II. 16. 4 (R^D, ‖ 2 Chr. 28. 4); Deut. 12. 2; Ezek. 6. 13; Jer. 3. 6, 13; 17. 2; Isa. 57. 5.

24. ככל התועבת . . . ישראל] So II. 16. 3 (‖ 2 Chr. 28. 3); 21. 2 (‖ 2 Chr. 33. 2) both R^D. הוריש with יהוה as subj., used of driving out the nations of Canaan, occurs in JE Ex. 34. 24; Num. 32. 21; Josh. 3. 10, but elsewhere appears to belong entirely to D and to passages influenced by D:—Deut. 4. 38; 9. 4, 5; 11. 23; 18. 12; Josh. 13. 6; 23. 5, 9, 13; Judg. 2. 21, 23; *ch.* 21. 26; II. 17. 8; Ps. 44. 3†. ככל תועבת הג׳ cf. Deut. 18. 9; 2 Chr. 36. 14.

22. ויעש יהודה וג׳] LXX, Luc. καὶ ἐποίησε Ῥοβοὰμ . . . καὶ παρεζήλωσεν αὐτὸν κ.τ.λ. is inconsistent with the context which lapses into the pl. (LXX οἱ πατέρες αὐτῶν, *v.* 23, LXX, Luc. καὶ ᾠκοδόμησαν) as in MT. Luc. οἱ πατέρες αὐτοῦ (David and Solomon) is scarcely possible in view of the manner in which R^D treats David as his standard of piety (*ch.* 3. 14 *note*).

23. במות] Cf. *ch.* 3. 2, 3 *note.*

מצבות] 'Pillars.' מַצֵּבָה is 'something set up,' i. e. a stone pillar or obelisk, doubtless representing the sacred stone which in primitive times was thought to be the abode of the deity. Cf. R. Sm. *Rel.*

Sem.[2] 203 *ff.* Thus Jacob sets up a rough stone as a Maççēba to mark the scene of a Theophany, and anoints it with oil, calling it the house of God, Gen. 28. 18, 22; 31. 13 (E); and Maççēbōth are raised by him and by Moses to indicate that Yahwe is witness or party to a covenant or agreement, Gen. 31. 44, 45, 51 *ff.* (E); Ex. 24. 3, 4 (JE); cf. also Isa. 19. 19, 20. The Maççēba played a prominent part in the worship of the Canaanites, standing, like the Ashēra, beside the altar at the Bāma. Its destruction is strictly enjoined in the Book of the Covenant, Ex. 23. 24, and in Deut. 7. 5; 12. 3, this latter code also forbidding its use for the worship of Yahwe, 16. 22. Jehu destroyed the Maççēbōth at the Temple of the Canaanite Ba'al, II. 10. 26 *f.*, while Maççēbōth of all kinds were demolished with the destruction of the Bāmōth at the reformations under Hezekiah and Josiah. Cf. further, for the use of the term in Phoenician to denote a commemorative obelisk, Dri. *Deut.* p. 204.

אשרים] Cf. *v.* 15 *note.*

רענן] Prob. 'spreading,' i.e. with branches hanging down and affording shelter for such worship. Cf. Verss.:—LXX, Luc. *συσκίου*, Vulg. *frondosam*, Pesh. ܟܒܝܟ 'thick,' Targ. עבוף 'shady.' Etym. doubtful.

24. קדש] 'Temple prostitutes.' The word is here collective as in *ch.* 22. 47, and includes persons of both sexes, קְדֵשִׁים and קְדֵשׁוֹת, who were 'set apart' for the immoral rites of the Canaanites, carried on within the precincts of their sanctuaries. A law against the introduction of these practices into Israel is found in Deut. 23. 18. Asa, *ch.* 15. 12, and Jehoshaphat, *ch.* 22. 47, effected a banishment of קדשים from Judah, and Josiah destroyed the houses of the קדשים which, during Manasseh's reign, had been established even at the Temple of Yahwe, II. 23. 7.

LXX, Luc. *σύνδεσμος* erroneously read קֶשֶׁר for קדש.

25. עלה שושק] Cf. *ch.* 11. 40 *note.* This invasion of Palestine by Sheshonk is recorded in an inscription upon the walls of the temple of Amon at Karnak. From the list of cities subjugated it appears that the expedition was directed not only against Judah

but also against the N. kingdom. The name of Jerusalem cannot be identified in the list. Cf. Dri. *Authority*, 87 *f.*; Sta. *Ges.* i. 353 *f.*

26. After ואת אצרות בית המלך LXX, Luc. have the insertion καὶ τὰ δόρατα τὰ χρυσᾶ ἃ ἔλαβεν Δαυεὶδ ἐκ χειρὸς τῶν παίδων ʽΑδραάζαρ βασιλέως Σουβὰ καὶ εἰσήνεγκεν αὐτὰ εἰς ʼΙερουσαλήμ. The reference is to 2 Sam. 8. 7, where also LXX, Luc. contain an addition stating that Shishak made booty of these shields in his expedition against Jerusalem recorded in our passage. Th., noticing that LXX in Samuel renders שִׁלְטֵי by χλιδῶνας, while in Kings addition the word used is δόρατα, infers thence that while Samuel addition is certainly a gloss (so Wellh.), Kings addition must be based upon an authentic text. Possibly, however, both additions are later cross-references derived from some independent source. If original, the sentence of LXX in our passage represents וְאֶת־שִׁלְטֵי הַזָּהָב אֲשֶׁר לָקַח דָּוִד מִיַּד עַבְדֵי הֲדַדְעֶזֶר מֶלֶךְ צוֹבָה וַיְבִיאֵם יְרוּשָׁלֶם.

ואת הכל לקח] LXX, Luc. omit ו, rightly. In Pesh. the whole is wanting.

27. והפקיד] We should expect וַיַּפְקֵד in continuation of ויעש, since the shields appear to have been given permanently into the charge of the שרי הרצים. Possibly, however, והפקיד is intended as a frequentative, like ישאום, והשיבום *v.* 28 which are used of the recurrent occasions upon which the רצים carried the shields.

על יד] 'Upon the hand,' i.e. '*into the possession* or *care of*.' So with נתן Gen. 42. 37, תנה אתו על ידי, 'Give him *into my care*.' Cf. the phrase הִגִּיר עַל־יְדֵי־חֶרֶב, 'deliver *into the power of* the sword,' Jer. 18. 21; Ezek. 35. 5; Ps. 63. 11.

שרי הרצים] Cf. *ch.* 1. 5 *note*.

28. מדי] Lit. 'out of the sufficiency of,' and so, 'as often as.' Followed thus by Infin. ‖ 2 Chr. 12. 11; 1 Sam. 1. 7; 18. 30; II. 4. 8; Isa. 28. 19; Jer. 31. 19†.

תא] Prob. 'guard room'; Vulg. *armamentarium*. The word is only elsewhere used in Ezek. 40. 7 *ff.*, where it denotes the small guard chambers at the gates of the outer court of Ezekiel's Temple.

30. ומלחמה וג׳] Cf. *note* on *ch.* 12. 1–24. For this summary statement by R^D of warfare recorded with some detail in the

Annals cf. *ch.* 15. 6, 16, 32, and *v.* 19, *ch.* 22. 46; II. 13. 12; 14. 15, 28.

כל הימים] Cf. *ch.* 5. 15 *note.*

31. The mention of the name of the queen-mother, repeated from *v.* 21, occurs only here in the summary of a reign, and is rightly omitted by LXX, Luc., Pesh., ‖ 2 Chr.

אבים] So *ch.* 15. 1, 7 (twice), 8†. In every case, Luc. Ἀβιά, Pesh. ܐܒܝܐ presuppose אֲבִיָּה as in MT. 1 Chr. 3. 10; 2 Chr. 12. 16; 13. 1, 2, 3, 4, 15, 17, 19, 22, 23; LXX Ἀβιού, אֲבִיָּהוּ as in MT. 2 Chr. 13. 20, 21. We may therefore conclude that this latter name, either in its longer or shorter form, stood originally in the text of Kings, and was altered by a later hand into אבים, perhaps for the sake of making a distinction from אביה of *ch.* 14. 1.

15. 1–8. *Abijah, king of Judah.*

The whole account is framed by R^D. For *vv.* 1–3, 7, 8 cf. *Introd.*; *v.* 4 ניר cf. *ch.* 11. 36; *v.* 5 אשר עשה וג׳ cf. *ch.* 11. 33, and generally for reference to David *ch.* 3. 14.

1. אבים] Luc. adds υἱὸς Ῥοβοάμ, LXX υἱὸς Ἰεροβοάμ.

2. ושם אמו מעכה בת אבישלום] Precisely the same statement is made concerning Asa the *son* of Abijah *v.* 10; cf. *v.* 13. Hence Ew., Ke., Ber. suggest that the mother of Abijah continued to hold the position of גבירה or 'chief lady' during the reign of her *grandson* Asa. More probably there has occurred a very early confusion between the mothers of the two kings which cannot now be elucidated. Kit. (*Ges.*) supposes that both were named Maʿacha, and that the addition בת אבישלום in *v.* 10 is an erroneous insertion from *v.* 2. LXX, Luc. *v.* 2 Μααχά, θυγάτηρ Ἀβεσσαλώμ, *v.* 10 Ἀνά, θυγάτηρ Ἀβεσσαλώμ, so *v.* 10 Ἀνά; probably an alteration made to remove the difficulty, the repetition of the name Ἀβεσσαλώμ being against the originality of the reading. 2 Chr. 11. 20–22, which gives the name of Abijah's mother as מַעֲכָה and names her other sons, appears to be derived from an ancient source. In 2 Chr. 13. 2 she is called מִיכָיָהוּ, and so Vulg. *Michaia*, Jos. *Ant.* viii. 11, § 3 Μαχαία;

but LXX, Luc., Pesh. presuppose מעכה rightly, מיכיהו being elsewhere a male name. So Ew., Ber., Kamp., Kit., *Sieg. u. Sta.*

אבישלום] 2 Chr. 11. 20 אַבְשָׁלוֹם. Doubtless the son of David is here meant, and Jos. (*Ant.* viii. 10, § 1) is probably correct in saying that Ma'acha was really his *granddaughter*, her mother being Tamar the daughter of Absalom (2 Sam. 14. 27):—ἤγετο ὕστερον (Ῥοβόαμος) καὶ τὴν ἐκ τῆς Ἀψαλώμου θυγατρὸς Θαμάρης Μαχάνην ὄνομα καὶ αὐτὴν οὖσαν συγγενῆ. Thus Ma'acha bore the same name as her great-grandmother 2 Sam. 3. 3. The statement of 2 Chr. 13. 2 that she was the daughter of אוּרִיאֵל מִן־גִּבְעָה[1] perhaps implies (Ke., Ber.) that this Uriel married Tamar, Absalom's daughter.

4ª. בירושלם] LXX, Luc. omit.

4ᵇ. בנו] LXX, Luc. τὰ τέκνα αὐτοῦ rightly presuppose בָּנָיו. So Klo., Kamp.

5. רק בדבר וג׳] LXX omits. The words may perhaps be a qualification inserted by a later hand.

6. ומלחמה וג׳] LXX, Luc. omit. The words are an erroneous insertion from *ch.* 14. 30. Pesh. reads ܐܒܝܐ ܒܪ ܪܚܒܥܡ 'Abijah son of R.' for רחבעם, and omits the similar statement in *v.* 7.

15. 9–24. *Asa, king of Judah.*

Ch. 15. 13–22 = 2 Chr. 15. 16—16. 6.

R^D—introduction and summary; *v.* 14 (cf. *ch.* 3. 2, 3); casting of *v.* 12 (cf. *note* on הגללים below) and of *v.* 16 (cf. *ch.* 14. 30) from information derived from the Annals. From this source all further particulars of the reign are drawn.

12. הקדשים] LXX suitably renders τὰς τελετάς, for which Luc. by corruption reads τὰς στήλας. Cf. *note* on *ch.* 14. 24.

הגללים] '*The idol-blocks*'; a term of opprobrium. Probably lit. 'logs' or 'rolling things,' from גלל 'to roll'; so Ges., &c. Ew. (*Die Lehre der Bibel von Gott*, ii. 264) prefers to render '*doll-images*,' as rolled or wrapped up in clothes, dressed up. Smend's proposal to connect the word with גֵּל, גָּלָל 'dung' (Ezek. 6. 4), as is done

[1] Luc. Ἀβεσσαλώμ is clearly a correction in accordance with 11. 20.

by the Rabbinic interpreters, is improbable. The word occurs elsewhere in Kings, *ch.* 21. 26; II. 17. 12; 21. 11, 21; 23. 24 (all R[D]); and besides, Deut. 29. 16; Lev. 26. 30 (H), and thirty-nine times in Ezekiel †.

13. ויסרה] The ו *consec.* introduces the predicate after the *accus. pendens,* as in *ch.* 9. 21 (cf. *note*).

מגבירה] Cf. *ch.* 11. 19 *note.*

מפלצת לאשרה] 'A horrible thing for an ashera' (or 'for Ashera,' supposing the word here to denote a Canaanite goddess; cf. *note* on *ch.* 14. 15).

מפלצת only occurs again in ‖ 2 Chr. 15. 16, and its meaning, 'an object causing *shuddering* or *horror,*' must be determined from the use of the verb יִתְפַּלָּצוּן prob. 'tremble,' Job 9. 6†, and the substantive פַּלָּצוּת 'trembling' or 'horror,' Isa. 21. 4; Ezek. 7. 18; Ps. 55. 6; Job 21. 6†. The nature of this 'horrible thing' is not clear. It must have been some kind of idol or idolatrous symbol, and Vulg., Kings *in sacris Priapi, v.* 13[b] *simulacrum turpissimum*[1], Chr. *simulacrum Priapi,* finds reference to a *phallus* cult. This explanation is adopted by Ew., Th., Ber., Kit.; Ew., citing the somewhat obscure תִּפְלַצְתְּךָ, perhaps 'Oh, thy *wantonness!*' Jer. 49. 16. LXX, Luc., Pesh. misunderstand, and Targ. offers no elucidation.

15. וקדשו] Read וְקָדָשָׁיו with ‖ 2 Chr. 15. 18 and LXX, Luc., Pesh., Targ. 'And he brought the votive gifts of his father and his own votive gifts into the house of Yahwe—silver and gold and vessels.'

17. הרמה] *Er-Râm,* two hours north of Jerusalem, and a short distance to the west of Geba (*Jeba'*). Rob. *BR.* i. 576; Smith, *Hist. Geogr.* 251.

לבלתי תת יצא ובא] Cf. Josh. 6. 1.

18. בן הדד] Three Aramaean kings of this name are generally

---

[1] The rendering *ne esset princeps in sacris Priapi, et in luco eius quem consecraverat* seems to presuppose a wrong rearrangement of words in some such form as מהיות גבירה למפלצת ולאשרה אשר עשתה; *v.* 13[b], *subvertitque specum eius, et confregit simulacrum turpissimum,* is probably merely a paraphrastic expansion of ויכרת מפלצתה.

supposed to be mentioned in these books; cf. *ch.* 20. 1 *ff.;* II. 13. 24. Winckler, however, regards the Ben-hadad of this passage as one with the Ben-hadad of *ch.* 20; an identification which postulates a reign of not much more than forty years in length. Cf. *Alttest. Untersuchungen*, pp. 60 *ff.* הֲדַד, the Aram. weather-god, is the same as רִמּוֹן (II. 5. 18 *note*); cf. the compound name הֲדַדְרִמּוֹן Zech. 12. 11; Baethgen, *Semit. Relig.* pp. 67 *f.*

חזיון] LXX Ἀζείν, Luc., Cod. A Ἀζαήλ. Ew., Th., Klo., &c. plausibly suggest the identification of חזיון with רזון of *ch.* 11. 23, whose name appears in LXX (11. 14) as Ἐσρώμ, Luc. Ἐσρών, Pesh. ܗܕܪܘܢ. Klo. regards חֶזְרוֹן as the original form of the name.

19. ברית וג׳] '*There is* a covenant between me and thee, &c.' LXX διάθου διαθήκην κ.τ.λ. is self-condemned.

20. עיון] Mentioned again in connexion with אבל בית מעכה and other cities of the north, as taken by Tiglath-Pileser in the reign of Pekah (II. 15. 29). Rob. suggests as the site of עיון the modern مرج عيون 'the plain of *'Ayûn*,' a fertile basin lying to the north of the plain of the *Hûleh*, and south-west of the ancient Dan. To the south of *Merj 'Ayûn* lies *Âbil*, probably the site of אבל בית מעכה. *BR.* ii. 438; iii. 372 *f.*

ואת כל כנרות] Th. is right in noticing that the reference, thus phrased, is to a *district*, and not to a city. So, as here in plural, Josh. 11. 2, and singular כִּנֶּרֶת Deut. 3. 17. In Josh. 19. 35 the allusion seems to be to a *city* כִּנֶּרֶת in the land of Naphtali, while in Num. 34. 11; Josh. 13. 27 we find mention of the *Sea of Cinnereth* יָם כִּנֶּרֶת, Josh. 12. 3 יָם כִּנְּרוֹת. Targ., except Josh. 19. 35 where it preserves כנרת, renders גניסר, גינסר, this being the name adopted in later times; cf. 1 Macc. 11. 67 Γεννησάρ, S. Matt. 14. 34; S. Mark 6. 53; S. Luke 5. 1 Γεννησαρέτ. The region of Gennesaret is described by Josephus (*BJ.* iii. 10, § 8) as being of marvellous beauty and fertility, and accordingly is generally identified with the level plain *El-Ghuwêr* on the north-west shore of the lake of Galilee; Sta. *SP.* 374 *f.;* Rob. *BR.* iii. 348 *f.;* Smith, *Hist. Geogr.* 443. A city כִּנֶּרֶת may have lain in this district, but its site is unknown.

על כל ארץ נפתלי] RV., Kamp. '*with* all the land of Naphtali,' taking על in the sense '*in addition to*,' as in Gen. 32. 12 אם על בנים; Ex. 35. 22; Job 38. 32. But such a use of the preposition is here very unnatural, and LXX, Luc. ἕως, i. e. עַד '*even unto* the whole land of Naphtali,' preserve a superior reading.

‖ 2 Chr. 16. 4ᵇ reads, in place of *v.* 20ᵇ, וְאֵת כָּל־מִסְכְּנוֹת עָרֵי נַפְתָּלִי.

21. וַיֵּשֶׁב] LXX, Luc., Vulg. וַיָּשָׁב, incorrectly.

22. השמיע] 'Summoned.' In this special sense only again in Jer. 50. 29; 51. 27; Piʿel 1 Sam. 15. 4; 23. 8†.

אין נקי] 'Without exemption'; lit. 'none was exempted,' a circumstantial clause; Dri. *Tenses*, § 164. For נקי '*free*' *from obligation*, cf. Num. 32. 22 והייתם נקיים מיהוה ומישראל.

גבע] Now called *Jebaʿ;* south of *Mukhmâs* (Michmash) from which it is separated by the steep ravine called the *Wady es-Suweinet*, the scene of Jonathan's adventure 1 Sam. 14. 1 *ff.* Rob. *BR.* i. 440.

הַמִּצְפָּה] Also called הַמִּצְפֶּה Josh. 18. 26. No modern equivalent of the name has been discovered, but *Nebi Samwîl*, about five miles NNW. of Jerusalem, and visible therefrom, is plausibly regarded by Rob. (*BR.* i. 459 *f.*) and others as the site of the ancient city. Mizpah was well known in connexion with Samuel, 1 Sam. 7. 5 *ff.*, 16; 10. 17, and is described in 1 Macc. 3. 46 as being κατέναντι Ἰερουσαλήμ.

23. חלה את רגליו] 'He was diseased in his feet.' The accusative, as in Greek, specifies the part affected; cf. Gen. 3. 15 הוא ישופך ראש; Deut. 33. 11; *al.* Da. § 71; Ew. § 281, c. 3. Luc. after the words לעת זקנתו adds ἐποίησεν Ἀσὰ τὸ πονηρόν, καί—a gloss inserted to assign a cause for his disease, and perhaps with reference to the events described in 2 Chr. 16. 7–12.

15. 25–32. *Nadab, king of Israel.*

Rᴰ *vv.* 25, 26, 29ᵇ–32.

27. לבית יששכר] '*Belonging to* the house of Issachar.' In place of יששכר LXX reads Βελαάν, Luc. Βεδδαμά.

ויכהו בעשא] LXX ἐχάραξεν αὐτόν, Luc. ἐχαράκωσεν αὐτόν.

גבתון] Pesh. ܓܬ 'Gath,' an easy substitution of a well known for a less known place. So *ch.* 16. 15, 17.

28. לאסא מלך יהודה] LXX τοῦ 'Ασὰ υἱοῦ 'Αβιού.

תחתיו] Luc. Βαασὰ ἐπὶ τὸν 'Ισραήλ. LXX omits.

29. כל נשמה] 'Anything breathing'; lit. 'any breath.' So Deut. 20. 16; Josh. 10. 40; 11. 11, 14 (D^2); Ps. 150. 6†.

עד הִשמדו] Cf. II. 3. 25 *note* on עד הִשאיר.

כדבר י׳ אשר דבר] Reference to *ch.* 14. 14. Cf. *ch.* 13. 26 *note.*

ביד עבדו] Cf. *ch.* 8. 53 *note.*

30. בכעסו אשר הכעיס] Cf. *ch.* 14. 9 *note.*

י׳ אלהי ישראל] Cf. *ch.* 8. 15 *note.*

32. A repetition of *v.* 16, rightly omitted by LXX, Luc.

15. 33—16. 7. *Ba'asha, king of Israel.*

The whole is framed by R^{D}.

16. 1–4. Cf. phraseology of Aḥijah's speech *ch.* 14. 7–16 *notes.*

2. נגיד] Cf. *ch.* 1. 35 *note.*

בחטאתם] Read בְּהַבְלֵיהֶם 'with their vain things,' as in *vv.* 13, 26 (cf. Deut. 32. 21), with LXX, Luc. ἐν τοῖς ματαίοις αὐτῶν, and probably Pesh. ܒܥܒܕ̈ ܐܝܕܝܗܘܢ 'with the work of their hands.' So Klo.

7. ועל כל הרעה . . . ועל אשר הכה אתו] '*Both* because of all the evil, &c., *and* because he smote him.' The repeated ו, '*both . . . and*,' is, however, rare (poetical); Job 34. 29; Ps. 76. 7; except in the rather different class of instances cited *v.* 11. אתו refers to Jeroboam as personifying his house, and Vulg. is incorrect in paraphrasing *ob hanc causam occidit eum, hoc est, Iehu filium Hanani, prophetam.*

16. 8–14. *Elah, king of Israel.*

Framed throughout by R^{D}, with short notices from the Annals *vv.* 9, 10$^{a\alpha, b}$, 11^{a}.

9. שתה שכור] So *ch.* 20. 16. 'Drinking to excess'; lit. 'drinking, drunk,' the two words being in apposition, and the second making closer definition of the first. Cf. *ch.* 1. 2 *note* on נערה בתולה.

ארצא] LXX 'Ωσά, Luc. 'Ασά.

אשר על הבית] Cf. *ch.* 4. 6 *note.* Targ. strangely explains ארצא as the name of an *idol;*—בית ארצא טעותא די בביתא בתרצה.

11[a], 12[a]. LXX, Luc. omit, through homoioteleuton, את כל בית בעשא.

11. משתין בקיר] Cf. *ch.* 14. 10 *note.*

וגאליו ורעהו] '*Neither* kinsmen *nor* friends.' The repeated ו, '*neither . . . nor,*' or without preceding negative, '*both . . . and,*' is used idiomatically in connecting an exhaustive category on to a previous more general statement, of which it is epexegetical. So Num. 9. 14 חֻקָּה אַחַת יִהְיֶה לָכֶם וְלַגֵּר וּלְאֶזְרַח הָאָרֶץ; Gen. 34. 28 אֶת־צֹאנָם וגו׳ וְאֵת אֲשֶׁר־בָּעִיר וְאֶת־אֲשֶׁר בַּשָּׂדֶה לָקָחוּ; Josh. 9. 23; Jer. 13. 14; 21. 6; Neh. 12. 28. גֹּאֵל is one to whom pertain the duties of a kinsman—in this case, the prosecution of a blood-feud; cf. the phrase גֹּאֵל הַדָּם '*the blood-avenger,*' 2 Sam. 14. 11; Deut. 19. 6, 12, and in P Num. 35. 19, 21, 24, 25, 27; Josh. 20. 3, 5 (om. LXX), 9. For ורעהו sing. used collectively cf. Da. § 17.

12. כדבר וג׳] Cf. *ch.* 15. 29.

ביד יהוא] LXX καὶ πρὸς Εἰοὺ as in *v.* 1; MT. אל י׳, where, however, LXX reads ἐν χειρὶ E.

13. אל כל חטאות] אל for על; cf. *ch.* 13. 29 *note.* The sins of Ba'asha and his son are here spoken of in the terms usually applied by R^D to the sins of Jeroboam. See *Introduction.*

להכעים] Cf. *ch.* 14. 9 *note.*

י׳ אלהי ישראל] Cf. *ch.* 8. 15 *note.*

16. 15–20. *Zimri, king of Israel.*

R^D, *vv.* 15[a], 19, 20, frames a brief narrative drawn from the Annals.

15. והעם חנים] LXX, Luc. καὶ ἡ παρεμβολὴ Ἰσραήλ, if not a direct paraphrase, probably arose from omission of ע, which gave the reading וְהַמַּחֲנִם or וְהַמַּחֲנֶה, to which the translator added the explanatory Ἰσραήλ. העם is used here, as in *ch.* 20. 15; 1 Sam. 14. 26; 30. 21; 2 Sam. 15. 17, of an *army* or *military detachment:* cf. Vulg. *porro exercitus obsidebat.*

16. וישמע העם החנים לאמר] The use of לאמר with a subj.

different from that of the preceding clause is idiomatic after the verb שמע. Cf. II. 19. 9; ‖ Isa. 37. 9; Deut. 13. 13; 1 Sam. 13. 4; 2 Sam. 19. 3. The new subj. is really the *implied obj.* of the preceding וישמע, e.g. אֶת־הַשֶּׁמַע 'the report,' or אֶת־דִּבְרֵי פ׳ 'someone's words.' This is apparent from Gen. 31. 1 וישמע את דברי בני לבן לאמר; 1 Sam. 24. 10 למה תשמע את דברי אדם לאמר; and, after a verb other than שמע, II. 5. 6 וַיָּבֵא הספר אל מלך ישראל לאמר; so perhaps 2 Sam. 13. 33; Jer. 7. 4.

More peculiar and not to be classed are the cases in which the subj. of לֵאמר is quite indefinite, and lies in a loose sense of the connexion with the preceding clause;—2 Sam. 7. 26 ויגדל שמך עד עולם לאמר י׳ צבאות אלהים על ישראל; Deut. 30. 12, 13 לא בשמים הוא לאמר מי יעלה וג׳; Ex. 5. 19.

Quite a distinct class, however, is formed by cases in which a *passive* verb is employed in the clause preceding לאמר, and the substitution of an active gives the subj. of לאמר;—וַיֻּגַּד לאמר *ch.* 1. 51; II. 6. 13; 8. 7; Gen. 22. 20; 38. 13, 24; Josh. 10. 17; 1 Sam. 15. 12; 19. 19; 2 Sam. 6. 12; Isa. 7. 2†; Ex. 5. 14 וַיֻּכּוּ שטרי בני ישראל . . . לאמר; 1 Sam. 9. 24 כי למועד שָׁמוּר לך לאמר; Isa. 29. 12 וְנִתַּן הספר . . . לאמר (cf. *v.* 11 אשר יִתְּנוּ אתו . . . לאמר).

וימלכו כל ישראל] Luc. καὶ ἐβασίλευσαν ὁ λαός, LXX καὶ ἐβασίλευσαν ἐν Ἰσραήλ. MT. is favoured by *v.* 17[a].

18. ארמון בית המלך] 'the *keep* of the king's palace'; cf. II. 15. 25.

וישרף] Pesh. ܘܐܘܩܕܘ, i. e. וישרפו 'they (the besiegers) burnt &c.'

את בית מלך] Cf. *note* on *ch.* 12. 31.

16. 21, 22. *Civil war between the parties of rival aspirants to the throne of Israel, Tibni and Omri.*

The short notice comes from the Annals.

21. אז יחלק] Cf. *ch.* 3. 16 *note.*

העם ישראל] 'The people Israel'; a case of apposition exactly like הַמֶּלֶךְ דָּוִד; הָהָר שֹׁמְרוֹן *v.* 24. So Josh. 8. 33†; cf. Judg. 20. 22 העם איש ישראל.

לחצי] LXX, Luc. omit, and Klo., Kamp., Kit. regard as an erroneous dittography of the final letter of ישראל and the following חצי.

גינת] On form of name cf. *note* on טפת *ch.* 4. 11.

והחצי] 'And *the* half,' i.e. '*the other* half,' in sharply defined opposition to the previously mentioned חצי העם. LXX *καὶ τὸ ἥμισυ τοῦ λαοῦ γίνεται ὀπίσω Ζαμβρεί* (Luc. *'Αμβρί, τοῦ βασιλεῦσαι αὐτόν*) is probably due to desire for uniformity with the preceding clause.

22. ויחזק . . . את העם] חזק thus followed by accusative only here; '*were strong as regards* the people,' so *prevailed over* them. Cf. the similar (but poetic) use of accus. in יְכָלְתִּיו 'I have prevailed over him,' Ps. 13. 5. The construction is, however, somewhat harsh in prose, and the connexion almost demands (Kamp.) the emendation עַל־הָעָם or מֵהָעָם. LXX for *v.* 22ᵃ *καὶ ἡττήθη ὁ λαὸς ὁ ὢν ὀπίσω Θαμνεὶ υἱοῦ Γωνάθ*, a reading probably due in the first place to omission of ויחזק . . . אחרי עמרי through homoioteleuton with *v.* 21 end.

וימת תבני] LXX, Luc. add *καὶ 'Ιωρὰμ ὁ ἀδελφὸς αὐτοῦ ἐν τῷ καιρῷ ἐκείνῳ*, and then, after וימלך עמרי, *μετὰ Θαμνεί* (Luc. *τὸν Θαβεννεί*); i.e. *v.* 22ᵇ וַיָּמָת תִּבְנִי וְיוֹרָם אָחִיו בָּעֵת הַהִיא וַיִּמְלֹךְ עָמְרִי אַחֲרֵי תִבְנִי 'And Tibni died and his brother Joram at that time, and Omri reigned after Tibni.' The genuineness of this text is favoured by the fact that the additional words supply a detail unessential to the narrative, and thus not to be explained as a later invention. So Th., Kamp., Benz., Kiṭ., Maspero.

16. 23–28. *Omri, king of Israel.*

The work of Rᴰ, with short details from the Annals, *vv.* 23ᵇ, 24.

23. בשנת שלשים ואחת שנה] But Zimri, who reigned but seven days, is said, *v.* 15, to have come to the throne in the twenty-seventh year of Asa. It might therefore be supposed that the civil war, *vv.* 21, 22, lasted some three or four years; but this is precluded by the synchronism in the case of Aḥab's accession, *v.* 29 'the thirty-eighth year of Asa,' which harmonizes with *v.* 15, supposing the interregnum to have been merely a matter of a few days or months—as might be inferred from the absence of special detail—and the length of Omri's reign to be correctly stated as twelve years. It must therefore be concluded that in the synchronism

for Omri's accession thirty-first is an error for twenty-seventh or twenty-eighth.

עמרי] Mentioned in Mesha's inscription, ll. 4 *f.*, as king of Israel who 'afflicted Moab for many days' (*Append.* 1). In the Cuneiform inscriptions Jehu is called 'son of Omri' (*Append.* 4), and the northern kingdom named *mât Ḫu-um-ri-i*, 'Omri-land,' or *mât Bît-Ḫu-um-ri-a*, 'Beth-Omri-land.' Cf. *COT.* i. 179 *f.*

24. שמרון] Sta. (*ZATW.* v. 165 *ff.*) argues very plausibly for an original vocalization שַׁמְרוֹן or שַׁמְרַיִן, upon the following grounds:—

1. The form of the name from which שמרון is said to be derived.

First stating that שֹׁמְרוֹן cannot come from שֶׁמֶר but only from שֹׁמֵר, he goes on to prove the genuineness of the form שֶׁמֶר as against שֹׁמֵר, and its actual existence, together with the kindred שִׁמְרָת 1 Chr. 8. 21, שִׁמְרוֹן Gen. 46. 13; Num. 26. 24; 1 Chr. 7. 1, as a *clan* name[1]. שִׁמְרוֹן Josh. 19. 15; 11. 1 is also the name of a *city*, and this transference of a clan-name to a city has its analogy in חֶבְרוֹן (חֶבֶר clan name 1 Chr. 8. 17), אַיָּלוֹן, שַׁעַלְבִים[2], &c.

2. Ancient evidence for vocalization of שמרון.

(*a*) Cuneiform inscriptions. Three forms of the name occur: *Ša-mir-i-na*, *Ša-mí-ri-na*, *Ša-mí-ur-na*. These presuppose שַׁמְרוֹן or שַׁמְרֵן or שַׁמְרִן.

(*b*) LXX Σαμάρεια. ει may represent Hebrew *ai* or *ê* or *î*. So שַׁמְרַיִן or שַׁמְרֵין or שַׁמְרִין.

(*c*) Aramaic forms ܫܡܪܝܢ, שָׁמְרַיִן (Ezra 4. 10, 17).

---

[1] That שֶׁמֶר is preferable to שֹׁמֵר in the two cases where the latter form occurs in MT. appears from the following facts. שׁוֹמֵר is found 1 Chr. 7. 32 as a proper name, probably of a clan, but in *v.* 34 the name appears as שֶׁמֶר (שָׁמֶר in pause). Further, one of the murderers of Joash, II. 12. 22, is named יְהוֹזָבָד בֶּן־שֹׁמֵר; but that this vocalization does not rest upon ancient tradition is clear from 2 Chr. 24. 26, where the same man is said to be son of שִׁמְרִית, a form presupposing שֶׁמֶר and not שֹׁמֵר. And moreover, while LXX in II. 12. 22 reads Σωμήρ, Luc. has the form Σεμμήρ, as in *ch.* 16. 24, LXX, Luc. Σεμήρ, Σεμμήρ, Σαμήρ.

[2] From names of animals used as clan totems.

(*d*) Testimony of LXX in *ch.* 16. 24. To mark derivation from Σεμήρ, Σαμήρ, שמרון is represented, not as usually by Σαμάρεια, but by Σεμερών, Σαεμερών, of which Σομορών (Luc., Cod. A) is a correction in accordance with MT.

Supposing therefore שַׁמְרוֹן, שַׁמְרַיִן to be the original form, the termination ַיִן is illustrated by דּוֹתַיִן Gen. 37. 17 (Δωθαείμ), and answers to the more usual ַיִם which appears in the place-names רָמָתַיִם, מַחֲנַיִם. שַׁמְרַיִן may stand together with שַׁמְרוֹן, just as we find the two names עֶגְלַיִם (עֵין) and עֶגְלוֹן.

The reason why the name should have been altered in later times into שֹׁמְרוֹן Sta. is not prepared to explain. He suggests the possibility of an erroneous explanation of the Aramaic form with *å*, but admits that this merely postpones the question, since one must next inquire how the Aramaic form with *Qameç* is to be explained. That the form שֹׁמְרוֹן is, however, very young, appears from the LXX rendering in *ch.* 16. 24.

If, as seems to be the case, שֶׁמֶר was a clan-name, the hill upon which Omri built his city was probably already named Samaria, and bore this name as being the possession and residence of the clan שֶׁמֶר. But that this fact need not invalidate the statement that Omri bought the hill from a *man* named שֶׁמֶר may be argued from the many occurrences of clan-names used as personal names. Thus שִׁמְעִי, David's foe, bears a clan-name Num. 3. 21; *al.*, and the same is the case with חֶבֶר the Kenite; Saul's son 'Esh-ba'al has the name of the Benjamite clan אַשְׁבֵּל Gen. 46. 21; *al.*; אֵלָה, the name of Ba'asha's son, and also of the father of Hosea, is found as a clan-name Gen. 36. 41; גָּד the tribal-name is borne by a prophet in David's time; &c.

25. וירע וג׳] Cf. *ch.* 14. 9 *note.*

26. להכעים וג׳] Cf. *v.* 13.

28. At the close of Omri's reign LXX, Luc. insert the account of Jehoshaphat's reign=MT. *ch.* 22. 41–51 with certain variations, in accordance with the different system of synchronism which appears in Luc. See *Introduction.*

16. 29–34. **22.** 39, 40. *Aḥab, king of Israel.*

R^D embodies short notices from the Annals (substance of *v.* 31^b, *v.* 32, *v.* 34 to דלתיה).

29. אחאב] Mentioned once on the monolith of Shalmaneser II as *A-ḫa-ab-bu mâtu Sir-'-la-ai*, 'Aḥab of Israel'; cf. *Append.* 3, and *ch.* 20. 34 *note.*

30^b. מכל וג׳] LXX, Luc. prefix (Luc. *καὶ*) *ἐπονηρεύσατο*, i.e. וַיָּרַע, probably correctly. Cf. *v.* 25; *ch.* 14. 9 *note.*

31. ויהי הנקל וג׳] 'And it came to pass—was it a light thing his walking in the sins of Jeroboam?—and (that) he took &c.': so RV. 'And it came to pass, as if it had been a light thing &c., that he took &c.' For similar use of interrogative with נָקֵל, expressing surprise at the lengths to which any one can go in sinning, cf. Ezek. 8. 17 הֲנָקֵל לְבֵית יְהוּדָה מֵעֲשׂוֹת אֶת־הַתּוֹעֵבוֹת אֲשֶׁר עָשׂוּ־פֹה כִּי־מָלְאוּ וג׳ וְהִנָּם שֹׁלְחִים אֶת־הַזְּמוֹרָה אֶל־אַפָּם 'Is it a light thing to the house of Judah that they do all the abominations which they do here, for behold &c., that, lo, they are holding the branch to their nose?' i.e. they overleap moral offences, and indulge in definite idolatry (sun-worship).

אֶתְבַּעַל] The name is similarly vocalized by LXX Ἰεθεβάαλ, Luc. Ἰεθβάαλ, and would thus bear the meaning *with Ba'al*, i.e. under his protection. Jos., however, writes Ἰθώβαλος (*Ant.* viii. 13, § 1), i.e. אִתּוֹבַעַל *Ba'al is with him*, and this form is preferred by Th., Sta. According to Jos. (*C. Ap.* i. 18) Ittoba'al, who lived some fifty years after Ḥiram, was a priest of Astarte, who came to the throne by the murder of the usurper Phelles.

33. האשרה] Cf. *ch.* 14. 15 *note.*

לעשות וג׳] LXX, Luc. *τοῦ ποιῆσαι παροργίσματα τοῦ παροργίσαι* (Luc. adds *καὶ ποιῆσαι*) *τὴν ψυχὴν αὐτοῦ* (LXX *τοῦ*) *ἐξολοθρευθῆναι* (Luc. *ἀνθ' ὧν*) *ἐκακοποίησεν ὑπὲρ πάντας κ.τ.λ.*, i.e. apparently לַעֲשׂוֹת כְּעָסִים לְהַכְעִים [וְ]אֶת־נַפְשׁוֹ לְהַשְׁחִית וַיָּרַע מִכֹּל וג׳. Scarcely superior to MT. Elsewhere כעסים II. 23. 26, כעס *ch.* 15. 30; 21. 22 form the direct obj. of הכעים; and omission of את י׳ אלהי ישראל (R^D; cf. *ch.* 8. 15 *note*) is unfavourable.

34. Luc. omits.

בימיו] A phrase of R^D used in synchronizing an event with the preceding narrative. So II. 8. 20; 23. 29; 24. 1; and 15. 19 (emend after LXX). For similar phrases thus employed cf. *ch.* 3. 16 *note* on אז.

חיאל] LXX Ἀχειήλ, i.e. אֲחִיאֵל. Cf. *note* on חירם *ch.* 5. 15.

בית האלי] Cf. *note* on בן הימיני *ch.* 2. 8.

באבירם . . . ובשגיב] ב = '*at the cost of*'; ב *pretii*. Cf. *note* on בנפשו *ch.* 2. 23. The statement suggests the possibility that the builder *sacrificed* his sons, perhaps by enclosing them alive in the foundation and wall, in order by this costly blood-offering to secure the prosperity of his city. Or, the tradition may have been that, through failure to perform such a rite, his eldest and youngest born were claimed by the offended deity at the initiatory and final stages of the building. For instances from various sources of the wide-spread primitive custom of human sacrifice 'in order to furnish blood at the foundations of a house or of a public structure,' cf. H. C. Trumbull, *The Threshold Covenant*, pp. 46 *ff.*

כדבר וג'] Josh. 6. 26.

Narratives of the Northern Kingdom.

I. 17–19; 20; 21; 22. 1–38. II. 1. 2–17$^{a\alpha}$; 2. 1–18, 19–22, 23–25; 3. 4–27; 4. 1–7, 8–37, 38–41, 42–44; 5; 6. 1–7, 8–23, 24–33; 7; 8. 1–6, 7–15; 9. 1—10. 28; 13. 14–19, 20, 21; (14. 8–14).

This great group consists of narratives dealing with the affairs of the kingdom of Israel. The stories are in most cases of some length, their high descriptive power and sympathetic feeling indicating that they have their origin in the kingdom to which they relate; and this conclusion is substantiated by such touches as I. 19. 3 באר שבע אשר ליהודה; II. 14. 11 בבית שמש אשר ליהודה. No blame is anywhere attached to the calf-worship of Bethel and Dan, the efforts of Elijah and his successor being wholly directed to the rooting out of the foreign cult of the Tyrian Ba'al.

Certain peculiarities of diction probably belong to the dialect of North Palestine. The following may be noticed:—

Suff. 2 f. sing. ־ֵכִי, pl. ־ַיְכִי:—Kt. II. 4. 2 לְכִי, 3 שְׁכֵנָיְכִי, 7 נִשְׁיֵכִי, בָּנָיְכִי. Elsewhere, sing. Cant. 2. 3; Ps. 103. 3, 4; Jer. 11. 15 (text corrupt), pl. Ps. 103. 3, 4, 5; 116. 7. Cf. Syr. suff. 2 f. sing. ـܟܝ, pl. ـܟܝܢ.

Pers. pron. 2 f. sing. Kt. אַתִּי:—II. 4. 16, 23; 8. 1. Elsewhere *ch.* 14. 2 (cf. *note*); Judg. 17. 2; Jer. 4. 30; Ezek. 36. 13†. Cf. Syr. ܐܢ̱ܬܝ. So probably Kt. הֹלַכְתִּי II. 4. 23 stands for הֹלַכְתְּ אַתִּי, as in Syr. ܩܛܠܬܝ for ܩܛܠܬ ܐܢ̱ܬܝ; Duval, *Gramm. Syr.* pp. 174 *f.*

Demonstr. pron. f. זֹה II. 6. 19. Cf. Aram. דָּא.

Infin. constr. verb ל״ה with suff. בְּהִשְׁתַּחֲוָיָתִי II. 5. 18, perhaps presupposing form without suff. הִשְׁתַּחֲוָיָה with termination as in Aram. Cf. Dalman, *Gramm. Jud.-Pal. Aram.* pp. 289 *f.*

Rel. ·שֶׁ in מִשֶּׁלָּנוּ II. 6. 11. So Judg. 5. 7 (North Palestine); 6. 17; 7. 12; 8. 26 (prob. Ephraimitic), and uniformly in Cant. (exc. title 1. 1). Elsewhere only in exilic or post-exilic writings[1]. In Phoenician rel. is אש with prosthetic א.

---

[1] The particle שֶׁל 'of' is thought by some to occur upon a haematite weight from Samaria, bearing an inscription upon either side which was at first read as רבע של רבע נצג 'the fourth part of the fourth part of a *néçegh* (?),' and dated *cir.* 8th century B.C. Careful examination of the original weight convinces the writer that Prof. Robertson Smith (*Academy*, Nov. 18, 1893, pp. 443 *ff.*) is correct in his view (based upon a close study of the original) that the much worn רבע של upon the one side is of earlier date than the clearly cut רבע נצג upon the other, this fact being especially marked in the different workmanship of the two inscriptions. To add one point to others already noticed by the Professor—in the older inscription the ע (which in the old character usually takes the shape of a circle) is formed by four straight cuts, which give the letter nearly the appearance of a quadrilateral. In the newer inscription, upon the other hand, attempt has been made to render the rounded form of the letter, at the cost of more than one slip of the graving tool.

It is also extremely doubtful whether the first letter of the supposed של is really a ש. If, however, this be the true reading, and Prof. Smith be correct in regarding של as an abbreviation of שָׁלֵם, the word is most simply to be regarded as an adjective in agreement with רבע, and the inscription denotes

Preservation of ה of art. after prep. ב:—II. 7. 12 בְּהַשָּׂדֶה.

Kt. אֵיכֹה = *where?* II. 6. 13. Elsewhere only Cant. 1. 7 *bis*. Cf. Aram. אֵיכָא, ܐܝܟܐ.

עַד־אֲלֵיהֶם, עַד־הֵם II. 9. 18, 20.

Constr. with suff. pron. anticipating obj. (akin to Syr.):—I. 19. 21 בִּשְּׁלָם הַבָּשָׂר; 21. 13 וַיְעִדֻהוּ . . . אֶת־נָבוֹת.

Indefinite use of אחד *a certain*:—I. 19. 4, 5; 20. 13, 35; 22. 9 (cf. *v.* 8); II. 4. 1; 7. 8; 8. 6: add I. 21. 1, LXX, Luc. Elsewhere I. 13. 11 (perhaps for אַחֵר); II. 12. 10; Judg. 9. 53; 13. 2; 1 Sam. 1. 1; 7. 9, 12; 2 Sam. 18. 10, and late Ezek. 1. 15; 8. 7, 8; 9. 2; 17. 7; 33. 2; Zech. 5. 7; Dan. 8. 13, 3; 10. 5[1].

To these may be added a few roots which betray the influence of Aram.:—שָׂפַק I. 20. 10; מְדִינוֹת 20. 14, 15, 17, 19 (elsewhere only very late); חֹרִים 21. 8, 11; הִשְׁלָה II. 4. 28. There is also a fair number of ἅπαξ λεγγ., some of which take the place of ordinary words and thus may be dialectical; e. g. שִׁנֵּס *gird*, I. 18. 46 (for אזר, חגר), אֲכִילָה *food*, 19. 8 (for אֹכֶל, אָכְלָה, מַאֲכָל); but of others nothing can be affirmed.

The narratives are clearly not all by one author.

(i) Some are histories of Elijah and Elisha, or of movements which they instituted in the direction of religious reform. (ii) In others the fate of the kingdom is regarded from a political standpoint, and this as determined mainly by the action of the *king;* though here also prophets play an important part as advisers and announcers of the oracle of Yahwe. Thus both classes have a religious colouring or motive, and may equally be regarded as

'*a full* (i.e. *complete* or *accurate;* cf. Deut. 25. 15, Prov. 11. 1) *quarter*.' In this case the difficult נצב of the obverse may be a Niph'al participle נִצָּב '*set*' or '*appointed*'; so רבע נצב '*a standard quarter*.'

Prof. Smith's article, together with other correspondence upon the subject of the inscription, is collected in *PEF. Ay. St.*, July, 1894, pp. 220–231; October, 1894, pp. 284–287.

[1] אחד II. 25. 19 appears to have a certain force; '*One* Eunuch and five men, &c.' Cf. 1 Sam. 6. 7.

the work of men of prophetic training, perhaps members of the guilds which we see coming into prominence in some of the Elisha stories.

(i) To the former class belong I. 17–19; 21; II. 1. 2–17[a α]; 2. 1–18, 19–22, 23–25; 4. 1–7, 8–37, 38–41, 42–44; 5; 6. 1–7; 8. 1–6, 7–15; 9. 1—10. 28; 13. 14–19, 20, 21.

Of these, I. 17–19 forms a continuous narrative. From the abruptness of *v.* 1, no reason being assigned for Elijah's threat, and no point of connexion existing for מִזֶּה *v.* 3, it may be inferred that the commencement of the story has been omitted or abbreviated by R^D, and the specification אליהו התשבי מתשבי גלעד thus represents his summary introduction. The sequel also, in strict accordance with 19. 15, 16, is lacking, only one part of Yahwe's commission being fulfilled, *vv.* 19–21.

I. 21 is clearly out of place in MT., breaking the connexion between *ch.* 20 and its sequel *ch.* 22, and LXX, Luc. are no doubt correct in placing this narrative immediately after *ch.* 19. The dislocation may have been due to the desire to bring the prophecy of Aḥab's death (21. 19) nearer to the account of its occurrence (22. 35 *ff.*), and perhaps in a minor degree to the description of the king's mood as סר וזעף in 20. 43 as in 21. 4.

Most critics (Wellh., Dri., Kamp., Benz., Kit.; but Kue. is uncertain: *Ond.* § 25. 7) assign I. 21 to the same author as I. 17–19. Thus Wellh. cites as points of contact the central position occupied by Elijah, his eagle-like swoop upon Aḥab at the right moment, and the formulae ויהי אחר הדברים האלה 21. 1 (but cf. *note ad loc.*) as 17. 17, ויהי דבר י׳ אל א׳ 21. 17 as ודבר י׳ היה אל א׳ 18. 1.

On the other hand, it may be maintained that Elijah is not really the central figure as in I. 17–19. He does not appear upon the scene until *v.* 17, and then takes scarcely a more conspicuous position than Micaiah in 22. 8 *ff.* The king and his action form the centre of interest both at the beginning and end of the narrative. Further, Kue. notices the absence of any reference in 21 to 17–19 and *vice versâ*, the murder of Naboth forming the single crime of Aḥab and Jezebel in the one story, while in the other the sole pivot is the struggle between Yahwe and Ba'al. This, however, is a point of slight moment, and no definite conclusion can be reached as to the relative authorship of the two sections.

Of far greater interest and importance is the question of the connexion of I. 21 with its natural sequel II. 9. 1—10. 28. Critics generally argue or assume that the latter section is by a different author to the former, and most (Wellh., Dri., Kamp., Kit.) assign II. 9 *f.* to the writer of I. 20. 22; II. 3. 4–27, &c. (see below). The argument against identity of authorship of I. 21 and II. 9 *f.*, as stated by Wellh., is based upon supposed discrepancy in detail. While in I. 21 it is the *vineyard* of Naboth which is mentioned, and this is described as אצל היכל אחאב (*v.* 1), II. 9. 21–26 alludes to the חלקת נבות, i.e. his *portion* or *estate*, which lay outside the city. Again, I. 21. 13 records only the death of Naboth, while II. 9. 26 speaks also of the blood of his sons as calling for vengeance.

On the other hand, the following considerations clearly make for the unity of the two narratives:—

II. 9. 21^{b}, the meeting of Joram ben-Aḥab with Jehu actually upon the estate of Naboth, is a touch of high dramatic power which demands that the writer should not only have *known* the story of Naboth (proved by *vv.* 25, 26), but should actually have written it down himself as an introduction to the sequel II. 9 *f.*

Thus a presumption is created in favour of *our* Naboth narrative being the story thus written.

The parallels between the prediction I. 21. 19, 23 and the fulfilment II. 9. 25, 26, 36 cannot be insisted upon, because I. 21. 19 *ff.* has been largely amplified by R^{D} (see *notes ad loc.*), and it is not now possible certainly to determine the original kernel of Elijah's prediction. It should, however, be noticed that the usual method of R^{D} is to expand rather than to excise, and, if this plan has here prevailed, the original speech must be contained in *vv.* 19, 20, 23^{b}. The disagreement in points of fact between I. 21 and II. 9 proves upon examination to be non-existent. Aḥab's dispute with Naboth arose in the first instance about a vineyard adjoining the palace, but this was only a portion of Naboth's estate (חלקה), the whole of which would lapse to the king supposing that the family of Naboth became extinct. And I. 21. 15, where Jezebel tells Aḥab to go down and take possession of the vineyard, clearly implies the extirpation of the whole family: in the statement כי אין נבות חי כי מת the name נבות means Naboth *and his sons*, just as much as in *v.* 19 דמך גם אתה means the blood of Aḥab *and his son* (cf. *v.* 29[b]).

Most decisive, however, is the question of the supposed unity of II. 9. 1—10. 28 with I. 20. 22; II. 3. 4–27; 6. 8—7. 20. If this be granted, the diverse authorship of I. 21 and II. 9 *f.* seems necessarily to follow, since I. 21 can scarcely be regarded as of one piece with I. 20. 22. The place where the dogs lick the blood of Aḥab, 22. 38, is discordant with the prediction of 21. 19, and in general the interest of the writer of 20. 22—mainly, if not wholly, political—and his sympathetic feeling for the king of Israel, preclude the supposition that he is also the author of the Naboth story.

Wellh. cites the following coincidences in phraseology of II. 9 *f.* with I. 20. 22, &c.:—חדר בחדר II. 9. 2; I. 20. 30; 22. 25; חכה *tarry*, II. 9. 3; 7. 9; רכב הסוס 9. 18; 7. 14; הפך ידיו II. 9. 23; I. 22. 34; תפש חי II. 10. 14; 7. 12; I. 20. 18; חרא II. 10. 27; 6. 25. The importance of this collection is, however, open to doubt, since it contains no striking phrase, but such only as might be expected to occur in narratives nearly contemporaneous, and having, in the main, the same subjects in common.

On the other hand, a point of phraseology, apparently hitherto overlooked, sharply separates between II. 9 *f.* and I. 20. 22, &c., and seems absolutely to preclude the theory of a common authorship. This is the title which is ordinarily applied to the *king* in the course of the narrative.

I. 20. 22; II. 3. 4–27; 6. 8—7. 20 are, as might be expected, bound together by the use of a common title. In all the writer's phrase is מלך ישראל, and the proper name of the king, if it occurs at all, is in nearly every case reserved for the necessary specification at the commencement of a section. The facts are as follow:—

I. 20 אחאב מלך ישראל *vv.* 2, 13; מלך ישראל eleven times, viz. *vv.* 4, 7, 11, 21, 22, 28, 31, 32, 40, 41, 43; המלך *vv.* 38, 39 *bis*; אחאב simply *v.* 14.

I. 22 מלך ישראל seventeen times, viz. *vv.* 2, 3, 4, 5, 6, 8, 9, 10, 18, 26, 29, 30 *bis*, 31, 32, 33, 34; המלך *vv.* 15 *bis*, 16, 35, 37[b].

II. 3. 4–27 מלך ישראל eight times, viz. *vv.* 4, 5, 9, 10, 11, 12, 13 *bis*; אחאב simply *v.* 5 (probably from another source); המלך יהורם *v.* 6.

II. 6. 8—7. 20 מלך ישראל seven times, viz. 6. 8, 9, 10, 11, 12, 21, 26; המלך ten times, viz. 6. 28, 30; 7. 2, 6, 12, 14, 15, 17 *bis*, 18.

On the other hand, in II. 9 the king of Israel is called יורם or יהורם simply nine times, viz. *vv.* 14 *bis*, 16 *bis*, 17, 21, 22, 23, 24; once יהורם המלך *v.* 15; and once יהורם מלך ישראל in direct distinction from אחזיהו מלך יהודה *v.* 21; never מלך ישראל simply. The double occurrence of יורם simply in *v.* 16 is specially to be noticed, since, on account of the proximity of אחזיהו מלך יהודה, the specification מלך ישראל might have been expected.

Similarly, in I. 21 אחאב simply is usual; nine times (omitting the prophecy *vv.* 21–26), viz. *vv.* 2, 3, 4, 8, 15, 16, 20, 27, 29. אחאב מלך שמרון *v.* 1; אחאב מלך ישראל *v.* 18.

Now though this agreement in form of reference to the king cannot be pressed to prove *identity* of authorship for I. 21 and II. 9, any more than the fact that I. 17–19 always speaks of אחאב simply can be used to connect this section with I. 21, because different writers may easily have employed the same so obvious citation of the proper name; yet the fact of disagreement in form of reference between I. 21 and I. 20. 22, &c., ought to be emphasized as demonstrating *diversity* of authorship.

It is true that in I. 20. 22, &c., the general use of מלך ישראל may be explained as prompted to a large extent by contrast to מלך ארם; but this does not sufficiently account for the almost total omission of the king's proper name, which would certainly have occurred far more frequently had the author of II. 9 been the writer of these narratives. Contrast especially I. 22, II. 3. 4–27, where (excepting 3. 6) the names of Aḥab and Joram are never mentioned in spite of the close connexion with יהושפט מלך יהודה, with II. 9, where in connexion with אחזיהו מלך יהודה the usual form of citation is יורם, יהורם simply. And, again, notice the use of המלך simply five times in I. 22, ten times in II. 6. 8—7. 20, where the desire for distinction from מלך ארם cannot have been in the writer's mind, and the occasion might have been suitable for the use of the king's proper name.

By this point, therefore, the diverse authorship of I. 20. 22, &c., and II. 9 seems to be proved, and this dissociation adds weight to the arguments which have above been put forward in favour of the unity of II. 9. 1—10. 27 with I. 21.

II. 1. 2–17[aα] is from a different source to the preceding Elijah narratives. This fact is marked by the form of the name אֵלִיָּה *vv.* 3, 4, 8, 12, peculiar to this section, and generally by the inferior literary merit of the composition. The story is probably much later than I. 17–19, I. 21 and sequel.

II. 2. 1–18, Elijah's translation, links itself closely on to some of the longer Elisha narratives which follow, as their introduction; but also might have formed a suitable close to the Elijah history, of which we possess a fragment in I. 17–19, if this can be thought to have gone on to embody also a history of Elisha. The following coincidences between the narratives are worthy of notice, and suggest that I. 17–19; II. 2. 1–18; 4. 1–37, to which we may add II. 5, may be the work of one author. In the case of II. 8. 7–15; 13. 14–19 the evidence is too slight to build upon.

Elijah.	*Elisha.*
I. 17. 8–24. Miraculous provision for the widow of Zarephath during famine, and the raising of her son from death.	II. 4. 1–7. Miraculous provision for the wife of one of the sons of the prophets. II. 4. 8–37. Raising to life of the son of the Shunammite woman.
I. 18. 26. וְאֵין קוֹל וְאֵין עֹנֶה; 29. וְאֵין קוֹל וְאֵין עֹנֶה וְאֵין קָשֶׁב.	II. 4. 31. וְאֵין קוֹל וְאֵין קָשֶׁב.

Elijah.	*Elisha.*
I. 18. 42. וַיִּגְהַר אַרְצָה.	II. 4. 34, 35. וַיִּגְהַר עָלָיו.
I. 19. 13, 19. Mention of Elijah's אַדֶּרֶת.	II. 2. 8, 13, 14. *ib.*
II. 2. 2, 4, 6. חַי י׳ וְחֵי־נַפְשְׁךָ אִם־אֶעֶזְבֶךָּ.	II. 4. 30. *ib.*
II. 2. 7. וַיַּעַמְדוּ מִנֶּגֶד; 15 . . וַיִּרְאֻהוּ מִנֶּגֶד.	II. 4. 25. וַיְהִי כִּרְאוֹת אִישׁ הָאֱלֹהִים אֹתָהּ מִנֶּגֶד.
II. 2. 17. וַיִּפְצְרוּ־בוֹ עַד־בֹּשׁ.	II. 8. 11. וַיָּשֶׂם עַד־בֹּשׁ.
II. 2. 12. אָבִי אָבִי רֶכֶב יִשְׂרָאֵל וּפָרָשָׁיו.	II. 13. 14. *ib.*

The short Elisha stories are probably popular tales handed down orally at first, and not put into writing till some considerable time after the longer narratives.

(ii) The second class includes I. 20; 22. 1–38; II. 3. 4–27; 6. 8–23, 24–33; 7; (14. 8–14). All these, with the exception of 14. 8–14, deal in the same style with the same subject—Israel's relations with Aram, and may not improbably flow from one hand. Notice especially the close bond of connexion between I. 22. 4, 7 and II. 3. 7, 11.

II. 14. 8–14, which stands apart from the other narratives, is marked as probably North Palestinian in origin by its tone, and especially by the reference *v.* 11 בבית שמש אשר ליהודה. Cf. I. 19. 3.

17. *Elijah the prophet predicts three years of famine. He is supported at the brook Kerîth by ravens, and afterwards at Zarephath by a widow, whose means of subsistence he miraculously maintains. He raises the widow's son from death.*

17. 1. התשבי] So *ch.* 21. 17, 28; II. 9. 36; 1. 3, 8. On the place Tishbe see below.

מִתֹּשָׁבֵי גלעד] R.V. 'Of the sojourners of Gilead.' תּוֹשָׁב occurs thirteen times elsewhere—eleven times in the Pentateuch exclusively in P and H, and in 1 Chr. 29. 15; Ps. 39. 13. The word may thus, but for this occurrence in Kings, be judged to be late. תושב is found eight times ‖ גֵּר, viz. Gen. 23. 4; Lev. 25. 23, 35, 47 *bis;* Num. 35. 15; 1 Chr. 29. 15; Ps. 39. 13; ‖ שָׂכִיר four times, viz. Ex. 12. 45; Lev. 22. 10; 25. 6, 40; while the participle הַגָּרִים refers to התושבים Lev. 25. 45. Thus תושב has much the same meaning as גר—a foreigner dwelling in the midst of Israel, and, if it can be in any way distinguished from this latter, seems to denote residence of a more fortuitous or transitory character; cf. Gen. 23. 4; Ps. 39. 13; 1 Chr. 29. 15. Elijah is thus said to have been a foreigner who had been sojourning, probably for a short time merely, in the region east of Jordan—a statement which ill accords with his zeal in extirpating the foreign Ba'al cult, and confirming the worship of Yahwe in the kingdom of Israel.

It should be noticed further that the *scriptio defectiva* of the *Ḥolem* in תֹּשָׁבֵי is not found elsewhere among the thirteen other occurrences of the word, and is unusual in the case of *ō* arising out of the diphthong *aw*.

The difficulty thus apparent is met by the rendering of LXX ἐκ Θεσβῶν τῆς Γαλαάδ, Luc. ὁ ἐκ Θεσσεβῶν τῆς Γαλαάδ, i.e. מִתִּשְׁבֵּי (מִתִּשְׁבֵּה) גִּלְעָד '*of Tishbe in Gilead.*' Thus the gentilic הַתִּשְׁבִּי is further elucidated, and the native city or village of the prophet is named, as might have been expected; cf. *ch.* 19. 16; II. 14. 25; *al.* So Jos. (*Ant.* viii. 13, § 2) ἐκ πόλεως Θεσεβώνης τῆς Γαλαδίτιδος χώρας, and among moderns Ew., Th., Wellh., Kamp., Benz., Kit., *Sta. u. Sieg.*, &c. Klo., who reads 'aus Thisbe Gileads' in his text, suggests in the notes that LXX ὁ προφήτης (Θεσβίτης) ὁ ἐκ Θ.[1] stands for הַנָּבִי שֶׁמִּתשבי, and that this is a corruption of הַיָּבֵשִׁי מִיָּבֵשׁ גִּלְעָד 'the Jabeshite of Jabesh Gilead.' This, however, must presuppose that הַתִּשְׁבִּי is a corruption in all its six occurrences.

A place named Tishbe in Naphtali is mentioned Tobit 1. 2:—ὃς ᾐχμαλωτεύθη ἐν ἡμέραις Ἐνεμεσσάρου τοῦ βασιλέως Ἀσσυρίων ἐκ Θίσβης (Cod. A Θίβης), ἥ ἐστιν ἐκ δεξιῶν Κυδιὼς τῆς Νεφθαλεὶμ ἐν τῇ

[1] According to Field, in some texts ὁ προφήτης stands alone without Θεσβίτης. His note is:—'Sic Ald., Codd. III, XI, 44, 55, 64, 71, alii (inter quos 247), Syro-hex. (cum ܬܫܒܝܐ .ܣ in marg.), Arm. 1.'

Γαλειλαίᾳ ὑπεράνω Ἀσήρ. Thus the statement 'Tishbe *of Gilead*' may be intended to make distinction from this other place of the same name.

Van Kasteren (*Zeitschr. d. deutsch. Pal. Vereins XIII*, 207 *ff.*) identifies תשבה with *El-istib* upon the *Jebel Ajlûn*, some ten miles north of the Jabbok, and supports the metathesis (*st* for *ts*) by comparison of Ar. *Tell semak* = Sycaminos. To the south-east of *Istib* lie the ruins of a quadrangular chapel now bearing the name of *Mār Elyās*, and near to this is an insignificant grave which is said to be the grave of the prophet.

חי י׳ וג׳] Cf. *ch.* 18. 15; II. 3. 14; 5. 16.

י׳ אלהי ישראל] LXX Κύριος ὁ Θεὸς τῶν δυνάμεων, ὁ Θεὸς Ἰσραήλ. Luc. omits. In *v.* 14 LXX, Luc. Κύριος. Elijah's expression elsewhere *ch.* 18. 15; 19. 10, 14 is י׳ אלהי צבאות, and this, taken in connexion with the fact that י׳ אלהי ישראל is most generally a redactional phrase (cf. *ch.* 8. 15 *note*), favours the reading in *v.* 1 י׳ אלהי צבאות, and in *v.* 14 יהוה merely.

אשר עמדתי לפניו] 'Before whom I stand,' i.e. *whose servant I am*, the phrase being employed in the idiomatic sense noticed *ch.* 1. 2 *note*. The perfect is here used of an action commencing at some point of time indefinitely anterior, and continuing into the present.

אם יהיה השנים האלה וג׳] According to Jos. (*Ant.* viii. 13, § 2) this drought is mentioned by Menander the historian among the events of the reign of Ittoba'al of Tyre, and its duration is stated as one full year:—μέμνηται δὲ τῆς ἀνομβρίας ταύτης καὶ Μένανδρος ἐν ταῖς Ἰθωβάλου τῶν Τυρίων βασιλέως πράξεσι λέγων οὕτως· "ἀβροχία τ' ἐπ' αὐτοῦ ἐγένετο ἀπὸ τοῦ Ὑπερβερεταίου μηνὸς ἕως τοῦ ἐχομένου ἔτους Ὑπερβερεταίου, ἱκετείαν δ' αὐτοῦ ποιησαμένου κεραυνοὺς ἱκανοὺς βεβληκέναι, κ.τ.λ."

2. אליו] LXX, Luc. here and in *v.* 8 πρὸς Ἠλειού (Ἠλιάν), if not paraphrastic, seems to be an easy error אליהו (אל) for אליו. Cf. *v.* 11 where ויקרא אליה is rendered καὶ ἐβόησεν ὀπίσω αὐτῆς Ἠλειού. For MT. cf. *ch.* 19. 9.

4. והיה וג׳] The substantive verb merely serves loosely to

introduce what follows. Dri. *Tenses*, § 121 *Obs.* 1, quotes also Ex. 4. 16; Ezek. 47. 10, 22.

6. מביאים] 'Were bringing.' The stress is on the continuity of their action during a period of some length.

לחם ובשר וג׳] LXX, Luc. ἄρτους τὸ πρωὶ καὶ κρέα τὸ δείλης, favoured by Klo., Kamp., Kit. upon the ground (Klo.) of a supposed reference to Ex. 16. 8, 12.

7. מקץ ימים] 'At the end of *some* days'; undefined. So Gen. 4. 3; 2 Sam. 14. 26†. Cf. Neh. 13. 6. The use of ימים *v.* 15 is similar.

9. צרפתה] The modern *Ṣarafand*, a large village near the sea, and some eight miles below Zidon. Cf. Rob. *BR.* 474 *ff.* So Jos. (*Ant.* viii. 13, § 2):—πόλιν οὐκ ἄπωθεν τῆς Σιδῶνος καὶ Τύρου, μεταξὺ γὰρ κεῖται.

וישבת שם] LXX, Luc. omit.

10. ויבא] LXX, Luc. omit.

בַּכְּלִי] 'In *the* vessel.' So בַּכַּד, בַּצַּפַּחַת *v.* 12. Cf. *note* on בבגדים *ch.* 1. 1.

11. לקחי] The first radical is thus preserved only again in imperat. 2 sing. masc. לְקַח Ex. 29. 1; Prov. 20. 16; Ezek. 37. 16†.

12. מעוג] 'A cake'; only again in the doubtful passage Ps. 35. 16. The more usual word is עֻגָה *v.* 13; *al.*, possibly so named from its *rounded* or *twisted* shape, if we may suppose a connexion with Ar. عَوِجَ 'to be curved or distorted.' Pesh. ܐܢ ܐܝܬ ܠܝ ܡܕܡ, Targ. אם אית לי מידעם presuppose אם יש לי מְאוּמָה 'I have *nothing*,' a reading which, as Th. notices, agrees better than MT. with the following כי אם וג׳, and is therefore preferable. So Klo.

וְלִבְנִי] LXX, Luc. presuppose וּלְבָנַי 'and for my *children*'; and so *v.* 13 וּלְבָנַיִךְ for וְלִבְנֵךְ. So Th., upon the ground that the *pl.* agrees better with ביתה 'her *household*,' *v.* 15, and that MT. vocalization may be due to *vv.* 17 *ff.* These latter verses, however, certainly convey the impression that the boy was the widow's *only* son, and this perhaps gains confirmation from the parallel story of Elisha, II. 4. 8 *ff.*

14. תִּכְלָה] The final syllable anomalously vocalized after the

analogy of verbs ל״א; cf. יִקְרָה Dan. 10. 14[1]. For cases of the converse change—true ל״א vocalized as ל״ה, cf. נִשָּׂא *ch.* 9. 11; חֹטֶא Eccl. 8. 12; 9. 18; רִפֵּאתִי II. 2. 21; כָּלָאתִי Ps. 119. 101; G-K. § 75 *oo;* Sta. § 143 ε, *Rem.* 1 δ.

תתן] On Kt. cf. *ch.* 6. 19 *note.*

15. ותאכל הִוא־וָהִיא] Q're, which is postulated by the fem. verb, has the support of LXX, Luc., Pesh., Targ.

16. לא חסר] The predicate agrees with שמן, the principal number of the compound subj., and not with צפחת as in *v.* 14. Naturally it is the oil and not the cruse which is thought of as not failing. Cf. קשת גברים חתים 1 Sam. 2. 4; עיני גבהות אדם שפל Isa. 2. 11. Ew. § 317ᶜ; Da. § 116, *Rem.* 2.

17. בעלת הבית] 'The mistress of the house.' Similarly בעל הבית Ex. 22. 7 (E); Judg. 19. 22, 23. Klo.'s ingenious suggestion to emend בַּעֲלִיַּת הַבַּיִת 'in the upper chamber of the house,' regarding this as a gloss from *v.* 19, is in fact refuted by the statement of that verse, ויעלהו.

נשמה] Luc. πνοὴ ζωῆς suggests נִשְׁמַת חַיִּים as in Gen. 2. 7. For MT., supported by LXX, Vulg., Pesh., Targ., cf. Dan. 10. 17.

18. מה לי ולך] 'What have I and thou (in common)?' i.e. 'What concern hast thou with my affairs?' The phrase occurs again in II. 3. 13; Judg. 11. 12; 2 Chr. 35. 21; מה לי ולכם 2 Sam. 16. 10; 19. 23, and in each case deprecates outside interference. This is further illustrated by NT.; S. Matt. 8. 29 Τί ἡμῖν καὶ σοί, υἱὲ τοῦ Θεοῦ; ἦλθες ὧδε πρὸ καιροῦ βασανίσαι ἡμᾶς; S. Jo. 2. 4 Τί ἐμοὶ καὶ σοί, γύναι; οὔπω ἥκει ἡ ὥρα μου. Cf. also S. Matt. 27. 19 μηδέν σοι καὶ τῷ δικαίῳ ἐκείνῳ. By באת אלי וג׳ the woman seems to mean that the man of God, by living in her house, has directed God's attention to her, and that some secret sin, perhaps unknown to her and which might otherwise have escaped detection, has been the cause of her son's death.

19. מטתו] LXX, Luc., Pesh. seem to have read הַמִּטָּה.

[1] Here, however, the vocalization may have been determined by יִקְרָא of Gen. 49. 1, which seems to have suggested the words of Daniel. Cf. Bevan, *ad loc.*

20. מתגורר] *Hithpo'lel* only here, Hos. 7. 14 being probably corrupt. *Heb. Lex. Oxf.* cf. Ar. x. استجار 'seek hospitality with.'

21. ויתמדד] 'And he stretched himself out'; the only occurrence of the reflex *Hithpo'el*. Cf. the similar action of Elisha, II. 4. 34, and of S. Paul with Eutychus, καταβὰς δὲ ὁ Παῦλος ἐπέπεσεν αὐτῷ, Acts 20. 10. LXX, Luc. make the guess καὶ ἐνεφύσησεν.

על קרבו] על in place of אל; cf. *ch.* 1. 33 *note.*

22. וישמע . . . ויחי] LXX καὶ ἐγένετο οὕτως (Luc. adds καὶ ἐπεστράφη ἡ ψυχὴ τοῦ παιδαρίου εἰς αὐτόν), καὶ ἀνεβόησεν τὸ παιδάριον. Here, no doubt, the words of MT. have fallen out through the homoioteleuton על קרבו, while, as Klo. suggests, ויחי was read as ויהי, and possibly the first few words of *v.* 23 gave rise to וַיִּקְרָא הַיֶּלֶד. The additional words of Luc. represent a later attempt to restore the true text.

24. עתה זה] So II. 5. 22†. Cf. *ch.* 14. 6 *note.*

18. *Elijah's meeting with Aḥab in the third year of the famine. After the contest between Yahwe and Ba'al, and the destruction of Ba'al's prophets, the rain is sent by Yahwe.*

18. 1. ויהי ימים רבים וג'] 'And there were many days, and the word &c.,' i.e. 'And when many days had elapsed, the word &c.' For the sing. verb preceding the pl. subj., cf. *ch.* 11. 3 *note.* Elsewhere the phrase וַיְהִי מִיָּמִים occurs, Josh. 23. 1; Judg. 11. 4; 15. 1†, and so, according to Th., 3 Codd. in our passage; but the rendering of the Verss. is ambiguous as to the original text, and cannot be cited (Th., Klo.) in support of the alteration.

4. ויחביאם . . . וכלכלם] '*Hid them* (once for all) *and used to feed them* (at stated intervals).'

חמשים איש] LXX κατὰ (Luc. ἀνὰ) πεντήκοντα, Vulg. *quinquagenos et quinquagenos*, Pesh. ܚܡ̈ܫܝܢ ܚܡ̈ܫܝܢ, Targ. חמשין חמשין גברא presuppose the distrib. חֲמִשִּׁים חֲמִשִּׁים 'by fifty,' which is doubtless correct. Cf. *v.* 13.

בַּמְּעָרָה] Cf. *ch.* 13. 14 *note.*

5. לך בארץ] LXX Δεῦρο καὶ διέλθωμεν ἐπὶ τὴν γῆν (Luc. ἐν τῇ γῇ) presupposes לֵךְ וְנַעְבֹר בָּאָרֶץ, agreeably to the following נמצא, and to *v.* 6 לעבר בה. So Th., Klo., Kamp., Benz., Kit.

ולוא נכרית מן בהמה] Impossible. Even a forced translation can merely give the sense that Aḥab feared to lose *some* only of the beasts, while the context clearly demands expression of the apprehension lest the whole should perish. The true text is given by Luc. καὶ οὐκ ἐξολοθρευθήσεται ἀφ' ἡμῶν κτήνη, i. e. וְלֹא תִכָּרֵת מִמֶּנּוּ בְּהֵמָה '*that cattle be not cut off from us.*' So Wellh.

6. הארץ] LXX, Luc., Pesh. suggest הַדֶּרֶךְ; inferior to MT.

לבדו] LXX, Luc. omit in reference to Aḥab.

7. ויכרהו] LXX, Luc. καὶ ἔσπευσεν, i. e. וַיְמַהֵר, preferred by Th., Klo. MT., however, agrees well with the fact that Obadiah had not before seen Elijah (cf. his question in this verse, and his statements as to himself *vv.* 12^b^, 13), and must therefore have recognized him from popular description of his appearance.

האתה זה] The enclitic זה gives point and vivacity to the interrogation. So *v.* 17; 2 Sam. 2. 20, and in an indirect question Gen. 27. 21†. With omission of ה, אַתָּה זֶה Gen. 27. 24†. Cf. *note* on למה זה *ch.* 14. 6.

8. אני] Luc. omits.

10. ואמרו אין והשביע] 'And when they said, He is not (here), he would take an oath of &c.' LXX, Luc. render והשביע by καὶ ἐνέπρησεν, rightly recognized by Klo. as a corruption of καὶ ἐνέπλησεν, i. e. והשׂביע.

כי לא ימצאכה] 'That he *could* not find thee.' Dri. *Tenses*, § 37 β.

11. הנה אליהו] LXX omits.

12. ישאך על אשר וג׳] Unless על be merely used in place of אל (*ch.* 1. 38 *note*), the constr. is pregnant: 'carry thee off (up) and set thee down *upon*.' Cf. II. 2. 16 פֶּן־נְשָׂאוֹ רוּחַ י׳ וַיַּשְׁלִכֵהוּ בְּאַחַד הֶהָרִים וג׳.

13. הלא הגד וג׳] For impers. passive governing the accus., cf. *ch.* 2. 21 *note*.

את אשר עשיתי . . . ואחבא] 'That which I did . . . *how* I hid &c.' Cf. *ch.* 2. 5 *note*.

15. חי וג׳] Cf. *ch.* 17. 1 *note*.

כי היום וג׳] כי introducing the substance of the oath. *Ch.* 2. 23 *note*.

16. וילך אחאב] LXX, Luc. *καὶ ἐξέδραμεν* 'Αχαὰβ *καὶ ἐπορεύθη*, i. e. וַיָּרָץ וילך א׳. Th. notices that such haste is wholly conformable to the statement of *v.* 10.

18. הבעלים] 'The Ba'als.' Some contempt is conveyed by the use of the plural as contrasted with the one Yahwe. Cf. 1 Sam. 7. 4 'And the children of Israel put away the Ba'als and the Astartes, and served *Yahwe alone.*' The plural הבעלים has reference to the various local forms under which the Canaanite Ba'al was worshipped; cf. בַּעַל זְבוּב, בַּעַל בְּרִית, בַּעַל פְּעוֹר, and the place-names (local sanctuaries) בַּעַל חֶרְמוֹן, בַּעַל גָּד, בַּעַל שָׁלִשָׁה, *al.* For instances from *CIS.* of Phoenician titles of special Ba'als, cf. Dri. *Sam.*, pp. 49 *f.*

19. הבעל] LXX, Luc. *τῆς αἰσχύνης*, and so *v.* 25; i.e. הַבֹּשֶׁת '*the shameful thing*' substituted by a later hand, as in Hos. 9. 10 הֵמָּה בָּאוּ בַעַל־פְּעוֹר וַיִּנָּזְרוּ לַבֹּשֶׁת; Jer. 3. 24; 11. 13. Cf. also the same alteration in the proper names יְרֻבֶּשֶׁת 2 Sam. 11. 21 for יְרֻבַּעַל Judg. 6. 32; אִישׁ־בֹּשֶׁת 2 Sam. 2. 8[1] for אֶשְׁבַּעַל 1 Chr. 8. 33; מְפִיבֹשֶׁת 2 Sam. 4. 4 for מְרִיב בַּעַל 1 Chr. 8. 34; 9. 40^a^ or מְרִי־בַעַל 1 Chr. 9. 40^b^. In these latter cases בעל appears to have been used as a title of Yahwe, an ancient practice which was afterwards discouraged by the prophets (cf. Hos. 2. 18), and finally disappeared. Cf. Dri. *Sam.*, p. 95.

ונביאי האשרה ארבע מאות] Wellh. (so Sta., Kamp., Benz., Kit.), calling attention to the absence of את before נביאי and to the omission of any mention in *vv.* 22, 40[2], regards these words as a gloss, upon the ground that אשרה was not confused with the *goddess* עַשְׁתֹּרֶת until much later times. Cf. *ch.* 14. 15 *note.* Pesh. gives the number as 450.

20. בכל בני ישראל] LXX, Luc. are preferable in omission of בני; *εἰς πάντα* 'Ισραήλ.

את הנביאים] LXX, Luc. *πάντας τοὺς προφήτας.* Pesh. ܘܟܢܫ ܐܢܘܢ ܠܓܒܪ̈ܐ 'and gathered the men' may perhaps point to a reading וַיִּקְבְּצֵם, with suffix of indefinite reference.

---

[1] Εἰσβάαλ is the reading of Cod. 93 Holmes and οἱ λοιποί, i. e. 'A., Σ., Θ.

[2] LXX, Luc. make the addition in *v.* 22 *καὶ οἱ προφῆται τοῦ ἄλσους* (Luc. *τῶν ἀλσῶν*) *τετρακόσιοι.*

21. עַד מָתַי וג׳] 'How long are ye limping upon the two different opinions?' The attempt to combine two religions so incompatible as Yahwe-worship and Baʿal-worship is compared to the laboured gait of a man walking upon legs of different length. סְעִפִּים appears to mean *divisions*, as rendered by Pesh. ܦܠܓ̈ܘ, Targ. פּוּלְגוּן, Vulg. *partes*[1]; cf. סָעִיף 'cleft' or 'fissure' of a rock, Judg. 15. 8, 11; Isa. 2. 21; 57. 5; 'branch' Isa. 17. 6; 27. 10†. שְׂעִפִּים 'thoughts' (as dividing or distracting the mind, Ges.) Job 4. 13; 20. 2† may be the same word. LXX, Luc. render by ταῖς ἰγνύαις, and this is followed by Ew., Th., Benz., who explain סְעִפִּים as 'knee-cavities (Kniekehlen), the place where the bone is *divided*,' and regard the saying as a proverb of Elijah's time.

22. אֶל הָעָם] Pesh. omits. Targ. לְכָל עַמָא.

23. וַיִתְּנוּ] '*So* let them give.' The ו is, however, not expressed in the Verss., excepting Targ.

24. בְּשֵׁם יהוה] LXX, Luc., Pesh. presuppose additional אֱלֹהַי, probably an easy gloss in antithesis to the preceding אֱלֹהֵיכֶם.

הוּא הָאֱלֹהִים] 'He is *the* God,' i. e. *the true* God. Cf. *v.* 39.

טוֹב הַדָּבָר] LXX, Luc. add אֲשֶׁר דִּבַּרְתָּ; but for MT. cf. *ch.* 2. 38, 42.

25[b]. וְקִרְאוּ . . . תְשִׂימוּ] Pesh. omits.

26. הַבַּעַל עֲנֵנוּ] The repetition of LXX, Luc. Ἐπάκουσον ἡμῶν, ὁ Βάαλ, ἐπάκουσον ἡμῶν is probably an imitation of *v.* 37.

וַיְפַסְּחוּ עַל הַמִּזְבֵּחַ] 'And they limped around the altar.' וַיְפַסְּחוּ, the intensive of the word used in *v.* 21, describes with some scorn the *pantomimic dance* (Ke., Th.) of the priests. LXX, Luc. καὶ διέτρεχον, Vulg. *transiliebantque*, Pesh. ܘܡܦܠܗ݂ܕܝܢ 'exerted themselves,' Targ. וּמְשַׁתְּטַן 'leapt madly.' Klo.'s suggestion וַיְפַזְּזוּ 'and they danced' (2 Sam. 6. 16) is unnecessary. Baethgen (*Semit. Relig.* 25) compares a Greek inscription from the neighbourhood of Berytus (*CIG.* 4536) Εἴλαθί μοι, Βαλμαρκώς, κοίρανε κώμων. Here Βαλμαρκώς must represent בַּעַל מַרְקֵד 'Baʿal of the dance,' or מַרְקֵד 'causing to dance,' i. e. 'worshipped in the dance.'

---

[1] Σ. ἀμφιβόλως, perhaps a corruption of ἀμφιβόλοις, 'doubtful (opinions).'

אשר עשה] LXX, Luc., Vulg., Pesh. presuppose אֲשֶׁר עָשׂוּ 'which they had made,' correctly.

27. וַיְהַתֵּל] Usually regarded as imperf. Pi'el, and a secondary form from הֵתֵל Hiph'il of תלל. Cf. Sta. § 145 ε; *Heb. Lex. Oxf.*

G-K. § 67 *y*; Kö. *Lehrg.* I. i, p. 352, explain as imperf. Hiph. of תלל with doubling of first radical (Aramaïzing form) as in יִסֹּב, and without elision of ה as in the forms תְּהָתֵלּוּ Job 13. 9, יְהָתֵלּוּ Jer. 9. 4. Sta., in adopting the former view, considers that these latter forms ought properly to be vocalized יְהַתֵּלּוּ, תְּ׳.

אליהו] LXX, Luc. add the gloss ὁ Θεσβείτης. Cf. *ch.* 17. 1 *note*. So Luc. *v.* 29.

כי שיח וג׳] 'Surely meditation, or surely going aside occupies him, or surely a journey occupies him!' שיח '*meditation*,' as producing a condition of abstraction (Pesh. ܪܢܝܐ), is preferable here to '*conversation*' (LXX, Luc., Vulg., Targ.). שִׂיג (for סִיג from סוג 'turn back'; cf. נָשׂוֹג 2 Sam. 1. 22 for נָסוֹג) is usually explained, after Jarchi, as an euphemism. But omission of וכי שיג לו in LXX, Luc., suggests that these words may be an erroneous repetition of the former. So Klo. The meaning of וכי דרך לו is brought out by paraphrase of LXX, Luc. καὶ ἅμα μή ποτε χρηματίζει αὐτός, 'perhaps he has business to transact!'

ויקץ] The *nuance* is '*must* (or *should*) be awakened.'

28. כמשפטם] LXX omits; but Luc. κατὰ τὸν ἐθισμὸν αὐτῶν.

29. In place of MT., LXX reads καὶ ἐπροφήτευσαν ἕως οὗ παρῆλθεν τὸ δειλινόν, καὶ ἐγένετο ὡς ὁ καιρὸς τοῦ ἀναβῆναι τὴν θυσίαν, καὶ ἐλάλησεν Ἠλειοὺ πρὸς τοὺς προφήτας τῶν προσοχθισμάτων λέγων Μετάστητε ἀπὸ τοῦ νῦν, καὶ ἐγὼ ποιήσω τὸ ὁλοκαύτωμά μου· καὶ μετέστησαν καὶ ἀπῆλθον. This is not, with Th., to be regarded as genuine, but is marked as a gloss which has usurped the place of the true text by the use of τὸ δειλινόν for הצהרים compared with *vv.* 26, 27 μεσημβρία, and τοὺς προφήτας τῶν προσοχθισμάτων as against οἱ προφῆται τοῦ Βάαλ *vv.* 22, 40, or revised τῆς αἰσχύνης *vv.* 19, 25. In Luc. this text has undergone revision, the reading of MT. being partially combined:— καὶ οὐκ ἦν φωνή inserted after θυσίαν. A similar glossing is to be seen in *v.* 36, LXX, Luc.

עד לעלות המנחה] '*Up to* (the time of) the offering of the oblation'; but *v.* 36 בעלות '*at* the offering.' עד ל (exc. Josh. 13. 5 = Judg. 3. 3 עד לבוא) is elsewhere very late, being confined to Chr., Ezra, Neh. The occurrences are cited Dri. *LOT.*, p. 506. In the earlier language עד alone is usual, as in Gen. 32. 25 עד עלות השחר; 19. 22; Judg. 6. 18; *al.* The phrase כעלות המנחה '*about* (the time of) the offering, &c.,' is also found in II. 3. 20, of the early morning, and not, as here, of the afternoon. The reference can scarcely be to anything else than the morning and evening offering *at the Temple at Jerusalem;* nor need this, as coming from a writer of the northern kingdom, cause difficulty, in view of the statement of *v.* 31[a]; see *note.*

מנחה in P always denotes a *meal-offering*, and this, according to the regulations of Ex. 29. 38–42; Num. 28. 3–8, was the regular accompaniment of the lamb which was to be offered morning and evening. But our passage clearly refers to the offering *generally*, of whatever it consisted at that time, and not to such a special portion of it as the term denotes in P. From 1 Sam. 26. 19 יָרַח מִנְחָה 'let him *smell* an offering,' smell i.e. the sweet smoke from the burning (cf. Gen. 8. 21), Gen. 4. 4; 1 Sam. 2. 17 (cf. *vv.* 15, 16), it appears that מנחה in early times could denote even an animal sacrifice, and was thus a general term for an *offering*, like קָרְבָּן in P. The use of the word with the meaning *present* (*ch.* 5. 1 *note*) is closely allied. Cf. Wellh. *Prolegomena*, pp. 61 *f.* Upon the difficult passage II. 16. 15 cf. *note ad loc.*

30[b]. וירפא וג׳] 'And he *repaired* &c.': a use of רפא *heal* peculiar to this passage. In LXX, Luc. these words do not stand in this position, but appear between 32[a] and 32[b], 32[a] being somewhat abbreviated; *καὶ ᾠκοδόμησεν τοὺς λίθους* (LXX *ἐν ὀνόματι* Κυρίου), *καὶ ἰάσατο τὸ θυσιαστήριον* (Luc. *κυρίου*) *τὸ κατεσκαμμένον, κ.τ.λ.* This is a superficial rearrangement made because the altar could not be said to be repaired until the stones had been built up. But in MT., *v.* 30[b] states summarily what is re-stated in detail in *vv.* 31, 32, according to the diffuse but picturesque style of the writer. Gen. 27. 23, followed by the details of *vv.* 24–29, is similar.

מזבח י׳ ההרום] Thus the spot selected on Carmel by Elijah was the site of a בָּמָה or local sanctuary which had been destroyed at the idolatrous reaction which had been brought about by Jezebel. Cf. *ch.* 19. 10 את מזבחתיך הרסו. These passages show incidentally the wide diffusion of such high-places for the (unmixed) worship of Yahwe throughout the northern kingdom. Cf. *ch.* 19. 18.

Th. cites Tac. *Hist.* ii. 78[1]; Suet. *Vespas.* 5[2] as stating that down to Vespasian's time an altar existed on Carmel without temple or statues.

31ª. שתים עשרה אבנים וג׳] Cf. the setting up by Joshua at the crossing of the Jordan of two cairns, each consisting of twelve stones, one for each tribe, Josh. 4. 1 *ff.* (JE); and the erection of the twelve Maççēboth for the twelve tribes at the ratification of the 'Book of the Covenant,' Ex. 24. 1 *ff.* (JE).

This notice goes to show that the absence of any polemic on the part of Elijah against the calf-worship of the kingdom of Israel does not imply his tacit approval, but rather that while (so far as we know) tolerating it in face of the far more serious deflection caused by the introduction of the Phoenician Ba'al worship, he had in view as an ideal the ultimate union of the two kingdoms in the pure worship of Yahwe. Cf. *v.* 29 *note; ch.* 22. 7 *note.*

כמספר וג׳] LXX, Luc. κατ' ἀριθμὸν (Luc. τῶν δώδεκα) φυλῶν 'Ισραήλ, ὡς ἐλάλησεν Κύριος πρὸς αὐτὸν κ.τ.λ. The substitution of 'Ισραήλ for יעקב, however, makes the statement of 31ᵇ superfluous.

31ᵇ. אשר היה וג׳] The *precise words,* ישראל יהיה שמך, occur in Gen. 35. 10 (P), and this has caused Kue. and others to regard this half-verse as an addition under the influence of P. Kamp. goes further, taking the whole of *vv.* 31, 32ª as a later gloss, and finding in them a contradiction to *v.* 30ᵇ (the mere *repair* of the altar; but see *note*); and it is most probable that, if the narrative

[1] 'Est Iudaeam inter Suriamque Carmelus, ita vocant montem deumque, nec simulacrum deo aut templum—sic tradidere maiores—ara tantum et reverentia.'

[2] 'Apud Iudaeam Carmeli dei oraculum consulentem ita confirmavere sortes, ut quidquid cogitaret volveretque animo, quamlibet magnum, id esse proventurum pollicerentur.'

has received *any* addition, this is the correct view. But the *fact* recorded in *v.* 31^{b} appears also in Gen. 32. 28, 29 (J), and too much stress must not be laid upon such a very easy coincidence with the words of P.

32. תעלה] 'A channel.' Cf. II. 18. 17; 20. 20, where the word means a 'conduit' or 'aqueduct.'

כבית] '(Of) about the capacity of.'

33. After *v.* 33^{a}, LXX, Luc. add ἐπὶ τὸ θυσιαστήριον ὃ ἐποίησεν, and at the close of the verse, καὶ ἐστοίβασεν ἐπὶ τὸ θυσιαστήριον.

34. שלשו] 'Do it a third time.' Elsewhere this denom. Piʿel means *Do on the third day* 1 Sam. 20. 19; *Divide into three parts* Deut. 19. 3†.

35. מלא] LXX ἔπλησαν, under the influence of the plural verbs in the preceding verse.

36. After אברהם יצחק וישראל LXX, Luc. add the gloss ἐπάκουσόν μου, Κύριε, ἐπάκουσόν μου σήμερον ἐν πυρί, and then continue καὶ γνώτωσαν πᾶς ὁ λαὸς οὗτος (cf. *v.* 37) in place of היום יודע.

37^{a}. Luc. omits.

37^{b}. את לבם] LXX, Luc. τὴν καρδίαν τοῦ λαοῦ τούτου.

38. אש יהוה] LXX, Luc. πῦρ παρὰ Κυρίου, Targ. אשתא מן קדם י׳ suggest אֵשׁ מֵאֵת־י׳, and this is adopted by Th., Klo., Kamp., on the supposition that מאת has been lost through proximity to the similar אש. After י׳ LXX, Luc. add ἐκ τοῦ οὐρανοῦ, as in Gen. 19. 24 גפרית ואש מאת י׳ מן השמים.

ואת האבנים וג׳] The different order of LXX, Luc., ואת האבנים ואת העפר following בתעלה, is certainly wrong, since לחכה must refer to את המים.

40. להם] LXX, Luc. πρὸς τὸν λαόν.

41. קול המון הגשם] 'There is a sound of *the roar* of rain.' המון means the loud rushing noise of a heavy downpour, as heard by Elijah's 'prophetically sharpened ear' (Klo.). So Pesh. ܪܘܓܫܐ, Targ. איתרגושת. Cf. Jer. 10. 13; 51. 16 לקול תתו המון מים בשמים.

42. ויעלה אחאב . . . ואליהו עלה] On the contrasted order cf. *ch.* 5. 25 *note.*

ויגהר] 'And he crouched.' The meaning, here and in the only

other occurrence II. 4. 34, 35, must be determined by the context. So Verss. in both passages.

43[b]. שב שבע פעמים] LXX Καὶ σὺ ἐπίστρεψον ἑπτάκι, καὶ ἀπόστρεψον ἑπτάκι. καὶ ἀπέστρεψεν τὸ παιδάριον ἑπτάκι. Luc. Ἐπίστρεψον καὶ ἐπίβλεψον ἑπτάκις. καὶ ἐπέστρεψε τὸ παιδάριον ἑπτάκις. Here the first sentence of LXX appears to contain a doublet, while in Luc. the text has been worked over, and the verb of the second member altered into ἐπίβλεψον, in accordance with *v.* 43[a]. The emphatic καὶ σύ of LXX has the appearance of originality, and supposing (with Klo.) אַתָּה to be a corruption of עַתָּה, we may restore:— וְעַתָּה שֻׁב שֶׁבַע פְּעָמִים וַיָּשָׁב הַנַּעַר שֶׁבַע פְּעָמִים '"Now return seven times." And the lad returned seven times.'

44. עלה מים] LXX, Luc. ἀνάγουσα ὕδωρ a mistaken reading מַעֲלָה מַיִם.

45. עד כה ועד כה] 'In a very short while.' The repetition expresses both the brevity of the interval and its indeterminateness. Vulg. explains differently *Cumque se verteret huc atque illuc*, and so Pesh. ܘܟܕ ܗܘ ܡܬܦܢܐ ܠܗܪܟܐ ܘܠܗܪܟܐ. Similarly Targ. paraphrases עד דמזדרז 'while he was harnessing.'

46. ויד י׳ היתה אל] So Ezek. 33. 22; but עַל instead of אל is usual:—II. 3. 15; Ezek. 1. 3; 3. 22; 37. 1; 40. 1. The phrase describes the powerful access of prophetic inspiration. Cf. also Ezek. 8. 1 ותפל עלי שם יד אדני י׳ 'And the hand of the Lord Yahwe fell upon me there'; Ezek. 3. 14 ויד י׳ עלי חזקה 'And the hand of Yahwe was strong upon me'; Isa. 8. 11 כה אמר י׳ אלי בחזקת היד 'Thus said Yahwe unto me with strength of hand.'

ויישנס] The word is otherwise quite unknown. All Verss. give the meaning 'gird.'

19. *Jezebel seeks to take vengeance upon Elijah for the death of her prophets. Elijah flees into the wilderness of Judah, and then journeys on to Ḥoreb, where he receives Yahwe's further commission for the extirpation of Baʿal worship from Israel.*

19. 1. לאיזבל] LXX adds τῇ γυναικὶ αὐτοῦ, i. e. אִשְׁתּוֹ, which may have fallen out before the following את.

ואת כל אשר הרג] ‘And all the details of his slaying’; lit. ‘and all that he had slain.’ This, however, is extremely forced, and, since כל is omitted by all Verss. except Targ., it may be supposed to be an erroneous insertion from the first half of the verse. So Th., Klo., Kamp., Benz., Kit.

כל הנביאים] LXX, Luc. omit כל.

2. LXX, Luc. preface Jezebel's speech with the words Εἰ σὺ εἶ Ἠλειοὺ (Luc. Ἠλιὰς) καὶ ἐγὼ (Luc. adds εἰμι) Ἰεζάβελ, i. e. אִם אַתָּה אֵלִיָּהוּ וַאֲנִי אִיזֶבֶל ‘*As surely as you are Elijah and I am Jezebel.*’ The force and character of the words speak for their genuineness. So Th.

כה יעשון] Add לִי with all Verss. On the phrase cf. *ch.* 2. 23 *note.*

אַחַד מהם] With *st. const.* before the preposition, as in *ch.* 22. 13; 1 Sam. 9. 3; *al.* (Da. § 35, *Rem.* 2). Against the view that this shorter form אַחַד can ever represent *st. absol.* in ‘the flow of speech’ (Ew. § 267b), as appears from the vocalization of the Massoretes in four instances, cf. Dri. on 2 Sam. 17. 22.

3. וַיַּרְא] Read וַיִּרָא ‘*And he was afraid,*’ with all Verss. except Targ. So Th., Klo., Kamp., Benz., Kit.

וילך אל נפשו] ‘And he went *for* his life’; lit. *on account of.* So II. 7. 7†. With על, Gen. 19. 17 המלט על נפשך.

4. רתם אחת] ‘A broom.’ This shrub, which bears in Ar. the same name رَتَمٌ, is the *Retama roetam* of modern botanists, the *Genista roetam* of older authors. It occurs with great frequency near Sinai and Petra, abundantly round the Dead Sea and in the ravines leading down to the Jordan valley, and occasionally in the wilderness of Judaea. The flower, a delicate white or purplish-pink blossom, appears in February in advance of the tiny foliage, and the shrub reaches a height of ten to twelve feet, affording a grateful shade. Tristram, pp. 359*f.*; cf. Stanley, *Sin. Pal.*, p. 80. On the use of אחד cf. p. 209.

וישאל את נפשו למות] ‘And he asked that his soul might die.’ So exactly Jon. 4. 8. Ew. § 336b calls the constr. ‘a species of the Latin accusative with the infinitive.’

כי לא טוב וג׳] Rightly explained by Th.:—‘As human I must one day die, and now it is death that I desire.’

5. תחת רתם אחד] LXX ἐκεῖ ὑπὸ φυτόν, Luc. ὑπὸ τὸ φυτὸν ἐκεῖ. Here the variation in order, and the fact that רתם אחת in the previous verse is simply transliterated, LXX Ῥαθμέν, Luc. ῥαθαμείν, suggest that the original text read ἐκεῖ alone, and that the remaining words are a later insertion after MT. In MT. the indefinite רתם אחד is strange after the shrub has been already mentioned, and the words have the character of a gloss taken directly from *v.* 4 to explain שָׁם of the original text. We may therefore restore וישכב ויישן שָׁם 'And he lay and slept *there*.'

הנה זה] Isa. 21. 9; Song of Sol. 2. 8, 9†. Cf. *ch.* 14. 6 *note*.

מלאך] LXX, Luc. τις, but in *v.* 7 ἄγγελος.

6. מראשתיו] The word means 'the places *or* parts near his head,' and, used as an adverbial accusative, should be rendered '*At his head*.' So 1 Sam. 19. 13; 26. 7; *al.*

עגת רצפים] 'A cake of (i. e. baked on) hot stones.' Ar. رَضْفٌ means a stone heated in the fire, to be dropped into milk for the purpose of making it boil. רִצְפָּה Isa. 6. 6 denotes a glowing ember.

8ᵇ *ff.*] The writer appears to know, and to be influenced by, the narrative of JE relating to Moses at Ḥoreb. Thus, with the forty days' fast cf. Ex. 34. 28; with the Theophany cf. Ex. 33. 18—34. 8, and especially *v.* 11 והנה י׳ עבר with Ex. 34. 6 ויעבר י׳ על פניו. The name חֹרֵב in the Hexateuch is peculiar to E, Ex. 3. 1; 17. 6; 33. 6, and to Deut., while the expression הר האלהים, always with reference to Ḥoreb, occurs elsewhere only in Ex. 3. 1; 18. 5; 24. 13 (E); 4. 27 (JE).

Perhaps, however, he was dependent, not upon the written source, but upon oral tradition. Contrast the מְעָרָה of Elijah with the נִקְרַת הַצּוּר in which Moses was placed, Ex. 33. 22. Our writer's tradition may have spoken of this latter as a מערה, and המערה *v.* 9, unless merely an example of the use of the definite article noticed *ch.* 13. 14, may mean '*the* cave' thus rendered famous in former times.

הר האלהים] LXX, Luc. omit אלהים.

9. מה לך פה] 'What hast thou here?' (to concern thee), so 'What doest thou here?' Cf. Judg. 18. 3; Isa. 22. 16; 52. 5†.

10. עזבו בריתך] LXX, Luc. *ἐνκατέλιπόν σε*, עֲזָבוּךָ, and so *v.* 14, where, however, in LXX *τὴν διαθήκην σου* has been added by a later hand.

11. והנה י׳ עֹבֵר] The participle picturesquely describes the Theophany as in course of occurrence, and is not, with LXX, Luc., to be rendered as a *fut. instans*, 'Behold Yahwe *shall* pass by,' as if the words formed part of the preceding speech.

רוח גדולה וחזק] The second adjective, as more remote from its subject, lapses into the masculine, and is then followed by masculine participles. So Jer. 20. 9 כְּאֵשׁ בֹּעֶרֶת עָצֻר בְּעַצְמֹתָי; cf. Ezek. 2. 9 יָד שְׁלוּחָה אֵלָי וְהִנֵּה־בוֹ וג׳. 1 Sam. 15. 9, quoted by G-K. § 132 *d;* Da. § 32, *Rem.* 4, is certainly corrupt; cf. Dri. *ad loc.*

12. קול דממה דקה] 'The sound of *a light whisper*.' LXX, Luc. *φωνὴ αὔρας λεπτῆς*, and so Vulg. *sibilus aurae tenuis*, have excellently grasped the sense both of substantive and adjective. דממה is a gentle breeze Ps. 107. 29, or a murmur which can be compared with such a breeze Job 4. 16†. דקה *thin, fine*, and *small*, is only here used of a *sound*, but cf. the similar application of *λεπτός*. RV. marg. 'a sound of gentle *stillness*' is unsatisfactory, *stillness* being incompatible both with קול and דקה, and with כשמע of the following verse.

At the close of the verse, Cod. A adds the weak gloss *κἀκεῖ Κύριος*.

13. וילט] Hiph. only here. Qal particip. pass. 1 Sam. 21. 10; Isa. 25. 7. Cf. the similar action of Moses Ex. 3. 6 (E).

15. חזאל] Cf. *note* on II. 8. 15.

18. והשארתי וג׳] 'And I will spare in Israel seven thousand, even all the knees &c.'

וכל הפה וג׳] The kiss of homage offered to idols may be illustrated by Hos. 13. 2 זֹבְחֵי אָדָם עֲגָלִים יִשָּׁקוּן *kiss calves* of Bethel and Dan. Cf. Job 31. 27, which speaks of kissing the hand in worship of the heavenly bodies.

20. ויאמר אשקה וג׳] Cf. S. Luke 9. 61. LXX omits ולאמי by oversight.

אֶשֳּׁקָה] With ḥatef-qameç under the doubled sibilant. So with the emphatic letters ק, ט; אֲלַקֳּטָה Ruth 2. 2, 7; לְקֳחָה (for לקחה)

Gen. 2. 23; מִטֳּהָרוֹ Ps. 89. 45. Cf. G-K. § 10 *h;* Sta. § 104.

לך שוב וג׳] Elijah disclaims any special significance for his action, unless the call correspond with Elisha's own free impulse. The words לך שוב do not merely grant Elisha's request, but give permission to return, if he will, to his ordinary pursuits.

21. בשלם הבשר] 'He boiled them, the (pieces of) flesh.' The pronom. suffix anticipates the object, as commonly in Syriac. Cf. also *ch.* 21. 13 וַיְעִדֻהוּ . . . אֶת־נָבוֹת; II. 16. 15 Kt. וַיְצַוֵּהוּ הַמֶּלֶךְ אָחָז אֶת־אוּרִיָּה הַכֹּהֵן. Cf. Da. § 29, *Rem.* 7, where a number of instances are cited from other books. LXX, Luc., however, omit הבשר, and it is thus possible that it may have come in as an explanatory gloss from the margin.

20. *Narrative of two campaigns of Ben-hadad II (Hadadezer) against Israel in successive years. In the first the Aramaeans besiege Samaria, and are beaten off by an unexpected sortie. In the second a pitched battle takes place at Aphek, the Aramaeans are defeated, and Ben-hadad falls into the hands of Aḥab, who concludes a truce with him.*

1. בן הדד] The second Aramaean king of this name mentioned in Kings. Cf. *ch.* 15. 18 *note.* This Ben-hadad appears in the Cuneiform inscriptions under the name *Dad-'-id-ri, Dad-id-ri,* i. e. הֲדַדְעֶזֶר. Cf. further *v.* 34 *note; COT.* i. 190 *ff.*

ושלשים וג׳] Cf. the list of allied princes who are mentioned as taking the field with this Hadadezer at Qarqar against Shalmaneser II (*Append.* 3). Here, as in other cases (cited *COT. loc. cit.*), their total is given as twelve, perhaps a round number.

2. העירה] Luc., Pesh. omit.

3. הטובים] LXX omits.

5. כי שלחתי] כי introduces the direct oration: cf. *ch.* 1. 13 *note.*

ובניך] LXX, Luc. omit.

6. עיניך] LXX, Luc., Pesh., Vulg. presuppose עֵינֵיהֶם, correctly. The Aramaeans were to take whatever seemed worth taking *to them.* So Th., Klo., Kamp., Benz., Kit.

7. וּלְבְנִי] So 'A. καὶ εἰς υἱούς μου. LXX καὶ περὶ τῶν υἱῶν μου καὶ περὶ τῶν θυγατέρων μου, Luc. καὶ περὶ τῶν τέκνων μου.

8. אַל תִּשְׁמַע וְלוֹא תֹאבֶה] 'Obey not, *nor* consent.' Continuation by לֹא with imperf. secures an even flow to the sentence, which would have been broken by reinforcement by the more energetic אַל with jussive. So Am. 5. 5ª וְאַל־תִּדְרְשׁוּ בֵּית־אֵל וְהַגִּלְגָּל לֹא תָבֹאוּ וּבְאֵר שֶׁבַע לֹא תַעֲבֹרוּ. Cf. Ew. § 350ª.

10. כֹּה יַעֲשׂוּן וג'] With pl. verb in the mouth of a polytheist, as in *ch.* 19. 2.

יִשְׂפֹּק] 'Shall suffice.' The only occurrence of the verb. Subs. סִפְקוֹ 'his sufficiency,' Job 20. 22 †. The root is common in Aram. in the same sense.

לִשְׁעָלִים] 'For *handfuls.*' Ezek. 13. 19; Isa. 40. 12†. The boast implies that Samaria is unworthy of the prowess of a power like Aram, and at the same time promises its utter obliteration:—'So innumerable are my followers that they will be unable to secure even a handful each of the dust of the ruined city.' Jos. (*Ant.* viii. 14, § 2) explains strangely:—ἀπειλῶν ὑψηλότερον τῶν τειχῶν οἷς καταφρονεῖ χῶμα τούτοις ἐπεγείρειν αὐτοῦ τὴν στρατιὰν κατὰ δράκα λαμβάνουσαν.

בְּרַגְלִי] 'At my feet,' i.e. *following me.* So II. 3. 9; 1 Sam. 25. 27; 2 Sam. 15. 16, 17; Judg. 4. 10; Ex. 11. 8 (J); Deut. 11. 6.

11. דַּבְּרוּ] LXX, Luc. Ἱκανούσθω (Luc. ὑμῖν) must have read רַב; cf. *ch.* 19. 4; 12. 28.

אַל יִתְהַלֵּל וג'] 'Let not him who is girding boast himself as he who is ungirding'; i.e. as Targ. rightly paraphrases לָא יִשְׁתַּבַּח דִּמְזָרֵז וְנָחֵת בִּקְרָבָא כְּגַבְרָא דִּנְצַח וְסָלִיק מִנֵּיהּ 'Let not him who is girding himself and going down into the battle boast himself as the man who has conquered and is coming up from it.' חגר refers to the buckling on of the sword; cf. 1 Sam. 17. 39; 25. 13; Judg. 18. 11; *al.* מפתח may be illustrated by Isa. 45. 1 וּמָתְנֵי מְלָכִים אֲפַתֵּחַ 'and the loins of kings will I ungird,' i.e. render them defenceless. LXX, Luc. μὴ καυχάσθω ὁ κυρτὸς ὡς ὁ ὀρθός interpret חגר from Rabb. Heb. חִגֵּר *lame,* and then guess at מפתח as expressing the antithesis.

12. שימו וישימו על העיר] Clearly an order for the renewal of the hostilities which had been suspended during the negotiations previously described. Render, '*Set yourselves in array, and they set themselves in array against the city*.' So Ges., Ke., Kit., *Sieg. u. Sta.*, RV. text. The expression covers every device which could be used to secure the downfall of the city[1], and it is therefore incorrect to postulate the ellipse of any *special object* after the verb, as is done by LXX, Luc. Οἰκοδομήσατε χάρακα, and similarly Klo., Benz. 'build battering rams,' Th., Kamp., RV. marg. 'place the engines': cf. Ezek. 4. 2; 21. 27. For שים used, as in our passage, to denote military mobilization *generally* (and so without expressed obj.) cf. Ezek. 23. 24 יָשִׂימוּ עָלַיִךְ סָבִיב; 1 Sam. 15. 2 שָׂם לוֹ בַּדֶּרֶךְ.

13. נביא אחד] Upon אחד cf. p. 209.

אחאב] LXX, Luc., Pesh. omit.

וידעת וג׳] Cf. *v.* 28 with pl. verb וידעתם. The phrase is specially characteristic of Ezekiel (some sixty occurrences), and appears also six times in P[2]. Elsewhere it is found only in Ex. 10. 2 (JE); Isa. 49. 23, and + מוֹשִׁיעֵךְ 49. 26; 60. 16, + אֱלֹהֵיכֶם Joel 4. 17.

14. בנערי שרי המדינות] 'By the young men of the princes of the provinces.' These שרי המדינות ('Landvögte,' Ew., Th., Klo., Kamp., Kit.) were probably appointed to the prefecture of special districts, perhaps in the same way as the נִצָּבִים under Solomon *ch.* 4. 7 *ff.*[3], and bound, as a condition of their tenure, in times of emergency to provide the king with a certain number of warriors

---

[1] So Jos. (*Ant.* viii. 14, § 2) rightly expands the king's brief command:—*ὁ δ' εὐθέως τοῦτο προσέταξε καὶ περιχαρακοῦν τὴν πόλιν καὶ χώματα βάλλεσθαι καὶ μηδένα τρόπον ἀπολιπεῖν πολιορκίας.*

[2] In Ezek. the cases are:—וְיָדַעְתָּ 25. 7; 35. 4; וְיָדַעַתְּ 16. 62; 22. 16; וִידַעְתֶּם 6. 7, 13; 7. 4; 11. 10, 12; 12. 20; 13. 14; 14. 8; 15. 7; 20. 38, 42, 44; 25. 5; 35. 9; 36. 11; 37. 6, 13: 13. 9; 23. 49; 24. 24 (אֲדֹנָי י׳); 7. 9 (+ מַכֶּה); וִידַעְתֶּן 13. 21, 23; וְיָדְעוּ 6. 10, 14; 7. 27; 12. 15, 16; 24. 27; 25. 11, 17; 26. 6; 28. 22, 23; 29. 6, 9, 21; 30. 8, 19, 25, 26; 32. 15; 33. 29; 34. 27; 35. 15; 36. 23, 38; 38. 23; 39. 6; 28. 24; 29. 16 (אֲדֹנָי י׳); 28. 26; 34. 30; 39. 22, 28 (+ אֱלֹהֵיהֶם); 39. 7 (+ קָדוֹשׁ בְּיִשְׂרָאֵל). In P:—וִידַעְתֶּם Ex. 6. 7; 16. 12 (+ אֱלֹהֵיכֶם); וְיָדְעוּ 7. 5; 14. 4, 18; 29. 46 (+ אֱלֹהֵיהֶם).

[3] So Wellh. *Isr. u. Jud. Ges.* 66 *note.*

out of their own retinues. In contrast to these כל העם of *v.* 15
denotes the standing army; cf. *ch.* 16. 15 *note.* LXX in *v.* 14
Ἐν τοῖς παιδαρίοις τῶν ἀρχόντων τῶν χορῶν (Luc. χωρῶν), but *v.* 15
τοὺς ἄρχοντας, τὰ παιδάρια τῶν χ., and similarly *v.* 17 ἄρχοντες παιδάρια
τῶν χ., *v.* 19 ἄρχοντα τὰ παιδάρια ἄρχοντα τῶν χ., as though נַעֲרֵי were
a suspended *st. constr.* (cf. 1 Sam. 28. 7; Isa. 23. 12; *al.;* Da.
§ 28, *Rem.* 6) and the phrase meant 'the young men, the princes of
the provinces,' i. e. 'the young princes &c.' Luc. in *v.* 19 renders
as in *v.* 14, but *vv.* 15, 17 show signs of having first exhibited the
same rendering as LXX and then undergone emendation :—τοὺς
ἄρχοντας (οἱ ἄρχοντες) καὶ τὰ παιδάρια τῶν ἀρχόντων τῶν χωρῶν. Ἀ. *v.* 14
Ἐν παισὶν ἀρχόντων τῶν ἐπαρχιῶν, *v.* 15 τοὺς παῖδας ἀρχόντων τῶν ἐπ.,
v. 17 παῖδες ἀρχόντων . . ., *v.* 19 *deest.*

מִי יֶאְסֹר הַמִּלְחָמָה] 'Who shall *join* battle?' i. e. make the first
advance. So 2 Chr. 13. 3.

15. מֵאתִים שְׁנַיִם וּשְׁלֹשִׁים] LXX omits שנים.

כֹּל בְּנֵי יִשְׂרָאֵל] LXX, Luc. rightly presuppose כָּל־בְּנֵי חַיִל 'all the
mighty men,' the phrase being explanatory of כל העם.

שִׁבְעַת אֲלָפִים] LXX ἑξήκοντα, Luc. ἑξήκοντα χιλιάδας.

16. וַיֵּצְאוּ בַּצָּהֳרָיִם] LXX καὶ ἐξῆλθεν μεσημβρίας, Luc. καὶ ἐξῆλθεν
ὁ βασιλεὺς μετ' αὐτῶν μεσημβρίας, an expansion explanatory of the
sing. verb.

שֹׁתֶה שִׁכּוֹר] *Ch.* 16. 9.

17. וַיִּשְׁלַח בֶּן הֲדַד] LXX, Luc. καὶ ἀποστέλλουσιν, the implied
subj. being the outposts of the Aramaean host who observed the
sortie, while the king was engaged at his carouse. The orig. text,
if not וַיִּשְׁלְחוּ, was perhaps impers. וַיִּשְׁלַח 'and one sent,' rendered
correctly by LXX, and with subj. erroneously supplied in MT.

20. וַיַּכּוּ אִישׁ אִישׁוֹ] 'And they smote each his man.' LXX, Luc.
add καὶ ἐδευτέρωσεν ἕκαστος τὸν παρ' αὐτοῦ, and so Ew. restores
וַיִּשְׁנוּ אִישׁ אִישׁוֹ 'and they repeated &c.,' the whole passage meaning 'and they slew each his man *repeatedly.*' The repetition of
אִישׁ אִישׁוֹ is, however, extremely awkward, and the addition is
certainly a later gloss. Had the original writer wished to lay
stress upon the fact that each man slew more than one of the

opposing Aramaeans he would have added simply וַיַּשְׁנוּ or else הַכֵּה וְשָׁנֹה. But the point of the narrative is that *the first onslaught* was such that it immediately put the enemy to flight.

20b. וימלט וג׳] The sense of the last three words is obscure. The best rendering is that of RV. text, 'And Ben-hadad king of Aram escaped *on a horse with* (lit. *and*) *horsemen*.' פרשים must be thought to be loosely connected on to סוס by the ו as forming a concomitant factor to the king's escape. Cf. Cod. A ἐφ' ἵππων σου ἱππεῦσίν τισιν, Vulg. *in equo cum equitibus suis*. But the text would be greatly improved by the addition of עִמּוֹ after פרשים, as is suggested by Targ. על סוסון ועמיה תרין פרשין 'upon horses, two horsemen being with him.' Klo. emends עַל־סוּס הוּא וּפָרָשָׁיו.

21. ויך] LXX, Luc. καὶ ἔλαβεν, i.e. וַיִּקַּח. The king and his reserve availed themselves of the horses and chariots which had been abandoned by the Aramaeans in their panic, and were thus (Th.) able to effect the 'great slaughter' which the main body of the army, following the fugitives on foot, might have failed to accomplish. MT. describes a senseless waste of energy.

את הסוס] LXX πάντας τοὺς ἵππους.

וְהִכָּה] Apparently an irregular abandonment of the constr. of imperf. with ו *consec.* in favour of ו *simplex* with perf. Possibly, however, the vocalization is at fault, and the writer intended to use the infin. abs. וְהַכֵּה; cf. *ch.* 9. 25; Judg. 7. 19; *al.* Da. § 88.

22. לך התחזק] LXX, Luc., with omission of לך, Κραταιοῦ. In הִתְחַזַּק the original *pathaḥ* of the last syllable of the *Hithpa'el* is preserved; cf. G-K. § 54 *k*.

לתשובת השנה] 'At the return of the year'; i.e. when spring comes round again after the winter, and warfare becomes practicable. So *v.* 26. Cf. 2 Sam. 11. 1 where the phrase is explained לְעֵת צֵאת הַמְּלָכִים 'at the time when kings go forth (on campaign)'; 2 Chr. 36. 10.

23. אלהי הרים וג׳] 'Gods of hills are their gods, therefore were they (the gods) too strong for us.' RV., in rendering אלהי as a sing. and making subj. of חזקו to be the Israelites themselves, is

incorrect. The Aramaeans, in accordance with their own ideas, ascribe a plurality of deities to Israel, and it is these gods, as well as their worshippers, against whom they are fighting, and whom they hope to conquer if they can decoy them from their fastnesses. LXX Θεὸς Ἰσραὴλ followed by sing. verb ἐκραταίωσεν is an intentional alteration in order to avoid the use of phraseology offensive to the unity of God. So in *v.* 28 the Israelitish prophet, in quoting the words of the Aramaeans, naturally substitutes a singular:—אלהי הרים יהוה '*A God* of hills is *Yahwe*.'

אלהיהם] LXX, Luc. add καὶ οὐ Θεὸς κοιλάδος (Luc. κοιλάδων), a gloss made for the sake of strict conformity with *v.* 28. In *v.* 23, however, the words are certainly out of place, וְאוּלָם *but however*, introducing the idea that the gods may not be gods of the plain as a suggestion not previously mentioned except by implied antithesis in אלהי הרים.

אם לא וג׳] '*Surely* we shall be stronger than they.' So *v.* 25. The same form of asseveration is found in Josh. 14. 9; Isa. 5. 9; 14. 24; Job 1. 11, and with perf. II. 9. 26; Jer. 15. 11; Job 22. 20; Ps. 131. 2. Cf. *note* on *ch.* 2. 23.

24. ממקומו] 'From his place'; i. e. his appointed position in the line of battle. LXX, Luc. εἰς τὸν τόπον αὐτῶν (Luc. αὐτοῦ), and so Jos. (*Ant.* viii. 14, § 3) ἀπολῦσαι πρὸς τὰ οἰκεῖα, is inferior, and probably arose from the common confusion of מ with ב. But neither במקומו (Th.) nor למקומו (Klo.) could correctly stand with this signification, אֶל־מ׳ being the required phrase.

פחות] 'Commanders' or 'vicegerents.' These appear to be the same as the שרי הרכב שלשים ושנים *ch.* 22. 31; cf. 20. 1. Giesebrecht, taking the term פחה as Persian in origin, is obliged to regard this verse as an interpolation, and considers that it breaks the connexion, ואתה of *v.* 25 forming the right continuation to *v.* 23, and ויעש כן, *v.* 25 *end*, being satisfied by *v.* 26 (a doubtful contention). But cf. *note* on *ch.* 10. 15.

25. מֵאוֹתָךְ . . . אוֹתָם] This form of the particle for the usual מֵאִתָּךְ, אִתָּם, occurs repeatedly in these N. Pal. narratives up to II. *ch.* 8;—*ch.* 22. 7, 8, 24; II. 1. 15; 3. 11, 12, 26; 6. 16; 8. 8;

but can scarcely be counted dialectical, depending as it does upon vocalization and *scriptio plena*, and standing also beside the more ordinary form; cf. *ch.* 20. 23; 22. 4, 24; II. 3. 7; 6. 16, 32. The form אוֹת is found several times in Jer. and Ezek., but appears elsewhere only rarely.

26. אפקה] Several cities of this name are mentioned in O. T.; but this one, which occurs again in II. 13. 17, is doubtless the same as is mentioned in Josh. 12. 18; 1 Sam. 29. 1, in the neighbourhood of Jezreel. Assyr. *Ap-ḳu; COT.* i. 194.

27. הָתְפָּקְדוּ] The same form occurs Num. 1. 47; 2. 33; 26. 62, and is intended as passive of הִתְפָּקְדוּ Judg. 20. 15, 17; 21. 9. Both forms, however, have precisely the same reflexive sense, 'set themselves for muster,' 'were mustered,' and probably Wright (*Compar. Gramm.* 208 *n.*) is correct in thinking the pronunciation as a passive הָתְפָּקְדוּ to be due to a misunderstanding of the Massoretes. הִתְפָּקֵד, without doubling of the 2nd rad., stands alone in Heb., and appears to be a relic of the reflexive of the simple stem פָּקַד, corresponding to Aram. אִתְקְטֵל, ܐܶܬ݂ܩܛܶܠ, Aeth. *taqatla*, Ar. VIII with transposition of 1st rad. and preform. إِقْتَتَلَ *'iqtatala* for *'ithqatala*, and so on the Moabite stone, *ll.* 11, 15, 19, 32 הלתחם from root לחם. Cf. Wright, *loc. cit.;* G-K. § 54 *l;* Sta. § 162; and, for other views as to the form, König, *Lehrg.* I. i. p. 198.

וכלכלו] 'And were provisioned'; passive of the Pilpel which is found in *ch.* 17. 4, 9; 18. 13; *al.* So Vulg. *et acceptis cibariis*, LXX, Luc. omit. ו *simplex* co-ordinates the two facts. Dri. *Tenses*, § 132.

כשני חשפי עזים] The subs. חשיף is elsewhere quite unknown. LXX, Luc., Vulg., Pesh., Targ. give the meaning 'like two *small flocks* of goats,' and this is generally adopted. חשף = 'strip off,' and thus חשיף 'that which is stripped off' may possibly denote *segregatum* (*Heb. Lex. Oxf.*), but the inference is precarious. Klo. emends בְּשְׁפִי מִשְׁפַּט עִזִּים 'upon the bare height, after the manner of goats.'

28. ויאמר אל מלך י׳ ויאמר] The repetition of ויאמר is certainly superfluous. Pesh. omits the first occurrence, thus making the

passage to agree with *vv.* 13, 22; while LXX, Luc., Vulg. are without the second. This latter omission is correct, the addition in MT. being probably due, as is suggested by Pesh., to an attempt to gain agreement with the preceding passages.

וידעתם] LXX καὶ γνώσῃ, Luc. γνώσει, as in *v.* 13.

30. עשרים ושבעה אלף] Pesh. ܥܣܪܝܢ ܘܫܒܥܐ ܐܠܦܝܢ, 25,000.

חדר בחדר] 'A chamber within a chamber,' i.e. 'an *innermost* chamber'; here, as in *ch.* 22. 25 (‖ 2 Chr. 18. 24); II. 9. 2†, selected as most remote and private. Jos. (*Ant.* viii. 14, § 4) explains as an *underground house;*—εἰς ὑπόγειον οἶκον ἐκρύβη.

31. ויאמרו וג׳] LXX puts the suggestion into the mouth of Ben-hadad, reading καὶ εἶπεν τοῖς παισὶν αὐτοῦ Οἶδα κ.τ.λ. τὰς ψυχὰς ἡμῶν. So Luc., with the different Οἴδατε. That this, however, is incorrect is shown by *vv.* 32, 33, where the servants *without the king* form the embassy.

כי מלכי . . . כי וג׳] For the second כי resumptive of the first, cf. *ch.* 1. 30 *note.*

בְּרֹאשֵׁנוּ] LXX, Luc., Vulg., Pesh., pl. בְּרָאשֵׁינוּ as in *v.* 32.

נפשך] Vulg., Pesh., though agreeing with MT. in placing the speech in the mouth of the servants, yet like LXX, Luc., presuppose pl. נַפְשׁוֹתֵינוּ. This is an easy alteration induced by the preceding pls. נשימה וג׳, but inferior to MT. in which the saving of the *king's life* is rightly made the object of the proposed plan.

33. והאנשים ינחשו] Vulg. excellently, *quod acceperunt viri pro omine;* i.e. they *divined* the successful issue of their mission from the favourable response אחי הוא. Cf. Sta. *Ges.* i. 445*f.* For this use of the verb cf. Gen. 30. 27 נִחַשְׁתִּי וַיְבָרְכֵנִי י׳ בִּגְלָלֶךָ 'I have observed the omens, and Yahwe hath blessed me for thy sake.' The only explanation that can be placed upon the imperf. is that it emphasizes pictorially *the coming into being* of their consciousness of the king's mood;—'and the men *began to* divine'; cf. Dri. *Tenses,* § 27 γ. The emendation of Grä. וַיָּחִישׁוּ joined with וימהרו, as in Isa. 5. 19, is unnecessary.

ויחלטו הממנו] The verb occurs nowhere else, and הֲמִמֶּנּוּ is untranslateable, RV. 'whether it were his mind' (*marg.* Heb. 'from him') being indefensible. The Verss.—LXX καὶ ἀνέλεξαν τὸν λόγον ἀπὸ (Luc. καὶ ἀνελέξαντο τὸν λόγον αὐτοῦ ἐκ) τοῦ στόματος αὐτοῦ, Vulg. *rapuerunt verbum ex ore ejus,* Pesh. ܘܦܠܛܘܗܝ ܡܢܗ, Targ. וחטפוהא מיניה—are unanimous both in presupposing a different division of the words וַיַּחְלְטוּהָ מִמֶּנּוּ, and in supplying a plausible meaning for the verb;—'*and they caught it from him,*' i. e. they at once took up and repeated the title of *brother* which he had conferred upon Ben-hadad. ויחלטו being isolated, and its meaning purely conjectural, it is futile to dogmatize as to its being Qal (Sta. § 529[a]) or shortened Hiph'il form like וַיַּדְבִּקוּ, וַיַּדְרְכוּ (G-K. § 53 *n;* Kö., *Lehrg.* I. i. p. 251).

וַיַּעֲלֵהוּ] LXX, Luc. καὶ ἀναβιβάζουσιν αὐτὸν πρὸς αὐτόν. Here the subj. of the verb being wrongly conceived as pl. ויעלהו (הָאֲנָשִׁים 33[a]), πρὸς αὐτόν appears to be the translator's explan. addit. 'unto him' (Aḥab) which is thus rendered desirable to complete the sense. The view that LXX presupposes an orig. וַיַּעֲלֵהוּ אֵלָיו (Th., Kamp.) is therefore improbable.

34. חוצות] 'Streets,' i.e. doubtless, as explained by Ke., Th., Ges., *Heb. Lex. Oxf.*, &c., *bazaars* where trade might be freely carried on. Ew. 'fortified quarters' is strangely alien to the term employed.

ואני וג׳] The change of speaker is regarded as sufficiently marked by the content of his speech as a response to the preceding: cf. II. 10. 15.

בברית] RV. '*with* this covenant,' i. e. *at the price of* it; ב *pretii;* cf. *ch.* 2. 23 *note* on בנפשו. The fact of this alliance between Aḥab and Hadadezer is strikingly confirmed by the monolith of Shalmaneser II, where the two kings are mentioned as leagued against the Assyrian at the battle of Qarqar: cf. *Append.* 3.

וישלחהו] Luc. adds ἐκ τῆς οἰκίας αὐτοῦ καὶ ἀπῆλθεν ἀπ' αὐτοῦ.

35. איש אחד] Cf. p. 209. The identification by Jos. (*Ant.* viii. 14, § 5) of this prophet with Micaiah of *ch.* 22 is by no means improbable: cf. *vv.* 42, 43 with *ch.* 22. 8.

מבני הנביאים] 'Sons of the prophets' was the title of members of the prophetic guilds or schools which existed at Bethel, II. 2. 3;

Jericho, *vv.* 5, 15; Gilgal, 4. 38, and probably elsewhere, and were in some sense presided over by Elijah and Elisha; cf. II. 2. 15–18; 4. 1, 38 *ff.*; 6. 1 *ff.*; 9. 1. Such guilds seem to have flourished under Samuel, 1 Sam. 19. 20 (Naioth), cf. 10. 5, 10 (Gibeah), and may, perhaps, have been founded by him; cf. 7. 15–17 where *Bethel* and *Gilgal* are included with Mizpah among the cities visited by Samuel in his yearly round from his centre, Ramah. The force of the term בן נביא is well illustrated by Am. 7. 14, where Amos tells Amaziah of Bethel, לא נביא אנכי ולא בן נביא אנכי 'I was no prophet, neither was I *a prophet's son*,' i. e. I had not the advantage of any special training for the calling.

בדבר י׳] Cf. *ch.* 13. 1 *note*.

36. האריה] '*The* lion,' singled out for the part which he is to play, and already conjured up before the speaker's prophetic vision. Cf. especially *ch.* 22. 21 הָרוּחַ, and see *note* on *ch.* 13. 14.

37. ויכהו . . . ופצע] 'And the man smote him, *so as to wound him*.' Here the act denoted by פָּצֹעַ sharply limits the duration of that described by ויכהו הכה, as forming its *end* or *result*. So exactly Jer. 12. 17 ונתשתי את הגוי ההוא נתוש ואבד 'I will pluck up that nation, *so as to destroy it*.' The case cannot be classed, as by Da. (§ 86c; Jer. 12. 17 is made to fall under § 87), among cases where 'the inf. abs. after its verb suggests an indefinitely prolonged state of the action, and therefore expresses continuance, prevalence, &c.'; this being precisely what in the present instance it does not do. Cases where the second infin. expresses *concomitance of indefinite duration*, Judg. 14. 9; II. 2. 11, or simple addition of an event *in due sequence* (but *not* as the result aimed at by the previous action), Isa. 19. 22, are different in character.

38. למלך] LXX, Luc. τῷ βασιλεῖ Ἰσραήλ.

באפר] The word אפר occurs only here and in *v.* 41, but the meaning '*covering*' or '*bandage*,' given by LXX, Luc. τελαμῶνι, Targ. במעפרא, has the support of Assyr. in which *apâru* = 'to attire,' especially with a head-covering; *êpartu* = 'garment.' See Friedr. Delitzsch, *Assyr. Handwörterbuch*, *s. v.* I. אפר, and *Prolegomena*, 54; Zimmern, *Babylonische Busspsalmen*, 95; Barth,

Etym. Studien, 19. Vulg., Pesh. 'A., Σ. vocalize אֵפֶר 'ashes.' For use of art. בָּאפר cf. *ch.* 1. 1 *note* on בַּבְּגדים.

40. עבדך עֹשֶׂה הנה והנה] 'Thy servant was *a doer of hither and thither*' (הנה והנה as in II. 2. 8, 14; Josh. 8. 20†), an impossibly harsh construction. Vocalization עֹשֶׂה *st. abs.* gives the rendering '*was busy hither and thither*'; but that a man posing as having been set to guard a captive should represent himself as deliberately engaged in other matters seems scarcely probable. LXX περιεβλέψατο, Luc. περιεβλέπετο, Vulg. *me verterem*, Pesh. ܟܕ ܡܬܦܢܐ, Targ. מתפני, point to an orig. פֹּנֶה '*was turning* (looking) hither and thither,' and are followed by Th., Klo., *Heb. Lex. Oxf.* Cf. Ex. 2. 12 וַיִּפֶן כֹּה וָכֹה.

כן משפטך וג'] 'Such (*lit.* so) is thy verdict; thou thyself hast decided.' For sense of verb חרצת cf. esp. Niph. participle in the phrase כָּלָה וְנֶחֱרָצָה 'a consumption and *a strict decision*,' i.e. a consumption finally decided; Isa. 10. 23; 28. 22; Dan. 9. 27.

42. איש חרמי] 'The man of my ban'; i.e. the man devoted by me to destruction. Cf. Isa. 34. 5 עַם חֶרְמִי referring to Edom.

מיד] LXX, Luc., Vulg. suggest מִיָּדְךָ, and so Th., Klo., Kamp., Benz., Kit.; but MT. is supported by 1 Sam. 19. 9; 26. 23; 2 Chr. 25. 20; Isa. 28. 2; Ezek. 12. 7, where בְּיָד occurs without specific suffix[1]. An expression first used, as in Prov. 6. 5 הִנָּצֵל כִּצְבִי מִיָּד, with vague and general reference, may then come to be employed where closer specification might be expected. Cf. colloquial Eng. *in hand, out of hand.*

43. על ביתו] Cf. *ch.* 1. 38 *note* on על גחון.

סר וזעף] So *ch.* 21. 4. '*Chafing and sullen.*' סַר, used again in fem. *ch.* 21. 5 מה זה רוחך סרה, is connected with סרר 'be refractory.' The meaning of the adj. זָעֵף is well illustrated by the use of the participle זֹעֲפִים which in Gen. 40. 6 denotes an appearance *dejected* and *gloomy* as produced by perplexing thoughts (cf. Joseph's

[1] Cf. the renderings of LXX, Vulg. in 1 Sam. 19. 9 ταῖς χερσὶν αὐτοῦ, *manu sua*; 26. 23 εἰς χεῖράς μου, *in manum meam*; 2 Chr. 25. 20 Luc. εἰς χεῖρας Ἰωάς, *in manus hostium*; where, as in our passage, the translators are at pains to make the reference precise, but presuppose no different original to MT.

question in *v.* 7 מדוע פניכם רעים היום), in Dan. 1. 10 a countenance *haggard* through spare and coarse diet. The phrase is further elucidated by the description of the king's conduct in *ch.* 21. 4b.

21. *Aḥab covets the vineyard of Naboth the Jezreelite, and obtains it by the judicial murder of the owner, planned and executed by Jezebel. The prophet Elijah announces Yahwe's sentence upon Aḥab and his house because of the deed.*

1a. LXX καὶ ἀμπελὼν εἶς ἦν τῷ Ναβουθαὶ τῷ Ἰσραηλείτῃ, i. e. וְכֶרֶם אֶחָד היה לנבות היזרעאלי: probably original. The introductory formula of MT., copied from *ch.* 17. 17 but here somewhat ill-fitting, was probably added by the scribe who interposed this *ch.* between *chh.* 20 and 22; cf. p. 210. The words are found in Luc., but that they are there a later addition is shown by the presence also of καί before ἀμπελών, as in LXX. On כרם אחד cf. p. 209.

1b. אצל היכל א׳] LXX παρὰ τῇ ἅλῳ Ἀχαάβ, i. e. אצל גֹּרֶן א׳. MT. is to some extent favoured by *v.* 2 אצל ביתי.

2. כסף מחיר זה] 'The money-value of this one'; lit. 'the money of the price of this.' כסף is *st. constr.* before מחיר as in Job 28. 15 כסף מחירה, and is not, with RV., to be taken as an accus. of limitation, 'the worth of it *in money*.' LXX, Luc., expanding זה into (Luc. τοῦ) ἀμπελῶνός σου τούτου, then repeat καὶ ἔσται μοι εἰς κῆπον λαχάνων.

3. חלילה לי מיהוה] So 1 Sam. 24. 7; 26. 11; and 2 Sam. 23. 17 Luc., Pesh., Targ. (cf. ‖ 1 Chr. 11. 19 חלילה לי מאלהי). מיהוה LXX παρὰ θεοῦ μου. Luc. παρὰ κυρίου θεοῦ μου a combination of MT. and LXX.

4. ויבא . . . וזעף] LXX καὶ ἐγένετο τὸ πνεῦμα Ἀχαὰβ τεταραγμένον, probably an alteration for exact agreement with *v.* 5. Luc. embodies the two readings, following MT. in *v.* 4a, and placing LXX reading at the beginning of *v.* 4b. On סר וזעף cf. *ch.* 20. 43 *note*.

ויסב את פניו] Cf. II. 20. 2a. Vulg., as in this passage, makes the addition *ad parietem.* LXX, Luc. καὶ συνεκάλυψεν seem to have read וַיְכַס for ויסב.

5. מה זה] *Ch.* 14. 6 *note.*

6. כי אדבר] Not, as RV. '*Because* I spake,' but simply 'I spake,' כי introducing the direct narration. Cf. *ch.* 1. 13 *note.* The use of the imperf. is here somewhat strange, but may perhaps be explained as laying pictorial stress upon the *commencement* of the king's overtures, a usage resembling the Eng. *historical present;* 'I *speak*' or '*begin to speak*,' when immediately negotiations are cut short by a definite refusal. Cf. Dri. *Tenses*, § 27 γ; Da. § 45, *Rem.* 2, quoting Hitzig. The suggestion of a *frequentative* force for the imperf. (Dri. *loc. cit.*) is less probable, there being no hint of this in the preceding narrative.

את כרמי] LXX, Luc. κληρονομίαν πατέρων μου, an alteration after *v.* 3.

7. אתה עתה] 'Dost *thou* now govern Israel?' On the interrogative force of the sentence cf. *ch.* 1. 24 *note.*

ויטב לבך] 'And let thy heart be cheerful.' Cf. *note* on טובי לב *ch.* 8. 66.

8. הספרים] Kt. הַסְּפָרִים is correct; '*the* letters' already mentioned, *v.* 8a.

החרים] 'The nobles,' lit. '*freeborn*'; Ar. حُرٌّ, Aram. בר חורין, ܒܪ ܚܐܪܐ. The word doubtless belongs to the N. Pal. dialect (cf. p. 209), other occurrences in O. T. being late;—seven times in Neh. of the magnates of Judah, and so in Jer. 27. 20; 39. 6 (both passages omitted in LXX, and probably later interpolations; cf. Dri. *Introd.* pp. 248, 254 *f.*), of Edomite nobles Isa. 34. 12 (exilic); בן חורים as in Aram., Eccl. 10. 17†.

אשר בעירו וג׳] 'Who were in his city, who *presided* with Naboth.' So *v.* 11 אשר הישבים בעירו 'who were *those who presided* in his city.' Naboth himself was one of the elders and nobles in whose hands the civil government of the city lay. That ישב here has the sense of *presiding*, especially as judges, is rightly recognized by Th., and by Klo. who renders 'Beisitzer.' For this use of the verb, cf. Isa. 28. 6 לַיּוֹשֵׁב עַל־הַמִּשְׁפָּט 'for him who *sits* (presides) over the judgement'; Am. 6. 3 שֶׁבֶת חָמָס 'the *seat* of violence (i. e.

of unjust judgement)'; and of Yahwe Ps. 9. 8 where the clause answering to יֹשֵׁב used absolutely is כּוֹנֵן לַמִּשְׁפָּט כִּסְאוֹ; cf. Ps. 29. 10; Joel 4. 12. RV. '*and* that dwelt with Naboth' makes the sentence simply a repetition of the statement אשר בעירו. LXX, Luc. wrongly omit this former clause, while Pesh. combines with the following: ܕܝܬܒܝܢ ܒܡܕܝܢܬܐ ܥܡ ܢܒܘܬ 'who dwelt in the city with Naboth.'

9. קראו צום] An extraordinary day of humiliation to avert the wrath of Yahwe which for some cause (supposed to be as yet unascertained) was assumed to be threatening the community. Such a special fast is mentioned as proclaimed by Jehoshaphat, 2 Chr. 20. 1–4. Cf. Th., Sta. *Ges.* i. 527.

והשיבו וג׳] Not as the suspected culprit, but as a man of marked position and piety who would naturally take the lead upon such an occasion; so Jos. (*Ant.* viii. 13, § 8) *καὶ ποιησαμένους ἐκκλησίαν προκαθίσαι μὲν αὐτῶν* Νάβωθον, *εἶναι γὰρ αὐτὸν γένους ἐπιφανοῦς.* The prominence of his position would thus the more excite the popular indignation (Th.), when the crime had been fastened upon him.

10. שנים אנשים] '*Two* men,' as at least necessary to secure a conviction; cf. Deut. 17. 6; 19. 15; Num. 35. 30; S. Matt. 26. 60 *f.*

בני בליעל] 'Villains.' The derivation and exact meaning of בליעל are highly obscure. There are two rival explanations, both of which regard the word, according to its Massoretic vocalization, as a compound. (i) בְּלִי *not* + יַעַל which is supposed to mean *worth* or *use* (cf. Hiph'il הועיל). Thus בְּלִיַּעַל = 'worthlessness,' בְּנֵי בְלִיַּעַל 'base fellows' (cf. *Heb. Lex. Oxf.*, *s. v.*). (ii) בְּלִי *not* + יַעַל for יַעֲלֶה *that which comes up*;—'not coming up,' and so 'unsuccessful' or 'ne'er-do-well' (Kimḥi בַּל יַעֲלֶה וּבַל יַצְלִיחַ, followed by Hupfeld among moderns). It is no objection to either of these explanations that the use of the term proves the conception to be not negative but positive—*malignity* or *dangerous wickedness* (Cheyne, as cited below), since instances can be quoted from all languages in which terms originally negative have gained later a very definite positive significance; cf. e. g. ἀσεβής, Germ. 'Unheil,' Old Eng. 'naughty.'

But a real difficulty in the way of the acceptance of either is the fact that the use of such a compound term in ordinary phraseology is without a parallel; expressions such as בְּלִימָה 'nothingness,' Job 26. 7; בְּנֵי בְלִי־שֵׁם 30. 8; מִלִּין בְּלִי דָעַת 38. 2 being late poetical creations, and therefore not to the point. בְּלִיַּעַל, then, is probably to be classed with צַלְמָוֶת (for צַלְמוּת) as exhibiting merely a fancy vocalization based upon relatively late tradition.

The view of Cheyne is that בליעל is to be identified with the Babylono-Assyrian goddess *Belili*, as representing the underworld, and that in later times the word may have been popularly associated with the derivation בַּל יַעֲלֶה in the sense 'the depth which lets no man return.' The chief passage cited in favour of this explanation is Ps. 18. 5[b] נַחֲלֵי בְלִיַּעַל, rendered 'streams of the underworld,' in juxtaposition to חֶבְלֵי מָוֶת *v.* 5[a], חֶבְלֵי שְׁאוֹל *v.* 6[a] (*Expositor*, June 1895, pp. 435–439; *Expository Times*, June 1897, pp. 423 *f.*; Nov. 1897, pp. 91 *ff.*; Apr. 1898, p. 332). The identification of בליעל with *Belili* is, however, denied by Baudissin and Jensen, on the grounds that there is no evidence to show that the *earth*-goddess *Belili* was ever regarded as a deity ruling the underworld; that there is no O. T. passage in which the meaning 'underworld' for בליעל is clearly present; and that there is no analogous O. T. expression in which men are brought into connexion with the underworld in order to mark them out as destructive or wicked (*Expository Times*, Oct. 1897, pp. 40–45; March 1898, pp. 283 *f.*).

If בליעל be *not* a compound term, it is natural to refer it to the root בלע 'swallow up, engulf,' and to regard the ל as ל formative, cases of which are seen in גִּבְעֹל, קַרְסֹל, כַּרְמֶל, and perhaps עֲרָפֶל. The י may then conceivably mark the word as a diminutive, according to the common Ar. usage (Wright, *Ar. Gramm.* i. § 269), to be traced also in Syr. in the words ܒܟܣܘܢܐ, ܒܘܪܘܠܐ, ܫܒܝܪܐ (Duval, *Gramm. Syr.* § 235), and in Heb. זְעֵיר, and perhaps also in שְׁפִיפוֹן and אֲמִינוֹן 2 Sam. 13. 20 (cf. Dri. *ad loc.*). Thus an original *bulai'āl* might become בְּלִיעַל, a form resembling שְׁפִיפוֹן, אֲמִינוֹן, which may be thought to stand for *shufaifān*, *'umainān*, upon the analogy of vulgar Ar. *ḳ'fīfah*, 'little basket,' for *ḳufaifah*

(Wright, *Compar. Gramm.* p. 89). בְלִיַּעַל will then denote '*engulfing ruin*' or '*perdition*,' the diminutive marking the word as used in contempt and antipathy. Such a significance attached to the root בלע may be seen in Ps. 52. 6 כָּל־דִּבְרֵי־בָלַע, and the phrase בֶּן בְלִיַּעַל may be paralleled by ὁ υἱὸς τῆς ἀπωλείας S. John 17. 12 ; 2 Thess. 2. 3.

After בְנֵי בְלִיַּעַל LXX omits all that follows in MT. down to בְנֵי בְלִיַּעַל of *v.* 13, apparently through homoioteleuton.

בֵרַכְתָּ] 'Thou hast *cursed*'; lit. '*blessed*,' and so *v.* 13; Job 1. 5, 11 ; 2. 5, 9 ; Ps. 10. 3†. A sense so strangely opposed to the usual meaning of the verb is scarcely to be regarded as obtained from the idea 'greet at departing' (*ch.* 8. 66 ; Gen. 47. 10), so 'say farewell,' and then 'renounce' (Ges. *Thes.*, Ke., Dillmann on Job, &c., and so RV. *marg.*), there being no particle of evidence for such a transition in meaning ; nor does it seem probable that the notion is that of 'a blessing overdone and so really a curse as in vulgar English as well as in the Shemitic cognates' (*Heb. Lex. Oxf.*). Rather, the word is an euphemism deliberately substituted for its direct antithesis, viz. the most fearful form of curse such as it were a sin even to mention in direct terms. Cf. among the Greeks the title Εὐμενίδες, 'the gracious goddesses,' applied euphemistically to the Ἐρινύες or Furies, and the name ὁ Εὔξινος given to the Black sea as being ἄξενος *in*hospitable ;—'*Dictus ab antiquis Axenus ille fuit*,' Ovid, *Trist.* 4. 4, 56.

אֱלֹהִים וָמֶלֶךְ] The cursing of *God and the king* is prohibited in the Book of the Covenant, Ex. 22. 27 אֱלֹהִים לֹא תְקַלֵּל וְנָשִׂיא בְעַמְּךָ לֹא תָאֹר.

וּסְקָלֻהוּ] The same penalty (verb רגם) is imposed for blasphemy in Lev. 24. 10–16 (H).

11^b. כַּאֲשֶׁר כָּתוּב וְגֹ'] Luc. omits. The words are redundant after the statement immediately preceding, and may therefore be a gloss.

12. וְהֹשִׁיבוּ] Not to be explained as a perf. with ו *consec.*, nor can any reason be assigned for the use of ו *simplex*. The form is an unintentional lapse into the imperat. form used in *v.* 9, and

we may correct וַיּוֹשִׁיבוּ. That the passage is not a mere gloss (Klo.) appears from the suffix of נגדו *v.* 13, which points back to the name נבות of this verse.

13. LXX, Luc. omit אנשי הבליעל את נבות נגד העם. But the last two words at least give a touch to the narrative not to be dispensed with.

ויעדהו . . . את נבות] Cf. *ch.* 19. 21 *note* on בשלם הבשר.

15. ויהי וג׳] LXX *καὶ ἐγένετο ὡς ἤκουσεν Ἰεζάβελ, καὶ εἶπεν πρὸς Ἀ.*, i.e. וַיְהִי כִּשְׁמֹעַ אִיזֶבֶל וַתֹּאמֶר אֶל־א׳. This less burdened sentence has to some extent the support of Luc., where the words of MT., though present, are marked as a gloss by the strange *Κέχωσται* for סקל; and of Pesh. which varies from MT., abbreviating ܕܡܝܬ ܢܒܘܬ, i.e. כִּי מֵת נ׳.

16. After *v.* 16[a] LXX adds *καὶ διέρρηξεν τὰ ἱμάτια ἑαυτοῦ καὶ περιεβάλετο σάκκον· καὶ ἐγένετο μετὰ ταῦτα, κ.τ.λ.* So Luc. This, however, is scarcely consistent with *v.* 27 MT.; since it is improbable that Aḥab first made a show of mourning at Naboth's death, then proceeded to take possession of his estate, and finally, upon Elijah's rebuke, secured a remand of the threatened vengeance through a repetition of the same tokens of remorse, this time, it must be supposed, sincere. Hence LXX varies from MT. in *v.* 27, making this statement to refer back to the former show of repentance narrated by the Version in *v.* 16:—*καὶ ὑπὲρ τοῦ λόγου ὡς κατενύγη Ἀ. ἀπὸ προσώπου τοῦ κυρίου, καὶ ἐπορεύετο κλαίων καὶ διέρρηξεν τὸν χιτῶνα αὐτοῦ καὶ ἐζώσατο σάκκον ἐπὶ τὸ σῶμα αὐτοῦ καὶ ἐνήστευσεν· καὶ περιεβάλετο σάκκον ἐν τῇ ἡμέρᾳ ᾗ ἐπάταξεν N. τὸν Ἰσραηλείτην, καὶ ἐπορεύθη. καὶ ἐγένετο ῥῆμα Κυρίου κ.τ.λ.* So substantially Luc. But all this stands self-condemned. It is impossible that Aḥab's remand should have been granted as an afterthought on account of his *first exhibition of repentance* (*v.* 16 LXX), which was clearly insincere and had not in the first place served in any way to qualify the penalty pronounced by Elijah. MT., therefore, in making the king display no sign of remorse, real or assumed, until after the prophet's threatenings, is certainly correct; and the fact that LXX text is here spurious and late is recognized by Th., who points out that

Jos. (*Ant.* viii. 13, § 8) was acquainted with a narrative in no way different from MT.

18. הנה וג׳] On omission of subj. with הנה cf. II. 6. 13 *note.*

19 *ff.* The account of this interview has been amplified by R^{D}. Cf. Abijah's prophecy against Jeroboam, *ch.* 14. 7–16 *notes*, and, beside the phrases there enumerated as characteristic, notice *vv.* 20, 25 התמכרך (התמכר) לעשות הרע בעיני י׳, cf. II. 17. 17 R^{D}†; *v.* 26 הגלולים, cf. *ch.* 15. 12 *note;* אשר הוריש וג׳, cf. *ch.* 14. 24 *note.* The original elements of the narrative, so far as they can be distinguished, are to be found in *v.* 19^{a}, *v.* 20 to מצאתי, *vv.* 27–29, and probably also *v.* 19^{b}. Less certain is the somewhat awkwardly placed statement as to Jezebel *v.* 23, which would follow more easily *after v.* 24, since *v.* 24 clearly forms the direct continuation to *v.* 22.

19. הכלבים] In the first place LXX, Luc. read *αἱ ὕες καὶ οἱ κύνες* (so *ch.* 22. 38), but that the addition is of the nature of a gloss is rendered most probable by its omission in the second place: *οἱ κύνες* simply, as in MT.

את דמך גם אתה] 'Thy blood, even *thine*,' or '*thy* blood also.' For this re-enforcement of the suff. by the pers. pron., cf. the exactly similar case 2 Sam. 17. 5 ונשמעה מה בפיו גם הוא 'and let us hear what is in *his* mouth also.' Cf. *ch.* 1. 26 *note* with references. At the end of the verse LXX, Luc. add *καὶ αἱ πόρναι λούσονται ἐν τῷ αἵματί σου*, adopted by Th. as presupposing וְהַזֹּנוֹת תִּרְחַצְנָה בְדָמֶךָ. The reference, however, implies not the vineyard of Jezreel but the pool *of Samaria*, and is therefore doubtless a gloss derived from *ch.* 22. 38.

20. יען התמכרך] Luc. *δι' ὅτι πέπρασαι μάτην*, LXX *διότι μάτην πέπρασαι*, i. e. יען התמכרך לַשָּׁוְא 'because thou hast sold thyself *to no purpose*'; a pointed addition in view of what follows. For לשוא cf. Jer. 2. 30; 4. 30; 46. 11. The suggestion of Th., חִנָּם, is less probable, since this would rather signify '*for nought*,' i. e. without *expecting* a return.

לעשות . . . י׳] LXX, Luc. add (Luc. *τοῦ*) *παροργίσαι αὐτόν*, i. e. לְהַכְעִיסוֹ, correctly. Cf. II. 17. 17; 2 Chr. 33. 6; Deut. 4. 25; 9. 18.

21. ועצור ועזוב] Cf. *ch.* 14. 10 *note.*

23. הכלבים וג׳] Cf. II. 9. 10, 36.

בחל] RV. 'by the rampart,' and so LXX, Luc. ἐν τῷ προτειχίσματι. Vulg., Pesh., Targ., however, presuppose בְּחֵלֶק '*in the district*' of Jezreel, according to II. 9. 10, 36, 37, and this ought certainly to be adopted. The prediction was not fulfilled 'by the rampart,' but outside the palace *within* the city. חלק is only here in this connexion used of the tract of land surrounding or appertaining to *a town*, being elsewhere employed of the territory or estate of a tribe or family.

25. אשר הסתה וג׳] Possibly with reminiscence of Deut. 13. 7 כי יסיתך . . . אשת חיקך . . . לאמר נלכה ונעבדה אלהים אחרים וג׳. הֵסַתָּה as though from verb ע doubled, in place of הֵסִיתָה.

27. On the variations of LXX, Luc. in this verse, cf. *v.* 16 *note.*

ויהלך אט] 'And went about *quietly*,' i.e. in the manner of one in penitence and grief. Pesh. ܚܦܝܐ, Targ. יחף explain 'barefoot'; cf. 2 Sam. 15. 30; Vulg. *demisso capite:* LXX, Luc. omit. אט is a subs., *quietness* or *gentleness*, used adverbially. Elsewhere always with ל expressing condition;—Isa. 8. 6; 2 Sam. 18. 5; Job 15. 11; with suff. לְאִטִּי Gen. 33. 14. Ar. أَطَّ means *to creak* (of a saddle), or *to make a low moaning or plaintive sound* (of a camel). So Isa. 19. 3† אִטִּים are *whisperers*, i.e. wizards of some description.

28. אל אליהו התשבי] LXX, Luc. ἐν χειρὶ (Luc. τοῦ) δούλου αὐτοῦ Ἡλειού.

29. על ביתו] LXX, Luc. omit.

22. 1–38. *Continuation of ch.* 20. *After seven years of peace between Israel and Aram, Aḥab, with the help of Jehoshaphat of Judah, determines to recover Rama of Gilead from the Aramaeans. He falls in the battle which takes place.*

Ch. 22. 2–37[a] = 2 Chr. 18. 2–34.

1. שלש שנים] After the 'covenant' described as concluded *ch.* 20. 34. The disastrous issue to which this led at Qarqar, where the confederate kings were defeated with great loss by

Shalmaneser (*Append.* 3), must have weakened the bonds of alliance, and led to a *rapprochement* between Israel and Judah. This new alliance made feasible the scheme to recover by force from the Aramaeans one of the most important cities which Ben-hadad had failed to cede according to compact. Cf. *COT.* i. 189*f.*

3. רָמֹת גלעד] Always with *script. defect.* except 2 Chr. 22. 5 רמות ג׳. Luc. in all occurrences transliterates Ῥαμὰθ Γ., while LXX varies between Ῥεμμὰθ Γ. and Ῥεμμὼθ Γ. Thus there is some presumption in favour of a vocalization רָמַת גִּלְעָד '*Rama of Gilead*,' the city being so called in distinction from other places of the same name west of Jordan; and in II. 8. 29 (‖ 2 Chr. 22. 6) רָמָה actually occurs. So Sta., Wellh. The form *Ramoth*, however, is substantiated as an existing form by the occurrence of the *st. absol.* רָמֹת בַּגִּלְעָד Josh. 21. 36; רָאמוֹת (רָאמֹת) בַּגִּלְעָד Deut. 4. 43; Josh. 20. 8; 1 Chr. 6. 65. The site of this Rama is doubtful. By most identification is sought with the modern *Es-Salṭ*, which would have formed a convenient point of vantage for an advance upon Samaria from an E.S.E. position. Dillmann (after Hitzig, Langer) on Gen. 31. 54 prefers the site *El-Jal'ûd*, six miles north of *Es-Salṭ*.

6. האלך על ר׳] Chr. הנלך אל ר׳. Cf. *ch.* 1. 38 *note*.

ויתן] LXX, Luc. καὶ (Luc. ὅτε) διδοὺς δώσει, i.e. וְנָתוֹן יִתֵּן. Cf. Num. 21. 2; Judg. 11. 30; 2 Sam. 5. 19.

אדני] ‖ 2 Chr. 18. 5 הָאֱלֹהִים. According to Th. many Codd. read יהוה, and this probably represents the original text, as in *vv.* 11, 12. The alteration probably arose (Th.) from the supposition suggested by Jehoshaphat's question *v.* 7, that the 400 were prophets of *Ba'al*.

7. האין פה וג׳] Render with AV. 'Is there not here a prophet of the Lord *besides?*' i.e. yet one more prophet of Yahwe in addition to these His (professed) prophets. The reason for Jehoshaphat's distrust of the 400 prophets can only be inferred. Jos. (*Ant.* viii. 15, § 4) συνεὶς ἐκ τῶν λόγων Ἰωσάφατος, ὅτι ψευδοπροφῆται τυγχάνουσιν, and similarly Ber., 'He shrewdly conjectured that Aḥab had only interrogated the prophets who were prepared to

give him a favourable answer.' RV. 'Is there not here *besides* a prophet of the Lord?' is an unwarrantable dislocation of עוד, intended apparently to imply that the speaker regarded the 400 not as prophets of Yahwe but of a strange god. This sense, not to be obtained from MT., is, *with omission of* עוד, given by LXX, Luc., Vulg., Pesh., 'Is there not here a prophet of Yahwe?' But against this is Aḥab's reply (*v.* 8) which presupposes that the 400 prophesied in the name of Yahwe, as is stated in *vv.* 11, 12.

This passage again points the inference (already drawn *ch.* 18. 31[a] *note*) that there were *two forms of Yahwe-worship* existent in the northern kingdom—that represented by the cult of the calves, and that of which such prophets as Elijah, Elisha, and Micaiah were the exponents; and that the view that the former was a perversion of the true religion was not merely the opinion of later (Deuteronomic) times, but was shared by the *contemporary* adherents of the purer form of religion. The 400 prophets cannot be thought to have belonged to the class which Jezebel used rigorous measures to extirpate (*ch.* 18. 4; 19. 10, 14; II. 9. 7), but must have been representatives of a form of Yahwe-religion which for some reason escaped attack during her persecution; and the reason for this escape may be assumed to have been that this professed Yahwe-worship could tolerate[1] the existence side by side with it of a definitely extraneous cult, even if it had not itself assimilated certain Canaanite elements[2].

On the other hand, the reason for Jezebel's vindictiveness against a certain section of Yahwe-worshippers must have been that these, by emphasis of *Yahwe's exclusive claim* (Ex. 20. 3), came into sharp collision with the form of religion which she desired to

[1] Cf. the indifferent attitude of the populace gathered at Mt. Carmel to the two diverse cults; *ch.* 18. 21.

[2] It may accordingly be conjectured that in II. 3. 13 Elisha's words to Joram לך אל נביאי אביך ואל נביאי אמך form not a pleonastic reference to the Ba'al prophets only, but couple together the perverted Yahwe prophets, described as the prophets of Aḥab, and the prophets of the Phoenician Ba'al who were under the special patronage of Jezebel; the former, as the latter, being really opposed to the pure religion of Yahwe.

naturalize. Such were those mentioned in *ch.* 19. 18—not merely an isolated prophet here and there, but a considerable body of the people whose number is reckoned as 7,000.

8. ימלה] Chr. יִמְלָא; 'probably more correct etymologically'; Th.

10. מלבשים בגדים] 'Clad *in robes*,' i. e. in robes of *state*. Cf. *v.* 30 לבש בגדיך 'put thou on *thy robes*,' in contrast to the preceding התחפש.

בגרן] 'In a *threshing-floor*.' Chr. ויושבים בגרן with explan. ref. of previous ישבים. Scarcely possible. RV. paraph. 'in an *open place*' is impermissible, there being no ground for assigning this general signification to גרן; and the same remark applies to the renderings of Vulg. *in area;* Luc. ἐν ὁδῷ[1]; LXX, Luc. in Chr. ἐν εὐροχώρῳ. In LXX (Kgs.) ἔνοπλοι answers to the whole מלבשים בגדים בגרן, i. e. בגרן is unrepresented, and may thus be regarded as mere dittography of בגדים. The emendations of Ew. בְּנֶשֶׁק '*in armour*,' Th., Ber. בְּרֻדִּים '*embroidered*' (?) have nothing to recommend them.

11. קרני ברזל] An emblem of offensive power; cf. Deut. 33. 17; Am. 6. 13; Jer. 48. 25; Dan. 8. 3 *f.*

12. ונתן וג׳] 'Yahwe shall give (it),' with obj. understood as in *vv.* 6, 15. LXX, Luc. wrongly supply as obj. καὶ τὸν βασιλέα Συρίας.

13. דברי הנביאים] LXX, Luc. λαλοῦσι πάντες οἱ προφῆται, in Chr. ἐλάλησαν κ.τ.λ., i. e. דִּבְּרוּ הנ׳ 'the prophets have, with one consent, spoken good &c.'; superior to the somewhat harsh MT. 'the words of the prophets &c. *are* good.' So Th., Kamp., Benz., Kit. Klo. מְדַבְּרִים, less simple.

פה אחד] So Josh. 9. 2. An accus. defining the *manner* of דִּבְּרוּ.

אַחַד מהם] Cf. *ch.* 19. 2 *note.*

17. ויאמר ראיתי] After ויאמר LXX inserts οὐχ οὕτως, Luc. Οὕτως, i. e. לָכֵן as in *v.* 19; 'I saw *then* all Israel &c.'; *then*, i. e. in case you wish really to hear the truth. Adopted by Klo.

---

[1] But perhaps this is a corruption of ἐν ἅλῳ. In Pesh. (Kgs. and Chr.) ܒܐܘܪܚܐ is clearly an error for ܒܐܕܪܐ, which answers to MT.

לא אדנים וג׳] Luc. in place of לֹא reads Eἰ, i. e. לוּ or לָא, and this is followed by Klo., 'If these had any master, they would return, &c.,' a reading incomparably poor by the side of MT. LXX Οὐ Κύριος τούτοις Θεός; presupposes a false repetition of לאלה as לֵאלֹהִים.

19. לכן שמע וג׳] The strange rendering of LXX, Luc. Οὐχ οὕτως, οὐκ ἐγώ· ἄκουε ῥῆμα Κυρίου· οὐχ οὕτως· εἶδον κ.τ.λ. represents at the beginning a doublet of לָכֵן, first read as לֹא כֵן, and then explained by the gloss οὐκ ἐγώ, 'Not I' (am responsible, but Yahwe). The second οὐχ οὕτως, which should not be followed by a stop, is an imitation of לכן ראיתי, *v.* 17.

שמע] Chr. שִׁמְעוּ, and so here 7 Codd. Kenn.

צבא השמים] 'The host of heaven'; an expression not used elsewhere in pre-exilic writings in the special sense of spiritual beings or angels. Cf., however, Josh. 5. 13 *ff.* (JE) where the 'man' who appears to Joshua describes himself as שַׂר צְבָא יהוה. In Isa. 34. 4 (prob. exilic) the phrase seems to describe the angels corresponding to or acting as guardians of 'all the nations' (*v.* 2), this being clearly the case in 24. 21 with the expression צבא המרום[1].

Elsewhere generally צבא הש׳ denotes the *stars*;—II. 17. 16; 21. 3, 5 (‖ 2 Chr. 33. 3, 5); 23. 4, 5; Deut. 4. 19; 17. 3; Jer. 8. 2; 19. 13; Zeph. 1. 5; cf. Gen. 2. 1; Ps. 33. 6; Isa. 40. 26; 45. 12. It is a late usage in which the term is used indefinitely to denote visible heavenly bodies and invisible agencies; Neh. 9. 6; Dan. 8. 10; cf. Ps. 103. 21; 148. 2.

20. מי יפתה וג׳] For the doctrine that Yahwe, in His displeasure, incites men to their own ruin or injury, cf. Ex. 4. 21b; 10. 1, 20, 27; 11. 9, 10 (J, E, or JE); 7. 3; 9. 12 (P); Deut. 2. 30 hardening of the heart ascribed to Yahwe (cf. Isa. 6. 10); Judg. 9. 23 Yahwe sends an evil spirit between Abimelech and the men of Shechem; 2 Sam. 24. 1 incites David to a pernicious action; Isa. 19. 2, 14 stirs up Egypt against Egypt and mingles a spirit of perverseness

---

[1] Cf. for this doctrine Dan. 10. 13, 20, 21; 12. 1; Ecclus. 17. 17; and Deut. 32. 8 LXX (reading אֵל for ישראל).

in the midst of her; Ezek. 14. 9 deceives the false prophet to his own ruin (the same verb as in our passage פִּתֵּיתִי).

אחאב] LXX, Luc., Vulg. presuppose אחאב מלך ישראל, and so Chr.

ויאמר זה וג׳] On the contrasted order cf. *ch.* 5. 25 *note.*

21. הרוח] '*The* spirit,' vividly pictured in the speaker's imagination through the part which he fulfilled. Cf. *ch.* 20. 36 *note.*

22. The variation of Luc. after *v.* 22ᵃ *καὶ ἀπατήσω αὐτόν. Καὶ εἶπεν Δυνήσει* is probably due merely to the dislocation of *εἶπεν* in the Greek text. LXX as MT. *καὶ εἶπεν Ἀπατήσεις καί γε δυνήσει.*

24. אי זה עבר] The interrog. אי זה is never elsewhere used with a verb, and Chr., in supplying הַדֶּרֶךְ before עבר, conforms to the usual constr. So Th., Klo., Kamp., Benz., Kit. On אי זה הדרך cf. *ch.* 13. 12 *note.* LXX Ποῖον πνεῦμα Κυρίου τὸ λαλῆσαν ἐν σοί suggests אֵי־זֶה רוּחַ יהוה הַמְדַבֵּר בָּךְ, i.e. not as rendered, 'What kind of spirit &c.[1]?' but '*where is the spirit of Yahwe that speaketh in thee?*' a direct challenge to Micaiah to avenge the insult, implying that, if he fails to do so, the spirit by which *he* speaks is a רוּחַ שֶׁקֶר. To this Micaiah replies, '*Behold thou shalt see* (*where it is;* i.e. the challenge shall be accepted; *not now, but*) *in that day &c.*' This is superior to the obscure sentence of MT., and probably represents the original text. Luc. exhibits a combination of LXX and MT.

26. קח את מ׳ והשיבֵהו] LXX, Luc., Pesh., Vulg. support pl. קחו את מ׳ והשיבֻהו, the reading of Chr. So Th., Klo. Sta., however, points out that in *v.* 27 LXX *εἶπον*, Luc. *εἰπέ*, like MT. וְאָמַרְתָּ, favour an original sing. in *v.* 26. The substitution of pl. for sing. may be explained as due to the influence of pl. imperat. *v.* 27 שימו . . . והאכלֻהו. These refer to two persons אמון and יואש, but the address of *v.* 26 is probably to the סרים אחד of *vv.* 9 *ff.* *ZATW.* V. 173 *ff.*

אל אמון] LXX *πρὸς Σεμήρ*, Luc. *πρὸς Σεμμήρ*. Chr. LXX *πρὸς Ἐμήρ*, Cod. A, Luc. *πρὸς Σεμμήρ*. The forms with Σ probably

[1] Adopted by Sta. *Ges.* i. 532: 'Was für ein Geist Jahwes hat denn aus *dir* gesprochen?'

exhibit a repetition of the last letter of πρός, and LXX Chr. represents the original form in the Greek. Accordingly Sta. favours the reading אֶל־אִמֵּר, 'Εμμήρ being the LXX form for MT. אִמֵּר in Jer. 20. 1; Ezr. 2. 37, 59; 10. 20; Neh. 3. 29; 7. 40; 11. 13; 1 Chr. 9. 12; 24. 14.

27. כה אמר המלך] LXX, Luc. omit.

את זה] With great contempt:—'*This fellow.*' So exactly, with את, 1 Sam. 21. 16; 2 Sam. 13. 17 (את זאת); cf. *ch.* 20. 7; II. 5. 7; 1 Sam. 10. 27; 25. 21; Ex. 10. 7.

לחם לחץ וג׳] 'Bread in scant measure and water in scant measure'; lit. 'bread—affliction and water—affliction,' a case of apposition. So Isa. 30. 20. Cf. Dri. *Tenses,* § 189. 1.

28. ויאמר שמעו וג׳] LXX, Luc. omit. The words are clearly a gloss derived from Mic. 1. 2, and inserted for the purpose of identifying Micaiah with Micah the Morashtite. The names מִיכָיְהוּ and מִיכָה are really identical, and the prophet of the later century bears the longer name מִיכָיָה in Jer. 26. 18 Kt. The pl. עמים occurs many scores of times with the signification of *foreign nations*, seldom or never of Israel[1].

30. התחפש ובא במלחמה] 'Let me *disguise myself and enter* the battle!' The infin. absol. presents the bare idea of the verb in exclamatory and excited speech. Cf. II. 4. 43 כֹּה אָמַר י׳ אָכוֹל וְהוֹתֵר 'Thus saith Yahwe, Ye shall *eat and leave over!*' II. 3. 16; Hos. 4. 2; *al.;* Da. § 88^b; Ew. § 328^c.

בגדיך] LXX, Luc. τὸν ἱματισμόν μου, an easy (but false) correction deduced from the fact that Aḥab himself was disguised.

31. ומלך ארם צוה] 'Now the king of Aram *had commanded.*' On order of sentence cf. *ch.* 14. 5 *note.*

את שרי הרכב וג׳] The military commanders who filled the place previously occupied by the thirty-two vassal princes. Cf. *ch.* 20. 24 *note.*

32. ויסרו עליו] 'They turned aside against him'; somewhat

---

[1] Supposed cases are Deut. 33. 3 where the better reading seems to be עַמּוֹ LXX; Gen. 28. 3; 48. 4 the promise to Jacob. With suffix Judg. 5. 14; Hos. 10. 14. Cf. Dri. on *Deut. loc. cit.*

harsh. LXX, Luc. *καὶ ἐκύκλωσαν αὐτόν* agree with Chr. וַיָּסֹבּוּ עָלָיו '*they surrounded him*,' a reading certainly to be preferred. So Th., Klo. סבב על as in Job 16. 13.

34. לתמו] Lit. '*in his simplicity*' (ל of norm), i. e. without being able to assign a reason for the selection of his mark. So AV., RV. suitably 'at a venture'; Luc. ἀφελῶς, 'artlessly.' That this is the meaning of the phrase is rendered clear by the context of its only other occurrence, 2 Sam. 15. 11 וְאֶת־אַבְשָׁלוֹם הָלְכוּ מָאתַיִם אִישׁ מִירוּשָׁלַםִ קְרֻאִים וְהֹלְכִים לְתֻמָּם וְלֹא יָדְעוּ כָּל־דָּבָר 'And with Absalom there went 200 men from Jerusalem, summoned and going in their simplicity, *and they knew not anything*' (of the projected conspiracy). Cf. also Gen. 20. 5, 6 בְּתָם־לְבָבִי. Vulg. *in incertum sagittam dirigens*, Pesh. ܠܡܘܟܟܗ (with doublet ܠܬܡܝܡܘܬܗ *id.* MT.), and so Targ. לקיבליה 'straight in front of him,' seem to have imagined that the phrase denoted the letting fly of an *aimless* shaft. LXX, guessing, *εὐστόχως*.

בין הדבקים וג׳] 'Between the attachments and between the coat of mail.' The subs. דֶּבֶק only elsewhere occurs in Isa. 41. 7, where it means *joining* or soldering. So *Heb. Lex. Oxf.*, following Th., Ber. *al.*, explains הדבקים 'the jointed *attachment* or *appendage* to the rigid breast-armour, which covered the abdomen.' Other explanations have merely the nature of guesses:—LXX, Luc. *ἀνὰ μέσον τοῦ πνεύμονος καὶ ἀνὰ μέσον τοῦ θώρακος*: Vulg. *inter pulmonem et stomachum;* Ew. the soft parts which *connect* the chest with the bottom of the back, so, 'between the *groin* and breastbone'; Ges. *Thes.* '*arm-pits*,' lit. joints of shoulder; Klo. '*helmet-appendages*.'

הפך ידיך] So II. 9. 23 with pl. ידיו as Kt.

המחנה] 'The army' *in action*, as in Judg. 4. 15, 16.

כי החליתי] RV. 'For I am sore wounded.' So 2 Chr. 35. 23.

35. ותעלה המלחמה] 'And the battle *waxed hotter*'; lit. *went up* or *increased*, the figure being perhaps drawn from a river which gathers force as it *rises* (Ke., Th., Ber.); cf. Isa. 8. 7; Jer. 46. 7, 8.

היה מָעֳמָד] 'Was propped up.' The participle with subs. verb expresses the *duration* of the action; Dri. *Tenses*, § 135. 5. Chr. act. היה מַעֲמִיד 'kept himself standing.'

After *v.* 35[a] LXX, Luc. add *ἀπὸ πρωὶ ἕως ἑσπέρας*, i.e. מִן־הַבֹּקֶר עַד־הָעָרֶב, and this is partially supported by Chr. עד הערב. In *v.* 35[b] LXX, Luc., which place וימת בערב *after* הרכב . . . ויצק, are superior.

וימת בערב] Chr. וַיָּמָת לְעֵת בּוֹא הַשָּׁמֶשׁ, either a summary conclusion formed by combining Kgs. *v.* 36[a] כבא השמש, or else the writer's eye passed to וימת of *v.* 37, and לעת וג׳ represents a corrupt reading of ויבוא שמרון.

וַיִּצֶק] '*And* the blood of the wound *flowed* &c.' This intrans. sense occurs only once besides, Job 38. 38 בְּצֶקֶת עָפָר לַמּוּצָק 'when dust *floweth* into the mass.' Imperf. Qal always elsewhere takes the form יִצֹּק.

36. ויעבר הרנה] 'And there passed the cry.' The verb, if not an error for ותעבר, is masc. as coming first in the sentence; cf. *ch.* 11. 3 *note* on ויהי לו נשים. LXX, Luc., Vulg., Pesh., Targ. interpret הרנה as *the herald*.

37. וימת המלך] LXX, Luc. *ὅτι τέθνηκεν ὁ βασιλεύς*, i.e. כִּי מֵת הַמֶּלֶךְ '*for the king is* dead'; certainly correct. The words are part of the רִנָּה, and assign a reason for *v.* 36[b]. So Th., Klo., Kamp., Benz., Kit. On the confusion of כ and ו, cf. *ch.* 12. 30 *note*.

ויבוא] LXX, Luc. *καὶ ἦλθον*, i.e. וַיָּבוֹאוּ, subj. being the same as the following ויקברו; correctly. So Th., Klo., Kamp., Benz., Kit. Targ., feeling the difficulty of sing. ויבוא, paraphrases ואתיוהי 'and they brought him.'

38. וישטף] Impers. '*one* washed,' and so 'the chariot *was washed*.'

והזנות רחצו] 'And the harlots washed themselves (there),' sc. in the pool into which the blood had drained. LXX, Luc. add *ἐν τῷ αἵματι* (Luc. *αὐτοῦ*). This is the only meaning of which the sentence is capable. The other Verss., probably for the sake of avoiding an objectionable statement, give to הזנות another interpretation and make it the obj. of רחצו;—Vulg. *et habenas laverunt*, Pesh. ܘܙܝܢܗ ܐܫܝܓܘ (transposed with וילקו וג׳), and so Targ. ומני

וזינא שטפו 'and they washed the (Pesh. his) armour.' But זַיִן *weapon* or *military equipment* of Rabb. Heb. and Aram. never occurs in Bib. Heb.; and verb רחץ is used exclusively of washing the body, whether *one's own person* (without obj.) or *some part of it* (obj. כַּפַּיִם, בָּשָׂר, *al.*) or *some one else* (Ex. 29. 4; 40. 12; Lev. 8. 6 P; Ezek. 16. 9†), or of washing the *flesh portions* of a sacrifice (Ex. 29. 17; Lev. 1. 9, 13; 8. 21; 9. 14 P†), never of washing any kind of inanimate object.

כדבר וג'] Cf. *ch.* 13. 26 *note.*

22. 39, 40. *Summary of Aḥab's reign.*

39. בית השן] 'The house of ivory.' The בתי השן of Am. 3. 15 perhaps contains an allusion to this. Cf. Ps. 45. 9 הֵיכְלֵי שֵׁן 'palaces of ivory.' Jer. 22. 15 speaks of Aḥab's fame as a builder, upon the reading of Cod. A 'Αχαάβ for ארז:—הֲתִמְלֹךְ כִּי אַתָּה מְתַחֲרֶה בְּאַחְאָב 'Shalt thou reign because thou competest with Aḥab?' (in magnificence of palace architecture; cf. *vv.* 13, 14).

22. 41–51. *Jehoshaphat, king of Judah.*

Ch. 22. 41–51 forms part of the material of 2 Chr. 20. 31–37. R[D] frames a collection of short notices from the Annals.

44. אך הבמות וג'] Cf. *ch.* 3. 2, 3 *note.*

47. הקדש] Cf. *ch.* 14. 24 *note.*

48, 49. ומלך וג'] Highly obscure as the text stands. RV. 'And there was no king in Edom: a deputy was king,' agrees with Targ.[1], and so Ke., Th., Kamp. But that a mere deputy, ostensibly appointed by Jehoshaphat, should be dignified with the title of *king* is incredible. Vulg. *nec erat tunc rex constitutus in Edom*, Pesh. ܘܡܠܟܐ ܠܝܬ ܒܐܕܘܡ ܕܡܩܝܡ give an intelligible sense: 'And there was no king in Edom appointed as king,' i. e. regularly constituted as such; but against this it may be urged (Sta.) that נצב

[1] Strictly speaking, Targ. ומלכא לית באדום ממנא אילהין איסטרטיגא מלכא 'And there was no king in Edom *appointed*, but *a general* was king,' exhibits a double rendering of נצב, the former '*appointed*' agreeing with Vulg., Pesh.

of the appointment of a king is unparalleled. LXX, Luc. simply transliterate נצב, and fail to afford any elucidation.

Probably, therefore, the text has suffered some corruption; and this inference is confirmed by the condition of *v.* 49[a], where עשר must be corrected עָשָׂה upon the authority of Q're, several Codd., and all Verss., and the reference of ולא הלך is, at best, highly obscure.

Sta. (*ZATW.* 1885, p. 178) by clever emendation obtains for the two verses a text which is at once lucid and but little divergent from MT. Connecting *v.* 48 with *v.* 49 he reads: וּמֶ֫לֶךְ אֵין בֶּאֱדוֹם וּנְצִיב· הַמֶּ֫לֶךְ יְהוֹשָׁפָט עָשָׂה אֳנִיַּת תַּרְשִׁישׁ לָלֶ֫כֶת אוֹפִירָה לַזָּהָב וְלֹא הָלָ֫כָה כִּי נִשְׁבְּרָה הָאֳנִיָּה (or אֳנִיָּתוֹ) בְּעֶצְיוֹן גָּ֫בֶר׃ 'Now there was no king in Edom. And the deputy of king Jehoshaphat made a ship of Tarshish to go to Ophir for gold; but it went not, for the ship (his ship) was wrecked at Ezion-geber.' For the constr. נציב המלך יהו׳ cf. 2 Sam. 16. 6; 19. 17; *ch.* 1. 38; 5. 7; 10. 13; II. 19. 5, and so נציב פלשתים 1 Sam. 13. 3. So Benz., Kit. Klo. agrees with Sta. as far as regards *v.* 48 and its connexion with *v.* 49, while in this latter verse he combines Q're and Kt. 'made *ten* ships,' and finds the reference of הלך to be to the projector of the expedition.

Upon אניות תרשיש cf. *ch.* 10. 22 *note.*

22. 52–54. *Aḥaziah, king of Israel.*

54. הבעל] LXX, Luc. pl. τοῖς Βααλείμ.

ככל וג׳] Luc. παρὰ πάντας τοὺς γενομένους ἔμπροσθεν αὐτοῦ is a correction in imitation of *ch.* 14. 9; 16. 25, 30, 33, but here inappropriate, since the editor would scarcely represent this king as *exceeding* his father in wickedness: cf. *ch.* 16. 30, 31; 21. 25, 26; R[D]. LXX κατὰ πάντα τὰ γενόμενα ἔμπροσθεν αὐτοῦ, i.e. doubtless כְּכֹל אֲשֶׁר הָיוּ לְפָנָיו is as good as, but not superior to MT., and may be a correction in view of the fact that the sins of Jeroboam as well as those of Aḥab are mentioned *v.* 53.

II. 1. 1. This verse clearly belongs to the series of short notices referring to the reign of Aḥaziah immediately preceding, I. 22. 52–54. The division of the Hebrew text of Kings into two books is not found in the MSS. nor in the early printed editions. It first occurs in the great Rabbinic Bible of Daniel Bomberg, published at Venice 1516–17, where an asterisk between I. 22. 54 and II. 1. 1 calls attention to a marginal note:—כאן מתחילים הלועזים ספר מלכי׳ רביעי: 'Here the non-Jews (i.e. Christians) begin the fourth book of Kings.' A similar note is found between 1 and 2 Sam. Cf. Ginsburg, *Introd. to the Massoretico-critical edit. of the Heb. Bible*, pp. 45, 930*f.* Thus the division in MT. appears to have been an innovation from LXX, Vulg. While in LXX no known MS. presents an undivided text of 1, 2 Kgs.; 3, 4 Kgs.; Chr.; it is noticeable that in Cod. B the first verse of each second book appears also at the close of each first book, a fact which shows that the divider of the books was desirous of indicating the inner connexion existing between the first and second divisions in each case. Cf. the manner in which in MT. Ezr. 1. 1–3[a] (to ויעל) repeats 2 Chr. 36. 22, 23, of which it originally formed the unbroken continuation.

ויפשע מואב וג׳] Cf. *ch.* 3. 4 *ff.* According to the inscription of Mesha' king of Moab (*Append.* 1) the rebellion took place *during* the reign of Omri's son. Aḥab is, however, nowhere mentioned by name in the inscription.

1. 2–18. *Aḥaziah, after an accidental fall through a lattice, appeals to the oracle of Ba'al-zebub, the god of Ekron, in order to learn whether he will recover. Elijah predicts his death, on account of his unfaithfulness to Yahwe.*

2. בעד השבכה] 'Out through (*lit.* away from) the lattice.' So LXX διὰ τοῦ δικτυωτοῦ, 'A. περὶ τὸν κιγχλιδωτόν, Vulg. *per cancellos*, Targ. מן סריגתא. For the other uses of שבכה cf. I. 7. 17 *note*. Luc. presents a slightly different form of *v.* 2[a]: καὶ ἀνέβη 'Οχ. εἰς τὸ δικτυωτὸν ὑπερῷον αὐτοῦ τὸ ἐν Σαμαρείᾳ καὶ ἔπεσε καὶ ἠρρώστησε—inferior to MT.

אם אחיה וג׳] Cf. *ch.* 8. 8, 9.

מחלי זה] The constr. חֳלִי זֶה (for the normal הֶחֳלִי הַזֶּה) is regular in Rabbinic Heb., but extremely uncommon in Bib. Heb. Other occurrences, cited by Kö. *Syntax*, § 334 β, are יוֹם הוּא Mic. 7. 12^{a} (text doubtful), גֶּפֶן זֹאת Ps. 80. 15. LXX, Luc., Vulg., Pesh., Targ. presuppose a reading חֳלָיִי זֶה 'this *my* sickness,' both here and in *ch.* 8. 8, 9. This constr., in which the demonstr. pronoun without the article follows a subs. with possessive suffix, is perfectly regular; cf. *v.* 13 עֲבָדֶיךָ אֵלֶּה; I. 8. 59; 10. 8; 22. 23; *al.*; Da. § 32 (2), *Rem.* 3; Ew. § 293; G-K. § 126 *y*.

At the end of the verse LXX, Luc. add καὶ ἐπορεύθησαν ἐπερωτῆσαι (LXX δι' αὐτοῦ), i.e. וַיֵּלְכוּ לִדְרֹשׁ מֵאִתּוֹ, an addition which forms a suitable introduction to *v.* 3^{a}, and which may be compared with *v.* 4^{b}.

3. דַּבֵּר] LXX ἐκάλεσεν . . . λέγων, Luc. ἐλάλησε . . . λέγων. Probably LXX is a corruption of Luc. The latter presupposes the reading of MT., λέγων being merely the translator's addition: cf. I. 13. 12 *note*.

מלך שמרון] So I. 21. 1†. Luc. Ὀχοζίου βασιλέως Ἰσραὴλ ἐν Σαμαρείᾳ.

המבלי אין] For the double negative, cf. *note* on I. 10. 21.

5. מה זה] Upon the enclitic זה, cf. I. 14. 6 *note*.

6. אתה שלח] LXX, Luc. presuppose אַתָּה הֹלֵךְ; cf. *v.* 3. MT., as the easier reading, appears to be a correction. A correction in the Greek would probably have run ὑμεῖς πορεύεσθε, i.e. אַתֶּם הֹלְכִים, in strict agreement with *v.* 3.

6^{b}. לכן] LXX, Luc. add τάδε λέγει Κύριος as in *v.* 4. At the end of the verse Luc. has a gloss, derived, in the main, from I. 21. (20) 21.

7. משפט] 'Description,' i.e. the summary of *distinctive characteristics*. Cf. Judg. 13. 12 מַה־יִּהְיֶה מִשְׁפַּט הַנַּעַר 'What shall be the description of the child?'

9^{b}. ויעל . . . וידבר אליו] The text is somewhat expanded in Luc.: καὶ ἐπορεύθησαν πρὸς αὐτόν. αὐτὸς δὲ ἐκάθητο ἐπὶ τῆς κορυφῆς τοῦ ὄρους. καὶ ἀνέβη ὁ ἡγούμενος καὶ οἱ πεντήκοντα αὐτοῦ καὶ ἦλθον ἕως τοῦ ἀνθρώπου τοῦ θεοῦ. καὶ ἐλάλησε πρὸς αὐτὸν ὁ πεντηκόνταρχος καὶ εἶπεν κ.τ.λ.

והנה ישֵׁב] Omission of the pronominal subject of the participle is not infrequent after הִנֵּה, which calls pointed attention to a subject closely preceding. Cf. Gen. 24. 30; 37. 15; *al.;* Dri. *Tenses*, § 135 (6); Da. § 100[a]. Such a use of הִנֵּה without expression of suffix of reference is idiomatic in other cases also; cf. e. g. *ch.* 6. 13; I. 2. 29; 21. 18.

דִּבֶּר] LXX ἐκάλεσέν σε, probably an alteration of ἐλάλησε; cf. *v.* 3 *note.* Luc. τάδε λέγει, in accordance with *v.* 11 כֹּה אָמַר.

10. ואם] *'And if.'* The ו, by emphasis of '*if*,' imparts a grim sarcasm to the prophet's words; the implication being, 'You glibly term me "man of God," while overlooking my power to withstand the king's command.' Cf. I. 2. 22 *note.* In *v.* 12 ו is omitted.

11. ויען] Luc., Cod. A are correct in reading καὶ ἀνέβη, i. e. וַיַּעַל as in *vv.* 9, 13. So Th., Kamp., Benz., Kit.

12. אליהם] LXX, Luc., Pesh., 3 Codd. read אֵלָיו. So Th., Kamp., Benz., Kit.

13. שלשים] Luc., Vulg., Targ. שְׁלִישִׁי, the reference being (as in clause *b*) to the captain; cf. אַחֵר 'another' (second) *v.* 11. So Th., Klo., Kamp., Benz., Kit. MT. שְׁלשִׁים has arisen by attraction to חמשים— 'a third fifty'; pl. as in 1 Sam. 19. 21 מַלְאָכִים שְׁלִשִׁים 'a third set of messengers.' LXX omits; Pesh. ܠܬܠܬ ܙܒܢܝܢ 'for the third time.'

ויעל ויבא] LXX, Luc. καὶ ἦλθεν, Vulg. *qui cum venisset,* omit the former verb, while Pesh. ܘܣܠܩ is without the latter. The subj. שר וג׳, following upon the second verb, occupies an awkward though not impossible position (cf. I. 10. 29[a]), and is omitted by Vulg. So Klo., Kamp., Benz.

עבדיך אלה חמשים] LXX, Vulg. omit the somewhat redundant חמשים.

14. ואת חמשיהם] LXX omits.

16. יען אשר] 'Forasmuch as' is answered by לכן 'therefore,' and the interjected question המבלי . . . בדברו destroys the construction of the sentence, and is rightly lacking in LXX, Luc. So Klo., Kamp., Benz., Kit. The words are a gloss from *vv.* 3, 6.

17. וימלך יהורם] Add אָחִיו with Luc., Θ. ὁ ἀδελφὸς αὐτοῦ, a specification presupposed by the statement of clause *b*. So Klo., Kamp., Kit.

בשנת . . . יהודה] This synchronism breaks the connexion between the statements preceding and following, and also conflicts with the synchronism of *ch.* 3. 1[a], which occupies the regular position in R[D]'s framework. As standing in MT. it is an erroneous insertion, and forms part of a distinct synchronistic system, which appears in Luc., but of which this notice and that of I. 16. 23 are the only traces in MT. See *Introduction.*

2. 1–18. *The translation of Elijah to heaven, and the gift of a double portion of his spirit to Elisha, his disciple and successor.*

1. בִּסְעָרָה] The *ḥatef-qameç* facilitates the pronunciation of the emphatic sibilant ס. Cf. Kö. *Lehrg.* I. i. 262; and *notes* on I. 13. 7; 19. 20.

הגלגל] It is the merit of Th. to have first noticed that this Gilgal, from which Elijah and Elisha *went down* (וַיֵּרְדוּ *v.* 2) to Bethel, cannot have been the Gilgal between Jericho and the Jordan, Josh. 4. 19; *al.;* and to have identified the place with *Jiljilia*, south-west of *Seilûn*, and 'near the high road between Bethel and Shechem'; cf. Smith, *Hist. Geogr.* 494. Rob. (*BR.* ii. 265 *f.*) describes the locality of *Jiljilia*, but fails to perceive the Biblical identification.

2. וחי נפשך] The vocalization חֵי is adopted by the punctuators for the sake of drawing artificial distinction between the sacred oath חַי יהוה and the non-sacred. Cf. *vv.* 4, 6; 4. 30; 1 Sam. 20. 3; 25. 26; 1. 26; 17. 55; 2 Sam. 11. 11; 14. 19; חֵי פַרְעֹה Gen. 42. 15, 16; חֵי אֲדֹנִי הַמֶּלֶךְ 2 Sam. 15. 21; חֵי אֱלֹהֶיךָ דָּן וְחֵי דֶּרֶךְ בְּאֵר־שָׁבַע Am. 8. 14.

3. אשר בית אל] 'Who were *at* Bethel.' The accusative of place, in answer to the question *where?* can thus be used in the case of proper names compounded with בַּיִת; so exactly 2 Sam. 2. 32 אשר בית לחם; cf. Hos. 12. 5; Da. § 69[a]. In contrast we have ביריחו 'in Jericho,' *v.* 5.

הֶחֱשׁוּ] According to norm we should expect הַחֲשׁוּ. Another instance of the imperat. of a verb פ gutt. vocalized after the analogy of the perf. is found in Jer. 49. 8, 30 הֶעֱמִקוּ, הֶעְמִיקוּ; so infin. constr. הֶחֱזִיקִי Jer. 31. 31.

8. ויגלם] 'And rolled (it) up.' The verb, which only occurs here in Bibl. Heb., is found in Rabbinic Heb. with the same significance. Other occurrences of the root in Bibl. Heb. are found in Ezek. 27. 24 גְּלוֹמֵי תְּכֵלֶת '*wrappings* of blue' (so Aram. גְּלִימָא, ܓܠܝܡܐ); Ps. 139. 16 גָּלְמִי 'my *unformed substance*' (*embryo;* so New Heb. id.; Aram. גּוּלְמָא).

9. יהי נא וג׳] 'Let there be now a share of two in thy spirit upon me!' Elisha claims the right of a firstborn son among the disciples of Elijah. פי שנים, as in Deut. 21. 17, lit. 'mouth (mouthful) of two,' is a share twice as large as that which is given to any one of the later-born sons. The explanation of Ew. 'two-thirds' is quite unwarranted[1]. In Zech. 13. 8 the expression has this meaning only through being brought into relationship with הַשְּׁלִשִׁית 'the third part.'

10. לֻקָּח] With dropping of מ preformative, for מְלֻקָּח. So אֻכַּל Ex. 3. 2; יוּלָּד Judg. 13. 8; מוֹרָט Isa. 18. 2, 7; הֻלָּלָה Ezek. 26. 17 (accent הֻלָּלָה). Ew. § 617[b]; G-K. § 52 *s.*

11. ויהי המה הלכים וג׳] Cf. I. 13. 20 *note.*

12. אבי וג׳] So *ch.* 13. 14, the words of king Joash to Elisha upon his death-bed. The expression seems to mean that Elijah, as after him Elisha, stands for Yahwe's invisible forces which should be Israel's true safeguard (cf. *ch.* 6. 16 *f.*), and to convey the apprehension lest this safeguard should be lost to the nation with the removal of the prophet. In the present case the use of the words naturally connects itself with the vision.

14. After the statement ויכה את המים in the first half-verse, Luc. inserts καὶ οὐ διῃρέθη, Vulg. *et non sunt divisae*—regarded by Hoo. as part of the original text, but more probably a gloss to explain

---

[1] Ew.'s words are (*Hist.* iv. p. 81), 'But although he had inherited Elijah's mantle, and many might esteem him equally great, yet it was always an essential feature of the representation of him that he had only received two-thirds of Elijah's spirit, and had indeed with difficulty obtained even that. In fact, in this sharp expression tradition expressed the most correct and striking judgement of his value, taken as a whole.' In contrast to this depreciatory estimate, cf. the words and action of the prophets, *v.* 15.

the repeated mention of the striking of the water which follows in clause *b*. Such a repeated reference to a single event, after an intervening clause or clauses, וַיַּכֶּה . . . וַיֹּאמַר . . . וַיַּכֶּה, may be paralleled by Gen. 27. 23^b–27^a וַיְבָרְכֵהוּ . . . וַיֹּאמֶר . . . וַיְבָרְכֵהוּ.

איה יהוה] LXX, Luc., Vulg. omit יהוה.

אף הוא] The accentuation connects אף הוא closely with ויכה וג׳, after the principal break in the verse, thus implying that the words mean 'and *he also* (like Elijah in *v.* 8) smote the waters, &c.' Had this meaning, however, been intended, we should certainly have read either וַיַּכֶּה אַף־הוּא (cf. Deut. 2. 11, 20; Lev. 26. 24, 28), or אַף־הוּא הִכָּה (cf. Lev. 26. 16, 41). As the text stands we must therefore (with Ke.) alter the accentuation, and, placing the principal break after הוא, render, 'Where is Yahwe, the God of Elijah, *even he?*' But this explanation is, as Th. notices, open to the objections that such an emphasis appears to be superfluous, and that אף (denoting properly *addition*) cannot be shown to have simply the force of a strengthened גַּם. While Pesh., Targ. support MT., Vulg. *etiam nunc*, Σ. καὶ νῦν, and perhaps LXX translit. ἀφφώ (cf. *ch.* 10. 10), suggest אֵפוֹא, connecting with the preceding interrogation, 'Where is Yahwe, the God of Israel, *now?*' This reading is followed by Th., Kamp., Benz., Kit., and some older commentators. It is true that אֵפוֹא, when used elsewhere with the interrog. אַיֵּה (Judg. 9. 38; Isa. 19. 12; Job 17. 15), immediately follows this particle, but cases can be cited in which the word, when used after other interrog. particles, occurs further on in the sentence; cf. Ex. 33. 16 וּבַמֶּה יִוָּדַע אֵפוֹא וג׳; Hos. 13. 10 אֱהִי מַלְכְּךָ אֵפוֹא.

If this emendation be not accepted, the only alternative seems to be to omit אף הוא with Luc., regarding the letters as an erroneous repetition of the preceding אליהו.

ויעבר אלישע] Luc. καὶ διῆλθε διὰ ξηρᾶς, as in *v.* 8.

15. Klo., followed by Kamp., Benz., Kit., omits ביריחו as an erroneous insertion after the pattern of *vv.* 3, 5. מִנֶּגֶד implies that the prophets were not *in Jericho*, but were standing near at hand as spectators of the scene—a fact which is clear from this verse and *v.* 7.

16. 'וישלכהו וג] After וישלכהו LXX adds ἐν τῷ Ἰορδάνῃ ἤ, i. e. בַּיַּרְדֵּן או 'and hath cast him *into the Jordan, or* upon one of the mountains, &c.' So Th., Klo. In view of the scene of Elijah's disappearance, the suggestion is very natural, and appropriately comes first.

הגיאות] Kt. הַגֵּיאוֹת as in Ezek. 6. 3, and in suff. form גֵּיאֹתֶיךָ Ezek. 35. 8. Q're הַגֵּאָיוֹת as in Ezek. 7. 16; 32. 5; 36. 4, 6. LXX, Luc. τῶν βουνῶν, i. e. הַגְּבָעוֹת, inferior to MT.

2. 19–25. *Elisha 'heals' the unwholesome water of Jericho* (19–22), *and vindicates his prophetic authority against the insults of children at Bethel* (23–25).

19. והארץ משכלת] 'And the land casts her young.' So Th., RV. הארץ is used of the *inhabitants* of the district, as in Lev. 19. 29; 1 Sam. 14. 29; 17. 46; 2 Sam. 15. 23; *al.* שִׁכֵּל as in Ex. 23. 26; Job 21. 10; Gen. 31. 38. Ges., Ke., Klo., Kamp., Benz., Kit. render, 'and the land causes untimely births'; but against this explanation it is to be noticed, with Th., that the misfortune is referred in *v.* 21 directly (מִשָּׁם) to the water.

21. רִפֵּאתִי] Vocalized after the analogy of a verb ל״ה as in Jer. 51. 9 רִפֵּאנוּ. Cf. *note* on I. 17. 14. An actual ל״ה form occurs in *v.* 22 וַיֵּרָפוּ. So נִרְפָּתָה Jer. 51. 9, and Pi'el וַיְרַפּוּ 8. 11 for וַיְרַפְּאוּ 6. 14.

ומשכלת] 'Nor any that casts her young.' It is more natural to take משכלת as a participle (as in *v.* 19) than to regard it, with Ges., Ke., Klo., Kamp., RV., as a subs. 'miscarriage.'

23. 'והוא עלה וג] On the constr. cf. I. 1. 14 *note.*

ויתקלסו בו] 'And reviled him.' The incident perhaps illustrates the unpopularity of Yahwe's true prophets in the chief centre of the calf-worship; cf. Am. 7. 10 *ff.* Luc. καὶ ἐλίθαζον αὐτόν, i. e. וַיְסַקְּלוּהוּ.

24. ותבקענה] 'And rent'; lit. '*cleft*' or '*tore open*,' as in *ch.* 8. 12; 15. 16.

3. *Jehoram, king of Israel. His campaign against Moab in alliance with the kings of Judah and Edom.*

2. מַצֵּבַת] LXX, Luc. τὰς στήλας, Vulg. *statuas* understand as pl. מַצְּבֹת, and so Klo., Kamp., Benz., Kit. In the passage with reference to Jehoram (‖ *vv.* 1–3) which follows in LXX, Luc. after *ch.* 1. 18 there is the addition καὶ συνέτριψεν αὐτάς, i. e. וַיְשַׁבְּרֵם. As Th. notices, the pillar (sing.) of MT. is probably intended to be brought into connexion with the statement of I. 16. 32. From the narrative of *ch.* 10. 18 *ff.* it is clear that Jehoram made no organized attempt to root out the worship of Baʿal-Melqart, such as is suggested by the reading of the pl. מַצְּבֹת, nor is such an attempt to be thought probable while Jezebel was still living and in possession of power.

3. בחטאות] Read sing. בְּחַטַּאת, in agreement with the suffix of מִמֶּנָּה following. So in *ch.* 13. 2, 6, 11; 17. 22. So Klo.

דבק] Cf. I. 11. 2 *note*.

לא סר ממנה] So, with reference to the sins of Jeroboam, *ch.* 13. 2, 6, 11; 14. 24; 15. 9, 24, 28; 17. 22: with מֵאַחֲרֵי 10. 29; with מֵעַל 10. 31; 15. 18. The phrase occurs in a favourable reference I. 15. 5; 22. 43 (מן); *ch.* 18. 6 (מאחרי).

4. נקד] 'A sheep-master,' or breeder of the kind of sheep called in Ar. نَقَدٌ, a breed of small size and ugly appearance[1], but highly esteemed on account of its wool. Amos, before his prophetic call, was one of the נֹקְדִים at Teḳoaʿ.

והשיב] 'And he used to render'; frequentative. So Targ. adds an explanatory שנא בשנא 'year by year.' LXX adds the gloss ἐν τῇ ἐπαναστάσει, regarding the tribute as the *single* payment of an indemnity after the rebellion.

צמר] An accusative more closely defining the manner in which Meshaʿ paid the rams, viz. '*in wool*,' i. e. the fleeces of 100,000 rams. Cf. Dri. *Tenses*, § 194.

5. ויהי כמות וג׳] Cf. *ch.* 1. 1, with *note*.

---

[1] Lane (Lex. 2836) quotes the saying أَذَلُّ مِنَ النَّقَدِ 'more abject than the sheep called *naqad*.'

7. יהושפט] Luc., here and in *v.* 9 Ὀχοζίας, i. e. אֲחַזְיָהוּ, in accordance with the different system of synchronism which appears in this Version. See *Introd.* In *vv.* 11, 12 *bis*, 14, the title ὁ βασιλεὺς Ἰούδα takes the place of the proper name.

8. אי זה הדרך] Cf. I. 13. 12 *note.*

9. אשר ברגליהם] For the idiom cf. I. 20. 10.

12ᵇ. ויהושפט] Add מֶלֶךְ יְהוּדָה with LXX, Luc., Vulg., Pesh., 2 Codd.

13. מה לי ולך] Cf. I. 17. 18 *note.*

לך וג׳] Cf. I. 22. 7 *footnote.* LXX wrongly omits ואל נביאי אמך.

אל] 'Nay!' אל is thus used absolutely in deprecation, *ch.* 4. 16; Judg. 19. 23; Gen. 19. 18; Ruth 1. 13; 2 Sam. 13. 16 (following Luc. μή, ἀδελφέ, i. e. אַל אָחִי; cf. Dri. *ad loc.*).

14. אשר עמדתי לפניו] Cf. I. 17. 1 *note.*

15. והיה] As the text stands, והיה introduces the statement of a single event in the past, and cannot be explained as a perf. with ו *consec.* On the other hand, the occurrence in our narrative of the perf. with weak ו, in place of the normal וַיְהִי, is inconceivable. Thus Klo. is probably correct in conjecturing that והיה 'and it shall come to pass' is the continuation of Elisha's speech, and that all that originally followed has fallen out through the scribe's eye confusing וְהָיָה with וַיְהִי, which introduced the statement כְּנַגֵּן הַמְנַגֵּן of clause *b.* The view that an omission has taken place is favoured (apart from the difficulty of והיה) by the fact that in MT. there is no mention of the bringing of a minstrel—an almost indispensable detail which is found in Luc. after clause *a*;—καὶ ἔλαβον αὐτῷ ψάλλοντα. Klo. suggests the following restoration: '"And it shall come to pass, when the hand of Yahwe comes upon me, that I will declare unto thee that which Yahwe saith." And they brought him a minstrel; and it came to pass, &c.'; i. e. וְהָיָה בִּהְיוֹת עָלַי יַד י׳ וְהִגַּדְתִּי אֵלֶיךָ אֶת־אֲשֶׁר יְדַבֵּר י׳ וַיִּקְחוּ־לוֹ מְנַגֵּן וַיְהִי וג׳.

16. עשה וג׳] 'I will make this torrent-bed nothing but cisterns!' Every depression, deep or shallow, in the dry bed of the *Wady* is to suddenly become a receptacle for water. The infin. absol. עָשֹׂה takes the place of the finite verb (הִנְנִי עֹשֶׂה) in the sudden

rush of the oracle upon the prophet, 'when the speaker is too full of his subject to mention the action in any other than an ejaculatory manner, and as briefly as possible' (Ew. § 328[a]). So exactly, in another oracle by Elisha, *ch.* 4. 43 'Thus saith Yahwe, Eating and leaving over!' i. e. '*There shall be* eating &c.,' or '*Ye shall* eat &c.'; cf. I. 22. 30 *note*. This explanation of the infin. abs. עָשֹׂה is implied by Pesh. ܢܬܥܒܕ ܢܚܠܐ ܗܢܐ, Targ. יתעבד נחלא הדין 'This torrent bed *shall be made* &c.'; so Ew. § 328[c] *end; Hist.* iv. p. 88.

On the other hand, LXX, Luc. Ποιήσατε, Vulg. *Facite* regard עָשֹׂה as equivalent to an *imperative:* 'Make this torrent-bed full of cisterns!' So RV., and most moderns. This explanation is, however, less in accord with *v.* 17[a], which seems to preclude the necessity of human intervention; and is also opposed by *vv.* 22, 23, where the phenomenon described must have been produced by the sun shining upon *natural* and so irregular and wide-spreading *pools of water*, and not upon *artificial* and so (presumably) symmetrically shaped *trenches*. For the repetition גבים גבים cf. Gen. 14. 10; G-K. § 123 *e;* Ew. 313[a].

17. ומקניכם] Luc. καὶ αἱ παρεμβολαὶ ὑμῶν, i. e. וּמַחֲנֵיכֶם, is certainly correct; cf. *v.* 9[b]. So Klo., Kamp., Benz., Kit.

18. ונקל . . . ונתן] 'And this shall be a light thing, &c., and he shall give &c.,' i. e. 'And this being a light thing, &c., he shall (further) give &c.' Cf. Isa. 49. 6.

19. וכל עיר מבחור] LXX, Luc. omit, and the words are regarded by Klo., Kamp., Benz., Kit. as a variant of the preceding כל עיר מבצר.

תכאבו] LXX ἀχρειώσετε, and so RV. '*ye shall mar.*' כאב, however, has always elsewhere the meaning *to be in pain*, Hiph'il *to pain*, and the use of the verb in this passage is unparalleled. Klo. emends תְּאַבְּדוּ 'ye shall destroy.'

20. כעלות המנחה] Cf. I. 18. 29 *note*.

21. וכל מואב שמעו] 'Now all Moab *had heard*.' So *v.* 22 והשמש זרחה 'and the sun *had risen*.' For the order, expressing the pluperfect, cf. *note* of I. 14. 5.

23. החרב נחרבו המלכים] Render, with RV. marg., 'The kings have surely fought together.' So Verss. הָחֳרֵב infin. abs. Pu'al

should probably be vocalized as Niph'al הֶחָרֵב. The verb חרב *slay*, occurs again in Qal, Jer. 50. 21, 27†, and is frequent in Syr. (in Pesh. generally as a rendering of הִכָּה; so e. g. *v.* 24 *bis*). Ar. حرب III. Klo. regards Targ. איתגראה איתגריאו and Luc. ἐρίσαντες γὰρ ἤρισαν (cf. *ch.* 14. 10) as presupposing an original הִתְגָּרֹה הִתְגָּרוּ; but this emendation, though adopted by Kamp., Benz., is scarcely necessary.

24. ויבו בה והכות] In place of the impossible MT., LXX, Luc. read καὶ εἰσῆλθον εἰσπορευόμενοι καὶ τύπτοντες, i.e. וַיָּבֹאוּ בֹא וְהַכּוֹת 'and they went forward smiting Moab as they went,' an emendation certainly to be adopted with Th., Klo., Kamp., Benz., Kit. הַכּוֹת appears to be a rare case of the infin. absol. with the termination ת as in the infin. constr.; so שָׁתוֹת Isa. 22. 13; אָלוֹת Hos. 10. 4; עָרוֹת Hab. 3. 13; and perhaps נִגְלוֹת 2 Sam. 6. 20. Cf. Kö. *Lehrg.* I. i. p. 536. Cases of the infin. constr. used *in place of* the infin. absol. are quoted by Da. § 86, *Rem.* 3.

25. יהרסו] 'They kept on overthrowing,' i. e. one after another. The imperfects are frequentative; cf. Dri. *Tenses*, § 113 β: 'a graphic picture of the way in which the people occupied themselves during their sojourn in Moab.'

עד השאיר וג׳] RV. 'until in Ḳir-ḥareseth (only) they left the stones thereof.' Had this meaning, however, been intended, the indispensable *only* (רַק) must have preceded בקיר חרשת, and the statement would naturally have followed immediately after the first clause of the verse, והערים יהרסו, to which it must be referred. LXX, Vulg., Pesh. presuppose the same text as MT., while in Luc., Targ. the addition of a negative before השאיר 'until there was not left, &c.,' is clearly an attempt at emendation, and limits to *one* city the thorough demolition which the context suggests to have been carried out in the case of *all*. Luc., however, has an additional statement preceding עד השאיר וג׳, viz. καὶ ἐξέσεισαν τὸν Μωάβ, i. e. probably, as Klo. suggests, וַיָּנִידוּ אֶת־מוֹאָב[1]. This seems

[1] The Hithpa'el of נוד, והתנודדה, is rendered by LXX σεισθήσεται in Isa. 24. 20. For the use of וַיָּנִידוּ in our passage, cf. Qal *wander about* or *flee away*, Gen. 4. 12, 14; Jer. 49. 30; 50. 3, 8; Hiph'il *drive about* or *scare*, *ch.* 21. 8; Ps. 36. 12.

to make plain the reference of עד השאיר. That which was left in Ḳir-ḥareseth after the ruthless expulsion of the Moabites from their territory, which is expressed by the strong term ἐξέσεισαν, was not the *stones* of the city, but, as is clear from *vv.* 26 *f.*, *the king of Moab and his immediate followers*. We may thus restore: וַיָּנִידוּ אֶת־מוֹאָב עַד־הִשְׁאִיר בָּנֶיהָ בַּקִּיר חֲרֶשֶׂת וג׳ 'and they harried Moab until *her sons* were left in Ḳir-ḥareseth, and the slingers encompassed and smote it.'

עַד־הִשְׁאִיר] הִשְׁאִיר, as in *ch.* 10. 11; Num. 21. 35; Deut. 3. 3; Josh. 8. 22; 10. 33; 11. 8 after עַד־בִּלְתִּי, and in Deut. 28. 55 after מִבְּלִי, may be regarded either as an impersonal perfect (understand subj. הַמַּשְׁאִיר; cf. *note* on יָלְדָה I. 1. 6), or as an infin. constr. vocalized with *Ḥireq* in place of *Pathaḥ*. Elsewhere in Kgs. we find עַד־הִכְרִית I. 11. 16; עַד־הִשְׁמִדוֹ I. 15. 29; *ch.* 10. 17. In this latter case the suffix indicates that the Massoretes recognized an infin. constr. form with *Ḥireq* under the preformative ה; and this is substantiated by the occurrence elsewhere of such forms as עַד־הִשְׁמִדְךָ Deut. 7. 24; 28. 48; Josh. 11. 14; אַחֲרֵי הִקְצוֹת Lev. 14. 43. Dri. (*Deut.* pp. 48, 105) rejects the hypothesis of Kö. (*Lehrg.* I. i. p. 212) that such a form can have *really* existed after the analogy of the perfect, and thinks it probable that the punctuation does not represent an original and true tradition, and that —הַ should therefore be throughout restored for —הִ.

קיר חרשת] The stronghold of Moab, mentioned again under the same name, Isa. 16. 7, and called קִיר חֶרֶשׂ 16. 11; Jer. 48. 31, 36; קִיר מוֹאָב Isa. 15. 1. Targ. in Isa. and Jer. renders by כרך, כרכא, i. e. the modern *El-Kerak* ('the fortress'), which gives its name to the surrounding district south-east of the Dead Sea. Cf. Rob. *BR.* ii. 166.

27. אשר ימלך] 'Who *was to* reign.' Cf. Dri. *Tenses*, § 39 β.

ויהי קצף גדול וג׳] 'And there came great wrath against Israel.' The 'great wrath' is that of Chemosh the Moabite deity, whom the writer supposes to have been induced by means of the costly offering to succour his worshipper and repulse the foe. Cf. Sta. *Ges.* i. p. 430; Wellh. *Prolegomena*, p. 23 *note*; Montefiore, *Hibbert*

Lectures, p. 35. Cf. the inscription of the Moabite stone, *ll.* 5 *ff.*, where Mesha' traces the affliction of Moab at the hand of Israel to the fact that 'Chemosh was angry with his land,' while so soon as the god overcomes his inertia the fortunes of his country change, and Moab is successful against Israel (*Append.* 1).

לארץ] Luc., Vulg., Pesh. presuppose לְאַרְצָם, correctly. So Klo., Kamp., Benz., Kit., Oort.

4. 1–7. *Elisha makes miraculous provision for the wife of one of the sons of the prophets.*

1. עבדך וג׳] Targ. expands the verse for the purpose of identifying the woman's husband with Obadiah of I. 18. 3 *ff.*, the ground of connexion probably being the resemblance of the statement ועבדך היה ירא את י׳ to I. 18. 3b, 12b.

2. לכי] On the form of suff. 2 fem. sing. here and in *vv.* 3, 7, cf. p. 208.

כי אם אסוך שמן] The ἅπαξ λεγ. אָסוּךְ is rendered by Pesh. ܡܫܘܚܬܐ, Targ. מנא, and so RV. 'pot.' Th.'s explanation, '*unctio*, i.e. *quantum ad unctionem sufficit*,' is more probably correct, as אָסוּךְ may thus, in accordance with its vocalization, be regarded as *stat. absol.* in apposition to שמן, 'an anointing measure—oil,' i.e. 'enough oil for an anointing.' Cf. Dri. *Tenses*, § 194.

LXX ἀλλ' ἢ ὃ ἀλείψομαι ἔλαιον, and probably Vulg. *parum olei, quo ungar*, regard אָסוּךְ as 1st sing. imperf. Qal of סוך, as though the sentence could be equivalent to כִּי־אִם הַשֶּׁמֶן אֲשֶׁר אָסוּךְ (בּוֹ). Luc. ἀλλ' ἢ ἀγγεῖον ἐλαίου . . . ὃ ἀλείψομαι exhibits a double rendering.

4. ויצקת על] 'And shalt pour *into*.' For this use of על (lit. *upon*, from above) cf. Nah. 3. 12 ונפלו על פי אוכל 'shall fall *into* the mouth of the eater.'

After *v.* 4a Luc. adds καὶ αὐτὸ οὐκ ἀποστήσεται, i.e. 'and it (the oil) shall not stay.' Cf. *v.* 6b ויעמד השמן 'and the oil stayed,' only when the vessels were exhausted.

תסיעי] So, of removing heavy objects, I. 5. 31; Eccles. 10. 9 (stones).

5. ותלך מאתו] Luc. adds καὶ ἐποίησεν οὕτως, i. e. וַתַּעַשׂ כֵּן, adopted by Klo., Kamp., Benz.

הם מגישים וג׳] On the constr. cf. I. 1. 14 *note*.

מיצקת] Kt. should probably be vocalized מֵיצֶקֶת Hiph'il, there being no occurrence of a Pi'el מְיַצֶּקֶת.

6. אל בנה] LXX, Luc. pl. πρὸς τοὺς υἱοὺς αὐτῆς, Ἐγγίσατε κ.τ.λ., probably a correction after *v.* 5.

7. ואת בניכי תחיי] All Verss. supply the needful copula before בניכי. Instances of the verb, when *following* a compound subj., agreeing with the principal member of the subj. are collected by Ew. § 340c. Cf. e.g. Ex. 21. 4b. As Klo. notices, the consonants of MT. can be vocalized וְאֶת־בָּנַיִכִי תְּחַיִּי 'and do thou keep thy sons alive &c.'

4. 8–37. *Elisha restores to life the son of the Shunammite woman.*

8. ויהי היום וג׳] 'And there came a day when Elisha passed over &c.' Lit. 'and *the* day was,' *day* being defined on account of the events which happened upon it, according to the idiom noticed, I. 13. 14 *note*. The phrase occurs elsewhere, *vv.* 11, 18; 1 Sam. 1. 4; 14. 1; Job 1. 6, 13; 2. 1.

The other explanation, which regards היום as used *adverbially*, 'and it came to pass, *on a day*, that &c.,' is less probably correct. Cf. Dri. on 1 Sam. 1. 4.

שונם] Cf. I. 1. 3 *note*.

מדי עברו] For the idiom cf. I. 14. 28 *note*.

13. מה לעשות לך] 'What (is one) to do for thee?' and so, 'What is to be done for thee?' The idiom occurs again Isa. 5. 4; 2 Chr. 25. 9; Est. 1. 15; 6. 6.

היש לדבר וג׳] Cf. Dri. *Tenses*, § 202 (1).

ותאמר וג׳] An assertion of independence. She has no need of patronage, being 'a great woman' (*v.* 8) within her own clan.

14. אבל] Cf. I. 1. 43 *note*.

15. ויאמר קרא לה] LXX omits.

16. למועד וג׳] 'At this season, next spring.' כעת חיה means

lit. 'about the time (when it is) reviving.' The phrase occurs again Gen. 18. 10, 14 (J), in the latter verse in conjunction with לַמּוֹעֵד. Cf. Gen. 17. 21 (P) לַמּוֹעֵד הַזֶּה בַּשָּׁנָה הָאַחֶרֶת 'at this time, *next year*.'

אתי] Cf. p. 208.

17. אשר] Read כַּאֲשֶׁר with LXX, Luc. ὡς, Pesh. ܐܝܟ ܕ, So Klo., Kamp., Benz., Kit.

19. שאהו] Vulg. *Tolle, et duc eum*, Pesh. ܫܩܘܠ ܘܐܝܬܝܘܗܝ, Targ. סבהי ואובלהי seem to presuppose the addition וַהֲבִיאֵהוּ. Cf. *v.* 20ª.

20. וישב] LXX καὶ ἐκοιμήθη, i. e. וַיִּשְׁכַּב.

23. אתי הלכתי] Cf. p. 208.

לא חדש ולא שבת] 'Not a new moon nor a Sabbath,' i. e. not a festive day. Cf. Am. 8. 5 and 1 Sam. 20. 5 with Dri.'s *note*. The universality of the festival of the new moon is illustrated by Dillmann on Lev. 23 (p. 578).

25. ותלך ותבוא] LXX δεῦρο καὶ πορεύσῃ καὶ ἐλεύσῃ, inferior to MT. Luc. exhibits a combination of the two readings.

הלז] Identical in form with Ar. *relative* اَلَّذْ, just as the fuller form הַלָּזֶה answers to Ar. اَلَّذِى. הַלָּז is equivalent to הַזֶּה or הַזֹּאת, with the additional demonstrative element *la*. The form is used only here with a fem. subs., but occurs elsewhere with a masc. subs. *ch.* 23. 17; Judg. 6. 20; 1 Sam. 14. 1; 17. 26; Zech. 2. 8. It should doubtless be restored with LXX הָאַרְגָּב הַלָּז in 1 Sam. 20. 19 (cf. Dri. *ad loc.*). Without a subs. Dan. 8. 16.

26. After *v.* 26ª Luc. adds καὶ ἔδραμεν εἰς ἀπάντησιν αὐτῆς καὶ εἶπεν Εἰρήνη σοι· εἰρήνη τῷ ἀνδρί σου· εἰρήνη τῷ παιδαρίῳ.

27. ויגש וג׳] Klo. compares the action of our Lord's disciples, S. Matt. 19. 13, 14.

ממני] LXX after ἀπ' ἐμοῦ makes the worthless addition καὶ σοῦ.

28. תשלה] 'Deceive' (lit. 'mislead'). שלה is frequent in Aram. in the sense 'go astray' or 'act in error,' occurring in Targ. as the equivalent of Heb. שָׁגַג or שָׁגָה. Cf. Aph'el,

Ps. 119. 10 לא תשלגני מפקודיך 'Cause me not to go astray from thy commandments.' The only other occurrence of the verb in Bib. Heb. is late, 2 Chr. 29. 11, and in our passage so marked an Aramaism must be regarded as dialectical (cf. pp. 208 *f.* and *note* on *ch.* 6. 11). In 2 Sam. 6. 7 a subs. שַׁל occurs, which has been explained as equivalent to Aram. שָׁלוּ 'error,' but here the text is probably at fault. Cf. Dri. *ad loc.*

29. כי תמצא וג׳] Cf. S. Luke 10. 4.

30. וחי נפשך] Cf. *ch.* 2. 2 *note.*

34. ויגהר עליו] 'And crouched upon him.' So *v.* 35; cf. I. 18. 42 †. The verb appears to describe the drawing up of the prophet's limbs that they might coincide with the short limbs of the child. Cf. I. 17. 21[a].

35. אחת הנה וג׳] 'Backwards and forwards'; lit. 'once here and once there.' For אַחַת fem. 'once' (for פַּעַם אַחַת Josh. 6. 3, 11, 14) cf. *ch.* 6. 10; Ps. 89. 36; *al.*

ויזורר] A ἅπαξ λεγ., rendered 'sneezed,' in accordance with Targ. Job 41. 10, where זרירוי represents Heb. עטישתיו 'his sneezings.' So apparently Targ. in our passage ואיתמקק (cf. Job 41. 10 *Edit. Regia* מקקוי). Vulg. *et oscitavit,* Pesh. ܘܐܬܦܩܥ give the meaning 'yawned.' LXX omits ויזורר together with the letters וי of the preceding עליו, thus reading וַיִּגְהַר עַל־הַיֶּלֶד עַד־שֶׁבַע פְּעָמִים καὶ συνέκαμψεν ἐπὶ τὸ παιδάριον ἕως ἑπτάκις. Thus Grä. is probably correct in regarding ויזורר as having arisen through dittography from ויגהר.

In the text of Luc. καὶ ἠνδρίσατο ἐπὶ τὸ παιδάριον seems to represent a marginal variant for LXX rendering of ויגהר על הילד, while καὶ ἐνέπνευσεν ἐπ' αὐτόν[1] . . . καὶ διεκινήθη τὸ παιδάριον is a second marginal reading answering to MT. ויגהר . . . הנער.

37. ותפל על רגליו] So exactly 1 Sam. 25. 24. In Est. 8. 3 the phrase is לִפְנֵי רַגְלָיו.

---

[1] Cf. the conjectural rendering of LXX, Luc. for ויתמדד in I. 17. 21 καὶ ἐνεφύσησεν. καὶ ἐνεφύσησεν εἰς (ἐπ') αὐτόν occurs also as a various rendering of ויגהר עליו in *v.* 34. Cf. Field.

4. 38–44. *Elisha makes wholesome a pot of poisoned broth* (38–41), *and miraculously increases a small supply of provisions* (42–44).

38. הגלגלה] Cf. *ch.* 2. 1 *note.*

הגדולה] LXX omits.

39. ארת] Probably 'herbs'; Vulg. *herbas agrestes*, Targ. ירקונין. So several authorities in Isa. 26. 19. There is a root ארה='pluck' which occurs Song 5. 1; Ps. 80. 13, and as Th. and Klo. notice, the translit. ἀριὼθ of LXX, Luc. suggests the form אֲרָיוֹת which might be derived from this root.

ידעו] Luc., Vulg., Pesh. sing. יָדַע, probably correctly.

41. וקחו] '*Then* take.' Cf. Ps. 4. 4.

וישלך] LXX, Luc., Pesh., Targ. וְהַשְׁלִיכוּ 'and cast.'

ויאמר] LXX, Luc. καὶ εἶπεν 'Ε. πρὸς Γιεζεὶ (LXX τὸ παιδάριον).

After ולא היה we should perhaps add עוֹד, with LXX, Luc. ἔτι (LXX doublet ἐκεῖ), Vulg. *amplius*.

42. בעל שלשה] LXX Βαιθσαρεῖσα, Luc. Βηθσαλισά, i.e. בֵּית-שָׁלִישָׁה, according to Eusebius (Βαιθσαρισάθ) fifteen Roman miles north of Diospolis (Lydda). The modern ruin *Kafr Tilt* (ثلث = שלש) seems to correspond with this situation. Cf. Buhl, p. 214.

כרמל] Probably 'garden-fruit.' So Lev. 2. 14; 23. 14, in each case in the enumeration of firstfruits. כרמל generally means 'garden-land.' RV. 'fresh ears of corn' follows Vulg. *frumentum novum*, Pesh. ܦܪ̈ܡܐ, Targ. פירוכין.

בצקלנו] The word is a ἅπαξ λεγ. RV. 'in his *sack*' agrees with Vulg. *in pera sua* in giving a meaning demanded by the context. Pesh. ܒܡܣܢܗ, Targ. בלבשיה interpret 'garment.' LXX, Luc. omit, but Cod. A transliterates βακελλέθ, and hence Lagarde (*Armen. Stud.* § 333) infers that, in place of בצקלנו, we should read בקלעת, קְלַעַת = קְלָעָה being explained by Ar. قَلَعَة *sack*, used for provisions, &c. Halévy, however (*Revue des Études Juives*, xi. 68), takes βακελλέθ to have been a marginal note transcribing the Aram. term (די לה) בקילת 'in his basket':—'קולתא is a very frequent word in the Rabbinic literature; its Arabic equivalent קֻלָּה is still at the present day very popular in the sense of *jar*, a large measure of capacity, which probably takes its origin from the Greek κόλαθος.'

43. אכול והותר] Cf. *ch.* 3. 16; I. 22. 30 *notes*.

44. ויתן לפניהם] LXX, Luc. omit.

5. *Elisha heals Naʿaman, the Aramaean, of his leprosy.*

It is an open question who is the nameless king of Israel to whom reference is made in *vv.* 5–8; and the same difficulty arises in connexion with the sections 6. 8–23; 6. 24—7. 20; 8. 1–6. Probably R^D, to judge by the position in which he has incorporated the narratives in Kings, assumed that the king in question was in every case Jehoram; but, since Elisha's death did not take place until the reign of Joash (*ch.* 13. 14 *ff.*), we have, after the reign of Jehoram, a period of 28 (Jehu) + 17 (Jehoaḥaz) + x (Joash) years during which he may be supposed to have been active.

There is not, however, any evidence sufficient to determine the question. Kue. (§ 25. 12) cites the expression בן המרצח in 6. 32 as an indication that the king thus characterized by Elisha is not Jehoram but Jehoaḥaz, the 'murderer' being Jehu, the father of the latter (cf. *chh.* 9, 10; Hos. 1. 4); but it is scarcely possible that Elisha would so stigmatize Jehu on account of a course of action of which he was himself the instigator (*ch.* 9. 1 *ff.*). Supposing בן המרצח to contain literally a reference to *the father* of the king in question, the reference is more naturally to Aḥab (cf. the use of רצח in I. 21. 19); but, as a matter of fact, the title explains itself as called forth by the hostile menace of *the king himself* against Elisha (6. 31; cf. *note* on בן המרצח 6. 32).

Thus, failing direct evidence, all that can be said is that in the single case of the narrative 6. 1–23 the friendly terms upon which Elisha stands to the king (cf. *vv.* 9, 21 *f.*) create a slight *presumption* against identification with Jehoram, to whom, in 3. 13, 14, he openly expresses his hostility, and in favour of some member of the dynasty which the prophet had been instrumental in placing upon the throne of Israel.

Upon the time-relationship of 5. 1–27 to 6. 24—7. 20; 8. 1–6, cf. *note* on 6. 25.

1. נשא פנים] So Isa. 3. 3; 9. 14; Job 22. 8.

והאיש וג׳] Luc. simply καὶ ὁ ἄνθρωπος ἦν λεπρός, omitting גבור חיל, which is probably to be regarded, with Benz., as a marginal gloss upon the preceding איש גדול.

2. יצאו גדודים] 'Had gone forth in (lit. *as*) marauding bands.' Cf. Dri. *Tenses*, § 161 (3).

3. אַחֲלֵי 'Would that!' Only again Ps. 119. 5, with vocalization אַחֲלַי. In our passage the punctuators seem to have regarded the word as a subs. plur. constr., and this view is taken by Pesh. ܛܘܒܘܗܝ ܠܡܪܝ ܐܢ ܐܙܠ ܠܘܬ ܢܒܝܐ, Targ. טובי ריבוני אם ייזיל קדם נבייא 'Oh, the benefits of my lord if he would go to the prophet!' Cf. the vocalization אַשְׁרֵי.

לפני הנביא] LXX ἐνώπιον τοῦ προφήτου τοῦ θεοῦ.

After *v.* 3[b] Luc. adds καὶ δεηθείη τοῦ προσώπου αὐτοῦ, i.e. וְחִלָּה אֶת־פָּנָיו. Cf. I. 13. 6 *note*.

4. ויבא וג׳] 'And he went in, &c.' The subject, as Vulg. rightly divines, is Na'aman (RV. marg.), and not some one unnamed, 'and one went in' (RV. text, Pesh.). LXX, Luc., Targ., against gender, take Na'aman's wife as subject: 'And she went in and told her lord,' and this necessitates in Luc. the addition καὶ ἀνήγγειλε τῷ βασιλεῖ, which is duplicated at the commencement of *v.* 5 in the form καὶ ἀνηγγέλη τῷ βασιλεῖ.

כזאת וכזאת] *Ch.* 9. 12; Josh. 7. 20 (JE); 2 Sam. 17. 15 (twice)†. Cf. כָּזֹה וְכָזֶה I. 14. 5 *note*.

6. ויבא . . . לאמר] On the constr. cf. *note* on I. 16. 16.

ועתה] 'And now.' The main point of the letter, to which that which precedes leads up, is all that is quoted. Cf. *note* on I. 1. 20.

7. זה] Cf. I. 22. 27 *note*.

דעו נא וג׳] Cf. I. 20. 7.

מתאנה] 'Seeks occasion against.' So Verss. Lit. 'causes himself to meet.'

8. אלישע איש האלהים] LXX omits איש האלהים, while Luc. omits אלישע.

10. וטהר] On the idiomatic use of the imperative with ו cf. *note* on I. 1. 12.

11. ועמד] LXX, Luc. omit.

והניף וג׳] Luc. *καὶ ἐπιθήσει τὴν χεῖρα αὐτοῦ ἐπὶ τὸν λεπρὸν καὶ ἀποσυνάξει αὐτὸ ἀπὸ τῆς σαρκός μου.*

אל המקום] אל in place of על; cf. I. 13. 29 *note.*

12. אבנה] Read אֲמָנָה with Q're, Pesh., Targ., i.e. probably 'the constant' (perennial) river. Cf. the use of the verb אמן in Isa. 33. 16.

The Amana is identified with the modern *Nahr Baradâ*, called by the Greeks Chrysorroas, which flows down from the gorges of the Anti-Libanus (cf. Song 4. 8); the Parpar is probably the *Nahr el-A'waj*, the only other important stream in the district. Cf. Rob. *B. R.* iii. 447; Baed. 183, 345.

13. אבי] Probably to be regarded, with Th., Kamp., Benz., Kit., Oort, as a corruption of אִם, which is scarcely to be dispensed with. Klo. emends הֲלֹא כִּי. LXX omits.

דבר גדול וג׳] The order—*object, subject, verb*—is very rare. Cf. *ch.* 6. 22; Dri. *Tenses*, 208 (2).

16. אשר עמדתי לפניו] Cf. I. 17. 1 *note.*

17. ולא] 'And (if) not.' So 2 Sam. 13. 26. וְיֵשׁ *ch.* 10. 15; cf. Judg. 6. 13.

יתן נא וג׳] The request is made upon the view that Yahwe, the national God of Israel, can only be worshipped aright upon the soil of Israel's land. Cf. the writer's *Outlines of O. T. Theology*, p. 35.

18. לדבר] LXX, Luc., Pesh. presuppose וְלַדָּבָר '*But* in this matter &c.,' correctly. So Th., Klo., Kamp., Benz.

רמן] The Assyrian *Rammânu*, 'the Thunderer,' the storm- or weather-god, apparently identical with הֲדַד; cf. I. 15. 18 *note;* Schrader, *COT.* i. p. 196; Baethgen, *Semit. Relig.* p. 75.

בהשתחויתי] On the form cf. p. 208. LXX, Luc. *ἐν τῷ προσκυνεῖν αὐτόν*, Vulg. *adorante eo*, i.e. בְּהִשְׁתַּחֲווֹתוֹ (בְּהִשְׁתַּחֲוָיָתוֹ), ought probably to be followed, with Th., Klo., Kamp., Benz., Kit.

19. כברת ארץ] RV. 'a little way'; *marg.* 'some way.' The expression occurs again Gen. 35. 16; 48. 7†; RV. 'some way.'

The distance denoted by כִּבְרָה (or כִּבְרַת) is quite indeterminate. Pesh. in all passages ܦܪܣܐ 'a parasang'; LXX, Luc. as one rendering in Gen. 48. 7 ἱππόδρομος, an expression perhaps equivalent to the Ar. شَوْطُ ٱلْفَرَسِ, i. e. as far as a horse can gallop; Targ. כרוב, explained as a piece of land of about an acre's extent (Aram. כרב, ܟܪܒ, Ar. كرب = 'to plough'), a rendering apparently obtained by transposition of ב and ר. In Assyrian, *kibrâtu* denotes a *region* of the earth or heaven; cf. e.g. *šàr kibrat arba'-i*, 'king of the four regions' (quarters of the earth); Delitzsch, *Assyr. Handwörterbuch*, 315. כברת also occurs in a Phoenician inscription from Ma'ṣûb, apparently with the same significance as in Assyr., in the expression כברת מצא שמש 'region of the sunrise'; cf. Halévy, *Revue des Études Juives*, xii (1886), p. 109; Lidzbarski, *Nordsemit. Epigraphik*, p. 419. E. Hoffmann, however (*Abhandlungen der Göttinger Gesellschaft der Wissenschaften*, xxxvi (1890), pp. 24 *f.*), explains the word in Phoen. and Heb. as meaning the tract of country which lies between the eye and the horizon; as much as one can see, rather than the direction in which one sees ('Sehweite, nicht Sehrichtung').

20. כי אם רצתי] '*I will surely run.*' רצתי is a perfect of certitude; cf. Jer. 51. 14 נִשְׁבַּע י׳ צְבָאוֹת בְּנַפְשׁוֹ כִּי אִם־מִלֵּאתִיךְ אָדָם וג׳ 'Yahwe Ṣebhā'oth hath sworn by himself, *Surely I will fill thee* with men, &c.'; Judg. 15. 7 אִם־תַּעֲשׂוּן כָּזֹאת כִּי אִם־נִקַּמְתִּי בָכֶם 'If ye act thus, *I will surely be avenged* of you.' The particles כי אם are connected closely together with a strong asseverative force, as is clear from the two passages above cited, and also from 1 Sam. 26. 10; 2 Sam. 15. 21 Kt. (in both cases after the oath חי י׳); Ruth 3. 12 Kt. (after כִּי אָמְנָם); 1 Sam. 21. 6. Cf. Dri. *Tenses*, § 139, *note* 1; Ew. § 356[b]; Kö. *Syntax*, § 391 *r*. The view which takes כי separately, as introducing the terms of the oath (cf. *note* on I. 2. 23), overlooks the fact that אם following could only, in such a case, introduce a *negation*, and not an assertion (אם לא).

21. ויפל מעל המרכבה] 'And he *lighted down from* the chariot. Cf. Gen. 24. 64 וַתִּפֹּל מֵעַל הַגָּמָל.

השלום] 'Is (all) well?' Vulg. *Recte ne sunt omnia?* or, understanding באך, as in I. 2. 13, 'Is *it* well?' i.e. 'Does *thy coming* portend no evil tidings?' Cf. *ch.* 9. 11, 17, 22, 31.

22. עתה זה] On זה cf. I. 14. 6 *note* on למה זה.

23. הואל וג׳] '*Consent*, take two talents,' or, as we should say, 'Consent to take &c.' Cf. *ch.* 6. 3 הוֹאֶל נָא וְלֵךְ; Judg. 19. 6 הוֹאֶל־נָא וְלִין; 2 Sam. 7. 29. When the verb is used of an action undertaken at one's own instance, and not at the suggestion of another, '*Resolve*' is a suitable rendering: cf. Gen. 18. 27, 31; Deut. 1. 5.

ויפרץ בו] 'And he urged him.' פרץ is used in the same sense in 1 Sam. 28. 23; 13. 25, 27, but the ordinary significance of this verb is *to break out* or *spread abroad*, and it is probable that we ought, with most critics, to substitute the verb פצר which occurs commonly with the meaning *urge* or *press upon*:—*v.* 16; *ch.* 2. 17; Gen. 19. 3, 9; 33. 11; Judg. 19. 7†.

חרטים] 'Bags.' The word only occurs again in Heb. Isa. 3. 22, where it is mentioned as an article of feminine adornment. In Ar. خَرِيطَةٌ denotes a bag or pouch made of leather, rag, or other material.

24. העפל] Probably '*the citadel*.' The universal explanation, however, among modern interpreters, seems to be 'the hill' or 'mound.' The verb עפל means *to swell*, and occurs twice in Heb., once in Puʿal עֻפְּלָה 'is puffed up,' Hab. 2. 4, and once in Hiphʿil וַיַּעְפִּילוּ 'and acted arrogantly' (internal Hiphʿil). The subs. עֹפֶל is used to denote a *swelling*, i.e. *tumour*, 1 Sam. 5. 6; *al.* (so in Ar.). When used in a topographical sense, the inference is generally drawn that עֹפֶל denotes a natural swelling of the earth's surface, i.e. conceivably, a low conical hill. But the connexion in which the term appears points with much greater probability to an artificial 'swelling,' i.e. a *bulging*, or *rounded keep*, or *enceinte*.

An עֹפֶל is mentioned as existing in three different localities:—(i) at Jerusalem; (ii) presumably at Samaria (here only); (iii) in the territory of Meshaʿ, king of Moab (Moabite stone, *ll.* 21 *f.*). In each case reference is made to הָעֹפֶל *the ʿophel*, well known as such, and so on a *prima facie* view *not* a hill marked out merely by its unimportant physical characteristics[1]. Accordingly, the *'ophel* at Jerusalem is a fortified place with walls, 2 Chr. 27. 3; Neh. 3. 27; is mentioned in close connexion with המגדל הגדול היוצא 'the great projecting tower,' Neh. 3. 27; and *in parallelism with* מגדל עדר 'tower of the flock,' Mic. 4. 8. In the same way Mesha' says ואנך בנתי . . . חמת העפל ואנך בנתי שעריה ואנך בנתי מגדלתה 'And I built the wall of the *'ophel*, and I built its gates, and I built its towers.'

25. ויעמד אל אדניו] 'And stood *by* his lord.' Cf. *ch.* 11. 14 וְהַשָּׂרִים וְהַחֲצֹצְרוֹת אֶל־הַמֶּלֶךְ.

מאן] Kt. אָן occurs again 1 Sam. 10. 14 and 27. 10 according to Pesh., Targ. (in place of אל), and in the expression עַד־אָן Job 8. 2.

26. לא לבי הלך] LXX, Luc. add μετὰ σοῦ, i. e. עִמְּךָ. The meaning of the expression is, 'Was not I present in spirit?' Ew.'s explanation, which makes לִבִּי an affectionate designation of Geḥazi, is strangely forced.

העת וג׳] 'Was it a time to take silver, &c.?' The miracle had served to emphasize before a representative of the rival nation the unique power of Israel's God (cf. *vv.* 15, 18), and the dignity of His prophet (cf. *vv.* 8ᵇ, 10, 16); Geḥazi's rapacity, representing itself as directed by Elisha, must have tended to weaken the impression. Klo., Kamp., Benz., Kit., Oort follow LXX καὶ νῦν ἔλαβες τὸ ἀργύριον, καὶ νῦν ἔλαβες τὰ ἱματια, κ.τ.λ., Luc. καὶ νῦν ἔλαβες τὸ ἀργύριον καὶ τὰ ἱματια καὶ λήψει ἐν αὐτῷ, κ.τ.λ.[2], Vulg. *nunc igitur accepisti argentum, et accepisti, &c.*, and read וְעַתָּה לָקַחְתָּ אֶת־הַכֶּסֶף וְלָקַחְתָּ בְגָדִים וג׳ 'And now thou hast taken the silver, and wilt take

---

[1] The kind of hill which עפל might be expected to describe, upon the supposition that the term was so used, would scarcely be outstanding and conspicuous, but rather with a low and rounded top, the less likely to attract attention as העפל if covered, wholly or partly, by buildings. And, again upon such a supposition, it is somewhat strange that the term is not more frequently employed, and that of hills not in towns but in the open country.

[2] The position of καὶ τὰ ἱματια has clearly been ignorantly altered in Luc. in order to agree with *vv.* 22, 23.

garments, &c.'; וְלָקַחְתָּ being a perfect with ו *consec.*, describing the use to which Geḥazi was already planning to put the money[1]. This emendation, though yielding a good sequence, is scarcely superior to MT.

6. 1–7. *Elisha causes iron to float.*

2. איש] LXX, Luc. *ἀνὴρ εἶς*, owing to the influence of the following קורה אחת. So Pesh. ܩܝܣܐ ܚܕ ܚܕ.

3. האחד] '*The* one' who, as a matter of fact, *did* so speak, but according to Eng. idiom simply '*one*.' Cf. *note* on I. 13. 14 with the instance 1 Sam. 9. 9 there quoted.

הואל] Cf. *ch.* 5. 23 *note.*

4. העצים] 'The timber,' in its natural condition, destined to become the קורות (prepared) 'beams' of *v.* 2.

5. ויהי . . . הקורה] As Kamp. remarks, a man cuts down tree-trunks (עֵצִים *v.* 4) and not *beams*. Klo.'s emendation הַקַּרְדֹּם, favoured by Kamp., Benz., Kit., Oort, is worthy of notice. Render, 'as one *was swinging his axe*.' This use of הִפִּיל cannot, however, be paralleled, while that implied by the reading of MT. has the support of *ch.* 3. 19.

ואת הברזל נפל] The use of את to introduce a new subject is sporadic, most of the certified instances belonging to the later and inferior style. Cf. Jer. 36. 22 וְהַמֶּלֶךְ יוֹשֵׁב בֵּית הַחֹרֶף . . . וְאֶת־הָאָח לְפָנָיו מְבֹעָרֶת. Other cases are cited by G-K. § 117 *m;* Ew. § 277[d]. G-K., however, considers that in our passage 'the את is probably derived from a text which read the Hiph'îl instead of נפל.'

Klo. regards אֵת as a substantive 'axe-head,' a suggestion which is favoured by Kamp., Benz., Kit., Kö. *Syntax*, § 270 *a*.

6. הרם לך] Luc. *Μετεώρισον καὶ λαβὲ σεαυτῷ.*

6. 8–23. *Elisha blinds and captures an Aramaean army.*

8. מקום פלני אלמני] 'Place of *so and so*,' i.e. '*such and such* a place.' So exactly 1 Sam. 21. 3, and, in addressing a person

---

[1] וְלָקַחְתָּ might in this sense be very idiomatically retained: 'and art for taking.' Cf. Gen. 30. 15; Dri. *Tenses*, § 204.

unnamed, Ruth 4. 1. פלני, upon comparison of Ar. فُلَانٌ, Aram. ܦܠܳܢ, is usually connected with the verb פלה in the sense *distinct, specific;* אלמני with אלם 'to be dumb,' as meaning *one whose name is withheld.* In Dan. 8. 13 the contraction פַּלְמֹנִי occurs, and this form appears to be presupposed by Luc. φελμούνι in our passage.

תחנתי] Apparently 'my camp.' So Targ. בית משרנא, and perhaps LXX παρεμβαλῶ. But the form is very strange (cf. Kö. *Lehrg.* I. ii. p. 192) and the context desiderates reference not to a camp but to an *ambush.* Accordingly, Luc. reads ποιήσωμεν ἔνεδρον, καὶ ἐποίησαν, Vulg. *ponamus insidias*, Pesh. ܟܡܢܘ ܘܐܬܛܫܘ 'place an ambush and conceal yourselves.' Thus Th., followed by Kamp., Benz., Kit., *Heb. Lex. Oxf.*, emends תֵּחָבְאוּ 'conceal yourselves' (cf. *ch.* 7. 12; I. 22. 25); Oort תִּתְחַבְּאוּ; Klo. נִתְחַבֵּא 'let us conceal ourselves.' This latter, as agreeing with Luc., Vulg., may be adopted[1]. Probably, with Luc., we should add וַיִּתְחַבְּאוּ, a suitable introduction to *v.* 9.

9. נְחִתִּים] An inexplicable form. RV. 'coming down,' i.e. נָחִתִים, a very pronounced Aramaism. We may safely follow Verss., and all moderns, in reading נֶחְבָּאִים or נֶחְבִּים 'concealed.'

10. והזהירה ונשמר] Perfects with ו *consec.* in a frequentative sense, after the summary statement וישלח. Cf. Dri. *Tenses*, § 114 *a.*

11. מי מִשֶּׁלָּנוּ אל מלך ישראל] 'Who of ours is for the king of Israel?' On the use of the relative ש cf. p. 208. The sense of אל '*towards,*' and so '*in support of,*' may be illustrated by Hos. 3. 3; Jer. 15. 1; Ezek. 36. 9; Hag. 2. 17. So Pesh., Targ. LXX, Luc., however, in place of משלנו presuppose a verb *betray*, προδίδωσίν με. Similarly, Vet. Lat. *prodet me*, Vulg. *proditor mei.* Accordingly Bö., retaining the consonants of MT., vocalizes מַשְׁלֵנוּ 'who *hath misled us*' (cf. *note* on תשלה *ch.* 4. 28). Change of one letter gives מְגַלֵּנוּ, which is adopted by Klo., Kamp., Benz. Kit. supposes that מְגַלֵּנוּ has fallen out after מִשֶּׁלָּנוּ, upon the view that the response (*v.* 12) presupposes the suggestion that there is a

[1] Possibly, if Luc. is correct in reading פלמני for פלני אלמני, the initial נ of נתחבא has been absorbed into אלמני.

traitor in the camp, 'one of ours.' But this is sufficiently implied by הלוא תגידו לי, i. e. substantially, 'One of you must know.'

12. את הדברים] LXX, Luc., Vulg. אֶת־כָּל־הַדְּבָרִים.

אשר תדבר וג׳] For the expression cf. Eccles. 10. 20.

13. איכה] Kt. אֵיכָה is probably correct. Cf. p. 209.

הנה בדתן] It is idiomatic to omit expression of the subject with הִנֵּה, when it may be readily inferred from the context. Cf. *v.* 20; I. 21. 18; Dri. *Tenses*, § 135 (6), *note* 4. So, with participle, 6. 25 *note*.

דתן] LXX, Luc. Δωθάειμ, i. e. דֹּתַיִם; cf. עֶגְלַיִם by the side of עֶגְלוֹן. Dothan is the modern *Tell Dôtân*, a green hill with a few ruins about ten miles north of Samaria. Cf. Eusebius, *Onom.*; Baed. 261; Buhl, 24 *f.*, 102.

15. וישכם וג׳] MT. is somewhat confused. The subj. of ויצא, in accordance with 15^b, must be Elisha, but following as it does upon what precedes, it can scarcely be different from that of וישכם, viz. in accordance with MT., משרת. Again, the servant is called משרת in 15^a, נערו in 15^b, and the expression וישכם . . . לקום 'and he got up early to arise,' is at best extremely harsh. Klo. happily restores order by emending מִמָּחֳרָת for מְשָׁרֵת (cf. Ex. 32. 6; Judg. 6. 38; 1 Sam. 5. 3), and substituting בַּבֹּקֶר for לָקוּם after Luc. τὸ πρωΐ[1], Vulg. *diluculo*:—'And the man of God arose early on the morrow in the morning, and went forth, &c.' So Kamp., Benz., and substantially Kit.[2]

17. את עיני הנער] LXX, Luc. τοὺς ὀφθαλμοὺς αὐτοῦ.

18. וירדו] Vulg. supplies the subj. *Hostes vero descenderunt*. 'They came down' from the hills surrounding the small valley in the midst of which *Tell Dôtân* lies.

סנורים] 'Blindness.' Only again Gen. 19. 11. The word is perhaps a Shaph'el formation from נור, *sanwara*, 'make blind' (lit. 'bright,' euphemistically). Cf. Kö. *Lehrg.* I. ii. 404.

19. זה] So again for זאת Ezek. 40. 45; Eccl. 2. 2, 24; 5. 15, 18;

---

[1] Luc. has also ἀναστῆναι, clearly as a gloss derived from LXX.

[2] Kit. reads וַיְהִי מִמָּחֳרָת וג׳, a reading which he apparently refers to Klo.

7. 23; 9. 13, and in the phrase כָּזֹה וְכָזֶה I. 14. 5; Judg. 18. 4; 2 Sam. 11. 25†. The form resembles Aram. דָּא, and may be dialectical. Cf. p. 208.

20. והנה וג׳] Cf. *v.* 13 *note.*

21. האכה אכה] Cf., for the repetition, Ezek. 14. 3^{b}, which should perhaps be vocalized הַאִדָּרֵשׁ אִדָּרֵשׁ לָהֶם. Most critics, however, restore an infin. absol. הִדָּרֹשׁ, and so in our passage LXX Εἰ πατάξας πατάξω, Pesh. ܡܩܛܠܘ ܐܩܛܘܠ ܐܢܘܢ suggest the reading הַהַכֵּה אַכֶּה.

22. האשר שבית וג׳] Klo. inserts a negative לא after Luc. οὓς οὐκ ᾐχμαλώτευσας . . . οὐ (read σύ LXX) τύπτεις; 'Wilt thou slay those whom thou hast not captured with thy sword and with thy bow?' So Benz., Kit. This is probably correct rather than MT. which is scarcely consonant with the frequent practice of the חֵרֶם, sanctioned and even enforced by members of the prophetic school; cf. e.g. I. 20. 42; 1 Sam. 15. 3, 33. Kamp. favours MT.

23. ויכרה וג׳] The context demands the meaning 'And he made them a great feast'; and so Vulg., Pesh., Targ.; but כרה with this meaning is not elsewhere found in Heb. Perhaps the root is the same as Assyr. *karû*, 'bring,' *kirêtu*, 'feast' (to which guests are *brought* or *invited*). So in the Balawat inscription, *ki-re-ti iškun*, 'he made a feast'; Delitzsch, *Assyr. Handwörterbuch*, p. 352. Klo. emends וַיַּעֲרֹךְ מַעֲרָכָה 'And he laid a spread,' after LXX, Luc. καὶ παρέθηκεν αὐτοῖς παράθεσιν, but this expression so used is unparalleled in Heb.[1] More probably the Greek represents a free guess at the unknown words.

6. 24—**7.** 20. *Samaria is besieged by the Aramaeans, and reduced to great straits through famine. The city is relieved through a panic which seizes the besieging army.*

24. בן הדד] Cf. *note* on I. 15. 18. If this narrative be wrongly assigned to the reign of Jehoram (cf. p. 278), the reference will be to the successor of Ḥazael (cf. *ch.* 13. 24).

[1] The regular phrase is עָרַךְ שֻׁלְחָן. Cf. Isa. 21. 5; Ps. 23. 5; 78. 19; Prov. 9. 2.

25. ויהי רעב גדול] It is not quite clear whether the writer regards the famine as simply due to the rigour of the siege, or as in a measure independent of it. The fact that the king of Israel considers Elisha as the main cause of the calamity (*v.* 31) favours the latter supposition, and the same inference is perhaps to be drawn from the reference to the opening of 'the windows of heaven,' *ch.* 7. 2. In this case the famine is probably the same as that mentioned in *ch.* 8. 1–6, which lasted seven years (*v.* 2). *Ch.* 8. 1–6 represents Geḥazi as still holding the position of Elisha's favoured servant; therefore 8. 1–6; 6. 24—7. 20 are presumably earlier than 5. 1–27 which relates the smiting of Geḥazi with leprosy.

והנה צרים] Expression of the subject is omitted in accordance with idiom. See cases cited by Dri. *Tenses*, § 135 (6), and cf. *note* on *v.* 13.

ראש חמור] Th. quotes a parallel from Plutarch, *Artaxerx.* 24: τὰ ὑποζύγια μόνον κατέκοπτεν, ὥστε ὄνου κεφαλὴν μόλις δραχμῶν ἑξήκοντα ὤνιον εἶναι.

בשמנים] LXX, Luc. πεντήκοντα.

הקב] The *kab* is only here mentioned in the OT., but occurs in New Heb. both as a dry and fluid measure. Josephus represents רֹבַע הַקַּב by ξέστης, a measure which is known to be equivalent to the Heb. לֹג. The fourth part of a *kab* was therefore about a pint. Cf. Benz. *Archäologie*, 182; Nowack, *Archäologie*, i. 202 *ff.*

חרייונים] The Verss. follow Kt., and, reading as two words חֲרֵי (חֲרֵי) יוֹנִים, render 'doves' dung.' Q're דִּבְיוֹנִים is of unknown derivation. The strangeness of such an article as used for food has aroused suspicion. Thus Ges. *Thes.* cites the view of Bochart that 'doves' dung' may have been the popular name for some vegetable product (roasted chick peas) just as in Ar. the name خرو العصافر 'sparrows' dung' is applied to the herb *kali*, and in German *assafoetida* is named *Teufelsdreck*. Klo. emends חֲרְצַנִּים 'sour wine' (? Num. 6. 4), Cheyne (*Expositor*, 1899, p. 32) חֲרוּבִים 'carob pods,' a word well known in New Heb. and Syriac, and restored by the same writer also in *ch.* 18. 27 = Isa. 36. 12 (חֲרוֹּבֵיהֶם for חריהם), Isa. 1. 20 (חֲרוֹּבִים תֹּאכֵלוּ for חֶרֶב תְּאֻכְּלוּ); cf. S. Luke 15. 16.

It is, however, by no means certain that MT., Kt., in its literal acceptation, is incorrect. A parallel in Jos. *Bell. Jud.* v. 13, § 7 depicts the extremities to which men may be brought by a prolonged siege:—μετὰ ταῦτα δ' ὡς οὐδὲ ποηλογεῖν ἔθ' οἷόν τ' ἦν περιτειχισθείσης τῆς πόλεως, προελθεῖν τινας εἰς τοσοῦτον ἀνάγκης, ὥστε τὰς ἀμάρας ἐρευνῶντας καὶ παλαιὸν ὄνθον βοῶν προσφέρεσθαι τὰ ἐκ τούτων σκύβαλα, καὶ τὸ μηδ' ὄψει φορητὸν πάλαι τότε γενέσθαι τροφήν. Again, Post (in Hastings, *BD.* i. 629) quotes, on the authority of Houghton, a statement from a Spanish author that in the year 1316 so great a famine distressed the English that 'men ate their own children, dogs, mice, and *pigeons' dung*.'

26. הושיעה וג'] Cf. 2 Sam. 14. 4b. Similarly *v.* 28a is exactly paralleled by 2 Sam. 14. 5a.

27. אל יושעך וג'] Difficult. As the text stands, it is best to render, 'If Yahwe help thee not, whence shall I help thee?' lit. 'Let not Yahwe help thee, whence &c.?' a case of the jussive used in the protasis of a hypothetical sentence. So Dri. *Tenses*, § 152 (3); G-K. § 109 *h*. The alternative is to regard אל as used absolutely in deprecation: 'Nay! let Yahwe help thee.' Cf. *note* on *ch.* 3. 13.

Pesh. is noticeable as suggesting the reading לָהּ for אַל: ܘܐܡܪ ܠܗ̇ ܢܦܪܩܟܝ ܡܪܝܐ 'And he said *to her*, Let Yahwe deliver thee!' Is it, however, possible (in view of the dialectical peculiarities of these narratives; pp. 208 *f.*) that we should find in אל the Aram. אֶלָּא '*except*'?

29. ותחבא את בנה] Luc. adds καὶ οὐκ ἔδωκεν αὐτὸν ἵνα φάγωμεν καὶ αὐτόν.

30. והוא עבר] Luc. καὶ αὐτὸς εἱστήκει, i. e. וְהוּא עֹמֵד, probably correct. So Klo., Kamp., Benz., Kit.

31. כה יעשה וג'] Cf. I. 2. 23 *note*.

32. והזקנים וג'] Cf. Ezek. 8. 1; 20. 1. Luc. καὶ πάντες οἱ πρεσβύτεροι.

וישלח איש מלפניו] RV. 'And [the king] sent a man from before him.' So Luc. inserts ὁ βασιλεύς. The sentence is probably a clumsy interpolation to explain the following reference המלאך and כי שלח. Wellh. (*C*. 360) drastically removes all reference to the messenger by excision both of this sentence and of ראו כבא ... אחריו, and emendation of המלאך in its first occurrence to הַמֶּלֶךְ, as also in *v*. 33.

בטרם] Read וּבְטֶרֶם with Luc., Vulg., Pesh.

בן המרצח הזה] As is remarked by Klo., Benz., Kit., the expression does not refer literally to the king's father (Aḥab? cf. p. 278), but characterizes the king himself. 'Mördersohn' = 'Mordbube.' Cf. 1 Sam. 20. 30 (reading בֶּן־נַעֲרַת הַמַּרְדּוּת; cf. Dri. *ad loc.*); Isa. 57. 3 בְּנֵי עֹנְנָה זֶרַע מְנָאֵף וַתִּזְנֶה.

ולחצתם וג׳] 'And press him with the door,' i.e., as we should say, 'Shut the door *in his face*.'

33. המלאך] Read הַמֶּלֶךְ with Ew., Wellh., Grä., Klo., Kamp., Kit., Benz., Oort. Mention of the king's arrival is presupposed by *ch*. 7. 2 (cf. *v*. 17 בְּרֶדֶת הַמֶּלֶךְ אֵלָיו), and the words of *v*. 33[b] are only explicable if placed in the king's mouth.

זאת הרעה] Cf. *note* on זה היום I. 14. 14.

7. 1. סאה] A *seä* contained about a peck, and was equivalent to six measures of the *kab* (*ch*. 6. 25), and twenty-four of the *log*. Cf. Benz. *Archäologie*, 181 *ff*.

וסאתים שערים בשקל] LXX omits through homoioteleuton.

2. השליש] Cf. I. 9. 22 *note*.

למלך] Read הַמֶּלֶךְ with several Codd., all Verss. and modern authorities.

נשען על ידו] Cf. *ch*. 5. 18.

ארבות בשמים] 'Windows *or* sluices (LXX, Luc. καταρράκτας) in the heavens,' through which the rain was thought to be poured down; Gen. 7. 11; 8. 2; Mal. 3. 10; cf. Isa. 24. 18. The point of the speech seems to be that, even if Yahwe were at once to send rain, it would be impossible for such a state of plenty to come about *by to-morrow*.

6. מלכי החתים] The kings of the Ḥittites are mentioned again in I. 10. 29 as providing themselves with horses from *Muṣri* (cf.

note ad loc.). The Ḥittite kingdom lay in north Syria, having its capital at Ḳadesh on the Orontes. In 2 Sam. 24. 6 David's northern boundary is said to have extended as far as 'the land of the Ḥittites to Ḳadesh[1].' The land of the Ḥittites is also mentioned in Judg. 1. 26, and in Judg. 3. 3 הַחִתִּי ought probably to be substituted for הַחִוִּי: 'the Ḥittites who inhabit the hill-country of the Lebanon' (cf. Moore, *ad loc.*). כל ארץ החתים Josh. 1. 4 is perhaps a later gloss, identifying the Ḥittites with the Canaanites. On the Ḥittites as they figure in the Egyptian and cuneiform inscriptions, cf. Sayce in Hastings, *DB.* ii. 390 *ff.*; Dri. *Authority*, 83 *ff.*

ואת מלכי מצרים] Probably we should vocalize מֻצְרִים or מֻצְרִים, and render, 'and the kings of Muṣri.' An alliance of the Ḥittites with Egypt would have been highly improbable, and could scarcely have suggested itself to the Aramaeans, while an alliance of the two north Syrian kingdoms for the purpose of turning their flank was a danger well calculated to cause a panic. On Muṣri, cf. I. 10. 28 *note.*

7. המחנה כאשר היא] RV. 'even the camp as it was.' But מחנה is always elsewhere masc. We may read בַּמַּחֲנֶה כַּאֲשֶׁר הֵמָּה with Luc. ὡς ἦσαν ἐν τῇ παρεμβολῇ: cf. *v.* 10[b]. The reading במחנה is also presupposed by LXX, Vulg., Pesh.

אל נפשם] Cf. I. 19. 3 *note.*

8[a]. ויטמנו] LXX omits.

9. לא כן אנחנו עשים] 'We are not doing *right.*' Cf. *ch.* 17. 9 דְּבָרִים אֲשֶׁר לֹא־כֵן.

עוון] 'Punishment.' So Gen. 4. 13. Cf. Num. 14. 34; Isa. 53. 11; *al.*

10. שֹׁעֵר] Pl. שֹׁעֲרֵי is demanded by the following לָהֶם, and by הַשֹּׁעֲרִים *v.* 11. So Th., Kamp., Kit., Oort.

אהלים] LXX, Luc. αἱ σκηναὶ αὐτῶν, i.e. וְאָהֳלֵיהֶם, correctly. So Klo., Kamp., Benz. Kit. הָאֹהָלִים.

---

[1] Reading אֶרֶץ הַחִתִּים קָדֵשָׁה, after Luc. εἰς γῆν Χεττιεὶμ Καδής, for the senseless ארץ תחתים חרשי of MT. Cf. Dri. *ad loc.*

11. ויקרא] Read וַיִּקְרְאוּ with LXX, Luc., Targ. Vulg. *Ierunt ergo*, Pesh. ܘܩܪܘ also presuppose a plural.

12. בהשדה] Cases in which the ה of the article remains unsyncopated after an inseparable preposition are cited by G-K. § 35 *n*. The occurrences are 'almost exclusively in the later Books.'

13. ויקחו וג׳] The text is seriously corrupted. The general resource is to regard the first אשר נשארו בה as a doublet of הנשארים, and to reject the second אשר נשארו בה down to ישראל as an error occasioned by repetition of the former. But even so the point of the remark, 'Lo, they are as all the multitude of Israel that are consumed,' is obscure. What we should expect is some statement such as that of the lepers in *v*. 4, viz. that, whatever may be the fate of the scouts, they will be no worse off than those who remain in the beleaguered city. Possibly therefore the text may have originally run:—שִׁלְחוּ אֲנָשִׁים וְיִקְחוּ חֲמִשָּׁה מִן־הַסּוּסִים הַנִּשְׁאָרִים אִם־יִחְיוּ הִנָּם כְּכָל־הֲמוֹן יִשְׂרָאֵל אֲשֶׁר נִשְׁאֲרוּ פֹה וְאִם־יֹאבְדוּ הִנָּם כְּכָל־הֲמוֹן יִשְׂרָאֵל אֲשֶׁר תָּמּוּ 'Send men, and let them take five of the horses which survive; if they live, lo, they are as all the multitude of Israel that survive here, and if they perish, lo, they are as all the multitude of Israel that are consumed.' The reading פֹּה for בָּהּ is suggested by LXX ὧδε, while the alternative ואם יאבדו וג׳ appears in Targ. ואם ייבדון הא אינון ככל המונא ישראל דספו; cf. Pesh. ܐܢ ܐܬܬܣܡܘ 'If they be taken, &c.'

14. רכב סוסים] LXX ἐπιβάτας ἵππων, Luc. ἀναβάτας ἵππων, i.e. רֹכְבֵי סוּסִים 'mounted men'; cf. *ch*. 9. 18. Scouts would naturally be sent out on horseback rather than in chariots.

15. בהחפזם] Kt. בְּהֵחָפְזָם is correct. The Niph'al is used elsewhere, 1 Sam. 23. 26; Ps. 48. 6; 104. 7.

16. כדבר י׳] Luc. adds ὃν ἐλάλησεν Ἐλισσαῖε.

17. כאשר דבר . . . אשר דבר] Scarcely original. Probably we have a combination of two different readings—כַּאֲשֶׁר דִּבֶּר simply, and כִּדְבַר . . . אֲשֶׁר דִּבֶּר. The former has the support of Vulg., Pesh., and is probably correct.

8. 1–6. *Elisha again assists the Shunammite woman.*

1. אֶל הָאִשָּׁה וג׳]‏ *Ch.* 4. 8–37.

וְגוּרִי בַּאֲשֶׁר תָּגוּרִי]‏ Dri. on Deut. 1. 46 calls the mode of expression 'the *idem per idem* idiom, often employed in the Semitic languages, when a writer is either unable or has no occasion to speak explicitly.' Cf. also Dri. on 1 Sam. 23. 13, where instances in Ar. are quoted from Lagarde, *Psalterium Hieronymi* (1874), 156 *f.;* Dri. *Tenses,* § 38 β *note.*

וְגַם בָּא וג׳]‏ 'And, moreover, it shall come &c.' בָּא is the participle, used as a *futurum instans.*

2. Luc. omits וַתָּקָם, and adds, after בָּאֶרֶץ פְלִשְׁתִּים, καθ᾽ ὡς εἶπεν αὐτῇ ὁ ἄνθρωπος τοῦ θεοῦ.

3. מֵאֶרֶץ פ׳]‏ LXX adds εἰς τὴν πόλιν.

5. אֵת הַמֵּת]‏ Luc. τὸν υἱὸν αὐτῆς τὸν τεθνηκότα, LXX υἱὸν τεθνηκότα, inferior to MT.

8. 7–15. *Elisha's interview with Ḥazael at Damascus.*

8. מָחֳלִי זֶה]‏ Cf. *ch.* 1. 2 *note.*

10. לֹא]‏ All Verss. agree with Q're לוֹ, which is certainly original. Cf. *v.* 14. Probably the alteration to the negative was due to a desire to remove from Elisha the imputation of falsehood.

וְהִרְאַנִי]‏ Perf. with ו simplex, co-ordinated with the preceding.

11. וַיַּעֲמֵד וג׳]‏ 'And he steadied his countenance, and set (it on him) till he was ashamed.' So RV. 'And he settled his countenance steadfastly (upon him), until he was ashamed.' The Hiph'il הֶעֱמִיד is here applied to a concentration of the gaze upon a single object to the exclusion of all extraneous distraction. After וַיָּשֶׂם we should expect אֵלָיו (cf. Ezek. 6. 2; 13. 17; *al.*) or עָלָיו (Ezek. 29. 2; 35. 2). The subject of עַד־בֹּשׁ is naturally Ḥazael. Elisha looked him out of countenance.

A variety of explanations of the passage have been suggested. LXX (vocalizing וַיַּעֲמֹד) καὶ παρέστη τῷ προσώπῳ αὐτοῦ, καὶ ἔθηκεν ἕως αἰσχύνης, expanded by Luc. καὶ ἔστη ʼΑζαὴλ κατὰ πρόσωπον αὐτοῦ, καὶ παρέθηκεν ἐνώπιον αὐτοῦ τὰ δῶρα ἕως ᾐσχύνετο. Vulg. *Stetitque cum eo, et conturbatus est* (i. e. וַיִּשֹּׁם) *usque ad suffusionem vultus.* Targ.

ואסחר ית אפוהי ואוריך עד סגי 'And he turned away his face and delayed a very long time.' Pesh. omits. Benz., Kit., reading וַיֵּשֶׁם or וַיָּשֹׁם (cf. Vulg.), explain, 'And he stared immoveably before him, and became horrified in the extreme,' understanding the first statement as referring to the setting in of the prophetic ecstasy, while the second depicts the effect produced upon the prophet by his vision. But the sense given to עד בש 'aufs äusserste' (*ch.* 2. 17; Judg. 3. 25) is improbable, since the naming of the subject in the following sentence ויבך איש האלהים seems to be intended to contrast with the implied different subject of בש (viz. Ḥazael), and is out of place if the subject of בש be the same as that of ויבך, וישם, ויעמד. Grä. emends וַיַּסְתֵּר for ויעמד (cf. Targ.) and וַיִּדֹּם for וישם, 'And he hid his face and was silent, &c.' Klo.'s explanation is strangely impossible.

13. כי] Cf. I. 1. 13 *note*.

מה עבדך וג׳] 'What is thy servant, the dog, that he should do this great thing?' LXX, Luc. ὁ κύων ὁ τεθνηκώς, as in 2 Sam. 9. 8; cf. 1 Sam. 24. 15; 2 Sam. 16. 9. So Klo., Oort, Winckler.

15. המכבר], RV. 'coverlet.' Cf. כְּבִיר הָעִזִּים 1 Sam. 19. 13, 16, spread by Michal over the head of Teraphim in David's bed. The word is a ἅπαξ λεγ., and seems to denote something of *intertwined* or *woven* workmanship. כְּבָרָה Am. 9. 9 = 'sieve.'

וימלך חזהאל] Shalmaneser II mentions two campaigns against '*Ḫa-za-'-ilu* of Damascus'; in the eighteenth year of his reign (B.C. 842; cf. *Append.* 4), and again in the twenty-first year (B.C. 839).

8. 16–24. *Jehoram, king of Judah.*

Ch. 8. 17–23 = 2 Chr. 21. 5–10ᵃ. Rᴰ *vv.* 16–19, 23.

16ᵃ. ויהושפט מלך יהודה] Rightly omitted by LXX, Pesh. The words have come in through error from the latter half of the verse.

17. שמנה שנה] Q're corrects to שנים, in accordance with the almost invariable rule that numerals from 2 to 10 take the object numbered in the pl. Other exceptions, cited by G-K. § 134 *e*, are *ch.* 22. 1 (שְׁמֹנֶה שָׁנָה uncorrected); 25. 17 (Q're pl.); Ex. 16. 22; Ezek. 45. 1. LXX τεσσαράκοντα ἔτη.

19. ולא אבה י׳ להשחית] So (without prep. ל) *ch.* 13. 23; Deut. 10. 10.

ניר] Cf. I. 11. 36 *note*.

לבניו] But the lamp was not given *for* the sons, since the sons are themselves the lamp. || 2 Chr. 21. 7, Luc., Vulg., Targ., feeling the difficulty, read וּלְבָנָיו; but this does not really effect any improvement. LXX omits. No doubt Klo., Kamp., Benz., Kit., Oort are right in emending לְפָנָיו; 'to give him a lamp *before Him* all the days.' Cf. I. 11. 36 לְפָנַי בִּירוּשָׁלַםִ.

20. בימיו] Cf. I. 16. 34 *note*.

21. צעירה] The place is unknown. Ew. would read צֹעֲרָה 'to Zoʿar,' but against this it is to be noticed with Buhl (*Edomiter*, p. 64 *f.*) that LXX, Luc. in our passage transliterate Σειώρ, Σιώρ, while צֹעַר is always represented by Σηγώρ, Σιγώρ; the inference being that ע in צָעִיר = ع, while in צֹעַר it = غ. Th. suggests שְׂעִירָה 'to Seʿir.' || 2 Chr. עִם־שָׂרָיו.

21^b. The half-verse seems to be seriously corrupt.

(1) The constr. ויהי הוא קם וג׳ is inexplicable. Accents connect ויהי closely with הוא קם (cf. || 2 Chr. 21. 9 ויהי קם); but the idea of *duration* usually conveyed by the constr. of participle with substantive verb (Dri. *Tenses*, § 135. 5) is out of harmony with the sense of the passage. The alternative, adopted by LXX, Luc., Pesh., Targ., is to make a break after ויהי, and to treat הוא קם לילה as a circumstantial clause, קם being a perfect. Upon this view, however, the analogy of the cases cited by Dri. *Tenses*, § 165, demands a change of subject in the (presumed) principal sentence which follows:—'And it came to pass, whilst he arose by night [some one else acted in such a way].'

(2) As the text stands, the statement is made that Joram, the subject of ויכה, smote את שרי הרכב. These, however, as is clear from *v.* 21^a, belonged to his own forces. The least correction, therefore, that can be made is to follow Kit. in reading וְאִתּוֹ שָׂרֵי הָרֶכֶב 'And the captains of the chariots were with him.'

(3) Verse 22 makes it plain that Joram's attempt to re-subjugate Edom was futile. What we therefore desiderate in *v.* 21^b is probably an account of the falling of Joram and his army into

an ambush laid by the Edomites, from which escape was only made by cutting a way through the surrounding enemy and beating a hurried retreat. As to the precise wording of such a narrative the passage in its present state affords no sufficient clue.

22. עד היום הזה] Cf. I. 8. 8 *note*.

אז] Cf. I. 3. 16 *note*.

לבנה] Cf. *ch.* 19. 8, from which it appears that the city was of strategical importance, probably lying south-west of Judah upon the way to Egypt. Eusebius places Libna among the cities in the neighbourhood of Eleutheropolis. Cf. Buhl, p. 193.

בעת ההיא] Cf. I. 14. 1 *note*.

8. 25–29. *Aḥaziah, king of Judah.*

Ch. 8. 26–29 forms the basis of 2 Chr. 22. 2–6. R[D] *vv.* 25–27.

25. שתים עשרה] *Ch.* 9. 29 אחת עשרה. So in the present passage, Luc., Pesh.

26. עשרים ושתים] ‖ 2 Chr. ארבעים ושתים.

בת עמרי] Luc. corrects θυγάτηρ Ἀχαάβ, in accordance with *v.* 18. בת, however, probably has here the more general sense of '*descendant*.' Cf. I. 15. 2.

27. כי חתן וג׳] LXX omits. ‖ 2 Chr. כִּי אִמּוֹ הָיְתָה יוֹעַצְתּוֹ לְהַרְשִׁיעַ.

28. ברמת גלעד] Cf. II. 22. 3 *note*.

ארמים] We should naturally expect הָאֲרַמִּים. ‖ 2 Chr. has the strange הָרַמִּים, which LXX, Luc. represent by οἱ τοξόται, i. e. הַמּוֹרִים '*the archers*'; cf. 1 Sam. 31. 3; 2 Sam. 11. 24. This reading is very probably original. So Klo.

29. יכהו] The use of the imperf. seems to be inexplicable; cf. Ew. § 346[c], *note* 2; Dri. *Tenses*, § 27 γ. ‖ 2 Chr. הִכֻּהוּ.

ארמים] LXX and ‖ 2 Chr. omit.

9. 1—10. 28. *Jehu, an officer of the host of Israel, is anointed king at the command of Elisha. He destroys the whole house of Aḥab, and extirpates Ba'al-worship from Israel.*

9. 2. יהוא] *Ja-u-a apal Ḫu-um-ri-i*, i. e. 'Jehu son of Omri' (cf. I. 16. 23 *note*), is twice mentioned in the cuneiform inscriptions of Shalmaneser II, as bringing tribute to the Assyrian king. The first inscription is found upon the obelisk, above a representation of the embassy presenting the tribute before Shalmaneser. In the second inscription (*Annals*, III, Rawlinson 5, no. 6, 40–65), after an account of the conquest of Ḥazael of Damascus, Shalmaneser states that 'at that time I received the tribute of the Tyrians, Sidonians, of Jehu son of Omri.' Cf. *Append.* 4. It may be inferred, therefore, that the aid of Assyria had been solicited by Jehu to meet the encroachments of Ḥazael, to which brief reference is made in *ch.* 10. 32, 33, just as in later times it was solicited by Aḥaz of Judah against the alliance of Israel and Aram; *ch.* 16. 6 *ff.*; cf. Isa. 7. 1–9.

חדר בחדר] Cf. I. 20. 30 *note.*

3. אל ישראל] A large number of Codd. read על for אל, both here and in *v.* 12. Other examples of the confusion between אל and על are noticed on I. 13. 29 *note.*

4. הנער הנביא] הנער *st. constr.* with the article, through erroneous approximation to the preceding הנער. Cf. Kö. *Syntax*, § 303 *c.*

6–10. The hand of R^D is very apparent in *vv.* 8, 9. Cf. *notes* on I. 14. 1–18.

7. והכיתה] LXX, Luc. καὶ ἐξολοθρεύσεις, i. e. probably וְהִכְרַתָּה [1]; cf. 2 Chr. 22. 7. So Klo., Kamp., Kit., Benz.

After אדניך LXX adds ἐκ προσώπου σου, Luc. ἐκ προσώπου μου.

ונקמתי] LXX, Luc. read 2nd pers. 'and thou shalt avenge,' making the same change in *v.* 8 והכרתי. MT. is preferable.

8. ואבד] Vulg., Pesh., Targ. presuppose וְאִבַּדְתִּי 'and I will destroy.' LXX, Luc. καὶ ἐκ χειρός, i. e. וּמִיַּד, accepted by Klo., Oort.

10. בחלק יזרעאל] Cf. I. 21. 23 *note.*

11. ויאמר] All Verss. presuppose וַיֹּאמְרוּ, correctly.

השלום] Luc. adds καὶ εἶπεν αὐτοῖς Εἰρήνη. καὶ εἶπον αὐτῷ—an unnecessary redundancy.

המשגע] Cf. Hos. 9. 7; Jer. 29. 26.

שיחו] 'His conversation.' Cf. Ps. 104. 34, and the use of the verb Job 12. 8; *al.*

---

[1] Ἐξολεθρεύειν occurs only once as a rendering of הִכָּה, viz. Josh. 11. 14, whereas it is constantly employed (as in *v.* 8) to represent הִכְרִית.

12. אל ישראל] Luc. ἐπὶ τὸν λαόν μου 'Ισραήλ. Cf. *v.* 6.

13. אל גרם המעלות] The meaning is very uncertain. Ges., Ew., Ke., upon the analogy of the use of עֶצֶם, suppose that the expression may mean 'upon the steps *themselves*,' i. e. 'upon the *bare* steps.' Grä. emends עַל־מְרוֹם המ׳ 'upon the elevation of the steps.'

14[b]. ויורם] Very probably Grä. is correct in substituting יֵהוּא for יוֹרָם:—'Now Jehu was keeping Ramoth Gilead . . . but Jehoram had returned to be healed &c.'

15. אם יש נפשכם] 'If it be your mind,' i. e. If ye are desirous of making me king. LXX, Luc. add μετ' ἐμοῦ, but this is unnecessary. Many Codd. read את נפשכם, as in Gen. 23. 8.

לגיד] Kt. לַגִּיד, with ה syncopated after the preposition ל. Cf. G-K. § 53 *q*.

16. שכב שמה] In place of these words LXX, Luc. present a second rendering of *v.* 15[a]—clearly a marginal gloss which has usurped the place of the true reading. Notice ἐθεραπεύετο for ἀπέστρεψεν . . . ἰατρευθῆναι—ἀπὸ τῶν τοξευμάτων ὧν κατετόξευσαν αὐτόν for ἀπὸ τῶν πληγῶν ὧν ἔπαισαν αὐτόν—οἱ 'Αραμιείν for οἱ Σύροι. LXX rounds off the gloss with ὅτι δυνατὸς καὶ ἀνὴρ δυνάμεως.

ואחזיה וג׳] On the order of sentence expressing the pluperfect cf. *note* on I. 14. 5.

17. שפעת אני ראה] שפעת is either a mistake for שפעה owing to the previous occurrence of the *st. constr.*, or else, as Klo., Kamp., Benz., Kit., Oort suggest, a genitive, *sc.* אֲנָשִׁים, has fallen out. שפעה probably denotes a *company* or *multitude*, agreeably to the use of the word in Isa. 60. 6; Ezek. 26. 10[1]. So Luc. ὄχλον, Vulg. *globum*, and most moderns. LXX, however, renders κονιορτόν[2], and so Kit.

18. השלום] Cf. *ch.* 5. 21 *note*.

מה לך וג׳] 'What hast thou (as an emissary of Aḥab's son)

---

[1] The root שפע in Aram. means *to overflow*, and accordingly the subs. שפעה is used in Heb. of *overflowing* or *abundance* of water, Job 22. 11; 38. 34; שֶׁפַע Deut. 33. 19.

[2] Luc. in the first occurrence has a doublet τὸν κονιορτὸν τοῦ ὄχλου. The original reading must obviously have been τὸν ὄχλον.

to do with peace?'—the implication (cf. *v.* 22) being 'How can peace exist so long as the house of Aḥab exists?' Cf. the phrase מה לי ולך I. 17. 18 *note*.

עַד־הֵם] We ought probably to read עָדֵיהֶם. Cf. Job 32. 12 עָדֵיכֶם.

20. עד אליהם] Cf. the phrase עַד לְ I. 18. 29 *note*.

בשגעון] 'Madly,' or, as RV., 'furiously.' So 'A. ἐν παραπληξίᾳ, Σ. ἀτάκτως, Vulg. *praeceps*, Pesh. ܡܫܬܓܢܐܝܬ, and probably LXX, Luc. ἐν παραλλαγῇ[1]. In contrast, Targ. renders בניח 'quietly,' and this interpretation is adopted by Jos. (*Ant.* ix. 6, § 3):—σχολαίτερον δὲ καὶ μετ' εὐταξίας ὥδευεν 'Ιηοῦς.

ינהג] Probably describing Jehu's habit:—'he is wont to drive.' In description of a (single) present event we should of course expect הוּא נֹהֵג.

22. מה השלום] For the sense 'What peace?' (RV.) we should expect מַה־שָּׁלוֹם, and this is adopted by Klo., Kit., who suppose that the ה before שלום has come in by dittography. Benz., following Targ., vocalizes מָה הַשָּׁלוֹם, explaining 'Jehu answers: Between us there can be no "How do you fare?" so long as &c.' But the sense assigned to הַשָּׁלוֹם is not that which it possesses in this connexion. Cf. *note* on *ch.* 5. 21.

עד זנוני וג'] The sense of עד is 'at' or '*during*.' Cf. Judg. 3. 26 עַד הִתְמַהְמְהָם '*During* their delay'; Jon. 4. 2 עַד־הֱיוֹתִי עַל־אַדְמָתִי 'Whilst I was (*during* my being) in my country.' Grä.'s emendation עִם for עַד is unnecessary. LXX ἔτι, i.e. עֹד (so Klo.), is greatly inferior to MT.

23. ויהפך י' ידיו] Cf. I. 22. 34.

24. מלא ידו בקשת] '*Armed* (lit. *filled*) his hand with the bow.' Cf. 2 Sam. 23. 7 יִמָּלֵא בַרְזֶל וְעֵץ חֲנִית 'arms himself with iron and a spear's shaft'—'lit. *fills himself*, viz. in so far as the hand using the weapon is concerned' (Dri. *ad loc.*)[2].

---

[1] The subs. occurs again in 'A.'s rendering of Job 4. 13ᵃ ἐν παραλλαγαῖς ἀπὸ ὁραματισμῶν νυκτός, i.e. probably 'In trances of visions of the night.' Cf. Σ. ἐν ἐκπλήξει ἀπὸ ὁραμάτων νυκτερινῶν.

[2] It should, however, be remembered that the context of this passage is very dubious, and that יִמָּלֵא disappears under Budde's emendation.

החצי] So in 1 Sam. 20. 36, 37 (twice), and 38 Kt. for the usual הַחֵץ.

25. שלשה] Cf. I. 9. 22 *note*.

כי זכר וג׳] LXX, Luc., Vulg., Pesh. presuppose כִּי זֹכֵר אֲנִי כִּי אֲנִי וג׳ 'For I remember that I and thou &c.' This is probably correct, MT. being due to homoioteleuton.

את רכבים צמדים] The impossible את must be rejected as dittography of the preceding אתה. The use of the pl. צְמָדִים 'pairs' is inexplicable. Ges.-Buhl, making a new division of the letters צמדמאחרי, reads צֶמֶד מֵאַחֲרֵי, and Kit., while rightly rejecting מֵאַחֲרֵי, favours the sing. צֶמֶד 'as a pair,' i. e. 'together,' and thinks that the pl. may have arisen through assimilation to the preceding pl. רכבים. Possibly צמדים ought to be vocalized as a passive participle צְמֻדִים (נִצְמָדִים) 'joined,' i. e. 'in company.'

26. אם לא וג׳] Cf. I. 20. 23 *note*.

27. גם אתו הכהו] It is necessary to follow Pesh. and add וַיַּכֻּהוּ, which has fallen out through similarity to the preceding word. So most moderns. Vulg. makes the insertion *after* אל המרכבה, and LXX, Luc. supply it *in place of* הכהו.

יבלעם] A city of Manasseh west of Jordan, Josh. 17. 11; Judg. 1. 27, called בִּלְעָם in 1 Chr. 6. 55; the modern *Bel'ame*, six hours north of *Nâblus*. Baed. 262; Buhl, 102, 201 *f.*

28. עם אבתיו] LXX, Luc. omit.

29. ובשנת וג׳] A redactional notice. Cf. *ch.* 8. 25 *note*. Luc. adds καὶ ἐνιαυτὸν ἕνα ἐβασίλευσεν ἐν Ἰερουσαλήμ after 8. 26.

30. ותשם וג׳] 'And set her eyes in *stibium*.' פּוּךְ is the *kohl* of the Arabs (cf. the verb כחל Ezek. 23. 40), i. e. sulphide of antimony reduced to a black powder which is mixed with oil and used for painting the eye-lashes and brows, in order to make the eyes appear large and dark. Cf. Jer. 4. 30 כִּי־תִקְרְעִי בַפּוּךְ עֵינַיִךְ 'though thou enlargest thine eyes with *stibium*.' Benz. *Archäologie*, 110.

31. השלום זמרי וג׳] RV. rightly, 'Is it peace, thou Zimri, thy master's murderer?' It is idiomatic in Heb. to change to the 3rd pers. after an opening vocative. Cf. cases cited by Dri. *Tenses*, § 198, *Obs.* 2, and add Isa. 51. 7 and Job 18. 4 (with inverted order).

הֲשָׁלוֹם, as Th. rightly emphasizes, must have the same sense as in *vv.* 17, 18, 19, 22. Jezebel reminds Jehu of the speedy fate of Zimri (I. 16. 9–18), and gives him the opportunity of making peace with *her*, the hitherto all-powerful mistress of the kingdom. To give to הֲשָׁלוֹם the meaning 'How fare you?' deprives the queen of her policy.

32. מי אתי מי] 'Who is *with me*, who?' i.e. *on my side*. For this use of את cf. *ch*. 6. 16; Isa. 43. 5; 63. 3; Jer. 1. 19; Ps. 12. 5. The reading of LXX, Luc. Τίς εἶ σύ; κατάβηθι μετ' ἐμοῦ (Luc. πρός μέ) probably has its origin in a double rendering of אתי, vocalized in the first place as אַתְּי, while κατάβηθι may answer to the second מי read as רְדִי. Klo. makes κατάβηθι the equivalent of תֵּרְדִי, a corrupt reading of תָּרִבִי, and so emends מִי אַתְּ תָּרִבִי עִמִּי 'Who art thou, that thou wouldest contend with me?'—a reading in no way comparable to MT.

שנים שלשה] 'Two *or* three.' Cf. Isa. 17. 6 . . . שְׁנַיִם שְׁלֹשָׁה גַּרְגְּרִים אַרְבָּעָה חֲמִשָּׁה 'Two *or* three berries . . . four *or* five.' LXX, Luc. omit שלשה.

33. וירמסנה] Verss. וַיִּרְמְסוּהָ, rightly making the horses the subject.

36. עבדו] LXX omits.

37. הָיְתָ] Kt. should probably be vocalized הָיָת, the older form of the 3rd fem. sing. perf. of verbs ל״ה which occurs in a few other cases:—עָשָׂת Lev. 25. 21; הִרְצָת Lev. 26. 34; הֶלְאָת Ezek. 24. 12; הָגְלָת Jer. 13. 19.

אשר לא יאמרו וג׳] Vulg., by omission of the negative, *ita ut praetereuntes dicant: Haeccine est illa Iezabel?* Luc. adds καὶ οὐκ ἔσται ὁ λέγων Οἴμοι.

10. 1. ולאחאב] According to the contents of Jehu's letter, *vv.* 2, 3, the seventy princes are sons of Jehoram rather than of Aḥab. Cf. the phrases בְּנֵי אֲדֹנֵיכֶם and עַל־כִּסֵּא אָבִיו. Thus Sta. (*ZATW.*, 1885, pp. 279 *f.*) regards *v.* 1ª as a later and erroneous gloss. It is not, however, unreasonable to suppose that בָּנִים is here used not in the strictly literal sense, but of *descendants* of Aḥab in any degree (cf. בֵּית אֲדֹנֵיכֶם *v.* 3), any one of whom might have been set up to resist the usurper. Cf. *note* following on the use of the number *seventy*. Jehu's commission (*ch.* 9. 7) is explicitly not against Jehoram but against *the house of Aḥab*, and to describe the members of this house no other term could have been chosen by the writer than בְּנֵי אַחְאָב.

שבעים בנים] It is remarkable that *seventy* is the number of the sons of Gideon-Jerubba'al, Judg. 8. 30 *ff.*, and of the relations of Bar-Çûr of Ya'di (Panammu inscription, *l.* 3: D. H. Müller, *Die altsemit. Inschr. von Sendschirli*), who, in each case as here, are massacred to secure succession to the throne. Possibly, therefore, as Müller (*op. cit.*, p. 9) suggests, seventy is a round number to denote the whole of the royal kin[1].

אל שרי יזרעאל הזקנים] Luc. πρὸς τοὺς στρατηγοὺς τῆς πόλεως καὶ πρὸς τοὺς πρεσβυτέρους[2], Vulg. *ad optimates civitatis, et ad maiores natu*, i. e. אֶל־שָׂרֵי הָעִיר וְאֶל־הַזְּקֵנִים—certainly correct: cf. *v.* 5 MT. יזרעאל of MT. has arisen from a mistaken combination of the letters העירואל. Jehu was himself at Jezreel, and would scarcely have sent a letter to the authorities of that city with regard to the royal princes who were in Samaria. So Klo., Kamp., Benz., Kit.

ואל האמנים אחאב] Luc. καὶ πρὸς τοὺς τιθηνοὺς τῶν υἱῶν Ἀχαάβ, i. e. וְאֶל־הָאֹמְנִים אֶת־בְּנֵי אַחְאָב, probably correct. So Klo., Kamp., Benz., Kit.

2. ועתה] Cf. *ch.* 5. 6 *note*.

עיר מבצר] LXX, Luc., Vulg., Pesh., Targ. עָרֵי מִבְצָר. So Jos., and Th., Klo., Kamp., Benz., Kit.

5. אשר על הבית] Cf. I. 4. 6 *note*.

עשה] LXX, Luc. ποιήσομεν.

6. שנית] Several Codd., and LXX, Luc. שֵׁנִי—'a *second* letter.'

אנשי בני אדניכם] As the text stands, the first *st. constr.* is in apposition to the second (suspended construct state)—'The men, the sons of your master.' Cf. Da. § 28, *Rem.* 6. Possibly אנשי is

---

[1] In Judg. 12. 13 *f.* the *descendants* of Abdon are seventy; forty sons and thirty grandsons, riding upon seventy asses.

[2] LXX agrees with Luc., except in the substitution of Σαμαρείας for τῆς πόλεως, an alteration made for the sake of precision.

merely a doublet of ראשי. Kamp., Oort omit the word. Sta. emends אַנְשֵׁי בֵית א׳. Luc. λαβέτο ἕκαστος τὴν κεφαλὴν τοῦ υἱοῦ τοῦ κυρίου αὐτοῦ, i. e. probably קְחוּ אִישׁ אֶת־רֹאשׁ בֶּן־אֲדֹנֵיכֶם; adopted by Benz., Kit. as far as regards the use of איש.

ובאו] LXX, Luc., Pesh. וְהָבִאוּ 'and bring (them).' So Th., Sta., Klo.

7. וישחטו] LXX, Luc., Pesh. וַיִּשְׁחָטוּם, correctly:—'slew them, even seventy men.'

בַּדּוּדִים] 'In baskets': so all Verss. On the use of the article cf. I. 1. 1 *note* on בַּבְּגָדִים.

8. המלאך] '*The* messenger.' Cf. I. 13. 14 *note*.

הביאו] LXX Ἤνεγκα—probably an easy alteration of MT.

9. ומי הכה וג׳] It is assumed that the populace know who were the perpetrators of the massacre, but not the fact that Jehu was the instigator of it. The inference is therefore clear to fair-minded men (צַדִּקִים אַתֶּם) that this is no case of the unscrupulous securing of his own interests by a single individual, but that circumstances are working together to bring about the destruction of the house of Aḥab (*v.* 10).

11. וכל גדליו] Luc. καὶ πάντας τοὺς ἀγχιστεύοντας αὐτοῦ, i. e. וְכָל־גֹּאֲלָיו 'even all *his kinsmen*':—probably correct; cf. I. 16. 11 *note*. So Klo.

הִשְׁאִיר] Cf. *ch.* 3. 25, *note* 2.

12. ויקם וג׳] By the side of וילך, ויבא is redundant; at least we should expect it to *follow* וילך and immediately precede שמרון, as in Pesh. LXX, Luc., Vulg. omit ויבא, probably correctly. Perhaps the word is a corruption of יֵהוּא. So Klo., Benz., Kit.

בית עקד] The rendering of RV. 'shearing house,' marg. 'house of gathering' (Targ. בית כנישת), is merely conjectural. The verb עקד, Gen. 22. 9†, means, as in New Heb., Ar., and Aram., *to bind*.

13. ויהוא] Read וְהוּא, with Dri. *Tenses*, § 169, *Obs.* 2. The events described by *v.* 12[b] and *v.* 13[a] are thus pointedly synchronized in accordance with the idiom of the language:—'He was at Beth-'eqed of the shepherds by the way, when he found &c.' Cf. 1 Sam. 9. 11; Judg. 18. 3; Gen. 38. 25. It is noticeable that

Luc., Vulg. omit the proper name, and may thus be regarded as supporting the emendation[1].

לשלום] The expression which ordinarily has the meaning 'to enquire after' is לִשְׁאֹל לְשָׁלוֹם פ׳; 2 Sam. 11. 7; 1 Sam. 10. 4; 17. 22; *al.* If this phrase in full was originally written in our passage, the omission of לשאל is earlier than the Verss., all of which agree with MT.

14. ויתפשום חיים] LXX omits; Luc., Pesh. apparently read ויתפשום simply.

אל בור בית עקד] LXX, Luc. omit בור.

15. לקראתו] Luc. *ἐν τῇ ὁδῷ ἐρχόμενον εἰς ἀπάντησιν αὐτοῦ.* בַּדֶּרֶךְ (if not a doublet of בֶּן־רֵכָב) may be original: *ἐρχόμενον*, like ܟܕ ܐܬܐ of Pesh., is due to the translator.

היש וג׳] Doubtless we ought to follow LXX, Luc. in reading הֲיֵשׁ לְבָבְךָ אֶת־לְבָבִי יָשָׁר, thus securing a perfect parallelism with the following clause. So Th., Klo., Benz., Oort. Kamp., Kit. adopt the less probable order הֲיֵשׁ לְבָבְךָ יָשָׁר אֶת־לְבָבִי.

ויש] '"If it be" (said he).' The writer regards it as sufficiently evident that וָיֵשׁ וג׳ is the *response* to the preceding יֵשׁ. Cf. I. 20. 34. Probably the additions of LXX, Luc. *καὶ εἶπεν* Εἰού, Luc. *καὶ εἶπεν αὐτῷ* 'Ιού, Vulg. *inquit*, Pesh. ܘܐܡܪ ܠܗ (*after* ויש, which is assigned to Jonadab as though יש ויש meant 'It is indeed!') are due in each case to the translator.

With וָיֵשׁ cf. וָלֹא *ch.* 5. 17 *note.*

16. וירכבו אתו] Read וַיַּרְכִּבֵ אֹתוֹ with LXX, Luc., Pesh. So Th., Oort. וַיַּרְכִּבֵ אֹתוֹ Klo., Kamp., Benz.; וַיַּרְכִּבוּ אֹתוֹ Kit.

17.* עַד־הִשְׁמִדוֹ] Cf. *note* 2 on 3. 25.

18. יהוא יעבדנו] Luc. *καὶ ἐγὼ δουλεύσω αὐτῷ*, Vulg. *ego autem colam eum*;—inferior to MT.

19. כל עבדיו] Klo., Kamp., Benz., Kit. cut out the two words as an erroneous insertion from *v.* 21. Jehu summons the *prophets*

[1] It is certain that Vulg., reading וְהוּא מָצָא, would have left the pronoun unexpressed, and rendered, as is actually the case, *invenit*. Cf. in Vulg. the other cases of the idiom cited. That the same course may have been followed in the Greek may be inferred from the rendering of Gen. 38. 25.

and *priests* of Baʿal, who are commanded to proclaim a solemn assembly, to which the *worshippers in general* are summoned (*v.* 20 *f.*). It is noticeable that in Luc. καὶ πάντας τοὺς δούλους αὐτοῦ *follows* καὶ τοὺς ἱερεῖς αὐτοῦ, as though inserted from the margin.

20. ויקראו] LXX, Luc., Vulg. sing. וַיִּקְרָא.

21. LXX erroneously expands the verse from *v.* 19.

פה לפה] *Ch.* 21. 16†.

22. המלתחה] The context demands the meaning 'wardrobe'; cf. Vulg. *vestes.* In Eth. አልታኅ: *'eltāḫ* denotes a kind of *tunic;* cf. Dillmann, *Lexicon,* 45 *f.*

המלבוש] LXX, Luc. ὁ στολιστής, i. e. הַמַּלְבִּישׁ.

23. מעבדי י׳] Luc. adds καὶ ἐξαποστείλατε αὐτούς. καὶ εἶπον Οὐκ εἰσὶν κ.τ.λ.; adopted by Klo.

24. ויבאו] LXX sing. καὶ εἰσῆλθεν. Cf. the sing. reference to Jehu as the chief offerer in *v.* 25 כְּכַלֹּתוֹ. So Klo., Sta., Kamp., Benz., Kit. Luc. places 24^a after 24^b, and adds, after εἰσῆλθον, the gloss εἰς τὸν οἶκον τοῦ προσοχθίσματος. Elsewhere in the context בעל = Βάαλ, never προσόχθισμα.

שמנים] Luc. τρισχιλίους, Pesh. ܬܠܬܡܐܐ ܘܬܡܢܝܢ, 380.

האיש וג׳] As יִמָּלֵט is vocalized, the sentence is extremely difficult. Read יְמַלֵּט with Th., Klo., Kamp., Benz., Kit.:—'The man *who suffers to escape* any of the men, &c., his life shall be for his life.'

על ידיכם] 'Into (lit. *upon*) your hands.' So, after נתן, Gen. 42. 37; after הִגִּיר, Jer. 18. 21; Ezek. 35. 5; Ps. 63. 11.

25. ככלתו] Pesh. ܟܕ ܫܠܡܘ, i. e. כְּכַלֹּתָם.

לרצים] Cf. I. 1. 5 *note.*

ולשלשים] Cf. I. 9. 22 *note.*

וישלכו] The object is missing. RV., 'cast them out,' finds the reference to be to the corpses of the slain; but it is reasonable to expect this to be more precisely indicated. Klo. is right in finding the object of וישלכו to lie concealed under הרצים והשלשים, the repetition in detail of the subject of the verb in MT. being scarcely less strange than the omission of the object. He ingeniously suggests וַיַּשְׁלִכוּ אַרְצָה הָאֲשֵׁרִים 'and they cast the Asherim down to the ground.' This restoration, however, is not very likely to represent the original if the emendation adopted in *v.* 26 be correct, which thus makes reference to the (single) Ashera of the temple.

עד עיר וג׳] 'To the *city* of the house of Ba'al' can hardly be correct. Klo.'s emendation עַד־דְּבִיר וג׳ 'to the *adytum*, &c.' (cf. I. 6. 16 *note*), is very suitable to the context, though it is illegitimate to cite the rendering of Luc. ἕως τοῦ ναοῦ τοῦ Βάαλ in support of the emendation[1]. The other Verss. agree with MT.

26. מצבות] The Verss. presuppose a sing. מַצֵּבַת, in accordance with the suffix of וישרפוה. But, as Sta. (*ZATW.*, 1885, p. 278) remarks, the *stone* Maççēba cannot have been burnt, and it is therefore probable that we ought to substitute אֲשֵׁרַת 'the Ashera of the house of Ba'al,' in accordance with I. 16. 33, וַיַּעַשׂ אַחְאָב אֶת־הָאֲשֵׁרָה: cf. *ch.* 23. 6. So Kamp., Benz., Kit., Oort. On the character of the Ashera cf. I. 14. 15 *note.*

27. מצבת] Sta., Kamp., Benz., Kit. emend מִזְבַּח, the first comparing I. 16. 32, and, for the expression נתץ מזבח, Ex. 34. 13; Deut. 7. 5; 12. 3; Judg. 2. 2; 6. 28 *ff.* Mention of the destruction of the *altar* is to be expected, supposing the clause to be not merely a doublet of that which follows (Klo.), which it resembles somewhat suspiciously.

למחראות] Kt. לְמַחֲרָאוֹת.

10. 29–36. *Summary of Jehu's reign: his character and his foreign relations.*

R^D *vv.* 28–31, 34–36; *vv.* 32, 33 summarized from the Annals.

29. עגלי הזהב] '(Namely) the golden calves,' in apposition to חטאי י׳. Vulg., with a view to make the connexion more clear, inserts *nec dereliquit*, Targ. אישתעבד ל.

32. בימים ההם] The same phrase is used by R^D in *ch.* 15. 37; 20. 1. Cf. *note* on I. 3. 16.

---

[1] דְּבִיר in I. 6. 5, 16, 19, 21, 23, 31; 7. 49; 8. 8 appears as δαβείρ; and, assuming that τοῦ ναοῦ could answer to דביר, as in Ps. 28 (LXX 27). 2, בית remains unrepresented, and דְּבִיר הַבַּעַל simply is scarcely likely to have been read by the translator.

לקצות בישראל] 'To cut Israel short,' lit. 'to cut off in Israel.' The expression is strange, though Hab. 2. 10 קְצוֹת עַמִּים רַבִּים affords an instance of the use of the verb קצה in this sense. The original reading is probably preserved by Vulg. *taedere super Israel*, i.e. לָקוּץ בְּיִשְׂרָאֵל 'to loathe Israel'; cf. Gen. 27. 46 קַצְתִּי בְחַיַּי, *Taedet me vitae meae*. So Klo. Targ. למתקף רוגזיה seems to have read לִקְצוֹף 'to be angry with,' and this is adopted by Th., Kamp., Benz., Kit.

33. מן הירדן וג׳] The double mention of הגלעד introduces confusion, and Grä., Buhl. (*Geogr.* 70) simplify the description by cutting out the first הגלעד, and also the ו before the second. The fact that, at the time of the fall of Omri's dynasty, Rama of Gilead appears to have been the most northern point of Israel's dominions east of Jordan causes some critics (cf. Sta. *ZATW.*, 1885, p. 279; Benz., Kit.) to regard the verse, either as a whole or in part, as a later addition.

33[b]. מערער וג׳] The same description of the position of עֲרֹעֵר, with the addition of שְׂפַת before נַחַל, is found in Deut. 2. 36; 3. 12; 4. 48; Josh. 12. 2; 13. 9, 16. The site of ʿAroʿer is found in a heap of ruins called *ʿArʿâîr*, south of *Dîbân*, and standing on a hill on the northern side of the ravine of Arnon. Buhl, 269.

והגלעד] Luc. adds καὶ Ἰαβόκ.

34. וכל גבורתו] LXX, Luc. add καὶ τὰς (Luc. αἱ) συνάψεις ἃς συνῆψεν, i.e. וְקִשְׁרוֹ אֲשֶׁר קָשַׁר. Cf. I. 16. 20; *ch.* 15. 15.

36. At the end of the verse Luc. adds ἐν ἔτει δευτέρῳ τῆς Γοθολίας βασιλεύει κύριος τὸν Ἰοὺ υἱὸν Ναμεσί, and then continues with a summary account of Aḥaziah's reign, derived in the main from *ch.* 8. 25 *ff.*, with a brief mention of the events of *ch.* 9 in so far as they concern the death of Aḥaziah.

11. *Athaliah the queen-mother usurps the throne of Judah. At the end of six years Jehoiada the priest effects a revolution, and sets Jehoash, the rightful heir, upon the throne.*

Ch. 11 forms the basis of 2 Chr. 22. 10—23. 21.

This chapter and its sequel, *ch.* 12. 5–17, form, with *chh.* 16.

10–16; 22. 3—23. 25, a series of Judaean narratives which reflect prominently the influence of the priests as conservators of the religion of Yahwe, and in which the interest centres to a great extent round the Temple at Jerusalem. Probably therefore, as Sta. suggests, the source from which the narratives were drawn may have been the Temple-archives.

Sta. (*ZATW.*, 1885, pp. 280 *ff.*) has pointed out that *ch.* 11 is probably a combination of two narratives. The first, *vv.* 4–12, 18^{b}–20, is a continuous whole; the second, *vv.* 13–18^{a}, merely a fragment. According to the first, Jehoiada effects the revolution by the aid of the royal bodyguard (הָרָצִים); in the second, it is the people (הָעָם) who are prominent. The insertion of הָרָצִין in *v.* 13 in apposition to הָעָם is clearly a redactional device, and traces of the redactor's hand are also to be found in *v.* 15 (see *ad loc.*).

The recognition of this composite character of the narrative explains certain difficulties which are patent if it be read as a continuous whole. Thus, it cannot be thought that the destruction of the temple of Ba'al (*v.* 18^{a}) took place between the anointing and enthronement of Jehoash. It would naturally occur *after* the measures taken against Athaliah, and not as an episode in their course. Again, it is difficult to understand why the setting of a guard over the Temple (*v.* 18^{b}) should have been necessary *after* the death of Athaliah (*vv.* 15, 16). The purpose of such a guard can only have been to protect the Temple against the danger of an attack by the queen and her adherents. It is strange, also, if the narrative be a whole, that there should be two accounts of the death of Athaliah; *vv.* 15, 16 and *v.* 20^{b}.

The main difference between the two narratives seems to be that while the fragment emphasizes the *religious* importance of the revolution, the continuous narrative regards it purely as an event of civil importance. This difference does not set the two accounts at variance; the religious revolution may well have followed in the train of the civil.

The parallel narrative of 2 Chr. has been considerably expanded in parts by the editor, the priests and Levites being introduced and made to take the place which is occupied in Kings by the royal bodyguard.

11. 1. וראתה] Omit ו with Q're and ‖ 2 Chr.

ותאבד] ‖ 2 Chr. וַתְּדַבֵּר, a scribal error.

2. יהושבע] ‖ 2 Chr. יְהוֹשַׁבְעַת. She is there stated to have been אֵשֶׁת יְהוֹיָדָע הַכֹּהֵן.

בן אחזיה] LXX υἱὸν ἀδελφοῦ αὐτῆς, i.e. בֶּן־אָחִיהָ. Luc. combines the two readings.

אתו ואת מנקתו] ‖ 2 Chr. prefixes וַתִּתֵּן, which is indispensable. So Ew., Th., Klo., Kamp., Benz., Kit.

ויסתרו אתו] LXX, Luc., Vulg., Pesh. וַתַּסְתֵּר אֹתוֹ. So ‖ 2 Chr. וַתַּסְתִּירֵהוּ.

4. יהוידע] Luc. adds ὁ ἱερεύς, i.e. הַכֹּהֵן, as in *vv.* 9 *ff.* The specification is necessary unless it be supposed that the narrative originally contained an earlier reference to Jehoiada, such as that of ‖ 2 Chr. noticed on *v.* 2.

המאיות] Kt. only again *vv.* 9, 10, 15. Kö. discusses the form and concludes that the י is merely euphonic, *mēyôth* for *mē'ôth*, representing the pronunciation adopted for the avoidance of hiatus, as in Aramaic. *Lehrg.* I. i. p. 217; cf. p. 481.

לכרי] So *v.* 19 and 2 Sam. 20. 23 Kt. Probably the *Carians* are denoted. Cf. R. Sm. *OTJC.*[2], p. 262 *note.*

ולרצים] Cf. I. 1. 5 *note.*

ויכרת . . . בבית י׳] LXX καὶ διέθετο αὐτοῖς διαθήκην Κυρίου καὶ ὥρκωσεν, i.e. וַיִּכְרֹת לָהֶם בְּרִית י׳ וַיַּשְׁבַּע אֹתָם, probably correct. בבית י׳ at the end is superfluous, while ברית י׳ may be paralleled from 1 Sam. 20. 8. So Klo.

5–7. As Wellh. (*C.* 361) points out, *v.* 6 is clearly a gloss, the שתי ידות וג׳ of *v.* 7 answering to השלשית וג׳ of *v.* 5. By removal of this insertion, and reading וְשֹׁמְרֵי (as in *v.* 5) for וְשָׁמְרוּ in *v.* 7, we obtain an intelligible text in *vv.* 5, 7, 8:—'And he commanded them, saying, This is the thing which ye shall do; the third part of you who go in on the Sabbath and keep the guard of the king's house, and the two divisions of you, even all who go forth on the Sabbath and keep the guard of the House of Yahwe about the king, ye shall compass the king round about, &c.' The point is obviously that all the bodyguard is to be concentrated at the Temple, no part of it being at Athaliah's disposal at the palace: cf. *v.* 9.

5. At the end LXX adds *ἐν τῷ πυλῶνι.*

6. בשער סור] ‖ 2 Chr. בְּשַׁעַר הַיְסוֹד.

הבית מסח] The unintelligible מסח is omitted by LXX, and by ‖ 2 Chr. in the free explanation, וְכָל־הָעָם בְּחַצְרוֹת בֵּית יְהוָֹה. Field cites a Schol. which states the existence of a reading *ἀμμελέχ*, i.e. הַמֶּלֶךְ, adopted by Kit.

8. אל השדרות] 'Up to the ranks,' i.e. the lines of men surrounding the king, suggested by the previous והקפתם וג׳. The word is the same as New Heb. סֵדֶר, Aram. סִדְרָא, ܣܶܕܪܳܐ. Vulg., *septum templi*, misunderstands. ‖ 2 Chr. אֶל־הַבַּיִת.

10. החנית] ‖ 2 Chr. הַחֲנִיתִים. So Th., Klo., Kamp., Benz., Kit.

השלטים] RV., here as in the other occurrences of the word, '*the shields.*' This rendering seems to be demanded by Song 4. 4, where כֹּל שִׁלְטֵי הַגִּבּוֹרִים stands in explanatory apposition to אֶלֶף הַמָּגֵן. Th. on 2 Sam. 8. 7 favours the more general meaning 'armour,' and the same view is taken by W. E. Barnes, who classifies the ancient renderings of the word: *Expos. Times*, Oct. 1898, pp. 43 *f.* The fact, however, that שלטים (here and in Jer. 51. 11) occurs in connexion with other specified items of military equipment is against the view that the term is used in a general and not a special sense. According to LXX, Luc. in I. 14. 26, the שִׁלְטֵי הַזָּהָב which David took from the servants of Hadadezer, king of Zoba, were carried off by Shishak, king of Egypt, during the reign of Rehoboam. Cf. *note ad loc.*

11. למזבח ולבית] RV. 'along by the altar and the house.' The meaning seems to be that the guards formed a semicircle extending from the south to the north corner of the Temple, and surrounding the brazen altar which stood before the Temple. Thus all the space between the porch and the altar would be enclosed. It is, however, highly doubtful whether ל can bear the sense '*along by*,' and whether, granted this sense, the writer would have chosen

to convey the explanation given above in so obscure a manner. Pesh. represents למזבח . . . סביב by ܘܐܩܦܘܗܝ ܥܠ ܡܕܒܚܐ ܘܥܠ ܒܝܬ ܡܠܟܐ. If we may regard ܒܝܬ ܡܠܟܐ as due to an erroneous explanation of הבית 'the house' (i.e. the Temple) as 'the king's house,' we obtain the good sense, סָבִיב לַמִּזְבֵּחַ וְלַבָּיִת 'round about the altar and the Temple.' סָבִיב seems to have been wrongly placed in MT., and then explained by the addition עַל־הַמֶּלֶךְ, a statement which at this stage of the proceedings is incorrect.

12. העדות] RV., following Verss., 'the testimony,' i.e., apparently, a written law-book, committed to the young king as head over the theocratic state; cf. Deut. 17. 18 *ff.* There is not, however, anywhere else allusion to such a custom as the laying of a book (?) upon (sc. the head of) a king at his coronation; the term עֵדוּת is a late one; and, if it represented the law of the kingdom embodied in a concrete form, it would be natural to expect that this fact would be more precisely indicated (e.g. סֵפֶר הָעֵדוּת). Thus it is reasonable to suspect the text of corruption. Wellh. (*C.* 361) makes the happy emendation הַצְּעָדוֹת '*the bracelets,*' which formed, with הַנֵּזֶר 'the diadem,' the royal insignia. Cf. 2 Sam. 1. 10[1].

13. הרצין העם] Obviously the two terms cannot stand together ἀσυνδέτως. הרצין is a gloss, roughly inserted for the purpose of connecting the narrative with that which precedes. Cf. *note* on the composition of the narrative. העם is probably used in a military sense. Cf. I. 16. 15 *note.*

14. אל המלך] '*By* the king.' For this sense of אל cf. *note* on I. 6. 18.

15. פְּקֻדֵי החיל] LXX τοῖς ἐπισκόποις, i.e. פְּקִידֵי, adopted by Sta., Kamp., Benz., Kit., is doubtless correct. MT. can only mean 'those of the army who were *mustered.*'

את שרי המאיות is superfluous by the side of פקידי החיל, and must be regarded as a gloss from *vv.* 4, 9, 10, of the same character as

---

[1] Reading הַצְּעָדָה for אֶצְעָדָה, with Wellh., Dri., Budde, &c.

that noticed in *v.* 13. The same is probably the case with the words אל מבית לשדרת, which seem to conflict with *v.* 15[b]. The queen is to be taken *outside* the Temple, and therefore not *inside* the ranks which, according to *v.* 8, surround the king within the Temple.

16. וישמו לה ידים] 'And they laid hands on her.' So LXX, Luc., Vulg., Kamp., Benz., Kit. The rendering, 'And they made way (lit. place) for her,' Pesh., Targ., adopted among moderns by Ke., Th., Klo., AV., RV., is not to be paralleled[1].

19. וישב] LXX, Luc. καὶ ἐκάθισαν αὐτόν. So ‖ 2 Chr. וַיּוֹשִׁיבוּ אֶת־הַמֶּלֶךְ.

12. 1–4. *Introduction by* R[D] *to the reign of Jehoash.*

Ch. 12. 1–3 = 2 Chr. 24. 1, 2.

12. 1, 2. Luc. reads יְהוֹאָשׁ בֶּן־אֲחַזְיָהוּ in the synchronism of *v.* 2, and inserts *v.* 1, the statement of the king's age at accession, *after* the synchronism, thus conforming to the order which is constant elsewhere in the introductory formula. See *Introduction.*

3. ויעש וג׳] 'And Jehoash did that which was right in the sight of Yahwe all his days, forasmuch as Jehoiada the priest instructed him.' So Ew., Th.[2], Kamp. The antecedent of אשר is found in יהואש; lit. '*he who* Jehoiada instructed.' Cf. e.g. Gen. 42. 21 אֲשֶׁר רָאִינוּ '*we who* saw' (or, '*in that* we saw'); *Heb. Lex. Oxf., s.v.* אשר, 8 *c.* AV., RV., Kit., following LXX, Luc., Vulg., render 'all his days wherein Jehoiada the priest instructed him,' thus limiting the period of the king's good living to the life-time of Jehoiada, in accordance with ‖ 2 Chr. 24. 2, כָּל־יְמֵי יְהוֹיָדָע הַכֹּהֵן, and the narrative of 2 Chr. 24. 17–22 which relates the defection of Jehoash from the religion of Yahwe and his murder of the son of Jehoiada. But the normal method of expressing such a sense

[1] יָדַיִם in Josh. 8. 20 does not mean *place* or *room* (Ges. *Thes.*), but *power*, as in Ps. 76. 6; singular יָד Deut. 32. 36. Cf. Dillmann, *ad loc.*; *Heb. Lex. Oxf.*

[2] Pesh., Targ. are ambiguous in meaning, and cannot be cited, as by Th., in favour of this rendering. The accentuation of MT., however, in placing the principal break upon יָמָיו, is certainly intended to convey the meaning adopted.

would have been כָּל־הַיָּמִים אֲשֶׁר וג׳, as e.g. in 1 Sam. 1. 28. כָּל־יָמָיו is elsewhere in every occurrence used absolutely, without further definition, in the sense '*all his life long*':—I. 15. 14, ‖ 2 Chr. 15. 17; *ch.* 15. 18; 2 Chr. 18. 17; 34. 33; Deut. 22. 19, 29; Eccl. 2. 23; 5. 16†. Moreover, as Ew. points out, it seems to be clear that R^D was unacquainted with any narrative of the king's defection, for 'had this been so, then the older historical work must have told us how Joash showed himself faithless afterwards; but so far is this from being the case, that the piety of his successor is afterwards compared with his own, and that of both regarded as inferior to David's alone, 2 Ki. 14. 3 (the Chronicles omit this passage); even Uzziah is only treated as their equal, 2 Ki. 15. 3; 2 Chr. 26. 4.'

It is, of course, possible that the statement אשר הורהו וג׳ may be an early marginal note intended to qualify the absolute כל ימיו, in accordance with the narrative of Chr. This supposition is perhaps favoured by the reading of ‖ 2 Chr. כל ימי יהוידע, which looks like a limited explanation of כל ימיו simply.

4. רק הבמות וג׳] Cf. I. 3. 2, 3 *note.*

12. 5–17. *Measures taken by Jehoash for the repair of the House of Yahwe.*

2 Chr. 24. 4–14 gives a different narrative of the same events.

5. כסף עובר וג׳] Very difficult. As the text stands, כסף עובר must mean 'current money' (RV.). Cf. Gen. 23. 16. Then the four following words are rendered by RV. 'the money of the persons for whom each man is rated'; *marg.* Heb. 'each man the money of the souls of his estimation.' The construction is here similar to that of Gen. 9. 5 אִישׁ אָחִיו 'each man his brother,' i.e. 'each man's brother'; Gen. 15. 10 אִישׁ בִּתְרוֹ 'each its half,' i.e. 'the half of each.'

Luc. represents כסף עובר . . . ערכו by *ἀργύριον συντιμήσεως ἀνδρός, ἀργύριον συντιμήσεως ψυχῶν*, i.e. כֶּסֶף עֶרֶךְ אִישׁ וג׳. It is certainly a great simplification of the text if we suppose, with Sta., Kamp., Benz., Kit., that these first three words, '*the money of each man's assessment'* (cf. Lev. 27. 2 *ff.*), represent the original text, and that כסף נפשות ערכו is an explanatory gloss which has come into the text as a doublet.

כל כסף] It is necessary to insert ו before כל, '*and* all the money &c.' The freewill offering of money which a man's heart prompts him to make is clearly distinct from the sum which is assessed by tariff.

6. איש מאת מכרו] Apparently, 'each from his acquaintance,' RV. The scope with which מַכָּר (only again *v.* 8) is employed is highly obscure, and the word is justly regarded with suspicion by Kamp., Benz. LXX ἀπὸ τῆς πράσεως αὐτοῦ (Luc. αὐτῶν) vocalizes מִכְרוֹ; Vulg. *juxta ordinem suum* (?).

בדק] 'Dilapidation.' Cf. *ch.* 22. 5; Ezek. 27. 9, 27.

לכל] 'For everything,' i. e. '*wherever*.'

9. קֶחַת] This form, in place of the ordinary קַחַת, appears here only. Kö. (*Lehrg.* II. i. 490) cites the similar segholate *st. constr.* forms חֲדַר, זֶרַע, נֶטַע, שֶׁבַע, תְּשַׁע, בְּעַד. Cf. G-K. § 93 *h*.

10. ארון אחד] אֲרוֹן, though vocalized as *st. constr.*, can only be regarded as *st. abs.*; Kimḥi's explanation, 'the chest of (*belonging to*) some one,' being excluded by ‖ 2 Chr. 24. 8 וַיַּעֲשׂוּ אֲרוֹן אֶחָד, and the statement of Ew., § 286[d], that 'the numeral אֶחָד *one,* though mostly used as an adjective, may nevertheless be subordinated to its noun, put in the construct state,' being in the present case inconceivable. Cf. Kö. *Syntax*, § 310 *d*. Probably the vocalization here and in Lev. 24. 22, מִשְׁפַּט אֶחָד, is merely an error of the punctuators. פַּחַת אַחַד וגו׳ II. 18. 24 (cf. *note*) is perhaps different.

אצל המזבח] The statement that the chest was placed *beside the altar* seems scarcely to accord with the fact that it was given into the charge of the keepers of the threshold, who placed in it the money which they received from persons entering the House of Yahwe. Hence Sta., following the suggestion of the LXX transliteration in Cod. A, αμμασβη, emends אֵצֶל הַמַּצֵּבָה, a suggestion favoured by Kamp., Kit., Oort. The fact that Maççēbōth existed subsequently in the Temple appears from *chh.* 18. 4; 23. 4 *ff.* Klo. emends אֵצֶל הַמְּזוּזָה '*beside the doorpost*,' and this agrees well with the following בַּיָּמִין Kt., and is favoured by Benz., who objects to the former suggestion on the ground that Maççēbōth usually stood in Semitic sanctuaries near the altar and not near the entrance.

|| 2 Chr. 24. 8 בְּשַׁעַר בֵּית י׳ חוּצָה.

ונתנו] Frequentative, '*used to place.*' So *v.* 12. Cf. the imperfects of *vv.* 14–17. For the reversion to the imperf. with ו *consec.* in *vv.* 11, 12ᵇ cf. Dri. *Tenses*, § 114.

המובא] LXX, Luc. *τὸ εὑρεθέν*, as in *v.* 11.

11. ויצרו] Luc. omits, while Pesh. places after וימנו.

13. אבני מחצב] So *ch.* 22. 6.

ולכל וג׳] 'And for all for which outlay should be made upon the house.' אשר יצא, lit. 'for which it (i.e. הכסף *v.* 12ᵃ) should go forth.'

לְחָזְקָה] 'For repair.' Probably the vocalization should be לְחַזְּקָהּ 'to repair it'; cf. Luc., Pesh., Targ. So Klo., Benz.

17. כסף אשם וג׳] The reference appears to be to fines in money. Cf. Wellh. *Prolegomena*, 73.

12. 18–22. *Closing events of the reign of Jehoash, summarized by* Rᴰ.

Ch. 12. 18–22 forms the substance of 2 Chr. 24. 23–27.

18. אז יעלה] Cf. I. 3. 16 *note.*

21. בית מלא] Cf. *note* on הַמִּלּוֹא I. 9. 15.

22. יוזכר וג׳] || 2 Chr. זָבָד בֶּן־שִׁמְעַת הָעַמּוֹנִית וִיהוֹזָבָד בֶּן־שִׁמְרִית הַמּוֹאָבִית.

13. 1–9. *Jehoaḥaz, king of Israel.*

Rᴰ frames short notices from the Annals.

13. 3. כל הימים] 'All the days,' viz. of Jehoaḥaz. Cf. *note* on I. 5. 15. The statement is made rather loosely if the events of *v.* 5 belong to this reign.

4. ויחל וג׳] For the expression cf. I. 13. 6 *note.*

5. ויצאו] Luc. *καὶ ἐξήγαγεν αὐτούς*, i.e. וַיֹּצִיאוּם.

מתחת יד ארם] Luc. adds *καὶ ἀπεστράφη ὅριον Ἰσραὴλ αὐτοῖς.*

באהליהם] Not strictly 'in their tents,' but '*in their homes.*' Cf. I. 8. 66; Judg. 19. 9, and the phrase of I. 12. 16; 2 Sam. 20. 1.

7. [כי לא השאיר וג׳] The reference of כי is to *v.* 4^b^, and the subject of השאיר is not Yahwe (Th., Kamp., Kit.) nor Ḥazael (Benz.), but is indefinite (הַמַּשְׁאִיר; cf. I. 1. 6 *note* on ילדה):—'For there was not left to Jehoaḥaz &c.' So LXX, Luc. οὐχ ὑπελείφθη, Vulg. *non sunt derelicti*, Pesh. ܠܐ ܐܫܬܒܩ ܗܘܐ.

[לדש] 'For treading.' Klo. emends לָדֹק after Luc. ἕως τοῦ λεπτυνθῆναι, and so Kamp., Benz., Oort. The change is unnecessary.

After *v.* 7 Luc. inserts *v.* 23 of MT. Probably this is correct. The mention of Jehoash's successes against Aram would form a reason for transferring the verse from its position in Luc. to that which it occupies in MT., whilst no reason can be cited for the converse change. Again, it is clear that the position assigned by Luc. to *vv.* 12, 13 MT. is correct; and this creates a strong presumption in favour of the position of *v.* 23 in Luc.

13. 10–25. *Jehoash, king of Israel.*

R^D^ *vv.* 10–13; two Elisha-narratives from North Palestinian sources, *vv.* 14–19, 20, 21; short notices from the Annals framed by R^D^ *vv.* 22–25.

Vet. Lat. (Cod. Vind.) places 13. 14–21 between 10. 30 and 10. 31, making the narrative refer not to Jehoash but to Jehu.

10. [בשנת שלשים ושבע] This synchronism disagrees with the statement of *v.* 1, that Jehoaḥaz, who reigned seventeen years, came to the throne in the twenty-third year of Jehoash. We should therefore expect the synchronism to be בשנת שלשים ותשע 'in the thirty-ninth year'; and this alteration agrees with *ch.* 14. 1, where the second year of Jehoash of Israel synchronizes with the accession of Amaziah.

[שש עשרה שנה] Pesh. ܠܬܠܬܥܣܪܐ ܫܢ̈ܝܢ 'thirteen years.'

12, 13. These two verses appear in Luc. at the close of the chapter, a position which, in accordance with the scheme of R^D^, is clearly correct. Luc. also replaces the unusual formula וירבעם ישב על כסאו in *v.* 13^a^ by the regular καὶ ἐβασίλευσεν Ἰ. υἱὸς αὐτοῦ ἀντ' αὐτοῦ at the end of *v.* 13^b^.

The formula for the close of this reign is repeated in *ch.* 14. 15, 16, where it is due to the preceding account of Jehoash in relationship to Amaziah. As this narrative, however, forms part of the history of the reign of Amaziah, the introduction of *vv.* 15, 16 breaks the connexion, and is probably the work of a later hand. The repetition is not found in Luc.

14. אשר ימות בו] Not, as RV., 'whereof he died,' but, 'whereof *he was to die.*' Cf. Dri. *Tenses*, § 39 β.

ויבך על פניו] Cf. Gen. 50. 1 וַיִּפֹּל יוֹסֵף עַל־פְּנֵי אָבִיו וַיֵּבְךְּ עָלָיו.

אבי וג'] Cf. *ch.* 2. 12 *note.*

17[b]. ויאמר . . . ויור] LXX omits through oversight.

באפק] Cf. I. 20. 26 *note.*

18. קח החצים] Luc. Λαβὲ πέντε βέλη.

19. להכות] '(It was) for smiting,' and so 'Thou shouldest have smitten.' Cf. 2 Sam. 4. 10 אֲשֶׁר לְתִתִּי לוֹ 'To whom (it was) for my giving,' i.e. 'To whom I should have given.' Dri. *Tenses*, § 204. Klo.'s emendation לוּ הִכִּתָ, after the rendering of LXX, Luc. εἰ ἐπάταξας, is unnecessary.

חמש או שש פעמים] Vulg. adds *sive septies.*

20. יבאו] Probably, 'kept on coming.'

בא שנה] The text gives no sense, but LXX, Luc. ἐλθόντος τοῦ ἐνιαυτοῦ suggest the emendation כְּבֹא הַשָּׁנָה 'when the (new) year came.' Cf. the phrase of I. 20. 22, 26 לִתְשׁוּבַת הַשָּׁנָה. Vulg. *in ipso anno*, Pesh. ܒܗ ܒܫܢܬܐ ܗܝ must have read בָּהּ שָׁנָה as though for בָּהּ בַּשָּׁנָה, an Aramaic construction. Benz. emends בַּשָּׁנָה 'yearly'(?); Kit. שָׁנָה בַּשָּׁנָה.

21. ויהי הם קברים וג'] Cf. I. 13. 20 *note.*

23. ולא השליכם וג'] Cf. *ch.* 17. 20 (R^D).

24. וימלך בן הדד בנו] Winckler (*Alttest. Untersuchungen*, 66) gives reasons for identifying this king with *Mari'*, king of Damascus, who was brought into subjection by the Assyrian king Rammân-nirari III in his campaign against the nations of the West, between B.C. 806–803. Cf. *KB.* i. 191; Winckler, *Keilinschrift. Textbuch*, 12 *f.*

25. את ערי ישראל] Luc. adds καὶ ὅσα ἔλαβεν.

14. 1–22. *Amaziah, king of Judah.*

Ch. 14. 1–14, 17–22 = 2 Chr. 25. 1–4, 11, 17–28; 26. 1, 2.

R^D embodies short notices from the Annals, together with a complete narrative (*vv.* 8–14; cf. p. 215) from an unknown source.

14. 2. יהועדין] ‖ 2 Chr. supports Q're יְהוֹעַדָּן. So Vulg., Pesh., Targ. LXX, Luc. Ἰωαδείμ. Cod. A. Ἰωαδείν.

3, 4. רק לא כדוד וג׳] ‖ 2 Chr. 25. 2^b sums up the limitations to the favourable verdict in the terse statement רַק לֹא בְּלֵבָב שָׁלֵם.

4. רק הבמות וג׳] Cf. I. 3. 2, 3 *note.*

5^b. המלך] LXX, Luc. omit.

6^b. ככתוב וג׳] Citation is made by R^D directly from Deut. 24. 16. For יומות Kt., יָמֻת Q're, Deut. reads יוּמְתוּ. ‖ 2 Chr. 25. 4 יָמוּתוּ.

7. הוא הכה] The emphatic הוא (almost '*It was he who* smote &c.') occurs again *vv.* 22, 25; 15. 35^b; 18. 4, 8, and may be regarded as a mark of the style of R^D in connecting together detached notices relating to one particular king.

בגי המלח] Kt. is supported by ‖ 2 Chr. 25. 11; 1 Chr. 18. 12; Q're בְּגֵי מֶלַח by 2 Sam. 8. 13; Ps. 60. 2.

ותפש] Perfect with weak ו, a mark of decadence in style, due not to R^D, but to his source. So elsewhere in later extracts from the Annals, *ch.* 18. 4; 21. 4, 6. The style of R^D is always, like that of Deuteronomy his model, of the best (cf. e.g. *ch.* 17); the style of the extracts is on a level with that of the lengthy narrative *ch.* 22. 3—23. 25, and may be taken as representing the popular style (as distinct from the prophetic or literary style) of the closing years of the kingdom of Judah.

הסלע] Cf. Judg. 1. 36; Isa. 16. 1; 42. 11 (סֶלַע without article). The usual identification with *Petra* (cf. Baed. 206) is denied by Buhl, *Edomites*, 34 *ff.* ‖ 2 Chr. 25. 11 finds reference to '*the crag*' from which ten thousand captive Edomites were thrown headlong. The name יָקְתְאֵל (LXX, Luc. Καθοήλ) as an Edomite city does not appear elsewhere.

8. אז] Cf. I. 3. 16 *note.*

10. ונשאך] Probably perf. with weak ו 'and thy heart *hath lifted*

thee up.' Another occurrence is found in *v.* 14 וְלָקַח. Cf. *note* on ותפש *v.* 7.

הכבד] 'Enjoy your honour' ('let yourself be honoured').

ולמה] The force of ו is sarcastic: '*Pray*, why?' Cf. I. 2. 22 *note.*

11. בית שמש] Cf. I. 4. 9 *note.*

13. ויבאו] Luc., Vulg. presuppose וַיְבִיאֵהוּ as in || 2 Chr. 25. 23, probably correctly.

בשער אפרים] Read מִשַּׁעַר א׳ with Luc., Vulg., Pesh., Targ., || 2 Chr.

שער הפנה] Cf. 2 Chr. 26. 9; Jer. 31. 38. A שַׁעַר הַפִּנִּים is mentioned in Zech. 14. 10.

14. ולקח] לקח is omitted in || 2 Chr. 25. 24, and it is therefore possible that the word may be a later insertion made to supply the missing verb, which may have been וַיִּקַּח, or לָקַח following after התערבות. Cf., however, ונשאך *v.* 10 *note.*

15, 16. Omitted in Luc. Cf. *note* on *ch.* 13. 12, 13.

18ª. After אמציהו, LXX adds *καὶ πάντα ἃ* (Luc. *ὅσα*) *ἐποίησεν.*

19. לכישה] An old Amorite city, several times named in the Tell el-Amarna inscriptions; probably the modern *Tell el-Ḥasi* some distance east of Gaza, and close to the south of *'Ajlân*, i. e. Eglon. Cf. Smith, *Geogr.* 234; Baed. 140; Buhl, 191 *f.*

21. את עזריה] Luc. adds *υἱὸν αὐτοῦ.* Pesh. ܥܘܙܝܐ conforms to || 2 Chr. 26. 1 עֻזִּיָּהוּ.

22. הוא בנה] Cf. *note* on הוא הכה *v.* 7.

14. 23–29. *Jeroboam II, king of Israel.*

R^D frames short notices from the Annals.

23. מלך ישראל בשמרון] The usual phrase is על ישראל בשמרון, and this appears in LXX, Targ., while Luc. combines the two readings.

ארבעים ואחת שנה] Luc. *καὶ τεσσαράκοντα καὶ ἓν ἔτος ἐβασίλευσεν ἐν Σαμαρείᾳ.*

25. מלבוא וג׳] Cf. I. 8. 65 *note.*

גת חפר] Mentioned again in the description of the territory assigned to the tribe of Zebulun, Josh. 19. 13. Tradition, both

Christian and Mohammedan, places the tomb of Jonah at *el-Meshhed*, about three miles to the north-east of Nazareth, and this village is therefore usually regarded as the site of Gath Ḥepher. Rob. *BR*. ii. 350; Baed. 285; Buhl, 219.

26. מרה מאד] As vocalized מֹרֶה 'rebellious' gives no sense. The Verss. render 'bitter,' which is doubtless the meaning intended, but fem. מָרָה is out of agreement with masc. עֳנִי. Hence Kamp. would emend כִּי מַר הוּא, a suggestion favoured by Benz., Kit. It is simpler to transpose the ה of מרה, and to read הַמַּר 'the very bitter affliction of Israel.'

ואפס עצור וג׳] Cf. I. 14. 10 *note*.

27. למחות וג׳] So Deut. 9. 14; 29. 19.

28. ואשר השיב וג׳] Certainly corrupt. The rendering of RV., Kamp., 'How he recovered Damascus, and Ḥamath, (which had belonged) to Judah, for Israel,' cannot be obtained from the text; reference in such terms to the state of affairs *under David* is impossible, since David's kingdom is never designated as 'Judah'; and, even if such reference could be substantiated, it would be untrue, since Ḥamath never formed part of David's kingdom (cf. 2 Sam. 8. 9 *ff*.). LXX, Luc., Vulg., Targ. present the same text as MT., but Pesh. reads ܘܐܗܦܟ ܕܪܡܣܘܩ ܘܚܡܬ ܠܐܝܣܪܝܠ, i.e. by substitution of לְיִשְׂרָאֵל for לִיהוּדָה בְּיִשְׂרָאֵל 'and restored Damascus and Ḥamath to Israel.' This text is adopted by Ew., Th., Kit., Oort[1], but is directly contradictory, as regards Ḥamath, to the statement of *v*. 25ᵃ. Winckler (*Ges*. i. 147 *f*.) takes הֵשִׁיב in the sense '*drove back*' (cf. Isa. 36. 9; השיב מלחמה Isa. 28. 6), and supposes that some words have fallen out after חמת which would have explained the connexion with יהודה; while Klo. disposes of the reference to Ḥamath, boldly emending וַאֲשֶׁר הֵשִׁיב אֶת־דַּמֶּשֶׂק מִתַּחַת לְיַד בֶּן־הֲדַד בֶּן־חֲזָאֵל.

If it might be supposed that את דמשק had been misplaced from the preceding sentence, very slight alteration would give the text וַאֲשֶׁר נִלְחַם אֶת־דַּמֶּשֶׂק וַאֲשֶׁר הֵשִׁיב אֶת־חֲמַת יְהוָֹה מִיִּשְׂרָאֵל 'and

[1] Schrader (*COT. ad loc.*) reads similarly לְמַלְכֵי יִשְׂרָאֵל.

how he fought with Damascus, and how he turned away the wrath of Yahwe from Israel.' Cf. *ch.* 10. 32.

29. Before עם מלכי ישראל the words וַיִּקָּבֵר בְּשֹׁמְרוֹן, in accordance with the usual formula, have probably fallen out. So Luc. καὶ ἐτάφη ἐν Σαμαρείᾳ, and, in part, Pesh. ܘܐܬܩܒܪ ܥܡ ܐܒܗܘܗܝ.

15. 1–7. *Azariah, king of Judah.*

Ch. 15. 2, 3, 5–7 = 2 Chr. 26. 3, 4, 21–23.

R^D^ frames short notices from the Annals.

15. 1. עזריה] This name appears in *ch.* 14. 21; 15. 1, 7, 17, 23, 27; and in the form עֲזַרְיָהוּ in *ch.* 15. 6, 8. עֻזִּיָּה is used in *ch.* 15. 13, 30; עֻזִּיָּהוּ in *ch.* 15. 32, 34. עֲזַרְיָה is read in place of עֻזִּיָּה in *v.* 13 by LXX, Luc., Vulg., Targ., and by LXX, Luc. in *v.* 32. In *v.* 30, LXX 'Αχάς, Luc. omits. עֻזִּיָּה is uniformly substituted for עֲזַרְיָה by Pesh. The form עֻזָּא occurs in *ch.* 21. 18; cf. *note ad loc.*

Outside Kings, with the exception of 1 Chr. 3. 12 עֲזַרְיָה, עֻזִּיָּהוּ is used in 2 Chr. 26. 1—27. 2 (13 times), and in Isa. 1. 1; 6. 1; 7. 1; עֻזִּיָּה in Hos. 1. 1; Am. 1. 1; Zech. 14. 5.

The supposed reference to this king in the Assyrian inscriptions under the name *Az-ri-ya-a-u* (*COT.* i. 208 *ff.*) is denied by Winckler (*Altorient. Forschungen*, i. 1 *ff.*): cf. also Maspero, iii. p. 150, *note* 3.

4. רק וג'] Cf. I. 3. 2, 3 *note.*

5. בבית החפשית] The meaning is obscure. RV. 'a several house,' i.e. lit. 'a house of separateness.' So Targ. paraphrases ויתב בר מן ירושלם 'and he dwelt *outside of Jerusalem*'; Pesh. ܘܝܬܒ ܒܒܝܬܐ ܡܛܫܝܐܝܬ 'and he dwelt in a house in privacy.' חפשית, however, according to the root-meaning, should denote not *separateness* but *freedom.* Klo.'s suggestion is noteworthy:—בְּבֵיתֹה חָפְשִׁית 'in his house at freedom,' i.e. not under restraint. חפשית is thus used adverbially, like אֲחֹרַנִּית Gen. 9. 23. Stade (*ZATW.* vi. 156 *ff.*) emends בְּבֵית הַחֹרֶף 'in the winter-house.'

על הבית] Cf. I. 4. 6 *note.*

15. 8–12. *Zechariah, king of Israel.*

R^D^ frames short notices from the Annals.

10. קבל עם] Senseless; the rendering 'before the people,'

adopted by RV. after Pesh., Targ., Vulg., being out of the question. We should, doubtless, follow Luc. ἐν Ἰεβλαάμ, and emend בְּיִבְלְעָם 'in Ibleam.' On the situation of Ibleam cf. *ch.* 9. 27 *note*.

12. הוא דבר י׳ וג׳] Cf. *ch.* 10. 30.

15. 13–16. *Shallum, king of Israel.*

R^D frames short notices from the Annals.

16. תפסח] Clearly not the תִּפְסַח of I. 5. 4 on the Euphrates. Th. emends תַּפּוּחַ, a town which lay in the territory of Ephraim near to the border of Manasseh; Josh. 16. 8; 17. 7, 8. This suggestion, which is borne out by Luc. Ταφωέ, is adopted by Buhl (*Geogr.* 178), Klo., Kamp., Benz., Kit.

כי לא פתח וג׳] Slightly corrupt. Read, after LXX, Pesh., כִּי לֹא פָתְחוּ לוֹ וַיַּךְ אֹתָהּ וְכָל־הָרוֹתֶיהָ בִּקֵּעַ.

15. 17–22. *Menaḥem, king of Israel.*

R^D frames short notices from the Annals.

17. מנחם] Mentioned by Tiglath-Pileser III as *Mí-ni-ḫi-im-mi* of Samaria in a list of tributary kings, B.C. 738; *COT.* i. 215; Dri. *Authority*, 98.

18. מעל] LXX ἀπὸ πασῶν, i. e. מִכָּל־—correct.

18, 19. כל ימיו : בא פול] Read, with LXX, Luc., בְּיָמָיו בָּא פול 'In his days came up Pul &c.' So moderns. כל ימיו at the end of *v.* 18 is an unusual addition; and *v.* 19 in MT. commences abruptly, and needs the mark of connexion which is supplied by בימיו as used elsewhere by R^D (cf. I. 16. 34 *note*).

19. פול] Identical with תִּגְלַת פִּלְאֶסֶר of *v.* 29; *ch.* 16. 7, 10. *Pûlu* of the Babylonian dynastic list corresponds to *Tukul-ti-abal-i-šar-ra* of the Babylonian chronicle. Cf. *KB.* ii. 290 *f.*; Dri. *Authority*, 97.

להחזיק וג׳] LXX omits.

20. ויצא וג׳] 'And Menaḥem *imposed* (lit. *brought forth*) the money *upon* Israel'; so RV. '*exacted . . . from.*' Such a use of the Hiph'il of יצא is, however, without a parallel; and probably Klo. is correct in emending וַיְצַו מ׳ אֶת־כָּל יִשְׂרָאֵל וְאֶת־כָּל־גִּבּוֹרֵי הַחַיִל.

So Benz., Kit. הכסף may then be supposed to have been introduced in imitation of *ch.* 12. 12, 13, after the corruption of ויצו into ויצא.

15. 23–26. *Pekaḥiah, king of Israel.*

R[D] frames a short notice (*v.* 25) from the Annals.

23. שנתים] Luc. δέκα ἔτη.

25. שלישו] Cf. I. 9. 22 *note.*

בארמון בית מלך] Cf. I. 16. 18. Probably Kt. is correct. Cf. את בית מלך of I. 16. 18, and *note* on I. 12. 31.

את ארגב ואת האריה] Scarcely possible. Even supposing that the place-name ארגב and the strange האריה with the article prefixed can be used as personal names, it is reasonable to expect some precise information as to the position of the men beyond the mere mention of their names, nor is it clear (supposing את to mean 'with') whether they were conspirators with Pekaḥ or victims together with Pekaḥiah. Klo. emends אֶת־אַרְבַּע מֵאֹת גִּבֹּרָיו 'with his 400 warriors,' the allusion being to the royal bodyguard which Pekaḥ with his small band managed by a *coup* to annihilate. Probably, however, Sta. (*ZATW.* vi. 160) is nearer the truth in regarding both names as place-names (cf. Vulg. *iuxta Argob et iuxta Arie*) which have come in by mistake from *v.* 29, and should be read as אֶת־אַרְגֹּב וְאֶת־חַוּוֹת יָאִיר.

15. 27–31. *Pekaḥ, king of Israel.*

R[D] frames notices from the Annals (*vv.* 29–30[a]).

27. עשרים שנה] The Assyrian inscriptions do not admit of a reign of such a length. Tiglath-Pileser mentions Menaḥem as his tributary in B.C. 738 (cf. *note* on *v.* 17), and also refers to the dethronement and execution of Pekaḥ in B.C. 734–732 (cf. *v.* 30 *note*). Thus, even supposing B.C. 738 to have been the last year of Menaḥem, we have at most six years for the reigns of Pekaḥiah and Pekaḥ. If Pekaḥiah reigned two years (i.e. possibly a little more than one year), Pekaḥ may have reigned from four to five years.

Hommel (Hastings, *BD.* i. 186) comments on the fact that exactly the same things are related of Pekaḥiah as of Pekaḥ, and that the names are virtually the same, and deduces the inference that there really existed only one king Pekaḥ (or Pekaḥiah), who reigned two years, between Menaḥem and Hoshea.

29. בא תגלת פלאסר] The account of this campaign is contained, in a somewhat mutilated condition, in the Annals of Tiglath-Pileser. Cf. Rost, 78 *ff.*; Dri. *Authority*, 98 *f.*

את עיון ואת אבל בית מעכה] Cf. I. 15. 20 *note*.

ינוח] The site is uncertain. Conder (*Lists*, 38; and in Hastings, *BD.*, *s. v.*) cites *Yanuḥ* near Tyre, but Buhl (*Geogr.* 229) maintains that this situation is too far west of the other places named. Guérin's identification with Hunîn, west of the Upper Jordan, is mentioned by Buhl (*Geogr.* 237). The place of the same name mentioned in Josh. **16.** 6, 7 on the border of Ephraim is too far south to be identical.

קדש] *Ḳades*, standing on a lofty plateau, west-north-west of the Lake of *Ḥûle*. Rob. *BR.* iii. 366 *ff.*; Baed. 297.

חצור] Cf. I. 9. 15 *note*.

הגלילה] Cf. I. 9. 11 *note*.

30. ויקשר וג׳] The statement of Tiglath-Pileser (cf. Rost, 80 *f.*), '*Pa-ḳa-ḫa* (Pekaḥ) their king they slew, *A-u-si-'* (Hoshea) to reign over them I appointed,' makes it clear that the revolution was effected under the auspices of Assyria.

בשנת עשרים ליותם] Clearly an erroneous statement. Pekaḥ's operations against Judah, in alliance with Rezin, which appear to have been begun during Jotham's reign (*v.* 37), were carried on into the reign of Aḥaz; *ch.* **16.** 5 *ff.*; Isa. 7. 1 *ff.*

15. 32–38. *Jotham, king of Judah.*

Ch. **15.** 33, 34, 35b, 36, 38 = 2 Chr. **27.** 1–3a, 7–9.

The whole account is cast by R^D.

32. At the end of the verse Luc. adds ἐπὶ Ἱερουσαλήμ.

35. רק וג׳] Cf. I. 3. 2, 3 *note*.

הוא בנה] Cf. *note* on הוא הכה *ch.* **14.** 7.

37. בימים ההם] Cf. *ch.* **10.** 32 *note*.

רצין] Frequently mentioned by Tiglath-Pileser as *Ra-ṣun-nu.*

Cf. *COT.* i. 252 *f.* His predecessor upon the throne of Damascus was perhaps טָבְאַל, or more correctly טָבְאֵל, to whom allusion is made in Isa. 7. 6[1]. Cf. Winckler, *Alttest. Untersuchungen*, 74.

16. *Aḥaz, king of Judah.*

Ch. 16. 2–4, 19, 20 = 2 Chr. 28. 1–4, 26, 27.

Verses 1–9, 17–20 contain notices from the Annals, framed by R^D. Verses 10–16 form a continuous narrative, probably derived from the same source as *ch.* 11; 12. 5–17. See p. 307.

16. 1. אחז] Tiglath-Pileser mentions, in a list of tributaries, *Ya-u-ḫa-zi* of Judah, i.e. יְהוֹאָחָז, the full form of the name אָחָז. The date is B.C. 728, the last year but one of Tiglath-Pileser. *KB.* ii. 20 *f.*; Rost, 72 *f.*; *COT.* i. 225; Dri. *Authority*, 100.

2. There is clearly some discrepancy between the statements of this verse and *ch.* 18. 2. If Aḥaz died at the age of thirty-six (20 + 16), and Ḥezekiah was twenty-five years old at his accession, then Aḥaz must have become a father at the age of eleven!

3. כתעבות וג׳] Cf. I. 14. 24 *note.*

4. ועל הגבעות וג׳] Cf. I. 14. 23 *note.*

5. אז יעלה] Cf. I. 3. 16 *note.*

6. בעת ההיא] Cf. I. 14. 1 *note.*

השיב רצין וג׳] It is quite clear that the Massoretes are correct in reading וַאֲדוֹמִים, and that this correction carries with it the correction of the preceding לַאֲרָם into לֶאֱדֹם (cf. I. 9. 26; 22. 48 *ff.*; II. 14. 7, 22). So Th., Sta., Kamp., Oort. Probability is also in favour of Klo.'s emendation מֶלֶךְ אֱדֹם in place of רְצִין מֶלֶךְ אֲרָם. So Benz., Kit. It is far more likely that the king of Edom should have seized the opportunity of Aḥaz's engagement with the northern confederacy in order to once more gain possession of his seaport town, than that the king of Aram should have despatched a purposeless expedition against the remote eastern point of Aḥaz's dominions.

עד היום הזה] Cf. I. 8. 8 *note.*

---

[1] The reference of 'the son of Ṭab'el' is most naturally to Rezin. The name Ṭab'el ('El is wise') is Aramaic, and identical in form with Ṭabrimmon, I. 15. 18.

7. הקומים] A rare form of participle act. Qal of the verb ע״ו. Cf. לוֹט Isa. 25. 7, בּוֹסִים Zech. 10. 5, and perhaps גֹּחִי Ps. 22. 10. See Wright, *Compar. Gramm.* 250; G-K. § 72 *p*.

8. שחד] So in I. 15. 19.

9. קירה] LXX omits; Luc. τὴν πόλιν (? קִרְיָה). Benz., Kit., Oort, on the ground of the omission, suppose that the name is a later insertion derived from Am. 1. 5. The situation of קיר is unknown. According to Am. 9. 7 the district was the original home of the Aramaeans.

10. דומשק] Probably an error for the form דַּרְמֶשֶׂק, which appears in Chr., and is regular in Syriac, and in the Targum of Pseudo-Jonathan.

אוריה הכהן] Cf. Isa. 8. 2.

11. LXX omits from כן עשה down to מדמשק in *v.* 12, probably through homoioteleuton, though the narrative runs quite smoothly without the words omitted. Luc. agrees with MT. except for the omission of the first מדמשק before כן עשה וג׳.

12. ויקרב . . . המזבח] LXX omits.

על המזבח] על for אל. Cf. I. 1. 38 *note* on על גחון.

ויעל עליו] 'And went up upon it.' Cf. I. 1. 53 *note* on מעל המזבח.

14. ואת המזבח . . . ויקרב] On constr. cf. I. 9. 21 *note*.

המזבח הנחשת] The original text must have read הַמִּזְבֵּחַ simply, and הנחשת is a gloss from *v.* 15ᵇ, correctly distinguishing the old altar from the new. LXX omits ואת המזבח, thus causing it to appear that the ritual described in *v.* 13 was still carried on upon the old (brazen) altar. This is adopted by R. Sm. (*Relig. Sem.*[2], *note L*), who further reads וַיִּקְרַב, as in *v.* 12, for וַיַּקְרֵב, thus making the verse from that point to be 'an elaborate description of the new ritual introduced by the king.' The context, however, desiderates the precise statement of MT. as to the new position of the brazen altar, which was clearly supplanted by the new altar (*v.* 15ᵃ), and devoted only to a special purpose (*v.* 15ᵇ). The LXX omission may thus be regarded as merely due to homoioteleuton.

15. ויצוהו וג׳] Kt. with pronoun-suffix anticipating the object, as in Syriac. Cf. I. 19. 21 *note*. Possibly, however, the words את אוריה הכהן may be a later explanatory insertion.

את עלת הבקר ואת מנחת הערב] The distinction appears to coincide with the ritual of Ezek. 46. 13–15, where there is only mention of a morning עולה. In *ch.* 3. 20 the term מנחה is applied to the morning sacrifice, and in I. 18. 29, 36 to the evening sacrifice. In the time of P the עולה has become both a morning and evening institution; Num. 28. 1 *ff.* Jer. 14. 12 draws a distinction, as in our passage, between עולה and מנחה; but it is by no means to be hence inferred (RV.) that מנחה therefore possesses the restricted sense of 'meal-offering,' as in P. Cf. *note* on מנחה I. 18. 29; Wellh. *Prolegomena*, 79, *note* 1.

כל עם הארץ] LXX, Luc., παντὸς τοῦ λαοῦ, omit הארץ. For the phrase of MT., *the people in general*, cf. *ch.* 11. 14, 18, 19, 20; 15. 5; 21. 24; 23. 30.

יהיה לי לבקר] The significance is obscure. בִּקֵּר means *to examine* (lit. *divide*, and so presumably *look at in detail;* cf. Ar. بَقَرَ *cleave, slit*). This meaning is clear for most of the occurrences in Bib. Heb.:—Lev. 13. 36 'The priest shall not *examine* (the suspected leper) for the yellow hair'; Lev. 27. 33 'he shall not *examine* (the tithe of the herd and flock) whether it be good or bad'; Ezek. 34. 11, 12 'will *look after* (or *look for*, i. e. *search out*) my flock'; Prov. 20. 25, probably 'after vowing, he begins *to make inquiry*,' i. e. *to examine* his financial position (cf. Toy *ad loc.*). Ps. 27. 4 לְבַקֵּר בְּהֵיכָלוֹ is involved in the same ambiguity as our passage; '*to look at* his Temple,' or '*to make inquiry in* his Temple.' In Rabb. Heb. בִּיקֵּר is used of *examining* sacrificial animals for blemishes.

Accordingly, the explanation of our passage least open to objection is that of AV., RV., R. Sm. (*Relig. Sem.*², *note L*), 'and the brazen altar shall be for me *to inquire by';* i. e. lit. *to investigate*, sc. the oracle, perhaps by examination of portions of the sacrifice. Cf. the action ascribed to the king of Babylon, Ezek. 21. 26 רָאָה בַּכָּבֵד. So approximately Pesh. ܢܗܘܐ ܠܝ ܠܡܫܐܠܘ 'shall be for me to make request by.' Less probable is the explanation of Klo., 'for me *to look at';* the idea of close scrutiny which is implied in the verb being inconsistent as applied to the altar, which must have been long familiar to the king, and which was (on this explanation) about to undergo degradation. Least probable, and without support from usage elsewhere, is the explanation of Kamp., Benz., Kit., 'shall be for me *to think of*,' i.e. 'I must decide at my leisure what is to become of it.' Cf. Vulg. *erit paratum ad voluntatem meam.*

17. המסגרות המכנות] The construction is impossible. Probably we should read מִסְגְּרוֹת הַמְּכֹנוֹת with Verss., or else emend הַמִּסְגְּרוֹת מֵהַמְּכֹנוֹת. Cf. Kamp. Klo., Benz. suppose that את המסגרות ought to follow מעליהם. On הַמִּסְגְּרוֹת cf. I. 7. 28 *note.*

הכיר] We should expect הַכִּיֹּרִים. Cf. I. 7. 38 *ff.*

הבקר הנחשת] הנחשת is probably, as in *v.* 14, a later addition.

מרצפת] 'A pediment.' Cf. the use of רִצְפָּה 'pavement,' 2 Chr. 7. 3; *al.;* and the participle רָצוּף Song 3. 10.

18. מיסך השבת] Highly obscure. Q're מוּסַךְ, if correct, should denote something *covered in;* hence RV. 'the covered way (*marg.* covered place) for the Sabbath.' LXX, however, reads τὸν θεμέλιον τῆς καθέδρας, i.e. מוּסַד הַשֶּׁבֶת; cf. I. 10. 19. Pesh. explains ܒܝܬ ܡܘܬܒܐ; Targ. שבתא (τεῖχος) טיכוס.

17. 1–6. *Hoshea, king of Israel. Fall of the kingdom.*

Winckler (*Alttest. Untersuchungen*, 15 *ff.*) argues with much cogency that in *vv.* 3–6 we have a combination of two narratives. Supposing the narrative to be single, the course of events can only have been as follows. Hoshea comes to the throne as the vassal of Tiglath-Pileser (*ch.* 15. 30 *note*); he revolts against Shalmaneser, and is again reduced to vassalage (*ch.* 17. 3); he again revolts, and is deposed and made prisoner (*ch.* 17. 4); the king of Assyria (Shalmaneser) besieges Samaria for three years (*ch.* 17. 5); at the end of three years (in the first year of Sargon; *v.* 6 *note*) Samaria falls, and the population is deported to Assyria. It is, however, highly improbable that Israel remained for three years without a king, after the deposition of Hoshea, and, as a matter of fact, *v.* 6 states that the fall of the capital took place 'in the ninth year of Hoshea,' i.e. in his ninth reigning year. *Ch.* 18. 9ᵇ–11 describes only one campaign of Assyria against Israel and the fall of Samaria after a three years' siege, and it is noticeable that this account is nearly verbally identical with *ch.* 17. 5, 6. Probably therefore *ch.* 17. 3, 4 represents another and independent account drawn from a different source to *ch.* 17. 5, 6=18. 9ᵇ–11 (Annals). The form of the statements of *v.* 3 suggests that the writer was ignorant of the true state of affairs, viz. that Hoshea was from the first a vassal of Assyria, and supposed that his dependence was the direct result of a campaign (עליו עלה וג׳) distinct from that in which he lost his throne (*v.* 4). Winckler meets the difficulty by the supposition that R^{D} read in his source והיה (frequentative?) in place of ויהי—'inasmuch as Hoshea was (already) his vassal, &c.'; but such a construction is impossible.

17. 1. בשנת וג׳] The synchronism is inconsistent with the preceding synchronisms of *chh.* 16, 17, but agrees, as Benz. notices, with the statement of Luc. in *ch.* 16. 23 as to the length of the reign of Pekaḥiah.

2. רק לא וג׳] Luc. *παρὰ πάντας τοὺς γενομένους ἔμπροσθεν αὐτοῦ*, i. e. מִכֹּל־אֲשֶׁר וג׳; cf. I. 14. 9; 16. 25, 30, 33. The reason why R^{D} should make exception in favour of Hoshea is not apparent from his narrative; while, on the other hand, it is eminently suitable to his scheme that the last king of Israel should be painted in the blackest colours of all. Cf. *vv.* 7 *ff.*

4. קשר] LXX *ἀδικίαν*, i.e. שֶׁקֶר, adopted by Th., Kamp., Benz., Kit.

סוא] Generally identified with *Šabaku*, who founded the twenty-fifth (Ethiopian) dynasty. Cf. *COT. ad loc.*; Dri. *Authority*, 100. Sargon (*KB.* ii. 54 *f.*) mentions *Sib'u* general (*turtan*) of Egypt as defeated by him, together with *Ḫanunu*, king of Gaza, at Raphiaḥ (B.C. 720), but he expressly distinguishes him from Pharaoh (*Pir'u*), *king* of Egypt. If, therefore, with Schrader, we vocalize סֶוֶא and identify with *Sib'u*, it is clear that the title מלך מצרים is at any rate inapplicable at the time when Hoshea's overtures were made. See, however, Winckler's note, *Keilschrift. Sargons*, p. 101.

Luc., in place of אל סוא וג׳, reads *πρὸς 'Αδραμέλεχ τὸν Αἰθίοπα τὸν κατοικοῦντα ἐν Αἰγύπτῳ. Καὶ ἦν Ὡσῆε φέρων δῶρα τῷ βασιλεῖ Ἀσσυρίων ἐνιαυτὸν κατ' ἐνιαυτόν, ἐν δὲ τῷ ἐνιαυτῷ ἐκείνῳ οὐκ ἤνεγκεν αὐτῷ μαναά. καὶ ὕβρισε τὸν Ὡσῆε ὁ βασιλεὺς Ἀσσυρίων καὶ ἐπολιόρκησεν αὐτὸν κ.τ.λ.*

6. לכד מלך אשור וג'] Not Shalmaneser, as in *v.* 3, but *Sargon;* cf. the great triumphal inscription *ll.* 23 *ff.*:—'Samaria I besieged and conquered; 27,290 of its inhabitants I carried into captivity, fifty chariots I seized from them; the rest of them I allowed to retain their possessions (?); I set my officers over them; the tribute of the former king I laid upon them.' *KB.* ii. 54 *f.;* Dri. *Authority*, 101. Schrader (*COT. ad loc.*) quotes evidence to show that the conquest of Samaria must have taken place in the year of Sargon's accession, i. e. B. C. 722.

וישב וג'] חבור is mentioned in the inscriptions as the *Ḥa-bur*, a tributary of the Euphrates; גוזן is *Gu-za-na*, which is assigned to the district of Mesopotamia. חלח is doubtful, but may be *Ḥalaḫḫu* in Mesopotamia. Cf. *COT. ad loc.*

17. 7–23. *Commentary by* R^D *upon the causes which brought about the downfall of the Northern Kingdom.*

The phraseology of R^D is very marked throughout the section. Notice אֱלֹהִים אֲחֵרִים *v.* 7 (I. 9. 6 *note*); הוֹרִישׁ *v.* 8 (I. 14. 24 *note*); עַל כָּל־גִּבְעָה וג' *v.* 10 (I. 14. 23 *note*); לְהַכְעִים *vv.* 11, 17 (I. 14. 9 *note*); הַגִּלֻּלִים *v.* 12 (I. 15. 12 *note*); שֻׁבוּ מִדַּרְכֵיכֶם הָרָעִים *v.* 13 (I. 13. 33 *note*); שִׁמְרוּ מִצְוֹתַי וג' *vv.* 13, 19 (I. 2. 3 *note*); עֲבָדַי הַנְּבִיאִים *vv.* 13, 23 (as in I. 9. 7; 21. 10; 24. 2); וַיַּקְשׁוּ אֶת־עָרְפָּם *v.* 14 *note;* וַיֵּלְכוּ אַחֲרֵי *v.* 15 (I. 11. 5 *note*); הַהֶבֶל *v.* 15 (I. 16. 2 *note*); וַיִּתְמַכְּרוּ וג' *v.* 17 (I. 21. 20, 25); לַעֲשׂוֹת הָרַע וג' *v.* 17 (I. 11. 6 *note*); וַיִּתְאַנַּף *v.* 18 (I. 11. 9 *note*); לֹא סָרוּ מִמֶּנָּה *v.* 22 (*ch.* 3. 3 *note*).

Verses 19, 20 are certainly a later insertion, subsequent to the commencement of the Judaean exile, and due to R^{D2}. The opening of *v.* 21, כי קרע וג' '*For* he rent &c.,' clearly refers immediately to the statement of *v.* 18, ויתאנף . . . ויסרם 'was very angry . . . and removed them'; but the sequence is destroyed by the interpolation, כי *v.* 21 being deprived of all point. The whole reference of the section is to the causes which brought about the rejection of the kingdom of *Israel*, no reference being elsewhere made to Judah except in *v.* 13, where וביהודה is probably by the same hand as *vv.* 19, 20.

Stade (*ZATW.* vi. 163 *f.*) regards *vv.* 7–17 as an exilic addition, later than R[D], upon the grounds that the writer of these verses ascribes Molech-worship (*v.* 17[a]) and Assyrian star-worship (*v.* 16[b]) to the Northern Kingdom—the abuses which later on were rife in the Southern Kingdom under Manasseh (*ch.* 21. 3, 6), and also because certain phrases appear to exhibit the influence of Jeremiah; cf. *v.* 13 שבו מדרכיכם הרעים with Jer. 18. 11; 25. 5; 35. 15; 36. 3, 7; ויעד י׳ וג׳ with Jer. 7. 25 *ff.*; 11. 7 *ff.*; *v.* 15[b] וילכו אחרי ההבל ויהבלו with Jer. 2. 5. The reflections embodied in these verses are, however, in strict accordance with R[D]'s plan which runs throughout his work, as the number of phrases above cited as characteristic of his hand sufficiently show, nor is it at all unnatural that the editor, who worked not many years after Josiah had removed from Judah the foreign abuses of Manasseh's reign, should ascribe the same kind of religious abuses to the kingdom of Israel, side by side with the worship of Yahwe under the form of a calf. Nor, again, need the phrases above mentioned imply dependence upon the written prophecies of Jeremiah, any more than need other phrases used by R[D] elsewhere, in common with Jeremiah[1], go to prove that R[D] and Jeremiah were one and the same person. All that clearly emerges from the fact of such resemblances is that the two writers were members of one prophetic school of thought, i.e. the Deuteronomic. Cf. Dri. *LOT.*[6] p. 203 at end.

7. ויהי כי חטאו] 'Now it (viz. the foregoing) came to pass because &c.' Luc. *καὶ ἐγένετο ὀργὴ κυρίου ἐπὶ τὸν Ἰσραήλ, δι' ὅτι ἥμαρτον κ.τ.λ.*, i. e. וַיְהִי אַף י׳ בְּיִשְׂרָאֵל כִּי חָטְאוּ—superior to MT.

---

[1] Cf. כי שמך נקרא וג׳ I. 8. 43 *note;* אשלח מעל פני I. 9. 7 *note;* כל עבר וג׳ I. 9. 8 *note;* לא שב מדרכו הרעה I. 13. 33 *note;* הנני מביא רעה אל (על) I. 14. 10 *note;* עבדי (עבדיו) הנביאים *ch.* 9. 7; 17. 13, 23; 21. 10; 24. 2; Jer. 7. 25; 25. 4; 26. 5; 29. 19; 35. 15; 44. 4. Other resemblances, from the later *chh.* of 2 Kings, are cited by Dri. *LOT.*[6] p. 203.

8. וילכו בחקות הגוים] Cf. Lev. 18. 3; 20. 23 (H).

ומלכי ישראל וג׳] Senseless. Cf. RV.'s attempt at a rendering. No doubt ומלכי ישראל is a corruption of מִלִּפְנֵי יִשְׂרָאֵל, a doublet of the preceding three words; and אשר עשו 'who performed (them,' sc. the statutes of the nations) is probably a marginal gloss made subsequently to the corruption to explain the occurrence of 'the kings of Israel' in this connexion.

9. ויחפאו] The rendering of RV. 'did secretly' can scarcely be maintained, and LXX ἠμφιέσαντο, 'clad themselves in,' in accordance with the use of חִפָּה 'overlay' in 2 Chr., is preferable, if the text be genuine. Pesh., Targ. render vaguely ܐܡܪܘ, אמרו; and Vulg. *offenderunt* seems only to be guessing. Klo. emends וַיְבַדְּאוּ 'devised'; cf. Job 13. 4 רֹפְאֵי אֱלִיל probably 'contrivers of nought' (‖ טֹפְלֵי שֶׁקֶר). So Benz., Kit.

לא כן] Cf. *ch.* 7. 9.

ממגדל וג׳] So *ch.* 18. 8. The expression, as here used, describes the smallest and largest of communities.

10. מצבות ואשרים] Cf. *notes* on I. 14. 15, 23.

13. כל נביאו כל חזה] Vulg. *omnium prophetarum et videntium*, Targ. כל ספר וכל מליף suggest כָּל־נָבִיא וְכָל־חֹזֶה. This is preferable to the supposition that the text originally read כָּל־נְבִיאָיו simply, and כָּל־חֹזֶה came in later as a gloss.

14. ויקשו את ערפם] So Deut. 10. 16; Jer. 7. 26; 17. 23; 19. 15; Neh. 9. 16, 17, 29; 2 Chr. 30. 8†. Cf. the expressions עָרְפְּךָ הַקָּשֶׁה Deut. 31. 27; קְשֵׁה עֹרֶף Deut. 9. 6, 13; Ex. 32. 9; 33. 3, 5; 34. 9 (JE).

כערף] LXX, Luc. ὑπὲρ τὸν νῶτον, Pesh. ܡܢ ܩܕܠ read מֵעֹרֶף.

17. ויקסמו וג׳] On the meaning of the terms used in Hebrew to describe various kinds of divination cf. Dri. on Deut. 18. 10. נחש is uncertain (probably applied in the case of Joseph's cup, Gen. 44. 5, 15, to *hydromancy*, but also used more generally): קסם = Ar. قَسَمَ *to divide*, x. إِسْتَقْسَمَ *to get a part allotted to oneself, to draw lots*, especially with headless arrows, as is described, in the case of the king of Babylon, in Ezek. 21. 26 *f.* After *v.* 17[b] Luc. adds καὶ ἐποίησαν ἐφοὺδ καὶ θεραφείμ.

18. לא נשאר רק] For the construction of רק with the negative,

'*not . . . except*,' cf. I. 8. 9 אֵין בָּאָרוֹן רַק שְׁנֵי לֻחוֹת הָאֲבָנִים. The negative is really redundant. Cf., with the same verb, Ex. 8. 5, 7; Deut. 3. 11; 1 Sam. 5. 4.

20. וימאס] Luc. presupposes וַיִּמְאֲסוּ בַיהוָֹה כָּל־זֶרַע יִשְׂרָאֵל וַיִּתְאַנַּף י׳ בָּם וַיְעַנֵּם וג׳.

21. וידא] Q're וַיַּדַּח is probably correct.

והחטיאם] Perf. with weak ו, unusual in R^D's own composition. Cf. *note* on ותפש *ch.* 14. 7.

23. עד היום הזה] Cf. I. 8. 8 *note*.

17. 24–41. *The foreign settlers in the district of Samaria.*

The narrative is certainly composite. Verses 32, 33, 41, in speaking of the races which were settled by the king of Assyria in the cities of Samaria, say that they 'feared Yahwe,' while retaining the worship of their own national deities. In *v.* 34, on the contrary, it is stated with great emphasis that they 'feared not Yahwe.' Again, while *vv.* 24–34^{a} refer exclusively to the *foreign* settlers, and only mention the introduction into their midst of a single priest of Israelitish nationality (*v.* 28 אֶחָד מֵהַכֹּהֲנִים), to whom was due their instruction in the worship of Yahwe, *vv.* 34^{b}–40 are couched in such terms as can only refer to *Israelites as such*, of however mixed and renegade a strain. Notice especially *vv.* 35, 38, the reference to the Deuteronomic covenant; *v.* 36 'Yahwe, who brought you up out of the land of Egypt.'

Thus this latter section must be regarded as a later addition to the narrative of Kings[1], referring probably to the Samaritans of post-exilic times. Verse 40^{b} rounds off the interpolation by the repetition of *v.* 34^{a}—the statement of the older narrative to which the later writer attaches his addition. Verses 24–34^{a}, 41, on the other hand, form, in part at least, an ancient narrative embodied by R^D. Stade (*ZATW.* vi. 167 *ff.*) regards *vv.* 24–28, 41 as the original kernel which has received the later extension, *vv.* 29–34^{a}. Possibly

---

[1] R^D 2; cf. תִּשְׁמְרוּן וג׳ וְאֶת־הַחֻקִּים *v.* 37 (I. 2. 3 *note*); בִּזְרוֹעַ נְטוּיָה *v.* 36 (I. 8. 42 *note*); כָּל־הַיָּמִים *v.* 37 (I. 9. 3 *note*); אֱלֹהִים אֲחֵרִים *vv.* 35, 37 (I. 9. 6 *note*).

this latter may be assigned to R^D himself:—*v.* 32^b resembles I. 12. 31, and in *v.* 34^a עַד הַיּוֹם הַזֶּה is an expression commonly employed by R^D (cf. I. 8. 8 *note*).

24. ויבא וג׳] The fact that Sargon imported foreign prisoners of war into Samaria is attested by his inscriptions, though the peoples mentioned are not those of our passage. A mutilated passage, however, in his annals refers to a campaign in his first year (subsequent to the conquest of Samaria) which (as read by Winckler, *Alttest. Untersuchungen*, 105) was directed against the tribe of Tu'muna, which had apparently allied itself 'with Merodach-Baladan, king of Kaldu, who against the will of the gods had usurped the sovereignty of Babylon.' This was followed by a deportation of prisoners into 'the land Ḫatti,' a term which may include Samaria. In another passage he states that he settled in Samaria 'men of Tamud, Ibâdid, Marsîman, Ḫayâpâ, the remote Arbâi inhabiting the desert.' This took place in his seventh year, i. e. B. C. 715. Cf. Delitzsch, *Paradies*, 304; *COT.* i. *ad loc.*; Winckler, *Keilschrifttexte Sargons*, i. 20 *f.*; *KB.* ii. 42 *f.*

כּוּתָה is *Kutû* of the inscriptions, the modern *Tell-Ibrâhîm*, north-east of Babylon. סְפַרְוַיִם probably denotes the two Sippars, *Sippar son of Šamaš* (the sun-god), and *Sippar of Anunitu(m)*, between Bagdad and Babylon. For this identification a form סִפָּרִים might have been expected, and this is perhaps to be found in *v.* 31^b Kt. Some critics, however, have been led by the reference to Sepharvaim in *ch.* 18. 34=Isa. 36. 19, in close connexion with Ḥamath, Arpad, and Samaria, to infer that its situation is to be sought in the west; and סִבְרַיִם Ezek. 47. 16 is cited as possibly identical. Cf. Dillmann on Isaiah *ad loc.* The unknown עַוָּה is doubtless the same as עִוָּה of *ch.* 18. 34—by inference a western state.

Winckler (*Alttest. Untersuchungen*, 95–107) conjectures that confusion has been introduced into the text between Sargon's importation and that of Assurbanipal, to which allusion is made in Ezra 4. 8–10. Sargon makes no mention of the capture of prisoners of war from Babylon and Kutha. Babylon was not besieged by him until B.C. 710, and then he came not as enemy to the Babylonians, but as deliverer from the Chaldean yoke of Merodach-Baladan. His successor, Sennacherib, cannot have formed such a settlement of Babylonian captives, and the same is the case with Esarhaddon, the reference to this king in Ezra 4. 2 being clearly an error for Assurbanipal (אסנפר as in Ezra 4. 10). Assurbanipal, however, carried out a successful campaign against Sippar, Kutha, and Babylon, all of which are mentioned in *ch.* 17. 24, supposing ספרוים to be an erroneous alteration of an original ספר. Winckler regards the inclusion of Ḥamath and Awwa as of a piece with this alteration, the reason being that the two names stand together with Sepharvaim (the *Syrian* city) in the speech of the Rabshakeh, *ch.* 18. 34. For 'no Assyrian king would have introduced settlers from Ḥamath into Samaria, since such a measure would have failed of its object, viz. the placing of unruly elements at a distance from their native soil. Ḥamathites would not have remained long in Samaria, but would soon have made their escape back to their home which lay so near.' Thus, according to Winckler, the narrative of Kings affords us no authentic account as to the nationality of the peoples introduced into Samaria by Sargon. These arguments are accepted by Benz. It may be doubted, however, whether there is evidence sufficient to substantiate Winckler's theory. For example, in default of precise information as to the reasons which may have influenced Sargon in the disposal of his prisoners of war, the argument by which Winckler rejects the mention of Ḥamath and Awwa appears to be highly arbitrary. Again, Assurbanipal, so far from mentioning any transportation of the people of Sippar, Kutha, and Babylon, definitely states that he allowed the remnant of them to remain in Babylonia (*KB*. ii. 192 *f*.).

Kit. accepts Winckler's argument with regard to Ḥamath and Awwa, but demurs to his main theory as without basis, either in the Old Testament or in the inscriptions.

25. האריות] On the use of the article cf. *note* on I. 13. 14.

26. ויאמרו] Impersonal; 'And it was told.'

27. הִגְלִיתֶם] Luc. ὧν ἀπῴκισα, i. e. הִגְלֵיתִם—certainly correct.

וילכו וישבו] Luc., Vulg., Pesh. וַיֵּלֶךְ וַיֵּשֶׁב, correctly.

30. סכות בנות] Uncertain. The interpretation of Delitzsch (*Paradies*, 215) *Sakkut-binûtu*, 'supreme judge of the Universe,' is rejected by Schrader (*COT. ad loc.*), who suggests identification with *Zîr-bânit* or *Zar-pa-ni-tuv*, the consort of *Marduk*. Jensen (*ZA.* iv. 352) regards בְּנוֹת as equivalent to *banîtu*, an epithet of *Ištar*. Cheyne (*Expos. Times*, x. 429) proposes to emend סַכּוּת כֵּיוָן, the two names which denote the Babylonian Saturn. Cf. Am. 5. 26.

נרגל] Nergal appears in the inscriptions as the god of Kutha. He is the lord of hell, and the god of war and pestilence. As a destructive agency his symbol is the lion. Jensen (*Kosmologie*, 476 *ff.*) explains the name as compounded of *Ni+uru+gal*= *Ni+unu+gal*='Lord of the great city,' or rather 'dwelling,' i. e. the Underworld. Cf. also *COT. ad loc.*

31. אדרמלך] Probably 'Adar is king' (*or* 'counsellor'). Adar appears as a west Semitic god in the name יתנאדר 'Adar has given' (Baethgen, *Semit. Religionsgeschichte*, 54), but is best known as an Assyrian god, the name, according to Schrader, being Akkadian in origin, and originally pronounced *A-tar*, 'father of decision.' אדרמלך occurs as the name of a son of Sennacherib in *ch.* 19. 37, a fact which favours the view that we have here the name of an *Assyrian* deity, and so lends weight to the view (above noticed) that ספרוים denotes Sippar rather than a western city.

ענמלך] Perhaps equivalent to ענומלך, i. e. 'Anu is king' (*or* 'counsellor'). Anu is the god of heaven, supreme among the deities of Assyria and Babylon.

אלה ספרים] Kt. (according to Ginsburg, אֱל הספרים) seems to make reference to one deity only, and similarly Luc. omits ענמלך, and reads τῷ 'Αδραμέλεχ Θεῷ Σεπφαρείμ.

32. מקצותם] 'From among the whole of them.' Cf. I. 12. 31 *note*. LXX, Luc. offer a double version of this verse, the second

corresponding to MT., while the first runs *καὶ ἦσαν φοβούμενοι τὸν κύριον, καὶ κατῴκισαν τὰ βδελύγματα αὐτῶν ἐν τοῖς οἴκοις τῶν ὑψηλῶν ἃ ἐποίησαν ἐν Σαμαρείᾳ, ἔθνος ἔθνος ἐν πόλει ἐν ᾗ κατῴκουν ἐν αὐτῇ*, i. e. probably וַיִּהְיוּ יְרֵאִים אֶת־י׳ וַיַּעֲשׂוּ לָהֶם (or וַיּוֹשִׁיבוּ) שִׁקֻּצֵיהֶם בְּבָתֵּי הַבָּמוֹת אֲשֶׁר עָשׂוּ בְּשֹׁמְרוֹן גּוֹי גּוֹי בָּעִיר אֲשֶׁר יָשְׁבוּ (or הֵמָּה יֹשְׁבִים) שָׁם. This reading bears the stamp of superiority, MT. probably representing the restoration of an imperfect text upon the lines of I. 12. 31.

18—20. *Ḥezekiah, king of Judah.*

Ch. 18. 1–8 is mainly the work of R^D^, based upon the notices of *vv.* 4, 7^b^, 8. The substance of *vv.* 7^b^, 8 is probably drawn from the Annals. With regard to *v.* 4 this is not so clear. The verse shows marks of a late style (perfect with weak ו, as in 21. 4, 6; 23. 4 *ff.*), and sketches the outline of a religious reformation which appears in all essentials to have resembled and anticipated the reformation of Josiah. Hence some critics regard the notice as a late and unhistorical interpolation (cf. Stade, *Ges.* i. 607 *f.; ZATW.* iii. 8 *ff.;* vi. 170 *ff.;* Wellh., *C.* 291).

The occurrence of a reformation under Ḥezekiah is supported by 18. 22 (which must, with the rejection of 18. 4, be likewise branded as a later misconception), and perhaps also by the statement of Jer. 26. 17–19^a^, which speaks of the influence exercised upon Ḥezekiah and all Judah by the preaching of Micah the Morashtite. Mic. 1. 5^b^ MT. mentions the בָּמוֹת of Jerusalem for reprobation; but this passage must not be pressed, because LXX, Pesh., Targ. presuppose a different reading[1]. Certainly Isaiah does not seem to have had in view any centralization of Yahwe's cultus, such as was prominent in Josiah's reformation; but his attacks upon the idol-worship (Isa. 2. 8, 18, 20; 31. 7; cf. 10. 10, 11), tree-worship (1. 29), and necromancy (8. 19), which seem to have been rife in the kingdom of Judah, are in agreement with

[1] חַטָּאת 'sin,' parallel to פֶּשַׁע 'transgression,' as in *v.* 4^a^. The reading of MT. is, however, accepted by Kit. (*Hist.* ii. 357), who regards the rendering of the Versions as merely a simplification.

such a movement in the direction of the pure worship of Yahwe. Probably, therefore, as is allowed by Sta. (*Ges.*, *loc. cit.*), the statement of *v.* 4^b is based upon authentic information as to such a reform, and this has been later on expanded in *v.* 4^a, under the influence of the accomplished fact of Josiah's reformation.

18. 2. אבי] Shortened form of אֲבִיָּה 2 Chr. 29. 1.

4. הוא הסיר] On the use of הוא cf. *ch.* 14. 7 *note.*

נחשתן] Vocalization connects the name with נְחֹשֶׁת, with a formative termination 'brazen one.' It seems certain, however, that the word is connected with נָחָשׁ; and, unless there is intended a play upon the similarity in name of the thing 'serpent,' *and* its material 'brass,' it is possible that the vocalization is incorrect. Cf. Luc. Νεεσθάν. For conjectures as to the form and its meaning cf. *Heb. Lex. Oxf.*, *s. v.*

5. ואחריו וג׳] Scarcely original. The clumsily connected sentence ואשר היו לפניו introduces a statement which we should have expected to occupy the first place (cf. I. 3. 12); and the statement ואחריו וג׳ is in direct contradiction to *ch.* 23. 25, where Josiah is regarded, from the standpoint of R^D, as the ideal of a religious king. Probably therefore we should omit אחריו and the ו before ואשר, and read וְלֹא הָיָה כָמֹהוּ בְּכָל־מַלְכֵי יְהוּדָה אֲשֶׁר הָיוּ לְפָנָיו.

6. וידבק ביהוה] On the use of דבק by R^D cf. *note* on I. 11. 2.

לא סר מאחריו] Cf. *ch.* 3. 3 *note.*

את משה] Luc. τῷ Μωσῇ παιδὶ αὐτοῦ.

7. והיה] Probably frequentative, in reference to the repeated occasions depicted by יֵצֵא.

9–12. A notice from the Annals, introduced by the synchronism of R^D, *v.* 9^a, and closed by his comment *v.* 12. The notice is identical with *ch.* 17. 5, 6.

18. 13—**20.** 19. *Sennacherib's campaign against Judah* (18. 13—19. 37): *sickness and recovery of Hezekiah* (20. 1–11): *embassy of Merodach-Baladan* (20. 12–19).

Chh. 18. 13, 17—20. 19 = Isa. 36. 1—38. 8; 38. 21—39. 8. The section *vv.* 14–16, which is not found in Isaiah, is distinguished from 18. 13, 17 *ff.* by the form of the name חִזְקִיָּה (instead of חִזְקִיָּהוּ) which occurs also in *vv.* 1, 10 (Annals). The notice appears to be in strict agreement with the Assyrian record (cf. *Append.* 5, col. iii. ll. 11 *ff.*), and is probably a genuine excerpt from the Annals.

It is generally agreed that the narrative of Isa. 36. 1—39. 8 cannot be traced to Isaiah himself, but must be of a considerably later date. Notice the mention of Sennacherib's death (Isa. 37. 38 || *ch.* 19. 37), which did not happen until B.C. 681, twenty years after the campaign against Jerusalem, and certainly later than the death of Isaiah. Again, it seems to be clear that the Isaiah section (except 38. 9–20, from another source) must have been extracted from our Book of Kings by the editor of Isa. 1—39. For certain phrases which are due to R^D in the Kings-narrative appear also in Isaiah:—cf. למען דוד עבדי *ch.* 19. 34 || Isa. 37. 35; את אשר התהלכתי . . . בעיניך *ch.* 20. 3 || Isa. 38. 3; and the redactional phrases בימים ההם *ch.* 20. 1 || Isa. 38. 1; בעת ההיא *ch.* 20. 12 || Isa. 39. 1. Kings is also superior to Isaiah in the account of Ḥezekiah's sickness. Isa. 38. 4–8 has been abbreviated; 38. 21, 22 is misplaced.

The Kings-narrative 18. 13, 17—20. 19 seems to represent a combination of three sources. Sta. (*ZATW.* vi. 174) notices that Isaiah's threat against Sennacherib occurs three times in similar terms: 19. 7; 19. 28^b; 19. 33. The contents of Sennacherib's letter (19. 10–13) merely repeat in brief that which has already been said by the Rabshakeh (18. 28–35). Again, it is highly improbable that Sennacherib, after hearing the news with regard to Tirhaḳah (19. 9^a), should have imagined that the mere dispatch of a letter would be likely to compel Ḥezekiah's submission, after the failure of previous verbal negotiations. The true sequel to 19. 9^a seems to be 19. 36 *f.*; upon receiving information of Tirhaḳah's hostile movement, Sennacherib raises the siege of Jerusalem and returns to Assyria. We have, then, two separate accounts of the Assyrian campaign, 18. 13, 17—19. 9^a, 36 *f.*, and 19. 9^b–35; 19. 9^b having probably been slightly modified by the redactor. Further, the section 19. 9^b–35 itself appears to be composite in character. The taunt-song *vv.* 21–28, with its accompanying sign *vv.* 29–31, stands apart from the prosaic statement *vv.* 32–34. לכן 'therefore' of *v.* 32 answers, not to anything in the prophecy preceding, but to *v.* $20^b \beta$, אשר התפללת ... שמעתי 'Whereas thou hast prayed... I have heard'; and, as has been noticed above, *vv.* 28^b, 33 are duplicates of the same statement. Thus *vv.* 21–31, generally regarded by critics as an authentic prophecy of Isaiah, appear to have been inserted into the midst of the prophetical history 19. 9^b–20, 32–34, *v.* 21^a representing the redactor's link.

The narrative of 20. 1–19 probably belongs to the author of one of the two preceding narrative sections. Cheyne, following Duhm, selects the second narrative, 19. 9^b *ff.* Notice, as a point of connexion, the occurrence of a prayer of Ḥezekiah in each section, 19. 15 *ff.*; 20. 2 *f.* Very possibly the chronological notice at the beginning of 18. 13, 'In the fourteenth year of king Ḥezekiah,' properly refers to the events of 20. 1–19, and occupies its present position upon the false assumption that Sennacherib's invasion took place in the same year as Ḥezekiah's sickness and recovery. This arrangement is probably due to R^D, who removed the note of time from its true position at the head of the narrative of 20. 1 *ff.*, replacing it by his synchronistic phrase, 'In those days[1].' Notice the reference to Assyria in 20. 6. The whole verse, from וּמִכַּף 'and from the hand &c.,' must be due to the author of the mistaken synchronism. Cf. the latter half with 19. 34.

13. ובארבע עשרה שנה] The sixth year of Ḥezekiah for the fall of Samaria, B.C. 722 (*v.* 10), cannot be reconciled with the fourteenth year for Sennacherib's campaign, B.C. 701, and it seems the best course to regard this latter date as true for the sickness of Ḥezekiah and the embassy of Merodach-Baladan (*ch.* 20), which will then fall cir. B.C. 714. Thus Ḥezekiah's reign may

[1] Cf. *note* on *ch.* 18. 13.

be supposed to have closed B.C. 699, i.e. some fifteen years after B.C. 714 (*ch.* 20. 6[a]).

על כל ערי וג׳] According to the inscription of the Taylor cylinder, col. iii. l. 13 (cf. *Append.* 5), Sennacherib captured forty-six fortified towns, besides innumerable fortresses and small places.

14. וישלח וג׳] LXX, Luc., Vulg. supply an object מַלְאָכִים.

לכישה] Cf. *ch.* 14. 19 *note.*

שלש מאות וג׳] The sum is given in the inscription (col. iii. l. 34) as thirty talents of gold and 800 talents of silver. Schrader quotes Brandis for the view that the difference in the statement of the amount of the silver is due to the difference in weight between the Babylonian *light* and the Palestinian *heavy* talent.

16. בעת ההיא] Cf. I. 14. 1 *note.*

17. תרתן] Assyr. *tartânu* or *turtânu,* title of the commander-in-chief of the Assyrian army. || Isa. 36. 2 omits this official and the one following.

רב סרים] Probably the Hebrew perversion ('chief of the eunuchs') of an Assyrian title which is unknown to us.

רב שקה] Probably in Assyr. *râb-šaḳê,* i.e. 'high officer.' Cf. *šud-šaḳû* or *šud-šaḳê,* 'high-lord, chieftain.' Delitzsch, *Assyr. HWB.* 685.

ויעלו ויבאו] Rightly omitted in the second place by LXX, Luc., Vulg., Pesh.

בתעלת וג׳] Cf. Isa. 7. 3. The site is unknown. For the conjectures which have been offered cf. Dillmann on Isa. 7. 3.

18. על הבית] Cf. I. 4. 6 *note.*

19. אשר בטחת] Luc. ἣν πέποιθας σὺ καὶ πᾶς Ἰούδα. Possibly the addition may be due to corruption of Σὺ εἶπας, i.e. אָמַרְתָּ, which is missing in Luc., at the beginning of the following verse. LXX εἶπας.

22. בירושלם] || Isa. 36. 7 omits.

24. פחת אחד וג׳] 'One satrap of the least of my lord's servants.' פַּחַת must be regarded as attracted into the construct state of its adjective אַחַד, as is the case in the expression אֵשֶׁת יְפַת תֹּאַר Deut.

21. 11. The general verdict is for the excision of פחת as a corrupt insertion, but the construction, though harsh, can scarcely be asserted to be impossible, in view of our limited knowledge of the possibilities of Hebrew syntax. Cf. Kö. *Syntax*, §§ 277 *o*, 337 *o*. On the meaning and use of פֶּחָה cf. *note* on I. 10. 15.

25. עליתי] LXX, Luc. ἀνέβημεν.

27. העל וג׳] Notice the confusion between על and אל:—על אדניך ואליך . . . על האנשים. ‖ Isa. 36. 12 reads האל אדניך. On this confusion between the prepositions cf. *note* on על גחון I. 1. 38, and the full list of instances given in *Heb. Lex. Oxf.*, *s. v.* על § 7 *c*.

29. מידו] Luc., Vulg., Pesh., Targ. rightly presuppose מִיָּדִי. ‖ Isa. 36. 14 omits.

31. עשו אתי ברכה] RV., following Targ., 'Make *your peace* with me.' This use of ברכה 'blessing,' in the sense of *a mutual well wishing* taking the form of a *treaty*, is unique.

32. וחיו] On the idiomatic use of the imperative in place of the cohortative cf. I. 1. 12 *note*.

34. איה וג׳] The allusion is perhaps to Sargon's defeat of *Ya'u-bi'di* king of Ḥamath, who had induced the Assyrian provinces of Arpad, Ṣimirra, Damascus, and Samaria to join with him in revolt. This coalition was crushed at Qarqar in B.C. 720. Cf. *KB*. ii. 56 *f*. אַרְפָּד the modern *Tell-Erfâd*, to the north of Aleppo, had been conquered by Tiglath-Pileser III, in B.C. 743–740. *KB*. i. 212 *f*. Upon סְפַרְוַיִם cf. *ch*. 17. 24 *note*. הֵנַע and עִוָּה (omitted in ‖ Isa. 36. 19) are unknown [1]. The latter is doubtless the same as עַוָּה of *ch*. 17. 24.

The second half of the verse runs in Luc. καὶ ποῦ εἰσὶν οἱ θεοὶ τῆς χώρας Σαμαρείας; μὴ ἐξείλαντο τὴν Σαμάρειαν ἐκ χειρός μου; וְאַיֵּה אֱלֹהֵי אֶרֶץ שֹׁמְרוֹן הֲכִי הִצִּילוּ וג׳. The insertion is indispensable, the subject presupposed by הצילו being obviously 'the gods of Samaria.' So Klo., Kamp., Benz., Kit., Oort.

---

[1] Targ. הלא טלטילינון ואגליאינון 'Has he not dispersed them and carried them captive?' takes the forms as verbs, Hiph'il of נוע and Pi'el of עוה. Similarly Σ. in Isa. 37. 13 ἀνεστάτωσε καὶ ἐταπείνωσε.

36. והחרישו] || Isa. 36. 21 וַיַּחֲרִישׁוּ, correctly.

העם] LXX, Luc. omit.

37. קרועי בגדים] Lit. 'rent as to garment.' Cf. *note* on I. 15. 23.

19. 2. After καὶ Σομναν τὸν γραμματέα Luc. has the curious insertion καὶ τὸν Σαιτην καὶ τὸν Σουμαιησουμαι καὶ τὸν Μακραπην τὸν γέροντα. Possibly Σαιτην and Σουμ. represent marginal notes of three various spellings of the name שבנא; the second perhaps Σουμα ἢ Σουμα by transposition of the letters of Σομνα.

3. ללדה] LXX, Luc., Vulg., Pesh. presuppose לַיֹּלֵדָה 'to her who is in travail,' probably correctly. So Klo. Cf. Mic. 4. 9, 10; Hos. 13. 13; Jer. 49. 24. The form לֵדָה as infin. constr. for the normal לֶדֶת occurs elsewhere Hos. 9. 11; Jer. 13. 21.

4. והוכיח] RV. 'And will rebuke the words which Yahwe thy God hath heard.' So Pesh., Targ. והוכיח is thus perf. with ו consec. in continuation of ישמע. LXX, Luc., Vulg. treat והוכיח as infin. constr., equivalent to וּלְהוֹכִיחַ, thus regarding מֶלֶךְ־אַשּׁוּר as the subject.

8. לבנה] Cf. *ch.* 8. 22 *note*.

9. וישמע אל וג׳] || Isa. 37. 9 reads על for אל.

תרהקה] Mentioned by Sennacherib not by name but as 'the king of *Miluḫḫi*,' Taylor cylinder, col. ii. ll. 69 *ff.* (cf. *Append.* 5). The name is given by Assurbanipal as *Tar-ḳu-u*, Egyptian *T-h-r-ḳ*.

וישב וישלח] || Isa. 37. 9 וישמע וישלח 'and when he had heard, he sent.' וישב was doubtless written by the hand which connected the following narrative with the preceding, i.e. presumably the hand of R^D (cf. p. 339): hence וישמע may be judged to be a corruption of וישב. LXX in Isaiah combines the two readings: καὶ ἀκούσας ἀπέστρεψεν καὶ ἀπέστειλεν.

10. LXX omits the introductory sentence down to the first לאמר, probably through homoioteleuton with the end of *v.* 9.

11. להחרימם] '*As regards* devoting them to destruction.'

12. אשר שחתו אבותי] Luc. οὓς διέφθειραν οἱ πατέρες μου αὐτοὺς καὶ τὰς χώρας αὐτῶν. The reading of LXX has arisen through corruption of οὓς into οὐ.

את גוזן וג׳] On גוזן cf. *ch.* 17. 6. חרן is *Ḥarran* of the inscriptions, Charrae of the Romans, in north-west Mesopotamia, situated on the Belias, a tributary of the Euphrates. רצף, mentioned in the inscriptions as *Ra-ṣa-ap-pa* or *Ra-ṣap-pa*, is the Ῥησάφα of Ptolemaeus (v. 15), and the modern *Ruṣâfa*, on the route from Sura to Palmyra in the Euphrates valley *Ez-Zôr* (cf. Delitzsch, *Paradies*, 297). The בני עדן belonged to the Aramaean state *Bît-Adini*, situated between the Euphrates and the Belias, which offered stubborn resistance to Assur-naẓir-pal, and was conquered by his successor Shalmaneser II in B.C. 856 (Hommel, *Assyria* in Hastings, *BD.* i. 183b, 184b; Maspero, iii. 30 *f.*, 66). The site of תלאשר (|| Isa. 37. 12 תְּלַשָּׂר) must naturally be sought for in the same neighbourhood, and is probably to be identified with *Til-aŝurri* in the land of the Ḥittites (cf. Winckler, *Geschichte Babyloniens*, 269, 335 *f.*).

Luc. separates תלאשר from necessary connexion with בני עדן by the insertion of *καί*, i. e. וַאֲשֶׁר בִּתְלַאשָּׂר.

13. איו וג׳] 'Where is *he*, (viz.) the king of Ḥamath?' So Isa. 19. 12 אַיָּם אֵפוֹא חֲכָמֶיךָ; Mic. 7. 10 אַיּוֹ י׳ אֱלֹהָיִךְ. || Isa. 37. 13 reads אַיֵּה.

מלך חמת וג׳] Cf. *ch.* 18. 34 *note*.

15. ויתפלל ח׳ לפני י׳] LXX omits.

י׳ אלהי ישראל] Luc. Κύριε παντοκράτωρ, ὁ Θεὸς Ἰσραήλ, Pesh. ܡܪܝܐ ܚܝܠܬܢܐ: ܐܠܗܗ ܕܐܝܣܪܝܠ presuppose the insertion of צְבָאוֹת after י׳, as in || Isa. 37. 16.

ישב הכרבים] Cf. 1 Sam. 4. 4; 2 Sam. 6. 2. || 1 Chr. 13. 6; Ps. 80. 2; 99. 1. The reference is primarily to the presence of the שְׁכִינָה above the כַּפֹּרֶת in the innermost sanctuary of the Temple.

אתה הוא האלהים] So 2 Sam. 7. 28. Probably '*Thou* (with emphasis; lit. 'Thou-He') art the God'; or else 'Thou art He, (namely) the God.' Cf. Dri. *Tenses*, § 200.

16a. וּשֲׁמַע] *Ḥatef-pathaḥ* frequently occurs under initial sibilants after ו copulative. Cf. I. 14. 21 וּשֲׁבַע; *ch.* 9. 17 וּשֲׁלַח; and other instances cited in G-K. § 10 *g*. Cf. *note* on I. 13. 7.

אשר שלחו] Read אֲשֶׁר שָׁלַח with LXX, Luc., Vulg., Pesh., and

‖ Isa. 37. 17; i. e. probably 'which he hath sent' (LXX, Luc.), or possibly 'who hath sent' (Vulg.).

17. החריבו] Probably we should read הֶחֱרִימוּ, in agreement with *v.* 11. So Benz., Kit., and (on Isa.) Duhm, Cheyne, Marti, and doubtfully Dillmann.

את הגוים] ‖ Isa. 37. 18 erroneously אֶת־כָּל־הָאֲרָצוֹת.

ואת ארצם] LXX omits. Luc. καὶ πᾶσαν τὴν γῆν αὐτῶν. Vulg. *et terras omnium.*

18. ונתנו] Irregular usage of the perfect with weak ו. ‖ Isa. 37. 19 is correct in reading infin. abs. וְנָתֹן, in accordance with idiom. Da. § 88[a].

19. כי אתה וג׳] ‖ Isa. 37. 20 omits אלהים erroneously.

20. י׳ אלהי ישראל] LXX, Luc. Κύριος (LXX adds ὁ Θεὸς) τῶν δυνάμεων Θεὸς Ἰσραήλ.

21. בתולת בת ציון] Suspended construct state. Cf. *note* on אַנְשֵׁי בְנֵי־אֲדֹנֵיכֶם *ch.* 10. 6.

ראש הניעה] A gesture of mockery. Cf. Ps. 22. 8; 109. 25; Lam. 2. 15; Job 16. 4.

22. חרפת וגדפת] Weak ו *co-ordinates* two synonymous ideas. Cf. Dri. *Tenses,* § 132.

23. ברכב] Q're בְּרֹב in agreement with the text of many Codd., all Verss. and ‖ Isa. 37. 24.

וְאֶכְרֹת] LXX, Luc., Vulg. are probably correct in reading וָאֶכְרֹת, and similarly וָאָבוֹא, and *v.* 24 וָאַחֲרִב, *v.* 25 (except Vulg.) וַתְּהִי. So most moderns.

מלון קצה] 'His farthest lodging-place'; lit. 'the lodging-place of his end.' מלון as in Isa. 10. 29. LXX μέσον, Cod. A, Luc. μέρος are doubtless emendations of a transliteration μέλων. Q're קִצּוֹ appears in the text of many Codd.

‖ Isa. 37. 24 offers the inferior reading מְרוֹם קִצּוֹ.

24. ואחרב] In reference to 'all the Nile-streams of Egypt,' וָאחרב must be regarded as a perfect of certitude; and this is quite consistent with the known intentions of Sennacherib, and the boastful tenour of the words which are put into his mouth.

מצור] Winckler (*Alttest. Untersuchungen*, 170) supposes that the original vocalization was מִיצוֹר or מִצּוֹר, on the ground that the form *Mi-iç-ça-ri* occurs twice on the Amarna tablets. The Massoretic vocalization will then be due to identification of the name with the Hebrew word meaning 'fortification.'

25. הלא וג'] Render as in RV., with the alteration וַתְּהִי 'that thou becamest,' in place of וּתְהִי, rendered 'that thou shouldest be,' and the addition of 'and' before 'now.' The thought of the verse is that of Isa. 10. 5 *ff*.

The first part of the verse down to למימי קדם is omitted by LXX.

ויצרתיה] Omit ו with LXX, Luc., Vulg., Pesh. So Marti.

עתה] Read וְעַתָּה with LXX, Luc., Vulg., Pesh.

לַהְשׁוֹת] Standing for לְהַשְׁאוֹת (‖ Isa. 37. 26) with syncope of ו. Cf. G-K. §§ 23 *f*., 75 *qq*.

נִצִּים] Participle Niph'al of נצה. The only other occurrence of the verb is in Jer. 4. 7, where תִּנָּצֶינָה should probably be restored for Qal תִּצֶּינָה.

26. קצרי יד] 'Short of hand,' i. e. unequal to the task of saving themselves. So, with the verb, Isa. 50. 2 הֲקָצוֹר קָצְרָה יָדִי מִפְּדוּת; 59. 1; Num. 11. 23.

ויבשו] ‖ Isa. 37. 27 וָבֹשׁוּ, perfect with ו co-ordinate.

ושדפה לפני קמה] RV., 'and as corn blasted before it be grown up,' follows the rendering of Vulg. *quae arefacta est antequam veniret ad maturitatem;* cf. Targ. דישלוק עד לא מטא למיהוי שובלין. Such a sense, however, cannot be extracted from the original as it stands; and, if we are to retain it, the least alteration will be הַשָּׁדוּף לִפְנֵי קָמוֹ, referring back to חֲצִיר גַּגּוֹת. But there can be no doubt that Wellh. (*C.* 360) is right in finding in לפני קמה a corruption of לְפָנַי קֻמְךָ which connects with וְשִׁבְתְּךָ of the following verse: 'Before me is thy rising up and thy lying down.' This supersedes the emendation of Th. לִפְנֵי קָדִים 'before the east wind.' Possibly, then, שְׁדֵפָה may stand by itself in the sense 'blasted' (sc. corn); and this is preferable to ‖ Isa. 37. 27 שְׁדֵמָה, which seems to give no sense in this connexion. Klo.'s emendation וּשְׁפָיִים is worthy of notice: 'grass of the house tops *and of the downs*.' So Cheyne. For שפיים as barren uplands, cf. Isa. 41. 18; Jer. 12. 12.

28. שאננך] RV. text, 'thine arrogance,' in agreement with LXX, Luc. τὸ στρῆνός σου, Vulg. *superbia tua*, a rendering perhaps to be justified by Ps. 123. 4. RV. marg., 'thy careless ease,' is the more usual meaning. This latter rendering, however, is unsuitable to the context and parallelism; and the same remark applies, in a less degree, to the former rendering. Probably the emendation שְׁאוֹנְךָ 'thy tumult,' adopted by Benz., Kit., Budde, Grätz, Cheyne, is correct.

ושמתי וג׳] The figure is that of a savage beast led captive by a ring in its nose. Cf. Ezek. 19. 4, and the similar figure of Ezek. 29. 4; 38. 4.

29. ספיח] 'That which groweth of itself'; from unused root equivalent to Ar. سَفَحَ *pour out*, and so, the produce of grain *spilled* or *self-sown*. סָחִישׁ (|| Isa. 37. 30 שָׁחִים) is by inference the self-sown produce of this natural crop in the second year. So Verss.

31. Q're צְבָאוֹת is supported by the text of many Codd., all Verss., and || Isa. 37. 32.

33. יבא] Read בָּא with || Isa. 37. 34.

34. להושיעה] LXX omits. In Luc. the whole of *v.* 34[a] has fallen out.

ולמען דוד עבדי] Cf. I. 11. 12 *note*.

35. The catastrophe, as might have been expected, is passed over in silence in the Assyrian inscriptions; but the fact that Sennacherib does not make claim to have captured Jerusalem is in agreement with our narrative. Herodotus (ii. 141) records an Egyptian tradition, according to which Sennacherib's army was easily routed at Pelusium because innumerable field-mice had during the night gnawed through its bow-strings and the thongs of its shields.

36. וילך וישב] Luc. omits.

37. נסרך] No such god is known in the Assyrian inscriptions.

Halévy (*Mélanges de crit.* 177) plausibly conjectures that the name should be נסוך, i.e. *Nusku,* a solar deity.

ויהי הוא משתחוה וג׳] On the construction cf. I. 13. 20 *note.*

אדרמלך] Cf. *note* on *ch.* 17. 31.

שׂראצר] According to Schrader (*COT. ad loc.*) the name is shortened from *Nergal-šar-uṣur* (cf. Jer. 39. 3, 13). He refers to Abydenus, as quoted by Eusebius, who states that Sennacherib was assassinated by *Adramelus,* and succeeded by *Nergilus,* and that this latter was put to death by *Axerdis.* If, as seems obvious, Adramelus corresponds to אדרמלך and Axerdis to אסרחדן, then Nergilus may be thought to answer to שׂראצר.

בניו] Q're has the support of many Codd., all Verss., and ‖ Isa. 37. 38.

אררט] Assyr. *Urarṭu,* the land of Armenia.

20. 1. בימים ההם] Cf. *ch.* 10. 32 *note.*

צו לביתך] Cf. I. 2. 1 *note.*

כי מת אתה] 'For thou art *about to die*'; the participle denoting the *futurum instans.* The same idiomatic expression occurs Gen. 20. 3; 48. 21; 50. 5, 24; Deut. 4. 22; Jer. 28. 16. Cf. also Deut. 17. 6 הַמֵּת 'the doomed man.'

2. וַיַּסֵּב] On the Aramaizing form cf. G-K. § 67 *y.*

4. ויהי וג׳] On the construction cf. Dri. *Tenses,* § 165. ‖ Isa. 38. 4 is much abbreviated.

העיר] Read חָצֵר with the text of several Codd., and all Verss. On חָצֵר used definitely without the article cf. I. 7. 8 *note.* The middle court was the courtyard of the palace, called חָצֵר הָאַחֶרֶת I. 7. 8 in contrast to the Temple (innermost) court. Cf. *note* on I. 6. 36.

5. נגיד] Cf. I. 1. 35 *note.*

6. למעני וג׳] ‖ Isa. 38. 6 omits.

7. קחו וג׳] LXX, Luc., Pesh. presuppose the reading יִקְחוּ . . . וְיָשִׂימוּ . . . וְיֶחִי 'Let them take . . . and place . . . that he may recover.' This is probably original, Ḥezekiah's request for the sign in *v.* 8 naturally presupposing that recovery is only as yet promised and not accomplished. וַיִּקְחוּ *v.* 7ᵇ must have been

inserted after וישימו וג׳ had been taken as describing a completed sequence of events.

|| Isa. 38. 21 (which, with *v.* 22, is misplaced) reads יִשְׂאוּ . . . וְיִמְרְחוּ . . . וְיֶחִי. The verb מרח, a ἅπαξ λεγ. in Heb., is explained from the Ar. مَرَخَ *anoint, smear.*

8. מה אות וג׳] || Isa. 38. 22 מה אות כי אעלה בית י׳.

9. הלך וג׳] The only possible rendering is that of RV. marg. 'The shadow is gone forward &c.' But it is evident from Ḥezekiah's reply, *v.* 10, that an alternative is offered to him. We must therefore emend הֲיֵלֵךְ, which is expressed by Targ. היהך, and presupposed by the other Verss. So Th. (doubtfully), Klo., Kamp., Benz., Kit., Oort.

11^b. As the text stands, יָרְדָה can only refer to the *masc.* הַצֵּל. The true subj. of the verb is, however, preserved by Pesh., Targ., viz. הַשֶּׁמֶשׁ, which should be inserted after יָרְדָה, or after אָחָז as in Isaiah (see below). The statement then runs:—'And he brought back the shadow on the steps by which the sun had gone down on the step-clock of Aḥaz, ten steps.' This slight correction (Th., Oort) is more obvious than the supposition that במעלות אשר ירדה is an erroneous insertion from || Isa. 38. 8.

The Isaianic account omits the offer of an alternative sign; *v.* 8 with the emendations הַצֵּל for צֵל, הַשֶּׁמֶשׁ for בַּשֶּׁמֶשׁ (Kautzsch and others) reading as follows:—הִנְנִי מֵשִׁיב אֶת־הַצֵּל הַמַּעֲלוֹת אֲשֶׁר יָרְדָה בְּמַעֲלוֹת אָחָז הַשֶּׁמֶשׁ אֲחֹרַנִּית עֶשֶׂר מַעֲלוֹת וַתָּשָׁב הַשֶּׁמֶשׁ עֶשֶׂר מַעֲלוֹת בַּמַּעֲלוֹת אֲשֶׁר יָרָדָה׃ 'Behold I will bring back the shadow so many steps as the sun has gone down upon the step-clock of Aḥaz, even ten steps. And the sun returned ten steps upon the steps by which it had gone down.'

The character of the sun-clock called מעלות can only be conjectured. Most probably it was 'a pointed pillar (obelisk) upon a (round or square) plinth, to which a flight of steps led up. This pillar cast the shadow of its point at midday upon the highest, and at morning and evening upon the lowest step (west or east), and thus indicated the time of day.' Cf. Dillmann on Isaiah *ad loc.* The clock may have been introduced by Aḥaz from Assyria (cf. *ch.* 16. 10 *ff.*). According to Herodotus (ii. 109) the Babylonians were the inventors of the πόλος or concave sun-dial upon which the shadow was cast by the γνώμων, and of the division of the day into twelve hours.

12. בעת ההיא] Cf. I. 14. 1 *note.*

בראדך בלאדן] Read מראדך בלאדן with several Codd., LXX, Luc., Pesh., Targ., and ‖ Isa. 39. 1. The Assyrian form is *Marduk-abal-idinna.* Merodach-Baladan appears at first as king of the *Kaldu.* His kingdom is called *Bît-Yakin,* 'by the salt waters,' i.e. the Persian Gulf. He paid homage and tribute to Tiglath-Pileser in B.C. 729 (Rost, 60 *f.*), but seems to have seized the opportunity of the death of Shalmaneser and the accession of Sargon to constitute himself king of Babylon. His principal ally was *Ḫumbanigaš* king of Elam. Sargon directed an expedition against the allies (B.C. 721); but little is known about it, and it seems to have met with ill success. *Ḫumbanigaš* of Elam died in B.C. 717, and was succeeded by his less able son *Šutur-naḫundi.* Merodach-Baladan retained the sovereignty of Babylon for twelve years, until Sargon, having settled his affairs in the west and north, was able to direct his arms against him. After a campaign which occupied B.C. 710–709, Sargon entered Babylon in triumph. He claims to have taken Merodach-Baladan prisoner (Winckler, *Sargon,* 84 *f.*, 122 *f.*, 150 *f.*), but elsewhere (Winckler, *Sargon,* 58 *f.*) seems to state that he fled away and could not be found. The latter alternative seems to be the more probable, since a Merodach-Baladan appears some years later as king of Babylon for nine months, until conquered and driven out by Sennacherib (B.C. 704: cf. Tiele, *Bab. Gesch.* i. 246). Cf. Winckler, *Sargon,* pp. xv *f.*, xvii, xxxi–xxxix; Maspero, iii. 222 *ff.*, 254 *ff.*

There can be no doubt that Merodach-Baladan's embassy to Ḥezekiah took place some time prior to B.C. 710, whilst he was forming alliances in order to meet the advance of Sargon, which he must have foreseen as inevitable so soon as the latter should find himself free to operate against him. According to the chronology of Kings, Ḥezekiah's sickness happened in B.C. 714

(cf. *ch.* 18. 13 *note*), and the embassy arrived shortly afterwards, i. e. probably any time between the end of B. C. 714 and the beginning of B. C. 712.

בן בלאדן] In the inscriptions he appears as 'son of *Yakin*,' doubtless a dynastic title. Cf. the title 'son of Omri,' applied by Shalmaneser II to Jehu, as king of the land which was known to Assyria as *Bît-Ḫu-um-ri-a*. Cf. *notes* on *ch*. 9. 2; I. 16. 23.

ספרים] Duhm, Cheyne, Marti emend סָרִיסִים 'eunuchs,' a correction which is suitable to the suffix objects in *v.* 13 וישמע עליהם וג׳.

כי שמע] ‖ Isa. 39. 1 incorrectly וַיִּשְׁמַע, through confusion of כ and ו. Cf. *note* on I. 12. 30.

13. וישמע] Read וַיִּשְׂמַח 'And Ḥezekiah *was glad* because of them,' with several Codd., LXX, Luc., Vulg., Pesh.[1], and ‖ Isa. 39. 2. So moderns.

את כל בית נכתה] כל is omitted by many Codd., Vulg., Pesh., and ‖ Isaiah. The meaning of בית נכתה can only be guessed from the context; so Luc. τὸν οἶκον τῆς ὑπάρξεως αὐτοῦ, Pesh. ܒܝܬ ܓܙܗ, Targ. בית גנזוהי, '*his treasure-house*'; Vulg. *domum aromatum*, and so 'A., Σ. in ‖ Isa. τὸν οἶκον τῶν ἀρωμάτων. In Assyr. *bît nakanti* denotes 'treasure-house,' *nakantu* or *nakamtu*, plural *nakamâti*, meaning 'treasure,' and *nakâmu*, 'to heap up.' Cf. Delitzsch, *Assyr. HWB.* 462. Hence some authorities (cf. *Heb. Lex. Oxf.*) propose to read בֵּית נְכוֹתָיו, making the word equivalent to *nakavâti* for *nakamâti*.

ובכל ממשלתו] Luc. καὶ ἐν παντὶ θησαυρῷ αὐτοῦ.

14. ומאין יבאו] 'And from whence *may they come?*' A more polite form of question than the categorical מֵאַיִן בָּאוּ. Cf. Dri. *Tenses*, § 39 γ.

15. לא היה דבר] LXX, Luc., Pesh. add בְּבֵיתִי.

באצרתי] LXX, Luc. וּבְאֹצְרֹתָי.

16–18. No kind of allusion is found elsewhere in the known prophecies of Isaiah to a Babylonian captivity, the prophet's

[1] Also Targ., according to de Rossi, in one MS. and in *Edit. Venet.*

political horizon being bounded by the great powers of his times, Assyria and Egypt. Thus it is probable that these verses have been worked over by R^{D2} in exilic or post-exilic times.

16. יהוה] Luc. Κυρίου παντοκράτορος.

17. הנה ימים באים] Luc. adds φησὶ Κύριος, i. e. נְאֻם י׳; cf. e. g. *ch.* 19. 33; 22. 19 in Luc.

18. ממך] Sta. emends מִמֵּעֶיךָ 'from thy bowels,' after Gen. 15. 4; 2 Sam. 7. 12, and regards the following אשר תוליד as a gloss which owes its origin to the corruption ממך.

19^b. הלוא וג׳] LXX omits. Pesh. ܢܗܘܐ ... ܕܢܗܘܐ ܫܠܡܐ, Luc. γενέσθω, Vulg. *sit*, agree with ‖ Isa. 39. 8 כי יהיה וג׳, properly 'There shall be &c.'

20. ואשר עשה וג׳] 2 Chr. 32. 30 describes the method adopted by Ḥezekiah in order to provide a water-supply for Jerusalem: וְהוּא יְחִזְקִיָּהוּ סָתַם אֶת־מוֹצָא מֵימֵי גִיחוֹן הָעֶלְיוֹן וַיַּשְּׁרֵם לְמַטָּה מַעְרָבָה לְעִיר דָּוִיד. There exists an ancient tunnel which was cut in order to supply the pool of Siloam from the spring now called the Virgin's Fountain (cf. *note* on עין רגל I. 1. 9). 'The distance in a straight line is 368 yards, but by the rocky channel 586 yards.' In the mouth of this tunnel, where it opens into Siloam, there was discovered in 1880 an inscription which records the manner in which two parties of workmen quarried at either end, and met in the middle (cf. *Append.* 2; Baed. 97 *f.*). Both tunnel and inscription may reasonably be supposed to be due to Ḥezekiah. Sta., however (*Ges.* i. 592 *ff.*), thinks that the tunnel was already in existence in the time of Aḥaz, and quotes Isa. 8. 6 in support of his contention.

21. After *v.* 21^b Luc. adds καὶ ἐτάφη μετὰ τῶν πατέρων αὐτοῦ ἐν πόλει Δαυίδ.

21. 1–18. *Manasseh, king of Judah.*

Ch. 21. 1–9, 18 = 2 Chr. 33. 1–9, 20.

The narrative throughout is the work of R^D, based upon very brief notices (*vv.* 3, 4^a, 5, 6^a, 7^a, 16^a), derived, presumably, from the Annals. The section *vv.* 10–15 appears to presuppose the captivity of Judah, and must therefore, in its present form, be assigned to R^{D2}. The following phrases of R^D have in most cases already been noticed:—

2. כתועבת הגוים וג׳] I. 14. 24 *note*.

4, 7. אשים את שמי] I. 9. 3 *note*.

7. ובירושלם אשר בחרתי] I. 8. 16 *note*.

8. אשר נתתי לאבותם] I. 8. 34 *note*.

אם ישמרו לעשות] So I. 11. 10 (*note*); *ch.* 17. 37; 2 Chr. 33. 8; 1 Chr. 22. 12; Deut. 5. 1, 29; 6. 3, 25; 7. 11; 8. 1; 11. 22, 32; 12. 1; 13. 1; 15. 5; 17. 10; 19. 9; 24. 8; 28. 1, 15, 58; 31. 12; 32. 46; Josh. 1. 7, 8; 22. 5 (D^2).

10. עבדיו הנביאים] Cf. *ch.* 9. 7; 17. 13, 23; 24. 2; Jer. 7. 25; 25. 4; 26. 5; 29. 19; 35. 15; 44. 4. Elsewhere Am. 3. 7; Zech. 1. 6; Ezra 9. 11; Dan. 9. 10.

11. הרע וג׳] I. 14. 9 *note*.

11, 21. גלולים; בגלוליו] I. 15. 12 *note*.

12. הנני מביא רעה על] I. 14. 10 *note*.

21. 1. מנשה] Both Esar-haddon and Assurbanipal refer to this king as *Mí-na-si-í* or *Mi-in-si-í*, king of Judah, in a list of twenty-two kings of the land of Ḫatti. Cf. *COT. ad loc.*

2. כתועבת] Luc. καὶ ἐπορεύθη κατὰ πάντα τὰ βδελύγματα κ.τ.λ.

3. צבא השמים] The stars; cf. *note* on I. 22. 19. The worship of the heavenly bodies was indigenous in Babylon in the earliest times, and was no doubt introduced into Judah through intercourse with Assyria. Whether this Babylonian cult was known and practised in the Northern Kingdom also before its fall, as is affirmed in *ch.* 17. 16ᵇ, has been questioned. Cf. p. 331.

4. ובנה] The use of perfect with weak ו, here and in *v.* 6, must be ascribed to the decadent style of the Annalist. Cf. *note* on ותפש *ch.* 14. 7.

מזבחת] LXX, Luc. sing. θυσιαστήριον. So LXX in *v.* 5.

5. בשתי חצרות וג׳] The House of Yahwe seems to have had only one courtyard; cf. I. 6. 36 *note*; *ch.* 20. 4. Possibly the reference may include the חָצֵר הָאַחֶרֶת or חָצֵר הַתִּיכֹנָה, properly

the Palace-courtyard, which, as Kit. remarks, passed over in the time of the second Temple into a wider Temple-courtyard.

6. ועשה] 'Appointed,' or 'instituted.' Cf. I. 1. 5 *note*.

אוב וידענים] 'Necromancers and wizards.' אוֹב seems to denote, in the first place, the ghost itself, which was said to dwell *in* the medium (Lev. 20. 27). Similarly, the witch of Endor is a בַּעֲלַת אוֹב 'possessor of a ghost' (1 Sam. 28. 7), and Saul's request to her is קָסֳמִי־נָא לִי בָּאוֹב 'Divine for me, I pray thee, through the ghost' (*v*. 8). In Deut. 18. 11 the diviner is called שֹׁאֵל אוֹב 'one who consults a ghost.' The voice of the אוֹב is low and thin, and appears to come from the ground (Isa. 29. 4).

The transference of the term from the ghost to the medium, as in our passage, ‖ 2 Chr. 33. 6; 1 Sam. 28. 3, 9, appears to be a secondary usage. According to Schwally, the reverse process took place in the case of יִדְּעֹנִי, the prime meaning being 'wizard,' and hence, as with Aram. זַכּוּרָא, a secondary application being made to the ghost. Cf. *Das Leben nach dem Tode*, 69 *f.* If, however, the meaning of יִדְּעֹנִי be either 'knowing one' or 'familiar,' it is more natural to find first reference to the ghost, as in the case of אוֹב. Cf. *Heb. Lex. Oxf.*, *s. v.* The root-meaning of אוֹב can only be remotely conjectured, and the distinction between אוב and ידעני is unknown.

7. את פסל האשרה] Cf. I. 14. 15 *note*.

אשר עשה] LXX, Luc. omit.

בבית הזה . . . אשר בחרתי . . . אשים] LXX, Luc. ἐν τῷ οἴκῳ τούτῳ . . . ἐξελεξάμην . . . καὶ θήσω (Luc. θεῖναι), omitting אֲשֶׁר before בָּחַרְתִּי, and reading וְאָשִׂימָה or לָשׂוּם for אָשִׂים.

8. ישמרו] Luc. ἀκούσωσι, i. e. יִשְׁמְעוּ.

9. את הרע] LXX adds ἐν ὀφθαλμοῖς Κυρίου, Luc. ἐνώπιον Κυρίου.

11. הרע] LXX, Luc., Vulg. omit.

מכל] Luc. κατὰ πάντα, i. e. כְּכֹל.

12. אשר כל שמעיו וג׳] Cf. 1 Sam. 3. 11; Jer. 19. 3.

13. ונטיתי וג׳] For the figure cf. Isa. 34. 11; Lam. 2. 8.

כאשר ימחה וג׳] Pesh., in place of this simile, reads ܘܐܘܒܕܝܗ̇

ܡܛܠ ܟܠܗ̇ ܒܝܫܬܐ ܕܥܒܕ ܡܢܫܐ ܒܝܗܘܕܐ 'and will destroy it, on account of all the evil which Manasseh wrought in Judah.'

מחה והפך] Read, with most moderns, מָחֹה וְהָפֹךְ 'wiping and turning (it).' The second infin. stands in simple sequence to the first, as e.g. in Isa. 19. 22, noticed under I. 20. 37 *note*.

18. עזא] Sta. (*Ges*. i. 569) quotes Wellh. for the suggestion that עֻזָּא (cf. 2 Sam. 6. 3) is a contracted form of עֲזַרְיָה, which was in later times confused with the name עֻזִּיָּה, so that this latter was written in place of the contraction. Cf. *ch*. 15. 1, *note* on עזריה.

On the narrative of 2 Chr. 33. 11–13, which relates the captivity, repentance, and restoration of Manasseh, cf. Dri. *Authority*, 114 *ff*.

21. 19–26. *Amon, king of Judah.*

Ch. 21. 19–24 = 2 Chr. 33. 21–25.

R^D frames brief notices from the Annals.

24. עם הארץ] Cf. *ch*. 16. 15 *note*.

26. בקברתו] Luc. ἐν τῷ τάφῳ τοῦ πατρὸς αὐτοῦ.

22. 1—**23.** 30. *Josiah, king of Judah. The finding of the Book of the Law, and the religious reformation to which it gave rise.*

Ch. 22. 1—23. 3 = 2 Chr. 34. 1, 2, 8–32.

Ch. 23. 4–20 is the probable source of the summary 2 Chr. 34. 3–7.

Ch. 23. 30^b = 2 Chr. 36. 1.

The lengthy narratives of the Chronicler which relate the keeping of the passover, 2 Chr. 35. 1–19 (cf. *ch*. 23. 21–23), and Josiah's defeat and death at the hands of Necho, king of Egypt, 2 Chr. 35. 20–27 (cf. *ch*. 23. 29, 30), appear to be based upon extraneous sources.

Ch. 22. 3—23. 25 is a continuous narrative, probably drawn from the Temple-archives (cf. *note* on *ch*. 11, pp. 307 *f*.). Deuteronomic phrases are found in 23. 3, 19, 25 [1], and in the speech of Ḥuldah,

[1] נפש . . . לשמר *v*. 3 (I. 2. 3, 4 *note*); להכעים *v*. 19 (I. 14. 9 *note*); וכמהו וג׳ *v*. 25 (I. 3. 12 *note*; I. 8. 48 *note*).

22. 15–20[1], which seems to show signs of revision by R^{D2} in exilic times. Certainly this later editor is responsible for the addition 23. 26, 27[2], at the close of the narrative, which strikes a note strangely alien to the enthusiasm of the pre-exilic author in view of Josiah's reformation (cf. especially 23. 22, 25).

Ch. 23. 29, 30 is probably drawn from the Annals.

22. 3. בשמנה . . . יאשיהו] LXX, Luc. add ἐν τῷ μηνὶ τῷ ὀγδόῳ.

4. ויתם] RV. 'that *he may sum* the money'; lit. 'may bring to an end,' and so, by inference, 'return the full amount of.' No parallel, however, can be cited for such a use of the verb. Comparison of *v.* 9, הִתִּיכוּ, suggests the emendation וְיַתֵּךְ, 'that he may pour out,' a reading which seems to be presupposed by Luc. καὶ χωνεύσατε, Vulg. *ut confletur*, and which is adopted by Ginsburg, Grä., Kit., Oort. LXX καὶ σφράγισον, i.e. וַחֲתֹם, is favoured by Th., Kamp., Benz., but appears less suitable. Klo. וְיִתַּכֵּן 'that he may weigh'; cf. הַמְתֻכָּן *ch.* 12. 12. ‖ 2 Chr. 34. 9 וַיִּתְּנוּ.

5. ויתנה על יד] Lit. 'And let them place it *upon the hand* &c.' So exactly Gen. 42. 37 תְּנָה אֹתוֹ עַל־יָדִי. Cf. also the expression הִגִּיר עַל־יַד Jer. 18. 21; Ezek. 35. 5; Ps. 63. 11.

ויתנו אתו] Luc. καὶ ἔδωκαν αὐτὸ κατὰ τὸ ῥῆμα τοῦ βασιλέως.

בבית] Q're בית, in agreement with *v.* 9. Cf. *ch.* 12. 12.

7. לא יחשב] Frequentative; 'there was not (from time to time) made audit of.' Cf. *ch.* 12. 16.

10. Before לאמר Luc. adds περὶ τοῦ βιβλίου.

12. עבד המלך] Apparently a special title, 'the servant of the king' *par excellence.* The title has been found in ancient Heb. character upon a seal. Cf. Benz. *Archäologie*, 310*f.*

13. עלינו] Luc. ἐν αὐτῷ, i.e. עָלָיו, the reading of two Codd., is probably correct. Cf. ‖ 2 Chr. 34. 21 עַל־הַסֵּפֶר הַזֶּה. So Th., Klo., Kamp., Benz., Kit., Oort.

---

[1] למען הכעסני *v.* 17 (I. 14. 9 *note*); אלהים אחרים *v.* 17 (I. 9. 6 *note*); הנני מביא רעה וג׳ *v.* 16 (I. 14. 10 *note*).

[2] הכעיסו *v.* 26 (I. 14. 9 *note*); אסיר מעל פני *v.* 27, cf. *ch.* 17. 18, 23; 24. 3; Jer. 32. 31; so with שִׁלַּח I. 9. 7; Jer. 15. 1; with הִשְׁלִיךְ *ch.* 13. 23; 17. 20 (מִן in place of מֵעַל); אשר בחרתי *v.* 27 (I. 8. 16 *note*).

14. אשת] LXX μητέρα.

במשנה] 'In the second (district).' Cf. Zeph. 1. 10, and, according to the probable interpretation, הָעִיר מִשְׁנֶה Neh. 11. 9. The precise significance with which the term is employed is unknown. According to Neh. 3. 9, 12 we find Jerusalem divided into two districts in post-exilic times for administrative purposes. Possibly the משנה may have been the new as distinct from the old city. So Ges.-Buhl.

18. הדברים וג׳] '(As regards) the words which thou hast heard.' Luc., however, offers the reading Ἀνθ' ὧν ἤκουσας τοὺς λόγους μου, καὶ ἡπαλύνθη ἡ καρδία σου, Vulg. *Pro eo quod audisti verba voluminis, et* &c., i.e. (יַ֫עַן) אֲשֶׁר שָׁמַעְתָּ הַדְּבָרִים וַיֵּרַךְ לְבָבְךָ.

19. ולקללה] Luc. omits.

20. על המקום הזה] Add וְעַל־יֹשְׁבָיו with Luc., and ‖ 2 Chr. 34. 28. So Klo. Oort וְיֹשְׁבָיו.

23. 1. ויאספו] LXX, Luc. presuppose sing. וַיֶּאֱסֹף, as in ‖ 2 Chr. 34. 29.

2. והנביאים] Six Codd. agree with ‖ 2 Chr. 34. 30 in reading וְהַלְוִיִּם. The mention of הַנְּבִיאִים is somewhat unexpected, in view of the fact that no mention is made of prophets in *ch.* 22, but only of Ḥuldah the prophetess. On the other hand, the fact that הלוים is the more obvious reading creates the suspicion that it is a correction, since no reason can be assigned for the substitution of הנביאים for הלוים.

4. כהני המשנה] RV. 'the priests of the second order.' In *ch.* 25. 18 a single כֹּהֵן מִשְׁנֶה, 'second (i.e. vice) priest,' is mentioned, in contrast to כֹּהֵן הָרֹאשׁ, and Targ. סגן כהניא is probably correct in making reference in the present passage also to a single individual.

ולאשרה] Cf. I. 14. 15 *note.*

בשדמות קדרון] RV. 'in the fields of Kidron.' Elsewhere שדמה is peculiar to poetry. Luc. ἐν τῷ ἐμπυρισμῷ, i.e. בְּמִשְׂרְפוֹת, adopted by Klo., Kamp., Benz., Kit., and interpreted as (*lime-*)*kilns*. Cf. Isa. 33. 12.

ונשא] Here and elsewhere in the narrative the use of the perfect with weak ו is a mark of decadence in style. Cf. *note* on ותפש *ch.* 14. 7.

5. ויקטר] Emend וַיְקַטְּרוּ with LXX, Targ. Luc., Vulg., Pesh. suggest לְקַטֵּר, but may equally be supposed to be reproducing in their renderings the idea of purpose implied in וַיְקַטְּרוּ.

ולמזלות] 'And for the heavenly mansions.' In Ar. مَنْزِل *manzil* denotes a *lodging-place* or *mansion;* and the pl. اَلْمَنَازِل is used of the twenty-eight *mansions* of the moon. In Assyr. (Delitzsch, *Assyr. Handwörterbuch*) *manzazu* denotes 'a place of standing,' from the root *nazâzu*, 'to stand.' This word occurs on the fifth table of the Babylonian Creation series, which begins, 'He made the mansions (*manzazi*) of the great gods' (Jensen, *Kosmologie*, 288 *ff.;* Schrader, *COT.* i. 15). Further, there is a fem. form of *manzazu*, viz. *manzaltu* (= *manzaztu*), *mazaltu*. For this Delitzsch quotes III Rawlinson, 59, 35[a]: 'The gods in heaven in their mansions (*man-zal-ti-šu-nu*) set me.' Jensen (*Kosmologie*, 347 *f.*) mentions the same facts. While, however, Delitzsch identifies these *manzalti* with the zodiacal stations (*Prolegomena*, 54), Jensen thinks that they were perhaps fifty in number[1], corresponding to the number of the great gods, and thus can scarcely denote merely the signs of the zodiac, but rather certain fixed stars and planets, lists of which are to be found in the inscriptions, but of which the identification seems to be possible in a few cases only (*Kosmologie*, 146 *ff.*)[2].

In Rabbinic Heb. מזלות is used to denote the twelve zodiacal signs (*Berachoth*, 32[b]; *Shabbath*, 75[a]), but also the planets, regarded as stars of good or ill fortune (*Bereshith rabba*, 10, 10[c]; *al.*). In agreement with this latter signification, we have, according to the restoration of de Vogüé, the dedication למזל נעם,

---

[1] The number of the *manzazi* appears to have originally existed on the Creation tablet.

[2] Jensen finds allusion to the zodiacal signs in the *maši* stars of l. 2 of the Creation tablet above cited. The word *miṣrāta* (not *mizrāta*) or *iṣrāta*, which occurs in l. 3, cannot, with Sayce (*Religion of Bab.*, 389), be identified with מַזָּרוֹת.

answering to the Greek Ἀγαθῇ τύχῃ in a Phoenician inscription from Larnaka of about the fourth century B.C. (*CIS.* 95).

It is doubtful whether מַזָּרוֹת of Job 38. 32 is identical with מַזָּלוֹת. LXX in both passages transliterates μαζουρώθ, while Targ., in accordance with Kings, uses in Job the rendering שטרי מזליא.

6. קבר בני העם] The common burial-place of those who were without name and memorial. Cf. Jer. 26. 23.

7. הקדשים] Cf. I. 14. 24 *note.*

בתים] Scarcely explicable in connexion with ארגים. RV. 'hangings' is unjustifiable; and 'tent-shrines' might have been called מִשְׁכָּנוֹת, but scarcely בָּתִּים. The transliteration of LXX χεττιείν suggests to Klo. an original כתנים for כֻּתְּנוֹת 'tunics,' a reading which is supported by Luc. στολάς, and may well be original. So Benz.

8. גבע] Cf. I. 15. 22 *note.*

את במות השערים] Emend, with most moderns after Hoffmann, *ZATW.* ii. 175, אֶת־בָּמוֹת (LXX, Luc. בֵּית) הַשְּׂעִירִים 'The high-places (*or* house) of the Satyrs.' Cf. 2 Chr. 11. 15; Lev. 17. 7.

בשער העיר] Luc. adds πύλην ἐκκεκεντημένων, and according to Field, Quinta τὴν πύλην τῶν τετρωμένων (or τετραυματισμένων), i.e. perhaps שַׁעַר הַדָּגִים 'the fish-gate'; cf. the rendering of LXX in Zeph. 1. 10, ἀπὸ πύλης ἀποκεντούντων.

9. לא יעלו] 'Did not go up'; frequentative. The regulation of Deut. 18. 6 *ff.* seems to have been intended to place the provincial priesthood upon a level with the priesthood of the central sanctuary, as regards service as well as maintenance. This regulation, so far as it concerned equality of service, appears from our passage to have remained a dead letter, doubtless owing to the exclusiveness of the Jerusalem priesthood. The provincial appears to have sunk at once into the subordinate position of the 'Levite,' as defined in the Priestly Code (I. 8. 4 *note*). Cf. also Ezek. 44. 10–16.

10. התפת] R. Sm. (*Rel. Sem.*[2], 377) conjectures that תפת is properly the Aram. name for a *fireplace*, upon the assumption of a variant ܬܦܬܐ, תְּפָת, for the Syr. ܐܬܦܝܐ. Cf. the use made of the

name in Isa. 30. 33. The vocalization תֹּפֶת, like that of מֹלֶךְ, עַשְׁתֹּרֶת, probably points to a later approximation to the vocalization of בֹּשֶׁת 'shameful thing.' Cf. the substitution of בֹּשֶׁת for בַּעַל in the text of Hos. 9. 10; Jer. 3. 24; 11. 13.

גי בני הנם] Elsewhere always גֵּי בֶן־הִנֹּם, or abbreviated גֵּי הִנֹּם. Q're is supported by many Codd., and by LXX, Luc., Vulg., Pesh., Targ.

לבלתי להעביר] לְבִלְתִּי לְ occurs only here. Cod. 304 de Rossi, LXX, Pesh. omit לבלתי, taking להעביר to express the purpose of the existence of the תפת:—'that a man might offer &c.' Thus it is possible that לבלתי is a later insertion, made by a scribe who understood the clause as explaining the purpose of וטמא.

11. בפרורים] RV. 'in the precincts.' הַפַּרְבָּר 1 Chr. 26. 18, doubtless the same, is stated to have been on the west of the Temple. New Heb. פַּרְוָר, Aram. פַּרְוָרָא denote a *suburb*. Ges. *Thes.* 1123 finds the origin of the term in Persian فَرْوَار, a *summer-house*, or *open kiosk* (lit. *light-possessing*). Dri. (*s. v. Parbar*, Hastings, *BD.* iii) remarks that, if the term is to be traced to the Persian, its occurrence in Kings must be regarded as a mark of post-exilic revision.

שרף באש] Luc. adds ἐν τῷ οἴκῳ ᾧ ᾠκοδόμησαν βασιλεῖς Ἰσραὴλ ὑψηλὸν τῷ Βάαλ καὶ πάσῃ τῇ στρατιᾷ τοῦ οὐρανοῦ.

12. הגג עלית אחז] הַגָּג clearly refers to the roof of the Temple, and עֲלִיַּת אָחָז, in apposition, must have come into the text as a gloss. Benz., Kit. conjecture that Aḥaz may have erected a shelter for the altars upon the Temple roof; cf. the עֲלִיַּת־קִיר of *ch.* 4. 10.

אשר עשו מלכי י׳] Luc. ἃ ἐποίησεν Ἀχάζ.

וַיָּרָץ] As the text stands, RV. 'and beat them down,' making the verb Imperf. Qal of רצץ, must be adopted. So Luc. καὶ συνέτριψε—apparently a third rendering of the word. Th., Oort follow Kimḥi in vocalizing וַיָּרֶץ (Imperf. Hiph'il of רוץ), 'and banished them,' in agreement with Targ. וארחק מתמן. Klo. cites the second rendering of Luc., καὶ ἐξήνεγκεν αὐτά, for the emendation וַיֹּצִאֵם, a suggestion favoured by Benz., Kit.

13. הר המשחית] 'The hill of the destroyer.' Only mentioned here. Klo. suggests that the name, if genuine, may have reference to 2 Sam. 24. 16. Targ. טור זיתיא 'mount of olives' suggests הַר הַמִּשְׁחָה 'mount of oil,' as occasionally in the Talmuds according to Neubauer, *Geographie du Talmud*, 147. So Hoffmann, *ZATW.* ii. 175; Perles, *Analekten*, 31 *f.*

15. וישרף את הבמה] Impossible. The במה itself, i. e. the *situation* of the altar, could not be burnt; nor can it be supposed that the term is used vaguely in place of בֵּית הַבָּמָה. LXX, Luc. read *καὶ συνέτριψεν τοὺς λίθους αὐτοῦ*, i. e. וַיְשַׁבֵּר אֶת־אֲבָנָיו—doubtless the original text. So Klo., Benz., Kit., Oort.

הדק וג׳] 'Crushing (them) to dust'; lit. 'he crushed &c.,' perf. used *asyndetos* in a circumstantial clause. Cf. Dri. *Tenses*, § 163.

אשרה] We ought probably to read הָאֲשֵׁרָה, or אֲשֵׁרָתָהּ.

16[b]. כדבר וג׳] After איש האלהים LXX, Luc. add *ἐν τῷ ἑστάναι Ἰεροβοὰμ ἐν τῇ ἑορτῇ ἐπὶ τὸ θυσιαστήριον. καὶ ἐπιστρέψας* (Luc. Ἰωσίας) *ἦρεν τοὺς ὀφθαλμοὺς αὐτοῦ ἐπὶ τὸν τάφον τοῦ ἀνθρώπου τοῦ θεοῦ*, i. e. בַּעֲמֹד יָרָבְעָם בֶּחָג עַל־הַמִּזְבֵּחַ וַיִּפֶן וַיִּשָּׂא אֶת־עֵינָיו עַל־קֶבֶר אִישׁ הָאֱלֹהִים. These words must have fallen out of the text through homoioteleuton. As MT. stands, the repeated אשר קרא וג׳ is awkward and redundant, while the details supplied by the missing words are felt to be wanting to the narrative. So Th. (וַיָּשָׁב for *καὶ ἐπιστρέψας*), Klo., Benz., Oort.

17. הציון הלז] 'Yonder tomb-stone.' ציון occurs again in Ezek. 39. 15 to denote a stone set up to mark the locality of an unburied body, and in pl. in Jer. 31. 21 of stones placed as way-marks. The word is used in the same sense in New Heb., together with a verb צִיֵּן *to mark*, e. g. the site of sepulchres as being unclean.

On הלז cf. *ch.* 4. 25 *note.*

הקבר איש האלהים] If the text be correct, הקבר can only be taken as an instance of the article with the *st. constr.* Benz., Kit. emend זֶה קֶבֶר 'This is the grave &c.' for הַקֶּבֶר; Klo., Da. (§ 20, *Rem.* b) הוּא קֶבֶר—a suggestion which is open to the objection that הוא would more naturally fall after איש האלהים.

הַמִּזְבַּח בית אל] The vocalization of MT., with the rendering of RV. 'the altar of Bethel,' is to be rejected. The correct vocalization is הַמִּזְבֵּחַ *st. absol.*, and בית אל is to be regarded as an accusative (cf. *ch.* 2. 3; 10. 29) defining the place of the event described by ויקרא וג׳ :—'and proclaimed these things which thou hast done against the altar at Bethel.' Cf. Dri. *Tenses*, § 191, *Obs.* 2.

18. וימלטו עצמתיו] Luc. *καὶ διεσώθη τὰ ὀστᾶ τοῦ προφήτου τοῦ πρεσβυτέρου τοῦ κατοικοῦντος ἐν Βαιθὴλ μετὰ κ.τ.λ.*, i.e. וַיְמַלְּטוּ עַצְמוֹת הַנָּבִיא הַזָּקֵן הַיֹּשֵׁב בְּבֵית־אֵל וג׳—probably original. Cf. I. 13. 31 *f.*

19. להכעים] LXX, Luc., Vulg., Pesh. add את יהוה.

20. אשר שם וג׳] Pesh., ܕܣܡܘ ܒܣ̈ܡܐ ܥܠ ܡܕܒ̈ܚܐ 'who placed sweet savours upon the altars,' appears to have read שָׂמוּ for שָׂם, a use of the verb which is justified by Deut. 33. 10b.

21. At the end of the *v.* Luc. adds *καὶ ἐποίησαν οὕτως*.

22. כי לא נעשה] RV. '*Surely* there was not kept &c.' It seems, however, preferable, in view of כי אם וג׳ of *v.* 23, to render 'For there had not been kept &c.'

כפסח הזה] 'Such a passover as this,' referring to ככתוב וג׳ of *v.* 21. LXX *τὸ πάσχα τοῦτο*, i.e. הַפֶּסַח הַזֶּה, seems to state that the passover was not kept at all during the period named.

24. את האבות וג׳] Cf. *ch.* 21. 6 *note*.

התרפים] A kind of idol, as is proved by the designation אלהים, Gen. 31. 30, 32; apparently of human form and size (1 Sam. 19. 13 *ff.*), though sometimes much smaller (Gen. 31. 34). Like אלהים, the plural תרפים may denote one image (cf. Sam. *l.c.*), or more than one (Gen. *l.c.*; *al.*). תרפים are found as household gods in the possession of the Aramaean Laban (Gen. 31. 19 *ff.*), the Ephraimite Micah (Judg. 17 *f.*), and Michal, David's wife (1 Sam. 19. 13 *ff.*). Ezekiel pictures them as consulted by the king of Babylon (21. 26). It is clear that תרפים were employed as oracle-givers. In Judg. 17 *f.*; Hos. 3. 4 they are mentioned in connexion with the oracular אֵפוֹד; in 1 Sam. 15. 23; Zech. 10. 2; Ezek. 21. 26, 27 with the form of divination called קֶסֶם (cf. *ch.* 17. 17 *note*). Their association in our passage with אֶת־הָאֹבוֹת וְאֶת־הַיִּדְּעֹנִים (cf. *ch.* 21. 6 *note*) appears to connect them with the practice of necromancy. The wide-spread character of the תרפים cult among the Semitic races (as attested by the Biblical references above cited) has led Schwally (*Das Leben nach dem Tode,* 36) to identify it with ancestor-worship; cf. also Sta. *Ges.* i. 467; Nowack, *Archäologie,* ii. 23. A strange Jewish tradition explains תרפים as the pickled head of a first-born son, which was fastened on the wall of a house, and worshipped as an oracle; cf. *Pirqê de R. Eliezer, ch.* 36 (eighth century A.D.); Jerus. Targ. on Gen. 31. 19; cited by Buxtorf, *s.v.* תרפים.

הגללים] Cf. I. 15. 12 *note.*

29. בימיו] Cf. I. 16. 34 *note.*

נכה] Necho II, son of Psammeticus I, was second king of the twenty-sixth dynasty, and reigned B.C. 610–595. Cf. Hastings, *BD.* iii. 504. The strange rendering of Pesh. ܚܓܝܪܐ, Targ. פרעה חגירא 'Pharaoh the lame,' connects נְכֹה with נְכֵה רַגְלַיִם.

במגדו] Cf. I. 4. 12 *note.* Herodotus (ii. 159) places the encounter at Μάγδωλος, i.e. מִגְדֹּל, probably the place of that name on the N.E. border of Egypt; Ex. 14. 2; Num. 33. 7; Jer. 44. 1; *al.*

After לקראתו Pesh. adds ܠܡܬܟܬܫܘ ܥܡܗ. ܘܐܡܪ ܠܗ ܦܪܥܘܢ. ܠܐ ܗܘܐ ܥܠܝܟ ܐܢܐ ܐܬܝܬ. ܗܦܘܟ ܡܢܝ. ܘܠܐ ܫܡܥܗ ܠܦܪܥܘܢ. ܘܡܚܝܗܝ ܦܪܥܘܢ. 'to fight with him; and Pharaoh said to him, I am not come against thee; turn aside from me. And he hearkened not unto Pharaoh, and Pharaoh smote him.' This is probably a reminiscence of 2 Chr. 35. 21 *ff.*

כראתו אתו] 'When he saw him,' i.e. when they joined battle. On the analogy of the use of the Hithpa'el in *ch.* 14. 8, Benz., following Winckler, proposes to read the Niph'al כְּהֵרָאֹת אִתּוֹ—scarcely a necessary emendation.

30. עם הארץ] Cf. *ch.* 16. 15 *note.*

23. 31–35. *Jehoaḥaz, king of Judah.*

Ch. 23. 31–34 forms the source of 2 Chr. 36. 2–4. Short notices, probably from the Annals, are framed by R^D (R^{D2}).

31. חמוטל] In *ch.* 24. 18; Jer. 52. 1 †Kt. חֲמִיטַל. This form of

the name is given in our passage also by LXX Ἀμειταί, Cod. A, Luc. Ἀμιτάλ, Vulg. *Amital.*

לבנה] Cf. *ch.* 8. 22 *note.*

33. ויאסרהו . . . במלך] LXX, Luc. καὶ μετέστησεν αὐτὸν . . . τοῦ μὴ βασιλεύειν (Luc. αὐτόν), i.e. וַיְסִרֵהוּ . . . מִמְּלֹךְ. Cf. ‖ 2 Chr. 36. 3. So Oort. It is, however, scarcely possible to suppose that ברבלה וג׳ originally followed וַיְסִרֵהוּ, and does not properly belong to MT. וַיַּאַסְרֵהוּ. Thus the passage seems to be involved by the combination of two readings :—'bound him in Ribla in the land of Ḥamath,' and, 'removed him from reigning in Jerusalem.' Klo., Kamp., Benz., Kit. retain MT. ויאסרהו, and regard ממלך בירושלם as a gloss introduced from 2 Chr. 36. 3.

וככר זהב] Luc., Pesh. presuppose עֶשֶׂר כִּכְּרֵי זָהָב 'ten talents of gold.'

34. וַיָּבֹא] LXX, Luc., Vulg. וַיָּבֵא.

35. את עם הארץ] The sentence is awkward in the extreme if these words be regarded as in apposition to איש כעֶרכו; and the alternative suggested by Benz., '*With* (i.e. by the help of) the people of the land' (cf. LXX, Luc. μετὰ τοῦ λαοῦ τῆς γῆς), is out of the question. Doubtless Klo. is right in regarding את עם הארץ as a gloss explanatory of את הארץ of the first half of the verse.

23. 36—**24.** 7. *Jehoiakim, king of Judah.*

Chh. 23. 36—24. 6 are summarized in 2 Chr. 36. 5–8. R^{D} (R^{D2}) frames short notices, probably drawn from the Annals.

24. 1. בימיו] Cf. I. 16. 34 *note.*

After נבכדנאצר Luc. adds ἐπὶ τὴν γῆν, while Pesh. adds ܥܠ ܐܘܪܫܠܡ 'against Jerusalem' after מלך בבל.

Nebuchadnezzar's campaign against Egypt (cf. *v.* 7) took place, according to Berossus, in the last year of his father Nabopolassar, i.e. B.C. 605. The news of Nabopolassar's death caused him to hasten back to Babylon, after he had brought his campaign to a successful issue. According to Jer. 46. 2 the defeat of the Egyptian army at Carchemish took place in Jehoiakim's fourth year (B.C. 604), and Jer. 25. 1 co-ordinates the fourth year of Jehoiakim with the first year of Nebuchadnezzar.

That Jehoiakim became 'servant' to Nebuchadnezzar through this campaign seems to follow both from the fragmentary account of Kings and also from the fact that Berossus speaks of τοὺς αἰχμαλώτους τῶν 'Ιουδαίων among other prisoners of war. Thus, if the 'three years' of *ch.* 24. 1ᵇ be correct, and if the length of Jehoiakim's reign extended to eleven years (*ch.* 23. 36), Jehoiakim must have remained in rebellion against Nebuchadnezzar for four years.

The reference to Egypt's loss of Syria in *v.* 7 demands that in the original narrative an account of Nebuchadnezzar's victory at Carchemish must have followed *v.* 1ᵃ. Cf. Winckler, *Alttest. Untersuchungen*, 81 *f.*

2. וְאֵת גְּדוּדֵי אֲרָם] אֱדֹם rather than אֲרָם is to be expected in connexion with מוֹאָב and בְּנֵי עַמּוֹן, and this emendation is favoured by Grä., Klo., Benz.

After בני עמון Luc. adds καὶ ἐκ τῆς Σαμαρείας, i.e. וּמִשֹּׁמְרוֹן— possibly original, though not (with Klo.) to be substituted for וַיִּשְׁלָחֵם.

3. עַל פִּי י'] LXX, Luc., Pesh., Targ. seem to have read עַל־אַף י' 'on account of the anger of Yahwe,' as in *v.* 20. The introductory אַף appears to be characteristic of this editor; cf. *ch.* 23. 26, 35.

4. וְגַם דַּם הַנָּקִי וג'] 'And also (because of) the innocent blood which he shed.' If the text is correct, the force of the בּ of בַּחַטֹּאת (*v.* 3) must be carried over into this clause.

6. וַיִּשְׁכַּב וג'] These words are omitted in 2 Chr. 36. 8 MT., but appear in the LXX text, with the addition καὶ ἐτάφη ἐν γανοζαὴ μετὰ τῶν πατέρων αὐτοῦ, i.e. וַיִּקָּבֵר בְּגַן עֻזָּא עִם־אֲבֹתָיו (cf. *ch.* 21. 26). Sta. *Ges.* i. 679 *note* conjectures that this reference to the burial-place originally stood in Kings, and was derived thence by the Chronicler, but that the notice was subsequently struck out in view of the prediction of Jer. 22. 19. So Wellh. (*C.* 359), Benz.

7. מִנַּחַל מִצְרָיִם] Cf. *note* on גְּבוּל מִצְרָיִם I. 5. 1.

24. 8–17. *Jehoiachin, king of Judah.*

Ch. 24. 8–17 is briefly summarized in 2 Chr. 36. 9, 10. No reference is made to the Annals, and it is possible that R^{D2} may be writing from personal knowledge of events, independently of a written source. Sta. (*ZATW.* iv. 271 *ff.*) regards *vv.* 13, 14 as a later insertion, properly referring to the events of 586 B.C. It is difficult to reconcile the 10,000 of *v.* 14 with the numbers given in *v.* 16; מִשָּׁם in *v.* 13 has no antecedent to which to refer back[1], whilst וַיֶּגֶל in *v.* 15 refers directly to *v.* 12. The chief objection, however, to the reference of these verses to 597 B.C. is to be found in their contents. Verse 13 speaks of *all* the treasures of the City and Temple as carried off by Nebuchadnezzar, and the golden vessels as melted down. But from *ch.* 25 (‖ Jer. 52) and Jer. 27. 18–20, 28. 2 *f.* the inference is that only a part of the City and Temple treasures were carried off on this occasion, and that the greater part was seized by the Chaldeans in 586 B.C. Thus the contents of *v.* 13 are suitable as a description of the events of 586 B.C., but not of those of 597 B.C. The same inference is to be drawn from the contents of *v.* 14. *All* Jerusalem was first deported in 586, and a characteristic of this deportation was that only the דלת הארץ remained (25. 12). On the other hand, as appears from Jer., the deportation at the close of Jehoiachin's reign consisted only of the higher classes (cf. e.g. Jer. 27. 20 את יכניה . . . ואת כל חרי יהודה וירושלם) and the men who bore arms, i.e. practically the same category as is named in *v.* 16.

8. ושלשה חדשים] 2 Chr. 36. 9 adds וַעֲשֶׂרֶת יָמִים.

10. בעת ההיא] Cf. I. 14. 1 *note.*

12. על מלך בבל] על for אל. Cf. *note* on על גחון I. 1. 38.

בשנת שמנה למלכו] B.C. 597. Jer. 52. 28 places the event in the seventh year of Nebuchadnezzar.

13. Luc. prefixes the statement καὶ εἰσῆλθε βασιλεὺς Βαβυλῶνος εἰς τὴν πόλιν, i.e. וַיָּבֹא מֶלֶךְ בָּבֶל אֶל־הָעִיר—an addition desiderated by מִשָּׁם of the following sentence.

[1] But cf. *note* on *v.* 13.

14. גֹּולָה] The participle singular is used of *a single exile* 2 Sam. 15. 19; fem. Isa. 49. 21. It is clear, however, from *vv.* 15, 16 that we should vocalize גּוֹלָה a collective, 'captives.'

הַמַּסְגֵּר] Probably 'the lock-smiths.' So *v.* 16; Jer. 24. 1; 29. 2; in each case collective sing., and in connexion with הֶחָרָשׁ, by inference 'the workers in *wood*.' Elsewhere (Isa. 24. 22; 42. 7; Ps. 142. 8 *f.*) מַסְגֵּר denotes '*place* of locking,' i. e. 'dungeon.'

דלת עם הארץ] 'The poorest of the people of the land.' Cf. Jer. 39. 10 וּמִן־הָעָם הַדַּלִּים אֲשֶׁר אֵין־לָהֶם מְאוּמָה. On the fem. collective cf. Da. § 14. 2.

15. ואת אולי הארץ] RV. 'and the *chief men* of the land.' Q're אֵילֵי, as in Ezek. 17. 13. The word is perhaps from a root אול 'to be foremost'; but it is possible that the insertion of the ו or י is an intentional alteration to distinguish from the divine title אֵל. Cf. *Heb. Lex. Oxf.*, *s. v.* אֵל § 1.

24. 18—**25.** 7. *Zedekiah, king of Judah.*

Ch. 24. 18—25. 7 = Jer. 52. 1–11.

18. חמיטל וג׳] Cf. *ch.* 23. 31 *note.*

20. עַד־הִשְׁלִכוֹ] Cf. *note* on עַד־הִשְׁאִיר *ch.* 3. 25.

25. 1. בעשור לחדש] LXX, Luc. omit.

3. בתשעה לחדש] It is impossible that mention should be made of the day of the month when the month itself has not been specified. Pesh. ܘܒܫܢܬ ܚܕܥܣܪ̈ܐ ܠܡܠܟܘܬܗ ܕܨܕܩܝܐ. ܒܝܪܚܐ ܚܡܝܫܝܐ. ܒܬܫܥܣܪܐ ܒܗ ܒܝܪܚܐ:, i. e. וּבְעַשְׁתֵּי עֶשְׂרֵה שָׁנָה לַמֶּלֶךְ צ׳ בַּחֹדֶשׁ הַחֲמִשִׁי בְּתִשְׁעָה לַחֹדֶשׁ. This, however, conflicts with the earlier date given in *v.* 8 for a subsequent event. Th., Klo., Kamp., Benz., Kit., Oort supply בַּחֹדֶשׁ הָרְבִיעִי after Jer. 39. 2; 52. 6.

4. וכל אנשי המלחמה וג׳] The missing verb is supplied by ‖ Jer. 52. 7 יִבְרְחוּ וַיֵּצְאוּ מֵהָעִיר; cf. Jer. 39. 4. So exactly Pesh. ܥܪܩܘ ܘܢܦܩܘ ܡܢ ܡܕܝܢܬܐ; while LXX, ἐξῆλθον, supplies the latter verb, Vulg., *fugerunt*, the former. We are still, however, confronted by the difficulty of the sing. וַיֵּלֶךְ in *v.* 4^b, without specified subj. This appears as plur. וַיֵּלְכוּ in ‖ Jer. 52. 7, and Pesh. in our passage is again in agreement. This is scarcely satisfactory, because the

king is only mentioned for the first time in *v.* 5 as having left the city with the men of war. The solution of the difficulty is probably to be found in Luc., which supplies in *v.* 4ª before וכל אנשי וג׳ καὶ ἐξῆλθεν ὁ βασιλεύς. We may thus read in *v.* 4ª וַיֵּצֵא הַמֶּלֶךְ וְכָל־אַנְשֵׁי הַמִּלְחָמָה, retaining sing. וַיֵּלֶךְ in *v.* 4ᵇ as referring to the principal actor. The plur. of Luc. καὶ ἐπορεύθησαν is probably the translator's alteration.

6. רבלתה] ‖ Jer. adds בְּאֶרֶץ חֲמָת, as in *ch.* 23. 33.

וידברו] Many Codd., all Verss., and ‖ Jer. 52. 9 read sing. וַיְדַבֵּר. The phrase דבר משפטים את פ׳ occurs again in Jer. 1. 16; 4. 12; 12. 1; 39. 5, and pl. משפטים (as in ‖ Jer. 52. 9) is the reading of several Codd. in our passage.

7. שחטו] Emend שָׁחַט, after LXX, Luc., Vulg., Pesh. Cf. ‖ Jer. 52. 10 וַיִּשְׁחַט.

ויביאהו בבל] ‖ Jer. 52. 11 adds וַיִּתְּנֵהוּ בְבֵית־הַפְּקֻדֹּת עַד־יוֹם מוֹתוֹ.

25. 8–26. *Destruction of the Temple and City of Jerusalem. Gedaliah, governor of Judah.*

Ch. 25. 8–21 = Jer. 52. 12–27.

Ch. 25. 22–26 is a much abbreviated account of the events described in Jer. 40. 7—43. 6, to which source R^{D2} clearly owes his information. Jer. 52, on the other hand, seems to be a later addition to the prophet's book excerpted from Kings[1], naturally with omission of 25. 22–26, as having been already related in fuller detail.

8. בשבעה לחדש] Three Codd., Luc., Pesh. בְּתִשְׁעָה לַחֹדֶשׁ; ‖ Jer. 52. 12 בֶּעָשׂוֹר לַחֹדֶשׁ. Klo., Benz. make the erroneous statement that Luc. agrees with ‖ Jer.

היא שנת וג׳] B.C. 586.

9. ואת כל בית גדול] 'And every house of a great one.' So Pesh., Targ. The statement is superfluous after the preceding ואת כל בתי ירושלם, and is regarded by Benz., Kit. as an explanatory gloss.

---

[1] Notice the closing words of Jer. 51, 'Thus far are the words of Jeremiah.'

10. אשר רב טבחים] Read אֲשֶׁר אֶת־רַב־טַבָּחִים, with || Jer. 52. 14. Luc. omits אשר וג׳, while the whole *v.* is wanting in LXX.

11. ההמון] 'The remnant of *the multitude*' is indistinguishable from 'the remnant of the people' mentioned just previously. || Jer. is doubtless correct in reading הָאָמוֹן '*the artificers*,' or '*master-workmen*.' Cf. *ch.* 24. 14.

At the end of the *v.* Pesh. adds ܘܐܘܒܠ ܐܢܘܢ ܠܒܒܠ 'and brought them to Babylon.'

12. ולגבים] Q're יֹגְבִים, as in || Jer. 52. 16, is supposed to mean 'husbandmen.' Kt. גָּבִים 'ploughmen' (lit. 'diggers') is preferred by Kö., *Lehrg.* I. ii. 105. Q're is to some extent supported by Jer. 39. 10[b] וַיִּתֵּן לָהֶם כְּרָמִים וִיגֵבִים; though here also it is possible that יְגֵבִים, of uncertain meaning (RV. 'fields'), is an alteration of גֵּבִים 'cisterns' (*ch.* 3. 16; Jer. 14. 3).

13–17. Cf. *notes* on I. 7. 15 *ff.*

15. אשר זהב וג׳] 'That which was of gold he took in gold, and that which was of silver in silver'; i.e. all the vessels &c. of these precious metals, as so much gold and silver.

18. כהן משנה] Cf. *ch.* 23. 4 *note.*

19. אשר הוא פקיד] || Jer. 52. 25 reads הָיָה for הוּא.

מראי פני המלך] So Est. 1. 14. Cf. 2 Sam. 14. 24, 28. The expression denotes a privileged position of intimate attendance upon the king.

ואת הספר וג׳] Read *st. constr.* סֹפֵר, with || Jer. 52. 25. Luc., καὶ τὸν Σαφάν, takes the word as a proper name סָפָן (or שָׁפָן), and this is adopted by Klo. But the statement המצבא וג׳, 'who *mustered* the people of the land,' makes it clear that the reference is not to the שר הצבא himself, but to an official who had charge of the *conscription*, and so appropriately a סֹפֵר.

23. והאנשים] Read וְאַנְשֵׁיהֶם, with LXX, Pesh., Targ., as in *vv.* 23[b], 24. So || Jer. 40. 7.

המצפה] Cf. I. 15. 22 *note.*

25. 27–30. *Kindness shown to the captive Jehoiachin by Evil-Merodach, king of Babylon.*

Ch. 25. 27–30 = Jer. 52. 31–34.

27. בשנת מלכו] B.C. 561.

מבית כלא] LXX, Luc., Pesh. are probably correct in reading וַיֹּצֵא אתו מִבֵּית כֶּלֶא, as in || Jer.

28. מעל כסא] || Jer. מִמַּעַל לְכִסֵּא is preferable.

30. ארחתו] 'His allowance' (&c. of food). So Jer. 40. 5; cf. Prov. 15. 17. In Assyr. *iaraḫtu* denotes a portion of corn.

דבר יום ביומו] Cf. I. 8. 59 *note*.

APPENDIX

1.

Inscription of Mesha', king of Moab[1].

1 אנך . משע . בן . כמשכן . מלך . מאב . הד

2 יבני | אבי . מלך . על . מאב . שלשן . שת . ואנך . מלכ

3 תי . אחר . אבי | ואעש . הבמת . זאת . לכמש . בקרחה | בנסך

4 שע . כי . השעני . מכל . השלכן . וכי . הראני . בכל . שנאי | עמר

5 י . מלך . ישראל . ויענו . את . מאב . ימן . רבן . כי . יאנף . כמש . באר

6 צה | ויחלפה . בנה . ויאמר . גם . הא . אענו . את . מאב | בימי . אמר . כדבר

7 וארא . בה . ובבתה | וישראל . אבד . אבד . עלם . וירש . עמרי . את [אר]

8 ץ . מהדבא | וישב . בה . ימה . וחצי . ימי . בנה . ארבען . שת . ויש

9 בה . כמש . בימי | ואבן . את . בעלמען . ואעש . בה . האשוח . ואב[ן]

10 את . קריתן | ואש . גד . ישב . בארץ . עטרת . מעלם . ויבן . לה . מלך . י

11 שראל . את . עטרת | ואלתחם . בקר . ואחזה | ואהרג . את . כלה[עם]

12 הקר . רית . לכמש . ולמאב | ואשב . משם . את . אראל . דודה . וא[ס]

13 חבה . לפני . כמש . בקרית | ואשב . בה . את . אש . שרן . ואת . אש

14 מחרת | ויאמר . לי . כמש . לך . אחז . את . נבה . על . ישראל | וא

15 הלך . בללה . ואלתחם . בה . מבקע . השחרת . עד . הצהרם | ואח

16 זה . ואהרג . כלה . שבעת . אלפן . גברן . וגרן | וגברת . ו[גר]

17 ת . ורחמת | כי . לעשתר . כמש . החרמתה | ואקח . משם . א[ת . כ]

18 לי . יהוה . ואסחב . הם . לפני . כמש | ומלך . ישראל . בנה . את

19 יהץ . וישב . בה . בהלתחמה . בי | ויגרשה . כמש . מפני ו

20 אקח . ממאב . מאתן . איש . כל . רשה | ואשאה . ביהץ . ואחזה .

---

[1] The readings adopted in doubtful places are those of Lidzbarski, *Ephemeris für Semit. Epigr.* I. i. Upon the language of the inscription cf. Dri. *Notes on the Hebrew Text of Samuel*, pp. lxxxv *ff.*; *Encyc. Bibl.* iii. *s.v.* Mesha.

21 לספת . על . דיבן | אנך . בנתי . קרחה . חמת . היערן . וחמת

22 העפל | ואנך . בנתי . שעריה . ואנך . בנתי . מגדלתה | וא

23 נך . בנתי . בת . מלך . ואנך . עשתי . כלאי . האשו[ח . למ]ין . בקרב

24 הקר | ובר . אן . בקרב . הקר . בקרחה . ואמר . לכל . העם . עשו . ל

25 כם . אש . בר . בביתה | ואנך . כרתי . המכרתת . לקרחה . באסר

26 י . ישראל | אנך . בנתי . ערער . ואנך . עשתי . המסלת . בארנן . [ו]

27 אנך . בנתי . בת . במת . כי . הרס . הא | אנך . בנתי . בצר . כי . עין .

28 ש . דיבן . חמשן . כי . כל . דיבן . משמעת | ואנך . מלכ

29 ת[י] מאת . בקרן . אשר . יספתי . על . הארץ | ואנך . בנת

30 י . [את .] מהדבא . ובת . דבלתן | ובת . בעלמען . ואשא . שם . את . נקד

31 צאן . הארץ | וחורנן . ישב . בה . בת וק . אש

32 ויאמר . לי . כמש . רד . הלתחם . בחורנן | וארד

33 [ויש]בה . כמש . בימי . ועל דה . משם . עש

34 שת . שדק | ואנ

1. I am Mesha', son of Chemosh[kān ?], king of Moab, the Daibonite.

2. My father reigned over Moab for thirty years, and I reigned

3. after my father, and I made this high-place to Chemosh in QR[Ḥ]H, . . .

4. . . . because he had saved me from all the . . ., and because he had caused me to see my desire upon all my haters. Omri

5. king of Israel afflicted Moab many days, because Chemosh was angry with his

6. land; and his son succeeded him, and he also said, I will afflict Moab. In my days said he [thus ?];

7. but I saw (my desire) upon him and upon his house, and Israel perished with an everlasting destruction. And Omri had taken possession of the [land ?]

8. of Mĕhēdĕba, and one (i.e. Israel) dwelt therein during his days and half his son's days, even forty years; but

9. Chemosh restored it in my days. And I built Ba'al-Me'on, and I made therein the reservoir (?), and I built

10. Qiryathên. And the men of Gad had dwelt in the land of 'Aṭaroth from of old; and the king of Israel had built for himself
11. 'Aṭaroth. And I fought against the city and took it, and I slew the whole of it, [the people of ??]
12. the city, a gazingstock (?) to Chemosh, and to Moab. And I took captive thence the altar-hearth of Dawdoh (?), and I dragged
13. it before Chemosh in Qeriyyoth. And I settled therein the men of SRN and the men of
14. MḤRT. And Chemosh said to me, Go, take Nebo against Israel, and I
15. went by night and fought against it from break of dawn until noon, and I took
16. it, and I slew the whole of it, 7,000 men, and male strangers, and [female strangers],
17. and female slaves; for to 'Ashtor-Chemosh had I devoted it, and I took thence the
18. vessels of Yahwe, and I dragged them before Chemosh. Now the king of Israel had built
19. Yahaṣ, and he abode therein when he fought with me. But Chemosh drove him out from before me; and
20. I took from Moab 200 men, even all its chiefs, and I took them up against Yahaṣ, and took it,
21. to add (it) unto Daibon. I built QRḤH, the wall of Ye'ārin, and the wall of
22. the keep. And I built its gates, and I built its towers, and
23. I built the king's house, and I made the sluices of the reservoir for water in the midst of
24. the city. Now there was no cistern in the midst of the city in QRḤH. And I said to all the people, Make
25. yourselves every man a cistern in his house; and I cut out the cutting for QRḤH by means of the
26. prisoners of Israel. I built 'Aro'er, and I made the highway by the Arnon.

27. I built Beth-Bamoth; for it was pulled down. I built Beṣer, for ruins

28. . . . . . . of Daibon (were) fifty, for all Daibon was obedient. And I ruled

29. over . . . 100 in the cities which I had added to the land. And I built

30. Mĕhēdĕba, and Beth-Diblathên, and Beth-Ba'al-Me'on, and I took thither the *naqad*-keepers,

31. . . . . sheep of the land. And as for Ḥoronên, there dwelt therein . . . . . .

32. . . . . . . and Chemosh said to me, Go down, fight against Ḥoronên. So I went down . . .

33. . . . . and Chemosh restored it in my days, and . . . thence . . .

34. . . . . And I . . . . .

2.

The Siloam Inscription[1].

1 . . . הנקבה . וזה . היה . דבר . הנקבה . בעוד . . . .
2 הגרזן . אש . אל . רעו . ובעוד . שלש . אמת . להב̄[ת נשמ]ע . קל . אש . ק̄
3 רא . אל . רעו . כי . הית . זדה . בצר . מימן . . . . . . ובים . ה
4 נקבה . הכו . החצבם . אש . לקרת . רעו . גרזן . על [. ג]רזן . וילכו .
5 המים . מן . המוצא . אל . הברכה . במאתים . ואלף . אמה . ומא̄
6 ת . אמה . היה . גבה . הצר . על . ראש . החצב̄ם̄ .

1. [Behold] the piercing through! And this was the manner of the piercing through. Whilst yet [the miners were lifting up]

2. the pick each towards his fellow, and whilst yet there were three cubits to be [cut through, there was heard] the voice of each call-

---

[1] Text as in Lidzbarski, *Nordsemit. Epigr.* p. 439. Translation, with conjectural supplement, from Dri. *Notes on the Hebrew Text of Samuel*, p. xvi.

3. ing to his fellow, for there was a fissure (?) in the rock on the right-hand . . . . And on the day of the
4. piercing through, the miners (lit. hewers) smote each so as to meet his fellow, pick against pick; and there flowed
5. the water from the source to the pool, 1,200 cubits; and one hun-
6. dred cubits was the height of the rock over the head of the miners.

3.

Inscription of the Monolith of Shalmaneser II, ll. 78–102[1].

78 In the Eponym-year of Daian-Asshur (B.C. 854), in the month Airu, on the 14th day, I left Nineveh, crossed the Tigris, advanced against the cities 79 of Giammu on the Baliḥ. Before the terror of my lordship, the panic of my mighty weapons, they were afraid, and with their own weapons Giammu their lord 80 they slew. Into Kitlala and Til-ša-apli-aḫi I advanced, my gods in his palaces I set up, revelling in his palaces I instituted. 81 His treasure-house I opened, his treasure I found, of his goods (and) possessions I made spoil, to my city Asshur I brought (them). From Kitlala I departed; to Kar-Šulman-ašarid 82 I drew nigh; on boats of sheep-skin for the second time the Euphrates at high water I crossed. The tribute of the kings on that side of the Euphrates, (namely) of Sangar of 83 Gargamiš (Carchemish), of Kundašpi of Qummuḥ, of Arami son of Gûši, of Lalli of Milida, of Ḥaiâni son of Gabar, 84 of Kalparuda of Patin, of Kalparuda of Gurgum, silver, gold, lead, copper, copper vessels,—85 at Asshur-utir-aṣbat on that side of the Euphrates, which is above (the river) Sagur, (and) which the Ḥittites Pitru (Pethor ?) 86 name, (even) there I received. From the Euphrates I departed; to Ḥalman (Aleppo) I drew nigh. Battle with me they dreaded; my feet they embraced. 87 Silver

[1] Nos. 3, 4, and 5 are based upon the text and translation of *KB.*, and Winckler, *Keilschrift. Textbuch*, and upon Delitzsch, *Assyrisches Handwörterbuch*.

(and) gold as their tribute I received; offerings before Rammân of Ḥalman I brought.

From Ḥalman I departed; to the two cities [88] of Irḥulini of Ḥamath I drew nigh. Adinnu, Mašgâ, Arganâ, the city of his kingship, I conquered. His spoil, his goods, [89] the possessions of his palaces I brought forth; to his palaces I set fire. From Arganâ I departed; to Qarqar I drew nigh; [90] Qarqar, the city of his kingship, I laid waste, I destroyed, with fire I burned. 1,200 chariots, 1,200 horsemen, 20,000 men of Hadadezer [91] of Damascus; 700 chariots, 700 horsemen, 10,000 men of Irḥulini of Ḥamath; 2,000 chariots, 10,000 men of Aḥab [92] of Israel; 500 men of Guai (Coa); 1,000 men of (the land) Muṣri; 10 chariots, 10,000 men of (the land) Irqanat; [93] 200 men of Matinu-ba'li (Mattan-ba'al) of Armada (Arvad); 200 men of (the land) Usanata; 30 chariots, 10,000 men [94] of Adunu-ba'li (Adoni-ba'al) of Šiana; 1,000 camels of Gindibu' of Arba . . . . . . 1,000 men [95] of Ba'sa, son of Ruḥubi (Reḥob), of Ammon;—these twelve kings to his assistance he took; for [96] battle and combat against me they advanced. With the exalted succour which Asshur, the lord, rendered, with the mighty power which Nergal, who marched before me, [97] bestowed, with them I fought; from Qarqar unto Gilzân their defeat I accomplished; 14,000 [98] of their troops with weapons I laid low; like Rammân upon them a flood I rained down; I scattered their corpses; [99] the surface of the wilderness (?) I filled with their numerous troops; with weapons I caused their blood to flow . . . [100] . . . . . . [101] the river Orontes . . . I dammed (?). In the midst of that battle their chariots, their horsemen, [102] their horses, their teams I captured.

4.

Fragment of the Annals of Shalmaneser II.

[1] In the eighteenth year of my reign for the sixteenth time the Euphrates [2] I crossed. Ḥazael of Damascus [3] in the multitude of his troops [4] placed confidence, and his troops [5] without number assembled. [6] Senir, a mountain-peak [7] in the neighbourhood of

Lebanon, his stronghold [8] he made. With him I fought, [9] his siege I conducted. 6,000 [10] of his men of war with weapons [11] I laid low; 1,121 of his chariots, [12] 470 of his war-horses, together with his baggage, [13] I took from him. For the saving [14] of his life he betook himself off. [15] In Damascus, the city of his kingship, I besieged him; [16] his plantations I cut down. To the mountains [17] of Ḥauran I went; cities [18] without number I destroyed, I laid waste, [19] with fire I burned; their prisoners [20] without number I carried off. [21] Unto the mountains of the range Ba'li-ra'si, [22] a promontory, I went; the image of my kingship [23] there did I set up. At that time [24] the tribute of the Tyrians, [25] of the Zidonians, of Ja-u-a (Jehu) [26] the son of Omri I received.

Descriptive Inscription from the Obelisk of Shalmaneser.

Tribute of Ja-u-a (Jehu) son of Omri; silver, gold, a bowl (? *šaplu* [1]) of gold, goblets (? *zuqût*) of gold, a ladle (? *qabuâti* [2]) of gold, pitchers (? *dalâni* [3]) of gold, bars of lead, a staff (? *ḫuṭartu* [4]) for the hand of the king, spear-shafts (? *budilḫâti*) I received of him.

5.

Narrative of Sennacherib's Third Campaign (B.C. 701), *from the Taylor Cylinder*, Col. II. l. 34–Col. III. l. 41.

[34] In my third campaign to the land Ḥatti (Ḥittite land) I went. [35] Lulî (Elulaeus), king of Zidon—the dread of the majesty [36] of my lordship overwhelmed him, and to a far-off spot [37] in the midst of the sea he fled, and his land I reduced to subjection. [38] Great Zidon, Little Zidon, [39] Beth-Zitti, Zarepta, Maḫalliba, [40] Ušû, Akzib, Akko, [41] his strong cities, the fortresses, the spots for pasture (?) [42] and for watering, his intrenchments (?), were overwhelmed by the might of the arms [43] of Asshur, my lord, and submitted themselves [44] under my feet. Tuba'lu (Ittoba'al) upon the royal throne [45] over them I seated, and the payment of the tribute of my lordship, [46] yearly without intermission, I laid upon him. [47] Minḫimmu

---

[1] Heb. סֵפֶל. [2] Heb. קֻבַּעַת. [3] Heb. דְּלִי. [4] Heb. חֹטֶר.

(Menaḥem) of Samsimuruna, [48] Tuba'lu of Zidon, [49] Abdili'ti of Arvad (Arados), [50] Urumilki of Gebal (Byblos), [51] Mitinti of Ashdod, [52] Buduilu of Beth-Ammon, [53] Kammušunadbi (Chemosh-nadab) of Moab, [54] Malikrammu (Malkiram) of Edom, [55] all the kings of the West country (Martu), [56] rich presents, weighty tribute, moveable (?) possessions [57] before me brought, and kissed my feet. [58] But Zidqâ, king of Ashqelon, [59] who had not bowed himself under my yoke—the gods of his father's house, himself, [60] his wife, his sons, his daughters, his brothers, the seed of his father's house [61] I dragged forth, and to Assyria I conveyed them.

[62] Šarruludâri, son of Rukibti, their former king, [63] over the people of Ashqelon I placed, and the tribute-offering [64] of subjection to my lordship I imposed upon him, and he became subject (?) to me. [65] In the course of my campaign Beth-Dagon, [66] Joppa, Bene-baraq, Azuru, [67] the cities of Zidqâ, which under my feet [68] had not speedily submitted, I besieged, conquered, carried off their spoil. [69] The leaders, nobles, and people of Amqarruna (Eqron), [70] who had cast Padî (their king by virtue of a sworn covenant [71] with Assyria) into fetters of iron, and to Ḥazaqiyau (Ḥezekiah) [72] of Judah had delivered him with hostile intent, (he shut him up in darkness;)—[73] their heart trembled. The kings of Egypt—[74] the archers, the chariots, the horses of the king of Miluḥḥi, [75] forces innumerable they summoned together, and came [76] to their aid. Before Altaqu (Elteqeh) [77] the battle-array was set against me; they lifted up (?) [78] their weapons. In reliance upon Asshur, my lord, I fought [79] with them, and effected their defeat; [80] the commander of the chariots and the sons of the king of Egypt, [81] together with the commander of the chariots of the king of Miluḥḥi, alive [82] in the midst of the battle my hand took prisoners. Altaqu [83] (and) Tamnâ (Timnath) I attacked, conquered, and carried forth their booty.

Col. III. [1] Against Amqarruna (Eqron) I advanced, and the chief officers, [2] the magnates who had offended, I slew; [3] and on stakes around the city I impaled their corpses. [4] The inhabitants of the town, who had practised wickedness and mischief, [5] as prisoners

I counted; the rest of them, [6] who had not practised wickedness and misdeed, who in their transgression [7] had not shared, their amnesty I proclaimed. Padî, [8] their king, from Jerusalem [9] I brought, and on the throne of lordship over them [10] I installed him, and the tribute of my lordship [11] I imposed upon him. But Ḥezekiah [12] of Judah, who had not bowed himself under my yoke, [13] 46 of his fortified towns, fortresses, and small cities [14] in their neighbourhood innumerable, [15] with casting down of battering-rams and assault of siege-engines, [16] with attack of infantry, of mines, ... , [17] I besieged, I captured. 200,150 souls, young, old, male, and female, [18] horses, mules, asses, camels, oxen, [19] and sheep, without number, from the midst of them I brought forth, and [20] as spoil I counted them. Himself, like a bird in a cage, in the midst of Jerusalem, [21] the city of his kingship, I shut up. Fortifications against him [22] I erected, and those coming forth from the gates of his city [23] I turned back. His cities, which I had plundered, from his territory [24] I severed, and to Mitinti king of Ashdod, [25] Padî king of Amqarruna (Eqron), and Zilbel [26] king of Ḥaziti (Gaza) I gave them, and diminished his territory. [27] To the former payment—their yearly tribute—[28] the tribute of subjection to my lordship I added, and [29] I laid it upon them. Himself, Ḥezekiah, [30] terror of the glory of my lordship overwhelmed him; and [31] the *Urbi* and his trusty soldiers, [32] which for the defence of Jerusalem, the city of his kingship, [33] he had introduced, laid down their arms (?). [34] Together with 30 talents of gold (and) 800 talents of silver, precious stones (?), [35] sparkling . . . -stones, great lapislazuli-stones (?), [36] couches of ivory, thrones of state of elephant-skins (and) [37] ivory, . . . -wood, . . . -wood, everything available, an enormous treasure, [38] and his daughters, the women of his palace, his male [39] and female servants (?), to Nineveh, the city of my lordship, [40] after me I caused to be brought; and for the payment of tribute [41] and the rendering of homage he despatched his envoy.

ADDITIONS

I. 1. 9. עין רגל] In favour of the view as to the site taken in the *note ad loc.*, and against the rival identification with *Bîr Eyûb*, cf. J. F. Stenning, art. *En-Rogel* in Hastings, *BD.* i. 711.

2. 10. עיר דוד] For further authorities for finding the site upon the south-east hill, cf. G. A. Smith, art. *Jerusalem* in *Encyc. Bibl.* ii. 2417 *f.*

10. 28. ומוצא וג׳] Further arguments for the view that Solomon's supply of horses was drawn, not from Egypt, but from the North-Syrian Muṣri are given by T. K. Cheyne, *Encyc. Bibl.* iii. 3162.

II. 3. 20. מדרך אדום] Luc. ἐξ ὁδοῦ τῆς ἐρήμου Σοὺδ ἐξ Ἐδώμ. So Vet. Lat. with *Sur* (שׁוּר Ex. 15. 22) for Σοὺδ.

13. 17. וחץ תשועה בארם] Luc. καὶ βέλος σωτηρίας ἐν Ἰσραήλ, Vet. Lat. *et sagitta salutis in israel*—superior to M.T.

באפק] Vet. Lat. *in aseroth quae est contra faciem samariae.* At the end of the verse Vet. Lat. continues *et aperuit fenestram secundam. Et dixit sagittare et sagittavit sagittam salutis dm̄i et sagittam salutis israel. Et dixit helisseus percuties syriā totam.* This looks like a doublet, introduced into the text with the gloss *et aperuit fenestram secundam.* That this is the case cannot, however, be affirmed with certainty, in view of the repetition of the second symbolic action which is desiderated by Elisha in *v.* 19. If the addition be genuine, we must suppose ויאמר [אלישע] to have fallen out after ויור.

INDEX

Abstract subs. for adj., page 18, 144.
Accusative of limitation, 48, 56, 199, 230, 253, 264, 268.
Adverbial use of subs., 250.
Agreement of subj. and adj., 231.
— of subj. and predicate, 53, 156, 219, 220, 258, 274.
Apposition, 2, 45, 56, 65, 97, 200, 256.
Article, idiomatic use of, 1, 81, 181, 241, 255.
— as relative, 156.
— omitted with demonstr. pronoun, 262.
— omitted with subs. when used with adj., 81.

Casus pendens, 69.
Circumscription of genitive, 5, 8, 26.
Circumstantial clause, 6, 11, 12, 70, 102, 126, 182, 189, 199, 295.
Construct state, suspended, 302.
Co-ordination in time, 6.

Dialect of North Palestine, 208.
Diminutives, 246.

Geographical sites:—
Abel-beth-ma'achah, 198.
Amana, 280.
Anathoth, 22.
Aphek̤, 238.
Argob, 45.
Aro'er, 307.
Arpad, 342.
Avva, 334.

Ba'alath, 138.
Ba'al-shalishah, 277.
Bethel, 177.
Beth-Ḥanan, 41.
Beth-Ḥoron, 137.
Beth-Shan, 44.
Beth-Shemesh, 41.

Cabul, 135.
Cinnereth, 198.
Coa, 151.
Cuthah, 334.

David, city of, 17, 380.
Dothan, 286.

Eden, 344.
En-Rogel, 5.

Gath-Ḥepher, 319.
Geba, 199.
Gezer, 137.
Giḥon, 8.
Gilgal, 264.
Gozan, 330.

Ḥabor, 330.

Ḥalaḥ, 330.
Ḥaran, 343.
Ḥazor, 136.

Ible'am, 300.
Ijjon, 198.

Januaḥ, 324.
Jarmuth, 42.
Joḳme'am, 44.
Jordan, circuit of, 102.

Ḳir-ḥareseth, 272.

Lachish, 319.
Libnah, 296.

Megiddo, 43.
Millo, the, 136.
Mizpah, 199.
Muṣri, 151, 291.

Pharpar, 280.

Ramah, 197.
Ramoth-Gilead, 251.
Reshef, 344.

Sela, 318.
Sepharvaim, 334.
Shechem, 173.
Shephelah, the, 151.
Shiloh, 188.
Shunem, 3.
Socoh, 42.
Succoth, 102.

Tappuaḥ, 322.
Telasshur, 344.
Tishbeh, 217.

Zarephath, 218.
Zarethan, 44.
Zeredah, 169.
Zion, 17.

Ḥatef-shewa with a sibilant, 180, 231, 264, 344.
Hebrew words and phrases :—
אֲבָל, 11.
אוֹב, 354.
אוֹת־ for אֹת־, 237.
אָז, 35.
אֶחָד as indefinite article, 209.
אֵי־זֶה, 255.
אַל used absolutely, 289.
אֶל, peculiar use of, 72, 182, 311.
אֶל for עַל, 72, 184, 201, 228, 297.
אִם in single direct questions, 7.
אָמְנָם, 116.
אָמַר = *assign*, 161.
אָמַר לְ, 54.
אַף־כִּי, 117.
אֲרוֹן בְּרִית י׳, 31.
אֲשֵׁרָה, 190.
אֲשֶׁר לְ, 5, 8.
אֵת, sign of accusative, before indef. obj., 178.
— sign of accusative, marking new subj., 284.
אֵת = *with*, 142.

ב pretii, 22, 207, 240.
בְּלִיַּעַל, 245.
בֶּן־הַיְמִינִי, 16.
בְּנֵי־קֶדֶם, 50.
בִּקֵּר, 327.
בֵּרֵךְ = *curse*, 247.

גֹּאֵל, 201.

גְּבִירָה, 161.

הַלָּז, 275.

הֵשִׁיב פָּנִים, 19.

ו consecutive epexegetical, 15.
— consecutive introducing predicate, 169.

זְבֻל, 110.
זֶה enclitic, 189.
זָחַל, 5.

יִדְּעֹנִי, 354.

כִּבְרַת אֶרֶץ, 280.
כִּי introducing direct narration, 6, 244.
— introducing oath, 21.
כִּי . . . כִּי, resumptive, 8.
כָּרָה, 287.

ל formative, 246.
ל = *at*, 142.
ל of norm, 257.
לֹא used absolutely, 162.
— with jussive, 16.
לֵאמֹר, subject of, 201.

מ preformative in substantives, signification of, 143.
מַזָּלוֹת, 358.
מִן, idiomatic uses of, 3, 12, 177. מֵאֵת, 8, 52. מֵעַל, 13, 15, 24. מֵעִם, 24. מִקְצֵה, 178.
מִנְחָה, 48, 225, 327.
מַצֵּבָה, 192.

סֹכֵן, 2.

עֵבֶר, 49. מֵעֵבֶר, 44.
עַל for אֶל, 10, 131, 220, 221, 242.
עַל = *incumbent upon*, 40.
עִם, idiomatic uses of, 5, 33, 35, 115, 157.
עֹפֶל, 282.
עָצַב, 3.
עָצוּר וְעָזוּב, 186.
עָשָׂה used absolutely, 118.

פֶּחָה, 147, 237.
פַּרְוָרִים, 360.

קָסַם, 332.

שׁ relative, 208.
שָׁלָה, 275.
שְׁלָטִים, 310.
שָׁלִישׁ, 139.

תְּרָפִים, 362.

'Idem per idem' idiom, 293.
Imperative with ו in place of cohortative, 6.
Imperfect, with frequentative force, 1, 32, 194, 268, 338, 359.
— pictorial, 239.
Impersonal construction, 4, 20, 48, 180, 187.
Infinitive absol., use of, 241, 256, 269.
— in ות-, 271.
Infinitive constr., use of, 317.
— Hiph'il with Ḥireq under preformative ה, 272.

Negative duplicated, 148.
Nomen unitatis, 12.

Oath, 12, 21, 281.
Omission of pronom. subject of participle, 262.
Order of sentence, 4, 18, 55, 120, 280.

Participle, agreement of, with suffix of antecedent subject, 189.
— force of, 3, 47, 218, 257.
Perfect with article prefixed, 156.
— with ו consecutive as imperative, 13.
Perfect with weak ו, 77, 124, 157, 236, 238, 293, 318, 345, 353, 357. Cf. 194, 247, 269.
Personal pronoun reinforcing suffix pronoun, 7, 249.
Pluperfect, 188, 270.

Question indicated by tone of voice, 7.

Relative omitted, 33.
Resumption, 8, 14, 118, 239.

Termination תַ‎ in proper names, 42.

Vocative continued by third person, 300.